AUSTRALASIAN BUSINESS STATISTICS

4TH EDITION

AUSTRALASIAN
BUSINESS STATISTICS

4TH EDITION

Ken BLACK

John ASAFU-ADJAYE

Paul BURKE

Nazim KHAN

Gerard KING

Nelson PERERA

Andrew PAPADIMOS

Carl SHERWOOD

Saleh WASIMI

Reetu VERMA

WILEY

Fourth edition published 2016 by
John Wiley & Sons Australia, Ltd
42 McDougall Street, Milton Qld 4064

First edition published 2007
Second edition published 2010
Third edition published 2013

Typeset in Minion Pro 10/12

National Library of Australia
Cataloguing-in-Publication entry

Creator:	Black, Ken (Kenneth Urban), author.
Title:	Australasian business statistics / Ken Black, John Asafu-Adjaye, Paul Burke, Nazim Khan, Gerard King, Nelson Perera, Andrew Papadimos, Carl Sherwood, Saleh Wasimi.
Edition:	4th edition.
ISBN:	9780730312932 (paperback) 9780730324836 (e-text)
Notes:	Includes index.
Subjects:	Commercial statistics — Australasia — Textbooks.
Other Creators/ Contributors:	Asafu-Adjaye, John, author. Burke, Paul, author. Khan, Nazim, author. King, Gerard, author. Perera, Nelson, author. Papadimos, Andrew, author. Sherwood, Carl, author. Wasimi, Saleh A. (Saleh Ahmed), author.
Dewey Number:	519.5

Typeset in India by Aptara

Printed in China by
Printplus Ltd

10 9 8 7 6 5 4 3 2 1

Brief contents

CHAPTER 1 Introduction to statistics 1
CHAPTER 2 Charts and graphs 13
CHAPTER 3 Descriptive summary measures 47
CHAPTER 4 Probability 93
CHAPTER 5 Discrete distributions 135
CHAPTER 6 The normal distribution and other continuous distributions 169
CHAPTER 7 Sampling and sampling distributions 193
CHAPTER 8 Statistical inference: estimation for single populations 227
CHAPTER 9 Statistical inference: hypothesis testing for single populations 261
CHAPTER 10 Statistical inferences about two populations 311
CHAPTER 11 Analysis of variance and design of experiments 367
CHAPTER 12 Chi-square tests 409
CHAPTER 13 Simple regression analysis 435
CHAPTER 14 Multiple regression analysis 479
CHAPTER 15 Time-series forecasting and index numbers 513

Contents

About the authors xi
Key features xiii
Real-world issues at a glance xiv
Acknowledgements xv

CHAPTER 1

Introduction to statistics

Learning objectives 1
Opening vignette: The search for information 2
Introduction 2
1.1 Basic statistical concepts 3
1.2 Types of data 4
Categorical data 4
Numerical data 5
Cross-sectional and time-series data 5
1.3 Obtaining data 6
Obtaining secondary data 6
Obtaining primary data 6
1.4 Statistical analysis using Excel 7
Getting started with Excel and KaddStat 7
Excel's Analysis ToolPak add-in 7
KaddStat 8
Using Excel with this book 9
1.5 When things go wrong 9
Space shuttle *Challenger* 9
The Sally Clark case 9
The 1936 US presidential election 10
Summary 10
Key terms 11
Review problems 11

CHAPTER 2

Charts and graphs

Learning objectives 13
Opening vignette: Red tape 14
Introduction 14
Chapter case: Electronic games 15
2.1 Frequency distributions 16
Class midpoint 17
Relative frequency 17
Cumulative frequency 17
2.2 Graphical display of data 22
Histograms 22
Frequency polygons 28
Ogives 30
Pie charts 32
Stem and leaf plots 33
Pareto charts 35
2.3 Graphical display of two-variable continuous data: scatter plots 39
Chapter case revisited: Electronic games 41
Summary 42
Key terms 43
Review problems 43

CHAPTER 3

Descriptive summary measures

Learning objectives 47
Opening vignette: Are you being followed? 48
Introduction 48
Chapter case: Location, location, location! 49
3.1 Measures of central tendency 51
Mode 51
Median 51
Mean 53
3.2 Measures of location 56
Percentiles 57
Quartiles 58
3.3 Measures of variability 61
Range 61
Interquartile range 61
Variance and standard deviation 62
Variance 63
Standard deviation 64
Population versus sample variance and standard deviation 68
Computational formulas for variance and standard deviation 69
z-scores 71
Coefficient of variation 72
3.4 Measures of shape 74
Skewness 74
Skewness and the relationship of the mean, median and mode 75
Coefficient of skewness 75
Kurtosis 76
Box and whisker plots 76
3.5 Measures of association 80
Correlation 80
Misuse of statistics 85
Chapter case revisited: Location, location, location! 85
Summary 86
Key terms 87
Key equations 88
Review problems 89
Maths appendix 91

CHAPTER 4

Probability

Learning objectives 93
Opening vignette: A conditional workout 94
Introduction 95

Chapter case: Too many leaders 96
4.1 Methods of determining probabilities 97
Classical method 97
Relative frequency of occurrence method 98
Subjective probability method 99
4.2 Structure of probability 100
Experiment 100
Event 100
Elementary events 100
Sample space 101
Set notation, unions and intersections 102
Mutually exclusive events 103
Independent events 103
Collectively exhaustive events 104
Complementary events 104
4.3 Contingency tables and probability matrices 105
Marginal, union, joint and conditional probabilities 106
Probability matrices 107
4.4 Addition laws 109
General law of addition 109
Exclusive or 112
Complement of a union 113
Special law of addition 114
4.5 Multiplication laws 116
General law of multiplication 116
Special law of multiplication 117
4.6 Conditional probability 120
Assessing independence 122
Tree diagrams 124
Revising probabilities and Bayes' rule 126
Misuse of statistics 129
Chapter case revisited: Too many leaders 129
Summary 130
Key terms 131
Key equations 131
Review problems 132

CHAPTER 5

Discrete distributions

Learning objectives 135
Opening vignette: Binge drinking 136
Introduction 136
Chapter case: Mental health and young people 137
5.1 Discrete versus continuous distributions 137
5.2 Describing a discrete distribution 138
Mean, variance and standard deviation of discrete distributions 139
Mean or expected value 140
Variance and standard deviation of a discrete distribution 140
5.3 Binomial distribution 143
Assumptions about the binomial distribution 143
Solving a binomial problem 144
Using the binomial table 147
Mean and standard deviation of a binomial distribution 150
Graphing binomial distributions 152
5.4 Poisson distribution 155
Solving Poisson problems by formula 156
Mean and standard deviation of a Poisson distribution 160
Graphing Poisson distributions 160
Poisson approximation of the binomial distribution 161
Misuse of statistics 164
Chapter case revisited: Mental health and young people 165
Summary 166
Key terms 166
Key equations 166
Review problems 167

CHAPTER 6

The normal distribution and other continuous distributions

Learning objectives 169
Opening vignette: Healthy body temperature 170
Introduction 170
Chapter case: Prawn farm continues to grow 171
6.1 The normal distribution 172
History and characteristics of the normal distribution 172
6.2 The standardised normal distribution 175
6.3 Solving normal distribution problems 177
Misuse of statistics 181
6.4 The normal distribution approximation to the binomial distribution 181
6.5 The uniform distribution 184
6.6 The exponential distribution 186
Probabilities for the exponential distribution 187
Chapter case revisited: Prawn farm continues to grow 189
Summary 190
Key terms 190
Key equations 190
Review problems 191

CHAPTER 7

Sampling and sampling distributions

Learning objectives 193
Opening vignette: Detecting accounting fraud 194
Introduction 194
Chapter case: Prawn farm success tied to strict quality control 195
7.1 Sampling 196
Reasons for sampling 196
Reasons for taking a census 197
Sampling frame 197

7.2 Random versus nonrandom sampling 198
Random sampling techniques 198
Simple random sampling 198
Stratified random sampling 201
Systematic sampling 202
Cluster (or area) sampling 203
Nonrandom sampling 204
Convenience sampling 204
Judgement sampling 204
Quota sampling 205
Snowball sampling 205
7.3 Types of errors from collecting sample data 205
Sampling error 205
Nonsampling errors 206
7.4 Sampling distribution of the sample mean, $\bar{x}$ 207
Central limit theorem 211
Sampling from a finite population 215
7.5 Sampling distribution of the sample proportion, $\hat{p}$ 218
Misuse of statistics 220
Chapter case revisited: Prawn farm success tied to strict quality control 221
Summary 222
Key terms 223
Key equations 223
Review problems 224

CHAPTER 8

Statistical inference: estimation for single populations

Learning objectives 227
Opening vignette: Rural obesity in Queensland on the rise 228
Introduction 228
Chapter case: Prawn farm up for sale 228
8.1 Estimating the population mean using the *z* statistic (σ known) 229
Finite population correction factor 235
Estimating the population mean using the *z* statistic when the sample size is small 236
8.2 Estimating the population mean using the *t* statistic (σ unknown) 238
The *t* distribution 238
Robustness 239
Characteristics of the *t* distribution 239
Reading the *t* distribution table 240
Confidence intervals to estimate the population mean using the *t* statistic 241
8.3 Estimating the population proportion 245
8.4 Estimating the population variance 248
8.5 Estimating sample size 252
Sample size when estimating μ 252
Determining sample size when estimating *p* 254
Misuse of statistics 256
Chapter case revisited: Prawn farm up for sale 256
Summary 257
Key terms 258
Key equations 258
Review problems 259

CHAPTER 9

Statistical inference: hypothesis testing for single populations

Learning objectives 261
Opening vignette: Australian childcare — enough to make you cry? 262
Introduction 262
Chapter case: Prawn farm expects a bright future 263
9.1 Hypothesis-testing fundamentals 263
Rejection and nonrejection regions 266
Type I and Type II errors 269
Type I error 269
Type II error 270
How are alpha and beta related? 271
9.2 The six-step approach to hypothesis testing 272
STEP 1. Set up H_0 and H_a 272
STEP 2. Decide on the type and direction of the test 273
STEP 3. Decide on the level of significance (α), determine the critical value(s) and region(s), and draw a diagram 273
STEP 4. Write down the decision rule 273
STEP 5. Select a random sample and do relevant calculations 273
STEP 6. Draw a conclusion 273
Misuse of statistics 273
9.3 Hypothesis tests for a population mean: large sample case (*z* statistic, σ known) 274
STEP 1. Set up H_0 and H_a 274
STEP 2. Decide on the type and direction of the test 275
STEP 3. Decide on the level of significance (α), determine the critical value(s) and region(s), and draw a diagram 275
STEP 4. Write down the decision rule 275
STEP 5. Select a random sample and do relevant calculations 275
STEP 6. Draw a conclusion 275
Testing the mean with a finite population 276
The critical value method 276
The *p*-value method 278
9.4 Hypothesis tests about a population mean: small sample case (*t* statistic, σ unknown) 282
9.5 Testing hypotheses about a proportion 288
9.6 Testing hypotheses about a variance 292
9.7 Solving for Type II errors 296
Some observations about Type II errors 301
Operating characteristic and power curves 301

Effect of increasing sample size on the rejection limits 302
Chapter case revisited: Prawn farm expects a bright future 304
Summary 306
Key terms 307
Key equations 307
Review problems 308

CHAPTER 10

Statistical inferences about two populations

Learning objectives 311
Opening vignette: Saving for retirement 312
Introduction 313
Chapter case: Life insurance premiums 314
10.1 Hypothesis testing and confidence intervals for the difference between two means (*z* statistic, population variances known) 315
Hypothesis testing 316
Confidence intervals 322
10.2 Hypothesis testing and confidence intervals for the difference between two means (*t* statistic, population variances unknown) 326
Hypothesis testing 326
Confidence intervals 333
10.3 Statistical inferences about two populations with paired observations 337
Hypothesis testing 337
Confidence intervals 343
10.4 Statistical inferences about two population proportions 347
Hypothesis testing 347
Confidence intervals 351
10.5 Statistical inferences about two population variances 353
Hypothesis testing 354
Confidence intervals 359
Misuse of statistics 361
Chapter case revisited: Life insurance 361
Summary 362
Key terms 362
Key equations 362
Review problems 364
Maths appendix 366

CHAPTER 11

Analysis of variance and design of experiments

Learning objectives 367
Opening vignette: Australian teens and luxury brands 368
Introduction 368
Chapter case: Cyberbullying amongst Australian adolescents 369
11.1 Introduction to design of experiments 370
11.2 The completely randomised design (one-way ANOVA) 372
Reading the *F* distribution table 376
11.3 Multiple comparison tests 380
Tukey's honestly significant difference (HSD) test: the case of equal sample sizes 380
Tukey–Kramer procedure: the case of unequal sample sizes 383
11.4 The randomised block design 385
11.5 A factorial design (two-way ANOVA) 390
Advantages of the factorial design 391
Factorial designs with two treatments 391
Statistically testing a factorial design 392
Interaction 392
Misuse of statistics 400
Chapter case revisited: Cyberbullying amongst Australian adolescents 401
Summary 401
Key terms 402
Key equations 402
Review problems 403
Maths appendix 406

CHAPTER 12

Chi-square tests

Learning objectives 409
Opening vignette: Social media is now crucial for business 410
Introduction 410
Chapter case: Job security at Combaro Ltd 411
12.1 Chi-square goodness-of-fit test 412
12.2 Contingency analysis: chi-square test of independence 423
Misuse of statistics 428
Chapter case revisited: Job security at Combaro Ltd 429
Summary 430
Key terms 431
Key equations 431
Review problems 431

CHAPTER 13

Simple regression analysis

Learning objectives 435
Opening vignette: Teenage smoking in pregnancy and birth weight 436
Introduction 436
Chapter case: Predicting the selling price of houses in the city of Baycoast 437

13.1 Introduction to simple regression analysis 437
13.2 Determining the equation of the regression line 440
13.3 Residual analysis 449
Using residuals to test the assumptions of the regression model 452
13.4 Standard error of the estimate 455
13.5 Coefficient of determination 459
Relationship between r and r^2 462
13.6 Hypothesis tests for the slope of the regression model and testing the overall model 462
Testing the slope 462
13.7 Estimation and prediction 466
Confidence (prediction) intervals to estimate the conditional mean of y: $\mu_{y/x}$ 466
Prediction intervals to estimate a single value of y 467
13.8 Interpreting the output 472
Misuse of statistics 472
Chapter case revisited: Predicting the selling price of houses in the city of Baycoast 472
Summary 473
Key terms 474
Key equations 475
Review problems 476

CHAPTER 14

Multiple regression analysis

Learning objectives 479
Opening vignette: Video gaming and gambling in Australian adolescents 480
Introduction 480
Chapter case: Predicting the prices of houses in Baycoast: using additional variables 481
14.1 The multiple regression model 481
Multiple regression model with two independent variables (first-order) 482
Determining the multiple regression equation 483
14.2 Significance tests of the regression model and its coefficients 488
Testing the overall model 488
Significance tests of the regression coefficients 490
14.3 Residuals, standard error of the estimate and R^2 493
Residuals 493
SSE and standard error of the estimate 497
Coefficient of multiple determination (R^2) 499
Adjusted R^2 500
14.4 Interpreting multiple regression computer output 501
A re-examination of the multiple regression output 501
Misuse of statistics 504
Chapter case revisited: Predicting the selling price of houses in the city of Baycoast: using additional variables 505
Summary 507
Key terms 507
Key equations 508
Review problems 508

CHAPTER 15

Time-series forecasting and index numbers

Learning objectives 513
Opening vignette: The power of tourism 514
Introduction 515
Chapter case: Forecasting at Combaro Ltd 516
15.1 Components of a time series 518
Trend component 518
Seasonal component 518
Cyclical component 519
Irregular (or random) component 519
15.2 Time-series smoothing methods 520
The moving average method 520
The exponential smoothing method 523
Seasonal indices 525
Deseasonalising time series 528
15.3 Least squares trend-based forecasting models 532
The linear trend model 532
The quadratic trend model 535
The exponential trend model 537
15.4 Autoregressive trend-based forecasting models 539
Testing for autocorrelation 540
Ways to overcome the autocorrelation problem 543
Addition of independent variables 543
Transforming variables 543
15.5 Evaluating alternative forecasting models 547
15.6 Index numbers 550
Simple price index 550
Aggregate price indices 551
Unweighted aggregate price index 551
Weighted aggregate price index 552
Changing the base period 556
Applications of price indices 557
Misuse of statistics 559
Chapter case revisited: Forecasting at Combaro Ltd 559
Summary 562
Key terms 563
Key equations 563
Review problems 564

Appendix: Tables 569
Sources 605
Glossary 609
Index 615

Ken Black is Professor of Decision Sciences in the School of Business and Public Administration at the University of Houston–Clear Lake. He earned a Bachelor of Arts in mathematics from Graceland College; a Master of Arts in mathematics education from the University of Texas at El Paso; a Doctor of Philosophy in business administration in management science; and a Doctor of Philosophy in educational research from the University of North Texas.

Ken has taught all levels of statistics courses: forecasting, management science, market research and production/operations management. He has published 20 journal articles, over 20 professional papers and two textbooks: *Business statistics: an introductory course* and *Business statistics: for contemporary decision making*. Ken has consulted for many different companies, including Aetna, the City of Houston, NYLCare, AT&T, Johnson Space Centre, Southwest Information Resources, Connect Corporation and Eagle Engineering.

John Asafu-Adjaye is an Associate Professor in the School of Economics at the University of Queensland (UQ). He obtained a Bachelor of Science (Honours) in agricultural economics from the University of Ghana and then earned a Master of Science in operations research from the Aston Business School, UK. He completed a Doctor of Philosophy in natural resource economics at the University of Alberta, Edmonton, Canada.

At UQ John teaches business and economic statistics at both the undergraduate and postgraduate levels. His research activities include policy analysis of economic and environmental issues in Africa and the Asia–Pacific region. John is the author or co-author of over 80 research-based publications, including 7 books and monographs, 5 book chapters, 63 peer-reviewed journal articles and 11 commissioned reports.

Paul Burke is a Research Fellow in the School of Marketing and Centre for the Study of Choice (CenSoC) at the University of Technology Sydney (UTS). He obtained a Bachelor of Economics (First Class Honours in Marketing) from the University of Sydney. He holds a Doctor of Philosophy and Graduate Certificate in Higher Education Teaching & Learning from UTS. Paul has won teaching awards for his work in business statistics and large class teaching from UTS as well as national recognition with citations from the Carrick Institute and the Australian Learning Teaching Council. He has published in many international journals including *Research Policy*, *Educational Researcher*, *International Journal of Research in Marketing*, *Journal of Operations Management* and *Journal of Product Innovation Management*. His research interests are in choice modelling, experimental design and consumer behaviour applied in the fields of education, ethical consumerism and innovation. He has been chief investigator on many large-scale grants including Discovery and Linkage grants from the Australian Research Council (ARC), working with many international companies and organisations.

Nazim Khan is a Lecturer and Consultant in the School of Mathematics and Statistics at the University of Western Australia. He earned a Bachelor of Engineering in electrical engineering from the University of Western Australia, a Technical Teachers Certificate from the Fiji Institute of Teaching, and a Bachelor of Science (Honours) in mathematics and a Doctor of Philosophy from the University of Western Australia.

Nazim has taught decision theory at the MBA level, financial mathematics, forecasting and statistics. Nazim is an active researcher in statistics and applications. He has also presented several papers and published several articles in mathematics and statistics education. Nazim has consulted for various companies and research groups in his capacity as Consultant with the UWA Statistical Consulting Group.

Andrew Papadimos is a Lecturer in international business, statistics and economics on the Brisbane campus of Australian Catholic University. His main research interests are the Chinese economy and International Business in the Asia–Pacific region. Apart from a PhD in International Relations and Economics, Andrew also has a Masters in Applied Law from the University of Queensland, and a Graduate Certificate in Higher Education from ACU. Andrew has lived and worked for many years in Taiwan and the People's Republic of China, and is fluent in speaking and reading Mandarin Chinese. He has also had a great deal of real-world experience with international business, having acted as a consultant on the Chinese economic and legal climate for international corporations conducting business with China.

Carl Sherwood is a Lecturer in the School of Economics at the University of Queensland. He obtained a Bachelor of Engineering (Civil), Master of Business Administration (MBA) and a Graduate Certificate in Higher Education from the University of Queensland. With twenty years of professional experience as an engineer, Carl has crafted his teaching by capturing this wealth of business experience to make courses relevant to students.

Carl has been teaching a variety of subjects at the University of Queensland for more than a decade. He has primarily concentrated on teaching statistics, at both the undergraduate and postgraduate level, as well as teaching business economics to managers studying at MBA level. As a result of his teaching efforts, Carl has won the University of Queensland School of Economics Teaching Excellence Award on four occasions, a University of Queensland Citation for Outstanding Contributions to Student Learning and a National Teaching Citation for Outstanding Contributions to Student Learning. One of Carl's areas of research centres on exploring how statistics can be made more meaningful, practical and engaging for students.

Saleh A Wasimi is an Associate Professor at Central Queensland University, Melbourne, Australia. He earned his Doctor of Philosophy degree from the University of Iowa, US, and his Masters and Bachelor degrees in water resources engineering from Bangladesh University of Engineering & Technology, Dhaka. He has worked in Bangladesh, the US and Australia as an academic and has conducted research and consultancy works in those countries as well as in Italy, Denmark, Sweden and Ireland. Saleh's current research interests include stochastic processes, optimisation, water resources planning and development, disaster management, hydrology, and hydraulics. He has authored in excess of 50 refereed articles and won awards for his publications.

Key features

Opening vignettes are concise case studies showing students the relevance of statistics and how data are used in business and the world they live in.

Chapter cases are brief business-world issues that introduce students to scenarios that use the techniques covered in the chapter to make a business decision. These are based on all-new data sets with a greater focus on cross-sectional data. At the end of each chapter, the **chapter case revisited** uses the techniques and concepts from the chapter to help make the business decision and reinforce the information presented in the text.

Excel-based data analysis is integrated throughout each chapter. Most businesses have access to Microsoft Excel and, accordingly, this text focuses on analysing data using Excel with the techniques learned in each chapter.

Misuse of statistics helps students avoid the pitfalls of using statistics incorrectly in business scenarios by highlighting their potential misuse in easy-to-understand terms.

Problems are included at the end of every section of the text. They usually follow demonstration problems and reinforce the concept learned in that section.

Going further with KaddStat is an online guide with stepped instructions to perform the textbook demonstration problems using enhanced KaddStat Excel functionality. Going further with KaddStat can be downloaded for free from the student website, www.johnwiley.com.au/highered/black4e/kaddstat.

Real-world issues at a glance

Chapter	Opening vignette	Chapter case
1 Introduction to statistics	The search for information	
2 Charts and graphs	Red tape	Electronic games
3 Descriptive summary measures	Are you being followed?	Location, location, location!
4 Probability	A conditional workout	Too many leaders
5 Discrete distributions	Binge drinking	Mental health and young people
6 The normal distribution and other continuous distributions	Healthy body temperature	Prawn farm continues to grow
7 Sampling and sampling distributions	Detecting accounting fraud	Prawn farm success tied to strict quality control
8 Statistical inference: estimation for single populations	Rural obesity in Queensland on the rise	Prawn farm up for sale
9 Statistical inference: hypothesis testing for single populations	Australian childcare — enough to make you cry?	Prawn farm expects a bright future
10 Statistical inferences about two populations	Saving for retirement	Life insurance premiums
11 Analysis of variance and design of experiments	Australian teens and luxury brands	Cyberbullying amongst Australian adolescents
12 Chi-square tests	Social media is now crucial for business	Job security at Combaro Ltd
13 Simple regression analysis	Teenage smoking in pregnancy and birth weight	Predicting the selling price of houses in the city of Baycoast
14 Multiple regression analysis	Video gaming and gambling in Australian adolescents	Predicting the prices of houses in Baycoast: using additional variables
15 Time-series forecasting and index numbers	The power of tourism	Forecasting at Combaro Ltd

The authors and publisher would like to thank the following copyright holders, organisations and individuals for their permission to reproduce copyright material in *Australasian Business Statistics*, 4th edition.

Images

• Google: **2** © Google. • Shutterstock: **14** © filmfoto; **15 (top)** © auremar; **48** © Twin Design; **49** © bikeriderlondon; **94, 436** © Syda Productions; **96, 228 (top)** © Monkey Business Images; **136** © Piotr Marcinski; **137** © luxorphoto; **170** © AVAVA; **194** © Andrey_Popov; **195** © Dream79; **262 (top)** © Goran Bogicevic; **262 (bottom)** © Mati Nitibhon; **312** © Jerry Sliwowski; **314** © Rawpixel; **368** © william casey; **369** © SpeedKingz; **410** © Ttatty; **411** © Kzenon; **437** © Ekaterina Kamenetsky; **480** © Photosani; **481** © Yulia von Eisenstein; **514** © zhu difeng; **516** © gemphoto. • Interactive Games & Entertainment Association: **15 (bottom), 42** © iGEA 2014. • Alamy: **171** © PhotoStock-Israel. • Picture Media: **228 (bottom)** © REUTERS/Andrea Hopkins/Picture Media.

Text

• Oxford University Press: **601–4** © Durbin, J & Watson, GS 1951, 'Testing for serial correlation in least squares regression II', *Biometrika*, vol. 38, pp. 159–78.

Every effort has been made to trace the ownership of copyright material. Information that will enable the publisher to rectify any error or omission in subsequent editions will be welcome. In such cases, please contact the Permissions Section of John Wiley & Sons Australia, Ltd.

John Wiley & Sons, Australia: Terry Burkitt (Publishing Manager), Kylie Challenor (Managing Content Editor), Beth Klan (Project Editor), Tara Seeto (Senior Publishing Assistant), Delia Sala (Graphic Designer), Jo Hawthorne (Senior Production Controller), Rebecca Cam (Digital Content Editor).

CHAPTER

1 Introduction to statistics

LEARNING OBJECTIVES

After studying this chapter, you should be able to:

1. define some basic statistical concepts
2. classify data by type and explain why doing so is important
3. describe some common sources of data used in business statistics
4. outline the appropriate use of computers in statistical analysis
5. discuss some examples of the potential consequences of incorrect data analysis.

OPENING VIGNETTE

The search for information

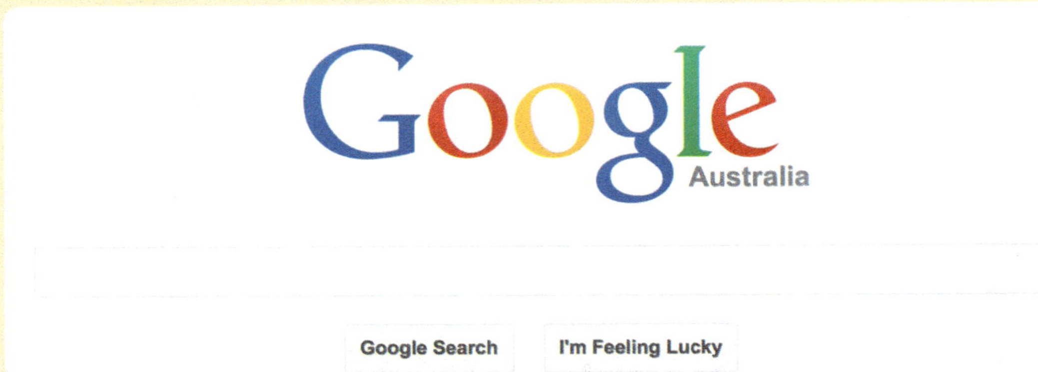

Every day hundreds of millions of people use Google to search for information on the internet. The number of searches per year has been growing exponentially since Google was founded in 1998, and reached a total of 2.2 trillion searches in 2013, or almost 6 billion searches per day. In 1999 it took Google a month to build an index of 50 million pages. Now this task takes less than a minute. Currently Google has 68% of total web search volume. Its nearest rival is Baidu with 19.1%. Google's revenue has grown from $0.5 billion in the first quarter of 2008 to almost $16 billion in the second quarter of 2014.

- What algorithms are used to provide fast searches and data retrieval?
- How are algorithms measured for search quality?
- How does Google optimise advertisement quality?

Answering all of these questions depends on statistical analysis of data. Such analysis is essential for Google to maintain its market dominance and revenue.

It will come as no surprise to learn that Google employs many statisticians. Some are specialists, but many have dual qualifications. Most of them work in the advertising division ('Ads') or the search engine division ('Search'). In the advertising division, quantitative analysts design tools and processes to measure the effectiveness of Google's advertising service and in turn to improve those services. In the search division, statisticians analyse the quality of the results returned by Google's search engine. That information then feeds back to the software engineers to improve the search engine.

With perhaps the biggest collection of data in the world, Google requires its statisticians to work with multi-disciplinary teams to solve a wide range of business problems.

Introduction

Every minute of the working day, businesses around the world make decisions that determine whether they will profit and grow or whether they will stagnate and die. Most of these decisions are made with the assistance of information about the marketplace, economic and financial environments, workforce, competition and other factors. Such information usually comes in the form of data. Business statistics provides the tools through which data are collected, analysed, summarised, interpreted and presented to facilitate the decision-making process. Thus, business statistics plays an important role in decision making within the dynamic world of business.

In this text, we first introduce basic statistical concepts. We then discuss how to organise and present data so they are meaningful and useful to decision makers. We will learn techniques for sampling (from a population) that allow studies of the business world to be conducted promptly at lower cost. We will explore various ways to forecast future values and examine techniques for determining trends. This text also includes many statistical tools for testing hypotheses and for estimating population parameters. These and many other useful statistical techniques await us on this journey through business statistics. Let us begin.

1.1 Basic statistical concepts

In this section some basic concepts will be discussed so that statistical problems can be put into context. These concepts will be covered in detail in later chapters.

Two important concepts in statistics are population and sample. A **population** is a collection of objects (often called units or subjects) of interest. Examples of populations include:

1. all small businesses
2. all workers currently employed by BHP Billiton
3. all dishwashers produced by Fisher & Paykel in Auckland in the past 12 months.

A population (and unit) can be very widely defined, such as 'all cars', or narrowly defined such as 'all red Toyota Corolla hatchbacks produced in 2015'.

Collection of data on a whole population is called a **census**. A **sample** is a subset of the units in a population. If selected using the principles of sampling, a sample can be expected to be representative of the whole population. Sampling has several advantages over a census. In particular, sampling is simpler and cheaper. Further, some forms of data collection are destructive. For example, crash test statistics for a particular model of car are obtained by destroying the car. This makes it impossible to collect crash data on all cars, so sampling is the only option.

There are two steps in analysing data from a sample: exploratory data analysis and statistical inference. These are related and both should be performed for any given data. **Exploratory data analysis**, or **EDA**, is the first step, in which numerical, tabular and graphical summaries (such as frequency tables, means, standard deviations and histograms) of data are produced to summarise and highlight the key aspects or any special features of the data. Often, such analysis is sufficient for the purpose of the study. However, more often this is a precursor to more formal and extensive analysis of the data.

Statistical inference uses sample data to reach conclusions about the population from which the sample was drawn. This is usually the main aim of any statistical exercise and involves more formal data analysis techniques. An inference is a conclusion that patterns observed in the data (sample) are present in the wider population from which the data were collected. A **statistical inference** is an inference based on a probability model linking the data to the population. Clearly such conclusions assume that the sample data are representative of the population; appropriate data collection is vital for such assumptions to hold true.

As an example, in pharmaceutical research, tests must be limited to a small sample of patients since new drugs are expensive to produce. Researchers design experiments with small, representative samples of patients and draw conclusions about the whole population using techniques of statistical inference.

Note that no inference is required for census data, since a census collects data on the whole population. In this case, EDA is all that is possible. Any inference will be based on simple comparisons of numerical and graphical summaries with a previous census.

A descriptive measure of the *population* is called a **parameter**. Parameters are usually denoted by Greek letters. Examples of parameters are population mean (μ), population standard deviation (σ) and population variance (σ^2). A descriptive measure of a *sample* is called a **statistic**. Statistics are usually denoted by Roman letters. Examples of statistics are sample mean ($\bar{x}$), sample standard deviation (s) and sample variance (s^2).

Distinction between the terms *parameter* and *statistic* is important. A business researcher often wants to estimate the value of a parameter or draw inferences about the parameter. However, the calculation of parameters is usually either impossible or infeasible because of the amount of time and money required to conduct a census. In such cases, the business researcher can take a representative sample of the population and use the corresponding sample statistic to estimate the population parameter. Thus, the sample mean, $\bar{x}$, is used to estimate the population mean, μ. The basis for inferential statistics, then, is the ability to make decisions about parameters without having to complete a census of the population.

For example, Fisher & Paykel may want to determine the average number of loads that its 8 kg LCD washing machines can wash before needing repairs. The population here is *all* the 8 kg LCD washing machines, and the parameter is the population mean: that is, the average number of washes per machine before repair. A company statistician takes a representative sample of these machines, conducts trials on this sample, recording the number of washes before repair for each machine, and then computes the sample average number of washes before repair. The (population) mean number of washes for this type of washing machine is then estimated from this sample mean.

Inferences about parameters are made under uncertainty. Unless parameters are computed directly from a census, the statistician never knows with certainty whether the estimates or inferences made from samples are true. In an effort to estimate the level of confidence in the result of the process, statisticians use probability statements. Therefore, part of this text is devoted to probability.

1.2 Types of data

Most available data are numerical. Before we analyse data we need to know what the numbers represent. For example, the data could be the dollar cost of items produced, the geographical location of retail outlets, weights of shipments or rankings of sales staff. These data are of different types and cannot be analysed the same way. Which exploratory techniques and which inferential methods we use are largely determined by the type of data. Data can be broadly classified as qualitative (also known as categorical) or quantitative (also known as numerical). Categorical data can be further subclassified as nominal or ordinal, and numerical data can be subclassified as discrete or continuous. Figure 1.1 shows this pictorially.

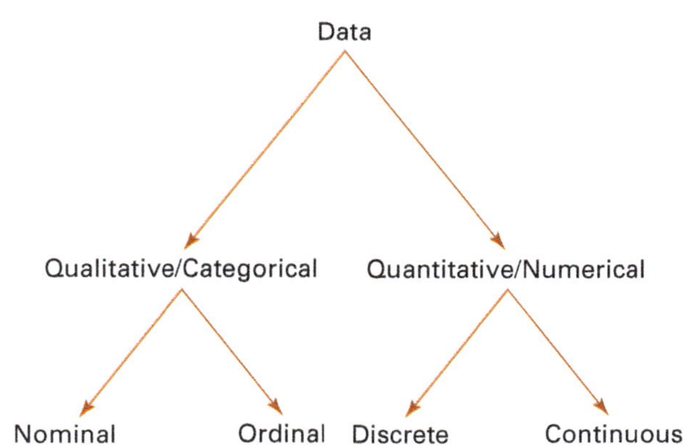

FIGURE 1.1
Types of data

Categorical data

A data type that is simply an identifier or label and has no numerical meaning is **categorical data**. Indeed, such data are often not numbers. For example, the employment of a person (teacher, doctor, lawyer, engineer, business executive, other) is a categorical data type. As another example, the grade in a test (A, B, C, D, E, F) is again simply a label and is a categorical data type. Notice that the two examples are slightly different, in that employment of a person cannot be ranked in any meaningful way, but the test grades have a natural ordering. Thus, the first example is a *nominal* data type, while the second is an *ordinal* data type.

Numerical data

Numerical data have a natural order and the numbers represent some quantity. Two examples are the number of heads in ten tosses of a coin and the weights of rugby players. Note that in the first example we know in advance exactly which values the data may take, namely 0, 1, . . . , 10, whereas in the second example all we can give is perhaps a range (say, 80–140 kg). The first example is that of a *discrete* data type, where we can list the possible values. The second example is that of a *continuous* data type, where we can give only a range of possible values for the data. Discrete data often arise from counting processes, while continuous data arise from measurements.

Some data that may be considered to be discrete are often taken as continuous for the purposes of analysis. For example, a person's salary is discrete (that is, in dollars and cents), but because the range of the data is large and often the number of observations is also large, such data are considered to be continuous.

DEMONSTRATION PROBLEM 1.1

PROBLEM: Shoppers in a city are surveyed by the chamber of commerce. Some of the questions in the survey are listed below. What type of data will result from each of the following questions?

1. What is your age (in years)? _____
2. Which mode of transport did you use to travel to the city today?
   ☐ Public ☐ Private
3. How far did you travel to the city today (in kilometres)? ______
4. How much did you spend in the city today? _____
5. What did you spend most of your money on today? (choose one)
   ☐ Clothes ☐ Shoes ☐ Food ☐ Electronic goods ☐ Services ☐ Other
6. How satisfied are you with your shopping experience in the city? (circle one)
   Very satisfied Satisfied Neutral Unsatisfied Very unsatisfied

SOLUTION: Question 1 is age in years, so it is a discrete variable. However, for the purpose of analysis age, like salary, is often regarded as continuous.

In question 2, the shopper is asked to categorise the type of transport they used. The responses to this question cannot be ranked or ordered in any meaningful way. Therefore the mode of transport data are categorical, nominal.

Questions 3 and 4 involve measurement and so provide continuous data.

Question 5 results in categorical, nominal data. The data cannot be ranked or ordered.

Question 6 provides categorical ordinal data, as the responses can be ranked or ordered in a sensible and natural way.

Cross-sectional and time-series data

Data that are collected at a fixed point in time are called **cross-sectional data**. Such data give a snapshot of the measured variables at that point in time. For example, Roy Morgan Research conducts and publishes monthly surveys of consumer confidence. The monthly survey provides information on consumer confidence for the given month.

Often data are collected over time. Such data are called **time-series data**. For example, data that consist of consumer confidence over several months or years are time-series data. Note that, unlike cross-sectional data, time-series data are time dependent. Such dependence needs to be appropriately modelled and accounted for in the data analysis.

1.3 Obtaining data

Decisions such as how many units of a product to produce, which processes should be changed to improve quality and which export market to target, can all be better informed through statistics. Statistical analysis begins with data. Deciding what data are needed and how to obtain them are essential for any person or organisation seeking to make an informed business decision. Assessing the quality of data is also important, because it is impossible to produce high-quality statistical analyses — and thus make good decisions — from poor-quality data.

Data that were collected for some other purpose and are already available are known as **secondary data**. Secondary data are available from external and internal sources. External sources of secondary data include government departments, industry associations, academic institutions and commercial research organisations. Internal sources might include sales figures, production records or customer evaluations. In business, the decision maker should always look for secondary data before conducting a data-collecting exercise. Where the required information already exists, further data gathering will likely be a waste of the organisation's time and money. However, secondary data may not adequately fit the purpose, may be out of date or may have been obtained or processed in some way that is not statistically valid.

Data collected to address a specific need are known as **primary data**. Primary data might be collected using a survey, experiment or some other study.

Obtaining secondary data

Government and government-related organisations are the largest source of secondary data. Most Asia–Pacific nations have a national statistics agency. The types of data typically available from these agencies include key economic, social and demographic indicators. In Australia the agency is the Australian Bureau of Statistics, and in New Zealand it is Statistics New Zealand. Other agencies in the region include the Statistics Bureau of Japan, Korea National Statistical Office, Statistics Indonesia, National Statistical Office of Thailand, Department of Statistics Malaysia and Statistics Singapore. Key economic data are also provided by the Reserve Bank of Australia and equivalent bodies in other countries, such as the Monetary Authority of Singapore, Bank Negara Malaysia, Bank of Indonesia and Reserve Bank of New Zealand. In addition to these national agencies, local government authorities often have significant data holdings in relation to their areas of responsibility.

A number of peak multinational organisations publish secondary data. The United Nations, Organisation for Economic Co-operation and Development (OECD), World Bank, and Association of Southeast Asian Nations (ASEAN) are good sources of data.

Industry associations such as the Australian Recording Industry Association and Horticulture New Zealand are also often excellent sources of secondary data specific to their industries. In the commercial domain, market reports on subjects such as market trends and financial indicators are available for purchase or on a subscription basis from organisations such as Dun and Bradstreet or ANZ Bank. Universities are also great sources of secondary data from their research programs.

When evaluating secondary data, it is extremely important to consider the reliability of the data collection agency (some countries, for example, have better collection capabilities than others), the data's relevance to your situation, the comparability of the data and the currency of the data.

Obtaining primary data

If a decision has been made to obtain primary data, the necessary research can be done in-house or by an external supplier of research services. Large businesses might have a dedicated research department; smaller ones might have someone with adequate research skills; others might have no in-house research expertise. Even if there is research expertise within a business, it would still be common for an outside service to be engaged, subject to the availability of funds. External research suppliers range from small consultancy operations to large multinationals such as Nielsen and BIS Shrapnel.

Another common way to obtain data is by customer surveys. Surveys need particular care as the results are unreliable unless the sample is taken at random and represents the target population. For example, *voluntary response surveys*, where the subject chooses to be in the survey, suffer from what is called *self-selection bias*; that is, individuals select themselves into the sample, thus producing a biased sample and consequently biasing any statistics based on the sample. Such samples do not represent the target population, and so the results are very unreliable. In particular, 'phone-in' surveys conducted by radio and television stations are extremely unreliable, even if the results seem very clear from what are relatively large samples. See section 1.5 for an example of a voluntary response survey.

1.4 Statistical analysis using Excel

Computers offer many opportunities for statistical analyses. Calculations for advanced statistical techniques are tedious and cumbersome to perform. In the business environment, decision makers will almost always be dealing with very large data sets and will commonly use a computer to analyse the data.

Business statisticians use statistical software packages including SPSS, MINITAB and SAS. Some of these specialist packages are quite expensive and require substantial user training. Fortunately, many spreadsheet software packages can analyse data statistically. In this book, when it is appropriate to use a computer, we will use Microsoft Excel for data analysis; it is the most commonly used package in the business environment and is the package you are most likely to use in your professional life. It must be noted, however, that Excel was not specifically designed for statistical analysis and there are some important limitations. In particular, Excel cannot perform every type of statistical analysis, and some charts produced by Excel are of poor quality from a statistical point of view.

We will use Excel's statistical add-in component and the KaddStat add-in that is provided with this text to give extra functionality. It is important to remember, however, that a statistical package is not a replacement for a thorough understanding of correct statistical methods. The statistician must analyse each business or statistical problem to determine the most appropriate statistical methods. Simply relying on convenient software tools that may be at hand without thinking through the best approach can lead to errors, oversights and poor decisions. This book aims to teach you when and how to use statistical methods to provide information that can be used in business decisions.

Getting started with Excel and KaddStat

Excel is part of the Microsoft Office suite. We assume you have this software installed. We give concise instructions for each Excel statistics function as you encounter it for the first time. We do, however, assume a basic familiarity with Excel. If you are not familiar with Excel or the Windows operating system, please refer to Microsoft's online documentation. The instructions in this book are for Microsoft Office 2013.

Excel's Analysis ToolPak add-in

Excel comes with a number of add-ins to provide extra functionality. To use Excel for statistical analysis you will need to load the Analysis ToolPak add-in.

1. To determine whether the Analysis ToolPak add-in is already loaded, click the Data tab. If Data Analysis is listed on the Analysis group, the add-in is already loaded and you can skip to the next section. If Data Analysis does not appear, you will need to follow the steps below to load the add-in.

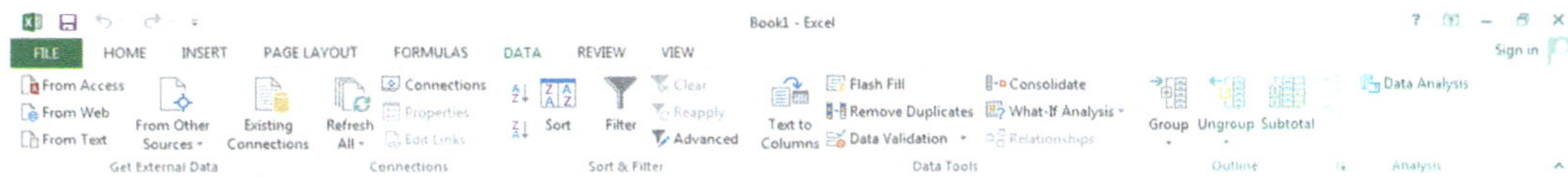

2. Click the File tab at the top left of the screen and select Options.
3. Select Add-ins from the left-hand menu.
4. Choose Excel Add-ins from the Manage drop-down menu and click Go . . .
5. Check the Analysis ToolPak box and click OK.

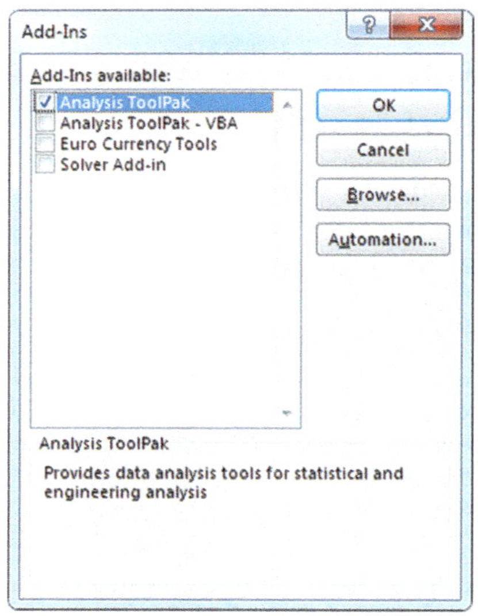

6. If Analysis ToolPak is not listed in the Add-Ins available box, click Browse in the Add-ins dialogue box, and then locate the add-in. If the add-in is not currently installed on your computer, click Yes to install it and follow the instructions for the setup program.
7. Data Analysis will now be listed on the Data tab.

KaddStat

Even with the Analysis ToolPak add-in, Excel's statistical functions are limited. This book comes with the KaddStat statistical analysis add-in to provide further functionality. To perform some of the statistical procedures in this book, you will need to install KaddStat.

1. Download the add-in from the student website, www.johnwiley.com.au/highered/black4e/kaddstat.
2. Unzip the file.
3. Within Excel, click the File tab at the top left of the screen and then click Open.
4. Click Computer and then the Browse icon.
4. Navigate to the downloaded Kadd.xla file. Select it and click Open. If you get a security dialogue box concerning macros, click Enable Macros.
5. If you get an Install KADDstat Option dialogue box, select Install KADDstat as Addin and click Update.
6. Kadd will appear under the Add-Ins tab.

Alternatively, you can copy the Kadd.xla file to a folder on your computer and install it using the same procedure used for installing the Analysis ToolPak add-in.

Using Excel with this book

Most of the demonstration problems in this textbook feature detailed instructions for both a manual solution and one that uses Excel functions, the Analysis ToolPak add-in or the KaddStat add-in. As your knowledge of statistics builds, you may wish to explore KaddStat more fully.

You may note that some of the Excel-generated graphs vary slightly in appearance from your own outputs. These are only cosmetic differences due to individual user settings and can be adjusted via the options on the Home or Page Layout tabs. Should you encounter any cells in scientific notation (i.e. those displaying E+ or E–), they can be reformatted by right-clicking the cell and selecting Format Cells . . . You can then select Number from the Category list, adjust the number of decimal places in the Decimal places field and then click OK.

The role of the software is to facilitate calculations. This is very important, as it allows a statistician to explore more complex models and to perform extended analyses of the data. The statistician's role is then to select the best model, interpret it and discuss its implications in the context of the question to be answered.

1.5 When things go wrong

Analysing data correctly is important. Incorrect analysis can have disastrous consequences. The following three examples of incorrect statistics and the ensuing consequences are presented for you to consider.

Space shuttle *Challenger*

The *Challenger* space shuttle launch on 28 January 1986, from the Kennedy Space Center in Florida, went disastrously wrong and the shuttle exploded 73 seconds into its flight. The launch was on a particularly cold morning, with subzero temperatures. Some engineers argued that low temperatures could cause the failure of the rubber O-rings that sealed the solid rocket boosters. Data on the performance of these O-rings at different temperatures were available, but some flights were omitted from the analysis. This led to an underestimation of the probability of failure of the O-rings at low temperatures. The launch went ahead with disastrous consequences, costing the lives of all seven crew members and billions of dollars.

The Sally Clark case

Sally Clark was the victim of a miscarriage of justice when incorrect statistics were used to convict her of the murder of her two children. Clark's first son died a few weeks after his birth. Two years later, when her second son also died at just a few weeks of age, Clark was arrested and charged with the murder of both children. At her trial, a paediatrician appeared as an expert medical witness and testified that there was only a 1 in 73 million chance that two children from such a family could die of sudden infant death syndrome (SIDS). This statistic was calculated by taking the probability of one such death (the paediatrician quoted 1 in 8543) and squaring it (to give 1 in 73 million). The figure of 1 in 8543 was for a particular set of circumstances that were not entirely applicable to the case. Further, the technique of squaring the probability assumes that the SIDS deaths would be totally independent, meaning there was no family or environmental link involved in SIDS — this is not a valid assumption.

Clark was convicted and sentenced to prison. She was released after three years when evidence came to light that suggested one of the children had died of natural causes. A couple of years after Clark's conviction, the Royal Statistical Society released a statement pointing out the invalidity of the paediatrician's testimony and calling for the courts to rely only on expert statisticians in such cases. Hundreds of other cases were reviewed after Clark was released from prison and two other women convicted of murdering their children were also released.

The 1936 US presidential election

In the 1932 US presidential election, Democrat candidate Franklin D Roosevelt won a sweeping election victory over the sitting Republican president, Herbert Hoover. During Roosevelt's reelection campaign in 1936, the *Literary Digest* conducted a survey by sending out 10 million ballots to voters selected from telephone books and motor vehicle registrations. More than 2.3 million ballots were returned, which is comparatively a very large sample. The results were published and indicated a landslide victory for the Republican challenger, Alf Landon. However, the election was actually won by Roosevelt with a large margin.

The magazine had run a poll for every election since 1920 and correctly predicted the election outcome in each case. The magazine tried to determine what had gone wrong. Polls of this nature suffer from the problem of *voluntary response bias*; that is, people choose whether they will respond, and this can lead to a very biased sample. For example, the people who respond to online surveys or phone-in surveys conducted by television and radio stations are predominantly those who feel strongly about the issue. The results of such surveys are not reliable, even if the sample size is large.

These examples show that it is important to use statistics correctly, as otherwise the results are at best doubtful and at worse simply incorrect. There can be serious consequences of incorrect statistical analysis, from both business and human cost points of view.

While this first course in statistics will prepare you for conducting many types of statistical analyses, you must be aware of the limitations of your knowledge. It is advisable to seek expert advice for more advanced data analysis and interpretation.

SUMMARY

1 Statistics is a mathematical science concerned with the collection, presentation, analysis and interpretation or explanation of data. Two important concepts in statistics are *population* and *sample*. A population is a set of units of interest and a sample is a subset of the population. A sample should be selected in such a way that it is representative of the population. A census is the process of collecting data on the whole population at a given point in time.

The two steps in analysing data are exploratory data analysis (EDA) and inferential statistics. EDA aims to summarise and describe data whereas inferential statistics uses sample data to reach conclusions about the population from which the sample was drawn.

2 Data are broadly classified as qualitative (also called categorical) and quantitative (also called numerical). Qualitative data can be further classified into nominal or ordinal, while quantitative data are further classified into discrete or continuous. The type of data and how they were collected determine which EDA and inference techniques should be used.

Data that are collected at a fixed point in time are called cross-sectional data, while data that are collected over time are called time-series data.

3 Various sources of data are available for answering business questions. Data that are already available are called secondary data. Various agencies routinely collect data and these are useful sources of data for statistical analysis. Data that are collected for a specific purpose are known as primary data.

4 Computers enable fast and accurate statistical analyses of very large amounts of data. In fact, new statistical techniques have become possible due to the increase in computing power. Business statisticians use software packages including SPSS, MINITAB and SAS. Many spreadsheet software packages can also analyse data statistically. Microsoft Excel is the most widely used package for business statistics due to its ease of use, but it is limited in its range of techniques. Remember that software cannot replace a thorough understanding of correct statistical methods.

5 Incorrect data analysis can have disastrous consequences, with large human and business costs. It is important to seek expert help for more complicated statistical analyses.

KEY TERMS

categorical data p. 4
census p. 3
cross-sectional data p. 5
exploratory data analysis (EDA) p. 3
numerical data p. 5
parameter p. 3
population p. 3
primary data p. 6
sample p. 3
secondary data p. 6
statistic p. 3
statistical inference p. 3
time-series data p. 5

REVIEW PROBLEMS

Testing your understanding

1.1 Give a specific example of data that might be gathered from each of the following business disciplines: finance, human resources, marketing, production and management. An example in the marketing area might be 'the number of sales per month by each salesperson'.

1.2 For each of the following companies, give examples of data that could be gathered and what purpose the data would serve: Bluescope Steel, AAMI, Jetstar, IKEA, Telstra, ANZ Bank, Sydney City Council, and Black and White Taxis.

1.3 Give an example of *descriptive* statistics in the recording industry. Give an example of how *inferential* statistics could be used in the recording industry.

1.4 Suppose you are an operations manager for a plant that manufactures batteries. Give an example of how you could use *descriptive* statistics to make better managerial decisions. Give an example of how you could use *inferential* statistics to make better managerial decisions.

1.5 Classify each of the following as nominal, ordinal, discrete or continuous data.

a. The RBA interest rate
b. The return from government bonds
c. The customer satisfaction ranking in a survey of a telecommunications company
d. The ASX 200 index
e. The number of tourists arriving in Australia each month
f. The airline a tourist flies by into Australia
g. The time to serve a customer in a bank queue

1.6 Classify each of the following as nominal, ordinal, discrete or continuous data.

a. The ranking of a company on *BRW*'s top 1000 list
b. The number of tickets sold at a cinema on any given night
c. The identification number on a questionnaire
d. Per capita income
e. The trade balance in dollars
f. Socioeconomic class (low, middle, upper)
g. Profit/loss in dollars
h. A company's ABN
i. Standard & Poor's credit ratings of countries based on the following scale

Rating	Grade
Highest quality	AAA
High quality	AA
Upper medium quality	A
Medium quality	BBB
Somewhat speculative	BB
Low quality, speculative	B
Low grade, default possible	CCC
Low grade, partial recovery possible	CC
Default, recovery unlikely	C

1.7 Powerkontrol Australia designs and manufactures power distribution switchboards and control centres for hospitals, bridges, airports, tunnels, highways and water treatment plants. Powerkontrol's director of marketing wants to determine client satisfaction with its products and services. He developed a questionnaire that yields a satisfaction score between 10 and 50 for participant responses. A random sample of 35 of the company's 900 clients is asked to complete a satisfaction survey. The satisfaction scores for the 35 participants are averaged to produce a mean satisfaction score.

a. What is the population for this study?
b. What is the sample for this study?
c. What is the statistic for this study?
d. What would be a parameter for this study?

1.8 Cricket Australia wants to run a marketing campaign to increase attendance at test matches. You have been hired as a consultant to conduct a survey and prepare a report on your findings.

a. What variables do you consider affect a person's interest in cricket test matches?
b. Design a questionnaire of 10 to 15 questions that will enable you to decide which section of the population the marketing campaign should target.

CHAPTER

2 Charts and graphs

LEARNING OBJECTIVES

After studying this chapter, you should be able to:

1. distinguish between grouped and ungrouped data
2. produce graphical summaries of univariate data — histograms, frequency polygons, ogives, pie charts, stem and leaf plots and Pareto charts
3. produce graphical summaries of two-variable continuous data — scatter plots.

OPENING VIGNETTE

Red tape

Government regulations, sometimes known as 'red tape', can be daunting for businesses. Regulations reflect society's expectations of how a business will operate, and non-compliance can lead to heavy penalties. Many businesses spend considerable time and resources complying with regulations. The table below shows Statistics New Zealand data on businesses' perceptions of their compliance burdens.

Type of regulation	Percentage
None	34.0
Border	4.0
Business and trade laws	13.0
Other industry specific	15.0
Environmental	16.0
Product standard and product safety	19.0
Employment	34.0
Workplace safety	40.0

These data can be displayed as a graph in several ways. Shown here are a pie chart and a vertical bar chart of the data. It may be easier to visually compare categories that are similar in size using a bar chart or a histogram rather than a pie chart. Equally, a Pareto chart could be produced.

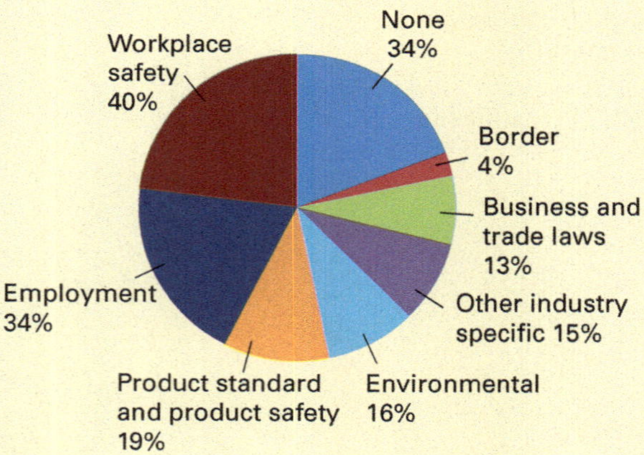

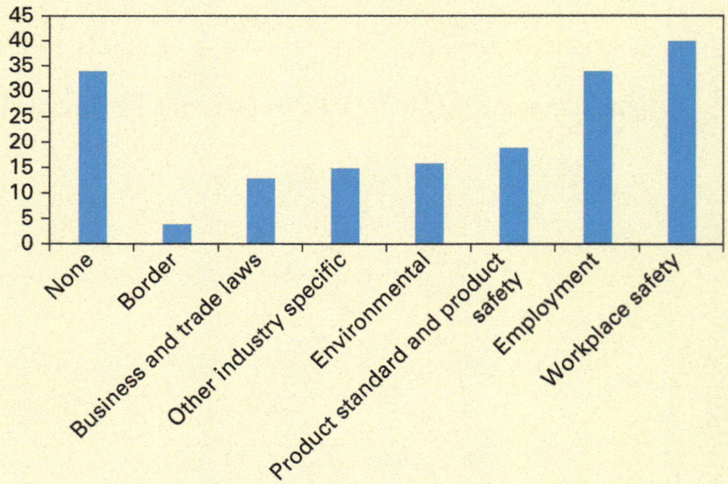

Introduction

The first step in any analysis is summarising and presenting the data in such a way that key features of the data can be identified, such as central location, spread, symmetry, distribution and groupings in the data. Two useful techniques for exploratory data analysis (EDA) are graphical presentation and numerical summaries of data. The methods used to display data and the numerical summaries depend on the type of data.

In this chapter we will focus on presenting data as graphs. Continuous data are usually presented as histograms and categorical data as bar charts or pie charts. In each case, often some grouping of the data is required first.

Note that often data that are not continuous are treated as if they were when analysed. For example, salary is a discrete variable, but due to its wide range of values it is treated as continuous. Most data dealing with money are discrete but are treated as continuous.

CHAPTER CASE

Electronic games

The first interactive video game, 'Tennis for Two', was invented by physicist William Higinbotham in 1958, to entertain visitors to an open day at his research lab. Since then computer and electronic games have come a long way — today they are a part of human culture around the globe.

Computer games have evolved over the decades. A growing market in recent years has been games for mobile phones and other handheld devices. This has led to many opportunities in the 'app' market for mobile devices and some app developers have become very wealthy from successful games.

As in any type of business, marketing is an essential part of raising the profile of a game. Important considerations for marketing are the profile of gamers, price and platform. A survey by Bond University shows that 75% of gamers are older than 18 years, with the average age being 32. Some 47% of gamers are female. More data from the report are presented in the table and chart below.

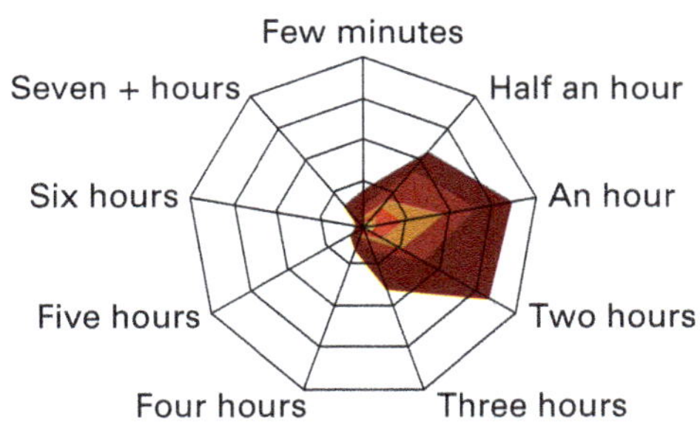

Age (years)	Percentage of total gamers
1 to 5	5
6 to 10	5
11 to 15	10
16 to 25	24
26 to 35	18
36 to 50	19
51 plus	19

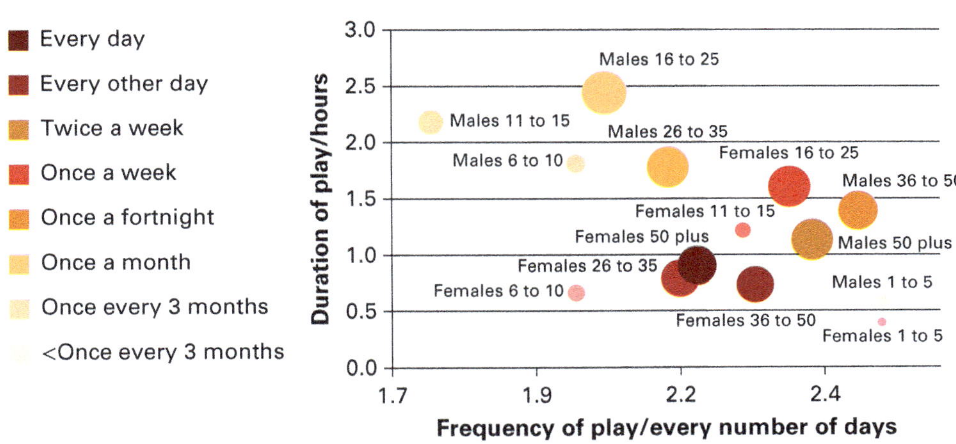

Questions to help managers make decisions

1. The analyst wishes to obtain some insights into the age profile of gamers. If you were preparing a report on these data, what sorts of graph would you include?
2. Study the graph on the previous page. What are the key features of this graph and how will this assist and guide marketing?

2.1 Frequency distributions

Raw data, or *data that have not been summarised in any way*, are sometimes referred to as **ungrouped data**. Table 2.1 contains raw data on the top 50 countries as measured by per capita gross domestic product (GDP). Such a table of data is difficult to interpret and obtain insights from.

TABLE 2.1 Per capita GDP (in international dollars) for the top 50 countries

88 222	39 761	35 059	28 496	22 607
81 466	39 492	34 918	28 073	22 195
56 694	39 171	33 910	27 130	21 460
51 959	38 775	33 885	26 932	19 743
48 333	38 204	30 049	25 492	18 981
47 439	36 730	29 997	24 950	18 841
46 860	36 443	29 830	24 833	18 527
41 950	36 274	29 602	23 308	18 209
40 973	36 081	29 480	23 262	17 819
39 764	35 604	28 960	22 776	17 235

Frequency distributions are a convenient way to group *continuous* data. A **frequency distribution** is a *summary of the data presented as non-overlapping class intervals covering the entire range of data and their corresponding frequencies. Data that have been organised into a frequency distribution* are called **grouped data**. Table 2.2 presents a frequency distribution for the data displayed in table 2.1. The distinction between ungrouped and grouped data is important because the calculation of statistics is different for the two types of data.

TABLE 2.2 Frequency distribution of per capita GDP data

Class interval	Frequency
(0, 20 000]	7
(20 000, 40 000]	34
(40 000, 60 000]	7
(60 000, 80 000]	0
(80 000, 100 000]	2

Before we begin to construct a frequency distribution, some summary statistics of the data are needed. In particular, we need the minimum and maximum data values, from which we can obtain the range. The **range** is defined as the *difference between the largest and smallest data values.*

For the data in table 2.1, the minimum and maximum values are 17 235 and 88 222 respectively (the last and the first data points), so the range is 70 987. Next, we need to decide how many class intervals to use. The number of class intervals will determine the shape of the frequency distribution, so this needs to be chosen carefully so that the key features of the data are revealed. Too many class intervals will fragment the data too much and produce a distribution with too many gaps, while too few class intervals will hide any structure in the data. Some experimentation will usually be required here. The best advice is to experiment with different numbers of class intervals and select a histogram (discussed later in the chapter) according to how well it communicates the distribution of the data for the given context. For the data of table 2.1, we chose five class intervals.

Finally, the width of each class interval needs to be determined. Since we will almost always use class intervals of equal width, we determine the width of each class interval by dividing the range of the data by the number of class intervals and then suitably rounding the result. For the GDP data, we get $\frac{70\,987}{5} = 14\,197.4$, which we round up to 20 000. Since the smallest data point is 17 235, we take the first class interval to be (0, 20 000], and the rest follow from this. *The notation* (0, 20 000] *indicates that the lower end is not included in this interval, but the upper end is included. An alternative way to select class intervals is* [0, 20 000), *so that the lower end is included in the interval and the upper end is not. Another common notation used to indicate class intervals is* 0–under 20 000, *where the lower end is included but the upper end is not. Throughout this text, we will use the notation* (0, 20 000], and this is consistent with Excel outputs.

Note that the intervals need to cover the full range of data, and each data value falls in exactly one class interval.

Class midpoint

The *midpoint of each class* is called the **class midpoint**, also sometimes referred to as the **class mark**. It is calculated by simply taking the midpoint or, equivalently, the average of the class endpoints. For the data in table 2.2, the class midpoint for the first class is $\frac{(0+20\,000)}{2} = 10\,000$. The third column in table 2.3 contains the class midpoint for the data of table 2.2.

The class midpoint is important, as it is taken as the representative value for the class interval.

Relative frequency

Relative frequency is *the ratio of the frequency of the class interval to the total frequency*. This gives the proportion of the total data that lie in the class interval. For the data in table 2.2, the relative frequency for the first interval is $\frac{7}{50}$, or .14. Column four of table 2.3 contains the relative frequencies for the per capita GDP data.

Relative frequencies pave the way for the study of probability. Indeed, if the values were randomly selected from the data in table 2.1, then an estimate of the probability of drawing a given number from the first interval is .14.

Cumulative frequency

The **cumulative frequency** is *the running total of frequencies through the classes of a frequency distribution*. The cumulative frequency of each class interval is found by adding the frequency of that interval to the cumulative frequency of the previous class interval, where the cumulative frequency of the first class interval is simply the frequency of that interval. Column five of table 2.3 (overleaf) gives the cumulative frequencies for the per capita GDP data of table 2.1.

The concept of cumulative frequency is used for many purposes, including sales accrued over a fiscal year, sports scores during a season, years of service, points earned in a reward scheme and business expenses over a period of time.

TABLE 2.3 Class midpoints, relative frequencies and cumulative frequencies for per capita GDP data

Class interval	Frequency	Class midpoint	Relative frequency	Cumulative frequency
(0, 20 000]	7	10 000	.14	7
(20 000, 40 000]	34	30 000	.68	41
(40 000, 60 000]	7	50 000	.14	48
(60 000, 80 000]	0	70 000	.00	48
(80 000, 100 000]	2	90 000	.04	50
Total	**50**		**1.00**	

DEMONSTRATION PROBLEM 2.1

PROBLEM: The dividend yield for 40 ASX-listed companies is given below. Construct a frequency distribution for this data set. Also calculate the class midpoints, relative frequencies and cumulative frequencies.

6.39	5.08	4.28	3.53
5.99	5.07	4.27	3.49
5.97	5.02	4.15	3.20
5.79	4.98	4.00	3.14
5.67	4.93	3.97	2.81
5.60	4.87	3.98	2.75
5.30	4.77	3.86	2.56
5.20	4.68	3.73	2.36
5.19	4.51	3.64	2.35
5.15	4.50	3.59	2.27

SOLUTION: The minimum value is 2.27 and the maximum value is 6.39, so the range of the data is 4.12. We will take class intervals of width 2, with (2.00, 4.00] as the first interval and (6.00, 8.00] as the last. The resulting frequency distribution, class midpoints, relative frequencies and cumulative frequencies are listed in the following table.

Class interval	Frequency	Class midpoint	Relative frequency	Cumulative frequency
(2.0, 4.0]	17	3.0	.425	17
(4.0, 6.0]	22	5.0	.55	39
(6.0, 8.0]	1	7.0	.025	40
Total	**40**		**1.000**	

The frequencies and relative frequencies reveal the most prevalent dividend interval. More than half the companies (57.5%) pay a dividend of more than $4.

USING EXCEL

Frequency tables

DP02-01

1. If you have already installed the Analysis ToolPak, skip to step 2. If you have not already installed the Analysis ToolPak (p. 7), do so now.
   a. Click on the File tab (at the top left-hand corner of the worksheet). Select Options in the list on the left-hand side.

b. Select Add-ins from the menu at the left. Select Excel Add-ins from the Manage dropdown menu near the bottom of the screen, and click Go . . .

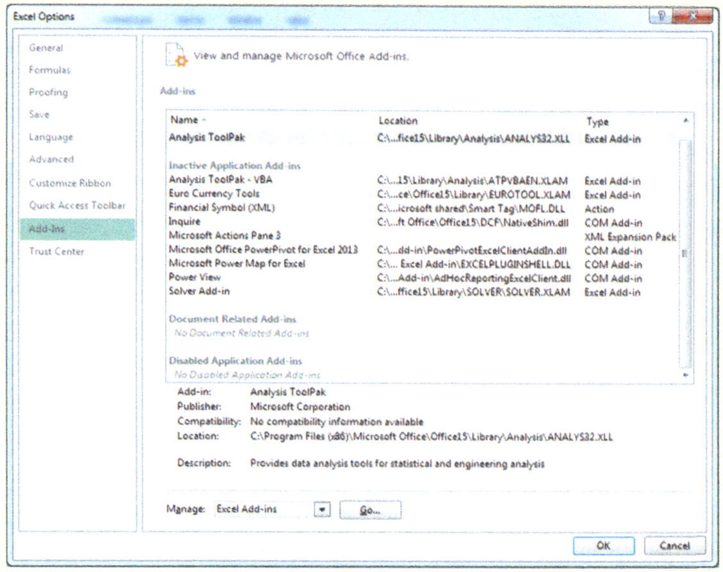

c. Select Analysis ToolPak (if not already selected) and click OK.

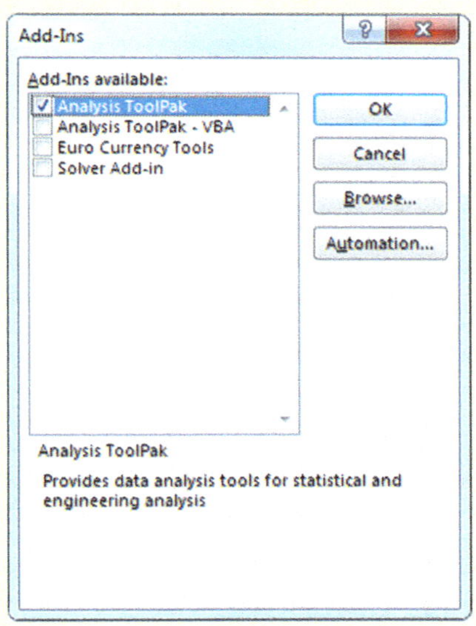

2. In Excel, the class intervals are called bins. If you do not specify bins, Excel will automatically determine the number of bins. To specify the bins, enter the class endpoints in a column of the spreadsheet. In the DP02-01.xls worksheet from the student website, define a set of bins by entering the word Bin in cell E1 and the numbers 2, 4, 6, 8 below it in cells E2 to E5.
3. From the Data tab, click Data Analysis. Choose Histogram from the dialogue box and click OK.
4. In the Histograms dialogue box:
   a. enter the data range, cells A1 to A41, in the Input Range field
   b. enter the bin range, cells E1 to E5, in the Bin Range field
   c. check the Labels box, as you have included labels for the data and the bins

d. select New Worksheet Ply under Output options

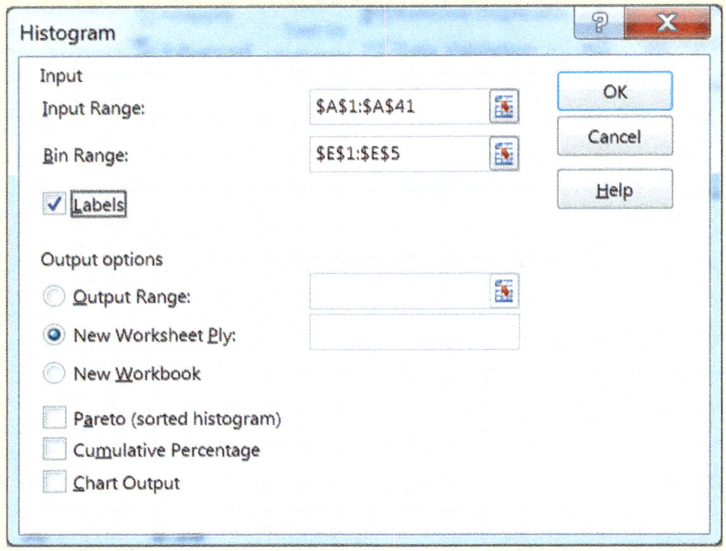

e. click OK.

The Excel output follows.

	A	B	C	D	E	F	G	H
1	*Bin*	*Frequency*						
2	4	17						
3	6	22						
4	8	1						
5	More	0						
6								
7								
8								
9								
11								
12								
13								

From this table, cumulative and relative frequencies can be produced.

PRACTICE PROBLEMS

Practising the calculations

P02-01 **2.1** The average monthly after-tax salary (in dollars) in 2014 for 162 countries is given opposite.

a. Construct a frequency distribution for the data using five class intervals.

b. Construct a frequency distribution for the data using 10 class intervals.

c. Examine the results of (a) and (b) and comment on the usefulness of the frequency distributions in summarising these data.

6301.73	2693.05	1250.00	713.11	502.19	350.00
4479.80	2650.03	1226.79	712.50	500.00	350.00
4330.98	2564.89	1081.73	710.22	492.13	346.48
4323.25	2495.86	1080.44	701.28	491.37	340.22
4250.00	2495.43	1020.48	686.16	487.08	334.60
4215.43	2470.36	1018.58	667.58	481.21	330.73
4038.08	2457.33	1017.82	650.00	474.66	312.89
3990.69	2236.71	979.60	644.09	466.74	304.25
3780.69	2228.21	953.44	636.99	464.89	299.37
3313.01	2176.15	949.50	633.02	460.00	281.62
3269.62	2174.36	947.95	632.67	452.11	281.33
3258.85	2117.76	937.16	627.30	447.61	274.10
3200.00	2087.14	914.97	614.24	434.19	267.21
3181.11	1911.78	905.62	592.50	425.61	264.33
3081.34	1874.63	869.71	589.82	421.11	251.75
3025.00	1786.07	862.60	572.85	415.59	249.00
2991.21	1704.12	808.02	570.79	400.00	244.09
2960.54	1703.52	786.93	564.76	393.03	243.94
2937.58	1635.15	779.04	564.23	386.85	239.31
2924.10	1625.00	770.21	562.45	379.79	229.00
2851.85	1618.85	757.92	533.33	365.00	213.58
2833.33	1562.20	757.22	528.84	360.72	209.33
2782.43	1441.00	756.06	524.84	359.29	200.00
2773.50	1400.01	731.68	522.86	357.71	191.18
2761.99	1337.74	731.14	507.08	352.62	166.49
2759.38	1307.43	729.94	506.76	351.83	39.37
2731.12	1275.66	719.49	502.78	351.22	25.05

P02-02 **2.2** Data were collected on the number of passengers at each train station in Melbourne. The numbers for the weekday peak time, 7 am to 9:29 am, are given below. Construct a frequency distribution for these data. What does the frequency distribution reveal about train usage in Melbourne?

456	1189	410	318	648	399	382	248	379	1240	2268	272
267	1113	733	262	682	906	338	1750	530	1584	7729	323
1311	1632	1606	982	878	169	583	548	429	658	344	2630
538	494	1946	268	435	862	866	579	1359	1022	1618	1021
401	1181	1178	637	2830	1000	2958	962	697	401	1442	115
454	2837	789	1396	603	2400	970	596	1841	1005	603	1386
867	692	245	1187	1548	697	656	1494	103	750	2199	647
987	528	337	874	1508	1630	148	883	1086	256	1443	309
487	278	1101	2286	1559	477	981	422	694	174	1245	647
497	1042	875	1028	208	1435	1420	1136	641	401	104	472
934	574	388	242	1222	95	742	1393	930	707	1117	339
1430	1616	1284	856	1079	362	1461	1120	909	1199	677	163
349	513	2447	593	669	244	1115	1112	367	721	640	287
746	364	254	239	348	514	519	1864	695	187	698	221
346	1180	643	4604	803	434	563	1365	661	649	528	1131
547	663	631	3074	767	1058	216	1406	814	1209	303	380
515	2521	343	2746	1018	686	750	537	1554	438	380	1292

2.3 The owner of a fast-food restaurant ascertains the ages of a sample of customers. From these data, the owner constructs the frequency distribution shown. For each class interval of the frequency distribution, determine the class midpoint, relative frequency and cumulative frequency.

Class interval	Frequency
(0, 5]	6
(5, 10]	8
(10, 15]	17
(15, 20]	23
(20, 25]	18
(25, 30]	10
(30, 35]	4

What does the relative frequency tell the fast-food restaurant owner about customer ages?

Testing your understanding

2.4 The human resources manager for a large company commissions a study in which the employment records of 500 company employees are examined for absenteeism (days off work) during the past year. The consultant conducting the study organises the data into a frequency distribution, shown below, to assist the human resources manager in analysing the data. For each class of the frequency distribution, determine the class midpoint, relative frequency and cumulative frequency. Write a brief statement interpreting this information regarding absenteeism in the company during the past year.

Class interval	Frequency
(0, 2]	218
(2, 4]	207
(4, 6]	56
(6, 8]	11
(8, 10]	8

2.5 List three specific uses of cumulative frequencies in business.

2.2 Graphical display of data

Graphical displays are an effective way of presenting data and showing key features of the data, such as shape, distribution, spread, central location, presence of groups in the data and outliers. Graphs and charts provide an overall picture of the data and some useful conclusions can be reached merely by studying the chart or graph. Converting data to graphics requires judgement and experimentation. Often the most difficult step in this process is to reduce important and sometimes extensive data to a graph that is both clear and concise, and yet consistent with the message of the original data. One of the most important uses of graphical displays in statistics is in determining the shape of a distribution. Six types of graphic displays are presented here: (1) histogram, (2) frequency polygon, (3) ogive, (4) pie chart, (5) stem and leaf plot and (6) Pareto chart.

Histograms

Histograms are the most useful and common graphs for displaying *continuous* data. A **histogram** is a vertical bar chart, where the *area* of the bar is equal to the frequency of the corresponding interval. This then gives a visual representation of the number of data points in each interval. When the intervals are of equal width, the area of each bar is proportional to the height of the bar, so in this case the height of the bar represents the frequency of the corresponding interval.

Note that bar charts (also called column graphs) are also used for categorical data. The difference is that histograms, representing continuous data, have no gaps between the bars, whereas bar charts, representing categorical data, have gaps between the bars.

A histogram can show the shape of the distribution, spread or variability, central location of data and any unusual observations such as outliers. Histograms are very sensitive to the selection of class intervals. In practice one will prepare several histograms and select the one that represents data the best, that is, the one that highlights the key features of the data most clearly.

Figure 2.1 shows a histogram of per capita GDP data, corresponding to the frequency distribution in table 2.2. Note that the labels in the *centres of the bars are the right-hand endpoints of the intervals*, a quirk of Excel. From the histogram we see that the GDP values are between $0 and $100 000. Most of the GDP values fall between $20 000 and $40 000. The histogram is not symmetrical; that is, the right half is not the mirror image of the left half. Most of the data lie below $40 000, with only a few values above it. We call such data *right skewed* or *positively skewed*. Two countries have rather large per capita GDP values. These are away from the bulk of the data and are considered to be **outliers**.

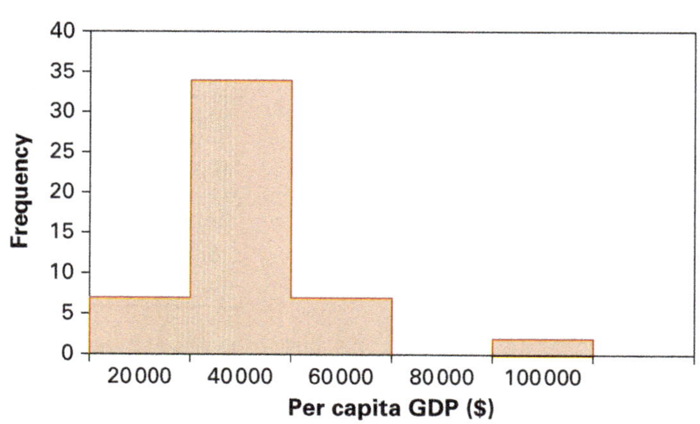

FIGURE 2.1 Histogram of per capita GDP data

Figure 2.2 shows another histogram of the same data with a different selection of interval width. This provides more detail and more information. The second histogram is a better representation of these data, as it gives a more smooth appearance and a better representation of the distribution. It is also clear that there are two outliers between 80 000 and 90 000.

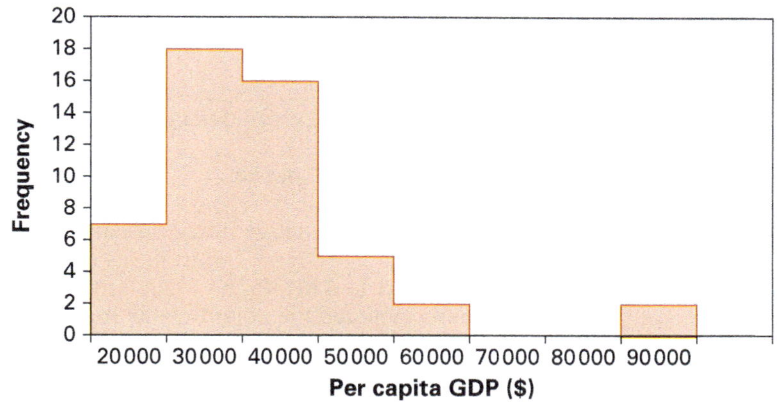

FIGURE 2.2
Histogram of per capita GDP data using different class intervals

As another example, consider the national debt as a percentage of GDP for 132 countries. Figure 2.3 shows a histogram of these data. What can we learn from this histogram? Virtually all national debts fall between 0 and 100%. There are a few values that are much larger than the rest of the data. The data are right or positively skewed, a common feature of most financial data.

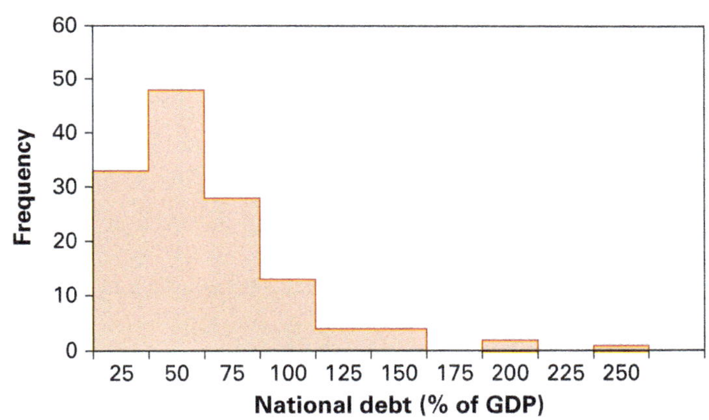

FIGURE 2.3
Histogram of per capita GDP

In statistics, it is often useful to determine whether data are approximately normally distributed (bell shaped) as shown in figure 2.4. We can see by examining the histogram in figure 2.3 that the national debt data are not normally distributed. In addition, the histogram shows some outliers in the upper end of the distribution. Outliers are data points that appear outside of the main body of observations; they may indicate phenomena that differ from those represented by other data points and should be investigated further. In these data, the extreme outlier represents the debt as a percentage of GDP for Zimbabwe (234.1%). These and other insights can be gleaned by examining the histogram and show that histograms play an important role in the initial analysis of data.

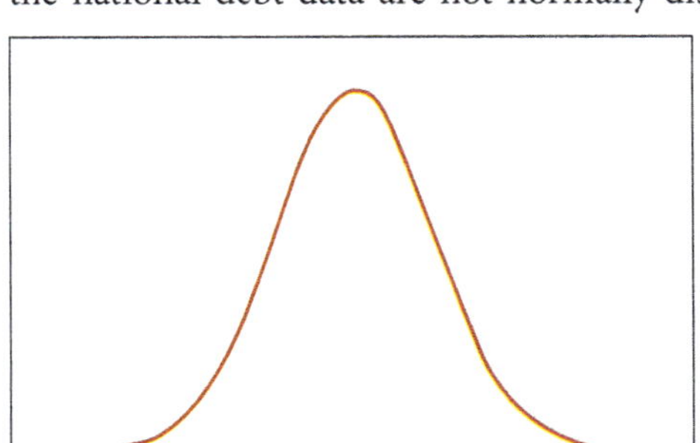

FIGURE 2.4
Normal distribution

DEMONSTRATION PROBLEM 2.2

The file DP02-02.xls on the student website contains the minimum salaries (in $000) offered for 130 accounting-related jobs advertised on the Seek website. Produce a histogram of the data.

USING EXCEL

Histograms

We will first produce a histogram using Excel's default bin settings.

DP02-02

1. Access DP02-02.xls from the student website.
2. From the Data tab, select Data Analysis.
3. From the Data Analysis dialogue box, select Histogram and click OK.
4. In the Histogram dialogue box:
   a. enter the data range, cells A1 to A131, in the Input Range field
   b. check Labels as you have included the column label in the input range
   c. select New Worksheet Ply under Output options
   d. check Chart Output to generate a histogram

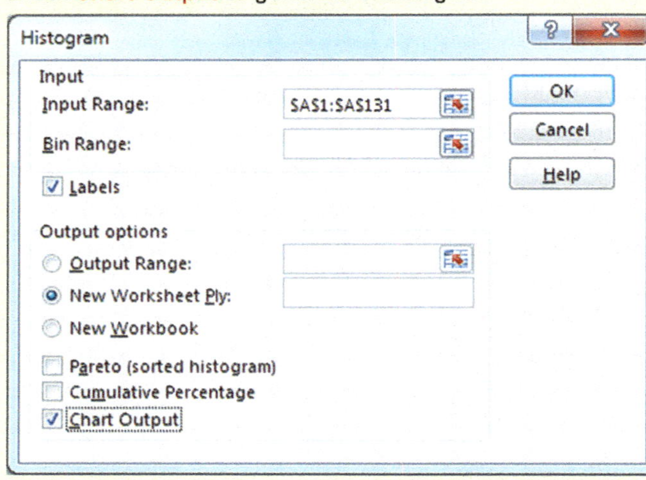

   e. click OK.

The Excel output follows.

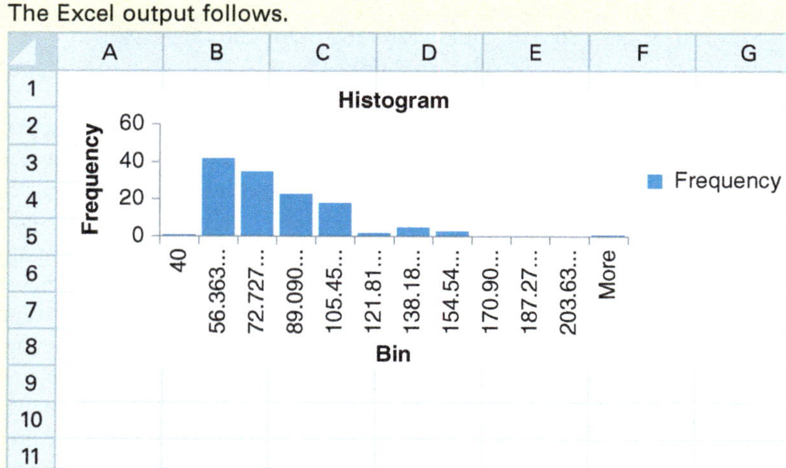

The histogram that Excel produces is really a bar chart and has gaps between the bars. Note also that the last class interval (or Bin as it is referred to in Excel) is always labelled 'More' by Excel, and this class contains all the data above the last class interval. In the histogram, the 'More' category always appears next to the last class interval, regardless of the *actual data values*. Consequently, this histogram hides the true location of any outliers that may be present far above the rest of the data and masks the relativity of the data values.

We next eliminate the gaps and convert this chart into a histogram:

5. Place the cursor over any of the bars.
6. Now right-click on the bar and select Format Data Series . . .
7. In the Series Options task pane, reduce the Gap Width to 0%.

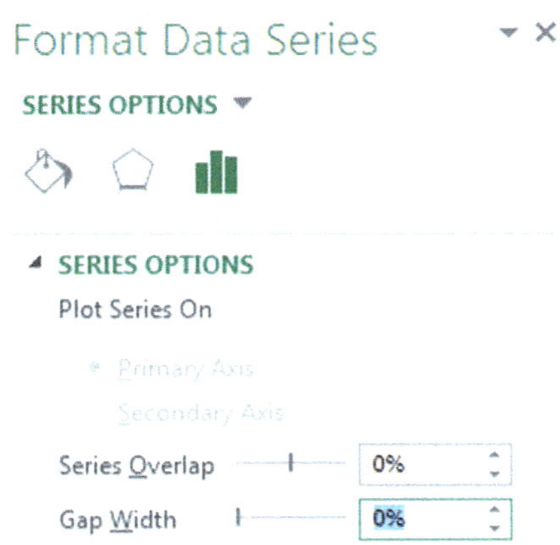

8. You can also put a border around the histogram. Right-click on the white space near the edge of the chart and select Format Chart Area . . . In the Format Chart Area task pane, click on Border and select Solid line. You can also select the colour of the line via the Color drop-down menu.

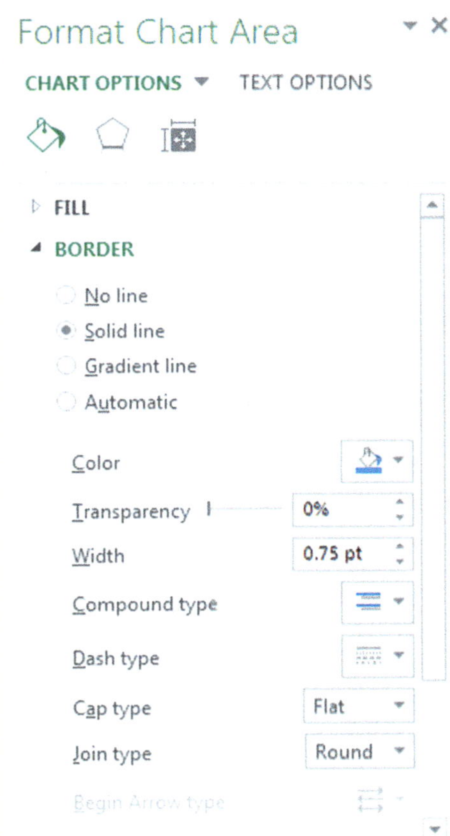

9. Remove the legend (Frequency) from the graph by selecting it and pressing the Delete key.
10. Select the *x* axis title (Bin) by clicking on it and change it to Salaries ($000) simply by typing over it.

11. The *x* axis has labels to several decimal places. To change this, select the numerical data from the Bin range in column A. Right-click and select Format Cells... Choose the Number tab, and then select Number in the Category menu. Choose the desired number of Decimal places, say 1, and click OK.
12. Finally, give the chart a more meaningful title (say, Accounting salaries) by selecting the current title (Histogram) and simply typing over it.

    Note that you can change the fonts of any of the text on the chart by selecting it and making amendments via the standard buttons in the Font group within the Home tab. Also note that there are more layout options within the Layout tab.

    The final output follows.

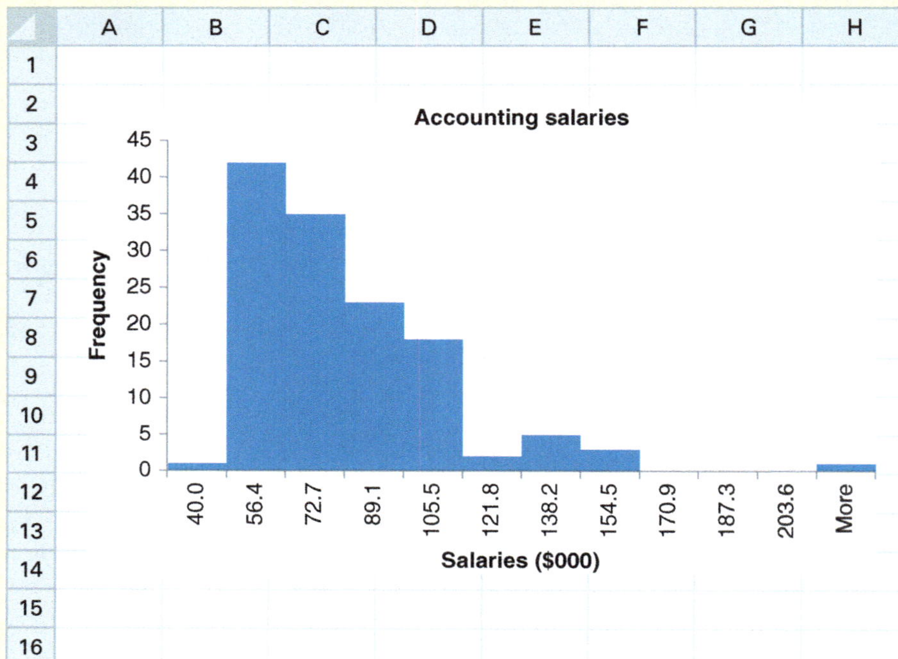

As mentioned earlier, this chart has several problems, the worst of which is the More class interval, which hides the actual values of the data points. To fix this, we will redo the histogram with our own choice of bins.

13. First, we need to obtain the minimum value, maximum value and range of the data. These are found by clicking Data Analysis from the Data tab, selecting Descriptive Statistics and clicking OK.
14. Enter the data range, cells A2 to A131, as the Input Range and check the Summary Statistics box. Then click OK.
15. This produces a variety of statistics. The minimum and maximum values are 40 and 220 respectively, so the range is 180. Class intervals (bins) of width 20 will give 10 intervals. Thus we define the bins to start from 50 (this is the upper end of the first bin so the lowest data point is included) in intervals of 20, ending at 230 (so the last data point is included). In column C, enter Bin in cell C1 and 50 in cell C2, and fill in the column using an appropriate formula. Alternatively, select cell C2 (containing the first bin value of 50) and then, from the Home tab's Editing group, click Fill and then select Series... Select Columns under Series in. Enter 20 for the Step value and 230 for the Stop value. Click on OK.

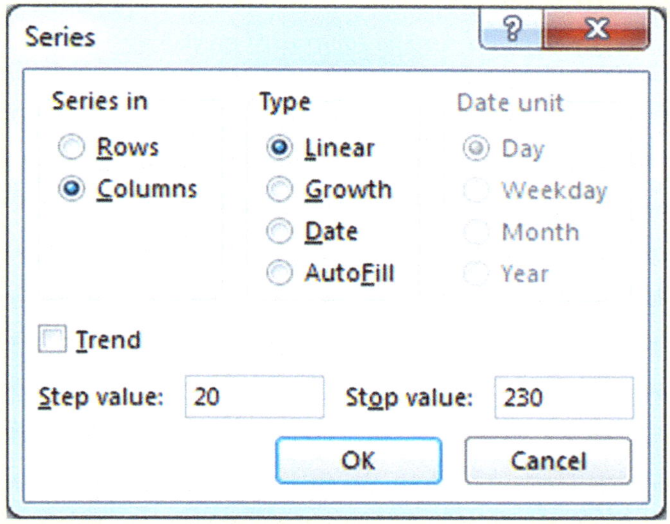

16. The method for producing the histogram is the same as before, except that now we will need to provide the location of the bins in the histogram dialogue box as we did for the frequency distribution in demonstration problem 2.1. Note that the More label for the last interval remains, but there are no data points in it. To delete this from the chart, simply delete the row corresponding to More from the Bin output produced by Excel. After tidying up the chart as previously, the following output is obtained.

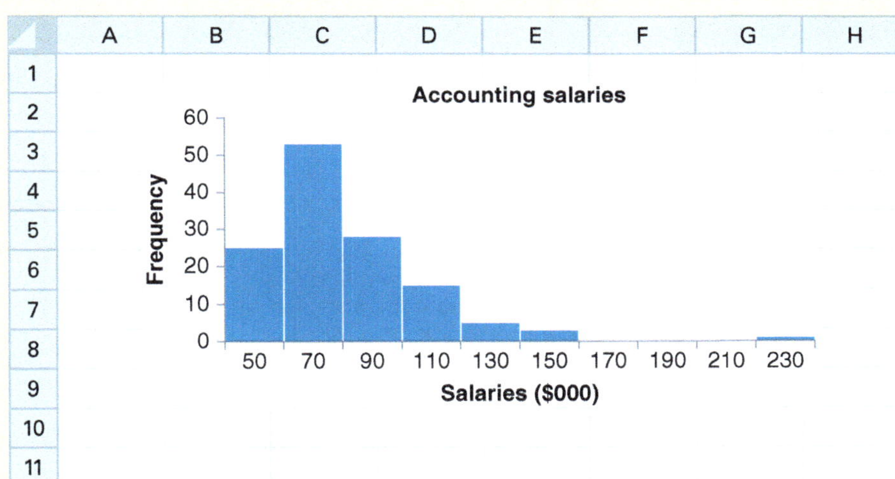

Clearly, most salaries are between $30 000 and $70 000 and almost all of them are below $110 000. There is one outlier corresponding to a salary between $210 000 and $230 000. The salaries are right skewed, typical of financial data.

Our recommendation is to use Excel's default choice of bin (class intervals) *only as a guide* and to obtain some initial impressions. Some adjustments will often be required to capture the key features of the data. Thus, the final histogram should be produced using your own bin ranges and Data Analysis in Excel.

Frequency polygons

A **frequency polygon** is *a graph constructed by plotting a dot for the frequencies at the class midpoints and connecting the dots.*

Construction of a frequency polygon begins, as with a histogram, by plotting the class endpoints along the *x* axis and the frequency values along the *y* axis. A dot is plotted for the frequency value at the midpoint of each class interval (class midpoint). Connecting these midpoint dots completes the graph. Figure 2.5 shows a frequency polygon of the distribution data in table 2.2. The information gleaned from frequency polygons and histograms is similar. As with the histogram, changing the scales of the axes can compress or stretch a frequency polygon, which affects the user's impression of what the graph represents.

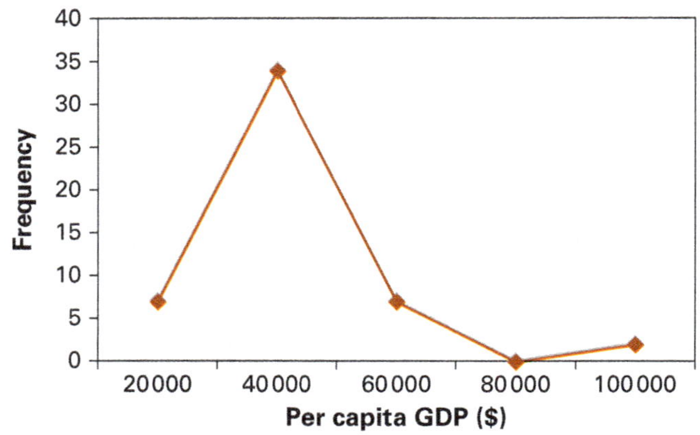

FIGURE 2.5 Frequency polygon of per capita GDP data

DEMONSTRATION PROBLEM 2.3

Use Excel to produce a frequency polygon for the accounting salaries data in demonstration problem 2.2.

USING EXCEL

Frequency polygons

To produce a frequency polygon, first a frequency distribution has to be obtained using the histogram feature described in demonstration problems 2.1 and 2.2.

As you learned in demonstration problem 2.1, Excel's Data Analysis feature is used to produce the frequency distribution.

DP02-03

1. Access DP02-03.xls from the student website.
2. From the Insert tab, select Line in the Charts group.
3. Select the first 2-D Line chart sub-type.
4. Right-click on the Chart Area and choose Select Data.
5. In Chart data range, select cells B2 to B11 in the Frequency column (do not include the column label).

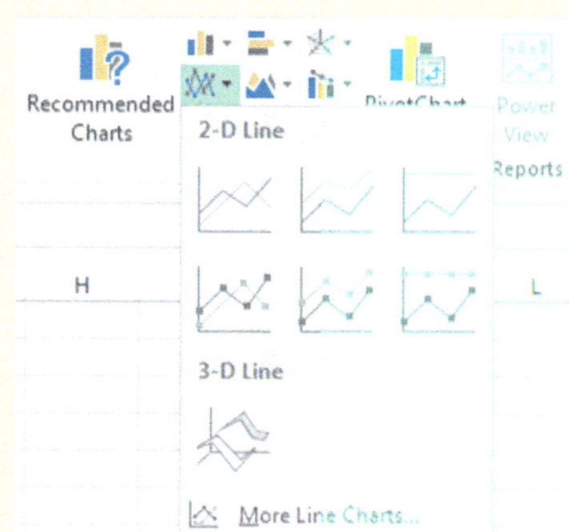

6. Select Edit in the Horizontal (Category) Axis Labels box.
7. In Axis label range, select cells A2 to A11 in the Bin column (do not include the column name), and click OK.

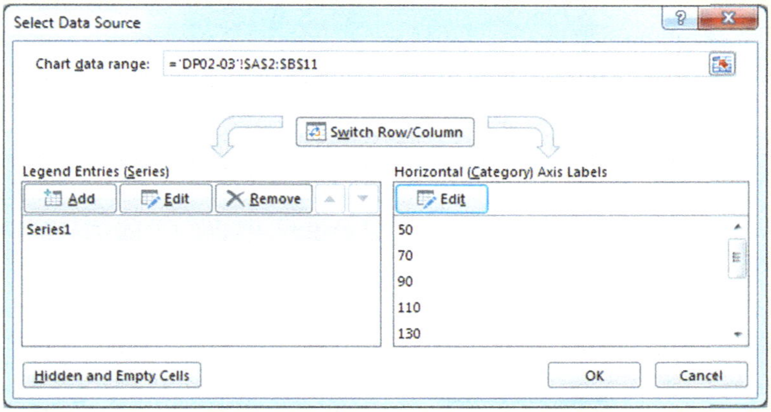

8. Click OK again in the Select Data Source dialogue box.
9. Click on the Chart Elements button (the large plus sign) next to the chart and ensure Axis Titles is checked. In the Axis Titles sub-menu, ensure Primary Horizontal and Primary Vertical are checked.
10. In the chart area, type Salaries ($000) over the *x* axis title and type Frequency over the *y* axis.
11. In the Chart Elements box, ensure Chart Title is checked and choose Above Chart in the sub-menu.
12. In the chart area, type Frequency polygon of accountant salaries over Chart Title. The font size can be reduced in the usual way (in the Font group under the Home tab).
13. Click on the legend, which reads Series1, and delete it.

You can explore additional options in the Chart Elements box, and on the Chart Tools Format tab.

The Excel output follows.

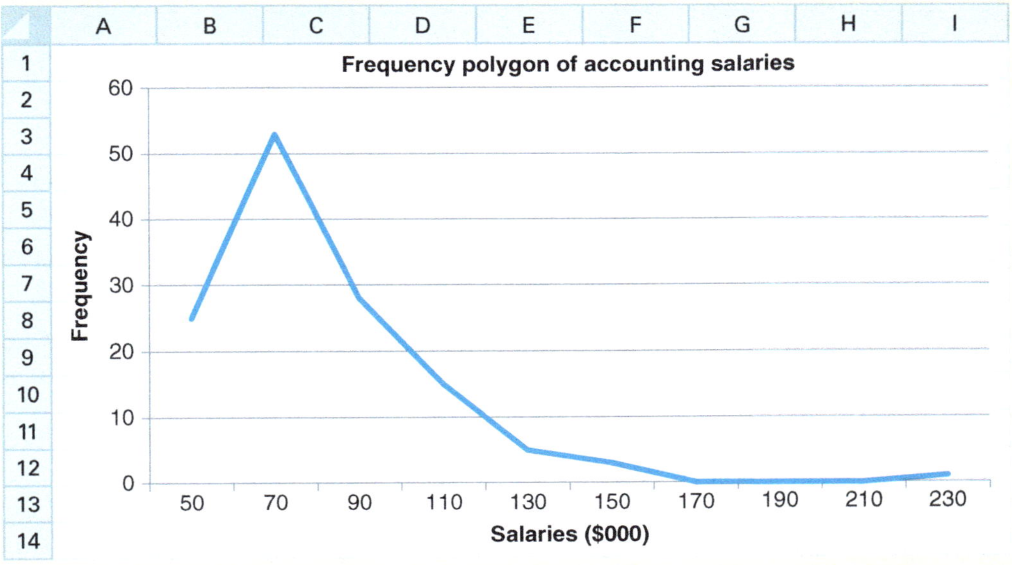

Ogives

An **ogive** (pronounced *o-jive*) is *a cumulative frequency polygon*. Again, construction begins by labelling the x axis with the class endpoints and the y axis with the frequencies. However, the use of cumulative frequency values requires that the scale along the y axis be large enough to include the frequency total. A dot of zero frequency is plotted at the beginning of the first class and construction proceeds by marking a dot at the *end* of each class interval for the cumulative value. Connecting the dots then completes the ogive. Figure 2.6 presents an ogive for the per capita GDP data in table 2.3.

Ogives are most useful when the decision maker wants to see *running totals*. For example, if a controller is interested in controlling costs, an ogive could depict cumulative costs over a fiscal year.

Steep slopes in an ogive can be used to identify sharp increases in frequencies. In figure 2.6 the steepest slope occurs in the (20 000, 40 000] class.

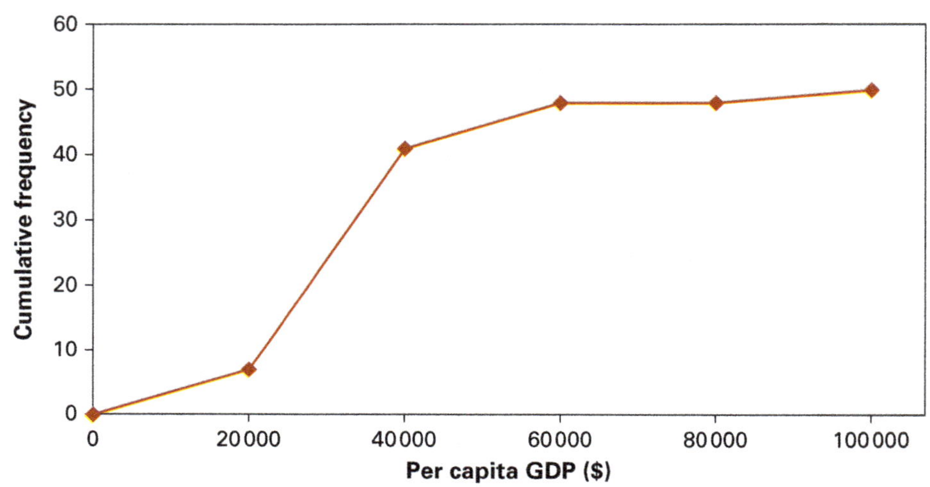

FIGURE 2.6
Ogive of per capita GDP data

DEMONSTRATION PROBLEM 2.4

Use Excel to produce an ogive for the accounting salaries data in demonstration problems 2.2 and 2.3.

USING EXCEL

Ogives

A frequency distribution has been obtained for the accounting salaries data using the method described in demonstration problem 2.1. These data are given in DP02-04.xls, available from the student website.

To create an ogive, we will produce a line graph as for the frequency polygon in demonstration problem 2.3, but include in the data range the class endpoints (bins) and the cumulative frequencies. Note that another class interval is required at the low end to start the ogive at zero.

DP02-04

1. Access DP02-04.xls from the student website.
2. Insert a blank row before the first class endpoint. In cells A2 to C2 enter the numbers 0, 0 and 0, corresponding to the first values of bins, Frequency and Cumulative Frequency respectively (see output on the following page).

3. In cell C3, enter the formula =C2+B3 and copy the formula down column C until cell C12.

	A	B	C
1	*Bins*	*Frequency*	Cumulative Frequency
2	0	0	0
3	50	25	25
4	70	53	78
5	90	28	106
6	110	15	121
7	130	5	126
8	150	3	129
9	170	0	129
10	190	0	129
11	210	0	129
12	230	1	130

4. From the Charts group in the Insert tab, choose the line chart icon and select the first graph on the second row of the options.
5. Right-click on the graph template that appears and click Select Data. For the Chart data range select the Cumulative frequencies from C2 to C12.
6. Click Edit under Horizontal (Category) Axis Labels, and select the bins data from A2 to A12. Click OK and then OK again.
7. Add chart and axis labels and delete the legend as in demonstration problem 2.3. The Excel output follows.

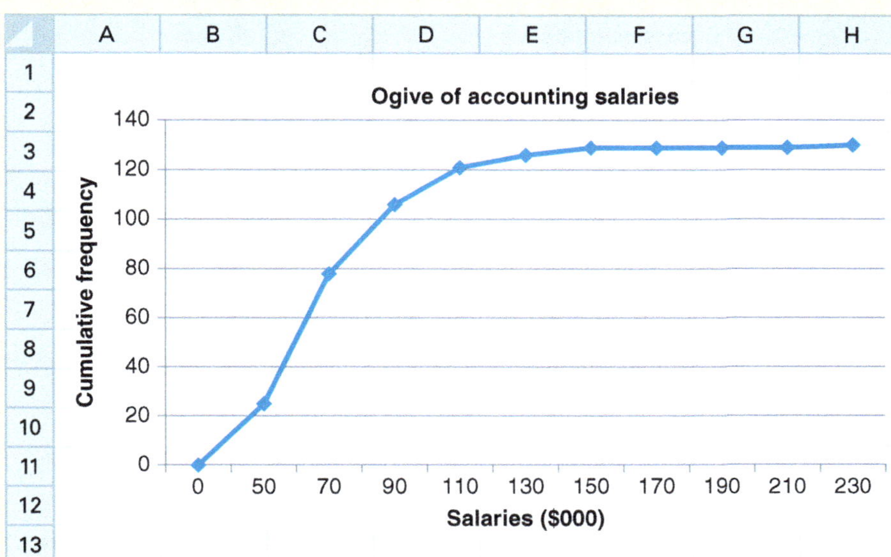

Pie charts

A **pie chart** is used to display categorical data. It is *a circular display of data where the area of the whole pie represents 100% of the data being studied and slices represent percentage contributions of the sublevels.* Pie charts show the relative magnitudes of parts to the whole. They are widely used in business, particularly to depict such things as budget categories, market share, and time and resource allocations. However, the use of pie charts is minimised in science and technology because pie charts can lead to less accurate judgements than are possible with other types of graphs. Generally, it is more difficult for the viewer to interpret the relative sizes of angles in a pie chart than to judge the lengths of rectangles in a histogram or the relative distance of a frequency polygon dot from the x axis. In the Opening vignette feature at the beginning of the chapter, graphical depictions of the percentage of tourists by origin are displayed using both a pie chart and a vertical bar chart, also called a column graph or chart.

To construct a pie chart by hand, first calculate the angle for each slice. This is simply the corresponding fraction of the total angle in a circle. For example, in the business regulations data given in the opening vignette, None accounts for 19% of the regulations, so the angle corresponding to None is $0.19 \times 360° = 68.4°$. The angles for the other regulations are calculated similarly.

DEMONSTRATION PROBLEM 2.5

The Australian Government Insolvency and Trustee Service prepares a profile of debtors. Its data on business reasons for bankruptcy are given below. Prepare a pie chart of the data.

Reason	Percentage
Gambling or speculation	1
Seasonal conditions	2
Inability to collect debts	2
Failure to keep proper books	2
Lack of capital	3
Excessive drawings	4
Lack of business ability	5
Excessive interest	6
Personal reasons	6
Other	28
Economic conditions	42

USING EXCEL

Pie charts

DP02-05

1. Access DP02-05.xls from the student website.
2. Select the data without the column labels.
3. From the Charts group in the Insert tab, click the pie chart icon and select the first option from the list of pie charts.
4. A pie chart immediately appears on the worksheet. We can format this chart to include more information and improve its presentation.
5. Remove the chart legend by clicking on it and deleting it.
6. Next, click on the chart to select it. Click on the Chart Elements button (the large plus sign) next to the chart and ensure that Data Labels is checked. Choose the Center option in the sub-menu. The default labels that are added to the chart are the data values themselves.

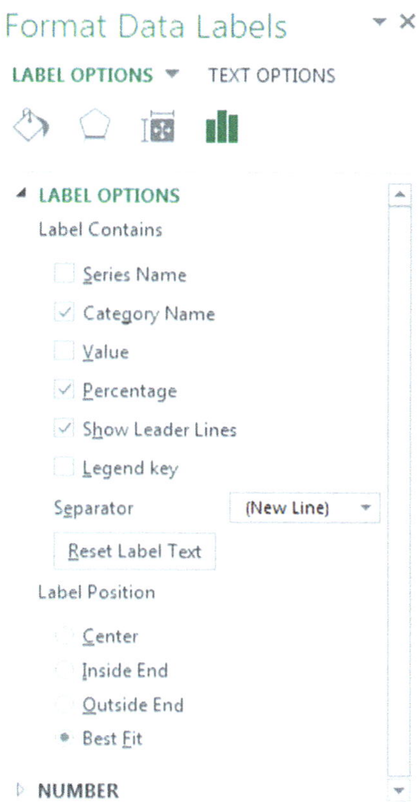

7. Right-click any of the labels to bring up the formatting menu. Select Format Data Labels... In the Format Data Labels task pane, click on Label Options, and check Category Name, Percentage and Show Leader Lines under Label Contains, and Best Fit under Label Position. Uncheck any other options. This adds the category names and corresponding percentages to the chart. If you drag any of the labels away from the pie chart, a line will appear linking the label to its slice.
8. Add and format the chart title as in demonstration problem 2.3. Enter the title Reasons for bankruptcy. The output follows.

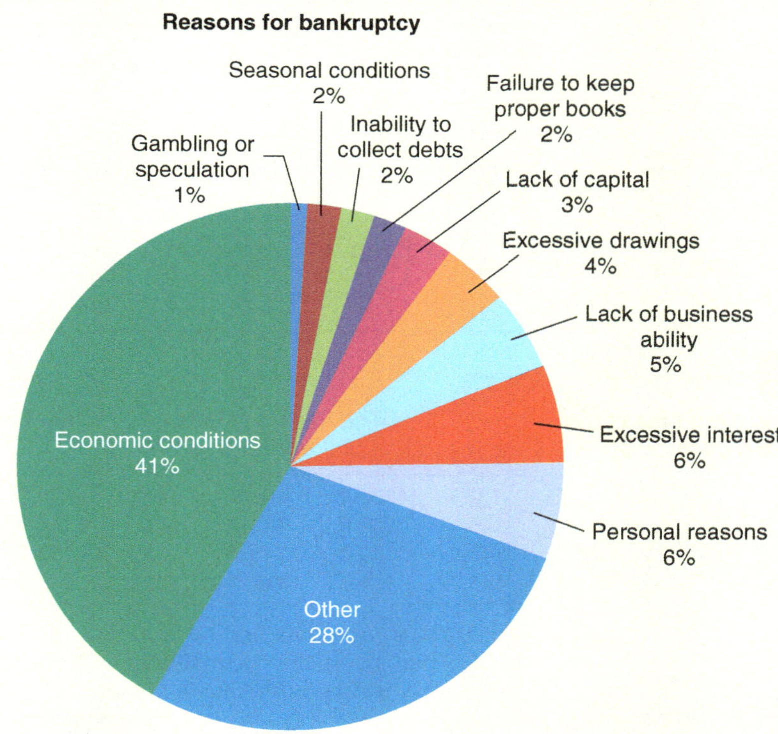

Note that pie charts can be converted to bar charts (and vice versa) simply by right-clicking on the chart, selecting Change Chart Type . . . and then choosing Column.

Stem and leaf plots

Another way to display *continuous* data is by using a **stem and leaf plot**. Each data point is split into a stem and a leaf. The leaf is the rightmost digit of the data, and the rest of the digits form the stem. Thus for the data value 34, 3 is the stem and 4 is the leaf, while for 123, 12 is the stem and 3 is the leaf. The plot is constructed by writing the stem values vertically and then writing the leaf values next to each stem equally spaced horizontally in increasing order. The major advantage of stem and leaf plots is that the original data are preserved on the plot. Otherwise, the stem and leaf plot displays information in a similar way to a histogram.

Table 2.4 (overleaf) contains scores from an examination on plant safety policy and rules given to a group of 35 job trainees. A stem and leaf plot of these data is displayed in figure 2.7 (overleaf). Be sure you understand how the stem and leaf plot was created. For example, for the data item 23,

3 is the leaf and 2 is the stem. For the data item 47, 7 is the leaf and 4 is the stem. There is another data item with 4 as the stem, so its leaf is also included on that line of the plot.

TABLE 2.4 Scores for plant safety examination

86	77	91	60	55
76	92	47	88	67
23	59	72	75	83
77	68	82	97	89
81	75	74	39	67
79	83	70	78	91
68	49	56	94	81

FIGURE 2.7 Stem and leaf plot for plant safety examination scores

Stem	Leaf									
2	3									
3	9									
4	7	9								
5	5	6	9							
6	0	7	7	8	8					
7	0	2	4	5	5	6	7	7	8	9
8	1	1	2	3	3	6	8	9		
9	1	1	2	4	7					

DEMONSTRATION PROBLEM 2.6

PROBLEM: The following data are the monthly telephone bills for 38 households. Construct a stem and leaf plot of the data.

137.9	136.4	142.6	146.0	145.4	145.3	143.5	137.3	132.2	141.8
145.1	144.9	143.7	144.9	144.9	136.9	139.1	137.8	135.8	136.6
144.6	140.3	143.2	133.2	139.2	140.5	142.9	138.8	144.6	145.4
146.7	144.0	142.4	132.8	145.9	141.6	138.9	139.8		

SOLUTION: The data first need to be sorted (you may wish to use Excel's sort feature; see p. 36). Then, using the decimal digit as the leaf (each leaf unit = 0.1) and the rest of the price as the stem, we obtain the following plot.

Stem	Leaf
132	2 8
133	2
134	
135	8
136	4 6 9
137	3 8 9
138	8 9
139	1 2 8
140	3 5
141	6 8
142	4 6 9
143	2 5 7
144	0 6 6 9 9 9
145	1 3 4 4 9
146	0 7

Pareto charts

An important concept gaining popularity in business is total quality management. One of the important aspects of total quality management is the constant search for causes of problems in products and processes. A graphical technique for displaying causes of problems is Pareto analysis. This is a quantitative tallying of the number and types of defects that occur in a product or service. Analysts use this tally to produce *a vertical bar chart that displays the most common types of defects, ranked in order of occurrence from left to right.* This bar chart is called a **Pareto chart** and is a special way of displaying categorical data.

Pareto charts were named after an Italian economist, Vilfredo Pareto, who observed more than 100 years ago that most of Italy's wealth was controlled by a few families who were the major drivers behind the Italian economy. Quality expert JM Juran applied this notion to the quality field by observing that poor quality can often be addressed by attacking a few major causes that result in most of the problems. A Pareto chart enables quality control officers to separate the most important defects from trivial defects, which helps them to set priorities for quality improvement work.

Suppose the number of electric motors being rejected by inspectors for a company has been increasing. Company officials examine the records of several hundred of the motors in which at least one defect was found to determine which defects occurred more frequently. They find that 40% of the defects involved poor wiring, 30% involved a short circuit in the coil, 25% involved a defective plug and 5% involved seizure of bearings. Figure 2.8 is a Pareto chart constructed from this information. It shows that the main three problems in defective motors — poor wiring, a short in the coil and a defective plug — account for 95% of the problems. From the Pareto chart, decision makers can formulate a logical plan for reducing the number of defects.

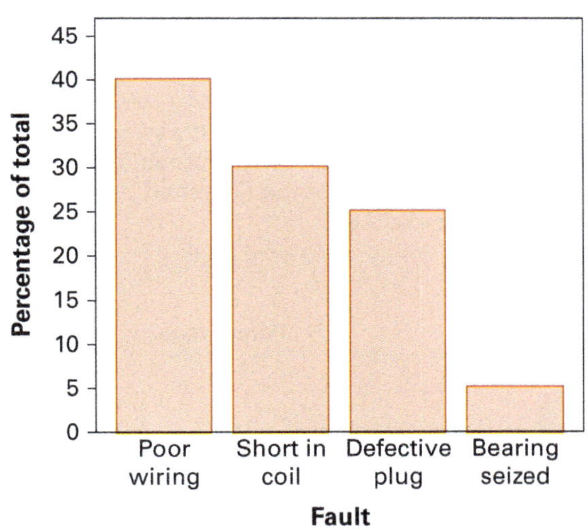

FIGURE 2.8 Pareto chart for electric motor problems

Company officials and workers should first examine and improve the processes that involve wiring. Then data should be re-collected and another Pareto chart constructed to determine the major fault. The reason for re-collecting the data is that fixing the wiring problem may also fix other problems, such as shorts in coils. In this case, there would be no need to waste resources dealing with the coil problem if it is no longer a major cause of faults. This sequence of collecting data, plotting a Pareto chart and addressing the major cause of faults should be a continual process.

DEMONSTRATION PROBLEM 2.7

The following are the reasons people give for returning items at a large variety store, with the corresponding percentages.

- Changed my mind: 25%
- Exchange: 45%
- Unwanted gift: 5%
- No reason: 20%
- Defective item: 5%

Produce a Pareto chart of these data using Excel.

USING EXCEL

Pareto charts

The simplest way to produce a Pareto chart in Excel is to sort the categories into descending percentage order and produce a bar chart.

DP02-07

1. Access DP02-07.xls from the student website.
2. Click on any cell containing the data.
3. From the Data tab, select Sort from the Sort & Filter group.
4. The data will be automatically selected and highlighted on the worksheet. Excel inserts the first row as column names. In the Sort by field, select Percentage, and in the Order field, select Largest to Smallest.

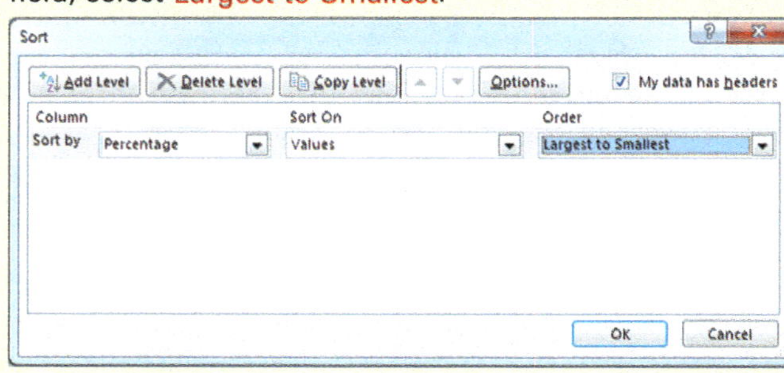

5. Click OK. The data are now sorted in descending order.
6. Select any cell containing the data. From the Insert tab, go to the Charts group, then choose the Column chart icon and select the first chart type. The following bar chart of the data will appear on the worksheet.

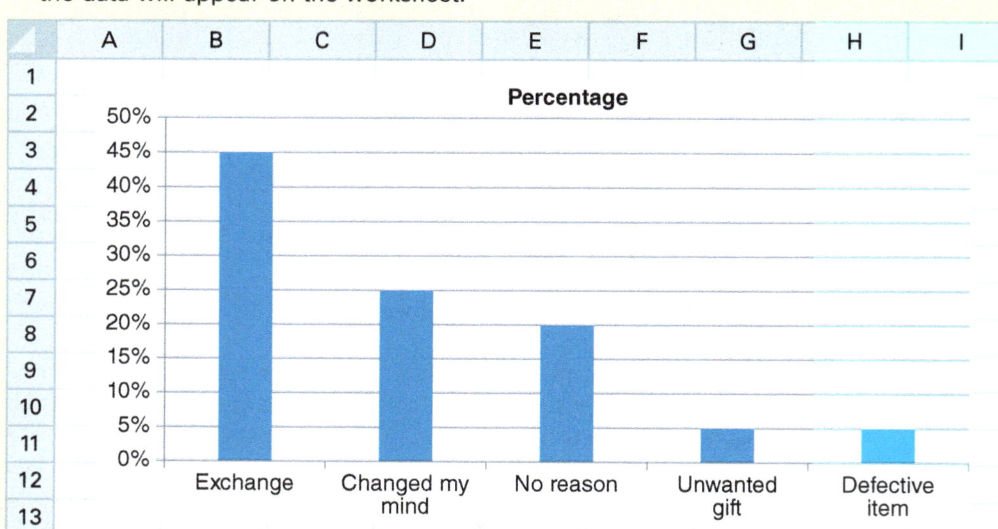

7. Remove the horizontal grid lines by clicking on one of them and pressing the Delete key.
8. You can also put a border around the chart. Right-click at the edge of the chart to show the formatting menu. Select Format Chart Area . . ., then in the Format Shape task pane, click the Border options and choose Solid line and your preferred colour.
9. Finally, select the chart title by clicking on it and change it to one that is more meaningful by simply typing over it. Reduce the font size by highlighting the title and selecting 12 from the drop-down menu in the Font group on the Home tab.

The final chart follows.

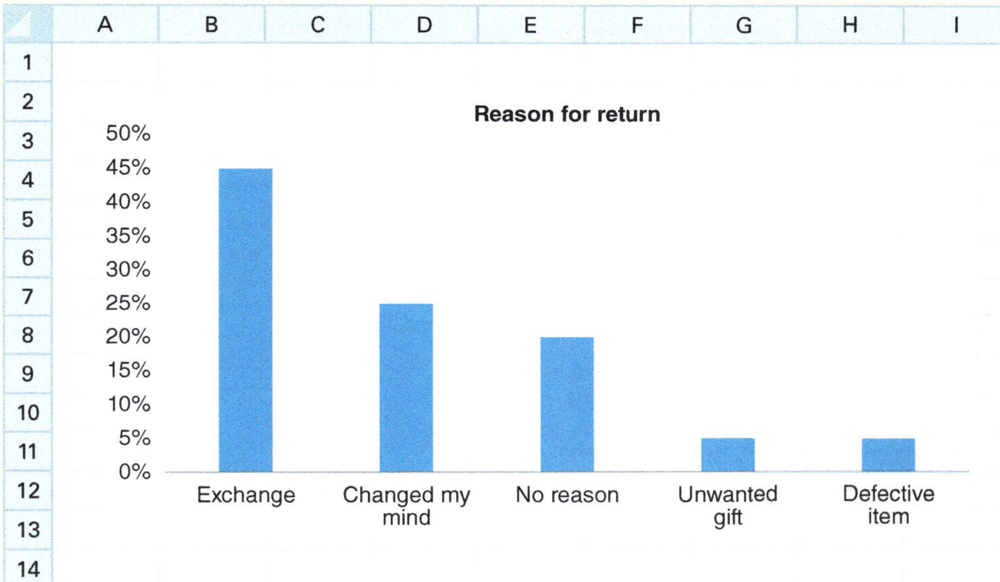

PRACTICE PROBLEMS

Practising the calculations

2.6 Construct a histogram and a frequency polygon for the following data.

Class interval	Frequency
(30, 32]	5
(32, 34]	7
(34, 36]	15
(36, 38]	21
(38, 40]	34
(40, 42]	24
(42, 44]	17
(44, 46]	8

2.7 Construct a histogram and a frequency polygon for the following data.

Class interval	Frequency
(10, 20]	9
(20, 30]	7
(30, 40]	10
(40, 50]	6
(50, 60]	13
(60, 70]	18
(70, 80]	15

2.8 Construct an ogive for the following data.

Class interval	Frequency
(3, 6]	2
(6, 9]	5
(9, 12]	10
(12, 15]	11
(15, 18]	17
(18, 21]	5

2.9 Construct a stem and leaf plot using two digits for the stem.

212	239	240	218	222	249	265	224
257	271	266	234	239	219	255	260
243	261	249	230	246	263	235	229
218	238	254	249	250	263	229	221
253	227	270	257	261	238	240	239
273	220	226	239	258	259	230	262
255	226						

P02-10 **2.10** The table below shows the value (in A$ million) of Australian exports to the top 10 buyers of Australian goods in 2013, according to the Department of Foreign Affairs and Trade. Construct a pie chart to represent these data. Label the slices with the corresponding percentages and give the chart an appropriate title. Comment on the effectiveness of using a pie chart to display these data.

Export market	A$ million
China	94 655
Japan	47 501
Republic of Korea	19 610
United States	9 580
India	9 517
New Zealand	7 399
Singapore	5 659
Taiwan	7 356
United Kingdom	3 859
Malaysia	5 561

P02-11 **2.11** The table above right shows the value (in A$ million) for the top 10 import sources of goods into Australia in 2013, according to the Department of Foreign Affairs and Trade. Use Excel to produce a bar chart for these data. On the basis of the charts for this and the previous problem, comment on Australia's major business partners.

Import source	A$ million
China	49 329
United States	39 181
Japan	21 221
Singapore	17 878
Thailand	13 832
Germany	13 099
United Kingdom	12 044
Malaysia	10 944
Republic of Korea	10 813
New Zealand	10 532

P02-12 **2.12** The Bureau of Infrastructure, Transport and Regional Economics (BITRE) publishes transport statistics. The table below shows the number of sectors flown by each domestic airline in September 2014. Construct a pie chart for these data and comment on your findings.

Airline	Number of sectors flown
Jetstar	7 315
Qantas	9 520
QantasLink	10 243
Regional Express	5 715
Tiger Airways	1 872
Virgin Australia	10 850
Virgin Australia Regional airlines	2 533

Testing your understanding

2.13 The following data are monthly downloads (megabytes) on a handheld device. Construct a stem and leaf plot of the data, using whole part for the stem and the decimal part for the leaf. What does this plot tell you about monthly downloads on handheld devices?

137.6	138.7	138.9	138.9	139.5	139.5	139.9	139.9
139.9	139.9	138.5	138.5	138.9	139.9	139.9	142.9
143.9	147.9	137.5	138.5	138.5	138.7	138.9	139.5
139.9	139.9	139.9	139.9	138.5	138.5	138.5	138.5
138.9	138.9	139.9	139.9	139.9	139.9	139.5	139.9
139.9	139.9	149.9	151.9	139.3	139.3	139.9	139.9
138.4	138.5						

P02-14 **2.14** An airline company uses a central telephone bank and a semi-automated telephone process to take reservations. It has been receiving an unusually high number of customer complaints about its reservation system. The company conducted a survey of customers, asking them whether they had encountered any of the following problems in making reservations: busy signal, disconnection, poor connection, too long a wait to talk to someone, not connected to an agent, or transferred to the wrong person. Suppose a survey of 744 complaining customers resulted in the following frequency tally.

Complaint	Number of complaints
Too long a wait	184
Transferred to the wrong person	10
Not connected to an agent	85
Disconnection	37
Busy signal	420
Poor connection	8

Construct a Pareto chart from this information to display the various problems encountered in making reservations.

2.3 Graphical display of two-variable continuous data: scatter plots

Often in business it is important to quantify the relationship between two (or more) continuous variables. This is often achieved by regression analysis. A first step to such analysis is data exploration. Here we present the **scatter plot** (also called a scatter graph or a scattergram), a graphical technique for qualitatively exploring the relationship between two continuous variables. A scatter plot is a *graph of pairwise data from two continuous variables.*

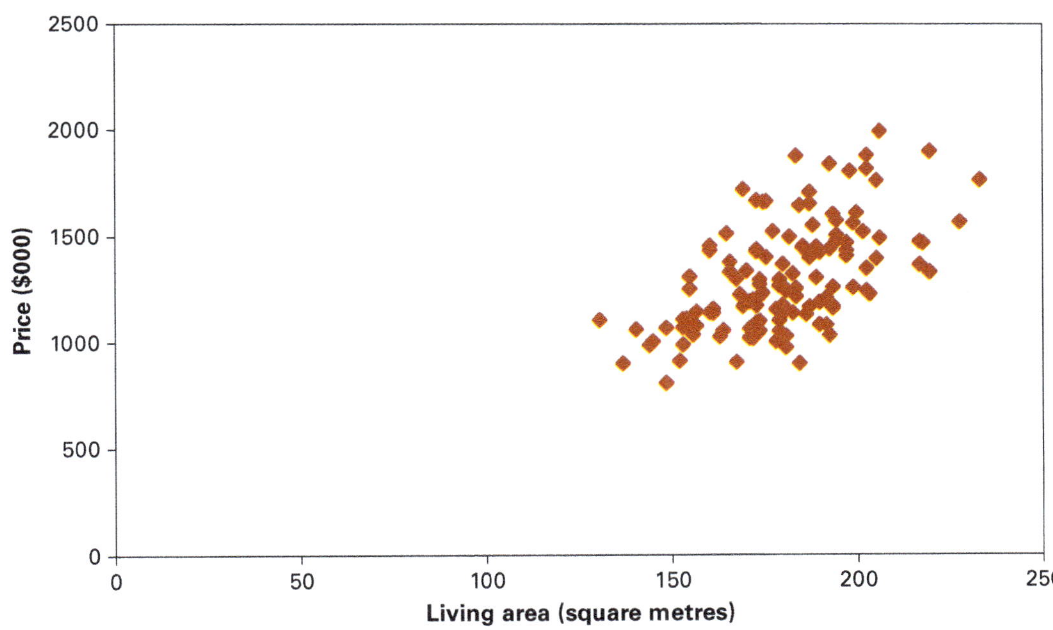

FIGURE 2.9 Scatter plot of price against living area of houses in two suburbs in Perth

As an example, consider the relationship between the price of a house and the size of the living area for houses in two exclusive suburbs of Perth. The data relate to 128 houses, with the living area in square metres and the price in thousands of dollars. The scatter plot of price against living area is displayed in figure 2.9. It can be seen that there is a strong *positive* linear relationship between price and size of living area; that is, as the living area increases, so does price.

DEMONSTRATION PROBLEM 2.8

The following data are the measurements of gas usage and minimum outside temperature (°C) over 26 days. Produce a scatter plot of the data, using gas usage as the response variable.

Temperature	Gas usage	Temperature	Gas usage
−0.8	7.2	6.0	4.4
−0.7	6.9	6.2	4.5
0.4	6.4	6.3	4.6
2.5	6.0	6.9	3.7
2.9	5.8	7.0	3.9
3.2	5.8	7.4	4.2
3.6	5.6	7.5	4.0
3.9	4.7	7.5	3.9
4.2	5.8	7.6	3.5
4.3	5.2	8.0	4.0
5.4	4.9	8.5	3.6
6.0	4.9	9.1	3.1
6.0	4.3	10.2	2.6

USING EXCEL

Scatter plots

DP02-08

1. Access DP02-08.xls from the student website.
2. Select the data in cells A2 to B27.
3. From the Insert tab, select the Scatter plot icon from the Charts group, and click on the first option.
4. A scatter plot appears on the worksheet. This can be tidied up as previously for other charts. Delete the horizontal and vertical gridlines. Right-click a data marker, and select Format Data Series... In the Format Data Series task pane, choose Series Options and then Marker Options. Select your preferred style of marker and colour. You can then insert axis labels using the Chart Elements button next to the chart. The final output is given below.

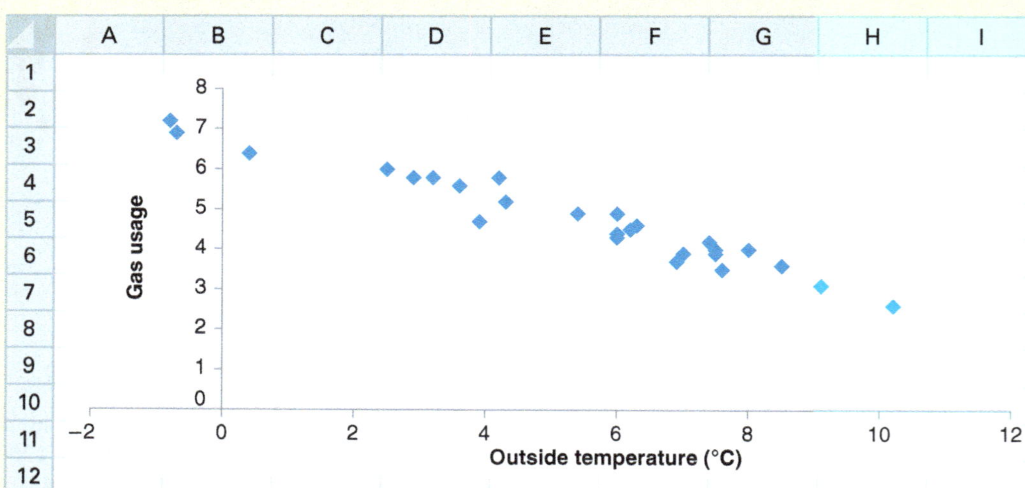

PRACTICE PROBLEMS

Practising the calculations

P02-15 **2.15** A researcher wants to determine if the number of international students studying in New Zealand and the number of visitors from their corresponding countries are related. Data on these variables for eight Asian countries are shown in the following table.

Country	Students	Visitors
China (mainland)	44 700	74 329
Hong Kong	1 183	27 779
India	1 569	15 834
Japan	14 303	160 844
Malaysia	1 008	25 801
South Korea	16 509	118 229
Taiwan	2 189	26 689
Thailand	2 923	21 071

Construct a scatter plot of the data. Examine the plot and discuss the strength of the relationship between the number of international students and the number of visitors from their countries.

Testing your understanding

P02-16 **2.16** Is the total sales revenue related to the advertising dollars spent by a company? The following data represent the advertising dollars and the sales revenues for various companies in a given industry during a recent year. Construct a scatter plot of the data from the two variables and discuss the relationship between the two variables.

Advertising ($ million)	Sales ($ million)	Advertising ($ million)	Sales ($ million)
4.2	155.7	10.4	168.2
1.6	87.3	7.1	136.9
6.3	135.6	5.5	101.4
2.7	99.0	8.3	158.2

CHAPTER CASE REVISITED

Electronic games

Raw data are rarely presented in reports, except in appendices. The age profile of gamers can be presented as a bar graph or pie chart. The bar graph is shown below.

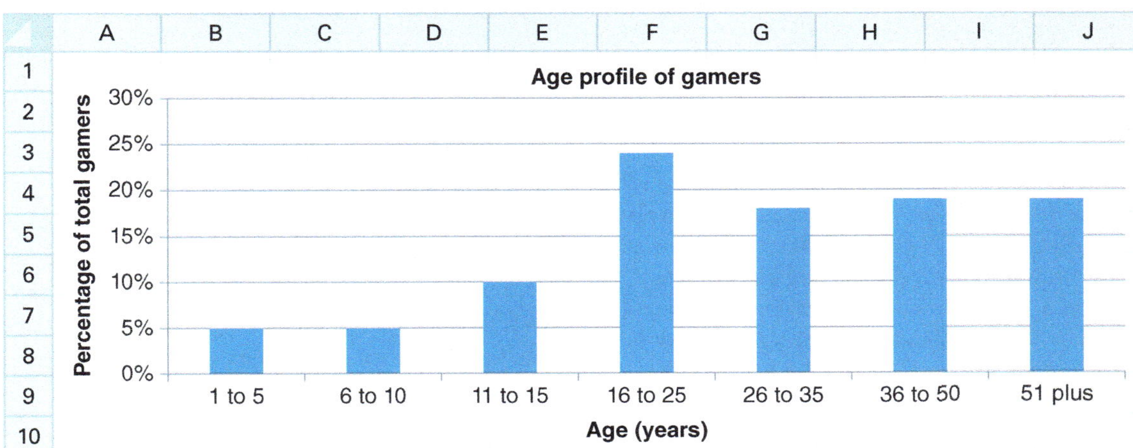

The chart shows that the 16 to 25 age group is the largest percentage of gamers. Beyond that the percentage of gamers is almost steady at around 19%.

From a marketing perspective the age group to target would be the 16 to 25 group, as it seems that those who become gamers at this stage continue to be so in later life.

The graph of duration of play versus frequency of play is reproduced below. This graph contains a lot of information and is a clever way of superimposing more than two variables on a graph with only two axes. The size of the circle for each point indicates the percentage of gamers at that point. From this graph we see that males aged 16 to 25 have the highest duration of play and also make up the largest percentage. The most frequent players are males and females aged 1 to 5, but their duration of play is only about half an hour at a time. A general observation is that males play for longer periods and more often than females. Other similar observations can be made from this graph.

Frequency and duration of play

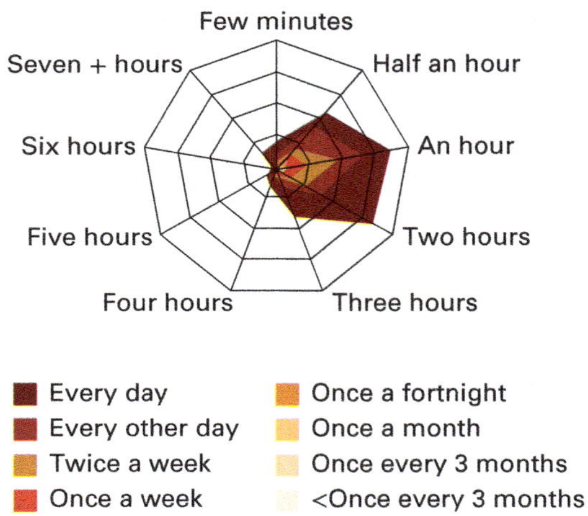

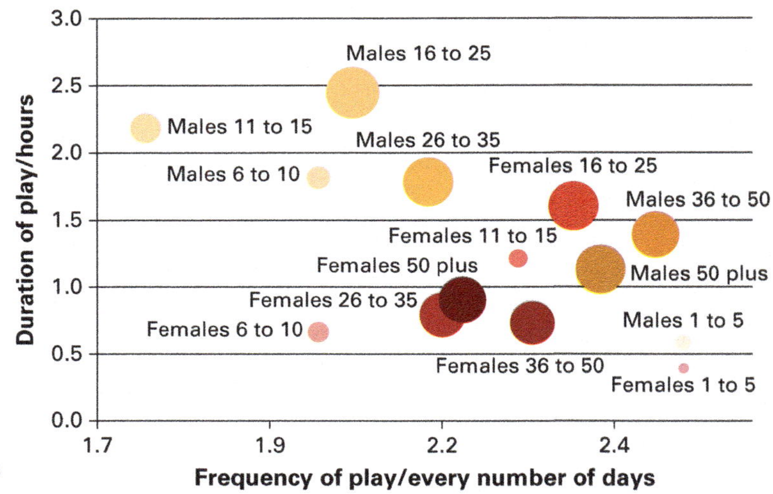

SUMMARY

1 Graphical analysis and summary of data is a first step to further data analysis. It is primarily used to highlight key aspects of the data and to reveal any special features, such as outliers or other unusual observations. Data can be displayed as a graph in several ways. Data that have not been summarised in any way are called raw or ungrouped data. Data that are organised into a frequency distribution are called grouped data. For some displays, a frequency distribution of the data must first be obtained. For others, the raw data can be used.

2 Histograms show the spread and shape of a data distribution. It is important to note that histograms are very sensitive to the selection of class intervals. A frequency polygon is a line graph of a frequency distribution, giving the same information as a histogram. An ogive is a cumulative frequency polygon. A stem and leaf plot is similar to a histogram, except that it plots the actual data and the data do not need to be grouped.

Categorical data can be represented as a pie chart or a bar chart. Although both of these contain the same information, visual interpretation may be easier with a bar chart. A Pareto chart is a bar chart plotted in descending order of proportion. It is frequently used in quality control to identify the major causes of problems.

3 In business there is often interest in the relationship between two variables. Scatter plots are used to investigate relationships between pairs of continuous variables. Unusual points, such as outliers, can be identified from this plot. Such a plot is usually a precursor to a regression analysis.

KEY TERMS

class mark p. 17
class midpoint p. 17
cumulative frequency p. 17
frequency distribution p. 16
frequency polygon p. 28
grouped data p. 16
histogram p. 22
ogive p. 30
outlier p. 22
Pareto chart p. 35
pie chart p. 32
range p. 16
raw data p. 16
relative frequency p. 17
scatter plot p. 39
stem and leaf plot p. 33
ungrouped data p. 16

REVIEW PROBLEMS

Practising the calculations

P02-17 **2.17** For the following data, construct a frequency distribution table with six classes.

114	46	70	36	42
52	102	94	58	42
92	86	58	46	78
100	82	36	72	56
62	84	104	58	36
112	92	66	56	40

2.18 For each class interval of the frequency distribution given, determine the class midpoint, relative frequency and cumulative frequency. Construct a histogram, a frequency polygon and an ogive for the frequency distribution.

Class interval	Frequency
(20, 25]	7
(25, 30]	6
(30, 35]	21
(35, 40]	25
(40, 45]	14
(45, 50]	12

P02-19 **2.19** Construct a pie chart from the following data.

Label	Value
A	55
B	121
C	83
D	46

2.20 Construct a stem and leaf plot for the following data. Let the leaf contain one digit.

312	324	289	335	298
314	309	294	326	317
290	311	317	301	316
306	286	308	284	324

P02-21 **2.21** An examination of items in a production line shows at least 10 different types of problems. A frequency tally of the problems follows. Construct a Pareto chart for these data.

Problem	Frequency
1	673
2	29
3	108
4	379
5	73
6	564
7	12
8	402
9	54
10	202

P02-22 **2.22** Construct a scatter plot for the following two numerical variables.

x	*y*
12	5
17	3
9	10
6	15
10	8
14	9
8	8

2.23 An Auckland-based distribution company surveyed 53 of its mid-level managers. The survey obtained the ages of these managers, which were later organised into the frequency distribution shown. Determine the class midpoint, relative frequency and cumulative frequency for these data.

Class interval	Frequency
(20, 25]	8
(25, 30]	6
(30, 35]	5
(35, 40]	12
(40, 45]	15
(45, 50]	7

Testing your understanding

P02-24 **2.24** A company manufactures a metal ring, which usually weighs about 1.4 kg, for industrial engines. A random sample of 50 of these metal rings produced the following weights (in kg).

1.51	1.59	1.42	1.25	1.34	1.51	1.51	1.19	1.62	1.31
1.56	1.16	1.25	1.48	1.59	1.42	1.62	1.25	1.31	1.16
1.48	1.96	1.51	1.62	1.45	1.53	1.79	1.19	1.34	1.34
1.48	1.51	1.31	1.02	1.65	1.45	1.08	1.39	1.42	1.76
1.11	1.25	1.56	1.22	1.48	1.22	1.19	1.62	1.39	1.45

Construct a frequency distribution for these data using eight classes. What can you observe about the data from the frequency distribution?

2.25 In a medium-sized New Zealand city, 90 houses are for sale, each having about 180 m^2 of floor space. The asking prices vary. The frequency distribution shown contains the price categories for the 90 houses. Construct a histogram, a frequency polygon and an ogive from these data.

Asking price ($000)	Frequency
(120, 130]	21
(130, 140]	27
(140, 150]	18
(150, 160]	11
(160, 170]	6
(170, 180]	3
(180, 190]	4

P02-26 **2.26** The following figures are type and corresponding proportion of expense required to create a new processed food product, ready to introduce to the market.

Expense	Proportion (%)
Technical support	8
Project management	5
Administrative support	4
Other overhead	2
Development	56
Research	25

Produce a pie chart and a Pareto chart for these data and comment on your findings.

P02-27 **2.27** The table below shows the total weekly expenses for a family of four.

Item	Expense ($)
Mortgage repayments	450
Other housing costs	15
Education	100
Cars	125
Groceries	250
Dining out	100
Sport, recreation and other entertainment	55

Construct a pie chart displaying this information.

P02-28 **2.28** A manufacturing company produces cardboard boxes for the car parts industry. Some of the boxes are rejected because of poor quality. Causes of poor-quality boxes include tears, labelling errors, discolouration and incorrect thickness. The following data for 400 boxes that were rejected include the problems and the frequencies of the problems. Use these data to construct a Pareto chart. Discuss the implications of the chart.

Problem	Number
Discolouration	32
Incorrect thickness	117
Tears	221
Labelling errors	30

2.29 Sometimes when we create a stem and leaf plot, we find that we get too many leaves per stem to give a good representation of the data. In such a case, we can further split the data space for each stem equally.

Suppose 100 CPA firms are surveyed to determine how many audits they perform over a certain time. In this case, the best representation of the data is given by splitting each stem into five ranges. This results in the stem and leaf plot shown in the next column. The first stem, 1, has been split into five, the first of which contains data in the range 10 to 11 inclusive (and there are no data points in this range), the second in the range 12 to 13, the third in the range 14 to 15, the fourth in the range 16 to 17 and the fifth in the range 18 to 19. Similarly, the other stems have been divided into five ranges. This method is similar to how we define intervals for histograms.

What can you learn from this plot about the number of audits being performed by these firms?

Stem	Leaf
1	
1	2 2 2 3 3 3 3 3 3
1	4 4 4 5 5 5 5
1	6 6 6 6 6 6 7 7 7 7
1	8 8 8 8 9 9 9 9 9
2	0 0 0 1
2	2 2 3 3 3
2	5 5 5 5 5
2	6 7 7 7 7 7 7 7 7
2	8 8 8 8 8 9 9
3	0 0 0 1 1 1
3	2 2 3 3 3 3
3	4 4 4 5 5 5 5 5
3	6 7 7 7 7
3	8 8 9
4	0 0 1 1
4	2 2 2

2.30 The following Excel ogive shows toy sales by a company over a 12-month period. What conclusions can you reach about toy sales at this company?

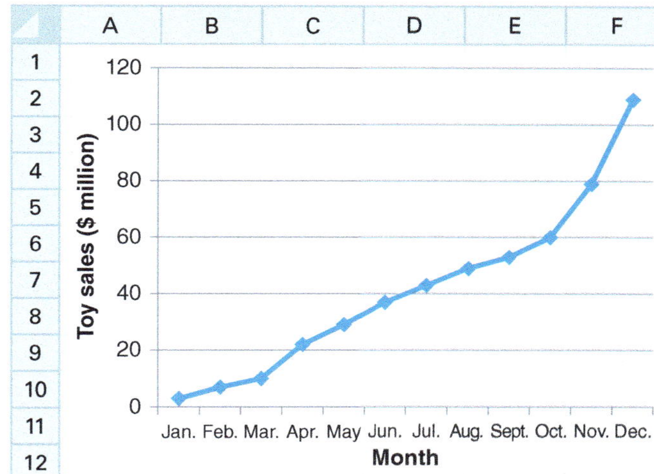

CHAPTER

3 Descriptive summary measures

LEARNING OBJECTIVES

After studying this chapter, you should be able to:

1. understand and calculate measures of central tendency, particularly the mean, median and mode
2. appreciate and determine measures of location, particularly percentiles and quartiles
3. distinguish between measures of variability — particularly the range, interquartile range, variance, standard deviation and coefficient of variation — and apply the empirical rule, Chebyshev's theorem and *z*-scores
4. consider shape and symmetry using measures of skewness and kurtosis and understand key features of a set of data by interpreting box and whisker plots
5. calculate and interpret a measure of association, particularly the Pearson product–moment correlation coefficient.

OPENING VIGNETTE

Are you being followed?

The world of social media is of interest to many businesses and other organisations as a means of interacting with their stakeholders in new ways. Descriptive statistics are a useful way of painting a picture about how often social media is used, by whom and for what purposes. However, in many instances, the summary statistics used to describe the data need to be carefully evaluated in terms of the properties of the distribution from which the data were drawn. Consideration should also be given to the representativeness of the sample before making conclusions from such statistics.

For example, a study of 36 million Twitter user profiles by Beevolve reveals that, of those accounts sampled:

- the highest proportion of users were from the United States (51% of users worldwide), followed by the United Kingdom (17%), and Australia (4%)
- the age of Twitter users is positively skewed with 74% of users aged 15–25 years of age and only 6% of users aged 46 or over.

As in many instances where descriptive statistics are used, the integrity of the data behind these results needs to be considered. Age was determined using information publicly disclosed in users' biographies and their tweets. Since younger people are suspected to be relatively more likely to disclose their age on social media, the adequacy of the sample data to be representative of the population of users needs to be considered. Indeed, Beevolve indicates that only 0.45% of Twitter users disclose their age.

Jon Bruner, a data journalist at O'Reilly Radar, used a sample of 400 000 tweets to reveal that the distribution describing the number of followers reveals an extremely positively skewed distribution. In fact, Bruner determined that the median number of followers of a Twitter account is just one. Given that many user accounts are inactive, Bruner further examined those accounts that were deemed active — that is, having posted to Twitter in the last 30 days. Among these accounts, the median was much higher at 61 followers. For the 90th percentile, the number of followers was 458. This implies that 90% of active account holders have 458 or fewer followers. The top 1% of active account holders had 3000 or more followers. At the lower end of the distribution, the 10th percentile was found to be 3 followers among active account holders. That is, 10% of active accounts had 3 or fewer followers.

Bruner further demonstrated how Twitter is much less conversational, but rather a consumption medium. Not surprisingly, 76% of users follow more people than follow them. Specifically, in terms of the median, 50% of active account holders follow 117 or fewer users, while the top 10% follow 542 or more users.

Introduction

Chapter 2 described tabular and graphical techniques for organising and presenting data. Even though these tables and graphs allow the researcher to make some general observations about key features of the data, such as the shape and spread, a more complete understanding of the data can be obtained by using numerical summaries. This chapter presents such descriptive measures, including measures of central tendency and location, measures of variability and measures of shape. In addition, we illustrate a descriptive summary measure, called the correlation coefficient, which can be used to examine the existence, direction and relative strength of a linear relationship between two numerical variables.

Often, companies must gauge how they are performing or perceived on a number of dimensions, such as their quality of service or consumers' awareness of a company's current product offerings.

Such an assessment may involve collecting data about consumers or their experiences, and then summarising them to describe what is generally happening and how this varies between customers. These summaries ultimately inform managers about what is occurring and may result in operational changes or reconsideration of a company's overall business strategy.

For example, the manager of a bank branch located in the CBD is concerned that a large number of customers have changed their habits and are now visiting the branch in the morning to avoid the peak lunchtime periods. In turn, this may have led to customers waiting an unacceptably long time and the manager wonders if there is a need to change staffing arrangements, particularly with regard to casual employees. To make a more informed assessment, the manager decides to record the waiting times of randomly selected customers visiting the bank during the morning period over several weeks. The waiting times data are listed in table 3.1. In this chapter, we will examine various ways in which the bank manager can summarise these data.

TABLE 3.1 Customer waiting times during morning period

Observation	1	2	3	4	5	6	7	8	9	10	11	12	13	14	15	16
Waiting time (min)	9	14	11	10	10	8	10	9	14	8	15	12	9	9	7	9

These responses show the waiting times of an individual customer in the sample range from a reasonably short period of time (observation 15) to waiting times that are much longer (observations 2, 9 and 11). Rather than looking at any individual waiting time, the bank manager is now interested in summarising these data to get a better feel for the general experience of the bank's customers in relation to waiting times. As you will see, the bank can use the mode to assess the most frequently occurring observation and the median and mean to summarise where the data are centred. The manager may want to see the waiting times of a certain percentage of customers (e.g. 75%), so measures of location could be used. The bank manager may also wish to see how waiting times vary and see whether the concept of an average is a good representation of customers' experiences. The manager may like to determine whether there are any unusual or extreme observations in the data (sometimes called outliers). With this example in mind, this chapter will explore measures of central tendency, location, spread, shape and outliers.

CHAPTER CASE

Location, location, location!

'Location, location, location!' is a common phrase used in real estate circles. It implies that the value of a property is higher when it is located in a beautiful street or has lovely views. However, also important is being close to schools, shops and transport options such as buses and trains. As the cost of running a private vehicle increases, people are gravitating to areas where their reliance on a car can be lessened. For people who do not drive, or have stopped driving, living close to public transport and shopping centres is essential.

The managers of Baycoast City Real Estate Agents (BCREA) believe that people choose to purchase or rent properties in Baycoast because the city stretches for several kilometres along lovely beaches. However, they also wonder whether being able to commute to the city via public transport and live within walking distance of shops is another factor by which to promote the area to potential buyers from outside the region. Using a sample of 120 recent sales, BCREA was able to provide the following summary statistics that describe how people living in the Baycoast City local government area potentially have transport and shops on their doorsteps.

Distance to nearest service (in kilometres)

Summary statistic	Train	Bus	Shops
Mode	1.40	0.10	1.50
Average	0.91	0.90	0.93
Standard deviation	0.49	0.60	0.53
First quartile	0.50	0.30	0.50
Median	0.90	0.80	0.90
Third quartile	1.35	1.50	1.45
Minimum	0.10	0.00	0.10
Maximum	1.90	2.00	1.80

Questions to help managers make decisions

BCREA

1. The statistics presented on the previous page can be obtained using the Baycoast data set and Excel. Use these statistics to write a short report to BCREA management about whether Baycoast provides transport services to its residents that are within a reasonable walking distance. Take into consideration that walking a kilometre takes approximately 15 minutes, depending on terrain and a person's fitness.
2. The maximum distance that a property in the sample data is from any shopping centre is 1.8 km. Suppose that the sample had instead included someone who lived in a remote part of Baycoast that was over 4 km from any such services. How would this affect the mode, median and mean?
3. The following scatter plot shows the relationship between the distance of a property from the nearest train station (in kilometres) and the selling price of the house. Does there appear to be a relationship? What does this imply about BCREA's decision to entice people to buy in the Baycoast area on the basis of its proximity to public transport? You may like to calculate a correlation coefficient using the Baycoast data to quantify what the graph shows.

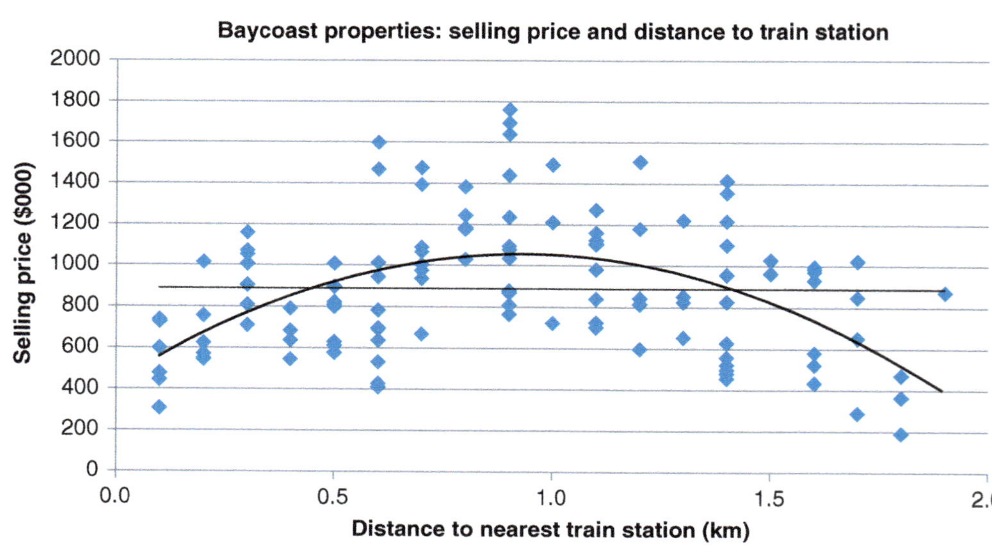

3.1 Measures of central tendency

Measures of central tendency *yield information about the centre, or middle part, of a set of numbers.* Table 3.1 displayed waiting times in a bank as recorded by the manager for a sample of its customers. For these data, measures of central tendency can yield such information as the average waiting time, the middle waiting time and the most frequently occurring waiting time. Measures of central tendency do not focus on the span of the data set or how far values are from the middle numbers. The measures of central tendency presented here are the mode, the median and the mean.

Mode

The **mode** is *the most frequently occurring value in a set of data.* For the data in table 3.1, the mode in relation to waiting time is 9 minutes because this value occurred most often (5 observations of the 16 recorded). Organising the data into an ordered array (an ordering of the numbers from smallest to largest) helps to locate the mode.

Waiting time (min)	7	8	8	**9**	**9**	**9**	**9**	**9**	10	10	10	11	12	14	14	15

This grouping makes it easier to see that 9 is the most frequently occurring number of the 16 observations. In other words, the most commonly occurring experience for the customers in the sample was to wait 9 minutes to be served when visiting the CBD branch of the bank in the morning period. This occurred in 31.25% of the cases listed in table 3.1.

In *the case of a tie for the most frequently occurring value*, two modes are listed. When this occurs, the data are said to be **bimodal**. If a set of data is not exactly bimodal but contains two values that are more dominant than others, some researchers take the liberty of referring to the data set as bimodal even without an exact tie for the mode. For example, a data set may describe the number of semesters a student has taken to complete their degree, but not be able to distinguish between whether a student has studied part-time, full-time or a mixture of both study patterns. One mode is likely to represent those who have studied predominantly part-time, while another mode will likely represent those who have studied predominantly full-time. *Data sets with two or more modes* are referred to as **multimodal**.

In the world of business, the concept of mode is often used in determining sizes. For example, shoe manufacturers might produce inexpensive shoes in three widths only: small, medium and large. Each width represents a modal width of feet. In reducing the number of sizes to a few modal sizes, companies reduce total product costs by limiting machine setup costs. Similarly, the garment industry produces shirts, dresses, suits and many other clothing products in modal sizes. For example, all men's size M shirts in a given lot are produced in the same size. This size is some modal size for medium-sized men.

The mode is an appropriate descriptive summary measure for categorical data. It can be used to determine which category occurs most frequently. In the bank survey, the manager may have recorded the gender of the customer waiting in line. In this case, the mode would represent whether it was more frequently observed that men or women waited in line. For these and similar types of categorical data that cannot be sorted, it would be inappropriate to consider the next measure examined, namely the median.

Median

The **median** is *the middle value in an ordered array of numbers.* For an array with an odd number of observations, the median is the middle number. For an array with an even number of observations, the median is the average of the two middle numbers.

Returning to our example of the waiting times of a sample of customers in a bank, the location of the median becomes clear when the observations are arranged in an ordered array and then divided into two groups of equal size.

Ordered position	1	2	3	4	5	6	7	8	9	10	11	12	13	14	15	16
Waiting time	7	8	8	9	9	9	9	9	10	10	10	11	12	14	14	15

Because the array contains 16 observations (an even number of terms), the median is the average of the two middle values, in the 8th and 9th positions, or 9.5 minutes.

If the last value in the ordered array (a waiting time of 15 minutes) is eliminated from the list, the array would contain only 15 observations. The array becomes:

Ordered position	1	2	3	4	5	6	7	8	9	10	11	12	13	14	15
Waiting time	7	8	8	9	9	9	9	9	10	10	10	11	12	14	14

For an odd number of observations, the median is the middle value in the array: in this case, the value in the 8th position. The resulting median value is 9 minutes. This means that 50% of the customers waited 9 minutes or less and 50% waited 9 minutes or more.

Another way to locate the median is by finding the $\frac{(n+1)}{2}$th term in the ordered array. For example, if an ordered data set contains 77 observations (an odd number of terms), the median is the 39th term.

$$\frac{n+1}{2}=\frac{77+1}{2}=\frac{78}{2}=39\text{th term}$$

If an ordered data set contains 78 observations (an even number of terms), the median is the average of the 39th and 40th terms.

$$\frac{n+1}{2}=\frac{78+1}{2}=\frac{79}{2}=39.5\text{th term}$$

This formula is helpful when a large number of observations must be considered.

The median is unaffected by the magnitude of extreme values. In other words, large and small values do not inordinately influence the median. For this reason, the median is often the best measure of location to use in the analysis of variables in which extreme but acceptable values at just one end of the data can legitimately occur, such as house prices, people's income or ages of pensioners. Suppose, for example, that a real estate agent wants to determine the median of the selling prices of 10 houses (given at left).

\$320 000	\$420 000
\$350 000	\$420 000
\$360 000	\$440 000
\$380 000	\$450 000
\$400 000	\$2 200 000

The median is the average of the two middle terms, \$400 000 and \$420 000: that is, \$410 000. This price is a reasonable representation of the prices of the 10 houses. In calculating the median, not all the information from the data set is used. For example, information about the selling price of the most expensive house (\$2.2 million) does not enter into the computation of the median other than to identify it as the highest value in the ordered array of selling prices. If the price of the 10th house was \$500 000, the median would still be the same.

For a median to be meaningful, the data must be quantitative or able to be ranked. For example, a bank may collect information on the ages of its customers when they apply for a new account, credit card or home loan by requesting the date of birth of each applicant. The median age of a customer is meaningful because customers can be sorted from youngest to oldest. Calculating the median of the type of account that these same customers have would be meaningless, as the various account types have nominal properties that cannot be sorted from lowest to highest in any useful way. Even the numbers used in a database to identify the type of account each customer has are arbitrary labels for which a median would be inappropriate.

Mean

The **arithmetic mean** is *the average of a set of numbers* and is computed by summing all numbers and dividing the sum by the count of numbers. Because the arithmetic mean is so widely used, most statisticians refer to it simply as the *mean* or *average*.

In the example presented in table 3.1, we can calculate the average waiting time of a customer to be 10.25 minutes, by adding the responses (a total of 164 minutes) and dividing by the number of responses (16). Because these data were obtained by observing a sample of customer waiting times, we refer to the 10.25 minutes as the sample mean. The sample mean is represented by $\bar{x}$, pronounced 'x-bar'.

If the data being considered represent a census, where all the population values are included in the calculations, the average would be calculated in the same way but be referred to as the population mean. The population mean is represented by the Greek letter *mu* (μ). Separate symbols for the population mean and sample mean are necessary because often the sample mean will be used to infer what is occurring at the population level.

Refer to maths appendix

The capital Greek letter *sigma* (Σ) is commonly used in mathematics to represent a summation of all the numbers in a grouping. For more information about summation notation, refer to the maths appendix at the end of this chapter. The algorithm for computing a mean is to sum all the numbers in the population or sample and divide the sum by the number of observations. N is used to represent the number of terms in a population, and n is the number of observations in a sample. Formulas 3.1 and 3.2 are used to compute the population mean and sample mean, respectively.

Population mean (3.1)

$$\mu = \frac{\Sigma x}{N} = \frac{x_1 + x_2 + x_3 + \cdots + x_N}{N}$$

Sample mean (3.2)

$$\bar{x} = \frac{\Sigma x}{n} = \frac{x_1 + x_2 + x_3 + \cdots + x_n}{n}$$

As the data need to be summed, it is inappropriate to use the mean to analyse data that are not quantitative in nature. For example, it would be suitable for a bank to calculate the average ages of its customers; it would not be appropriate, however, to calculate the average gender, even if we use the value 0 to represent male and the value 1 to represent female. The average waiting time of the sample of customers presented in table 3.1 is calculated using formula 3.2 by obtaining the total waiting time of all 16 customers:

$$\Sigma x = 9 + 14 + 11 + 10 + 10 + 8 + 10 + 9 + 14 + 8 + 15 + 12 + 9 + 9 + 7 + 9 = 164$$

and dividing this by the number of customers to determine the average waiting time of the 16 customers:

$$\bar{x} = \frac{\Sigma x}{n} = \frac{164}{16} = 10.25 \text{ minutes}$$

DEMONSTRATION PROBLEM 3.1

PROBLEM: A firm of architects was attempting to get a feel for the sizes of houses in the suburb of Colton in the city of Baycoast, the same suburb for which they had been commissioned to design a house. Using their contacts at the Baycoast City Real Estate Agents, the architects were provided information on a sample of 13 houses. Compute the mode, median and mean for the number of bedrooms. Calculate the mean, median and modal number of bathrooms and number of all rooms.

House no.	Suburb	Bedrooms	Bathrooms	All rooms
110	Colton	2	1	5
112	Colton	2	1.5	5
108	Colton	2	1	5
117	Colton	2	1.5	6
100	Colton	2	1	5
89	Colton	2	2	6
96	Colton	3	1.5	6
94	Colton	3	1	7
93	Colton	3	1.5	6
113	Colton	3	1.5	6
102	Colton	3	1.5	7
114	Colton	4	2	8
115	Colton	5	2	9

SOLUTION: The mode is 2 bedrooms, since this is the most commonly occurring number: 6 of the 13 houses have 2 bedrooms.

With 13 houses in this group, $n = 13$. The median is located at the $\frac{(13+1)}{2} = 7$th position. Because the data are already ordered by number of bedrooms, the 7th term is 3 bedrooms, which is the median. (To calculate the median number of bathrooms, we have to sort the table by number of bathrooms.)

The total number of bedrooms in the sample of 13 houses is $36 = \Sigma x$. Therefore, the mean is:

$$\bar{x} = \frac{\Sigma x}{n} = \frac{36}{13} = 2.77 \text{ bedrooms}$$

Similarly, the total number of bathrooms in the sample of 13 houses is $19 = \Sigma x$. Therefore, the mean is $\frac{19}{13} = 1.46$ bathrooms. The modal number of bathrooms is 1.5, and the median is 1.5. The total number of rooms in the sample of 13 houses is 81. Therefore, the mean is $\frac{81}{13} = 6.23$ rooms per house. The modal number of rooms is 6 and the median number of rooms is also 6.

USING EXCEL

Descriptive statistics

DP03-01

1. Access DP03-01.xls from the student website.
2. From the Data tab, select Data Analysis.
3. From the Data Analysis dialogue box, select Descriptive Statistics and click OK.
4. In the Descriptive Statistics dialogue box:
   a. enter the range of cells containing the numeric data and their column headings in the Input Range field
   b. check Grouped By: Columns
   c. check Labels in First Row because you have included the column labels in the input range
   d. choose an output option

e. check Summary statistics

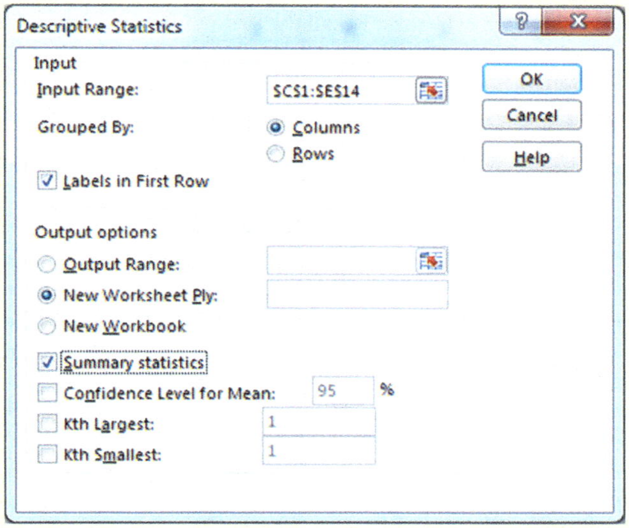

f. click OK.

The Excel output follows.

	A	B	C	D	E	F
1	*Bedrooms*		*Bathrooms*		*All rooms*	
2						
3	Mean	2.769231	Mean	1.461538	Mean	6.230769
4	Standard Error	0.25705	Standard Error	0.105331	Standard Error	0.342574
5	Median	3	Median	1.5	Median	6
6	Mode	2	Mode	1.5	Mode	6
7	Standard Deviation	0.926809	Standard Deviation	0.379777	Standard Deviation	1.235168
8	Sample Variance	0.858974	Sample Variance	0.144231	Sample Variance	1.525641
9	Kurtosis	1.524332	Kurtosis	−1.05261	Kurtosis	0.722761
10	Skewness	1.273684	Skewness	0.135646	Skewness	1.053911
11	Range	3	Range	1	Range	4
12	Minimum	2	Minimum	1	Minimum	5
13	Maximum	5	Maximum	2	Maximum	9
14	Sum	36	Sum	19	Sum	81
15	Count	13	Count	13	Count	13
16						

The Excel output includes many useful descriptive summary measures. For now, we are interested in the mean, median and mode. The mode informs the architects that houses with 2 bedrooms occur more frequently than houses with any other number of bedrooms. Likewise, the mode for bathrooms indicates that houses with 1.5 bathrooms are more frequently observed than a house with any other number of bathrooms. The median indicates that 50% of houses have 3 or fewer bedrooms, while 50% have 3 or more. A house has, on average, 2.77 bedrooms, 1.46 bathrooms and 6.23 rooms in total. These summary measures are useful if the architectural team wants to design a house that is similar in size to others or one that is larger, on average, than other houses in Colton.

The mean is affected by each and every value, which may be an advantage because it reflects all the data. A problem with the mean is that it is affected by extreme values at just one end of the data, and is pulled towards those extremes. Recall the preceding discussion of the 10 house prices. The total price of all 10 houses is $5 740 000, and the mean price is $574 000; the mean price is higher than the prices of nine of the houses because the house worth $2.2 million is included in the calculation.

The mean is the most commonly used measure of location because it uses each data item in its computation, it is a familiar measure, and it has mathematical properties that make it attractive to use in inferential statistics.

PRACTICE PROBLEMS

Practising the calculations

P03-01 **3.1** Determine the mode, median and mean of the following data.

16	9	19	10	16	16	4	18	19	10	8	2	20	8	17

Testing your understanding

P03-02 **3.2** The owner of a new Indian restaurant is wondering how its prices compare with others in the local area. Use the following price information on a sample of Rogan Josh main dishes to write a short report to the restaurant owner about the central tendency of the data.

Outlet	Price	Outlet	Price
Naan Place	$14.50	Spice of India	$14.90
Vindaloo Palace	$13.90	Tasty Biryani	$14.50
Chole Now	$10.90	Jimmy's	$11.90
Sounds of India	$13.50	House of Spice	$11.50
Café India	$12.90	Malai Village	$11.50
Kings	$14.50	Lassi Palace	$14.50
Metro	$13.90	Tasty Tandoori	$12.50
Saffron Plaza	$11.50	Second Avenue	$10.50

3.3 A fitness consultant working with a leading rugby league team measured the height of a sample of 100 male players. The output is broken down by position in terms of summary measures associated with a sample of 50 players who predominantly play in the forwards and a sample of 50 players who predominantly play in the backs. Explain in plain language what the figures imply.

Measure	Height of Backs (cm)	Height of Forwards (cm)
Mode	172	179
Median	175	181
Mean	177.8	180.5

3.4 A university has collected data to summarise the method of transportation that students use to predominantly travel to the main campus. Students were asked to respond to one category only. In cases where multiple modes were used, students were asked to indicate the method that represents the majority of their travel time.

Code	Predominant method used to travel to main campus
1	By private vehicle as the driver
2	By private vehicle as a passenger
3	Public transport
4	Walk
5	Intercampus shuttle bus
6	Other form of transportation

Data were collected for each case using the above coding scheme. Of the mean, median and mode, which summary measure(s) are appropriate to describe the data? Justify your answer.

3.2 Measures of location

Measures of location *yield information about certain sections of a set of numbers when ranked into an ascending array.* For instance, we may wish to divide the data into quarters and see what value makes up the first 25% of our data. The first quartile tells us the location that the bottom 25% of data are equal to or less than in value and the location that the top 75% of data are equal to or more than in value. We may wish to divide the data into percentiles and identify which values make up the top 10% of our data. The median is both a measure of central tendency and a specific location: the middle of the data. The median identifies the location that allows the data to be split into halves. Even the minimum can be considered to be a measure of location as it informs us that 100% of values are greater than or equal to it. Conversely, 100% of values are equal to or below the maximum. The measures of location presented here are percentiles and quartiles.

Percentiles

Percentiles are *measures of location that divide a set of data so that a certain fraction of data can be described as falling on or below this location.* The *P*th percentile is the value such that *P*% of the data are equal to or below that value and (100 – *P*)% are above or equal to that value. Equivalently, the *P*th percentile is a value such that *P*% of the data are equal to or below the value and no more than (100 – *P*)% are above the value. For example, the 87th percentile is a value such that 87% of the data are equal to or below the value and no more than 13% are above the value.

Percentiles are widely used in reporting test results. Most university students in Australia take exams at school to achieve a score to enter university. The results of these exams are reported in percentile form and also as raw scores. There are various methods for calculating percentiles. The following steps are one way to determine the location of a percentile.

1. Organise the numbers into an ascending-order array.
2. Calculate the percentile location (i) by:

$$i = \frac{P}{100}(n)$$

   where:
   i = the percentile location
   P = the percentile of interest
   n = the number of observations in the data set.
3. Determine the location by the following.
   a. If i is a whole number, the *P*th percentile is the average of the value at the ith location and the value at the $(i + 1)$th location.
   b. If i is not a whole number, the *P*th percentile value is found by rounding i up to the next integer and reporting the value at this location. This is equivalent to the value at the location given by the whole number part of $i + 1$.

   For example, suppose you want to determine the 80th percentile of 1240 numbers. P is 80 and n is 1240. First, order the numbers from lowest to highest. Next, calculate the location of the 80th percentile.

$$i = \frac{80}{100}(1240) = 992$$

Because $i = 992$ is a whole number, follow step 3(a). The 80th percentile is the average of the 992nd and 993rd numbers.

$$P_{80} = \frac{(992\text{nd number} + 993\text{rd number})}{2}$$

DEMONSTRATION PROBLEM 3.2

DP03-02 PROBLEM: Determine the 15th percentile of the waiting times of the sample of bank customers presented in table 3.1.

SOLUTION: For these 16 customers, we want to find the value of the 15th percentile, so $n = 16$ and $P = 15$.

First, organise the data into an ascending-order array.

7	8	8	9	9	9	9	9	10	10	10	11	12	14	14	15

Next, compute the value of i.

$$i = \frac{15}{100}(16) = 2.4$$

Because i is not an integer, use step 3(b). Rounding i up to the next integer is 3 and indicates that the 15th percentile is located at the 3rd value in the ordered array. Equivalently, the value of $i + 1$ is 2.4 + 1, or 3.4; the integer part of 3.4 is 3. The 3rd value is 8, so 8 minutes is the 15th percentile.

There are a variety of other methods used to calculate percentiles, but these will usually generate similar answers, particularly with a large number of observations. The method demonstrated in the previous section is consistent with computer software, such as KaddStat and SAS. It expresses a percentile as either a specific value in the data or halfway between two adjacent values in the data (as determined by their average). Averaging two data values to infer another is a simple, but usually less accurate, form of interpolation. **Interpolation** is *a prediction of the value of something that is hypothetical or unknown based on other values that are known*, such as other values in the data. Other software packages, such as Excel and MINITAB, use different interpolation methods and slightly different formulas to locate the ranking term.

For example, Excel uses a method that is equivalent to calculating the percentile location as:

$$i = \frac{P}{100}(n - 1) + 1$$

Using the decimal component of this result provides information on how to interpolate the location of the percentile value in a more precise fashion. For example, Excel would calculate the location of the 85th percentile as:

$$i = \frac{85}{100}(16 - 1) + 1 = 13.75$$

To more accurately determine the 85th percentile by interpolation, the value of the 13.75th term can be inferred. It is a value between the 13th and 14th terms, interpolated as a distance of 0.75 units above the 13th term and 0.25 units below the 14th term. In other words, the 85th percentile relating to the customer waiting times in table 3.1 would be reported by Excel as $12 + 0.75(14 - 12) = 13.5$ minutes.

MINITAB uses a different formula from Excel but a similar method of interpolation. MINITAB determines the location of a percentile using $\frac{P}{100}(n+1)$. This formula gives rise to a common method for locating the median term, which was introduced earlier. The median, the 50th percentile, is the term at the location given by $\frac{50}{100}(n+1)$ in the ordered array. In other words, the median is the $\frac{(n+1)}{2}$th term in an ordered array. In general, while all methods may report slightly different percentile values, the median value is identical for all methods as the more precise approaches involving interpolation are equivalent to taking the average of two adjacent data values.

Quartiles

Quartiles are *measures of location that divide a set of data into four subgroups or parts*. The three quartiles are denoted as Q_1, Q_2 and Q_3. The first quartile, Q_1, separates the first, or lowest, one-quarter of the data from the upper three-quarters and is equal to the 25th percentile. The second quartile, Q_2, separates the second quarter of the data from the third quarter. Q_2 is located at the 50th percentile and equals the median of the data. The third quartile, Q_3, divides the first three-quarters of the data from the last quarter and is equal to the value of the 75th percentile. These three quartiles are shown in figure 3.1.

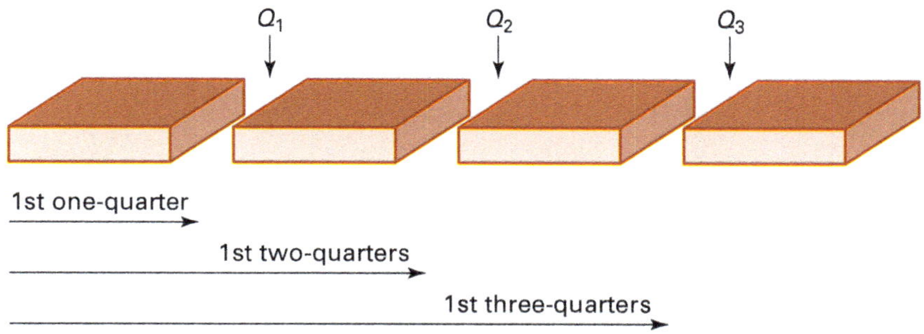

FIGURE 3.1 Quartiles

Suppose we want to determine the values of Q_1, Q_2 and Q_3 for the following numbers representing the observed waiting times of customers sorted from the shortest waiting time to the longest waiting time.

7 8 8 9 9 9 9 9 10 10 10 11 12 14 14 15

The value of Q_1 is found at the 25th percentile, P_{25}, by:

$$\text{For } n=16,\ i=\frac{25}{100}(16)=4$$

Because i is an integer, P_{25} is found as the average of the fourth and fifth numbers.

$$P_{25}=\frac{(9+9)}{2}=9 \text{ minutes}$$

The value of Q_1 is $P_{25}=9$. Notice that one-quarter, or four, of the customers waited 9 minutes or less. The remaining three-quarters, or 75%, of the customers in the sample have waited 9 minutes or more.

The value of Q_2 is equal to the median. Because the array contains an even number of terms, the median is the average of the two middle terms.

$$Q_2=\text{median}=\frac{(9+10)}{2}=9.5 \text{ minutes}$$

Notice that exactly half of the terms are less than Q_2 and half are greater than Q_2.

The value of Q_3 is determined by P_{75} as follows.

$$i=\frac{75}{100}(16)=12$$

Because i is an integer, P_{75} is the average of the 12th and 13th numbers.

$$P_{75}=\frac{(11+12)}{2}=11.5 \text{ minutes}$$

The value of Q_3 is $P_{75}=11.5$. Notice that the waiting times of three-quarters, or twelve, of the customers are less than 11.5 minutes, and the waiting times of four of the customers are greater than 11.5 minutes.

DEMONSTRATION PROBLEM 3.3

PROBLEM: An investor in the telecommunications industry has been provided some questionable information in a prospectus regarding market potential in New Zealand, particularly in relation to potentially over-optimistic statements made about the average monthly download usage for broadband connections. The investor obtains data from recent reports on usage from a variety of sources. The average monthly data usage by a household with broadband connection listed in a random sample of 12 such reports is stated as follows, sorted by usage.

Average monthly data usage (GB)	10	11	12	13	14	15	16	16	17	18	19	19

Determine the first, second and third quartiles for these data.

SOLUTION: For a sample of 12 reports, $n = 12$. $Q_1 = P_{25}$ is found by:

$$i = \frac{25}{100}(12) = 3$$

Because i is an integer, Q_1 is the average of the third and fourth values.

$$Q_1 = \frac{12 + 13}{2} = 12.5 \text{ GB}$$

$Q_2 = P_{50}$ = median; with 12 items, the median is the average of the sixth and seventh values.

$$Q_2 = \frac{15 + 16}{2} = 15.5 \text{ GB}$$

$Q_3 = P_{75}$ is solved by:

$$i = \frac{75}{100}(12) = 9$$

Q_3 is found by averaging the ninth and tenth terms.

$$Q_3 = \frac{17 + 18}{2} = 17.5 \text{ GB}$$

The results imply that 25% of the sampled reports indicate average monthly household usage to be 12.5 GB or less, half report it to be 15.5 GB or less and a quarter of the sampled reports indicate usage to be 17.5 GB or more. The investor can now compare this information with what is in the prospectus to better evaluate its claims about the average data usage by a household with broadband access.

PRACTICE PROBLEMS

Practising the calculations

P03-05 **3.5** Compute the 20th percentile, the 60th percentile, Q_1, Q_2 and Q_3 for the following data.

820	298	280	918	964	800	356	146
445	320	204	470	849	786	450	957

P03-06 **3.6** Compute P_{35}, P_{65}, P_{90}, Q_1, Q_2 and Q_3 for the following data.

21	10	18	13	22	29
18	11	11	29	42	27
30	12	42	41	46	30
30	21	23	23	16	

Testing your understanding

3.7 A hairdresser franchisor is concerned about the time taken by staff to complete a standard haircut for male customers at one of its newly opened stores. The franchisor decides to visit the store and record the time taken for such a category of haircut on 30 random occasions. A benchmark of 20 minutes has been set as a reasonable objective based on the franchisors' experience at their other stores. Interpret the following output to help the franchisor understand the time taken to provide male customers with a standard haircut in relation to this benchmark.

Summary measure	Time taken (minutes)
10th percentile	8.2
Quartile 1	10.5
Median	12.5
Quartile 3	19.7
90th percentile	32

3.3 Measures of variability

Measures of central tendency and location yield useful information about the values in a particular data set. However, they do not tell the whole story. In particular, because they are measures of central tendency, the mean, median and mode are often presented as being average values; that is, that they are typical of the data. However, the more variability there is in a set of data, the less typical they are of the whole set. Thus we need tools that are **measures of variability**, which *describe the spread or the dispersion of a set of data*. Using measures of variability in conjunction with measures of central tendency makes possible a more complete numerical description of the data.

For example, a company has 25 salespeople in the field, and the median annual sales figure for these people is $1.2 million. Are the salespeople being successful as a group or not? The median provides information about the sales of the person in the middle, but what about the other salespeople? Are all of them selling $1.2 million annually, or do the sales figures vary widely, with one person selling $5 million annually and another selling only $150 000 annually? Measures of variability provide the additional information necessary to answer that question.

Figure 3.2 shows three distributions in which the mean of each distribution is the same ($\mu = 50$) but the variability in the data differs; a measure of variability is necessary to complement the mean value when describing data. This section focuses on several measures of variability: range, interquartile range, variance, standard deviation and coefficient of variation.

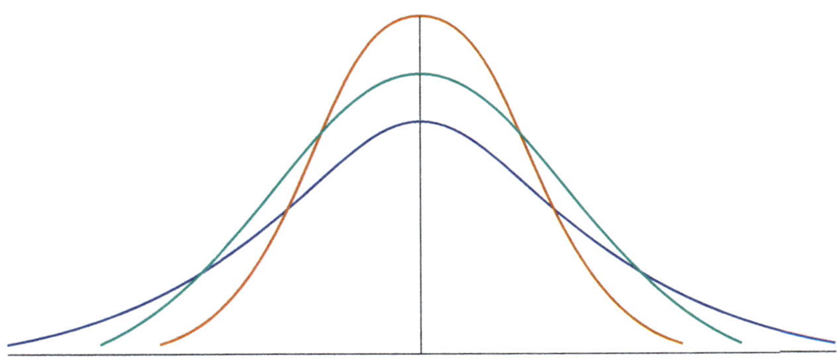

FIGURE 3.2 Three distributions with the same mean but different variability

Range

The **range** is *the difference between the maximum and minimum values of a data set*. It is a crude measure of variability. An advantage of the range is its ease of calculation. One important use of the range is in quality assurance, where the range is used to construct control charts. A disadvantage of the range is that, because it is calculated with the values that are on the extremes of the data, it is affected by extreme values. Therefore, its application as a measure of variability is limited.

The data in table 3.1 (p. 49) represent the waiting times of customers. The shortest waiting time for any customer was 7 minutes and the longest waiting time was 15 minutes. The range of waiting times can be calculated as the difference between the highest and lowest values:

$$\text{Range} = \text{maximum} - \text{minimum} = 15 - 7 = 8 \text{ minutes}$$

Interquartile range

Another measure of variability is the interquartile range. The **interquartile range**, or **IQR**, is *the distance between the first and third quartiles*. Essentially, it is the range of the middle 50% of the data and is determined by computing the value of $Q_3 - Q_1$, as in formula 3.3 (overleaf). The interquartile range is especially useful in situations where data users are more interested in values toward the middle and less interested in extremes. In describing a real estate housing market, realtors might use the interquartile range as a measure of the variability of housing prices when describing the middle half of the market for buyers who are interested in houses in the mid range. In addition, the interquartile range is used in the construction of box and whisker plots, explained later.

Interquartile range (3.3)

$$IQR = Q_3 - Q_1$$

The waiting times experienced by the random sample of bank customers presented in table 3.1 can be summarised using the quartiles calculated earlier.

Quartile	Waiting time (min)
Quartile 1	9.0
Quartile 2 (median)	9.5
Quartile 3	11.5

The interquartile range is:

$$Q_3 - Q_1 = 11.5 - 9 = 2.5 \text{ minutes}$$

The waiting times of the middle 50% of the 16 randomly selected bank customers spans a range of 2.5 minutes.

Variance and standard deviation

Two other measures of variability are variance and standard deviation. Because one is obtained from the other, they are presented together. The variance and standard deviation are widely used in statistics, often in conjunction with other statistical techniques. The calculation of variance and standard deviation involves considering how far each data value is from the mean and describing this dispersion on average. This differs from the two previously examined measures, range and interquartile range, which describe spread in terms of the range between two values with no reference to the mean.

To illustrate these measures of variability, consider a company that specialises in obtaining repossessed office equipment from businesses that have gone bankrupt or into liquidation, and reselling this stock to the public after it has been reconditioned. To make a decision about hiring another employee, the owner monitors how long it takes to repair a particular make and model of photocopier. The times taken for five separate repairs were 17, 9, 16, 5 and 18 hours. Which descriptive summary measures could the owner use to measure repair time? In an attempt to summarise these figures, the owner could calculate a mean. For the moment, we will assume that these five values represent the population of repair times, so the population mean is calculated as:

$$\begin{aligned}\mu &= \frac{\Sigma x}{N} \\ &= \frac{17+9+16+5+18}{5} \\ &= \frac{65}{5} \\ &= 13 \text{ hours}\end{aligned}$$

What is the variability in these five observations? One way for the owner to look at the spread of the data is to subtract the mean from each data value. *Subtracting the mean from each value of data* yields the **deviation from the mean** $(x - \mu)$. Table 3.2 shows these deviations for the photocopier repair times.

TABLE 3.2 Deviations from the mean for photocopier repair times

Repair time (x)	Deviations from the mean ($x - \mu$)
17	17 − 13 = +4
9	9 − 13 = −4
16	16 − 13 = +3
5	5 − 13 = −8
18	18 − 13 = +5
$\Sigma x = 65$	$\Sigma(x - \mu) = 0$

Figure 3.3 shows these same deviations graphically. Note that some deviations from the mean are positive and some are negative. Negative deviations represent values that are below (to the left of) the mean and positive deviations represent values that are above (to the right of) the mean.

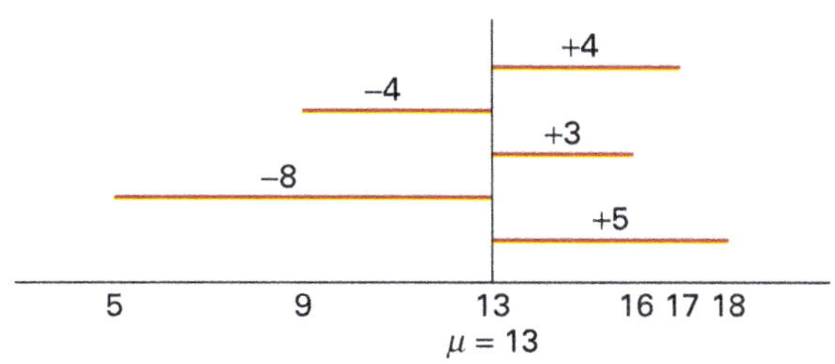

FIGURE 3.3 Geometric distances from the mean (from table 3.2)

An examination of deviations from the mean can reveal information about the variability of the data. However, the deviations are used mostly as a tool to calculate other measures of variability. Note that in table 3.2 these deviations total zero. For any set of data, the sum of all deviations from the arithmetic mean is always zero, as given in formula 3.4. This property requires considering alternative ways of obtaining measures of variability from the mean that are averaged over the set of all observations.

Sum of deviations from the arithmetic mean is always zero (3.4)

$$\Sigma(x - \mu) = 0$$

One obvious way to force the sum of deviations to have a non-zero total is to take the absolute value of each deviation from the mean. Because absolute values are not conducive to easy manipulation, mathematicians have developed an alternative mechanism for overcoming the zero-sum property of deviations from the mean. This approach uses the squares of the deviations from the mean. The result is the variance, an important measure of variability.

Variance

The **variance** is *the average of the squared deviations from the mean for a set of numbers*. The population variance is denoted by σ^2, which is read as 'sigma-squared', and is calculated using formula 3.5.

Population variance (3.5)

$$\sigma^2 = \frac{\Sigma(x - \mu)^2}{N}$$

Table 3.3 (overleaf) shows the original repair times for photocopiers of a particular make and model, the deviations from the mean and the squared deviations from the mean.

TABLE 3.3 Computing the variance and standard deviation of the photocopier repair time data

x	$x - \mu$	$(x - \mu)^2$
17	+4	16
9	−4	16
16	+3	9
5	−8	64
18	+5	25
$\Sigma x = 65$	$\Sigma(x - \mu) = 0$	$\Sigma(x - \mu)^2 = SS_x = 130$

$$\text{Variance} = \sigma^2 = \frac{SS_x}{N} = \frac{\Sigma(x-\mu)^2}{N} = \frac{130}{5} = 26$$

$$\text{Standard deviation} = \sigma = \sqrt{\frac{SS_x}{N}} = \sqrt{\frac{\Sigma(x-\mu)^2}{N}} = \sqrt{\frac{130}{5}} = \sqrt{26} = 5.1$$

The sum of the squared deviations from the mean of a set of values — called the **sum of squares of x**, sometimes abbreviated to SS_x — is used throughout statistics. For the company repairing repossessed office equipment, this value is 130. Dividing it by the number of data values (5 repairs) yields the variance for repair time.

$$\sigma^2 = \frac{130}{5} = 26$$

Because the variance is computed from squared deviations, the final result is expressed in terms of squared units of measurement. Statistics measured in squared units are problematic to interpret. Consider, for example, Darrell Lea attempting to interpret production costs in terms of squared dollars or Masport measuring production output variation in terms of squared lawn mowers. Therefore, when used as a descriptive measure, variance can be considered as an intermediate calculation in the process of obtaining the standard deviation. The main value of the variance is its use in more sophisticated statistical work such as analysis of variance.

Standard deviation

The standard deviation is arguably the most useful and most important measure of variability. It is used both as a separate entity and as a part of other analyses, such as calculating confidence intervals and in hypothesis testing.

The **standard deviation** is *the square root of the variance*. The population standard deviation is denoted by the lowercase Greek letter sigma, σ, and is calculated using formula 3.6.

Population standard deviation (3.6)

$$\sigma = \sqrt{\sigma^2} = \sqrt{\frac{\Sigma(x-\mu)^2}{N}}$$

Like the variance, the standard deviation uses the sum of the squared deviations from the mean (SS_x). It is calculated by averaging these squared deviations ($\frac{SS_x}{N}$) and taking the square root of that average. One feature of the standard deviation that distinguishes it from the variance is that the standard deviation is expressed in the same units as the raw data, whereas the variance is expressed in those units squared. Table 3.3 shows the standard deviation for the time taken to repair photocopiers for resale: $\sqrt{26}$ or 5.1 hours.

What does a standard deviation of 5.1 hours mean? The meaning of standard deviation is more readily understood from its use, which is explored below.

Meaning of standard deviation

What is a standard deviation? What does it do, and what does it mean? The most precise way to define standard deviation is by reciting the formula used to compute it; however, that does not have an intuitive practical meaning. Instead, one can think of a standard deviation as an estimate of the average distance that individual values are away from the mean. Further insight into the concept of standard deviation can be gleaned by viewing the manner in which it is applied. Two ways of applying the standard deviation are the empirical rule and Chebyshev's theorem.

Empirical rule

The **empirical rule** is an important rule of thumb that *is used to state the approximate percentage of values that lie within a given number of standard deviations from the mean of a set of data if the data are normally or approximately normally distributed.* The empirical rule is used only for three numbers of standard deviations: 1σ, 2σ and 3σ (see table 3.4). The **normal distribution** is *a unimodal and symmetrical distribution that is often referred to as the bell-shaped distribution.* When a normal distribution has an unusually large or small variance, the bell (or mound) shape of the distribution may appear less pronounced. The bell shape is more obvious in the standardised normal distribution, which has a mean of zero and standard deviation of 1 and is an important distribution used in statistical analysis.

TABLE 3.4 Empirical rule for normally or approximately normally distributed data

Distance from the mean	Values within distance
$\mu \pm 1\sigma$	68%
$\mu \pm 2\sigma$	95%
$\mu \pm 3\sigma$	99.7%

If a set of data is normally distributed, or bell shaped, approximately 68% of the data values are within one standard deviation of the mean, 95% are within two standard deviations, and almost 100% are within three standard deviations (table 3.4).

Suppose a recent report states that, for New South Wales, the average statewide price of a litre of regular unleaded petrol on a given day was \$1.50. Suppose regular unleaded petrol prices varied across the state with a standard deviation of \$0.08 and were normally distributed. According to the empirical rule, approximately 68% of prices should fall within $\mu \pm 1\sigma$ or 1.50 ± 1(\$0.08). That is, approximately 68% of the prices would be between \$1.42 and \$1.58, as shown in figure 3.4(a). Approximately 95% of prices should fall within $\mu \pm 2\sigma$ or 1.50 ± 2(\$0.08) = \$1.50 ± \$0.16, or between \$1.34 and \$1.66, as shown in figure 3.4(b). Nearly all regular unleaded petrol prices (99.7%) should fall between \$1.26 and \$1.74 ($\mu \pm 3\sigma$).

Note that with 68% of the regular unleaded petrol prices falling within one standard deviation of the mean, approximately 32% are outside this range. Because the normal distribution is symmetrical, the 32% can be split in half such that 16% lie in each tail of the distribution. Thus, approximately 16% of the regular unleaded petrol prices should be less than \$1.42 and approximately 16% of the prices should be greater than \$1.58.

Many phenomena are distributed approximately in a bell shape, including most human characteristics such as height and weight; therefore the empirical rule applies in many situations and is widely used.

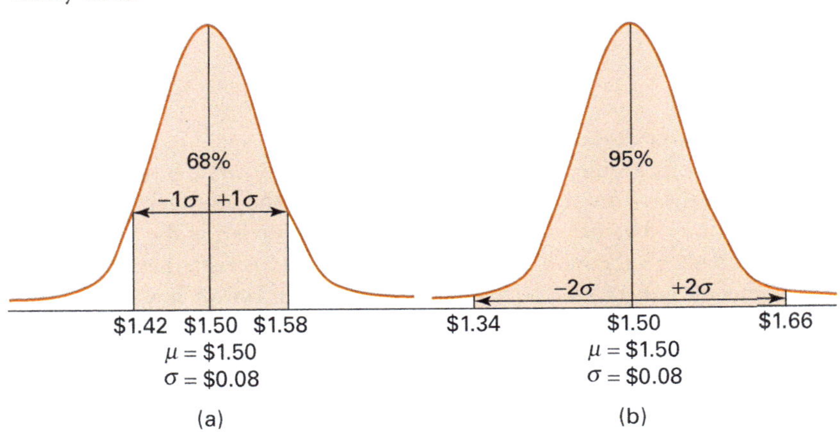

FIGURE 3.4 Empirical rule for one and two standard deviations of petrol prices

Another useful application of the empirical rule is in detecting potential **outliers**. Outliers are *observations that are unusually large or small values* that appear to be inconsistent with the rest of the data. The empirical rule suggests that, for normally distributed data, nearly all (99.7%) observations should fall within three standard deviations of the mean. In other words, only a small number (less than 0.3%) of data are expected to fall outside these ranges if the data are normally distributed. In the example on the previous page, the report suggested that 99.7% of regular unleaded petrol prices should be between \$1.26 and \$1.74. If a person examining a sample of petrol prices noted that a price of \$1.99 was recorded, this observation may be double-checked to see if an error was made or if anything unusual had occurred when this recording took place (such as a petrol strike or natural disaster).

True outliers can arise for a number of reasons, such as human error or measurement error. For example, a person may respond to an online survey and intend to indicate their age of 22 years, but accidentally type in an extra '2' and indicate their age to be 222 years. An instrument located outside that is used to record the weight of freight may be damaged by rainfall and report unusual weights to operators. In other cases, outliers may be genuine but extreme responses. For example, someone may report that they have more than 10 children; such cases are rare but do occur. In any case, it is important to check for the occurrence of outliers and investigate the legitimacy of the observation. In some cases, some researchers believe that extreme but genuine values are so unlike the other values that they should not be considered in the same analysis as the rest of the distribution, as they distort the summary measures in their intention to represent typical outcomes. For other researchers, including those working in insurance and other industries where rare events occur legitimately, the occurrence of extreme but genuine values is an important consideration in any analysis.

DEMONSTRATION PROBLEM 3.4

PROBLEM: A company produces a lightweight valve that is specified to weigh 130 grams. Unfortunately, because of natural variation in the manufacturing process, not all of the valves produced weigh exactly 130 grams. In fact, the weights of the valves produced are normally distributed with a mean weight of 130 grams and a standard deviation of 4 grams. Within what range of weights would approximately 95% of the valve weights fall? Approximately 16% of the weights would be more than what value? Approximately 0.15% of the weights would be less than what value?

SOLUTION: Because the valve weights are normally distributed, the empirical rule applies. According to the empirical rule, approximately 95% of the weights should fall within $\mu \pm 2\sigma = 130 \pm 2(4) = 130 \pm 8$ grams. Thus, approximately 95% should fall between 122 and 138 grams. Approximately 68% of the weights should fall within $\mu \pm 1\sigma$ and 32% should fall outside this interval. Because the normal distribution is symmetrical, approximately 16% should lie above $\mu + 1\sigma = 130 + 4 = 134$ grams. Approximately 99.7% of the weights should fall within $\mu \pm 3\sigma$ and, 0.3% should fall outside this interval. Half of these or 0.15% should lie below $\mu - 3\sigma = 130 - 3(4) = 130 - 12 = 118$ grams. Likewise, 0.15% should lie above $\mu + 3\sigma = 130 + 3(4) = 130 + 12 = 142$ grams.

Chebyshev's theorem

The empirical rule applies only when data are known to be approximately normally distributed. This is not always the case as data come in many shapes other than a bell shape. What do researchers use when data are not normally distributed or when the shape of the distribution is unknown? Chebyshev's theorem applies to all distributions regardless of their shape and thus can be used whenever the data distribution shape is unknown or is non-normal. If the data are bell shaped, even though Chebyshev's theorem can in theory be applied to such data, we should always apply the empirical rule as it gives better approximations to the ranges of values in the data. As shown in formula 3.7, **Chebyshev's theorem** states that *at least* $1-\frac{1}{k^2}$ *values fall within* $\pm k$ *standard deviations of the mean regardless of the shape of the distribution.*

Chebyshev's theorem
(3.7)

The proportion of values lying within k standard deviations of the mean, $\mu \pm k\sigma$, is at least:

$$1-\frac{1}{k^2}$$

where:

$k > 1$

Figure 3.5 provides a graphic illustration of a strangely shaped set of data — it is certainly not bell shaped. Applying Chebyshev's theorem, at least 75% of all values relating to these data will be within $\pm 2\sigma$ of its mean, regardless of its unusual shape. This is because, when $k = 2$, $1-\frac{1}{k^2}=1-\frac{1}{2^2}=1-\frac{1}{4}=\frac{3}{4}=.75$. In contrast, the empirical rule states that, if the data are normally distributed, 95% of all values are within $\mu \pm 2\sigma$. According to Chebyshev's theorem, the percentage of values within three standard deviations of the mean is at least 89%, in contrast to 99.7% for the empirical rule.

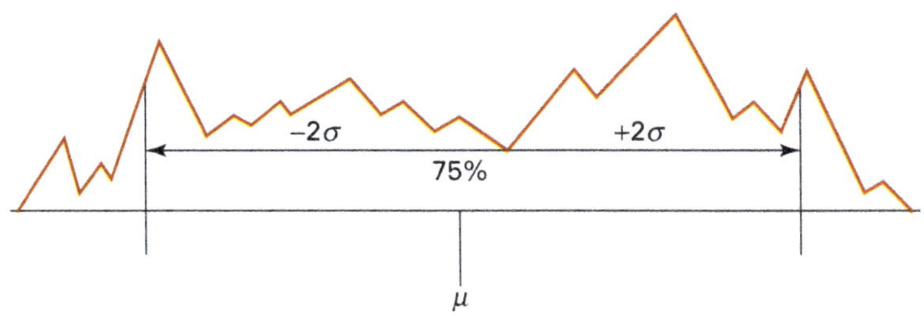

FIGURE 3.5 Application of Chebyshev's theorem for two standard deviations

Because a formula is used to calculate proportions for Chebyshev's theorem, any value of k greater than 1 can be used. For example, if $k = 2.5$, at least 84% of all values are within $\mu \pm 2.5\sigma$, because $1-\frac{1}{k^2}=1-\frac{1}{(2.5)^2}=.84$.

DEMONSTRATION PROBLEM 3.5

PROBLEM: In the IT industry, the average age of professional employees tends to be lower than in many other business professions. Suppose the average age of a professional employed by a particular computer firm is 28 years with a standard deviation of 5 years. A histogram of professional employee ages in this firm reveals that the data are not normally distributed but, rather, that the bulk of employees are in their twenties and that few workers are over 40. Apply Chebyshev's theorem to determine within what range of ages at least 85% of the workers' ages fall.

SOLUTION: Because the ages are not normally distributed, it is not appropriate to apply the empirical rule; therefore, Chebyshev's theorem must be applied to answer the question.

Chebyshev's theorem states that at least $1-\frac{1}{k^2}$ of the values are within $\mu \pm k\sigma$. Because 85% of the values are within this range:

$$1-\frac{1}{k^2}=.85$$

Solving for k yields:

$$.15=\frac{1}{k^2}$$

$$k^2 = 6.667$$

$$k = 2.58$$

Chebyshev's theorem says that at least 85% of the values are within $\pm 2.58\sigma$ of the mean. For $\mu = 28$ and $\sigma = 5$, at least .85, or 85%, of the values are within $28 \pm 2.58(5) = 28 \pm 12.9$ years of age, or between 15.1 and 40.9 years old.

Population versus sample variance and standard deviation

In statistics we often want to make decisions about population parameters such as μ, the population mean, or σ, the population standard deviation; however, we are often unable to do so because it requires observation of every member of the population, which can be expensive in terms of time, money and other resources. Instead, we observe a subset of the population, a sample, and summarise what we have observed in the form of sample statistics. We tend to use sample statistics to provide estimates or make inferences about equivalent population parameters.

The sample variance is denoted by s^2 and the sample standard deviation by s. The main use for sample variances and standard deviations is as estimators of population variances (σ^2, sigma squared) and standard deviations (σ, sigma). The computation of the sample variance, using formula 3.8, and sample standard deviation, using formula 3.9, differs slightly from calculation of the population variance and standard deviation. Both the sample variance and sample standard deviation use $n - 1$ in the denominator instead of n, because using n in the denominator of a sample variance results in a statistic that tends to underestimate the population variance. While discussion of the properties of good estimators is beyond the scope of this text, one of the properties of a good estimator is being unbiased. Whereas using n in the denominator of the sample variance makes it a biased estimator, using $n - 1$ allows it to be an unbiased estimator, which is a desirable property in inferential statistics.

Sample variance (3.8)

$$s^2 = \frac{\Sigma(x-\bar{x})^2}{n-1}$$

Sample standard deviation (3.9)

$$s = \sqrt{s^2} = \sqrt{\frac{\Sigma(x-\bar{x})^2}{n-1}}$$

Suppose a firm is interested in the expenditure that staff incur on entertainment for potential clients. A sample of six staff members reveals the following monthly expense amounts: $433, $259, $438, $376, $345 and $399.

The sample variance and sample standard deviation are computed as follows.

x	$(x-\bar{x})$	$(x-\bar{x})^2$
433	58	3 364
259	−116	13 456
438	63	3 969
376	1	1
345	−30	900
399	24	576
$\Sigma x = 2\,250$	$\Sigma(x-\bar{x}) = 0$	$\Sigma(x-\bar{x})^2 = 22\,266$

$$\bar{x} = \frac{2\,250}{6} = 375$$

$$s^2 = \frac{\Sigma(x-\bar{x})^2}{n-1} = \frac{22\,266}{5} = 4453.2$$

$$s = \sqrt{s^2} = \sqrt{4453.2} = 66.73$$

The sample variance is 4453.2 and the sample standard deviation is $66.73. We can interpret the standard deviation as a measure of the average distance individual values in the data are from the mean. Using Chebyshev's theorem, at least 75% of all values are within 2 standard deviations of the mean. In this case, Chebyshev's theorem tells us that at least 75% of monthly expenses are within 2(66.73) = \$133.46 of the mean of \$375: that is, in the range \$241.54 to \$508.46. In fact, however, we find 100% of our six values are in this range — this illustrates that while Chebyshev's theorem is an approximation showing the minimum percentages in a given range, in practice we may have more, especially if the data are bell shaped.

DEMONSTRATION PROBLEM 3.6

DP03-06 PROBLEM: Table 3.1 (p. 49) lists the waiting times of a random selection of customers at a busy bank during the morning period. It was previously stated that the manager believes that the potential increase in waiting times is arising because customers are moving away from doing their banking during the lunchtime period. The manager decides to verify this and collects data related to the number of customers arriving during lunchtime for five randomly selected days over a month. The results are as follows.

25	30	15	35	45

Compute the variance and the standard deviation for the number of customers during lunchtime, assuming that the data are sample data.

SOLUTION: The manager computes the variance and the standard deviation for these data in the following manner.

x	$(x-\bar{x})$	$(x-\bar{x})^2$
25	−5	25
30	0	0
15	−15	225
35	5	25
45	15	225
$\Sigma x = 150$	$\Sigma(x-\bar{x}) = 0$	$\Sigma(x-\bar{x})^2 = 500$

$$\bar{x} = \frac{\Sigma x}{n} = \frac{150}{5} = 30$$

$$s^2 = \frac{\Sigma(x-\bar{x})^2}{n-1} = \frac{500}{4} = 125$$

$$s = \sqrt{s^2} = 11.18$$

Computational formulas for variance and standard deviation

An alternative method of calculating variance and standard deviation, sometimes referred to as the computational method or shortcut method, is available. Because:

$$\Sigma(x-\mu)^2 = \Sigma x^2 - \frac{(\Sigma x)^2}{N}$$

and:

$$\Sigma(x-\bar{x})^2 = \Sigma x^2 - \frac{(\Sigma x)^2}{n}$$

these equivalent expressions can be substituted into the original formulas 3.5, 3.6, 3.8 and 3.9 for variance and standard deviation, yielding the computational formulas 3.10 and 3.11 (overleaf).

Computational formulas for population and sample variance (3.10)

$$\sigma^2 = \frac{\Sigma x^2 - \frac{(\Sigma x)^2}{N}}{N}$$

$$s^2 = \frac{\Sigma x^2 - \frac{(\Sigma x)^2}{n}}{n-1}$$

Computational formulas for population and sample standard deviation (3.11)

$$\sigma = \sqrt{\sigma^2} = \sqrt{\frac{\Sigma x^2 - \frac{(\Sigma x)^2}{N}}{N}}$$

$$s = \sqrt{s^2} = \sqrt{\frac{\Sigma x^2 - \frac{(\Sigma x)^2}{n}}{n-1}}$$

These computational formulas use the sum of the x values and the sum of the x^2 values instead of the difference between the mean and each value and computed deviations. Before calculators and computers were available, this method was usually faster and easier than using the original formulas.

For situations in which the mean is already computed or is given, alternative forms of these formulas are:

$$\sigma^2 = \frac{\Sigma x^2 - N\mu^2}{N}$$

$$s^2 = \frac{\Sigma x^2 - n(\bar{x})^2}{n-1}$$

Using the computational method, the owner of the company that reconditions and resells office equipment can compute a population variance and standard deviation for the photocopier repair data (in table 3.2, p. 63). The calculations are shown in table 3.5 and can be compared with those results in table 3.3 (p. 64).

TABLE 3.5 Computational formula calculations of variance and standard deviation for photocopier repair data

x	x^2
17	289
9	81
16	256
5	25
18	324
$\Sigma x = 65$	$\Sigma x^2 = 975$

$$\sigma^2 = \frac{\Sigma x^2 - \frac{(\Sigma x)^2}{N}}{N} = \frac{975 - \frac{(65)^2}{5}}{5} = \frac{975 - 845}{5} = \frac{130}{5} = 26$$

$$\sigma = \sqrt{26} = 5.1$$

Demonstration problem 3.6 showed how the sample variance and standard deviation can be calculated using the original formulas presented. Using computational formulas, the variance and standard deviation can be computed as follows.

x	x^2
25	625
30	900
15	225
35	1 225
45	2 025
$\Sigma x = 150$	$\Sigma x^2 = 5\,000$

$$s^2 = \frac{\Sigma x^2 - \frac{(\Sigma x)^2}{n}}{n-1} = \frac{5000 - \frac{(150)^2}{5}}{4} = \frac{5000-4500}{4} = \frac{500}{4} = 125$$

$$s = \sqrt{s^2} = 11.18$$

The results are the same. The sample standard deviation obtained by both methods is 11.18.

z-scores

A **z-score** represents *the number of standard deviations that a value (x) is above or below the mean of a set of numbers*. Using z-scores, as shown in formula 3.12, allows translation of a value's raw distance from the mean into units of standard deviations.

z-score
(3.12)

$$z = \frac{x-\mu}{\sigma} \text{ for population data}$$

$$z = \frac{x-\bar{x}}{s} \text{ for sample data}$$

If a z-score is negative, the raw value (x) is below the mean. If the z-score is positive, the raw value (x) is above the mean.

For example, suppose a teacher determines that her students' marks are normally distributed with a mean of 60 and a standard deviation of 5. Suppose she wants to determine the z-score for a student with a mark of 70. This value ($x = 70$) is 10 units above the mean, so the z-score is:

$$z = \frac{70-60}{5} = +2.00$$

This z-score signifies that the student's mark is two standard deviations above the mean.

Recall that the empirical rule is useful to determine the approximate percentage of data that lie within a given number of standard deviations from the mean when data are normally or approximately normally distributed. For example, if data are normal, or bell shaped, 68% of the data values are within one standard deviation of the mean; 95% are within two standard deviations; and, 99.7% are within three standard deviations. Because a z-score is the number of standard deviations that an individual data value is from the mean, the empirical rule can be restated in terms of z-scores.

In the example involving student grades, a raw mark of $x = 50$ is two standard deviations below the mean, or $z = \frac{(50-60)}{5} = -2$. Figure 3.6 (overleaf) shows that, because the value of 50 is two standard deviations below the mean and 70 is two standard deviations above the mean ($z = +2$), approximately 95% of the students' marks should be between 50 and 70. Because 5% of the values are outside the range of two standard deviations from the mean and the normal distribution is symmetrical, 2.5% ($\frac{1}{2}$ of the 5% outside two standard deviations) are below the value of 50. Thus 97.5% of the students' marks are below the value of 70.

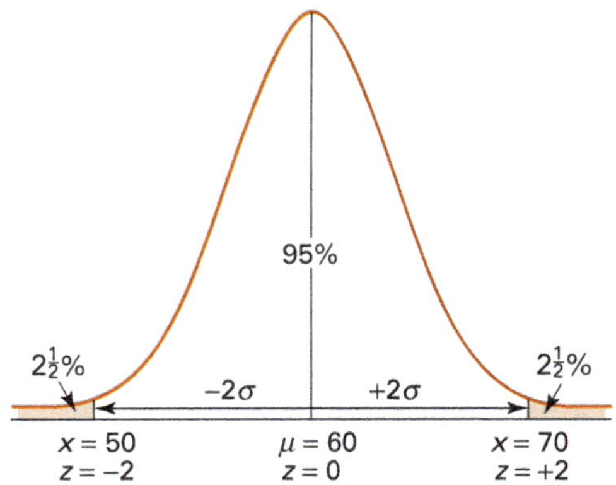

FIGURE 3.6 Percentage breakdown of scores two standard deviations from the mean

Approximately 68% of the values are between $z = -1$ and $z = +1$.
Approximately 95% of the values are between $z = -2$ and $z = +2$.
Approximately 99.7% of the values are between $z = -3$ and $z = +3$.

What does a *z*-score of 1.2 or −2.4 mean? In the student marks example, a *z*-score equal to 1.2 represents a student with a mark that is 1.2 standard deviations above the mean, a mark of 60 + 1.2(5) = 66. A *z*-score of −2.4 represents a student with a mark that is 2.4 standard deviations below the mean, a mark of 60 − 2.4(5) = 48.

Coefficient of variation

The **coefficient of variation (CV)** is a descriptive summary measure that is *the ratio of the standard deviation to the mean expressed as a percentage* and is calculated using formula 3.13.

Coefficient of variation (3.13)

$$CV = \frac{\sigma}{\mu}(100) \text{ for population data}$$

$$CV = \frac{s}{\bar{x}}(100) \text{ for sample data}$$

The coefficient of variation essentially is a relative comparison of a standard deviation with its mean. The coefficient of variation can be useful in comparing standard deviations that have been calculated from data with different magnitudes or which are in different units.

Suppose a sample of the closing prices for stock A for five days selected randomly over the past month are \$25, \$27, \$35, \$34 and \$36. To compute a coefficient of variation for these prices, first determine the sample mean and sample standard deviation: $\bar{x} = \$31.40$ and $s = \$5.03$. The coefficient of variation for the sample is:

$$CV_A = \frac{s_A}{\bar{x}_A}(100) = \frac{5.03}{31.40}(100) = 16.02\%$$

The standard deviation is 16.02% of the mean.

Sometimes financial investors use the coefficient of variation, the standard deviation or both as measures of risk. Imagine a stock with a price that never changes. An investor bears no risk of losing money from the price going down because no variability occurs in the price. Suppose, in contrast, that the price of the stock fluctuates wildly. An investor who buys at a low price and sells for a high price can make a nice profit. However, if the price drops below what the investor paid for it, the stock owner is subject to a potential loss. The greater the variability is, the greater is the potential for profits and losses. Hence, investors use measures of variability such as standard deviation and coefficient of variation to determine the risk of a stock. What does the coefficient of variation tell us about the risk of a stock that the standard deviation does not?

Suppose a sample of closing prices for a second stock, stock B, on these same five days were $3, $4, $7, $10 and $9. The sample mean for stock B is $6.60 with a sample standard deviation of $3.05. The coefficient of variation can be computed for stock B as:

$$CV_B = \frac{s_B}{\bar{x}_B}(100) = \frac{3.05}{6.60}(100) = 46.21\%$$

The standard deviation for stock B is 46.21% of the mean.

With the standard deviation as the measure of risk over this period of time, stock A is more risky because it has a larger standard deviation. However, the average price of stock A is almost five times as much as that of stock B. Relative to the amount invested in stock A, the standard deviation of $5.03 may not represent as much as the standard deviation of $3.05 for stock B, which has an average price of only $6.60. The coefficient of variation reveals the risk of a stock in terms of the size of its standard deviation relative to the size of its mean (as a percentage). Stock B has a coefficient of variation that is more than double the coefficient of variation for stock A. Using the coefficient of variation as a measure of risk indicates that stock B is riskier.

PRACTICE PROBLEMS

Practising the calculations

P03-08 **3.8** A data set contains the following seven values.

6	2	4	7	8	3	5

a. Calculate the range.
b. Calculate the population variance.
c. Calculate the population standard deviation.
d. Calculate the interquartile range.
e. Calculate the *z*-score for each value.
f. Calculate the coefficient of variation.

P03-09 **3.9** A data set contains the following eight values.

4	3	0	5	2	9	4	5

a. Calculate the range.
b. Calculate the sample variance.
c. Calculate the sample standard deviation.
d. Calculate the interquartile range.
e. Calculate the coefficient of variation.

3.10 According to Chebyshev's theorem, at least what proportion of the data is within $\mu \pm k\sigma$ for each of the following values of *k*?

a. 2
b. 2.5
c. 1.6
d. 3.2

Testing your understanding

3.11 A car fleet manager working for a local council is thinking of gradually replacing the current fleet of vehicles used by the council with vehicles that use LPG (gas) rather than unleaded petrol. The concern is not so much the average price of petrol but rather the variability in price that occurs, as this becomes problematic for budgeting and managing reimbursements to employees. The fleet manager will upgrade the fleet to LPG-powered vehicles so long as the variability in the LPG price is lower than that of unleaded petrol. The fleet manager uses a website that collates data on fuel prices in the council region to produce the following summary statistics based on a random sample of prices drawn from the past year.

	Price of unleaded petrol (cents)	Price of LPG (cents)
Average	150.43	79.82
Standard deviation	6.19	5.44

Interpret the output and comment on the variability observed for the price of each fuel. If you make this comparison using the standard deviation for each fuel type, what conclusion can you reach? Suppose the fleet manager tells you that they prefer to compare variability relative to the size of each fuel's mean price. Make a recommendation to the fleet manager about which vehicles should be used in the upgrade.

3.12 A wine industry association reported in its magazine that a particular wine was being marketed by online wine distributors with an average market price of $125 and standard deviation of $12, with the distribution of prices being approximately bell shaped. One boutique wine distributor is concerned by this report as they are charging $50 per bottle for this particular wine.

Between what two price points would approximately 68% of prices fall? Between what two numbers would 95% of the prices fall? Between what two values would 99.7% of the prices fall? Write a short report informing the distributor whether the current price being charged is comparable to others.

3.13 An employment agency is concerned that some of its clients for whom it has found part-time work are not receiving enough hours of employment. It examines a sample of clients and asks them to report how many hours they had worked in the last month. The agency notes that the data are not normally distributed.

If the mean hours worked is 38 and the standard deviation is 6 hours, what proportion of values would fall between 26 hours and 50 hours? What proportion of values would fall between 14 hours and 62 hours? Between what two values would 89% of the values fall? Explain your findings in simple terms to the employment agency's management team.

BCREA **3.14** Baycoast City Real Estate Agents has been approached by a government organisation to examine rental affordability in the Baycoast area. The organisation seeks information on the weekly rental price, particularly information about the average weekly rental for a house and the range of rental amounts that defines where 95% of rentals will fall. Using the Baycoast data set, calculate the necessary statistics and write a short report to the government organisation in answer to their question (assuming the data are bell shaped).

3.4 Measures of shape

Measures of shape are *tools that can be used to describe the appearance of a distribution of data.* In this section, we examine two numerical measures of shape: skewness and kurtosis. The box and whisker plot, a graphical measure of variation, is also examined.

Skewness

A distribution of data where the right half is a mirror image of the left half is said to be *symmetrical.* One example of a symmetrical distribution is the normal distribution, or bell curve.

A distribution is skewed when it *is asymmetrical or lacks symmetry.* The distribution in figure 3.7 has no **skewness** because it is symmetrical. Figure 3.8 shows a distribution that is skewed to the left, or negatively skewed. It shows that a greater number of observations occur in the left tail of the distribution relative to the normal distribution. These observations would have negative z-scores as they occur below (or to the left of) the mean. Figure 3.9 shows a distribution that is skewed to the right, or positively skewed. In this case, a greater number of observations appear in the right tail (above the mean) of the distribution relative to what occurs in a normal distribution.

The skewed portion is the long, thin part of the curve. Many researchers use the term 'skewed distribution' to indicate that the data are sparse at one end of the distribution and piled up at the other end. Teachers sometimes refer to a grade distribution as skewed, meaning that few students scored at one end of the grading scale, and many students scored at the other end. Skewness can occur when the data have extreme values, which can appear to pull the distribution in a particular direction. For example, the time to travel to the city on a train may consistently occur around a certain set of values and the distribution describing travel times may appear bell shaped. If the data, however, contain journeys that take unusually longer, due to bad weather or track maintenance, the distribution of travel times will be skewed by these extreme values and appear similar to figure 3.9.

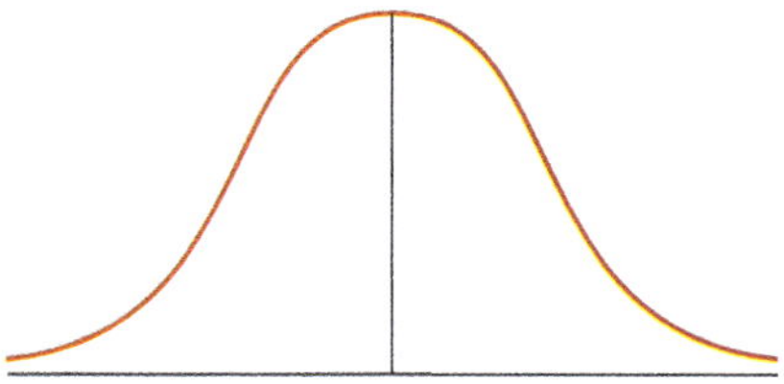

FIGURE 3.7 Symmetrical distribution

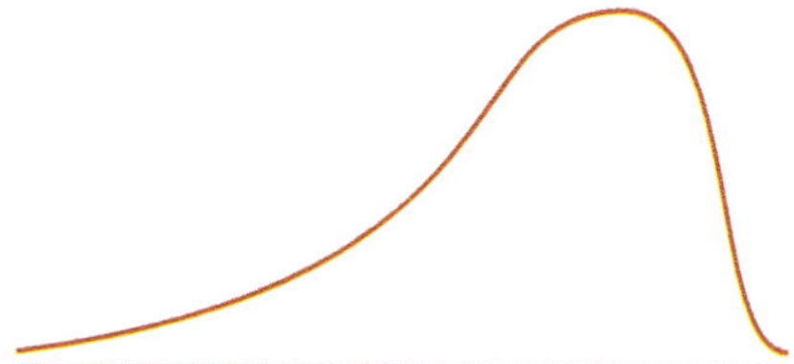

FIGURE 3.8 Distribution skewed left, or negatively skewed

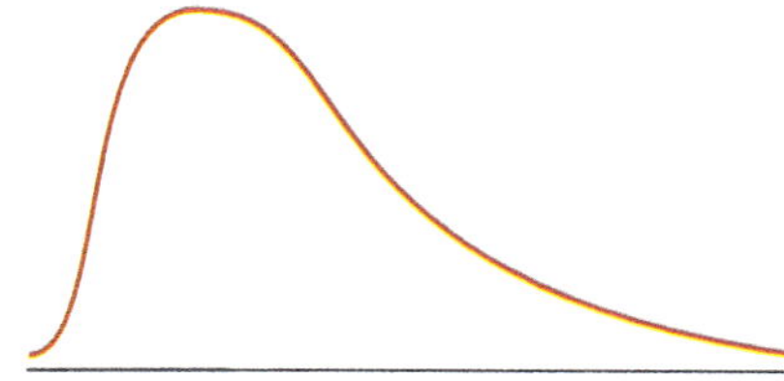

FIGURE 3.9 Distribution skewed right, or positively skewed

Skewness and the relationship of the mean, median and mode

The concept of skewness helps us to understand the relationship between the mean, median and mode. In a unimodal distribution (distribution with a single peak or mode) that is skewed, the mode is the value on the horizontal axis where the apex (high point) of the curve occurs. The mean tends to be located toward the tail of the distribution, because the mean is drawn towards the extreme values. The median is generally located somewhere between the mode and the mean. A bell-shaped or normal distribution, with the mean, median and mode all at the centre of the distribution, has no skewness. Figure 3.10 displays the relationship between the mean, median and mode for different types of skewness.

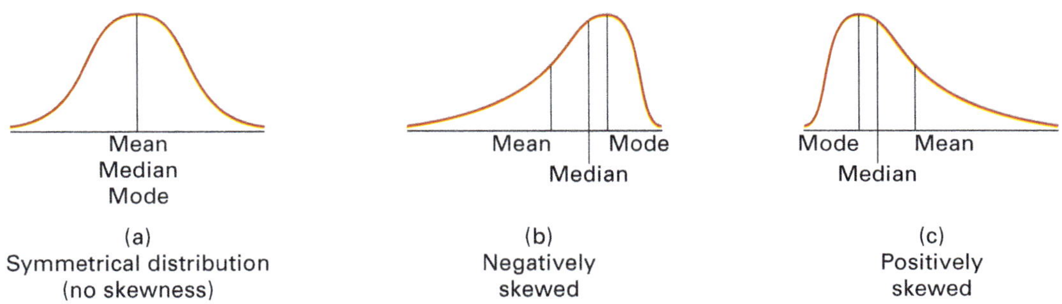

FIGURE 3.10 Relationship between mean, median and mode

Coefficient of skewness

Statistician Karl Pearson is credited with developing at least two coefficients of skewness that can be used to determine the degree of skewness in a distribution. One of these coefficients, the Pearsonian **coefficient of skewness**, can be calculated using formula 3.14. This coefficient *compares the mean and median in light of the magnitude of the standard deviation.* Note that, if the distribution is symmetrical, the mean and median are the same value and hence the coefficient of skewness is equal to zero.

Pearsonian coefficient of skewness **(3.14)**

$$s_k = \frac{3(\mu - M_d)}{\sigma} \text{ for population data}$$

$$s_k = \frac{3(\bar{x} - M_d)}{s} \text{ for sample data}$$

where:

M_d = the median

Suppose, for example, that a distribution has a mean of 29, median of 26, and standard deviation of 12.3. The coefficient of skewness is:

$$s_k = \frac{3(29-26)}{12.3} = +0.73$$

Because the value of s_k is positive, the distribution is positively skewed. If the value of s_k is negative, the distribution is negatively skewed. The greater the magnitude of s_k, the more skewed is the distribution.

Kurtosis

In 1905, Karl Pearson originally defined the concept of **kurtosis** to *describe the amount of peakedness of a distribution.* Pearson first used the concept of kurtosis to compare the shape of a distribution with the shape of a normal distribution that has the same variance. The normal distribution is often described as having zero 'excess' kurtosis. Distributions with excess (sometimes called positive) kurtosis are **leptokurtic** distributions, from the prefix 'lepto-' meaning slender. Such distributions arise when a higher frequency of values occur nearer the mean relative to a normal distribution. Some definitions of kurtosis also recognise that, relative to a normal distribution with the same variance, changes in the number of observations moving from the 'shoulders' of the distribution to the centre of the distribution often occur with changes in the tails of distribution. For example, the leptokurtic distribution is also described as having longer (heavier) tails relative to the normal distribution. In this way, kurtosis is a measure related to both peakedness and tail heaviness of a distribution. The tails of distributions are important to many researchers and those working in finance and economics because they often provide additional insights into risk and uncertainty.

Distributions that are flatter and spread out relative to a normal distribution with the same variance are referred to as **platykurtic** distributions, from the prefix 'platy-' meaning broad. Distributions that are relatively flat and plateau shaped are sometimes described as having negative excess kurtosis and arise when values in the data occur with similar frequencies. Between these two types are distributions that are more 'normal' in shape, referred to as **mesokurtic** distributions. These three types of kurtosis are illustrated in figure 3.11.

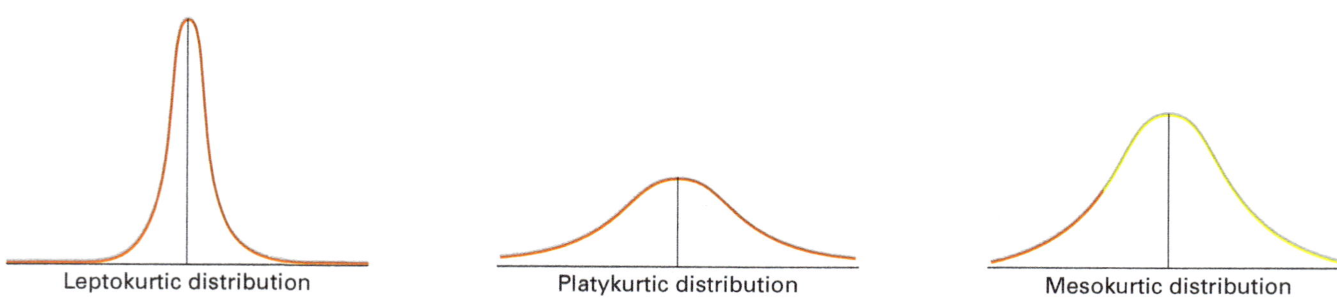

FIGURE 3.11 Types of kurtosis

Box and whisker plots

Another way to describe a distribution of data is by using a box and whisker plot. A **box and whisker plot**, sometimes called a *boxplot*, is *a diagram that uses five summary measures (the first and third quartiles, along with the median and the two most extreme values not deemed outliers) to depict a distribution graphically.* The plot is constructed by using a box to represent the middle 50% of the data and lines to indicate the remaining 50%. This *box* begins at the first quartile and extends to the third quartile. These box endpoints (Q_1 and Q_3) are referred to as the *hinges* of the box. A line within the box represents the location of the median. From the first and third quartiles, lines referred to as *whiskers* are extended out from the box toward the outermost data values that are not deemed outliers. If there are no outliers in the data, the whiskers extend to the minimum and maximum values. Box and whisker plots may be drawn vertically (as in this chapter) or horizontally.

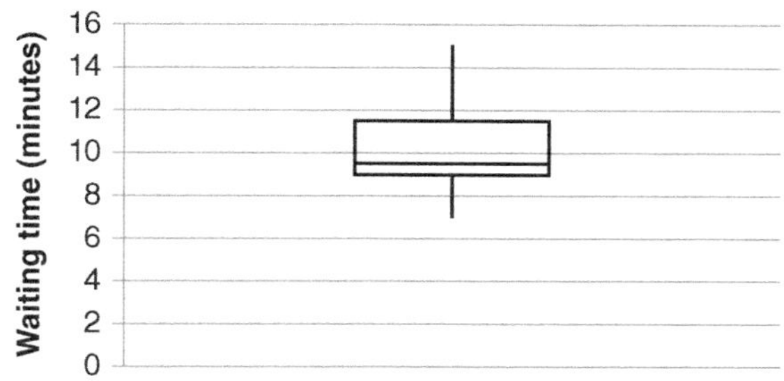

FIGURE 3.12 Box and whisker plot of bank customer waiting times during the morning

To demonstrate, a box and whisker plot is presented in figure 3.12 to depict the distribution of observed waiting times for a random selection of bank customers visiting a bank during the morning period, with the original time data presented in table 3.1 (p. 49). The box and whisker plot shows the box extending from the first quartile (9 minutes) to the third quartile (11.5 minutes) and a line within the box representing the median waiting time of a bank customer (9.5 minutes). The two whiskers extend to the two outermost observations that are not considered outliers. In this example, as will be discussed in more detail, no outliers are detected so the two outermost observations are the minimum and maximum waiting times. One whisker extends from the edge of the box at the first quartile to the minimum waiting time observed in the sample (7 minutes) and another extends from the third quartile to the maximum value observed (15 minutes).

The box extends from the first quartile, Q_1, to the third quartile, Q_3. This distance is referred to as the interquartile range (IQR) and is computed by $Q_3 - Q_1$ as in formula 3.3. The interquartile range includes the middle 50% of the data and always equals the length of the box. In the banking example, the interquartile range is calculated as $11.5 - 9.0 = 2.5$ minutes.

The empirical rule suggests that researchers can construct a range of values to detect whether observations are potential outliers. This method is based on detecting values that are three or more standard deviations above or below the mean. Box and whisker plots enable a different approach to detecting potential outliers based on constructing ranges using the quartile values. At a distance of 1.5 IQR outward from the lower and upper quartiles are what are referred to as *inner fences.* The inner fences are established as follows.

$$Q_1 - 1.5\,\text{IQR}$$
$$Q_3 + 1.5\,\text{IQR}$$

Outer fences can be constructed based on a distance that is 3.0 IQR from the lower and upper quartiles:

$$Q_1 - 3.0\,\text{IQR}$$
$$Q_3 + 3.0\,\text{IQR}$$

Figure 3.13 (overleaf) shows the features of a box and whisker plot.

The whiskers of a boxplot extend to the most extreme values that are not considered outliers. In other words, the whiskers extend to the two outermost values that are inside the inner fences. Values in the data distribution that are outside the inner fences, but within the outer fences, are referred to as *moderate outliers.* Values that are outside the outer fences are called *extreme outliers.* Thus, one use of a box and whisker plot is to identify outliers. In some computer-produced box and whisker plots, the whiskers are drawn to the largest and smallest data values within the inner fences. An unshaded triangle (or similar symbol such as an asterisk) is then printed for each data value located between the inner and outer fences to indicate a moderate outlier. Values outside the outer fences are indicated by a solid triangle (or similar symbol such as a zero) on the graph. These values are extreme outliers.

If we re-examine the waiting times of banking customers, as presented in table 3.1 (p. 49), we can identify moderate outliers as those values being outside the inner fences and extreme outliers being those values outside the outer fences. The inner fence is constructed by:

$$Q_1 - 1.5\,\text{IQR} = 9 - 1.5(2.5) = 5.25 \text{ minutes}$$
$$Q_3 + 1.5\,\text{IQR} = 11.5 + 1.5(2.5) = 15.25 \text{ minutes}$$

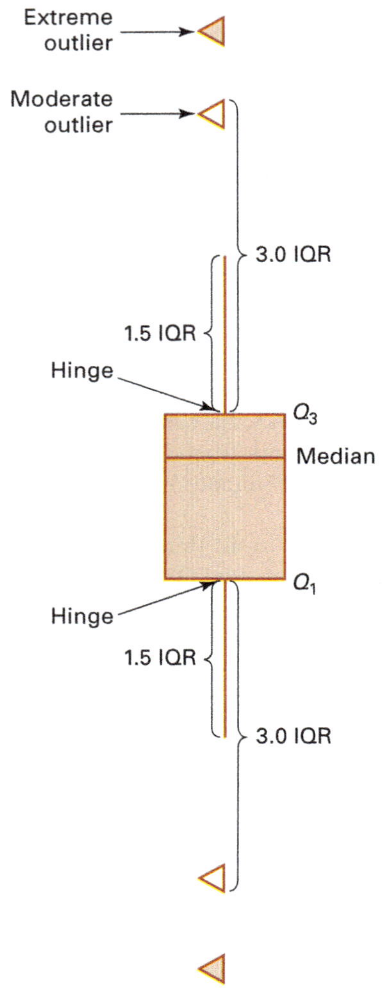

FIGURE 3.13 Box and whisker plot features

The outer fence is constructed by:

$$Q_1 - 3.0\,\text{IQR} = 9 - 3(2.5) = 1.5 \text{ minutes}$$
$$Q_3 + 3.0\,\text{IQR} = 11.5 + 3(2.5) = 19 \text{ minutes}$$

In this example, we can see that there are no outliers identified (either moderate or extreme) as all the reported waiting times are inside these boundaries. As a result, the whiskers extend to the minimum and maximum waiting times in the sample.

DEMONSTRATION PROBLEM 3.7

DP03-07 One of the factors that universities are judged by in the *Good University Guide* is the starting salary of university graduates. To check the statistics reported by the *Good University Guide,* a regional university decided to survey recent graduates. The survey asked graduates their starting salary and degree. A random selection of 50 responses from each degree can be found on the student website in file DP03-07.xls. Draw boxplots to compare the starting salaries of graduates with different degrees.

Please refer to 'Going further with KaddStat' at www.johnwiley.com.au/highered/black4e/kaddstat for KaddStat instructions.

PRACTICE PROBLEMS

Practising the calculations

3.15 The size in square metres of properties sold by a major real estate firm in Australia in the last year was analysed using descriptive summary measures. The mean size of a one-bedroom residential apartment sold by this firm was 60 square metres, the median was 55 square metres, and the standard deviation was 12 square metres. Compute the value of the Pearsonian coefficient of skewness and interpret the result.

P03-16 **3.16** A survey of drivers asked respondents to list the age in years of the vehicle that they predominantly drive. The following data represent a sample of 18 responses provided. Use the data to construct a box and whisker plot. List the median, Q_1, Q_3, the endpoints of the inner fences and the endpoints of the outer fences. Are any outliers present in the data?

1	3	8	5	8	4	9	11	4
3	17	3	15	9	7	5	4	2

Testing your understanding

3.17 An online retailer that sells board games and puzzles has produced summary measures, shown in the right-hand column, describing the cost charged to consumers for shipping. Write a short description of the data incorporating a discussion of symmetry and skewness to inform the retail owners whether the data related to shipping charges are bell shaped and how this is reflected in the measures of central tendency, particularly the median and mean.

Cost of shipping charges	
Mean	10.5331
Standard error	0.171893
Median	9.8
Mode	8
Standard deviation	2.881457
Sample variance	8.302794
Kurtosis	3.002015
Skewness	1.855815
Range	13
Minimum	7.7
Maximum	20.7
Sum	2959.8
Count	281

3.18 A manufacturer of solar power systems is doing some comparative testing of two differently designed 1.9 kWh (10 module) systems. On the basis of a sample of 52 observations, both systems, on average, produce 8.18 kWh per day. The company is seeking to further develop the system that appears to produce a fairly stable amount of output above and below this measure of central tendency. System B was rejected as it displayed too much variation in output relative to system A and did so with noticeable negative skewness. Based on the data and the plots below, do you agree with this decision?

	A	B	C
1	**Boxplot Output**	System A	System B
2	First Quartile	7.9092	7.3904
3	Median	8.1898	8.5002
4	Third Quartile	8.5112	8.8811
5	Interquartile Range	0.6020	1.4907

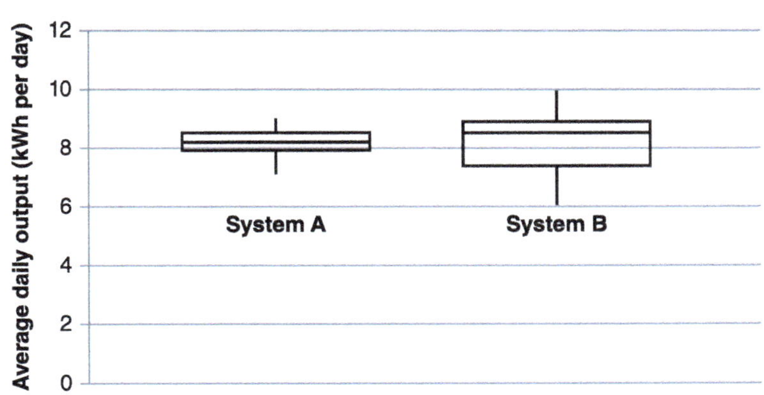

3.5 Measures of association

Measures of association are numerical descriptors that yield information about the relatedness of numerical variables. In this chapter, we discuss only one measure of association between two numerical variables, correlation.

Correlation

Correlation is *a measure of the degree of relatedness of variables.* It can help a business researcher in the real estate sector determine, for example, the extent to which house price is related to the number of bedrooms. Logically, the two variables, price of a house and number of bedrooms, should be related. For a sample of pairs of data, correlation analysis can yield a numerical value that represents the degree of relatedness between the two variables. In the advertising industry, businesses make decisions to buy and sell advertising on the basis that sales are correlated with certain variables. For example, advertisers may ask whether any correlation is evident between the size of an advertisement and the sales of the product being advertised. Do sales and the frequency with which a product is advertised show any correlation? How strong are the correlations? In other settings, similar questions about the association between two variables often arise. In economics and finance, how strong is the correlation between the official interest rate and the unemployment rate? In human resource management, what variables are related to whether an individual employee expresses an interest in working with the same firm in the future? Is this related to how much the employee is currently paid, the number of employees they currently manage, or other variables?

Ideally, researchers would like to calculate the population coefficient of correlation (ρ). However, because researchers virtually always deal with sample data, this section introduces the sample coefficient of correlation, r. This measure is applicable only if both variables being analysed are quantitative data.

The statistic r is the **Pearson product–moment correlation coefficient**, named after Karl Pearson (1857–1936), an English statistician who developed several coefficients of correlation along with other significant statistical concepts. The term r is a *measure of the linear association* between two variables and is calculated using formula 3.15. It is a number that ranges from −1 to +1, representing the direction and relative strength of the linear relationship between the variables. An r value of +1 denotes a perfect (linear) positive relationship between two sets of numbers. An r value of −1 denotes a perfect (linear) negative relationship, which indicates an inverse relationship between two variables; as one variable gets larger, the other gets smaller. An r value of 0 means no linear relationship is present between the two variables.

Pearson product–moment correlation coefficient (3.15)

$$r = \frac{\Sigma(x-\bar{x})(y-\bar{y})}{\sqrt{\Sigma(x-\bar{x})^2\,\Sigma(y-\bar{y})^2}} = \frac{\Sigma xy - \dfrac{(\Sigma x \Sigma y)}{n}}{\sqrt{\left[\Sigma x^2 - \dfrac{(\Sigma x)^2}{n}\right]\left[\Sigma y^2 - \dfrac{(\Sigma y)^2}{n}\right]}}$$

Figure 3.14 depicts five different degrees of correlation; (a) represents strong negative correlation, (b) represents moderate negative correlation, (c) represents moderate positive correlation, (d) represents strong positive correlation, and (e) represents virtually no correlation.

Suppose a small retailer that sells books online believes that older customers tend to purchase more books during a single online visit while younger customers tend to add fewer items to their online cart on any one shopping occasion. If such a relationship is found, the retailer intends to talk to a marketing consultant about how younger customers might be encouraged to purchase additional books before finalising their purchases. To do so, the retailer asks what is the correlation between the number of books a customer purchases and their age? In table 3.6 (p. 82), the data for 16 customers is shown, along with the steps for calculating r.

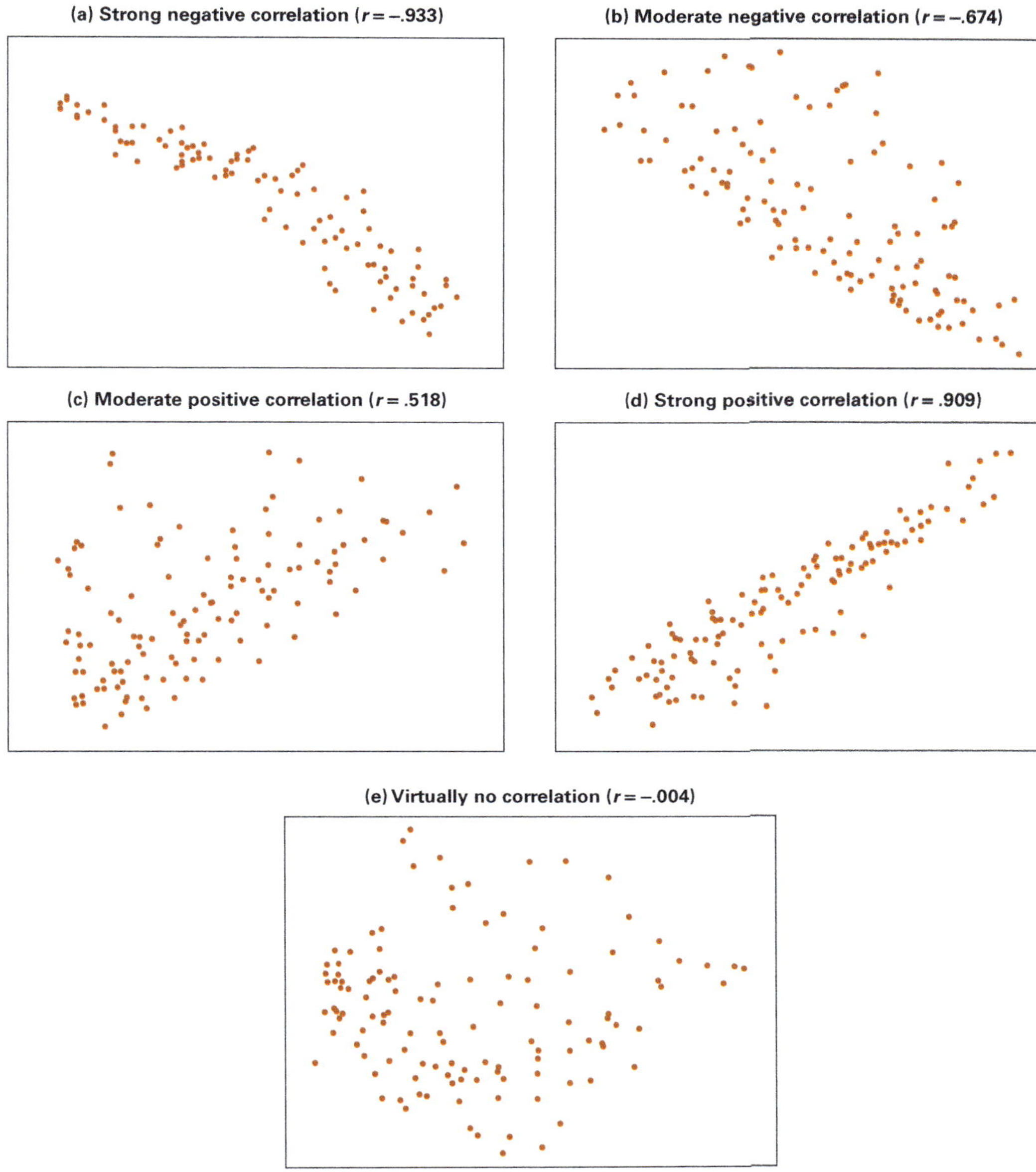

FIGURE 3.14
Five correlations

Examination of the formula for computing a Pearson product–moment correlation coefficient reveals that the following values must be obtained: Σx, Σy, Σx^2, Σy^2, Σxy and n. The terms with capital sigma, Σ, are simply the totals or summation of each column in the table, and n is the number of observations. In correlation analysis, it does not matter which variable is designated x and which is designated y. Substituting each value in table 3.6 (overleaf) into the formula allows the correlation coefficient to be calculated as follows.

$$r = \frac{2789 - \frac{(52)(768)}{16}}{\sqrt{\left[(226) - \frac{(52)^2}{16}\right]\left[(42\,534) - \frac{(768)^2}{16}\right]}} = .515$$

The r value obtained ($r = +.515$) represents a moderate positive linear relationship between the number of books a customer purchases on a single occasion from the online retailer and the age of the customer.

TABLE 3.6 Books purchased online and age of customer

Customer	Books purchased x	Age of customer y	x^2	y^2	xy
1	6	36	36	1 296	216
2	7	65	49	4 225	455
3	5	60	25	3 600	300
4	1	18	1	324	18
5	4	35	16	1 225	140
6	2	34	4	1 156	68
7	2	64	4	4 096	128
8	4	56	16	3 136	224
9	1	33	1	1 089	33
10	2	20	4	400	40
11	5	80	25	6 400	400
12	5	75	25	5 625	375
13	3	48	9	2 304	144
14	3	52	9	2 704	156
15	1	27	1	729	27
16	1	65	1	4 225	65
	$\Sigma x = 52$	$\Sigma y = 768$	$\Sigma x^2 = 226$	$\Sigma y^2 = 42\,534$	$\Sigma xy = 2\,789$

DEMONSTRATION PROBLEM 3.8

PROBLEM: A marketing manager is concerned about a forthcoming reduction in his annual advertising budget. He manages many products that all require separate marketing strategies, predominantly supported by advertising. To justify his request for a higher advertising budget, he collected data on annual sales of a random sample of 12 of the products he manages and the corresponding annual advertising expenditure for each. Calculate the correlation coefficient between annual sales and advertising expenditure.

Product	Annual sales ($000)	Annual advertising expenditure ($000)
1	200	80
2	200	80
3	240	120
4	180	50
5	170	40
6	160	40
7	210	50
8	230	90
9	230	110
10	200	60
11	210	50
12	190	80

SOLUTION

Advertising expenditure x	Sales y	x^2	y^2	xy
80	200	6 400	40 000	16 000
80	200	6 400	40 000	16 000
120	240	14 400	57 600	28 800
50	180	2 500	32 400	9 000
40	170	1 600	28 900	6 800
40	160	1 600	25 600	6 400
50	210	2 500	44 100	10 500
90	230	8 100	52 900	20 700
110	230	12 100	52 900	25 300
60	200	3 600	40 000	12 000
50	210	2 500	44 100	10 500
80	190	6 400	36 100	15 200
$\Sigma x = 850$	$\Sigma y = 2\,420$	$\Sigma x^2 = 68\,100$	$\Sigma y^2 = 494\,600$	$\Sigma xy = 177\,200$

$$r = \frac{177\,200 - \frac{(850)(2420)}{12}}{\sqrt{\left[(68\,100) - \frac{(850)^2}{12}\right]\left[(494\,600) - \frac{(2420)^2}{12}\right]}} = 0.803$$

USING EXCEL

Correlation

DP03-08

1. Access DP03-08.xls from the student website.
2. From the Data tab, select Data Analysis.
3. From the Data Analysis dialogue box, select Correlation and click OK.
4. In the Correlation dialogue box:
   a. enter the data range in the Input Range field
   b. check Grouped By: Columns
   c. check Labels in First Row if you have included the column headings. Otherwise leave it unchecked.
   d. choose an output option

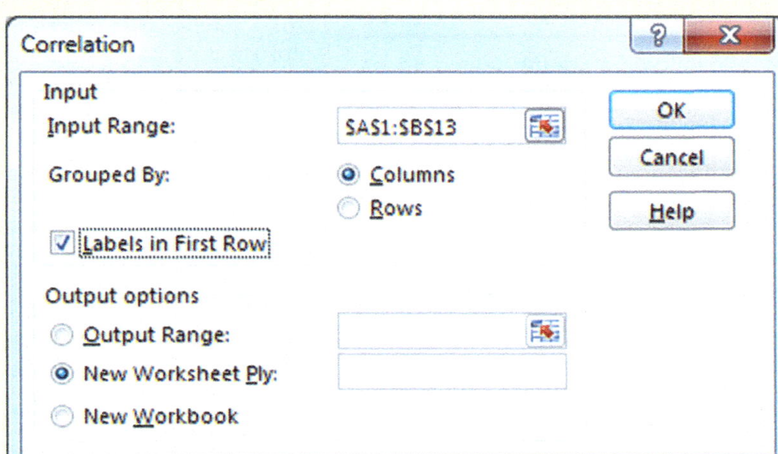

   e. click OK.

The Excel output follows.

	A	B	C
1		*Annual sales ($000)*	*Annual advertising expenditure ($000)*
2	Annual sales ($000)	1	
3	Annual advertising expenditure ($000)	0.803381	1

The r value obtained (r = .803) represents a relatively strong positive linear association between annual sales and advertising expenditure over the 12 products sampled. It implies that, when advertising expenditure is higher than average, this is associated with a product that has higher than average sales. Likewise, the result implies that, when advertising expenditure is lower, this is associated with a product with lower sales. So, the marketing manager may be able to use this to argue against the proposed decrease in his advertising budget for the next year.

The result, however, indicates only an association between the two variables and not whether there is a causal relationship or whether the relationship may be arising for some other reason. For example, products with existing higher sales are often allocated even larger amounts of resources (including money to spend on advertising) or may do well for other reasons beyond the amount spent on advertising. Successful products with higher sales may be given more prominent shelf space by retailers, or consumers may have developed a habitual buying pattern with an established product.

PRACTICE PROBLEMS

Practising the calculations

P03-19 **3.19** Determine the value of the coefficient of correlation, r, for the following data.

x	4	6	7	11	14	17	21
y	18	12	13	8	7	7	4

P03-20 **3.20** Determine the value of r for the following data.

x	158	296	87	110	436
y	349	510	301	322	550

P03-21 **3.21** The following data are the selling prices of houses (in $000) and the land size (in square metres) for an outer suburb of Sydney.

Land size (square metres)	Price ($000)
553	530
496	531
548	588
559	510
547	680
569	610
554	555
529	845
566	750
556	625
907	925

Use the data to compute a correlation coefficient, r, to determine the correlation between house price and the size of the land. Interpret your results.

Testing your understanding

3.22 The chief financial officer (CFO) for the producer of a well-known fashion line has recently come under fire for suggesting that retailers should hire younger people as frontline employees to improve sales. A human resource manager working for a retailer that stocks this fashion line is able to collate data gathered by an independent survey company for a sample of employees on a number of variables. These include the weekly sales the employee achieves, their age, years employed by the company and an average rating of friendliness on a scale of 1 to 10 (10 = most friendly). The human resource manager generates output in Excel that shows the correlation between these variables (see the opposite page).

Use the information to write a response to the CFO stating whether the analysis supports their assertion. You may like to comment on associations between other variables that appear in this output, such as whether people who have worked with the retailer for a longer period are friendlier or generate better sales.

	A	B	C	D	E
1		*Sales*	*Friendliness*	*Age*	*Years Employed*
2	Sales	1			
3	Friendliness	0.8656501	1		
4	Age	–0.0241143	0.041261521	1	
5	Years Employed	0.4414954	–0.007922502	0.657305507	1

Combaro **3.23** The CEO of Combaro Ltd is interested in seeing whether employees who are paid more have a greater level of job satisfaction and take fewer days off. Using the data set provided, examine whether this is the case.

BCREA **3.24** An investor in real estate wonders whether there is any evidence to support her belief that older houses tend to sell for less, while newer houses can command higher selling prices. Using the Baycoast City Real Estate Agents data set of recent house sales, examine whether there is an association between the selling price of a house and the age of the house in years. Write a short interpretation of this result for the real estate investor.

MISUSE OF STATISTICS

In describing a body of data to an audience, it is advisable to investigate all summary measures to ensure a 'full' picture of the data. By limiting the descriptive measures used or by providing only selected graphs and tables, the business researcher might give the audience only part of the picture and could bias the way the audience interprets the data. For example, if a researcher presents only the mean, the audience will have no insight into the variability of the data; in addition, the mean might be inordinately large or small because of extreme values. Likewise, the choice of just the median or mode precludes a picture that includes the extreme values. Using the mode can cause the receiver of the information to focus only on values that occur more often. In particular, it is advisable that any attempt at providing typical results should be accompanied by an assessment of the variability in the data set and its shape.

In summarising the association between two variables using correlation, it is important to consider that a strong correlation does not necessarily indicate a strong cause-and-effect relationship. That is, in the absence of any theory about how two variables may be related such that changes in one variable cause changes in another, correlation is a measure of association not causation. Also, the measure of correlation presented in this chapter indicates linear association; a zero correlation does not rule out the presence of a nonlinear association.

CHAPTER CASE REVISITED

Location, location, location!

The descriptive statistics presented in this chapter cover the most widely used measures for summarising and presenting data sets in more concise formats. For example, the chapter case presented statistics that describe how a sample of 120 houses within the Baycoast region is situated in terms of their distances to a train station, a bus stop and a shopping centre. On average, residents are 900 metres from a bus stop, 910 metres from a train station and 930 metres from a shopping centre — all within about a 15-minute walk. The first quartile suggests that 25% of residents have 300 metres or less to walk to a bus stop and 500 metres or less to walk to a train station or shopping centre. The median suggests that 50% of residents can walk 900 metres or less to arrive at their nearest train station or shopping centre. The closeness of the median and average demonstrates that the data for all three variables are fairly symmetrical, although the distance that people are from a bus stop is slightly positively skewed with the median lower than the mean. The variation in the distance of Baycoast properties from bus stops is much larger than the variation in the distances of properties from train stations and shops, as indicated by the larger standard deviation, coefficient of variation and interquartile range. The measures of central location imply that services are typically around the same distance away, but the measures of spread imply that there is more variation between residents in their proximity to a bus stop than to a train station or shopping centre; this is shown in the boxplots for each variable.

Variation in data can affect some summary statistics but not others. An unusual or extreme observation, such as a property that is over 4 km away from any of these services, would introduce an outlier to the data. How would it affect the summary measures used to describe the data? In this case, the outlier is quite large so it would increase the mean but would not affect the median or mode. Including this observation would also result in greater variability in the data; the standard deviation and range would both increase.

To interpret any of the original statistics, the BCREA management would need to consider whether the typical experience of being within about 900 metres of such services is attractive to all segments; while active people may enjoy this convenience, it could prove more troublesome for those who have difficulty walking this far. Also, the statistics do not take into account the potential variation in terrain that could make walking harder. The correlation coefficient between distance from a train station and selling price is $r = 0.003$, indicating that there is no linear relationship between the two variables. This would suggest that BCREA should not pursue marketing Baycoast properties on this basis. However, the scatter plot demonstrates one of the reasons why numerical summaries of data must be evaluated in conjunction with graphical summaries. While there is no linear relationship, there appears to be a nonlinear relationship: Selling prices appear to be lower for those houses that are situated very close to a station and those that are very distant from a station. Properties neither very close to nor very far from a train station appear to command a higher selling price.

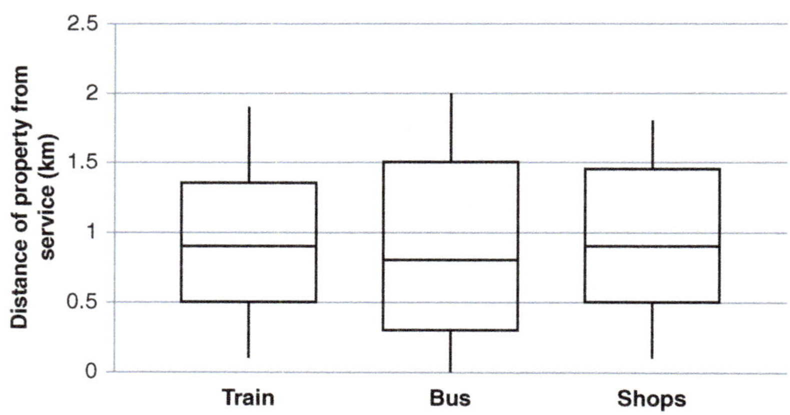

SUMMARY

1 The most common measures of central tendency are the three Ms: mode, median and mean. The mode is the most frequently occurring value in a set of data. The median defines the middle of an ordered array of numbers; the median is unaffected by the magnitude of extreme values, and therefore is an appropriate measure of location when reporting such things as income, age and prices of houses, where there can be extreme values at just one end of the data set. The arithmetic mean or common average is widely used and is usually what researchers are referring to when they use the terms mean and average. The arithmetic mean is affected by every value and can be inordinately influenced by extreme values at one end of the data.

2 Measures of location extending beyond those that describe central location include percentiles and quartiles. Percentiles divide data into two groups, with a given percentage of observations equal to or below a certain value and the remaining percentage being above this value. Quartiles divide data into four groups. The three quartiles are Q_1, which is the lower quartile, Q_2, which is the middle quartile and equals the median, and Q_3, which is the upper quartile.

3 Measures of variability include the range, variance, standard deviation, interquartile range and coefficient of variation. One of the most elementary measures of variability is the range, the difference between the maximum and minimum values. The interquartile range is the difference between the third and first quartiles and represents the range of the middle 50% of the data. The variance is a widely used tool in statistics but is used little as a stand-alone descriptive measure of variability. The variance is the average of the squared deviations from the mean. The square root of the variance is the standard deviation, which is in the same units as the original data. The standard deviation describes how far observations typically are from the mean, with a higher standard deviation indicating that observations tend to be spread out and typically not very close to the mean. The standard deviation, arguably the most important measure of variability, allows the spread of the data to be described further when used in conjunction with a number of other rules, theorems and measures. The empirical rule reveals the percentage of values that are within one, two or three standard deviations of the mean for a set of data from a bell-shaped distribution. For example, according to the empirical rule, approximately 95% of all values are within two standard deviations either side of the mean. Chebyshev's theorem reveals the percentage of values that are within a given number of standard deviations from the mean; it applies to any distribution regardless of its shape. According to Chebyshev's theorem, at least $1-\frac{1}{k^2}$ values are within k standard deviations of the mean. A z-score represents the number of standard deviations a value is from the mean. The coefficient of variation is a ratio of a standard deviation to its mean, given as a percentage. It is especially useful in comparing standard deviations that represent data with different means or in different units.

4 There are number of measures and methods to summarise the shape of a set of observations. Skewness is the lack of symmetry in a distribution. If a distribution is skewed, it is stretched in one direction. Kurtosis is the degree of peakedness of a distribution. A box and whisker plot is a graphical depiction of the shape of a distribution. Outliers are extreme observations that are unusual or inconsistent with the rest of the data so warrant further investigation about their validity. The empirical rule can be applied to identify potential outliers in the case of data from a bell-shaped distribution. Boxplots can be useful for identifying outliers, even in cases where the data are not bell shaped.

5 Association between two variables can be analysed using several different measures. In this chapter, the Pearson product–moment correlation coefficient, r, was presented. This value ranges from −1 to +1. An r value of +1 indicates perfect positive correlation, and an r value of −1 indicates perfect negative correlation. Negative correlation means that, as one variable increases in value, the other variable tends to decrease. For r values near zero, little or no linear relationship is present.

KEY TERMS

arithmetic mean p. 53
bimodal p. 51
box and whisker plot p. 76
Chebyshev's theorem p. 66
coefficient of skewness p. 75
coefficient of variation (CV) p. 72
correlation p. 80
deviation from the mean p. 62
empirical rule p. 65
interpolation p. 58
interquartile range (IQR) p. 61
kurtosis p. 76
leptokurtic p. 76
measures of central tendency p. 51
measures of location p. 56
measures of shape p. 74
measures of variability p. 61
median p. 51
mesokurtic p. 76
mode p. 51
multimodal p. 51
normal distribution p. 65
outliers p. 66
Pearson product–moment correlation coefficient (*r*) p. 80
percentiles p. 57
platykurtic p. 76
quartiles p. 58
range p. 61
skewness p. 74
standard deviation p. 64
sum of squares of *x* p. 64
variance p. 63
***z*-score** p. 71

KEY EQUATIONS

EQUATION	DESCRIPTION	FORMULA
3.1	Population mean	$\mu = \dfrac{\Sigma x}{N}$
3.2	Sample mean	$\bar{x} = \dfrac{\Sigma x}{n}$
3.3	Interquartile range	$\text{IQR} = Q_3 - Q_1$
3.4	Sum of deviations from the arithmetic mean is always zero	$\Sigma(x-\mu) = 0$
3.5	Population variance	$\sigma^2 = \dfrac{\Sigma(x-\mu)^2}{N}$
3.6	Population standard deviation	$\sigma = \sqrt{\sigma^2} = \sqrt{\dfrac{\Sigma(x-\mu)^2}{N}}$
3.7	Chebyshev's theorem	$1 - \dfrac{1}{k^2}$ fall within $\mu \pm k\sigma$
3.8	Sample variance	$s^2 = \dfrac{\Sigma(x-\bar{x})^2}{n-1}$
3.9	Sample standard deviation	$s = \sqrt{s^2} = \sqrt{\dfrac{\Sigma(x-\bar{x})^2}{n-1}}$
3.10	Computational formulas for population and sample variance	$\sigma^2 = \dfrac{\Sigma x^2 - \frac{(\Sigma x)^2}{N}}{N} = \dfrac{\Sigma x^2 - N\mu^2}{N}$ $s^2 = \dfrac{\Sigma x^2 - \frac{(\Sigma x)^2}{n}}{n-1} = \dfrac{\Sigma x^2 - n(\bar{x})^2}{n-1}$
3.11	Computational formulas for population and sample standard deviation	$\sigma = \sqrt{\sigma^2} = \sqrt{\dfrac{\Sigma x^2 - \frac{(\Sigma x)^2}{N}}{N}} = \sqrt{\dfrac{\Sigma x^2 - N\mu^2}{N}}$ $s = \sqrt{s^2} = \sqrt{\dfrac{\Sigma x^2 - \frac{(\Sigma x)^2}{n}}{n-1}} = \sqrt{\dfrac{\Sigma x^2 - n(\bar{x})^2}{n-1}}$
3.12	*z*-score	$z = \dfrac{x-\mu}{\sigma}$ for population data $z = \dfrac{x-\bar{x}}{s}$ for sample data
3.13	Coefficient of variation	$\text{CV} = \dfrac{\sigma}{\mu}(100)$ for population data $\text{CV} = \dfrac{s}{\bar{x}}(100)$ for sample data

EQUATION	DESCRIPTION	FORMULA
3.14	**Pearsonian coefficient of skewness**	$s_k = \frac{3(\mu - M_d)}{\sigma}$ for population data $s_k = \frac{3(\bar{x} - M_d)}{s}$ for sample data
3.15	**Pearson's product–moment correlation coefficient**	$r = \frac{\Sigma(x-\bar{x})(y-\bar{y})}{\sqrt{\Sigma(x-\bar{x})^2\Sigma(y-\bar{y})^2}} = \frac{\Sigma xy - \frac{(\Sigma x \Sigma y)}{n}}{\sqrt{\left[\Sigma x^2 - \frac{(\Sigma x)^2}{n}\right]\left[\Sigma y^2 - \frac{(\Sigma y)^2}{n}\right]}}$

REVIEW PROBLEMS

Practising the calculations

P03-25 **3.25** The Australian Census of Population and Housing asks every household to report information on each person living in the house. Suppose that, for a sample of 30 households, the number of persons living in each was reported as follows.

2	3	1	2	6	4	2	1	5	3	2	3
3	1	2	3	1	3	1	2	2	4	2	1
1	2	8	3	2	1						

Compute the mean, median, mode, range, lower and upper quartiles, and interquartile range for these data and interpret them in a brief plain-language report.

P03-26 **3.26** The Australian Census of Population and Housing asks for each resident's age. Suppose that a sample of 40 households taken from the census data showed the age of the first person recorded on the census form as follows.

42	29	31	38	55	27	28	33	49	70	25	21
25	38	47	63	22	38	52	50	41	19	22	29
34	81	52	26	35	38	29	31	48	26	33	42
24	58	40	32								

Compute P_{10}, P_{80}, Q_1, Q_3, the interquartile range and the range of these data.

P03-27 **3.27** Determine the Pearson product–moment correlation coefficient for the following data.

x	6	3	2	2	4	4	3	0
y	40	95	82	95	38	45	35	90

Testing your understanding

3.28 Financial analysts like to use the standard deviation as a measure of risk for a stock. The greater the deviation in a stock price over time, the more risky it is to invest in the stock. However, the average prices of some stocks are considerably higher than the average prices of others, allowing for the potential of a greater standard deviation of price. For example, a standard deviation of $5.00 on a $10.00 stock is considerably different from a $5.00 standard deviation on a $40.00 stock. In this situation, a coefficient of variation might provide insight into risk. Suppose stock X costs an average of $13.21 per share and has shown a standard deviation of $5.28 for the past 30 days. Suppose stock Y costs an average of $2.52 per share and has shown a standard deviation of $0.50 for the past 30 days. Use the coefficient of variation to determine the variability for each stock. Based on the coefficient of variation, which is the riskier stock?

3.29 An NRMA report stated that the average age of a car in Australia is 10.5 years. Suppose the distribution of ages of cars on Australian roads is approximately bell shaped. If the standard deviation is 2.4 years, between what two values would 95% of the car ages fall?

3.30 According to a *Human Resources* report, a worker in the IT industry spends on average 419 minutes (or 6.98 hours) a day on the job. Suppose the standard deviation of time spent on the job is 27 minutes.

a. If the distribution of time spent on the job is approximately bell shaped, between what two times would 68% of the data fall? 95%? 99.7%?

b. If the shape of the distribution of times is unknown, approximately what percentage of the times would be between 359 and 479 minutes?

c. Suppose a worker spent 400 minutes on the job. What would that worker's *z*-score be and what would it tell the researcher?

3.31 According to the Australian Taxation Office, the average taxable income in an affluent suburb of Sydney is $94 720. Suppose the median taxable income in this area is $90 050 and the mode is $89 200. Is the distribution in this area skewed? If so, how? Which of these measures of central tendency would you use to describe these data? Why?

3.32 A hire car company is interested in summary statistics that are useful in describing travel times between the central business district and the domestic terminal at Sydney Airport. They locate a report that indicates that the average total time for travel by car is 14 minutes. The shape of the distribution of travel times is unknown, but in addition it is reported that 35% of travel times are between 10.5 and 17.5 minutes. Use Chebyshev's theorem to determine the value of the standard deviation associated with travel times.

3.33 The *Monthly Banking Statistics* published by the Australian Prudential Regulation Authority provides selected information on the banking business of individual banks within the domestic market. It contains high-level breakdowns of the domestic assets and liabilities of each bank as well as more detail on loans and advances to and deposits by different sectors of the economy. Total resident assets refer to all assets on the banks' domestic books that are due from residents. The following Excel descriptive statistics output lists the variable total domestic assets of banks in Australia ($ million). Study the output and describe in your own words what you can learn about the domestic assets of banks in Australia.

	A	B
1	*Total resident assets*	
2	Mean	37020
3	Standard Error	11212
4	Median	6478
5	Mode	N/A
6	Standard Deviation	83148
7	Sample Variance	6913656116
8	Kurtosis	9
9	Skewness	3
10	Range	357051
11	Minimum	96
12	Maximum	357147
13	Sum	2036076
14	Count	55

Combaro **3.34** The CEO of Combaro would like to know whether employees are satisfied in their positions. In particular, the CEO would like to know about the central tendency of the data and whether the data are skewed in some way. For instance, the CEO suspects that there may be many employees who are quite satisfied, but average satisfaction levels are being distorted by a few individuals who are extremely unhappy. Use a boxplot to investigate whether this is the case. Write a report to the CEO on your findings, including supporting numerical measures such as skewness.

Combaro **3.35** The following scatter plot examines the potential association between years of education and weekly salary. The data come from the Combaro data set. Write short descriptions about what you would expect to see in the graph and what you actually see. In examining both descriptions, estimate the correlation coefficient in each case. Using the Combaro data set, calculate the correlation coefficient. What does your analysis suggest about the years of education an employee has completed and the amount they are paid?

BCREA **3.36** A recent article in the *Baycoast City Times* states that the days of large backyards have disappeared, and that larger properties are in short supply. In turn, the journalist writes that the Baycoast region provides the perfect place for those wishing to find houses on larger lots and property developers to have a greater number of options for subdivision. This article was based on a report by Baycoast City Real Estate Agents that the mean lot size of recent properties sold was 1175 square metres. The journalist interpreted this to imply that 50% of properties are equal to or bigger than 1175 square metres. The journalist also claimed that this is made even more exciting because larger lot sizes always mean higher house prices.

a. Using the BCREA data set and KaddStat, construct a box and whisker plot to verify how representative this mean lot size is and verify the journalist's claims about lot sizes

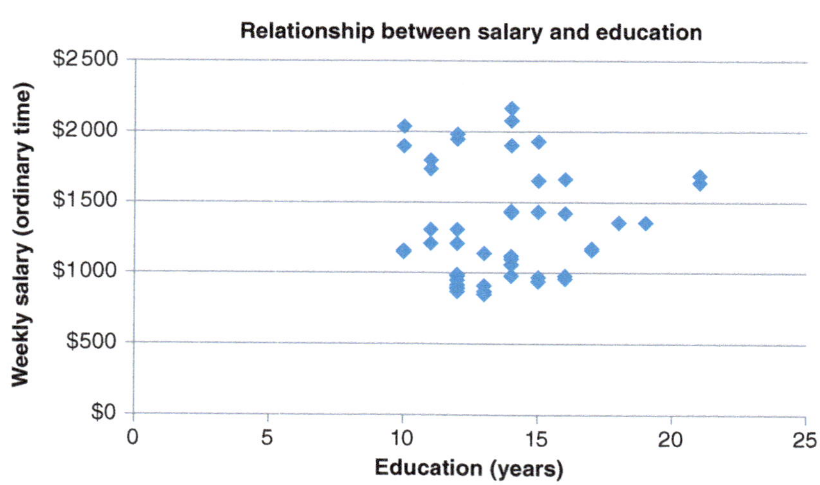

in the Baycoast region. Write a short report to explain how to interpret different summary measures of central tendency and how the journalist may have misinterpreted the original summary measure.

b. Use an appropriate measure of linear association to determine whether house prices and lot sizes are related. Interpret this measure to determine whether it supports the journalist's claims.

c. Which other factors in the Baycoast data set could also be associated with higher house prices? Pick one these and see whether the sample data in the Baycoast data set support your suspicions.

P03-37 **3.37** A sales report describes the current price of various digital cameras on the market with 16-megapixel resolution and 10× optical zoom using z-scores. Prices are described as following a normal distribution with an average price of \$219 and a standard deviation of \$13. The z-score associated with one particular model is 1.5. What is its sales price? How much more expensive is this camera compared to another camera with a z-score of −2.5?

MATHS APPENDIX

Summation notation

In mathematics, the symbol Σ (the Greek letter sigma) is an instruction to sum a set of values as described by the notation following it. The value given below Σ is the first subscript value and the value given above Σ is the final subscript value used in the sum. Generally:

$$\sum_{i=1}^{n} x_i = x_1 + x_2 + x_3 + \cdots + x_n \qquad \text{(Rule 1)}$$

For example, if $x_1 = 3$, $x_2 = 5$, $x_3 = 7$ and $x_4 = 12$:

$$\sum_{i=1}^{4} x_i = x_1 + x_2 + x_3 + x_4 = 3 + 5 + 7 + 12 = 27$$

The second summation rule is:

$$\sum_{i=1}^{n} cx_i = c\sum_{i=1}^{n} x_i \qquad \text{(Rule 2)}$$

For example, if $c = 8$, $x_1 = 3$, $x_2 = 5$, $x_3 = 7$ and $x_4 = 12$:

$$\sum_{i=1}^{4} 8x_i = 8x_1 + 8x_2 + 8x_3 + 8x_4 = 8(3) + 8(5) + 8(7) + 8(12)$$
$$= 24 + 40 + 56 + 96 = 216$$

and:

$$\sum_{i=1}^{4} 8x_i = 8\sum_{i=1}^{4} x_i = 8(x_1 + x_2 + x_3 + x_4) = 8(3 + 5 + 7 + 12)$$
$$= 8(27) = 216$$

The third summation rule is:

$$\sum_{i=1}^{n} (x_i + y_i) = \sum_{i=1}^{n} x_i + \sum_{i=1}^{n} y_i \qquad \text{(Rule 3)}$$

For example, if $x_1 = 2$, $x_2 = 4$, $x_3 = 5$, $y_1 = 1$, $y_2 = 3$ and $y_3 = 6$:

$$\sum_{i=1}^{3} (x_i + y_i) = (x_1 + y_1) + (x_2 + y_2) + (x_3 + y_3)$$
$$= (2 + 1) + (4 + 3) + (5 + 6) = 3 + 7 + 11 = 21$$

and:

$$\sum_{i=1}^{n}(x_i + y_i) = \sum_{i=1}^{n}x_i + \sum_{i=1}^{n}y_i = (x_1 + x_2 + x_3) + (y_1 + y_2 + y_3)$$
$$= (2 + 4 + 5) + (1 + 3 + 6) = 11 + 10 = 21$$

The fourth summation rule is:

$$\sum_{i=1}^{n}c = nc \qquad \text{(Rule 4)}$$

For example, if $c = 12$ and $n = 5$:

$$\sum_{i=1}^{5}12 = 12 + 12 + 12 + 12 + 12 = 60$$

but 60 = 5(12), so:

$$\sum_{i=1}^{5}12 = 5(12) = 60$$

CHAPTER

4 Probability

LEARNING OBJECTIVES

After studying this chapter, you should be able to:

1. distinguish between the different ways of assigning probabilities
2. describe the structure of probability using terms such as experiments, events and sample space, and explain the concepts of mutually exclusive events, independent events, collectively exhaustive events and the complement of an event
3. use contingency tables and probability matrices to calculate marginal, union, joint and conditional probabilities
4. use the general law of addition to solve problems, including the complement of a union
5. apply the general law of multiplication, and know when to use the special law of multiplication
6. use the concept of conditional probability to consider whether two events are independent and appreciate how Bayes' rule may be useful for revising the calculation of conditional probabilities.

OPENING VIGNETTE

A conditional workout

Probability plays an important role in many aspects of business. For example, it can be useful in describing the likelihood that a customer will buy a particular product. The value of probability becomes even more pronounced when companies use conditional probabilities to account for how the tendency for certain people to undertake certain behaviours can be related to various factors. This approach may provide better insights into those segments that have higher demand for a company's products or services. In turn, this can inform marketing strategies aimed at specific groups.

For example, a report by the Gemba Group on gym workouts and fitness used a sample of 27 826 New Zealanders to examine the reasons for visiting gyms and the activities undertaken at the gym. The data revealed that during the past 12 months, 21% of sampled participants had participated in a gym workout while 10% had participated in group exercise. Such participation rates are high, with both among the top five activities examined in the study. The other activities in the top five included swimming (25%), running (15%) and cycling (12%).

These figures are determined by counting the number of people who indicated they had participated in a given activity and dividing by the total sample size ($n = 27\,826$). In this way, the figures can be viewed as probabilities. Of course, these probabilities are based on historical information and are subject to various response and measurement biases, including whether participants were able to accurately recall or were truthful in accounting for what activities they had participated in over a 12-month period.

While 51% of respondents were female, among those individuals who participated in group exercise in the past 12 months, 79% were female. Letting F refer to the event that an individual is female, the marginal probability of this event can be written as $P(\text{F}) = .51$. Letting G refer to the event that an individual participated in group exercise in the last year, the conditional probability that an individual is female given that they participated in group exercise can be written as $P(\text{F}|\text{G}) = .79$. The difference between the marginal and conditional probabilities indicates some level of dependence between gender and group exercise. Similarly, in comparing the marginal probability that a respondent is from a particular age group to conditional probabilities associated with participation in gym workouts or group exercise given an individual's age indicates that age and participation are related. Specifically, younger persons, particularly those aged 16 to 24, have higher levels of participation relative to persons over the age of 35.

Among those participating in a gym workout, the most important reason for participation was fitness (74%), followed by relaxation (13%), competition (7%) and social (6%). In contrast, among those participating in group exercise, the most important reason for participation was fitness (68%), followed by social (15%), relaxation (11%) and competition (6%). These results indicate that the motivating reason for participation is conditional upon the activity being undertaken. For those operating in the sport and fitness industry, insights such as these can be useful in selecting and communicating with target markets.

Introduction

In business, most decision making involves uncertainty. For example, an operations manager does not know definitely whether a valve in a machine is going to malfunction or continue to function. If it is currently functioning well, how long will it be before it malfunctions? When should it be replaced? What is the chance that the valve will malfunction within the next week? In the banking industry, what are the prospects of a loans customer defaulting on their mortgage? In the telecommunications industry, will a customer buy a prepaid plan or a postpaid plan? Are men more likely to buy a prepaid plan than women? The answers to these questions are uncertain. In an attempt to answer these and many other questions, businesses rely on samples to infer what is happening at the population level, a process that is associated with uncertainty. For example, to ensure quality, a bakery can only taste and assess the inside texture of its bread using a sample of loaves; otherwise it would not have any remaining loaves to sell. Is the bakery going to come to the correct conclusion about all the loaves its sells on the basis of sampling just a small number of loaves? Businesspeople must address these and thousands of similar questions daily. Because most such questions do not have definite answers, decision making is based on uncertainty. In many of these situations, a probability can be determined to indicate the likelihood of an outcome. This chapter is about learning how to determine or assign probabilities.

In descriptive statistics, the objective is to describe what is occurring, such as using an average, a numeric measure that summarises the central tendency of the data. Inferential statistics involves using sample data to describe and make conclusions about what is occurring at the population level. Probability is the basis for inferential statistics. Inferential statistics involves taking a sample from a population, computing a statistic related to the sample (such as the sample mean, $\bar{x}$) and inferring from the statistic the value of the corresponding parameter of the population (such as the population mean, μ). The reason for doing so is that the value of the parameter is unknown. Because it is unknown, the analyst conducts the inferential process under uncertainty. However, by applying rules and laws, the analyst can often assign a probability of obtaining the sample results and assess the error that is likely to occur. Figure 4.1 depicts this process.

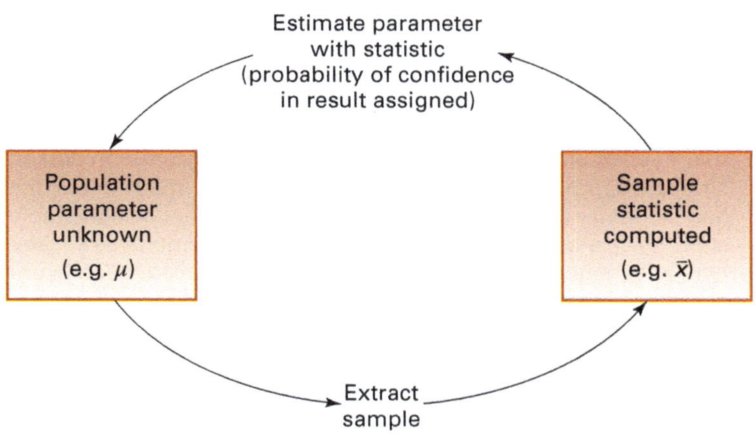

FIGURE 4.1 Probability in the process of inferential statistics

Suppose a marketer is interested in promoting the light bulbs a company produces on the basis of how long they will last and wishes to estimate the mean life of a bulb. To assist in answering this question, a quality control inspector selects a random sample of 40 light bulbs from a population of bulbs the company produces, and computes the average number of hours of luminance for the sample bulbs. By using techniques discussed later in this text, the specialist estimates the average number of hours of luminance for the population of light bulbs from this sample information. Because the light bulbs being analysed are only a sample of the population, the average number of hours of luminance for the 40 bulbs may not accurately reflect the average for all bulbs in the population. The results are uncertain. By applying certain laws, the inspector can assign a value of probability to this estimate.

In addition, probabilities are used directly in certain industries and industry applications. For example, the insurance industry uses probabilities in actuarial tables to determine the likelihood of certain outcomes in order to set specific insurance premiums and coverage. The gaming industry uses probability values to establish charges and payoffs. In designing new products and how to market them, companies consider market research information about what consumers are likely to buy and which consumers will do so. In industries such as manufacturing and aerospace, in order to protect the business from the effects of major breakdowns, it is important to know the estimated life of a particular mechanised part and the probability that any part could malfunction in any given length of time.

CHAPTER CASE

Too many leaders

When the economic climate takes a downturn, such as the global financial crisis (GFC) of the late 2000s, businesses must adapt. This can see many companies finding it necessary to restructure and implement redundancies. Rearranging an organisation can take time and leave a company exposed on a number of levels during such a transition period. Combaro Ltd, a provider of low-cost loans for housing and other purposes, is concerned that a recent period of restructuring has led to an imbalance of staff in some of its divisions. Management at Combaro aims to employ staff such that 75% are at the consultant level (junior staff) and 25% are in supervisory (senior) roles. Senior staff can hold a great deal of tacit knowledge about company practices and policies and may have much historical insight into the market. They also provide valuable mentorship and leadership to the company's rising stars.

Combaro offers three types of loans: home loans, car loans and personal loans. The manager of one of Combaro's divisions is concerned that his division has too many senior staff, which he claims is creating difficulties in determining a succinct strategic approach and will lead to budgetary shortfalls for his division. On the other hand, another division manager is worried that her division employs too many junior staff, which she claims has led to lower levels of employee satisfaction as many of her staff are undertaking tasks for which they are inadequately trained. Both division managers have asked that some level of balance across divisions be maintained. Unfortunately, the various databases that contain information on employees' levels of appointment and the areas in which they are employed have not been completely updated to reflect all changes. However, the results (below) of a recent survey of 48 employees collected for another purpose reveal information that may offer some preliminary insights.

	Division			
Employee level	**Home**	**Car**	**Personal**	**Total**
Supervisor/senior staff	3	6	3	12
Consultant/junior staff	8	15	13	36
Total employees	11	21	16	48

Questions to help managers make decisions

Combaro

1. What is an alternative way to present the information contained in the contingency table on the opposite page so that management can easily determine the probability that someone works in a certain division and has a particular appointment?
2. The management of Combaro attempts to hire and place staff in each division based on customer demand. What does the probability of someone working in each division suggest about the types of loans that customers are looking for from Combaro Ltd?
3. Combaro Ltd hopes that consultant employees outnumber supervisors such that one in four employees, or 25% of total employees, would be a senior staff member in a supervisory role. Using the survey of 48 staff members, is this being achieved?
4. Using the values presented in the case study, what is the probability that a staff member would be employed in a supervisory role, given that the employee is employed in the home loans division? the car loans division? the personal loans division?
5. What do the responses to questions 3 and 4 suggest about the relationship between the level of appointment of a staff member and the division in which they are employed? If the sample size was increased and the probabilities calculated were the same, how concerned should Combaro management be about the restructuring that has occurred? To which division should their concerns be directed? How can these concerns be addressed?

4.1 Methods of determining probabilities

The three general methods of assigning probabilities are (1) the classical method, (2) the relative frequency of occurrence method and (3) the subjective probability method.

Classical method

The **classical method of assigning probabilities** *involves assuming that each outcome is equally likely to occur, with no assumed knowledge or historical basis for what will occur.* For example, if a customer walks into a store that offers a \$59 phone plan, a \$79 plan, a \$99 plan and a \$129 plan, what is the probability that they choose the \$99 plan? Without any other information, we would assume that each plan has an equal chance of being chosen. In other words, the probability of choosing the \$99 plan would be $\frac{1}{4} = .25 = 25\%$. Likewise, without any other information, the probability that the customer is male would be $\frac{1}{2} = .50 = 50\%$, since there are only two possible outcomes (male and female) and we have no way of knowing if the customer base is predominantly male or female.

When we assign probabilities using the classical method, the probability of an individual event occurring is determined using formula 4.1 (overleaf), the ratio of the number of times the event could occur (n_i) to the total number of possible events (N_E); that is, $P(E_i) = \frac{n_i}{N_E}$. For example, if a company has 200 workers and 70 are female, the probability of randomly selecting a female worker from this company is $\frac{70}{200} = .35$. Probability values can be converted to percentages by multiplying by 100. In other words, there is a 35% chance that the employee chosen is female if each and every worker is given an equal opportunity to be selected.

Classical method of assigning probabilities (4.1)

$$P(E_i) = \frac{n_i}{N_E}$$

where:

E_i = the event of interest

n_i = the number of outcomes in which the event of interest could occur

N_E = the total number of possible outcomes

Because the number of times something could occur, n_i, can never be greater than the total number of possible outcomes, N_E, the highest value of any probability is 1. If the probability of an outcome occurring is 1, the event is certain to occur. The smallest possible probability is 0. If none of the outcomes of the N_E possibilities has the desired characteristic, the probability is $\frac{0}{N_E} = 0$, and the event is certain not to occur. The range of possible probabilities is given in formula 4.2.

Range of possible probabilities (4.2)

$$0 \leq P(E_i) \leq 1$$

Probabilities can be stated as decimals, percentages or fractions. Thus, probabilities are positive values that cannot be greater than 1 (when stated in decimal form or as a fraction) or 100% (when stated in percentage form). Meteorologists often report weather forecasts in percentage form, such as forecasting a 60% chance of rainfall tomorrow. In decimal form, they are saying the probability of rain tomorrow is .60. It would be impossible for meteorologists to forecast a value that is below 0% or above 100%.

Relative frequency of occurrence method

The **relative frequency of occurrence method** of assigning probabilities is based on cumulated historical data. With this method, given in formula 4.3, *the probability of an event occurring is equal to the number of times the event has occurred in the past divided by the total number of opportunities for the event to have occurred.* This method is sometimes called empirical probability.

Probability by relative frequency of occurrence (4.3)

$$P(E_i) = \frac{x_i}{N_E}$$

where:

x_i = the number of times an event has occurred

N_E = the total number of opportunities for the event to occur

Relative frequency of occurrence is not based on rules or laws but on what has occurred in the past. For example, a company may want to determine the probability that its inspectors are going to reject the next batch of raw materials from a supplier. Data gathered from company record books show that the supplier sent the company 90 batches in the past, and inspectors rejected 10 of them. By the method of relative frequency of occurrence, the probability of the inspectors rejecting the next batch is $\frac{10}{90} = .1111 = 11.11\%$. If the next batch is rejected, the relative frequency of occurrence probability for the subsequent shipment would change to $\frac{11}{91} = .1209 = 12.09\%$. The probability assigned using the relative frequency method, based on what actually occurs, is often compared with what could occur if everything was equally likely. For example, suppose that, in our phone plan example, a random sample of 1200 sales was recorded and the number of units sold at each price point is presented in table 4.1.

TABLE 4.1 Number of units of each phone plan sold

Cost of plan	Units sold
$59	180
$79	300
$99	420
$129	300
Total	1200

Using the relative frequency of occurrence method to assign probabilities, the probability that a customer will choose the $99 plan out of the four available is $\frac{420}{1200} = .35 = 35\%$. Recall that, using the classical method of assigning probabilities, the probability of selecting any plan was one in four or 25%. Based on these historical outcomes, the $99 plan appears to be more popular than if people were choosing at random. Likewise, the probability of a customer selecting the $59 plan based on the relative frequency method is $\frac{180}{1200} = .15 = 15\%$, which suggests that the plan is being selected at a rate that is less than chance (25%).

Subjective probability method

The **subjective probability method** of *assigning probability is based on the feelings or insights of the person determining the probability*. Subjective probability comes from the person's intuition or reasoning. Although not a scientific approach to probability, the subjective method often is based on the accumulation of knowledge, understanding and experience stored and processed in the human mind. At times it is merely a guess. Subjective probability can be used to capitalise on the background of experienced workers and managers in decision making.

Suppose a director of transportation for an oil company is asked the probability of getting a shipment of oil out of Saudi Arabia to Australia within four weeks. The director, who has scheduled many such shipments, has knowledge of Saudi Arabia's political and economic climate, as well as an awareness of the current weather conditions, may be able to give an accurate probability that the shipment can be made on time.

Subjective probability also can be a potentially useful way of tapping a person's experience, knowledge and insight, and using them to forecast the occurrence of some event. An experienced airline mechanic can usually assign a meaningful probability to whether a particular plane has a certain type of mechanical difficulty based on characteristics that it exhibits when it comes in for repair. Physicians sometimes assign subjective probabilities to the life expectancy of people who have cancer.

PRACTICE PROBLEMS

Practising the calculations

4.1 Suppose event A occurs 1050 times, event B occurs 720 times, event C occurs 120 times and event D occurs 1110 times. Calculate the relative frequency of each event and report the probabilities of each event.

a. $P(A) =$ ___
b. $P(B) =$ ___
c. $P(C) =$ ___
d. $P(D) =$ ___

4.2 If X is the set of events that lists the seven days of a week, what is the probability that any single day chosen from X will be:

a. a Monday
b. not a Monday
c. a weekday
d. a weekend day?

Testing your understanding

4.3 A company advertising used cars for sale classifies vehicles, based on their shape, into one of eight mutually exclusive categories. The following table summarises the company's current range of advertised vehicles.

Body type	Number of vehicles for sale
4WD/SUV	8 330
Coupe	1 190
Hatchback	17 850
People mover	9 520
Sedan	47 600
Ute	5 950
Van	4 760
Wagon	23 800

What is the probability that a randomly selected vehicle will be:

a. a ute
b. a sedan
c. a sedan or a hatchback?

4.4 A superannuation company offers seven different types of funds that members can choose to invest in. Two of these funds involve a portfolio that exposes investors to a high level of risk. Using only this information, what method of assigning probabilities can be used to determine the probability that a member will invest in a fund that is deemed to be of a high risk? Determine this probability. Write a short paragraph that describes the advantages and disadvantages of the method used to determine the probability.

4.5 A train has been delayed by a fallen tree. The train driver can see the extent of the damage and estimates the probability that the tree will be removed and the train will be able to carry on its journey within the next hour is 90%. This information is communicated to other rail employees at train stations that may be affected by any delays. What method has been used to assign a probability to the train delay? Use the aforementioned context to write a short paragraph that reflects on occasions when this method may be appropriate relative to other methods of assigning probability.

4.2 Structure of probability

The structure of probability provides a common framework within which the topics of probability can be explored. In the study of probability, developing a language of terms and symbols is helpful. Many of the concepts in probability are based on an understanding of how the occurrence of events, or outcomes of an experiment, can be described and listed using various key words, symbols and notation. This structure then enables a description of the probability relating to particular types of events, such as independent and mutually exclusive events, to be made in a more precise fashion. The notation will be used to present key formulas throughout this chapter. An understanding of these key terms, notation and formulas can assist in calculating other probabilities that may be required to answer a particular managerial question.

Experiment

An **experiment** is *a process or activity that produces outcomes*. Examples of business-oriented experiments with outcomes that can be statistically analysed might include:

- interviewing 20 randomly selected consumers and asking them which brand of appliance they prefer
- sampling every 200th bottle of tomato sauce from an assembly line and weighing the contents
- testing new pharmaceutical drugs on samples of cancer patients and measuring the patients' improvement
- auditing every 10th account to detect errors.

Event

Because an **event** is *an outcome of an experiment*, the experiment defines the possibilities of the event. If the experiment is to randomly sample five bottles coming off a production line to check their quality, an event could be that one bottle is defective and the other four in the sample are not. In an experiment to roll a die, one event could be to roll an even number and another event could be to roll a number greater than two.

Elementary events

Events that cannot be decomposed or broken down into other events are called **elementary events**. Suppose the experiment is to roll a die. The elementary events for this experiment are to roll a 1, to roll a 2, to roll a 3 and so on. Rolling an even number is an event, but it is not an elementary event because the event of rolling an even number can be broken down further into events where a 2, 4 or 6 is rolled.

In the experiment of rolling a die, there are six elementary events: {1, 2, 3, 4, 5, 6}. Rolling a pair of dice results in 36 possible elementary events (outcomes). For each of the six elementary events possible on the roll of one die, there are six possible elementary events on the roll of the second die, as depicted in the tree diagram in figure 4.2. Table 4.2 contains a list of these 36 outcomes.

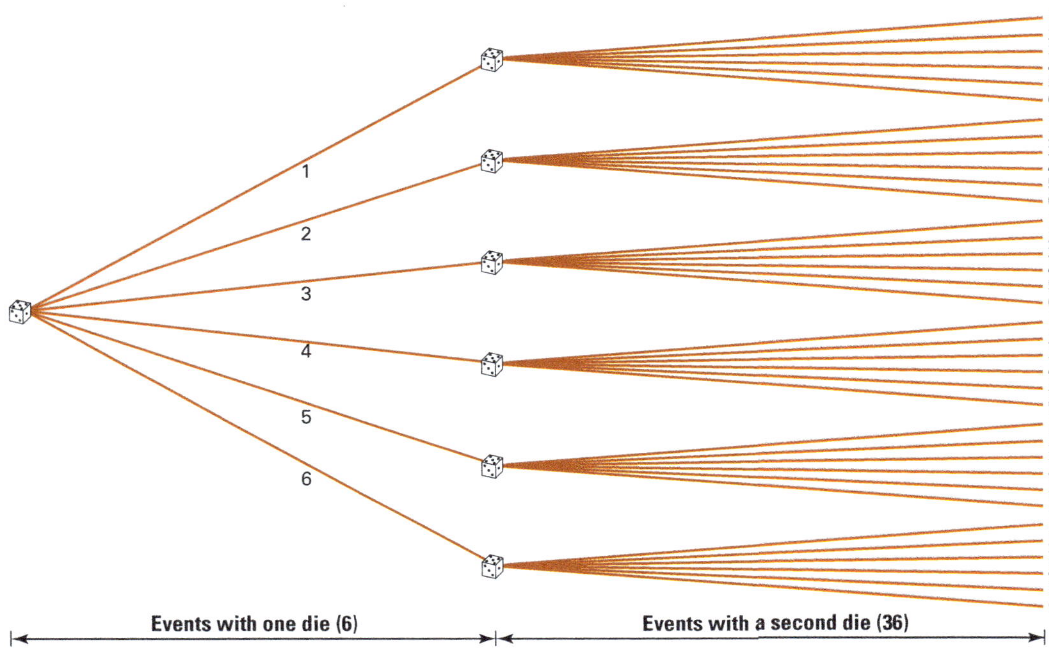

FIGURE 4.2 Possible outcomes for the roll of a pair of dice

In the experiment of rolling a pair of dice, other events could include outcomes such as two even numbers, a sum of 10 or a sum greater than five. However, none of these events is an elementary event because each can be broken down into several of the elementary events displayed in table 4.2.

TABLE 4.2 All possible elementary events in the roll of a pair of dice (sample space)

(1, 1)	(2, 1)	(3, 1)	(4, 1)	(5, 1)	(6, 1)
(1, 2)	(2, 2)	(3, 2)	(4, 2)	(5, 2)	(6, 2)
(1, 3)	(2, 3)	(3, 3)	(4, 3)	(5, 3)	(6, 3)
(1, 4)	(2, 4)	(3, 4)	(4, 4)	(5, 4)	(6, 4)
(1, 5)	(2, 5)	(3, 5)	(4, 5)	(5, 5)	(6, 5)
(1, 6)	(2, 6)	(3, 6)	(4, 6)	(5, 6)	(6, 6)

Sample space

A **sample space** is *a complete roster or listing of all elementary events for an experiment*. Table 4.2 is the sample space for the roll of a pair of dice. The sample space for the roll of a single die is {1, 2, 3, 4, 5, 6}.

A sample space can aid in finding probabilities. Suppose an experiment is to roll a pair of dice. What is the probability that the dice will sum to 7? An examination of the sample space shown in table 4.2 reveals that there are six outcomes in which the dice sum to 7 — {(1, 6), (2, 5), (3, 4), (4, 3), (5, 2), (6, 1)} — in the total possible 36 elementary events in the sample space. Using this information, we can conclude that the probability of rolling a pair of dice that sum to 7 is $\frac{6}{36}$, or 16.67%. However, using the sample space to determine probabilities is unwieldy and cumbersome when the sample space is large. Hence, in such situations, statisticians usually use other more effective methods of determining probability.

Set notation, unions and intersections

Set notation is the *use of various mathematical symbols to define a group or set of events, as well as describe outcomes relating to their occurrence with other sets of events*. Recall that the set of outcomes relating to the roll of a die was represented as {1, 2, 3, 4, 5, 6}; the use of braces to group numbers is an example of set notation. Throughout this chapter, set notation is used as a symbolic tool to represent various concepts such as the union and intersection of two events.

The **union** of two or more sets is *formed by combining elements from each set*. Using set notation, the union of X and Y is denoted by $X \cup Y$. An element qualifies for the union of X and Y if it is in either X or Y or in both X and Y. The union expression $X \cup Y$ can be translated to 'X or Y'. For example, if:

$$X = \{1, 4, 7, 9\} \text{ and } Y = \{2, 3, 4, 5, 6\}$$

$$X \cup Y = \text{'}X \text{ or } Y\text{'} = \{1, 2, 3, 4, 5, 6, 7, 9\}$$

Note that all the values of X and all the values of Y qualify for the union. However, none of the values is listed more than once in the union. In figure 4.3, the shaded region of the Venn diagram denotes the union.

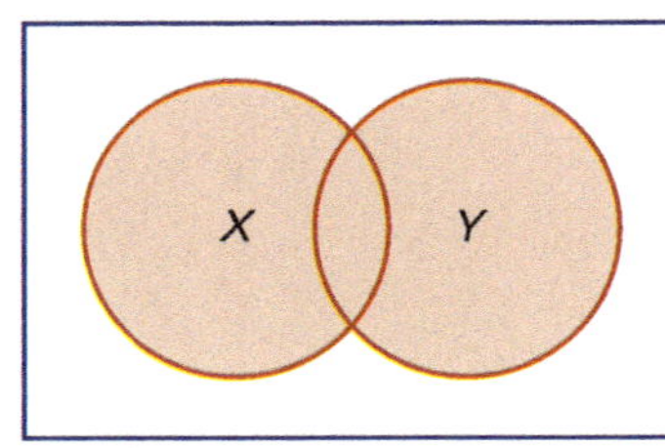

FIGURE 4.3 A union

A **Venn diagram** is *a graphical representation of how any event may occur in terms of its possible co-occurrence with any other event*. Often a Venn diagram is adapted to refer to the probability that events will occur. The area inside any one circle indicates that this event will occur or, in the context of probability, the probability that this event will occur. The area outside of the circle indicates the non-occurrence of the event. Where two circles overlap, both events are said to occur and are often referred to as an intersection.

The **intersection** of two or more sets *contains the elements common to all sets*. Using set notation, the intersection of X and Y is denoted $X \cap Y$. As it contains elements that are in both X and Y, the intersection symbol, $\cap$, is often read as 'and'. For example, if:

$$X = \{1, 4, 7, 9\} \text{ and } Y = \{2, 3, 4, 5, 6\}$$

$$X \cap Y = \text{'}X \text{ and } Y\text{'} = \{4\}$$

Note that only the value 4 is common to both sets X and Y. Elements must be a characteristic of both X and Y to qualify. In figure 4.4, the shaded region denotes the intersection.

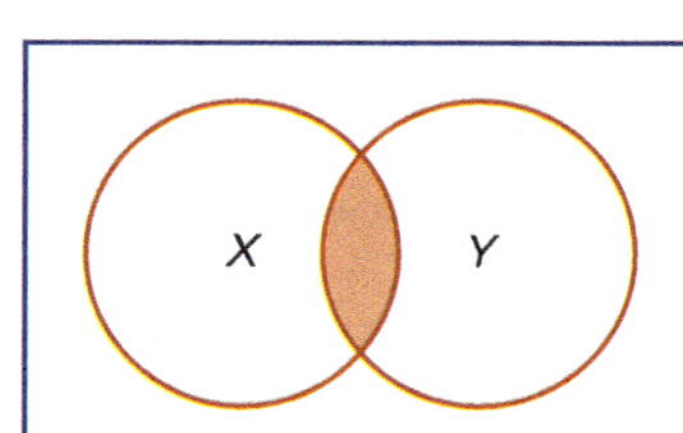

FIGURE 4.4 An intersection

Mutually exclusive events

Two or more events are **mutually exclusive events** if *the occurrence of one event precludes the occurrence of the other event(s)*. This characteristic means that mutually exclusive events cannot occur simultaneously and therefore can have no intersection or overlap.

The variable 'gender' presents two mutually exclusive outcomes, male and female. An employee randomly selected to be part of a study is either male or female and cannot be both. In a random sample of manufactured products, the event of selecting a defective part is mutually exclusive of the event of selecting a nondefective part. A manufactured part is either defective or acceptable; the part cannot be both acceptable and defective at the same time because 'acceptable' and 'defective' are mutually exclusive categories. Suppose an office building is for sale and two different potential buyers have placed bids on the building. It is not possible for both buyers to purchase the building; therefore, the event of buyer A purchasing the building is mutually exclusive of the event of buyer B purchasing the building. On a roll of a pair of dice, the event (6, 6), 'boxcars', is mutually exclusive of the event (1, 1), 'snake eyes'. Getting both boxcars and snake eyes on the same roll of the dice is impossible. Getting two numbers that are identical and even is possible with the same outcome, so this would be an example of two events that are not mutually exclusive.

The probability of two mutually exclusive events occurring at the same time is zero, as shown in formula 4.4.

Mutually exclusive events *X* and *Y*
(4.4)

$$P(X \cap Y) = P(X \text{ and } Y) = 0$$

Independent events

Two or more events are **independent events** if *the occurrence or non-occurrence of one of the events does not affect the occurrence or non-occurrence of the other event(s)*. Certain experiments, such as rolling dice, yield independent events; each die is independent of the other and each roll is independent of the other. Whether a 6 is rolled on the first die has no influence on whether a 6 is rolled on the second die. Coin tosses are also always independent of each other. The event of getting a head on the first toss of a coin is independent of getting a head on the second toss. Certain human characteristics are independent of other events. For example, left-handedness is independent of the method of transportation a person uses to travel to work. Whether a person wears glasses is independent of the brand of milk they prefer.

Many experiments using random selection can produce either independent or non-independent events. In these experiments, the outcomes are independent if sampling is done with replacement; that is, after each item is selected and the outcome is determined, the item is restored to the population and the population is shuffled. This way, each draw becomes independent of the previous draw. Suppose an inspector is randomly selecting bolts from a bin that contains 5% defects. If the inspector randomly samples a defective bolt and returns it to the bin, there are still 5% defects in the bin on the second draw regardless of the fact that the first outcome was a defective bolt. If the inspector does not replace the first draw, the second draw is not independent of the first; in this case, less than 5% defects remain in the population. Thus the probability of the second outcome is dependent on the first outcome. However, for small samples from very large populations (e.g. two bolts from 10 000 bolts), the probabilities are changed in only a very small way; hence, in this and similar situations, statisticians sometimes assume events to be independent of each other.

If *X* and *Y* are independent, the symbolic notation shown in formula 4.5 is used.

Independent events *X* and *Y*
(4.5)

$$P(X \mid Y) = P(X \text{ given } Y) = P(X) \quad \text{and} \quad P(Y \mid X) = P(Y \text{ given } X) = P(Y)$$

The vertical stroke '|' is notation that means 'conditional upon' and can be read simply as 'given'. Hence, $P(X|Y)$ denotes the probability of X occurring given that Y has occurred. If X and Y are independent, the probability of X occurring given that Y has occurred is just the probability of X occurring. Knowledge that Y has occurred does not affect the probability of X occurring because X and Y are independent. For example, P(prefers Pepsi | person is right-handed) = P(prefers Pepsi) because a person's brand preference is independent of handedness. A more in-depth discussion of conditional probability and independent events occurs later in this chapter.

Collectively exhaustive events

A list of **collectively exhaustive events** contains *all possible elementary events for an experiment.* Thus, all sample spaces are collectively exhaustive lists. The list of possible outcomes in table 4.2 for the rolling of a pair of dice is a collectively exhaustive list. The sample space for an experiment can be described as a list of events that are mutually exclusive and collectively exhaustive. Sample space events do not overlap or intersect, and the list is complete. When contemplating how to measure the outcomes of an experiment, it is important to consider all possible outcomes and ensure these do not inadvertently overlap. For example, if a market research company asks whether a person's employment status is full-time or part-time or in which profession they are employed, it is important to recognise that one possible outcome is that a person may be unemployed.

Complementary events

The **complement** of an event *represents all the elementary events of an experiment that occur when a specified event does not occur.* For example, if in rolling one die, event A is getting an even number, the complement of A is getting an odd number. The complement of A is denoted by A', pronounced 'not A'. If event A is getting a 5 on the roll of a die, the complement of A is getting a 1, 2, 3, 4 or 6. The complement of event A contains whatever portion of the sample space that event A does not contain, as the Venn diagram in figure 4.5 shows.

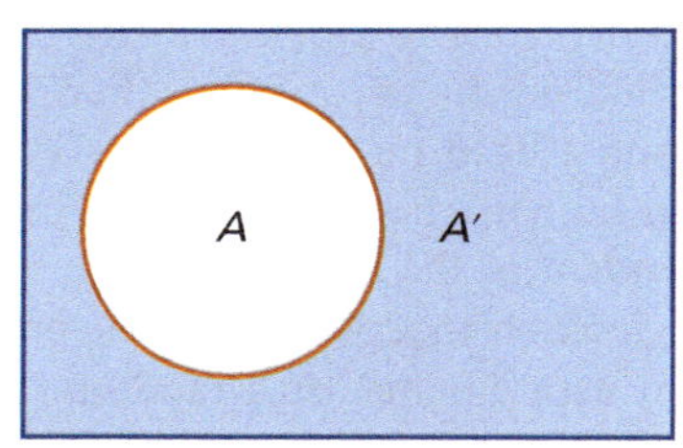

FIGURE 4.5 The complement of event *A*

Using the complement of an event can sometimes be helpful in solving for probabilities because of the rule represented by formula 4.6.

Probability of the complement of *A* **(4.6)**

$$P(A') = 1 - P(A)$$

Suppose 32% of the employees of a company have a university degree. If an employee is randomly selected from the company, the probability that the person does not have a university degree is 1 − .32 = .68 or, simply, 68%. Suppose 42% of all parts produced in a plant are moulded by machine A and 31% are moulded by machine B. Each part is moulded by one machine only. Thus, P(A or B) = .42 + .31 = .73 or 73%. If a part is randomly selected, the probability that it was moulded by neither machine A nor machine B is 1 − .73 = .27 or 27%.

PRACTICE PROBLEMS

Practising the calculations

4.6 Given $A = \{1, 4, 7\}$, $B = \{3, 4, 6, 8, 9\}$ and $C = \{1, 3, 4, 5, 6, 7\}$, solve the following.

a. $A \cup B =$ ___
b. $A \cap C =$ ___
c. $B \cap C =$ ___
d. $A \cup B \cup C =$ ___
e. $A \cap B \cap C =$ ___
f. $(A \cup B) \cap C =$ ___
g. $(A \cap B) \cup (B \cap C) =$ ___

4.7 If a population consists of the positive even numbers up to 30, and if $A = \{2, 6, 12, 24\}$, what is A'?

Testing your understanding

4.8 A white goods manufacturer is sourcing parts for its air conditioning units. Management are currently putting together a timeline for the next stages of manufacturing. To do so they consider that one set of parts relating to the motor are coming from Germany and one set of parts relating to the casing will come from the united States. Past experience suggests that there is an 8% probability that the German parts will arrive late due to disruptions in shipping. The probability of parts arriving late from the United States is deemed to be 5%.

a. What is the probability that parts from Germany will not be delayed?
b. What is the probability that parts from the United States will not be delayed?
c. Assume that the events in the two previous questions are independent. What is the probability that the parts from Germany will arrive late given that parts from the United States arrived late?

4.9 An external agency monitors and measures the number of listeners of radio stations in a number of different regions. For one particular region in which there are 20 radio stations, it claims that listeners are fairly random in choosing which station to listen to. Station ABC and station XYZ are just two of the stations in this particular region. A person driving in their car switches on the radio and chooses one station to listen to.

a. If listening behaviour was as random as the external agency claims, what would be the probability of the driver tuning into station ABC when choosing one station to listen to?
b. What would be the probability of the driver choosing XYZ?
c. What is the probability of the driver listening to either ABC or XYZ?
d. What is the probability of the driver listening to both ABC and XYZ at the same time? Use your answer to explain how the concept of a mutually exclusive event is relevant in this particular context.

4.10 A government department investigating the issues of tax avoidance and evasion determines that the following outcomes have occurred in a random sample of 400 cases.

Tax return assessment	Returns
Not filed	80
Filed with no evasion to be investigated	260
Filed with minor level of possible evasion to be investigated	40
Filed with major level of possible evasion to be investigated	20

a. What is the probability that a tax return will be filed? Show how considering the complement of this event provides at least two methods of answering this question.
b. Using the information provided, explain why the event of some form of evasion requiring further investigation occurring among those who do file an assessment is not an elementary event.

4.3 Contingency tables and probability matrices

When discussing probabilities that involve two or more variables, there are several concepts of probability to consider. For example, as will be explored in this section, we can discuss one of the variables using the concept of marginal probability, we can discuss both events using the concepts of union and joint probabilities, and we can discuss the likelihood of one event given that the other has occurred using the concept of conditional probability. To further improve understanding of these four concepts, it is useful to consider that data for summarising how two variables co-occur can be presented in the form of a cross-tabulation or contingency table.

For example, suppose further information becomes available about the 1200 sales relating to phone plans; not just the type of plan bought (a \$59, \$79, \$99 or \$129 plan) but also whether the plan was bought by a male or female customer. Table 4.3 summarises the joint outcomes of these two events: gender and cost of plan bought.

TABLE 4.3 Sales of each phone plan broken down by gender

	Gender		
Cost of plan	**Male**	**Female**	**Total units sold**
\$59	72	108	180
\$79	84	216	300
\$99	324	96	420
\$129	180	120	300
Total customers	660	540	1200

Table 4.3 is an example of a contingency table. A **contingency table** is *a table that presents the frequency with which two or more events occur and co-occur*. A contingency table is sometimes referred to as a cross-tabulation, or cross-tab, since the cell where a row and column cross represents a tabulation of the number of times both events occurred. In this table, we can see information about outcomes relating to gender, cost of plan or both. For example, of the 1200 purchases recorded, 180 people bought a \$59 plan. Breaking this down further, we can see that 72 customers who purchased a \$59 plan were male. In total, we can see that 660 purchases were made by male customers.

Marginal, union, joint and conditional probabilities

To see the usefulness of contingency tables, we can now consider four particular types of probability presented in this chapter. The first type is marginal probability. **Marginal probability** is *the probability that a single event occurs without reference to any other event*. It is denoted $P(E)$, where E is some event. A marginal probability is usually *computed by dividing some subtotal by the whole*. In the phone plan example, the marginal probability of purchasing a \$99 plan is found by dividing the number of people buying this plan (420) by the total number of people purchasing any of the four plans available (1200), a probability of $\frac{420}{1200} = .35 = 35\%$. Likewise, the probability that the person purchasing any plan is male is found by dividing the subtotal of 660 that represents the number of male customers by the 1200 customers in total, a probability of $\frac{660}{1200} = .55 = 55\%$. Marginal probabilities refer to one event only, in this case either to the cost of plan or the gender of the customer. In turn, notice that the figures to calculate marginal probabilities come from the margins of the contingency table where various subtotals appear.

A second type of probability is the union of two events. **Union probability** is *the probability that at least one of the events of interest will occur*. Using set notation, it is denoted by $P(E_1 \cup E_2)$, where E_1 and E_2 are two events. $P(E_1 \cup E_2)$ is the probability that E_1 will occur or that E_2 will occur or that both E_1 and E_2 will occur. An example of union probability is the probability a person purchases a \$99 plan or is a male customer. It would include three sets of customers: those who purchased a \$99 plan and were male (324 customers); those who purchased a \$99 plan but were female (96 customers); and those who did not purchase the \$99 plan but were male customers (72 + 84 + 180 = 336 customers). In total this is 324 + 96 + 336 = 756 customers out of our 1200 customers. The union probability of a customer purchasing a \$99 plan or is male is $\frac{756}{1200} = .63 = 63\%$. Another example is the probability of a person wearing glasses or having red hair. All people wearing glasses are included in the union, along with all redheads and all redheads who wear glasses. In a company, the probability that a person is male or a clerical worker is a union probability. A person qualifies for the union by being male or by being a clerical worker or by being both (a male clerical worker).

A third type of probability is the probability relating to the intersection of two events, or joint probability. Recall that the intersection of two events was introduced earlier and refers to the set of outcomes where both events occur simultaneously; the joint probability is the probability that this happens. That is, **joint probability** is *the probability that two events will co-occur as an outcome of an experiment*. The joint probability of events E_1 and E_2 occurring is denoted by $P(E_1 \cap E_2)$. $P(E_1 \cap E_2)$ is read as 'the probability of E_1 and E_2'. An example of joint probability in the context of our phone plan discussion would be the joint probability that a customer purchases a $99 plan and is male, occurring with a probability of $\frac{324}{1200} = .27 = 27\%$. Notice that the figures used to calculate joint probabilities come from the cells in the body of the contingency table (table 4.3). A second example of joint probability is the probability that a person is a redhead and wears glasses.

The fourth type of probability is conditional probability. **Conditional probability** is *the probability of one event given that the occurrence of another event is known*. It is denoted by $P(E_1 | E_2)$. This expression is read as 'the probability that E_1 will occur given that E_2 has occurred'. Conditional probabilities involve knowledge of some prior information. The information that is known or given is written to the right of the vertical line in the probability statement.

Conditional probabilities are computed by determining the number of items that have an outcome out of some subtotal of the population. An example of conditional probability in the context of the phone example would be the probability that a customer purchases a $99 plan given they are male. In this case, we would express our probability with respect to the 660 male customers rather than all 1200 customers. In other words, the conditional probability would be equivalent to asking what proportion of male customers purchased a $99 plan? Examining the contingency table, we can see that 324 out of the 660 male customers sampled purchased the $99 plan, a conditional probability of $\frac{324}{660} = .49 = 49\%$.

Of the four probability types, only conditional probability does not have the overall total as its denominator. Conditional probabilities have a subtotal as the denominator. Figure 4.6 summarises these four types of probability.

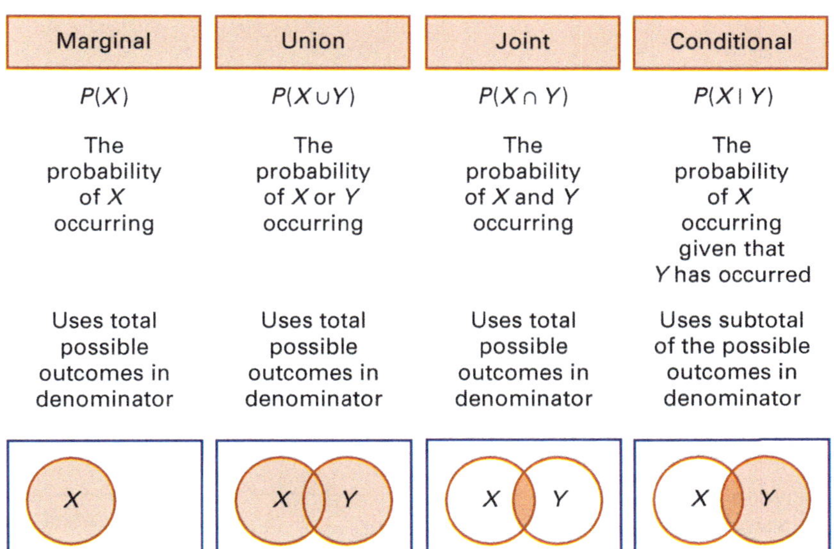

FIGURE 4.6
Marginal, union, joint and conditional probabilities

Probability matrices

In addition to using formulas, another useful tool in solving probability problems is a joint probability matrix or, simply, probability matrix. A **probability matrix** is generally derived directly from a contingency table and *displays the marginal probabilities and the joint (intersection) probabilities of* *a given problem in a table*. Sometimes information may already be presented in probability form. If, on the other hand, the information is presented in the form of a contingency table, which presents the frequency of each event, the probabilities can be calculated by determining the relative frequency of each event as discussed earlier.

Probability matrices can be produced by dividing every entry in the contingency table by the total number of outcomes observed. In the phone plan example, the marginal and joint probabilities of each phone plan being bought by each gender of customer are calculated by dividing each entry in the table of joint frequencies by the total number of customers sampled (1200). Table 4.4 presents the outcome of these calculations.

TABLE 4.4 Probability matrix representing probability of phone plan purchases by gender

	Gender		
Cost of plan	**Male (%)**	**Female (%)**	**Total sold (%)**
$59	6	9	15
$79	7	18	25
$99	27	8	35
$129	15	10	25
Total customers (%)	55	45	100

All the information is now presented in a probability or percentage form. Marginal and joint probabilities can be read straight from the table. For example, the marginal probability of purchasing a $99 plan is 35%, which can be verified using the calculations performed earlier. Likewise, the joint probability that a customer purchases a $99 plan and is male occurs with a probability of 27%, and again confirms the previous calculation using the information from entries in the contingency table. Union probabilities and conditional probabilities, however, require further calculations, which are helped by several laws discussed in the next section.

PRACTICE PROBLEMS

Practising the calculations

4.11 Use the values in the following contingency table to solve the equations given.

	A	B	C
X	42	48	36
Y	54	30	18
Z	21	39	12

a. $P(A) =$ ___

b. $P(Z) =$ ___

c. $P(A \cap X) =$ ___

d. $P(B \cap Z) =$ ___

e. $P(A \cup C) =$ ___

f. $P(A \cap B)$

4.12 Convert the following contingency table to a probability matrix to solve the equations given.

	D	E
A	16	8
B	10	6
C	8	2

a. $P(A) =$ ___

b. $P(E) =$ ___

c. $P(A \cap E) =$ ___

d. $P(A = E) =$ ___

Testing your understanding

4.13 A company is wondering whether a consumer's preferred brand among its own and competing brands is related to the age of the consumer. The company conducts a survey on 2000 consumers, asking participants to indicate which brand they most prefer and to indicate to which age group they belong. The responses to these two questions are summarised using a contingency table.

	Most preferred brand			
Age (years)	**Brand A**	**Brand B**	**Brand C**	**Brand D**
18 to 34	210	110	100	80
35 to 54	176	280	144	200
55 or more	126	126	266	182

For each set of respondents in a particular age group, use the information in the table to determine the probability that a consumer most prefers Brand A. Do the same for Brand B, C and D. Arrange the probabilities that you have calculated into a suitable table. Write a short report to the company discussing these results and whether you think the preference towards a particular brand is related to a consumer's age.

4.14 The operations manager of a cinema complex is currently interested in how patrons using a retail outlet purchase food and drinks in various combinations. In particular, the manager would like to know the probability that a patron will purchase water and popcorn, juice and popcorn, soft drink and popcorn, and popcorn with no drink. The table lists a random sample of 730 purchase outcomes recently made by patrons. To simplify the experiment, only outcomes in which no beverage or one beverage was purchased were examined. Hence, any event in any row is mutually exclusive of an event in any other row (e.g. a single purchase could be listed as purchasing water only, but outcomes relating to a single purchase involving water *and* juice were not recorded). Transform this table to list probability information of purchases and use it to respond to the manager's questions. Overall, what is the probability that popcorn will be purchased?

Drink	Popcorn	Food other than popcorn	No food
Water	12	8	120
Juice	25	35	260
Soft drink	163	7	70
No drink	20	5	5

4.4 Addition laws

Several tools are available for use in solving probability problems. These tools include sample space, tree diagrams, contingency tables and insight. Because of the individuality and variety of probability problems, some techniques apply more readily in certain situations than in others. The selection of one tool over another often depends on what information is available or how it is presented. No best method is available for solving all probability problems. Each tool can be used in conjunction with others. The laws of probability provide another useful method for solving probability problems.

Three groups of laws of probability are presented in this chapter: the addition laws, the multiplication laws and the laws of conditional probability. The groups of addition laws and multiplication laws each have a general law and a special law.

General law of addition

The general law of addition, shown in formula 4.7, is used to find the probability of the union of two events, $P(X \cup Y)$. The expression $P(X \cup Y)$ denotes the probability of X occurring or Y occurring or both X and Y occurring.

General law of addition (4.7)

$$P(X \cup Y) = P(X) + P(Y) - P(X \cap Y)$$

$$P(X \text{ or } Y) = P(X) + P(Y) - P(X \text{ and } Y)$$

where:

X and Y = the two events of interest

$(X \cap Y)$ = the intersection of X and Y

Suppose a wine merchant was interested in the combinations of the types of wine being sold (red and white) and the regions in which the wines were produced (domestic and overseas). The wine merchant examined a random sample of wines during a recent stocktake and presented the information in percentage form as listed in table 4.5 (overleaf).

TABLE 4.5 Probability matrix representing stock levels of wine in percentage form

	Wine type		
Region	**Red**	**White**	**Total (%)**
Domestic	25	45	70
Overseas	10	20	30
Total (%)	35	65	100

Let D represent the event 'domestically produced'. Let R represent the event 'red wine'. Suppose the merchant is searching for various wines to display at the front of the store and wonders what the probability is that a wine available for selection is domestically produced or a red wine. The probability of a wine with D *or* R can be symbolised statistically as a union probability such that the question becomes:

$$P(\mathrm{D} \cup \mathrm{R}) = ?$$

To successfully satisfy the search for a wine that is domestically produced or a red wine, the merchant need only find a wine that satisfies at least one of those two events. Because 70% of the stocked wine is domestically produced, $P(\mathrm{D}) = .70$. In addition, because 35% of wines are red, $P(\mathrm{R}) = .35$. Either of these would satisfy the requirement of the union. Thus, the solution to the problem may appear to be:

$$P(\mathrm{D} \cup \mathrm{R}) = P(\mathrm{D}) + P(\mathrm{R}) = .70 + .35 = 1.05$$

However, we have already established that probabilities cannot be more than 1. What is the problem here? Notice that, among the wines randomly sampled, those that were *both* domestically produced *and* red would be included in *both* of the marginal probabilities $P(\mathrm{D})$ and $P(\mathrm{R})$. In other words, some of the wines have been counted twice. For that reason, the general law of addition subtracts the intersection probability, $P(\mathrm{D} \cap \mathrm{R})$. The Venn diagrams in figure 4.7 illustrate this discussion. Notice that the intersection area of D and R is double shaded in figure 4.7(a), indicating that it has been counted twice. In figure 4.7(b), the shading is consistent throughout D and R because the intersection area has been subtracted. Thus figure 4.7(b) illustrates the proper application of the general law of addition.

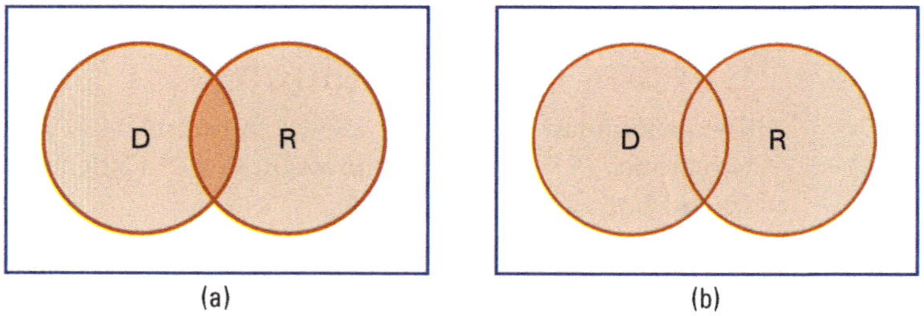

FIGURE 4.7 Solving for the union in the wine merchant problem

So what is the answer to the union probability question? In the probability matrix, it can be seen that 25% of wines for sale are *both* domestically produced *and* red: $P(\mathrm{D} \cap \mathrm{R}) = .25$. We can use the general law of addition to solve for the probability that a wine for sale is *either* domestically produced *or* red.

$$P(\mathrm{D} \cup \mathrm{R}) = P(\mathrm{D}) + P(\mathrm{R}) - P(\mathrm{D} \cap \mathrm{R}) = .70 + .35 - .25 = .80$$

Hence, 80% of the wines selected by the merchant for display at the front of the store would be *either* domestically produced *or* red.

DEMONSTRATION PROBLEM 4.1

PROBLEM: A company that produces software for managing investments is interested in the relationship between gender and the type of investment portfolios that self-managed investors hold. To find out about this relationship, the company commissions a survey of 1200 self-managed investors. The contingency table lists the frequency counts for each category and for subtotals and totals. In this way it breaks down investors by their gender and by the predominant type of investment portfolio they have held over the past 12 months. Investors could nominate one type of portfolio only, so the outcomes relating to type of portfolio are mutually exclusive. If a self-managed investor is selected randomly, what is the probability that the investor is female or predominantly uses an aggressive investment portfolio?

	Gender		
Type of portfolio	**Male**	**Female**	**Total**
Aggressive	260	232	492
Defensive	19	42	61
Hybrid	131	46	177
Income	58	25	83
Speculative	166	75	241
Other	86	60	146
Total	720	480	1200

SOLUTION: Let F denote the event of 'female' and A denote the event of 'aggressive investment portfolio'. The question is:

$$P(\mathrm{F} \cup \mathrm{A}) = ?$$

By the general law of addition:

$$P(\mathrm{F} \cup \mathrm{A}) = P(\mathrm{F}) + P(\mathrm{A}) - P(\mathrm{F} \cap \mathrm{A})$$

Of the 1200 surveyed investors, 480 are female. Therefore:

$$P(\mathrm{F}) = \frac{480}{1200} = 0.40 = 40\%$$

The 1200 surveyed investors include 492 predominantly holding an aggressive investment portfolio. Therefore:

$$P(\mathrm{A}) = \frac{492}{1200} = 0.41 = 41\%$$

Because 232 surveyed investors are both female and predominantly hold an aggressive investment portfolio:

$$P(\mathrm{F} \cap \mathrm{A}) = \frac{232}{1200} = 0.1933 = 19.33\%$$

The union probability is solved as:

$$P(\mathrm{F} \cup \mathrm{A}) = .4000 + .4100 - .1933 = .6167 = 61.67\%$$

Alternatively, to solve this probability, the contingency table can be converted to a probability matrix by dividing every value in the matrix by the value of N_E (1200). This produces the following table listing joint and marginal probabilities.

Type of portfolio	Gender		Total
	Male	Female	
Aggressive	0.2167	0.1933	0.4100
Defensive	0.0158	0.0350	0.0508
Hybrid	0.1092	0.0383	0.1475
Income	0.0483	0.0208	0.0692
Speculative	0.1383	0.0625	0.2008
Other	0.0717	0.0500	0.1217
Total	0.6000	0.4000	1.0000

In this way, the joint probability and the two marginal probabilities required to calculate the union probability can be read straight from the table and substituted into the formula.

DEMONSTRATION PROBLEM 4.2

PROBLEM: The following probability matrix summarises information about new vehicle sales during the past 12 months in Australia with respect to where the sale took place and the type of vehicle sold. The types of vehicles sold are passenger, SUV and commercial; the locations of these sales are New South Wales, Victoria, Queensland and other.

Vehicle type	Geographic location				Total (%)
	NSW (N)	Vic. (V)	Qld (Q)	Other (OG)	
Passenger (P)	15	12	9	11	47
SUV (S)	10	9	7	7	33
Commercial (C)	6	5	4	5	20
Total (%)	31	26	20	23	100

Suppose a new vehicle sale is selected randomly from the data used to create the probability matrix.

a. What is the probability that the new vehicle sale took place in Queensland (Q)?
b. What is the probability that the new vehicle sold is a passenger vehicle (P) or the sale took place in New South Wales (N)?
c. What is the probability that the sale of the new vehicle took place in Victoria (V) or is a commercial vehicle (C)?

SOLUTION:

a. $P(\text{Queensland}) = P(\text{Q}) = 20\%$
b. $P(\text{P} \cup \text{N}) = P(\text{P}) + P(\text{N}) - P(\text{P} \cap \text{N}) = 47\% + 31\% - 15\% = 63\%$
c. $P(\text{V} \cup \text{C}) = P(\text{V}) + P(\text{C}) - P(\text{V} \cap \text{C}) = 26\% + 20\% - 5\% = 41\%$

Exclusive or

The union of two events, $X \cup Y$, refers to the set of outcomes where X occurs, Y occurs, or both X and Y occur. That is, the union includes the outcome where both events occur. However, in everyday speech, the use of the word 'or' is ambiguous, having multiple meanings. It is used by many people to describe cases where only one of the two events of interest has occurred, excluding the case where both events have occurred, even when events are not mutually exclusive. This would be inconsistent with the definition of the union of two events. In turn, replacing the symbol for union with the word 'or' must be done with care, especially when communicating to others who may not appreciate this potential ambiguity. For example, a manager may request information about the probability of two events occurring, but may or may not wish to include outcomes where both events occur. In turn, the law of addition is useful in creating a clear understanding of what is precisely implied by the word 'or' when it is used in statistics to describe the union of two events.

Nonetheless, the dual interpretation of the word 'or' that arises in natural language is problematic for a range of settings where comparisons about the occurrence of two events are made, such as in computer science. In computer science, many programs rely on expressing such outcomes as being true or false, relying on a concept referred to as Boolean logic. To overcome the possible confusion and also to present a shortcut in computer programming, many computer languages used to write programs incorporate two logic operators, 'or' and 'exclusive or'. 'Exclusive or' (sometimes written XOR) refers to the set of outcomes where X occurs or Y occurs but X and Y do not occur together. Figure 4.8 presents this in the form of a Venn diagram.

To calculate the probability that only one of two events occurs, it is useful to reconsider how the union of two events is calculated. In calculating the union by using the general law of addition, the intersection probability is subtracted because it is already included in both marginal probabilities. This adjusted probability leaves a union probability that properly includes both marginal values and the intersection value. If the intersection probability is subtracted a second time, the intersection is removed, leaving the probability of X or Y but not both (as shown in figure 4.8).

$$\begin{aligned} P(X \text{ or } Y \text{ but not both}) &= P(X) + P(Y) - P(X \cap Y) - P(X \cap Y) \\ &= P(X \cup Y) - P(X \cap Y) \end{aligned}$$

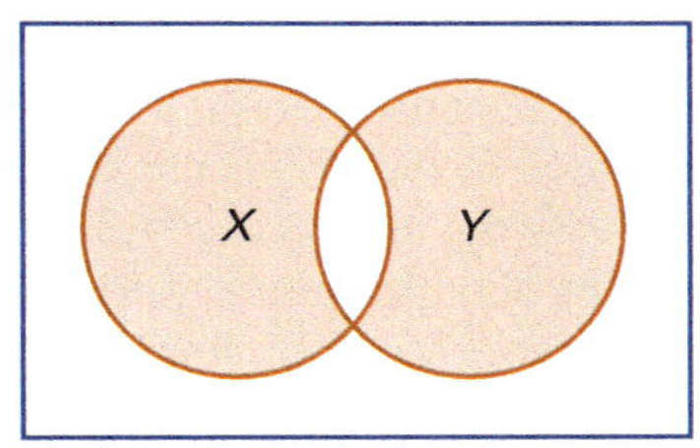

FIGURE 4.8 The *X* or *Y* but not both case

Complement of a union

The probability of the union of two events X and Y represents the probability that the outcome is X *or* it is Y *or* it is *both* X and Y. The union includes everything except the possibility that it is *neither* X *nor* Y, which can be represented symbolically as $P(\text{not } X \cap \text{not } Y)$. Because it is the only possible case other than the union of X or Y, it is the **complement of a union**. Stated more formally:

$$P(\text{neither } X \text{ nor } Y) = P(\text{not } X \cap \text{not } Y) = 1 - P(X \cup Y)$$

That is:

$$P(\text{neither } X \text{ nor } Y) = P(\text{not } X \text{ and not } Y) = 1 - P(X \text{ or } Y)$$

Examine the Venn diagram in figure 4.9. Note that the complement of the union of X and Y is the shaded area outside the circles. This area represents the neither X nor Y region.

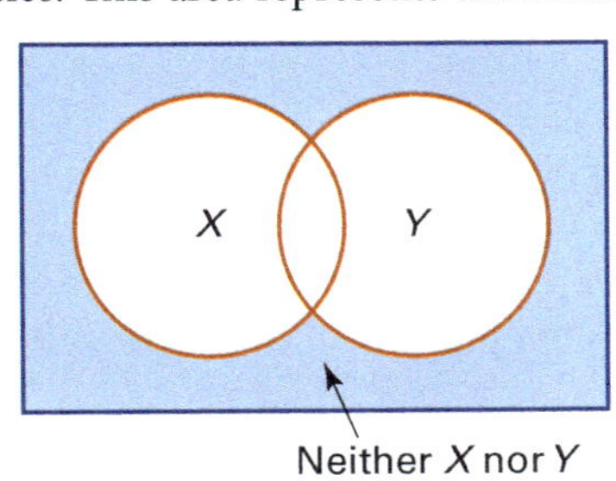

FIGURE 4.9 The complement of a union: the neither/nor region

In the example involving the wine merchant selecting a bottle for display at the front of the store, the probability that a randomly selected wine would be domestically produced *or* a red wine was determined to be:

$$P(\mathrm{D} \cup \mathrm{R}) = P(\mathrm{D}) + P(\mathrm{R}) - P(\mathrm{D} \cap \mathrm{R}) = .70 + .35 - .25 = .80 = 80\%$$

The probability that a wine selected would be *neither* domestically produced *nor* a variety of red is calculated as the complement of this union.

$$P(\text{neither D nor R}) = P(\text{not D} \cap \text{not R}) = 1 - P(\mathrm{D} \cup \mathrm{R}) = 1 - .80 = .20 = 20\%$$

In table 4.5, this *neither/nor* probability is found in the cell representing the joint probability of a wine being both a variety of white and one that is sourced from overseas.

Special law of addition

If two events are mutually exclusive, the probability of the union of the two events is the probability of the first event plus the probability of the second event, as shown in formula 4.8. Because mutually exclusive events do not intersect, nothing has to be subtracted.

Special law of addition (4.8)

$$\text{If } X \text{ and } Y \text{ are mutually exclusive, } P(X \cup Y) = P(X) + P(Y)$$

The special law of addition is a special case of the general law of addition. In a sense, the general law fits all cases. However, when the events are mutually exclusive, a zero is inserted into the general law formula for the intersection, resulting in the special law formula.

In a survey about improving productivity, workers were asked what most hinders their productivity and were given the following selections from which to choose only one answer or nominate another factor that was not listed.

- Lack of direction
- Lack of support
- Too much work
- Inefficient process
- Not enough equipment/supplies
- Low pay/chance to advance

Lack of direction was cited by the most workers (20%), followed by lack of support (18%), too much work (18%), inefficient process (8%), not enough equipment/supplies (7%), low pay/chance to advance (7%) and a variety of other factors nominated by respondents. If a worker who responded to this survey is selected (or if the survey actually reflects the views of the working public and a worker in general is selected) and that worker is asked which of the given selections most hinders his or her productivity, what is the probability that the worker will respond that it is either too much work or inefficient process?

Let M denote the event 'too much work' and I denote the event 'inefficient process'. The question is:

$$P(\mathrm{M} \cup \mathrm{I}) = ?$$

18% of the survey respondents said 'too much work':

$$P(\mathrm{M}) = .18$$

8% of the survey respondents said 'inefficient process':

$$P(\mathrm{I}) = .08$$

It was not possible to select more than one answer; therefore:

$$P(\mathrm{M} \cap \mathrm{I}) = .00$$

Implementing the special law of addition gives:

$$P(\mathrm{M} \cup \mathrm{I}) = P(\mathrm{M}) + P(\mathrm{I}) = .18 + .08 = .26 = 26\%$$

DEMONSTRATION PROBLEM 4.3

PROBLEM: If an investor is randomly selected from the set of data described in demonstration problem 4.1, what is the probability that the investor holds a portfolio categorised as either income or speculative? What is the probability that the investor is holding a portfolio categorised as either aggressive or speculative?

SOLUTION: Examine the software company's self-managed investor profile data shown in demonstration problem 4.1. In matrices like this one, the rows are non-overlapping or mutually exclusive, as are the columns. In this matrix, an investor was classified as holding only one type of investment portfolio and as either male or female but not both. Thus, in this example, the categories of type of investment portfolio are mutually exclusive, as are the categories of gender, and the special law of addition can be applied to the self-managed investor profile data to determine the union probabilities.

Let 'A' denote an aggressive portfolio, 'I' denote an income portfolio and 'S' denote a speculative portfolio. The probability that a self-managed investor holds either an income or speculative investment portfolio is:

$$P(\text{I} \cup \text{S}) = P(\text{I}) + P(\text{S}) = \frac{83}{1200} + \frac{241}{1200} = \frac{324}{1200} = 0.2700 = 27.00\%$$

The probability that a self-managed investor holds either an aggressive or speculative investment portfolio is:

$$P(\text{A} \cup \text{S}) = P(\text{A}) + P(\text{S}) = \frac{492}{1200} + \frac{241}{1200} = \frac{733}{1200} = 0.6108 = 61.08\%$$

PRACTICE PROBLEMS

Practising the calculations

4.15 Given $P(\text{A}) = .10$, $P(\text{B}) = .12$, $P(\text{C}) = .21$, $P(\text{A} \cap \text{C}) = .05$ and $P(\text{B} \cap \text{C}) = .03$, solve the following equations.

a. $P(\text{A} \cup \text{C}) =$ ___
b. $P(\text{B} \cup \text{C}) =$ ___
c. If A and B are mutually exclusive, $P(\text{A} \cup \text{B}) =$ ___

4.16 Use the values in the following matrix to solve the equations given.

	D	E	F
A	5	8	12
B	10	6	4
C	8	2	5

a. $P(\text{A} \cup \text{D}) =$ ___
b. $P(\text{E} \cup \text{B}) =$ ___
c. $P(\text{D} \cup \text{E}) =$ ___
d. $P(\text{C} \cup \text{F}) =$ ___

Testing your understanding

4.17 According to a recent survey, 40% of adult Millennials (those aged 18 to 29 years) viewed themselves more as 'spenders' than 'savers'. The survey also revealed that 25% of adult Millennials viewed social networking as important to find out about products and services. A social media expert would like to determine the probability that a randomly selected adult Millennial either views themselves as a 'spender' or views social networking as important to find out about products and services. Can this question be answered? Under what conditions can it be solved? If the problem cannot be solved, what information is needed to make it solvable?

4.18 According to the ABS, 73% of women aged 25 to 54 participate in the labour force. Suppose that 78% of the women aged 25 to 54 are married. Suppose also that 61% of all women aged 25 to 54 are married and are participating in the labour force. What is the probability that a randomly selected woman aged 25 to 54:

a. is married or is participating in the labour force
b. is married or is participating in the labour force but not both
c. is neither married nor participating in the labour force?

4.19 According to a consumer report, approximately 3% of New Zealanders bought a new vehicle in the past 12 months. The report also indicated that 10% had commenced a new job in the same period. The report further revealed that in the past 12 months, 2% had bought a new vehicle and commenced a new job. A New Zealander is randomly selected.

a. What is the probability that in the past 12 months the individual has purchased a new car or commenced a new job?

b. What is the probability that in the past 12 months the individual has purchased a new car or commenced a new job but not both?

c. What is the probability that in the past 12 months the individual has neither bought a new car nor commenced a new job?

d. Why does the special law of addition not apply to this problem?

4.20 A survey conducted by Roy Morgan Research asked 1116 Australians to nominate health issues they consider important. Sixty per cent of respondents nominated cancer as an important health issue, and only 29% mentioned heart disease. Assume that these percentages are true for the population of Australia and that 25% of all respondents mentioned both cancer and heart disease as important health issues.

a. What is the probability that a randomly selected Australian nominates either cancer, heart disease or both as important health issues?

b. What is the probability that a randomly selected Australian nominates either cancer or heart disease but not both as important health issues?

c. What is the probability that a randomly selected Australian nominates neither cancer nor heart disease as an important health issue?

d. Construct a probability matrix for this problem and indicate the locations of your answers to parts (a), (b) and (c) on the matrix.

4.5 Multiplication laws

General law of multiplication

As stated earlier, the probability of the intersection of two events $P(X \cap Y)$ is called the *joint probability*. If we have constructed a probability matrix, sometimes called a joint probability table, we can just read the joint probabilities from the inner cells of the matrix. The general law of multiplication, shown in formula 4.9, is used to find the joint probability that *both* event X and event Y will occur when information is not provided in this format.

General law of multiplication (4.9)

$$P(X \cap Y) = P(X)P(Y \mid X) = P(Y)P(X \mid Y)$$

For example, according to the ABS, 55% of the Australian labour force is male. In addition, 15% of the males in the labour force work part time. What is the probability that a randomly selected member of the Australian labour force is a male *and* works part time? This question is one of joint probability and, since we cannot construct a joint probability matrix directly, the general law of multiplication can be applied to answer it.

Let M denote the event that the member of the labour force is a man. Let T denote the event that the member is a part-time worker. The question is:

$$P(\text{M} \cap \text{T}) = ?$$

According to the general law of multiplication, this problem can be solved by:

$$P(\text{M} \cap \text{T}) = P(\text{M})P(\text{T} \mid \text{M})$$

Since 55% of the labour force are males, $P(\text{M}) = .55$. $P(\text{T} \mid \text{M})$ is a conditional probability that can be stated as 'the probability that a worker is a part-time worker given that the worker is a male'.

This condition is what was given in the statement that *15% of the males in the labour force work part time*. Hence, $P(T|M) = 0.15$. It follows that:

$$P(M \cap T) = P(M)P(T|M) = (.55)(.15) = .0825 = 8.25\%$$

It can be stated that 8.25% of the Australian labour force are males *and* work part time. The Venn diagram in figure 4.10 shows these relationships and the joint probability.

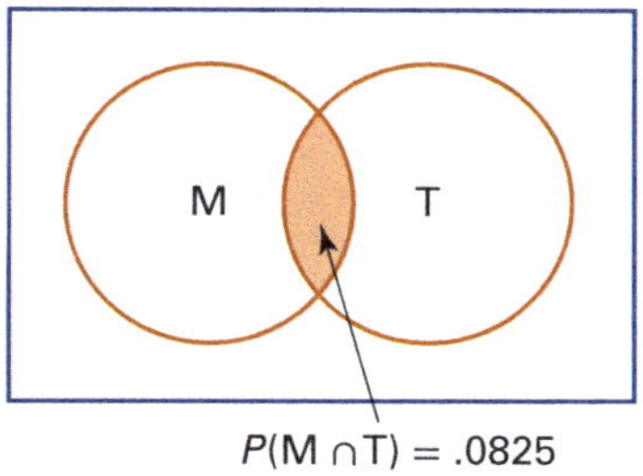

FIGURE 4.10 Joint probability that a member of the labour force is a male and a part-time worker

DEMONSTRATION PROBLEM 4.4

PROBLEM: A company has 140 employees, of whom 30 are supervisors. Eighty of the employees are married, and 20% of the married employees are supervisors. If a company employee is randomly selected, what is the probability that the employee is married and is a supervisor?

SOLUTION: Let M denote married and S denote supervisor. The question is:

$$P(M \cap S) = ?$$

First, calculate the marginal probability:

$$P(M) = \frac{80}{140} = .5714$$

Then, note that 20% of the married employees are supervisors, which is the conditional probability $P(S|M) = .20$. Finally, applying the general law of multiplication gives:

$$P(M \cap S) = P(M)P(S|M) = (.5714)(.20) = .1143$$

Hence, the probability of a randomly selected employee being married and a supervisor is .1143. That is, 11.43% of the 140 employees are married and are supervisors.

Special law of multiplication

If events X and Y are independent, a special law of multiplication, given in formula 4.10, can be used to find the joint probability of X and Y. This special law uses the fact that, when two events X and Y are independent, $P(X|Y) = P(X)$ and $P(Y|X) = P(Y)$. Thus, the general law of multiplication:

$$P(X \cap Y) = P(X)P(Y|X)$$

becomes:

$$P(X \cap Y) = P(X)P(Y)$$

when X and Y are independent.

Special law of multiplication (4.10)

If X and Y are independent, $P(X \cap Y) = P(X \text{ and } Y) = P(X)P(Y)$

DEMONSTRATION PROBLEM 4.5

PROBLEM: A manufacturing company produces pads of bound paper. Three per cent of all paper pads produced are improperly bound. An inspector randomly samples two pads of paper, one at a time. A large number of pads are being produced during the inspection (over 10 000) so the sampling is assumed to be effectively the same as sampling with replacement. What is the probability that the two pads selected are both improperly bound?

SOLUTION: Let I denote 'improperly bound'. The question is:

$$P(I_1 \cap I_2) = ?$$

The probability of I = .03, or 3% are improperly bound. Because the sampling can be assumed to be done with replacement, the two events are independent. Hence:

$$P(I_1 \cap I_2) = P(I_1)P(I_2) = (.03)(.03) = .0009$$

This can be interpreted to mean the probability that both pads are improperly bound is 0.09%.

The special law of multiplication can be extended to examine the joint probability of two or more events that are assumed or known to be independent. For example, in demonstration problem 4.5 the manager may additionally ask about the probability that five pads selected are improperly bound. The law can also be used to consider cases where various combinations of events occur, such as the probability that, out of five pads examined, two pads are improperly bound and three pads are not. The ability to examine probabilities across multiple events where the assumption of independence can be made and various combinations could occur will be revisited under the topic of binomial distributions later in the text.

Most matrices that show the outcomes of historical data, such as those constructed using relative frequencies, refer to events that are not independent. If a probability matrix contains independent events, the special law of multiplication can be applied. If not, the special law cannot be used.

DEMONSTRATION PROBLEM 4.6

PROBLEM: The wine merchant discussed in section 4.4 decides to re-examine the information that was collated on stock broken down by region of production and wine type. This information was presented in table 4.5. The wine merchant observes that the joint probability that a wine is white and was domestically produced is 45%. The merchant wonders if there is a relationship between region of production and wine type. The wine merchant asks what percentage of wines would be both white and produced domestically if these events were independent.

SOLUTION: The wine merchant's question can be answered by determining $P(\text{D and W})$ where D represents the event that the wine was domestically produced and W represents the event that the wine is white. If the colour of the wine was independent of the region of production, the special law of multiplication would hold, such that:

$$P(D \cap W) = P(D)P(W) = (.70)(.65) = .4550 = 45.50\%$$

The joint probability of what the wine merchant observed by examining the actual stock in the store (exactly 45%) is very close to what would be expected if there was no relationship (i.e. independence) between wine colour and region (45.5%).

The special law of multiplication provides a method of determining joint probabilities when the events being examined are independent. Assessing whether events are independent is discussed in more detail in the next section of this chapter.

PRACTICE PROBLEMS

Practising the calculations

4.21 A hardware store determines that 70% of its customers do not use the self-checkout system to make their purchases. It also determines that 80% of its customers pay by cash. Among those using the self-checkout system, however, only 60% pay by cash.

a. Use this information to determine the probability that a customer uses the self-checkout system and pays by cash.

b. If use of the self-checkout system and payment by cash are independent, what would the probability in part (a) be?

4.22 Given $P(A) = .40$, $P(B) = .25$, $P(C) = .35$, $P(B \mid A) = .25$ and $P(A \mid C) = .80$, solve the following.

a. $P(A \cap B) =$ ___

b. $P(A \cap C) =$ ___

c. If A and B are independent, $P(A \cap B) =$ ___

d. If A and C are independent, $P(A \cap C) =$ ___

4.23 A batch of 50 parts contains six defects.

a. If two parts are drawn randomly one at a time without replacement, what is the probability that both parts are defective?

b. If this experiment is repeated with replacement, what is the probability that both parts are defective?

Testing your understanding

4.24 According to the ABS, 64% of Australian adults live in capital cities. Further, the ABS reports that about 3% of all Australian adults care for ill relatives. Suppose that, of those adults living in capital cities, 2% care for ill relatives.

a. Use the general law of multiplication to determine the probability of randomly selecting an adult from the Australian population who lives in a capital city area and is caring for an ill relative.

b. What is the probability of randomly selecting an adult from the Australian population who lives in a capital city area and does not care for an ill relative?

c. Construct a probability matrix and confirm that your answers to parts (a) and (b) are listed in the matrix.

d. From the probability matrix, determine the probability that an adult does not live in a capital city area but cares for an ill relative.

4.25 A study by the ASX revealed that 39% of the Australian adult population are shareholders. In addition, the study determined that 7.1% of all Australian adult shareholders have postgraduate education. Suppose 5% of all Australian adults have postgraduate education. An Australian adult is randomly selected. What is the probability that the adult:

a. does not own shares

b. owns shares and has postgraduate education

c. owns shares or has postgraduate education

d. has neither postgraduate education nor owns shares

e. does not own shares or has no postgraduate education

f. has postgraduate education and owns no shares?

4.26 the Land transport Safety Authority of New Zealand conducted a survey on public attitudes to road safety in New Zealand and found that 78% of New Zealanders agreed that New Zealand roads are safer to travel on. Sixty-six per cent of New Zealanders believe that drink-driving laws aimed at reducing the road death toll are effective. Suppose that 57% of New Zealanders who say that New Zealand roads are safer to travel on believe that drink-driving laws aimed at reducing the road death toll are effective. What is the probability of randomly selecting a New Zealander who:

a. says that New Zealand roads are safer to travel on and believes that drink-driving laws aimed at reducing the road death toll are effective

b. neither says that New Zealand roads are safer to travel on nor believes that drink-driving laws aimed at reducing the road death toll are effective

c. says that New Zealand roads are not safer to travel on but believes that drink-driving laws aimed at reducing the road death toll are effective?

4.27 The ABS energy survey reports that 45% of all Australian households have an air conditioner and that 30% of all Australian households have a dishwasher. An Australian household is randomly selected.

a. Assume that whether a household has a dishwasher is unrelated to whether the same household has an air conditioner. Use the special law of multiplication to determine the probability that the household has both an air conditioner and a dishwasher.

b. Suppose another report states that if an Australian household has a dishwasher the probability of this household having an air conditioner is 80%. Use the general law of multiplication to determine the probability that the household has both an air conditioner and a dishwasher. Does it appear that whether a household has a dishwasher may be related to whether the same household has an air conditioner?

4.6 Conditional probability

Conditional probabilities are computed based on the prior knowledge that a statistician has on one of the two events being studied. If X and Y are two events, the conditional probability of X occurring given that Y is known or has occurred is expressed as $P(X|Y)$ and is given in the *law of conditional probability*, as shown in formula 4.11.

Law of conditional probability (4.11)

$$P(X|Y)=\frac{P(X\cap Y)}{P(Y)}=\frac{P(X)P(Y|X)}{P(Y)}$$

The *conditional probability* of $(X|Y)$ is the probability that X will occur given Y. The formula for conditional probability is derived by dividing both sides of the general law of multiplication by $P(Y)$.

Suppose a company that offers emergency breakdown services to its members is interested in whether the type of call-out incident, particularly those relating to flat batteries, is conditional upon whether the call-out occurs on a weekday or on a weekend. Table 4.6 presents information about the occurrence of such events sourced from the company's annual report.

TABLE 4.6 Probability matrix representing breakdown of type of call-out and time of call

	Time of call		
Type of call-out	**Weekday (%)**	**Weekend (%)**	**Total (%)**
Flat battery	44	9	53
Keys locked in car	15	14	29
Out of petrol	6	5	11
Other	2	5	7
Total call outs (%)	67	33	100

The company may believe that the rate of call-outs relating to flat batteries appears to be higher on weekdays than on weekends; however, a greater percentage of call-outs occur on weekdays as this represents five out of the seven days in a week. In any case, 53% of call-outs are made in relation to a flat battery. The company can confirm its suspicions by asking whether the probability of a flat battery incident is higher *given* that the call-out is made on a weekday. Let F represent incidents relating to a call-out involving a flat battery and D represent call-outs made on a weekday. In mathematical notation, the question is:

$$P(\mathrm{F}|\mathrm{D}) = ?$$

Note that the given part of the information is listed to the right of the vertical line in the conditional probability. The formula solution is:

$$P(\mathrm{F}|\mathrm{D})=\frac{P(\mathrm{F}\cap \mathrm{D})}{P(\mathrm{D})}$$

$$P(\mathrm{D}) = .67 \text{ and } P(\mathrm{F}\cap \mathrm{D}) = .44$$

$$P(\mathrm{F}|\mathrm{D})=\frac{P(\mathrm{F}\cap \mathrm{D})}{P(\mathrm{D})}=\frac{.44}{.67}=.6567=65.67\%$$

The conditional probability implies that the probability of a flat battery call-out being made is 65.67% given the call-out is made on a weekday. This is higher than $P(\mathrm{F}) = 53\%$, the probability that a call-out relates to a flat battery regardless of when the call-out is made. In this regard, it suggests that the incidence of flat battery call-outs is higher during the week than on weekends. This can be confirmed by examining the probability that a call-out relates to a flat battery given that the call is made on the weekend. If D represents call outs being made on a weekday, the complement of this event, D′, represents call-outs being made on the weekend. The formula for the solution in this case is:

$$P(\mathrm{F}|\mathrm{D}') = \frac{P(\mathrm{F} \cap \mathrm{D}')}{P(\mathrm{D}')}$$

$$P(\mathrm{D}') = 1 - .67 = .33 \text{ and } P(\mathrm{F} \cap \mathrm{D}') = .09$$

$$P(\mathrm{F}|\mathrm{D}') = \frac{P(\mathrm{F} \cap \mathrm{D}')}{P(\mathrm{D}')} = \frac{.09}{.33} = .2727 = 27.27\%$$

The conditional probability in this case implies that the probability of a flat battery call-out being made is 27.27% given that the call-out is made on a weekend. In other words, the call-out incidence relating to flat batteries appears to rise on weekdays and fall on weekends; about two in three call-outs relate to flat batteries during the week, while only one in three call-outs require such assistance on the weekend. This type of information would be beneficial to the company in efficiently managing its support services for its members, especially if the service vehicles used to help members with flat batteries are different from those used to give mechanical assistance of another type. For example, the conditional probabilities inform them that they would need a greater proportion of vehicles on the road during the week that are dedicated to assisting people with flat batteries, whereas the weekend would relate more to incidents not requiring a battery installation.

The second version of the conditional probability law formula is:

$$P(X|Y) = \frac{P(X)P(Y|X)}{P(Y)}$$

This version is more complex than the first version of the formula for conditional probability that was presented. However, sometimes the second version must be used because of the information given in the problem — for example, when solving for $P(X|Y)$ but $P(X)$ and $P(Y|X)$ are given rather than $P(X \text{ and } Y)$. Even though $P(X \text{ and } Y)$ may not be known directly, such as from a joint probability matrix, we may be able to use the formula relating to multiplication; the second version of the conditional probability formula is obtained by substituting $P(X \cap Y) = P(X)P(Y|X)$ into the first version.

Data relating to the Australian labour force were presented in section 4.5. Included in this information is the fact that 55% of the Australian labour force is male and that 15% of the men in the Australian labour force work part time. In addition, 28% of all Australian workers are known to be part-time workers. What is the probability that a randomly selected Australian worker is male if that person is known to be a part-time worker? Let M denote the event of selecting a male and T denote the event of selecting a part-time worker. In symbols, the question to be answered is:

$$P(\mathrm{M}|\mathrm{T}) = ?$$

The first form of the law of conditional probability is:

$$P(\mathrm{M}|\mathrm{T}) = \frac{P(\mathrm{M} \cap \mathrm{T})}{P(\mathrm{T})}$$

Note that this version of the law of conditional probability requires knowledge of the joint probability $P(\mathrm{M} \cap \mathrm{T})$, which is not given here. We, therefore, try the second version of the law of conditional probability, which is:

$$P(\mathrm{M}|\mathrm{T}) = \frac{P(\mathrm{M})P(\mathrm{T}|\mathrm{M})}{P(\mathrm{T})}$$

For this version of the formula, all required information is given in the problem.

$$P(\mathrm{M}) = .55$$

$$P(\mathrm{T}) = .28$$

$$P(\mathrm{T}\,|\,\mathrm{M}) = .15$$

The probability of a worker being a man given that the person works part time can now be computed.

$$P(\mathrm{M}|\mathrm{T}) = \frac{P(\mathrm{M})P(\mathrm{T}|\mathrm{M})}{P(\mathrm{T})} = \frac{(.55)(.15)}{(.28)} = .295$$

Hence, 29.5% of the part-time workers are men.

DEMONSTRATION PROBLEM 4.7

PROBLEM: An online advertiser is interested in whether a brand manager's perception that the role of social media is critical to their marketing efforts is related to the type of consumer product or service being sold. A survey of brand managers is completed and the following table lists the percentages of responses regarding strategy and whether the product or service being managed is categorised as a convenience, shopping, specialty or unsought offering.

	Critical reliance on social media		
Type of offering	**Disagree (D)**	**Agree (A)**	**Total (%)**
Convenience (C)	18	7	25
Shopping (SH)	14	21	35
Speciality (SP)	8	17	25
Unsought (U)	7	8	15
Total (%)	47	53	100

Use the table to calculate $P(\mathrm{A}|\mathrm{SP})$, the probability that a brand manager agrees that a critical reliance on social media is required for their product, given that they manage a product or service categorised as a speciality offering. Interpret this conditional probability and compare it with $P(\mathrm{A})$.

SOLUTION: Because the joint probability matrix contains the joint and marginal probabilities required in the formula, determining the conditional probability required by using the formula is straightforward. In this case, the joint probability $P(\mathrm{A} \cap \mathrm{SP})$ appears in the inner cell of the matrix that represents the managers who responded that manage a speciality product and agreed that social media is critical in their marketing efforts (17%); the marginal probability $P(\mathrm{SP})$ appears in a margin and represents the probability that the brand manager looks after a speciality offering (25%). Using these two probabilities, the desired conditional probability can be calculated as:

$$P(\mathrm{A}\,|\,\mathrm{SP}) = \frac{P(\mathrm{A} \cap \mathrm{SP})}{P(\mathrm{SP})} = \frac{17}{25} = .68$$

This means that 68% of the brand managers looking after speciality offerings agree that social media is critical to their marketing strategies. If we did not know whether a brand manager was looking after a speciality offering, we would have assigned the probability of the brand manager agreeing that social media plays a critical role in their marketing efforts to be $P(\mathrm{A}) = 53\%$.

Assessing independence

Independent events are those in which one event does not influence the outcome of another. For instance, it is unlikely that people born on a Tuesday are more likely to listen to classical music than people born on another day of the week. As outlined previously, knowing whether two events are independent influences whether the general or special law of multiplication can be used to calculate joint probabilities. In business, it is useful to know whether events are independent. For instance, a cinema may determine that whether a person buys popcorn depends on whether the outside temperature is above average. Knowing that a movie is running on a particularly hot day may change how many people will be assigned to staff the popcorn stand or whether to offer a special deal at this time to entice more sales. Likewise, determining that outside temperature and popcorn sales are independent implies that operational decisions about popcorn sales can be made without concern for how hot or cold it is outside the cinema complex.

To determine whether X and Y are independent events, the following assessment can be made.

$$P(X \mid Y) = P(X) \text{ and } P(Y \mid X) = P(Y)$$

When events are independent, each conditional probability is identical in value to its corresponding marginal probability. If *any* combination of two events fails to indicate that this equality exists, the two events are not independent. Determining that two events are not independent is the same as saying the two events are dependent.

DEMONSTRATION PROBLEM 4.8

PROBLEM: The owner of the store that collected data on phone plan sales, as presented in table 4.3, would like to determine if the cost of a plan is independent of the gender of the customer intending to purchase the plan. The following table presents the same information about the cost of a plan and the gender of the person purchasing the plan in the form of a probability matrix.

	Gender		
Cost of plan	**Male**	**Female**	**Total sold (%)**
$59	6	9	15
$79	7	18	25
$99	27	8	35
$129	15	10	25
Total customers (%)	55	45	100

SOLUTION: Select one plan and one gender: say, $79 plan (B) and female (F). Does $P(\text{B} \mid \text{F}) = P(\text{B})$?

$$P(\text{B}|\text{F}) = \frac{P(B \cap F)}{P(F)} = \frac{18}{45} = .40 = 40\% \text{ and } P(\text{B}) = 25\%$$

In this one example, the probability of purchasing the $79 plan (25%) is quite different if the owner knows that the customer considering purchasing the plan is female (40%). Cost of plan and gender are not independent because at least one clear exception to the test exists. This implies that the retailer will market the plans differently depending on whether the customer walking into the store is male or female.

One way to see how the store owner might approach the decision about which product to market, given that gender is known, is to produce a table that lists a set of conditional probabilities. In the table below, the probabilities relating to the cost of the phone plan are listed, conditional upon the gender of the customer. For example, the first entry, 10.9%, is the probability that a $59 plan will be purchased, given that the customer is male, or $P(\$59 \mid \text{male})$.

Cost of plan	*P*(plan | male)	*P*(plan | female)	*P*(plan) (%)
$59 plan	10.9	20.0	15.0
$79 plan	12.7	40.0	25.0
$99 plan	49.1	17.8	35.0
$129 plan	27.3	22.2	25.0
Total (%)	100.0	100.0	100.0

This table may allow the retailer to consider a different sales strategy in talking to customers, conditional on knowing the gender of the customer. For example, if the customer is male, the table shows that they are more likely to purchase the $99 plan with $P(\$99 \text{ plan} | \text{male}) = 49.1\%$. The $99 plan is a lot less attractive to women with $P(\$99 \text{ plan} | \text{female}) = 17.8\%$. Instead, women appear to be more interested in the $79 plan with $P(\$79 \text{ plan} | \text{female}) = 40\%$.

Assessing whether two events are independent by comparing various conditional probabilities with their corresponding marginal probabilities is less precise than other approaches for assessing the independence of two events. In some cases, such a comparison allows a clear conclusion to be drawn about whether two events influence each other and are, therefore, not independent. In other cases, however, it is less clear whether the differences in probabilities are significant, thereby indicating a relationship between the two events. The differences between observed experimental outcomes and what would be expected to occur if the two events were independent can be used to calculate a statistic; a formal test comparing this statistic with a specific (critical) value allows a clear conclusion about independence to be made. This comparison, however, requires a knowledge of how the two events occur, using a contingency table of raw frequency data. In some cases only the relative frequency or probability information is available and the methods outlined in this chapter become useful for assessing independence.

Tree diagrams

A **tree diagram** is a *graphical representation of the outcomes of an experiment listing all the possible outcomes that could occur.* A tree diagram may or may not present additional information about the probability that each event occurs; those that do are often referred to as probability trees. An example of a tree diagram was presented in figure 4.2 to list all the possible outcomes that occur when rolling two dice. Tree diagrams and probability trees can become very large and impractical when the number of outcomes increases. For example, if the tree diagram presented in figure 4.2 was redrawn to represent a roll involving three dice, this would require an additional 216 branches to indicate all outcomes. Tree diagrams that contain probability information, however, are particularly useful for illustrating conditional probability and the general law of multiplication.

For example, suppose that a particular type of printer cartridge available in the market is produced by two companies: company A and company B. A parent company sells the cartridges, with company A producing 65% of the cartridges for sale and company B producing the remaining 35%. The parent company conducts an audit of both companies to examine the rate of defective cartridges following several incidents relating to product quality. Random sampling at each location reveals that 4% of the cartridges produced by company A are defective and that 6% of the cartridges produced by company B are defective. What is the joint probability that a cartridge is defective and is produced by company A? What is the joint probability that a cartridge is defective and is produced by company B? What is the marginal probability that a cartridge is defective?

These questions can be answered by representing the two events in a tree diagram and applying the law of multiplication. Figure 4.11 represents the outcomes relating to where a cartridge was produced and the rate of defective production, conditional upon where the cartridge was produced. Probability information relating to each event is also presented.

The first event in the tree diagram indicates the company that produced the cartridge. This reflects the marginal probability that a cartridge sold by the parent company is produced by company A, $P(A) = .65$, and the complement of this event, $P(B) = P(A') = .35$. The second event in the tree diagram indicates the conditional probability that a cartridge is defective, D, given which company produced the cartridge. If the cartridge was produced by company A, this conditional probability is $P(D | A) = .04$. If the cartridge was produced by company B, this conditional probability is $P(D | B) = P(D | A') = .06$. The tree diagram indicates how probabilities of one event may change depending on what has occurred in relation to other events.

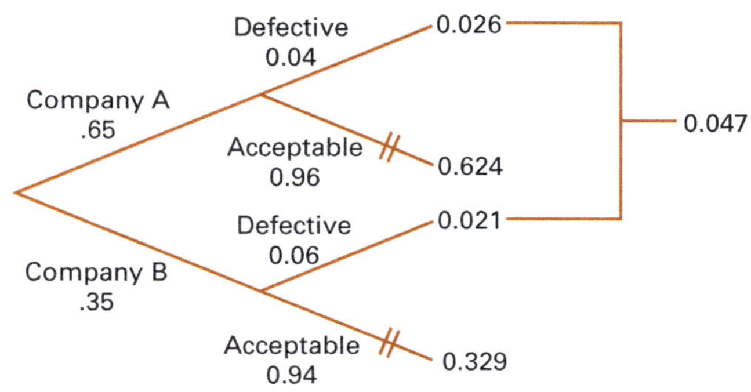

FIGURE 4.11 Tree diagram for probabilities of cartridges being defective

The tree diagram also allows the law of multiplication to be illustrated. The joint probability that a cartridge sold by the parent company is produced by company A and that it is defective is calculated as:

$$P(\text{A} \cap \text{D}) = P(\text{A})P(\text{D} \mid \text{A}) = (.65)(.04) = .026$$

Similarly, the joint probability that a cartridge is defective and it is produced not by company A, but by company B, is calculated as:

$$P(\text{A}' \cap \text{D}) = P(\text{A}')P(\text{D} \mid \text{A}') = (.35)(.06) = .021$$

In other words, 2.6% of all cartridges are made by company A and are defective; 2.1% of all cartridges are made by company B and are defective. Since the cartridges are produced at only two locations, the addition of these two probabilities allows the overall rate of defective cartridges to be determined.

$$P(\text{D}) = P(\text{A} \cap \text{D}) + P(\text{A}' \cap \text{D}) = .026 + .021 = .047$$

The probability that the parent company sells a cartridge that is defective is 4.7%. This corresponds to the value presented in figure 4.11.

With knowledge of the overall defect rate, the parent company can now use the information to calculate other probabilities. For example, suppose a cartridge is returned by a customer and found to be defective yet it is unclear which company produced the cartridge. The parent company may like to determine the probability that the cartridge was produced by company A, that is, $P(\text{A} \mid \text{D})$, in order to appropriately calculate the loss of revenue associated with sourcing cartridges from company A. If the parent company determines that \$10 000 is the loss in revenue due to faulty cartridges being returned, should it attribute 65% of this loss, or \$6500, to company A, given that company A produces 65% of the cartridges for sale? This appears particularly unfair given that the auditing process revealed that the rate of defective production at company A is lower than at company B.

Instead, the parent company may use a conditional probability combining prior knowledge about how much each company produces with the additional knowledge from the audits of the overall rate of defectiveness at each company. The probability that company A produced a cartridge, given it is known to be defective, is found by:

$$P(\text{A}|\text{D}) = \frac{P(\text{A} \cap \text{D})}{P(\text{D})} = \frac{P(\text{A})P(\text{D}|\text{A})}{P(\text{D})} = \frac{.026}{.047} = .553$$

Similarly, the probability that company B produced a cartridge, given it is known to be defective, is found by:

$$P(\text{A}'|\text{D}) = \frac{P(\text{A}' \cap \text{D})}{P(\text{D})} = \frac{.021}{.047} = .447$$

Before the audit, which determined the rate of defectiveness, prior knowledge that the parent company held was that 65% of cartridges were produced by company A and 35% were produced by company B. The audit revealed new knowledge allowing the parent company to revise its judgement about the probability that a particular company produced a cartridge given that it is defective. Given a cartridge is known to be defective, the probability that it was produced by company A is 55.3% and by company B is 44.7%. Hence, management at company A should argue that the $10 000 in revenue lost due to defective production should be attributed based on these percentages. In this regard, company A would be associated with more of the cost as it supplies more of the cartridges, but this cost allocation is revised downward to reflect the lower rate of defectiveness being achieved at company A. In other words, rather than $6500 of the losses being attributed to company A, the figure would be closer to $5530.

Revising probabilities and Bayes' rule

The process of revising probabilities based on prior knowledge combined with new information is often associated with a more general theorem called **Bayes' rule**. Bayes' rule was developed by Thomas Bayes (1702–1761) to *extend the law of conditional probability to cases where it is desirable to examine a conditional probability in light of new information*. While the original conditional probability formulas express the denominator as a marginal probability, Bayes' rule recognises that this event may be conditional upon a series of other events. In doing so, the denominator is expanded to be expressed in terms of two or more events.

To illustrate, consider the approach that was used to calculate the conditional probability that company A produced a cartridge, given it is known to be defective, $P(\mathrm{A} \mid \mathrm{D})$. In order to calculate this, the marginal probability relating to overall defectiveness, $P(\mathrm{D})$, was expanded to include additional knowledge about the different rates of defectiveness at each company. Specifically the overall rate of defectiveness was based on knowledge about how defectiveness was conditional upon whether the cartridge was produced at company A, $P(\mathrm{D} \mid \mathrm{A})$, and conditional on whether the cartridge was produced at company B, $P(\mathrm{D} \mid \mathrm{A}')$. The approach that was used can be rewritten in greater detail by expanding the marginal probability in the denominator of the original conditional probability formula:

$$P(\mathrm{A}|\mathrm{D}) = \frac{P(\mathrm{A} \cap \mathrm{D})}{P(\mathrm{D})} = \frac{P(\mathrm{A})P(\mathrm{D}|\mathrm{A})}{P(D)} = \frac{P(\mathrm{A})P(\mathrm{D}|\mathrm{A})}{P(\mathrm{A})P(\mathrm{D}|\mathrm{A}) + P(\mathrm{A}')P(\mathrm{D}|\mathrm{A}')}$$

Substituting the values from the tree diagram in figure 4.11, the calculations become:

$$P(\mathrm{A}|\mathrm{D}) = \frac{(.65)(.04)}{(.65)(.04)+(.35)(.06)} = \frac{.026}{.026+.021} = \frac{.026}{.047} = .553$$

In general, where only two events occur, Bayes' rule can be expressed as $P(X \mid Y)$ and is given as an extension to the law of conditional probability, as shown in formula 4.12.

Bayes' rule for two events (4.12)

$$P(X|Y) = \frac{P(X \cap Y)}{P(X \cap Y) + P(X' \cap Y)} = \frac{P(X)P(Y|X)}{P(X)P(Y|X) + P(X')P(Y|X')}$$

Bayes' rule can be extended for the case where more than two events occur. In this case, the more general version, given in formula 4.13, involves expanding the denominator so that it reflects the sum of all joint probabilities involving event Y, which is known to have occurred.

Bayes' rule for more than two events (4.13)

$$P(X_i|Y) = \frac{P(X_i)P(Y|X_i)}{P(X_1)P(Y|X_1) + P(X_2)P(Y|X_2) + \cdots + P(X_n)P(Y|X_n)}$$

DEMONSTRATION PROBLEM 4.9

PROBLEM: A company is considering launching one of two new products, product X and product Y, for its existing market. Prior market research suggests that this market is made up of three consumer segments: segment A, representing 60% of consumers, is primarily interested in the functionality of products; segment B, representing 30% of consumers, is extremely price sensitive; and segment C, representing 10% of consumers is primarily interested in the appearance and style of products. To be more certain about which product to launch and how it will be received by each segment, market research is conducted. It reveals the following new information.

- The probability that a person from segment A prefers product X is 40%.
- The probability that a person from segment B prefers product X is 50%.
- The probability that a person from segment C prefers product X is 70%.

The company would like to know the probability that a consumer comes from segment A if it is known that this consumer prefers product X over product Y. Overall, what is the probability that a consumer prefers product X over product Y?

SOLUTION: The size of each segment can be written in terms of marginal probabilities with $P(A) = .6$, $P(B) = .3$ and $P(C) = .1$. The new information obtained by market research about preferences of each segment can be written as conditional probabilities with $P(X|A) = .4$, $P(X|B) = .5$ and $P(X|C) = .7$. The probability that a person is from segment A given that they prefer product X is a conditional probability written as $P(A|X)$. The law of conditional probability would calculate this as:

$$P(A|X) = \frac{P(A \cap X)}{P(X)} = \frac{P(A)P(X|A)}{P(X)}$$

Using the general law of multiplication, the joint probability in the numerator can be calculated as $P(A \text{ and } X) = P(A)P(X|A) = (.6)(.4) = .24$. The overall marginal probability in the denominator, $P(X)$, which refers to whether a consumer prefers product X, is unknown. It can, however, be calculated by adding the various joint probabilities involving X. This is the approach outlined in Bayes' rule. Since the events unrelated to X involve more than two events, the desired conditional probability can be calculated as:

$$P(A|X) = \frac{P(A)P(X|A)}{P(A)P(X|A) + P(B)P(X|B) + P(C)P(X|C)}$$

$$P(A|X) = \frac{(.6)(.4)}{(.6)(.4) + (.3)(.5) + (.1)(.7)} = \frac{.24}{.24 + .15 + .07} = \frac{.24}{.46} = .52$$

In other words, 52% of consumers are from segment A, given that they prefer product X. The denominator also reveals the overall preference for product X; 46% of consumers prefer it over product Y regardless of which segment they are from. All of the information that was used in the calculation of the conditional probability $P(A|X)$ is presented in the tree diagram below.

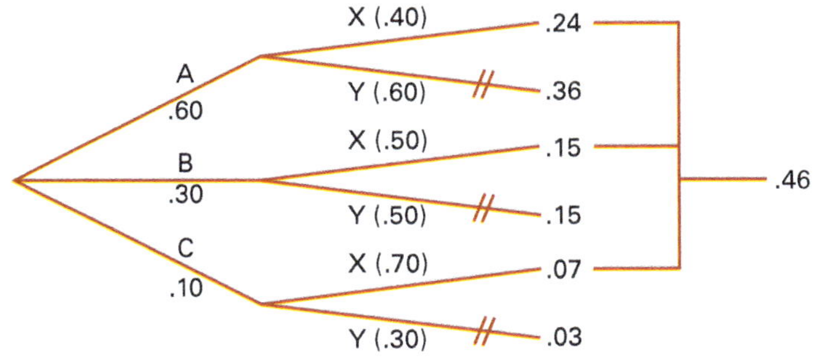

PRACTICE PROBLEMS

Practising the calculations

4.28 use the values in the contingency table to solve the equations given.

	E	F	G
A	15	12	8
B	11	17	19
C	21	32	27
D	18	13	12

a. $P(G \mid A) =$ ___
b. $P(B \mid F) =$ ___
c. $P(C \mid E) =$ ___
d. $P(E \mid G) =$ ___

4.29 Use the values in the probability matrix to solve the equations given.

	C	D
A	.36	.44
B	.11	.09

a. $P(C \mid A) =$ ___
b. $P(B \mid D) =$ ___
c. $P(A \mid B) =$ ___

4.30 Consider the following results of a survey asking, 'Have you visited a museum in the past 12 months?' and 'Do you have a child less than 10 years of age?'

	Visited museum in last year		
Child under 10	**Yes**	**No**	**Total**
Yes	160	80	240
No	40	120	160
Total	200	200	400

Is the variable 'Museum visitor' independent of the variable 'Child under 10'? Why or why not?

Testing your understanding

4.31 CPA Australia under the sponsorship of American Express conducted a national survey of small-business owners to determine the issues affecting employment in their businesses. According to the study, 40% of the small-business owners believe that payroll tax was a barrier to employment in the sector. Twenty-five per cent of the small-business owners see workers compensation insurance as a barrier to employment in the sector. Suppose 15% of the small-business owners selected both payroll tax and workers compensation insurance as barriers to employment in the sector. A small-business owner is selected randomly.

a. What is the probability that the owner believes that payroll tax is a barrier to employment if the owner believes that workers compensation insurance is a barrier to employment?
b. What is the probability that the owner believes that workers compensation insurance is a barrier to employment if the owner believes that payroll tax is a barrier to employment?
c. Given that the owner does not believe that payroll tax is a barrier to employment, what is the probability that the owner believes that workers compensation insurance is a barrier to employment?
d. What is the probability that the owner believes that neither payroll tax nor workers compensation insurance is a barrier to employment?

4.32 Many organisations, including the Cancer Society of New Zealand, endorse the recommendation that people consume three servings of vegetables and two servings of fruit per day as this provides some protection from heart disease and cancer. A report states that 49% of New Zealanders regularly eat fresh fruit and vegetables and that, among this same group, 80% agree that it is good for their health. Interestingly, the report also states that 94% of those who do not eat fresh fruit and vegetables regularly believe that eating fresh fruit and vegetables regularly is good for their health. If a New Zealander is selected randomly, determine the probability that this person:

a. regularly eats fresh fruit and vegetables and believes this to be a dietary practice that is good for their health.
b. does not regularly eat fresh fruit and vegetables.
c. does not regularly eat fresh fruit and vegetables and yet believes this to be a dietary practice that is good for their health.
d. believes that regularly eating fresh fruit and vegetables is a dietary practice that is good for their health.
e. regularly eats fresh fruit and vegetables given they believe this to be a dietary practice that is good for their health.

4.33 A company has recently undertaken a program to replace the desktop computers of its staff. The new computers have a different operating system and newer associated software. Initially, employees appeared disgruntled about having to learn how to use the computers. The company offered, at great cost, a series of training programs; unfortunately, some employees still appear to be unsatisfied, although management suspects this stems from part-time employees who have had fewer opportunities to use the new computers.

Assess the survey that was conducted on a random sample of 200 employees to report on the interest in training overall, but also determine whether the additional training sought by employees is conditional upon their employment status being full-time or part-time. Write a short summary to help management decide whether to offer more training and whether this arises from the part-time cohort.

	Employment status		
Interest in training	**Part-time**	**Full-time**	**Total**
Seek more training	16	54	70
Satisfied with skills	64	66	130
Total employees	80	120	200

MISUSE OF STATISTICS

One of the potential misuses of probability information occurs when it is based on unreliable or limited amounts of data. Recall that probability is an important concept because sample data are often used to infer what is happening at the population level. If this inference process is based on too few observations, it is likely that there will be a larger error in using what is learnt from a sample to describe what is happening at the population level. Likewise, when professionals report information in the form of a probability, it may be based on relative frequencies, usually calculated on the basis of historical figures. If only a few historical figures are available or the figures exclude certain periods that are unfavourable, the historical information may be inaccurate and unreliable. For example, if a company states that four out of five, or 80%, of its customers feel its service was excellent and all its future customers can expect the same, as a potential customer you would feel disheartened to learn that this was based on a survey of only five customers, or that respondents were selected because they were likely to provide a favourable response.

CHAPTER CASE **REVISITED**

Too many leaders

It is possible to use the techniques presented in this chapter to answer the managerial questions about Combaro Ltd.

1. The probability that a worker at Combaro Ltd is employed in the home loans division is $P(\text{H}) = \frac{11}{48}$ or 22.92%. This is a marginal probability calculated using the relative frequency method of assigning probabilities. Other probabilities can be constructed similarly. For example, the joint probability that an employee is employed in the home loans division and is a supervisor is $P(\text{S and H}) = \frac{3}{48} = 6.25\%$. A probability matrix captures these and other joint and marginal probabilities.

	division			
employee level	**Home**	**Car**	**Personal**	**Total (%)**
Supervisor	6.25	12.50	6.25	25.00
Consultant	16.67	31.25	27.08	75.00
Total employees (%)	22.92	43.75	33.33	100.00

2. The bottom row of the table displays marginal probabilities, detailing the probability that someone works in the home loans division (22.92%), car loans division (43.75%) or personal loans division (33.33%). This implies that, if the proportion of staff employed reflects the demand for loans offered by Combaro, more customers are looking for car loans.
3. The values in the probability matrix show that the probability of an employee being a supervisor is $P(\text{S}) = 25\%$.
4. Given that an employee is working in the home loans division, the probability that this employee is in a supervisory role is $P(\text{S} \mid \text{H}) = \frac{3}{11} = \frac{6.25\%}{22.92\%} = 27.27\%$. This is a conditional probability and can be calculated using values in either the contingency table or the joint probability matrix. The conditional probability of an employee being a supervisor in the other divisions are $P(\text{S} \mid \text{C}) = 28.57\%$ and $P(\text{S} \mid \text{P}) = 18.75\%$.
5. Overall the probability of an employee being a supervisor is $P(\text{S}) = 25\%$, but this is slightly higher if the employee is known to be working in the home loans division or car loans division, and lower if the employee is known to be working in the personal loans division. Hence, the probability that an employee is a supervisor appears to be conditional, or dependent, upon which division they are employed in. While the overall target of hiring a

balance of supervisory and consultant employees is being met, the restructuring appears to have created an imbalance in some of the divisions.

These probabilities were calculated using relative frequencies based on 48 observations only. This may affect the confidence with which one can make conclusions about whether an employee's role is independent of which division they are employed in. If more data generate similar results, it appears that Combaro should consider addressing this staffing issue. One solution could be to swap some of the senior staff in the car loans division with junior staff in the personal loans division. Of course, this should be examined in conjunction with other decision criteria, such as how further restructuring may affect morale and team dynamics and whether it takes experienced employees from a division for which they may have specialised knowledge.

SUMMARY

1 The study of probability addresses ways of assigning probabilities, types of probabilities and laws of probabilities. Probabilities support the notion of inferential statistics. Using sample data to estimate and test hypotheses about population parameters is done with uncertainty. If samples are taken at random, probabilities can be assigned to outcomes of the inferential process. Three methods of assigning probabilities are (1) the classical method, (2) the relative frequency of occurrence method and (3) the subjective probability method. The classical method involves forming probabilities by giving each element an equal chance of being selected. The relative frequency of occurrence method assigns probabilities based on historical data or empirically derived data. Subjective probabilities are based on the feelings, knowledge and experience of the person determining the probability.

2 Many business occurrences can be classified as experiments, or processes that produce outcomes for which the probability can be calculated. The topic of probability is explored using various symbols and notation to ensure a clearer understanding of its related concepts and an ability to define and calculate desired probabilities using formulas based on this structure and notation. For example, the co-occurrence of two events can be represented using the symbol for intersection, $\cap$; mutually exclusive events are events that do not co-occur or intersect. The occurrence of at least one event or both events is sometimes represented by $\cup$, the union of two events. The complement of an event is the set of events that occur when a specified event does not occur.

3 A contingency table, sometimes referred to as a cross-tab or cross-tabulation, represents the frequency with which events occur and co-occur with one another. A probability matrix, or joint probability table, captures the probability of these same events. There are several concepts in probability that refer to the occurrence of one event or how two events co-occur. Marginal probabilities refer to the probability that a single event will occur. Union probabilities refer to the probability that two events will occur or where one of the events will occur. Joint probability is the probability that two events occur together. Conditional probabilities refer to the probability of one event given that some other event has occurred.

4 When contingency tables and joint probability matrices are unable to be formed, several laws of probability may be useful to determine probabilities. The general law of addition is used to compute the probability of a union. The probability of a union of two events is specified as the sum of the two marginal probabilities relating to each event, adjusted by subtracting the joint probability relating to the co-occurrence of the two events. When two events are mutually exclusive the joint probability is zero and gives rise to the special law of addition. The complement of a union represents the case where neither of the two events has occurred.

5 The general law of multiplication is used to compute joint probabilities. The joint probability of two events is calculated as the marginal probability of one of the events multiplied by the probability of the other event conditional upon the occurrence of the first event. When two events are independent, the occurrence of one has no influence on the occurrence of the other. Certain experiments, such as those involving coins or dice, naturally produce independent events. If events are independent, the joint probability is computed by multiplying the individual marginal probabilities, which is a special case of the law of multiplication.

6 The computation of conditional probabilities involves dividing the joint probability describing the probability that two events co-occur by the marginal probability for the event that is known or assumed to have occurred. A conditional probability can be compared with a corresponding marginal probability

to assess whether two events are independent. Independent events can be interpreted as those having no relationship; dependent events imply that some relationship exists and that the prediction of one event is helped by knowing the outcome of another. Tree diagrams, and probability trees in particular, are useful in graphically representing how the probability of one event depends upon, or is conditional upon, the occurrence of another event. Bayes' rule is a method that can be useful in extending the law of conditional probability in cases where new information reveals the nature of this dependence.

KEY TERMS

Bayes' rule p. 126
classical method of assigning probabilities p. 97
collectively exhaustive events p. 104
complement p. 104
complement of a union p. 113
conditional probability p. 107
contingency table p. 106
elementary events p. 100
event p. 100
experiment p. 100
independent events p. 103
intersection p. 102
joint probability p. 107
marginal probability p. 106
mutually exclusive events p. 103
probability matrix p. 107
relative frequency of occurrence method p. 98
sample space p. 101
set notation p. 102
subjective probability method p. 99
tree diagram p. 124
union p. 102
union probability p. 106
Venn diagram p. 102

KEY EQUATIONS

EQUATION	DESCRIPTION	FORMULA
4.1	Classical method of assigning probabilities	$P(E_i)=\frac{n_i}{N_E}$
4.2	Range of possible probabilities	$0 \le P(E_i) \le 1$
4.3	Probability by relative frequency of occurrence	$P(E_i)=\frac{x_i}{N_E}$
4.4	Mutually exclusive events X and Y	$P(X \cap Y) = P(X \text{ and } Y) = 0$
4.5	Independent events X and Y	$P(X \mid Y) = P(X \text{ given } Y) = P(X)$ and $P(Y \mid X) = P(Y \text{ given } X) = P(Y)$
4.6	Probability of the complement of A	$P(A') = 1 - P(A)$
4.7	General law of addition	$P(X \cup Y) = P(X) + P(Y) - P(X \cap Y)$
4.8	Special law of addition	If X and Y are mutually exclusive, $P(X \cup Y) = P(X) + P(Y)$
4.9	General law of multiplication	$P(X \cap Y) = P(X)P(Y \mid X) = P(Y)P(X \mid Y)$
4.10	Special law of multiplication	If X and Y are independent, $P(X \cap Y) = P(X \text{ and } Y) = P(X)P(Y)$
4.11	Law of conditional probability	$P(X \mid Y)=\frac{P(X \cap Y)}{P(Y)}=\frac{P(X)P(Y \mid X)}{P(Y)}$
4.12	Bayes' rule for two events	$P(X \mid Y)=\frac{P(X \cap Y)}{P(X \cap Y)+P(X' \cap Y)}=\frac{P(X)P(Y \mid X)}{P(X)P(Y \mid X)+P(X')P(Y \mid X')}$
4.13	Bayes' rule for more than two events	$P(X_i \mid Y)=\frac{P(X_i)P(Y \mid X_i)}{P(X_1)P(Y \mid X_1)+P(X_2)P(Y \mid X_2)+\cdots+P(X_n)P(Y \mid X_n)}$

REVIEW PROBLEMS

Practising the calculations

4.34 Use the values in the contingency table to solve the equations given.

	Variable 1	
Variable 2	**E**	**F**
A	85	75
B	40	55
C	40	85
D	95	25

a. $P(F) =$ ___
b. $P(B \cup F) =$ ___
c. $P(D \cap F) =$ ___
d. $P(B | F) =$ ___
e. $P(A \cup B) =$ ___
f. $P(B \cap C) =$ ___
g. $P(F | B) =$ ___
h. $P(A | B) =$ ___
i. $P(B) =$ ___
j. Based on your answers to these calculations, parts a, d, g and i, are variables 1 and 2 independent? Why or why not?

4.35 Use the values in the contingency table to solve the equations given.

	E	F	G	H
A	88	66	198	66
B	198	220	176	88
C	154	110	154	176
D	176	132	132	66

a. $P(A \cap G) =$ ___
b. $P(A | G) =$ ___
c. $P(A) =$ ___
d. $P(A \cup G) =$ ___
e. $P(F | B) =$ ___
f. $P(B | F) =$ ___
g. $P(A \cup B) =$ ___
h. $P(F) =$ ___

4.36 The following probability matrix contains a breakdown of the age and gender of general practitioners working in Australia.

	Age (years)				
Gender	**< 35**	**35–44**	**45–54**	**> 54**	**Total**
Male	0.036	0.129	0.194	0.261	0.620
Female	0.054	0.122	0.130	0.074	0.380
Total	0.090	0.251	0.324	0.335	1.000

What is the probability that one randomly selected general practitioner:

a. is 35–44 years old
b. is both female and 45–54 years old
c. is male or is 35–44 years old
d. is less than 35 years old or more than 54 years old
e. is female if they are 45–54 years old?

Testing your understanding

4.37 A survey company asked purchasing managers what traits in a sales representative impressed them most. Seventy-eight per cent selected 'thoroughness'. Forty per cent responded 'knowledge of your own product'. The purchasing managers were allowed to list more than one trait. Suppose 27% of the purchasing managers listed both 'thoroughness' and 'knowledge of your own product' as traits that impressed them most. A purchasing manager is sampled randomly.

a. What is the probability that the manager selected 'thoroughness' or 'knowledge of your own product'?
b. What is the probability that the manager did not select 'thoroughness' and did not select 'knowledge of your own product'?
c. If it is known that the manager selected 'thoroughness', what is the probability that the manager also selected 'knowledge of your own product'?
d. What is the probability that the manager did not select 'thoroughness' but did select 'knowledge of your own product'?

4.38 A university conducted a study into students' perceived usability of a proposed upgrade to their existing learning management system (LMS). Students were asked to visit a test site and evaluate the proposed LMS relative to their perceptions of the existing LMS. To further evaluate the results, participants were asked to nominate one field that represents their primary area of study. Some 84% of students perceived the proposed LMS to be superior in usability relative to the existing system. Of all the students sampled, 45% were primarily studying business and rated the proposed system to be superior in usability. Of those students primarily studying science, 95% found the proposed LMS easier to use. Students primarily studying science represented 30% of the surveyed participants. Together, those students primarily studying science or those primarily studying business made up 85% of the sample. If a student is selected randomly, determine the probabilities of the following.

a. The student rates the proposed system as superior in usability given that the student primarily studies in the area of business.

b. The student rates the proposed system as superior in usability given that the student primarily studies in an area other than business.
c. The student is studying in science given they do not believe the proposed system to be superior in usability.
d. The student is primarily studying science and believes the proposed system to be superior in usability.

4.39 A large bank reports that 30% of families have a MasterCard, 20% have an American Express card, and 25% have a Visa card. Eight per cent of families have both a MasterCard and an American Express card. Twelve per cent have both a Visa card and a MasterCard. Six per cent have both an American Express card and a Visa card.
a. What is the probability of selecting a family that has either a Visa card or an American Express card?
b. If a family has a MasterCard, what is the probability that it also has a Visa card?
c. If a family has a Visa card, what is the probability that it also has a MasterCard?
d. Is possession of a Visa card independent of possession of a MasterCard? Why or why not?
e. Is possession of an American Express card mutually exclusive of possession of a Visa card?

4.40 A poll was conducted by a television network to evaluate public opinion on the state of the economy in New Zealand using a countrywide representative sample. It was found that 35% of the respondents believed the economy is in an acceptable position. Of the respondents who are living in rural areas, 75% did not believe the economy to be in an acceptable position. Assume that, of the people surveyed, 85% were not living in a rural area. One New Zealander is selected randomly.
a. What is the probability that the person is living in a rural area?
b. What is the probability that the person is not living in a rural area and does not believe the economy is in an acceptable position?
c. If the person selected does not believe the economy is in an acceptable position, what is the probability that the person is living in a rural area?
d. What is the probability that the person is living in a rural area or believes the economy is in an acceptable position?

4.41 Octopus Travel studied the types of work-related activity that Australians did while on holidays. Among other things, 20% take their work with them on holidays. Fifteen per cent negotiate new deals or contracts on holidays. Respondents to the study were allowed to select more than one activity. Suppose that, of those who take their work on holidays, 68% negotiated new deals or contracts. One of these survey respondents is selected randomly.
a. What is the probability that while on holiday this respondent negotiated a new deal or contract and took their work?
b. What is the probability that while on holiday this respondent did not take their work and did not negotiate a new deal or contract?
c. What is the probability that while on holiday this respondent took their work given that the respondent negotiated a new deal or contract?
d. What is the probability that while on holiday this respondent did not negotiate a new deal or contract given that the respondent took their work?
e. What is the probability that while on holiday this respondent did not negotiate a new deal or contract given that the respondent did not take their work?
f. Construct a probability matrix for this problem.

4.42 A study of tweeting behaviour revealed that among 36- to 45-year-olds, the number one tweeted topic related to family, with 28% making some reference of it among those tweets that could be categorised in a mutually exclusive manner. Other tweets were categorised as referring to the arts (22%), entertainment (18%), education (17%), and sports (11%), while 4% referred to some other topic. If a tweet by a 36- to 45-year-old is randomly selected and able to be categorised in the same way, determine the probabilities of the following.
a. The tweet is about family.
b. The tweet is not about sports.
c. The tweet is about the arts or entertainment.
d. The tweet is neither about family nor about education.

4.43 Companies use employee training for various reasons including employee loyalty, certification, quality and process improvement. In a national survey of companies, it was reported that 56% of the responding companies named employee retention as a top reason for training. Suppose 36% of the companies replied that they use training for process improvement and for employee retention. In addition, suppose that, of the companies that use training for process improvement, 90% use training for employee retention. A company that uses training is selected randomly.
a. What is the probability that the company uses training for employee retention and not for process improvement?
b. If it is known that the company uses training for employee retention, what is the probability that it uses training for process improvement?
c. What is the probability that the company uses training for process improvement?

d. What is the probability that the company uses training for employee retention or process improvement?

e. What is the probability that the company uses training neither for employee retention nor for process improvement?

f. Suppose it is known that the company does not use training for process improvement. What is the probability that the company uses training for employee retention?

4.44 Marketing managers and directors at large and medium-sized New Zealand companies were surveyed to determine what they believe is the best vehicle for educating decision makers on complex issues when selling products and services. The highest percentage (38%) of companies chose direct mail/catalogues, followed by direct sales/sales rep. None of the companies selected both direct mail/catalogues and direct sales/sales rep. Suppose also that 41% selected neither direct mail/catalogues nor direct sales/sales rep. If one of these companies is selected randomly, and their top marketing person is interviewed about this matter, determine the probabilities of the following.

a. The marketing person selected direct mail/catalogues but did not select direct sales/sales rep.

b. The marketing person selected direct sales/sales rep.

c. The marketing person selected direct sales/sales rep given that they selected direct mail/catalogues.

d. The marketing person did not select direct mail/catalogues given that they did not select direct sales/sales rep.

4.45 A person decides to go to the movies and has a choice between several movies starting at 3 pm. The person is thinking of seeing one of two action films that are now showing. What is the probability that they see both action films at this time? Explain your answer noting what concept of probability this is an example of.

4.46 A local GP is concerned that the other doctors in the general practice that she works at provide a proportionally higher number of short consultations. A random sample of 200 consultations is extracted from the records and the results are detailed in the following contingency table. Calculate the conditional probability that a short consultation is provided, given that the patient sees Dr Howell. Repeat the calculations for each other doctor. Overall, what is the probability that the consultation is short? Does there appear to be a relationship between the doctor a person sees and whether the consultation is short or long? Write a short interpretation of your findings for the local GP.

	Consultation		
Doctor	**Short**	**Long**	**Total**
Dr Howell	38	33	71
Dr Tran	22	33	55
Dr Jackson	38	36	74
Total patients	98	102	200

4.47 A company that invests heavily in shopping centres conducts a study to determine whether there is a relationship between the type of retailer a customer encounters and whether this occurs on the ground floor of a shopping complex. A random sample of 550 outlets is tabulated across a number of multistorey shopping centres with the following details provided in a joint probability matrix.

	Floor		
Type of retailer	**Ground**	**Other**	**Total (%)**
Food	26	10	36
Fashion	8	22	30
Other	10	24	34
Total (%)	44	56	100

Construct a table identical to the one above but, in each of the cells where the joint probabilities occur, calculate the percentage of retailers that would appear on a certain floor if floor and type of retailer are independent. Compare the two tables, and write a short interpretation advising whether any relationship appears to exist and the nature of this relationship.

CHAPTER

5 Discrete distributions

LEARNING OBJECTIVES

After studying this chapter, you should be able to:

1. explain the concept of a random variable and distinguish between discrete and continuous random variables
2. determine the mean and variance of a discrete random variable
3. identify the types of situations that can be described by the binomial distribution and know how to solve such problems
4. decide when to use the Poisson distribution and know how to solve such problems.

OPENING VIGNETTE

Binge drinking

Alcohol is the most widely used recreational drug in Australia and New Zealand. According to a report from the Australian Institute of Health and Welfare, alcohol is second only to tobacco as a preventable cause of drug-related death and hospitalisation. The rise in overall alcohol consumption has been accompanied by a rise in binge drinking among teenagers. A survey of Australian students found that one in ten admitted to binge drinking or drinking unsafe amounts of alcohol. For teenagers aged between 16 and 17, the figure was one in five. This means that in every average classroom of 30, six students are binge drinkers.

To try to change teenagers' behaviour, the Australian Government funded an advertising campaign aimed at confronting 15–25-year-olds with the costs and consequences of binge drinking. A part of this campaign was to conduct a survey of the drinking history of 18–21-year-olds, and ask them the number of standard drinks they consumed the last time they drank. The results were as follows.

21 to 25 drinks	5%
16 to 20 drinks	7%
11 to 15 drinks	11%
7 to 10 drinks	16%
5 to 6 drinks	13%
Up to 4 drinks	33%
No drinks in the last three months	15%

Introduction

As you probably realise, many business situations have uncertain outcomes: the demand for products is uncertain; the quality of a product is uncertain; the number of phone calls to call centres is uncertain; and changes to interest rates are uncertain. In this chapter, we examine the probabilities of various outcomes that can occur in experiments involving chance; that is, where outcomes are random. As an example of such an experiment, suppose a battery manufacturer randomly selects three batteries from a large batch of batteries to test for quality. Each selected battery is to be rated as good or defective. The batteries are numbered from 1 to 3. A defective battery is designated with a D, and a good battery is designated with a G. All possible outcomes are shown in table 5.1. The expression $D_1\ G_2\ D_3$, for example, denotes one particular outcome in which the first and third batteries are defective and the second battery is good.

TABLE 5.1 All possible outcomes for the battery experiment

G_1	G_2	G_3
D_1	G_2	G_3
G_1	D_2	G_3
G_1	G_2	D_3
D_1	D_2	G_3
D_1	G_2	D_3
G_1	D_2	D_3
D_1	D_2	D_3

CHAPTER CASE

Mental health and young people

Mental health is one of the key issues facing today's youth in Australia, and it is vital that services treating the early stages of mental health issues be offered. Currently, the health system in Australia is not able to deal with young Australians suffering mental health issues, meaning that young people cannot receive the early treatment necessary to cater to their needs.

Problems especially arise when young people do not know who to approach, thereby delaying treatment even further. Usually, good friends or family members are the first avenue for help. However, these people too may be unsure of where to go for help next, and may not know what support options are available.

Included in mental issues is alcohol and substance abuse, with approximately 14% of 12–17-year-olds, and 27% of 18–25-year-olds experiencing such problems each year. About 75% of mental health problems emerge before the age of 25, and up to 50% of alcohol and substance abuse problems are preceded by mental health issues. In total, mental health and substance abuse disorders account for 60–70% of all diseases among 15–24-year-old Australians, and only one in four is receiving professional help.

Questions to help managers make decisions

1. The above article mentions that 14% of 12–17-year-olds experience some sort of mental health issue. If you randomly selected 20 Australians between those ages, what is the probability that more than 5 have experienced a mental health issue?
2. Our study reports that only 1 in 4 young Australians with a mental health issue are seeking professional support. Based on this, if you randomly selected 20 young people experiencing a mental health issue, what is the probability that more than 6 have sought professional help?
3. Suppose a survey of a youth health clinic shows that, on average, they receive 5 calls for help a day. If this figure is correct, what is the probability that a youth health clinic will receive no calls in a day? What is the probability that a youth health clinic receives more than 10 calls in a day?

5.1 Discrete versus continuous distributions

A **random variable** is a variable that contains the outcomes of a chance experiment. For example, suppose an experiment measures the arrival of cars at a tollbooth during a 30-second period. The possible outcomes are: 0 cars, 1 car, 2 cars, . . ., n cars. The numbers (0, 1, 2, . . ., n) are the values of a random variable. Suppose another experiment measures the time between the completion of two tasks in a production line. The values will range 0 seconds to n seconds. These time measurements are the values of another random variable. The two categories of random variables are (1) discrete random variables and (2) continuous random variables.

A random variable is a **discrete random variable** if the set of all possible values is a finite or, at most, countably infinite number of possible values. In most statistical situations, discrete random variables produce values that are non-negative whole numbers. For example, if six people are randomly selected from a population and we wish to determine how many of them are left-handed, the random variable produced is discrete. The only possible numbers of left-handed people in the sample of six are 0, 1, 2, 3, 4, 5 and 6. For example, there cannot be 2.75 left-handed people in a group of six people; it is impossible to obtain a value that is not a whole number. Other examples of experiments that yield discrete random variables include:

1. randomly selecting 25 people who consume soft drinks and determining how many of them prefer diet soft drinks
2. determining the number of defects in a batch of 50 items
3. counting the number of people who arrive at a shop during a five-minute period.

The battery experiment described in the introduction produces a distribution that has discrete outcomes. Any one trial of the experiment will contain 0, 1, 2 or 3 defective batteries. It is not possible to have 1.58 defective batteries, for example. It could be said that discrete random variables are usually generated from experiments in which things are 'counted', not 'measured'.

Continuous random variables take values at every point over a given interval. Thus, continuous random variables have no gaps or unassumed values. It could be said that continuous random variables are generated from experiments in which things are 'measured', not 'counted'. For example, if a person is assembling a product component, the time it takes to accomplish that feat could be any value within a reasonable range, such as 3 minutes 36.4218 seconds or 5 minutes 17.5169 seconds. A list of measures for which continuous random variables might be generated would include time, height, weight and volume. Other examples of experiments that yield continuous random variables include:

1. sampling the volume of liquid nitrogen in a storage tank
2. measuring the time between customer arrivals at a retail outlet
3. measuring the lengths of newly designed vehicles
4. weighing grain in a grain elevator at different times.

Once continuous data are measured and recorded, they become discrete data because the data are rounded to a discrete number. Thus, in practice, virtually all business data are discrete. However, for practical reasons, data analysis is facilitated greatly by using continuous distributions for data that were originally continuous.

The outcomes for random variables and their associated probabilities can be organised into two types of distributions: discrete distributions and continuous distributions.

In the text, we present two discrete distributions:

1. binomial distribution
2. Poisson distribution.

In addition, six continuous distributions are discussed:

1. uniform distribution
2. normal distribution
3. exponential distribution
4. *t* distribution
5. chi-square distribution
6. *F* distribution.

5.2 Describing a discrete distribution

How can we describe a discrete distribution? One way is to construct a graph of the distribution and study the graph. The histogram is probably the most common graphical way to depict a discrete distribution.

Observe the discrete distribution in table 5.2. An executive is considering out-of-town business travel for a given Friday. She recognises that at least one crisis could occur on the day that she is gone and she is concerned about that possibility. Table 5.2 shows a discrete distribution that contains the number of crises that could occur during the day that she is gone and the probability that each number will occur; for example, there is a .31 probability of one crisis.

TABLE 5.2 Discrete distribution of occurrence of daily crises

Number of crises	Probability
0	.37
1	.31
2	.18
3	.09
4	.04
5	.01

The probability that no more than two crises occur is:

$$P(x \leq 2) = P(x = 0) + P(x = 1) + P(x = 2)$$
$$= .37 + .31 + .18 = .86$$

The probability that at least one crisis will occur is:

$$P(x \geq 1) = 1 - P(x = 0)$$
$$= 1 - .37 = .63$$

The bar chart in figure 5.1 depicts the distribution given in table 5.2. Notice that the x axis of the bar chart contains the possible outcomes of the experiment (the number of crises that might occur), and the y axis contains the probabilities of these occurring.

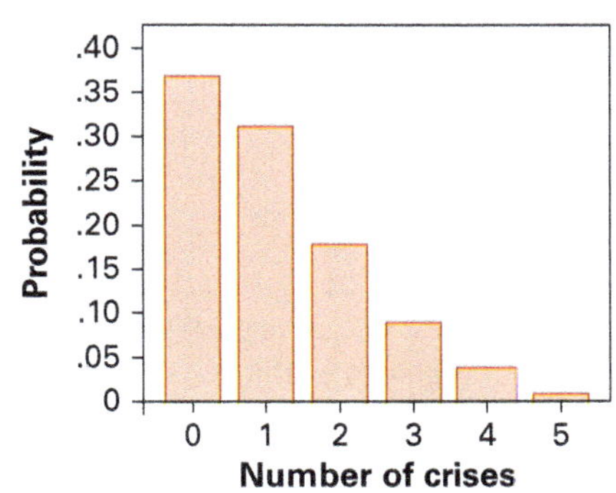

FIGURE 5.1 Bar chart of crises distribution

It is apparent from figure 5.1 that the most likely number of crises is 0. In addition, we can see that the distribution is discrete; no probabilities are shown for values between the whole numbers of crises.

Mean, variance and standard deviation of discrete distributions

What additional mechanisms can be used to describe discrete distributions besides depicting them graphically? Measures of central tendency and measures of variability can be applied to discrete distributions to compute a mean, a variance and a standard deviation. Each of these three descriptive measures is computed for group data by using class midpoints to represent data in class intervals. However, for discrete distributions, it is not necessary to use class midpoints because each outcome is represented by its discrete value (e.g. 0, 1, 2, 3, . . .). Thus, whereas we would use the values of class midpoints to compute the descriptive measures for group data, for discrete distributions we use the discrete values of the experiment's outcomes (x). In computing descriptive measures for group data, the frequency is used to weight the class midpoint. When analysing discrete distributions, the probability of each occurrence is used as the weight.

Mean or expected value

The **mean or expected value** of a discrete distribution is the long-run average of occurrences. We must realise that any one trial using a discrete random variable yields only one outcome. However, if the process is repeated enough times, the average of the outcomes is most likely to approach a long-run average, expected value or mean value. Formula 5.1 is used to calculate the mean, or expected, value of a discrete distribution.

Mean or expected value of a discrete distribution (5.1)

$$\mu = E(x) = \Sigma[xP(x)]$$

where:

$E(x)$ = the long-run average
x = an outcome
$P(x)$ = the probability of outcome x

As an example, let us compute the mean or expected value of the distribution given in table 5.2. The results are shown in table 5.3. In the long run, the mean or expected number of crises on a Friday for this executive is 1.15 crises. Of course, the executive can never have exactly 1.15 crises.

TABLE 5.3 Computing the mean of the crises data

x	P(x)	xP(x)
0	.37	.00
1	.31	.31
2	.18	.36
3	.09	.27
4	.04	.16
5	.01	.05
		$\Sigma[xP(x)] = 1.15$
	$\mu = 1.15$ crises	

Variance and standard deviation of a discrete distribution

The variance and standard deviation of a discrete distribution are solved by using the outcomes (x) and probabilities of outcomes [$P(x)$] in a manner similar to that of computing the mean. In addition, the computations for variance and standard deviation use the mean of the discrete distribution. Formula 5.2 is used to compute the variance of a discrete distribution.

Variance of a discrete distribution (5.2)

$$\sigma^2 = \Sigma[(x - \mu)^2 P(x)]$$

where:

x = an outcome
$P(x)$ = the probability of outcome x
μ = the mean

The standard deviation is computed by taking the square root of the variance, as shown in formula 5.3.

Standard deviation of a discrete distribution (5.3)

$$\sigma = \sqrt{\Sigma[(x-\mu)^2 P(x)]}$$

where:

x = an outcome

$P(x)$ = the probability of outcome x

μ = the mean

The variance and standard deviation of the crises data are shown in table 5.4. The standard deviation is 1.19, and the variance is 1.41.

TABLE 5.4 Calculation of variance and standard deviation on crises data

x	$P(x)$	$(x-\mu)^2$	$(x-\mu)^2P(x)$
0	.37	$(0-1.15)^2 = 1.32$	$(1.32)(.37) = 0.49$
1	.31	$(1-1.15)^2 = 0.02$	$(0.02)(.31) = 0.01$
2	.18	$(2-1.15)^2 = 0.72$	$(0.72)(.18) = 0.13$
3	.09	$(3-1.15)^2 = 3.42$	$(3.42)(.09) = 0.31$
4	.04	$(4-1.15)^2 = 8.12$	$(8.12)(.04) = 0.32$
5	.01	$(5-1.15)^2 = 14.82$	$(14.82)(.01) = 0.15$
			$\Sigma[(x-\mu)^2P(x)] = 1.41$

The variance is $\sigma^2 = \Sigma[(x-\mu)^2P(x)] = 1.41$.

The standard deviation is $\sigma = \sqrt{1.41} = 1.19$ crises.

DEMONSTRATION PROBLEM 5.1

PROBLEM: A lottery sells 80 million tickets at $1 each. Let the random variable x denote the amount won for a ticket that is purchased. Shown below is the distribution of x. Compute the mean and standard deviation of the amount won per ticket. Interpret the mean value. What is the expected profit from the lottery?

Distribution of lottery winnings

Prize (x)	Probability $P(x)$
$1000	.000 03
100	.000 71
20	.005 20
10	.007 01
4	.023 03
2	.091 77
1	.123 67
0	.761 23

SOLUTION: The mean winnings are computed as follows.

Prize (x)	Probability $P(x)$	$xP(x)$
$1000	.000 03	.030 00
100	.000 71	.071 00
20	.005 20	.104 00
10	.007 01	.070 10
4	.023 03	.092 12
2	.091 77	.183 54
1	.123 67	.123 67
0	.761 23	.000 00
		$\Sigma[xP(x)] = .674\,43$

The expected payoff for a $1 ticket is 67.4 cents. If a person plays the game for a long time, they can expect to average about 67 cents in winnings. In the long run, the participant will lose about $1.00 − .674 43 = .326 or about 33 cents per game. Of course, an individual will never win 67 cents in any one game.

Using this mean, $\mu = .674\,43$, the variance and standard deviation can be computed as follows.

x	$P(x)$	$(x-\mu)^2$	$(x-\mu)^2 P(x)$
$1000	.000 03	998 651.594 86	29.959 55
100	.000 71	9 865.568 86	7.004 55
20	.005 20	373.477 66	1.942 08
10	.007 01	86.966 26	0.609 63
4	.023 03	11.059 42	0.254 70
2	.091 77	1.757 14	0.161 25
1	.123 67	0.106 00	0.013 11
0	.761 23	0.454 86	0.346 25
			$\Sigma[(x-\mu)^2 P(x)] = 40.291\,13$

The variance is $\sigma^2 = \Sigma[(x-\mu)^2 P(x)] = 40.291\,13$.

The standard deviation is $\sqrt{40.291\,13} = 6.347\,53$.

The total amount collected from ticket sales is $80 million and the expected payment (or prize winnings) from each ticket is $0.674 43. So, the expected profit from the venture is $80 000 000 − (80 000 000 × $0.674 43) = $53 954 400.

PRACTICE PROBLEMS

Practising the calculations

5.1 Determine the mean, variance and standard deviation of the following discrete distribution. Interpret the mean value.

x	$P(x)$
1	.268
2	.314
3	.256
4	.167
5	.124

5.2 Determine the mean, variance and standard deviation of the following discrete distribution. Explain the results.

x	$P(x)$
0	.091
1	.124
2	.276
3	.283
4	.162
5	.054
6	.072
7	.003

Testing your understanding

5.3 The following data are the result of a historical study of the number of flaws found in a porcelain cup produced by a manufacturing company. Use these data and the associated probabilities to compute the expected number of flaws and the standard deviation of the number of flaws. Explain your findings.

Flaws	Probability
0	.461
1	.285
2	.129
3	.087
4	.038

5.4 Suppose 20% of the people in a city choose to travel to work by bus. If a random sample of six people is chosen, the number of bus commuters could range from 0 to 6. Shown here are the possible numbers of bus commuters in a sample of six people and the probability of each number of bus commuters occurring in the sample. Use the data to determine the mean number of bus commuters in a sample of six people in the city and also compute the standard deviation. Explain the results.

Number of bus commuters	Probability
0	.270
1	.346
2	.259
3	.104
4	.017
5	.004
6	.000

5.3 Binomial distribution

Perhaps the most widely known of all discrete distributions is the **binomial distribution**. The binomial distribution has been used for hundreds of years. One characteristic of the binomial distribution is that there are only two possible outcomes of a particular trial or experiment. For example, a product may be classified as either acceptable or not acceptable by a quality-control inspector; a person may be classified as employed or unemployed; a customer may be either happy with services provided or not; and a sales call may result in a customer either purchasing the product or not purchasing the product.

Assumptions about the binomial distribution

The following important assumptions underlie the use of the binomial distribution.

- The experiment involves n identical trials, where n is fixed before the trials are conducted.
- Each trial has only two possible outcomes, denoted as success or failure.
- Trials are independent.
- The probability of a success in any one trial remains constant throughout the experiment. We denote the probability of success by p. Then $q = 1 - p$ is the probability of failure.

If we let the random variable x denote the number of successes in n trials, x has a binomial distribution with parameters n and p.

As the term 'binomial' indicates, any single trial of a binomial experiment contains only two possible outcomes. These two outcomes are labelled 'success' and 'failure'. Usually, the outcome of interest to the researcher is labelled a success. For example, if a quality-control analyst is looking for defective products, they would consider finding a defective product a success, even though the company would not consider a defective product a success. If researchers are studying left-handedness, the outcome of finding a left-handed person in a trial of an experiment is a success. The other possible outcome of a trial in a binomial experiment is called a failure. The term 'failure' is used only in opposition to success. In the preceding experiments, a failure could be to find an acceptable product (rather than a defective part) or to find a right-handed person (rather than a left-handed person). In a binomial experiment, any one trial can have only two possible, mutually exclusive outcomes (right-handed/left-handed, defective/good, male/female etc.).

The binomial distribution is a discrete distribution. In n trials, only x successes are possible; where x is a whole number from 0 to n. For example, if five parts are randomly selected from a batch of parts, only 0, 1, 2, 3, 4 or 5 defective parts are possible in that sample; in a sample of five parts, it is not possible to find 2.714 defective parts or to find eight defective parts.

In a binomial experiment, the trials must be independent. A requirement of an independent trial is that p, the probability of a success in one trial, remains constant from trial to trial. This constraint means that either the experiment is by nature one that produces independent trials (such as tossing coins or rolling dice) or the experiment is conducted with replacement. For example, suppose 5% of all parts in a bin are defective. The probability of obtaining a defective part on the first draw is $p = .05$. If the first part drawn is not replaced, the second draw is not independent of the first, and the value of p will change for the next draw. The binomial distribution does not allow for p to change from trial to trial within an experiment. However, if the population is large in comparison with the sample size, the effect of sampling without replacement is minimal, and the independence assumption is essentially met; that is, p remains relatively constant.

Generally, if the sample size, n, is less than 5% of the population, the independence assumption is not of great concern. Therefore, the acceptable sample size for using the binomial distribution with samples taken *without* replacement is:

$$n < .05N$$

where:
n = the sample size
N = the population size

For example, suppose that 10% of the population of the world is left-handed and that a sample of 20 people is selected randomly from the world's population. If the first person selected is left-handed — and the sampling is conducted without replacement — the value of $p = .10$ is virtually unaffected because the population of the world is so large. In addition, in many experiments, the population is continually being replenished even as the sampling is being done. This is often the case with quality-control sampling of products from large production runs. Here are some further examples of binomial distribution problems.

1. Suppose a machine producing computer chips has a 6% defective rate. If a company purchases 30 of these chips, what is the probability that none is defective?
2. A survey on workplace behaviour found that one in four workers steals stationery from work. From a random sample of 15 workers, what is the probability that at least 10 have stolen stationery from work?
3. Suppose a brand of car battery has a 35% market share. If 70 cars are selected at random, what is the probability that at least 30 cars have this brand of battery?
4. A survey found that 67% of company buyers stated that their company had programs for preferred buyers. If a random sample of 50 company buyers is taken, what is the probability that 40 or more have companies with programs for preferred buyers?
5. The manufacturer of a machine claims that only 1% of items it produces are defective. A random sample of 20 items is selected from a demonstration machine and 4 are found to be defective. What conclusion would you draw?

Solving a binomial problem

A survey by relocation administrators revealed several reasons why workers reject relocation offers. Included in the list were family considerations and financial reasons. Four per cent of the respondents said they rejected relocation offers because they would have received too little relocation help. Suppose five workers who have just rejected relocation offers are randomly selected and interviewed. Assuming the 4% figure holds for all workers being offered relocation, what is the probability that the first worker interviewed rejected the offer because of too little relocation help and the next four workers rejected the offer for other reasons?

Let T represent 'too little relocation help' and R represent 'other reasons'. The sequence of interviews for this problem is:

$$T_1, R_2, R_3, R_4, R_5$$

The probability of getting this sequence of workers is calculated by using the special rule of multiplication for independent events (assuming the workers are selected independently from a large population of workers). If 4% of the workers rejecting relocation offers did so because of too little relocation help, the probability of one person being randomly selected from workers rejecting relocation offers for that reason is .04, which is the value of p. The other 96% of workers who rejected relocation offers did so for other reasons. Thus, from those who rejected relocation offers, the probability of randomly selecting a worker who did so for other reasons is $1 - .04 = .96$, which is the value of q. The probability of obtaining this sequence of five workers who rejected relocation offers is:

$$P(T_1 \cap R_2 \cap R_3 \cap R_4 \cap R_5) = (.04)(.96)(.96)(.96)(.96) = .03397$$

Obviously, in the random selection of workers who rejected relocation offers, the worker who did so because of too little relocation help could have been the second, third, fourth or fifth worker. All possible sequences of selecting one worker who rejected relocation because of too little help and four workers who did so for other reasons are:

$$T_1, R_2, R_3, R_4, R_5$$

$$R_1, T_2, R_3, R_4, R_5$$

$$R_1, R_2, T_3, R_4, R_5$$

$$R_1, R_2, R_3, T_4, R_5$$

$$R_1, R_2, R_3, R_4, T_5$$

The probability of each of these sequences occurring is:

$$(.04)(.96)(.96)(.96)(.96) = .03397$$

$$(.96)(.04)(.96)(.96)(.96) = .03397$$

$$(.96)(.96)(.04)(.96)(.96) = .03397$$

$$(.96)(.96)(.96)(.04)(.96) = .03397$$

$$(.96)(.96)(.96)(.96)(.04) = .03397$$

Note that in each case the final probability is the same. Each of the five sequences contains the product of .04 and four .96s. The commutative property of multiplication allows for the reordering of the five individual probabilities in any one sequence. The probabilities in each of the five sequences may be reordered and summarised as $(.04)^1(.96)^4$. Each sequence contains the same five probabilities, which makes recomputing the probability of each sequence unnecessary. What *is* important is to determine how many different ways the sequences can be formed and multiply that figure by the probability of one sequence occurring. There are five sequences for this problem, so the total probability of selecting exactly one worker who rejected relocation because of too little relocation help in a random sample of five workers who rejected relocation offers is:

$$5(.04)^1(.96)^4 = .16987$$

An easier way to determine the number of sequences, rather than by listing all possibilities is to use *combinations* to calculate them. Five workers are sampled, so $n = 5$; the problem is to select one worker who rejected a relocation offer because of too little relocation help, so $x = 1$. Hence $\binom{n}{x}$ will yield the number of possible ways to get x successes in n trials. For this problem, $\binom{5}{1}$ is the number of possible sequences:

$$\binom{5}{1} = \frac{5!}{1!(5-1)!} = 5$$

Now suppose 70% of all New Zealanders believe cleaning up the environment is an important issue. What is the probability of randomly sampling four New Zealanders and having exactly two of them say that they believe cleaning up the environment is an important issue? Let E represent the success of selecting a person who believes cleaning up the environment is an important issue. For this example, $p = .70$. Let N represent the failure to select a person who believes cleaning up is an important issue. The probability of selecting one of these people is $q = .30$.

The various sequences of getting two Es in a sample of four are:

$$E_1, E_2, N_3, N_4$$
$$E_1, N_2, E_3, N_4$$
$$E_1, N_2, N_3, E_4$$
$$N_1, E_2, E_3, N_4$$
$$N_1, E_2, N_3, E_4$$
$$N_1, N_2, E_3, E_4$$

Two successes in a sample of four can occur six ways. Using combinations, the number of sequences is:

$$\binom{4}{2} = 6$$

The probability of selecting any individual sequence is:

$$(.70)^2(.30)^2 = .0441$$

Thus the overall probability of getting exactly two people who believe cleaning up the environment is important out of four randomly selected people, when 70% of New Zealanders believe cleaning up the environment is important, is:

$$\binom{4}{2}(.70)^2(.30)^2 = .2646$$

Generalising from these two examples yields the binomial formula 5.4, which summarises the steps presented so far for calculating probabilities for a binomial distribution.

Binomial formula (5.4)

$$P(x) = \binom{n}{x} p^x q^{n-x} = \frac{n!}{x!(n-x)!} p^x q^{n-x}$$

where:

n = the number of trials (or the number being sampled)
x = the number of successes
p = the probability of a success in any one trial
$q = 1 - p$ = the probability of a failure in any one trial

DEMONSTRATION PROBLEM 5.2

PROBLEM: A customer satisfaction survey of Australia's four largest mobile phone carriers found that 80% were either very satisfied or fairly satisfied with their mobile service. Suppose a random sample of 50 customers of the four carriers is taken. If 80% of their customers are still satisfied with their service, what is the probability that exactly 42 of the 50 are satisfied with their service?

SOLUTION: Let the random variable x denote the number of people in the sample of 50 who are satisfied with their home loans. Here $p = .80$ (satisfied), $q = 1 - p = .20$ (not satisfied), $n = 50$ and $x = 42$. We need $P(x = 42)$, which is given by:

$$\binom{50}{42}(.80)^{42}(.20)^8 = 0.1169$$

If 80% of the customers are satisfied with their mobile service, then about 12% of the time the researcher would find that exactly 42 out of 50 customers of the four biggest mobile carriers are satisfied with their service. The expected number of satisfied customers in a random sample of 50 is 50 × .80 = 40, and the probability of getting this number is:

$$\binom{50}{40}(.80)^{40}(.20)^{10} = 0.1398$$

Therefore, the probability of getting 42 satisfied customers is not as small as it may at first seem.

DEMONSTRATION PROBLEM 5.3

PROBLEM: According to the Australian Bureau of Statistics, the current unemployment rate in Australia is 6.1%. If you were conducting a random telephone survey, what would be the probability of getting three or fewer unemployed workers in a sample of 30?

SOLUTION: Let the random variable x denote the number of unemployed people in the sample of 30. The requirement of getting three or fewer unemployed people is satisfied by getting 0, 1, 2 or 3 unemployed workers. Thus, this problem must be solved as the union of four problems: (1) zero unemployed, $x = 0$; (2) one unemployed, $x = 1$; (3) two unemployed, $x = 2$; and (4) three unemployed, $x = 3$.

In each problem, $p = .061$, $q = .939$ and $n = 30$. Whenever the binomial formula 5.4 is used to solve for cumulative success (not an exact number), the probability of each x value must be found and the probabilities summed.

The binomial formula gives the following result:

$$P(x = 0) + P(x = 1) + P(x = 2) + P(x = 3)$$

$$= \binom{30}{0}(.061)^0(.939)^{30} + \binom{30}{1}(.061)^1(.939)^{29}$$

$$+ \binom{30}{0}(061)^2(.939)^{28} + \binom{30}{3}(.061)^3(.939)^{27}$$

$$= 0.1513 + 0.2950 + 0.2778 + 0.1685 = 0.8926$$

Therefore, with an unemployment rate of 6.1%, the random survey would get three or fewer unemployed workers 89.26% of the time in a random sample of 30 workers.

Using the binomial table

Anyone who encounters a large number of binomial problems will begin to recognise that the probability of getting $x = 5$ successes from a sample size of $n = 30$ when $p = .10$ is the same no matter whether the five successes are left-handed people, defective parts, brand Y purchasers or any other variable. Whether the sample involves people, parts or products does not affect the final probabilities. The essence of the problem is the same: $n = 30$, $x = 5$ and $p = .10$. Recognising this fact, mathematicians constructed binomial probability tables.

Two parameters, n and p, describe or characterise a binomial distribution. Binomial distributions are actually a family of distributions. Every different value of n gives a different binomial distribution, as does every different value of p, and tables are available for various combinations of n and p values. Because of space limitations, the binomial tables presented in this text are limited. Table A.1 in the appendix contains binomial tables. Each table is headed by a value of n. Nine values of p are presented in each table. In the column below each value of p is the binomial distribution for that combination of n and p. Table 5.5 (overleaf) contains a segment of table A.1 with the binomial probabilities for $n = 20$.

TABLE 5.5 Extract from table A.1

	$n = 20$								
	Probability								
x	.1	.2	.3	.4	.5	.6	.7	.8	.9
0	.122	.012	.001	.000	.000	.000	.000	.000	.000
1	.270	.058	.007	.000	.000	.000	.000	.000	.000
2	.285	.137	.028	.003	.000	.000	.000	.000	.000
3	.190	.205	.072	.012	.001	.000	.000	.000	.000
4	.090	.218	.130	.035	.005	.000	.000	.000	.000
5	.032	.175	.179	.075	.015	.001	.000	.000	.000
6	.009	.109	.192	.124	.037	.005	.000	.000	.000
7	.002	.055	.164	.166	.074	.015	.001	.000	.000
8	.000	.022	.114	.180	.120	.035	.004	.000	.000
9	.000	.007	.065	.160	.160	.071	.012	.000	.000
10	.000	.002	.031	.117	.176	.117	.031	.002	.000
11	.000	.000	.012	.071	.160	.160	.065	.007	.000
12	.000	.000	.004	.035	.120	.180	.114	.022	.000
13	.000	.000	.001	.015	.074	.166	.164	.055	.002
14	.000	.000	.000	.005	.037	.124	.192	.109	.009
15	.000	.000	.000	.001	.015	.075	.179	.175	.032
16	.000	.000	.000	.000	.005	.035	.130	.218	.090
17	.000	.000	.000	.000	.001	.012	.072	.205	.190
18	.000	.000	.000	.000	.000	.003	.028	.137	.285
19	.000	.000	.000	.000	.000	.000	.007	.058	.270
20	.000	.000	.000	.000	.000	.000	.001	.012	.122

DEMONSTRATION PROBLEM 5.4

PROBLEM: Find the binomial probability for $n = 20$, $p = .40$ and $x = 10$ by using table A.1 in the appendix.

SOLUTION: To use table A.1, first locate the required value of *n*. Because $n = 20$ for this problem, the extract of the binomial tables containing values for $n = 20$ presented in table 5.5 can be used. After locating the value of *n*, search horizontally across the top of the table for the appropriate value of *p*. In this problem, $p = .40$. The column under .4 contains the probabilities for the binomial distribution of $n = 20$ and $p = .40$. To get the probability of $x = 10$, find the value of *x* in the leftmost column and locate the probability in the table at the intersection of $p = .40$ and $x = 10$. The answer is .117. Solving this problem using the binomial formula yields the same result.

$$\binom{20}{0}(.40)^{10}(.60)^{10} = .1171$$

Excel can be used to produce the probabilities for virtually any binomial distribution and offers yet another option for solving binomial problems. Excel produces essentially a column of the binomial table. The advantages of using Excel for this purpose are convenience (if the binomial tables are not readily available but a computer is) and the potential for generating tables for many more values than those printed in this book.

DEMONSTRATION PROBLEM 5.5

PROBLEM: Sparkle Group Limited, a Hong Kong cleaning products company, has a 40% share of the Hong Kong cleaning products market. Suppose 20 new cleaning products buyers are selected at random from the Hong Kong population. What is the probability that fewer than five bought Sparkle cleaning products?

SOLUTION: Let the random variable x denote the number of people out of 20 who bought Sparkle cleaning products. Then x has a binomial distribution with $n = 20$ and $p = .4$. Because $n = 20$, the extract of the binomial tables presented in table 5.5 can be used to solve this problem. Search along the row of values of p for .40. Determining the probability of getting $x < 5$ involves summing the probabilities for $x = 0, 1, 2, 3$ and 4. This gives $P(x < 5) = .125$.

Therefore, if Sparkle has a 40% market share of the Hong Kong cleaning products market and 20 cleaning products buyers are randomly selected, about 5% of the time, fewer than five of the 20 buyers will have purchased Sparkle cleaning products.

x value	Probability
0	.000
1	.000
2	.003
3	.012
4	.035
	$P(x < 5) = .125$

USING EXCEL

Producing a binomial distribution

1. From the Formulas tab, select Insert Function.
2. In the Insert Function dialogue box, select Statistical from the drop-down menu and BINOM.DIST from the Select a function options.

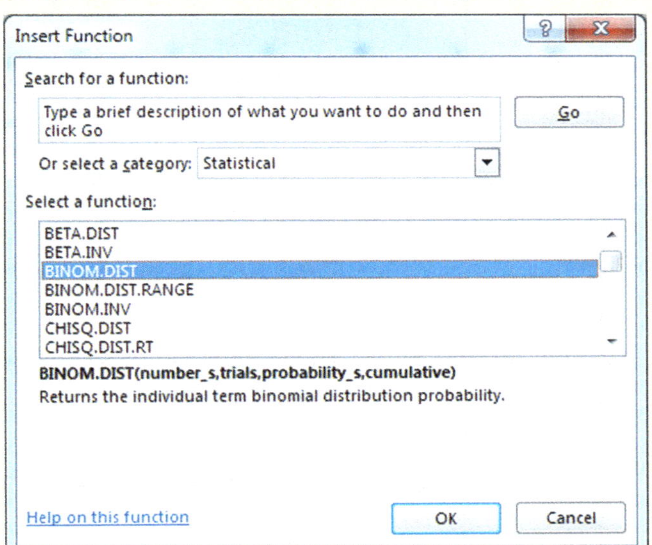

3. Click OK.
4. In the Function Arguments dialogue box:
   a. enter 4 in the Number_s field
   b. enter 20 in the Trials field
   c. enter .4 in the Probability_s field

d. enter TRUE in the Cumulative field to compute the cumulative probabilities for the binomial distribution. (Entering FALSE in this field would return the individual probability and the process would need to be done for 0, 1, 2 and 3 separately, producing a table similar to the one in the manual solution.)

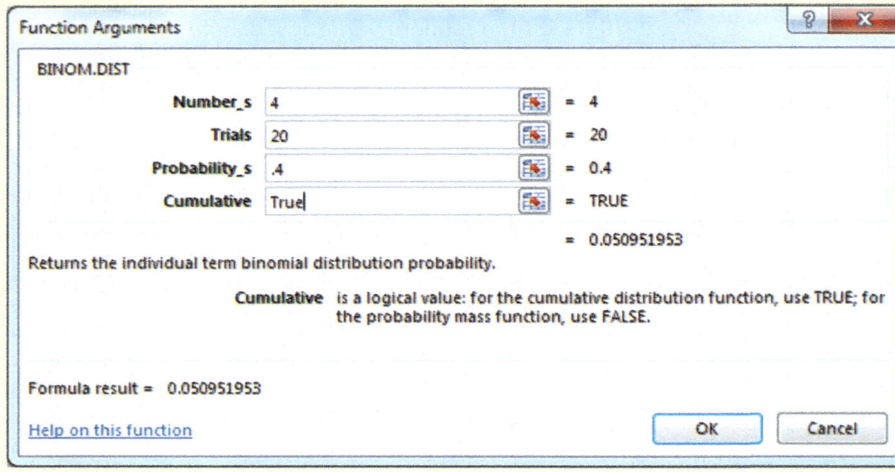

5. Click OK to paste the function into a cell on the worksheet.

K ***Please refer to 'Going further with KaddStat' for KaddStat instructions at www.johnwiley.com.au/highered/black4e/kaddstat.***

Mean and standard deviation of a binomial distribution

Suppose a brand of car battery has a 30% market share. If 70 cars are selected at random many times, how many cars on average would be found to be using this brand of battery? In this case, we are looking for the average value of the binomial distribution. A binomial distribution has an expected value or a long-run average, which is denoted by μ. Formula 5.5 shows that the value of μ is determined by np. For example, if $n = 10$ and $p = .4$, then $\mu = np = (10)(.4) = 4$. The long-run average or expected value means that, if n items are sampled many times, and if p is the probability of a success in one trial, the average number of successes per sample is expected to be np. Therefore, in the car battery example, if 70 cars are selected at random many times, on average $\mu = np = (70)(.30) = 21$ cars will be found to have this brand of battery. In another example, if 40% of all graduate business students at a large university are women, and if random samples of 10 graduate business students are selected many times, on average, four of the 10 students would be women.

Mean of a binomial distribution (5.5)

$$\mu = np$$

Examining the mean of a binomial distribution gives an intuitive feeling about the likelihood of a given outcome. For example, researchers may generally agree that 10% of all people are left-handed. However, suppose a researcher wishes to test whether this figure is higher for children who are born to women over the age of 35. To gather evidence, she randomly selects 100 children who were born to women over the age of 35, and 20 of these children are left-handed. How likely is it that she would have found 20 left-handed people in a sample of 100 from the general population? How many would she have expected in a sample of 100? The mean or expected value for $n = 100$ and $p = .10$ is $(100)(.10) = 10$ left-handed people. Did the 20 left-handed children in a sample of 100 happen by chance, or is the researcher drawing from a population that is different from the general population that produces 10% left-handed people? She can investigate this outcome further by examining the binomial probabilities for this problem. The mean of the distribution gives her an expected value from which to work.

According to one study, 64% of all financial consumers believe that banks are more competitive today than they were five years ago. If 23 financial consumers are selected randomly, what is the expected number who believe banks are more competitive today than they were five years ago? This problem can be described by the binomial distribution of $n = 23$ and $p = .64$ given in table 5.6. The mean of this binomial distribution yields the expected value for this problem.

$$\mu = np = 23(.64) = 14.72$$

In the long run, if 23 financial consumers are selected randomly over and over, and if indeed 64% of all financial consumers believe banks are more competitive today, then the experiment should average 14.72 financial consumers out of 23 who believe banks are more competitive today. (Note that, because the binomial distribution is a discrete distribution, you will never actually get 14.72 people out of 23 who believe banks are more competitive today.) The mean of the distribution does reveal the relative likelihood of any individual occurrence. Examine table 5.6. Notice that the highest probabilities are those near $x = 14.72$; for example, $P(x = 15) = .1712$, $P(x = 14) = .1605$ and $P(x = 16) = .1522$. All other probabilities for this distribution are less than these.

TABLE 5.6 Binomial distribution for $n = 23$, $p = .64$

x	$P(x)$
0	0.0000
1	0.0000
2	0.0000
3	0.0000
4	0.0000
5	0.0000
6	0.0002
7	0.0009
8	0.0031
9	0.0090
10	0.0225
11	0.0473
12	0.0840
13	0.1264
14	0.1605
15	0.1712
16	0.1522
17	0.1114
18	0.0660
19	0.0309
20	0.0110
21	0.0028
22	0.0005
23	0.0000

The mean value tells us only half of the story behind the data. To understand the complete story, spread and maximum likely spread of the data as described by the standard deviation are needed. The standard deviation of a binomial distribution is denoted by the symbol σ and is equal to $\sqrt{npq}$, as given in formula 5.6. For the left-handedness example, $\sigma = \sqrt{100(.10)(.90)} = 3$. The standard deviation for the financial consumer problem described by the binomial distribution in table 5.6 is:

$$\sigma = \sqrt{npq} = \sqrt{23(.64)(.36)} = 2.30$$

Standard deviation of a binomial distribution (5.6)

$$\sigma = \sqrt{npq}$$

Some binomial distributions are nearly bell-shaped and can be approximated by using the normal distribution. The mean and standard deviation of a binomial distribution are the tools used to convert these binomial problems to normal distribution problems.

Graphing binomial distributions

The graph of a binomial distribution can be constructed by using all the possible x values of the distribution and their associated probabilities. The x values usually are graphed along the x axis and the probabilities are graphed along the y axis.

Table 5.7 lists the probabilities for three different binomial distributions: $n = 8$ and $p = .20$; $n = 8$ and $p = .50$; and $n = 8$ and $p = .80$. Figure 5.2 displays graphs for these three binomial distributions. Observe how the shape of the distribution changes as the value of p increases. For $p = .50$, the distribution is symmetrical. For $p = .20$, the distribution is skewed to the right, and for $p = .80$, the distribution is skewed to the left. This pattern makes sense because the mean of the binomial distribution $n = 8$ and $p = .50$ is 4, which is in the middle of the distribution. The mean of the distribution $n = 8$ and $p = .20$ is 1.6, which results in the highest probabilities being near $x = 2$ and $x = 1$. This graph peaks early and stretches toward the higher values of x. The mean of the distribution $n = 8$ and $p = .80$ is 6.4, which results in the highest probabilities being near $x = 6$ and $x = 7$. Thus the peak of the distribution is nearer to 8 than to 0 and the distribution stretches back towards $x = 0$.

In any binomial distribution, the largest x value that can occur is n and the smallest value is zero. Thus the graph of any binomial distribution is constrained by zero and n. If the value of p is not .50, this constraint will result in the graph 'bunching up' at one end and being skewed at the other end.

TABLE 5.7 Probabilities for three binomial distributions with $n = 8$

	Probabilities for		
x	$p = .20$	$p = .50$	$p = .80$
0	.1678	.0039	.0000
1	.3355	.0312	.0001
2	.2936	.1094	.0011
3	.1468	.2187	.0092
4	.0459	.2734	.0459
5	.0092	.2187	.1468
6	.0011	.1094	.2936
7	.0001	.0312	.3355
8	.0000	.0039	.1678

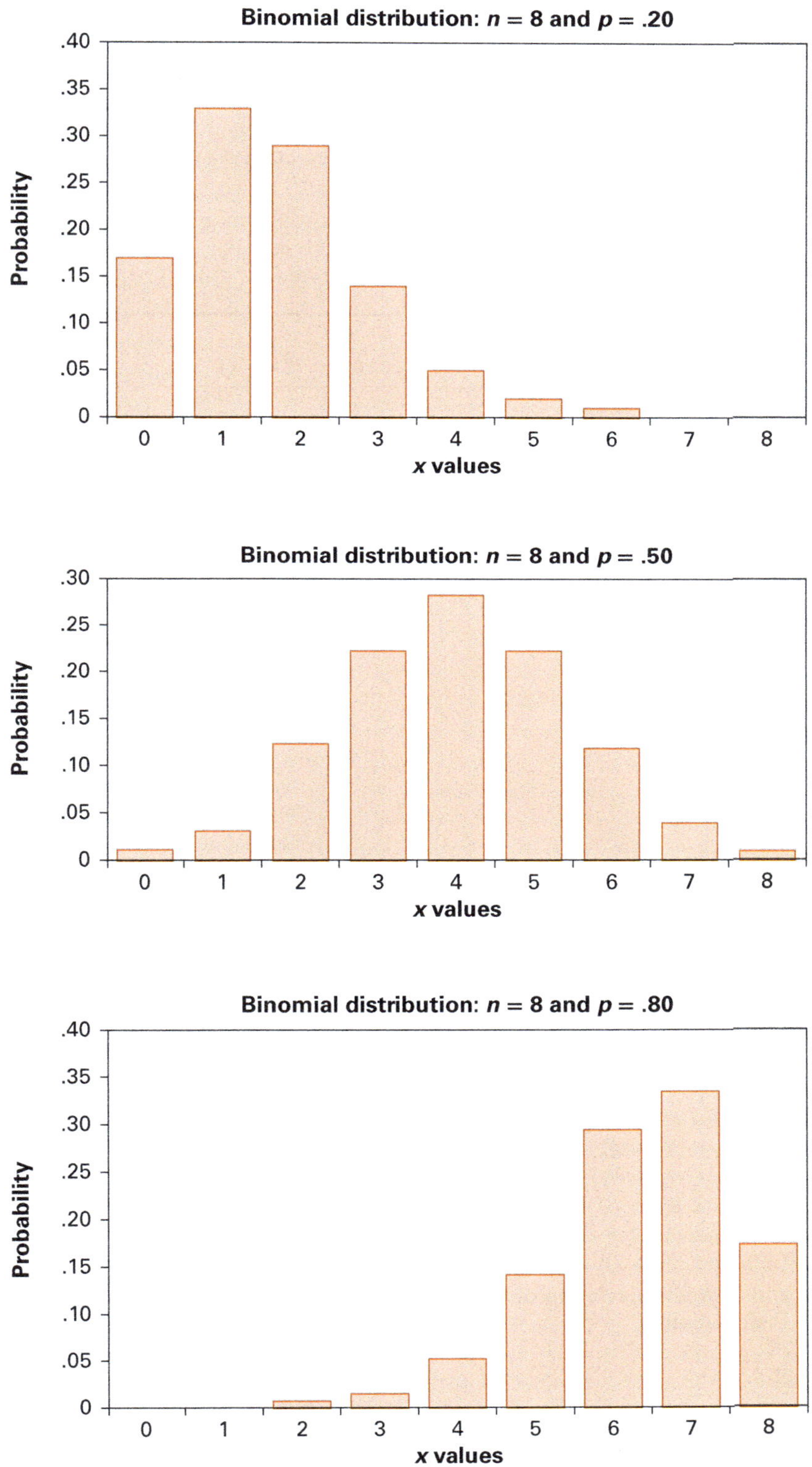

FIGURE 5.2 Graphs of three binomial distributions with $n = 8$

DEMONSTRATION PROBLEM 5.6

PROBLEM: A manufacturing company produces 10 000 plastic cups per week. This company supplies cups to another company, which packages the cups as part of picnic sets. The second company randomly samples 10 cups sent from the supplier. If two or fewer of the sampled cups are defective, the second company accepts the lot. What is the probability that the lot will be accepted if the proportion of defective cups produced by the cup manufacturing company is actually 10%? 20%? 30%? 40%?

SOLUTION: In this series of binomial problems, $n = 10$ and $x \leq 2$, and p ranges from .10 to .40. From table A.1 — and cumulating the values — we have the following probability of $x \leq 2$ for each value of p and the expected value ($\mu = np$).

p	Lot accepted $P(x \leq 2)$	Expected number of defective cups (μ)
.10	.930	1.0
.20	.677	2.0
.30	.382	3.0
.40	.167	4.0

These values indicate that, if 10% of the cups produced are defective, the probability is relatively high (.930) that the lot will be accepted by chance. For higher values of p, the probability of accepting the lot decreases. In addition, as p increases, the expected number of defective cups moves away from the acceptable values, $x \leq 2$. This reduces the chance of the lot being accepted.

PRACTICE PROBLEMS

Practising the calculations

5.5 Solve the following problems by using the binomial formula.

a. If $n = 5$ and $p = .10$, find $P(x = 2)$.
b. If $n = 8$ and $p = .80$, find $P(x = 5)$.
c. If $n = 10$ and $p = .70$, find $P(x \geq 6)$.
d. If n = 13 and p = .50, find $P(4 \leq x \leq 6)$.

5.6 Solve the following problems by using the binomial tables (table A.2).

a. If $n = 20$ and $p = .50$, find $P(x = 12)$.
b. If $n = 20$ and $p = .30$, find $P(x > 8)$.
c. If $n = 20$ and $p = .70$, find $P(x < 12)$.
d. If $n = 20$ and $p = .90$, find $P(x \leq 16)$.
e. If $n = 15$ and $p = .40$, find $P(4 \leq x \leq 9)$.
f. If $n = 10$ and $p = .60$, find $P(x \geq 7)$.

5.7 Find the mean and standard deviation of the following binomial distributions.

a. $n = 20$ and $p = .70$
b. $n = 70$ and $p = .35$
c. $n = 100$ and $p = .50$

5.8 Use the probability tables in table A.2 to sketch the graph of each of the following binomial distributions. Note on each graph where the mean of the distribution falls.

a. $n = 6$ and $p = .70$
b. $n = 20$ and $p = .50$
c. $n = 8$ and $p = .80$

Testing your understanding

5.9 The 2 most popular majors in a business degree are marketing and international business, with 30% of students enrolled in marketing, and 18% enrolled in international business. Suppose 20 students are selected at random.

a. What is the probability that:
   i. at least half of them are studying a marketing major
   ii. no more than a quarter are studying an international business major
   iii. between 10 and 15 are studying a marketing major?
b. Find the mean and variance of the number of students studying a marketing major. Find the mean and variance of the total number of people who are studying a marketing or international business major.

5.10 A survey of holiday accommodation in New Zealand showed that in Auckland, excluding caravan parks and camping grounds, 42% were full (i.e. had no vacancies). A random sample of 25 holiday accommodation facilities (of the same capacity) in Auckland is selected at random. Assume that the probability that a particular holiday accommodation facility is full is 0.42.

a. What is the probability that at most 10 of these are full?
b. What is the probability that no more than 15 of these are full?
c. What is the probability that less than one-quarter of them are full?

5.11 Graph the distribution for problem 5.10. For which values of *x* are the probabilities highest? Determine the expected value of this distribution. How does the expected value compare with the values of *x* that have the highest probabilities? Compute the standard deviation. Determine the interval $\mu \pm 2\sigma$ for this distribution. Between which two values of *x* does this interval lie? What is the percentage of values within this interval? How does this answer compare with what Chebyshev's theorem or the empirical rule would yield?

5.12 A survey conducted by Certified Practising Accountants Australia to investigate the reaction to new audit standards issued by the Australian Auditing and Assurance Standards Board found that only 53% of auditors believed that the new standards had improved audit quality. Fifty-eight per cent of auditors felt that the standards had improved confidence in financial reporting. Assume that these two events (improved quality and improved confidence) are independent. Suppose 20 auditors from Australia are selected at random.

a. What is the probability that fewer than 15 of them believe that the standards have improved confidence in financial reporting?
b. What is the expected number of auditors who believe that the standards have improved confidence in financial reporting?
c. What is the probability that more than 10 of them believe that the new standards have improved audit quality?
d. On average, how many of them feel that the new standards have improved audit quality?
e. What is the probability that exactly 10 of them believe that the new standards have improved both confidence in financial reporting and audit quality?
f. What is the probability that at least 10 of them believe that the new standards have improved both confidence in financial reporting and audit quality?
g. What is the expected number of auditors who believe that the new standards have improved both confidence in financial reporting and audit quality?

5.13 An importer of shirts made in China buys items in lots of 100 from a supplier who guarantees that no more than 2% of the items are faulty. On a given day, 15 lots are delivered to the assembler.

a. What is the probability that, in a given lot of 100 shirts, more than five shirts are faulty?
b. What is the expected number of faulty shirts in a lot selected at random?
c. A lot is rejected if it has more than four faulty shirts. What is the probability that a lot is rejected?
d. What is the probability that more than three lots out of the 15 are rejected?
e. On average, how many lots out of the 15 will be rejected?

5.4 Poisson distribution

The Poisson distribution is named after Simeon-Denis Poisson (1781–1840), a French mathematician, who published its essentials in a paper in 1837. The Poisson distribution and the binomial distribution have some similarities, but also several differences. The binomial distribution describes a distribution of two possible outcomes designated as successes and failures from a given number of trials.

The **Poisson distribution** *focuses only on the number of discrete occurrences over some interval or continuum.* A Poisson experiment does not have a given number of trials (n) as a binomial experiment does. For example, whereas a binomial experiment might be used to determine how many Japanese-made cars are in a random sample of 20 cars, a Poisson experiment might focus on the number of cars randomly arriving at a service station during a 10-minute interval.

The Poisson distribution is often used to describe the number of random arrivals in some time interval such as the number of customer arrivals per five-minute interval at a small boutique on weekday mornings. This information is useful to the owner of a shop planning the number of staff who need to be employed during the morning.

The Poisson distribution also has applications in the field of management science. Models used in queuing theory (theory of waiting lines) are usually based on the assumption that the Poisson distribution is the proper distribution to describe random arrivals over a period of time. Waiting in queues is a common occurrence of everyday life; for example, waiting in a queue to buy a train ticket, waiting in a queue at a bank branch for service and waiting in a queue to get a response from a call centre. Examples are not limited to people spending time in queues; planes wait to take off or land, and products queue up in warehouses, as do cars for service at a service station.

The Poisson distribution has the following characteristics.

- It is a discrete distribution; its possible values are whole numbers (e.g. 0, 1, 2).
- Each occurrence is independent of other occurrences.
- It describes occurrences over an interval.
- The number of occurrences in each interval can range from zero to infinity.
- The expected number of occurrences remain constant throughout the experiment.

The following are examples of Poisson-type situations:

1. the number of telephone calls per minute at a small business
2. the number of customer arrivals at a bank in an hour
3. the number of arrivals at Sydney Harbour Bridge toll points between 8.00 am and 9.00 am in January
4. the number of paint spots per new vehicle
5. the number of units of product demanded per week.

Each of these examples represents an occurrence of events for some interval. Note that, although time is a more common interval for the Poisson distribution, intervals can range from a city in New Zealand to a pair of jeans. Some of the intervals in these examples might have zero occurrences. Moreover, the average occurrence per interval for many of these examples is in the single digits (0, 1, 2, . . . , 9).

The Poisson distribution is characterised by lambda (λ), the mean number of occurrences in the interval. We expressed this as 'x has a Poisson distribution with parameter λ'. If a Poisson-distributed phenomenon is studied over a long period of time, λ is the *long-run average* of the process. The Poisson formula 5.7 is used to compute the probability of occurrences over an interval for a given value of lambda.

Poisson formula
(5.7)

$$P(x)=\frac{\lambda^x e^{-\lambda}}{x!}$$

where:

$x = 0, 1, 2, 3, \ldots$
λ = the mean number of occurrences in the interval
$e = 2.718282$

Solving Poisson problems by formula

Suppose bank customers arrive randomly on weekdays at an average of 3.2 customers every 5 minutes. What is the probability of exactly five customers arriving in a 5-minute interval on a weekday?

Let the random variable x denote the number of customers arriving in a 5-minute interval on a weekday. The variable x can take values 0, 1, 2, 3, . . . Therefore, x is distributed as a Poisson distribution with a mean value of 3.2, and:

$$P(x=5)=\frac{(3.2^5)(e^{-3.2})}{5!}=.1140$$

If a bank averages 3.2 customers every 5 minutes, the probability of five customers arriving during any one 5-minute interval is .1140.

DEMONSTRATION PROBLEM 5.7

PROBLEM: Bank customers arrive randomly on weekdays at an average of 3.2 customers every 5 minutes.

a. What is the probability of more than 3 customers arriving in a 5-minute interval on a weekday?
b. What is the probability of exactly 10 customers arriving during a 10-minute interval?

SOLUTION: Let the random variable x denote the number of customers arriving in a 5-minute interval on a weekday. The variable x can take values 0, 1, 2, 3, . . . Therefore, x is distributed as a Poisson distribution with a mean value of 3.2.

a. We need $P(x > 3) = 1 - P(x \leq 3)$
First find $P(x \leq 3) = P(x = 0) + P(x = 1) + P(x = 2) + P(x = 3)$

$$P(x = 0) = \frac{(3.2^0)(e^{-3.2})}{0!} = .0408$$

$$P(x = 1) = \frac{(3.2^1)(e^{-3.2})}{1!} = .1304$$

$$P(x = 2) = \frac{(3.2^2)(e^{-3.2})}{2!} = .2087$$

$$P(x = 3) = \frac{(3.2^3)(e^{-3.2})}{3!} = .2226$$

Then $P(x > 3) = 1 - (.0408 + .1304 + .2087 + .2226)$
$= .3975$

If the bank has been averaging 3.2 customers every 5 minutes on weekdays, then more than three people would arrive in a randomly chosen 5-minute period about 40% of the time.

b. This is different from part (a) since the interval is different. The correct way to approach this dilemma is to adjust the interval for λ so that it and x have the same interval.

The interval for x is 10 minutes, so λ should be adjusted to a 10-minute interval. Logically, if the bank averages 3.2 customers every 10 minutes, it should average twice as many, or 6.4 customers, every 10 minutes. The wrong approach to this dilemma is to equalise the intervals by changing the x value. Never adjust or change x in a problem. Just because 10 customers arrive in one 10-minute interval does not mean that there would necessarily have been five customers in a 5-minute interval. There is no guarantee how the 10 customers are spread over the 10-minute interval. Always adjust the lambda value. After λ has been adjusted for a 10-minute interval, the solution is:

$$P(x = 10) = \frac{(6.4^{10})(e^{-6.4})}{10!} = .0528$$

Bank officers could use these results to roster enough staff to serve customers and reduce waiting times.

DEMONSTRATION PROBLEM 5.8

PROBLEM: Bank customers arrive randomly on weekdays at an average of 3.2 customers every 5 minutes.

a. What is the probability of more than 7 customers arriving in a 5-minute interval on a weekday?
b. What is the probability of more than 2 customers arriving in a 5-minute interval on a weekday?

SOLUTION:

a. In theory, the solution requires obtaining the values of $x = 8, 9, 10, 11, 12, 13, 14, \ldots, \infty$. In practice, each x value is determined until the values are so far away from $\lambda = 3.2$ that the probabilities approach zero. The exact probabilities are then summed to find $x > 7$.

$$P(x = 8) = \frac{(3.2^8)(e^{-3.2})}{8!} = .0111$$

$$P(x = 9) = \frac{(3.2^9)(e^{-3.2})}{9!} = .0040$$

$$P(x = 10) = \frac{(3.2^{10})(e^{-3.2})}{10!} = .0013$$

$$P(x = 11) = \frac{(3.2^{11})(e^{-3.2})}{11!} = .0004$$

$$P(x = 12) = \frac{(3.2^{12})(e^{-3.2})}{12!} = .0001$$

$$P(x = 13) = \frac{(3.2^{13})(e^{-3.2})}{13!} = .0000$$

Then $P(x > 7) = .0111 + .0040 + .0013 + .0004 + .0001$
$= .0169$

If the bank has been averaging 3.2 customers every 5 minutes on weekdays, it is unlikely that more than 7 people would randomly arrive in any one 5-minute period. This answer indicates that more than 7 people would randomly arrive in a 5-minute period only 1.69% of the time.

b. The required probability is $P(x > 2)$. This probability is equal to $1 - P(x \leq 2)$.

$$P(x > 2) = 1 - P(x = 0) + P(x = 1) + P(x = 2)$$

As calculated in demonstration problem 5.7:

$$P(x = 0) = \frac{(3.2^0)(e^{-3.2})}{0!} = .0408$$

$$P(x = 1) = \frac{(3.2^1)(e^{-3.2})}{1!} = .1304$$

$$P(x = 2) = \frac{(3.2^2)(e^{-3.2})}{2!} = .2087$$

$$P(x > 2) = 1 - (.0408 + .1304 + .2087)$$

$$= .6201$$

DEMONSTRATION PROBLEM 5.9

PROBLEM: If a real estate agency sells on average 1.6 houses per day and sales of houses per day are Poisson distributed, what is the probability of selling exactly four houses in one day? What is the probability of selling no houses in one day? What is the probability of selling more than five houses in a day? What is the probability of selling 10 or more houses in a day? What is the probability of selling exactly four houses in two days?

SOLUTION: $\lambda = 1.6$ houses/day; $P(x = 4)$?

The table on the opposite page gives the probabilities for $\lambda = 1.6$. The left column contains the x values. The row for $x = 4$ yields the probability .0551. If a real estate agency has been averaging 1.6 houses sold per day, only on 5.51% of the days would it sell exactly four houses. The first row of the table shows that the probability of selling no houses in a day is .2019; that is, on 20.19% of the days, the agency would sell no houses if sales are Poisson distributed with $\lambda = 1.6$ houses per day.

Poisson table for $\lambda = 1.6$

x	Probability
0	.2019
1	.3230
2	.2584
3	.1378
4	.0551
5	.0176
6	.0047
7	.0011
8	.0002
9	.0000

The table is not cumulative. To determine $P(x > 5)$, more than five houses sold in a day, find the probabilities of $x = 6$, $x = 7$, $x = 8$, $x = 9, \ldots$ However, at $x = 9$, the probability to 4 decimal places is zero, and the table ends when the probability is zero at four decimal places. The answer for $P(x > 5)$ is:

$$P(x > 5) = .0047 + .0011 + .0002 = .0060$$

As the table shows zero probability at $x = 9$, the probability of $x \geq 10$ is essentially .0000; that is, if the real estate agency has been averaging 1.6 houses sold per day, it is virtually impossible to sell 10 or more houses in a day.

What is the probability of selling exactly four houses in two days? In this case, the interval has been changed from one day to two days. Lambda is for one day, so an adjustment must be made: A lambda of 1.6 for one day converts to a lambda of 3.2 for two days. The table no longer applies, so the answer is found by looking up $\lambda = 3.2$ and $x = 4$ in table A.2; the probability is .1781.

USING EXCEL

Generating Poisson distributions

DP05-09

1. Access DP05-09.xls from the student website.
2. Click on the first cell under the Probability heading.
3. From the Formulas tab, select Insert Function.
4. In the Insert Function dialogue box, select Statistical from the drop-down menu and POISSON.DIST from the Select a function options.

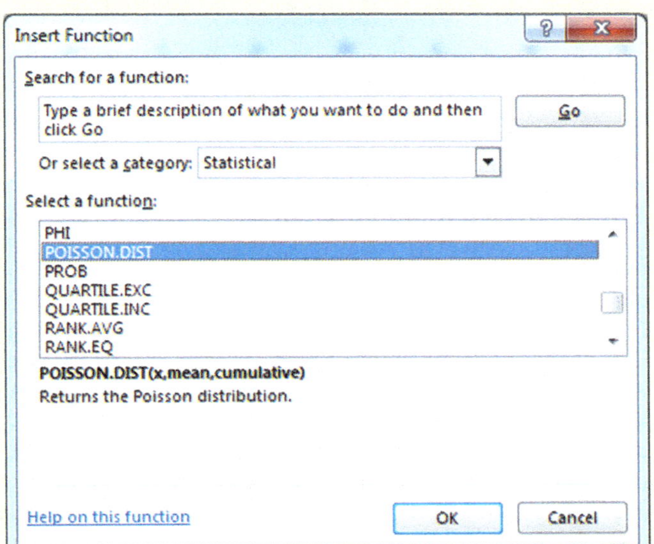

5. Click OK.
6. In the Function Arguments dialogue box:
   a. enter A2 as the first value of x in the X field
   b. enter 1.6 in the Mean field
   c. enter FALSE in the Cumulative field to calculate the individual Poisson probability. (Entering TRUE would return the cumulative Poisson probability.)

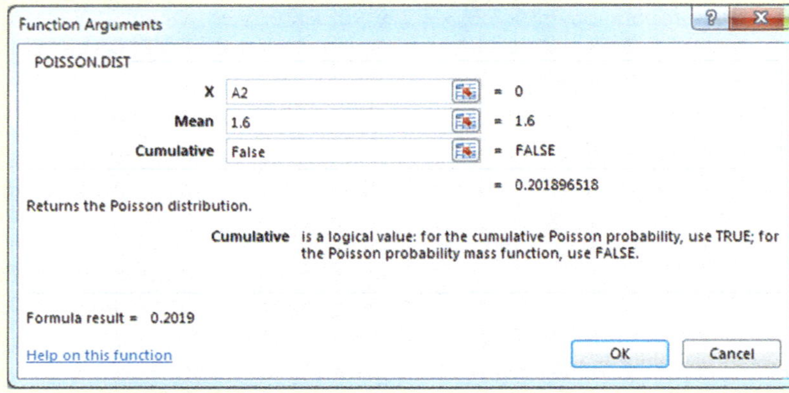

d. click OK to paste the function into the worksheet.

7. To complete the Poisson table, fill the second column with the pasted function.

	A	B
1	*x*	*Probability*
2	0	0.2019
3	1	0.3230
4	2	0.2584
5	3	0.1378
6	4	0.0551
7	5	0.0176
8	6	0.0047
9	7	0.0011
10	8	0.0002
11	9	0.0000

Mean and standard deviation of a Poisson distribution

The mean or expected value of a Poisson distribution is λ. It is the long-run average of occurrences for an interval. Lambda is usually not a whole number, so most of the time it is not possible to observe lambda occurrences in an interval. Understanding the mean of a Poisson distribution gives a feel for the actual occurrences that are likely.

The standard deviation of a Poisson distribution is the square root of λ. This means that, if you are working with a Poisson distribution, reducing the mean can also reduce the variability.

For example, if $\lambda = 6.5$, the standard deviation is 2.55. Chebyshev's theorem states that at least $1-\frac{1}{k^2}$ values are within k standard deviations of the mean. The interval $\mu \pm 2\sigma$ contains at least $1-\frac{1}{2^2}=1-\frac{1}{4}=.75$ of the values. For $\mu = \lambda = 6.5$ and $\sigma = 2.55$, at least 75% of the values should be within the range $6.5 \pm 2(2.55) = 6.5 \pm 5.1$. That is, the range from 1.4 to 11.6 should include at least 75% of all the values. An examination of the 20 values randomly generated for a Poisson distribution with $\lambda = 6.5$ shows that actually 100% of the values are within this range.

Graphing Poisson distributions

The values in table A.2 can be used to graph a Poisson distribution with the x values on the x axis and the probabilities on the y axis. Figure 5.3 shows the distribution for $\lambda = 1.6$. The graph reveals a distribution skewed to the right. With a mean of 1.6 and a possible range of x from zero to infinity, the values will obviously 'bunch up' between 1 and 2. Consider, however, the graph of the Poisson distribution for $\lambda = 6.5$ in figure 5.4. Note that, with $\lambda = 6.5$, the probabilities are greatest for the values of 5, 6, 7 and 8. The graph is less skewed because the probability of occurrence of values near zero is small, as are the probabilities of large values of x.

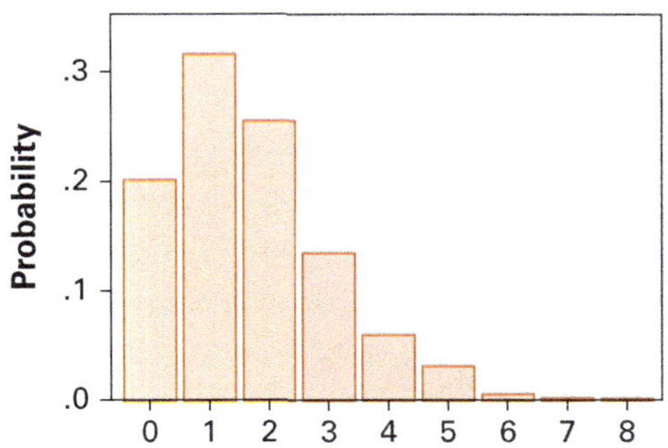

FIGURE 5.3 Graph of the Poisson distribution for $\lambda = 1.6$

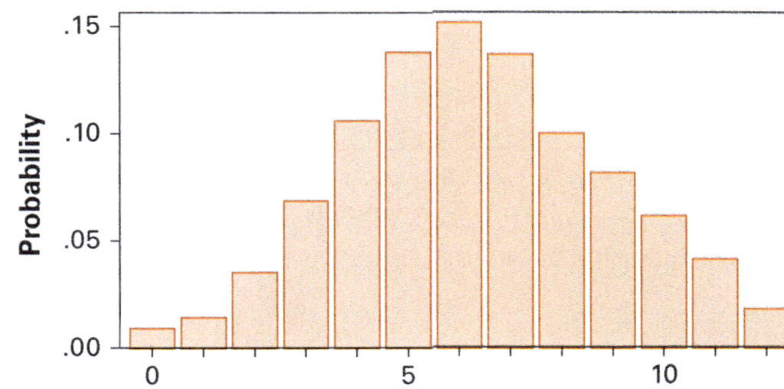

FIGURE 5.4 Graph of the Poisson distribution for $\lambda = 6.5$

Poisson approximation of the binomial distribution

Certain binomial distributions can be approximated by using the Poisson distribution. This is possible since the two distributions are related. The intervals of a Poisson distribution can be subdivided into n very small subintervals; the probability of success in any subinterval is given by $p = \frac{\lambda}{n}$, and this has an approximately binomial distribution.

Binomial distributions with large number of trials, n, and small values of p, which then generate rare events, are potential candidates for use of the Poisson distribution. As a rule of thumb, if $n > 20$ and $np \leq 7$, the approximation is close enough to use the Poisson distribution for binomial problems. If these conditions are met and the binomial distribution is a candidate for this process, the procedure begins with computation of the mean of the binomial distribution, $\mu = np$. The expected value of the binomial distribution approximates the expected value, λ, of the Poisson distribution, allowing the approximation of binomial probabilities using probabilities from a Poisson table or by using the Poisson formula 5.7.

As an example, the following binomial distribution problem can be solved by using the Poisson distribution. If $n = 50$ and $p = .03$, what is the probability that $x = 4$; i.e. $P(x = 4) = ?$

To solve this problem, first determine lambda:

$$\lambda = \mu = np = (50)(.03) = 1.5$$

As $n > 20$ and $np \leq 7$, this problem is a candidate for the Poisson approximation. For $x = 4$, table A.2 yields a probability of .0471 for the Poisson approximation.

For comparison, solving the problem exactly by using the binomial formula 5.4 yields:

$$\binom{50}{4}(.03^4)(.97^{46}) = .0459$$

The Poisson approximation is .0012 greater than the result obtained by using the binomial formula to solve the problem.

A graph of this binomial distribution is shown in figure 5.5 (overleaf) and a graph of the Poisson distribution with $\lambda = 1.5$ is shown in figure 5.6 (overleaf). In comparing the two graphs, it is difficult to see a difference between the binomial distribution and the Poisson distribution because the approximation of the binomial distribution by the Poisson distribution is very close.

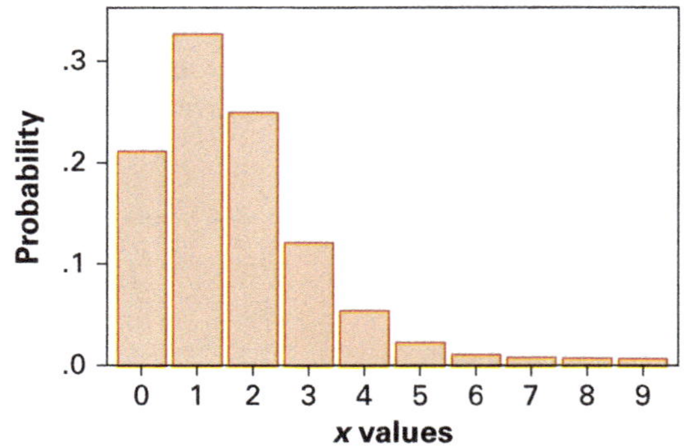

FIGURE 5.5 Graph of the binomial distribution with $n = 50$ and $p = 0.03$

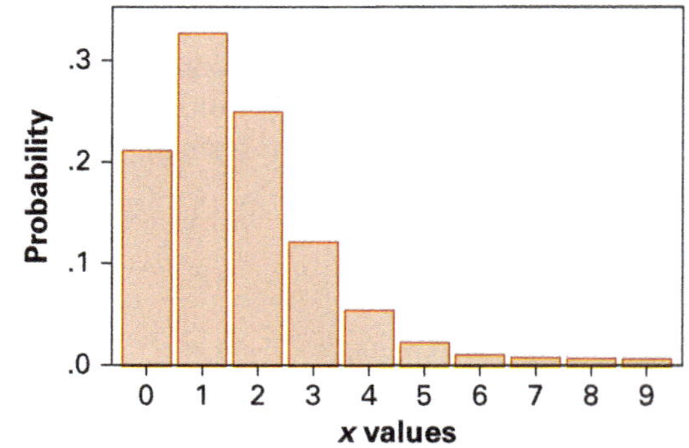

FIGURE 5.6 Graph of the Poisson distribution with $\lambda = 1.5$

DEMONSTRATION PROBLEM 5.10

PROBLEM: Suppose the probability of a bank making a mistake in processing a deposit is .0003. If 10 000 (n) deposits are audited, what is the probability that more than six mistakes will be found?

SOLUTION:

$$\lambda = \mu = np = (10\,000)(.0003) = 3.0$$

Because $n > 20$ and $np \leq 7$, the Poisson distribution is a good approximation of the binomial distribution. The extract below of table A.2 shows the probabilities.

$\lambda = 3.0$	
x	**Probability**
7	.0216
8	.0081
9	.0027
10	.0008
11	.0002
12	.0001
	$x > 6 = .0335$

To solve this problem by using the binomial formula requires starting with $x = 7$.

$$\binom{10000}{7}(.0003)^7(.9997)^{9993}$$

This process would continue for x values of 8, 9, 10, 11, . . . until the probabilities approach zero. Obviously, the process using the binomial formula requires more calculations, making the Poisson approximation an attractive alternative.

PRACTICE PROBLEMS

Practising the calculations

5.14 Find the following values by using the Poisson formula.

a. $P(x = 4|\lambda = 3.2)$
b. $P(x = 3|\lambda = 2.3)$
c. $P(x \leq 4|\lambda = 5.1)$
d. $P(x = 0|\lambda = 3.5)$
e. $P(x = 2|\lambda = 3.7)$
f. $P(2 < x < 5|\lambda = 3.6)$

5.15 Find the following values by using table A.3.

a. $P(x = 6|\lambda = 3.8)$
b. $P(x > 7|\lambda = 2.9)$
c. $P(3 \leq x \leq 9|\lambda = 4.2)$
d. $P(x = 0|\lambda = 1.9)$
e. $P(x \leq 6|\lambda = 2.9)$
f. $P(5 < x \leq 8|\lambda = 5.7)$

5.16 Sketch the graphs of the following Poisson distributions. Compute the mean and standard deviation for each distribution. Locate the mean on the graph. note how the probabilities are grouped around the means.

a. $\lambda = 6.3$
b. $\lambda = 1.3$
c. $\lambda = 8.9$
d. $\lambda = 0.6$

Testing your understanding

P05-17 **5.17** In any given month, a busy port can have many cargo ships arriving. The following table displays the data collected over a month of ship arrivals at a particular port, with a total of 76. The following data will allow the managers of the port to formulate staffing plans for crews to load and unload the vessels.

Day	Arrivals	Day	Arrivals	Day	Arrivals
1	3	11	5	21	6
2	2	12	6	22	2
3	4	13	0	23	0
4	1	14	1	24	3
5	0	15	2	25	4
6	2	16	2	26	3
7	0	17	3	27	2
8	3	18	0	28	1
9	2	19	4	29	4
10	4	20	5	30	2

Assume that the number of arrivals per day has a Poisson distribution.

a. What is the probability of zero arrivals in any given day?
b. What is the probability of two arrivals in any given day?
c. The manager's standard plan should provide a 90% service rate — it should include adequate manpower and other resources to service 90% of the vessels on their arrival date. How many arrivals per day should the standard plan anticipate?

P05-18 **5.18** A restaurant manager is interested in predicting customer load and has been advised that a statistical approach can be applied in this case. She begins the process by gathering data. Restaurant staff count customers every 5 minutes from 7.00 pm until 8.00 pm every Saturday night for three weeks. the data are shown below. Assume that customer arrivals have a Poisson distribution with mean λ for a 5-minute interval. After the data are gathered, the manager computes λ using the data from all three weeks as a single data set. What value of λ did she find? use the value of λ computed by the manager and help the manager calculate the probabilities in parts (a) to (e) for the given interval between 7.00 pm and 8.00 pm on Saturday night.

Number of arrivals		
Week 1	**Week 2**	**Week 3**
3	1	5
6	2	3
4	4	5
6	0	3
2	2	5
3	6	4
1	5	7
5	4	3
1	2	4
0	5	8
3	3	1
3	4	3

a. Using λ, what is the probability that no customers arrive during any given 5-minute interval?
b. What is the probability that six or more customers arrive during any given 5-minute interval?
c. What is the probability that during a 10-minute interval fewer than four customers arrive?
d. What is the probability that between three and six (inclusive) customers arrive in any 10-minute interval?
e. What is the probability that exactly eight customers arrive in any 15-minute interval?
f. Write a short non-technical report to assist the manager make decisions related to predicting the customer load.

5.19 According to the United nations Environmental Program and the World Health Organization, in Bombay, India, air pollution standards for particulate matter are exceeded on an average of 5.6 days in every 3-week period. Assume that the distribution of the number of days exceeding the standards per 3-week period is Poisson distributed.

a. What is the probability that the standard is not exceeded on any day during a 3-week period?
b. What is the probability that the standard is exceeded exactly 6 days in a 3-week period?
c. What is the probability that the standard is exceeded 15 or more days during a 3-week period? If this outcome actually occurred, what might you conclude?

5.20 The average number of annual trips per family to the beach in new Zealand is Poisson distributed, with a mean of 0.6 trips per year. What is the probability of randomly selecting a new Zealand family and finding the following?

a. The family did not make a trip to the beach last year.
b. The family took exactly one trip to the beach last year.

c. The family took two or more trips to the beach last year.
d. The family took three or fewer trips to the beach over a three-year period.
e. The family took exactly four trips to the beach during a six-year period.

5.21 Tropical cyclones are quite common in northern Australia during the summer months. Suppose the number of cyclones are Poisson distributed with a mean of 4.5 per cyclones season.

a. What is the probability of having no cyclones over a season?
b. What is the probability of having between three and four cyclones in a given season?
c. What is the probability of having over six cyclones in a given season? If this actually occurred, could you make any conclusions to support the argument for global warming? What might you conclude about lambda?

5.22 A pen company averages 1.2 defective pens per carton produced (200 pens). the number of defects per carton is Poisson distributed.

a. What is the probability of selecting a carton and finding no defective pens?
b. What is the probability of finding eight or more defective pens in a carton?
c. Suppose a purchaser of these pens will stop buying from the company if a carton contains more than three defective pens. What is the probability that the purchaser stops buying pens from the company?

5.23 A medical researcher estimates that the proportion of the population that has a rare blood disorder is 0.000 04. If the researcher randomly selects 100 000 people from the population, what is the probability that seven or more people have the rare blood disorder? What is the probability that more than 10 people have the rare blood disorder? Suppose the researcher finds more than 10 people who have the rare blood disorder in the sample of 100 000 that was taken from a particular geographic region. What might the researcher conclude from the results?

5.24 A data-management company records a large amount of data. Historically, 0.8% of the pages of data recorded by the company contain errors. If 150 pages of data are randomly selected, what is the probability that:

a. five or more pages contain errors
b. more than 15 pages contain errors
c. none of the pages contain errors
d. fewer than four pages contain errors?

MISUSE OF STATISTICS

Several points must be emphasised about the use of discrete distributions to analyse data. The independence and/or size assumptions must be met when using the binomial distribution in situations where sampling is done without replacement. Size and λ assumptions must be satisfied when using the Poisson distribution to approximate binomial problems. In either case, failure to meet such assumptions can result in spurious conclusions, leading to misuse of statistical results.

As n increases, the use of binomial distributions to compute exact x value probabilities becomes questionable in decision making. Although the probabilities are mathematically correct, as n becomes larger the probability of any particular x value becomes lower because there are more values among which to split the probabilities. For example, if $n = 100$ and $p = .50$, the probability of $x = 50$ is .0796. This probability of occurrence appears quite low, even though 50 is the expected value of this distribution and is also the value most likely to occur. It is more useful to decision makers and, in a sense, probably more informative to present an interval of values for larger sizes of n. In this example, it is probably more useful to examine $P(x > 50)$ than $P(x = 50)$.

In this chapter, the value of λ is assumed to be constant in a Poisson distribution experiment. Researchers may produce spurious results because the λ value changes during a study. For example, suppose the value of λ is obtained for the number of customer arrivals at a toy store between 7 pm and 9 pm in the month of December. Because a toy store is likely to have a high traffic volume in December, the use of this value of λ to analyse arrivals at the same store between noon and 2 pm in February would be inappropriate and, in a sense, unethical.

CHAPTER CASE
REVISITED

Mental health and young people

1. The study reports that 14% of 12–17-year-olds experience some sort of mental health issue. If 20 people between those ages are randomly selected, what is the probability that *more than 5* people have experienced a mental health issue? Converting 14% to a proportion, the value of p is .14, and this is a classic binomial distribution problem with $n = 20$ and $x = 6, 7, 8, 9$ and so on through to 20 (because the question asks for the probability of *more than 5*). Because the binomial distribution probability tables (table A.1) do not include $p = .14$, the problem is solved using the binomial formula for each of $x = 6, 7, 8, 9 \ldots, 20$.

$$\text{For } x = 6\text{: } \binom{20}{6}(.14)^6(.86)^{14} = 0.0353$$

   Solving for $x = 7, 8, 9, 10$ and 11 in a similar manner results in probabilities of 0.0115, 0.0030, 0.0007, 0.0001 and 0.0000, respectively. Since the probabilities approach zero at $x = 11$, we need not proceed on to $x = 12, 13, 14, \ldots, 20$. The answer to the question is therefore 0.0506. To further understand these probabilities, we calculate the expected value of this distribution as:

$$\mu = np = 20(.14) = 2.8$$

   In the long run, one would expect to average about three Australians between 12 and 17 years of age out of every 20 to have experienced some sort of mental health issue. In light of this, there is a very small probability that more than 5 in a random selection of 20 would do so.

2. The study also reported that only 1 in 4 young Australians experiencing a mental health issue seek professional support. Converting this to $p = .25$ and using $n = 20$ and $x > 6$, this, too, is a binomial problem and can be solved in the same way as question 1, obtaining the values below.

x	Probability
7	.112
8	.061
9	.003
10	.001

   The total of these probabilities is .177. Probabilities for all other values ($x > 10$) approach zero and are not included here. If 25% of young Australians experiencing a mental health issue are seeking professional support, the probability is 17.7% that, out of 20 randomly selected young Australians experiencing a mental health issue, more than 6 are seeking professional help. The expected number in any random sample of 20 is $(20)(.25) = 5$.

3. Suppose a survey of a youth health clinic shows that, on average, they receive 5 calls for help in a day. If this figure is correct, what is the probability that a youth health clinic will receive no calls in a day? Since random calls are generally thought to be Poisson distributed, this problem can be solved by using either the Poisson probability formula or the Poisson tables (table A.2). In this problem, $\lambda = 5$ and $x = 0$, and the probability associated with this is:

$$P(x) = \frac{\lambda^x e^{-\lambda}}{x!} \quad (e = 2.718\,282)$$

$$P(x = 0) = \frac{(5^0)(e^{-5})}{0!} = 0.0067$$

   What is the probability that a youth health clinic receives more than 10 calls in a day? Since this is a cumulative probability question ($x > 5$), the best option is to use the Poisson probability tables (table A.2) to obtain the values below.

x	Probability
10	.0181
11	.0082
12	.0034
13	.0013
14	.0005
15	.0002
Total	**.0317**

   There is a 3.17% chance that a youth health clinic receives more than 10 calls in a day if, on average, such a clinic averages 5 calls per day.

SUMMARY

1 Probability experiments produce random outcomes. A variable that represents the outcomes of a random experiment is called a random variable. Random variables, such that the set of all possible values is a finite or a countably infinite number of possible values, are called discrete random variables. Random variables that take on values at all points over a given interval are called continuous random variables. Discrete distributions are constructed from discrete random variables. Continuous distributions are constructed from continuous random variables. Two discrete distributions are the binomial distribution and Poisson distribution.

2 Measures of central tendency and measures of variability can be applied to discrete distributions to compute a mean and a variance. The mean value of a discrete distribution is the long-run average of occurrences. This mean is calculated as the sum of the products of the value of the random variable and the probability of the random variable. The variance of a discrete distribution is determined by using the outcomes and probabilities of outcomes in a manner similar to that of computing a mean.

3 The binomial distribution fits experiments when only two mutually exclusive outcomes are possible. In theory, each trial in a binomial experiment must be independent of the other trials. However, if the population size is large enough in relation to the sample size ($n < 5\%N$), the binomial distribution can be used where applicable in cases where the trials are not independent. The probability of getting a desired positive outcome in any one trial is denoted as p, which is the probability of a success. The binomial formula is used to determine the probability of obtaining x successes in n trials. Binomial distribution problems can be solved more rapidly using binomial tables than by using a formula. Table A.1 contains binomial tables for selected values of n and p. In the absence of tables, any problem using binomial distribution can be solved with Excel. The binomial distribution is used in statistical quality control situations to determine upper and lower limits of defective items in the manufacturing environment and to determine risks to producers and consumers when a lot of a product is accepted by the consumer.

4 The Poisson distribution is usually used to analyse phenomena that produce rare occurrences. The only information required to generate a Poisson distribution is the long-run average, which is denoted by lambda (λ). The Poisson distribution is related to occurrences over some intervals. The assumptions are that each occurrence is independent of other occurrences and that the value of lambda remains constant throughout the experiment. Poisson probabilities can be determined by either the Poisson formula or the Poisson tables in table A.2. The Poisson distribution can be used to approximate a binomial distribution when n is large ($n > 20$), p is small and $np \leq 7$. The Poisson distribution is used in the design of customer service operations and allocation of workloads in customer call centres.

KEY TERMS

binomial distribution p. 143
continuous random variables p. 138
discrete random variable p. 137
mean or expected value p. 140
Poisson distribution p. 155
random variable p. 137

KEY EQUATIONS

EQUATION	DESCRIPTION	FORMULA
5.1	**Mean or expected value of a discrete distribution**	$\mu = E(x) = \Sigma[xP(x)]$
5.2	**Variance of a discrete distribution**	$\sigma^2 = \Sigma[(x-\mu)^2 P(x)]$
5.3	**Standard deviation of a discrete distribution**	$\sigma = \sqrt{\Sigma[(x-\mu)^2 P(x)]}$

EQUATION	DESCRIPTION	FORMULA
5.4	**Binomial formula**	$P(x)=\binom{n}{x}p^x q^{n-x}=\frac{n!}{x!(n-x)!}p^x q^{n-x}$
5.5	**Mean of a binomial distribution**	$\mu=np$
5.6	**Standard deviation of a binomial distribution**	$\sigma=\sqrt{npq}$
5.7	**Poisson formula**	$P(x)=\frac{\lambda^x e^{-\lambda}}{x!}$

REVIEW PROBLEMS

Practising the calculations

5.25 Solve the following binomial distribution problems by using the binomial formula.

a. If $n = 12$ and $p = .33$, what is the probability that $x = 5$?
b. If $n = 7$ and $p = .60$, what is the probability that $x \geq 1$?
c. If $n = 8$ and $p = .80$, what is the probability that $x > 9$?
d. If $n = 12$ and $p = .75$, what is the probability that $x \leq 5$?

5.26 Use table A.1 to find the values of the following binomial distribution probabilities.

a. $P(x = 14 \mid n = 20 \text{ and } p = .60)$
b. $P(x < 5 \mid n = 10 \text{ and } p = .30)$
c. $P(x \geq 12 \mid n = 15 \text{ and } p = .60)$
d. $P(x > 20 \mid n = 25 \text{ and } p = .40)$

5.27 Use the Poisson formula to solve the following Poisson distribution problems.

a. If $\lambda = 1.10$, what is the probability that $x = 3$?
b. If $\lambda = 7.57$, what is the probability that $x \leq 1$?
c. If $\lambda = 3.6$, what is the probability that $x > 6$?

5.28 Use table A.2 to solve the following Poisson distribution probabilities.

a. $P(x = 3 \mid \lambda = 1.8)$
b. $P(x < 5 \mid \lambda = 3.3)$
c. $P(x \geq 3 \mid \lambda = 2.1)$
d. $P(2 < x \leq 5 \mid \lambda = 4.2)$

Testing your understanding

5.29 Suppose that 20% of all sharemarket investors are retired people. Suppose a random sample of 25 sharemarket investors is taken.

a. What is the probability that exactly seven are retired people?
b. What is the probability that 10 or more are retired people?
c. How many retired people would you expect to find in a random sample of 25 sharemarket investors?

5.30 In a manufacturing plant, two machines (A and B) produce a particular part. Machine B is newer and faster. In a 5-minute period, a lot consisting of 32 parts is produced. Twenty-two parts are produced by machine B and the rest by machine A. Suppose an inspector randomly samples a dozen parts from this lot.

a. What is the probability that exactly three parts were produced by machine A?
b. What is the probability that half of the parts were produced by each machine?
c. What is the probability that all of the parts were produced by machine B?
d. What is the probability that seven, eight or nine parts were produced by machine B?
e. Using the calculations in parts (a) to (d), determine whether one machine is better than the other.

5.31 Suppose that for every lot of 100 computer chips a company produces, an average of 1.4 are defective. Another company buys many lots of these chips at a time, from which one lot is selected randomly and tested for defects. If the tested lot contains more than three defects, the buyer will reject all the lots sent in that batch. What is the probability that the buyer will accept the lots? Assume that the defects per lot are Poisson distributed.

5.32 According to ABS data, 40% of Australians above the age of 65 have chronic heart disease. Suppose you live in a state where the environment is conducive to good health and low stress, and you believe the conditions in your state promote healthy hearts. To investigate this theory, you conduct a random telephone survey of 20 persons over 65 years of age in your state.

a. On the basis of the figure from the ABS, what is the expected number of persons in your survey who have a chronic heart condition?

b. Suppose only one person in your survey has a chronic heart condition. What is the probability of finding one or fewer people with a chronic heart condition in a sample of 20 if 40% of the population in this age bracket has this health problem? What do you conclude about your state from the sample data?

5.33 According to an industry survey, women make more digital photo prints than men. Eighty per cent of users of digital photo printing kiosks are women. Sixty-three per cent of women think that digital prints are important, compared with only 53% for men. Also, 19% of women use an online photo printing service, compared with 15% for men.

a. Suppose a random sample of 10 people who use a particular digital photo printing kiosk is selected. What is the probability that more than seven of them are women? What is the expected number of women in the sample?

b. If a random sample of 15 women is selected, what is the probability that all of them think that digital prints are important? What is this probability for a random sample of 15 men?

c. A random sample of 20 men is selected. What is the probability that none of them use an online photo printing service? If this event actually occurred, what might you conclude about the percentage of men who use an online photo printing service?

d. In each of parts (a) to (c), interpret your results in relation to this particular printing kiosk.

5.34 Suppose that, for every family holiday trip of more than 2000 km by car, an average of 0.60 flat tyres occurs. Suppose also that the number of flat tyres per trip of more than 2000 km is Poisson distributed.

a. What is the probability that a family taking a trip of more than 2000 km will have no flat tyres?

b. What is the probability that the family will have three or more flat tyres on such a trip?

c. Suppose trips are independent and the rate of flat tyres is the same for all trips of more than 2000 km. If a family takes two trips of more than 2000 km during a summer, what is the probability that the family will have no flat tyres on either trip?

5.35 One of the most useful applications of the Poisson distribution is in analysing visitor numbers on websites. Analysts generally believe that visitor number numbers are Poisson distributed. Suppose a large e-commerce website averages 12 600 visits per minute.

a. What is the probability that there will be 13 000 hits in any given minute?

b. If a server can handle a maximum of 15 000 hits per minute, what is the probability that it will be unable to handle the calls in any 1-minute period?

c. What is the probability that between 12 000 and 13 000 hits will occur in any given minute?

d. What is the probability that 5000 or fewer hits will arrive in a 15-second interval?

CHAPTER

6 The normal distribution and other continuous distributions

LEARNING OBJECTIVES

After studying this chapter, you should be able to:

1. describe the important features of the normal distribution
2. explain what is meant by the standardised normal distribution
3. recognise and solve problems involving the normal distribution
4. use the normal distribution to approximate binomial distributions in solving problems
5. understand concepts relating to the uniform distribution
6. know how and when to use the exponential distribution to solve problems.

OPENING VIGNETTE

Healthy body temperature

Various medical journals have reported that the human body temperature is normally distributed with an average temperature of 36.8 °C and a standard deviation of 0.7 °C. This information has been invaluable for doctors over the years as it has allowed them to treat and monitor their patients' health successfully.

For example, based on health and wellbeing studies, 'ideally healthy' people have a body temperature somewhere between 36.2 °C and 37.4 °C. A large percentage of people will lie somewhere within this 'ideally healthy' body temperature range.

However, doctors also set both upper and lower body temperature limits that alert them to possible health-related issues for their patients. Any patient who approaches these limits would likely be considered unwell, with something perhaps not quite right. The doctor might then recommend the patient undergo further tests or possibly see a specialist.

Then there are those patients presenting to a doctor that have a fever. In these instances, a patient's body temperature would be at the very upper limit of possible values for the normal distribution of human body temperature. Temperatures at these very upper limits would prompt cause for concern from a doctor and likely result in immediate medical attention and treatment of the patient.

Introduction

This chapter discusses continuous distributions. **Continuous distributions** *are associated with random variables that can take values at every point over a given interval*. They are usually generated from experiments where things are measured. For example, continuous variables can include items or products involving height, weight, length and time. The values given to these variables will need to be measured. In contrast, discrete distributions typically assign variables a value that can be counted.

Continuous distributions are fundamental to understanding and applying inferential statistical techniques. In particular, the normal distribution is a continuous distribution that provides the basis for much inferential statistics work involving probabilities. Inferential statistics is of importance to business managers as it can be one of the tools used to help make decisions. In business situations, the normal distribution has been found to approximate many practical distributions of variables observed in everyday life. Hence, with an understanding of the normal distribution, techniques involving inferential statistics can be developed. The normal distribution is, therefore, the emphasis of this chapter. In addition, two other continuous distributions are also presented toward the end of this chapter. They are the uniform and exponential distributions. The general shape of these three distributions can be seen in figure 6.1. Other continuous distributions also exist, including the t distribution, chi-square distribution and F distribution.

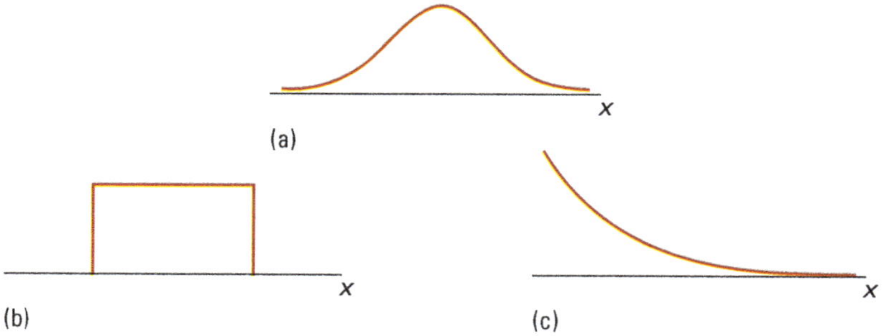

FIGURE 6.1 (a) Normal, (b) uniform and (c) exponential distributions

CHAPTER CASE

Prawn farm continues to grow

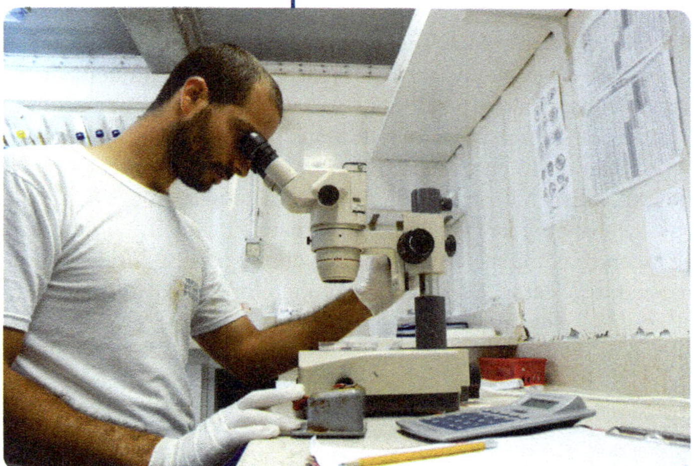

Sunny Bay Prawn Farm has grown prawns commercially in Australia since 1990. It sells a large quantity of prawns to Japan where it has an enviable reputation for quality. As part of their operations, management carefully control all elements of the farming process. One of the crucial areas of the business is to closely monitor the growth of the prawns from the larval stage. Investing in monitoring of prawn growth rates over many years at various points in the prawn life cycle has resulted in increasing business success. This success has convinced management that they are close to finding the ideal growing conditions for the prawns on their farm. They also believe that the data they have collected over the years provide them with a valuable resource and competitive advantage. These historical data enable management to monitor the health of the prawns at all stages of the prawn life cycle.

Management continue to place great importance on monitoring the larval stage of the prawns. Changes in observed features or behaviour of larvae, compared with the previously collected data, provide management with an early warning indicator of possible changes to growing conditions. For example, changes can indicate possible problems with equipment controlling water temperature, water quality, food supply or some other process. Having detected a problem, and using appropriate statistical techniques, management can investigate, identify and correct any production process problems. This can then help in saving an otherwise endangered batch of prawn larvae. So, with strategic use of historical data combined with statistical analysis, management at Sunny Bay Prawn Farm have continued to grow more profitable prawns, as well as more and more prawns!

Questions to help managers make better decisions

1. Management have observed that, based on years of historical data, the lengths of their prawn larvae at two weeks of age are normally distributed. They use this observation when performing statistical analysis to make various decisions. Describe some of the characteristics that would be observed in a normal distribution of two-week-old prawn larvae.
2. Management believe the lengths of their two-week-old prawn larvae are normally distributed with $\mu = 7$ mm and $\sigma = 0.5$ mm. What percentage of prawn larvae would have lengths between 6.5 mm and 7.5 mm?
3. An employee on the farm visits one of the farm ponds where larvae are two weeks old and decides to perform a quick check of their health. The basis of this investigation is to use the information provided by management that the lengths of two-week-old prawn larvae are normally distributed with $\mu = 7$ mm and $\sigma = 0.5$ mm. The employee decides to select a single larva at random and measure its length. This single larva is 5 mm long. Based on management's values of μ and σ, what is the probability of catching a larva shorter than 5 mm? Is it likely that there is a problem with the larvae in this pond? What could the worker do to be more confident about any conclusions relating to the health of all the larvae in the pond?

6.1 The normal distribution

The **normal distribution** *has a bell-shaped appearance*. The shape of the normal distribution is shown in figure 6.2. This normal distribution is arguably the most widely known continuous distribution used in statistics. In our everyday lives, many continuous variables take values that follow a normal distribution. For example, various human characteristics such as height, weight and IQ have values that follow this distribution. Similarly, characteristics of trees, animals and insects also take values that can be seen to follow this distribution. In addition, many situations arise in business where values of variables can be seen to be normally (or approximately normally) distributed. For example, this could be the time taken to complete a task, or the volume of liquid injected into a bottle by a machine during a production process. Experience has therefore revealed many situations where values of a particular variable follow a normal distribution.

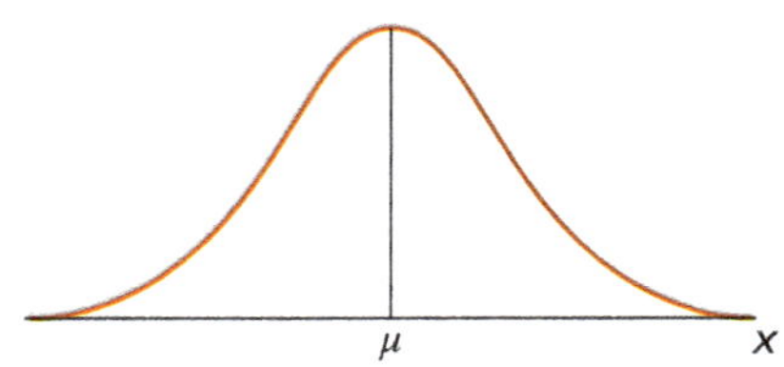

FIGURE 6.2 The normal distribution

This chapter will demonstrate how the normal distribution can be used to calculate probabilities. However, before doing so, it is important to note a clear distinction between calculating probabilities relating to discrete variables and continuous variables. When probabilities are calculated for discrete variable values such as 0, 1 and 2, a discrete distribution such as the binomial or Poisson distribution may be used. If the range of possible likely values is relatively small, it makes sense to talk about the probability of a single value occurring; for example, it is possible to calculate $P(x = 10)$ in a binomial distribution with $n = 20$ and $p = .4$. However, with a continuous distribution, it makes less sense to talk about the probability of a specific value occurring: for example, what is the probability of selecting one person, from a particular group, having a height of exactly 173.412 cm? This is most unlikely. Therefore, when using continuous distributions, a specified range of values needs to be used; for example, what is the probability that a person selected will have a height somewhere in the range of 170 cm to 175 cm? Importantly, when using continuous distributions, the probability of an outcome between two specified values occurring is determined by calculating the area under the curve between these two values. As a result, when dealing with continuous variables, the probability of an exact value is equal to zero; for example, if x is a continuous variable, $P(x = 173.412) = 0$. Hence, $P(a \le x \le b)$ and $P(a < x < b)$ are equal in value and can be used interchangeably.

To calculate a particular probability using the normal distribution, the area under the normal distribution curve over a specific range of values is required. From first principles, this area can be found using integral calculus involving complex calculations. This particular approach is not presented in this book. Instead, the solution techniques presented make use of tabulated z-scores. Using tabulated z-scores greatly simplifies the probability calculations. Alternatively, Excel can be used to quickly find probabilities between specific values.

History and characteristics of the normal distribution

The German mathematician and astronomer Karl Gauss (1777–1855) was one of the first to extensively use the normal distribution. Thus the normal distribution is sometimes referred to as the Gaussian distribution. To a lesser extent, some credit has been given to Pierre-Simon de Laplace

(1749–1827) for discovering the normal distribution. However, many people now believe that Abraham de Moivre (1667–1754), a French mathematician, first understood the normal distribution. De Moivre determined that the binomial distribution approached the normal distribution as a limit. De Moivre worked with remarkable accuracy. His published table values for the normal curve are only a few ten-thousandths off the values of currently published tables.

In order to understand how to apply the normal distribution to solve statistical problems, appreciating the important characteristics of this distribution is a good starting point. The key characteristics can be summarised as follows.

1. The normal distribution is referred to as being bell-shaped (see figure 6.2). It is a continuous distribution.
2. This bell-shape curve can be represented by formula 6.1, called the normal probability density function.

Probability density function of the normal distribution (6.1)

$$f(x)=\frac{1}{\sigma\sqrt{2\pi}}e^{-\left(\frac{1}{2}\right)\left[\frac{x-\mu}{\sigma}\right]^2}$$

where:

μ = mean of x

σ = standard deviation of x

π = 3.141 59 . . .

e = 2.718 28 . . .

It is from this function that areas under any normal probability distribution curve, over a specified range, can be calculated using integral calculus. These areas represent probabilities. However, since this formula is quite complex, using it to determine areas under the curve can be time consuming. To simplify things, specific area values under the normal probability distribution curve can be found in tables A.4 and A.5 in the appendices. These tabulated values will be used throughout this chapter (and others) to calculate probabilities.

3. The defining parameters of the normal distribution, as can be seen in the probability density function (formula 6.1), are the mean (μ) and standard deviation (σ). There are an infinite number of possible combinations of these two parameters. As a result, there are an infinite number of different normal distributions. This is sometimes referred to as a 'family' of distributions. Some distributions may have the same centre value (or mean) but different spreads (standard deviations). This is shown in figure 6.3. Alternatively, some distributions may have different means but the same standard deviation (see figure 6.4, overleaf).

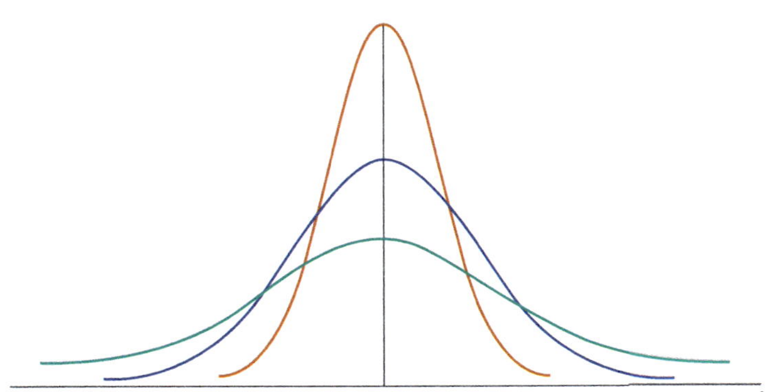

FIGURE 6.3 Three normal distributions with the same μ but different σ

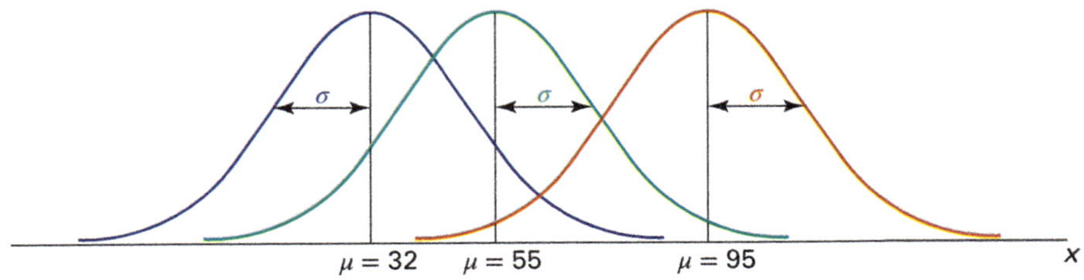

FIGURE 6.4 Three normal distributions with different μ but the same σ

4. The normal distribution is symmetrical and centred on the mean, with the mean also being equal to the median and mode. The distribution is unimodal (one mode), with the highest point on the normal distribution occurring at the value of the mean, median and mode.
5. As a result of the symmetrical nature of the normal probability distribution function, the shape of the curve to the right of the mean is identical to the shape of the curve to the left of the mean.
6. The total area under the curve of any normal probability distribution equals 1.
7. The area under the normal probability distribution to the left of the mean is .5 (or 50%). Since the curve is symmetrical, the area to the right of the mean is also .5.
8. The normal distribution is a continuous distribution where the ends of the curve (tails) extend horizontally to an infinite value in both directions but never touch the horizontal axis (i.e. asymptotic to the x axis). In reality, however, most applications of the normal distribution relate to experiments with finite limits of potential outcomes. For example, even though heights of people are taken to have a normal distribution, the range of heights of adults is bounded, with the shortest recorded adult height of 0.546 m (Chandra Bahadur Dangi, Nepal) and the tallest recorded adult height of 2.72 m (Robert Wadlow, USA, who died in 1940).
9. The empirical rule states the approximate percentage of values that lie within a given number of standard deviations from the mean if the data are normally distributed. This rule is used only for three multiples of the standard deviation: 1σ, 2σ and 3σ. For one standard deviation either side of the mean, the area under the normally distributed curve is approximately 68%. For two standard deviations either side, the area is approximately 95%, and, for three standard deviations, the area is 99.7%. Diagrammatically, this is shown in figure 6.5.

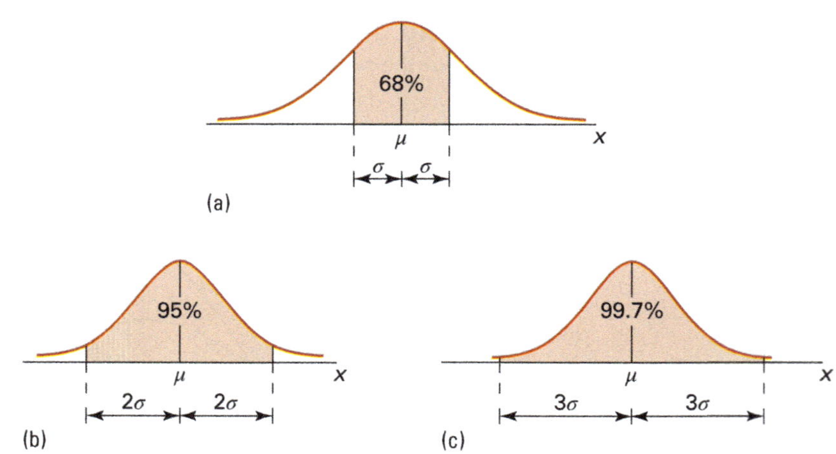

FIGURE 6.5 Areas under the normal distribution curve for (a) 1σ, (b) 2σ and (c) 3σ either side of the mean

PRACTICE PROBLEMS

Testing your understanding

6.1 The normal distribution can model many real-world characteristics that can be measured. Explain why the height of 18-year-old boys, the volume contained in 2-litre bottles of a particular brand of soft drink, and the time taken for marathon runners to complete a race would be expected to show characteristics that relate to a normal distribution.

6.2 Free range eggs are produced on a farm. The weight of eggs is found to be normally distributed with a mean of 55 g and a standard deviation of 1 g. Using the empirical rule and no calculations, determine whether a randomly chosen egg from the farm could have the following weight.

a. 51 g
b. 53 g
c. 56 g
d. 60 g

6.2 The standardised normal distribution

A characteristic of the normal distribution is that an infinite number ('family') of distributions can result from specifying different combinations of μ and σ. This implies that an infinite number of tables would be required if the probabilities relating to every normal distribution were to be calculated and tabulated. This is clearly not feasible. Fortunately, all normal probability distributions have the characteristic that the area under the curve equals 1. With this knowledge, and by selecting only one specific normal probability distribution, it is possible to calculate probabilities for this one specific distribution over various ranges of values. The particular normal distribution selected, as the basis for calculating probabilities for any other normal distribution, has a mean $\mu = 0$ and a standard deviation $\sigma = 1$. This distribution is called the **standardised normal distribution** or the z distribution. The probability values calculated over specific ranges of z-scores are typically presented in tabular form. These tabulated values provide a valuable tool for doing statistical calculations for any normal probability distribution. Two versions of the standardised normal distribution can be found in the appendix (tables A.4 and A.5).

To use the standarised normal distribution tabulated values, a given normal distribution with mean μ and standard deviation σ needs any x value of the given normal distribution to be transformed to a z-score using formula 6.2.

Standardisation (6.2)

$$z = \frac{x - \mu}{\sigma} \qquad (\sigma \neq 0)$$

This calculated value of z is referred to as the z-score. The interpretation of a z-score is the number of standard deviations that a value of x is above or below the mean.

- If the value of x is less than the mean, the z-score is negative.
- If the value of x is greater than the mean, the z-score is positive
- If the value of x equals the mean, the z-score equals zero.

This z formula allows conversion of the distance of any x value from its mean into standard deviation units (standardisation). A standard z-score table can be used to find probabilities for any normal distribution problem that has been converted to z-scores. This is because of the characteristic that all normal distributions have exactly the same area under the curve for 1, 1.46, 2, 2.5 etc. standard deviations away from the mean.

Recall that the empirical rule is based on the normal distribution, where about 68% of all values are within one standard deviation of the mean. It can be observed that, in the z distribution, about 68% $(= .3413 + 0.3413)$ of the z values are between $z_1 = -1$ and $z_1 = +1$, which is one standard deviation either side of the mean. This probability can be found in table A.4 in the appendix (which is reproduced in table 6.1 overleaf). Table A.4 gives probabilities for the standard normal distribution for positive values of z. The symmetry of the distribution can be used to find probabilities for negative values of z.

TABLE 6.1 The standardised normal distribution ($\mu = 0, \sigma = 1$)

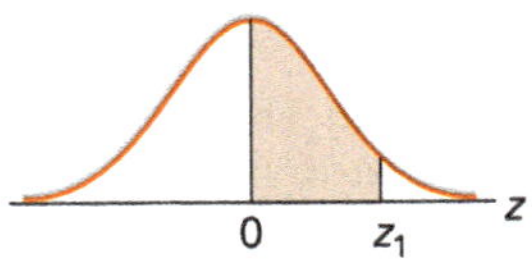

The entries in this table are the probabilities that a standard normal random variable is between 0 and z_1 (the shaded area).

z_1	0.00	0.01	0.02	0.03	0.04	0.05	0.06	0.07	0.08	0.09
0.0	.0000	.0040	.0080	.0120	.0160	.0199	.0239	.0279	.0319	.0359
0.1	.0398	.0438	.0478	.0517	.0557	.0596	.0636	.0675	.0714	.0753
0.2	.0793	.0832	.0871	.0910	.0948	.0987	.1026	.1064	.1103	.1141
0.3	.1179	.1217	.1255	.1293	.1331	.1368	.1406	.1443	.1480	.1517
0.4	.1554	.1591	.1628	.1664	.1700	.1736	.1772	.1808	.1844	.1879
0.5	.1915	.1950	.1985	.2019	.2054	.2088	.2123	.2157	.2190	.2224
0.6	.2257	.2291	.2324	.2357	.2389	.2422	.2454	.2486	.2517	.2549
0.7	.2580	.2611	.2642	.2673	.2704	.2734	.2764	.2794	.2823	.2852
0.8	.2881	.2910	.2939	.2967	.2995	.3023	.3051	.3078	.3106	.3133
0.9	.3159	.3186	.3212	.3238	.3264	.3289	.3315	.3340	.3365	.3389
1.0	.3413	.3438	.3461	.3485	.3508	.3531	.3554	.3577	.3599	.3621
1.1	.3643	.3665	.3686	.3708	.3729	.3749	.3770	.3790	.3810	.3830
1.2	.3849	.3869	.3888	.3907	.3925	.3944	.3962	.3980	.3997	.4015
1.3	.4032	.4049	.4066	.4082	.4099	.4115	.4131	.4147	.4162	.4177
1.4	.4192	.4207	.4222	.4236	.4251	.4265	.4279	.4292	.4306	.4319
1.5	.4332	.4345	.4357	.4370	.4382	.4394	.4406	.4418	.4429	.4441
1.6	.4452	.4463	.4474	.4484	.4495	.4505	.4515	.4525	.4535	.4545
1.7	.4554	.4564	.4573	.4582	.4591	.4599	.4608	.4616	.4625	.4633
1.8	.4641	.4649	.4656	.4664	.4671	.4678	.4686	.4693	.4699	.4706
1.9	.4713	.4719	.4726	.4732	.4738	.4744	.4750	.4756	.4761	.4767
2.0	.4772	.4778	.4783	.4788	.4793	.4798	.4803	.4808	.4812	.4817
2.1	.4821	.4826	.4830	.4834	.4838	.4842	.4846	.4850	.4854	.4857
2.2	.4861	.4864	.4868	.4871	.4875	.4878	.4881	.4884	.4887	.4890
2.3	.4893	.4896	.4898	.4901	.4904	.4906	.4909	.4911	.4913	.4916
2.4	.4918	.4920	.4922	.4925	.4927	.4929	.4931	.4932	.4934	.4936
2.5	.4938	.4940	.4941	.4943	.4945	.4946	.4948	.4949	.4951	.4952
2.6	.4953	.4955	.4956	.4957	.4959	.4960	.4961	.4962	.4963	.4964
2.7	.4965	.4966	.4967	.4968	.4969	.4970	.4971	.4972	.4973	.4974
2.8	.4974	.4975	.4976	.4977	.4977	.4978	.4979	.4979	.4980	.4981
2.9	.4981	.4982	.4982	.4983	.4984	.4984	.4985	.4985	.4986	.4986
3.0	.4987	.4987	.4987	.4988	.4988	.4989	.4989	.4989	.4990	.4990
3.1	.4990	.4991	.4991	.4991	.4992	.4992	.4992	.4992	.4993	.4993
3.2	.4993	.4993	.4994	.4994	.4994	.4994	.4994	.4995	.4995	.4995
3.3	.4995	.4995	.4995	.4996	.4996	.4996	.4996	.4996	.4996	.4997
3.4	.4997	.4997	.4997	.4997	.4997	.4997	.4997	.4997	.4997	.4998
3.5	.4998									
4.0	.49997									
4.5	.499997									
5.0	.4999997									
6.0	.499999999									

PRACTICE PROBLEMS

Practising the calculations

6.3 Using $\mu = 25$ and $\sigma = 3$, calculate the corresponding *z*-scores for each of the following values of x.

a. 16
b. 20
c. 24
d. 28

6.4 Using $\mu = 100$ and $\sigma^2 = 25$, calculate the corresponding *z*-scores for each of the following values of *x*.

a. 85
b. 92
c. 103
d. 113

6.3 Solving normal distribution problems

Many statistical problems require finding the area under part of a normal distribution for a specified range of the variable. This is illustrated in the following demonstration problems. The first problem uses the standard normal distribution to provide practice in reading the standard normal tables. The next two problems require the transformation of a variable to a *z*-score and then finding probabilities from the standard normal tables.

DEMONSTRATION PROBLEM 6.1

PROBLEM: Using the *z* distribution, find:

a. $P(z < 1.5)$
b. $P(z > -1.5)$
c. $P(z > 1.5)$
d. $P(z < -2.3)$
e. $P(-1.5 < z < 2.3)$

SOLUTION: It is helpful to sketch a diagram of the normal distribution and shade the required area.

a. The solution to this question is not found directly using table 6.1. However, by using the properties of the normal distribution outlined in section 6.1 (see page 174, points 5, 6 and 7), the area to the left of $z = 0$ under the *z* distribution we know is .5. The area under the *z* distribution to the right of $z = 0$ and left of $z = 1.5$ is given in table 6.1 as .4332. So we can now calculate:

$$P(z < 1.5) = .5 + .4332 = .9332$$

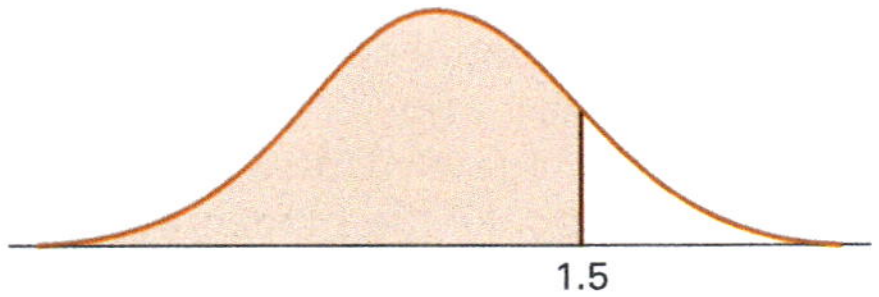

b. Using the symmetrical nature of the *z* distribution, and the solution to a. above, then:

$$P(z > -1.5) = P(z < 1.5) = .9332$$

c. Using the result from part a. where the area to the left of $z = 1.5$ equals .9332, and knowing that the total area under the normal distribution equals 1, the area to the right of $z = 1.5$ is:

$$P(z > 1.5) = 1 - P(z < 1.5) = 1 - .9332 = .0668$$

Alternatively, this problem can be solved by noting the area under the *z* distribution to the right of $z = 0$ equals .5. Also, the area between $z = 0$ and $z = 1.5$ from table 6.1 equals 0.4332, so the area to the right of $z = 1.5$ and under the *z* distribution must be:

$$P(z > 1.5) = .5 - P(0 < z < 1.5) = .5 - .4332 = .0668$$

d. $P(z < -2.3) = P(z > 2.3) = 1 - P(z < 2.3) = 1 - .9893 = .0107$

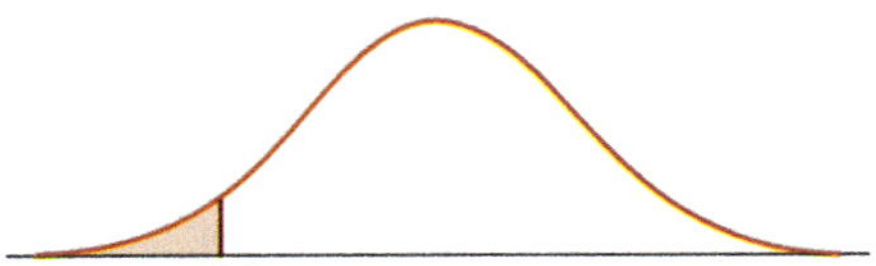

e. $P(-1.5 < z < 2.3) = P(-1.5 < z < 0) + P(0 < z < 2.3)$
$= P(0 < z < 1.5) + P(0 < z < 2.3)$
$= .4332 + .4893 = .9225$

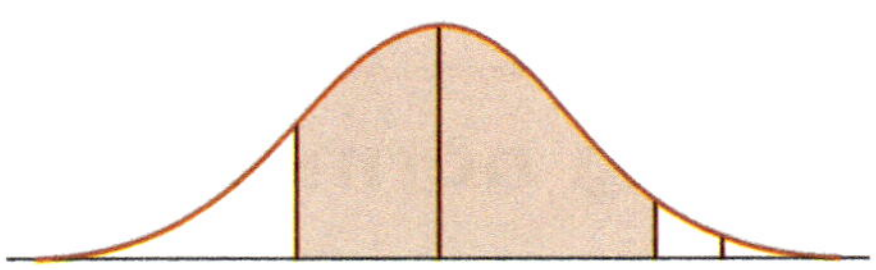

DEMONSTRATION PROBLEM 6.2

PROBLEM: For a variable x that is normally distributed with $\mu = 100$, $\sigma^2 = 36$, find:

a. $P(x > 110)$ b. $P(88 < x < 105)$

SOLUTION:

a. $P(x > 110) = P\left(z > \frac{110 - 100}{\sqrt{36}}\right) = P(z > 1.67) = .5 - P(0 < z < 1.67)$
$= .5 - .4525 = .0475$

b. $P(88 < x < 105) = P\left(\frac{88 - 100}{\sqrt{36}} < z < \frac{105 - 100}{\sqrt{36}}\right)$
$= P(-2 < z < .83)$
$= P(0 < z < 2) + P(0 < z < .83)$
$= .4772 + .2967 = .7739$

DEMONSTRATION PROBLEM 6.3

PROBLEM: A machine fills miniature bottles of wine to a mean volume of 210 ml with a standard deviation of 10 ml. The volumes of the bottles are known to be normally distributed. The label on the bottle specifies a volume of 200 ml. A bottle is underfilled if it contains less than this specified value.

a. What percentage of bottles are underfilled?
b. In order to reduce the percentage of underfilled bottles to 1%, the company decides to adjust the standard deviation of the volumes filled by the machine. What should the standard deviation be?

SOLUTION:

a. Let the random variable x denote the volume of the bottles. With the mean bottle volume being 210 ml and the standard deviation being 10 ml, we need:

$$P(x < 200) = P\left(z < \frac{200 - 210}{10}\right) = P(z < -1) = .5 - .3413 = .1587$$

So, 15.87% of the bottles are underfilled.

b. Let σ denote the new standard deviation of the volumes. We need:

$$P(x < 200) = P\left(z < \frac{200 - 210}{\sigma}\right) = P\left(z < \frac{-10}{\sigma}\right) = .01$$

Then $P\left(z > \frac{10}{\sigma}\right) = .01$, and $P\left(0 < z < \frac{10}{\sigma}\right) = .49$

From table 6.1, the z-score corresponding to a probability of .49 is 2.33, so we need:

$$\frac{10}{\sigma} = 2.33 \text{ and } \sigma = \frac{10}{2.33} = 4.3 \text{ ml}$$

USING EXCEL

Normal distribution

Excel can compute cumulative normal probabilities for particular values of x. For demonstration problem 6.3a, Excel can be used to solve the problem as follows.

1. From the Formulas tab, select Insert Function.
2. In the Insert Function dialogue box, select Statistical from the drop-down menu and then select the function NORM.DIST.

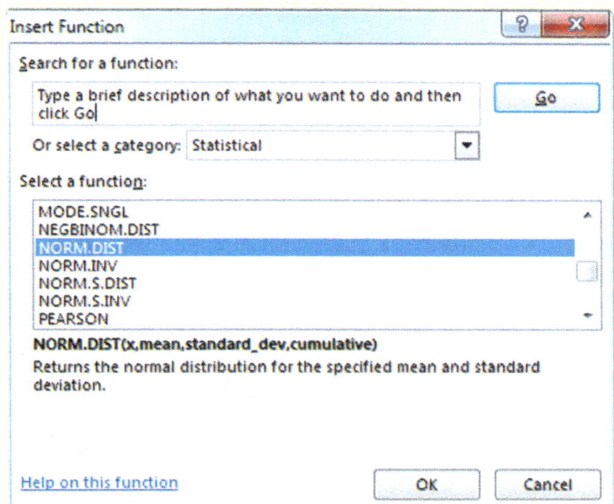

3. Click OK.
4. In the Function Arguments dialogue box:
   a. enter the value of x on the first line
   b. enter the mean on the second line
   c. enter the standard deviation on the third line
   d. enter TRUE on the fourth line to obtain cumulative probabilities for all values up to x. (If FALSE is entered on the fourth line, the value of the probability density function $f(x)$ is obtained for the specific value of x and a combination of mean and standard deviation. In this chapter, we are interested in probabilities, so we choose TRUE.)

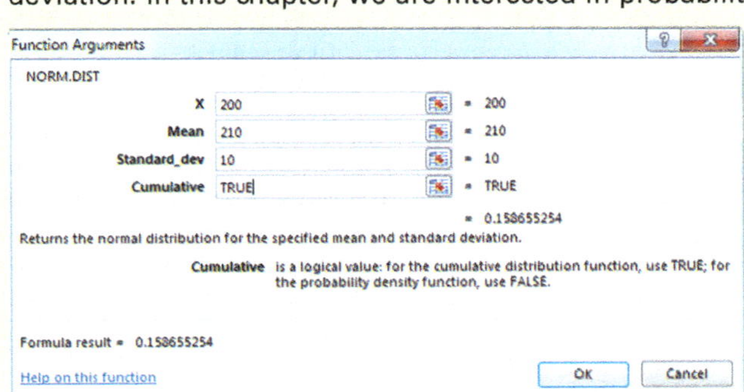

   e. click OK.

Excel will paste the formula into the spreadsheet and display the result.

DEMONSTRATION PROBLEM 6.4

PROBLEM: A biscuit manufacturer packs its biscuits into individual boxes using a machine. The weight is advertised on each box as 200 g. The machine has been operating for many years and is regularly inspected during production to ensure that it is operating correctly. A quality-control worker at the factory has used historical data from many previous production runs. It is known that the weight of packed boxes follows a normal distribution with a mean weight of 200 g and a standard deviation of 2.1 g. During a particular production run, a quality-control worker randomly selects one box and finds that the weight is 208.1 g. Using the empirical rule and the data from the machine's historical operational performance, would this box weight of 208.1 g be considered unusual?

SOLUTION: Using $\mu = 200$ g and $\sigma = 2.1$ g, the empirical rule indicates that 99.7% of all values for a normally distributed variable lie between $\mu - 3\sigma$ and $\mu + 3\sigma$. This implies that 99.7% of biscuit boxes packed by the machine, if it is performing as specified, should lie somewhere in the range:

$$\mu - 3\sigma = 200 - 3 \times 2.1 = 193.7 \text{ g}$$

$$\mu + 3\sigma = 200 + 3 \times 2.1 = 206.3 \text{ g}$$

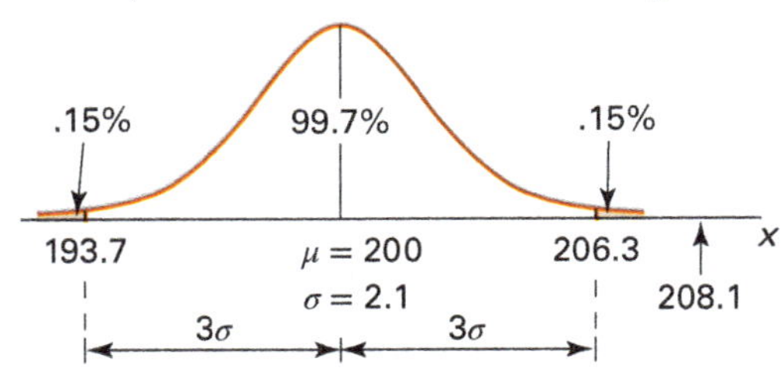

This indicates that the probability of any one particular box having a weight of 206.3 g or more is very low (.15%) if the machine is working correctly. It can also be noted that a box weighing 208.1 g is almost 4σ above the mean. The probability of a box with this weight or more is even lower than .15%. Therefore, it would be very unusual to select a box of biscuits weighing 208.1 g if the machine was operating as specified. These observations are shown in the graph above.

PRACTICE PROBLEMS

Practising the calculations

6.5 Determine the probability for the following intervals of the standard normal distribution.

a. $z \geq 1.96$
b. $z < 0.73$
c. $-1.46 < z \leq 2.84$
d. $-2.67 \leq z \leq 1.08$
e. $-2.05 < z \leq -0.87$

6.6 Determine the probabilities for the following normal distribution problems.

a. $\mu = 604, \sigma = 56.8, x \leq 635$
b. $\mu = 48, \sigma = 12, x < 20$
c. $\mu = 111, \sigma = 33.8, 100 \leq x < 150$
d. $\mu = 264, \sigma = 10.9, 250 < x < 255$
e. $\mu = 37, \sigma = 4.35, x > 35$
f. $\mu = 156, \sigma = 11.4, x \geq 170$

6.7 The values of investment properties in Brisbane are normally distributed with mean \$360 000 and standard deviation \$60 000. An investment property is randomly selected.

a. What is the probability that the property is worth less than \$300 000?
b. What is the probability that the property is worth more than half a million dollars?
c. What proportion of investment properties are worth between \$200 000 and \$400 000?

6.8 The age of real estate investors is found to be normally distributed with a mean of 40 years and a standard deviation of 10 years. What proportion of investors are below the age of 25?

6.9 Consider the average home mortgage in New Zealand of \$283 000 where the standard deviation of the mortgages is \$50 000 and home mortgages are normally distributed.

a. What proportion of home loans are more than \$250 000?
b. What proportion of home loans are between \$250 000 and \$300 000?
c. If a home loan is known to be more than \$250 000, what is the probability that it is less than \$280 000?

6.10 The Royal Automobile Club of Victoria estimates that the cost of running a small car is $150 per week, based on driving 15 000 km per year. Taking the cost to be normally distributed with a standard deviation of $10 per week, answer the following questions.

a. What proportion of small cars cost more than $170 per week to run?

b. What proportion of small cars cost between $120 and $180 per week to run?

c. You want to be 95% certain that the weekly cost of running your small car will not exceed your budgeted amount. How much should you budget?

6.11 You are working with a data set where the variable is normally distributed, with a mean of 200 and a standard deviation of 47. In each of the following cases, determine the value of x_1.

a. 60% of the values are greater than x_1.

b. 17% of the values are greater than x_1.

c. 22% of the values are less than x_1.

d. x_1 is greater than 55% of the values.

6.12 Solve the following problems, assuming that the data are normally distributed.

a. The standard deviation of the distribution is 12.56, and 71.97% of the values are greater than 56. What is the value of μ?

b. The mean of the distribution is 352, and only 13.35% of the values are less than 300. What is the value of σ?

MISUSE OF STATISTICS

In business situations, managers may make the assumption that a population variable of interest is normally distributed. However, this assumption may or may not be true. If the assumption is not valid, the results obtained can result in misleading conclusions being reached or poor decisions being made. Worse still, knowingly basing calculations on the assumption that a variable is normally distributed, when it is known not to be, is unethical. Some form of exploratory evaluation to assess the assumption that a variable is normally distributed should be made where important decisions are being based on this assumption. It is therefore important to be aware of any implications of making the assumption of normality when performing calculations.

6.4 The normal distribution approximation to the binomial distribution

The normal distribution can be used to approximate the probabilities for certain types of binomial distribution problems. As sample sizes become large, binomial distributions approach the normal distribution in shape regardless of the value of p. When p is near .50, this phenomenon is observed to occur for a smaller value of n compared with when p is larger or smaller than .50. This can be seen by examining the three binomial distributions in figures 6.6, 6.7 and 6.8 (overleaf). Note in figure 6.6 (n = 10 and p = .50) that, even though the sample size is only 10, the binomial distribution bears a strong resemblance to a normal distribution. The graph in figure 6.7 (n = 10 and p = .20) is skewed to the right because of the low value of p and the small value of n. For this distribution, the expected value is only 2 and the probabilities 'bunch up' at x = 0 and 1. However, when n becomes large enough, as in the binomial distribution in figure 6.8 (n = 100 and p = .20), the graph is relatively symmetrical around the mean ($\mu = np = 20$) because enough possible outcome values to the left of x = 20 allow the distribution to fall back to the x axis. For large n values, the binomial distribution is cumbersome to use without a computer. Note that table A.1 in the appendix provides values of n only to 25, so if n is larger than this, the necessary hand calculation of probabilities becomes time consuming and cumbersome. Fortunately, the normal distribution is a good approximation for the binomial distribution for large values of n.

To solve a binomial problem using the normal distribution requires a translation process. The first part of this process is to convert the two parameters of a binomial distribution, n and p, into the two parameters of the normal distribution, μ and σ.

Mean of a binomial distribution (6.3)

$$\mu = np$$

Standard deviation of a binomial distribution (6.4)

$$\sigma = \sqrt{npq}$$

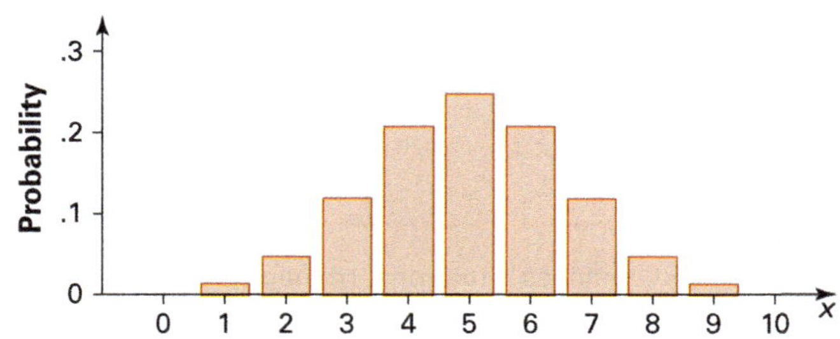

FIGURE 6.6 The binomial distribution for $n = 10$ and $p = .50$

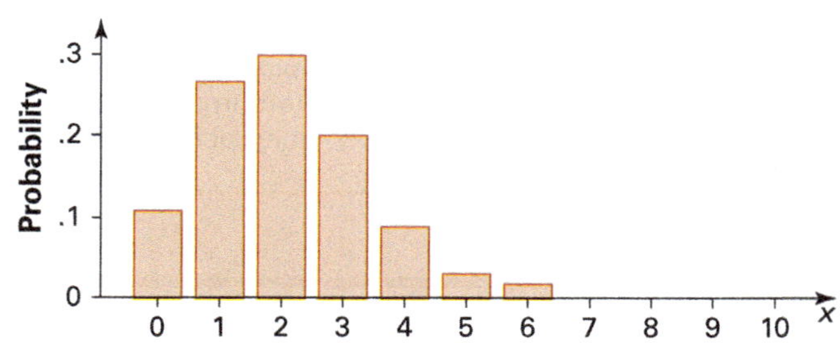

FIGURE 6.7 The binomial distribution for $n = 10$ and $p = .20$

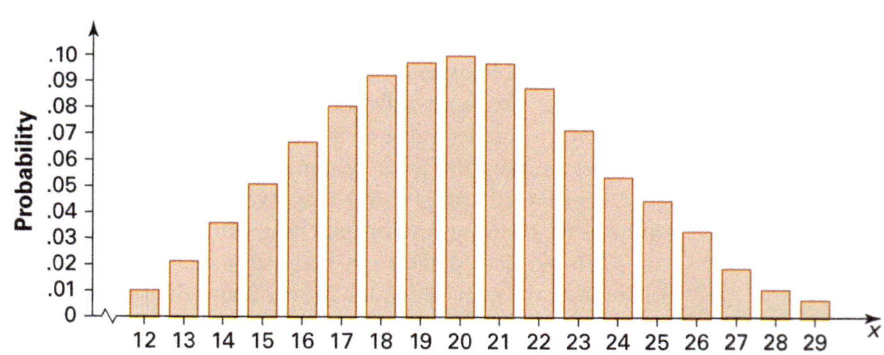

FIGURE 6.8 The binomial distribution for $n = 100$ and $p = .20$

Having established the parameters for the normal distribution, a test must now be performed to determine if the normal distribution is a good enough approximation to the particular binomial distribution of interest. To do this, the following question needs to be answered. Does the interval

$\mu \pm 3\sigma$ lie between 0 and n? Recall that the empirical rule states that approximately 99.7% of the values of a normal distribution are within three standard deviations of the mean. For a normal distribution approximation of a binomial distribution problem to be acceptable, all possible x values should be between 0 and n, which are the lower and upper limits, respectively, of a binomial distribution. If $\mu \pm 3\sigma$ is not between 0 and n, do not use the normal distribution to solve a binomial problem because the approximation is not good enough. However, if this condition is satisfied, then the normal distribution is a good approximation for a binomial problem and the procedure can continue. Another rule of thumb for determining when to use the normal distribution to approximate a binomial problem is that the approximation is good enough if both $np > 5$ and $nq > 5$.

The process can be illustrated in the solution of the following binomial distribution problem:

$$P(x \geq 25 \mid n = 60 \text{ and } p = .30) = ?$$

Note that this binomial problem contains a relatively large sample size and that none of the binomial tables in appendix A.2 can be used to solve the problem. This problem is therefore a potentially good candidate for using the normal distribution approximation. Firstly, the translation from a binomial problem to a normal distribution problem is required, giving:

$$\mu = np = (60)(.30) = 18$$

$$\sigma = \sqrt{npq} = \sqrt{60(.30)(.70)} = 3.55$$

The binomial problem becomes a normal distribution approximation problem:

$$P(x \geq 25 \mid \mu = 18 \text{ and } \sigma = 3.55) = ?$$

Next, a test is required to determine whether this normal distribution sufficiently approximates this binomial distribution:

$$\mu \pm 3\sigma = 18 \pm 3(3.55) = 18 \pm 10.65$$

$$7.35 \leq \mu \pm 3\sigma \leq 28.65$$

This interval $\mu \pm 3\sigma$ does lie between 0 and 60, so the approximation is sufficient to allow use of the normal curve. Alternatively, both $np = (60)(.30) = 18 > 5$ and $nq = (60)(.70) = 42 > 5$, so the binomial distribution can be approximated by the the normal distribution with $\mu = 18$ and $\sigma = 3.55$. Figure 6.9 shows the binomial distribution when $n = 60$ and $p = .30$. Figure 6.10 shows the continuous normal probability distribution for when $\mu = 18$ and $\sigma = 3.55$. Notice how closely the discrete binomial distribution approximates the graph of the continuous normal distribution in this situation where n is large.

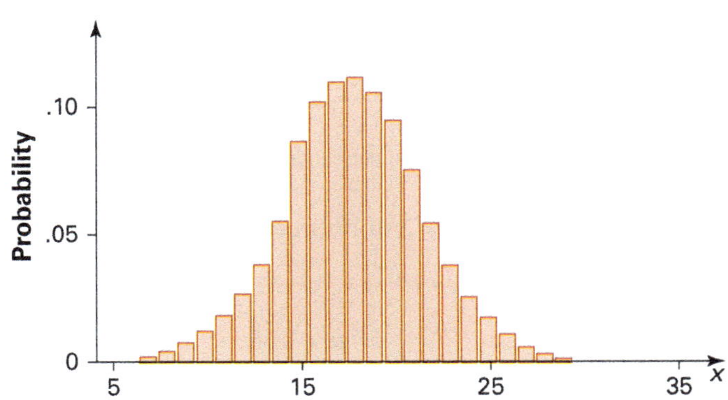

FIGURE 6.9 Graph of the binomial problem: $n = 60$ and $p = .30$

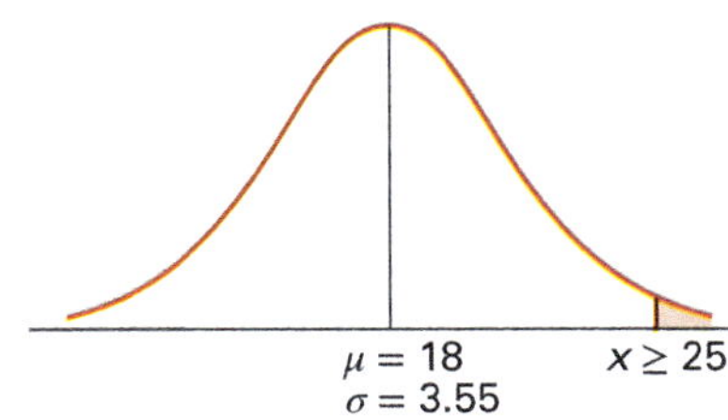

FIGURE 6.10 Graphical solution of the binomial problem approximated by the normal distribution

PRACTICE PROBLEMS

Practising the calculations

6.13 Determine whether the following binomial distributions can be adequately approximated by a normal distribution.

a. $p = .1$, $n = 10$
b. $p = .2$, $n = 30$
c. $p = .6$, $n = 15$
d. $p = .8$, $n = 15$
e. $p = .9$, $n = 60$

6.14 If each of the following binomial distributions can be approximated by a normal distribution, what are the values of the mean and standard deviation?

a. $p = .2$, $n = 25$
b. $p = .5$, $n = 25$
c. $p = .7$, $n = 40$
d. $p = .8$, $n = 40$
e. $p = .8$, $n = 100$

6.5 The uniform distribution

The **uniform distribution**, sometimes referred to as the rectangular distribution, is a relatively simple continuous distribution. The probability density function, *f(x)*, is constant over a specified range of values. The following probability density function (formula 6.5) defines a uniform distribution.

Probability density function of a uniform distribution (6.5)

$$f(x) = \begin{cases} \dfrac{1}{b-a} & \text{for } a \le x \le b \\ 0 & \text{for all other values} \end{cases}$$

Figure 6.11 is an example of a uniform distribution. Since the distribution is a probability density function, by definition, the total area under the curve is equal to 1. In this case, the area can be found by calculating the product of the side lengths of a rectangle.

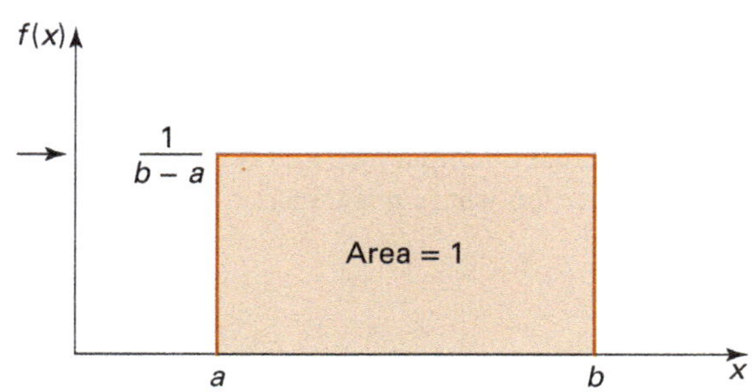

FIGURE 6.11 Uniform distribution

The mean and standard deviation of a uniform distribution are given below.

Mean of a uniform distribution (6.6)

$$\mu = \frac{a+b}{2}$$

Standard deviation of a uniform distribution (6.7)

$$\sigma = \frac{b-a}{\sqrt{12}}$$

To demonstrate how to calculate probabilities using the uniform distribution, consider the following example.

The ages of managers in an organisation range from 41 to 47 years and follow a uniform distribution. What is the probability that a randomly chosen manager is between 42 and 45 years old?

Since the continuous variable of age is indicated to follow a uniform distribution, and age ranges from 41 to 47, the base (horizontal axis) of the rectangular distribution is 6 years. For the distribution to be a uniform probability distribution, the other (vertical) side of the rectangle must be so that the product of the rectangle side lengths gives an area under the curve = 1. This is shown in figure 6.12.

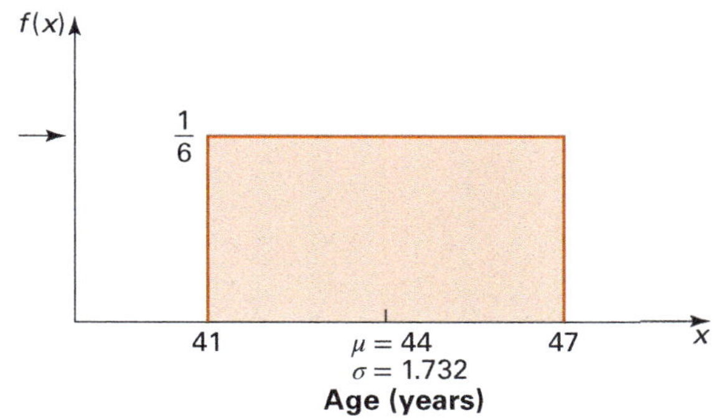

FIGURE 6.12 Distribution of ages of managers

Note that the mean and standard deviation of this distribution are:

$$\text{Mean} = \frac{a+b}{2} = \frac{41+47}{2} = \frac{88}{2} = 44$$

$$\text{Standard deviation} = \frac{b-a}{\sqrt{12}} = \frac{47-41}{\sqrt{12}} = \frac{6}{3.464} = 1.732$$

Using the probability distribution in figure 6.12 allows the following question to be answered: 'What is the probability that a randomly chosen manager is between 42 and 45 years old?'

The probability required is the rectangular area shaded in figure 6.13 over the range of x values from 42 to 45. The base of the rectangular area is 3 and the vertical side of the rectangle is $\frac{1}{6}$. Hence, the shaded area of the rectangle in figure 6.13 is:

$$\frac{1}{6} \times (45-42) = \frac{1}{6} \times 3 = .5$$

Therefore, the probability of selecting a manager with an age between 42 and 45 is .5 given that the distribution of ages follows a uniform distribution. Note that the probability of a manager being more than 47 years old is zero. Similarly, the probability that a manager is less than 41 years old is also zero.

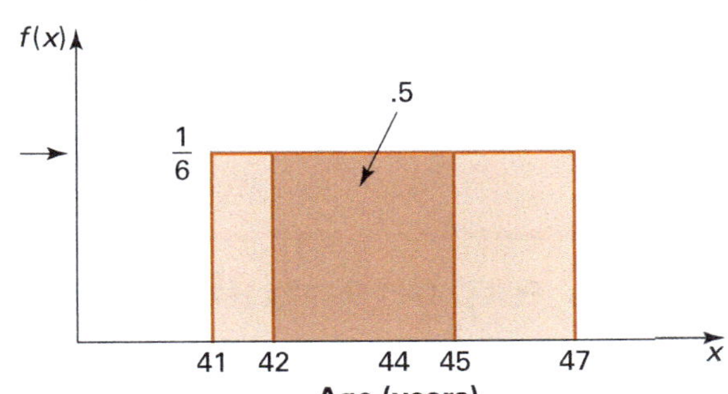

FIGURE 6.13 Calculating probabilities in a uniform distribution

DEMONSTRATION PROBLEM 6.5

PROBLEM: Annual home insurance costs in Australia are reported to be uniformly distributed between \$200 and \$1182. What are the mean and the standard deviation of this uniform distribution? What is the height of the distribution? What is the probability that a person's annual cost for home insurance in Australia is between \$410 and \$825?

SOLUTION: The value of $a = \$200$ and $b = \$1182$.

$$\mu = \frac{a+b}{2} = \frac{200+1182}{2} = \$691$$

$$\sigma = \frac{b-a}{\sqrt{12}} = \frac{1182-200}{\sqrt{12}} = \$283.48$$

The height of the distribution is:

$$\frac{1}{1182-200} = \frac{1}{982} = .001$$

$$P(410 \le x \le 825) = \frac{825-410}{1182-200} = \frac{415}{982} = .4226$$

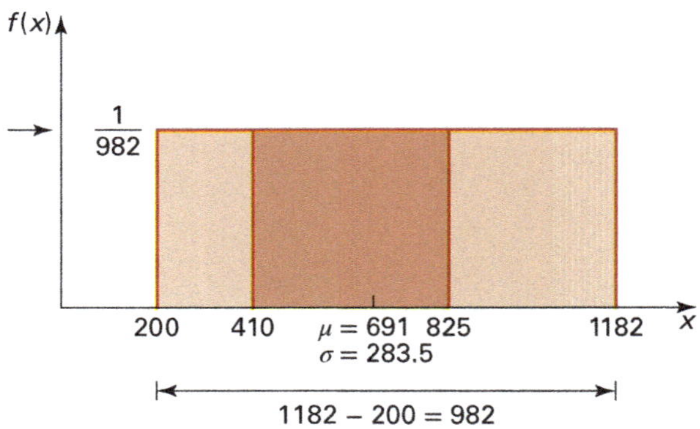

The probability that a randomly selected person pays between \$410 and \$825 annually for home insurance in Australia is .4226. That is, about 42% of all people in Australia pay home insurance in that range. This is the darker shaded area shown in the diagram at left.

PRACTICE PROBLEMS

Practising the calculations

6.15 The random variable x is uniformly distributed between 200 and 240.

a. What is the value of $f(x)$ for this distribution?
b. Determine the mean and standard deviation of this distribution.
c. What is the probability of $(x > 230)$?
d. What is the probability of $(205 \le x \le 220)$?
e. What is the probability of $(x \le 225)$?

6.16 The random variable x is uniformly distributed between 8 and 21.

a. What is the value of $f(x)$ for this distribution?
b. Determine the mean and standard deviation of this distribution.
c. Probability of $(10 \le x < 17) = ?$
d. Probability of $(x > 22) = ?$
e. Probability of $(x > 7) = ?$

6.17 In the TV game show *The Price is Right*, two players spin a wheel. The wheel is divided into 100 equal segments numbered 1 to 100. After each contestant spins the wheel and it stops, the contestant who lands on a number closest to 100 wins a prize. If the first contestant spins the number 80, what is the probability that the second contestant will win the prize?

6.18 The retail price of a medium-sized box of a well-known brand of cornflakes ranges from \$2.80 to \$3.14. Assume these prices are uniformly distributed. What are the average price and standard deviation of the prices? What is the probability that a randomly selected box of cornflakes is priced between \$3.00 and \$3.10?

6.19 In the TV game show *Temptation*, one of the temptations is the 'Temptation Vault', in which the leading contestant presses the buzzer to win a dollar amount from \$1 up to \$10 000. What is the probability that a contestant wins more than \$4000? What is the probability that more than \$4000 is won every day in a week (5 days)?

6.6 The exponential distribution

The **exponential distribution** is closely related to the Poisson distribution. Whereas the Poisson distribution is discrete and describes the probability of random occurrence of events over an interval, the exponential distribution is continuous and describes the probability distribution of the times between these random occurrences. In business applications, the exponential distribution can be used to solve problems that relate to quality control or manufacturing processes. The Poisson and exponential distributions are used together to solve queuing problems (theory of waiting times) among others. For example, the random variable in the exponential distribution can be used to describe the successive time between arrivals of defects on a production line.

The following are characteristics of the exponential distribution.

1. It is a continuous distribution.
2. It is a family of distributions.
3. It is skewed to the right.
4. The x values range from zero to infinity.
5. Its apex is always at $x = 0$.
6. The curve steadily decreases as x gets larger.

The exponential distribution has the probability density function given in formula 6.8.

Exponential probability density function (6.8)

$$f(x) = \lambda e^{-\lambda x}$$

where:

$x \geq 0$

$\lambda > 0$

$e = 2.718\,28\ldots$

An exponential distribution is characterised by the single parameter λ, which is the average number of occurrences in an interval. The mean of an exponential distribution is given by $\mu = \frac{1}{\lambda}$ and the standard deviation by $\sigma = \frac{1}{\lambda}$. Each unique value of λ determines a different exponential distribution, resulting in a family of distributions. Figure 6.14 shows graphs of the probability density functions for exponential distributions for four values of λ.

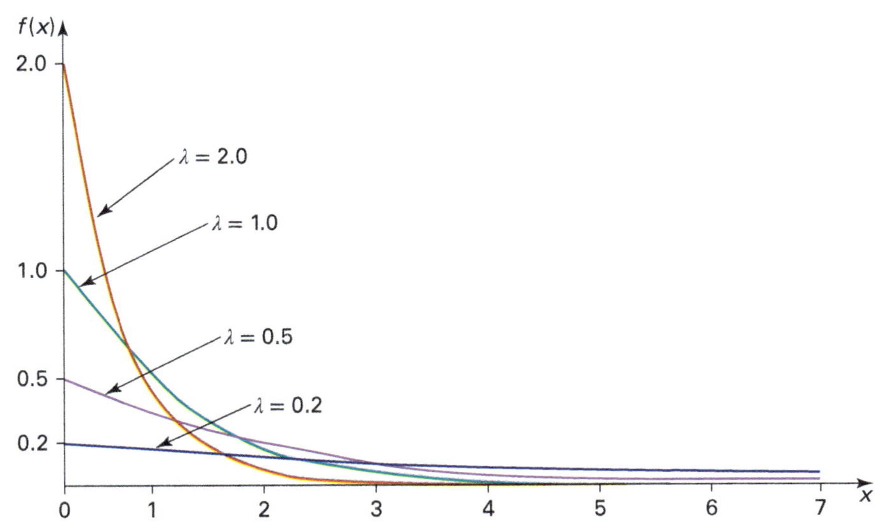

FIGURE 6.14 Graphs of some exponential distributions

Probabilities for the exponential distribution

As with all continuous probability distributions, the area under the curve formed between two endpoints gives the probability of the random variable occurring in that interval.

For the exponential distribution, the probability that a random variable (x) will take a value larger than a specific value x_0 is given by:

Probabilities of the right tail of the exponential distribution (6.9)

$$P(x \geq x_0) = e^{-\lambda x_0}$$

where:

$x_0 \geq 0$

For example, arrivals at a bank are Poisson distributed with a λ of 1.2 customers every minute.

1. What is the average time between arrivals?
2. What is the probability that at least 2 minutes will elapse between one arrival and the next arrival?

To answer the first question, since the arrival rate is 1.2 per minute, the interarrival time follows an exponential distribution with $\lambda = 1.2$. Therefore, the mean of this exponential distribution is $\mu = \frac{1}{\lambda} = \frac{1}{1.2} = 0.833$ minutes per arrival (50 seconds).

On average, 0.833 minutes, or 50 seconds, will elapse between arrivals at the bank.

For the second question, the probability of an interval of two minutes or more between arrivals can be calculated by:

$$P(x \geq 2 \mid \lambda = 1.2) = e^{-1.2(2)} = 0.0907$$

The interpretation of this probability is that when the rate of random arrivals is 1.2 per minute at the bank, two minutes or more will elapse between arrivals 9.07% of the time, as shown in figure 6.15. This problem underscores the potential of using the exponential distribution in conjunction with the Poisson distribution to solve problems. The Poisson distribution can be used to analyse the arrivals to the queue, and the exponential distribution can be used to analyse the interarrival time.

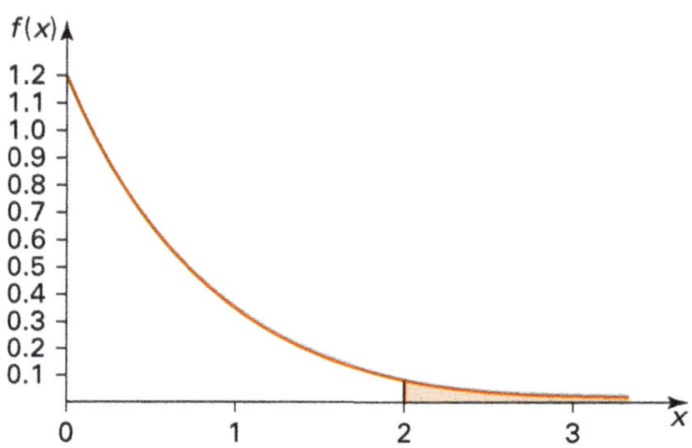

FIGURE 6.15 $P(x \geq 2)$ for the exponential distribution for $\lambda = 12$

PRACTICE PROBLEMS

6.20 Sketch the graphs of the probability density function of the following exponential distributions.

a. $\lambda = .1$
b. $\lambda = .3$
c. $\lambda = .8$
d. $\lambda = 3$

6.21 Determine the mean and standard deviation of the following exponential distributions.

a. $\lambda = 3.25$
b. $\lambda = .7$
c. $\lambda = 1.1$
d. $\lambda = 6$

6.22 Let x follow an exponential distribution. Determine the following probabilities.

a. $P(x \geq 5 \mid \lambda = 1.35)$
b. $P(x < 3 \mid \lambda = .68)$
c. $P(x > 4 \mid \lambda = 1.7)$
d. $P(x < 6 \mid \lambda = .80)$

6.23 The average length of time between arrivals at a motorway tollbooth is 23 seconds. Assume that the time between arrivals at the tollbooth is exponentially distributed.

a. What is the probability that a minute or more will elapse between arrivals?
b. If a car has just passed through the tollbooth, what is the probability that no car will show up for at least 3 minutes?

6.24 A busy restaurant determined that between 6.30 pm and 9.00 pm on Friday nights, the arrival of customers is Poisson distributed with an average arrival rate of 2.44 per minute.

a. What is the probability that at least 10 minutes will elapse between arrivals?

b. What is the probability that at least 5 minutes will elapse between arrivals?

c. What is the probability that at least 1 minute will elapse between arrivals?

d. What is the expected length of time between arrivals?

6.25 During the dry month of December, Perth has measurable rain on average only 2 days per month. If the arrival of rainy days is Poisson distributed in Perth during the month of December, what is the average number of days that will pass between measurable rain? What is the standard deviation? What is the probability that there will be a period of less than 2 days between rain during December?

CHAPTER CASE
REVISITED

Prawn farm continues to grow

1. Management have many years of historical data relating to the growth rates of prawns at various stages of their life cycle under ideal growing conditions. If specific information collected on two-week-old prawn larvae lengths are normally distributed, various characteristics of the larvae length distribution should be able to be observed. The first and most striking feature to observe in a normal distribution of larvae lengths would be the smooth, symmetrical, bell-shaped appearance of the distribution. The most frequently observed larva length (mode) will occur at the centre of the distribution, making the distribution unimodal. The mean (and median) larva length is at the centre of the distribution of lengths. The distribution should also have a reduction in the observed number of larvae length the further the distance is from the centre of the distribution, with very few larvae lengths in the tails (ends) of the distribution.
2. To demonstrate how management can put the normal distribution to use, consider the two-week-old prawn larvae is normally distributed with $\mu = 7$ mm and $\sigma = 0.5$ mm. Management are interested to know what percentage of prawn larvae would have lengths between 6.5 mm and 7.5 mm long. This range of prawn lengths can be observed to be one standard deviation either side of the mean of 7 mm. Using the empirical rule outlined in this chapter, approximately 68% of all two-week-old prawn larvae are between 6.5 mm and 7.5 mm long. Alternatively, this problem can be solved using the standard normal distribution and z-scores. The first step is to transform the individual prawn lengths into z-scores as follows:

$$P(6.5 < x < 7.5) = P\left(\frac{6.5-7}{.5} < z < \frac{7.5-7}{.5}\right)$$
$$= P(-1 < z < 1)$$
$$= .3413 + .3413 = .6826$$

Therefore, management can conclude that 68% of two-week-old prawn larvae are between 6.5 mm and 7.5 mm long.
3. Using the parameters of a normal distribution with $\mu = 7$ mm and $\sigma = 0.5$ mm, it is possible to calculate the probability of selecting a prawn larva being smaller than 5 mm long. The standardised normal distribution can be used once again, and the problem can be transformed to z-scores. The probability required can be written as:

$$P(x < 5) = P\left(z < \frac{5-7}{.5}\right)$$
$$= P(z < -4) = P(z > 4)$$
$$= .5 - .49997$$
$$= .00003$$

(Refer to table A.4 in the appendix.)

In other words, the chance of an employee selecting a single prawn larva 5 mm or less is very, very small (0.003%) or effectively zero. Note that a prawn larva of length 5 mm is four standard deviations from the population mean. Very few prawn larvae lengths are expected to be observed beyond three standard deviations of the mean (only 0.15%). Therefore, given that the employee did find a prawn larva of 5 mm in length, a length that is highly improbable if $\mu = 7$ mm and $\sigma = 0.5$ mm, it seems most unusual and could indicate something is wrong with this batch of two-week-old prawn larvae. Given only one prawn larva was measured, a much better method of identifying if there is a possible health problem with the larvae would be to take a sample, measure each larva's length, and then find a sample average length.

SUMMARY

1 This chapter has focused on continuous probability distributions. In particular, the emphasis has been on the normal distribution. The normal distribution has applications in solving many practical and business-related problems.

2 The standardised normal distribution is one of a family of normal distributions. It is uniquely defined by the parameters $\mu = 0$ and $\sigma = 1$. The areas under the standard normal distribution are published in the standardised normal distribution table (see tables A.4 and A.5 in the appendix).

3 Any normal distribution with mean μ and standard deviation σ can be transformed to the standardised normal distribution involving *z*-scores. The use of *z*-scores allows probabilities to be calculated for any other normal distribution.

4 A discrete binomial distribution can be approximated by a specific continuous normal distribution under certain conditions. This normal approximation can then make use of the standardised normal distribution. The standardised normal distribution can be used to calculate probabilities that relate to the original binomial distribution.

5 Another continuous probability distribution reviewed in this chapter was the uniform distribution. This distribution has a constant probability over a range of variable values. This probability distribution shows a clear contrast to the smooth, bell-shaped pattern of the normal distribution.

6 The final continuous distribution covered was the exponential distribution. It too is a continuous probability distribution. Overall, an ability to recognise when to use the normal, uniform or exponential distributions to solve real-world problems involving probabilities is an important learning outcome from this chapter.

KEY TERMS

continuous distributions p. 170
exponential distribution p. 186
normal distribution p. 172
standardised normal distribution p. 175
uniform distribution p. 184

KEY EQUATIONS

EQUATION	DESCRIPTION	FORMULA
6.1	**Probability density function of the normal distribution**	$f(x) = \frac{1}{\sigma\sqrt{2\pi}} e^{-\left(\frac{1}{2}\right)\left[\frac{x-\mu}{\sigma}\right]^2}$
6.2	**Standardisation**	$z = \frac{x-\mu}{\sigma} \quad (\sigma \neq 0)$
6.3	**Mean of a binomial distribution**	$\mu = np$
6.4	**Standard deviation of a binomial distribution**	$\sigma = \sqrt{npq}$
6.5	**Probability density function of a uniform distribution**	$f(x) = \begin{cases} \frac{1}{b-a} & \text{for } a \leq x \leq b \\ 0 & \text{for all other values} \end{cases}$

EQUATION	DESCRIPTION	FORMULA
6.6	**Mean of a uniform distribution**	$\mu = \frac{a+b}{2}$
6.7	**Standard deviation of a uniform distribution**	$\sigma = \frac{b-a}{\sqrt{12}}$
6.8	**Exponential probability density function**	$f(x) = \lambda e^{-\lambda x}$
6.9	**Probabilities of the right tail of the exponential distribution**	$P(x \geq x_0) = e^{-\lambda x_0}$

REVIEW PROBLEMS

Practising the calculations

6.26 Assume x has a normal distribution and find the following probabilities.

a. $P(x < 210 \mid \mu = 250 \text{ and } \sigma = 35)$
b. $P(x \geq 31 \mid \mu = 25 \text{ and } \sigma = 4)$
c. $P(x > 41 \mid \mu = 30 \text{ and } \sigma = 7)$
d. $P(18 < x < 21 \mid \mu = 27 \text{ and } \sigma = 5)$
e. $P(x \geq 366 \mid \mu = 350 \text{ and } \sigma = 10.7)$

6.27 Data are uniformly distributed between the values of 6 and 14. Determine the value of $f(x)$. What are the mean and standard deviation of this distribution? What is the probability of randomly selecting a value greater than 11? What is the probability of randomly selecting a value between 7 and 12?

6.28 Find the probabilities for the following exponential distribution problems.

a. $P(x \geq 3 \mid \lambda = 1.3)$
b. $P(x < 2 \mid \lambda = 2)$
c. $P(1 \leq x \leq 3 \mid \lambda = 1.65)$
d. $P(x > 2 \mid \lambda = .405)$

Testing your understanding

6.29 Australian Bureau of Statistics data show that young full-time students work an average of 15 hours per week. If the number of hours worked is normally distributed with this mean and 10% of students work more than 25 hours a week, what is the standard deviation of the number of hours worked by students?

6.30 A survey showed that one in five people aged 16 years or older do some volunteer work. If this figure holds for the entire population, and if a random sample of 150 people aged 16 years or older is taken, what is the probability that more than 40 of them do some volunteer work?

6.31 Truck freight delivery times between Brisbane and Sydney have been found to be approximately normally distributed. If the average freight delivery time is 12.5 hours, with a standard deviation of .45 hours, what is the probability that a delivery arrives after 13.5 hours?

6.32 Egg production per year in Malaysia can be closely approximated as being normally distributed, with a standard deviation of 83 million eggs. If during the year only 3% of the egg farmers produce more than 2655 million eggs, what is the mean egg production by Malaysian farmers?

6.33 According to the Department of Building and Housing, the average rent for a one-bedroom Auckland City apartment was \$314 with a standard deviation of \$88. Given the rents are normally distributed, what is the probability that a student can find a one-bedroom apartment that rents for:

a. less than \$200 per week
b. more than \$400 per week
c. between \$280 and \$350 per week?

6.34 The weight of a medium size loaf of homemade bread in Australia, using high-grade baking flour and a bread-making machine, has been found to be normally distributed with an average weight of 750 g and standard deviation of 10 g. What is the probability that a homemade loaf of bread will be:

a. less than 745 g
b. more than 795 g
c. between 725 g and 785 g?

6.35 The average speeds of passenger trains travelling from Kyoto to Tokyo have been found to be normally distributed, with a mean of 250 km per hour and a standard deviation of 30 km per hour.

a. What is the probability that a train will average less than 200 km per hour?
b. What is the probability that a train will average more than 300 km per hour?
c. What is the probability that a train will average between 210 and 280 km per hour?

CHAPTER

7 Sampling and sampling distributions

LEARNING OBJECTIVES

After studying this chapter, you should be able to:

1. determine when to use sampling instead of a census
2. distinguish between various random and nonrandom sampling techniques and know how to use them
3. describe the different types of errors that can occur in a survey
4. use the sampling distribution of the sample mean
5. use the sampling distribution of the sample proportion.

OPENING VIGNETTE

Detecting accounting fraud

A physicist named Frank Benford became famous in 1938 when he discovered a pattern (or distribution) existed in the frequency of the first digit — from 1 through to 9 — of any naturally occurring large list of numbers. This is now referred to as Benford's Law (or sometimes the First-digit Law). The law states that 30.1% of any large list of naturally occurring numbers will begin with the number 1, 17.6% with the number 2, and so on, continuing to decline to 4.5% of numbers beginning with the number 9. It applies, for example, to a large list of numbers that might be obtained from a firm's invoices to clients.

As a practical application of Benford's Law, consider a forensic auditor who decides to use the law to detect systematic fraud. The auditor knows the population proportion of numbers that naturally begin with the digit 2 in any large data set of invoices should be 17.6%. The auditor selects a random sample of 505 invoices issued by a firm and then counts the number of invoices with a value beginning with the digit 2. Having done this, the auditor can now calculate the sample proportion of invoices beginning with the digit 2. The auditor decides further investigation of systematic fraud by the organisation is warranted if the sample proportion of invoices selected is in the highest or lowest 0.5% of all possible sample proportions.

In this scenario, it can be shown that if the sample proportion is higher than 22% or lower than 13%, the auditor would conduct further investigation. In other words, from the sample of 505 invoices and using the upper and lower proportion limits, the auditor would investigate further if it was found there were more than 111 invoices or fewer than 66 invoices beginning with the number 2.

It must be noted, however, that even if the auditor finds more than 111 or less than 66 invoices in the sample beginning with the number 2, it is not possible to be 100% certain that fraud has occurred — the possibility of sampling error cannot be eliminated entirely.

Introduction

Decision makers and researchers use statistical techniques to draw conclusions about a particular population characteristic at a given point in time. Very often, however, it is not possible to investigate every single item of the population. Hence, even though the objective is to understand a particular population characteristic, decision makers and researchers must resort to using a random sample. As a result, only some items from a population are included in an investigation. The sample selected can be quite small, both in terms of the actual number of items in the sample and as a fraction of the overall population size.

Clearly a relatively small sample is almost certain not to be perfectly representative of the population from which it is drawn. Therefore, if the results from a sample are used to draw conclusions about the population from which it was selected, the results are almost certain to be in error. However, statisticians have been able to develop methods, provable by mathematics, that enable this sampling error to be managed. By managing sampling error, meaningful conclusions can be confidently drawn about populations based on relatively small samples.

This chapter begins by examining how data are collected using various random and nonrandom sampling techniques. It then explores the distribution of two statistics: the sample mean and the sample proportion. Both of these sampling distributions are approximately normally distributed under certain conditions. The understanding of these two sampling distributions is the basis for developing inferential statistics techniques.

CHAPTER CASE

Prawn farm success tied to strict quality control

Since 1990, Sunny Bay Prawn Farm has grown prawns using holding pond techniques. It has an enviable reputation for quality and sells a large quantity of prawns to Japan, Korea and China.

A principal reason for this market position is that, from the outset, management has carefully controlled all elements of the farming process and meticulously recorded data for various activities at different farming stages. One critical area of the business is to closely monitor the prawns' health from the larval stage through to adulthood. The company continually trials new farming processes and adopts those that prove successful. As a result of years of testing, monitoring and implementing improved processes, management are convinced they have found the optimal growing conditions for the prawns on their farm. They believe the years of experience in farming prawns, combined with statistical analysis of the data collected, give them a significant advantage over current and potential competitors.

An example of how management use statistical analysis can be seen in how they observe changes in behavioural characteristics and appearance of the prawns from the larval stage to adulthood. Comparing current observations with previously collected data provides management with early warning indicators of possible problems with growing conditions. For example, changes in the prawns could be a result of faulty equipment, incorrect water temperature or problems with the water quality or food supply. Similarly, enforcement of strict quality-control procedures while packing the prawns for export limits the chance of inferior prawns being sent to key markets.

Questions to help managers make decisions

1. An employee noted that the prawn larvae at a particular location on the farm seemed rather small. These prawns were being grown in pond G. To investigate if there is a problem in pond G, a sample of 20 larvae is randomly selected and then analysed by the farm's quality-control centre (QCC). Historical data have shown that the lengths of two-week-old prawn larvae are normally distributed with $\mu = 7$ mm and $\sigma = 0.5$ mm. After each of the 20 larvae were measured at the QCC, the sample average length was calculated to be 6.5 mm. Using this sample average length and historical data for prawn larvae length at two weeks of age, determine whether it is reasonable for the QCC to suspect that something is wrong with the growing conditions in pond G.
2. A new prawn larvae food was used in pond K for the first six weeks of their life. It was hoped that the new food would produce larger prawns. A sample of 20 prawns was randomly selected after six weeks and found to have a sample average length of 79.95 mm. The prawns at this age have historically had lengths that are normally distributed with a mean length of 80 mm and standard deviation of 3 mm. Based on these sample data and historical information, would it seem reasonable for the QCC manager to consider discontinuing the new type of food on the basis that there is very little change in the lengths of the prawns?

   In addition to assessing the length of the prawns eating this new type of food, a member of the QCC decided to weigh the sample of 20 prawns and found that the sample average weight was 51 g. Historical data showed that prawns at six weeks of age had weights that are normally distributed with a mean of 48 g and standard deviation of 2 g. Based on this information, would the QCC be justified in allowing the new prawn larvae food experiment to continue with the aim of adopting the new food on the farm in the future? Why?

3. Japanese importers are happy to accept up to 10% of prawns in any one shipment, on arrival in Japan, to have some kind of defect. For example, some prawns may have broken feelers. Thousands of live prawns are transported to Japan in tanks of water slurry by air every few days. The QCC has a standard procedure of inspecting 400 randomly selected prawns in any particular shipment. The prawns are shipped while still alive. If more than 7.5% of prawns are found to be defective in the sample, the shipment is halted and the prawns are sold to the local market. The reason for this procedure is that Sunny Bay does not want to risk sending a shipment with more than 10% of the prawns being defective. So, to be very conservative, they aim for no more that 5% of the prawns in any one shipment to be defective. By stipulating 30 as the maximum number of defective prawns in a batch of 400, they can be 99% confident that their goal of 5% is being met, and that there is also an acceptably high level of confidence that they are well under the 10% standard. Using the sampling distribution of the proportion, how can the QCC arrive at these conclusions?

7.1 Sampling

Sampling is widely used in business as a means of gathering useful information about a population. Data are gathered from samples and conclusions are drawn about the population as a part of the inferential statistics process. For example in the chapter case, Sunny Bay Prawn Farm's success is believed to be built around quality-control measures the farm has implemented. Researchers on the farm can take a random sample of prawn larvae, for example, to determine the average length, weight or other characteristic. The researchers can then compile the data obtained from their observations and analyse them. Findings can be summarised and a report provided to management. The report could enable management to make decisions that perhaps relate to future planning needs on the farm or how to improve the quality of prawns they grow. Hence, it is often the case that a sample can provide a method for gathering useful decision-making information that might otherwise be more time consuming or impossible to obtain.

Reasons for sampling

Taking a sample instead of conducting a census offers several advantages.

1. Sampling can save money.
2. Sampling can save time.
3. For given resources, sampling can broaden the scope of the study.
4. Since the research process is sometimes destructive, sampling does not destroy all the product.
5. If accessing the population is impossible, sampling is the only option.

It can be cheaper and quicker to obtain a sample than to conduct a census for a given number of questions. For example, it obviously is less expensive to conduct eight-minute telephone interviews with a sample of 100 customers rather than with a population of 100 000 customers. In addition to the cost savings, the significantly smaller number of interviews usually requires less total time. Thus, if obtaining the results is a matter of urgency, sampling can provide them more quickly. With the volatility of some markets and the constant barrage of new competition and new ideas, sampling has a strong advantage over a census in terms of research turnaround time.

If the resources allocated to a research project are limited, more detailed information can be gathered by taking a sample than by conducting a census. With resources concentrated on fewer individuals or items, the study can be broadened in scope to allow for more specialised questions. One organisation budgeted $100 000 for a study and opted to take a census instead of a sample by using a mail survey. The researchers mass-mailed thousands of copies of a computer card containing

20 questions to which the respondent could answer yes or no by punching a perforated hole. The information retrieved amounted to the percentage of respondents who answered yes and no to the 20 questions. For the same amount of money, the company could have taken a random sample of the population, held interactive one-on-one sessions using highly trained interviewers and gathered detailed information about the process being studied. By using the money for a sample, the researchers could have spent significantly more time with each respondent and thus increased the potential for gathering useful information.

Some research processes are destructive to the product or item being studied. For example, if light bulbs are being tested to determine how long they burn or if lollies are being taste tested to determine whether the taste is acceptable, the product is destroyed during testing. If a census were conducted for this type of research, no product would be left to sell. Hence, taking a sample is the only realistic option for testing such products.

Sometimes a population is virtually impossible to access for research. For example, some people refuse to answer sensitive questions, and some telephone numbers are unlisted. Some items of interest (such as a 1957 model Holden) are so scattered that locating all of them would be extremely difficult. When the population is inaccessible for these or other reasons, sampling is the only option.

Reasons for taking a census

Sometimes taking a census makes more sense than using a sample. One reason to take a census is to eliminate the possibility that by chance a randomly selected sample might not be representative of the population. Even when all the proper sampling techniques are implemented, a sample that is not representative of the population can be selected by chance. For example, if the population of interest is all ute owners in far north Queensland, a random sample of owners could yield mostly farmers, when in fact many of the ute owners in far north Queensland are urban dwellers. This situation could arise if the sampling frame was based in a geographic location rather than, say, a random selection from an electoral roll.

A second reason to take a census is that the client (person authorising and/or underwriting the study) does not have an appreciation for random sampling and feels more comfortable with conducting a census. Both of these reasons for taking a census are based on the assumption that enough time and money are available to conduct such a census.

Sampling frame

Every research study has a target population that consists of the individuals, institutions or entities that are the objects of investigation. The sample is taken from a population list, map, directory or other source used to represent the population. This list, map or directory is called the **sampling frame**, which can be school lists, trade association lists or even lists sold by list brokers. Ideally, a one-to-one correspondence exists between the frame units and the population units. In reality, the frame and the target population are often different. For example, suppose the target population is all families living in Adelaide. A feasible frame would be the residential pages of the Adelaide telephone books. How would the frame differ from the target population? Some families have no telephone. Other families have unlisted numbers. Still other families might have moved and/or changed their numbers since the directory was printed. Some families even have multiple listings under different names. Also, since 2007, the Australian government has maintained a 'Do not call' register where households who do not want to be contacted by telemarketers can register their telephone numbers.

Frames that have over-registration contain all the target population units plus some additional units. Frames that have under-registration contain fewer units than does the target population. Sampling is done from the frame, not the target population. In theory, the target population and the frame are the same. In reality, a researcher's goal is to minimise the differences between the frame and the target population.

7.2 Random versus nonrandom sampling

The two main types of sampling are random and nonrandom sampling. In **random sampling** every unit of the population has a known probability of being selected in the sample. This is sometimes called **probability-based sampling**. Such a sample can be analysed using probability theory and statistical theory. In simple random sampling (discussed shortly), every unit of the population has an equal probability of being selected in the sample. Random sampling implies that chance governs the process of selection. For example, lottery winners are selected by some random draw of numbers, allowing selections to be made by chance.

In **nonrandom sampling**, not every unit of the population has a known probability of being selected in the sample. Members of nonrandom samples are not selected by chance. For example, they might be selected because they are at the right place at the right time or because they know the people conducting the research.

Sometimes nonrandom sampling is called *nonprobability sampling*. Because units of the population have an unknown probability of being selected, assigning a probability of occurrence in nonrandom sampling is impossible. The statistical methods presented and discussed in this text are based on the assumption that the data come from random samples. *Nonrandom sampling methods are not appropriate techniques for gathering data to be analysed by most of the statistical methods presented in this text.* However, several nonrandom sampling techniques are described in this section, primarily to alert you to their characteristics and limitations.

Random sampling techniques

The four basic random sampling techniques are simple random sampling, stratified random sampling, systematic random sampling and cluster (or area) random sampling. Each technique offers advantages and disadvantages. Some techniques are simpler to use, some are cheaper, and others show greater potential for reducing sampling error.

Simple random sampling

The most elementary random sampling technique is **simple random sampling**. Simple random sampling can be viewed as the basis for the other random sampling techniques. In simple random sampling, every (possible) unit of the population has the same probability of being sampled and so every unit has an equal probability of being selected in the sample. To conduct a simple random sample, each unit of the frame is numbered from 1 to N (where N is the size of the population). Next, a table of random numbers or a random number generator is used to select n items in the sample. A random number generator is usually a computer program that allows computer-calculated output to yield random numbers. Table 7.1 contains a brief table of random numbers. These numbers are random in all directions. The spaces in the table are there only for ease of reading the values. For each number, each of the 10 digits (0–9) is equally likely, so getting the same digit twice or more in a row is possible.

TABLE 7.1 A brief table of random numbers

47112	23038	65467	91365	90124	96445	15663	49288
88296	26282	35391	18313	17193	28468	33216	15885
38815	43783	61801	45005	46243	44853	92323	54302
50892	40429	97920	83454	99249	36352	95865	18995
74757	84298	97646	54329	40113	78622	44501	80801
20784	31403	19904	45088	56102	58170	46381	98792
17906	34166	14848	93679	23007	36389	80803	72584

To select the sample, we first number every member of the population. For example, if there were 2000 members, we would number them from 1 to 2000. We then use the table. We select as many digits for each unit sampled as there are in the largest number in the population. For a population of 2000 members, we would therefore select four-digit numbers. Often a researcher will start at some randomly selected location in the table and proceed in a predetermined direction to select numbers, but for ease of understanding we will begin at the start of the table. The first four digits in table 7.1 to form a four-digit number when reading from left to right are 4711. We would discard this because it is larger than 2000. The next four consecutive digits are 2230 (taking the last 2 in 4711**2** and the first three digits in **230**38). We would discard the number 2230 as it is also larger than 2000. We continue on to find the numbers 3865 and 4679, which would also be discarded. The next number would be 1365 and this would be the number of the first unit to be sampled, as it is the first number that is not greater than 2000. We continue until we have our desired sample size (n). Demonstration problem 7.1 helps explain this process.

DEMONSTRATION PROBLEM 7.1

PROBLEM: From the sampling frame of companies below, use simple random sampling to select a sample of six companies.

AVJennings	ABN Amro	Alcatel
ANZ	Avon	AXA
Bank of Queensland	BHP Billiton	Black & Decker
China Food Industries	Circuit City	Coca-Cola Amatil
Commonwealth Bank of Australia	David Jones	Del Monte Pacific
Ford Australia	Holden	Kraft Foods
McDonald's	Mattel	National Australia Bank
Siemens	Telstra	Time Warner
Toys"R"Us	Toyota	Venture Corporation
Vodafone	Woolworths	Xerox

SOLUTION: Because our population of companies contains 30 members, only two-digit numbers are needed. The population is numbered from 01 to 30, as shown below.

01 AVJennings	02 ABN Amro	03 Alcatel
04 ANZ	05 Avon	06 AXA
07 Bank of Queensland	08 BHP Billiton	09 Black & Decker
10 China Food Industries	11 Circuit City	12 Coca-Cola Amatil
13 Commonwealth Bank of Australia	14 David Jones	15 Del Monte Pacific
16 Ford Australia	17 Holden	18 Kraft Foods
19 McDonald's	20 Mattel	21 National Australia Bank
22 Siemens	23 Telstra	24 Time Warner
25 Toys"R"Us	26 Toyota	27 Venture Corporation
28 Vodafone	29 Woolworths	30 Xerox

The object is to sample six companies, so six different two-digit numbers must be selected from the table of random numbers. Since this population contains only 30 companies, all numbers greater than 30 (31–99) must be ignored. If for example the number 67 is selected, the process is continued until a value between 1 and 30 is obtained. If the same number occurs more than once, we proceed to another number. In the first row of table 7.1, the first two-digit number is 47. This number is out of range and so it is ignored. The next two-digit number is 11, which is the first usable number. From our numbered list of companies, we see that 11 is the number associated with Circuit City, so Circuit City is selected in the sample. The next two-digit number is 22, which is also usable. Twenty-two is the number for Siemens, so this company is selected. Continuing the process, the next usable number is 30, which is the value for Xerox. The next two digits are 38, which is ignored because it is outside the range.

For similar reasons, the next three two-digit numbers (65, 46, 79) are also discarded. The next usable number is 13, which is the value for the Commonwealth Bank of Australia. The following two two-digit numbers are 65 and 90, which are unusable. The next usable number is 12, the number associated with Coca-Cola Amatil. To select the sixth and final company for the sample, we skip over the next three sets of two-digit numbers (49, 64, 45) and select the number 15. This is the value for Del Monte Pacific. The following companies constitute the final sample: Circuit City, Siemens, Xerox, Commonwealth Bank of Australia, Coca-Cola Amatil and Del Monte Pacific. Note that this sample selection process is done efficiently using Excel as outlined below (rather than manually selecting the sample).

USING EXCEL

Selecting a random sample

You can use Excel to select a sample from a given list. Suppose the task is to randomly select six companies from the population of 30 companies.

DP07-01

1. Access DP07-01.xls from the student website.
2. From the Data tab, select Data Analysis.
3. Select Sampling and click OK.
4. In the Sampling dialogue box:
   a. enter the location of the data into the Input Range field
   b. select Random for the Sampling Method
   c. enter 6 in the Number of Samples field
   d. choose an output option
   e. click OK.

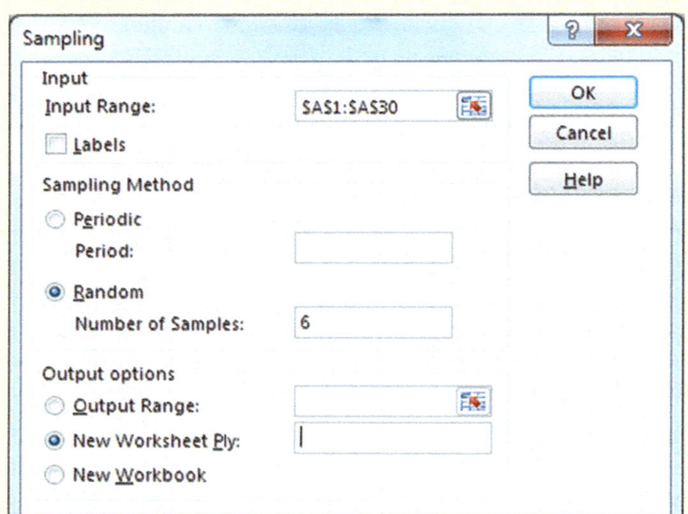

The computer generates a set of numbers (in our example 12, 17, 8, 4, 1 and 11, but you will of course get different numbers each time). Matching these numbers with their respective companies gives the sample (in our example, Coca-Cola Amatil, Holden, BHP Billiton, ANZ, AVJennings and Circuit City).

Generating random numbers

You can use Excel to generate random numbers using different distributions. For example, suppose you wish to generate a table of random numbers similar to table 7.1.

1. From the Data tab, select Data Analysis.
2. Select Random Number Generation and click OK.

3. In the Random Number Generation dialogue box:
   a. enter 1 in the Number of Variables field
   b. enter the number of random numbers required (e.g. 56) in the Number of Random Numbers field
   c. select uniform from the Distribution drop-down menu (other distributions will be dealt with later in the chapter)
   d. enter the range from which to choose the random numbers in the Parameters fields (i.e. *a* and *b* of the uniform distribution). For example, enter 14422 in the field after Between and 99999 in the field after and.
   e. choose an output option

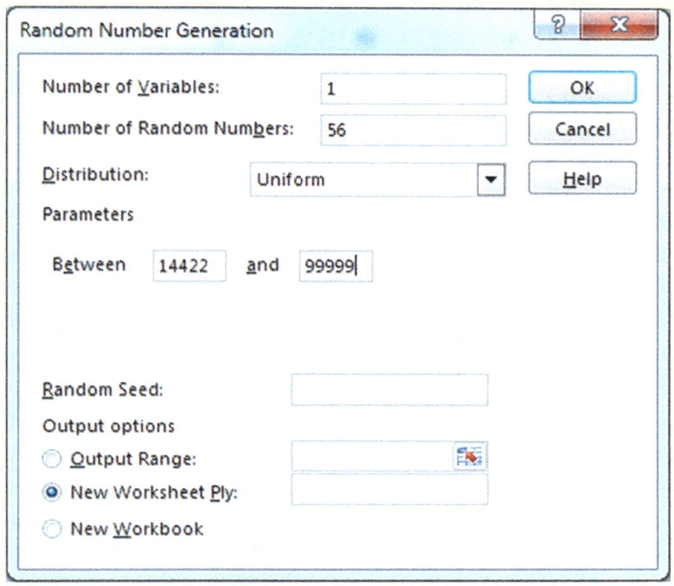

   f. click OK.

Excel will generate a list of random numbers. You should experiment with the other distributions.

Simple random sampling is easier to perform on small populations than on large ones. The process of numbering all the members of a population and selecting items is cumbersome for large populations, but computers do make the process easier.

Stratified random sampling

A second type of random sampling is **stratified random sampling**, in which the population is divided into non-overlapping subpopulations called strata. The researcher then extracts a simple random sample from each of the subpopulations. The main reason for using stratified random sampling is that it has the potential to reduce sampling error.

Sampling error occurs when we select a subset from a population. With stratified random sampling, the potential to match the sample closely to the population is greater than it is with simple random sampling because portions of the total sample are taken from different population subgroups. However, stratified random sampling is generally more costly than simple random sampling because each unit of the population must be assigned to a stratum before the random selection process begins.

Strata selection is usually based on available information. Such information may have been gleaned from previous censuses or surveys. Stratification benefits increase as the strata differ more.

Internally, a stratum should be relatively homogeneous; externally, strata should contrast with each other. Stratification is often done by using demographic variables, such as gender, socioeconomic class, geographic region, religion and ethnicity. For example, if an Australian federal election poll is to be conducted by a market research company, what important variables should be stratified? The gender of the respondent might make a difference because a gender gap in voter preference has been noted in past elections; that is, men and women have tended to vote differently in elections. Geographic region also provides an important variable in national opinion polls. For example, people living in regional areas where forestry is the main industry are more likely to be in favour of increased logging than people living in urban areas.

In FM radio markets, the age of listeners is an important determinant of the type of programming used by a station. Figure 7.1 contains a stratification by age with three strata, based on the assumption that age affects preference in radio programming. This stratification implies that listeners aged 20 to 29 years tend to prefer a particular type of programming, which is different from that preferred by listeners aged 30 to 49 and 50 to 59. Within each age subgroup (stratum), *homogeneity* or alikeness is present; between each pair of subgroups a difference, or *heterogeneity*, is present.

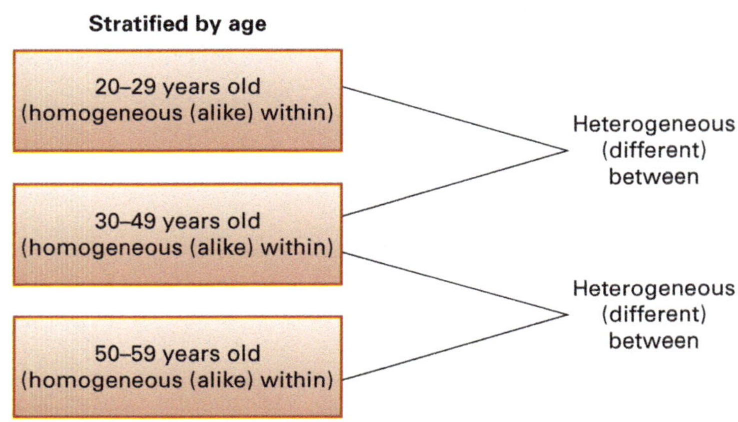

FIGURE 7.1 Stratified random sampling of FM radio listeners

Stratified random sampling can be either proportionate or disproportionate. **Proportionate stratified random sampling** occurs *when the percentage of the sample taken from each stratum is proportionate to the percentage that each stratum is within the whole population.* For example, suppose voters are being surveyed in Perth and the sample is being stratified by religion: Buddhist, Christian, Jewish, Muslim and others. If Perth's population is 90% Christian, and if a sample of 1000 voters is taken, the sample would require inclusion of 900 Christians to achieve proportionate stratification. Selecting any other number of Christians would be disproportionate stratification. The sample proportion of other religions would also have to follow population percentages. In another example, consider the Northern Territory, where 27.8% of the population were identified in a recent census as being of indigenous origin. If a researcher is conducting a territory-wide poll, and if the population is stratified by ethnicity, 27.8% of a proportionate stratified random sample should contain people of indigenous background. Hence, an ethnically proportionate stratified sample of 155 residents from the Northern Territory's 211 000 residents should contain 43 indigenous persons. **Disproportionate stratified random sampling** occurs *whenever the proportions of the strata in a sample are different from the proportions of the strata in the population.*

Systematic sampling

Systematic sampling is a third random sampling technique. Unlike stratified random sampling, systematic sampling is not used to reduce sampling error. Rather, systematic sampling is used because of its convenience and relative ease of administration. With **systematic sampling**, *every kth item is selected to produce a sample of size n from a population of size N.* The value of k, sometimes called the sampling cycle, can be determined by formula 7.1. If k is not an integer value, the whole number value should be used.

Determining the value of *k*
(7.1)

$$k = \frac{N}{n}$$

where:
n = the sample size
N = the population size
k = the size of the interval for selection

As an example of systematic sampling, a management information systems researcher wanted to sample Australian manufacturers, retailers and service providers. She had enough financial support to sample 150 companies (n). An online directory search found approximately 500 companies (N) in alphabetical order. The value of k was 3 ($\frac{500}{150} = 3.33$; using the whole number value, $k = 3$), so the researcher selected every third company in the directory for her sample.

Did the researcher begin with the first company listed or the third or one somewhere between? In selecting every kth value, a simple random number table should be used to select a value between 1 and k inclusive as a starting point. The second element for the sample is the starting point plus k. In the example, $k = 3$, so the researcher would have used a table of random numbers to determine a starting point between 1 and 3. Suppose she selected the number 2. She would have started with the 2nd company and then selected the 5th (2 + 3), the 8th and so on.

Besides convenience, systematic sampling has other advantages. Because systematic sampling is evenly distributed across the frame, a knowledgeable person can easily determine whether a sampling plan has been followed in a study. However, a problem with systematic sampling can occur if the data are subject to any periodicity and the sampling interval is in syncopation with it. In such a case, the sampling would be nonrandom. For example, if a list of 150 university students is actually a merged list of five classes with 30 students in each class and if each of the lists of the five classes has been ordered with the names of top students first and bottom students last, then systematic sampling of every 30th student could cause selection of all top students, all bottom students, or all mediocre students; that is, the original list is subject to a cyclical or periodic organisation. Systematic sampling methodology is based on the assumption that the source of population elements is random.

Cluster (or area) sampling

Cluster (or area) sampling is a fourth type of random sampling. Cluster (or area) sampling involves dividing the population into non-overlapping areas or clusters. However, in contrast to stratified random sampling, where strata are homogeneous, cluster sampling identifies clusters that tend to be internally heterogeneous. In theory, each cluster contains a wide variety of elements, and the cluster is a miniature, or microcosm, of the population. Examples of clusters are towns, companies, homes, universities, areas of a city and geographic regions. Often clusters are naturally occurring groups of the population and are already identified, such as states or ABS Statistical Districts. Although area sampling usually refers to clusters that are areas of the population, such as geographic regions and cities, the terms *cluster sampling* and *area sampling* are used interchangeably in this text.

After choosing the clusters, the researcher randomly selects individual elements in the sample from the clusters. Business research frequently makes use of cluster sampling in surveying consumer purchases of various products.

Sometimes the clusters are too large, and a second set of clusters is taken from each original cluster. This technique is called **two-stage sampling**. For example, a researcher could divide Australia into clusters of cities. She could then divide the cities into clusters of blocks and randomly select individual houses from the block clusters. The first stage is selecting the test cities and the second stage is selecting the blocks.

Cluster or area sampling offers several advantages. Two of the foremost advantages are convenience and cost. Clusters are usually convenient to obtain, and the cost of sampling from the entire population is reduced because the scope of the study is reduced to the clusters. The cost per element is usually lower in cluster or area sampling than in stratified sampling because of reduced element listing or locating costs. The time and cost of contacting elements of the population can be reduced, especially if travel is involved, because clustering reduces the distance between sampled elements. In addition, administration of the sample survey can be simplified. Sometimes cluster or area sampling is the only feasible approach because the sampling frames of the individual elements of the population are unavailable and therefore other random sampling techniques cannot be used.

Cluster or area sampling also has several disadvantages. If the elements of a cluster are similar, cluster sampling may be statistically less efficient than simple random sampling. In an extreme case — when the elements of a cluster are the same — sampling from the cluster may be no better than sampling a single unit from the cluster. Moreover, the costs and problems of statistical analysis are greater with cluster or area sampling than with simple random sampling.

Nonrandom sampling

Sampling techniques used to select elements from a population by any mechanism that does not involve a random selection process are called nonrandom sampling techniques. Because probability-based sampling methods are not used to select items from the population, these techniques are nonprobability techniques and are not desirable for use in gathering data to be analysed by the methods of inferential statistics presented in this text. Sampling error cannot be determined objectively for these sampling techniques. Four nonrandom sampling techniques are presented here: convenience sampling, judgement sampling, quota sampling and snowball sampling.

Convenience sampling

In **convenience sampling**, *elements for the sample are selected for the convenience of the researcher.* The researcher typically chooses elements that are readily available, nearby or willing to participate. The sample tends to be less variable than the population because in many environments the extreme elements of the population are not readily available. The researcher tends to select more elements from the middle of the population. For example, a convenience sample of homes for door-to-door interviews might include houses where people are at home, houses with no dogs, houses near the street, first-floor apartments and houses with friendly people. In contrast, a random sample would require the researcher to gather data only from houses and apartments that have been selected randomly, no matter how inconvenient or unfriendly the location. If a research company is located in a mall, a convenience sample might be selected by interviewing only shoppers who pass the shop and look friendly.

Judgement sampling

Judgement sampling occurs when *elements selected for the sample are chosen by the judgement of the researcher*. Researchers often believe they can obtain a representative sample by using sound judgement, which can save time and money. Sometimes, ethical, professional researchers might believe they can select a more representative sample than a random process will provide. They might be right! However, some studies show that random sampling methods outperform judgement sampling in estimating the population mean even when the researcher who is administering the judgement sampling is trying to put together a representative sample. When sampling is done by judgement, it is not possible to calculate the probability that an element will be selected in the sample. The sampling error cannot be determined objectively because probabilities are based on *nonrandom* selection.

Other problems are associated with judgement sampling. The researcher tends to make errors of judgement in one direction. These systematic errors lead to what are called *biases*. The researcher is also unlikely to include extreme elements. Judgement sampling provides no objective method for determining whether one person's judgement is better than another's.

Quota sampling

A third nonrandom sampling technique is **quota sampling**, which appears similar to stratified random sampling. Certain population subclasses, such as age group, gender and geographic region, are used as strata. However, instead of randomly sampling from each stratum, the researcher uses a nonrandom sampling method to gather data from one stratum until the desired quota of samples is filled. Quotas are described by quota controls, which set the sizes of the samples to be obtained from the subgroups. Generally, a quota is based on the proportions of the subclasses in the population. In this case, the quota concept is similar to that of proportional stratified sampling.

Quotas are often filled by using available, recent or applicable elements. For example, instead of randomly interviewing people to obtain a quota of Chinese Australians, the researcher might go to the Chinatown area of the city and interview there until enough responses are obtained to fill the quota. In quota sampling, an interviewer would begin by asking a few filter questions; if the respondent represents a subclass whose quota has been filled, the interviewer would terminate the interview.

Quota sampling can be useful if no frame is available for the population. For example, suppose a researcher wants to stratify the population into owners of different types of cars but fails to find any lists of Toyota van owners. Through quota sampling, the researcher would proceed by interviewing all car owners until the quota of Toyota van owners is filled.

Quota sampling is less expensive than most random sampling techniques because it is essentially a technique of convenience. However, cost may not be meaningful because the quality of nonrandom and random sampling techniques cannot be compared. Another advantage of quota sampling is the speed of data gathering. The researcher does not have to call back or send out a second questionnaire if they do not receive a response; they just move on to the next element. Also, preparatory work for quota sampling is minimal.

The main problem with quota sampling is that it is a *nonrandom* sampling technique. Some researchers believe that if the quota is filled by *randomly* selecting elements and discarding those not from a stratum, quota sampling is essentially a version of stratified random sampling. However, most quota sampling is carried out by the researcher selecting in areas where the quota can be filled quickly. The object is to gain the benefits of stratification without the high field costs of stratification. Ultimately, it remains a nonprobability sampling method.

Snowball sampling

Another nonrandom sampling technique is **snowball sampling**, in which *survey subjects are selected based on referral from other survey respondents*. The researcher identifies a person who fits the profile of subjects wanted for the study. The researcher then asks this person for the names and locations of others who would also fit the profile of subjects wanted for the study. Through these referrals, survey subjects can be identified cheaply and efficiently, which is particularly useful when survey subjects are difficult to locate. This is the main advantage of snowball sampling; its main disadvantage is that it is nonrandom.

7.3 Types of errors from collecting sample data

Sampling error

Sampling error is the difference between the value computed from a sample (a statistic) and the corresponding value for the population (a parameter). Sampling error occurs because the sampling process involves selecting a subset of the population and not the entire population. We can minimise sampling error by taking a larger sample or by using stratified random sampling. However, this has to be weighed against the extra cost involved in doing so. The results of opinion polls, typically published in newspapers and magazines or broadcast on TV, often include a statement similar to the following: the results are correct to within ±2 percentage points of their actual values. This is called the margin of error (a specified sampling error), which is an indicator of the accuracy of the estimates. A more detailed understanding of the concept of margin of error involves learning how to compute sampling error and how to select a sample size subject to a given sampling error. Sampling error computed in this manner assumes that a simple random sampling technique has been used. In general, sampling error formulas can be derived for each of the random sampling designs, which can then be incorporated into the expression for the sampling distribution. However, these formulas are not introduced in this text and we restrict our examples to the case of simple random sampling.

Nonsampling errors

All errors other than sampling errors are **nonsampling errors**. The many possible nonsampling errors include missing data, recording errors, input processing errors and analysis errors. Other nonsampling errors result from the measurement instrument, such as errors of unclear definitions, defective questionnaires and poorly conceived concepts. Improper definition of the frame is a nonsampling error. In many cases, it is impossible to find a frame that fits the population perfectly. This lack of fit is a nonsampling error.

Response errors are also nonsampling errors. They occur when people do not know or will not give an answer, or overstate their opinion. Virtually no statistical method is available to measure or control for nonsampling errors. The statistical techniques presented in this text are based on the assumption that none of these nonsampling errors are committed. The researcher must eliminate these errors through carefully planning and monitoring the execution of the research study.

PRACTICE PROBLEMS

Practising the calculations

7.1 For each of the following research projects, list three variables for stratification of the sample.

- **a.** A study of consumer gambling habits in the horse racing industry.
- **b.** Local government wants to understand the attitude of their ratepayers. A representative community group is to be selected and interviewed at various times during the year.
- **c.** A potato chip manufacturer wants to understand where their product is distributed but does not want to conduct a census.
- **d.** A university department wishes to create a new marketing campaign by sampling current students.

7.2 List some strata into which each of the following variables can be divided.

- **a.** Employee qualification
- **b.** Company value
- **c.** Car park size
- **d.** Degree program studied by university students
- **e.** Job description

7.3 A city's telephone book lists 100 000 people. if the telephone book is the frame for a study, how large would the sample size be if systematic sampling were done on every 200th person?

7.4 If a university employed 3500 academic staff, and a random sample of 175 academic staff was selected using systematic sampling, what value of k was used? Between what two values would the sampling selection process have started? Where would a frame for this sampling of academic staff have been obtained?

Testing your understanding

7.5 For each of the following research projects, list at least one area or cluster that could be used in obtaining the sample.

- **a.** A study of road conditions in the North Island of New Zealand
- **b.** A study of coalmining companies in Australia
- **c.** A study of the environmental effects of agricultural industries on the Murray–Darling river system

7.6 Give an example of how judgement sampling could be used in a study to determine how lawyers feel about other lawyers advertising on television.

7.7 Give an example of how convenience sampling could be used in a study of *BRW* Top 1000 CEOs to measure corporate attitude toward paternity leave for employees.

7.8 Give an example of how quota sampling could be used to conduct sampling by a company test marketing a new personal computer.

7.4 Sampling distribution of the sample mean, $\bar{x}$

In the inferential statistics process, the procedure is to select a random sample from a specified population, compute the desired statistic from the sample and then use the sample statistic to make an inference about the corresponding population parameter. For example, the sample mean, $\bar{x}$, is used to provide an estimate of the population parameter, μ. Logic tells us that, for a particular sample size, depending on which items from the population are selected, the value of the sample statistic could vary from one sample to the next. To analyse the sample statistic, it is essential to know the distribution of the statistic. If, for example, it was found that a sample statistic followed some mathematical distribution, such as the normal distribution, then the analysis of the sample statistic would become easier.

In this section we explore how the sample mean, $\bar{x}$, can be used to estimate the corresponding population parameter. The sample mean is arguably the most common statistic used in the inferential process. To fully appreciate how the mean of a single random sample can be used to draw a meaningfully conclusion about a population mean, an understanding of the sampling distribution of the sample mean is needed.

To describe the sampling distribution of the sample mean in simple terms, consider a situation where many different samples, all of the same size, have been randomly selected from a specific population and each sample mean has been calculated. If these sample averages are then plotted using a histogram, with the sample mean on the horizontal axis and frequency of occurrence on the vertical axis, what visual pattern would emerge? Would the pattern show the sample means to be uniformly distributed, concentrated around a common sample mean value or spread out in some other pattern? The way the sample means are spread out when plotted is what is referred to as the sampling distribution of the sample mean.

To explain further, consider a small finite population consisting of the following eight values.

54	55	59	63	64	68	69	70

The shape of the distribution of these values is shown in figure 7.2.

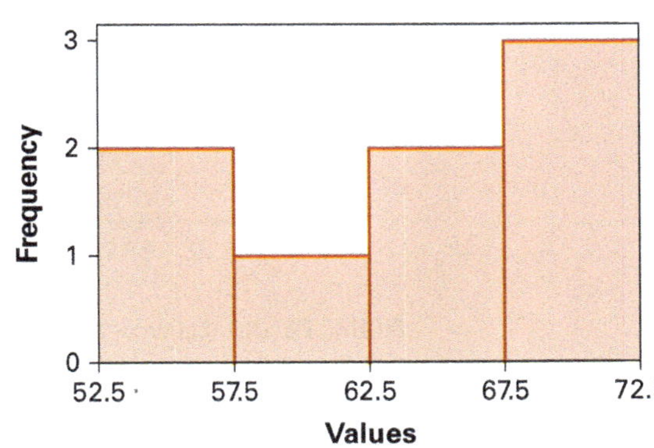

FIGURE 7.2 Distribution shape of population data

It is decided that two values are to be selected from this small population and not replaced once selected. In this case, the lowest possible sample mean expected is 54.5 if the two lowest numbers, 54 and 55, are selected. Similarly, if the two highest numbers, 69 and 70, are selected, the sample mean is 69.5. Notice that these two sample means are greater than the lowest individual value of 54 and lower than the highest individual value of 70. Hence, this will result in all other sample combinations of two values having sample means larger than 54.5 and smaller than 69.5. This highlights how samples that are randomly selected, even when selected and not replaced into the population, have a range of sample mean values that are spread out and follow some kind of distribution.

Now consider that all possible combinations of two values are sampled from the small population of eight values *with* replacement. All possible pairs of values that could be selected are shown in the table below.

(54, 54)	(55, 54)	(59, 54)	(63, 54)	(54, 55)	(55, 55)	(59, 55)	(63, 55)
(54, 59)	(55, 59)	(59, 59)	(63, 59)	(54, 63)	(55, 63)	(59, 63)	(63, 63)
(54, 64)	(55, 64)	(59, 64)	(63, 64)	(54, 68)	(55, 68)	(59, 68)	(63, 68)
(54, 69)	(55, 69)	(59, 69)	(63, 69)	(54, 70)	(55, 70)	(59, 70)	(63, 70)
(64, 54)	(68, 54)	(69, 54)	(70, 54)	(64, 55)	(68, 55)	(69, 55)	(70, 55)
(64, 59)	(68, 59)	(69, 59)	(70, 59)	(64, 63)	(68, 63)	(69, 63)	(70, 63)
(64, 64)	(68, 64)	(69, 64)	(70, 64)	(64, 68)	(68, 68)	(69, 68)	(70, 68)
(64, 69)	(68, 69)	(69, 69)	(70, 69)	(64, 70)	(68, 70)	(69, 70)	(70, 70)

The sample means of these pairs of values are shown below.

54	54.5	56.5	58.5	54.5	55	57	59
56.5	57	59	61	58.5	59	61	63
59	59.5	61.5	63.5	61	61.5	63.5	65.5
61.5	62	64	66	62	62.5	64.5	66.5
59	61	61.5	62	59.5	61.5	62	62.5
61.5	63.5	64	64.5	63.5	65.5	66	66.5
64	66	66.5	67	66	68	68.5	69
66.5	68.5	69	69.5	67	69	69.5	70

The histogram in figure 7.3 shows the shape of the distribution *for all possible sample mean values*. This plot is for all possible pairs of samples that can be selected from the small population.

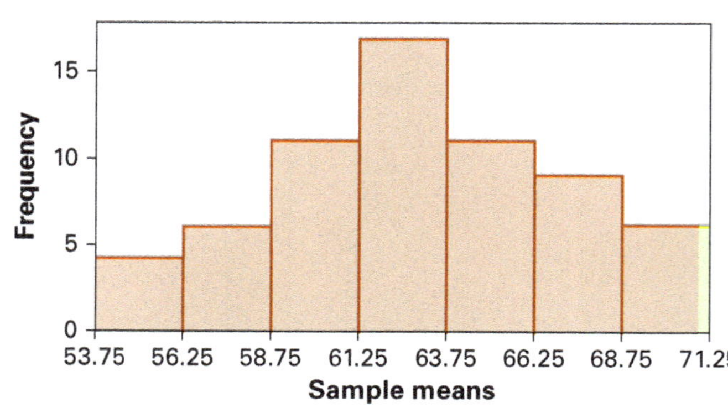

FIGURE 7.3 Distribution of all possible sample means of size $n = 2$

Notice the shape of the histogram in figure 7.3. When the sample means are plotted on the horizontal axis, the histogram shape is quite different from the shape of the histogram for the individual population values shown in figure 7.2. The sample means appear to cluster towards the middle of the distribution with fewer observations of sample means near the ends of the distribution. Importantly, by ensuring that all possible samples are taken using replacement, a bell-shaped pattern, resembling the normal distribution, appears in the distribution of the sample means. In addition, there is a concentration of sample mean values towards the centre of the distribution.

As a second example, consider the data in figure 7.4. The histogram shown is a Poisson distribution with $\lambda = 1.25$. Note that this histogram is skewed to the right. From this population distribution, take 90 random samples, each with size $n = 30$. The resulting distribution of sample means is displayed in figure 7.5. Notice that, although the samples were drawn from a distribution that is skewed to the right, the sample means form a distribution that approaches a symmetrical, normal distribution.

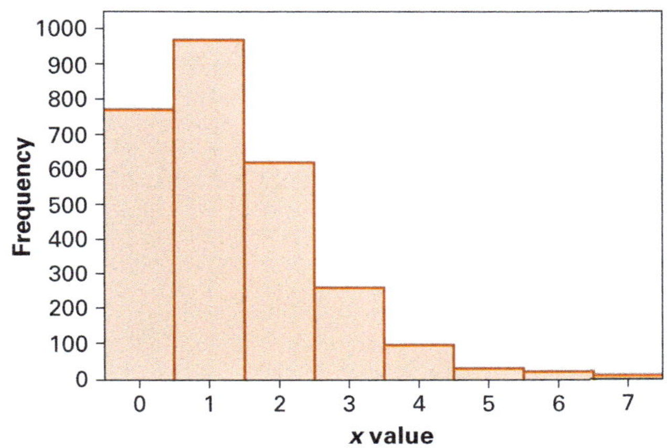

FIGURE 7.4 Histogram of a Poisson-distributed population, with $\lambda = 1.25$

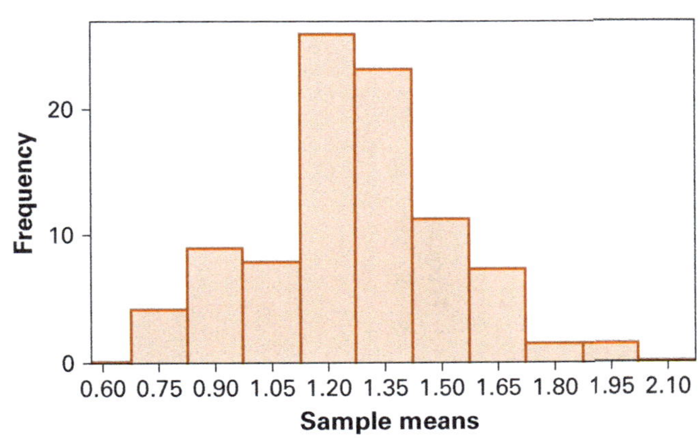

FIGURE 7.5 Histogram of sample means of size $n = 30$

Now consider a population that is uniformly distributed. If samples are selected randomly from this population, how would the sample means be distributed? Figure 7.6 (overleaf) displays the histogram distributions of sample means using five different sample sizes. Each of these histograms represents a sampling distribution of the sample mean, where 90 samples of varying sample sizes were selected. The uniform distribution used had $a = 10$ and $b = 30$. Some interesting observations can be made about the shapes of the distributions plotted in figure 7.6.

Notice that, even for small samples, the distributions of sample means tend to concentrate toward the middle of the distribution. Further, as the sample size increases, the sampling distributions approach a normal distribution and the spread of the sample means decreases.

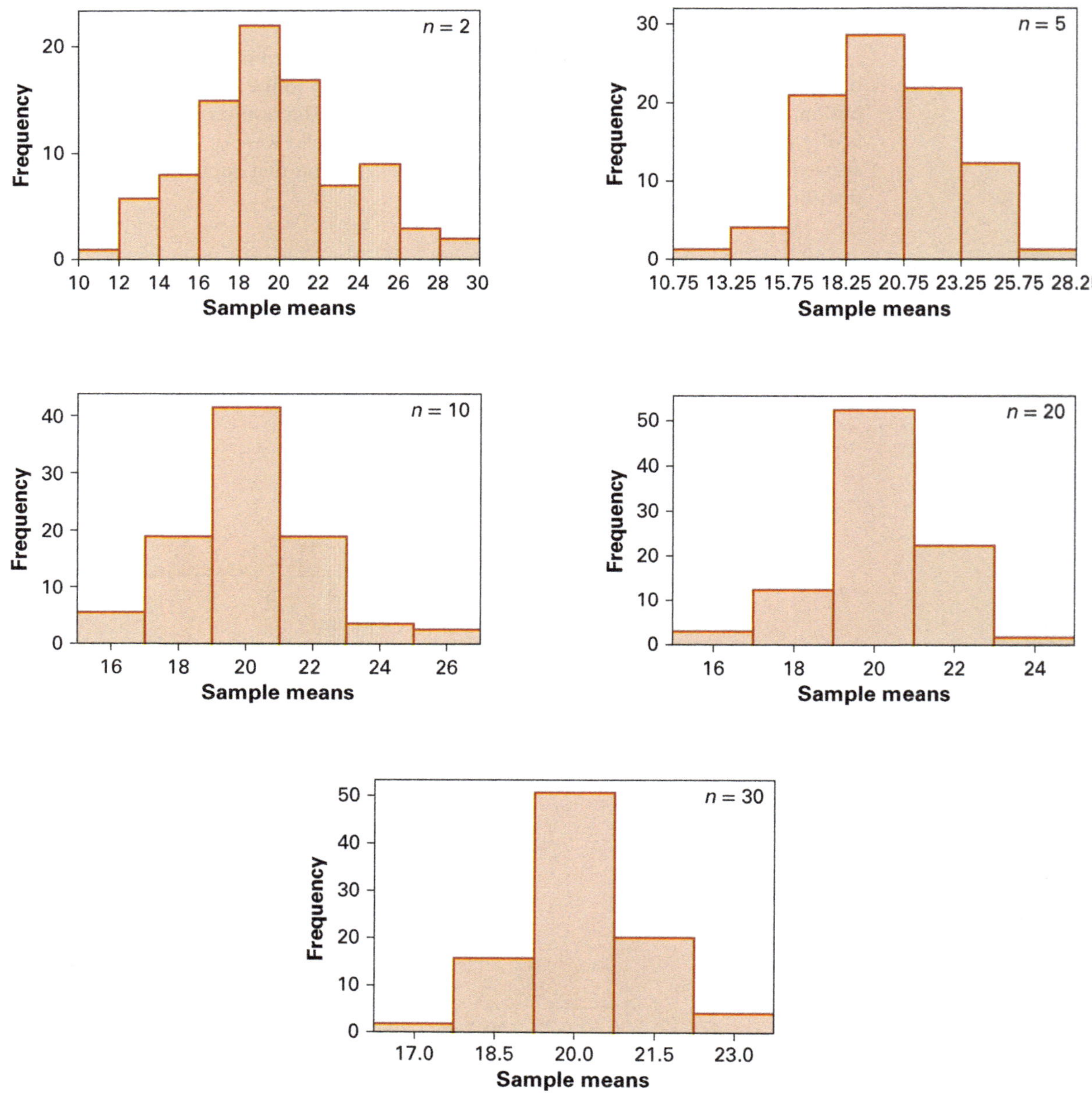

FIGURE 7.6 Histograms for sample means of 90 samples ranging in size from $n = 2$ to $n = 30$ from a uniformly distributed population with $a = 10$ and $b = 30$

So far, we have examined three populations with different shaped distributions. In all three cases the distributions of sample means appear to be approximately normally distributed, especially as the sample sizes increase. What would happen to the distribution of sample means if we studied populations with other shaped distributions? The answer to this question is given by the **central limit theorem**.

Central limit theorem

If samples of size n are drawn randomly from a population with a mean μ and standard deviation σ, the sample means $\bar{x}$ are approximately normally distributed for sufficiently large samples ($n \geq 30$) regardless of the shape of the population variable distribution. If the population variable is normally distributed, the sample means are normally distributed for any sample size.

From mathematical expectation (the derivations are beyond the scope of this text and are not shown), it can be shown that the mean of the sample means is the population mean:

$$\mu_{\bar{X}} = \mu$$

and the standard deviation of the sample means (called the **standard error of the mean**, $SE_{\bar{x}}$) is the standard deviation of the population divided by the square root of the sample size:

$$SE_{\bar{x}} = \sigma_{\bar{X}} = \frac{\sigma}{\sqrt{n}}$$

The central limit theorem creates the potential to apply our knowledge of the normal distribution to many problems when the sample size is sufficiently large. How large must a sample be for the central limit theorem to apply? The sample size necessary varies according to the shape of the distribution of the population variable. However, in this book a sample size of *30 or larger* will suffice. (Note that if the population variable is normally distributed the sample means are normally distributed for any size sample: that is, for $n \geq 1$.)

In practice, the central limit theorem is used when the distribution of a variable in a population is unknown. According to the central limit theorem, as long as a sample size of 30 or more is selected from any shaped population distribution, the sampling distribution of the sample mean will be approximately normally distributed. This is a powerful conclusion. It allows inferences to be made about a population variable using knowledge of the normal distribution and a single sample taken from a population where the variable is not normally distributed. To appreciate this, consider the first column in figure 7.7 (overleaf), which shows four different population distributions. It can be seen that, as the sample size increases, the shape of the sampling distribution of the sample mean from each population changes. The distributions of the sample means in all cases begin to approximate the normal distribution as n becomes larger and larger. For each of the population distributions, the distribution of sample means can be seen to be approximately normal distributed when $n = 30$. Note that, for the normally distributed population in the last row, the sample means are normally distributed for a sample size as small as $n = 2$.

The distributions in figure 7.7 were generated using random sampling from the population in a similar way to that used to generate figures 7.5 and 7.6. Notice that the sampling distribution of the sample mean becomes narrower (and more peaked) as the sample size increases. This makes sense because the standard deviation of the sampling distribution of the sample mean is calculated using $\frac{\sigma}{\sqrt{n}}$. Hence, as the sample size n increases, the value of the standard deviation of the sampling distribution becomes smaller, indicating that the distribution becomes narrower.

In table 7.2 (overleaf), the means and standard deviations of the sample means are displayed for random samples of various sizes ($n = 2$ to $n = 30$) drawn from a uniform distribution where $a = 10$ and $b = 30$. For this distribution, the population mean is 20 and the population standard deviation is 5.774. Note that the mean of the sample means for each sample size is approximately 20 and that the standard deviation of the sample means for each set of 90 samples is approximately equal to $\frac{\sigma}{\sqrt{n}}$. A small discrepancy occurs between the standard deviation of the sample means and $\frac{\sigma}{\sqrt{n}}$ because not all possible samples of a given size were taken from the population (only 90 samples were selected).

Note that, to find $\mu_{\bar{x}}$ without using a mathematical derivation, all possible samples of the same size would have to be selected randomly from a population. Then, each sample average would have to be calculated. Finally, the average of all the sample averages would be calculated to find $\mu_{\bar{x}}$. This task is virtually impossible to accomplish and is certainly out of the question if a practical problem involves a population size of 100 or more.

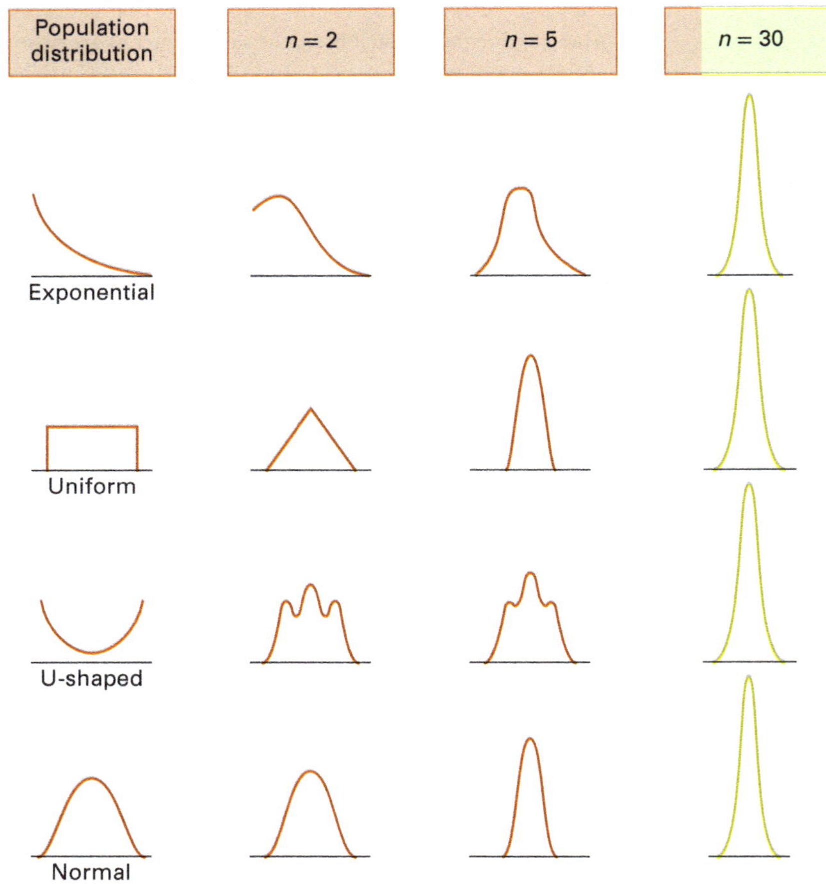

FIGURE 7.7 Shapes of various distributions of sample means, where three different sample sizes are used and samples are selected from four different population distributions

TABLE 7.2 $\mu_{\bar{x}}$ and $SE_{\bar{x}}$ of only 90 random samples of five different sizes (randomly generated from a uniform distribution with $a = 10$, $b = 30$)

Sample size	$\mu_{\bar{x}} = \mu$	Average of only 90 sample means	σ	Standard deviation of only 90 sample means	$SE_{\bar{x}} = \frac{\sigma}{\sqrt{n}}$
$n = 2$	20	19.92	5.774	3.87	4.08
$n = 5$	20	20.17	5.774	2.65	2.58
$n = 10$	20	20.04	5.774	1.96	1.83
$n = 20$	20	20.20	5.774	1.37	1.29
$n = 30$	20	20.25	5.774	0.99	1.05

The central limit theorem states that, regardless of the shape of the distribution of individual values of a variable in the population, the distribution of sample means is approximately normally distributed for sufficiently large sample sizes ($n \geq 30$). Thus, sample means can be analysed using our knowledge of the normal distribution and, in particular, by using z-scores. The formula to determine z-scores for individual values from a normal distribution is given by:

$$z = \frac{x - \mu}{\sigma}$$

If the variable of interest is now taken to be the sample mean, $\bar{x}$, instead of x, and the central limit theorem is applied to the sampling distribution of the sample means, the z-score formula applicable to the sampling distribution of the sample means would be:

$$z = \frac{\bar{x} - \mu_{\bar{x}}}{\sigma_{\bar{x}}}$$

Using the central limit theorem with $\mu_{\bar{x}} = \mu$ and $\sigma_{\bar{x}} = \text{SE}_{\bar{x}} = \frac{\sigma}{\sqrt{n}}$, and then making these substitutions into the z formula for the sampling distribution of the sample means gives formula 7.2, the z formula for sample means.

***z* formula for sample means** **(7.2)**

$$z = \frac{\bar{x} - \mu}{\text{SE}_{\bar{x}}} = \frac{\bar{x} - \mu}{\frac{\sigma}{\sqrt{n}}}$$

Note that, when a population variable is normally distributed and the sample size is one ($n = 1$), the z formula for the sampling distribution of the sample means becomes exactly the same as the z formula for individual values in the population. The reason is that, if $n = 1$, the sample mean of a single value is the same as that value, and the value of $\text{SE}_{\bar{x}} = \frac{\sigma}{\sqrt{n}} = \sigma$. Hence the sampling distribution of the sample mean is exactly the same as the distribution of the variable of interest in the population only when, and in the most unlikely situation, $n = 1$.

To understand how to apply the sampling distribution of the sample means, consider a hardware store owner who has decided to sell the store. As part of the promotional details provided to potential buyers, the store owner states that the average expenditure for a customer visiting this store is \$85 per customer with a standard deviation of \$9 per customer. Based on previous experience with other stores, the prospective buyer thinks this hardware store should be achieving an average expenditure per customer of at least \$87 and wonders if the shop owner is underselling the business. To assess this, the prospective buyer decides to take a random sample of 40 customers visiting the store. What is the probability that the average expenditure in this random sample will be at least \$87 per customer? In other words, what is $P(\bar{x} \geq 87)$?

To answer this question, it is worth noting that the sample size of 40 is greater than 30. Hence, the central limit theorem can be used. This allows the sampling distribution of the sample means to be taken to be approximately normally distributed and the z distribution to be used. In order to transform the sampling distribution of the sample means into z-scores, we first calculate $\text{SE}_{\bar{x}}$ where σ = \$9 and $n = 40$. Hence, $\text{SE}_{\bar{x}} = \frac{\sigma}{\sqrt{n}} = 1.42$. Now the z-score can be calculated where μ = \$85 and $\bar{x}$ = \$87 using formula 7.2:

$$z = \frac{\bar{x} - \mu}{\text{SE}_{\bar{x}}} = \frac{87 - 85}{1.42} = 1.41$$

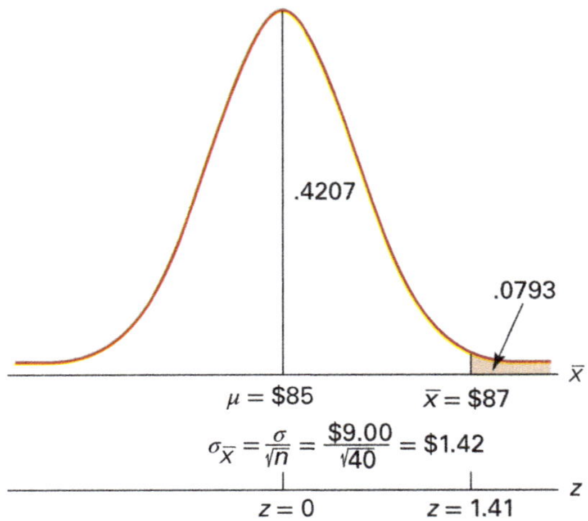

FIGURE 7.8 Graphical solution to the hardware store example

Using the z distribution and probabilities shown in table A.4, when $z = 1.41$, the probability of getting a z-score between 0 and 1.41 is .4207. This is the same as the probability of getting a sample mean between \$85 per person and \$87 per person. Hence, to calculate the probability of obtaining a sample mean of at least \$87 per person, this requires finding the area in the upper tail of the sampling distribution (which is the same as in the z distribution). The area in the upper tail = .5 − .4207 = .0793 = 7.93%. This is $P(\bar{x} \geq 87)$. That is, only 7.93% of all possible random samples of 40 customers selected from the population of customers who visit this hardware store will have a sample mean expenditure of \$87 per customer or more. Hence, if the prospective buyer uses the random sample of 40 customers as the basis for a purchase decision, there is only a 7.93% chance of wrongly concluding that the average expenditure per customer at the store is \$87 or more. This information would be useful in making a purchase decision, especially if the sample mean was \$87 per customer or more. Figure 7.8 shows diagrammatically the solution to this problem.

DEMONSTRATION PROBLEM 7.2

PROBLEM: Having used people-counting devices at the entry to a particular department store, it is known that the average number of shoppers visiting this store during any one-hour period is 448 shoppers, with a standard deviation of 21 shoppers. What is the probability that a random sample of 49 different one-hour shopping periods will yield a sample mean between 441 and 446 shoppers?

SOLUTION: For this problem, $\mu = 448$, $\sigma = 21$ and $n = 49$. The problem is to determine $P(441 \leq \bar{x} \leq 446)$. The following diagram depicts the problem.

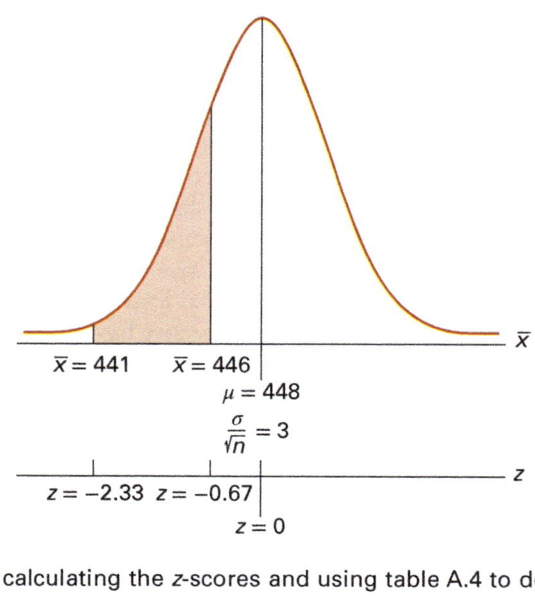

Solve this problem by calculating the z-scores and using table A.4 to determine the probabilities. Firstly:

$$SE_{\bar{x}} = \frac{\sigma}{\sqrt{n}} = \frac{21}{\sqrt{49}} = 3$$

Then:

$$z = \frac{441 - 448}{3} = \frac{-7}{3} = -2.33$$

and:

$$z = \frac{446 - 448}{3} = \frac{-2}{3} = -0.67$$

The probability of z falling between −2.33 and 0 is .4901, while the probability of z falling between −0.67 and 0 is .2486. Therefore, the probability of a value being between $z = -2.33$ and −0.67 is .4901 − .2486 = .2415; that is, there is a 24.15% chance of randomly selecting 49 one-hour periods for which the sample mean is between 441 and 446 shoppers.

DEMONSTRATION PROBLEM 7.3

PROBLEM: Referring to the department store in demonstration problem 7.2, how would the standard error of the mean be affected if the sample size was initially 49 and then increased to 196?

SOLUTION: In demonstration problem 7.2, $n = 49$ gave a standard error of 3. If n increases to 196, the standard error of the mean is:

$$SE_{\bar{x}} = \frac{\sigma}{\sqrt{n}} = \frac{21}{\sqrt{196}} = 1.5$$

This demonstrates that an increase in the sample size by a factor of 4 (from 49 to 196) reduces the standard error of the sampling distribution of the sample mean by half (from 3 to 1.5). This indicates taking larger samples reduces the distribution of the sample mean values.

Sampling from a finite population

The hardware store example and demonstration problem 7.2 were both based on the assumption that the population was infinitely large (or at least extremely large). In cases of a finite population, a *statistical adjustment can be made to the z formula for sample means*. The adjustment is called the **finite population correction (fpc) factor**:

$$\text{fpc} = \sqrt{\frac{N-n}{N-1}}$$

It operates on the standard deviation of sample means, $SE_{\bar{x}}$. Formula 7.3 is the z formula for sample means when samples are drawn from a finite population.

z formula for sample means for a finite population (7.3)

$$z = \frac{\bar{x} - \mu}{SE_{\bar{x}}} = \frac{\bar{x} - \mu}{\frac{\sigma}{\sqrt{n}}\sqrt{\frac{N-n}{N-1}}}$$

If a random sample of size 35 is taken from a finite population of only 500, the sample mean would be less likely to deviate from the population mean than if a sample of size 35 is taken from an infinite population. For a sample of size 35 taken from a finite population of 500, the fpc factor is:

$$\sqrt{\frac{500-35}{500-1}} = \sqrt{\frac{465}{499}} = .965$$

Thus, the standard error of the mean, $SE_{\bar{x}}$, for a finite population is adjusted downward by multiplying the infinite population standard error of the mean by .965. As the size of the finite population becomes larger in relation to the sample size, the fpc factor approaches 1. In theory, whenever researchers are working with a finite population, they can use the fpc factor. However, many researchers check to see if the sample size is less than 5% of the finite population size (meaning $\frac{n}{N} < .05$). If this is the case, then the fpc factor will have little effect on the standard error of the mean and so can be disregarded in any calculations. Table 7.3 contains some illustrative finite correction factors.

TABLE 7.3 Finite population correction factor for various sample sizes

Population size	Sample size	Value of correction factor
2000	30 (= 0.015*N*)	.993
2000	500 (= 0.25*N*)	.866
500	30 (= 0.06*N*)	.971
500	200 (= 0.4*N*)	.775
200	30 (= 0.15*N*)	.924
200	75 (= 0.375*N*)	.793

DEMONSTRATION PROBLEM 7.4

PROBLEM: An engineering firm employs 235 staff. Consider the ages of the firm's employees are normally distributed, with the average age of all staff being 40.5 years and standard deviation being 7.1 years. If a random sample of 40 staff is selected, what is the probability that the sample will have an average age of less than 43 years?

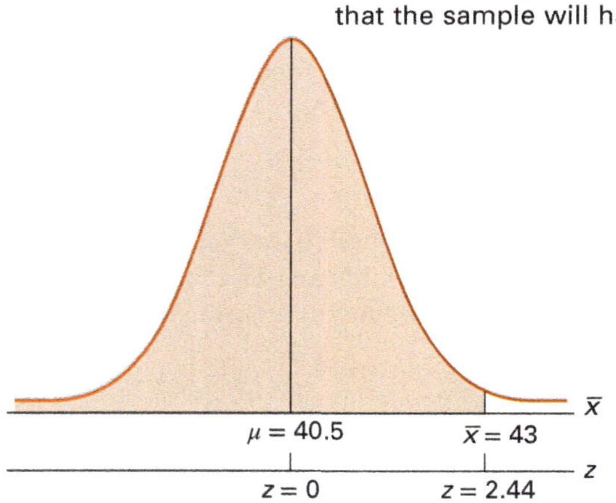

SOLUTION: The population mean is 40.5, with a population standard deviation of 7.1; that is, $\mu = 40.5$ and $\sigma = 7.1$. The sample size is 40, but it is drawn from a finite population of 235; that is, $n = 40$ and $N = 235$. The sample mean under consideration is 43, or $\bar{x} = 43$. The accompanying diagram depicts the problem on a normal curve.

Using the *z* formula with the finite correction factor, we first find $SE_{\bar{x}}$:

$$SE_{\bar{x}} = \frac{\sigma}{\sqrt{n}}\sqrt{\frac{N-n}{N-1}} = \frac{7.1}{\sqrt{40}}\sqrt{\frac{235-40}{235-1}} = 1.0248$$

$$z = \frac{\bar{x}-\mu}{SE_{\bar{x}}} = \frac{43-40.5}{1.0248} = 2.44$$

This *z*-score yields a probability of .4927 (table A.4). Therefore, the probability of getting a sample average age of less than 43 years is .4927 + .5000 = .9927. Had the finite correction factor not been used, the *z*-score would have been 2.23, and the final answer would have been .9871.

DEMONSTRATION PROBLEM 7.5

PROBLEM: At a major city airport, it is known that the average number of taxis departing the taxi rank between 7 am and 9 am on a weekday is 268, with a standard deviation of 12 taxis. Find an interval around the population mean that includes 95% of the sample means, based on using samples of 36 different weekdays between 7 am and 9 am.

SOLUTION: The 95% area around the population mean can be divided into two equal parts: 47.5% below the mean and 47.5% above the mean. From the standard normal distributions in table A.4, the *z*-scores corresponding to these areas are −1.96 and +1.96, respectively. The solution to the problem is to find the values of $\bar{x}$ corresponding to these *z*-scores.

First, find $SE_{\bar{x}}$ for the sampling distribution of the mean.

$$SE_{\bar{x}} = \frac{\sigma}{\sqrt{n}} = \frac{12}{\sqrt{36}} = 2$$

Hence, by using the z formula:

$$z = \frac{\bar{x} - \mu}{SE_{\bar{x}}}$$

and letting $\bar{x}_1$ be the lower value and $\bar{x}_2$ the upper value of $\bar{x}$, cross-multiplying and rearranging gives:

$$\begin{aligned}\bar{x}_1 &= zSE_{\bar{x}} + \mu \\ &= -1.96 \times 2 + 268 \\ &= -3.92 + 268 \\ &= 264.08\end{aligned}$$

Similarly:

$$\bar{x}_2 = zSE_{\bar{x}} + \mu = 1.96 \times 2 + 268 = 3.92 + 268 = 271.92$$

Therefore, 95% of all sample means, based on samples of 36 different weekdays between 7 am and 9 am, have values lying between 264 and 272 for the number of taxis leaving the rank.

PRACTICE PROBLEMS

Practising the calculations

7.9 A population has a mean of 150 and a standard deviation of 21. If a random sample of 49 is taken, what is the probability that the sample mean is:

a. greater than 154
b. less than 153
c. less than 147
d. between 152.5 and 157.5
e. between 148 and 158?

7.10 A population is normally distributed, with a mean of 14 and a standard deviation of 1.2. What is the probability of each of the following?

a. Taking a sample of 26 and obtaining a sample mean of 13.7 or more
b. Taking a sample of 15 and getting a sample mean of more than 15.7

7.11 A random sample of 81 is drawn from a population with a standard deviation of 12. If a sample mean greater than 300 is obtained only 18% of the time, what is the mean of the population?

7.12 Find the probability in each of the following cases. Consider each population as being finite and therefore apply the finite population correction factor.

a. $P(\bar{x} < 76.5)$ if $N = 1000$, $n = 60$, $\mu = 75$ and $\sigma = 6$
b. $P(107 < \bar{x} < 107.7)$ if $N = 90$, $n = 36$, $\mu = 108$ and $\sigma = 3.46$
c. $P(\bar{x} \geq 36)$ if $N = 250$, $n = 100$, $\mu = 35.6$ and $\sigma = 4.89$
d. $P(\bar{x} \leq 123)$ if $N = 5000$, $n = 60$, $\mu = 125$ and $\sigma = 13.4$

Testing your understanding

7.13 According to the ABS, the average length of stay by tourists in Queensland's hotels, motels and serviced apartments is 2.2 days, with a standard deviation of 1.2 days. A sample of 65 randomly selected tourists is taken.

a. What is the probability that the average length of stay for the 65 chosen in the sample is less than 2.2 days?
b. What is the probability that the average length of stay for the 65 chosen in the sample is between 2.1 days and 2.4 days?
c. What is the probability that the average length of stay for the 65 chosen in the sample is between 2.4 and 3 days?
d. What would be the minimum value for the average length of stay, for the chosen sample of 65, for the 5% of tourists who stayed longest?

7.14 A new estate contains 1500 houses. A sample of 100 houses is selected randomly and evaluated by a real estate agent. If the mean appraised value of a house for all houses in this area is $300 000, with a standard deviation of $10 500, what is the probability that the sample average is greater than $303 000?

7.15 The monthly mobile phone bill for all customers at a large telecommunications company has been found to be normally distributed with a mean of $145.55 per month and standard deviation of $15.22 per month. What value would be exceeded by 65% of sample means if the sample size was 40?

7.16 A recent survey of Australians found that mean sleep time was 8 hours, with a standard deviation of 3 hours. Assume sleep time is normally distributed.

a. What is the probability that a randomly selected population member sleeps more than 9 hours?
b. What is the probability that, in a random sample of 42 people, the sample mean is more than 9 hours?
c. What is the probability that, in a random sample of 42 people, the sample mean is between 7.5 and 9 hours?

7.5 Sampling distribution of the sample proportion, $\hat{p}$

If a sample involving a categorical variable is analysed, the frequency of occurrence of a particular category can be found. If a researcher uses a sample to analyse a categorical variable, the statistic called the sample proportion, denoted $\hat{p}$, can be used. For example, when categorical items, such as how many people in a sample choose Pepsi as their preferred soft drink or how many people in a sample have a flexible work schedule, the sample proportion is the statistic to use. The **sample proportion** is calculated by dividing the frequency with which a given characteristic occurs in a sample by the total number of items in the sample, as shown in formula 7.4.

Sample proportion (7.4)

$$\hat{p} = \frac{x}{n}$$

where:

x = the number of items in a sample with a particular characteristic of interest
n = the number of items in the sample

For example, in a sample of 100 factory workers, 30 workers might belong to a union. The value of the sample proportion for the characteristic of union membership is $\frac{30}{100} = .30$. In a sample of 500 businesses in suburban malls, if 10 are shoe stores, then the sample proportion of shoe stores is $\frac{10}{500} = .02$. The sample proportion is a widely used statistic and can be used for questions involving yes/no answers. For example, do you have at least a high school education? Are you predominantly right-handed? Are you female? Do you belong to the student accounting association?

How does a researcher use the sample proportion in analysis? The central limit theorem applies to sample proportions in that the normal distribution approximates the shape of the distribution of sample proportions. This approximation holds if both $np > 5$ and $nq > 5$ (where p is the population proportion and $q = 1 - p$). The mean of all possible sample proportions of the same size n randomly drawn from a population is p (the population proportion). The standard deviation of this distribution of sample proportions is $\sqrt{\frac{pq}{n}}$, referred to as the **standard error of the proportion**, $SE_{\hat{p}}$. Sample proportions also have a z formula, as shown in formula 7.5.

***z* formula for sample proportions when $np > 5$ and $nq > 5$ (7.5)**

$$z = \frac{\hat{p} - p}{SE_{\hat{p}}} = \frac{\hat{p} - p}{\sqrt{\frac{pq}{n}}}$$

where:

$\hat{p}$ = the sample proportion
n = the sample size
p = the population proportion
$q = 1 - p$

For example, it is known that 60% of the electrical contractors in a region use a particular brand of wire. What is the probability of taking a random sample of 120 of these electrical contractors and finding that 50% or less use that brand of wire?

For this problem, $p = .60$, $\hat{p} = .50$ and $n = 120$ so:

$$SE_{\hat{p}} = \sqrt{\frac{pq}{n}} = \sqrt{\frac{(.60)(.40)}{120}} = .0447$$

The z formula yields:

$$z = \frac{\hat{p} - p}{SE_{\hat{p}}}$$
$$= \frac{.50 - .60}{.0447}$$
$$= -2.24$$

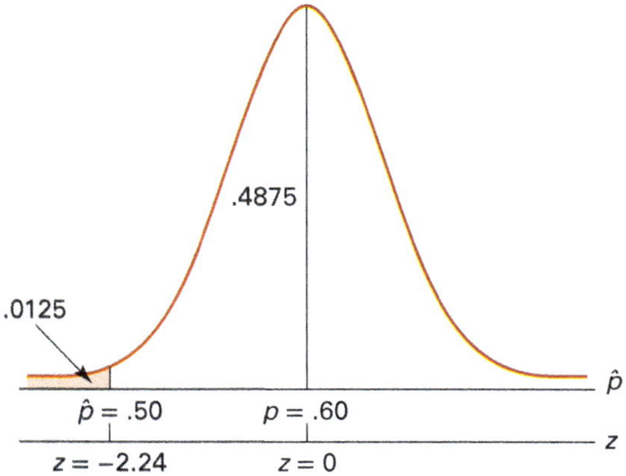

FIGURE 7.9 Graphical solution to the electrical contractor example

From table A.4, the probability of getting a z-score between 0 and -2.24 is .4875. For $z < -2.24$ (the tail of the distribution), the answer is $.5000 - .4875 = .0125$. Figure 7.9 shows the solution graphically.

This answer indicates that a researcher would have difficulty (a probability of .0125) finding that 50% or less of a sample of 120 contractors use a given brand of wire if indeed the population market share for that wire is .60. If this sample result actually occurred, it may have been a rare chance result, the .60 proportion may not hold for this population, or the sampling method may not have been random.

DEMONSTRATION PROBLEM 7.6

PROBLEM: If 10% of a population of parts is defective, what is the probability of randomly selecting 80 parts and finding that 12 or more parts are defective?

SOLUTION: Here, $p = .10$, $\hat{p} = \frac{12}{80} = .15$ and $n = 80$, so:

$$SE_{\hat{p}} = \sqrt{\frac{pq}{n}} = \sqrt{\frac{(.10)(.90)}{80}} = .03354$$

Entering these values in the z formula yields:

$$z = \frac{\hat{p} - p}{SE_{\hat{p}}}$$
$$= \frac{.15 - .10}{.03354}$$
$$= 1.49$$

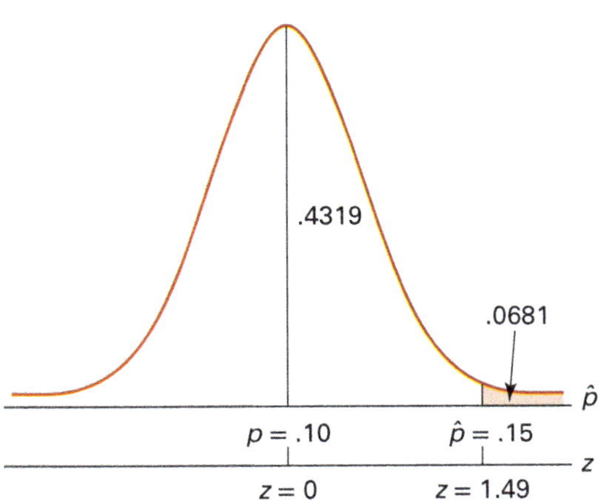

Table A.4 gives a probability of .4319 for a z-score of 1.49, which is the area between the sample proportion .15, and the population proportion .10. The solution to this problem is:

$$P(\hat{p} \geq .15) = .5000 - .4319 = .0681$$

Thus, 6.81% of the time, 12 or more defective parts would appear in a random sample of 80 parts when the population proportion is .10. If 12 or more defective parts in a sample were actually found, the assumption that 10% of the population is defective would be open to question. The diagram shows the problem graphically.

PRACTICE PROBLEMS

Practising the calculations

7.17 For a population with $p = 0.6$, find the probability for each sample proportion and given sample size.

a. $n = 12$ and $\hat{p} < .77$
b. $n = 30$ and $\hat{p} > .56$
c. $n = 65$ and $.54 < \hat{p} < .56$
d. $n = 100$ and $\hat{p} < .69$
e. $n = 240$ and $\hat{p} > .53$

7.18 A population proportion is .32. Suppose a random sample of 40 items is sampled randomly from this population. What is the probability that the sample proportion is:

a. greater than .42
b. between .18 and .51
c. greater than .30
d. between .38 and .48
e. less than .39?

7.19 Suppose a population proportion is .40, and 80% of the time when you draw a random sample from this population you get a sample proportion of .35 or more. How large a sample were you taking?

7.20 If a population proportion is .28 and the sample size is 140, 30% of the time the sample proportion will be less than what value if you are taking random samples?

Testing your understanding

7.21 According to a study undertaken in a large rural town, 15% of children aged from 10 to 16 years were found to exercise less than one hour per day. If a random sample of 35 children in this age group was selected from this town, what is the probability that more than 7 children would be found to exercise less than one hour per day?

7.22 According to a survey by Accountemps, 48% of executives believe that employees are most productive on Tuesdays. Suppose 200 executives are randomly surveyed.

a. What is the probability that fewer than 90 of the executives believe employees are most productive on Tuesdays?
b. What is the probability that more than 100 of the executives believe employees are most productive on Tuesdays?
c. What is the probability that more than 80 of the executives believe employees are most productive on Tuesdays?

7.23 A survey asked business travellers about the purpose of their most recent business trip. Nineteen per cent responded that it was for an internal company visit. Suppose 950 business travellers are randomly selected.

a. What is the probability that more than 25% of the business travellers say that the reason for their most recent business trip was an internal company visit?
b. What is the probability that between 15% and 20% of the business travellers say that the reason for their most recent business trip was an internal company visit?
c. What is the probability that between 133 and 171 of the business travellers say that the reason for their most recent business trip was an internal company visit?

MISUSE OF STATISTICS

The application to business of the sampling distribution of the sample mean and sample proportion requires, among other things, an understanding of the normal distribution and sampling techniques. For example, it involves understanding the central limit theorem for the sampling distribution of the mean and the assumption that both *np* and *nq* are larger than 5 for the sampling distribution of the proportion. If, during research, a sample is selected and a researcher knowingly disregards any underlying assumptions related to the sampling distribution of the sample mean or sample proportion, this would be unethical. Such behaviour may occur as a result of pressure to arrive at specific conclusions that satisfy a client's needs or maintain head office funding for future projects. For example, consider that you are responsible for analysing company data to assess future projects. You have been provided with statistics by upper management, along with some conclusions based on these data. You review the data and have some doubts about the findings. For example, the sample was clearly not selected in an appropriate way to arrive at the stated conclusions. The statistics look 'good' and you sense that management wants to make an important investment decision based on the reported findings from the statistics. You have two options. You could play on management's ignorance and tell them what you think they want to hear, or you could act professionally and recommend that improved data collection and statistical analysis be done. Proper ethical behaviour demands that you go for the second option. This is the ethically correct thing to do and will likely save the company money in the long run.

CHAPTER CASE
REVISITED

Prawn farm success tied to strict quality control

1. The first thing to note in assessing whether there is something wrong with the growing conditions is that historical data show that the lengths of two-week-old prawn larvae are normally distributed. This means that, no matter the sample size, the sampling distribution of the sample mean of lengths of two-week-old prawn larvae is normally distributed. Hence, the z formula for the sampling distribution of the mean can be used in this situation with $n = 20$ and a standard error given by:

$$SE_{\bar{x}} = \frac{\sigma}{\sqrt{n}} = \frac{.5}{\sqrt{20}} = .1118$$

We need to determine the probability that a sample of size 20, with a sample mean of 6.5 mm, could be drawn from a population with a mean length of 7 mm and standard deviation of 0.5 mm. First we find:

$$z = \frac{\bar{x} - \mu}{SE_{\bar{x}}} = \frac{6.5 - 7}{.1118} = -4.47$$

Since the absolute value of this z-score is much larger than 3, the area in the tail of the z distribution for $z = -4.47$ is very small and effectively zero. Recall that 99% of all observations in the normal distribution are within three standard deviations either side of the population mean. Hence, this implies that the chance of selecting a random sample of 20 larvae with an average length of 6.5 mm (when μ is 7 mm) or smaller is effectively impossible (probability zero). Hence, the fact that a sample with an average length of 6.5 mm was randomly selected implies that μ is almost certainly less than 7 mm.

2. To assess findings on the new type of food, the concept of the sampling distribution of the sample mean can be used once again. Firstly, we can examine whether the lengths of the prawns have become larger using the new food. The standard error of the mean is:

$$SE_{\bar{x}} = \frac{\sigma}{\sqrt{n}} = \frac{3}{\sqrt{20}} = .671$$

If the new prawn food has no significant effect on the length of six-week-old prawns, 99% of the sample means will be between three standard errors either side of the population mean length: that is, between $80 - .671 \times 3 = 77.99$ mm and $80 + .671 \times 3 = 82.01$ mm. Since the sample average weight of the 20 prawns was 79.95 mm, well within the limits of 77.99 mm and 82.01 mm, there is no clear evidence that the sample average length has changed. It looks as though the new food does not make the prawns any longer.

However, in assessing the weight of six-week-old prawns, the standard error is:

$$SE_{\bar{x}} = \frac{\sigma}{\sqrt{n}} = \frac{2}{\sqrt{20}} = .447$$

If the new prawn food has no effect on the weight of six-week-old prawns, 99% of the sample means will be between three standard errors either side of the population mean weight; that is, between $48 - .447 \times 3 = 46.66$ g and $48 + .447 \times 3 = 49.34$ g. Since the sample average weight of the 20 prawns was 51 g, well outside the limits of 46.66 g and 49.34 g, it appears that the new food makes the prawns heavier.

3. The sampling distribution of the proportion can be used to understand how management aims to control the number of defective prawns in any one shipment. Using the tighter QCC restriction that aims to have no more than 5% defective prawns in any shipment, $p = .05$. Hence, when using a sample of 400 to test for the proportion of defective prawns in a shipment, the standard error of the proportion is:

$$SE_{\hat{p}} = \sqrt{\frac{pq}{n}} = \sqrt{\frac{(.05)(.95)}{400}} = .0109$$

If the sample of 400 is selected and the sample proportion of defective prawns is .075, the probability of finding a sample proportion of this value or larger can be found by calculating the corresponding z-score:

$$z = \frac{\hat{p} - p}{SE_{\hat{p}}} = \frac{.075 - .05}{.0109} = 2.29$$

The solution is illustrated in the following diagram.

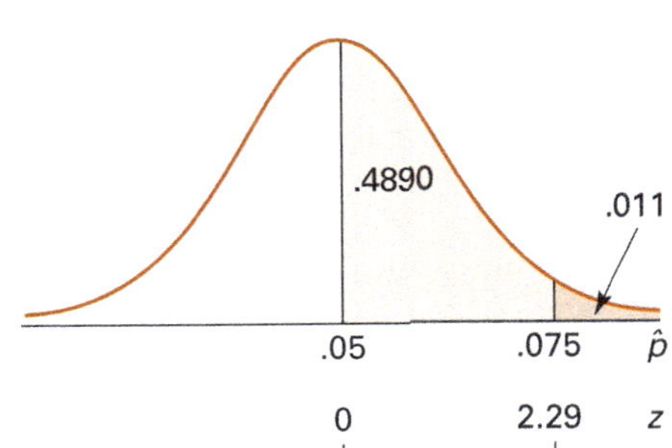

This calculation shows that there is only about a 1% chance (a very low probability) of selecting a random sample of 400 with more than 7.5% defect prawns. This procedure, while not guaranteeing that all shipments will have 10% or fewer defective prawns, has a very low risk of allowing a shipment to be sent overseas where the percentage of defective prawns exceeds 10%. Hence, if a selected sample has more than 7.5% defective prawns, it would be reasonable to conclude that the shipment has more than 5% defective prawns and should not be sent to Japan. Note that, by limiting shipments to 5% defective prawns, the QCC has set a stricter standard than the 10% limit that customers will accept.

SUMMARY

1 For much business research, successfully conducting a census is virtually impossible so sampling is a feasible alternative. Other reasons for sampling include cost reduction, potential for broadening the scope of the study and reduction of losses when the testing process destroys the product.

To take a sample, a population must be identified. Often the researcher cannot obtain an exact roster or list of the population and so must find some way to identify the population as closely as possible. The final list or directory used to represent the population from which the sample is drawn is called the frame.

2 The two main types of sampling are random and nonrandom sampling. Random sampling occurs when each unit of the population has a known probability of being selected in the sample. The four main types of random sampling are simple random sampling, stratified sampling, systematic sampling and cluster or area sampling. Nonrandom sampling is any sampling that is not random. Four types of nonrandom sampling are convenience, judgement, quota and snowball sampling.

In simple random sampling, every unit of the population has an equal (and known) probability of being selected in the sample. Stratified random sampling uses the researcher's prior knowledge of the population to stratify the population into subgroups. Each subgroup is internally homogeneous but different from the others. Stratified random sampling is an attempt to reduce sampling error and ensure that at least some of each of the subgroups appears in the sample. After the strata are identified, units can be sampled randomly from each stratum. If the proportions of units in the sample selected from each subgroup are the same as the proportions of the subgroups in the population, the process is called proportionate stratified sampling. If not, it is called disproportionate stratified sampling. With systematic sampling, every kth item of the population is sampled until n units have been selected. Systematic sampling is used because of its convenience and ease of administration. Cluster or area sampling involves subdividing the population into non-overlapping clusters or areas. Each cluster or area is a microcosm of the population and is usually heterogeneous within the group. Individual units are then selected randomly from the clusters or areas to get the final sample. Cluster or area sampling is usually done to reduce costs. If a second set of clusters or areas is selected from the first set, the method is called two-stage sampling.

Four types of nonrandom sampling are convenience, judgement, quota and snowball sampling. In convenience sampling, the researcher selects units from the population for convenience. In judgement sampling, units are selected according to the judgement of the researcher. Quota sampling is similar to stratified sampling, with the researcher identifying subclasses or strata. However, the researcher selects units from each stratum by some nonrandom technique until a specified quota from each stratum is filled. In snowball sampling, the researcher obtains additional sample members by asking current sample members for referrals.

3 Sampling errors occur because the sampling process involves selecting from a subset of the population. With random sampling, sampling errors occur by chance. Nonsampling errors include all other research and analysis errors that occur in a study, such as recording errors, input errors, missing data and incorrect definition of the frame.

4 According to the central limit theorem, if the sample is large ($n \geq 30$), the sample mean is approximately normally distributed, regardless of the distribution of the variable of interest in the population. Also, if the population variable is normally distributed, the sample means for samples taken from that population are normally distributed for any sample size. The central limit theorem is extremely useful because it enables researchers to analyse sample data using the normal distribution for virtually any type of study where the sample mean is the appropriate statistic.

5 The sampling distribution of the proportion is also approximately normally distributed provided the sample size is large enough such that both $np > 5$ and $nq > 5$.

KEY TERMS

central limit theorem p. 210
cluster (or area) sampling p. 203
convenience sampling p. 204
disproportionate stratified random sampling p. 202
finite population correction (fpc) factor p. 215
judgement sampling p. 204
nonrandom sampling p. 198
nonsampling error p. 206
probability-based sampling p. 198
proportionate stratified random sampling p. 202
quota sampling p. 205
random sampling p. 198
sample proportion p. 218
sampling error p. 205
sampling frame p. 197
simple random sampling p. 198
snowball sampling p. 205
standard error of the mean p. 211
standard error of the proportion p. 218
stratified random sampling p. 201
systematic sampling p. 203
two-stage sampling p. 203

KEY EQUATIONS

EQUATION	DESCRIPTION	FORMULA
7.1	Determining the value of k	$k = \frac{N}{n}$
7.2	z formula for sample means	$z = \frac{\bar{x} - \mu}{SE_{\bar{x}}} = \frac{\bar{x} - \mu}{\frac{\sigma}{\sqrt{n}}}$
7.3	z formula for sample means for a finite population	$z = \frac{\bar{x} - \mu}{SE_{\bar{x}}} = \frac{\bar{x} - \mu}{\frac{\sigma}{\sqrt{n}}\sqrt{\frac{N-n}{N-1}}}$
7.4	Sample proportion	$\hat{p} = \frac{x}{n}$
7.5	z formula for sample proportions when $np > 5$ and $nq > 5$	$z = \frac{\hat{p} - p}{SE_{\hat{p}}} = \frac{\hat{p} - p}{\sqrt{\frac{pq}{n}}}$

REVIEW PROBLEMS

Practising the calculations

7.24 The mean of a population is 54 and the standard deviation is 10. The shape of the population is unknown. Determine the probability of each of the following occurring for this population.

a. A random sample of 38 yielding a sample mean of 56 or less

b. A random sample of 120 yielding a sample mean between 52.6 and 55.4

c. A random sample of 180 yielding a sample mean greater than 52

7.25 Forty-six per cent of a population possesses a particular characteristic. Random samples are taken from this population. Determine the probability of each of the following occurrences.

a. The sample size is 60 and the sample proportion is between .41 and .53.

b. The sample size is 458 and the sample proportion is less than .40.

c. The sample size is 1350 and the sample proportion is greater than .49.

Testing your understanding

7.26 Suppose the age distribution in a city is as follows.

Under 18	16%
18–25	19%
26–50	29%
51–65	22%
Over 65	14%

A researcher is conducting proportionate stratified random sampling with a sample size of 300. Approximately how many people should they sample from each stratum?

7.27 Candidate Jones believes she will receive .55 of the total votes cast in her electorate. However, in an attempt to validate this figure, her pollster contacts a random sample of 600 registered voters in the electorate. The poll results show that 298 of the voters say they are committed to voting for her. If she actually does have .55 of the total vote, what is the probability of getting a sample proportion this small or smaller? Do you think she actually has 55% of the vote? Why or why not?

7.28 Determine a possible frame for conducting random sampling in each of the following studies.

a. The average amount of overtime per week for production workers in a plastics company in Queensland

b. The average number of employees in all Coles supermarkets in New South Wales

c. A survey of commercial lobster catchers in Tasmania

7.29 The average fee charged by suburban accountants to do a basic tax return in Brisbane was found to be normally distributed with a mean of \$110 and standard deviation of \$15. If a random sample of 45 basic tax returns completed by suburban accountants was selected, what is the probability the sample mean fee charged will be:

a. larger than \$105

b. larger than \$115

c. between \$106 and \$116?

7.30 A survey of 2645 consumers by a public relations agency showed that how a company handles a crisis when at fault is one of the top influences in consumer-buying decisions, with 73% claiming it is an influence. However, the quality of its product was the number one influence, with 96% of consumers stating that quality influences their buying decisions. How a company handles complaints was number two, with 85% of consumers reporting it as an influence in their buying decisions. Suppose a random sample of 1100 consumers is taken and each is asked which of these three factors influence their buying decisions.

a. What is the probability that more than 810 consumers claim that how a company handles a crisis when at fault is an influence in their buying decisions?

b. What is the probability that fewer than 1030 consumers claim that quality of product is an influence in their buying decisions?

c. What is the probability that between 82% and 84% of consumers claim that how a company handles complaints is an influence in their buying decisions?

7.31 As part of a research study, you send questionnaires to a randomly selected sample of 100 managers. The frame for this study is the membership list of the Australian Institute of Management. The questionnaire contains demographic questions about the company and its top manager. In addition, it asks questions about the manager's leadership style. Research assistants are to score and enter the responses into the computer as soon as they are received. You are to conduct a statistical analysis of the data. Name and describe four non-sampling errors that could occur in this study.

7.32 A researcher is conducting a study of a *large* company that has factories, distribution centres and retail outlets across the country. How can she use cluster or area sampling to take a random sample of employees of this company?

7.33 A directory of personal computer retail outlets in Australia contains 12 080 alphabetised entries. Explain how systematic sampling could be used to select a sample of 300 outlets.

7.34 In an effort to cut costs and improve profits, many companies in the United States, Australia and New Zealand have been turning to outsourcing. Suppose that 54% of companies surveyed outsourced some part of their manufacturing process in the past two to three years and that 565 of these companies are contacted.

a. What is the probability that 339 or more companies outsourced some part of their manufacturing process in the past two to three years?
b. What is the probability that 288 or more companies outsourced some part of their manufacturing process in the past two to three years?
c. What is the probability that 50% or less of these companies outsourced some part of their manufacturing process in the past two to three years?

7.35 The Department of Housing can provide apartment accommodation in a particular city. The average cost of renting a two-bedroom apartment in this city is $800 per month. What is the probability of randomly selecting a sample of 50 two-bedroom apartments in this city and getting a sample mean of rental costs of less than $750 per month? Assume the population standard deviation to be $100 per month.

7.36 According to ABS figures, average weekly total earnings of all employees in Australia is $1105 per week. Take this population standard deviation to be $45 per week. If a representative random sample of 70 Australian employees is surveyed, what is the probability the sample average weekly total earnings will be:

a. less than $1115
b. more than $1100
c. between $1110 and $1120
d. less than $1098?

7.37 The marketing team of a major video rental company has found that 68% of its customers returned rented movies before the third night. A random sample of 500 customers is taken. What is the probability that the proportion returning a video before the third night is:

a. 65% or less
b. 75% or more
c. between 60% and 72%?

7.38 It is estimated that 80% of occupants use electricity as their principal heating fuel during winter in newly constructed apartments in Auckland. A random sample of 100 homes was selected to determine whether this figure was correct. It was found 92 of the 100 apartments sampled used electricity as their principal heating fuel. What is the probability of getting a sample proportion larger than this amount if the population estimate is correct?

CHAPTER

8 Statistical inference: estimation for single populations

LEARNING OBJECTIVES

After studying this chapter, you should be able to:

1. estimate a population mean from a sample mean when the population standard deviation is known
2. estimate a population mean from a sample mean when the population standard deviation is unknown
3. estimate a population proportion from a sample proportion
4. estimate a population variance from a sample variance
5. estimate the minimum sample size necessary to achieve particular statistical goals.

OPENING VIGNETTE

Rural obesity in Queensland on the rise

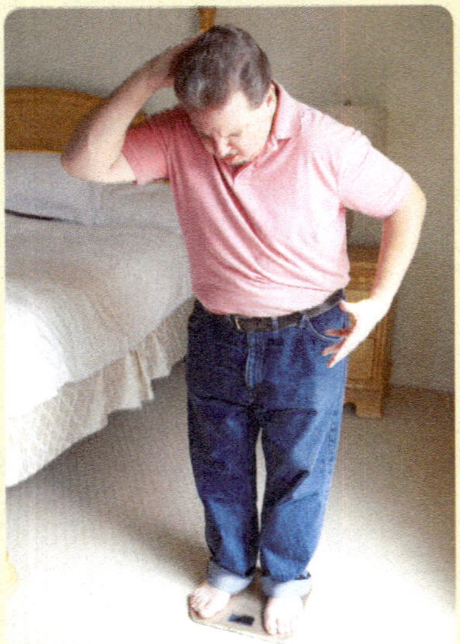

In July 2014, the Australian Medical Association's branch in Queensland (AMAQ) announced a campaign called 'Lighten your Load' to address the large proportion of rural Queenslanders considered to be overweight. The AMAQ president reported that 'on average, 67 per cent of regional Queenslanders are overweight or obese'. Further, AMAQ noted that 'statistics are even higher around Townsville and Mackay regions with 75 per cent overweight or obese. That's 226 000 adults carrying too much weight.' By comparison, figures from the Australian Institute of Health and Welfare suggest that in the Australian population 60% of adults and 25% of children are classified as overweight or obese.

In addition, the AMAQ reported that men aged 45–65 who live in a regional area are, compared to their city counterparts:

- 30% more likely to smoke
- up to 1.5 times as likely to drink heavily
- 44% more likely to die of heart disease
- at 31% greater risk of suffering a stroke.

The AMAQ clearly indicate that as obesity-related diseases increase, life expectancy decreases. They are concerned for Queenslanders living away from urban areas. Men are more at risk than women. The 'Lighten your Load' campaign aims to address these health-related issues.

Introduction

In this chapter, the concepts of the normal distribution and sampling distributions are applied to develop estimation, an inferential statistics technique. Knowledge of inferential statistics provides decision makers and researchers with a powerful analytical tool. It enables conclusions to be made about a much larger population by analysing a smaller representative sample thereby saving time and money, and often being more practical. The focus of this chapter is to outline the techniques used to estimate a population mean and a population proportion. Attention is also given to explaining how to calculate the sample size that is needed to draw meaningful conclusions about a population parameter using a specified margin of error and level of confidence.

CHAPTER CASE

Prawn farm up for sale

In 2015, the owner of Sunny Bay Prawn Farm decided it was time to retire and sell the prawn farming business. An investor was thinking about making an offer. Prior to making the offer and parting with a very large amount of money, the investor wanted to investigate specific aspects of the business. Of particular interest was the quality of prawns the farm actually delivered to its customers. Since Japan was Sunny Bay Prawn Farm's largest market, the investor decided to travel to Japan, meet existing customers and assess the quality of the prawns being delivered there.

Questions to help managers make decisions

1. At the fish market in Japan, the investor decides to take a random sample of Sunny Bay prawns from unopened boxes that have been delivered. The owner at Sunny Bay has advised the investor that the prawns sent to Japan have lengths that are normally distributed, with a specified average length of 15 cm (the length that consumers prefer) and a standard deviation of 0.8 cm. The investor randomly selects 25 prawns from the unopened boxes and obtains a sample average of 14.8 cm. The investor decides to construct a 95% confidence interval using the sample data to get a better estimate of the population mean. Does the stated population mean of 15 cm lie within the confidence interval constructed, and what does this indicate to the investor?
2. Sunny Bay has advised potential investors that Japanese importers are happy to accept up to 10% of prawns in any one shipment having some kind of defect; for example, some prawns may have broken feelers. The investor wished to estimate the percentage of damaged prawns in a shipment and be 95% confident. It is decided to test the claim made by Sunny Bay that they aim for 5% defective prawns in any shipment. The investor decides that an acceptable margin of error would be 3%. To estimate the population proportion of damaged prawns, how large a sample should the investor select to meet the specified level of confidence and margin of error? Assume that, after discussions with some Japanese clients, the investor determines that 6% is a good estimate of the population proportion of damaged prawns.
3. The investor finally decides to use a sample size of 250 and finds that 11 prawns in the sample are damaged. Construct a 95% confidence interval for the proportion of damaged prawns arriving in Japan based on this sample proportion. Based on this confidence interval, what conclusions can the investor make about the proportion of damaged prawns?

8.1 Estimating the population mean using the z statistic (σ known)

Managers frequently need to understand more about a whole group (population) of items or individuals. This may involve taking a random sample to then draw conclusions about the whole group. For example, the manager of human resources in a company might want to estimate the average number of days of work employees miss per year because of illness. If the company has thousands of employees, direct calculation of a population mean such as this may be practically impossible. Instead, a random sample of employees can be taken, and the sample mean number of sick days can be used to estimate the population mean number of sick days. Quality control and quality assurance is another area where sampling is needed to draw conclusions about a population. For example, suppose a company develops a new process for prolonging the shelf life of a loaf of bread. The company wants to be able to indicate a use-by date on each loaf. However, company officials do not know exactly how long the bread will stay fresh. By taking a random sample of loaves and determining the sample mean shelf life, they can estimate the average shelf life for the population of bread.

To illustrate how decision makers use sample data, consider the example of a mobile phone company wishing to rethink its pricing structure as the mobile phone market matures. Users appear to be spending more time on the phone. To improve planning, the company wants to ascertain the average number of minutes used per week by each of its residential users but does not have the resources available to examine all bills and extract the information. The company decides to take a random sample of customer bills and estimate the population mean from sample data. A researcher for the company takes a random sample of 85 recent bills and uses these bills to compute a sample mean of 153 minutes per week. This sample mean (a statistic) is used to estimate the population mean (the parameter). If the company uses the sample mean of 153 minutes as an estimate of the population mean, then this sample mean is a **point estimate** for the population mean.

A point estimate is a statistic calculated from a sample that is used to estimate a population parameter. Since a sample is unlikely to be perfectly representative of a population, a sample mean is unlikely to be exactly the same as the population mean. Hence, the sample mean could overestimate or underestimate the population mean. Since the value of a sample statistic is likely to vary from sample to sample, estimating a population parameter with an **interval estimate** is often preferable to simply using a point estimate. An interval estimate, the **confidence interval**, is a range of values within which the analyst can declare, with a particular level of confidence, the population parameter lies.

The absolute difference between the point estimate and the parameter is called the **error of estimation**. For example, when using the sample mean $\bar{x}$ and the population mean μ, then:

$$\text{error of estimation} = |\bar{x} - \mu|$$

The maximum value assigned to the error of estimation is called the **margin of error (ME)** of the confidence interval. In other words, the margin of error specifies the upper limit of the sampling error that is associated with a particular confidence interval. The upper and lower limits of the confidence interval are determined by adding the margin of error to and subtracting it from the point estimate. We often use intervals in everyday life. For example, if you ask for 200 g of cheese at a delicatessen, you are generally willing to accept something close to that amount — perhaps 10 g either side of 200 g. The 10 g represents the lower and upper bounds of an interval that would be 190 g to 210 g. So, having introduced various terminologies and concepts, it can now be demonstrated how a confidence interval for the population mean can be found.

According to the central limit theorem, the z distribution for sample means can be used when sample sizes are large, regardless of the shape of the population distribution. In addition, the z distribution can be used for smaller sample sizes if the population is normally distributed. The z formula for sample means is:

$$z = \frac{\bar{x} - \mu}{\text{SE}_{\bar{x}}}$$

where $\text{SE}_{\bar{x}} = \frac{\sigma}{\sqrt{n}}$

Rearranging this formula algebraically and solving for μ gives:

$$\mu = \bar{x} - z\text{SE}_{\bar{x}}$$

Since a sample mean can be greater than or less than the population mean, z can be either positive or negative. Thus, the preceding expression takes the following form.

$$\bar{x} \pm z\frac{\sigma}{\sqrt{n}}$$

Rewriting this expression as shown in formula 8.1 yields the confidence interval formula for estimating μ with large sample sizes where σ is known.

100(1 − α)% confidence interval to estimate μ
(8.1)

$$\bar{x} - z_{\alpha/2}\mathrm{SE}_{\bar{x}} \le \mu \le \bar{x} + z_{\alpha/2}\mathrm{SE}_{\bar{x}}$$
$$\bar{x} - z_{\alpha/2}\frac{\sigma}{\sqrt{n}} \le \mu \le \bar{x} + z_{\alpha/2}\frac{\sigma}{\sqrt{n}}$$
$$\bar{x} - \mathrm{ME} \le \mu \le \bar{x} + \mathrm{ME}$$

where:

ME = the margin of error for the confidence interval = $z_{\alpha/2}\frac{\sigma}{\sqrt{n}}$

α = the area under the normal curve in the tails of the distribution, i.e. outside the confidence interval

$\alpha/2$ = the area in one tail (end) of the distribution, i.e. outside the confidence interval, $P(z > z_{\alpha/2}) = \frac{\alpha}{2}$

Alpha (α), called the **level of significance**, is the area under the normal curve in the tails of the distribution, that is, outside the confidence interval. This can be seen in figure 8.1. The area under the normal curve between the limits of the confidence interval is called the **level of confidence** and has an area = 1 − α. Typically, the level of confidence for an interval is denoted as a percentage = 100% × (1 − α) rather than in the decimal form 1 − α. For example, when α = .05 the level of confidence is 95%. Note that, throughout this book, α is used in both decimal and percentage forms. For example, it may be stated to use 'a 5% level of significance' or 'α = .05'. Specifying a value for α sets the margin of error acceptable for the confidence interval as it allows $z_{\alpha/2}$ to be found. Since the standard normal table (table A.4) provides areas between a z-score of 0 and $z_{\alpha/2}$, the value of $z_{\alpha/2}$ is found by locating the area of .5000 − $\alpha/2$ within the table and then reading the z-score from the edges of the table. Another way to find the z-score for $z_{\alpha/2}$ is to convert the confidence level percentage to a decimal, divide this decimal value by 2, find this value within table A.4, and read the z-score from the edges of the table to get the value of $z_{\alpha/2}$. The value of $z_{\alpha/2}$ can also be found in Excel by typing into any cell the Excel command '=NORMSINV(1 − α/2)'. For example, typing =NORMSINV(1−.05/2) or the equivalent =NORMSINV(0.975) calculates that $z_{0.025}$ = 1.959 964.

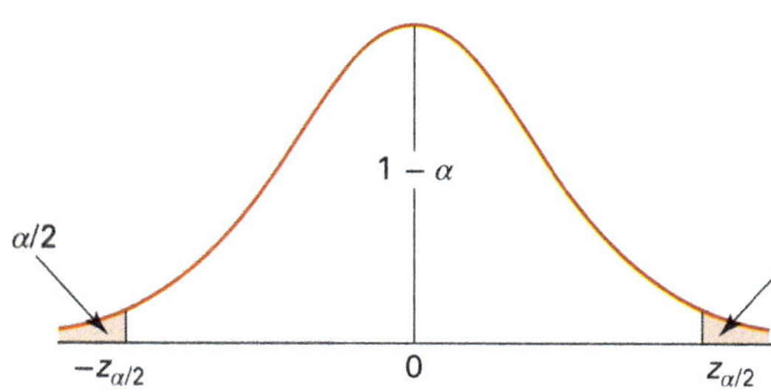

α = the sum of the two shaded tail areas

FIGURE 8.1 z-scores for confidence intervals

The confidence interval formula:

$$\bar{x} - z_{\alpha/2}\frac{\sigma}{\sqrt{n}} \le \mu \le \bar{x} + z_{\alpha/2}\frac{\sigma}{\sqrt{n}}$$

gives a range of values where we can be reasonably confident the value of the population mean will be located. However, by forming a confidence interval using just one sample mean, it is not possible to be certain the population mean will be located within this interval. Certainty could be achieved only if a 100% confidence interval is formed, and this would result in the interval being infinitely wide. However, if a 95% confidence interval is constructed, with say 100 intervals from 100 random samples from the population, then it is likely that 95 of the intervals constructed, using each sample mean, would include the population mean somewhere within each interval. The five remaining intervals constructed would not include the population mean within these intervals.

Having explained the logic behind confidence intervals, the application of a confidence interval can now be detailed using an example. Consider the mobile phone problem described earlier, which required an estimate of the population mean number of minutes called per residential user per week. A business researcher selected a random sample of 85 bills and the sample mean was found to be 153 minutes per week. Using this sample mean, a confidence interval can be calculated within which the business researcher is relatively confident the actual population mean is located.

To calculate the confidence interval using formula 8.1, the value of the population standard deviation, value of z, sample mean and the sample size must be known. In this mobile phone problem, similar previous studies and past historical data indicate that the population standard deviation is 46 minutes per week. The value of z is determined by the level of confidence required. Some of the more common levels of confidence used by business researchers are 90%, 95%, 98% and 99%. Why would a business researcher not just select the highest confidence and always use that level? The reason is that trade-offs between sample size, interval width and level of confidence must be considered. For example, if a business researcher chooses a larger sample size, this will reduce the margin of error and so reduce the width of the confidence interval for a given level of confidence. The estimate of the population mean in this situation will be more precise for the chosen level of confidence. However, there is a trade-off for this increased precision (a narrower interval) in that it will require additional time and money to obtain the larger sample. Alternatively, if the level of confidence is required to be increased, then the value of z will increase. If at the same time the sample size and standard deviation both remain the same for this increased level of confidence, then the confidence interval constructed must get wider and so be less precise. Hence, the information a researcher gains through the construction of a confidence interval will require a trade-off to be made between an increased level of confidence and a corresponding reduction in precision.

Continuing with the mobile phone example, consider that the researcher decides on a 95% level of confidence. Figure 8.2 shows a normal distribution of the sampling distribution of sample means about the population mean. To construct a 95% confidence interval for the population mean, the researcher would need to randomly select a sample from the population and calculate the sample mean. This sample mean could be any of the sample means that form the sampling distribution of sample means in figure 8.2. Once a 95% level of confidence is specified, the business researcher can look up the $z_{\alpha/2}$ value in table A.4.

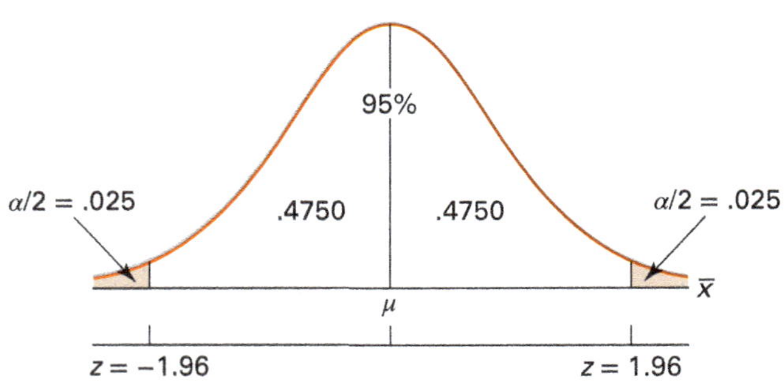

FIGURE 8.2 Distribution of sample means for a 95% level of confidence

For a 95% level of confidence, $\alpha = .05$ and $\alpha/2 = .025$. The value of $z_{\alpha/2}$ or $z_{.025}$ is found by locating the value of the area $.5000 - .0250 = .4750$ in table A.4. This area in the table is associated with a z-score of 1.96. This then is the value for $z_{\alpha/2}$. Another way to find $z_{\alpha/2}$ is to make use of the fact that the normal distribution is symmetrical and the intervals are equal on each side of the population mean. That is, $.95/2 = .4750$ of the area is on each side of the population mean, and this is the area given in table A.4; this gives a z-score of 1.96, which is the value of $z_{\alpha/2}$. The z-score for a 95% confidence interval is always 1.96. In other words, of all the possible $\bar{x}$ values along the horizontal axis of the sampling distribution of the sample mean shown in figure 8.3, 95% of the $\bar{x}$ values should be within a z-score of 1.96 from the population mean. So, with a sample mean of 153 minutes, a value for $z_{\alpha/2}$ of 1.96, a population standard deviation α of 46 minutes, and a sample size $n = 85$, the margin of error (ME) for the confidence interval can be calculated as:

$$\begin{aligned} \text{ME} &= z_{\alpha/2}\frac{\sigma}{\sqrt{n}} \\ &= 1.96\frac{(46)}{\sqrt{85}} \\ &= 9.78 \text{ minutes} \end{aligned}$$

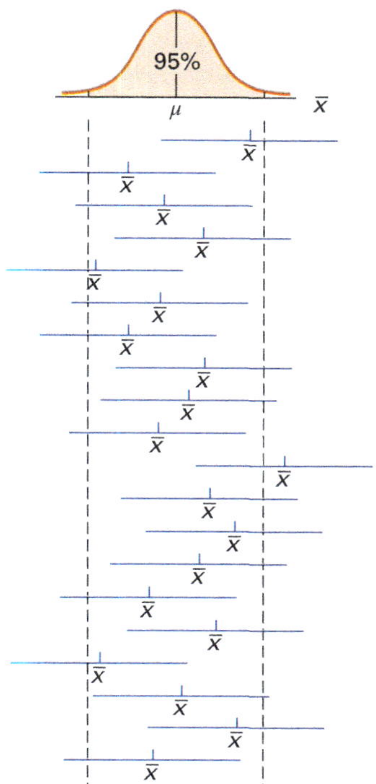

FIGURE 8.3 Sampling distribution of the sample mean showing 19 out of 20 different 95% confidence intervals, constructed using each sample mean, having μ within the intervals

The confidence interval that is constructed using the point estimate of 153 minutes, with a margin of error of 9.78 minutes, calculated using formula 8.1 is:

$$\bar{x} - z_{\alpha/2}\frac{\sigma}{\sqrt{n}} \le \mu \le \bar{x} + z_{\alpha/2}\frac{\sigma}{\sqrt{n}}$$

$$\bar{x} - \text{ME} \le \mu \le \bar{x} + \text{ME}$$

$$153 - 9.78 \le \mu \le 153 + 9.78$$

$$143.22 \le \mu \le 162.78$$

The interpretation of this statement can be seen by referring to figure 8.3. This interval indicates that, based on the sample, the mobile phone company can be 95% confident that the population mean number of minutes called per residential user per week is estimated to be between 143.22 and 162.78 minutes.

What does being 95% confident that the population mean lies within an interval actually indicate? It indicates that, if the mobile phone company was to randomly select 100 samples, with each sample having 85 customers, and use the results of each sample to construct a 95% confidence interval, then approximately 95 of the 100 intervals constructed would each contain the population mean somewhere within the interval. It also indicates that 5% of the intervals constructed would not contain the population mean somewhere within the interval. The business researcher is likely to take only a single sample and compute the confidence interval from that sample information. The interval constructed either contains the population mean or it does not. Figure 8.3 depicts the meaning of a 95% confidence interval for the mean. Note that if 20 random samples are taken from the population, 19 of the 20 are likely to contain the population mean if a 95% confidence interval is used ($\frac{19}{20} = 95\%$). If a 90% confidence interval is constructed, only 18 of the 20 intervals are likely to contain the population mean.

DEMONSTRATION PROBLEM 8.1

PROBLEM: A random sample of 18 Australian fresh fruit and vegetable farmers was selected and surveyed. These farmers all supply large Australian supermarkets. One survey question asked farmers to indicate how many years they had been supplying their fresh produce to the large Australian supermarkets. From this sample, the average number of years was calculated to be 9.2 years. This particular survey has been ongoing for many years. Based on historical data, it is believed that the standard deviation for all Australian fresh fruit and vegetable farmers in Australia supplying large supermarkets is 2.5 years.

Using this information, construct a 95% confidence interval for the population mean number of years that Australian fresh fruit and vegetable farmers have been supplying their produce to the large Australian supermarkets.

SOLUTION: Here, $n = 18$, $\bar{x} = 9.2$ years and $\sigma = 2.5$ years. To determine the value of $z_{\alpha/2}$, divide the 95% confidence in half by taking $.5000 - \alpha/2 = .5000 - .0250 = .4750$. The z distribution of $\bar{x}$ around μ contains .4750 of the area on each side of μ, or $\frac{1}{2}(95\%)$. Table A.4 yields a z-score of 1.96 for the area of .4750. Hence:

$$\text{SE}_{\bar{x}} = \frac{\sigma}{\sqrt{n}} = \frac{2.5}{\sqrt{18}} = .589$$

$$\bar{x} \pm z_{\alpha/2}\text{SE}_{\bar{x}} = \bar{x} \pm 1.96(.589) = \bar{x} \pm 1.154$$

The confidence interval is:

$$9.2 - 1.154 \le \mu \le 9.2 + 1.154$$

$$8.0 \le \mu \le 10.4$$

Hence, it is concluded with 95% confidence that if a census of all Australian fresh fruit and vegetable farmers who supply their produce to large Australian supermarkets was taken at the time of the survey, the population mean number of years for supplying large Australian supermarkets would be between 8.0 years and 10.4 years.

USING EXCEL

Confidence interval for the mean, assuming σ is known

1. From the Formulas tab, select Insert Function.
2. In the Insert Function dialogue box, select the function category Statistical and the function CONFIDENCE.NORM.

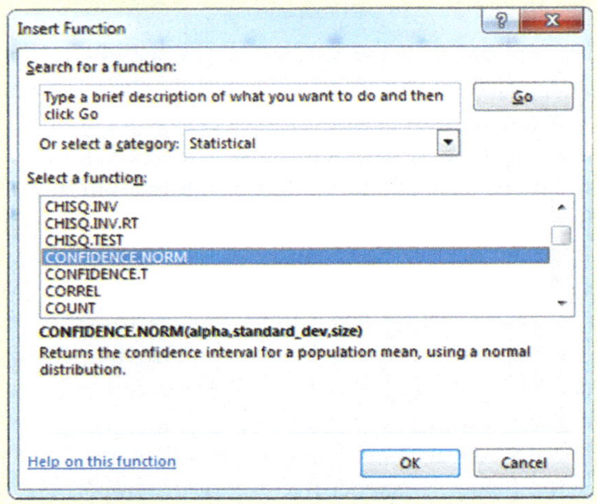

3. Click OK.
4. In the Function Arguments dialogue box:
   a. enter .05 in the Alpha field
   b. enter 2.5 in the Standard_dev field
   c. enter 18 in the Size field.

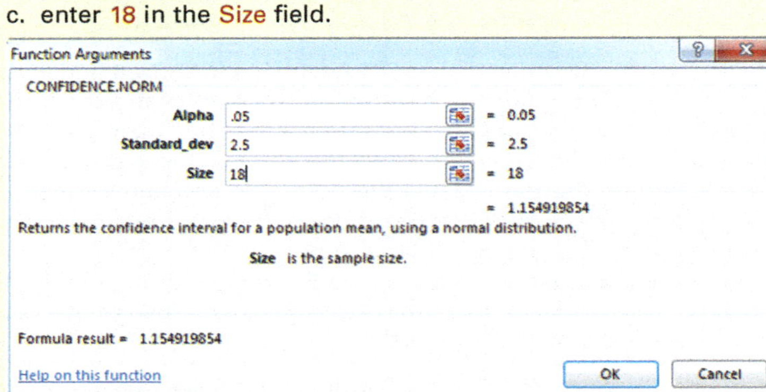

5. Click OK to paste the function into a cell on the worksheet.
6. The Excel output from step 4 is the margin of error used to create the confidence interval. The margin of error needs to be subtracted from and added to the sample mean to construct the confidence interval when using Excel. Note that the margin of error is equal to 'half the width' of the confidence interval that is constructed. Note also that the Excel solution, when rounded to three decimal places is 1.155. This is different to the 1.154 found when using the manual calculations in demonstration problem 8.1. This is because the manual calculation uses a rounded *z*-score to two decimal places from table A.4, whereas Excel uses a *z*-score to more than two decimal places.

TABLE 8.1 Values of z-scores for commonly used levels of confidence

Confidence level	z-score
90%	1.645
95%	1.960
98%	2.330
99%	2.575

For convenience, table 8.1 contains some common levels of confidence and their associated z-scores.

Finite population correction factor

If a sample is taken from a finite population, a finite population correction factor may be used to increase the accuracy of the solution. In the case of interval estimation, the finite population correction factor is used to reduce the width of the interval. If the sample size is less than 5% of the population, the finite population correction factor does not significantly alter the solution. If the standard error for the sampling distribution of the mean is adjusted to account for the fact that the population is finite, then the standard error becomes:

$$SE_{\bar{x}} = \frac{\sigma}{\sqrt{n}}\sqrt{\frac{N-n}{N-1}}$$

Hence, the confidence interval for the mean is given by:

$$= \bar{x} \pm zSE_{\bar{x}}$$

$$= \bar{x} \pm z\frac{\sigma}{\sqrt{n}}\sqrt{\frac{N-n}{N-1}}$$

Formula 8.1 can then be modified to give formula 8.2, which reflects the fact that a finite population exists.

Confidence interval to estimate μ using the finite population correction factor (8.2)

$$\bar{x} - z_{\alpha/2}SE_{\bar{x}} \leq \mu \leq \bar{x} + z_{\alpha/2}SE_{\bar{x}}$$

$$\bar{x} - z_{\alpha/2}\frac{\sigma}{\sqrt{n}}\sqrt{\frac{N-n}{N-1}} \leq \mu \leq \bar{x} + z_{\alpha/2}\frac{\sigma}{\sqrt{n}}\sqrt{\frac{N-n}{N-1}}$$

$$\bar{x} - ME \leq \mu \leq \bar{x} + ME$$

where:

$$ME = z_{\alpha/2}\frac{\sigma}{\sqrt{n}}\sqrt{\frac{N-n}{N-1}}$$

Demonstration problem 8.2 shows how the finite population correction factor can be used.

DEMONSTRATION PROBLEM 8.2

PROBLEM: A study is conducted in a company that employs 800 engineers. A random sample of 50 engineers reveals that the average sample age is 34.3 years. Historically, the population standard deviation of the age of the company's engineers is approximately 8 years. Construct a 98% confidence interval to estimate the average age of all the engineers in this company.

SOLUTION: This problem has a finite population. The sample size, 50, is greater than 5% of the population, so the finite population correction factor may be helpful. In this case, $N = 800$, $n = 50$, $\bar{x} = 34.3$ and $\sigma = 8$. The z-score for a 98% confidence interval is 2.33 (0.98 divided into two equal parts gives an area of .4900; the z-score of 2.33 is obtained from table A.4 and gives an area of .4901. This area is closer to 0.4900 than a z-score of 2.32, which gives an area of 0.4898. Using formula 8.2 and solving for the confidence interval gives:

$$\bar{x} - z_{\alpha/2}SE_{\bar{x}} \leq \mu \leq \bar{x} + z_{\alpha/2}SE_{\bar{x}}.$$

where:

$$SE_{\bar{x}} = \frac{\sigma}{\sqrt{n}}\sqrt{\frac{N-n}{N-1}} = \frac{8}{\sqrt{50}}\sqrt{\frac{800-50}{800-1}} = 1.096$$

The confidence interval is therefore:

$$34.3 - 2.33(1.096) \le \mu \le 34.3 + 2.33(1.096)$$
$$34.3 - 2.55 \le \mu \le 34.3 + 2.55$$
$$31.75 \le \mu \le 36.85$$

Without the finite population correction factor, the resulting confidence interval would have been:

$$34.3 - 2.64 \le \mu \le 34.3 + 2.64$$
$$31.66 \le \mu \le 36.94$$

Notice that the margin of error is 2.55 if the finite population correction factor is used, but is 2.64 (and larger) if the finite population correction factor is not used. The finite population factor takes into account the fact that the population is only 800 instead of being infinitely large. The sample size $n = 50$ is a greater proportion of a population of 800 than it would be for a very much larger population. Thus the width of the confidence interval is *reduced* by using the finite population correction factor.

Estimating the population mean using the *z* statistic when the sample size is small

In the formulas and problems presented so far in this section, the sample size was sufficiently large ($n \ge 30$) that the central limit theorem applies. However, quite often in the business world sample sizes are small. The distribution of sample means is normally distributed for small sample sizes *provided the population variable is normally distributed.* Thus, if it is known that the population variable from which the sample is being drawn is normally distributed and σ is known, the z formula presented can still be used to estimate a population mean even if the sample size is small ($n < 30$). (Note that, if the sample size is small and the normal population assumption is *invalid*, a nonparametric approach should be considered.)

As an example of estimating the population mean when the sample size is small, consider a car-rental company that wants to estimate the average number of kilometres travelled per day by each of its cars rented in Adelaide. A random sample of 20 cars rented in Adelaide gives a sample mean travel distance of 85.5 kilometres per day. Previous historical records have shown that the population standard deviation is 19.3 kilometres per day. Compute a 99% confidence interval to estimate μ.

Here, $n = 20$, $\bar{x} = 85.5$ and $\sigma = 19.3$. For a 99% level of confidence, the z-score is 2.575. Consider that the number of kilometres travelled per day is normally distributed in the population. Then the standard error $SE_{\bar{x}}$ for this problem is:

$$SE_{\bar{x}} = \frac{\sigma}{\sqrt{n}} = \frac{19.3}{\sqrt{20}} = 4.316$$

The confidence interval can therefore be calculated using:

$$\bar{x} - z_{\alpha/2}SE_{\bar{x}} \le \mu \le \bar{x} + z_{\alpha/2}SE_{\bar{x}}$$

$$85.5 - 2.575(4.316) \le \mu \le 85.5 + 2.575(4.316)$$

$$85.5 - 11.1 \le \mu \le 85.5 + 11.1$$

$$74.4 \le \mu \le 96.6$$

The point estimate indicates that the average distance travelled by a rental car in Adelaide is 85.5 kilometres per day. We cannot attach confidence to using this single point estimate. However, with the calculated confidence interval, we can say with 99% confidence that the population mean distance travelled by all the cars of the rental company in Adelaide is estimated to be between 74.4 and 96.6 kilometres per day.

PRACTICE PROBLEMS

Practising the calculations

8.1 Use the following information to construct the confidence intervals specified to estimate μ.

a. 99% confidence for $\bar{x} = 35$, $\sigma = 5.2$ and $n = 55$
b. 95% confidence for $\bar{x} = 85$, $\sigma = 6.3$ and $n = 35$
c. 90% confidence for $\bar{x} = 6.4$, $\sigma = 0.8$ and $n = 42$
d. 85% confidence for $\bar{x} = 22.3$, $\sigma = 2.1$, $N = 600$ and $n = 72$

8.2 A random sample of size 70 is taken from a population that has a variance of 49. The sample mean is 90.4. What is the point estimate of μ? Construct a 94% confidence interval for μ.

8.3 A random sample of size 39 is taken from a population of 200 members. The sample mean is 66 and the population standard deviation is 11. Construct a 96% confidence interval to estimate the population mean. What is the point estimate of the population mean?

Testing your understanding

8.4 A company sells 25 gram boxes of sultanas that are promoted as a healthy snack food option for children. The company wants to estimate the number of sultanas that is packed into a box. To do so, a random sample of 30 boxes of sultanas is selected during a production run. The number of sultanas in each box is counted. Using this sample, the average number of sultanas per box is calculated to be 50.3. If the standard deviation is known to be 1.2 sultanas per box, what is the point estimate of the number of sultanas per box? Construct a 95% confidence interval to estimate the mean number of sultanas packed per box during the production process.

P08-05 **8.5** The average total dollar purchase at a convenience store is less than that at a supermarket. Despite smaller purchases, convenience stores can still be profitable because of the size of operation, volume of business and the mark-up. A researcher is interested in estimating the average purchase amount for convenience stores in suburban Melbourne. To do so, she randomly samples 24 purchases from several convenience stores in suburban Melbourne and tabulates the amounts to the nearest dollar. Use the following data to construct a 90% confidence interval for the population average amount of purchases. Assume that the population standard deviation is 3.23 dollars and the population is normally distributed.

2	11	8	7	9	3
5	4	2	1	10	8
14	7	6	3	7	2
4	1	3	6	8	4

P08-06 **8.6** A community health association is interested in estimating the average number of days women stay in a local maternity hospital. A random sample is taken of 36 women who had babies in the hospital during the past year. The following numbers of days each woman was in the hospital are rounded to the nearest day.

3	3	4	3	2	5	3	1	4	3
4	2	3	5	3	2	4	3	2	4
1	6	3	4	3	3	5	2	3	2
3	5	4	3	5	4				

Use these data and a population standard deviation of 1.17 days to construct a 98% confidence interval to estimate the average stay for all women who have babies in this hospital.

P08-07 **8.7** A toothbrush company sells a particular model of toothbrush nationally. The company is interested in knowing the average retail price across the country. A researcher employed by the company randomly selects 25 retailers from a data base that contains all the retailers that sell this particular toothbrush. The price the retailer sells the toothbrush for is recorded. The toothbrush company believes the population standard deviation in price for this toothbrush can be taken as 25 cents based on previous investigations. Using the following price data (in dollars), determine a point estimate for the national retail price of this particular toothbrush and then construct a 95% confidence interval to estimate this price.

2.40	2.45	2.50	2.55	2.55	2.70	2.70	2.75	2.80
2.80	2.95	2.95	3.00	3.00	3.00	3.10	3.20	3.20
3.25	3.25	3.30	3.40	3.40	3.45	3.50		

P08-08 **8.8** According to a study, the average travel time to work in Perth is 27.4 minutes. A business researcher wants to estimate the average travel time to work in Brisbane using a 95% level of confidence. A random sample of 45 Brisbane commuters is taken and the travel time (minutes) to work is obtained from each. The data follow. Assuming a population standard deviation of 5.124 minutes, compute a 95% confidence interval on the data. What is the point estimate and what is the margin of error of the interval? Explain what these results mean in terms of Perth commuters.

27	25	19	21	24	27	29	34	18	29	16	28
20	32	27	28	22	20	14	15	29	28	29	33
16	29	28	28	27	23	27	20	27	25	21	18
26	14	23	27	27	21	25	28	30			

8.2 Estimating the population mean using the *t* statistic (σ unknown)

In section 8.1, we learned how to estimate a population mean by using the sample mean when the population standard deviation is known. In most instances, if a business researcher wants to estimate a population mean, the population standard deviation will be unknown and thus the techniques presented in section 8.1 will not be applicable. When the population standard deviation is unknown, the sample standard deviation must be used in the estimation process. In this section, a statistical technique is presented to estimate a population mean using the sample mean when the population standard deviation is unknown.

Consider a business researcher who is interested in estimating the average flying time of a 747 jet from Perth to Melbourne. Since the business researcher does not know the population mean or average time, it is likely that they do not know the population standard deviation either. From recent data on flights from Perth to Melbourne, the researcher can randomly select a sample of flights and note the time taken to travel between Perth and Melbourne. From this sample, a sample mean and a sample standard deviation can be calculated, and then an estimate of the population mean can be constructed.

The *z* formula presented in section 8.1 is inappropriate to use when the population standard deviation is unknown. Instead, another mechanism to handle such cases was developed by William S Gosset, a British statistician. Gosset was born in 1876 in Canterbury, England. He studied chemistry and mathematics, and in 1899 he went to work for the Guinness Brewery in Dublin, Ireland. Gosset was involved in quality control at the brewery, studying variables such as raw materials and temperature. As a result of the circumstances of his experiments, Gosset conducted many studies where the population standard deviation was unavailable. He discovered that using the *z* formula with a sample standard deviation, instead of the population standard deviation, produced inexact and incorrect distributions. This finding led to his development of the distribution of the sample standard deviation and the *t* test.

Gosset was a student and close personal friend of Karl Pearson. When Gosset's first work on the *t* test was published, he used the pen name 'Student'. As a result, the *t* test is sometimes referred to as the Student's *t* test. Gosset's contribution was significant because it led to more exact statistical tests, which some scholars say marked the beginning of the modern era in mathematical statistics.

The *t* distribution

Gosset developed the ***t* distribution**. This distribution is used instead of the *z* distribution for doing inferential statistics on the population mean when both:

1. the population standard deviation is unknown
2. the population variable of interest is normally distributed.

The formula for the *t* value is:

$$t = \frac{\bar{x} - \mu}{SE_{\bar{x}}}$$

where $SE_{\bar{x}} = \frac{s}{\sqrt{n}}$ and s = the sample standard deviation.

This formula is essentially the same as the *z* formula. It is different only in that the population standard deviation, σ, is replaced by the sample standard deviation, s. However, it is important to note that the *t* distribution is not a normal distribution and the distribution table values in the *z* table and *t* table are different. We interpret *t* in a similar way to *z*, being the number of standard errors a particular sample mean is away from the population mean.

The t distribution is actually a series of distributions because every sample size has a different distribution, thereby creating the potential for many t tables. To make these t values more manageable, only select key values are presented in table A.6 in the appendix; each line in the table contains values from a different t distribution. An assumption underlying the use of the t statistic is that the population variable, from which the sample is taken, is normally distributed. However, if the distribution of the population is unknown or the population standard deviation is unknown, but the sample size is large (at least 30), then z is often used as a good estimate of t, with s used as a good estimate of σ. Alternatively, if the distribution of the variable of interest in the population is not normal, or is unknown, nonparametric techniques may also be used.

Robustness

Most statistical techniques have one or more underlying assumptions. If a statistical technique is relatively insensitive to minor violations in one or more of its underlying assumptions, the technique is said to be **robust** to that assumption. The t statistic for estimating a population mean is relatively robust to the assumption that the population is normally distributed. Therefore, the confidence interval created using t will be quite accurate even if the population is only approximately normal.

Some statistical techniques lack robustness (e.g. the chi-square distribution; see section 8.4). In these cases, extreme caution should be used to be certain that the assumptions underlying a technique are being met before using the technique or interpreting statistical output resulting from its use. A business analyst should always be aware of statistical assumptions and the robustness of techniques being used in any analysis.

Characteristics of the *t* distribution

Figure 8.4 displays three t distributions superimposed on the standard normal distribution. Like the standard normal curve, t distributions have a mean equal to 0 and are symmetrical, unimodal and a family of curves. The t distributions are flatter in the middle and have more area in their tails than the standard normal distribution.

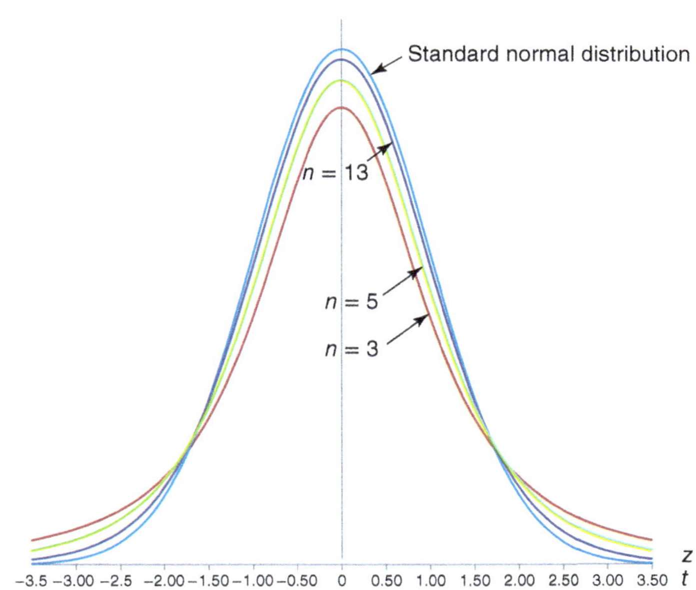

FIGURE 8.4 Comparison of three *t* distributions with the standard normal curve

An examination of t distribution values reveals that the t distribution approaches the z distribution (standard normal curve) as n becomes large. Sample sizes of 120 or more have t values that are almost identical to the z-scores. Hence, the z distribution is a very close approximation to the t distribution for sample sizes of about 120 or more. However, if the population standard deviation is unknown and the population variable of interest is normally distributed (or approximately so), then the t distribution is the more appropriate distribution to use when the sample size is small.

Reading the *t* distribution table

To find a value in the t distribution table requires knowing the degrees of freedom; each different value of degrees of freedom is associated with a different t distribution. The t distribution table presented in table A.6 in the appendix is a compilation of many t distributions. Each line of this table has a different number of degrees of freedom and contains t values for different t distributions. The degrees of freedom used to calculate the t statistic in this section equals $n - 1$. **Degrees of freedom (df)** refers to *the number of independent observations for a source of variation minus the number of independent parameters estimated in computing the variation.* In this section, one independent parameter, the population mean, μ, is being estimated by $\bar{x}$ in computing s. Thus, the degrees of freedom formula is n independent observations minus one independent parameter being estimated $(n - 1)$. For other types of problems involving the t distribution, different t formulas are used and the calculation of degrees of freedom differs. Therefore, the formula to calculate the degrees of freedom is given with each specific t formula in this book.

In table A.6, the degrees of freedom are located in the left column. The t distribution table in this book does not use the area between the statistic and the mean as does the z distribution (standard normal distribution). Instead, the t table uses the area in the tail of the distribution. The emphasis in the t table is on α. Note that, when using the t table to calculate a confidence interval, each tail of the distribution contains $\alpha/2$ of the area under the curve. Hence, for confidence intervals, the required t value can be found in table A.6 at the intersection of the column headed 'upper tail area', with the value being $\alpha/2$ in the upper tail when a confidence interval is considered, and the row matching the value for the degrees of freedom (df).

For example, if a 90% confidence interval for the mean is being computed, the total area in the two tails is 10%. Therefore, α is 10% and $\alpha/2$ is 5% as indicated in figure 8.5 (an extract from table A.6). The t distribution table shown in table A.6 (an extract is shown in table 8.2) contains only six values of $\alpha/2$ (.10, .05, .025, .01, .005 and .001). The t value is located at the intersection of the selected $\alpha/2$ value in the upper tail and the df value. So, if the selected $\alpha/2$ value is .05 and a sample size of 25 is used giving df = 24 for the t statistic, then the t value is 1.711. Mathematically, the t value is written generally as $t_{\alpha/2,\, n-1}$ when it is used for constructing a confidence interval for the mean. In the example used here, the t value is written as $t_{0.05,\, 24} = 1.711$.

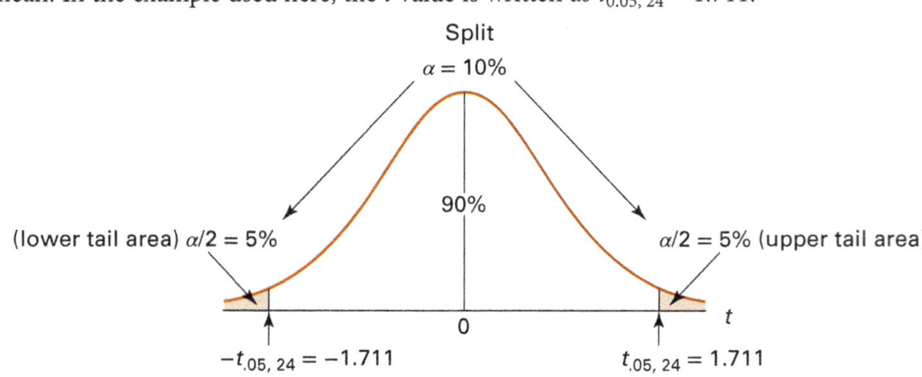

FIGURE 8.5 t value for when a 90% confidence interval is required using $n = 25$ (upper tail area = .05 and df = 24)

TABLE 8.2 Extract of the *t* distribution table A.6

Degrees of freedom	.10	.05	.025	.01	.005	.001
23		1.714				
24	1.318	**1.711**	2.064			
25						

The value of $t_{\alpha/2,\, n-1}$ can also be found using Excel by typing into any cell the Excel command '=TINV(α, $n-1$)'. For example, typing =TINV(.1, 24) calculates $t_{0.05,\, 24} = 1.71088$. Be careful when using this Excel command as you will notice the value of $\alpha = .1$ has been used and *not* $\alpha/2 = .05$. Using α will produce the correct t value needed for a confidence interval, which is $t_{\alpha/2,\, n-1}$. (Note that the input for TINV(α, $n-1$) uses α, while the Excel command NORMSINV($1-\alpha/2$) uses $\alpha/2$, as outlined in section 8.1.)

Confidence intervals to estimate the population mean using the *t* statistic

The t formula is:

$$t = \frac{\bar{x} - \mu}{\mathrm{SE}_{\bar{x}}}$$

where $\mathrm{SE}_{\bar{x}} = \frac{s}{\sqrt{n}}$ and s = the sample standard deviation.

Rearranging this formula algebraically and solving for μ gives:

$$\mu = \bar{x} - t\,\mathrm{SE}_{\bar{x}}$$

Since a sample mean can be greater than or less than the population mean, t can be either positive or negative. Thus, the preceding expression takes the form:

$$\bar{x} \pm t\frac{s}{\sqrt{n}}$$

Formula 8.3 is used for estimating the population mean when σ is unknown and the population is normally distributed.

Confidence interval to estimate μ: population standard deviation unknown and population normally distributed (8.3)

$$\bar{x} - t_{\alpha/2,n-1}\mathrm{SE}_{\bar{x}} \le \mu \le \bar{x} + t_{\alpha/2,n-1}\mathrm{SE}_{\bar{x}}$$

$$\bar{x} - t_{\alpha/2,n-1}\frac{s}{\sqrt{n}} \le \mu \le \bar{x} + t_{\alpha/2,n-1}\frac{s}{\sqrt{n}}$$

$$\bar{x} - \mathrm{ME} \le \mu \le \bar{x} + \mathrm{ME}$$

where

$\mathrm{df} = n - 1$

$$\mathrm{ME} = t_{\alpha/2,n-1}\frac{s}{\sqrt{n}}$$

To show how formula 8.3 can be used to construct a confidence interval estimate of μ, consider the situation where many public servants are allowed to accumulate time-off-in-lieu (TOIL) by working unpaid overtime. A researcher wants to estimate the average amount of TOIL (in hours) accumulated per week by all public servants. A random sample of 18 public servants is selected and the amount of unpaid overtime they each work during a specific week is measured. The results, in hours, are shown below.

6	21	17	20	7	0	8	16	29	3	8	12	11	9	21	25	15	16

The researcher decides to construct a 90% confidence interval to estimate the average amount of TOIL accumulated per week by all public servants. It is assumed that TOIL is normally distributed. Since the population standard deviation is unknown, and the sample standard deviation can be calculated from the data collected, the t distribution can be used. Since the sample size is 18, df = 17. For a 90% level of confidence (with $\alpha = 10\%$), $\alpha/2 = .05$ is the area in each tail of the t distribution. The t value from table A.6 is:

$$t_{.05,\,17} = 1.740$$

The subscripts in the t value denote to other researchers the area in the right tail of the t distribution (for confidence intervals $\alpha/2$) and the number of degrees of freedom. The sample mean is 13.56 hours, and the sample standard deviation is 7.8 hours. The confidence interval is computed using:

$$\text{SE}_{\bar{x}} = \frac{s}{\sqrt{n}} = \frac{7.8}{\sqrt{18}} = 1.838$$

$$\bar{x} - t_{\alpha/2,n-1}\text{SE}_{\bar{x}} \le \mu \le \bar{x} + t_{\alpha/2,n-1}\text{SE}_{\bar{x}}$$

$$13.56 - 1.74(1.838) \le \mu \le 13.56 - 1.74(1.838)$$

$$13.56 - 3.20 \le \mu \le 13.56 + 3.20$$

$$10.36 \le \mu \le 16.76$$

The point estimate for this problem is 13.56 hours, with a margin of error of ±3.20 hours. The researcher is 90% confident that the average amount of TOIL accumulated per week, for all public servants, is estimated to be between 10.36 and 16.76 hours. From these figures, managers could attempt to build a reward system for the unpaid overtime that workers do each week. Alternatively, managers could evaluate the working week to determine how to use regular working hours more effectively and thus reduce TOIL.

DEMONSTRATION PROBLEM 8.3

PROBLEM: A rental car company promotes cheap, affordable, old cars to backpackers. The company is interested in estimating the average number of days its cars have been rented for over the past few years. The company has the records for all its cars, but to use all this data would be very time consuming. To make a quick estimate, a random sample of 32 hire cars is selected from the company records. The number of days each car was hired is noted below (in days).

2	3	7	5	8	2	1	5
9	6	3	2	5	10	1	2
4	8	4	3	7	5	8	2
5	3	7	4	9	11	4	3

Using these data, construct a 95% confidence interval to estimate the average number of days a car is rented out. Assume that the number of days a car is rented is normally distributed in the population.

SOLUTION: As $n = 32$, df = 31. The 95% level of confidence results in $\alpha/2 = .025$ area in each tail of the distribution. The t value from table A.6 is:

$$t_{.025,\,31} = 2.040$$

The sample mean is 4.94 days and the sample standard deviation is 2.75 days. The confidence interval is calculated using:

$$\mathrm{SE}_{\bar{x}} = \frac{s}{\sqrt{n}} = \frac{2.75}{\sqrt{32}} = .486$$

$$\bar{x} - t_{\alpha/2,\, n-1}\mathrm{SE}_{\bar{x}} \le \mu \le \bar{x} + t_{\alpha/2,\, n-1}\mathrm{SE}_{\bar{x}}$$

$$4.94 - 2.040(.486) \le \mu \le 4.94 + 2.040(.486)$$

$$4.94 - .99 \le \mu \le 4.94 + .99$$

$$3.95 \le \mu \le 5.93$$

The point estimate of the average length of time per rental is 4.94 days. As noted previously, we cannot attach confidence to using a single point estimate. However, with the calculated confidence interval and a margin of error of ±.99 days, we can say with a 95% level of confidence that the rental car company can estimate that the average number of days a car is rented out is between 3.95 days and 5.93 days. For the rental car company owner, this information, together with variables such as frequency of car rentals each year, can help estimate the potential profit or loss from renting the cars.

USING EXCEL

t confidence interval for the mean, assuming σ is unknown

DP08-03

1. Access DP08-03.xls from the student website.
2. From the Data tab, select Data Analysis.
3. From the Data Analysis dialogue box, select Descriptive Statistics and click OK.
4. In the Descriptive Statistics dialogue box:
   a. enter the data range in the Input Range field
   b. choose Grouped by: Columns
   c. select Labels in First Row if you have included a column label in the Input Range. If not, leave it unchecked.
   d. choose an output option
   e. select Summary statistics
   f. select Confidence Level for Mean and enter the level of confidence.

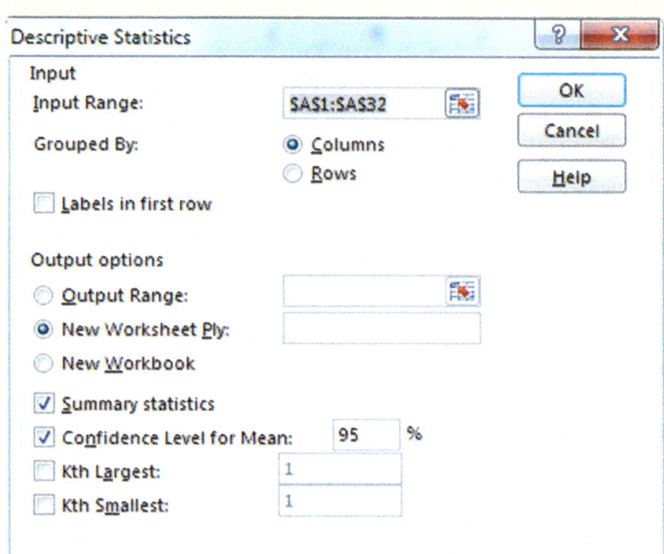

5. Click OK.
The Excel output follows.

	A	B
1	*Column1*	
2	Mean	4.9375
3	Standard Error	0.485552
4	Median	4.5
5	Mode	2
6	Standard Deviation	2.746699
7	Sample Variance	7.544355
8	Kurtosis	−0.70074
9	Skewness	0.517837
10	Range	10
11	Minimum	1
12	Maximum	11
13	Sum	158
14	Count	32
15	Confidence Level(95.0%)	0.990291

6. The confidence level of 0.99 given by Excel is the margin of error used to create the confidence interval. More precisely, the confidence function used in Excel calculates the confidence interval half-width value. This value must be subtracted from, and added to, the sample mean to construct the confidence interval. This is shown in the last two steps of the worked solution to demonstration problem 8.3.

PRACTICE PROBLEMS

Practising the calculations

P08-09 **8.9** The following data are selected randomly from a population of normally distributed values.

20.5	24.8	22.3	23.7	22.2	27.8	27.6
19.7	21.0	24.3	23.1	20.6	20.5	35.3

Construct a 90% confidence interval to estimate the population mean.

P08-10 **8.10** Assuming x is normally distributed, use the following data to compute a 90% confidence interval to estimate μ.

313	320	319	340	325	310
321	329	317	311	307	318

8.11 If a random sample of 41 items produces $\bar{x} = 128.4$ and $s = 20.6$, what is the 98% confidence interval for μ? Assume x is normally distributed for the population. What is the point estimate?

8.12 A random sample of 15 items is taken, producing a sample mean of 2.364 with a sample variance of .81. Assuming that x is normally distributed, construct a 90% confidence interval for the population mean.

Testing your understanding

P08-13 **8.13** Use the following data to construct a 99% confidence interval for μ.

16.4	17.1	17.0	15.6	16.2
14.8	16.0	15.6	17.3	17.4
15.6	15.7	17.2	16.6	16.0
15.3	15.4	16.0	15.8	17.2
14.6	15.5	14.9	16.7	16.3

Assume that x is normally distributed. What is the point estimate for μ?

8.14 According to Runzheimer International, organisations are investing an average of $1436 each year per mobile device. A researcher randomly selects 28 organisations and calculates the average amount they invested during the year on mobile devices to be $1295. The sample standard deviation is calculated to be $245. Construct a 99% confidence interval for the population mean amount invested by organisations each year on mobile devices using these sample data. Assume the data are normally distributed in the population. Does the $1436 figure, reported by Runzheimer International, fall within the confidence interval calculated using the researcher's sample data? What does this tell you?

P08-15 **8.15** Some fast-food chains offer a lower priced combination meal in an effort to attract budget-conscious customers. One chain tested a burger, chips and drink combination for $6.95. The weekly sales volume for these meals was impressive. Suppose the chain wants to estimate the average amount its customers spent (in dollars) on a meal at their restaurant while this combination offer was in effect. An analyst gathers data from 28 randomly selected customers. The following data represent the sample meal totals in dollars.

7.25	8.80	6.50	7.75	9.25	7.40	6.50	8.50	7.95	8.70
7.10	9.20	7.20	6.90	8.70	7.00	6.75	8.50	7.95	9.00
8.00	7.50	8.95	7.70	6.50	8.70	7.95	8.25		

Use these data to construct a 90% confidence interval to estimate the population mean value in dollars. Assume that the amounts spent are normally distributed.

8.16 The marketing director of a large department store wants to estimate the average number of customers who enter the store every 5 minutes. She randomly selects 5-minute intervals and counts the number of arrivals at the store. She obtains the figures 58, 32, 41, 47, 56, 80, 45, 29, 32 and 78. The analyst assumes that the number of arrivals is normally distributed. Using these data, the analyst computes a 95% confidence interval to estimate the mean value for all 5-minute intervals. What interval values does she get?

8.3 Estimating the population proportion

Business decision makers and researchers often need to be able to estimate a population proportion. For example, business decisions can be based on estimated market share (a company's proportion of the market), the proportion of defective goods produced, or knowledge relating to the proportion of various demographic characteristics among potential customers or clients. Methods similar to those in section 8.1 can be used to estimate the population proportion. Consider the following formulas (where both np and nq are greater than 5).

$$z = \frac{\hat{p}-p}{\mathrm{SE}_{\hat{p}}} = \frac{\hat{p}-p}{\sigma_{\hat{p}}} = \frac{\hat{p}-p}{\sqrt{\frac{pq}{n}}}$$

where $q = 1 - p$.

Algebraically manipulating this z formula to estimate p involves solving for p. However, p is in both the numerator and the denominator of this formula, which makes solving for p complicated. Therefore, to estimate p for large sample sizes, p and q in the denominator of the z formula are replaced by $\hat{p}$ and $\hat{q}$ respectively. This gives:

$$z = \frac{\hat{p}-p}{\sqrt{\frac{\hat{p}\hat{q}}{n}}}$$

where $\hat{q} = 1 - \hat{p}$. Rearranging and solving for p results in the confidence interval in formula 8.4.

Confidence interval to estimate p
(8.4)

$$\hat{p}-z_{\alpha/2}\text{SE}_{\hat{p}} \le p \le \hat{p}+z_{\alpha/2}\text{SE}_{\hat{p}}$$

$$\hat{p}-z_{\alpha/2}\sqrt{\frac{\hat{p}\hat{q}}{n}} \le p \le \hat{p}+z_{\alpha/2}\sqrt{\frac{\hat{p}\hat{q}}{n}}$$

$$\hat{p}-\text{ME} \le p \le \hat{p}+\text{ME}$$

where:

$\hat{p}$ = the sample proportion
$\hat{q} = 1-\hat{p}$
p = the population proportion
n = the sample size

$\text{ME} = z_{\alpha/2}\sqrt{\frac{\hat{p}\hat{q}}{n}}$

In formula 8.4, $\hat{p}$ is the point estimate of the population proportion and the margin of error is $z_{\alpha/2}\sqrt{\frac{\hat{p}\hat{q}}{n}}$. As an example, a study of 87 randomly selected companies with a telemarketing operation revealed that 39% of the sampled companies used telemarketing to assist them in processing orders. Using this information, how could a researcher estimate the *population* proportion of telemarketing companies that use their telemarketing operation to assist them in processing orders?

The sample proportion $\hat{p}$ = .39 is the *point estimate* of the population proportion p. For n = 87 and $\hat{p}$ = .39, a 95% confidence interval can be computed to determine the interval estimation of p. The z-score for 95% confidence is 1.96. The value of $\hat{q} = 1-\hat{p} = 1-.39 = .61$. To construct the confidence interval estimate, first calculate $\text{SE}_{\hat{p}}$:

$$\text{SE}_{\hat{p}} = \sqrt{\frac{\hat{p}\hat{q}}{n}} = \sqrt{\frac{(.39)(.61)}{87}} = .0523$$

So the confidence interval is:

$$\hat{p}-z_{\alpha/2}\text{SE}_{\hat{p}} \le p \le \hat{p}+z_{\alpha/2}\text{SE}_{\hat{p}}$$

$$.39 - 1.96(.0523) \le p \le .39 + 1.96(.0523)$$

$$.39 - .10 \le p \le .39 + .10$$

$$.29 \le p \le .49$$

This interval suggests that the population proportion of telemarketing companies that use their telemarketing operation to assist in processing orders is estimated to be between .29 and .49, based on the point estimate of .39 with a margin of error of .10. This result has a 95% level of confidence.

DEMONSTRATION PROBLEM 8.4

PROBLEM: In a survey of 210 chief executives of small companies, 51% had a management succession plan. Succession plans aim to minimise negative impacts to a company's performance following the unexpected loss of its chief executive. Using this data, compute a 92% confidence interval to estimate the proportion of *all* small companies that have a management succession plan.

SOLUTION: The point estimate is the sample proportion of .51. It is estimated that .51, or 51%, of all small companies have a management succession plan. Realising that the point estimate might change with the selection of another sample, we calculate a confidence interval.

The value of n is 210, $\hat{p}$ is .51, and $\hat{q} = 1-\hat{p} = .49$. Since the level of confidence required is 92%, α = .08 so $z_{\alpha/2} = z_{.04}$ = 1.75. The value of the standard error for this problem is:

$$\text{SE}_{\hat{p}} = \sqrt{\frac{\hat{p}\hat{q}}{n}} = \sqrt{\frac{(.51)(.49)}{210}} = .0345$$

Hence, the confidence interval is computed as:

$$\hat{p} - z_{\alpha/2}\text{SE}_{\hat{p}} \le p \le \hat{p} + z_{\alpha/2}\text{SE}_{\hat{p}}$$
$$.51 - 1.75(.0345) \le p \le .51 + 1.75(.0345)$$
$$.51 - .06 \le p \le .51 + .06$$
$$.45 \le p \le .57$$

It is estimated with 92% confidence that the proportion of the population of small companies that have a management succession plan is between 45% and 57%.

DEMONSTRATION PROBLEM 8.5

PROBLEM: A clothing company produces men's jeans. The jeans are made and sold with either a regular cut or a boot cut. In an effort to estimate the proportion of their men's jeans market in Wellington that prefers boot-cut jeans, an analyst takes a random sample of 120 jeans sales from the company's two Wellington retail outlets. Only 11 of the sales were boot-cut jeans. Construct a 95% confidence interval to estimate the proportion of the company's Wellington customers who prefer the company's boot-cut jeans.

SOLUTION: The sample size is 120 and the number preferring boot-cut jeans is 11. The sample proportion is $\hat{p} = \frac{11}{120} = .092$. A point estimate for boot-cut jeans in the population is .092 or 9.2%. The z-score for a 95% level of confidence is 1.96, and $\hat{q} = 1 - \hat{p} = 1 - .092 = .908$. The value of the standard error for this problem is:

$$\text{SE}_{\hat{p}} = \sqrt{\frac{\hat{p}\hat{q}}{n}} = \sqrt{\frac{(.092)(.908)}{120}} = .026$$

The confidence interval estimate is:

$$\hat{p} - z_{\alpha/2}\text{SE}_{\hat{p}} \le p \le \hat{p} + z_{\alpha/2}\text{SE}_{\hat{p}}$$
$$.092 - 1.96(.026) \le p \le .092 + 1.96(.026)$$
$$.092 - .051 \le p \le .092 + .051$$
$$.041 \le p \le .143$$

The analyst estimates that the population proportion of boot-cut jeans purchased from the company is between 4.1% and 14.3%. The level of confidence in this result is 95%.

Please refer to 'Going further with KaddStat' for KaddStat instructions at www.johnwiley.com.au/highered/black4e/kaddstat.

PRACTICE PROBLEMS

Practising the calculations

8.17 Use the information about each of the following samples to compute the confidence interval to estimate p.

a. $n = 25$ and $\hat{p} = .24$; 98% confidence interval
b. $n = 142$ and $\hat{p} = .61$; 92% confidence interval
c. $n = 213$ and $\hat{p} = .38$; 95% confidence interval
d. $n = 62$ and $\hat{p} = .73$; 80% confidence interval

8.18 Use the following sample information to calculate the confidence interval to estimate the population proportion. Let x be the number of items in the sample with the characteristic of interest.

a. $n = 116$ and $x = 57$, with 99% confidence
b. $n = 800$ and $x = 479$, with 97% confidence
c. $n = 240$ and $x = 106$, with 85% confidence
d. $n = 60$ and $x = 21$, with 90% confidence

Testing your understanding

8.19 A candidate is considering nominating for an election to become Mayor of a country town. Prior to officially nominating, the candidate decides to conduct a survey to assess their chances of being elected. Ninety voters are randomly selected, with 55 indicating they will vote for the candidate. Find a 95% confidence interval for the proportion of voters in the town that will vote for this candidate. Based on this confidence interval, can the candidate determine whether or not to nominate for the election to become Mayor?

8.20 A regional town planning department wanted to determine the proportion of residential houses in their region that have air-conditioning. To do so, a random sample of 80 residential houses across the region was selected, and 56 of those houses were found to have air-conditioning. From these data, what is the 95% confidence interval for the proportion of residential houses that have air-conditioning in this region? What effect would an increase in the confidence level have on this estimate?

8.21 VicRoads wants to estimate the proportion of vehicles on the Hume Highway between the hours of midnight and 5.00 am that are semitrailers. The estimate will be used to determine highway repair and construction considerations and in highway patrol planning. Suppose researchers for VicRoads counted vehicles at different locations on the highway for several nights during this time period. Of the 3481 vehicles counted, 927 were semitrailers.

a. Determine the point estimate for the proportion of vehicles travelling the Hume Highway during this time period that are semitrailers.

b. Construct a 99% confidence interval for the proportion of vehicles on the Hume Highway during this time period that are semitrailers.

8.22 What proportion of commercial airline pilots are more than 40 years of age? A researcher has access to a list of all pilots who are members of the Australian Federation of Air Pilots. If this list is used as a frame for the study, she can randomly select a sample of pilots, contact them and ascertain their ages. From 89 of these pilots so selected, she learns that 48 are more than 40 years of age. Construct an 85% confidence interval to estimate the population proportion of commercial airline pilots who are more than 40 years of age.

8.23 In a survey of relocation administrators, 63% of all workers who rejected relocation offers did so for family considerations. This figure was obtained by using a random sample of the files of 672 workers who had rejected relocation offers. Use this information to construct a 95% confidence interval to estimate the population proportion of workers who rejected relocation offers for family considerations.

8.4 Estimating the population variance

At times in statistical analysis, the researcher is more interested in the population variance than in the population mean or population proportion. For example, in the field of total quality management, suppliers who want to earn world-class supplier status, and even those who just want to maintain customer contracts, are often asked to show continual reduction in the variation of supplied parts. Tests are conducted on samples to determine batch variation and to determine whether variability goals are being met.

Estimating the variance is important in many other instances in business. For example, variations between aeroplane altimeter readings need to be minimal. It is not enough just to know that, on average, a particular brand of altimeter produces the correct altitude reading. It is also important that the variation between altimeter readings be small. Thus, measuring the variation of altimeter readings is critical. As another example, parts used in engines must fit tightly on a consistent basis. A wide variability among engine parts can result in parts being too large to fit into the required slots, or parts that are too small resulting in too much tolerance and engine vibration. Even many basic household items such as batteries must be made with minimal variation. If a torch battery is too large it will not fit, and if it is too small it will not make contact with the points. How then can this population variance be estimated?

You may recall that sample variance is computed by using the formula:

$$s^2 = \frac{\Sigma(x-\bar{x})^2}{n-1}$$

Sample variances are typically used as estimators of the population variance. A mathematical adjustment is made in the denominator by using $n - 1$, as in the formula above, to make the sample variance an unbiased estimator of the population variance.

Suppose a researcher wants to estimate the population variance from the sample variance. This can be done in a manner similar to the estimation of the population mean from a sample mean. In this instance, the relationship of the sample variance to the population variance is captured by the **chi-square distribution** (χ^2). The ratio of the sample variance (s^2) multiplied by $n - 1$ to the population variance (σ^2) is approximately chi-square distributed, as shown in formula 8.5. This approximation holds if the population from which the values are selected is normally distributed.

χ^2 formula for variance (8.5)

$$\chi^2 = \frac{(n-1)s^2}{\sigma^2}$$
$$\text{df} = n - 1$$

Caution: The chi-square statistic to estimate the population variance is extremely sensitive to violations of the assumption that the population variable of interest is normally distributed. For that reason, some researchers do not include this technique among their statistical repertoire. Although the technique is still rather widely presented as a mechanism for constructing confidence intervals to estimate a population variance, you should proceed with extreme caution and apply the technique only in cases where the population variable is known to be normally distributed. We can say that this technique lacks robustness.

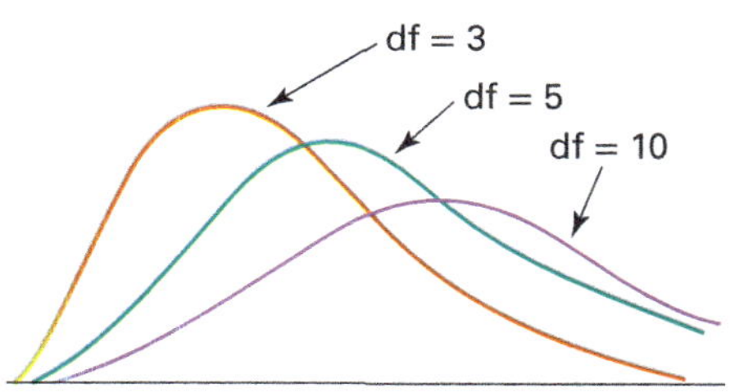

FIGURE 8.6 Three chi-square distributions

Like the t distribution, the chi-square distribution varies with sample size and contains a degrees of freedom value. The number of degrees of freedom for the chi-square formula (formula 8.5) is $n - 1$.

The chi-square distribution is not symmetrical, and its shape depends on the degrees of freedom. Figure 8.6 shows the shapes of chi-square distributions for three different degrees of freedom.

Formula 8.5 can be rearranged algebraically to produce formula 8.6, which can be used to construct a confidence interval for a population variance.

Confidence interval to estimate the population variance (8.6)

$$\frac{(n-1)s^2}{\chi^2_{\alpha/2}} \le \sigma^2 \le \frac{(n-1)s^2}{\chi^2_{1-\alpha/2}}$$
$$\text{df} = n - 1$$

A sample variance is needed to use formula 8.6 to make an inference about a population variance. To demonstrate how to use this formula, consider a production process where batteries are being manufactured. Eight batteries, specified to be 50 mm long, are selected at random and measured. The values measured (in mm) are tabulated below.

49.91	49.93	50.01	50.02
50.05	50.00	49.98	50.01

From this sample, the sample variance value $s^2 = .0022125$ mm squared (note that the units of variance are squared, so 'mm squared' could be written as 'mm^2'). If a point estimate is all that is required, the point estimate is the sample variance of .0022125 mm^2. However, realising that the point estimate will probably change from sample to sample, we need to construct an interval estimate to have a certain level of confidence. To do this, we must know the degrees of freedom and the table values of the chi-square distributions. Since $n = 8$, the degrees of freedom are $\text{df} = n - 1 = 7$. What are the chi-square values necessary to complete the information needed in formula 8.6?

Assume that the population of battery lengths is normally distributed, and consider that a 90% confidence interval is required. The value of α is $1 - .90 = .10$. This is the portion of the area under the chi-square curve that is outside the confidence interval. This outside area is needed because the chi-square values given in table A.8 are listed according to the area in the right tail of the

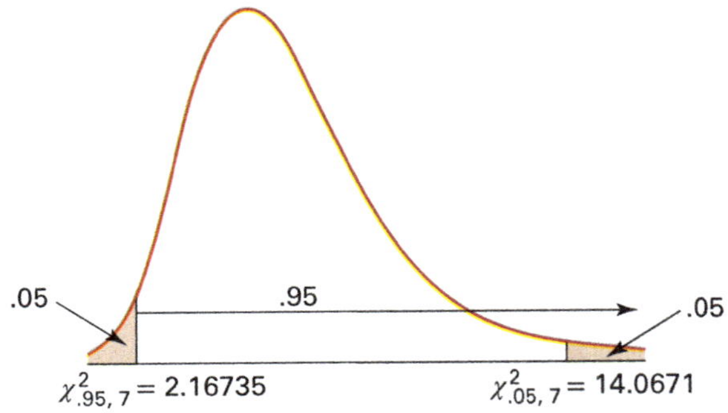

FIGURE 8.7 Two table values of chi-square

distribution. In a 90% confidence interval, $\alpha/2$ or .05 of the area is in the right tail of the distribution and .05 is in the left tail of the distribution. The chi-square value for the .05 area on the right tail of the distribution can be obtained directly from the table by using the degrees of freedom. For this example, df = 7. Thus the right-side chi-square value, $\chi^2_{.05,7}$, is 14.0671. Since table A.8 lists chi-square values for areas in the right tail, the chi-square value for the left tail must be obtained by determining how much area lies to the right of the left tail. If .05 is to the left of the confidence interval, then $1 - .05 = .95$ of the area is to the right of the left tail. This calculation is consistent with the $1 - \alpha/2$ expression used in formula 8.6. Thus the chi-square value for the left tail is $= \chi^2_{.95,7} = 2.16735$. Figure 8.7 shows these two table values of χ^2 on a chi-square distribution.

Incorporating these values into formula 8.6, we can construct the 90% confidence interval to estimate the population variance of the battery lengths.

$$\frac{(n-1)s^2}{\chi^2_{\alpha/2}} \le \sigma^2 \le \frac{(n-1)s^2}{\chi^2_{1-\alpha/2}}$$

$$\frac{(7)(.0022125)}{14.0671} \le \sigma^2 \le \frac{(7)(.0022125)}{2.16735}$$

$$.001101 \le \sigma^2 \le .007146$$

Hence, it is estimated with 90% confidence that the population variance of battery lengths is somewhere between .001101 and .007146 mm^2. It is worth noting that the confidence interval for the population standard deviation can be found from this interval. Note that the standard deviation σ is the square root of the variance σ^2; that is, the standard deviation can be found using:

$$\sigma = \sqrt{\sigma^2}$$

By taking the square root of both sides of the confidence interval for the variance, the confidence interval for the standard deviation becomes:

$$\sqrt{.001101} \le \sigma \le \sqrt{.007146}$$

$$.033 \le \sigma \le .085$$

Hence, it is estimated with 90% confidence that the population standard deviation of battery lengths is somewhere between .033 mm and .085 mm. Notice that the units are mm for standard deviation and mm^2 for variance.

DEMONSTRATION PROBLEM 8.6

PROBLEM: A study found that the average hourly wage in Greece for a production worker in manufacturing is $7.55. The business council of Greece wants to know how consistent this figure is. It randomly selects 31 production workers in manufacturing from across the country and determines that the standard deviation of hourly wages for these workers is $1.22. Use this information to develop a 90% confidence interval to estimate the population standard deviation for the hourly wages of production workers in manufacturing in Greece. Assume that the hourly wages for production workers across the country in manufacturing are normally distributed.

SOLUTION: By squaring the standard deviation, $s = 1.22$, we can obtain the sample variance, $s^2 = 1.4884$. This figure provides the point estimate of the population variance. Since the sample size $n = 31$, the degrees of freedom $df = n - 1 = 30$. A 90% confidence means that alpha is 1 – .90 = .10. This value is split to determine the area in each tail of the chi-square distribution: $\alpha/2$ = .05. The values of the chi-squares obtained from table A.8 are:

$$\chi^2_{.05,\,30} = 43.7730 \text{ and } \chi^2_{.95,\,30} = 18.49267$$

From this information, the confidence interval for the variance is given by:

$$\frac{(n-1)s^2}{\chi^2_{\alpha/2}} \le \sigma^2 \le \frac{(n-1)s^2}{\chi^2_{1-\alpha/2}}$$

$$\frac{(30)(1.4884)}{44.7730} \le \sigma^2 \le \frac{(30)(1.4884)}{18.492\,67}$$

$$0.9973 \le \sigma^2 \le 2.4146$$

Therefore, the confidence interval for the standard deviation is:

$$\sqrt{0.9973} \le \sigma \le \sqrt{2.4146}$$

$$1.00 \le \sigma \le 1.55$$

The business council can estimate with 90% confidence that the population variance of the hourly wages of production workers in manufacturing in Greece is between 1.0201 and 2.4146 dollars^2. Therefore, it can be estimated with 90% confidence that the population standard deviation for the hourly wage for a production worker is somewhere between $1.01 and $1.55.

PRACTICE PROBLEMS

Practising the calculations

8.24 For each of the following sample results construct the requested confidence interval. Assume that the data come from normally distributed populations.

a. $n = 14$, $\bar{x} = 30$, $s^2 = 17.2$; 98% confidence for σ^2

b. $n = 9$, $\bar{x} = 7.2$, $s = 1.53$; 90% confidence for σ^2

c. $n = 22$, $\bar{x} = 136$, $s = 6.5$; 85% confidence for σ^2

d. $n = 19$, $s^2 = 22.15$; 80% confidence for σ^2

Testing your understanding

P08-25 **8.25** Use the following sample data to estimate the population variance. Produce a point estimate and a 98% confidence interval. Assume that the data come from a normally distributed population.

27	40	32	41	45	29	33	39
30	28	36	32	42	40	38	46

8.26 A study revealed that the average amount withdrawn at automatic teller machines (ATMs) is $160 per withdrawal. This figure was determined using a random sample of 91 withdrawals at ATMs. The sample standard deviation was calculated to be $10 per withdrawal. Assume the dollar values of the withdrawals are normally distributed. Using the sample information, find a 90% confidence interval for the population variance of the withdrawal amount at an ATM.

P08-27 **8.27** A random sample of 14 people aged between 30 and 39 years produced the household incomes shown below (in dollars). Use these data to determine a point estimate for the population variance of household incomes for people 30–39 years of age and construct a 95% confidence interval. Assume that household income is normally distributed.

47 500	54 800
43 500	46 900
52 300	42 400
38 000	51 200
56 600	48 500
50 200	42 000
45 500	46 800

P08-28 **8.28** C-type batteries have a nominal diameter of 26.2 mm. Producing batteries with this value will ensure they fit properly into all toys and appliances that require C-type batteries. A tolerance variation of .000225 mm^2 (σ = .015 mm) is allowable. After repair, a machine produces a batch of 12 C-type batteries with the following diameters in mm.

26.22	26.19	26.24	26.21	26.16	26.18
26.21	26.20	26.22	26.19	26.20	26.18

a. Construct a 95% confidence interval for σ^2.

b. Does this variation appear acceptable?

8.5 Estimating sample size

In business decision making and research, we have seen that sample statistics can be used to make inferences about a population. However, to be able to draw meaningful conclusions from sample statistics, it is important to be able to estimate the sample size needed before actually selecting the sample. In other words, there is a need for **sample size estimation** so the sample size used is able to fulfil the requirements of a particular level of confidence and to be within a specified margin of error. Without a good estimate of the desired sample size, the sample could be too small to allow meaningful conclusions to be drawn about the population parameter of interest. Alternatively, selecting a sample much larger than is necessary can waste time and money.

The need to estimate the sample size before actually taking the sample is the same for a large corporation investing thousands of dollars into a study of consumer preference as it is for students wanting to send out questionnaires to local businesspeople. For example, if a large corporation is undertaking a market study of consumer preference, should it sample 40 people or 4000 people? Similarly, should a study being undertaken by students of local businesspeople sample 10 or 100 businesspeople? In most cases, as a result of cost considerations, business researchers do not want to sample any more units or individuals than necessary. However, at the same time, any sample that is selected must not be so small that it is of no use.

Sample size when estimating μ

In research studies when μ is being estimated, the size of the sample can be determined using the z formula for sample means. From this z formula, recall formula 8.1 for a confidence interval estimate of μ is:

$$\begin{aligned}&\bar{x} \pm z_{\alpha/2}\frac{\sigma}{\sqrt{n}}\\&= \bar{x} \pm \text{ME}\end{aligned}$$

where ME is the margin of error. To specify the value for ME, the words 'to be within' are typically used. For example, if it is specified that a confidence interval for the mean is to be constructed so as to be within 10 g of the population value, then ME = 10 g. By specifying a margin of error, it is possible to then calculate the sample size needed for a specified level of confidence using:

$$\text{ME} = z_{\alpha/2}\frac{\sigma}{\sqrt{n}}$$

By rearranging this equation:

$$\text{ME}\sqrt{n} = z_{\alpha/2}\sigma$$

$$\sqrt{n} = \frac{z_{\alpha/2}\sigma}{\text{ME}}$$

$$n = \frac{z_{\alpha/2}^2\sigma^2}{(\text{ME})^2} = \left(\frac{z_{\alpha/2}\sigma}{\text{ME}}\right)^2$$

Therefore, formula 8.7 can be used to determine the sample size n prior to undertaking an experiment or survey if the following conditions apply.

1. A level of confidence is specified which allows the value of $z_{\alpha/2}$ to be determined.
2. The population standard deviation is known.
3. An acceptable margin of error is specified.

Sample size when estimating μ (8.7)

$$n = \frac{z_{\alpha/2}^2\sigma^2}{(\text{ME})^2} = \left(\frac{z_{\alpha/2}\sigma}{\text{ME}}\right)^2$$

In estimating the sample size, the population standard deviation is sometimes known or can be determined from past studies. At other times, the population standard deviation is unknown and must be estimated to determine the sample size. When σ is unknown, it is acceptable to use the following approximation of σ:

$$\sigma = \frac{\text{range}}{4}$$

Using formula 8.7, the business researcher can estimate the sample size needed to achieve the goals of the study before gathering data. For example, suppose a researcher wants to estimate the average number of loaves of bread a Brisbane family buys each month. It is known from similar previous studies that the standard deviation of average monthly bread purchases is 4 loaves. The business researcher wants to be 90% confident of the results and to have an estimate that is within 1 loaf of bread of the population mean. What sample size is required to achieve this outcome?

Using formula 8.7 with the value of z for a 90% level of confidence being $z_{\alpha/2} = 1.645$, ME = 1 loaf, and $\sigma = 4$ loaves, gives:

$$n = \frac{z^2_{\alpha/2}\sigma^2}{(\text{ME})^2} = \frac{(1.645)^2(4)^2}{1^2} = 43.3$$

In practice, sampling 43.3 families does not make sense, so this value is rounded up to $n = 44$ families. This rounding-up process is needed to find the sample size that can be used in formula 8.1. This will ensure that the value of ME is less than the specified 1 loaf of bread when the confidence interval for the population mean number of loaves of bread is constructed.

DEMONSTRATION PROBLEM 8.7

PROBLEM: Suppose you want to estimate the average age of all Boeing 727 aeroplanes now in active domestic service. You want to be 95% confident, and you want your estimate to be within 2 years of the actual figure. The 727 was first placed into service about 30 years ago, but you believe that no active 727s in the domestic fleet are more than 25 years old. How large a sample should you take?

SOLUTION: Here, ME = 2 years and the z-score for a 95% confidence interval is 1.96. Since α is unknown, it must be estimated by using the approximation $\sigma = \frac{\text{range}}{4}$. As the range of ages is 0 to 25 years, $\sigma = \frac{25}{4} = 6.25$ years. Using formula 8.7:

$$n = \frac{z^2_{\alpha/2}\sigma^2}{(\text{ME})^2} = \frac{(1.96)^2(6.25)^2}{2^2} = 37.52$$

Since you cannot sample 37.52 aeroplanes, the required sample size needs to be 38. If you randomly sample 38 aeroplanes, you have an opportunity to estimate the average age of active 727s to within 2 years and be 95% confident of the result. If you want to be within 1 year of the estimate (ME = 1), the sample size estimate changes to:

$$n = \frac{z^2_{\alpha/2}\sigma^2}{(\text{ME})^2} = \frac{(1.96)^2(6.25)^2}{1^2} = 150.1$$

Note that halving the margin of error from 2 years to 1 year increases the required sample size by a factor of 4. The reason is that ME is squared and is in the denominator of formula 8.7. Hence, this shows that if the margin of error needs to be reduced by half, giving increased precision for a given level of confidence, extra costs will need to be incurred to obtain a sample that is four times larger.

Please refer to 'Going further with KaddStat' for KaddStat instructions at www.johnwiley.com.au/highered/black4e/kaddstat.

Determining sample size when estimating *p*

To derive a formula for the sample size needed to construct a confidence interval estimate for a population proportion with a specified margin of error, recall the confidence interval for the proportion in formula 8.4:

$$\hat{p} \pm z_{\alpha/2}\sqrt{\frac{\hat{p}\hat{q}}{n}}$$
$$= \hat{p} \pm \text{ME}$$

By specifying a margin of error and level of confidence, the required sample size can be found as follows.

$$\text{ME} = z_{\alpha/2}\sqrt{\frac{\hat{p}\hat{q}}{n}}$$
$$(\text{ME})^2 = \frac{z^2_{\alpha/2}\hat{p}\hat{q}}{n}$$
$$n = \frac{z^2_{\alpha/2}\hat{p}\hat{q}}{(\text{ME})^2}$$

Therefore, formula 8.8 is used to calculate the sample size for a given level of confidence, an estimated population proportion, $\hat{p}$, and a specified margin of error.

Sample size when estimating *p*
(8.8)

$$n = \frac{z^2_{\alpha/2}\hat{p}\hat{q}}{(\text{ME})^2}$$

where:
$\hat{p}$ = the estimated population proportion
$\hat{q} = 1 - \hat{p}$
ME = the margin of error
n = the sample size

TABLE 8.3 $\hat{p}\hat{q}$ values for various selected values of $\hat{p}$

$\hat{p}$	$\hat{q}$	$\hat{p}\hat{q}$
.1	.9	.09
.2	.8	.16
.3	.7	.21
.4	.6	.24
.5	.5	.25
.6	.4	.24
.7	.3	.21
.8	.2	.16
.9	.1	.09

To solve for n using formula 8.8, the values of $\hat{p}$ and $\hat{q}$ are needed. However, these values are not known since a sample has to be taken to be able to calculate them. This poses a dilemma. To calculate the sample size, we need to know the values of $\hat{p}$ and $\hat{q}$ without actually taking a sample. How can this be achieved? It turns out that there are two possible approaches to solving this problem.

The first approach is to rely on previous studies that might have generated good approximations of the values of $\hat{p}$ to use in formula 8.8. If there is no previous information available to approximate the value of $\hat{p}$, the most conservative approach to use is to let $\hat{p}$ = .5. As can be seen in table 8.3, this particular choice of $\hat{p}$ gives the largest possible value of $\hat{p}\hat{q}$ = .25. Since $\hat{p}\hat{q}$ is in the numerator of formula 8.8, using an estimate of $\hat{p}$ = .5 will result in the largest possible sample size. This is therefore a conservative approach for calculating the sample size so as to be within a specified margin of error for a chosen level of confidence.

DEMONSTRATION PROBLEM 8.8

PROBLEM: Hewitt Associates conducted a national survey to determine the extent to which employers are promoting health and fitness among their employees. One of the questions asked was 'Does your company offer on-site exercise classes?' Calculate the sample size Hewitt Associates would need in order to estimate the population proportion to ensure 98% confidence that the results are within .03 of the true population proportion if:

1. it was estimated before the study that no more than 40% of the companies would answer yes
2. there was no previous information available to make an approximation of the value of $\hat{p}$.

SOLUTION:

1. The value of ME for this problem is .03. Since it is estimated that no more than 40% of the companies would say yes, $\hat{p} = .40$ can be used. A 98% confidence interval results in a *z*-score of 2.33 (table A.4). Inserting these values into formula 8.8 yields:

$$n = \frac{(2.33)^2(.40)(.60)}{(.03)^2} = 1447.7$$

   Hewitt Associates would have to sample 1448 companies to be 98% confident in the results and maintain a margin of error of .03.

2. The value of ME = .03. However, since there is no previous information available to estimate $\hat{p}$, the conservative approach is to let $\hat{p} = .5$. Using a 98% confidence interval results in a *z*-score of 2.33 (table A.4). Inserting these values into formula 8.8 yields:

$$n = \frac{(2.33)^2(.50)(.50)}{(.03)^2} = 1508.03$$

   Hewitt Associates would have to sample 1509 companies to be 98% confident in the results and maintain a margin of error of .03. Notice that the sample size is larger in this case (and will increase sampling costs) because an estimate of $\hat{p} = .5$ is used instead of $\hat{p} = .4$.

Please refer to 'Going further with KaddStat' for KaddStat instructions at www.johnwiley.com.au/highered/black4e/kaddstat.

PRACTICE PROBLEMS

Practising the calculations

8.29 Determine the sample size necessary to estimate μ for the following information.

a. $\sigma = 20$ and ME = 2.5 at 99% confidence
b. $\sigma = 10.2$ and ME = 1.5 at 95% confidence
c. Values range from 60 to 460, error is to be within 15, and the confidence level is 99%.
d. Values range from 30 to 90, error is to be within 5, and the confidence level is 90%.

8.30 Determine the sample size necessary to estimate *p* for the following information.

a. ME = .02, *p* is approximately .40, and the confidence level is 96%.
b. ME is to be within .04, *p* is unknown, and the confidence level is 95%.
c. ME is to be within 5%, *p* is approximately 55%, and the confidence level is 90%.
d. ME is to be no more than .01, *p* is unknown, and the confidence level is 99%.

Testing your understanding

8.31 A bank manager wants to determine the average total monthly deposits per customer at the bank. He believes an estimate of this average amount using a confidence interval is sufficient. How large a sample should he take to be within $200 of the actual average with 99% confidence? He assumes that the standard deviation of total monthly deposits for all customers is about $1000.

8.32 Suppose you have been following a particular mining stock for many years. You are interested in determining the average daily price of this stock over a 10-year period and you have access to the stock reports for these years. However, you do not want to average all the daily prices over 10 years because there are more than 2500 data points, so you decide to take a random sample of the daily prices and estimate the average. You want to be 90% confident of your results, you want the estimate to be within $2.00 of the true average, and you believe the standard deviation of the price of this stock is about $12.50 over this period of time. How large a sample should you take?

8.33 A group of investors wants to develop a chain of fast-food restaurants. In determining potential costs for each facility, they must consider, among other expenses, the average monthly electricity bill. They decide to sample some fast-food restaurants currently operating to estimate the monthly cost of electricity. They want to be 90% confident of their results and want the error of the interval estimate to be no more than $100. They estimate that such bills range from $600 to $2500. How large a sample should they take?

8.34 Suppose a production facility purchases a particular component in large lots from a supplier. The production manager wants to estimate the proportion of defective parts received from this supplier. She believes the proportion defective is no more than .20

and wants to be within .02 of the true proportion of defective parts with a 90% level of confidence. How large a sample should she take?

8.35 What proportion of secretaries of *BRW's* Top 500 public companies has a personal computer at his or her workstation? You want to answer this question by conducting a random survey. How large a sample should you take if you want to be 95% confident of the results and you want the error of the confidence interval to be no more than .05? Assume no one has any idea of what the proportion actually is.

8.36 A fuel company wishes to determine the proportion of cars that fill up using unleaded petrol. This population proportion needs to be estimated to within 5% and with a 99% level of confidence. Assuming there is no information regarding this population proportion, how large a sample should be selected?

MISUSE OF STATISTICS

Using sample statistics to estimate population parameters can pose a couple of ethical concerns. Firstly, survey reports and advertisers can at times wrongly state that the value of a point estimate, such as a sample mean, is the value of the population parameter. It is in fact most unlikely that a point estimate will be equal to the population parameter. To overcome this, an allowance should be made for a margin of error when using point estimates. In other words, it is much better to provide a point estimate of the value of the population parameter along with a margin of error in any reported findings.

Secondly, the application of the *t* formula when data are not normally distributed in the population is also of concern. Although some studies have shown that the *t* formula in analyses is robust, a researcher should be careful not to violate the assumptions underlying the use of the *t* formula. Similarly, it is equally unethical, when using the *t* formula for small sample sizes, to report the results without an allowance for the margin of error.

CHAPTER CASE REVISITED

Prawn farm up for sale

1. This example highlights the potential problems that can arise if a point estimate (in this case the sample mean of 14.8 cm) is used to directly compare with the population parameter (the population average of 15 cm). A better estimate of the population mean is to use the sample mean, with an allowance for a margin of error, to construct a confidence interval for the population mean. In this case, the length of prawns is stated to be normally distributed, $\bar{x}$ = 14.8 cm, the population standard deviation is known from historical data σ = .8 cm, the level of confidence required is 95% (giving $z_{.025}$ = 1.96), and the sample size is 25. The confidence interval for the population mean length of prawns for sale at the markets in Japan is:

$$\bar{x} - z_{\alpha/2}\text{SE}_{\bar{x}} \le \mu \le \bar{x} + z_{\alpha/2}\text{SE}_{\bar{x}}$$

where

$$\text{SE}_{\bar{x}} = \frac{\sigma}{\sqrt{n}} = \frac{.8}{\sqrt{25}} = .16$$

so

$$14.8 - 1.96(.16) \le \mu \le 14.8 + 1.96(.16)$$
$$14.8 - .3136 \le \mu \le 14.8 + .3136$$
$$14.49 \text{ cm} \le \mu \le 15.11 \text{ cm}$$

The margin of error for 95% level of confidence can be seen to be .3136 cm. Therefore, based on the sample selected, the average length of all prawns in the shipment is estimated, with 95% confidence, to be between 14.5 cm and 15.1 cm long. Since the specified average length of 15 cm is within this interval, the investor can have a high level of confidence In the average length claim of 15 cm made by the owner of Sunny Bay Prawn Farm.

2. To find the sample size required, the following formula relating to the sampling distribution of the proportion is used.

$$n = \frac{z^2_{\alpha/2}\hat{p}\hat{q}}{(\text{ME})^2}$$

where, for 95% level of confidence, $z_{.025}$ = 1.96.

From discussions with Japanese clients, the investor believes that a good estimate of $\hat{p}$ is .06, so $\hat{q} = 1 - \hat{p} = .94$. Using ME = .03, this gives a required sample size of:

$$n = \frac{1.96^2(.06)(.94)}{.03^2} = 240.7$$

Hence, the sample size required would be 241 prawns.

3. A sample of 250 is selected and 11 damaged prawns are found in this sample. Therefore, $\hat{p} = \frac{11}{250} = .044$. Using a level of confidence of 95%, the margin of error is:

$$\text{ME} = z_{\alpha/2}\sqrt{\frac{\hat{p}\hat{q}}{n}}$$

$$\text{ME} = 1.96\sqrt{\frac{(.044)(.956)}{250}} = .0254 = 2.54\%$$

Hence, the 95% confidence interval for the proportion of defective prawns in the population (shipment) is:

$$\hat{p} - z_{\alpha/2}\sqrt{\frac{\hat{p}\hat{q}}{n}} < p < \hat{p} + z_{\alpha/2}\sqrt{\frac{\hat{p}\hat{q}}{n}}$$

$$.044 - .0254 < p < .044 + .0254$$

$$.019 < p < .069$$

Therefore, based on the sample selected, the proportion of damaged prawns in the shipment is estimated, with 95% confidence, to be somewhere between 1.9% and 6.9%. The investor can have a high level of confidence that the population proportion of defective prawns in shipments arriving in Japan is less than 10%.

SUMMARY

1 An interval estimate for the population mean can be constructed around a point estimate of the population mean when σ is known. This interval estimate is called a confidence interval. The confidence interval provides more information about a population parameter than simply the point estimate. The value of σ can come from past experience or historical data. By using the z distribution, specifying a level of confidence, knowing the value of σ and specifying a sample size, a confidence interval can be constructed around a point estimate for the population mean. The confidence interval estimation for the population mean when σ is known is:

$$\bar{x} \pm z_{\alpha/2}\text{SE}_{\bar{x}} = \bar{x} \pm z_{\alpha/2}\sigma_{\bar{x}} = \bar{x} \pm z_{\alpha/2}\frac{\sigma}{\sqrt{n}}$$

2 A second confidence interval for the population mean can be constructed when σ is unknown. In this case, the sample standard deviation must be calculated and the t distribution is used. By specifying a level of confidence, knowing the value of the sample standard deviation and specifying a sample size, a confidence interval can be constructed around a point estimate for the population mean. The confidence interval estimation for the population mean when σ is unknown is:

$$\bar{x} \pm z_{\alpha/2,n-1}\text{SE}_{\bar{x}} = \bar{x} \pm z_{\alpha/2,n-1}s_{\bar{x}} = \bar{x} \pm t_{\alpha/2,n-1}\frac{s}{\sqrt{n}}$$

3 A third estimate of a population parameter is for the population proportion. Using the z distribution, a level of confidence and a specified sample size, a confidence interval can be constructed around a point estimate of the population proportion. The confidence interval estimation for the population proportion is:

$$\hat{p} \pm t_{\alpha/2}\text{SE}_{\hat{p}} = \hat{p} \pm z_{\alpha/2}s_{\hat{p}} = \hat{p} \pm z_{\alpha/2}\sqrt{\frac{\hat{p}\hat{q}}{n}}$$

4 A fourth estimate is for the population variance from a sample variance. Using the chi-square distribution, a specified level of confidence and a sample variance, a confidence interval for the population variance can be constructed. The confidence interval estimation for the population variance is:

$$\frac{(n-1)s^2}{\chi^2_{\alpha/2}} \leq \sigma^2 \leq \frac{(n-1)s^2}{\chi^2_{1-\alpha/2}} \quad \text{with df} = n - 1$$

5 To minimise any expense in collecting a sample, as well as collecting a sample that is large enough to provide meaningful information, methods to calculate a sample size prior to collecting data were explained. By specifying an acceptable margin of error, along with a desired level of confidence, two formulas to calculate a sample size can be derived.

- To estimate the population mean:

$$n = \frac{z^2_{\alpha/2}\sigma^2}{(\text{ME})^2} = \left(\frac{z_{\alpha/2}\sigma}{\text{ME}}\right)^2$$

- To estimate a population proportion:

$$n = \frac{z^2_{\alpha/2}\hat{p}\hat{q}}{(\text{ME})^2}$$

KEY TERMS

chi-square distribution p. 249
confidence interval p. 230
degrees of freedom (df) p. 240
error of estimation p. 230
interval estimate p. 230
level of confidence p. 231
level of significance p. 231
margin of error (ME) p. 230
point estimate p. 230
robust p. 239
sample size estimation p. 252
t distribution p. 238

KEY EQUATIONS

EQUATION	DESCRIPTION	FORMULA
8.1	100(1 – α)% confidence interval to estimate μ	$\bar{x} - z_{\alpha/2}\frac{\sigma}{\sqrt{n}} \le \mu \le \bar{x} + z_{\alpha/2}\frac{\sigma}{\sqrt{n}}$
8.2	Confidence interval to estimate μ using the finite population correction factor	$\bar{x} - z_{\alpha/2}\frac{\sigma}{\sqrt{n}}\sqrt{\frac{N-n}{N-1}} \le \mu \le \bar{x} + z_{\alpha/2}\frac{\sigma}{\sqrt{n}}\sqrt{\frac{N-n}{N-1}}$
8.3	Confidence interval to estimate μ: population standard deviation unknown and population normally distributed	$\bar{x} - t_{\alpha/2,n-1}\frac{s}{\sqrt{n}} \le \mu \le \bar{x} + t_{\alpha/2,n-1}\frac{s}{\sqrt{n}}$ $\text{df} = n - 1$
8.4	Confidence interval to estimate p	$\hat{p} - z_{\alpha/2}\sqrt{\frac{\hat{p}\hat{q}}{n}} \le p \le \hat{p} + z_{\alpha/2}\sqrt{\frac{\hat{p}\hat{q}}{n}}$
8.5	χ^2 formula for variance	$\chi^2 = \frac{(n-1)s^2}{\sigma^2}$ $\text{df} = n - 1$
8.6	Confidence interval to estimate the population variance	$\frac{(n-1)s^2}{\chi^2_{\alpha/2}} \le \sigma^2 \le \frac{(n-1)s^2}{\chi^2_{1-\alpha/2}}$ $\text{df} = n - 1$
8.7	Sample size when estimating μ	$n = \frac{z^2_{\alpha/2}\sigma^2}{(\text{ME})^2} = \left(\frac{z_{\alpha/2}\sigma}{\text{ME}}\right)^2$
8.8	Sample size when estimating p	$n = \frac{z^2_{\alpha/2}\hat{p}\hat{q}}{(\text{ME})^2}$

REVIEW PROBLEMS

Practising the calculations

P08-37 **8.37** Use the following data to construct 90%, 95% and 99% confidence intervals to estimate μ. Assume that σ is 4.9. State the point estimate.

15	17	17	17	19	20	20	21
22	23	23	25	26	26	26	26
27	28	29	29	30	30	31	31
32							

P08-38 **8.38** Construct 90%, 95% and 99% confidence intervals to estimate μ from the following data. State the point estimate. Assume that the data come from a normally distributed population.

12.3	11.6	11.9	12.8	12.5	11.4	12.0
11.7	11.8	12.3				

8.39 Use the following information to compute the confidence interval for the population proportion.

a. $n = 715$ and $x = 329$, with 95% confidence
b. $n = 284$ and $\hat{p} = .71$, with 90% confidence
c. $n = 1250$ and $\hat{p} = .48$, with 95% confidence
d. $n = 457$ and $x = 270$, with 98% confidence

P08-40 **8.40** Use the following data to construct 90% and 95% confidence intervals to estimate the population variance. Assume the data come from a normally distributed population.

212	229	217	216	223
219	208	214	232	219

8.41 Determine the sample size necessary to estimate:

a. μ with $\sigma = 44$, ME = 3 and 95% confidence
b. μ with a range of values from 20 to 88 with ME = 2 and 90% confidence
c. p with p unknown, ME = .04 and 98% confidence
d. p with ME = .03, 95% confidence and p thought to be approximately .70.

Testing your understanding

P08-42 **8.42** In planning both market opportunity and production levels, being able to estimate the size of a market can be important. Suppose a nappy manufacturer wants to know how many nappies a 1-month-old baby uses during a 24-hour period. To determine this usage, the manufacturer's analyst randomly selects 15 parents of 1-month-olds and asks them to keep track of nappy usage for 24 hours. The results are shown. Construct a 95% confidence interval to estimate the average daily nappy usage of a 1-month-old baby. Assume that nappy usage is normally distributed.

11	9	9	10	12	12
11	9	8	14	12	7
10	14	11			

8.43 You want to estimate the proportion of cars that are sports utility vehicles being driven in Melbourne at rush hour by standing on the corner of Flinders Street and Swanston Street and counting sports utility vehicles. You believe the figure is no higher than .40. If you want the error of the confidence interval to be no greater than .03, how many cars should you randomly sample? Use a 90% level of confidence.

8.44 A book publisher wished to estimate the average number of printed pages in textbooks used by university students. A random sample of 65 university textbooks was selected. The average number of printed pages for this sample of textbooks was 562 pages. The sample standard deviation was found to be 97 pages. Using this information, construct a 95% confidence interval to estimate the mean number of printed pages in textbooks used by university students.

8.45 Is global warming a major issue for Australians? To answer that question, a researcher conducts a survey of 1255 randomly selected Australians. Of the selected people, 714 replied that global warming is a major issue. Construct a 95% confidence interval to estimate the proportion of Australians who feel that global warming is a major issue. What is the point estimate of this proportion?

8.46 According to a survey by Topaz Enterprises, a travel auditing company, the average error by travel agents is \$128. Suppose this figure was obtained from a random sample of 41 travel agents and the sample standard deviation is \$21. What is the point estimate of the national average error for all travel agents? Compute a 98% confidence interval for the national average error based on these sample results. Assume that the errors are normally distributed in the population. How wide is the interval? Interpret the interval.

8.47 A coin operated laundromat is for sale. An investor would like to determine the average daily revenue generated by this business. An estimate of the average daily revenue is to be found using a random sample. A good estimate of the population standard deviation has been determined to be \$85 per day for this business. If the investor wishes to be within \$25 of the actual population average daily revenue, how large a sample would the investor need to select if the level of confidence is to be 90%?

8.48 According to a survey, the average cost of a fast-food meal (cheeseburger, large chips, medium soft drink) in Christchurch is $7.25. Suppose this figure was based on a sample of 27 different establishments and the standard deviation was $0.60. Construct a 95% confidence interval for the population mean cost for all fast-food meals in Christchurch. Assume that the costs of a fast-food meal in Christchurch are normally distributed. Using the interval as a guide, is it likely that the population mean is really $7? Why or why not?

8.49 A regional survey of 560 companies asked the operations manager how satisfied they were with the software support received from the computer staff of the company. Suppose 33% of the 560 managers said they were satisfied. Construct a 99% confidence interval for the proportion of the population of managers who would have said they were satisfied with the software support if a census had been taken.

8.50 A research company has been asked to determine the proportion of all restaurants in Western Australia that serve alcoholic beverages. The company wants to be 98% confident of its results but has no idea what the actual proportion is. The company would like to report an error of no more than .05. How large a sample should it take?

P08-51 **8.51** A national survey of a large supermarket chain was undertaken. Data were collected for the price of a particular brand of natural yoghurt. The data are shown below. Assuming the prices of natural yoghurt are normally distributed, find a 95% confidence interval for the population variance of prices for this particular brand of natural yoghurt.

4.99	5.25	5.30	5.50	5.20	4.95	5.00
4.50	4.99	5.25	4.50	4.99	5.25	5.30
5.25	5.60	4.75	4.90	5.30	5.25	5.50
5.00	4.75	5.50	5.25	5.35	4.75	5.30

CHAPTER

9 Statistical inference: hypothesis testing for single populations

LEARNING OBJECTIVES

After studying this chapter, you should be able to:

1. explain the logic involved in hypothesis testing and be able to establish null and alternative hypotheses
2. implement the six-step approach to test hypotheses
3. perform a hypothesis test about a single population mean when σ is known
4. perform a hypothesis test about a single population mean when σ is unknown
5. test hypotheses about a single population proportion
6. test hypotheses about a single population variance
7. explain Type II errors in hypothesis testing.

OPENING VIGNETTE

Australian childcare — enough to make you cry?

Various stakeholders have claimed the childcare industry in Australia is in crisis. Government reports indicate a shortage of skilled staff to fill vacancies. In Queensland, for example, only 71% of childcare worker vacancies were filled within six weeks of advertising. While more than 90% of regional vacancies were filled, only 58% of metropolitan vacancies were filled. In addition, of those applying, almost 40% lacked qualifications, were still studying, or did not have the higher level qualification (such as a diploma) sought by employers. Similarly in Tasmania, only 23% of vacancies were filled, with employers reportedly receiving an average of 2.3 applicants per vacancy, of whom fewer than one per vacancy were suitable. Some employers claimed they received no applications at all. This lack of suitable childcare workers is routinely blamed on low wages.

Combined with this shortage of childcare workers, research and media reports also focus on the increasing demand by parents for childcare services. The *Sydney Morning Herald* (August 2013) reported that in Melbourne 84 childcare centres out of 621 had no available places for children aged under two during that month. The article also reported the results of a survey that revealed 20% of parents had to wait more than a year for a childcare place. Similarly, *The Australian* (January 2013) reported 'three in every four long-day care centres in Australia's capital cities do not have vacancies for babies, with two-thirds having no places left for toddlers'.

Consequently, politicians find themselves under constant pressure to provide practical solutions to address these childcare issues. Recent funding cutbacks to the sector have only generated more pain for government, with media reports highlighting how childcare centres have been forced to recruit qualified staff from overseas. It has been reported that 775 foreign workers applied for positions in Australia in the 2012–13 financial year, with less than 50% approved (38% from the UK and Ireland, 22% from New Zealand). Government policy relating to paid parental leave has also come under fire from some researchers who find 'increasing investment in childcare is twice as effective as investing in paid parent leave in increasing women's workforce participation'. Whatever policies are finally proposed and eventually implemented by the Australian Government in relation to childcare, claims as to their success or otherwise will surely be under the spotlight.

Introduction

The inferential technique of estimation involves making a conclusion about a population parameter from a sample statistic by stating a confidence interval. In this chapter, we introduce an inferential technique called **hypothesis testing**.

Hypothesis testing lies at the heart of inferential statistics. By following a series of well-defined steps, conclusions about a population parameter can be made. The status quo (an existing condition) is defined where the value of a parameter is known. Something may then occur or change in some way to change the status quo, so that a new value of the parameter exists. Hypothesis testing is a procedure used to assess whether there is sufficient evidence to conclude that the status quo has changed. For example, consider that management know that customers wait in a queue at their supermarket checkouts for an average of 8.5 minutes before being served. Management feel this is too long and decide to install new checkout scanning equipment and self-serve checkouts to reduce this average waiting time. Using hypothesis testing, management can test whether they have been successful in significantly reducing the average waiting time by introducing the new equipment.

Also in this chapter, hypothesis testing involving a population proportion and population variance are explored. It also highlights how hypothesis testing is not able to provide 100% certainty in any conclusion that is reached. In other words, hypothesis testing can result in possible errors occurring when reaching a conclusion that is based on sample data. Awareness, understanding and implications of these possible errors are addressed.

CHAPTER CASE

Prawn farm expects a bright future

The owner of Sunny Bay Prawn Farm is in the final stages of negotiations to sell their farm to an investor. Management promotes their farming techniques as a source of competitive advantage. With years of experience, it has allowed the business to constantly outperform their competitors in terms of the quality of prawns produced. A potential investor wants to test a particular claim made by management about the weight of the prawns on the farm when they are six weeks of age.

Questions to help managers make decisions

1. Management at Sunny Bay Prawn Farm introduced a new feed for their prawns and believe that, at six weeks of age, the prawns' average weight is higher than when the previous type of feed was used. They consider that this observed increased weight at six weeks of age is one of the highest in the industry. This claim is based on a sample of 20 prawns taken by a member of the quality-control centre on the farm that was found to have an average weight 51 g. Historical data for the farm's output over many years, before the new prawn food was introduced, show that prawns at six weeks of age had weights that were normally distributed with a mean of 48 g and a standard deviation of 2 g. What conclusions can the investor make, using hypothesis testing, regarding Sunny Bay's claim about the increased average weight of their six-week-old prawns?
2. Suspicious of using data supplied by Sunny Bay Prawn Farm, the investor decides to randomly select a sample of 50 prawns that are six weeks of age and weigh each of them. The historical mean of 48 g, prior to introducing the new prawn food, is considered reasonable as it compares well with other prawn farming businesses. The standard deviation of the sample was 3.2 g and the sample mean 50.2 g. Using hypothesis testing and the sample's standard deviation, is there sufficient evidence for the investor to conclude that the average weight of six-week-old prawns is higher after introducing the new prawn food?
3. Aware that errors can be made in drawing conclusions from hypothesis testing, the investor wonders what the risk is that the average weight is concluded to have increased when in fact it has not. Comment on this using the conclusions from the hypothesis tests conducted in questions 1 and 2.

9.1 Hypothesis-testing fundamentals

Sample information can be used for estimation purposes to draw conclusions about a population parameter. In this chapter, sample information is used to explore another major area of inferential statistics called hypothesis testing. This procedure also enables conclusions about a population to be made based on a representative sample. For instance, by using sample data, a manager or researcher can aim to answer the following questions.

- Is our soft-drink bottling machine correctly delivering 1.5 litres per bottle?
- Has our market share increased above 60% after a three-month advertising campaign?
- Is the average motel room rate on the Gold Coast $120 per night this winter?
- Is the proportion of Brisbane teenagers with an iPhone 27%?
- Has the average crop yield increased above 5 kg/m^2 after introducing the new fertiliser?

In order to answer such questions scientifically, it is possible to conduct formal statistical hypothesis testing for a population parameter. Expressed simply, hypothesis testing aims to test if a population parameter has remained as it has been in the past (the status quo has been maintained) or if the parameter has changed significantly. **Statistical hypotheses,** therefore, consist of what is called the **null hypothesis** (the status quo has been maintained) and the **alternative hypothesis** (the parameter has changed). Together these two hypotheses contain all the possible outcomes of any experiment or investigation. The alternative hypothesis is also known as the research hypothesis. Usually, the researcher uses the procedure of hypothesis testing to try to reject the null hypothesis in favour of the alternative hypothesis. If the null hypothesis cannot be rejected, then the null hypothesis holds. Understanding the intuition behind hypothesis testing is really the key to appreciating this inferential technique. Using an example is a good way to get a feel for this intuition.

For example, consider a situation where a chicken farmer decides to change the grain mixture that is fed to the chickens. The farmer wants to know if the new grain mixture will increase the average chicken weight above the current 1.6 kg when they are ten weeks old and ready for sale. By using hypothesis testing, the farmer can make an informed decision as to whether the new grain mixture increases the average weight of the chicken population at ten weeks old compared with the previous grain mixture. Note that the status quo is that the chickens remain at 1.6 kg after feeding them the new grain mixture. Alternatively, what the farmer is hoping to find is an average weight above 1.6 kg. This highlights the fundamental intuition behind hypothesis testing. That is, using sample statistics, a conclusion is made that finds either that the status quo regarding the parameter is maintained or that sufficient statistical evidence exists to conclude that the status quo regarding the parameter has changed. In other words, generally, the null hypothesis states that the 'null' condition exists; that is, nothing has changed, the old theory is still true, the old standard is correct, things are performing as intended. The alternative hypothesis, on the other hand, states that the 'alternate' condition exists; that is, something has changed, the new theory is true, there are new standards, the system is not performing as intended.

Consider another example. A manager wants to check the performance of a machine required to fill 1.5-litre bottles of soft drink. The null hypothesis is that the average fill amount is 1.5 litres (the machine is operating as intended). The alternative hypothesis is that the average fill amount is not 1.5 litres (the machine is not working as intended). The symbol used to represent the null hypothesis is H_0 and the alternative hypothesis is H_a. The null and alternative hypotheses in this soft-drink bottling example can be restated using these symbols. Importantly, it should be noted that the hypothesis statements are made in terms of a parameter and not a statistic. In this example, the parameter is μ for the population mean of the fill amount per bottle. Hence the hypotheses are written as:

$$H_0\text{: } \mu = 1.5 \text{ litres (machine working correctly)}$$
$$H_a\text{: } \mu \neq 1.5 \text{ litres (machine not working correctly)}$$

In a different situation, a company wants to determine if their market share has increased above a previously known value of 60% after an extensive three-month advertising campaign. The keyword in the previous sentence is 'increased', which can be represented mathematically by the symbol >. This relates to the alternative hypothesis; if the advertising campaign was successful, the market share would have increased above 60%. Therefore, the null hypothesis is that the market share (population proportion) has remained at 60% (or perhaps has dropped below 60% if the campaign was poorly run). Using p to represent the population proportion, the parameter in the hypothesis statements, gives:

$$H_0: p \leq .60 \text{ (marked share is unchanged or has decreased)}$$
$$H_a: p > .60 \text{ (marked share has increased)}$$

Note that, if a researcher is interested in testing a 'new idea' or 'new theory', this new theory is always stated in the alternative hypothesis. In this example, the aim is to test if the market share has increased (>) above 60% after the advertising campaign. Note that the null hypothesis states the 'old idea' or the 'status quo'.

In statistical hypothesis testing, the formal hypothesis structure always consists of both the null hypothesis and the alternative hypothesis. Importantly, these two statements alone should contain all the possible outcomes of any research experiment or study and have no overlap. In other words, the null and alternative hypotheses are collectively exhaustive (all cases included) and mutually exclusive (no overlap). In the market share example above, the alternative hypothesis tests if the market share has increased (>). The null hypothesis tests whether nothing has changed and that the status quo remains (=). However, because the two hypotheses must cover all possible outcomes with no overlap, there is a need to introduce the less than sign (<) somewhere. This can logically be used only in the null hypothesis. By introducing the < symbol, it indicates the market share has in fact decreased; now all possible outcomes are covered. Note that a decrease in market share could be an outcome after an advertising campaign takes place but certainly not one intended by a company promoting itself. Hence, the symbol to use in the null hypothesis in this example should be ≤. So, the combinations of symbols that will be used in the hypothesis statements through this textbook will be one of the following three combinations (with the appropriate parameter used):

$H_0: p = .60$	$H_0: p \leq .60$	$H_0: p \geq .60$
$H_a: p \neq .60$	$H_a: p > .60$	$H_a: p < .60$

Note that a distinguishing feature here is that the H_0 statement *always* contains an equals sign. The H_a statement *never* contains an equals sign. Other examples of statistical hypotheses are:

$H_0: \mu = 1.5$ litres	$H_0: \mu \leq 1.5$ litres	$H_0: \mu \geq 1.5$ litres
$H_a: \mu \neq 1.5$ litres	$H_a: \mu > 1.5$ litres	$H_a: \mu < 1.5$ litres

Having now established the possible formal hypothesis statements for a particular problem, it is possible to classify any test as being either a **two-tailed test** or **one-tailed test**.

By definition, a two-tailed hypothesis test tests for deviations, in either direction, away from the parameter in the null hypothesis (the status quo). For example, if a manager believes a machine filling 1.5-litre bottles of soft drinks is *not* filling the bottles correctly, a two-tailed test is used. The way to identify that this is a two-tailed test is the use of the word 'not'. If the machine is not working correctly, it could be underfilling or overfilling the bottles (hence ≠ is used). Underfilling or overfilling does not specify which direction the bottles are being filled. Hence, a two-tailed test is called a non-directional test. The hypotheses in this example would be written as:

$$H_0: \mu = 1.5 \text{ litres}$$
$$H_a: \mu \neq 1.5 \text{ litres}$$

So any two-tailed tests will always involve = and ≠ in the statistical hypotheses. It is directionless in that the alternative hypothesis test for the parameter could be either greater than or less than the value stated in the null hypothesis.

In contrast to the non-directional, two-tailed test, a one-tailed hypothesis test is designed to test for deviations from the parameter in the null hypothesis (status quo) in one direction only. For example, consider the example investigating if market share has increased above a previously known value of 60% following an advertising campaign. The keyword here is 'increased', which can be represented by the symbol >. Since there is no equals sign (=) involved, 'increased' implies an alternative hypothesis. It is also very specific in that it is testing to see if the market share has become larger, a very clear directional indicator. For this reason, this type of hypothesis test is called a directional test or a one-tailed hypothesis test. In this example, the symbol to use in the alternative hypothesis is > (indicating 'increased'), and so the sign to use in the null hypothesis must be ≤. Hence, with the parameter being the proportion, the hypothesis statements are written as:

$$H_0\text{: } p \leq .60$$
$$H_a\text{: } p > .60 \text{ (market share increased)}$$

So, any one-tailed tests will always involve only > or < signs in the alternative hypothesis. This makes the alternative hypothesis test directional because it tests for the parameter either being greater than a specific value or less than a specific value.

When determining whether a hypothesis test is two-tailed or one-tailed, identifying keywords and phrases helps make this task easier. For example, some typical keywords and phrases are associated with the following symbols:

For H_0 statements:

= equal to, is, remains the same, no change

≥ greater than or equal to, at least, an amount or more

≤ less than or equal to, at most, not exceeding, no more than

For H_a statements:

≠ not equal to, not, is different from, has changed

> greater than, more than, exceeds, increased, larger

< less than, fewer than, below, decreased, smaller

As a final comment on two-tailed and one-tailed tests, a conservative approach in business research is to conduct a two-tailed test. Sometimes research results can be the opposite of what is anticipated. For example, in the market share problem discussed earlier, it is possible that the company has lost market share, to be below 60% after the advertising campaign was completed. Even though the company managers may not have expected a reduction in market share from the advertising campaign, they would still like to know this if this had occurred. In this case, the managers would be interested to see if market share has changed from 60%: in other words, has market share increased or decreased? This test would require a non-directional, two-tailed test. Hence, if in doubt, it is recommended that researchers conduct a two-tailed test.

Rejection and nonrejection regions

In hypothesis testing, there are two possible statistical decisions that can be made from a research study: *reject* H_0 or *do not reject* H_0. This wording is quite deliberate and the intuition behind it is the key to the understanding of hypothesis testing. Notice, for example, that the wording in the decision does not state the null hypothesis is proven correct (true) or that it should be accepted. Hypothesis testing is not able to *prove* anything (or find that it is 100% certain) as the test procedure is based on calculations that rely on sample data and probabilities. However, by using sample data and probability concepts, the hypothesis-testing procedure is able to assess whether a particular outcome is likely. Hence, the decision made is either reject H_0 or do not reject H_0.

The basis then of any hypothesis test is to examine whether there is sufficient evidence, based on sample data and probability, to conclude that the status quo has changed or has not changed. If there is sufficient evidence that there has been a change in the status quo, then the decision is to reject H_0 in favour of H_a. Otherwise, if there is insufficient evidence, the null hypothesis is not rejected and the status quo is taken to still hold. Importantly, an explanation is needed here to clearly explain what is meant by the term 'sufficient evidence'. This key concept in hypothesis testing is required to understand how a conclusion about a population parameter is made using a sample.

In order to understand what is meant by sufficient evidence, some further elements of hypothesis testing need to be introduced here. It has been mentioned that the process of rejecting H_0 or not rejecting H_0 relies on using sample data. Having randomly selected a representative sample, statistics such as the mean, proportion, standard deviation and standard error can be calculated. Using sample statistics, it is possible to calculate what is called the test statistic (such as z_{test} and t_{test}). The test statistic indicates how many standard errors the sample statistic is from the parameter in the hypothesis H_0. The test statistic can then be compared with the **critical value** (z_{crit} or t_{crit}). It is the critical values that divide the nonrejection region from the rejection region, and the test statistic is then used to indicate if there is sufficient or insufficient evidence to reject H_0. The critical value and test statistic are, therefore, used to make the decision to either *reject the null hypothesis* or *not reject the null hypothesis*. This technique of comparing the critical value with the test statistic to make a decision is called the **critical value method** of hypothesis testing.

Now it is possible to describe what is meant by sufficient evidence in statistics. If the test statistic lies beyond the critical value and in the tail of the distribution, we conclude there is sufficient evidence to reject H_0, since the sample statistic is far enough away from the parameter based on a **level of significance** for the test. Conversely, if the test statistic is not beyond the critical value, we conclude that there is insufficient evidence to reject H_0, since the sample statistic is not far enough away from the parameter based on a level of significance for the test.

In summary, the decision rule using the critical value method in hypothesis testing is:

1. if the test statistic exceeds the critical value in magnitude and direction, reject H_0
2. if the test statistic is less than the critical value in magnitude and direction, do not reject H_0.

An alternative method for making a decision is called the ***p*-value** method of hypothesis testing (explained further in section 9.3). This method uses the value of **alpha (α)** as a critical probability value. By definition, the p-value is equal to the area in the tail(s) beyond the test statistic (such as z_{test} or t_{test}). The decision rule using the p-value method is:

1. if the p-value is larger than α, do not reject H_0 (since this means the test statistic must have fallen relatively close to the parameter in H_0)
2. if the p-value is less than α, reject H_0 (since this means the test statistic must have been in the tail(s) beyond the critical value).

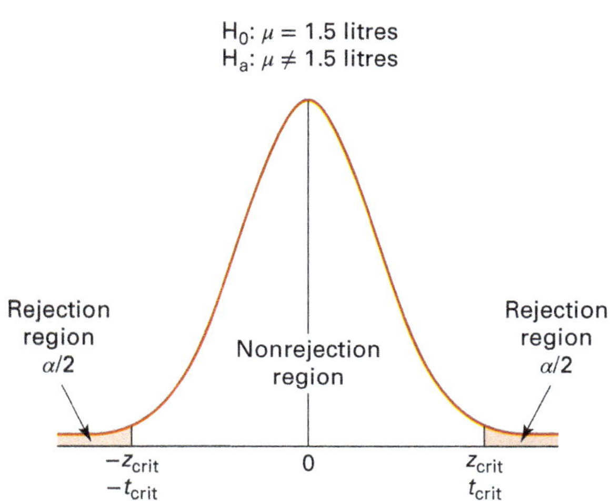

FIGURE 9.1 Rejection and nonrejection regions for a two-tailed test

Having outlined the basis of hypothesis testing, this decision-making procedure can be directly compared to the justice system. For example, in a court of law a defendant is assumed to be innocent until proven guilty. That is, H_0 is that the status quo holds (innocent) and H_a is the alternative to innocent (guilty). Prosecutors present evidence against the defendant (analogous to gathering data). At some point, if enough evidence is presented against the defendant and analysed, the jury may no longer believe that the defendant is innocent (analogous to calculating a test statistic and comparing it with the critical value). At this point, a critical level of evidence must be reached to reject the null hypothesis. The jury then reaches a decision that the defendant is guilty (analogous to the test statistic exceeding the critical value).

Conceptually and graphically, a statistical decision to reject H_0 relates to the **rejection region**. A statistical decision to not reject H_0 relates to the **nonrejection region**. Figures 9.1 to 9.3 show the possible rejection and nonrejection regions for two-tailed and one-tailed hypothesis tests. Note that these regions are based on the value of α, which in turn defines the critical values (such as z_{crit} or t_{crit}).

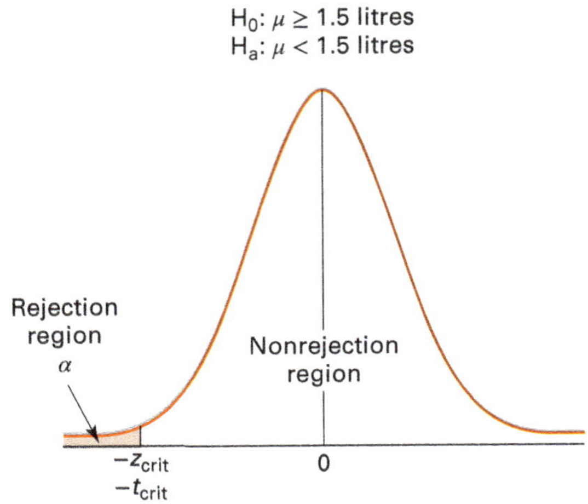

FIGURE 9.2 Rejection and nonrejection regions for a one-tailed (left tail) test

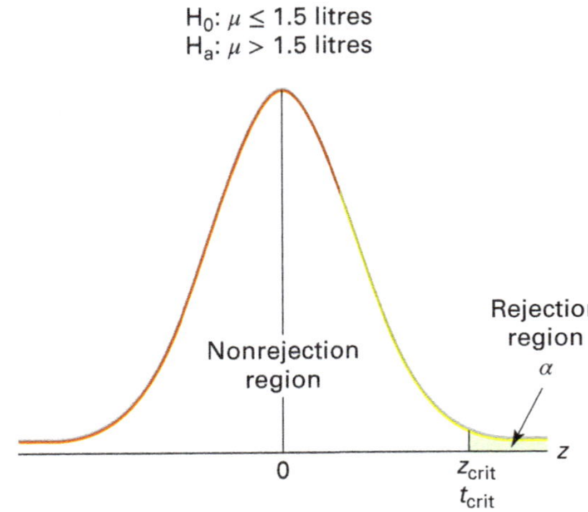

FIGURE 9.3 Rejection and nonrejection regions for a one-tailed (right tail) test

To demonstrate the decision-making process of rejecting H_0 or not rejecting H_0, consider the soft-drink bottling machine example used earlier. The quality-control manager needs to ensure that the bottling machine is filling 1.5-litre bottles correctly. Both underfilling and overfilling bottles will present problems; production will need to be stopped, the machine will need to be adjusted, and the company is likely to suffer a financial loss. This situation requires a two-tailed test to be performed as the specified fill amount could be either side of 1.5 litres. Therefore, the null hypothesis is that the average fill amount for all the bottles is 1.5 litres, and the alternative hypothesis is that the fill amount is not 1.5 litres.

To test the fill amount being delivered by the machine, a quality-control manager randomly selects a sample of 100 bottles and calculates a sample mean of 1.51 litres per bottle. Since this sample average is not 1.5 litres, does this mean the the null hypothesis should be rejected in favour of the alternative hypothesis? In the hypothesis test process, sample statistics are used (in this case, the sample mean of 1.51 litres) to make decisions about a population parameter (in this case, the population mean of 1.5 litres). It makes sense that, in taking random samples from a population with a mean of 1.5 litres, not all sample means will equal exactly 1.5 litres. In fact, the central limit theorem states that, for large sample sizes, sample means are normally distributed around the population mean. So, even though the population mean should be 1.5 litres, a random sample with a mean of 1.48, 1.51 or 1.6 is possible and this could be considered close enough to the population mean that the decision is to not reject H_0. It is also possible that, from a sample of 100 bottles, the calculated sample mean could be 1.2 litres. In this case, the sample mean might be considered to be far enough away from the population mean of 1.5 litres that the decision is to reject H_0. This then begs the question: When is the sample mean far enough away from the population mean to reject the null hypothesis? This can be explained using the critical values.

Recall that the critical values are used to divide the distribution of sample means into the regions of rejection and nonrejection of H_0. Figure 9.4 displays a normal distribution of sample means around a population mean of 1.5 litres. Note the critical values $\bar{x}_{\text{lower crit}}$ and $\bar{x}_{\text{upper crit}}$ in the tails of the distribution. Sample means that fall between these critical values are considered close enough to the population mean, μ = 1.5 litres, that there is insufficient evidence to reject H_0 (the nonrejection region). In each direction beyond the critical values lie the rejection regions. Any sample mean that falls beyond these critical values is considered far enough away from the population mean of μ = 1.5 litres that there is sufficient evidence to reject H_0.

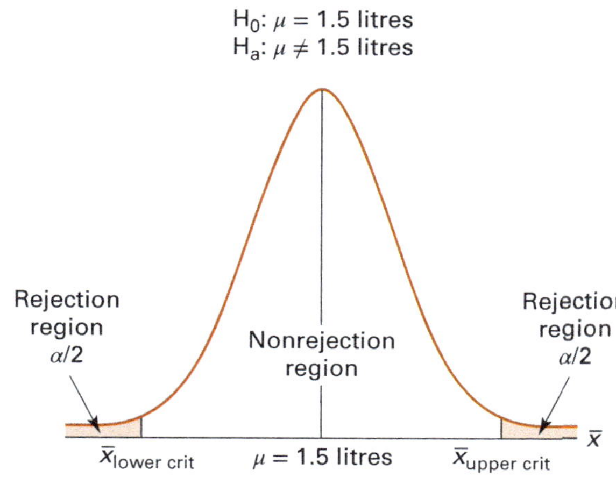

FIGURE 9.4 Rejection and nonrejection regions (two-tailed test) using the critical values of the sample mean

Type I and Type II errors

The hypothesis-testing procedure uses a sample statistic to draw conclusions about a population parameter. With decisions about the null hypothesis based on a level of significance (α) and a random sample statistic, it is possible to reach an incorrect decision. For example, the test statistic based on the sample may be beyond the critical value and the decision will be to reject the null hypothesis. Having defined a level of significance, there is a possibility that an unusually large or small value of a sample statistic is used in arriving at a decision. In doing so, by using an atypical sample statistic with a low probability of occurring, an incorrect conclusion about a parameter will occur and hence an error made. There are two types of errors that can be made in testing hypotheses: Type I error and Type II error.

Type I error

The hypothesis-testing procedure relies on using a sample statistic to draw conclusions about a population parameter. A **Type I error** is committed by *rejecting a 'true' null hypothesis*. In other words, a Type I error occurs in hypothesis testing when a decision is made, by using sample data, that there is sufficient evidence to reject the null hypothesis when in fact the null hypothesis is true and should not be rejected. For example, consider a soft-drink filling machine that is working correctly and delivering an average a specified amount of 1.5 litres per bottle. To routinely test whether this machine is working correctly, a quality-control manager randomly selects 100 bottles and measures the volume in each and then calculates the sample mean. It is possible by chance to randomly select a large number of atypical bottles in a sample of 100 bottles that are mostly overfilled or mostly underfilled. If this occurs, a sample mean much larger or much smaller than the population mean will be found. Any atypical sample means will therefore lie in the tails of the sampling distribution of the sample mean and be beyond the critical values of the sample mean. Hence, atypical sample means will fall in the rejection region and any decision made using an atypical sample would be to reject the null hypothesis. The conclusion would be that the machine is not delivering, on average, 1.5 litres per bottle. However, if the machine *is* actually working correctly and *is* delivering, on average, 1.5 litres per bottle, an incorrect decision would be made if based on an atypical sample. In this instance a Type I error occurs.

Another way to help understand Type I errors is to consider some decisions made in everyday life. For example, a manager has decided to sack an employee. Evidence gathered and given to the manager indicated that the employee was stealing from the company. In fact, it is later discovered that the employee was not stealing from the company but someone else was. In this example, the null hypothesis (and status quo) is that the employee was not stealing, and sufficient evidence should therefore be found to show they were stealing (the alternative hypothesis). Given that the employee was sacked, this indicates that the null hypothesis was rejected in favour of the alternative hypothesis. However, since it was later found that the employee was not stealing, the null hypotheses should not have been rejected as it was true. Here, the manager rejected a 'true' null hypothesis and, therefore, made a Type I error. This is analogous to sending an innocent person to jail.

As another example, an inspector on a vehicle assembly line hears an unusual noise as cars are being manufactured. The appropriate sample data are collected and the inspector then makes the decision to stop the assembly line (that is, reject the null hypothesis that the machine is working correctly). After checking the assembly line equipment, the noise is found not to be related to this equipment and everything is found to be operating correctly (the null hypothesis is 'true'). Here, the inspector has rejected a 'true' null hypothesis and made a Type I error.

In figure 9.4, the rejection regions represent the possibility of committing a Type I error. Sample means that fall beyond the critical value(s) and in the tail(s) of the distribution are considered atypical and therefore unlikely to be found using a random sampling. If a sample mean is found that lies in this region then the decision is to reject the null hypothesis. The probability of a sample mean being in the rejection region is equal to level of significance (α). If the null hypothesis is actually 'true', any sample mean that falls in a rejection region will result in a decision to reject the null hypothesis and, therefore, a Type I error. In other words, the *probability of committing a Type I error* is equal to the level of significance. Alpha is the area under the curve in the rejection region(s) beyond the critical value(s). The value of alpha is always set before the experiment or study is undertaken. Common values of alpha are .10, .05, .01 and .001.

Type II error

A **Type II error** occurs when a decision is made to not *reject a 'false' null hypothesis*. In this case, the null hypothesis is 'false' but, based on a random sample, the decision is to not reject the null hypothesis. For example, consider a sugar-packaging machine that is intended to deliver on average 2 kg per bag. From a random sample of 100, the sample mean is calculated to be 2.01 kg. For a specified level of significance, it is found that this sample mean falls in the nonrejection region. Hence the decision is to not reject the null hypothesis. However, it is later found that the machine was *actually* delivering 2.07 kg on average per bag for all the bags produced. The decision should have been to reject the null hypothesis as the machine was not delivering exactly 2 kg per bag on average. This is an example of a Type II error. The packaging machine was not working as specified to deliver on average 2 kg per bag. Hence, based on the sample it shows how the hypothesis-testing procedure did not correctly identify that the packaging machine was not working correctly.

As another example, a manager is presented with some evidence indicating that an employee is stealing from the company. In this example, the null hypothesis (and status quo) is that the employee is not stealing and sufficient evidence must therefore be found to show they are stealing (the alternative hypothesis). The evidence gathered is not sufficient to draw the conclusion that the employee is stealing. Hence, the manager decides not to sack the employee. If it is later discovered that the employee was actually stealing from the company, the manager made a Type II error by not rejecting a 'false' null hypothesis.

In a similar situation, consider an inspector on a vehicle assembly line who heard an unusual noise as cars are being manufactured. The appropriate sample data were collected and the inspector then made the decision not to stop the assembly line. However, it was later found that the noise was coming from a vibrating and damaged steel support bracket. To prevent a possible serious workplace accident, the inspector should have identified this problem and had it repaired urgently. Having not detected the problem and believing that assembly line was working correctly, the inspector made a Type II error by not rejecting a 'false' null hypothesis. This is analogous to a courtroom situation where a guilty person is declared innocent.

The probability of committing a Type II error is **beta (β)**. Since beta occurs only when the null hypothesis is false, the calculated value of beta will depend on the value of the parameter used. For example, with the sugar-packaging machine, if the population mean is not 2 kg, then what is it? It could be 1.98, 2.07 or 2.2 kg, for example. A value of beta is associated with each of these alternative means. This is covered in more detail in section 9.7.

How are alpha and beta related?

From the analysis of Type I and Type II errors, the following observations can be made.

1. A Type I error (α) can be committed only when the null hypothesis is rejected and a Type II error (β) can be committed only when the null hypothesis is not rejected. Therefore, it is not possible to make a Type I error and a Type II error at the same time.
2. Generally alpha and beta are inversely related. That is, if alpha is reduced, then beta will be increased (and vice versa). For example, if alpha is reduced then the rejection regions in figures 9.1 to 9.3 are made smaller. At the same time, this also makes it harder to reject the null hypothesis thereby making it is less likely to identify a change in the status quo. Using the vehicle assembly line example, if management makes it harder for workers to shut down the assembly line (by reducing the chance of a Type I error), then there is a greater chance that defective product will be made or that a serious problem with the assembly line will arise (increased chance of Type II errors). In the context of law, if the courts make it harder to send innocent people to jail, then they make it easier to let guilty people go free.
3. One way to reduce both errors is to increase the sample size. For example, if a larger sample is selected, it is more likely that the sample will be representative of the population and that the sample mean will be closer to the population mean. This will then translate into a better chance of making the correct decision regarding the null hypothesis.
4. Table 9.1 shows the relationship between Type I and Type II errors. The statistical decision (represented by the rows in the table) is the decision made from the hypothesis-testing procedure using sample information. Note that each statistical decision alternative (across the rows) contains only one type of error and one possibility for making a correct decision. The columns in table 9.1 represent the actual or real condition (that is unknown and being tested) relating to the null hypothesis. Note also that the **power** of the test is *the probability of a test rejecting the null hypothesis when the null hypothesis is false*. The power is equal to $1 - \beta$.

TABLE 9.1 Outcomes of hypothesis testing

Statistical decision (using a sample)	Actual (real) situation	
	H_0 true	H_0 false
Do not reject H_0	Correct decision Confidence = $1 - \alpha$	Type II error P(Type II error) = β
Reject H_0	Type I error P(Type I error) = α	Correct decision Power = $1 - \beta$

PRACTICE PROBLEMS

Testing your understanding

9.1 For each of the following, state the null and alternative hypotheses.

a. The mean length increased to above 15 cm.

b. The population proportion is the same as the historical value of 50%.

c. The average height of a 32-year-old male in a community is claimed to be at most 180 cm.

d. The proportion of healthy children in a community is believed to be less than 75%.

e. The average weight of people in a community is 85 kg.

9.2 For each of the hypothesis statements in problem 9.1, is a two-tailed test or one-tailed test needed? If it is a one-tailed test, indicate if it is a left-tailed or right-tailed test.

9.3 The critical values for a particular two-tailed hypothesis test are given to be −1.96 and 1.96. Depending on the sample selected, the calculated test statistic can vary. For each of the following possible test statistics, indicate whether to reject the null hypothesis.

a. −2.8   b. −1.97   c. 0   d. 1.5   e. 2

9.4 The critical value for a specific left-tailed hypothesis test is given as −1.645. Depending on the sample selected for the hypothesis test, the calculated test statistic can vary. For each of the following test statistics, indicate whether to reject reject the null hypothesis.

a. −2.8   b. −1.7   c. 0   d. 1.63

9.5 From the information given, indicate if a correct decision, a Type I error or a Type II error was made.

a. $H_0 : \mu = 1.5$ litres. The decision was to not reject H_0 and μ is actually 1.5 litres.

b. $H_0 : \mu = 1.5$ litres. The decision was to not reject H_0 and μ is actually 1.6 litres.

c. $H_0 : \mu = 1.5$ litres. The decision was to reject H_0 and μ is actually 1.5 litres.

d. $H_0 : \mu = 1.5$ litres. The decision was to reject H_0 and μ is actually 1.6 litres.

9.2 The six-step approach to hypothesis testing

Having established the fundamentals of hypothesis testing, a detailed six-step procedure is now presented to illustrate how hypothesis testing is performed. The procedure presented in this section will be adopted throughout this book.

STEP 1. Set up H_0 and H_a (in symbols and words).
STEP 2. Decide on the type and direction of the test.
STEP 3. Decide on the level of significance (α).
Determine critical values and regions for the test.
Draw a diagram for the problem.
STEP 4. Write down the decision rule.
STEP 5. Select a random sample and do relevant calculations.
STEP 6. Draw a conclusion.

STEP 1. Set up H_0 and H_a

State the null and alternative hypotheses in symbol form (by identifying keywords in the problem and then translating them into mathematical symbols). Keep in mind that the null hypothesis must have an equals sign in its formulation (=, ≤ or ≥) and the alternative hypothesis must have no equals sign in its formulation (≠, < or >). This will ensure that between them the null and alternative hypotheses cover all possibilities. In setting up the null and alternative hypotheses, remember the two types of errors that can be made. In deciding on the null hypothesis, it is usual to try and minimise the chance of making the more serious error. Hence, a conservative attitude is usually adopted towards the decision to be made.

STEP 2. Decide on the type and direction of the test

From the null and alternative hypotheses, determine if a two-tailed test, upper-tail test or lower-tail test is needed.

STEP 3. Decide on the level of significance (α), determine the critical value(s) and region(s), and draw a diagram

The level of significance chosen will depend on how serious it would be to commit a Type I error (to reject H_0 when in fact it is true). The critical region (for a one-tailed test) or regions (for a two-tailed test) can now be specified (in terms of z or t, for example). Using these critical value(s), the critical region(s) of the sampling distribution can be shaded. This shaded region can also be later compared with the p-value.

STEP 4. Write down the decision rule

This can be done using one of two methods:

1. the critical value method
2. the p-value.

This decision rule is used to act once a sample is taken and analysed. (*Note:* Steps 1 to 4 should usually be done *before* the sample is taken in step 5 and before the conclusion is drawn in step 6.)

STEP 5. Select a random sample and do relevant calculations

When the sample results become available, calculate the appropriate statistic and estimate the standard error. From this, calculate the required test statistic (such as z_{test} or t_{test}). This will indicate how many standard errors the sample statistic is from the parameter in H_0. The test statistic is then compared with the critical value (such as z_{crit} or t_{crit}) established in step 3. If the test statistic exceeds the critical value (in magnitude and direction), then H_0 is rejected in favour of H_a. If the test statistic is less than the critical value, then H_0 is not rejected. Alternatively, using the p-value method, if the p-value is less than the level of significance, α, then H_0 is rejected. If the p-value is larger than α, then H_0 is not rejected.

STEP 6. Draw a conclusion

Decide to *reject* H_0 or to *not reject* H_0. A full conclusion in words should then be stated in terms of the problem being solved.

MISUSE OF STATISTICS

The hypothesis-testing procedure relies on a chosen level of significance to arrive at a conclusion. The process is clear in that it requires the level of significance be chosen prior to any analysis of sample data (refer to step 3 of the six-step hypothesis-testing approach). It can be tempting, however, to analyse the sample data first, look at the results and then choose a level of significance. If this is done, it can help ensure that a predetermined outcome is achieved. This is not how hypothesis testing is intended to be conducted. To overcome any potential problems of analysing data first and then defining a value of alpha so as to reach a desired conclusion, the hypothesis-testing procedure is very specific. The level of significance is to be chosen *before* any analysis of sample data is done and *before* any conclusion is made.

9.3 Hypothesis tests for a population mean: large sample case (z statistic, σ known)

Having established a six-step procedure for hypothesis testing, various situations can now be explored where this procedure can be applied. A useful situation to begin illustrating this procedure is to consider the hypothesis test for a population mean. For example, in the past it was known that callers to a call centre had to wait an average of 37 minutes to speak to an operator. Management realised this waiting time was too long and so decided to introduce a new system with the aim of reducing this average waiting time. After introducing the new system, they wanted to test whether there had been a reduction in the average waiting time for callers.

Other business examples where a hypothesis test of a single population mean could apply are:

1. a manufacturing company wants to test if the average thickness of a particular plastic bottle they produce is 2.4 mm
2. a retail store wants to determine whether the average age of its customers is less than 40 years
3. a survey of Certified Practising Accountants (CPAs) done 5 years ago found that a sole proprietor CPA's average net income was \$74 914. The Institute of Chartered Accountants wanted to test if this average net income had increased since the survey.

Formula 9.1 can be used to calculate the test statistic in hypothesis testing for a single population mean involving any population where the standard deviation (σ) is known and when either:

1. the sample size is large ($n \geq 30$)
2. the sample size is small ($n < 30$) and the variable of interest is known to be normally distributed.

z_{test} for a single mean (9.1)

$$z_{test} = \frac{\bar{x} - \mu}{SE_{\bar{x}}}$$

where:

$$SE_{\bar{x}} = \frac{\sigma}{\sqrt{n}}$$

Consider the example where the average net income for all sole proprietor CPAs was found to be \$74 914 in a survey done 5 years ago. A new survey is conducted by taking a random sample of 112 currently practising sole proprietor CPAs to determine if this average net income figure has changed. The sample average net income is calculated to be \$78 695, and it is known that the population standard deviation of net incomes for sole proprietor CPAs is \$14 530. We can use this example to illustrate the six-step approach to hypothesis testing. The hypothesis-testing procedure will use the sample data to establish if there is sufficient evidence to conclude that the average net income for sole proprietor CPAs has changed in the last 5 years. The detailed steps of the process to arrive at a conclusion follow.

STEP 1. Set up H_0 and H_a

Since a test is needed to determine whether the figure has changed, the alternative hypothesis is that the average net income is not ($\neq$) \$74 914. This implies that the figure may be higher or lower than \$74 914. The null hypothesis is that the mean net income is still the same as (=) \$74 914. These hypotheses can be written as:

$$H_0: \mu = \$74\,914 \text{ (remains unchanged)}$$
$$H_a: \mu \neq \$74\,914 \text{ (has changed)}$$

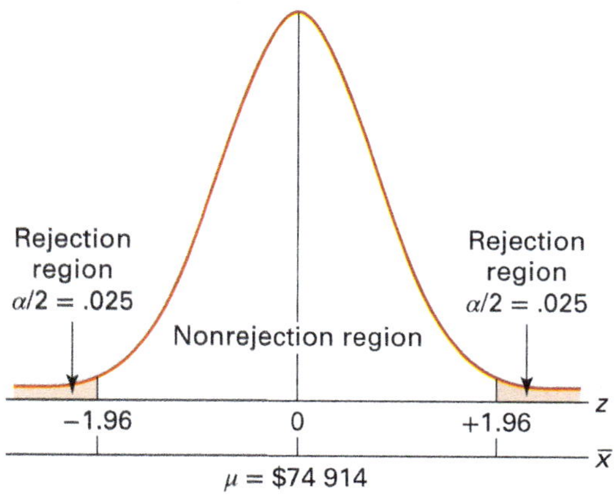

FIGURE 9.5 Sole proprietor CPA average net income example

STEP 2. Decide on the type and direction of the test

Since the alternative hypothesis contains the ≠ sign, this requires a two-tailed test (see figure 9.5).

STEP 3. Decide on the level of significance (α), determine the critical value(s) and region(s), and draw a diagram

It is decided that the level of significance (α) for this problem (the chance of making a Type I error) is to be .05. Since the population standard deviation (σ) is known, the test statistic will be z. So the critical value is $z_{crit} = z_{\alpha/2}$. Since the test is two-tailed and alpha is .05, there is an area of $\alpha/2$ or .025 in each of the tails of the distribution. Thus, the rejection region in the two ends of the distribution has an area of .025. There is a .4750 area between the mean and each of the critical values that separates the tails of the distribution (the rejection region) from the nonrejection region. By using this .4750 area and table A.4, the critical z-score can be obtained:

$$z_{crit} = z_{\alpha/2} = z_{.025} = \pm 1.96$$

Observe the different notations that are used to represent the critical value. Throughout this book, these various notations to represent the critical value will be used interchangeably. Note that figure 9.5 displays the problem with the rejection regions and the critical values of z.

STEP 4. Write down the decision rule

The decision rule is that, if the data gathered produces a z-score greater than 1.96 or less than −1.96, the test statistic is in one of the rejection regions and the null hypothesis will be rejected. If the z-score calculated from the data is between −1.96 and +1.96, the decision is to not reject the null hypothesis because the calculated z-score is in the nonrejection region.

STEP 5. Select a random sample and do relevant calculations

The sample mean for the net income was found to be \$78 695. The value of the test statistic is calculated by using $\bar{x} = \$78\,695$, $n = 112$, $\sigma = \$14\,530$ and a hypothesised $\mu = \$74\,914$:

$$z_{test} = \frac{\bar{x} - \mu}{SE_{\bar{x}}}$$

where

$$SE_{\bar{x}} = \frac{\sigma}{\sqrt{n}} = \frac{14\,530}{\sqrt{112}} = 1372.96$$

so

$$z_{test} = \frac{78\,695 - 74\,914}{1372.96} = 2.75$$

Here the test statistic, $z_{test} = 2.75$, is greater than the critical value of $z_{crit} = 1.96$ in the upper tail of the z distribution, so the decision is to reject the null hypothesis.

STEP 6. Draw a conclusion

The problem was formulated to test if the average net income of sole proprietor CPAs had changed. Hence, the following conclusion can be stated:

At the 5% level of significance, there is sufficient evidence to conclude that the average net income of sole proprietor CPAs has changed.

Note: The sample mean of \$78 695 is a point estimate of the current population average net income for sole proprietor CPAs. This point estimate is higher than the previous population mean. If it is required to test that the population average net income had *increased* over the 5-year period, a different hypothesis test would be required. An upper-tail (one-tailed) test would be needed with the hypotheses being:

$$H_0: \mu \le \$74\,914$$
$$H_a: \mu > \$74\,914$$

An example of how a one-tailed test is performed can be found in demonstration problem 9.1.

Testing the mean with a finite population

If the hypothesis test for the population mean is being conducted with a known finite population, the population information can be incorporated into the hypothesis-testing formula. Doing so can increase the potential for rejecting the null hypothesis. However, if the sample size is less than 5% of the population, the finite population correction factor does not significantly alter the solution. Formula 9.1 can be amended to formula 9.2 to include the finite population information.

Formula to test hypotheses about μ with a finite population (9.2)

$$z_{test} = \frac{\bar{x} - \mu}{SE_{\bar{x}}}$$

where:

$$SE_{\bar{x}} = \frac{\sigma}{\sqrt{n}}\sqrt{\frac{N-n}{N-1}}$$

In the CPA net income example, consider that there are only 600 practising sole proprietor CPAs. A sample of 112 CPAs taken from a population of only 600 CPAs represents 18.7% of the population. This particular sample is much more likely to be representative of the population than the same size sample of 112 CPAs taken from a population of 20 000 CPAs (0.6% of the population). The finite population correction factor takes this observation into consideration and allows for an increase in the test statistic z-score. The test statistic z-score using the finite population factor would be:

$$z_{test} = \frac{\bar{x} - \mu}{SE_{\bar{x}}}$$

where

$$SE_{\bar{x}} = \frac{\sigma}{\sqrt{n}}\sqrt{\frac{N-n}{N-1}} = \frac{14\,530}{\sqrt{112}}\sqrt{\frac{600-112}{600-1}} = 1239.23$$

$$z_{test} = \frac{78\,695 - 74\,914}{1239.23}$$
$$= \frac{3781}{1239.23}$$
$$= 3.05$$

Use of the finite population correction factor increased the test statistic z-score from 2.75 to 3.05. The decision to reject the null hypothesis does not change with this new information. However, occasionally, the finite population correction factor can make the difference between rejecting and not rejecting the null hypothesis.

The critical value method

In the CPA net income example above, the critical value method of hypothesis testing was used. The null hypothesis was rejected because the computed value of the test statistic z_{test} of 2.75 in step 5 was larger than the critical value z_{crit} of 1.96, placing the test statistic in the rejection zone. As noted in section 9.1, critical values divide the nonrejection region from the rejection region. By comparing the critical values of the test statistic (such as z_{crit} or t_{crit}) with the sample test statistic (such as z_{test} or t_{test}), a decision can be made to reject or to not reject the null hypothesis. This approach to hypothesis testing is called the critical value method. It is also possible to use the critical value method in a slightly different manner. This is done by calculating the critical value of the sample mean, $\bar{x}_{crit}$, and then comparing it with the sample mean, $\bar{x}$, of a randomly selected sample. This method is particularly attractive in industrial settings where standards can be set ahead of time so that quality-control technicians can gather data and compare actual measurements of products with specifications. Rather than calculating a critical value of the test statistic (such as z_{crit} or t_{crit}), a critical value of the sample statistic, $\bar{x}_{crit}$, can be calculated. The critical value of the sample mean then defines the rejection and nonrejection regions and can be used to test the sample mean, $\bar{x}$, obtained from a production process.

To demonstrate the technique of using critical values of the sample mean to define the rejection and nonrejection regions, consider once again the example regarding the net income of sole proprietor CPAs. Since the level of significance was .05 and a two-tailed test is required, the critical values of $z_{crit} = \pm 1.96$. The formula to solve this problem is

$$z_{crit} = \frac{\bar{x}_{crit} - \mu}{SE_{\bar{x}}}$$

where

$$SE_{\bar{x}} = \frac{\sigma}{\sqrt{n}} = \frac{14\,530}{\sqrt{112}} = 1372.96$$

Substituting values from the CPA net income example gives:

$$\pm 1.96 = \frac{\bar{x}_{crit} - 74\,914}{1372.96}$$

Hence

$$\bar{x}_{crit} = 74\,914 \pm 1.96\,(1372.96) = 74\,914 \pm 2691$$

$$\bar{x}_{lower\ crit} = \$72\,223 \text{ and } \bar{x}_{upper\ crit} = \$77\,605$$

These values of \$72 223 and \$77 605 represent the lower and upper critical values of the sample means that define the rejection and nonrejection regions of the null hypothesis. This is shown in figure 9.6.

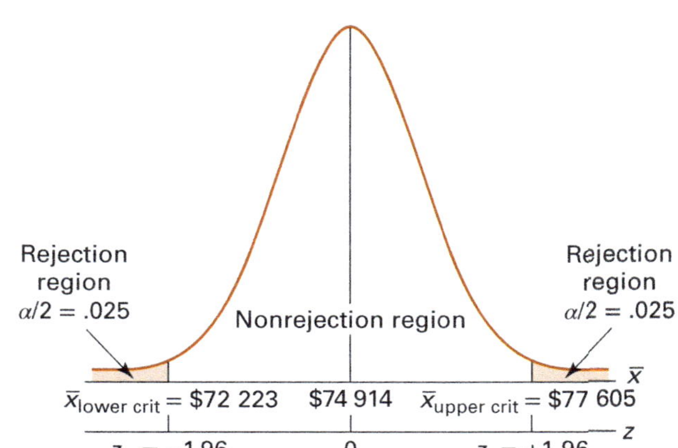

FIGURE 9.6 Rejection and nonrejection regions for the critical value methods

No matter which approach is taken when using the critical value method, most of the computational work is done ahead of time. In this CPA net income problem, before any sample mean is computed, it is known that a sample with a mean value of less than \$72 223 or greater than \$77 605 must be selected to reject the hypothesised population mean. Since the sample mean for this problem was \$78 695, which is greater than \$77 605, the decision is to reject the null hypothesis. This is the same answer as was obtained using the critical values of z_{crit} and the test statistic value of z_{test}. Figure 9.6 depicts graphically the rejection and nonrejection regions in terms of the both the critical values of the z-scores and critical values of the sample means.

The *p*-value method

Another way to reach a statistical conclusion in hypothesis-testing problems is to use the p-value method. This is an alternative to using the critical value method of hypothesis testing. Both methods always lead to the same conclusion and both methods are equally important (however, the p-value method has the advantage that the p-value is directly comparable to alpha). To calculate the p-value, it is required to first calculate the test statistic (such as z_{test} or t_{test}) in step 5 using the six-step approach to hypothesis testing. The area in the tail(s) beyond the test statistic is then calculated. This area equals the p-value.

So rather than comparing the test statistic with a critical value, as in the critical value method, the p-value method makes a comparison of the tail area with the level of significance (α). If the p-value is less than α, then the decision is to reject H_0 (since this means that the sample test statistic must be located in the tail). If the p-value is larger than α, the decision is to not reject H_0 (since this means that the sample test statistic must be located relatively close to the parameter hypothesised in H_0). For example, if the p-value $= .03$ and $\alpha = .05$, then the decision is to reject H_0 since the p-value is less than alpha. However, if the p-value $= .12$ and $\alpha = .05$, the decision is to not reject H_0 since the p-value is greater than alpha.

Consider an example where an upper one-tailed test is conducted with a test statistic of $z_{test} = 2.04$. Using the critical value method, the z test statistic can be compared directly with the critical value of z to make a decision. Using the p-value method, the test statistic is used to calculate the area in the tail beyond the test statistic to give the p-value (since a one-tailed test is being done). This tail area beyond the test statistic is then compared with α to make a decision. Using the standard normal distribution table A.4 in the appendix, the probability of randomly obtaining a z-score greater than or equal to 2.04 is $.5000 - .4793 = .0207$. This is the area in the tail beyond the test statistic. Therefore, the p-value is .0207. Using this information, the decision in a hypothesis test would be to reject the null hypothesis, for example, if $\alpha = .05$ or .10 (p-value $< \alpha$). Alternatively, the decision would be to not reject the null hypothesis for $\alpha = 0.01$ or .005 (p-value $> \alpha$).

Now consider an example where a two-tailed test is conducted and the test statistic of $z_{test} = 2.04$. In this instance, more care is needed in calculating and interpreting the p-value. When the decision is to not reject the null hypothesis, the sample statistic could be either larger or smaller than the hypothesised value of the parameter. To allow for this possibility, the area in the tail beyond the test statistic (the one-sided probability) is calculated first, and then this tail area is doubled to determine the p-value. So, if a two-tailed test is conducted and the sample statistic yields a test statistic value of $z_{test} = 2.04$, the p-value equals $2 \times .0207 = .0414$. This p-value is compared with α in the usual way.

As a final comment on the p-value method, it is important to take care when interpreting p-values generated from various computer packages. Some computer packages always assume a two-tailed test is to be performed when computing the p-value. In other words, the tail area beyond the test statistic is calculated and this area is then doubled to get the p-value. Other packages, however, assume a one-tailed test is needed and the tail area beyond the test statistic is calculated and this is reported as the p-value. The reason there is a difference in the way the p-value is reported is that the computer does not know whether the problem at hand is a one-tailed or two-tailed test. A researcher must be very clear on the approach the software has taken before interpreting any p-value that appears in the computer output.

DEMONSTRATION PROBLEM 9.1

PROBLEM: A vehicle dealership has experienced increased demand for its car maintenance services over recent years. It decided to expand by doubling the size of the maintenance garage. Prior to the expansion, the average waiting time to have a car serviced was 4.3 weeks. Six months after the expansion of the garage was completed, the owner wanted to test whether the average waiting time for customers had been reduced below 4.3 weeks. The owner had doubts that this would be the case as demand for car servicing had continued to increase after the expansion. To test whether the average waiting time had been reduced, the owner randomly selected 32 customers and found that the average waiting time in this sample was 4.156 weeks. From previous studies at other dealerships within Australia undertaking similar expansions to reduce customer waiting times, the population standard deviation can be taken to be 0.574 weeks. Using $\alpha = .05$, test whether the average waiting time has been reduced after expanding the maintenance garage.

SOLUTION:

STEP 1. Set up H_0 and H_a

Since the garage owner is testing to determine whether the average waiting time has been reduced, the alternative hypothesis is that the mean waiting time is less than (<) 4.3 weeks. Therefore, the null hypothesis is that the mean is still the same or more than (≥) 4.3 weeks. These hypotheses can be written as:

$$H_0\text{: } \mu \geq 4.30$$
$$H_a\text{: } \mu < 4.30 \text{ (waiting time reduced)}$$

STEP 2. Decide on the type and direction of the test

Since the alternative hypothesis contains the < sign, this requires a one-tailed test (to the left).

STEP 3. Decide on the level of significance (α), determine the critical value(s) and region(s), and draw a diagram

Alpha is .05. Since the test is a one-tailed test to the left, the critical z-score is found by looking up $.5 - .05 = .45$ as the area in table A.4. The critical value of the test statistic is $-z_{crit} = -1.645$. The test statistic must be less than −1.645 to reject the null hypothesis. The rejection region and critical value are shown in figure 9.7.

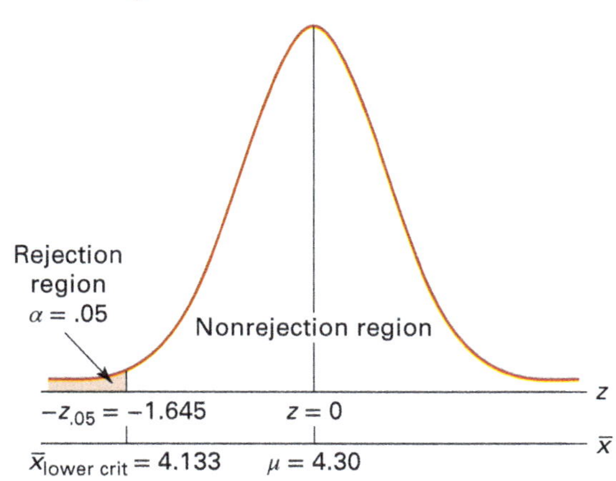

FIGURE 9.7. Rejection and nonrejection regions for the vehicle dealership problem

STEP 4. Write down the decision rule

The decision rule is that if the data gathered produce a z-score less than −1.645, then the test statistic is in the rejection region and the decision is to reject the null hypothesis. If the z-score calculated from the data is more than −1.645, the decision is to not reject the null hypothesis because the calculated z-score is in the nonrejection region.

STEP 5. Select a random sample and do relevant calculations

The mean waiting time for the sample is 4.156 weeks. The value of the test statistic is calculated by using $\bar{x} = 4.156$ weeks, $\sigma = 0.574$ weeks, $n = 32$ and a hypothesised $\mu = 4.30$ weeks.

$$z_{test} = \frac{\bar{x} - \mu}{SE_{\bar{x}}}$$

where

$$SE_{\bar{x}} = \frac{\sigma}{\sqrt{n}} = \frac{.574}{\sqrt{32}} = .10147$$

so

$$z_{test} = \frac{4.156 - 4.30}{.10147} = -1.42$$

Here the test statistic, $z_{test} = -1.42$, is greater than the critical value of $z_{crit} = -1.645$ in the lower tail of the distribution, so the decision is to not reject the null hypothesis.

STEP 6. Draw a conclusion

At the .05 level of significance, there is insufficient evidence to conclude that the average waiting to book into the garage has been reduced below 4.3 weeks after the expansion.

Using the p-value method

The test statistic is $z = -1.42$. From table A.4, the probability of getting a z-score at least this extreme when the null hypothesis is true is $.5000 - .4222 = .0778$ (the area in the tail beyond the test statistic). This means that the p-value is .0778. Hence, the p-value is greater than $\alpha = .05$ so the decision is to not reject the null hypothesis.

Using the critical value (sample mean) method

Another method for solving this problem is to use the critical value method by first finding the critical sample mean. That is, determine the sample mean (or more extreme value) at which the null hypothesis would be rejected. This critical sample mean can be determined by using the critical z-score associated with $\alpha = .05$, namely $-z_{.05} = -1.645$.

$$z_{crit} = \frac{\bar{x}_{crit} - \mu}{SE}$$

$$-1.645 = \frac{\bar{x}_{crit} - 4.30}{.10147}$$

$$\bar{x}_{crit} = 4.3 - 1.645\,(.10147)$$

$$\bar{x}_{crit} = 4.133$$

The decision rule is that a sample mean less than 4.133 would be necessary to reject the null hypothesis. Since the mean obtained from the sample data was 4.156, the decision is to not reject the null hypothesis. Note that, in all three methods used to analyse this problem, the same decision is made — do not reject the null hypothesis.

USING EXCEL

Testing hypotheses about a single population mean using the z statistic

Excel has somewhat limited capability for doing hypothesis testing with single samples. However, it can produce the p-value.

DP09-01

1. Access DP09-01.xls from the student website.
2. From the Formulas tab, select Insert Function.

3. In the Insert Function dialogue box, select Statistical from the category options and Z.TEST from the function options, and click OK.

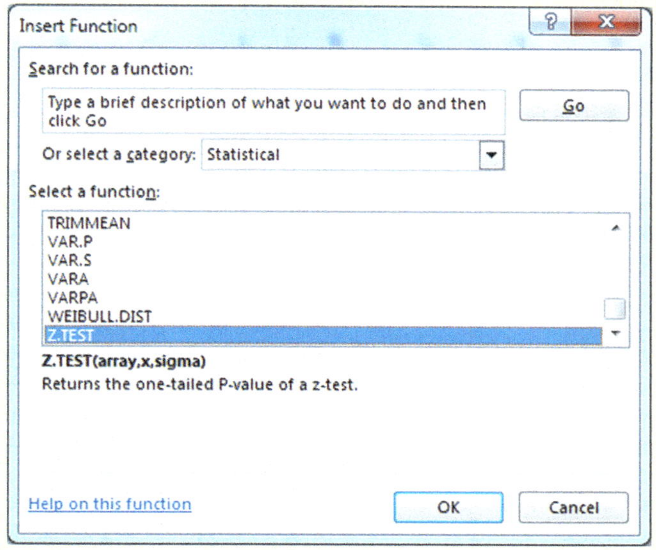

4. In the Function Arguments dialogue box:
   a. enter the data range in the Array field
   b. enter the hypothesised value of the mean in X field
   c. enter the population standard deviation in the Sigma field.

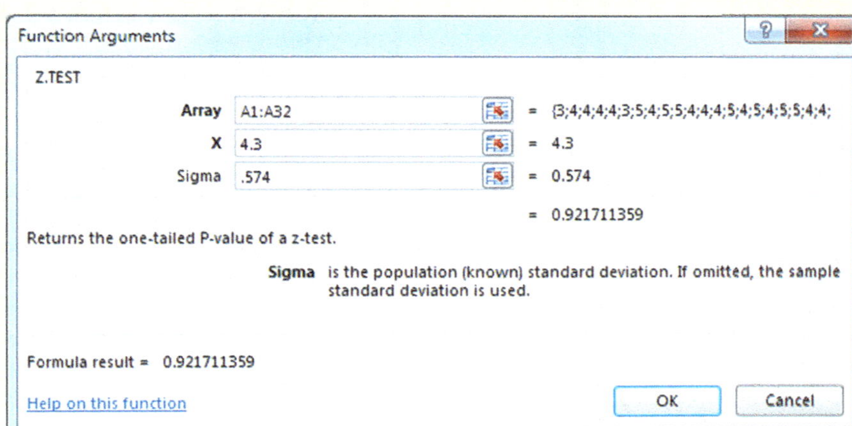

5. Click OK.

The Excel output is the right-tailed (one-tailed) *p*-value for the test statistic. If the *z*-score is negative, subtract this output value from 1 to obtain the *p*-value for the left tail (i.e. 1 – .9217 = .0783). Notice that this *p*-value from Excel is slightly different from the calculation value of .0778 shown at step 6 in demonstration problem 9.1. This is because Excel uses the *z*-score to more than two decimal places. Finally, notice that, to obtain the *p*-value for a two-sided test, simply multiply the *p*-value output from Excel by 2.

PRACTICE PROBLEMS

Practising the calculations

9.6 a. Use the data given to test the following hypotheses.

$$H_0: \mu = 18 \quad H_a: \mu \neq 18$$
$$\bar{x} = 16.7 \quad n = 31 \quad \sigma = 4.2 \quad \alpha = .05$$

b. Use the *p*-value to reach a statistical conclusion.
c. Using the critical value method, what are the critical sample mean values?

9.7 Use the data given to test the following hypotheses. Assume the data are normally distributed in the population.

$$H_0: \mu \geq 7.48 \quad H_a: \mu < 7.48$$
$$\bar{x} = 6.91 \quad n = 24 \quad \sigma = 1.21 \quad \alpha = .01$$

9.8 a. Use the data given to test the following hypotheses.

$$H_0: \mu \leq 1200 \quad H_a: \mu > 1200$$
$$\bar{x} = 1215 \quad n = 113 \quad \sigma = 100 \quad \alpha = .10$$

b. Use the *p*-value to draw a statistical conclusion.
c. Using the critical value method, find the critical value of the sample mean and draw a statistical conclusion.

Testing your understanding

P09-09 **9.9** Research has found that the average number of suspended particles of air in a particular city is currently 80 micrograms per cubic metre. Suppose city officials work with businesses, commuters and industries and introduce initiatives to try to reduce this figure. These officials hire an environmental company to take random measurements of suspended particles, in micrograms per cubic metre of air, over a period of several weeks. The resulting data follow. Take the population standard deviation to be 10.25 micrograms per cubic metre of air. Use these data to determine whether the city's average number of suspended particles is significantly lower than it was when the initial measurements were taken. Let α =.05.

63	64	64	65	66	66	66	68
71	71	72	74	74	75	75	75
76	76	76	77	77	78	78	78
78	79	79	80	80	80	81	82
85	88	88	89	89			

9.10 The average annual income for Australian childcare workers five years ago was \$38 100. It is believed this average annual income has essentially remained the same since then. To test this hypothesis, a random sample of 22 Australian childcare workers was selected and the average annual salary found to be \$40 200. Taking the population standard deviation for annual income to be \$2500 per year, using α = .01, and assuming annual incomes of the workers are normally distributed, test the researcher's hypothesis.

9.11 A manufacturing company makes steel wire. One particular steel wire is very thin and has a designed breaking load of 5 kg. The company tests a random sample of 42 lengths of wire and finds the mean breaking load is 5.0611 kg. The wire production machine has a specification such that the standard deviation is 0.2803 kg. Using α = .10, test whether the steel wire has an average breaking load different from 5 kg.

9.12 A manufacturing company has been averaging 18.2 orders per week for several years. However, during a recession, weekly orders have appeared to slow. Suppose the company's production manager randomly samples 32 weeks during the recession period and finds a sample mean of 15.6 orders per week. The population standard deviation is 2.3 orders per week. Test to determine whether the average number of weekly orders decreased in the recession period, using α = .10.

9.13 A report indicated the many health benefits of consuming cheese as part of a healthy diet. It also claimed that the average sodium content in cheese is 1000 mg per 100 g. Thinking this figure seemed high, a researcher decided to test this claim. A random sample of 14 different types of cheese was selected and the sodium content on the packaging recorded. This sample average sodium content was found to be 955 mg per 100 g. If the population standard deviation of sodium content in cheese is 120 mg per 100 g, using a 5% level of significance, test if the claim in the report has been overstated.

9.4 Hypothesis tests about a population mean: small sample case (t statistic, σ unknown)

We have seen that, when gathering data to test hypotheses about a single population mean, the value of the population standard deviation can be found from previous similar studies or historical records. However, it is very often the case in practice that the population standard deviation is unknown and the researcher must use the sample standard deviation as an estimate.

In general, the t distribution can be used in hypothesis testing if a researcher is drawing a single random sample to test the value of a population mean when the sample size is small, the population standard deviation is unknown, and the variable of interest in the population is normally distributed. In this section, the t test for a single population mean is explained.

When the standard deviation σ of a population is unknown, formula 9.3 is used to test hypotheses about a population mean involving the t distribution.

t test for μ
(9.3)

$$t_{\text{test}} = \frac{\bar{x} - \mu}{\text{SE}_{\bar{x}}}$$

where:

$$\text{SE}_{\bar{x}} = \frac{s}{\sqrt{n}}$$

degrees of freedom (df) $= n - 1$

As an example, consider a machine that produces solid steel plates. The average weight of the plates produced by the machine is specified to be 25 kg and the weights are normally distributed. During a routine inspection of the plate manufacturing process, a supervisor wants to check if the machine is producing plates of the specified weight. To test this, a random sample of 20 steel plates is selected and weighed. Table 9.2 shows the weights obtained, along with the computed sample mean and sample standard deviation.

TABLE 9.2 Weights in kilograms of a sample of 20 steel plates

22.6	22.2	23.2	27.4	24.5
27.0	26.6	28.1	26.9	24.9
26.2	25.3	23.1	24.2	26.1
25.8	30.4	28.6	23.5	23.6

$\bar{x} = 25.51$, $s = 2.1933$, $n = 20$

In this problem, if the machine is operating according to specification, it would produce steel plates with a population mean equal to 25 kg. If it is not operating as specified, the steel plates could be heavier or lighter than 25 kg; that is, the weight is not equal to 25 kg. Thus, a two-tailed test is needed. The hypotheses are:

$$H_0: \mu = 25 \text{ kg}$$
$$H_a: \mu \neq 25 \text{ kg}$$

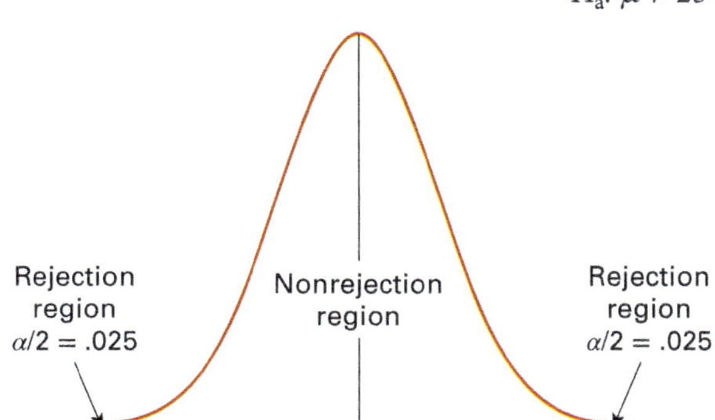

FIGURE 9.8 Rejection regions for the machine plate example

A level of significance of .05 is chosen. Figure 9.8 shows the rejection regions. Since $n = 20$, the degrees of freedom for this test are 19 (df = 20 − 1). The t distribution is in table A.6. The upper tail area for this problem is $\alpha/2 = .025$, giving the value in each tail. (When using table A.6 for a two-tailed test, always use $\alpha/2$ as the upper tail area to look up the t value.) The t value from the table for this example is 2.093 for the upper tail area of .025 and df = 19. Table values such as this are often written in the following form:

$$t_{.025,\,19} = 2.093$$

Figure 9.9 depicts the t distribution for this example, along with the critical values, the test statistic value and the rejection regions. In this case, the decision rule is to reject the null hypothesis if the test statistic value of t is less than −2.093 or greater than +2.093; that is, the test statistic is in the tails of the distribution. Computation of the test statistic yields:

$$t_{\text{test}} = \frac{\bar{x} - \mu}{\text{SE}_{\bar{x}}}$$

where $$\text{SE}_{\bar{x}} = \frac{2.1933}{\sqrt{20}} = .4904$$

so $$t_{\text{test}} = \frac{25.51 - 25}{.4904} = 1.04$$

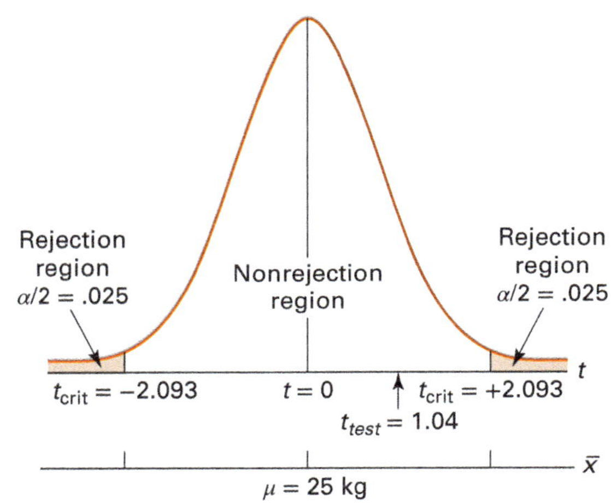

FIGURE 9.9 Graph of test statistic and critical t values for a machine producing 25 kg steel plates

Since the test statistic t value is 1.04, the null hypothesis is not rejected and we continue to believe that the machine is operating as specified. In other words, there is insufficient evidence to conclude that average weight of steel plates produced by the machine is not 25 kg.

DEMONSTRATION PROBLEM 9.2

PROBLEM: Records show that the average farm size in a particular region has increased over the last 70 years. This trend might be explained, in part, by the inability of small farms to compete with the prices and costs of large-scale operations and to produce a level of income necessary to support the farmers' desired standard of living. An agribusiness researcher believes the average size of farms has continued to increase since 2009 from a mean of 515 hectares. To test this, a random sample of 24 farms was selected from official government sources and their sizes recorded. The data gathered are shown in the table 9.3. Use $\alpha = .01$ to test the hypothesis.

TABLE 9.3 Farm size (hectares) for a sample of 24 farms

438	465	480	498	505	525	532	540	555	562	570	600
452	473	492	500	515	530	535	554	560	565	580	625

SOLUTION:

STEP 1. Set up H_0 and H_a

The researcher's hypothesis is that the average size of a farm is more than 515 hectares. Since 'more than' implies >, this gives the alternative hypothesis. The null hypothesis is that the mean is still 515 hectares (or less).

$$H_0: \mu \leq 515$$
$$H_a: \mu > 515 \text{ (increased farm size)}$$

STEP 2. Decide on the type and direction of the test

Since the alternative hypothesis contains the > sign, this requires a one-tailed test (to the right).

STEP 3. Decide on the level of significance (α), determine the critical value(s) and region(s), and draw a diagram

Alpha is .01. Since the test is a one-tailed test to the right, the sample size is small and α is unknown, the critical t value with 24 data points has $df = n - 1 = 24 - 1 = 23$. The critical t value is:

$$t_{.01,\,23} = 2.500$$

The rejection and nonrejection regions and critical value are depicted in the diagram below.

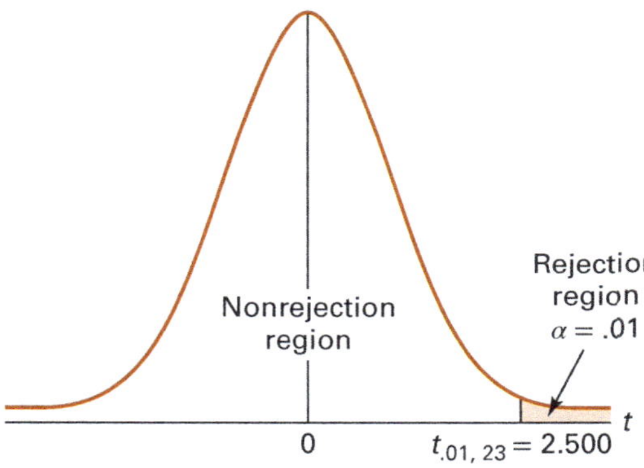

STEP 4. Write down the decision rule

The decision rule is that, if the data gathered produce a test statistic t value greater than 2.500, then the test statistic is in the rejection region and the decision is to reject the null hypothesis. If the test statistic t value is less than 2.500, the decision is to not reject the null hypothesis because the calculated t value is in the nonrejection region.

STEP 5. Select a random sample and do relevant calculations

The sample mean is 527.125 and the sample standard deviation is 47.12. The test statistic t value is:

$$t_{\text{test}} = \frac{\bar{x} - \mu}{SE_{\bar{x}}}$$

where

$$SE_{\bar{x}} = \frac{s}{\sqrt{n}} = \frac{47.12}{\sqrt{24}} = 9.6183$$

so

$$t_{\text{test}} = \frac{527.125 - 515}{9.6183} = 1.26$$

Here the test statistic $t_{\text{test}} = 1.26$ is less than the critical value of $t_{\text{crit}} = 2.500$, so the decision is to not reject the null hypothesis.

STEP 6. Draw a conclusion

At the .01 level of significance, there is insufficient evidence to conclude that the average farm size has increased to more than 515 hectares.

USING EXCEL

Testing hypotheses about a mean using the *t* test

Excel does not have a one-sample *t* test function. However, by using the two-sample *t* test for means with unequal variances, the results for a one-sample test can be obtained.

DP09-02

1. Access DP09-02.xls from the student website. Note that the sample data appears in the first column and the value of the parameter being tested ($\mu = 515$) appears in the second column. The second column is used as the second sample.
2. From the Data tab, select Data Analysis.
3. From the Data Analysis dialogue box, select t-Test: Two-Sample Assuming Unequal Variances and click OK.
4. In the t-Test: Two-Sample Assuming Unequal Variances dialogue box:
   a. enter the Sample data range in the Variable 1 Range field
   b. enter the range of Value of the parameter being tested in the Variable 2 Range field
   c. enter 0 in the Hypothesised Mean Difference field
   d. if you have included the column labels in the variable range fields, check Labels. If not, leave it unchecked.
   e. enter the value of Alpha
   f. choose an output option.

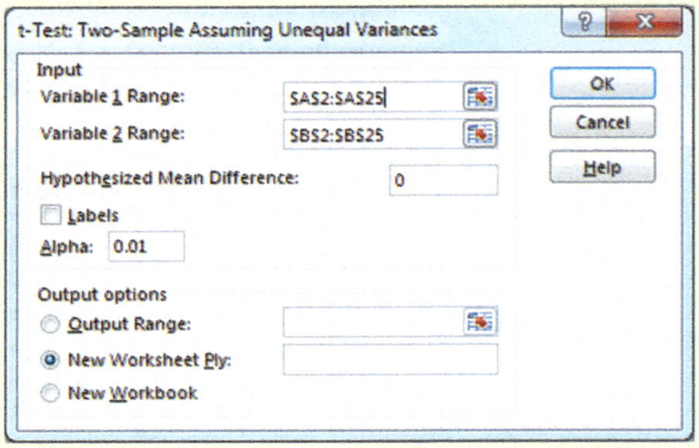

5. Click OK.

The Excel output follows (ignoring the output for variable 2, as we are performing a one-sample test). The output shown in the column headed Variable 1 is based on the sample data.

	A	B
1	*t*-Test: Two-Sample Assuming Unequal Variances	
2		
3		*Variable 1*
4	Mean	527.125
5	Variance	2220.462
6	Observations	24
7	Hypothesized Mean Difference	0
8	df	23
9	t Stat	1.260566
10	P(T<=t) one-tail	0.110052
11	t Critical one-tail	2.499867
12	P(T<=t) two-tail	0.220104
13	t Critical two-tail	2.807336

Please refer to 'Going further with KaddStat' for KaddStat instructions at www.johnwiley.com.au/highered/black4e/kaddstat.

PRACTICE PROBLEMS

Practising the calculations

9.14 A random sample of size 20 is taken, resulting in a sample mean of 16.45 and a sample standard deviation of 3.59. Assuming that x is normally distributed, use this information and $\alpha = .05$ to test the following hypotheses.

$$H_0: \mu = 16 \quad H_a: \mu \neq 16$$

9.15 A random sample of 51 items is taken, with $\bar{x} = 58.42$ and $s^2 = 25.68$. Use these data to test the following hypotheses, assuming you want to take only a 1% risk of committing a Type I error and that x is normally distributed.

$$H_0: \mu \geq 60 \quad H_a: \mu < 60$$

P09-16 **9.16** The following data were gathered from a random sample of 11 items.

1200	1175	1080	1275	1201	1387
1090	1280	1400	1287	1225	

Use these data and a 5% level of significance to test the following hypotheses, assuming that the data come from a normally distributed population.

$$H_0: \mu \geq 1160 \quad H_a: \mu < 1160$$

Testing your understanding

P09-17 **9.17** The following data represent the recorded weights (g) of a randomly selected sample of a particular car component. The manufacturing specifications require this car component to have an average weight of 6 g. The weights of this car component can be taken to be normally distributed. Use these data and $\alpha = .05$ to test the hypothesis that the manufacturing process is producing the car component with an average weight of 6 g.

5.85	5.90	5.90	5.95	5.98	5.98
5.99	6	6	6.05	6.08	6.11
6.12	6.15	6.17	6.18	6.18	

P09-18 **9.18** A hole-punch machine is set to punch a hole 1.84 cm in diameter in a strip of sheet metal in a manufacturing process. The strip of metal is then creased and sent on to the next phase of production, where a metal rod is slipped through the hole. It is important that the hole be punched to the specified diameter of 1.84 cm. To test punching accuracy, technicians have randomly sampled 12 punched holes and measured the diameters. The data follow. Use $\alpha = .10$ to determine whether the holes are being punched with an average diameter of 1.84 cm. Assume that the diameters of the punched holes are normally distributed in the population.

1.81	1.89	1.86	1.83
1.85	1.82	1.87	1.85
1.84	1.86	1.88	1.85

P09-19 **9.19** Across the country, families of two adults and two children currently have an average weekly shopping bill at a large supermarket chain of $255. However, you believe the weekly bill for this type of family in your local area is more than the national average figure. You decide to test your claim by randomly selecting 21 families of two adults and two children who shop at this supermarket chain in your local area. The data collected is presented in the table below. Assuming the bill amounts for families shopping at this supermarket chain are normally distributed, and using a 5% level of significance, is there evidence to support your belief?

212	220	225	234	241	249	255	262
270	288	289	295	296	299	304	315
320	323	328	331	334			

9.20 In previous years, the average market price of warehouses in a particular city equates to $322.80 per m² of usable floor space. An investor wants to determine whether this figure has changed. A researcher is hired who randomly samples 19 warehouses that are for sale in the city and finds that the mean price is $316.70 per m² of usable floor space, with a standard deviation of $12.90 per m². If the researcher uses a 5% level of significance, what statistical conclusion can be reached?

9.21 According to a survey, the average commuting time from home to the city is 19.0 minutes if the population is between 1 and 3 million people. A researcher lives in a city with a population of 2.4 million people and wants to test the claim. A random sample of commuters is gathered, and the data are collected and analysed using Excel. The Excel output is shown here. Using $\alpha = .05$, what statistical conclusion can be reached?

	A	B
4	Mean	19.534
5	Variance	16.813
6	Observations	26
7	Hypothesized Mean Difference	0
8	df	25
9	t Stat	0.66
10	P(T<=t) one-tail	0.256
11	t Critical one-tail	1.71
12	P(T<=t) two-tail	0.513
13	t Critical two-tail	2.06

9.5 Testing hypotheses about a proportion

Business decisions can often be made using information relating to a proportion. For example, an increase or decrease in market share can provide information to a company regarding the success or otherwise of an advertising campaign. Similarly, the proportion of defective items produced from a production process can influence company profitability. In addition, business surveys can often produce information expressed as a proportion. For example, it might be found that 45% of all businesses offer flexible hours to employees, or 88% of all businesses have websites.

In analysing data that relate to a single proportion, hypothesis testing can be used to test whether there has been a significant change. For example:

- management believe their market share has increased above 26% after an extensive marketing campaign in the last two years
- a market researcher wants to determine whether the proportion of women purchasing a new car has decreased
- a financial researcher believes the proportion of first home buyers had significantly increased from previous years after the introduction of the First Home Buyers Grant by the Australian government
- a quality-control manager for a large manufacturing company wants to test whether the proportion of defective items in a large production run is less than 4%.

Formula 9.4 relates to the analysis of a proportion. Recall that $\hat{p}$ denotes a sample proportion and p denotes the population proportion. (Note that p used here has a different meaning from the p-value and they should not be confused.) To justify using formula 9.4, the sample size needs to be large enough. The sample size can be considered large enough if both $np > 5$ and $nq > 5$.

z test of a population proportion (9.4)

$$z_{\text{test}} = \frac{\hat{p} - p}{\text{SE}_{\hat{p}}}$$

where:

$$\text{SE}_{\hat{p}} = \sqrt{\frac{pq}{n}}$$

$\hat{p}$ = sample proportion
p = population proportion
$q = 1 - p$

As an example of the application of hypothesis testing about a single population proportion, consider a manufacturing company that believes that exactly 8% of their products are defective. A researcher wanting to test this belief would write the null and alternative hypotheses as:

$$\text{H}_0\text{: } p = .08 \text{ (proportion defective is 8\%)}$$
$$\text{H}_a\text{: } p \neq .08 \text{ (proportion defective is not 8\%)}$$

This test is two-tailed because the hypothesis being tested is that the proportion of defective products is 8%. A level of significance of $\alpha = .10$ is selected. Figure 9.10 shows the distribution with the rejection regions. Since α is divided by 2 for a two-tailed test, the tail area $= \frac{.10}{2} = .05$. Therefore, $z_{\text{crit}} = z_{\alpha/2} = z_{.05} = \pm 1.645$.

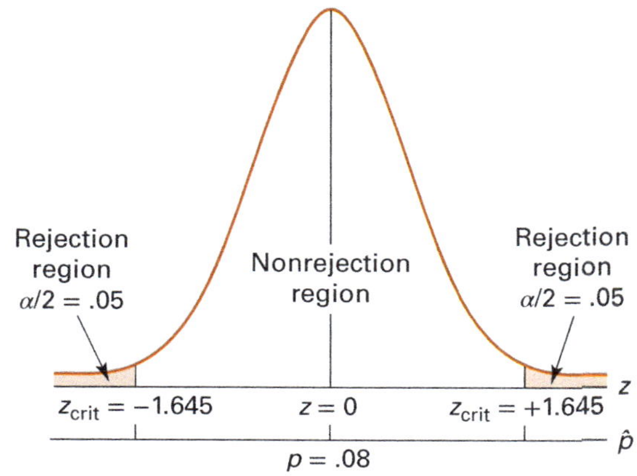

FIGURE 9.10 Distribution with rejection regions for the defective product example

For the researcher to reject the null hypothesis, the test statistic *z*-score must be greater than 1.645 or less than −1.645. The researcher randomly selects a sample of 200 products, inspects each item for any defect and determines that 33 items are defective. Calculating the sample proportion gives:

$$\hat{p} = \frac{33}{200} = .165$$

The test statistic for *z* is calculated as:

$$SE_{\hat{p}} = \sqrt{\frac{pq}{n}} = \sqrt{\frac{(.08)(.92)}{200}} = .01918$$

so

$$z_{test} = \frac{\hat{p} - p}{SE_{\hat{p}}} = \frac{.165 - .08}{.01918} = 4.43$$

The test statistic for *z* is in the rejection region ($z = 4.43$, which is greater than $z_{crit} = 1.645$), so the company rejects the null hypothesis. There is sufficient evidence at the .10 level of significance for the researcher to conclude that the proportion of defective products in the population from which the sample of 200 was drawn is not 8%. Note that with $\alpha = .10$ the risk of committing a Type I error in this example is .10. In addition, note that the test statistic value of $z = 4.43$ is outside the range of values in table A.4. Thus, if the researcher were using the *p*-value to arrive at a decision about the null hypothesis, the *p*-value would be approximately .0000, and the decision would be to reject the null hypothesis, since it is less than $\alpha = .10$. Importantly, in arriving at this conclusion, it is useful to take a closer look at how z_{test} is calculated.

In calculating z_{test}, note that the standard error $SE_{\hat{p}}$ used to calculate the test statistic of 4.43 contains the population proportion, *p*. Although the researcher does not know the actual population proportion, the test is being done for a specific population proportion value of 8%. Hence, this hypothesised population proportion value of 8% is used as *p* in calculating the standard error in hypothesis test. However, it is worth noting here that the formula for the standard error of the proportion in hypothesis testing is different from the formula for the standard error of the proportion used to construct a confidence interval. This difference is quite subtle. When finding the confidence interval for the proportion, the formula for the standard error for the proportion is:

$$SE_{\hat{p}} = \sqrt{\frac{\hat{p}\hat{q}}{n}}$$

Notice that the sample proportion $\hat{p}$ (not population proportion, p) is used in the calculation of the standard error of the proportion for confidence intervals. When constructing a confidence interval, unlike in hypothesis testing, no information is available about the population proportion (as this is being estimated by the confidence interval). Hence, we use the sample proportion as the best estimate of the population proportion to calculate the standard error of the proportion when constructing a confidence interval.

As a final observation, it is worth noting that the critical value method, using the critical sample proportions $\hat{p}_{\text{crit}}$, can be used to solve this defective items problem. Using the table value of $z_{\text{crit}} = 1.645$ in the z formula for single sample proportion, along with the values for the hypothesised population proportion and sample size, the critical values $\hat{p}_{\text{crit}}$ can be found using:

$$z_{\text{crit}} = \frac{\hat{p}_{\text{crit}} - p}{\text{SE}_{\hat{p}}}$$

where

$$\text{SE}_{\hat{p}} = \sqrt{\frac{pq}{n}}$$

$$\begin{aligned}\hat{p}_{\text{crit}} &= p \pm z_{\text{crit}}\text{SE}_{\hat{p}} \\ &= .08 \pm 1.645(.01918) \\ &= .08 \pm .032 \\ &= .048 \text{ and } .112\end{aligned}$$

From examining the value of the sample proportion $\hat{p} = .165$ and figure 9.11, it is clear that the sample proportion is in the rejection region using the critical value method. The statistical conclusion again is to reject the null hypothesis. Hence, there is sufficient evidence to conclude that the proportion of defective products in the population is not 8% at the .10 level of significance.

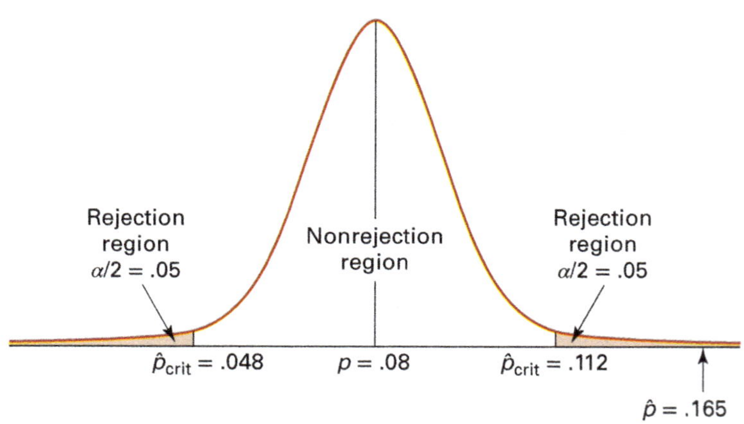

FIGURE 9.11 Distribution using critical value method for the defective product example

DEMONSTRATION PROBLEM 9.3

PROBLEM: A national survey found that 17% of Australians consume milk with their breakfast. However, in Victoria, a large milk producer believes that more than 17% of Victorians consume milk with their breakfast. To test this idea, a marketing organisation randomly selected 550 Victorians and asked if they consume milk with their breakfast. It was found that 115 did. Using a .05 level of significance, test the idea that more than 17% of Victorians consume milk with their breakfast.

SOLUTION:

STEP 1. Set up H_0 and H_a

The milk producer's idea is that the proportion of Victorians who drink milk with their breakfast is higher than the national proportion. 'Higher' implies >, and this therefore is the alternative hypothesis. Therefore, the null hypothesis is that the proportion in Victoria does not differ from, or is less than, the national average. The hypotheses for this problem are:

$$H_0: p \leq .17$$
$$H_a: p > .17$$

STEP 2. Decide on the type and direction of the test

Since the alternative hypothesis contains the > sign, this requires a one-tailed test (to the right).

STEP 3. Decide on a level of significance (α), determine the critical value(s) and region(s), and draw a diagram

Alpha is .05. Since the test is a one-tailed test to the right, the critical *z*-score (the problem involves proportion) is found by looking up .5 − .05 = .45 as the area in table A.4. The critical value of the test statistic is $z_{.05} = 1.645$. The test statistic must be greater than 1.645 to reject the null hypothesis. The rejection region and critical value are shown in the following diagram.

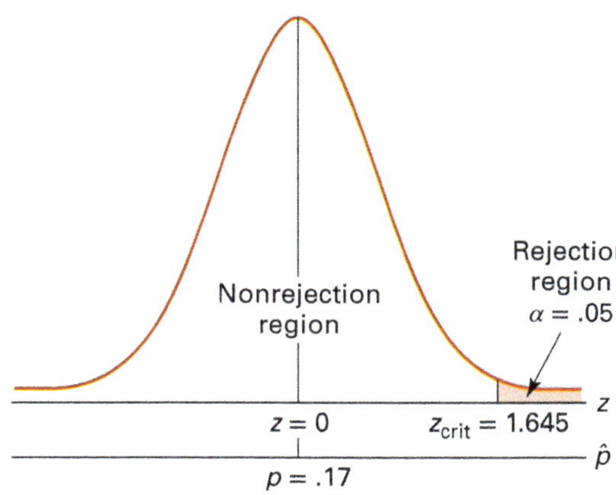

STEP 4. Write down the decision rule

The decision rule is that, if the data gathered produce a *z*-score greater than 1.645, then the test statistic is in the rejection region and the decision is to reject the null hypothesis. If the *z*-score calculated from the data is less than 1.645, then the test statistic is in the nonrejection region and the decision is to not reject the null hypothesis.

STEP 5. Select a random sample and do relevant calculations

$$n = 550 \text{ and } x = 115$$

$$\hat{p} = \frac{115}{550} = .20909$$

$$SE_{\hat{p}} = \sqrt{\frac{pq}{n}} = \sqrt{\frac{(.17)(.83)}{550}} = .01602$$

so

$$z_{test} = \frac{\hat{p} - p}{SE_{\hat{p}}} = \frac{.20909 - .17}{.01602} = 2.44$$

Here the test statistic, $z_{test} = 2.44$ is larger than the critical value of $z_{crit} = 1.645$ in the upper tail of the distribution, so the decision is to reject the null hypothesis.

STEP 6. Draw a conclusion

At the 5% level of significance, there is sufficient evidence to conclude that the proportion of Victorians who consume milk with their breakfast is more than the national average of 17%.

As an alternative approach using the *p*-value method, the probability of obtaining a $z_{test} \geq 2.44$ by chance is .0073. This equals the *p*-value. Since the *p*-value = .0073 is less than $\alpha = .05$, the null hypothesis is rejected.

Another approach is to determine the critical proportion value by solving:

$$z_{crit} = \frac{\hat{p}_{crit} - p}{SE_{\hat{p}}}$$

$$1.645 = \frac{\hat{p}_{crit} - .17}{.01602}$$

$$\hat{p}_{crit} = .17 + (1.645)(.01602)$$
$$= .17 + .026 = .196$$

With the critical value method, a sample proportion greater than 19.6% must be obtained to reject the null hypothesis. The sample proportion using the data for this problem is 20.9%, so the null hypothesis is rejected using this critical value method. Hence, all three approaches show how the same decision will be reached. In this problem, the decision is to reject the null hypothesis.

K ***Please refer to 'Going further with KaddStat' for KaddStat instructions at www.johnwiley.com.au/highered/black4e/kaddstat.***

PRACTICE PROBLEMS

Practising the calculations

9.22 You are testing H_0: $p \geq .25$ versus H_a: $p < .25$. A random sample of 146 people gives a value of $\hat{p} = .21$. Using $\alpha = .10$, test this hypothesis.

9.23 You are interested in testing H_0: $p \geq .63$ versus H_a: $p < .63$. From a random sample of 100 people, there are 55 people with a particular characteristic of interest that you are testing. Use a .01 level of significance to test this hypothesis.

9.24 You are testing H_0: $p = .29$ versus H_a: $p \neq .29$. A random sample of 740 items shows that 207 have a characteristic of interest. With a .05 probability of committing a Type I error, test the hypothesis using the critical value method. Check your result by using the *p*-value method.

Testing your understanding

9.25 A survey of insurance policy holders found that 48% of them read their policy document when it is renewed each year. An insurance company decided to invest considerable time and money into rewriting their policies to make them easier for their policy holders to read. After using the newly written policies for one year, company managers wanted to determine if the rewriting had significantly changed the proportion of policyholders who read their insurance policy upon renewal. They decided to randomly contact 380 of the company's policy holders who renewed a policy in the past year and ask them whether they had read their current policy; 164 responded that they had read the policy. Use a 1% level of significance to test the appropriate hypothesis.

9.26 The banking industry claimed that 80% of their customers aged over 65 used computers at home to make regular bill payments online for such things as electricity, gas and telephone. An independent research company decided to test this claim. A random sample of 150 bank customers over age 65 was selected, with 109 found to make regular bill payments online. Using a 5% level of significance, is there sufficient evidence to conclude that the proportion is significantly less than the 80% claimed by the banking industry?

9.6 Testing hypotheses about a variance

At times a researcher needs to test hypotheses about a population variance. For example, in the area of statistical quality control, manufacturers try to produce equipment and parts that are consistent in measurement. Suppose a company produces industrial wire that is specified to be a particular thickness. As a result of the production process, the thickness of the wire will vary slightly from one end to the other and from batch to batch. Even if the average thickness of the wire as measured from batch to batch meets the specification, the variance of the measurements might be too great to be acceptable. In other words, on average, the wire is the correct thickness, but some portions of the wire might be too thin and others unacceptably thick. By conducting hypothesis tests for the variance of the thickness measurements, quality control measures can be put in place to monitor variations in thicknesses from the process that are too great.

The procedure for testing hypotheses about a population variance is similar to the techniques for estimating a population variance from the sample variance. Formula 9.5, which is used to conduct these tests, assumes a population variable of interest is normally distributed.

Formula for testing hypotheses about a population variance (9.5)

$$\chi^2_{\text{test}} = \frac{(n-1)s^2}{\sigma^2}$$

where:

df = $n - 1$

(Note that the chi-square test of a population variance is extremely sensitive to violations of the assumption that the variable of interest in the population is normally distributed.)

As an example of hypothesis testing involving variance, consider a manufacturing company that has been working diligently to implement a just-in-time inventory system for its production line. The final product requires the installation of a pneumatic tube at a particular workstation on the assembly line. With the just-in-time inventory system, the company's goal is to minimise the number of pneumatic tubes stored at the workstation waiting to be installed. Ideally, the tubes would arrive at the workstation just as the operator needs them. However, it has been observed that generally there is a build-up of tubes and, on average, about 20 pneumatic tubes are stored at the workstation. The production superintendent does not want the variance of this inventory to be greater than 4. On a given day, the number of pneumatic tubes stored at the workstation is counted on eight separate occasions. The results are:

23 17 20 29 21 14 19 24

Using these sample data, and assuming that the number of tubes is normally distributed, a test can be performed to determine whether the variance of the inventory is greater than 4. This requires a one-tailed hypothesis test where the alternative hypothesis is that the variance is greater than 4. The null hypothesis is that the variance is acceptable (with no problems) if the variance is less than or equal to 4.

$$H_0: \sigma^2 \leq 4$$
$$H_a: \sigma^2 > 4$$

The value of alpha is .05. Since the sample size is eight, the degrees of freedom for the critical table chi-square value are 8 – 1 = 7. Using table A.8, the critical chi-square value is:

$$\chi^2_{.05,\,7} = 14.0671$$

Since the alternative hypothesis is greater than 4, the rejection region is in the upper tail of the chi-square distribution. The sample variance is calculated from the sample data to be:

$$s^2 = 20.9821$$

The test statistic value is calculated as:

$$\chi^2_{\text{test}} = \frac{(8-1)(20.9821)}{4} = 36.72$$

This test statistic for the chi-square value, $\chi^2_{test} = 36.72$, is greater than the critical chi-square table value, $\chi^2_{.05,7} = 14.0671$; therefore, the decision is to reject the null hypothesis. On the basis of this sample of eight data measurements, there is sufficient evidence at the .05 level of significance to conclude that the population variance of inventory at this workstation is greater than 4. Company production personnel and managers might want to investigate further to determine whether they can find a cause for this unacceptable variance. Figure 9.12 shows a chi-square distribution with the critical value, rejection region, nonrejection region, value of α and test statistic value of chi-square.

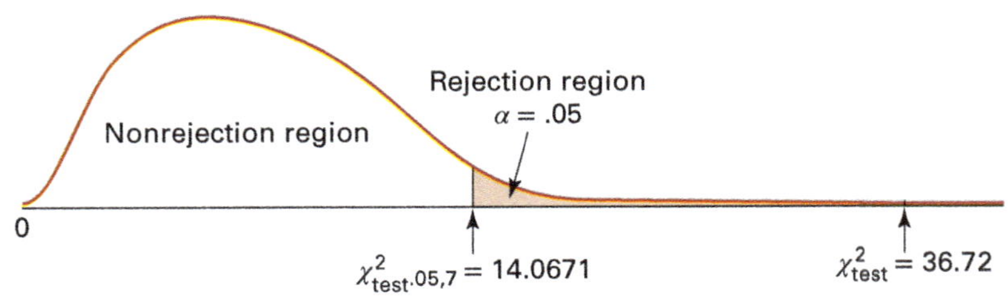

FIGURE 9.12 Hypothesis test distribution for the pneumatic tube example

Using Excel, the p-value of the observed chi-square value of 36.72 is determined to be .0000053. Since this value is less than $\alpha = .05$, the conclusion is to reject the null hypothesis using the p-value. In fact, using this p-value, the null hypothesis could be rejected for $\alpha = .00001$.

This null hypothesis can also be tested using the critical value method. Instead of solving for the test statistic value of chi-square, the critical chi-square value for α is inserted into formula 9.5 along with the hypothesised value of σ^2 and the degrees of freedom $(n - 1)$. Solving for s^2 yields a critical sample variance value, s^2_{crit}.

$$\chi^2_{crit} = \frac{(n-1)s^2_{crit}}{\sigma^2}$$

$$s^2_{crit} = \frac{\chi^2_{crit}\sigma^2}{(n-1)} = \frac{(14.0671)(4)}{7} = 8.038$$

The critical value of the sample variance is $s^2_{crit} = 8.038$. Since the sample variance was 20.9821, which is larger than the critical variance, the null hypothesis is rejected.

DEMONSTRATION PROBLEM 9.4

57	56	52	44
46	53	44	44
48	51	55	48
63	53	51	50

PROBLEM: A small business has 37 employees. As a result of the uncertain demand for its product, the company usually pays overtime in any given week. The company estimates that 50 total hours of overtime per week has usually been required and that the variance on this figure is 25 hours per week squared. (Note that the units of variance are squared, so 25 hours per week squared could also be written as 25 (hours per week)^2.) Company officials want to know whether the variance of overtime hours has changed. A sample of 16 weeks of overtime data (in hours per week) is given at left. Assume that hours of overtime are normally distributed. Use these data to test the null hypothesis that the variance of overtime data is 25 hours per week squared. Let $\alpha = .10$.

SOLUTION:

STEP 1. Set up H_0 and H_a

Since the company officials are testing whether the variance has changed, the alternative hypothesis is that the variance in overtime is not equal to 25. Therefore, the null hypothesis is that the variance is unchanged and equals 25. These hypotheses can be written as:

$$H_0: \sigma^2 = 25$$
$$H_a: \sigma^2 \neq 25$$

STEP 2. Decide on the type of the test

Since the alternative hypothesis contains the ≠ sign, this requires a two-tailed test.

STEP 3. Decide on a level of significance (α), determine the critical value(s) and region(s), and draw a diagram

Alpha is .10. Since the test is a two-tailed test, there must be $\alpha/2 = .05$ in each tail. The degrees of freedom are 16 – 1 = 15. The two chi-square critical values from table A.8 are:

$$\chi^2_{.95,15} = 7.26093$$
$$\chi^2_{.05,15} = 24.9958$$

The rejection and nonrejection regions, as well as the critical values, are shown in the diagram.

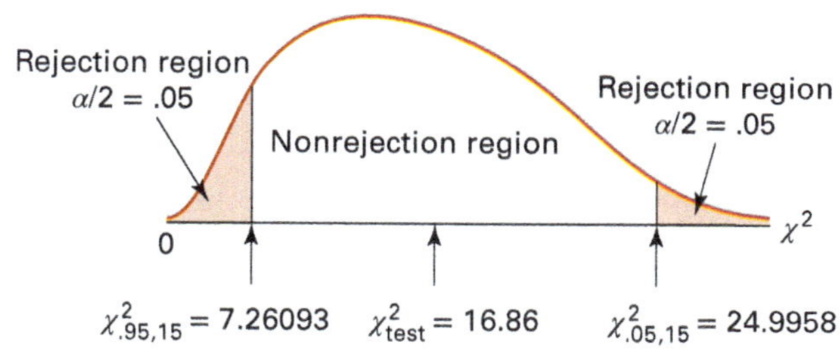

STEP 4. Write down the decision rule

The decision rule is that, if the data gathered produce a test statistic value of χ^2 greater than 24.9958 or less than 7.26093, then the test statistic is in the rejection region and the decision is to reject the null hypothesis. If the test statistic value of χ^2 is between these two values, then the decision is to not reject the null hypothesis because the calculated χ^2 value is in the nonrejection region.

STEP 5. Select a random sample and do relevant calculations

The test statistic for the chi-square value is calculated using $n = 16$, a sample variance of $s^2 = 28.1$ and the hypothesised variance $\alpha^2 = 25$:

$$\chi^2_{\text{test}} = \frac{(n-1)s^2}{\sigma^2} = \frac{(15)(28.1)}{25} = 16.86$$

Here the test statistic, $\chi^2_{\text{test}} = 16.86$, is in the nonrejection region, since it is between the critical values of 7.26093 and 24.9958. Hence the decision is to not reject the null hypothesis.

STEP 6. Draw a conclusion

At the 10% level of significance, there is insufficient evidence to conclude that the variance of overtime hours has changed from 25 hours per week squared.

PRACTICE PROBLEMS

Practising the calculations

9.27 Test each of the following hypotheses using the given information. Assume that the populations are normally distributed.

a. H_0: $\sigma^2 \leq 20$, H_a: $\sigma^2 > 20$, $\alpha = .05$, $n = 15$, $s^2 = 32$

b. H_0: $\sigma^2 = 8.5$, H_a: $\sigma^2 \neq 8.5$, $\alpha = .10$, $n = 22$, $s^2 = 17$

c. H_0: $\sigma^2 \geq 45$, H_a: $\sigma^2 < 45$, $\alpha = .01$, $n = 8$, $s = 4.12$

d. H_0: $\sigma^2 = 5$, H_a: $\sigma^2 \neq 5$, $\alpha = .05$, $n = 11$, $s^2 = 1.2$

Testing your understanding

P09-28 **9.28** A production process is known to produce output with a variance of 4 units^2. Management are concerned that the variance in the production process has changed. Data collected from a random sample of units produced during the production process are shown below. Using a 1% level of significance, test if the variance of the output from the production process has changed. Assume the measurements are normally distributed.

5	6	8	8	9	11	11	12
12	12	13	13	14	14	15	

P09-29 **9.29** A manufacturing company produces bearings. One line of bearings is specified to be 1.64 cm in diameter. A major customer requires that the variance of the bearings be no more than .001 cm^2. The producer is required to test the bearings before they are shipped, and so the diameters of 16 bearings are measured with a precise instrument, resulting in the following values.

1.69	1.64	1.62	1.69	1.63	1.57	1.70	1.64
1.66	1.59	1.63	1.66	1.65	1.63	1.71	1.65

Assume that bearing diameters are normally distributed. Use the data and α = .01 to test the data to determine whether the population of these bearings is to be rejected because of too high a variance.

P09-30 **9.30** A retail store manager knows the average weekly sales revenue for last year was $42 000. The store manager also knows that weekly sales are subject to many factors and show a large amount of variability. The standard deviation for all weekly sales recorded last year was $7500. The manager was interested to determine whether the variance in weekly sales had changed during the course of the current year. A random sample of 15 weekly sales figures (in dollars) was selected for the current year and is shown below. Assuming that weekly sales are normally distributed, use the data and α = .05 to determine whether the variance for weekly sales has changed.

24 000	27 000	28 000	32 000	33 000
37 000	39 000	41 000	43 000	44 000
46 000	48 000	49 000	52 000	53 000

9.31 A company produces industrial wiring. One batch of wiring is specified to be 2.16 cm thick. A company inspects the wiring in seven locations and determines that, on average, the wiring is about 2.16 cm thick. However, the measurements vary. It is unacceptable for the variance of the wiring to be more than .04 cm^2. The standard deviation of the seven measurements on this batch of wiring is .34 cm. Use α = .01 to determine whether the variance on the sample wiring is too great to meet specifications. Assume wiring thickness is normally distributed.

9.7 Solving for Type II errors

If a researcher reaches the statistical conclusion to not reject a null hypothesis, either a correct decision is made or a Type II error is made. If the null hypothesis is true, the researcher has made a correct decision. If the null hypothesis is false, a Type II error has been made.

In business, failure to reject a null hypothesis may mean staying with the status quo, not implementing a new process or not making adjustments. If the null hypothesis relates to a new process, product, theory or adjustment that is not significantly better than currently accepted practice, this would mean that the decision maker makes a correct decision. However, if the new process, product, theory or adjustment would significantly improve profits, sales, business climate, costs or morale, it would mean that the decision maker makes an error (Type II) in judgement. In business, Type II errors can translate to lost opportunities, poor product quality (as a result of failure to discern a problem in a process) or failure to react to the marketplace. Sometimes the ability to react to changes, new developments or new opportunities is what allows a business to grow. The Type II error plays an important role in business statistical decision making.

Determining the probability of committing a Type II error is more complex than finding the probability of committing a Type I error. The probability of committing a Type I error (level of significance, α) is either given in a problem or stated by the researcher before proceeding with the study. A Type II error, β, varies with different possible values of the alternative population parameter. For example, a researcher wants to determine if the average amount of a brand of motor oil sold in a particular container is less than the advertised 12 litres. The hypotheses would be:

$$H_0: \mu \geq 12 \text{ litres}$$
$$H_a: \mu < 12 \text{ litres}$$

A Type II error can be committed only when the researcher does not reject the null hypothesis and the null hypothesis is false. In these hypotheses, if the null hypothesis $\mu \geq 12$ litres is false, what is the true value of the population mean? Is the mean really 11.99 or 11.90 or 11.5 or 10 litres? The researcher can compute the probability of committing a Type II error for each of these possible values of the population mean. Often, when the null hypothesis is false, the value of the alternative mean is unknown, so the researcher will compute the probability of committing Type II errors for several alternative possible values. How can the probability of committing a Type II error be computed for some specific alternative value of the mean? To answer this, consider the motor oil example above where the containers are advertised as containing 12 litres of motor oil.

It is required to test if the average fill amount of the motor oil containers is less than 12 litres. A sample of 60 containers of motor oil gives a sample mean of 11.985 litres. Assume that the population standard deviation is $\sigma = .10$ litres. From $\alpha = .05$ and a one-tailed test, the table z_{crit} value is −1.645. The test statistic value of z from the sample data is:

$$z_{test} = \frac{11.985 - 12.00}{\frac{.10}{\sqrt{60}}} = -1.16$$

From this test statistic value of z, the researcher decides to not reject the null hypothesis. By not rejecting the null hypothesis, the researcher either makes a correct decision or commits a Type II error. What is the probability of committing a Type II error in this problem if the alternative population mean is actually 11.99 litres? The first step in determining the probability of a Type II error is to calculate a critical value for the sample mean, $\bar{x}_{crit}$.

In testing the null hypothesis by the critical value method, this value is used as the cut-off for the nonrejection region. For this one-tail motor oil problem for any sample mean obtained that is less than $\bar{x}_{crit}$ (or greater for an upper-tail rejection region), the null hypothesis is rejected. Any sample mean greater than $\bar{x}_{crit}$ (or less for an upper-tail rejection region) causes the researcher to not reject the null hypothesis. Solving for the critical value of the sample mean gives:

$$z_{crit} = \frac{\bar{x}_{crit} - \mu}{\frac{\sigma}{\sqrt{n}}}$$

$$-1.645 = \frac{\bar{x}_{crit} - 12}{\frac{.10}{\sqrt{60}}}$$

$$\bar{x}_{crit} = 11.979$$

Figure 9.13(a) (overleaf) shows the distribution of values when the null hypothesis is true. It contains a critical value of the sample mean, $\bar{x}_{crit} = 11.979$ litres, below which the null hypothesis will be rejected. Figure 9.13(b) shows the distribution when the alternative mean, $\mu_1 = 11.99$ litres, is true. How often will the business researcher fail to reject that distribution (a) is true when, in reality, distribution (b) is true? If the null hypothesis is false, the researcher will fail to reject the null hypothesis whenever $\bar{x}$ is in the nonrejection region, $\bar{x} \geq 11.979$ litres. If μ actually equals 11.99 litres, what is the probability of failing to reject $\mu = 12$ litres when 11.979 litres is the critical value? The business researcher calculates this probability by extending the critical value ($\bar{x}_{crit} = 11.979$ litres) from distribution (a) to distribution (b) and solving for the area to the right of $\bar{x}_{crit} = 11.979$.

$$z_1 = \frac{\bar{x}_{crit} - \mu_1}{\frac{\sigma}{\sqrt{n}}} = \frac{11.979 - 11.99}{\frac{.10}{\sqrt{60}}} = -.85$$

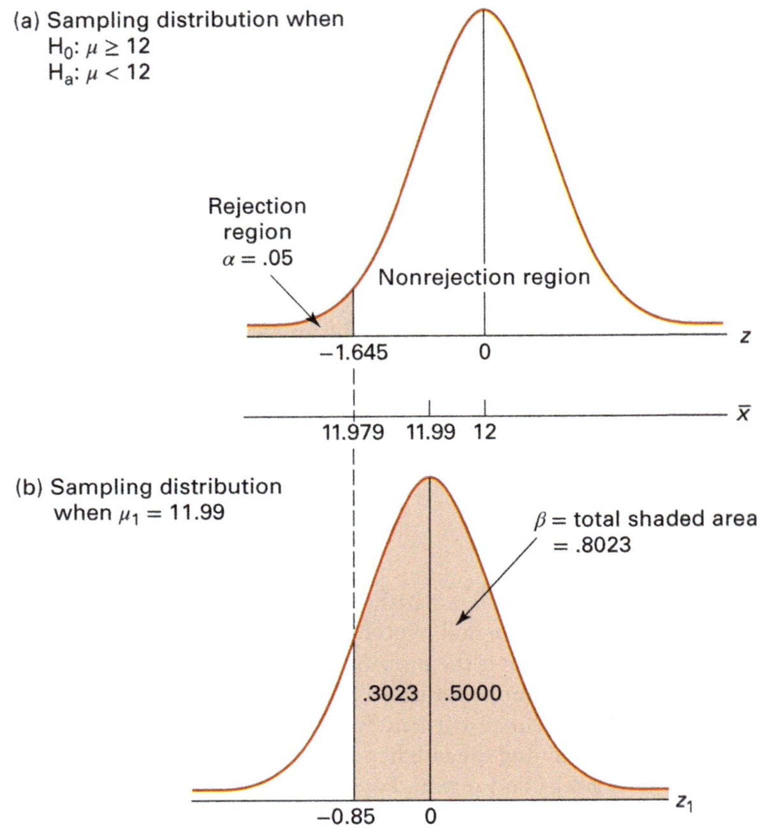

FIGURE 9.13 Type II error for motor oil example with alternative mean = 11.99 litres

This z-score of $-.85$ yields an area of .3023. The probability of committing a Type II error is all the area to the right of $\bar{x}_{crit} = 11.979$ in distribution (b), or .3023 + .5000 = .8023. Hence there is an 80.23% chance of committing a Type II error if the alternative mean is 11.99 litres. Using notation, we write $\beta = .8023$ when $\mu = 11.99$.

DEMONSTRATION PROBLEM 9.5

PROBLEM: Recompute the probability of committing a Type II error for the motor oil example if the alternative mean is 11.96 litres.

SOLUTION: The distribution in figure 9.13(a) does not change. The null hypothesised mean is still 12 litres, the critical value is still 11.979 litres and $n = 60$. However, distribution (b) of figure 9.13 changes with $\mu_1 = 11.96$ litres, as the following diagram shows.

The z formula used to solve for the area of distribution (b), $\mu_1 = 11.96$, to the right of 11.979 is:

$$z_1 = \frac{\bar{x}_{crit} - \mu_1}{\frac{\sigma}{\sqrt{n}}} = \frac{11.979 - 11.96}{\frac{.10}{\sqrt{60}}} = 1.47$$

Using table A.4, only .0708 of the area is to the right of the critical value of 1.47. Thus the probability of committing a Type II error is only .0708, as illustrated in the following diagram. So $\beta = .0708$ when $\mu = 11.96$.

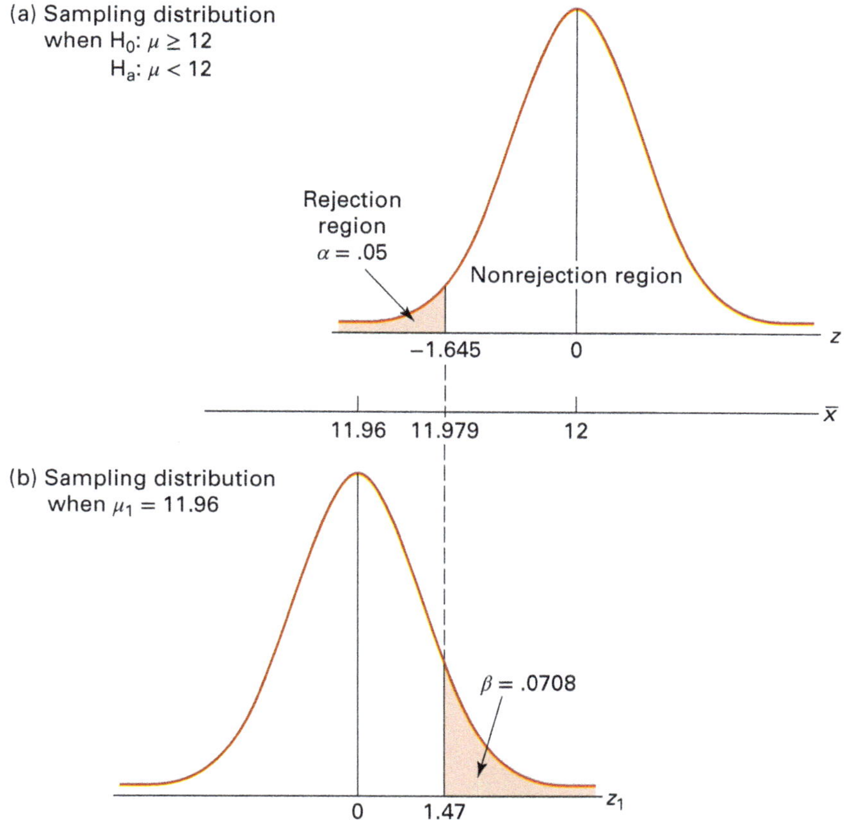

DEMONSTRATION PROBLEM 9.6

PROBLEM: Suppose you are conducting a two-tailed hypothesis test for a proportion. The null hypothesis is that the population proportion is 40%. The alternative hypothesis is that the population proportion is not 40%. A random sample of 250 produces a sample proportion of 44%. With alpha of .05, the table *z*-score for $\alpha/2$ is 1.96. The test statistic *z* from the sample information is:

$$SE_{\hat{p}} = \sqrt{\frac{pq}{n}} = \sqrt{\frac{(.40)(.60)}{250}} = .031$$

so

$$z_{test} = \frac{\hat{p} - p}{SE_{\hat{p}}} = \frac{.44 - .40}{.031} = 1.29$$

Thus the null hypothesis is not rejected. Either a correct decision is made or a Type II error is committed. Suppose the alternative population proportion really is 36%. What is the probability of committing a Type II error?

SOLUTION: Solve for the critical value of the proportion.

$$z_{crit} = \frac{\hat{p}_{crit} - p}{SE_{\hat{p}}}$$

$$\pm 1.96 = \frac{\hat{p}_{crit} - .40}{.031}$$

$$\hat{p}_{crit} = .40 \pm .06$$

The critical values are 34% on the lower end and 46% on the upper end. The alternative population proportion is 36%. The following diagram illustrates these results and the remainder of the solution to this problem.

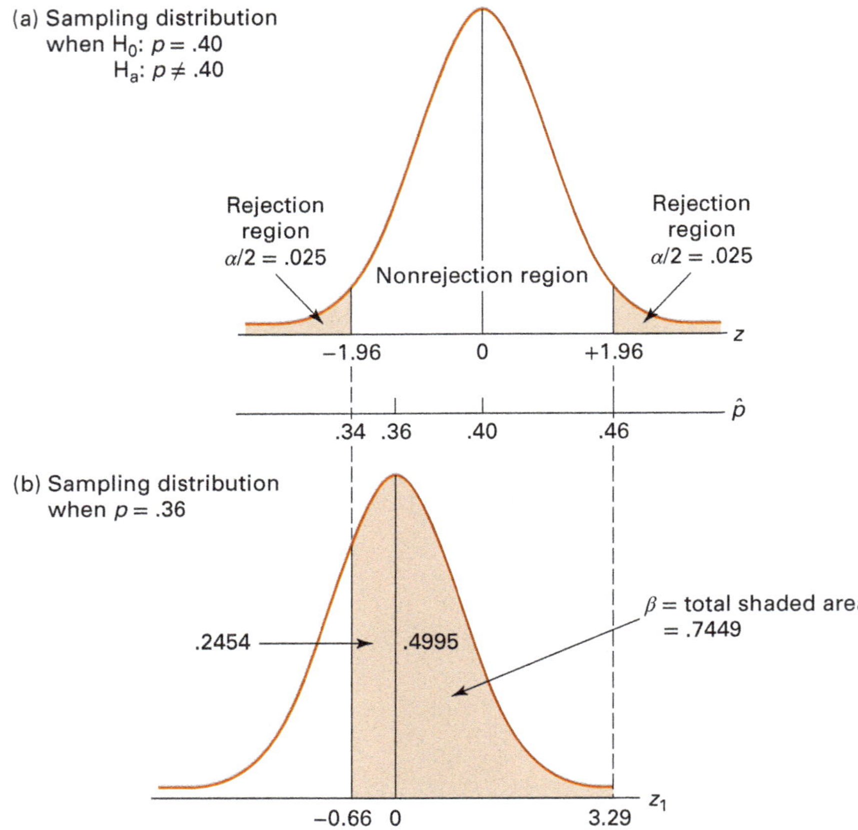

Solving for the area between $\hat{p}_{\text{crit}} = .34$ and $p_1 = .36$ yields:

$$z_1 = \frac{.34 - .36}{\sqrt{\frac{(.36)(.64)}{250}}} = -0.66$$

The area associated with $z_1 = -0.66$ is .2454.

The area between 36% and 46% of the distribution shown in diagram (b) can be solved for by using the following *z*-score.

$$z_1 = \frac{.46 - .36}{\sqrt{\frac{(.36)(.64)}{250}}} = 3.29$$

The area from table A.4 associated with $z = 3.29$ is .4995. Adding this value to the .2454 obtained from the left side of the distribution in graph (b) yields the total probability of committing a Type II error:

$$.2454 + .4995 = .7449$$

So $\beta = .7449$ when $p = 36\%$.

With two-tailed tests, both tails of the distribution contain rejection regions. The area between the two tails is the nonrejection region and the region where Type II errors can occur. In this problem, note that the right critical value is so far away from the alternative proportion ($p_1 = .36$) that the area between the right critical value and the alternative proportion is near .5000 (.4995), and virtually no area falls in the upper right tail of the distribution (.0005).

Some observations about Type II errors

Type II errors are committed only when the researcher fails to reject a null hypothesis when the alternative hypothesis is true. If the alternative mean or proportion is close to the hypothesised value, the probability of committing a Type II error is high. If the alternative value is relatively far away from the hypothesised value, as in the problem with $\mu = 12$ litres and $\mu_1 = 11.96$ litres, the probability of committing a Type II error is small. The implication is that, when a value is being tested in a null hypothesis against a true alternative value that is relatively far away, the sample statistic obtained is likely to show clearly which hypothesis is true. For example, a researcher is testing whether a company really is filling 2-litre bottles of cola with an average of 2 litres. If the company decides to underfill the bottles by filling them with only 1 litre, a sample of 50 bottles is likely to average a quantity near 1 litre rather than near 2 litres. Committing a Type II error is highly unlikely. Even a customer could probably see by looking at the bottles on the shelf that they are underfilled. However, if the company fills 2-litre bottles with 1.99 litres, the bottles appear close in fill volume to those filled with 2 litres. In this case, the probability of committing a Type II error is much greater. A customer would probably not notice the underfill simply by looking at the bottle.

In general, if the alternative value is relatively far from the hypothesised value, the probability of committing a Type II error is smaller than it is when the alternative value is close to the hypothesised value. The probability of committing a Type II error decreases as alternative values of the hypothesised parameter move farther away from the hypothesised value. This observation can be shown graphically in what are referred to as operating characteristic curves and power curves.

Operating characteristic and power curves

Since the probability of committing a Type II error changes for each different value of the alternative parameter, it is best in managerial decision making to examine a series of possible alternative values. For example, table 9.4 shows the probabilities of committing a Type II error (β) for several possible alternative means for the motor oil example discussed in demonstration problem 9.5, in which the null hypothesis was H_0: $\mu = 12$ litres and $\alpha = .05$.

Power is the probability of rejecting the null hypothesis when it is false and represents the correct decision of selecting the alternative hypothesis when it is true. Power is equal to $1 - \beta$. Table 9.4 contains the power values for the alternative means. Note in this table that the β probabilities and power probabilities add up to 1 for each particular alternative mean chosen.

TABLE 9.4 β values and power values for the motor oil example

Alternative mean (μ_1)	Probability of committing a Type II error (β)	Power ($1 - \beta$)
11.999	.94	.06
11.995	.89	.11
11.99	.80	.20
11.98	.53	.47
11.97	.24	.76
11.96	.07	.93
11.95	.01	.99

These values can be displayed graphically as shown in figures 9.14 and 9.15 (overleaf). Figure 9.14 is an **operating characteristic (OC) curve** *constructed by plotting the β values against the various values of the alternative hypothesis*. Notice that, when the alternative means are near the value of the null hypothesis, $\mu = 12$, the probability of committing a Type II error is high because it is difficult to discriminate between a distribution with a mean of 12 and a distribution with a mean of 11.999. However, as the values of the alternative means move away from the hypothesised value, $\mu = 12$, the value of β decreases. This visual representation underscores the notion that it is easier to discriminate between a distribution with $\mu = 12$ and a distribution with $\mu = 11.95$ than between distributions with $\mu = 12$ and $\mu = 11.999$.

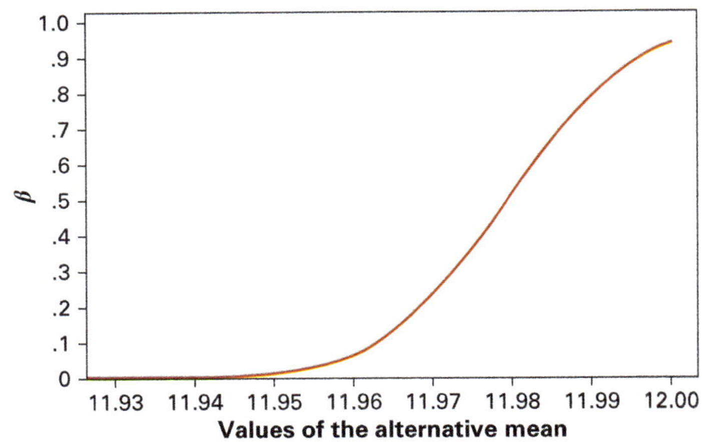

FIGURE 9.14 Operating characteristic curve for the motor oil

Figure 9.15 is a **power curve** constructed by *plotting the power values (1 − β) against the various values of the alternative hypotheses.* Note that the power increases as the alternative mean moves away from the value of μ in the null hypothesis. This relationship makes sense. As the alternative mean moves further and further away from the mean in the null hypothesis, a correct decision to reject the null hypothesis becomes more likely.

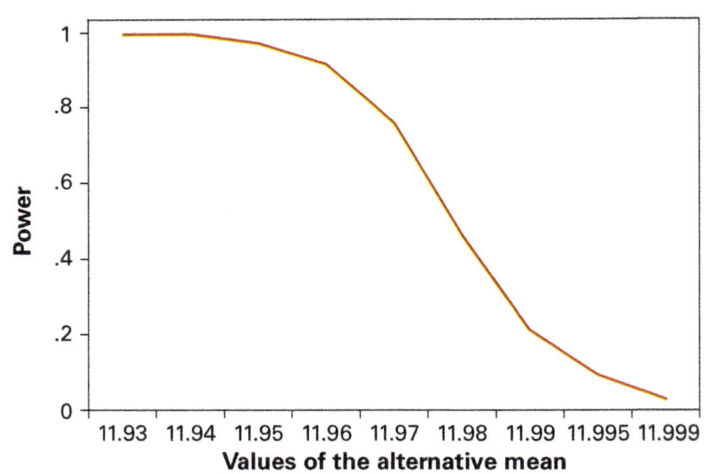

FIGURE 9.15 Power curve for the motor oil example

Effect of increasing sample size on the rejection limits

The size of the sample affects the location of the rejection limits. Consider the motor oil example in which we were testing the following hypotheses:

$$H_0: \mu \geq 12 \text{ litres}$$
$$H_a: \mu < 12 \text{ litres}$$

Sample size was 60 (n = 60) and the population standard deviation was .10 (σ = .10). With α = .05, the critical value of the test statistic was $z_{.05} = -1.645$. From this information, a critical sample mean value was computed:

$$z_{crit} = \frac{\bar{x}_{crit} - \mu}{\frac{\sigma}{\sqrt{n}}}$$

$$-1.645 = \frac{\bar{x}_{crit} - 12}{\frac{.10}{\sqrt{60}}}$$

$$\bar{x}_{crit} = 11.979$$

In the process of testing the hypothesis, any sample mean obtained that is less than 11.979 will result in a decision to reject the null hypothesis.

Suppose the sample size is increased to 100. The critical sample mean value is:

$$-1.645 = \frac{\bar{x}_{crit} - 12}{\frac{.10}{\sqrt{100}}}$$

$$\bar{x}_{crit} = 11.984$$

Notice that the critical sample mean value is nearer to the hypothesised value μ = 12 for the larger sample size than it was for a sample size of 60. Since n is in the denominator of the standard error of the mean $\left(\frac{\sigma}{\sqrt{n}}\right)$, an increase in n results in a decrease in the standard error of the mean (implying less error around the mean), which when multiplied by the critical value of the test statistic (z_{crit}) results in a critical sample mean that is closer to the hypothesised value. For n = 500, the critical sample mean value for this problem is 11.993.

Increased sample size not only affects the distance of the critical sample mean value from the hypothesised value of the distribution, but also can result in reducing β for a given value of α. Examine figure 9.13. Note that the critical sample mean value is 11.979 with alpha equal to .05 for n = 60. The value of β for an alternative mean μ_1 11.99 is .8023. Now consider the sample size is increased to 100. The critical sample mean value shown above is 11.984. The value of β is calculated as follows using an alternative mean of 11.99.

$$z = \frac{11.984 - 11.99}{\frac{.10}{\sqrt{100}}} = -0.60$$

The area under the standard normal curve for z = −.60 is .2257. Adding .2257 + .5000 results in β = .7257. Figure 9.16 shows the sampling distributions with α and β for this problem. In addition, by increasing sample size a business researcher could reduce α without necessarily increasing β. It is possible to reduce the probabilities of committing Type I and Type II errors simultaneously by increasing sample size.

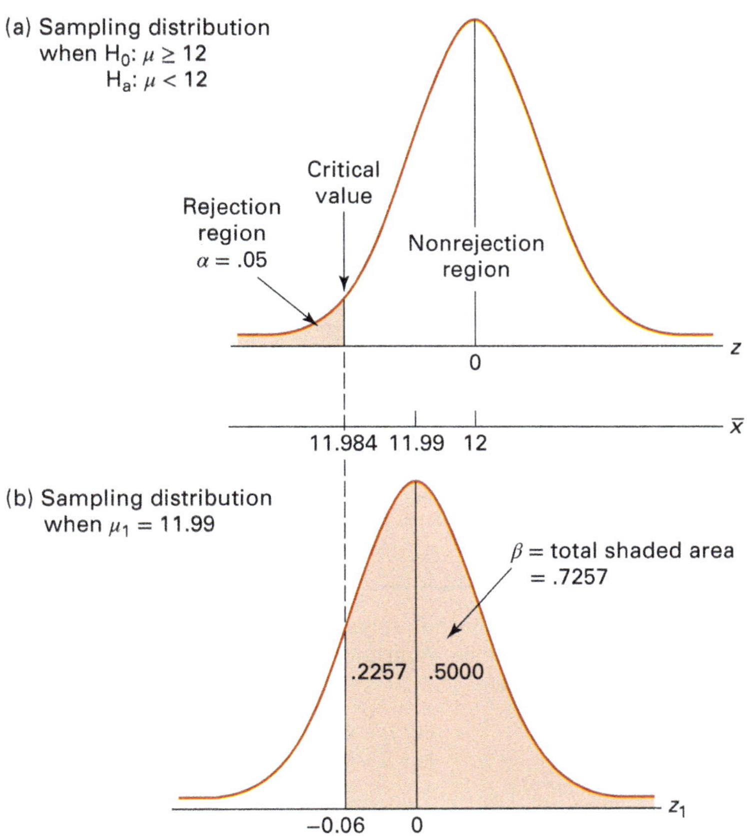

FIGURE 9.16 Type II error for motor oil example with n increased to 100

PRACTICE PROBLEMS

Practising the calculations

9.32 Suppose a null hypothesis is that the population mean is greater than or equal to 40. Suppose further that a random sample of 52 items is taken and the population standard deviation is 8. For each of the following α values, compute the probability of committing a Type II error if the population mean is actually 39.

a. $\alpha = .10$
b. $\alpha = .05$
c. $\alpha = .01$
d. Based on the answers to parts (a), (b) and (c), what happens to the value of β as α gets smaller?

9.33 For problem 9.32, use $\alpha = .05$ and solve for the probability of committing a Type II error for the following possible true alternative means.

a. $\mu_1 = 98.5$
b. $\mu_1 = 98$
c. $\mu_1 = 97$
d. $\mu_1 = 96$
e. What happens to the probability of committing a Type II error as the alternative value of the mean gets farther from the null hypothesised value of 100?

9.34 Suppose a hypothesis states that the mean is exactly 50. If a random sample of 35 items is taken to test this hypothesis, what is the value of β if the population standard deviation is 7 and the alternative mean is 53? Use $\alpha = .01$.

9.35 An alternative hypothesis is that $p < .65$. To test this hypothesis, a random sample of size 360 is taken. What is the probability of committing a Type II error if $\alpha = .05$ for each of the following alternative proportions?

a. $p_1 = .60$ b. $p_1 = .55$ c. $p_1 = .50$

Testing your understanding

9.36 A national study recently reported that the average age of a female shareholder is 44 years. A broker in Adelaide wants to know whether this figure is accurate for the female shareholders in Adelaide. The broker secures a master list of shareholders in Adelaide and takes a random sample of 58 women. Suppose the average age of female shareholders in the sample is 45.1 years, with a population standard deviation of 8.7 years. Test whether the broker's sample data differ significantly enough from the average of 44 years released by the earlier study to declare that the age of Adelaide's female shareholders is different from the national average. Use $\alpha = .05$. If no significant difference is noted, what is the broker's probability of committing a Type II error if the average age of a female Adelaide shareholder is actually 45 years, 46 years, 47 years or 48 years? Construct an OC curve for these data. Construct a power curve for these data.

9.37 A poll was taken to determine which of 13 major industries are doing a good job of serving their customers. Among the industries rated most highly for serving their customers were computer hardware and software companies, car manufacturers and airlines. The industries rated lowest on customer service were tobacco companies, managed-care providers and health insurance companies. Seventy-one per cent of those polled responded that airlines are doing a good job of serving their customers. Suppose, due to rising ticket prices, a researcher feels that this figure is now too high. He takes a poll of 463 people, and 324 say that the airlines are doing a good job of serving their customers. Does the survey show enough evidence to declare that the proportion of people saying that the airlines are doing a good job of serving their customers is significantly lower than stated in the original poll? Let alpha equal .10. If the researcher fails to reject the null hypothesis and if the figure is actually 69% now, what is the probability of committing a Type II error? What is the probability of committing a Type II error if the figure is really 66% or 60%?

CHAPTER CASE REVISITED

Prawn farm expects a bright future

1. The six-step hypothesis approach can be used to make conclusions regarding Sunny Bay's claim that the average weight of their six-week-old prawns has increased after changing the feed.

STEP 1. Set up H_0 and H_a
The investor wishes to test Sunny Bay's claim that the average weight of the prawns has increased to more than 48 g. Since 'increased' implies >, this allows the alternative hypothesis to be written. The null hypothesis must then be that the mean is still 48 g (or less).

H_0: $\mu \leq 48$
H_a: $\mu > 48$ (increased weight)

STEP 2. Decide on the type and direction of the test
Since the alternative hypothesis contains a > sign, this requires a one-tailed test (to the right).

STEP 3. Decide on a level of significance (α), determine the critical value(s) and region(s), and draw a diagram
Alpha has not been specified. The level of α chosen will depend on how serious it would be to commit a Type I error (i.e. to reject H_0 when in fact it is true). In this situation, the investor decides that a 5% level of significance is an acceptable level based on the investment outlay.

Since $\sigma = 2$ g, and a one-tailed test to the right is needed with $\alpha = .05$, the critical z-score is $z_{crit} = 1.645$. The rejection and nonrejection regions and critical value are shown in the following diagram.

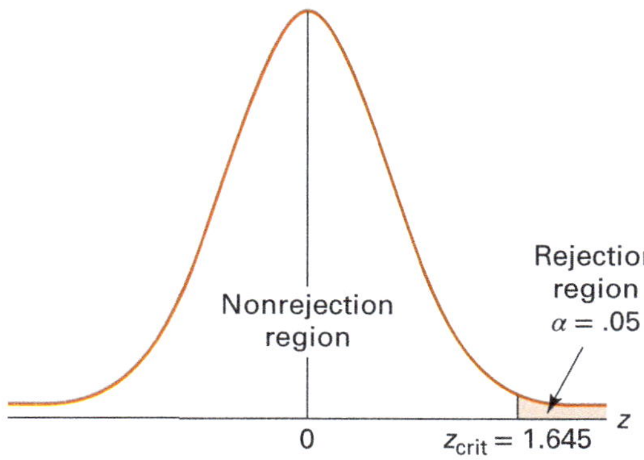

STEP 4. Write down the decision rule
The decision rule is that, if the data gathered produce a z-score greater than 1.645, then the test statistic is in the rejection region and the decision is to reject the null hypothesis. If the z-score calculated from the data is less than 1.645, the decision is to not reject the null hypothesis because the calculated z-score is in the nonrejection region.

STEP 5. Select a random sample and do relevant calculations
The sample mean is 51 g, $n = 20$ and the population standard deviation is 2 g. The test statistic z-score is:

$$z_{test} = \frac{\bar{x} - \mu}{SE_{\bar{x}}}$$

where $$SE_{\bar{x}} = \frac{\sigma}{\sqrt{n}} = \frac{2}{\sqrt{20}} = .447$$

$$z_{test} = \frac{\bar{x} - \mu}{SE} = \frac{51 - 48}{0.447} = 6.71$$

Here the test statistic, $z_{test} = 6.71$, is far greater than the critical value of $z_{crit} = 1.645$ in the upper tail of the distribution, so the decision is to reject the null hypothesis.

STEP 6. Draw a conclusion
At the .05 level of significance, there is sufficient evidence to conclude that the average weight of six-week-old prawns has increased above 48 g.

Using the sample standard deviation

2. To determine whether there is sufficient evidence to conclude that the average weight of six-week-old prawns has increased after the new prawn food was introduced, the following calculations can be performed using the six-step hypothesis procedure and t distribution.

STEP 1. Set up H_0 and H_a
The average weight of the prawns is to be tested for an increase above 48 g, so the hypotheses are the same as for the previous solution:

$$H_0: \mu \le 48$$
$$H_a: \mu > 48$$

STEP 2. Decide on the type and direction of the test
Since the alternative hypothesis contains the > sign, this requires a one-tailed test (to the right).

STEP 3. Decide on a level of significance (α), determine the critical value(s) and region(s), and draw a diagram
Alpha is .05. Since the test is a one-tailed test to the right, and α is taken to be unknown, the critical t value with 50 data points has $df = n - 1 = 50 - 1 = 49$. The critical t value is:

$$t_{.05,\,49} = 1.677$$

The rejection and nonrejection regions and critical value are shown in the following diagram.

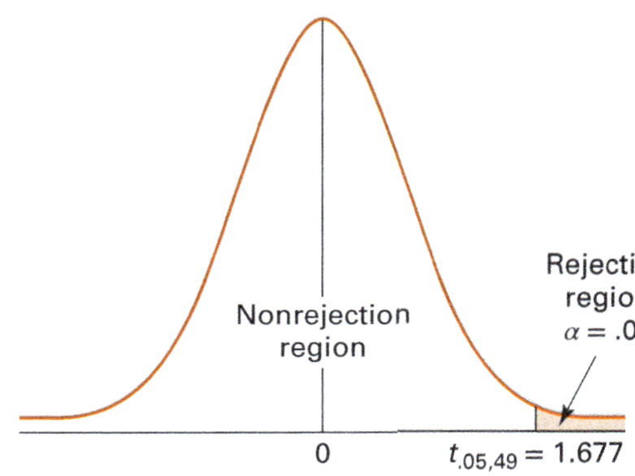

STEP 4. Write down the decision rule
The decision rule is that, if the data gathered produce a t value greater than 1.677, then the test statistic is in the rejection region and the decision is to reject the null hypothesis. If the t value calculated from the data is less than 1.677, the decision is to not reject the null hypothesis because the calculated t value is in the nonrejection region.

STEP 5. Select a random sample and do relevant calculations
The sample mean is 50.2 g, $n = 50$ and the sample standard deviation is 3.2 g. The test statistic t value is:

$$t_{test} = \frac{\bar{x} - \mu}{SE_{\bar{x}}}$$

where $$SE_{\bar{x}} = \frac{s}{\sqrt{n}} = \frac{3.2}{\sqrt{50}} = .4525$$

Here the test statistic, $t_{test} = 4.86$, is far greater than the critical value of $t_{crit} = 1.677$ in the upper tail of the distribution, so the decision is to reject the null hypothesis.

STEP 6. Draw a conclusion

At the .05 level of significance, there is sufficient evidence to conclude that the average weight of prawns at six weeks of age has increased above 48 g.

Errors in stating conclusions

3. Is there a chance that the average prawn weight is found to have increased when it really has not? In hypothesis testing, it is possible to make a Type I or Type II error (but not both at the same time). In this particular situation, the investor would like to buy the prawn farm knowing that the prawns are on average heavier than the industry standard of 48 g. The investor would, therefore, not want a hypothesis test to conclude that the average weight of six-week-old prawns is greater than 48 g when in actual fact it is not. This would be a Type I error. This would occur if the decision was to reject the null hypothesis (based on the sample data indicating that the weight had increased) when in fact the null hypothesis should not have been rejected (indicating that the average weight had not changed). For the calculations shown by the previous two methods, the test statistic is well beyond three standard errors of the mean and far into the tail of the distribution. The *p*-value in both cases is therefore very close to zero. This indicates that the results are significant for a very low value of alpha. A low value of alpha indicates that the probability of making a type I error is very low.

SUMMARY

1 The focus of this chapter was to understand the logic of the inferential statistic technique called hypothesis testing. Hypothesis testing draws conclusions about a population parameter using sample statistics. It requires an understanding of how to establish the null and alternative hypotheses. The null hypothesis always contain an equals sign (=, ≤, ≥) while the alternative hypothesis never contains an equals sign (≠, <, >). Being able to identify the keywords within any problem involving hypotheses testing is the key to solving problems. Keywords allow hypothesis statements to be written using the appropriate mathematical symbols. This allows regions of rejection and nonrejection to be defined and problems then solved.

2 To conduct a hypothesis test, a six-step approach is used. These steps initially involve setting up the hypothesis test using mathematical symbols and deciding whether a one- or two-tailed test is required, along with a level of significance. A diagram is then sketched to show the critical value(s) of the test statistic and a decision rule is written in terms of the critical value(s) of the test statistic. Then, using the sample data, the relevant calculations are done to determine the test statistic, which is then compared with the critical value(s). A decision is then made to either reject or not reject the null hypothesis based on the sample data. Finally, a conclusion should be stated in everyday language that makes it clear what the hypothesis test findings are.

3 Testing hypotheses involving a single population mean, when σ is known, was demonstrated. The decision to reject or not reject the null hypothesis was explained using three methods. First, the critical value method compares the test statistic of z or t with the critical value of z or t. The second method, the p-value method, uses the decision rule to reject the null hypothesis if the p-value is less than α (for both one-tailed and two-tailed tests). The third method also uses critical values but compares the critical value of the statistic (such as $\bar{x}_{crit}$) with the sample statistic value (such as $\bar{x}$) to make a decision.

4 Testing hypotheses involving a single population mean when σ is unknown was demonstrated. When small samples are involved, the variable of interest is normally distributed, and the sample standard deviation, s, is used instead of σ and the t distribution is used instead of the z distribution.

5 Testing hypotheses involving a single population proportion was demonstrated using the six-step approach. When calculating the standard error of a proportion, the hypothesised value of p is used in the calculation of $SE_{\hat{p}}$ where:

$$SE_{\hat{p}} = \sqrt{\frac{pq}{n}}$$

This is different from the calculation of the standard error of the proportion used in constructing confidence intervals, where $\hat{p}$ is used instead of p.

6 Testing hypotheses involving a single population variance was demonstrated using the six-step approach. This test makes use of the chi-squared distribution to find the critical values that define the rejection and nonrejection regions.

7 Hypothesis testing can result in two possible errors: Type I and Type II. The chance of making a Type I error is alpha (α) and the chance of a Type II error is beta (β). In analysing Type II errors, an operating characteristic (OC) curve is used to depict values of β that can occur for various values of the alternative hypothesis. The power curve plots power values against various values of the alternative hypothesis and allows researchers to observe the increase in power as values of the alternative hypothesis diverge from the value of the null hypothesis.

KEY TERMS

alpha (α) p. 267
alternative hypothesis p. 264
beta (β) p. 271
critical value p. 267
critical value method p. 267
hypothesis testing p. 263
level of significance p. 267
nonrejection region p. 267
null hypothesis p. 264
one-tailed test p. 265
operating characteristic (OC) curve p. 301
power p. 271
power curve p. 302
***p*-value** p. 267
rejection region p. 267
statistical hypotheses p. 264
two-tailed test p. 265
Type I error p. 269
Type II error p. 270

KEY EQUATIONS

EQUATION	DESCRIPTION	FORMULA
9.1	z_{test} for a single mean	$z_{test} = \dfrac{\bar{x} - \mu}{SE_{\bar{x}}}$ where: $SE_{\bar{x}} = \dfrac{\sigma}{\sqrt{n}}$
9.2	Formula to test hypotheses about μ with a finite population	$z_{test} = \dfrac{\bar{x} - \mu}{SE_{\bar{x}}}$ where: $SE_{\bar{x}} = \dfrac{\sigma}{\sqrt{n}}\sqrt{\dfrac{N-n}{N-1}}$
9.3	t test for μ	$t_{test} = \dfrac{\bar{x} - \mu}{SE_{\bar{x}}}$ where: $SE_{\bar{x}} = \dfrac{s}{\sqrt{n}}$ $df = n - 1$

EQUATION	DESCRIPTION	FORMULA
9.4	**z test of a population proportion**	$z_{\text{test}} = \dfrac{\hat{p} - p}{\text{SE}_{\hat{p}}}$ where: $\text{SE}_{\hat{p}} = \sqrt{\dfrac{pq}{n}}$
9.5	**Formula for testing hypotheses about a population variance**	$\chi^2_{\text{test}} = \dfrac{(n-1)s^2}{\sigma^2}$ where: $\text{df} = n - 1$

REVIEW PROBLEMS

Practising the calculations

9.38 Use the information given and the six-step approach to test the following hypotheses. Let $\alpha = .10$.

H_0: $\mu = 17$ $\quad$ H_a: $\mu \neq 17$ $\quad$ $n = 37$ $\quad$ $\bar{x} = 16.2$ $\quad$ $\sigma = 3.1$

9.39 Use the information given and the six-step approach to test the following hypotheses. Let $\alpha = .05$. Assume the population is normally distributed.

H_0: $\mu \geq 7.82$ $\quad$ H_a: $\mu < 7.82$ $\quad$ $n = 17$ $\quad$ $\bar{x} = 7.1$ $\quad$ $s = 1.69$

9.40 For each of the following problems, test the hypotheses using the six-step approach.

a. H_0: $p \leq .28$ $\quad$ H_a: $p > .28$ $\quad$ $n = 783$ $\quad$ $x = 230$ $\quad$ $\alpha = .10$

b. H_0: $p = .61$ $\quad$ H_a: $p \neq .61$ $\quad$ $n = 401$ $\quad$ $\hat{p} = .56$ $\quad$ $\alpha = .05$

9.41 Test the following hypotheses by using the information given and the six-step approach. Let $\alpha = .01$. Assume that the population is normally distributed.

H_0: $\sigma^2 \leq 15.4$ $\quad$ H_a: $\sigma^2 > 15.4$ $\quad$ $n = 18$ $\quad$ $s^2 = 29.6$

9.42 Solve for the value of beta (β) in each of the following problems.

a. H_0: $\mu \leq 130$ $\quad$ H_a: $\mu > 130$ $\quad$ $n = 75$ $\quad$ $\sigma = 12$ $\quad$ $\alpha = .01$. The alternative mean is actually 135.

b. H_0: $p \geq .44$ $\quad$ H_a: $p < .44$ $\quad$ $n = 1095$ $\quad$ $\alpha = .05$. The alternative proportion is actually .42.

Testing your understanding

9.43 A property developer proposed to construct a new shopping centre in an environmentally sensitive area. It was believed 80% of residents in the community were opposed to the development. The developer therefore decided to undertake an extensive advertising campaign in order to try to get popular support for the project. The campaign focused heavily on promoting the many community benefits the shopping centre would deliver. After a period of time, another survey was conducted by randomly selecting a sample of 125 residents, with 70% of residents indicating they support the construction of the shopping centre. Is there sufficient evidence to conclude the proportion of residents opposed to the construction of the shopping centre has decreased? Use a 1% level of significance.

9.44 According to a recent survey, the average urban person consumes 1.5 kg of food per day. Is this figure also true for rural people? Suppose 64 rural people are identified by a random procedure and their average consumption per day is 1.57 kg of food. Assume a population variance of 0.52 kg^2 of food per day. Use a 5% level of significance to determine whether the survey figure for urban people is also true for rural people on the basis of the sample data.

P09-45 **9.45** Road workers are painting white stripes on a highway. The stripes are supposed to be approximately 3 m long. However, because of the machine, the operator and the motion of the vehicle carrying the equipment, considerable variation occurs among the stripe lengths. Workers claim that the variance of stripes is not more than 0.009 m^2. Use the sample lengths given here from 12 measured stripes to test the variance claim. Assume stripe length is normally distributed. Let $\alpha = .05$.

Stripe lengths in metres

3.09	2.76	2.79	2.82
3.12	2.94	2.94	3.21
3.15	3.03	2.97	3.12

P09-46 **9.46** Suppose the number of beds filled per day in a medium-sized hospital is normally distributed. A hospital administrator tells the board of directors that, on average, at least 185 beds are filled on any given day. One of the board members believes this figure is inflated, and she manages to secure a random sample of figures for 16 days. The data are shown below. Use $\alpha = .05$ and the sample data to test whether the hospital administrator's statement is false. Assume the number of filled beds per day is normally distributed in the population.

Number of beds occupied per day			
173	149	166	180
189	170	152	194
177	169	188	160
199	175	172	187

9.47 Changes in lifestyles over the years are believed to now see families eat more takeaway food at home for dinner than previously. It is claimed the proportion of families who now eat at least one takeaway meal per week as the family dinner is 75%. To test this claim, a random sample of 250 families was selected. 192 families indicated that they eat at least one takeaway meal per week as the family dinner. Using a 5% level of significance, what conclusion can be made? If the actual proportion of families who eat at least one takeaway meal per week as the family dinner was later found to be 83%, what error if any would have been made?

CHAPTER

10 Statistical inferences about two populations

LEARNING OBJECTIVES

After studying this chapter, you should be able to:

1. test hypotheses about and construct confidence intervals for the difference between two population means when population variances are known
2. test hypotheses about and construct confidence intervals for the difference between two population means when population variances are unknown
3. test hypotheses about and construct confidence intervals for the mean difference between two populations with paired observations
4. test hypotheses about and construct confidence intervals for the difference between two population proportions
5. test hypotheses about and construct confidence intervals for the ratio of two population variances.

OPENING VIGNETTE

Saving for retirement

To help Australians provide for their retirement, employers are required to pay an amount equivalent to 9.5% (as of 2014) of an employee's salary into a complying superannuation fund. Superannuation savings are made available to employees after they reach retirement age. Many workers make additional contributions because of tax concessions and other government benefits, and to provide for a more comfortable retirement.

However, many workers find choosing a superannuation fund and selecting an investment option to be a difficult decision. In any super fund there are high-growth, high-risk investment options as well as low-growth, low-risk investment options. Many people need high growth for a reasonable standard of living in retirement, but they seek a low-risk option to avoid the chance they will lose their life's savings. This is the kind of dilemma that can have heart-wrenching consequences when there is a financial crisis.

A little statistical analysis can help in making informed decisions. To illustrate, let's consider two investment options in Unisuper.

Investment composition	Growth (high return, high risk)	Capital stable (low return, low risk)
Australian shares	44.00%	15.00%
Cash and fixed interest	15.00%	70.00%
International shares	26.00%	8.50%
Property	10.00%	6.50%
Infrastructure and private equity	5.00%	0.00%

The performances of the two investment options over six years are given below.

Financial year ended	Growth (% return)	Capital stable (% return)
June 2009	–12.68	–0.94
June 2010	9.85	8.56
June 2011	9.45	6.67
June 2012	0.03	5.97
June 2013	18.75	8.73
June 2014	15.91	8.50

As we can see, the *growth* option generally had very high returns after 2012 and the same was true before 2008 (though the values are not shown in the table). The 2008 global financial crisis saw growth funds lose a lot of money — with much greater losses than the *capital stable* option. If we exclude the 2008–09 financial year, the compound 5-year average return from the *growth* option was 10.61% but that of the *capital stable* option was 7.68%. One can find the portfolio risk of an investment option from the probabilities of various returns. Financial advisers continually do these tasks.

The average return from an investment option is estimated using the geometric mean. (Geometric mean is described in the maths appendix at the end of this chapter.) Unisuper's compound 5-year average returns have been given earlier. Here we show the computations for the given six years:

- for the growth option:

$$[(1-.1268)(1+.0985)(1+.945)(1+.0003)(1+.1875)(1+.1591)]^{\frac{1}{6}}-1=.06333$$

- for the capital stable option:

$$[(1-.0094)(1+.0856)(1+.0667)(1+.0597)(1+.0873)(1+.0850)]^{\frac{1}{6}}-1=.06193$$

The returns considering the six-year period is not very different. The difference is significant *if* we exclude the 2008–2009 financial year. One can randomly select a few super funds from hundreds of available super funds, such as REST, AustralianSuper, Sunsuper, HESTA and MLC, and calculate their returns in *growth* and *capital stable* options. However, the names of these two investment options vary from one fund to another; for example, in REST they are called *high growth* and *capital stable*, and in HESTA they are called *shares plus* and *conservative pool*, respectively. The returns also vary from year to year and from fund to fund, and, thus, the average returns have to be calculated for each fund separately. For instance, the returns from REST given below illustrate the differences between annual returns.

Financial year ended	High growth (% return)	Capital stable (% return)
June 2009	−12.71	−2.78
June 2010	13.72	10.07
June 2011	7.35	6.60
June 2012	−0.39	4.21
June 2013	23.13	10.94
June 2014	15.17	7.58

Once we have a sample of average returns, we can test the hypothesis that a growth option has a higher average return than a capital stable option over the long term at a given level of significance assuming that the variables are approximately normally distributed with similar variances (here we are not taking into account the risks). We can also test if a group of super funds such as industry super funds performed significantly differently from non-industry super funds. Based on the analyses, we can make an informed decision.

Introduction

It is important, on many occasions, to determine if there is a significant difference in a characteristic of two populations. This can be assessed with the statistical tools we introduced earlier. Confidence interval construction and hypothesis testing in relation to making inferences about a single population use different approaches to achieve similar objectives. The application of these two techniques can be further extended to situations where we are confronted with the problem of establishing if there is a significant difference between two population distributions. To illustrate this with an example, suppose an engineer claims that he has successfully modified the engine of a car to obtain greater fuel efficiency. One way to test his claim is to conduct an experiment, in which several cars of the same make and model are driven with original engines under different road conditions and the distance travelled per litre of fuel consumed by each car is recorded. This forms the sample data for one population. Next, each car should be fitted with the modified engine and driven under similar conditions. The observed kilometres per litre consumed by the modified engine form the second sample. Through hypothesis testing or confidence interval construction we can then evaluate if the two samples originate from two distinct population distributions, or the differences are not significant enough to be considered as distinct population distributions. This is the scientific way of verifying the veracity of the engineer's claim.

The techniques described in this chapter are applicable when we focus on one characteristic or variable of the populations measured in the same units (or dimensionless). Quite often we need to investigate only the difference between the mean values of this variable of the populations.

In general, to proceed with the inference about the difference between two population means, the following assumptions are required.

1. Each set of sample data follows an approximately normal distribution, or the central limit theorem applies.
2. The two distributions have almost identical variabilities, or the sample sizes are large, nearly equal and their variances are similar.
3. Each observation is a random sample from its population (or the experimental design is such that the observed values are representative of the population).
4. Observations are independent of each other, which means that the occurrence of any one (or a matched pair) observation in no way affects the occurrence of any other (or another matched pair) observation.

CHAPTER CASE

Life insurance premiums

A life insurance policy is a contract between you and a company to pay your designated beneficiary a sum of money upon your death in exchange for a premium. Depending on the policy the payout could be for other reasons such as critical illness. The premium can be paid monthly, quarterly or annually.

Although it is important to know exactly how life insurance premiums are calculated — as the premium is one of the biggest deciding factors when choosing a life insurance policy — insurance companies are not fully transparent as to how they decide on the premiums. However, there are some guidelines that all life insurance providers follow in quoting premiums rather consistently.

Here is a look at the major factors that determine your life insurance premium.

- *Age:* Generally, the younger a person, the lower his or her premium will be. The rationale behind this is that a young person has many years to go before the company may have to make payouts for him or her. And since, in all these years, the individual will keep making regular premium payments, his or her premium could be low, but the total will still be high. But an older person is likely to pass away earlier making lesser total contributions to the insurer. Older people are also more liable to contract fatal diseases than younger people. Hence, the premiums for older people are higher so as to offset the increased risk that the insurance company is willing to expose itself to.
- *Nature of profession:* The nature of a person's job or profession also has an impact on the life insurance premium. For instance, if you work in an office and sit at a desk all day, your risk of death at your job is quite low. Thus, your insurance premium will be low. If you have a high-risk job such as a miner, a builder or a stuntman, your risk of death on the job is much higher than an office executive. Hence, your insurance premium will be higher.
- *Individual lifestyle:* A person's lifestyle is another factor that determines his or her life insurance premium. If you are a chain smoker, or if you drink often, you will be considered at high risk for earlier than normal death and your insurance premium will be higher than someone who does not smoke or drink. Similarly, if you are into adventure sports and put your life at risk doing things such as mountain climbing and paragliding then your life insurance premium will be more than someone who does not indulge in such risky activities.
- *Pre-existing conditions:* If you have any pre-existing medical conditions such as diabetes, high blood pressure or a family history of heart problems, you will be deemed as a high-risk individual and the insurance company will charge you a higher insurance premium than healthier individuals.

Questions to help managers make decisions

Assume an employer pays life insurance premiums as one of the benefits it offers its employees.

1. Are the differences in premiums that insurance companies charge for smokers and nonsmokers significant? If so, should the employer provide different levels of cover to its employees based on lifestyle? To make a decision, a manager based in Sydney, Australia in 2014 obtained quotes for monthly premiums from several insurance companies selected randomly. The quotes for a 40-year-old male for a death cover of $500 000 (ignoring the fact that terms and conditions vary from company to company) are provided in the table below.

Company name	Smoker	Nonsmoker
ANZ	$118	$57
Allianz	$129	$53
AAMI	$105	$52
Suncorp	$110	$55
Zurich	$ 76	$40
AMP	$124	$58
TAL	$121	$58
AIA	$123	$56
OnePath	$121	$58
MLC	$119	$54

2. Would the employer make significant savings in premiums if younger and healthier people were assigned to risky jobs and older people to desk jobs?
3. Is it worthwhile to the employer to invest in improving the workplace environment to save on insurance premiums?

10.1 Hypothesis testing and confidence intervals for the difference between two means (*z* statistic, population variances known)

When we are required to check if two population distributions are similar, we frequently collect data from each of the two populations and test statistically whether their means are significantly different. This type of analysis can be used to determine, for example, whether the effectiveness of two brands of skin lotion differ or whether two brands of tyre wear differently. Business research might be conducted to study the difference in the productivity of men and women on an assembly line under certain conditions. An engineer might want to determine differences in the strength of aluminium produced under two different temperatures. Does the average cost of a two-bedroom, one-storey house differ between Perth and Adelaide? If so, what is the difference? These and many other interesting questions can be addressed by comparing the difference between two sample means.

How does a researcher analyse the difference between two sample means? The central limit theorem states that the difference between two sample means, $\bar{x}_1 - \bar{x}_2$, is normally distributed for large sample sizes (both n_1 and $n_2 \geq 30$) regardless of the shape of the parent population distributions. It can also be shown that:

$$\mu_{\bar{x}_1-\bar{x}_2} = \mu_1 - \mu_2$$

$$\sigma_{\bar{x}_1-\bar{x}_2} = \sqrt{\frac{\sigma_1^2}{n_1} + \frac{\sigma_2^2}{n_2}}$$

These expressions lead to the z formula (formula 10.1) for the difference between two sample means.

z formula for the difference between two sample means (independent samples and population variances known) (10.1)

$$z = \frac{(\bar{x}_1 - \bar{x}_2) - (\mu_1 - \mu_2)}{\sqrt{\frac{\sigma_1^2}{n_1} + \frac{\sigma_2^2}{n_2}}}$$

where:

μ_1 and σ_1^2 = the mean and variance of population 1, respectively
μ_2 and σ_2^2 = the mean and variance of population 2, respectively
n_1 = size of sample 1
n_2 = size of sample 2

This formula is the basis for statistical inferences about the difference between two population means using two random **independent samples**.

Note: If the populations can be assumed to be normally distributed on the variable being studied, and if the population variances are known, formula 10.1 can be used for small samples.

Hypothesis testing

Hypothesis testing involves constructing null and alternative hypotheses and testing those against observed data. The Latin word 'null' means zero, which implies there is nothing new from what people already know. The alternative hypothesis challenges this notion. One example might be to challenge the notion of equality in men and women for employment or income. A consumer organisation might want to test two brands of light bulbs to determine whether one burns longer than the other. A company planning to relocate might want to determine whether a significant difference separates the average rent of a commercial property in Ipswich, Queensland from that in Dunedin, New Zealand. Formula 10.1 can be used to test the difference between two population means.

As a specific example, suppose we want to conduct a hypothesis test to determine whether the average annual salary for an advertising manager is different from the average annual salary of an auditing manager. Because we are testing to determine whether the means are different, it might seem logical that the null and alternative hypotheses would be:

$$H_0: \mu_1 = \mu_2$$
$$H_a: \mu_1 \neq \mu_2$$

where advertising managers are population 1 and auditing managers are population 2. Remember that the null hypothesis should always reflect the 'business-as-usual scenario' or the conventional wisdom, because null means zero, which implies there is nothing unusual. The two hypotheses above can be rearranged as:

$$H_0: \mu_1 - \mu_2 = 0$$
$$H_a: \mu_1 - \mu_2 \neq 0$$

A simple random sample of 32 advertising managers from across Australia is taken. The advertising managers are contacted by telephone and asked their annual salary. A similar random sample is taken of 34 auditing managers. The resulting salary data are listed in table 10.1, along with the sample means, the population standard deviations and the population variances. (It is a mere coincidence that the population variances are the same as the sample variances for this given problem.)

In this problem, the business analyst is testing whether there is a difference between the average salaries of an advertising manager and an auditing manager; therefore the test is two-tailed. If the business analyst had hypothesised that one was paid more than the other, the test would have been one-tailed.

Suppose $\alpha = .05$. Because this test is a two-tailed test, each of the two rejection regions has an area of .025, leaving .475 of the area in the distribution between each critical value and the mean of the distribution. The associated critical table value for this area is $z_{.025} = \pm 1.96$. Figure 10.1 shows the critical table z value along with the rejection regions.

TABLE 10.1 Wages for advertising managers and auditing managers ($000)

Advertising managers		Auditing managers	
74.256	64.276	69.962	67.160
96.234	74.194	55.052	37.386
89.807	65.360	57.828	59.505
93.261	73.904	63.362	72.790
103.030	54.270	37.194	71.351
74.195	59.045	99.198	58.653
75.932	68.508	61.254	63.508
80.742	71.115	73.065	43.649
39.672	67.574	48.036	63.369
45.652	59.621	60.053	59.676
93.083	62.483	66.359	54.449
63.384	69.319	61.261	46.394
57.791	35.394	77.136	71.804
65.145	86.741	66.035	72.401
96.767	57.351	54.335	56.470
77.242		42.494	67.814
67.056		83.849	71.492
$n_1 = 32$		$n_2 = 34$	
$\bar{x}_1 = 70.700$		$\bar{x}_2 = 62.187$	
$\sigma_1 = 16.253$		$\sigma_2 = 12.900$	
$\sigma_1^2 = 264.164$		$\sigma_2^2 = 166.411$	

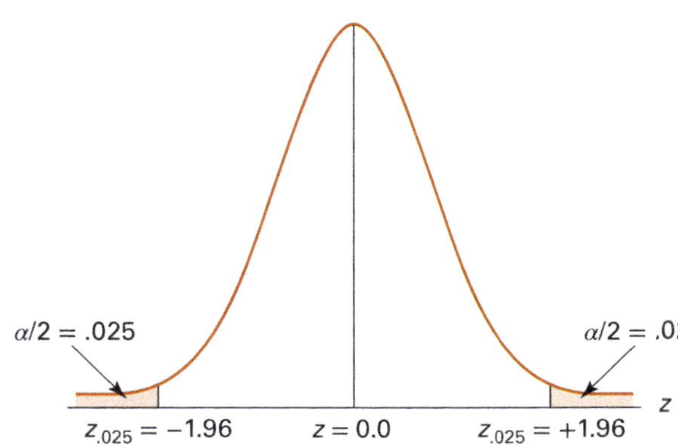

FIGURE 10.1 Critical values and rejection regions for the salary example

Formula 10.1 and the data in table 10.1 yield a z value to complete the hypothesis test:

$$z = \frac{(70.700 - 62.187) - (0)}{\sqrt{\frac{264.164}{32} + \frac{166.411}{34}}} = 2.35$$

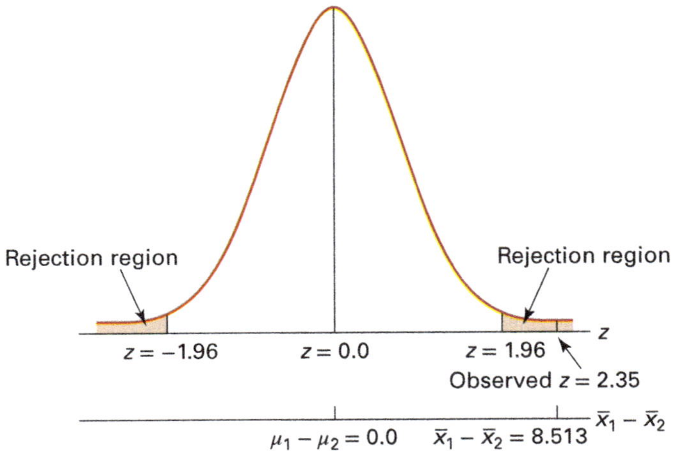

FIGURE 10.2 Location of observed z value for the salary example

The estimated value of 2.35 is greater than the critical value obtained from the z table, 1.96. The business researcher rejects the null hypothesis and can say that there is evidence of a significant difference between the average annual salary of an advertising manager and the average annual salary of an auditing manager. The business researcher then examines the sample means (70.700 for advertising managers and 62.187 for auditing managers) and uses common sense to conclude that advertising managers earn more, on average, than do auditing managers. Figure 10.2 shows the relative positions of the observed z and $z_{\alpha/2}$ in the normal curve.

This conclusion could have been reached by using the p-value. Looking up the probability of $z \geq 2.35$ in the z distribution table in table A.4 yields an area of $.5000 - .4906 = .0094$. The p-value for this two-tailed problem is $2 \times .0094 = .0188$, which is less than $\alpha = .05$. The decision is to reject the null hypothesis.

DEMONSTRATION PROBLEM 10.1

PROBLEM: Sue Taylor, an automotive engineer with Nord Motor Company, claims that she has been able to modify the engine of the Revel model car so that it is now more fuel efficient. To verify her claim she took four new identical cars from the factory, and along with her co-workers drove each car for 500 km under similar road conditions and found that all four cars consumed exactly the same amount of fuel. Being convinced that the cars have exactly the same fuel consumption, she replaced the engines of two of the cars with her modified engine. Over the next few days, Sue and her co-workers drove the cars under different road conditions but under similar exposures in accordance with the principles of experimental design that accounted for atmospheric temperature, wind, uphill and downhill conditions, surface roughness, acceleration etc. to produce unbiased and representative results. (Experimental design has become an important branch of statistics for representative sample data collection in controlled experiments.) For each trip, they recorded the number of kilometres each car travelled per litre of fuel consumed. Their observations are given in the following table.

Original engine fuel efficiency (km/L)

11.8	9.7	12.8	13.1	10.2	10.5	11.8	10.7	10.8
11.3	11.4	13.0	11.6	11.8	9.5	10.5	11.9	12.2
12.4	12.5	12.7	9.9	12.8	11.5	10.1	13.2	

Modified engine fuel efficiency (km/L)

13.8	10.9	11.4	11.5	12.5	11.7	11.8	12.0	13.1
12.1	13.4	12.3	12.5	11.5	14.0	12.8	13.1	12.0
13.2	12.2	13.6	10.8	14.0	12.7	14.6	14.4	

It is also known that the original engine has a population standard deviation of 1.1072 km/L, but the modified engine has a population standard deviation of 1.0345 km/L. Perform a hypothesis test of Sue's claim. Use $\alpha = .01$.

SOLUTION: As with any statistical analysis, the first approach should always be to get a graphical or visual impression of the data sets. A stem and leaf plot and histogram of each data set are given in the following figures.

Original car engine

Steam	Leaf
9	5 7 9
10	1 2 5 5 7 9
11	3 4 5 6 8 8 8 9
12	2 4 5 7 8 8
13	0 1 2

Stem and leaf plot

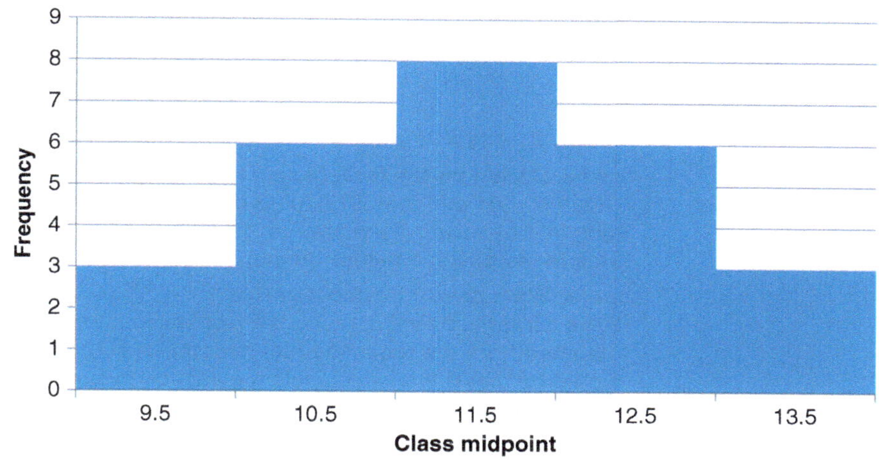

Histogram

Modified engine

Steam	Leaf
10	8 9
11	4 5 5 7 8
12	0 0 1 2 3 5 5 7 8
13	1 1 2 4 6 8
14	0 0 4 6

Stem and leaf plot

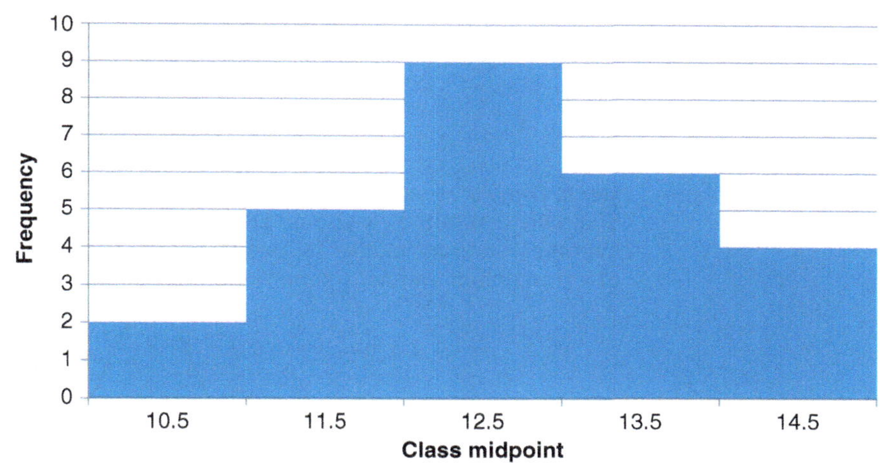

Histogram

From the figures it can be concluded that the data sets do not have very different central values and variability, and their distribution shapes look fairly normally distributed. Thus, formula 10.1 can be used for hypothesis testing.

STEP 1. Set up H_0 and H_a

This test is one-tailed because Sue wants to establish that her engine is superior to the original engine. Let μ_m be the mean of the modified engine and μ_o be the mean of the original engine in kilometres per litre. Then the null and alternative hypotheses would be:

$$H_0: \mu_m - \mu_o \leq 0$$
$$H_a: \mu_m - \mu_o > 0$$

STEP 2. Decide on the type of test

The test statistic is:

$$z = \frac{(\bar{x}_m - \bar{x}_o) - (\mu_m - \mu_o)}{\sqrt{\frac{\sigma_m^2}{n_m} + \frac{\sigma_o^2}{n_o}}}$$

where $\bar{x}_m$ and $\bar{x}_o$ are the sample means for the modified and original engines, respectively.

STEP 3. Decide on the level of significance, α, and determine the critical value(s) and region(s)

Given $\alpha = .01$ and that .01 ($= \alpha$) is contained in the right tail, determine the critical value from table A.4 by locating the area of .49 in the body of the table; therefore, $z_{.01} = 2.33$. (The total area in the positive half of the normal curve is .50.)

STEP 4. Write down the decision rule

If the computed z value using the test statistic formula exceeds the critical z value of 2.33 as obtained from the table, the null hypothesis should be rejected. Otherwise, the conclusion would be that there is insufficient evidence to support Sue's claim.

STEP 5. Select a random sample and do relevant calculations

From the information provided, the following values can be obtained.

Modified engine	Original engine
$\bar{x}_m = 12.61$	$\bar{x}_o = 11.53$
$\sigma_m = 1.0345$	$\sigma_o = 1.1072$
$n_m = 26$	$n_o = 26$

Solving for z gives:

$$z = \frac{(12.61 - 11.53) - (0)}{\sqrt{\frac{1.0345^2}{26} + \frac{1.1072^2}{26}}} = 3.65$$

STEP 6. Draw a conclusion

Since the computed z value of 3.65 is greater than the critical z value of 2.33, we reject the null hypothesis and conclude that Sue Taylor has valid reason to claim that the fuel consumption of her modified engine is superior to the original engine.

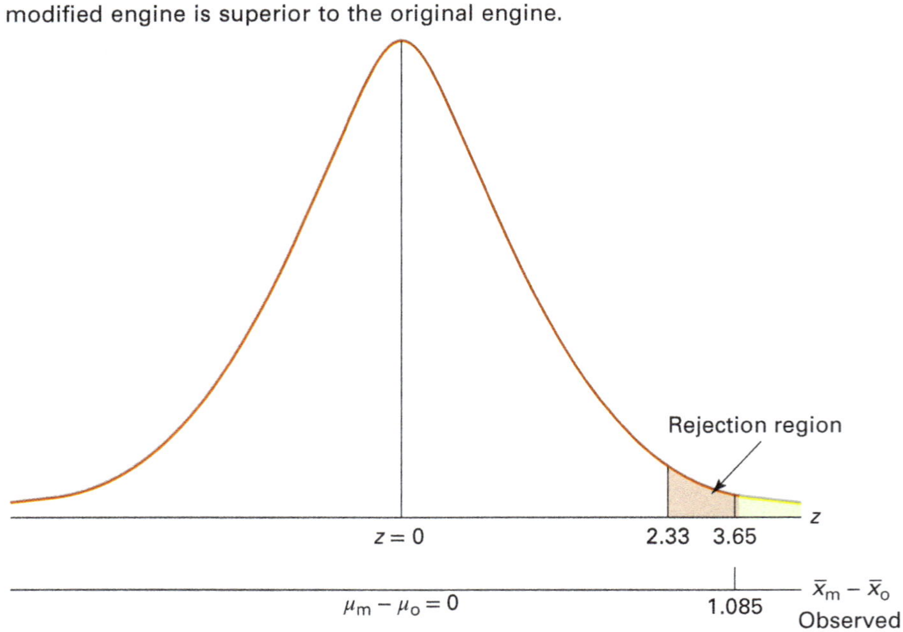

If the null hypothesis is true, the probability of obtaining an observed z value of 3.65 by chance is virtually zero (only .000 13 by Excel function NORM.DIST). Using the p-value, the null hypothesis is rejected because the probability is .000 13, or less than $\alpha = .01$.

If this problem is solved using the critical value method, what critical value of the difference between the two means would have to be exceeded to reject the null hypothesis for a table z value of 2.33? The answer is:

$$(\bar{x}_m - \bar{x}_o)_{crit} = (\mu_m - \mu_o) + z_{crit}\sqrt{\frac{\sigma_m^2}{n_m} + \frac{\sigma_o^2}{n_o}}$$

$$= 0 + 2.33(0.29717) = 0.6924$$

The difference between sample means would need to be at least 0.6924 to reject the null hypothesis. The actual sample difference in this problem was 1.085(12.612 − 11.527), which is considerably larger than the critical value of difference. Thus, with the critical value method also, the null hypothesis is rejected.

USING EXCEL

z-test: two-sample for means

DP10-01

1. Access DP10-01.xls from the student website.
2. From the Data tab, select Data Analysis.
3. In the Data Analysis dialogue box, select z-Test: Two Sample for Means and click OK.
4. In the z-Test: Two Sample for Means dialogue box:
   a. enter the data range for the modified engine performance into the Variable 1 Range field
   b. enter the data range for the original engine performance into the Variable 2 Range field
   c. enter 0 in the Hypothesized Mean Difference field
   d. enter the variance of the modified engine performance into the Variable 1 Variance (known) field. (Note that the standard deviations need to be squared to obtain the variances.)
   e. enter the variance of the original engine performance into the Variable 2 Variance (known) field
   f. check the Labels box if you have included the column titles in the data ranges. Otherwise, leave it unchecked.
   g. enter 0.01 in the Alpha field
   h. choose an output option or leave the default option New Worksheet Ply:

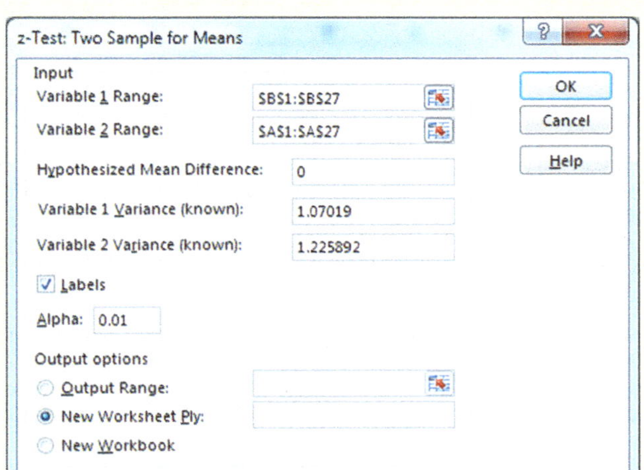

   i. click OK.

The Excel output follows.

	A	B	C
1	*z*-Test: Two Sample for Means		
2		*Modified*	*Original*
3	Mean	12.6115385	11.52692
4	Known Variance	1.07019	1.225892
5	Observations	26	26
6	Hypothesized Mean Difference	0	
7	Z	3.64979723	
8	P(Z<=z) one-tail	0.00013122	
9	*z* Critical one-tail	2.32634787	
10	P(Z<=z) two-tail	0.00026245	
11	*z* Critical two-tail	2.5758293	

The value of the test statistic is the same as we calculated manually earlier. Note that Excel gives the *p*-values and critical values of both one-tailed and two-tailed tests. It is up to you to determine which of these is appropriate. In this case we are performing a one-tailed test.

Confidence intervals

Sometimes it is valuable to be able to estimate the upper and lower bounds of the difference between the means of two populations. By how much do two populations differ in size, weight or age? By how much do two products differ in effectiveness? Do two different methods produce different mean results? The answers to these questions are often difficult to obtain through census techniques. The alternative is to take a random sample from each of the two populations and study the difference between the sample means.

Algebraically, formula 10.1 can be manipulated, considering a two-tailed situation, to produce formula 10.2, which constructs the confidence intervals for the difference between two population means.

Confidence interval to estimate $\mu_1 - \mu_2$
(10.2)

$$(\bar{x}_1 - \bar{x}_2) - z\sqrt{\frac{\sigma_1^2}{n_1} + \frac{\sigma_2^2}{n_2}} \le \mu_1 - \mu_2 \le (\bar{x}_1 - \bar{x}_2) + z\sqrt{\frac{\sigma_1^2}{n_1} + \frac{\sigma_2^2}{n_2}}$$

Demonstration problem 10.1 on fuel efficiency can be used to construct a 98% confidence interval on the difference between fuel consumption of the original and modified Revel cars. A 98% confidence interval implies that there is a 1% area in each tail of the normal curve. The corresponding z value is 2.33. Substituting all of the relevant information in formula 10.2, we get:

$$(12.612 - 11.527) - 2.33\sqrt{\frac{1.0345^2}{26} + \frac{1.1072^2}{26}} \le (\mu_m - \mu_o)$$

$$\le (12.612 - 11.527) + 2.33\sqrt{\frac{1.0345^2}{26} + \frac{1.1072^2}{26}}$$

$$1.085 - 2.33(0.2972) \le \mu_m - \mu_o \le 1.085 + 2.33(0.2972)$$

$$0.392 \le \mu_m - \mu_o \le 1.777$$

Thus the confidence interval is (0.392, 1.777).

There is a 98% level of confidence that the actual difference between the population means of the fuel consumption of the original and modified engine Revel cars is between 0.392 km/L and 1.777 km/L. That is, the difference could be as little as 0.392 km/L or as great as 1.777 km/L. The point estimate for the difference between the means is 1.085 km/L. Note that a zero difference between the population means of these two groups is unlikely, because zero is not in the 98% confidence interval. Therefore, we can conclude that the difference is significant, which is the same inference we have made using the hypothesis-testing technique but with an entirely different approach. In most circumstances the application of either of the techniques is adequate, and there is seldom any need to apply both techniques. However, both techniques remain popular in different areas of statistical analysis. The prominent British statistician Sir Ronald Fisher popularised hypothesis testing, whereas an eminent American statistician George Snedecor popularised confidence interval construction. These days, where there is a preconceived notion such as 'Smoking during pregnancy reduces a child's IQ', hypothesis testing is usually done; where there is no preconceived notion, such as in opinion polls, a confidence interval is constructed.

DEMONSTRATION PROBLEM 10.2

PROBLEM: A motoring organisation wants to determine the difference between the fuel economy of cars using regular unleaded petrol and cars using premium unleaded petrol. The organisation's researchers tested a fleet of 100 cars on one tank of petrol each. Fifty of the cars were filled with regular unleaded petrol and 50 were filled with premium unleaded petrol. The sample average for the regular group was 7.59 litres per 100 kilometres. The sample average for the premium group was 8.71 litres per 100 kilometres. Assume that the population standard deviation of the regular unleaded petrol group is 1.22 litres per 100 kilometres and that the population standard deviation of the premium unleaded petrol group is 1.06 litres per 100 kilometres. Construct a 95% confidence interval to estimate the difference in the mean fuel economy between the cars using regular unleaded petrol (r) and the cars using premium unleaded petrol (p).

Regular	Premium
$n_r = 50$	$n_p = 50$
$\bar{x}_r = 7.59$	$\bar{x}_p = 8.71$
$\sigma_r = 1.22$	$\sigma_p = 1.06$

SOLUTION: The z value for a 95% confidence interval is 1.96 from table A.4.

Based on this information, the confidence interval is:

$$(7.59 - 8.71) - 1.96\sqrt{\frac{1.22^2}{50} + \frac{1.06^2}{50}} \le \mu_1 - \mu_2 \le (7.59 - 8.71) + 1.96\sqrt{\frac{1.22^2}{50} + \frac{1.06^2}{50}}$$

$$-1.12 - 0.45 \le \mu_1 - \mu_2 \le -1.12 + 0.45$$

$$-1.57 \le \mu_1 - \mu_2 \le -0.67$$

We are 95% confident that the actual difference in mean fuel economy between the two types of petrol is between −1.57 litres per 100 kilometres and −0.67 litres per 100 kilometres. The lower limit is −1.57 and the upper limit is −0.67. The point estimate is −1.12 litres per 100 kilometres.

Designating one group as group 1 and another group as group 2 is an arbitrary decision. If the two groups in demonstration problem 10.2 were reversed, the confidence interval would be the same, but the signs would be reversed and the inequalities would be switched. Thus the researcher must interpret the confidence interval in light of the sample information. For the confidence interval in demonstration problem 10.2, the population difference in mean fuel economy between regular and premium petrol could be as much as −1.57. This result means that the premium petrol could average 1.57 litres per 100 kilometres more than regular petrol. The other side of the interval shows that, on the basis of the sample information, the difference in favour of premium petrol could be as little as 0.67 litres per 100 kilometres.

If the confidence interval were being used to test the hypothesis that there is a difference in the average number of litres per 100 kilometres between regular and premium petrol, the interval would tell us to reject the null hypothesis because the interval does not contain zero. When both ends of a confidence interval have the same sign, zero is not in the interval. In demonstration problem 10.2, the interval signs are both negative. We are 95% confident that the true difference between population means is negative. Hence, we are 95% confident that there is a non-zero difference between means. For such a test, $\alpha = 1 - .95 = .05$. If the signs of the limits of confidence interval for the difference between the sample means are different, the interval includes zero, and finding no significant difference in population means is possible.

PRACTICE PROBLEMS

Practising the calculations

10.1 Test the following hypotheses of the difference between population means by using the following data and the six-step process.

a. H_0: $\mu_1 - \mu_2 \geq 0$; H_a: $\mu_1 - \mu_2 < 0$; $\alpha = 0.10$

Sample 1	Sample 2
$\bar{x}_1 = 51.3$	$\bar{x}_2 = 53.2$
$\sigma_1^2 = 52$	$\sigma_2^2 = 60$
$n_1 = 31$	$n_2 = 32$

b. H_0: $\mu_1 - \mu_2 = 0$; H_a: $\mu_1 - \mu_2 \neq 0$; $\alpha = 0.02$

Sample 1	Sample 2
$\bar{x}_1 = 129$	$\bar{x}_2 = 153$
$\sigma_1^2 = 108$	$\sigma_2^2 = 124$
$n_1 = 32$	$n_2 = 36$

c. H_0: $\mu_1 - \mu_2 \leq 0$; H_a: $\mu_1 - \mu_2 > 0$; $\alpha = 0.05$

Sample 1	Sample 2
$\bar{x}_1 = 47$	$\bar{x}_2 = 45$
$\sigma_1^2 = 16$	$\sigma_2^2 = 27$
$n_1 = 16$	$n_2 = 14$

d. H_0: $\mu_1 - \mu_2 \geq 0$; H_a: $\mu_1 - \mu_2 < 0$; $\alpha = 0.01$

Sample 1	Sample 2
$\bar{x}_1 = 28$	$\bar{x}_2 = 32$
$\sigma_1^2 = 36$	$\sigma_2^2 = 13$
$n_1 = 21$	$n_2 = 20$

e. H_0: $\mu_1 \leq \mu_2$; H_a: $\mu_1 > \mu_2$; $\alpha = 0.05$

Sample 1	Sample 2
$\bar{x}_1 = 85.24$	$\bar{x}_2 = 82.12$
$\sigma_1^2 = 90.51$	$\sigma_2^2 = 28.53$
$n_1 = 41$	$n_2 = 33$

10.2 Use the sample information provided below to construct the required confidence interval for the difference between the two population means.

a. a 90% confidence interval

Sample 1	Sample 2
$\bar{x}_1 = 106$	$\bar{x}_2 = 97$
$\sigma_1^2 = 111$	$\sigma_2^2 = 158$
$n_1 = 12$	$n_2 = 16$

b. a 95% confidence interval

Sample 1	Sample 2
$\bar{x}_1 = 136$	$\bar{x}_2 = 148$
$\sigma_1^2 = 900$	$\sigma_2^2 = 1060$
$n_1 = 102$	$n_2 = 133$

c. a 99% confidence interval

Sample 1	Sample 2
$\bar{x}_1 = 47$	$\bar{x}_2 = 45$
$\sigma_1^2 = 56$	$\sigma_2^2 = 67$
$n_1 = 19$	$n_2 = 17$

d. an 80% confidence interval

Sample 1	Sample 2
$\bar{x}_1 = 2\,208$	$\bar{x}_2 = 3\,127$
$\sigma_1^2 = 43036$	$\sigma_2^2 = 51300$
$n_1 = 71$	$n_2 = 112$

e. a 98% confidence interval

Sample 1	Sample 2
$\bar{x}_1 = 5.24$	$\bar{x}_2 = 3.12$
$\sigma_1^2 = 9.51$	$\sigma_2^2 = 8.53$
$n_1 = 11$	$n_2 = 13$

P10-03 **10.3** Examine the following data.

a. Determine the population means and variances.

b. Use the data to test the following hypotheses ($\alpha = .05$).

$$H_0: \mu_1 - \mu_2 = 0$$
$$H_a: \mu_1 - \mu_2 \neq 0$$

Population 1			Population 2		
54	79	63	99	72	45
95	48	57	68	71	63
90	88	80	78	85	82
88	87	91	90	80	76
81	84	84	77	75	79
88	90	91	82	83	88
89	95	97	80	90	74
88	83	94	81	75	76
81	83	88	83	88	77
87	87	93	86	90	75
88	84	83	80	80	74
95	93	97	89	84	79

c. Use the critical value method to find the critical difference between the mean values required to reject the null hypothesis.

d. What is the *p*-value for this problem?

Testing your understanding

P10-04 **10.4** A survey was conducted to determine why people go to trade shows. The respondents were asked to rate a series of reasons on a scale from 1 to 5, with 1 representing little importance and 5 representing great importance. One of the reasons suggested was general curiosity. The following responses for 50 people from the computers/electronics industry and 50 people from the food/beverage industry were recorded. Use these data and $\alpha = .01$ to determine whether there is a significant difference between people in these two industries on this question. Assume the variance for the computer/electronics population is 1.0188 and the variance for the food/beverage population is 0.9180.

Computers/electronics					Food/beverage				
1	2	1	3	2	3	3	2	4	3
0	3	3	2	1	4	5	2	4	3
3	3	1	2	2	3	2	3	2	3
3	2	2	2	2	4	3	3	3	3
1	2	3	2	1	2	4	2	3	3
1	1	3	3	2	2	4	4	4	4
2	1	4	1	4	3	5	3	3	2
2	3	0	1	0	2	0	2	2	5
3	3	2	2	3	4	3	3	2	3
2	1	0	2	3	4	3	3	3	2

P10-05 **10.5** The website www.domain.com.au lists houses for sale in Australia. In August 2014, the asking prices of established houses with 4 bedrooms, 2 bathrooms and 2 car spaces for sale in Bundaberg (central and adjoining suburbs), Queensland 4670 and in Gympie, Queensland 4570 are given in the accompanying table (in thousands of dollars). All listings have been accounted for and duplicate listings by different real estate agents have been removed; therefore, the data constitute the population. Listings without a proper address or asking price have been excluded. Assuming normality:

a. test the hypothesis that the mean house prices in the two Queensland cities are not significantly different. Use $\alpha = .05$.

b. construct a 95% confidence interval for the difference between mean house prices in Bundaberg and Gympie.

Bundaberg house prices ($000)									
442	389	365	349	279	749	585	495	449	439
475	359	309	299	315	300				

Gympie house prices ($000)									
312	399	379	340	339	334	349	334	370	329
299	339	348	295	329	305	289			

10.6 A survey shows that the average insurance cost to a company per employee per hour is $1.84 for managers and $1.99 for professional specialty workers. Suppose these figures were obtained from 35 managers and 41 professional specialty workers and that their respective population standard deviations are $0.38 and $0.51. Calculate a 98% confidence interval to estimate the difference between the mean hourly insurance costs per employee for these two groups.

10.7 A company's auditor believes the per diem cost in Darwin rose significantly between 2005 and 2012. To test this belief, the auditor samples 51 business trips from the company's records for 2005; the sample average was $190 per day, with a population standard deviation of $18.50. The auditor selects a second random sample of 47 business trips from the company's records for 2012; the sample average was $198 per day, with a population standard deviation of $15.60. If he uses a risk of committing a Type I error of .01, does the auditor find that the per diem average expense in Darwin has gone up significantly?

P10-08 **10.8** Suppose a market analyst wants to determine the difference between the average prices of a two-litre bottle of full-cream milk in Melbourne and Sydney. To do so, he takes a telephone survey of 31 randomly selected consumers in Melbourne. He first asks whether they have purchased a two-litre bottle of full-cream milk during the past 2 weeks. If they say no, he continues to select consumers until he selects $n = 31$ people who say yes. If they say yes, he asks them how much they paid for the milk. The analyst undertakes a similar survey in Sydney with 31 respondents. Using the resulting sample information that follows, compute a 99% confidence interval to estimate the difference between the mean prices of two litres of full-cream milk in the two cities. Assume the population variance for Melbourne is 0.03, and the population variance for Sydney is 0.015.

Melbourne ($)			Sydney ($)		
3.55	3.36	3.43	3.25	3.40	3.39
3.67	3.54	3.43	3.30	3.33	3.40
3.50	3.54	3.38	3.19	3.29	3.23
3.61	3.80	3.49	3.41	3.18	3.29
4.10	3.61	3.57	3.39	3.59	3.53
3.86	3.56	3.71	3.26	3.38	3.19
3.50	3.64	3.97	3.19	3.25	3.45
3.47	3.72	3.65	3.42	3.61	3.33
3.76	3.73	3.80	3.60	3.25	3.51
3.65	3.83	3.69	3.38	3.29	3.36
3.71			3.44		

10.9 Employee suggestions can provide useful and insightful ideas for management. Some companies solicit and receive more employee suggestions than others, and company culture influences the use of employee suggestions. Suppose a study is conducted to determine whether there is a significant difference in the mean number of suggestions a month per employee between company A and company B. The study shows that the average number of suggestions per month is 5.8 at company A and 5.0 at company B. Suppose these figures were obtained from random samples of 36 and 45 employees, respectively. If the population standard deviations of suggestions per employee are 1.7 and 1.4 for company A and company B, respectively, is there a significant difference between the population means? Use $\alpha = .05$.

10.2 Hypothesis testing and confidence intervals for the difference between two means (*t* statistic, population variances unknown)

The techniques presented in section 10.1 are for use whenever the population variances are known. That was more of a theoretical exercise to develop your basic understanding, rather than a realistic scenario. If we do not know the means of two populations, it is only on very rare occasions that we will know the variances of the two populations. On many occasions, statisticians test hypotheses or construct confidence intervals about the difference between two population means when the population variances are not known. If the population variances are not known, the z methodology is not appropriate. This section presents methodology for handling the situation when the population variances are unknown.

Hypothesis testing

The hypothesis test presented in this section is a test that compares the means of two samples to determine whether there is a difference between the population means of the two samples. This technique is used whenever the population variances are unknown (and hence the sample variances must be used) and the four assumptions stated in the introduction of this chapter hold. In section 10.1, the difference between means of large samples was analysed using formula 10.1:

$$z = \frac{(\bar{x}_1 - \bar{x}_2) - (\mu_1 - \mu_2)}{\sqrt{\frac{\sigma_1^2}{n_1} + \frac{\sigma_2^2}{n_2}}}$$

If $\sigma_1^2 = \sigma_2^2 = \sigma^2$, formula 10.1 algebraically reduces to:

$$z = \frac{(\bar{x}_1 - \bar{x}_2) - (\mu_1 - \mu_2)}{\sigma\sqrt{\frac{1}{n_1} + \frac{1}{n_2}}}$$

If the two population variances can be assumed to be nearly equal, then a better estimate would be a weighted average of the two, which is called a pooled sample standard deviation:

$$\text{Estimate of } \sigma = s_p = \sqrt{\frac{s_1^2(n_1 - 1) + s_2^2(n_2 - 1)}{n_1 + n_2 - 2}}$$

s_p^2 is the weighted average (by degrees of freedom) of the two sample variances, s_1^2 and s_2^2. Substituting the above expression for the standard deviation in the denominator and changing z to t produces formula 10.3 for testing the difference between means.

***t* formula to test the difference between means assuming $\sigma_1^2 = \sigma_2^2$**
(10.3)

$$t = \frac{(\bar{x}_1 - \bar{x}_2) - (\mu_1 - \mu_2)}{s_p\sqrt{\frac{1}{n_1} + \frac{1}{n_2}}}$$

where:

$$s_p = \sqrt{\frac{s_1^2(n_1 - 1) + s_2^2(n_2 - 1)}{n_1 + n_2 - 2}}$$

$$\text{df} = n_1 + n_2 - 2$$

A t distribution is similar to a normal distribution except that it is a little flatter or more spread out (has thicker tails), which should obviously be the case because we are introducing more uncertainty into the problem. Formula 10.3 is constructed by assuming that the two population variances, σ_1^2 and σ_2^2, are equal. However, the assumptions of normality and equal variances are not strict requirements. The t test is robust to moderate departures of the assumptions of normality and equal variances.

When you cannot assume that the distributions are approximately normal and the variances are approximately equal, you have two choices. You can either use a normalising transformation or use a nonparametric procedure. A normalising transformation frequently used in statistics is the logarithmic transformation. We often come across data sets that are skewed to the right; a logarithmic transformation can make those data sets approximately normal. In the logarithmic transformation, an original value of data is replaced by the logarithm of that value.

When a suitable normalising transformation cannot be found, the only available option is to use a nonparametric procedure. A nonparametric procedure does not use any parameter such as mean or variance, and, therefore, the question of normality or equal variance does not arise.

Since the assumptions of approximately normal and nearly equal variances are quite critical, especially with small sample sizes, for the techniques discussed in this chapter, it is imperative to know how to test for these in a given data set. The first approach should always be a visual inspection, which we have described in demonstration problem 10.1. Another tool frequently used for visual inspection is the box and whisker plot. If a distribution is approximately normal, the median in the box and whisker plot should be near the middle, the whiskers should be nearly equal, and the interquartile range should be roughly 1.33 times the standard deviation.

However, the most popular test for normality is the **normal probability plot**. Statistical packages such as SPSS and SAS have menus that routinely construct the normal probability plot. The construction of a normal probability plot by hand is cumbersome; nevertheless, we will explain here how the graph is produced to give you an understanding of what the statistical software is doing.

We revisit demonstration problem 10.1 for the modified engine data to explain the procedure in the following steps.

1. Rank the data from the smallest to the largest value, giving the smallest observation rank 1 and the largest observation rank, n, which is 26 in this case.
2. For each rank, $i = 1, \ldots, n$, find the percentile of order $\frac{i}{(n+1)}$. For example with the sample size $n = 26$, these values will be $\frac{1}{(26+1)} = 0.037, \frac{2}{(26+1)} = 0.074, \ldots, \frac{26}{(26+1)} = 0.963$ (up to 3 decimal places).
3. Find the standard normal distribution values, z_i, which correspond to the cumulative area of these values. For example, $z_{.037} = -1.787$, $z_{.074} = -1.447, \ldots, z_{.963} = 1.787$.
4. Produce a scatter plot of the ordered data values against the standardised normal scores. Figure 10.3 shows the normal probability plot for the given data. If the plotted points fall roughly along a straight line, the data can be assumed to be approximately normally distributed, which is the case with the given data. If the plotted points deviate too far from a straight line alignment, the data cannot be assumed to be normally distributed.

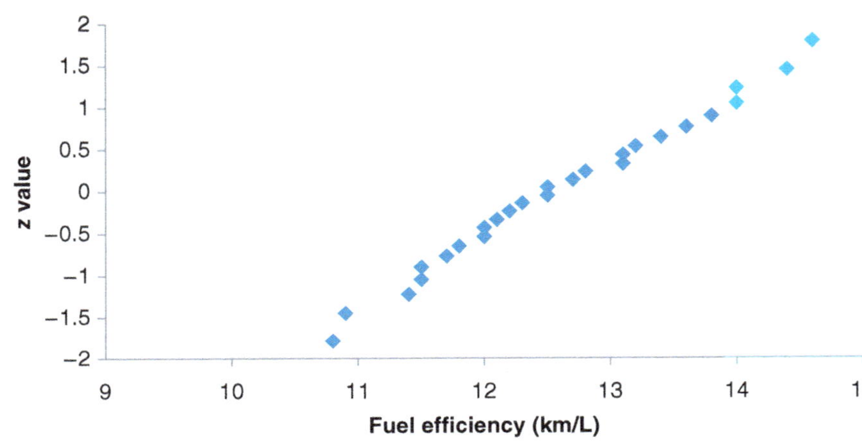

FIGURE 10.3 Normal probability plot of the performance of the modified car engine

The following shows hypothesis testing of the problem in demonstration problem 10.1 assuming that the population variances are unknown.

STEP 1. Set up H_0 and H_a

The test is one-tailed because Sue wants to show that her engine is superior to the original engine. Let μ_m be the mean of the modified engine and μ_o be the mean of the original engine in kilometres per litre. Then the null and alternative hypotheses are:

$$H_0\colon \mu_m - \mu_o \le 0$$
$$H_a\colon \mu_m - \mu_o > 0$$

STEP 2. Decide on the type of test

The test statistic is:

$$t = \frac{(\bar{x}_m - \bar{x}_o) - (\mu_m - \mu_o)}{s_p\sqrt{\frac{1}{n_m} + \frac{1}{n_o}}}$$

where

$$s_p = \sqrt{\frac{s_m^2(n_m - 1) + s_o^2(n_o - 1)}{n_m + n_o - 2}}$$

$\bar{x}_m$ and s_m, $\bar{x}_o$ and s_o are the sample mean and standard deviation of the modified and original engines, respectively, and the degrees of freedom (df) of the t distribution are $n_m + n_o - 2$.

STEP 3. Decide on the level of significance, α, and determine the critical value(s) and region(s)

Given $\alpha = .01$ and df = 50, the critical value from table A.6 is $t_{.01,\,50} = 2.403$.

STEP 4. Write down the decision rule

If the computed t value using the test statistic formula exceeds the critical t value of 2.403 as obtained from the table, the null hypothesis should be rejected. Otherwise, the conclusion would be that there is insufficient evidence to validate Sue's claim.

STEP 5. Select a random sample and do relevant calculations

From the data provided, the following values can be obtained.

Modified engine	Original engine
$\bar{x}_m = 12.61$	$\bar{x}_o = 11.53$
$s_m = 1.055$	$s_o = 1.129$
$n_m = 26$	$n_o = 26$

Solving for t gives:

$$s_p = \sqrt{\frac{1.055^2(26-1)+1.129^2(26-1)}{26+26-2}} = 1.0926$$

$$t = \frac{(12.61-11.53)-(0)}{1.0926\sqrt{\frac{1}{26}+\frac{1}{26}}} = 3.579$$

STEP 6. Draw a conclusion

Since the computed t value of 3.579 is more extreme (greater than) the critical t value of 2.403, we reject the null hypothesis and conclude that Sue Taylor has valid reason to claim that her modified engine is superior to the original engine. The change we notice in this solution from the previous solution in demonstration problem 10.1 is that the critical value has increased due to more uncertainty, but the computed statistic has decreased a little because of higher standard deviations. The result is that the difference has narrowed.

To investigate how different sample sizes may affect the results, let us look at another example. Is there a difference in the way Chinese cultural values affect the purchasing strategies of industrial buyers in Taiwan and mainland China? A study by researchers at the National Chiao Tung University in Taiwan attempted to determine whether there is a significant difference in the purchasing strategies of industrial buyers between the two countries based on the cultural dimension labelled 'integration'. Integration is defined as being in harmony with one's self, family and associates. For the study, 46 Taiwanese buyers and 26 mainland Chinese buyers were contacted and interviewed. Buyers were asked to respond to 35 items using a 9-point scale with possible answers ranging from no importance (1) to extreme importance (9). The resulting statistics for the two groups are shown in table 10.2. Using $\alpha = .01$, the researchers want to determine whether there is a significant difference between buyers of the two countries based on integration.

TABLE 10.2 Sample statistics of Taiwanese and mainland Chinese buyers

Integration

Taiwanese buyers	Mainland Chinese buyers
$n_1 = 46$	$n_2 = 26$
$\bar{x}_1 = 5.42$	$\bar{x}_2 = 5.04$
$s_1^2 = (.58)^2 = .3364$	$s_2^2 = (.49)^2 = .2401$
$df = n_1 + n_2 - 2 = 46 + 26 - 2 = 70$	

STEP 1. Set up H_0 and H_a

If a two-tailed test is undertaken, the hypotheses are as follows.

$$H_0\colon \mu_1 - \mu_1 = 0$$
$$H_a\colon \mu_1 - \mu_2 \neq 0$$

STEP 2. Decide on the type of test

The appropriate statistical test is formula 10.3.

STEP 3. Decide on the level of significance, α, and determine the critical value(s) and region(s)

The sample sizes are 46 and 26. Thus, there are 70 degrees of freedom (46 + 26 − 2). With these degrees of freedom and, given $\alpha = .01$, $\alpha/2 = .005$, a critical table t value can be determined.

$$t_{.005,\,70} = 2.648$$

STEP 4. Write down the decision rule

If the estimated t value is either less than −2.648 or greater than 2.648, we reject the null hypothesis and conclude that there is a significant difference. Otherwise, we do not reject the null hypothesis and conclude that there is insufficient evidence to infer that there is a difference.

STEP 5. Select a random sample and do relevant calculations

The observed t value can be estimated as follows with the data provided in table 10.2:

$$s_p = \sqrt{\frac{.3364 \times 45 + .2401 \times 25}{46 + 26 - 2}} = 0.5496$$

$$t = \frac{(5.42 - 5.04) - (0)}{0.5496\sqrt{\frac{1}{46} + \frac{1}{26}}} = 2.82$$

STEP 6. Draw a conclusion

Since the observed value of $t = 2.82$ is greater than the critical table value of $t = 2.648$, the decision is to reject the null hypothesis. Thus we can conclude that Taiwan industrial buyers scored significantly higher than mainland China industrial buyers based on integration.

Figure 10.4 shows the critical t values, the rejection regions, the observed t value and the difference between the raw means. A larger sample size lowers the value of the denominator thus increasing the magnitude of the observed t value.

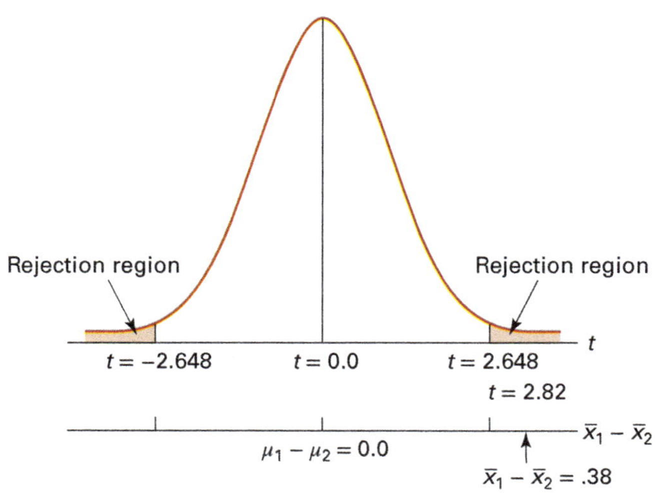

FIGURE 10.4 t values for the cultural values example

In a test of this sort, which group is group 1 and which is group 2 is an arbitrary decision. If the two samples had been designated in reverse, the observed t value would have been $t = -2.82$ (same magnitude but different sign), and the decision would have been the same.

DEMONSTRATION PROBLEM 10.3

PROBLEM: At the Allcutt Manufacturing Company, an application of the test of the difference between small sample means arises. New employees are expected to attend a three-day seminar to learn about the company. At the end of the seminar, they are tested to measure their knowledge about the company. The traditional training method has been a lecture and a question-and-answer session. Management decided to experiment with a different training procedure, which processes new employees in two days by using DVDs and having no question-and-answer session. If this procedure works, it could save the company thousands of dollars over a period of several years. However, there is some concern about the effectiveness of the two-day method, and company managers would like to know whether there is any difference between the effectiveness of the two training methods.

To test the difference between the two methods, the managers randomly select one group of 15 newly hired employees to take the three-day seminar (method A) and a second group of 12 new employees for the two-day DVD method (method B). The test scores of the two groups are shown in the following table.

Training method A					Training method B			
56	50	52	44	52	59	54	55	65
47	47	53	45	48	52	57	64	53
42	51	42	43	44	53	56	53	57

Using $\alpha = .05$, determine whether there is a significant difference between the mean scores of the two groups. Assume that the scores for this test are normally distributed and that the population variances are approximately equal.

SOLUTION:

STEP 1. Set up H_0 and H_a

The test is two-tailed. The null and alternative hypotheses for this test are:

$$H_0: \mu_1 - \mu_2 = 0$$
$$H_a: \mu_1 - \mu_2 \neq 0$$

STEP 2. Decide on the type of test

The statistical test to be used is formula 10.3.

STEP 3. Decide on the level of significance, α, and determine the critical value(s) and region(s)

The degrees of freedom are 25 (15 + 12 – 2 = 25). The *t* table requires an alpha value for one tail only. Because α = .05. and it is a two-tailed test, alpha should be divided evenly into .025 in each tail to obtain the table *t* value: $t_{.025,\,25} = \pm 2.060$ from table A.6.

STEP 4. Write down the decision rule

If the computed *t* value is less than –2.060 or greater than 2.060, the null hypothesis should be rejected. Otherwise, the conclusion would be that there is insufficient evidence to infer that the effectiveness of the two training methods is significantly different.

STEP 5. Select a random sample and do relevant calculations

From the data provided we can calculate the sample statistics. The sample means and variances are shown in the following table.

Training method A	Training method B
$\bar{x}_1 = 47.73$	$\bar{x}_2 = 56.5$
$s_1^2 = 19.495$	$s_2^2 = 18.273$
$n_1 = 15$	$n_1 = 12$

$$s_p = \sqrt{\frac{19.495 \times 14 + 18.273 \times 11}{15 + 12 - 2}} = 4.354$$

$$t = \frac{(47.73 - 56.50) - (0)}{4.354\sqrt{\frac{1}{15} + \frac{1}{12}}} = -5.20$$

STEP 6. Draw a conclusion

Because the observed value, $t = -5.20$, is less than the lower critical table value, $t = -2.06$, the observed value of *t* is in the rejection region. The graph overleaf shows the critical areas, the observed t value and the decision for this test. Since the computed t value is –5.20, it is enough to cause the managers of the Allcutt Manufacturing Company to reject the null hypothesis. Their conclusion would be that there is a significant difference between the effectiveness of the training methods. Upon examining the sample means, it can be seen that method B (the two-day DVD method) produced an average score that was more than eight points higher than that for the group trained with method A.

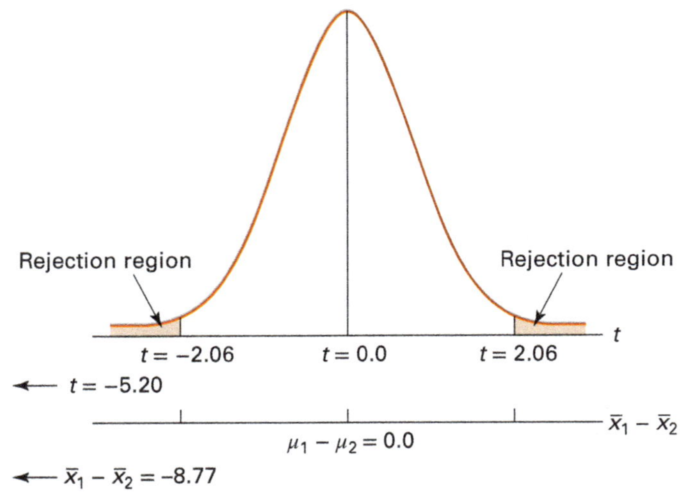

USING EXCEL

t-test: two-sample assuming equal variances

DP10-03

Access DP10-03.xls from the student website. Follow steps 2 to 4 used for DP10-01.xls previously except that, in the Data Analysis dialogue box, select *t*-Test: Two-Sample Assuming Equal Variances, and enter 0.05 in the Alpha field, as shown in the screenshot below.

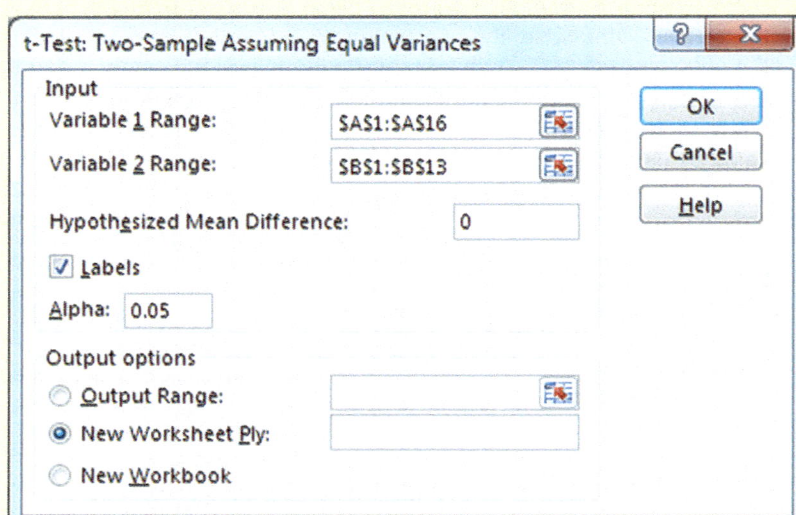

The Excel output follows. Note that the estimate of the pooled variance and the corresponding degrees of freedom are given, as well as one- and two-tailed p-values and critical values.

	A	B	C
1	*t*-Test: Two-Sample Assuming Equal Variances		
2			
3		*Method A*	*Method B*
4	Mean	47.733333	56.5
5	Variance	19.495238	18.27273
6	Observations	15	12
7	Pooled Variance	18.957333	
8	Hypothesized Mean Difference	0	
9	df	25	
10	t Stat	−5.1987657	
11	P(T<=t) one-tail	0.0000112	
12	t Critical one-tail	1.7081407	
13	P(T<=t) two-tail	0.0000223	
14	t Critical two-tail	2.0595385	

Confidence intervals

A confidence interval formula can be derived to estimate the difference between population means for independent samples when the population variances are unknown. However, the scope of this section is restricted to the construction of confidence intervals, using formula 10.4, when approximately equal population variances and normally distributed populations can be assumed.

Confidence interval to estimate $\mu_1 - \mu_2$ assuming similar variances
(10.4)

$$(\bar{x}_1 - \bar{x}_2) - t \cdot s_p \sqrt{\frac{1}{n_1} + \frac{1}{n_2}} \le \mu_1 - \mu_2 \le (\bar{x}_1 - \bar{x}_2) + t \cdot s_p \sqrt{\frac{1}{n_1} + \frac{1}{n_2}}$$

where:

$$s_p = \sqrt{\frac{s_1^2(n_1 - 1) + s_2^2(n_2 - 1)}{n_1 + n_2 - 2}}$$

$$\text{df} = n_1 + n_2 - 2$$

One group of researchers set out to determine whether there is a difference between 'average citizens' and those who are 'phone survey respondents'. (*Note:* This is part of a much larger study. The results in this portion of the study are about the same as those of the actual study except that the sample sizes were 500 to 600.) Their study was based on a well-known personality survey that attempted to assess the personality profile of both average citizens and phone survey respondents. Suppose they sampled nine phone survey respondents and 10 average citizens in this survey and obtained results for one personality factor, conscientiousness, which are displayed in table 10.3 (overleaf).

The table t value for a 99% level of confidence and 17 degrees of freedom is $t_{.005,\,17} = 2.898$. The confidence interval is:

$$(37.09 - 34.99) \pm 2.898\sqrt{\frac{(1.727)^2(8) + (1.253)^2(9)}{9 + 10 - 2}}\sqrt{\frac{1}{9} + \frac{1}{10}}$$

$$2.10 \pm 1.99$$

$$0.11 \le \mu_1 - \mu_2 \le 4.09$$

TABLE 10.3 Conscientiousness data on phone survey respondents and average citizens

Phone survey respondents	Average citizens
35.38	35.03
37.06	33.90
37.74	34.56
36.97	36.24
37.84	34.59
37.50	34.95
40.75	33.30
35.31	34.73
35.30	34.79
	37.83
$n_1 = 9$	$n_2 = 10$
$s_1 = 1.727$	$s_2 = 1.253$
df = 9 + 10 − 2 = 17	

The researchers are 99% confident that the true difference in population mean personality scores for conscientiousness between phone survey respondents and average citizens is between 0.11 and 4.09. Zero is not in this interval, so they can conclude that there is a significant difference between the average scores of the two groups. Higher scores indicate more conscientiousness. Therefore, it is possible to conclude from table 10.3 and this confidence interval that phone survey respondents are significantly more conscientious than average citizens. These results indicate that researchers should be careful in using phone survey results to reach conclusions about average citizens.

DEMONSTRATION PROBLEM 10.4

PROBLEM: A coffee manufacturer is interested in estimating the difference in the average daily coffee consumption between regular-coffee drinkers and decaffeinated-coffee drinkers. Its researcher randomly selects 13 regular-coffee drinkers and asks how many cups of coffee per day they drink. He randomly locates 15 decaffeinated-coffee drinkers and asks how many cups of coffee per day they drink. The average for the regular-coffee drinkers is 4.35 cups, with a standard deviation of 1.20 cups. The average for the decaffeinated-coffee drinkers is 6.84 cups, with a standard deviation of 1.42 cups. The researcher assumes, for each population, that the daily consumption is normally distributed, and he constructs a 95% confidence interval to estimate the difference between the averages of the two populations.

SOLUTION: The table t value for this problem is $t_{.025,\,26} = 2.056$. The confidence interval estimate is:

$$(4.35 - 6.84) \pm 2.056\sqrt{\frac{(1.20)^2(12) + (1.42)^2(14)}{13 + 15 - 2}}\sqrt{\frac{1}{13} + \frac{1}{15}}$$

$$-2.49 \pm 1.03$$

$$-3.52 \le \mu_1 - \mu_2 \le -1.46$$

The researcher is 95% confident that the difference in population average daily consumption of cups of coffee between regular- and decaffeinated-coffee drinkers is between 1.46 cups and 3.52 cups. The point estimate for the difference in population means is 2.49 cups, with an error of 1.03 cups. Since zero is not in the confidence interval, the results indicate a significant difference between the two groups.

PRACTICE PROBLEMS

Practising the calculations

10.10 Use the data given and the six-step process to test the following hypotheses. Assume that the variables are normally distributed and their variances are approximately equal.

a. H_0: $\mu_1 - \mu_2 \geq 0$; H_a: $\mu_1 - \mu_2 < 0$; $\alpha = 0.10$

Sample 1	Sample 2
$\bar{x}_1 = 77.9$	$\bar{x}_2 = 80.1$
$s_1^2 = 52.2$	$s_2^2 = 65$
$n_1 = 24$	$n_2 = 25$

b. H_0: $\mu_1 - \mu_2 = 0$; H_a: $\mu_1 - \mu_2 \neq 0$; $\alpha = 0.02$

Sample 1	Sample 2
$\bar{x}_1 = 129$	$\bar{x}_2 = 153$
$s_1^2 = 108$	$s_2^2 = 124$
$n_1 = 12$	$n_2 = 16$

c. H_0: $\mu_1 - \mu_2 \leq 0$; H_a: $\mu_1 - \mu_2 > 0$; $\alpha = 0.05$

Sample 1	Sample 2
$\bar{x}_1 = 47$	$\bar{x}_2 = 45$
$s_1^2 = 16$	$s_2^2 = 27$
$n_1 = 18$	$n_2 = 20$

d. H_0: $\mu_1 - \mu_2 \geq 0$; H_a: $\mu_1 - \mu_2 < 0$; $\alpha = 0.01$

Sample 1	Sample 2
$\bar{x}_1 = 28$	$\bar{x}_2 = 32$
$s_1^2 = 36$	$s_2^2 = 13$
$n_1 = 28$	$n_2 = 28$

e. H_0: $\mu_1 \leq \mu_2$; H_a: $\mu_1 > \mu_2$; $\alpha = 0.05$

Sample 1	Sample 2
$\bar{x}_1 = 85.24$	$\bar{x}_2 = 82.12$
$s_1^2 = 90.51$	$s_2^2 = 28.53$
$n_1 = 41$	$n_2 = 33$

10.11 Use the sample information provided below to construct the required confidence interval for the difference between the two population means.

a. a 90% confidence interval

Sample 1	Sample 2
$\bar{x}_1 = 105$	$\bar{x}_2 = 97$
$s_1^2 = 131$	$s_2^2 = 118$
$n_1 = 13$	$n_2 = 16$

b. a 95% confidence interval

Sample 1	Sample 2
$\bar{x}_1 = 131$	$\bar{x}_2 = 149$
$s_1^2 = 950$	$s_2^2 = 1050$
$n_1 = 102$	$n_2 = 133$

c. a 99% confidence interval

Sample 1	Sample 2
$\bar{x}_1 = 46$	$\bar{x}_2 = 52$
$s_1^2 = 56$	$s_2^2 = 67$
$n_1 = 19$	$n_2 = 17$

d. an 80% confidence interval

Sample 1	Sample 2
$\bar{x}_1 = 2200$	$\bar{x}_2 = 3120$
$s_1^2 = 43\,030$	$s_2^2 = 51\,300$
$n_1 = 77$	$n_2 = 112$

e. a 98% confidence interval

Sample 1	Sample 2
$\bar{x}_1 = 5.24$	$\bar{x}_2 = 3.12$
$s_1^2 = 9.51$	$s_2^2 = 8.53$
$n_1 = 11$	$n_2 = 13$

P10-12 **10.12** Suppose that for years it has been accepted that the mean of population 1 is the same as the mean of population 2, but that now population 1 is believed to have a higher mean than population 2. Letting $\alpha = .05$ and assuming the populations have equal variances and are normally distributed, use the following data to test this belief.

Sample 1		Sample 2	
43.6	45.7	40.1	36.4
44.0	49.1	42.2	42.3
45.2	45.6	43.1	38.8
40.8	46.5	37.5	43.3
48.3	45.0	41.0	40.2

P10-13 **10.13** Suppose you want to determine whether the average values for populations 1 and 2 are different, and you randomly gather the following data.

Sample 1						Sample 2					
2	10	7	8	2	5	10	12	8	7	9	11
9	1	8	0	2	8	9	8	9	10	11	10
11	2	4	5	3	9	11	10	7	8	10	10

a. Test your conjecture, using a probability of .01 of committing a Type I error. Assume the population variances are the same and x is normally distributed in both populations.

b. Use these data to construct a 98% confidence interval for the difference between the two population means.

Testing your understanding

P10–14 **10.14** An investor on the Australian Securities Exchange (ASX) wants to check if there is a significant difference in dividend yields between stocks which have market capitals of over one billion dollars and stocks which have market capitals in the range 100 million to one billion dollars. To check, the investor randomly picks samples of stocks and records their dividend yields for the financial year ending in 2014 as given in the following table. Each dividend yield is followed in parentheses by the corresponding ASX code of the company. Use $\alpha = .05$ to test if there is a significant difference between the mean dividend yields of these two groups of stocks. Assume normality.

Dividend yield (%) of stocks each with market capital of over one billion dollars

4.3 (WES)	1.1 (NCM)	3.4 (RIO)	5.9 (WPL)	3.8 (FMG)
4.6 (AMP)	2.2 (STO)	5.6 (SUN)	5.3 (CCL)	4.6 (ORI)
3.3 (BHP)	3.4 (IPL)	4.9 (CBA)	4.2 (LLC)	3.6 (SHL)
4.8 (MGR)	0.0 (QAN)	5.1 (TOL)	5.3 (SVW)	3.1 (JHX)

Dividend yield (%) of stocks each with market capital between 100 million and one billion dollars

2.3 (ARP)	0.0 (ISU)	3.0 (GWA)	3.8 (SIP)	5.1 (BKN)
2.2 (ENE)	8.65 (SDM)	7.2 (SXL)	0.0 (APN)	5.5 (MGX)
5.4 (MRM)	4.2 (MMS)	5.5 (UXC)	6.3 (HLO)	3.5 (CIN)
6.3 (WAM)	0.0 (EWC)	6.1 (CAB)	0.9 (FNP)	

10.15 Based on an indication that mean daily car-rental rates may be higher for Melbourne than for Sydney, a survey of eight car-rental companies in Melbourne is taken and the sample mean car-rental rate is \$47, with a standard deviation of \$3. Further, suppose a survey of nine car-rental companies in Sydney results in a sample mean of \$44 and a standard deviation of \$3. Use $\alpha = .01$ to test whether the average daily car-rental rates in Melbourne are significantly higher than those in Sydney. Assume car-rental rates are normally distributed and the population variances are equal.

10.16 What is the difference in average daily hotel room rates between Christchurch (C) and Auckland (A)? Suppose we want to estimate this difference by taking hotel rate samples in each city and using a 98% confidence level. The data for such a study follow. Use these data to produce a confidence interval estimate for the mean difference in hotel rates between the two cities. Assume the population variances are approximately equal and hotel rates in any given city are normally distributed.

Christchurch	Auckland
$n_C = 22$	$n_A = 20$
$\bar{x}_C = \$112$	$\bar{x}_A = \$122$
$s_C = \$11$	$s_A = \$12$

P10–17 **10.17** A study was made to compare the cost of supporting a family of four for a year in different foreign cities. The lifestyle of living at home on an annual income of \$75 000 was the standard against which living in foreign cities was compared. A comparable living standard in Kuala Lumpur and Bangkok was attained for about \$64 000. Suppose an executive wants to determine whether there is any difference between Kuala Lumpur and Bangkok in the average annual cost of supporting her family of four in the manner to which they are accustomed. She uses the following data, randomly gathered from 11 families in each city, and $\alpha = .01$ to test this difference. She assumes the annual cost is normally distributed and the population variances are equal. What does the executive find?

Kuala Lumpur ($)		Bangkok ($)	
69 000	65 000	65 000	62 500
64 500	69 000	64 000	63 000
67 500	71 000	66 000	64 500
64 500	68 500	64 900	63 500
66 700	67 500	62 000	62 400
68 000		60 500	

10.18 Use the data in problem 10.17 to construct a 95% confidence interval to estimate the difference in average annual costs between the two cities.

10.3 Statistical inferences about two populations with paired observations

In section 10.2, hypotheses were tested and confidence intervals constructed to determine the difference between two population means of independent samples — the relative order of data sets for the two populations did not matter. In this section, a method is presented to analyse data sets where the populations have distinct entities (or identities), and if an entity is randomly selected it has to be observed in each population. Observations in one population cannot be made independently of observations in the other population, and that is why it is sometimes referred to as **dependent samples** or related samples. Some researchers refer to this test as the matched-pairs test.

What are some types of situations in which the two samples being studied are related or dependent? Let's begin with the before-and-after study. Sometimes, as an experimental control mechanism, the same person or object is measured both before and after a treatment. Certainly, the after measurement is not independent of the before measurement because the measurements are taken on the same person or object in both cases. Table 10.4 gives data from a hypothetical study in which people were asked to rate a company before and after viewing a 30-minute DVD of the company. The before scores are one sample and the after scores are a second sample, but each pair of scores is related because the two measurements apply to the same person and are dependent on each other. The before scores and the after scores of the same persons should be compared, because individuals bring their biases about businesses and the company to the study. These individual biases affect both the before scores and the after scores in the same way because each pair of scores is measured on the same person.

TABLE 10.4 Rating of a company (on a scale from 0 to 50)

Individual	Before	After
1	32	39
2	11	15
3	21	35
4	17	13
5	30	41
6	38	39
7	14	22

Other examples of related measures include studies in which twins, siblings or spouses are matched and placed in two different groups. For example, a medical researcher may administer a drug to one of a set of identical twins and compare his/her developments/reactions with the other. If the men and women selected for the study are identical twins, a built-in relatedness between the measurements of the two groups — treatment group and control group — in the study is likely. Because of similar genetic make-up, their paired scores are more likely to capture the real effects than those of randomly chosen independent groups of men and women.

Hypothesis testing

To ensure the use of the proper hypothesis-testing techniques, the researcher must determine whether the two samples being studied are dependent or independent. The approach to analysing two related samples is different from the techniques used to analyse independent samples. Use of the techniques in section 10.2 to analyse related group data can result in a loss of power and an increase in Type II errors. This would occur because related group data would have less variance, and, since the variance term is in the denominator, the computed t value would have a higher magnitude than when using the techniques in section 10.2.

The matched-pairs test for related samples requires that the two samples be the same size and that the individual related scores be matched. Formula 10.5 is used to test hypotheses about dependent populations.

t formula to test the difference between two dependent populations (10.5)

$$t = \frac{\bar{d} - \mu_D}{\frac{s_d}{\sqrt{n}}}$$

$$\text{df} = n - 1$$

where

n = number of pairs
d = sample difference in pairs
μ_D = mean population difference
s_d = standard deviation of sample difference
$\bar{d}$ = mean sample difference

This **paired t test** for dependent measures uses the sample difference, d, between individual matched sample values instead of individual sample values as the basic measurement of analysis. Analysis of the d values effectively converts the problem from a two-sample problem to a single sample of differences, which is an adaptation of the single-sample means formula. This test uses the sample mean of differences, $\bar{d}$, and the standard deviation of differences, s_d, which can be computed by using formulas 10.6 and 10.7.

Formula for $\bar{d}$ (10.6)

$$\bar{d} = \frac{\Sigma d}{n}$$

Formula for s_d (10.7)

$$s_d = \sqrt{\frac{\Sigma(d - \bar{d})^2}{n-1}} = \sqrt{\frac{\Sigma d^2 - \frac{(\Sigma d)^2}{n}}{n-1}}$$

If the two populations are approximately normally distributed, the differences between the two populations are also approximately normally distributed.

Analysing data by this method involves calculating a t value with formula 10.5 and comparing it with a critical t value obtained from table A.6. The critical t value is obtained from the t distribution table in the usual way, with the exception that, in the degrees of freedom ($n - 1$), n is the number of matched pairs of scores.

Suppose a stock market investor is interested in determining whether there has been a significant difference in the price earnings ratio (P/E) for big companies in Australia in the last five years. To study this question, the investor randomly samples nine companies from the S&P/ASX200 and records the average P/E ratios for each of these companies during the financial years July 2008 to June 2009 and July 2013 to June 2014. The data are shown in table 10.5.

These data are related data because each P/E ratio value for 2008–09 has a corresponding P/E ratio value for 2013–14 for the same company. Because no prior information indicates whether P/E ratios have gone up or down, the hypothesis is two-tailed. Assume $\alpha = .01$.

TABLE 10.5 P/E ratios for nine randomly selected companies

Company name	ASX code	P/E ratio (2008–09)	P/E ratio (2013–14)
BHP Billiton Limited	BHP	13.3	14.0
Commonwealth Bank of Australia	CBA	12.3	15.2
National Australia Bank Limited	NAB	11.7	13.1
Telstra Corporation Limited	TLS	11.5	14.8
Woolworths Limited	WOW	17.6	18.5
Wesfarmers Limited	WES	13.0	20.6
Origin Energy Limited	ORG	25.7	20.9
CSL Limited	CSL	20.2	24.2
Brambles Limited	BXB	14.5	22.1

STEP 1. Set up H_0 and H_a

The test is two-tailed. The null and alternative hypotheses for this test are:

$$H_0\text{: } \mu_D = 0$$
$$H_a\text{: } \mu_D \neq 0$$

STEP 2. Decide on the type of test

$$t = \frac{\bar{d} - \mu_D}{\frac{s_d}{\sqrt{n}}}$$

The appropriate test statistic is:

STEP 3. Decide on the level of significance, α, and determine the critical value(s) and region(s)

Because $\alpha = .01$ and this test is two-tailed, $\frac{\alpha}{2} = .005$ is used to obtain the table t value. With nine pairs of data, $n = 9$, df $= n - 1 = 8$. The table t value is $t_{.005,\,8} = \pm 3.355$.

STEP 4. Write down the decision rule

If the observed test statistic is greater than 3.355 or less than −3.355, the null hypothesis will be rejected. Otherwise, the conclusion will be that there is insufficient evidence to support the suggestion that P/E ratios change annually.

STEP 5. Select a random sample and do relevant calculations

Table 10.6 shows the sample data and the calculations required to obtain the observed value of the test statistic, which is $t = -2.073$.

TABLE 10.6 Analysis of P/E ratio data

ASX code	P/E ratio (2008–09)	P/E ratio (2013–14)	d
BHP	13.3	14.0	−0.7
CBA	12.3	15.2	−2.9
NAB	11.7	13.1	−1.4
TLS	11.5	14.8	−3.3
WOW	17.6	18.5	−0.9
WES	13.0	20.6	−7.6
ORG	25.7	20.9	4.8
CSL	20.2	24.2	−4.0
BXB	14.5	22.1	−7.6

$\bar{d} = -2.622 \quad s_d = 3.795 \quad n = 9$

$$\text{Observed } t = \frac{-2.622 - 0}{\frac{3.795}{\sqrt{9}}} = -2.073$$

STEP 6. Draw a conclusion

Since the observed t value is greater than the critical table t value in the lower tail ($t = -2.073 > t = -3.355$), it is in the nonrejection region. Thus, there is not enough evidence from the data to declare a significant difference in the average P/E ratio between the 2008–09 and 2013–14 financial years. The graph in figure 10.5 depicts the rejection regions, the critical values of t and the observed value of t for this example.

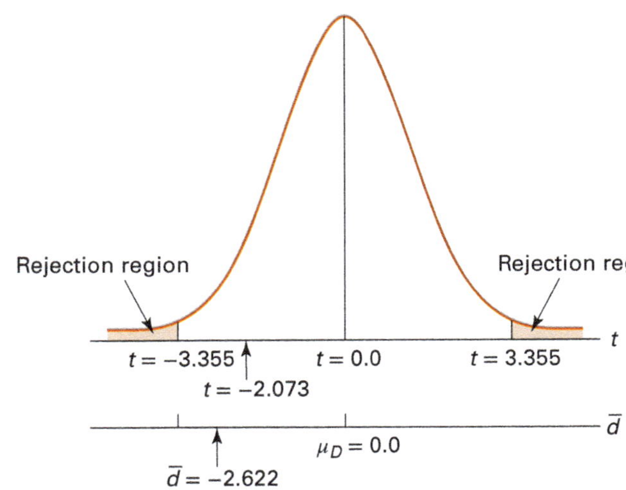

FIGURE 10.5 Graphical depiction of P/E ratio analysis

DEMONSTRATION PROBLEM 10.5

PROBLEM: A researcher wanted to test if grocery prices in August 2014 in Melbourne were significantly different from the grocery prices in Perth. A group of volunteers in Melbourne went out to various shops and noted the prices of different items. Another group of volunteers in Perth went out to various shops and recorded the prices of similar items. The shops were selected randomly and the average prices for each city are given in the table below. Test the hypothesis that the average grocery prices in the two cities are not significantly different. Use $\alpha = .05$.

	Melbourne		Perth	
Item	Average ($)	Range ($)	Average ($)	Range ($)
Milk, 1-litre whole milk	1.43	1.00 – 2.00	1.64	1.00 – 2.00
Bread, white loaf sliced (500 g)	2.89	2.00 – 4.00	3.14	2.20 – 4.00
Rice (white), (1 kg)	2.40	2.00 – 3.00	2.83	2.00 – 3.95
Eggs (large), (1 dozen)	4.17	3.40 – 5.00	4.68	4.00 – 5.80
Local cheese (1 kg)	11.48	8.00 – 17.00	11.03	8.00 – 13.00
Chicken breasts (boneless, skinless), (1 kg)	12.21	9.50 – 15.00	12.65	10.50 – 15.00
Apples (1 kg)	4.01	3.00 – 5.00	4.36	3.00 – 5.00
Oranges (1 kg)	3.54	3.00 – 4.00	4.05	3.00 – 5.00
Tomatoes (1 kg)	4.92	4.00 – 6.50	4.92	4.00 – 6.00
Potatoes (1 kg)	3.32	2.00 – 4.00	2.72	2.00 – 3.00
Lettuce (Iceberg), (1 head)	2.32	2.00 – 3.00	2.29	2.00 – 3.00

SOLUTION: Because it is logical to compare the prices of the same item, this is a paired study.

STEP 1. Set up H_0 and H_a

The desired objective is to check whether the prices are different, which means it is a two-tailed test. If μ_D is the mean population difference:

$$H_0: \mu_D = 0$$
$$H_a: \mu_D \neq 0$$

STEP 2. Decide on the type of test

The appropriate test statistic is:

$$t = \frac{\bar{d} - \mu_D}{\frac{s_d}{\sqrt{n}}}$$

STEP 3. Decide on the level of significance, α, and determine the critical value(s) and region(s)

Given $\alpha = .05$, the critical value of t with degrees of freedom $n - 1 = 11 - 1 = 10$ from table A.6 is $t_{.025,\,10} = 2.228$.

STEP 4. Write down the decision rule

The decision rule is to reject the null hypothesis if the computed t value is either less than −2.228 or greater than 2.228.

STEP 5. Select a random sample and do relevant calculations

From the observed values, $\bar{d} = -0.1473$, $s_d = 0.3811$ and so the computed t value is:

$$t = \frac{-0.1473}{\frac{0.3811}{\sqrt{11}}} = -1.28$$

STEP 6. Draw a conclusion

Since the observed t value of −1.28 is less extreme than the critical table value of −2.228, the decision is not to reject the null hypothesis.

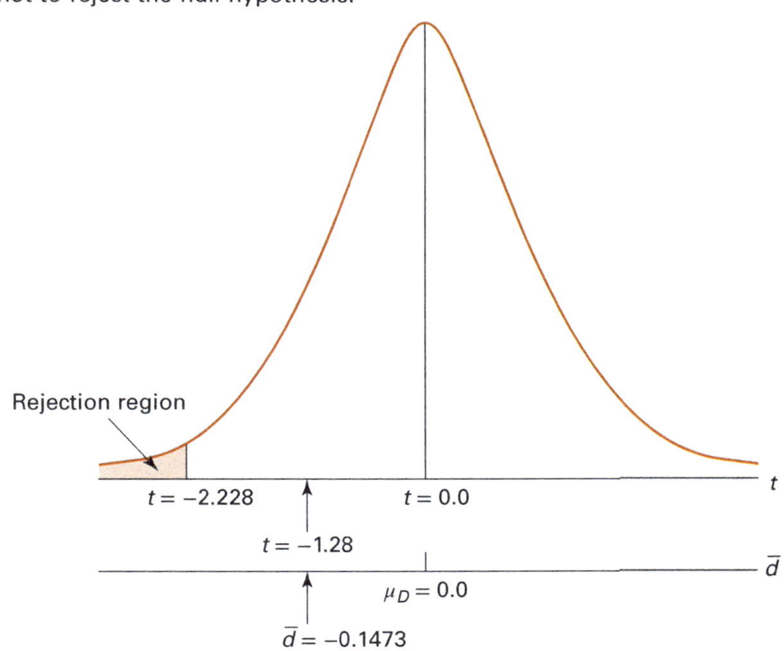

Thus there is not enough evidence to conclude that the grocery prices in the two major metropolitan areas of Australia were significantly different in August 2014.

t-test: paired two sample for means

DP10-05

Access DP10-05.xls from the student website. Follow steps 2 to 4 used for DP10-01 previously except that, in the Data Analysis dialogue box, select *t*-Test: Paired Two Sample for Means, and enter 0.05 in the Alpha field, as shown in the screenshot below.

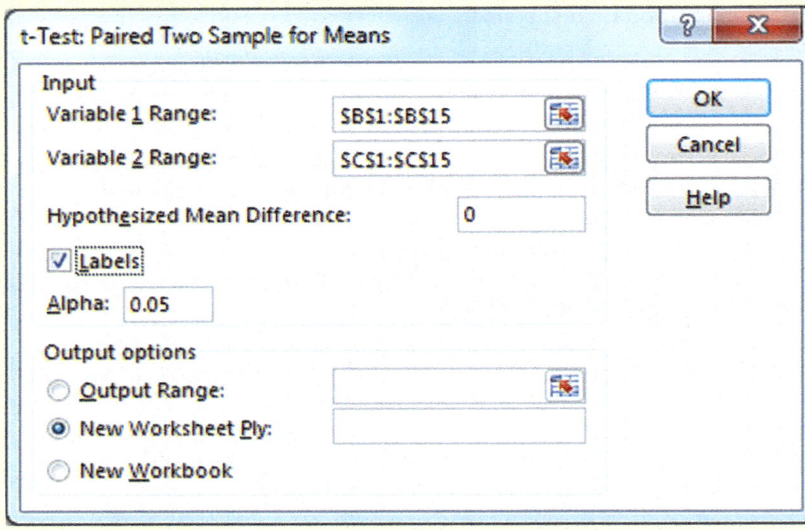

The Excel output follows. The output contains the t value, the p-values and critical values for one- and two-tailed tests.

	A	B	C
1	t-Test: Paired Two Sample for Means		
2			
3		*Melbourne*	*Brisbane*
4	Mean	5.512143	5.327857
5	Variance	14.38133	12.9929
6	Observations	14	14
7	Pearson Correlation	0.994409	
8	Hypothesized Mean Difference	0	
9	df	13	
10	t Stat	1.58992	
11	P(T<=t) one-tail	0.067934	
12	t Critical one-tail	1.770933	
13	P(T<=t) two-tail	0.135867	
14	t Critical two-tail	2.160369	

Confidence intervals

Sometimes a researcher is interested in estimating the mean difference between two populations for related samples. A confidence interval for μ_D, the mean population difference between two related samples, can be constructed by algebraically rearranging formula 10.5, which was used to test hypotheses about μ_D. This produces formula 10.8. Again the assumption is that, for small sample sizes, the population differences are normally distributed.

Confidence interval formula to estimate the difference between related populations, μ_D (10.8)

$$\bar{d} - t\frac{s_d}{\sqrt{n}} \le \mu_D \le \bar{d} + t\frac{s_d}{\sqrt{n}}$$

$$\text{df} = n - 1$$

The following housing industry example demonstrates the application of formula 10.8. Sales of new houses apparently fluctuate seasonally. Superimposed on this seasonality are economic and business cycles that also influence the sales of new houses. In certain parts of the country, new-house sales increase in the spring and early summer and drop off in autumn. Suppose a national real estate association wants to estimate the average difference between the number of new-house sales per company in Wellington between 2013 and 2014. To do so, the association randomly selects 18 real estate companies in the Wellington area and obtains their new-house sales figures for May 2013 and May 2014. The numbers of sales per company are shown in table 10.7. Using these data, the association's analyst estimates the average difference between the number of sales per real estate company in Wellington for May 2013 and May 2014 and constructs a 99% confidence interval.

TABLE 10.7 Number of new-house sales in Wellington

Realtor	May 2013	May 2014
1	8	11
2	19	30
3	5	6
4	9	13
5	3	5
6	0	4
7	13	15
8	11	17
9	9	12
10	5	12
11	8	6
12	2	5
13	11	10
14	14	22
15	7	8
16	12	15
17	6	12
18	10	10

The number of pairs, n, is 18, and the degrees of freedom are 17. For a 99% level of confidence and these degrees of freedom, the table t value is $t_{.005,\,17} = 2.898$. The values for $\bar{d}$ and s_d are shown in table 10.8.

TABLE 10.8 Differences in number of new-house sales, 2013–2014

Realtor	May 2013	May 2014	d
1	8	11	−3
2	19	30	−11
3	5	6	−1
4	9	13	−4
5	3	5	−2
6	0	4	−4
7	13	15	−2
8	11	17	−6
9	9	12	−3
10	5	12	−7
11	8	6	2
12	2	5	−3
13	11	10	1
14	14	22	−8
15	7	8	−1
16	12	15	−3
17	6	12	−6
18	10	10	0
	$\bar{d} = -3.39$	$s_d = 3.27$	

The point estimate of the difference is $\bar{d} = -3.39$. The 99% confidence interval is:

$$\bar{d} - t\frac{s_d}{\sqrt{n}} \le \mu_D \le \bar{d} + t\frac{s_d}{\sqrt{n}}$$

$$-3.39 - 2.898\frac{3.27}{\sqrt{18}} \le \mu_D \le -3.39 + 2.898\frac{3.27}{\sqrt{18}}$$

$$-3.39 - 2.23 \le \mu_D \le -3.39 + 2.23$$

$$-5.62 \le \mu_D \le -1.16$$

The analyst estimates with a 99% level of confidence that the average difference between new-house sales for a real estate company in Wellington in May 2013 and 2014 is between −5.62 and −1.16 houses. Because 2014 sales were subtracted from 2013 sales, the negative signs indicate more sales in 2014 than in 2013. Note that both ends of the confidence interval contain negative signs. This result means that the analyst can be 99% confident that zero is not the average difference. If the analyst were using this confidence interval to test the hypothesis that there was no significant mean difference between average new-house sales per company in Wellington in May 2013 and May 2014, the null hypothesis would be rejected for $\alpha = .01$. The point estimate for this example of the population mean difference in new-house sales is 3.39 fewer houses sold in 2013 than in 2014, with a margin of error of 2.23 houses.

PRACTICE PROBLEMS

Practising the calculations

P10-19 **10.19** Use the data given and a 1% level of significance to test the following hypotheses. Assume that the differences are normally distributed in the population.

$$H_0: \mu_D \leq 0$$
$$H_a: \mu_D > 0$$

Pair	Sample 1	Sample 2
1	138	122
2	117	98
3	130	121
4	141	138
5	136	118
6	138	126
7	133	119
8	135	131
9	144	125

P10-20 **10.20** Use the data given to test the following hypotheses ($\alpha = .05$). Assume that the differences are normally distributed in the population.

$$H_0: \mu_D = 0$$
$$H_a: \mu_D \neq 0$$

Individual	Before	After
1	107	102
2	99	98
3	110	100
4	113	108
5	96	89
6	98	101
7	100	99
8	102	102
9	107	105
10	109	110
11	104	102
12	99	96
13	101	100

10.21 Construct a 98% confidence interval to estimate μ_D from the following sample information. Assume that the differences are normally distributed in the population.

$$\bar{d} = 40.56 \quad s_d = 26.58 \quad n = 22$$

P10-22 **10.22** Construct a 90% confidence interval to estimate μ_D from the following sample information. Assume that the differences are normally distributed in the population.

Client	Before	After
1	32	40
2	28	25
3	35	36
4	32	32
5	26	29
6	25	31
7	37	39
8	16	30
9	35	31

Testing your understanding

P10-23 **10.23** Australia and New Zealand (ANZ) Banking Group regularly conducts job advertisement surveys in Australia. From their Job Advertisements Series, the average numbers of newspaper job advertisements per week in Australian states and territories in July 2013 and July 2014 are given in the following table. Test the hypothesis that the number of newspaper job advertisements in Australia did not change significantly during this period. Use $\alpha = .01$ and assume that the differences are normally distributed.

State/territory	July 2013	July 2014
New South Wales	1256	1202
Victoria	535	397
Queensland	446	375
South Australia	470	194
Western Australia	711	739
Tasmania	207	206
ACT	202	132
Northern Territory	349	502

P10-24 **10.24** Because of uncertainty in real estate markets, many home owners are considering remodelling and constructing additions rather than selling. Probably the most expensive room in the house to remodel is the kitchen, with an average cost of about $23 400. Given the resale value, is remodelling the kitchen worth the cost? The following cost and resale figures are published for 11 cities. Use these data to construct a 99% confidence interval for the difference between cost and added resale value of kitchen remodelling. Assume that the differences are normally distributed in the population.

City	Cost of remodelling ($)	Added resale value ($)
A	20 427	25 163
B	27 255	24 625
C	22 115	12 600
D	23 256	24 588
E	21 887	19 267
F	24 255	20 150
G	19 852	22 500
H	23 624	16 667
I	25 885	26 875
J	28 999	35 333
K	20 836	16 292

P10-25 **10.25** The economic prosperity of a nation is often reflected by the number of people in employment. The Australian Bureau of Statistics collects data on the number of people in employment in various sectors. The table below gives the total number of people employed in June 2009, just after the global financial crisis, and in June 2013 in various sectors. Test at the 1% level of significance whether the distribution of employment changed in four years since the global financial crisis. Assume normality of the difference in value in any industry.

Employment by industry (in '000)	June 2009	June 2013
Agriculture, forestry and fishing	491	499
Mining	135	190
Manufacturing	974	896
Electricity, gas, water and waste services	108	116
Construction	983	1047
Wholesale trade	531	569
Retail trade	1260	1313
Accommodation and food services	811	928
Transport, postal and warehousing	559	564
Information media and telecommunications	173	168
Rental, hiring and real estate services	368	395
Professional, scientific and technical services	893	964
Administrative and support services	685	877
Public administration and safety	66	81
Education and training	295	363
Health care and social assistance	846	1001
Arts and recreation services	184	199
Other services	447	437

10.26 Lawrence and Glover published the results of a study in the *Journal of Managerial Issues* in which they examined the effects of accounting company mergers on auditing delay. Auditing delay is the time between a company's fiscal year-end and the date of the auditor's report. The hypothesis is that, with the efficiencies gained through mergers, the length of the audit delay would decrease. Suppose, to test their hypothesis, they examined the audit delays on 27 clients of six companies before and after the merger of the companies (a span of 5 years). Suppose further that the mean difference in audit delay for these clients from before the merger to after the merger was a decrease in 3.71 days and the standard deviation of difference was 5 days. Use these data and $\alpha = .01$ to test whether the audit delays after the merger were significantly lower than before the merger. Assume that the differences in auditing delay are normally distributed in the population.

10.27 A supermarket decided to promote its own brand of soft drinks on TV for two weeks. Before the advertising campaign, the company randomly selected 21 of its stores to be part of a study to measure the campaign's effectiveness. During a specified half-hour period on a certain Monday morning, all the stores in the sample counted the number of cans of its own brand of soft drink sold. After the campaign, a similar count was made. The average difference was an increase of 75 cans, with a standard deviation of difference of 30 cans. Using this information, construct a 90% confidence interval to estimate the population average difference in soft-drink sales for this company's brand before and after the ad campaign. Assume the differences in soft-drink sales for the company's brand are normally distributed in the population.

10.4 Statistical inferences about two population proportions

Sometimes a researcher wishes to make inferences about the difference between two population proportions. This type of analysis has many applications in business, such as comparing the market share of a product for two different markets, studying the difference in the proportion of female customers between two geographic regions or comparing the proportion of defective products from one period to another. In making inferences about the difference between two population proportions, the statistic normally used is the difference between the sample proportions, $\hat{p}_1 - \hat{p}_2$. This statistic is computed by taking random samples and determining $\hat{p}$ for each sample for a given characteristic, and then calculating the difference between these sample proportions.

The central limit theorem states that, for large samples (each of $n_1\hat{p}_1$, $n_1\hat{q}_1$, $n_2\hat{p}_2$ and $n_2\hat{q}_2 > 5$, where $\hat{q} = 1 - \hat{p}$), the difference between sample proportions is normally distributed with a mean difference of:

$$\mu_{\hat{p}_1 - \hat{p}_2} = p_1 - p_2$$

and a standard deviation of the difference between sample proportions of:

$$\sigma_{\hat{p}_1 - \hat{p}_2} = \sqrt{\frac{p_1q_1}{n_1} + \frac{p_2q_2}{n_2}}$$

From this information, the z formula 10.9 for the difference between sample proportions can be developed.

***z* formula for the difference between two population proportions (10.9)**

$$z = \frac{(\hat{p}_1 - \hat{p}_2) - (p_1 - p_2)}{\sqrt{\frac{p_1q_1}{n_1} + \frac{p_2q_2}{n_2}}}$$

where:

$\hat{p}_1$ = proportion from sample 1
$\hat{p}_2$ = proportion from sample 2
n_1 = size of sample 1
n_2 = size of sample 2
p_1 = proportion from population 1
p_2 = proportion from population 2
$q_1 = 1 - p_1$
$q_2 = 1 - p_2$

Hypothesis testing

Formula 10.9 can be used to determine the probability of getting a particular difference between two sample proportions when given the values of the population proportions. In testing hypotheses related to the difference between two population proportions, particular values of the population proportions are not usually known or assumed. Rather, the hypotheses are about the difference between the two population proportions ($p_1 - p_2$). Note that formula 10.9 requires knowledge of the values of p_1 and p_2. Hence, a modified version of formula 10.9 is used when testing hypotheses related to $p_1 - p_2$. This formula uses a pooled value obtained from the sample proportions to replace the population proportions in the denominator of formula 10.9.

Since the population proportions are unknown, an estimate of the standard deviation of the difference between two sample proportions is made by using sample proportions as point estimates of the population proportions. The sample proportions are combined by using a weighted average, which, in conjunction with the sample sizes, produces a point estimate of the standard deviation of the difference between sample proportions. The result is formula 10.10, which we shall use to test hypotheses related to the difference between two population proportions.

z formula to test the difference between two population proportions (10.10)

$$z = \frac{(\hat{p}_1 - \hat{p}_2) - (p_1 - p_2)}{\sqrt{(\overline{p}\,\overline{q})\left(\frac{1}{n_1} + \frac{1}{n_2}\right)}}$$

where:

$$\overline{p} = \frac{x_1 + x_2}{n_1 + n_2} = \frac{n_1\hat{p}_1 + n_2\hat{p}_2}{n_1 + n_2}$$

$$\overline{q} = 1 - \overline{p}$$

Testing the difference between two population proportions is useful whenever the researcher is interested in comparing the proportion of one population that has a certain characteristic with the proportion of a second population that has the same characteristic. For example, a researcher might be interested in determining whether the proportion of people driving new cars (less than 1 year old) in Hobart is different from the proportion in Launceston. A study could be conducted with a random sample of Hobart drivers and a random sample of Launceston drivers to test this idea. The results could be used to compare the new-car potential of the two markets and the propensity of drivers in these areas to buy new cars.

Do consumers and CEOs have different perceptions of ethics in business? A group of researchers attempted to determine whether there was a difference between the proportion of consumers and the proportion of CEOs who believe that the fear of getting caught or losing one's job is a strong influence on ethical behaviour. In their study, they found that 57% of consumers said that fear of getting caught or losing one's job was a strong influence on ethical behaviour but only 50% of CEOs felt the same way.

Suppose these data were determined from a sample of 420 consumers and 345 CEOs. Does this result provide enough evidence to declare that a significantly higher proportion of consumers than of CEOs believe fear of getting caught or losing one's job is a strong influence on ethical behaviour? We can perform a hypothesis test as follows.

STEP 1. Set up H_0 and H_a

Suppose sample 1 is the consumer sample and sample 2 is the CEO sample. Because we are trying to establish that a higher proportion of consumers than of CEOs believe fear of getting caught or losing one's job is a strong influence on ethical behaviour, the alternative hypothesis should be $p_1 - p_2 > 0$. The following hypotheses are being tested.

$$H_0\text{: } p_1 - p_2 \leq 0$$
$$H_a\text{: } p_1 - p_2 > 0$$

where:

p_1 = the proportion of consumers who select the factor
p_2 = the proportion of CEOs who select the factor

STEP 2. Decide on the type of test

The appropriate statistical test is formula 10.10.

STEP 3. Decide on the level of significance, α, and determine the critical value(s) and region(s)

Let α = .05. Because this test is a one-tailed test, the critical table z value is $z_{crit} = 1.645$.

STEP 4. Write down the decision rule

If an observed value of z of more than 1.645 is obtained, the null hypothesis will be rejected. Figure 10.6 shows the rejection region and the critical value for this problem.

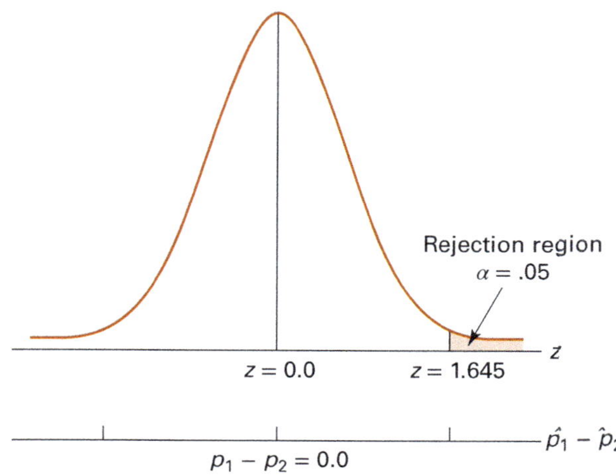

FIGURE 10.6 Rejection region for the ethics example

STEP 5. Select a random sample and do relevant calculations

The following sample information is given.

Consumers	CEOs
$n_1 = 420$	$n_2 = 345$
$\hat{p}_1 = .57$	$\hat{p}_2 = .50$

Using these values, we get:

$$\bar{p} = \frac{n_1\hat{p}_1 + n_2\hat{p}_2}{n_1 + n_2} = \frac{(420)(.57)+(345)(.50)}{420+345} = .54$$

If the statistics had been given as raw data instead of sample proportions, we would have used the following formula:

$$\bar{p} = \frac{x_1 + x_2}{n_1 + n_2}$$

The observed z value is:

$$z = \frac{(.57 - .50) - (0)}{\sqrt{(.54)(.46)\left(\frac{1}{420} + \frac{1}{345}\right)}} = 1.93$$

STEP 6. Draw a conclusion

Because $z = 1.93$ is greater than the critical z value of 1.645 and is in the rejection region, the null hypothesis is rejected. Thus, we can conclude that a significantly higher proportion of consumers than of CEOs believe that fear of getting caught or losing one's job is a strong influence on ethical behaviour. CEOs might want to take another look at how to influence ethical behaviour. If employees are more like consumers than CEOs, CEOs might be able to use fear of getting caught or losing one's job as a means of ensuring ethical behaviour on the job. By transferring the idea of ethical behaviour to the consumer, retailers might use fear of being caught and prosecuted to reduce shop-lifting in the retail trade.

Note that alpha was small and that a one-tailed test was conducted. If a two-tailed test had been used, z_{crit} would have been $z_{.025} = 1.96$, and the null hypothesis would not have been rejected. This result underscores the crucial importance when selecting alpha and determining whether to use a one-tailed or a two-tailed test in hypothesis testing. In making statistical inferences, it is only appropriate that the critical value and the type of test be decided before the analysis. Deciding on the critical value or on the type of test after analysing the data is known as **data snooping**, which is considered unethical behaviour.

DEMONSTRATION PROBLEM 10.6

PROBLEM: Every year, RedBalloon conducts research into workplace issues affecting the bottom line of businesses across Australia and New Zealand. Their research found that more than 1 in 5 employees do not receive any praise at all for the work they do. RedBalloon asked the question, 'Would you consider leaving your organisation if you weren't receiving any recognition for your contribution?' Of the 1282 randomly selected respondents from generation X (born between 1965 and 1980), 410 said Yes, and, of the 763 randomly selected respondents from the baby boomer generation (born between 1946 and 1964), 138 said Yes.

Use this information to determine whether there is a significant difference between the proportions of the two age groups in their willingness to quit their jobs if their achievements are not recognised. Use $\alpha = .01$.

SOLUTION:

STEP 1. Set up H_0 and H_a

You are testing to determine whether there is a difference between the two groups, so a two-tailed test is required. The hypotheses are:

$$H_0\text{: } p_1 - p_2 = 0$$
$$H_a\text{: } p_1 - p_2 \neq 0$$

STEP 2. Decide on the type of test

The appropriate statistical test is formula 10.10.

STEP 3. Decide on the level of significance, α, and determine the critical value(s) and region(s)

Given $\alpha = .01$, the critical z value from table A.4 for $\frac{\alpha}{2} = .005$ is $z_{.005} = \pm 2.575$.

STEP 4. Write down the decision rule

If the observed z value is more than 2.575 or less than −2.575, the null hypothesis is rejected.

STEP 5. Select a random sample and do relevant calculations

The given sample information follows.

Generation X	Baby boomers
$n_1 = 1282$	$n_2 = 763$
$x_1 = 410$	$x_2 = 138$
$\hat{p}_1 = \frac{410}{1282} = .32$	$\hat{p}_2 = \frac{138}{763} = .18$

$$\bar{p} = \frac{x_1 + x_2}{n_1 + n_2} = \frac{410 + 138}{1282 + 763} = \frac{548}{2045} = .27$$

x = the number of respondents who said Yes

The observed z value for the data provided is:

$$z = \frac{(\hat{p}_1 - \hat{p}_2) - (p_1 - p_2)}{\sqrt{(\bar{p}.\bar{q})\left(\frac{1}{n_1} + \frac{1}{n_2}\right)}} = \frac{(.32 - .18) - (0)}{\sqrt{(.27)(.73)\left(\frac{1}{1282} + \frac{1}{763}\right)}} = \frac{.14}{.02} = 7$$

STEP 6. Draw a conclusion

Since the computed z value is much higher than the critical z value, we reject the null hypothesis and conclude that generation X employees have a significantly different propensity from baby boomers to quit their jobs if their achievements are not recognised. The result can be interpreted in various ways; for example, generation Xers are more critical, or they are less tolerant.

The following diagram shows the critical values, the rejection regions and the observed value for this problem.

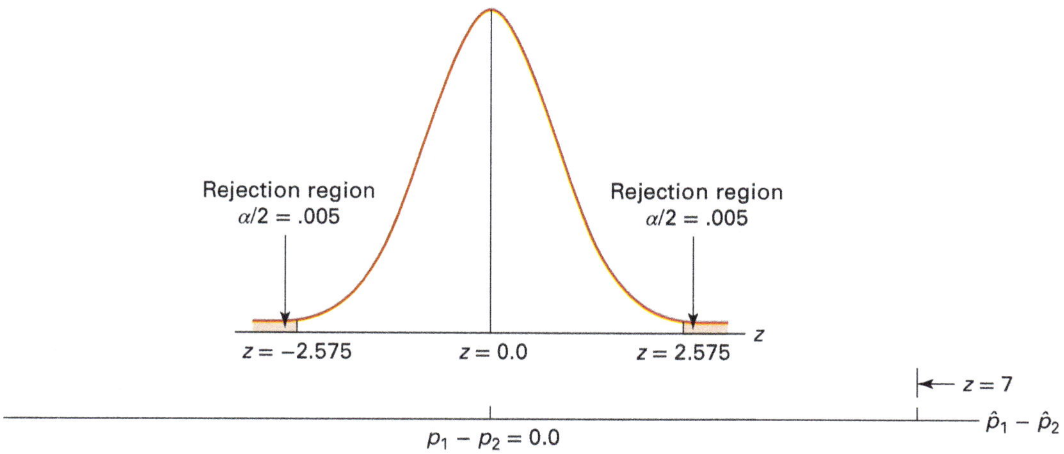

Confidence intervals

Sometimes in business research the investigator wants to estimate the difference between two population proportions. For example, what is the difference, if any, between the population proportions of workers in Western Australia who favour union membership and workers in Queensland who favour union membership? In studying two different suppliers of the same part, a large manufacturing company might want to estimate the difference between the proportions of parts that meet specifications. These and other situations requiring estimation of the difference between two population proportions can be solved by using confidence intervals.

The formula for constructing confidence intervals to estimate the difference between two population proportions is a modified version of formula 10.9. Formula 10.9 for two proportions requires knowledge of each of the population proportions. Because we are attempting to estimate the difference between these two proportions, we obviously do not know their value. To overcome this lack of knowledge in constructing a confidence interval formula, we substitute the sample proportions for the population proportions and use these sample proportions in the estimate, as follows:

$$z = \frac{(\hat{p}_1 - \hat{p}_2) - (p_1 - p_2)}{\sqrt{\frac{\hat{p}_1\hat{q}_1}{n_1} + \frac{\hat{p}_2\hat{q}_2}{n_2}}}$$

Solving this equation for $p_1 - p_2$ produces formula 10.11 (overleaf) for constructing confidence intervals for $p_1 - p_2$.

Confidence interval to estimate $p_1 - p_2$ **(10.11)**

$$(\hat{p}_1 - \hat{p}_2) - z\sqrt{\frac{\hat{p}_1 \cdot \hat{q}_1}{n_1} + \frac{\hat{p}_2 \cdot \hat{q}_2}{n_2}} \le p_1 - p_2 \le (\hat{p}_1 - \hat{p}_2) + z\sqrt{\frac{\hat{p}_1 \cdot \hat{q}_1}{n_1} + \frac{\hat{p}_2 \cdot \hat{q}_2}{n_2}}$$

To see how formula 10.11 is used, suppose we are interested in home ownership and want to test if the proportion of renters in New South Wales is different from that in Victoria. To perform the test, we can use data from the Australian Bureau of Statistics. The ABS sampled 1183 households in New South Wales and found 262 to be renters, and sampled 1193 households in Victoria and found 164 to be renters. Let us now construct a 98% confidence interval to estimate the difference between the population proportions of renters.

The given sample information follows.

New South Wales	Victoria
$n_1 = 1183$	$n_2 = 1193$
$x_1 = 262$ renters	$x_2 = 164$ renters
$\hat{p}_1 = .2215$	$\hat{p}_2 = .1375$
$\hat{q}_1 = .7785$	$\hat{q}_2 = .8625$

For a 98% level of confidence, $z = 2.33$. Using formula 10.11 yields:

$$(.2215 - .1375) - 2.33\sqrt{\frac{(.2215)(.7785)}{1183} + \frac{(.1375)(.8625)}{1193}} \le p_1 - p_2$$

$$\le (.2215 - .1375) + 2.33\sqrt{\frac{(.2215)(.7785)}{1183} + \frac{(.1375)(.8625)}{1193}}$$

$$.084 - .0365 \le p_1 - p_2 \le .084 + .0365$$

$$.0475 \le p_1 - p_2 \le .1205$$

There is a 98% level of confidence that the difference between population proportions is between 0.0475 and 0.1205. Since both the lower and upper limits are positive, zero is not in the range. Thus we can be 98% confident that the proportion of renters in New South Wales is higher than the proportion of renters in Victoria. This may lead to other conclusions, such as house prices in New South Wales are less affordable than in Victoria, but to establish such derivative inferences further analysis should be done.

PRACTICE PROBLEMS

Practising the calculations

10.28 Using the given sample information, test the following hypotheses.

a. H_0: $p_1 - p_2 = 0$
H_a: $p_1 - p_2 \neq 0$

Sample 1	Sample 2
$n_1 = 416$	$n_2 = 432$
$x_1 = 121$	$x_2 = 115$

Let $\alpha = .05$.

Note that x is the number in the sample having the characteristic of interest.

b. H_0: $p_1 - p_2 \le 0$
H_a: $p_1 - p_2 > 0$

Sample 1	Sample 2
$n_1 = 547$	$n_2 = 489$
$\hat{p}_1 = .36$	$\hat{p}_2 = .29$

Let $\alpha = .10$.

10.29 In each of the following cases, calculate a confidence interval to estimate $p_1 - p_2$.

a. $n_1 = 85$, $n_2 = 90$, $\hat{p}_1 = .75$, $\hat{p}_2 = .67$; level of confidence = 90%

b. $n_1 = 1100$, $n_2 = 1300$, $\hat{p}_1 = .19$, $\hat{p}_2 = .17$; level of confidence = 95%

c. $n_1 = 430$, $n_2 = 399$, $x_1 = 275$, $x_2 = 275$; level of confidence = 85%

d. $n_1 = 1500$, $n_2 = 1500$, $x_1 = 1050$, $x_2 = 1100$; level of confidence = 80%

Testing your understanding

10.30 According to a study conducted for Gateway Computers, 59% of men and 70% of women say that weight is an extremely/very important factor in purchasing a laptop computer. Suppose this survey was conducted using 374 men and 481 women. Do these data show enough evidence to declare that a significantly higher proportion of women than men believe that weight is an extremely/very important factor in purchasing a laptop computer? Use a 5% level of significance.

10.31 Does age make a difference in the amount of savings a worker feels is needed to be secure in retirement? A study found that .26 of workers aged 25–33 years feel that $744 000, as indicated by the Association of Superannuation Funds of Australia (ASFA) in 2014 for couples, is enough to be secure at retirement. However, .35 of the workers aged 34–52 years feel that this amount is enough. Suppose 124 workers aged 25–33 years and 146 workers aged 34–52 years were involved in this study. Use these data to construct a 90% confidence interval to estimate the difference between population proportions on this question.

10.32 Companies that recently developed new products were asked to rate which activities were most difficult to accomplish with new products. Options included such activities as assessing market potential, market testing, completing the design and developing a business plan. A researcher wants to conduct a similar study to compare the results between two industries: the computer hardware industry and the banking industry. He takes a random sample of 56 computer companies and 89 banks. The researcher asks whether market testing is the most difficult activity to accomplish in developing a new product. Some 48% of the sampled computer companies and 56% of the sampled banks respond that it is the most difficult activity. Use a level of significance of .20 to test whether there is a significant difference in the responses to the question between these two industries.

10.33 According to the Australian Government, in 2014 there were 485 job service providers listed in Victoria, of whom 41 provide job training, and in Queensland there are 382 listed job service providers of whom 62 provide job training. Test at 1% level of significance whether the difference in proportions of job service providers who offer training between these two states is significant.

10.34 In a survey of 64 land holdings in the Mossman River catchment, it was found 7.8% of land was used for agricultural production. The corresponding figure for the Daintree River catchment was 6.4% in the 106 holdings surveyed. Construct a 95% confidence interval for the difference in proportion of the agricultural land use between the two catchments.

10.5 Statistical inferences about two population variances

Sometimes we are interested in studying the variance of a population rather than the mean or proportion. Section 9.6 discussed how to test hypotheses related to a single population variance, but on some occasions business researchers are interested in comparing two population variances. In this section, we examine how to conduct such comparisons.

When would a business researcher be interested in the variances of two populations? In quality control, analysts often examine both a measure of central tendency (mean or proportion) and a measure of variability. Suppose a manufacturing plant made two batches of an item, produced items on two different machines or produced items in two different shifts. It might be of interest to management to compare the variances from two batches or two machines to determine whether there is more variability in one than another.

Variance is sometimes used as a measure of the risk of a stock in the stock market; the greater the variance, the greater is the risk. By using techniques discussed here, a financial researcher could determine whether the variances (or risks) of two stocks are the same.

In comparing two population variances, the sample variances are used. It makes sense that, if two samples come from the same population (or populations with equal variances), the ratio of the sample variances, $F = \frac{s_1^2}{s_2^2}$, should be about 1. However, because of sampling error, sample variances even from the same population (or from two populations with equal variances) will vary. This ratio of two sample variances creates what is called an **F value**:

$$F = \frac{s_1^2}{s_2^2}$$

These ratios, if computed repeatedly for pairs of sample variances taken from a population, are distributed as an **F distribution**. The distribution is named after an eminent statistician of the twentieth century, Sir Ronald Fisher. The concept of the *F* distribution can be understood as follows.

- If x_1 is a random variable that has a normal (Gaussian) distribution, then x_1^2 has a chi-square (χ^2) distribution. If another variable x_2 is also normally distributed, x_2^2 will have a chi-square distribution.
- The ratio $\frac{x_1^2}{x_2^2}$ will have an *F* distribution — that is, the ratio of two chi-square distributions has an *F* distribution.
- The *F* distribution will vary with the sizes of the samples, which are converted to degrees of freedom.

In an *F* distribution, there are degrees of freedom associated with both the numerator and the denominator of the ratio. The *F* test of two population variances is very sensitive to violations of the assumption that the populations are normally distributed. The statistician should carefully investigate the shape of the distributions of the populations from which the samples are drawn to be certain the populations are normally distributed.

Hypothesis testing

Formula 10.12 is used to test hypotheses comparing two population variances.

F test for two population variances (10.12)

$$F = \frac{s_1^2}{s_2^2}$$

$$df_{numerator} = v_1 = n_1 - 1$$
$$df_{denominator} = v_2 = n_2 - 1$$

The use of formula 10.12 rather strictly stipulates that the two populations are normally distributed; if that is not the case, a more elaborate expression, called Levene's test, is used, which also uses an *F* distribution. Table A.7 contains *F* distribution table values for α = .10, .05, .025, .01 and .005. Figure 10.7 shows an *F* distribution for $v_1 = 6$ and $v_2 = 30$. Notice that the distribution is skewed, which can be a problem when we are conducting a two-tailed test and want to determine the critical value for the lower tail; table A.7 contains *F* values for the upper tail only. The *F* distribution is not symmetric nor does it have a mean of zero, as the *z* and *t* distributions do; therefore, we cannot merely place a minus sign on the upper-tail critical value to obtain the lower-tail critical value. To determine the lower-tail critical value, formula 10.13 can be used. Notice how the degrees of freedom in formula 10.13 have changed from the numerator to the denominator.

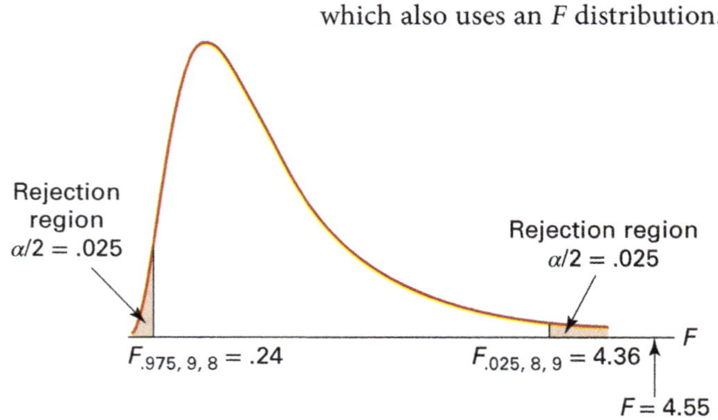

FIGURE 10.7 An *F* distribution for $v_1 = 6, v_2 = 30$

Formula for determining the lower-tail critical value for the *F* distribution (10.13)

$$F_{1-\alpha,\,\nu_1,\,\nu_2} = \frac{1}{F_{\alpha,\,\nu_2,\,\nu_1}}$$

A hypothesis test can be conducted using two sample variances and formula 10.12. The following example illustrates this process.

Suppose a machine produces metal sheets that are specified to be 22 millimetres thick. Because of the machine, operator, raw material, manufacturing environment and other factors, there is variability in the thickness. Two machines produce these sheets. Operators are concerned about consistency between the two machines. To test this consistency, they randomly sample ten sheets produced by machine 1 and nine sheets produced by machine 2. The thickness measurements of sheets from each machine are given in the following table. Assume that sheet thickness is normally distributed in the population. How can we determine whether the samples come from populations with the same or different variances?

Machine 1		Machine 2	
22.3	21.9	22.0	21.7
21.8	22.4	22.1	21.9
22.3	22.5	21.8	22.0
21.6	22.2	21.9	22.1
21.8	21.6	22.2	
$s_1^2 = .1138$		$s_2^2 = .0250$	
$n_1 = 10$		$n_2 = 9$	

STEP 1. Set up H_0 and H_a

In this case, we are conducting a two-tailed test (variances are either the same or different), so the following hypotheses are used.

$$H_0: \sigma_1^2 = \sigma_2^2$$
$$H_a: \sigma_1^2 \neq \sigma_2^2$$

STEP 2. Decide on the type of test

The appropriate statistical test is:

$$F = \frac{s_1^2}{s_2^2}$$

STEP 3. Decide on the level of significance, α, and determine the critical value(s) and region(s)

Let $\alpha = .05$. Since we are conducting a two-tailed test, $\frac{\alpha}{2} = .025$. Because $n_1 = 10$ and $n_2 = 9$, the degrees of freedom of the numerator for the upper-tail critical value are $\nu_1 = n_1 - 1 = 10 - 1 = 9$ and the degrees of freedom of the denominator for the upper-tail critical value are $\nu_2 = n_2 - 1 = 9 - 1 = 8$. The critical F value for the upper tail obtained from table A.7 is:

$$F_{.025,\,9,\,8} = 4.36$$

Table 10.9 (overleaf) shows a portion of the F distribution for a one-tailed test with $\alpha = .025$ (which yields equivalent values for a two-tailed test with $\alpha = .05$ where the upper tail contains .025 of the area). Locate $F_{.025,\,8,\,9} = 4.10$ in the table. The lower-tail critical value can be calculated from the upper-tail value by using formula 10.13.

$$F_{.975,\,9,8} = \frac{1}{F_{.025,\,8,\,9}} = \frac{1}{4.10} = .24$$

TABLE 10.9
A portion of the F distribution table

Percentage points of the F distribution

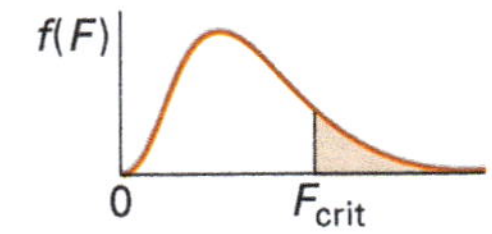

$\alpha = .025$

Numerator degrees of freedom (v_1); **Denominator degrees of freedom** (v_2)

v_2 \ v_1	1	2	3	4	5	6	7	8	9
1	647.8	799.5	864.2	899.6	921.8	937.1	948.2	956.7	963.3
2	38.51	39.00	39.17	39.25	39.30	39.33	39.36	39.37	39.39
3	17.44	16.04	15.44	15.10	14.88	14.73	14.62	14.54	14.47
4	12.22	10.65	9.98	9.60	9.36	9.20	9.07	8.98	8.90
5	10.01	8.43	7.76	7.39	7.15	6.98	6.85	6.76	6.68
6	8.81	7.26	6.60	6.23	5.99	5.82	5.70	5.60	5.52
7	8.07	6.54	5.89	5.52	5.29	5.12	4.99	4.90	4.82
8	7.57	6.06	5.42	5.05	4.82	4.65	4.53	4.43	4.36
9	7.21	5.71	5.08	4.72	4.48	4.32	4.20	4.10	4.03
10	6.94	5.46	4.83	4.47	4.24	4.07	3.95	3.85	3.78
11	6.72	5.26	4.63	4.28	4.04	3.88	3.76	3.66	3.59
12	6.55	5.10	4.47	4.12	3.89	3.73	3.61	3.51	3.44
13	6.41	4.97	4.35	4.00	3.77	3.60	3.48	3.39	3.31
14	6.30	4.86	4.24	3.89	3.66	3.50	3.38	3.29	3.21
15	6.20	4.77	4.15	3.80	3.58	3.41	3.29	3.20	3.12
16	6.12	4.69	4.08	3.73	3.50	3.34	3.22	3.12	3.05
17	6.04	4.62	4.01	3.66	3.44	3.28	3.16	3.06	2.98
18	5.98	4.56	3.95	3.61	3.38	3.22	3.10	3.01	2.93
19	5.92	4.51	3.90	3.56	3.33	3.17	3.05	2.96	2.88
20	5.87	4.46	3.86	3.51	3.29	3.13	3.01	2.91	2.84
21	5.83	4.42	3.82	3.48	3.25	3.09	2.97	2.87	2.80
22	5.79	4.38	3.78	3.44	3.22	3.05	2.93	2.84	2.76
23	5.75	4.35	3.75	3.41	3.18	3.02	2.90	2.81	2.73
24	5.72	4.32	3.72	3.38	3.15	2.99	2.87	2.78	2.70
25	5.69	4.29	3.69	3.35	3.13	2.97	2.85	2.75	2.68
26	5.66	4.27	3.67	3.33	3.10	2.94	2.82	2.73	2.65
27	5.63	4.24	3.65	3.31	3.08	2.92	2.80	2.71	2.63
28	5.61	4.22	3.63	3.29	3.06	2.90	2.78	2.69	2.61
29	5.59	4.20	3.61	3.27	3.04	2.88	2.76	2.67	2.59
30	5.57	4.18	3.59	3.25	3.03	2.87	2.75	2.65	2.57
40	5.42	4.05	3.46	3.13	2.90	2.74	2.62	2.53	2.45
60	5.29	3.93	3.34	3.01	2.79	2.63	2.51	2.41	2.33
120	5.15	3.80	3.23	2.89	2.67	2.52	2.39	2.30	2.22
∞	5.02	3.69	3.12	2.79	2.57	2.41	2.29	2.19	2.11

$F_{.025,\,8,\,9}$

STEP 4. Write down the decision rule

The decision rule is to reject the null hypothesis if the observed F value is greater than 4.36 or less than .24.

STEP 5. Select a random sample and do relevant calculations

Next we compute the sample variances as shown in the data table. The computed statistic is:

$$F = \frac{s_1^2}{s_2^2} = \frac{.1138}{.0250} = 4.55$$

Thus the ratio of the sample variances is 4.55.

STEP 6. Draw a conclusion

The observed F value is 4.55, which is greater than the upper-tail critical value of 4.36. As figure 10.8 shows, this F value is in the rejection region. Thus, the decision is to reject the null hypothesis. We conclude that the population variances are not equal.

An examination of the sample variances reveals that the variance of machine 1 measurements is greater than that of machine 2 measurements. The operators and process managers might want to examine machine 1 further; an adjustment may be needed or there may be another reason for the greater variation on that machine.

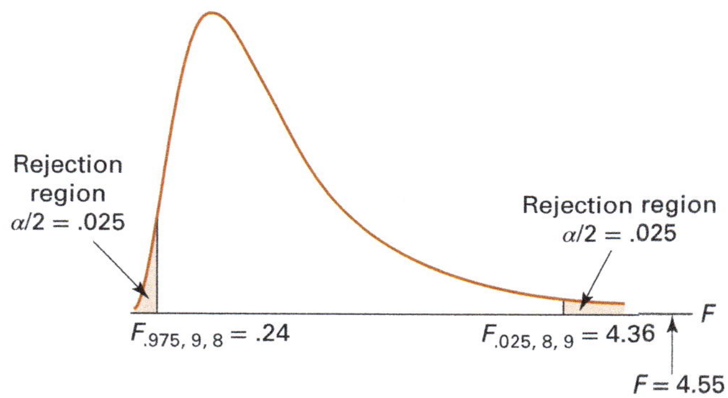

FIGURE 10.8 Graph of F values and rejection regions for the sheet metal example

DEMONSTRATION PROBLEM 10.7

PROBLEM: According to a study, a family of four in Sydney with $70 000 annual income spends more than $15 000 a year on groceries. Suppose we want to test to determine whether the variance of money spent per year on groceries by families across Australia is greater than the variance of money spent on groceries by families in Sydney — that is, whether the amounts spent by families of four in Sydney are more homogeneous than the amounts spent by such families nationally. Suppose a random sample of eight Sydney families produces the following data of average annual spending on groceries, which are given along with those reported from a random sample of seven families across Australia. Complete a hypothesis-testing procedure to determine whether the variance of values taken from across Australia can be shown to be greater than the variance of values obtained from families in Sydney. Let $\alpha = .01$. Assume the amount spent on groceries is normally distributed in the population.

Across Australia	Sydney
$17 500	$17 900
13 250	15 900
11 400	16 600
12 750	14 680
10 600	16 140
14 800	14 800
18 750	15 100
	16 300

SOLUTION:

STEP 1. Set up H_0 and H_a

This is a one-tailed test with the following hypotheses.

$$H_0: \sigma_1^2 \leq \sigma_2^2$$
$$H_a: \sigma_1^2 > \sigma_2^2$$

Note that we are trying to show that the variance for the Australian population (1) is greater than the variance for families in Sydney (2).

STEP 2. Decide on the type of test

The appropriate statistical test is:

$$F = \frac{s_1^2}{s_2^2}$$

STEP 3. Decide on the level of significance, α, and determine the critical value(s) and region(s)

This test is a one-tailed test, so we will use the F distribution table in table A.7 with $\alpha = .01$. The degrees of freedom for $n_1 = 7$ and $n_2 = 8$ are $v_1 = 6$ and $v_2 = 7$. The critical F value for the upper tail of the distribution is:

$$F_{.01,\,6,\,7} = 7.19$$

STEP 4. Write down the decision rule

The decision rule is to reject the null hypothesis if the observed value of F is greater than 7.19.

STEP 5. Select a random sample and do relevant calculations

The following sample variances are computed from the data.

$$s_1^2 = 9\,290\,000,\ n_1 = 7$$
$$s_2^2 = 1\,148\,564,\ n_2 = 8$$

The observed F value can be determined by:

$$F = \frac{s_1^2}{s_2^2} = \frac{9\,290\,000}{1\,148\,564} = 8.09$$

STEP 6. Draw a conclusion

Because the observed value of $F = 8.09$ is greater than the critical F value of 7.19, the decision is to reject the null hypothesis.

Thus the variance for families in Australia is greater than the variance for families in Sydney. Families in Sydney are more homogeneous in the amount spent on basics than families across Australia. Marketing managers need to understand this homogeneity as they attempt to find niches in the Sydney population. For example, Sydney may not contain as many subgroups as found across Australia, or the task of locating market niches may be easier in Sydney than in the rest of the country because fewer possibilities are likely. The following graph shows the rejection region as well as the critical and calculated values of F.

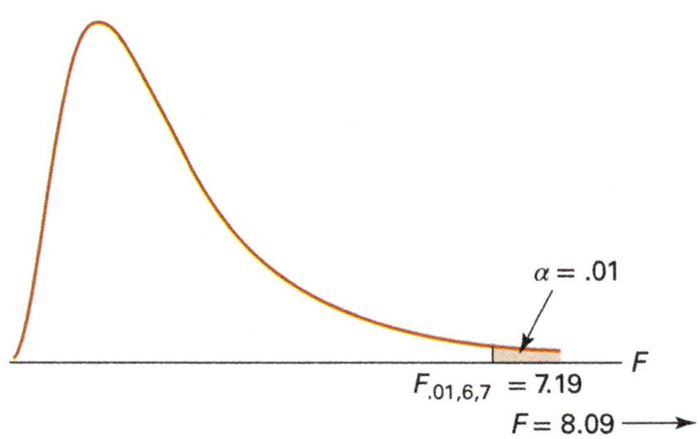

USING EXCEL

F-test two-sample for variances

DP10-07

Access DP10-07.xls from the student website. Follow steps 2 to 4 used for DP10-01 previously except that, in the Data Analysis dialogue box, select F-Test Two-Sample for Variances. The completed dialogue box is shown below.

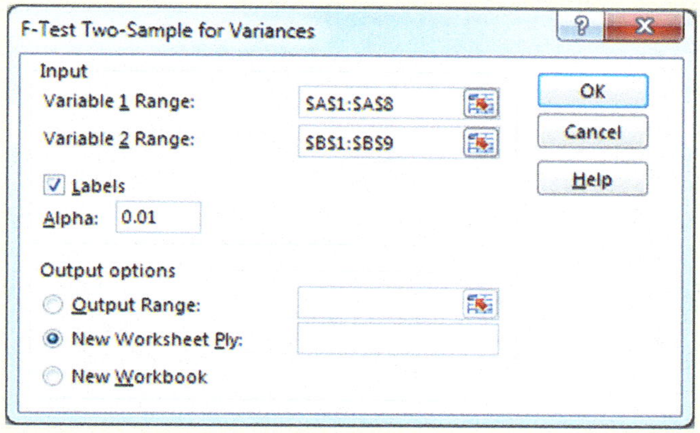

The Excel output follows.

	A	B	C
1	F-Test Two-Sample for Variances		
2			
3		*Across Australia*	*Sydney*
4	Mean	14150	15927.5
5	Variance	9290000.571	1148564
6	Observations	7	8
7	df	6	7
8	F	8.088359	
9	P(F<=f) one-tail	0.007164	
10	F Critical one-tail	7.191405	

Confidence intervals

If a variable x_1 has a normal (Gaussian) distribution, then $(n_1-1)\frac{s_1^2}{\sigma_1^2}$ has a χ^2 distribution with $(n_1 - 1)$ degrees of freedom. If another variable x_2 is normally distributed, then $(n_2-1)\frac{s_2^2}{\sigma_2^2}$ has also a χ^2 distribution with $(n_2 - 1)$ degrees of freedom. Thus the ratio of the two, $[(n_1-1)\frac{s_1^2}{\sigma_1^2}]/[(n_2-1)\frac{s_2^2}{\sigma_2^2}]$, has an F distribution.

In fact, it can be shown that:

$$P\left(F_{1-\alpha/2,\,n_1-1,\,n_2-1} \le \frac{\sigma_2^2 s_1^2}{\sigma_1^2 s_2^2} \le F_{\alpha/2,\,n_1-1,\,n_2-1}\right) = 1-\alpha$$

From the above equation we can obtain the $(1-\alpha)100\%$ confidence interval for $\frac{\sigma_1^2}{\sigma_2^2}$ as given in formula 10.14. Formula 10.13 is used to derive formula 10.14 (overleaf).

Confidence interval formula for the ratio of two population variances (10.14)

$$\frac{s_1^2}{s_2^2}\frac{1}{F_{\alpha/2,\,n_1-1,\,n_2-1}} \le \frac{\sigma_1^2}{\sigma_2^2} \le \frac{s_1^2}{s_2^2}F_{\alpha/2,\,n_2-1,\,n_1-1}$$

For the previous example related to machines that produce metal sheets, we can compute the 95% confidence interval as follows.

$$\frac{s_1^2}{s_2^2}\frac{1}{F_{\alpha/2,\,n_1-1,\,n_2-1}} \le \frac{\sigma_1^2}{\sigma_2^2} \le \frac{s_1^2}{s_2^2}F_{\alpha/2,\,n_2-1,\,n_1-1}$$

$$\frac{0.1138}{0.0250}\frac{1}{4.10} \le \frac{\sigma_1^2}{\sigma_2^2} \le \frac{0.1138}{0.0250}4.36$$

$$1.110 \le \frac{\sigma_1^2}{\sigma_2^2} \le 19.847$$

Since 1 is not in the confidence interval, we are 95% confident that the two variances are not equal. This is the same conclusion we arrived at earlier by hypothesis testing.

PRACTICE PROBLEMS

Practising the calculations

10.35 Test the following hypotheses by using the given sample information and $\alpha = .01$. Assume that the populations are normally distributed.

$$H_0\text{: } \sigma_1^2 \ge \sigma_2^2$$
$$H_a\text{: } \sigma_1^2 < \sigma_2^2$$

$$n_1 = 10 \quad n_2 = 12 \quad s_1^2 = 562 \quad s_2^2 = 1013$$

10.36 Test the following hypotheses by using the given sample information and $\alpha = .05$. Assume that the populations are normally distributed.

$$H_0\text{: } \sigma_1^2 \ge \sigma_2^2$$
$$H_a\text{: } \sigma_1^2 < \sigma_2^2$$

$$n_1 = 5 \quad n_2 = 19 \quad s_1 = 4.68 \quad s_2 = 2.78$$

Testing your understanding

10.37 G Jones et al. studied the effect of feed withdrawal on the live weight of pigs during the weaning phase. They weighed the pigs in the evening and the following morning, after a time lapse of 11 hours during which time food was withheld. The standard deviation of the weights of 52 pigs in the evening was 2.0704 and in the morning 1.9599. The authors believed that 'gut fill' is a component of the variability in weight and that feed withdrawal could reduce gut fill and, therefore, variability. Test the authors' belief at $\alpha = .01$ and assume normality.

P10-38 **10.38** The data shown here are the results of a survey to investigate petrol prices in Auckland and Adelaide. Ten days were selected randomly in each of two cities in the June quarter of 2014, and the figures represent the prices in dollars of a litre of unleaded regular petrol. Use the *F* test to determine whether there is a significant difference between the variances of the prices of unleaded regular petrol in these two cities. Let $\alpha = .10$. Assume petrol prices are normally distributed, and Australian and New Zealand dollars have a similar exchange rate.

Auckland			Adelaide		
2.10	2.12	2.24	1.36	1.40	1.44
2.12	2.28	2.16	1.49	1.51	1.39
2.03	2.09	2.14	1.45	1.42	1.38
2.19			1.47		

P10-39 **10.39** How long do houses for sale remain on the market? One survey reported that, in Sydney, houses for sale are on the market an average of 112 days. Of course, the length of time varies by market. Suppose random samples of 13 houses in Sydney and 11 houses in Brisbane that are for sale are traced. The data shown here represent the number of days each house was on the market before being sold. Use the given data and a 1% level of significance to determine whether the population variance for the number of days until sold is different in Sydney from that in Brisbane. Assume that the number of days houses for sale are on the market are normally distributed for both cities.

Sydney		Brisbane	
132	126	118	56
138	94	85	69
131	161	113	67
127	133	81	54
99	119	94	137
126	88	93	
134			

10.40 According to government figures, the average age of a male federal public servant is 43.6 years and that of a male state public servant is 37.3 years. Is there any difference between the variations of ages of men in the federal sector and men in the state sector? Suppose a random sample of 15 male federal workers is taken and the variance of their ages is 91.5. Suppose also that a random sample of 15 male state workers is taken and the variance of their ages is 67.3. Use these data and $\alpha = .01$ to answer the question. Assume that ages are normally distributed.

MISUSE OF STATISTICS

In any statistical research it is very important to identify the appropriate variables and select appropriate tools. The techniques presented in this chapter are valid when the assumptions outlined in the introduction of this chapter are satisfied. Not testing for those assumptions may lead to a conclusion that is far from the truth. The z and t tests are robust to moderate variations of normality and the equal variance assumption, but the F test is not.

The decision rule and significance level should be set before any data analysis is done. Changing the decision rule or critical value after an initial analysis of data, which is often referred to as data snooping, is unethical behaviour.

All statistical findings should be reported for general dissemination in plain English so that a person with no statistical background can understand the findings. Shrouding a statistical finding in statistical jargon is tantamount to misuse of statistics. For instance, the statement 'the decision should be to invest with alpha = .05 and not to invest with alpha = .01' should be reworded as 'the decision for an average risk taker should be to invest and for a risk averse investor not to invest'.

CHAPTER CASE REVISITED

Life insurance

1. The average of the quotes for premiums for smokers is $115 and that for nonsmokers is $54. The standard deviations are $15.21 and $5.04, respectively. Assuming normality, and since population standard deviation is unknown and the sample size is less than 30, we should use the t statistic. To check if the premiums are significantly different between smokers and nonsmokers, we can construct a confidence interval for the difference between the two means using formula 10.4. Using a value of alpha of .05 for a two-tailed situation with 18 (=10 +10 − 2) degrees of freedom, the critical t value from table A.6 is 2.101. The value of the pooled standard deviation is $11.41. Thus the confidence interval of the difference between the mean values using formula 10.4 is ($50, $71). The lower and upper boundaries of the confidence interval have positive signs. Thus, zero is not in the interval, which indicates that the difference in quotes is significant. In fact, if you look at the quotes, you will find that your premium almost doubles as soon as you mention that you smoke.
2. A manager should investigate the savings a company could make if it were to allocate tasks based on physical fitness, and whether it would be worthwhile. There are many other issues that a manager should consider such as job satisfaction, skill level and experience before making such a decision.
3. Workplace health and safety issues are important issues throughout Australia and New Zealand. It is important to ensure that adequate safety and precautionary measures are taken to minimise the risk of accidents. Otherwise, in addition to the harm suffered by workers, litigation could cost the company dearly. While addressing health and safety issues, it is always a good idea to investigate the amount of savings that can be made in insurance premiums and whether it is significant.

SUMMARY

1 Business research often requires the comparison of two populations. Statistical investigation into such comparisons is especially warranted when we cannot readily distinguish between the means and variances of the two populations through graphs and visual inspections of the data. When the sample data from each population can be assumed to be approximately normal, the observations are random and independent, and the variances of the populations are similar and assumed to be known, the test for significance of the difference between the means of the two populations can be done using the z statistic. The estimated z value from the data is always compared with the critical z value from the standard normal table to make a statistical inference.

2 Sometimes we are required to test whether the means of two population distributions are significantly different. Where the sample data from each population can be assumed to be approximately normal, the observations are random and independent, and the population variances are similar although unknown, the test can be done using the t statistic. The formula for the t statistic uses a pooled estimate of the variances from the sample data.

3 When there are distinct entities in a population, and observations are made in pairs, such as before and after a treatment, a t test can be performed to check if there has been a significant change due to the treatment. The t statistic is constructed by subtracting the average difference from the expected difference and dividing the result by the standard error of the differences.

4 When we are interested only in comparing the proportion of successes in two populations, we can use a z statistic. The z statistic is obtained by the normal approximation of the binomial distribution, and, thus, the number of observations should be fairly large.

5 There are times when instead of focusing on the means we need to test whether there is a significant difference between the variances of two populations. Such a test can be done using the F test.

The assumption of normality is critical for the F test. The most popular method of checking for normality is the normal probability plot. If the normality assumption cannot be satisfied and the variances are very different, a nonparametric procedure should be adopted instead of the procedures described in this chapter.

KEY TERMS

data snooping p. 350
dependent samples p. 337
***F* distribution** p. 354
***F* value** p. 354
independent samples p. 316
normal probability plot p. 327
paired *t* test p. 338

KEY EQUATIONS

EQUATION	DESCRIPTION	FORMULA
10.1	**z formula for the difference between two sample means (independent samples and population variances known)**	$z=\dfrac{(\bar{x}_1-\bar{x}_2)-(\mu_1-\mu_2)}{\sqrt{\dfrac{\sigma_1^2}{n_1}+\dfrac{\sigma_2^2}{n_2}}}$
10.2	**Confidence interval to estimate $\mu_1-\mu_2$**	$(\bar{x}_1-\bar{x}_2)-z\sqrt{\dfrac{\sigma_1^2}{n_1}+\dfrac{\sigma_2^2}{n_2}}\le\mu_1-\mu_2\le(\bar{x}_1-\bar{x}_2)+z\sqrt{\dfrac{\sigma_1^2}{n_1}+\dfrac{\sigma_2^2}{n_2}}$

EQUATION	DESCRIPTION	FORMULA
10.3	**t formula to test the difference between means assuming $\sigma_1^2 = \sigma_2^2$**	$t = \frac{(\bar{x}_1 - \bar{x}_2) - (\mu_1 - \mu_2)}{s_p\sqrt{\frac{1}{n_1} + \frac{1}{n_2}}}$ where: $s_p = \sqrt{\frac{s_1^2(n_1 - 1) + s_2^2(n_2 - 1)}{n_1 + n_2 - 2}}$ $\mathrm{df} = n_1 + n_2 - 2$
10.4	**Confidence interval to estimate $\mu_1 - \mu_2$ assuming similar variances**	$(\bar{x}_1 - \bar{x}_2) - t \cdot s_p\sqrt{\frac{1}{n_1} + \frac{1}{n_2}} \le \mu_1 - \mu_2 \le (\bar{x}_1 - \bar{x}_2) + t \cdot s_p\sqrt{\frac{1}{n_1} + \frac{1}{n_2}}$ where: $s_p = \sqrt{\frac{s_1^2(n_1 - 1) + s_2^2(n_2 - 1)}{n_1 + n_2 - 2}}$ $\mathrm{df} = n_1 + n_2 - 2$
10.5	**t formula to test the difference between two dependent populations**	$t = \frac{\bar{d} - \mu_D}{\frac{s_d}{\sqrt{n}}}$ $\mathrm{df} = n - 1$
10.6	**Formula for $\bar{d}$**	$\bar{d} = \frac{\sum d}{n}$
10.7	**Formula for s_d**	$s_d = \sqrt{\frac{\sum(d - \bar{d})^2}{n - 1}} = \sqrt{\frac{\sum d^2 - \frac{(\sum d)^2}{n}}{n - 1}}$
10.8	**Confidence interval formula to estimate the difference between related populations, μ_D**	$\bar{d} - t\frac{s_d}{\sqrt{n}} \le \mu_D \le \bar{d} + t\frac{s_d}{\sqrt{n}}$ $\mathrm{df} = n - 1$
10.9	**z formula for the difference between two population proportions**	$z = \frac{(\hat{p}_1 - \hat{p}_2) - (p_1 - p_2)}{\sqrt{\frac{p_1 q_1}{n_1} + \frac{p_2 q_2}{n_2}}}$
10.10	**z formula to test the difference between two population proportions**	$z = \frac{(\hat{p}_1 - \hat{p}_2) - (p_1 - p_2)}{\sqrt{(\bar{p}\bar{q})\left(\frac{1}{n_1} + \frac{1}{n_2}\right)}}$ where: $\bar{p} = \frac{x_1 + x_2}{n_1 + n_2} = \frac{n_1\hat{p}_1 + n_2\hat{p}_2}{n_1 + n_2}$ $\bar{q} = 1 - \bar{p}$

EQUATION	DESCRIPTION	FORMULA
10.11	Confidence interval to estimate $p_1 - p_2$	$(\hat{p}_1-\hat{p}_2)-z\sqrt{\frac{\hat{p}_1\cdot\hat{q}_1}{n_1}+\frac{\hat{p}_2\cdot\hat{q}_2}{n_2}}\le(p_1-p_2)\le(\hat{p}_1-\hat{p}_2)+z\sqrt{\frac{\hat{p}_1\cdot\hat{q}_1}{n_1}+\frac{\hat{p}_2\cdot\hat{q}_2}{n_2}}$
10.12	*F* test for two population variances	$F=\frac{s_1^2}{s_2^2}$ $\text{df}_{\text{numerator}}=v_1=n_1-1$ $\text{df}_{\text{denominator}}=v_2=n_2-1$
10.13	Formula for determining the lower-tail critical value for the *F* distribution	$F_{1-\alpha,\,v_1,\,v_2}=\frac{1}{F_{\alpha,\,v_2,\,v_1}}$
10.14	Confidence interval formula for the ratio of two population variances	$\frac{s_1^2}{s_2^2}\frac{1}{F_{\alpha/2,\,n_1-1,\,n_2-1}}\le\frac{\sigma_1^2}{\sigma_2^2}\le\frac{s_1^2}{s_2^2}F_{\alpha/2,\,n_2-1,\,n_1-1}$

REVIEW PROBLEMS

Practising the calculations

10.41 Test the following hypotheses with the data given. Let $\alpha = .10$.

$$H_0: \mu_1 - \mu_2 = 0$$
$$H_a: \mu_1 - \mu_2 \neq 0$$

Sample 1	Sample 2
$\bar{x}_1 = 340$	$\bar{x}_2 = 295$
$\sigma_1 = 80$	$\sigma_2 = 55$
$n_1 = 38$	$n_2 = 49$

10.42 Use the following data to construct a 98% confidence interval to estimate the difference between μ_1 and μ_2.

Sample 1	Sample 2
$\bar{x}_1 = 25$	$\bar{x}_2 = 29$
$\sigma_1^2 = 14.05$	$\sigma_2^2 = 9.80$
$n_1 = 83$	$n_2 = 71$

10.43 The following data come from independent samples drawn from normally distributed populations. Use these data to test the following hypotheses. Let the Type I error rate be .05, and assume $\sigma_1^2 = \sigma_2^2$.

$$H_0: \mu_1 - \mu_2 \le 0$$
$$H_a: \mu_1 - \mu_2 > 0$$

Sample 1	Sample 2
$\bar{x}_1 = 2.06$	$\bar{x}_2 = 1.93$
$s_1^2 = .176$	$s_2^2 = .143$
$n_1 = 12$	$n_2 = 15$

10.44 Construct a 95% confidence interval to estimate $\mu_1 - \mu_2$ by using the following data. Assume that the populations are normally distributed.

Sample 1	Sample 2
$\bar{x}_1 = 74.6$	$\bar{x}_2 = 70.9$
$s_1^2 = 10.5$	$s_2^2 = 11.4$
$n_1 = 18$	$n_2 = 19$

10.45 The following data have been gathered from two related samples. The differences are assumed to be normally distributed in the population. Use these data and an alpha of .01 to test the following hypotheses.

$$H_0: \mu_D \ge 0$$
$$H_a: \mu_D < 0$$
$$n = 21 \quad \bar{d} = -1.16 \quad s_d = 1.01$$

P10-46 **10.46** Use the following data to construct a 99% confidence interval to estimate μ_D. Assume that the differences are normally distributed in the population.

Respondent	Before	After
1	151	126
2	133	135
3	188	146
4	150	136
5	129	110
6	127	149
7	145	132
8	146	124
9	81	77

10.47 Test the following hypotheses by using the given data and an alpha equal to .05.

$$H_0: p_1 - p_2 = 0$$
$$H_a: p_1 - p_2 \neq 0$$

Sample 1	Sample 2
$n_1 = 783$	$n_2 = 896$
$x_1 = 345$	$x_2 = 421$

10.48 Use the following data to construct a 99% confidence interval to estimate $p_1 - p_2$.

Sample 1	Sample 2
$n_1 = 409$	$n_2 = 378$
$\hat{p}_1 = .71$	$\hat{p}_2 = .67$

10.49 Test the following hypotheses by using the given data. Let $\alpha = .05$.

$$H_0: \sigma_1^2 = \sigma_2^2$$
$$H_a: \sigma_1^2 \neq \sigma_2^2$$
$$n_1 = 8 \quad n_2 = 10 \quad s_1^2 = 46 \quad s_2^2 = 37$$

Testing your understanding

P10-50 **10.50** The table below gives the annual rainfall amounts in millimetres for Melbourne as published by the Australian Bureau of Meteorology (Station No. 086282). Draw a normal probability plot of annual rainfall amounts and comment whether the data can be considered to be normally distributed.

Year	Rainfall (mm)
1993	650.4
1994	382.8
1995	681.0
1996	595.8
1997	310.2
1998	461.8
1999	554.6
2000	558.2
2001	538.4
2002	474.0
2003	419.4
2004	508.2
2005	597.8
2006	555.4
2007	422.6
2008	405.6
2009	397.8
2010	727.4
2011	678.4
2012	482.8
2013	559.8

10.51 A tree nursery has been experimenting with fertiliser to increase the growth of seedlings. To gain more insight, 35 two-year-old pine trees are grown for three more years with a cake of fertiliser buried in the soil near the tree roots. A second group of 35 two-year-old pine trees are grown for three more years under identical conditions (soil, temperature, water) to the first group, except that they are not fertilised. Tree growth is measured over the three-year period with the following results.

Trees with fertiliser	Trees without fertiliser
$n_1 = 35$	$n_2 = 35$
$\bar{x}_1 = 97.5$ cm	$\bar{x}_1 = 58.7$ cm
$\sigma_1 = 24.9$ cm	$\sigma_2 = 18.8$ cm

Do the data support the theory that the population of trees with the fertiliser grew significantly larger during the period in which they were fertilised than the unfertilised trees? Use $\alpha = .01$.

10.52 A boutique confectioner wants to estimate the difference between the average weights of its handmade chocolates sold in Sydney and Melbourne. According to the confectioner's researcher, a random sample of 20 chocolates sold at stores in Sydney yielded a sample mean of 17.53 grams, with a standard deviation of 3.2 grams. Her random sample of 24 handmade chocolates sold at stores in Melbourne yielded a sample mean of 14.89 grams, with a standard deviation of 2.7 grams. Use a 1% level of significance to determine whether there is a difference between the mean weights of handmade chocolates sold in these two cities. Assume that the population variances are approximately the same and that the weights of handmade chocolates sold in the stores are normally distributed.

P10-53 **10.53** A study is conducted to estimate the average difference in bus use in a large city between the morning and afternoon rush hours. The transit authority's researcher randomly selects nine buses because of the variety of routes they represent. On a given day, the number of passengers on each bus is counted at 7.45 am and at 4.45 pm, with the following results.

Bus	Morning	Afternoon
1	43	41
2	51	49
3	37	44
4	24	32
5	47	46
6	44	42
7	50	47
8	55	51
9	46	49

Use the data to compute a 90% confidence interval to estimate the population average difference. Assume that the number of passengers is normally distributed.

10.54 A medical association monitoring two groups of physicians who agreed to participate in a study over a 7-year period found that, of 3420 physicians who took aspirin daily, 147 died from a stroke or heart attack during this period. For 1705 physicians who received a placebo instead of aspirin, 78 deaths were recorded. At the .01 level of significance, does the study indicate that taking aspirin is beneficial in reducing the likelihood of a stroke or heart attack?

P10-55 **10.55** As the prices of heating oil and natural gas increase, consumers become more careful about heating their homes. Researchers want to know how warm home owners keep their houses in July and how the results from Wollongong and Newcastle compare. The researchers randomly call 23 Wollongong households between 7 pm and 9 pm on 15 July and ask the respondent the temperature (°C) of the house according to the thermostat setting. The researchers then call 19 households in Newcastle on the same night and ask the same question. The results follow.

Wollongong	Newcastle
21.7	22.8
21.1	23.3
23.9	22.2
23.3	23.3
20.6	20.6
21.1	23.9
21.7	22.8
16.1	21.7
20.0	22.8
20.0	21.1
22.2	23.3
22.8	23.3
18.3	20.6
19.4	21.1
21.7	19.4
19.4	21.7
19.4	21.1
22.2	22.2
20.0	22.2
20.6	
22.8	
20.6	
22.2	

Assuming that the temperatures are normally distributed, construct a 95% confidence interval for the ratio of the variances of temperatures of houses in Newcastle and in Wollongong on the evening of 15 July.

MATHS APPENDIX

M

Geometric mean

If $x_1, x_2, \ldots, x_n$ are n observations, the geometric mean of these values is given by $\bar{x}_g = (x_1 \times x_2 \times \ldots \times x_n)^{\frac{1}{n}}$. The geometric mean rate of return for a return stream $r_1, r_2, \ldots, r_n$ gives the average percentage return of an investment expressed as $\bar{r}_g = [(1+r_1) \times (1+r_2) \times \ldots \times (1+r_n)]^{\frac{1}{n}} - 1$.

CHAPTER

11 Analysis of variance and design of experiments

LEARNING OBJECTIVES

After studying this chapter, you should be able to:

1. understand the differences between various experimental designs and when to use them
2. compute and interpret the results of a one-way ANOVA
3. know when and how to use multiple comparison techniques
4. compute and interpret the results of a randomised block design
5. compute and interpret the results of a two-way ANOVA.

OPENING VIGNETTE

Australian teens and luxury brands

Most teenagers want to 'belong' — to be part of a group. The down side is that they can experience a lot of pressure to act in certain ways. *Peer pressure* occurs when people are influenced to do something they would not usually do because they want to feel accepted by a certain group. Peer pressure can surface in many different forms. One of the most common is the pressure to dress in a certain way, or to wear particular brands of clothing and apparel.

Like teenagers everywhere, Australian teens believe that what they wear affects their popularity. In fact, a British study by Elliot and Leonard (2004) found that young children form stereotypes about people simply on the basis of the brand of trainers they wear. The study found that if the trainers are branded and expensive, children believe the owner to be rich and young. If the trainers are unbranded and cheap-looking, children perceive the owner to be poor and old. The researchers also found that children wearing branded trainers are seen as popular, and easily fit in with their peers.

An Australian study by Phau and Yip (2008) also researched this phenomenon, examining the attitudes of status-seeking and non-status-seeking teenagers toward domestic and foreign luxury brands. As part of their research, they surveyed 365 teenagers by way of a questionnaire. Once they collected the data, the researchers used ANOVA and *t*-tests to examine whether the groups had different views about buying luxury branded clothing. The clothing was differentiated by country of manufacture: 'Made in Australia', 'Made in Italy', 'Made in Japan' and 'Made in China'.

Phau and Yip's research found that among the status-seeking teenagers, there was a more positive attitude toward brands made in Italy and Japan, with Chinese brands being the least popular. However non-status-seeking teenagers had a more positive attitude towards brands made in Australia than those made in Italy, Japan or China.

This type of practical research has important business implications for the Australian apparel industry. Its findings suggest that Australian clothing manufacturers should concentrate on a marketing strategy that boosts the attributes of 'fashionable' and 'brand name' that both status-seeking and non-status-seeking teenagers prefer in foreign apparel. The study also suggested that the Australian clothing industry should cooperate with the Italian industry in using more Italian textiles and designs to reposition its brand name and image in the Australian market. Another alternative would be to use more Australian textiles (especially wool) in Italian clothing, so as to boost local industries.

Introduction

Sometimes business research entails more complicated hypothesis-testing scenarios than those presented to this point in the text. For example, instead of comparing the wear of tyre tread for two brands of tyres to determine whether there is a significant difference between the brands, a tyre researcher may choose to compare three, four or even more brands of tyres at the same time. In addition, the researcher may want to include different levels of quality of tyres in the experiment, such as low-quality, medium-quality and high-quality tyres. Tests may be conducted under different conditions of temperature, precipitation or road surface.

How does a researcher set up designs for such experiments? How can the data be analysed? These questions can be answered, in part, through the use of analysis of variance and the design of experiments.

Analysis of variance is a statistical test to determine whether the population means of a dependent variable for several groups are all equal. It therefore extends the t test to more than two groups. Doing multiple two-sample t tests would result in an increased chance of committing a type I error.

For this reason, analysis of variance tests are useful in comparing two, three, four or more means simultaneously. The test was first used in the 1920s to determine whether different treatments of fertiliser produced different crop yields.

CHAPTER CASE

Cyberbullying amongst Australian adolescents

It is a normal part of growing up that there will be conflicts between children. Because of this, adults can make the mistake of treating bullying or cyberbullying as a normal childhood conflict when in fact, such actions can be very serious and potentially very harmful for the child in the long run.

Headspace.org.au documents several forms of cyberbullying:

- *harassment* — sending offensive messages targeted to a group or individual
- *cyber stalking* — persistent behaviours, including threats of harm, that instil apprehension and fear
- *outing* — the public display, posting, or forwarding of personal messages or images. It includes behaviours such as reading out saved messages from someone's mobile phone, printing out an IM chat or copying others into email messages
- *flaming* — an intense argument which often uses offensive or rude language.

Increased internet usage, especially among teenagers, has seen an increase in cyberbullying, and has become a concern both in Australia and New Zealand, and internationally. As a result, there has been increasing research into the area of cyberbullying and its impact on the victims. The website Nobullying.com has found that older students (or those with more access to technology) are more likely to cyberbully than younger ones.

- Over 80% of those who bullied others online would also do so offline.
- 84% of those who were bullied online were also victims of bullying behaviour offline.
- One-quarter of all cyberbullies target people they do not even know.
- 64% of females in school years 6 to 12 reported being cyberbullied.
- Increased smartphone usage has made cyberbullying easier than ever before.

There are many factors which place students at risk of being bullied. Research published in the *American Journal of Public Health* found that children from poor families were more likely to be bullied than others. The study also concluded that schools with the largest economic inequality (or a big difference between how wealthy some families are and how poor other families are) had the highest rates of bullying. A similar study in Australia surveyed a total of 1000 young people, with 230 coming from higher socioeconomic backgrounds, 480 from a middle-class background, and 290 coming from a low socioeconomic background. The respondents were surveyed as to whether or not they had ever experienced cyberbullying. The measures were combined to give the overall score related to the participant's experience. Some of the data for further analysis in the study follow.

	Cyberbullying experiences	
Higher socioeconomic	**Middle socioeconomic**	**Lower socioeconomic**
30	41	34
34	35	33
32	37	32
35	37	34
34	40	35
35	39	35
32	43	34
31	39	32
	38	31
		30

The issue of cyberbullying among teenagers has become so prevalent that it requires a crucial response from schools, parents and advocacy organisations.

Questions to help managers make decisions

Cyber

1. Test whether there is a difference in cyberbullying experiences of young people according to their socioeconomic status.
2. From question 1, if you found differences in the cyberbullying experiences of young people, how do you test which group is significantly different from the others?
3. Do other demographic variables such as gender and age make a difference? If we record gender (or age) along with cyberbullying experiences for each of the three groups, is it possible to determine whether there is an interaction between each group and gender (or age)? What statistical techniques might be used to analyse the interaction of each of the groups and gender (or income). How do the results affect the other parts of the study?

11.1 Introduction to design of experiments

An **experimental design** is a plan and structure to test hypotheses in which the researcher either controls or manipulates the variables being studied. It contains one dependent and one or more independent variables. In an experimental design:

- a **dependent variable** is the variable of interest with a parameter, such as population mean, that we are trying to estimate or predict
- an **independent variable** may be either a treatment variable or a classification variable. Independent variables are also referred to as **factors**
- a **treatment variable** is a variable, such as dosage, that the experimenter controls or modifies in the experiment
- a **classification variable** is some characteristic of the experimental subjects, such as gender, that was present prior to the experiment and is not a result of the experimenter's manipulations or control.

Coles supermarket executives might request an in-house study to compare daily sales volumes for a given size store in four different demographic settings: inner-city stores (large city), suburban stores (large city), stores in a medium-sized city and stores in a small town. Managers might also decide to compare sales on the five different weekdays (Monday to Friday). In this study, the dependent variable is the daily sales volumes and the independent variables are store demographics and day of the week.

A finance researcher might conduct a study to determine whether there is a significant difference in application fees for home loans in five geographical regions of Australia, and he might include three different types of lending organisations. The dependent variable here is the fee charged for the loan application and the independent variables are geographical region and type of lending organisations.

In another example, suppose a manufacturing company produces a valve that is specified to have an opening of 6.5 cm. Quality controllers within the company might decide to test how the opening sizes in valves produced on four different machines vary in three different work shifts. This experiment includes the independent variables of type of machine and work shift. The dependent variable is the opening size of the valve.

Whether an independent variable can be manipulated by the researcher depends on the concept being studied. For example, the conditions of the independent variables of work shift and type of machine in the valve example existed prior to the study; therefore, they are known as classification variables. However, some independent variables can be manipulated by the researcher. For example, in the Hawthorne studies of the Western Electric Company in the 1920s, the amount of light in production areas was varied to determine the effect of light on productivity. In theory, this independent variable could be manipulated by the researcher to allow any level of lighting. Other examples of independent variables that can be manipulated include the size of bonuses offered to workers, level of humidity and temperature.

Each independent variable has two or more levels, or classifications. **Levels**, or *classifications*, of independent variables are the subcategories of the independent variable used by the researcher in the experimental design. For example, the different demographic settings listed for the Coles study have four levels, or classifications, of the independent variable (store demographics): inner-city store, suburban store, store in a medium-sized city and store in a small town. In the valve experiment, four levels or classifications of machines within the independent variable (machine type) are used: machine 1, machine 2, machine 3 and machine 4.

Experimental designs in this chapter are analysed statistically by a group of techniques referred to as **analysis of variance (ANOVA)**. ANOVA is a procedure that tests whether differences exist between two or more population means. Although we are testing whether the population means differ, the calculations are performed by analysing the variance of the data. The concept of ANOVA begins with the notion that individual items being studied are not all the same. For example, the measurements for the openings of 24 valves randomly selected from an assembly line are given in table 11.1. The mean valve opening measure is 6.34 cm. Only one of the 24 valve openings is actually the mean. Why do the valve openings vary? Notice that the total sum of squares of deviation of these valve openings around the mean is 0.39 cm^2. Why is this value not zero? Using various types of experimental designs, we can use ANOVA techniques to explore some possible reasons for this variance. As we explore each of the experimental designs and its associated analysis, note that the statistical technique is attempting to 'break down' the total variance among the objects being studied into possible causes. In the case of valve openings, this variance of measurements might be due to variables such as machine, operator, shift, supplier and production conditions.

TABLE 11.1 Valve opening measurements (in cm) of 24 valves produced on an assembly line

6.26	6.19	6.33	6.26	6.50
6.19	6.44	6.22	6.54	6.23
6.29	6.40	6.23	6.29	6.58
6.27	6.38	6.58	6.31	6.34
6.21	6.19	6.36	6.56	

$\bar{x} = 6.34$, total sum of squares of deviation $= SST = \Sigma(\bar{x}_i - \bar{x})^2 = 0.39$

Many different types of experimental designs are available to researchers. In this chapter, we will present and discuss three specific types of experimental designs: completely randomised design, randomised block design and factorial experiments.

PRACTICE PROBLEMS

Testing your understanding

11.1 Suppose an economist is interested in developing a model that predicts total household expenditure as a function of household disposable income.

a. State the independent variable.

b. List at least two levels, or classifications, for the variable in part (a).

c. Give the dependent variable for this study.

11.2 A market analyst for an online music store is analysing the relationship between sales in alternative music and the size of the teenage population. She gathers data from six Australian states.

a. State an independent variable for such a study.

b. What are some of the levels or classifications that might be studied under the variable in part (a)?

c. Give a dependent variable for this study.

11.3 A large multinational bank wants to determine whether there is a significant difference in the average dollar amounts purchased by users of different types of credit cards. Among the credit cards being studied are MasterCard, Visa and American Express.

a. If an experimental design is set up for such a study, what are some possible independent variables?

b. List at least three levels, or classifications, for each independent variable in part (a).

c. What are some possible dependent variables for this experiment?

11.4 Is there a difference in the family demographics of people who stay at motels? Suppose a study is conducted on three categories of motels: economy motels, modestly priced chain motels and exclusive motels. One of the dependent variables studied might be the number of children in the family of the person staying in the motel. Name three other dependent variables that might be used in this study.

11.2 The completely randomised design (one-way ANOVA)

One of the simplest experimental designs is the **completely randomised design**, where *subjects are randomly selected and then randomly assigned to treatments*. The completely randomised design contains only one independent variable, with two or more treatment levels, or classifications. If only two treatment levels, or classifications, of the independent variable are present, the design is the same as that used to test the difference between means of two independent populations, using the *t* test to analyse the data.

In this section, we will focus on completely randomised designs with three or more classification levels. A **one-way analysis of variance (one-way ANOVA)** will be used to analyse the data that result from the treatments. This process involves computing a ratio of the variance between treatment levels of the independent variable to the error variance. This ratio is an *F* value, which is then used to determine whether there are any significant differences between the population means of the treatment levels.

As an example of a completely randomised design, suppose a researcher decides to analyse the effects of the machine operator on the opening sizes of valves produced in a manufacturing plant, like those shown in table 11.1. The independent variable in this design is machine operator. Suppose that four different people operate the machines. These four machine operators are the treatment levels, or classifications, of the independent variable. Machines are randomly assigned to operators. The dependent variable is the opening size of the valve. Figure 11.1 shows the structure of this completely randomised design. Is there a significant difference between the mean valve openings of 24 valves produced by the four operators? Table 11.2 contains the valve opening sizes for valves produced by each operator.

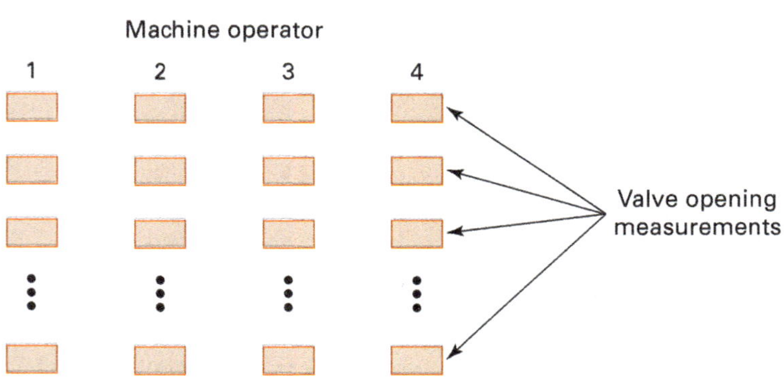

FIGURE 11.1 Completely randomised design

TABLE 11.2 Valve opening sizes (cm) by machine operator

Operator			
1	2	3	4
6.33	6.26	6.44	6.29
6.26	6.36	6.38	6.23
6.31	6.23	6.58	6.19
6.29	6.27	6.54	6.21
6.40	6.19	6.56	
	6.50	6.34	
	6.19	6.58	
	6.22		

In general, if k samples are being analysed, the following hypothesis is tested in a one-way ANOVA.

$$H_0: \mu_1 = \mu_2 = \mu_3 = \ldots = \mu_k$$

The null hypothesis states that the population means for all treatment levels are equal. This is tested against the alternative hypothesis that not all population means are equal,

$$H_a\text{: At least one of the means is different from the others.}$$

Because of the way the alternative hypothesis is stated, if even one of the population means is different from the others, the null hypothesis is rejected.

To test these hypotheses by using one-way ANOVA, split the total variance of the data into two variances:

1. the variance resulting from or explained by the treatment (columns)
2. the error variance, or that portion of the total variance unexplained by the treatment.

As part of this process, the total sum of squares of variation is partitioned into the sum of squares of the treatment (columns) and the sum of squares of the error. This relationship is shown in figure 11.2.

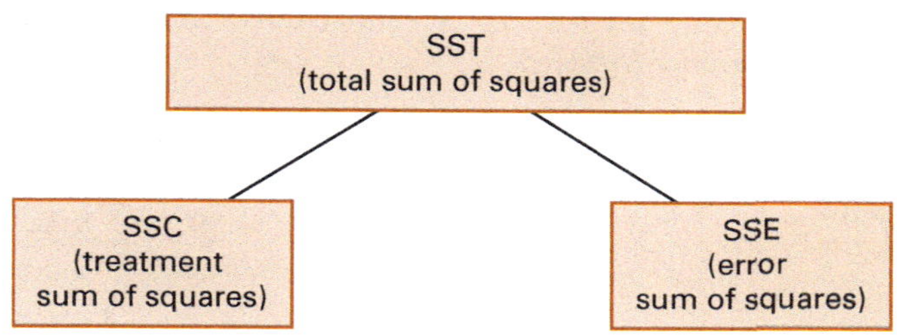

FIGURE 11.2 Partitioning the total sum of squares of variation

Figure 11.3 displays the data from the machine operator example in terms of treatment level. Note the variation of values (x) *within* each treatment level. Now examine the variation *between* the four levels (the difference between the machine operators). In particular, note that values for treatment level 3 seem to be located differently from those of levels 2 and 4. This difference also is underscored by the mean values for each treatment level:

$$\bar{x}_1 = 6.32 \quad \bar{x}_2 = 6.28 \quad \bar{x}_3 = 6.49 \quad \bar{x}_4 = 6.23$$

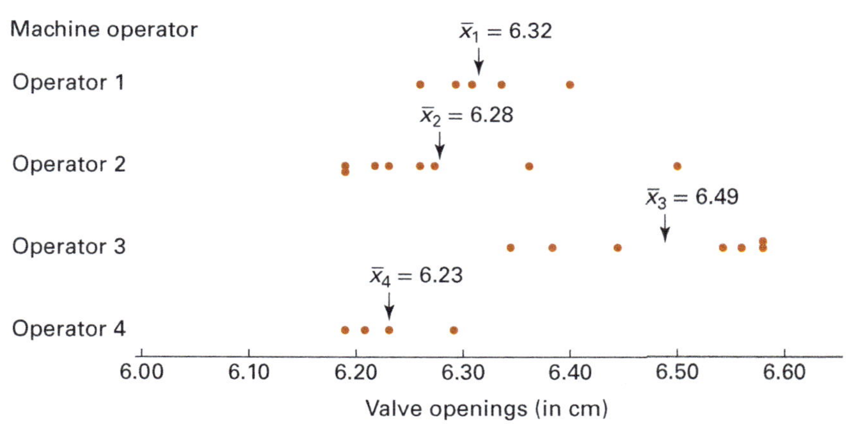

FIGURE 11.3 Location of mean value openings by operator

Analysis of variance is used to determine statistically whether the variance between the treatment level means is greater than the variances within levels (error variance). The following important assumptions underlie analysis of variance.

1. Observations are drawn from normally distributed populations.
2. Observations represent random samples from the populations.
3. Observations in the populations have equal variances.

These assumptions are similar to those for using the t test for small independent samples. It is assumed that the populations are normally distributed and that the population variances are equal. These techniques should be used only with random samples.

An ANOVA is computed using the three sums of squares: total, treatment (columns) and error. Formula 11.1 gives the calculations required to compute a one-way analysis of variance. The term SS represents 'sum of squares', and MS represents 'mean square'. SSC is the sum of squares of columns (often called sum of squares between), which yields the sum of squares of treatments; it measures the variation between columns or between treatments, since the independent variable treatment levels are presented in columns. SSE is the sum of squares of error (often called sum of squares within), which yields the variation within treatments (or columns); it is the variation that is unexplained by the treatment. SST is the total sum of squares and is a measure of all variation in the dependent variable. As shown previously, SST contains both SSC and SSE and can be partitioned into SSC and SSE. MSC, MSE and MST are the mean squares of columns, error and total, respectively. Mean square is an average and is computed by dividing the sum of squares by the degrees of freedom. F is a ratio of two variances. The **F value (ANOVA)** is the *ratio of the treatment variance (MSC) to the error variance (MSE)*.

Formulas for computing a one-way ANOVA
(11.1)

$$\text{SSC} = \sum_{j=1}^{C} n_j(\bar{x}_j - \bar{x})^2$$

$$\text{SSE} = \sum_{i=1}^{n_j}\sum_{j=1}^{C}(x_{ij} - \bar{x}_j)^2$$

$$\text{SST} = \sum_{i=1}^{n_j}\sum_{j=1}^{C}(x_{ij} - \bar{x})^2$$

$$\text{df}_C = C - 1$$

$$\text{df}_E = N - C$$

$$\text{df}_T = N - 1$$

$$\text{MSC} = \frac{\text{SSC}}{\text{df}_C}$$

$$\text{MSE} = \frac{\text{SSE}}{\text{df}_E}$$

$$F = \frac{\text{MSC}}{\text{MSE}}$$

where:

i = a particular member of a treatment level
j = a treatment level
C = number of treatment levels
N = total number of observations
n_j = number of observations in a given treatment level
$\bar{x}$ = grand mean
$\bar{x}_j$ = column mean
x_{ij} = a particular value for individual i in treatment j

Performing the calculations for the machine operator example (table 11.2) yields the following.

T_j: $T_1 = 31.59$	$T_2 = 50.22$	$T_3 = 45.42$	$T_4 = 24.92$	$T = 152.15$
n_j: $n_1 = 5$	$n_2 = 8$	$n_3 = 7$	$n_4 = 4$	$N = 24$
$\bar{x}_j : \bar{x}_1 = 6.32$	$\bar{x}_2 = 6.28$	$\bar{x}_3 = 6.49$	$\bar{x}_4 = 6.23$	$\bar{x} = 6.34$

$$\begin{aligned}\text{SSC} = \sum_{j=1}^{C} n_j (x_j - \bar{x})^2 &= 5(6.32-6.34)^2 + 8(6.28-6.34)^2 \\ &\quad + 7(6.49-6.34)^2 \\ &\quad + 4(6.23-6.34)^2 \\ &= 0.0020 + 0.0288 + 0.1575 + 0.0484 \\ &= 0.2367\end{aligned}$$

$$\begin{aligned}\text{SSE} = \sum_{i=1}^{n_j} \sum_{j=1}^{C} (x_{ij} - \bar{x}_j)^2 &= (6.33-6.32)^2 + (6.26-6.32)^2 \\ &\quad + (6.31-6.32)^2 + (6.29-6.32)^2 \\ &\quad + (6.40-6.32)^2 + (6.26-6.28)^2 \\ &\quad + (6.36-6.28)^2 + \cdots + (6.19-6.23) \\ &\quad + (6.21-6.23)^2 \\ &= 0.1550\end{aligned}$$

$$\begin{aligned}\text{SST} = \sum_{i=1}^{n_j} \sum_{j=1}^{C} (x_{ij} - \bar{x})^2 &= (6.33-6.34)^2 + (6.26-6.34)^2 \\ &\quad + (6.31-6.33)^2 + \cdots \\ &\quad + (6.19-6.34)^2 + (6.21-6.34)^2 \\ &= 0.3917\end{aligned}$$

$$\text{df}_C = C - 1 = 4 - 1 = 3$$

$$\text{df}_E = N - C = 24 - 4 = 20$$

$$\text{df}_T = N - 1 = 24 - 1 = 23$$

$$\text{MSC} = \frac{\text{SSC}}{\text{df}_C} = \frac{0.2367}{3} = 0.0789$$

$$\text{MSE} = \frac{\text{SSE}}{\text{df}_E} = \frac{0.1550}{20} = 0.0078$$

$$F = \frac{0.0789}{0.0078} = 10.12$$

From these computations, an analysis of variance chart can be constructed, as shown in table 11.3. The observed F value is 10.12. It is compared with a critical value from the F table to determine whether there are significant differences in treatment effects.

TABLE 11.3 Analysis of variance for the machine operator example

Source of variance	df	SS	MS	*F*
Between	3	0.2367	0.0789	10.12
Error	20	0.1550	0.0078	
Total	23	0.3917		

Reading the *F* distribution table

The *F* distribution table is in table A.7. Associated with every *F* value in the table are two unique degrees of freedom (df) values: degrees of freedom in the numerator (df_C) and degrees of freedom in the denominator (df_E).

The df_C values are the treatment (column) degrees of freedom, $C - 1$. The df_E values are the error degrees of freedom, $N - C$. Table 11.4 contains an abbreviated *F* distribution table for $\alpha = .05$. For the machine operator example, $df_C = 3$ and $df_E = 20$. $F_{.05,\,3,\,20}$ from table 11.4 is 3.10. Analysis of variance tests are always one-tailed tests with the rejection region in the upper tail. The decision rule is to reject the null hypothesis if the observed *F* value is greater than the critical *F* value ($F_{.05,\,3,\,20} = 3.10$). For the machine operator problem, as the observed *F* value of 10.12 is larger than the table *F* value of 3.10 (figure 11.4), the null hypothesis is rejected. Not all means are equal; i.e. there is a significant difference between the mean openings of valves produced by different machine operators. Figure 11.4 is a graph of an *F* distribution showing the critical *F* value and the rejection region for this example. Note that the *F* distribution begins at zero and contains no negative values because the *F* value is the ratio of two variances, and variances are always positive.

TABLE 11.4 An abbreviated *F* table for $\alpha = .05$

	Numerator degrees of freedom								
Denominator degrees of freedom	**1**	**2**	**3**	**4**	**5**	**6**	**7**	**8**	**9**
.									
.									
.									
19	4.38	3.52	3.13	2.90	2.74	2.63	2.54	2.48	2.42
20	4.35	3.49	3.10	2.87	2.71	2.60	2.51	2.45	2.39
21	4.32	3.47	3.07	2.84	2.68	2.57	2.49	2.42	2.37

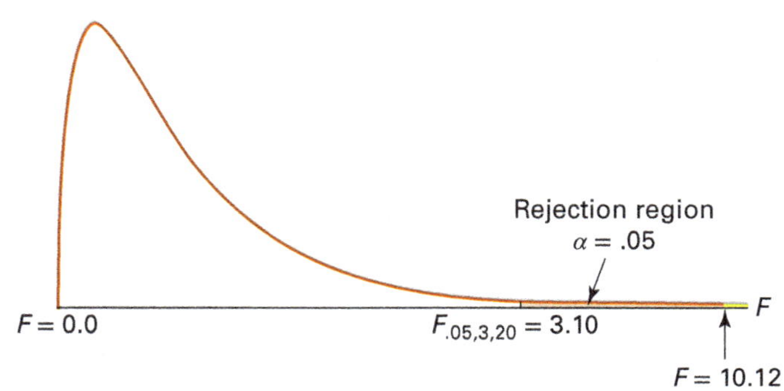

FIGURE 11.4 Graph of *F* values for the machine operator example

DEMONSTRATION PROBLEM 11.1

PROBLEM: A company has three manufacturing plants, and company officials want to determine whether there is a significant difference between the average ages of workers at the three locations. The following data are the ages of five randomly selected workers at each plant. Perform a one-way ANOVA to determine whether there is a significant difference between the mean ages of the workers at the three plants. Use $\alpha = .01$ and note that the sample sizes are equal.

Worker ages		
Plant 1	**Plant 2**	**Plant 3**
29	32	25
27	33	24
30	31	24
27	34	25
28	30	26

SOLUTION:

STEP 1. Set up H_0 and H_a

H_0: $\mu_1 = \mu_2 = \mu_3$

H_a: At least one of the population means is different from the others.

STEP 2. Decide on the type of test

The appropriate test is the F test calculated from one-way ANOVA

where. $F = \dfrac{\text{MSC}}{\text{MSE}}$.

STEP 3. Decide on the level of significance, α, and determine the critical value(s) and region(s)

The value of α is .01. The degrees of freedom for this problem are $3 - 1 = 2$ for the numerator (treatments – columns) and $15 - 3 = 12$ for the denominator (error). The critical F value is $F_{.01,\,2,\,12} = 6.93$. The ANOVA test is always a one-tail test with the rejection region in the upper tail.

STEP 4. Write down the decision rule

The decision rule is to reject the null hypothesis if the observed value of F is greater than the critical value of 6.93.

STEP 5. Select a random sample and do relevant calculations

The data were provided on the previous page. The following calculations are required to compute an ANOVA.

$T_j : T_1 = 141$	$T_2 = 160$	$T_3 = 124$	$T = 425$
$n_j : n_1 = 5$	$n_2 = 5$	$n_3 = 5$	$N = 15$
$\bar{x}_j : \bar{x}_1 = 28.2$	$\bar{x}_2 = 32.0$	$\bar{x}_3 = 24.8$	$\bar{x} = 28.33$

$$\text{SSC} = 5(28.2 - 28.33)^2 + 5(32.0 - 28.33)^2 + 5(24.8 - 28.33)^2 = 129.73$$
$$\text{SSE} = (29 - 28.2)^2 + (27 - 28.2)^2 + \cdots + (25 - 24.8)^2 + (26 - 24.8)^2 = 19.60$$
$$\text{SST} = (29 - 28.33)^2 + (27 - 28.33)^2 + \cdots + (25 - 28.33)^2 + (26 - 28.33)^2 = 149.33$$
$$df_C = 3 - 1 = 2$$
$$df_E = 15 - 3 = 12$$
$$df_T = 15 - 1 = 14$$

The Excel output for ANOVA is shown below.

	A	B	C	D	E
1	*Source of Variation*	*SS*	*Df*	*MS*	*F*
2	Between Groups	129.73	2	64.87	39.71
3	Within Groups	19.60	12	1.63	
4	Total	149.33	14		

STEP 6. Draw a conclusion

The decision is to reject the null hypothesis as the observed F value of 39.71 is greater than the critical table F value of 6.93. Thus, there is a significant difference between the mean ages of workers at the three plants. This difference can have hiring implications. Company leaders should understand that, because motivation, discipline and experience may differ with age, the differences between ages may call for different managerial approaches in each plant.

The following chart displays the dispersion of the ages of workers from the three samples, along with the mean age for each plant sample. Note the difference between group means. The significant F value implies that the variation between the mean ages is relatively greater than the variation in ages within each group.

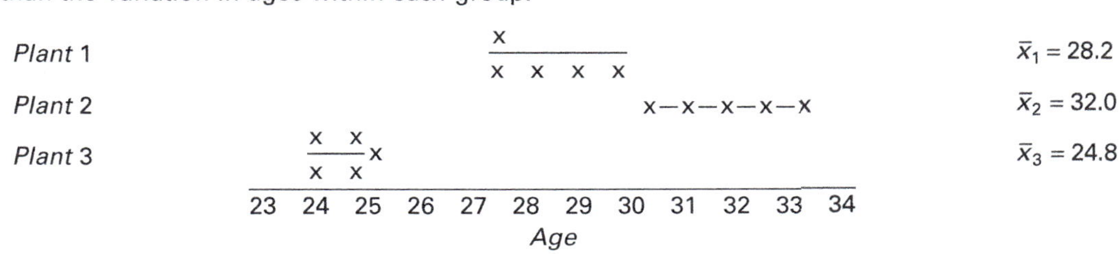

One-way ANOVA

DP11-01

1. Access DP11-01.xls from the student website.
2. From the Data tab, select Data Analysis.
3. From the Data Analysis dialogue box, select ANOVA: Single Factor and click OK.
4. In the ANOVA: Single Factor dialogue box:
   a. enter the data range in the Input Range field
   b. choose Grouped By: Columns
   c. check Labels in First Row if you have included the column labels in the Input Range. If not, leave it unchecked.
   d. enter .01 for Alpha
   e. choose an output option

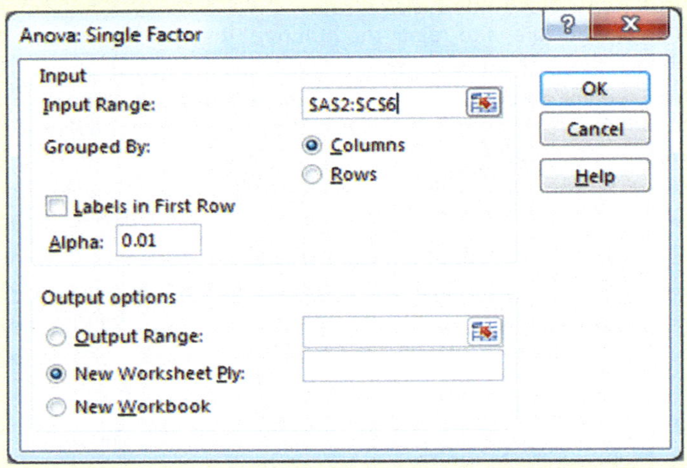

   f. click OK.

The Excel output follows.

	A	B	C	D	E	F	G
1	Anova: Single Factor						
2							
3	SUMMARY						
4	*Groups*	*Count*	*Sum*	*Average*	*Variance*		
5	Column 1	5	141	28.2	1.7		
6	Column 2	5	160	32.0	2.5		
7	Column 3	5	124	24.8	0.7		
8							
9							
10	ANOVA						
11	*Source of Variation*	*SS*	*df*	*MS*	*F*	*P-value*	*F crit*
12	Between Groups	129.73	2	64.87	39.71	0.00001	6.93
13	Within Groups	19.60	12	1.63			
14							
15	Total	149.33	14				
16							

PRACTICE PROBLEMS

Practising the calculations

P11-05 **11.5** Compute a one-way ANOVA of the following data.

A	B	C
3	6	4
2	4	5
4	8	7
5	5	8
3	7	2
2		4

Determine the observed *F* value. Compare the observed *F* value with the critical table *F* value and decide whether to reject the null hypothesis. Use $\alpha = .05$.

P11-06 **11.6** Develop a one-way ANOVA of the following data.

A	B	C	D
113	120	132	122
121	127	130	118
117	125	129	125
110	129	135	125

Determine the observed *F* value. Compare it with the critical *F* value and decide whether to reject the null hypothesis. Use a 1% level of significance.

11.7 Suppose you are using a completely randomised design to study some phenomenon. There are five treatment levels and a total of 55 people in the study. Each treatment level has the same sample size. Complete the following ANOVA table.

Source of variation	SS	df	MS	*F*
Treatment	688.66			
Error	1035.7			
Total	1887.32			

11.8 Suppose you are using a completely randomised design to study some phenomenon. There are three treatment levels and a total of 17 people in the study. Complete the following ANOVA table. Use $\alpha = .05$ to find the table *F* value and use the data to test the null hypothesis.

Source of variation	SS	df	MS	*F*
Treatment	29.64			
Error	68.42			
Total				

Testing your understanding

P11-09 **11.9** A market research firm is analysing the profits of its five largest clients in NSW, Queensland and Victoria to decide where it should prioritise its market. Use a one-way ANOVA to analyse the following data. Note that the data can be restated to make the computations easier (for example: $42 500 = 4.25). Use a 1% level of significance. Discuss the business implications of your findings.

NSW ($ million)	Victoria ($ million)	Queensland ($ million)
15 500	45 000	41 500
16 500	43 500	39 500
15 000	43 000	41 000
16 000	42 000	42 500
16 500	43 500	42 000

P11-10 **11.10** A management consulting company presents a three-day seminar on project management to various clients. The seminar is basically the same each time it is given. However, sometimes it is presented to high-level managers, sometimes to mid-level managers and sometimes to low-level managers. The seminar organisers believe evaluations of the seminar may vary with the audience. Suppose the following data are some randomly selected evaluation scores from different levels of managers who attended the seminar. The ratings are on a scale from 1 to 10, with 10 being the highest. Use a one-way ANOVA to determine whether there is a significant difference in the evaluations according to manager level. Assume $\alpha = .05$. Discuss the business implications of your findings.

High-level	Mid-level	Low-level
7	8	5
7	9	6
8	8	5
7	10	7
9	9	4
	10	8
	8	

11.11 Business is very good for a chemical company. In fact, it is so good that workers are averaging more than 40 hours per week at each of the chemical company's five plants. However, management is not certain whether there is a difference between the five plants in the average number of hours worked per week per worker. Random samples of data are taken at each of the five plants. The data are analysed using Excel. The results follow. Explain the design of the study and determine whether there is an overall significant difference between the means at $\alpha = .05$? Why or why not? What are the values of the means? What are the business implications of this study to the chemical company?

	A	B	C	D	E	F	G
1	Anova: Single Factor						
2							
3	SUMMARY						
4	*Groups*	*Count*	*Sum*	*Average*	*Variance*		
5	Plant 1	11	662	60.18	57.16		
6	Plant 2	12	674	56.17	52.70		
7	Plant 3	8	529	66.13	47.55		
8	Plant 4	5	255	51.00	67.50		
9	Plant 5	7	395	56.43	146.95		
10							
11							
12	ANOVA						
13	*Source of Variation*	*SS*	*df*	*MS*	*F*	*P-value*	*F crit*
14	Between Groups	872.85	4	218.21	3.15	0.02	2.62
15	Within Groups	2635.89	38	69.37			
16							
17	Total	3508.74	42				
18							

11.3 Multiple comparison tests

When the result of an analysis of variance yields an overall significant difference between the treatment means, we often need to know which treatment means are responsible for the difference.

Although many techniques are available, this text considers only a posteriori or *post hoc* pairwise comparisons. **A posteriori** or *post hoc* pairwise comparisons are made *after the experiment when the researcher decides to test for significant differences between the sample means based on a significant overall F value.* The two **multiple comparison tests** discussed here are Tukey's HSD test for designs with equal sample sizes and the Tukey–Kramer procedure for situations in which sample sizes are unequal.

Tukey's honestly significant difference (HSD) test: the case of equal sample sizes

Tukey's honestly significant difference (HSD) test, sometimes known as Tukey's T method, is a popular test for pairwise a posteriori multiple comparisons. This test, developed by John W Tukey and presented in 1953, is somewhat limited by the fact that it requires equal sample sizes.

Tukey's HSD test takes into consideration the number of treatment levels, the value of mean square error and the sample size. Using these values and a table value, q, the HSD determines the critical difference necessary between the means of any two treatment levels for the means to be significantly different. Once the HSD is computed, the researcher can examine the absolute value of any or all differences between pairs of means from treatment levels to determine whether there is a significant difference. Formula 11.2 is for Tukey's HSD test.

Tukey's HSD test (11.2)

$$\text{HSD} = q_{\alpha, C, N-C}\sqrt{\frac{\text{MSE}}{n}}$$

where:
C = number of treatment levels
N = total number of observations
MSE = mean square error
n = sample size
$q_{\alpha, C, N-C}$ = critical value of the studentised range distribution from table A.10

In demonstration problem 11.1, an ANOVA was used to determine that there was an overall significant difference between the mean ages of workers at three different plants, as evidenced by the F value of 39.71. The sample data are shown below, along with the group means and sample sizes:

	Plant		
	1	2	3
	29	32	25
	27	33	24
	30	31	24
	27	34	25
	28	30	26
Group means	28.2	32.0	24.8
n_j	5	5	5

Because the sample sizes are equal in this problem, Tukey's HSD test can be used for multiple comparisons between plants 1 and 2, 2 and 3, and 1 and 3. To compute the HSD, the values of MSE, n and q must be determined. From the solution presented in demonstration problem 11.1, the value of MSE is 1.63. The sample size, n_j, is 5. The value of q is obtained from table A.10 by using: number of populations = number of treatment means = C along with $\text{df}_E = N - C$.

In this problem, the values used to look up q are:

$$C = 3$$
$$\text{df}_E = N - C = 12$$

Table A.10 has a q table for α = .05 and one for α = .01. In this problem, α = .01. Shown in table 11.5 is a portion of table A.10 for α = .01.

TABLE 11.5 q values for $\alpha = .01$

	Number of populations			
Degrees of freedom	2	3	4	5
1	90	135	164	186
2	14	19	22.3	24.7
3	8.26	10.6	12.2	13.3
4	6.51	8.12	9.17	9.96
.				
.				
.				
11	4.39	5.14	5.62	5.97
12	4.32	5.04	5.50	5.84

For this problem, $q_{.01,\,3,\,12} = 5.04$. HSD is computed as:

$$\text{HSD} = q\sqrt{\frac{\text{MSE}}{n}} = 5.04\sqrt{\frac{1.63}{5}} = 2.88$$

Using this value of HSD, the business researcher can examine the differences between the means from any two plants. Any of the pairs of means that differ by more than 2.88 are significantly different at $\alpha = .01$. Here are the differences for all three possible pairwise comparisons.

$$|\bar{x}_1 - \bar{x}_2| = |28.2 - 32.0| = 3.8$$
$$|\bar{x}_1 - \bar{x}_3| = |28.2 - 24.8| = 3.4$$
$$|\bar{x}_2 - \bar{x}_3| = |32.0 - 24.8| = 7.2$$

All three comparisons are greater than the value of HSD, which is 2.88. Thus, the mean ages between any and all pairs of plants are significantly different.

DEMONSTRATION PROBLEM 11.2

PROBLEM: A foundry wants to test the tensile strength of a given metal under various heat treatments. Suppose that the metal is processed under five different heat treatments and that random samples of size 5 are taken under each temperature condition. The data follow.

Tensile strength of metal produced under five different temperature settings

1	2	3	4	5
2.46	2.38	2.51	2.49	2.56
2.41	2.34	2.48	2.47	2.57
2.43	2.31	2.46	2.48	2.53
2.47	2.40	2.49	2.46	2.55
2.46	2.32	2.50	2.44	2.55

A one-way ANOVA is performed on these data using Excel, with the resulting analysis shown below.

	A	B	C	D	E	F	G
1	Anova: Single Factor						
2							
3	SUMMARY						
4	*Groups*	*Count*	*Sum*	*Average*	*Variance*		
5	Column 1	5	12.23	2.446	0.00063		
6	Column 2	5	11.75	2.350	0.00150		
7	Column 3	5	12.44	2.488	0.00037		
8	Column 4	5	12.34	2.468	0.00037		
9	Column 5	5	12.76	2.552	0.00022		
10							
11							
12	ANOVA						
13	*Source of Variation*	*SS*	*df*	*MS*	*F*	*P-value*	*F crit*
14	Between Groups	0.108024	4	0.027006	43.70	1.3E–09	2.866081
15	Within Groups	0.012360	20	0.000618			
16							
17	Total	0.120384	24				
18							

Note from the ANOVA table that the *F* value of 43.70 is greater than the critical value of 2.87. There is an overall difference in the population means of metal produced under the five temperature settings. Use the data to compute a Tukey's HSD to determine which of the five groups are significantly different from the others.

SOLUTION: From the ANOVA table, the value of MSE is .000618. The sample size, n_j, is 5. The number of treatment means, *C*, is 5 and the df_E are 20. With these values and $\alpha = .01$, the value of *q* can be obtained from table A.10.

$$q_{.01,\,5,\,20} = 5.29$$

HSD can be computed as:

$$\text{HSD} = q\sqrt{\frac{\text{MSE}}{n}} = 5.29\sqrt{\frac{0.000618}{5}} = 0.0588$$

The treatment group means for this problem are:

Group 1 = 2.446
Group 2 = 2.350
Group 3 = 2.488
Group 4 = 2.468
Group 5 = 2.552

Computing all pairwise differences between these means (in absolute values) produces the following table.

	Group				
Group	**1**	**2**	**3**	**4**	**5**
1	—	0.096	0.042	0.022	0.106
2	0.096	—	0.138	0.118	0.202
3	0.042	0.138	—	0.020	0.064
4	0.022	0.118	0.020	—	0.084
5	0.106	0.202	0.064	0.084	—

Comparing these differences with the value of HSD = 0.0588, we can determine that the differences between groups 1 and 2 (0.096), 1 and 5 (0.106), 2 and 3 (0.138), 2 and 4 (0.118), 2 and 5 (0.202), 3 and 5 (0.064), and 4 and 5 (0.084) are significant at $\alpha = .01$.

The ANOVA shows that there is an overall significant difference between the treatment levels and also that there are significant differences in the tensile strength of the metal between seven pairs of levels. By studying the magnitudes of the means of individual treatment levels, the foundry can determine which temperatures result in the greatest tensile strength.

Tukey–Kramer procedure: the case of unequal sample sizes

Tukey's HSD was modified by CY Kramer in the mid-1950s to handle situations in which the sample sizes are unequal. The modified version of HSD is sometimes referred to as the **Tukey–Kramer procedure**. Formula 11.3 (overleaf) for computing the significant differences for this procedure is similar to formula 11.2 for equal sample sizes, with the exception that the mean square error is divided in half and weighted by the sums of the inverses of the sample sizes under the root sign.

Tukey–Kramer formula (11.3)

$$q_{\alpha,C,N-C}\sqrt{\frac{\text{MSE}}{2}\left(\frac{1}{n_r}+\frac{1}{n_s}\right)}$$

where:

C = number of treatment levels
N = total number of observations
MSE = mean square error
n_r = sample size for rth sample
n_s = sample size for sth sample
$q_{\alpha,\,C,\,N-C}$ = critical value of the studentised range distribution from table A.10

As an example of the application of the Tukey–Kramer procedure, consider the machine operator example in section 11.2. A one-way ANOVA was used to test for any difference between the mean valve openings produced by four different machine operators. An overall F of 10.12 was computed, which was significant at $\alpha = .05$. Because the ANOVA test was significant and the null hypothesis was rejected, this problem is a candidate for multiple comparisons. The sample sizes are not equal, so Tukey's HSD cannot be used to determine which pairs are significantly different. However, the Tukey–Kramer procedure can be applied. Shown in table 11.6 are the means and sample sizes for the openings of valves produced by the four different operators.

TABLE 11.6 Means and sample sizes for the valves produced by four operators

Operator	Sample size	Mean
1	5	6.3180
2	8	6.2775
3	7	6.4886
4	4	6.2300

The mean square error for this problem, MSE, is shown in table 11.3 as 0.0078. The four operators represent the four levels of the independent variable. Thus, $C = 4$, $N = 24$, and $N - C = 20$. The value of alpha in the problem is .05. With this information, the value of q is obtained from table A.10 as:

$$q_{.05,\,4,\,20} = 3.96$$

Because the sample sizes differ, it is necessary to compute the difference between the means of the two samples. This can be done using the Tukey–Kramer procedure separately for each pair. In this problem with $C = 4$, there are $\frac{C(C-1)}{2}$ or six possible pairwise comparisons. The computations follow.

For operators 1 and 2:

$$3.96\sqrt{\frac{.0078}{2}\left(\frac{1}{5}+\frac{1}{8}\right)} = 0.1405$$

The difference between the means of operator 1 and operator 2 is:

$$6.3180 - 6.2775 = 0.0405$$

As this result is less than the critical difference of 0.1405, there is no significant difference between the average openings of valves produced by machine operators 1 and 2.

Table 11.7 reports the critical differences for each of the six pairwise comparisons as computed by using the Tukey–Kramer procedure, along with the absolute values of the actual differences between the means. Any actual difference between means that is greater than the critical difference is significant. As shown in the table, the means of three pairs of samples — operators 1 and 3, operators 2 and 3, and operators 3 and 4 — are significantly different.

TABLE 11.7 Results of pairwise comparisons for the machine operator example using the Tukey–Kramer procedure

Pair	Critical difference	Actual difference
1 and 2	0.1405	0.0405
1 and 3	0.1443	0.1706*
1 and 4	0.1653	0.0880
2 and 3	0.1275	0.2111*
2 and 4	0.1509	0.0475
3 and 4	0.1545	0.2586*

*Significant at $\alpha = .05$

PRACTICE PROBLEMS

Practising the calculations

11.12 Suppose an ANOVA has been performed on a completely randomised design containing six treatment levels. The mean of group 3 is 20.25, and the sample size is 7. The mean of group 6 is 16.31, and the sample size is 7. MSE is 0.4231. The total number of observations is 46. Compute the significant difference for the means of these two groups by using the Tukey–Kramer procedure.

11.13 A completely randomised design has been analysed by using a one-way ANOVA. There are four treatment groups in the design, and each sample size is 6. MSE is equal to 2.389. Using $\alpha = .05$, compute Tukey's HSD for this ANOVA.

Testing your understanding

11.14 Using the results of problem 11.5, compute a critical value by using the Tukey–Kramer procedure for groups 1 and 2. Use $\alpha = .05$. Determine whether there is a significant difference between these two groups.

11.15 Using the results of problem 11.6, compute Tukey's HSD to determine whether there are any significant differences between group means. Let $\alpha = .01$.

11.16 Use Tukey's HSD test to compute multiple comparisons for the data in problem 11.9. Let $\alpha = .01$. State which regions, if any, are significantly different from other regions in mean starting salaries.

11.17 Using $\alpha = .05$, compute critical values using the Tukey–Kramer procedure for the pairwise groups in problem 11.10. Determine which pairs of groups are significantly different, if any.

11.18 Problem 11.11 analysed the number of weekly hours worked per person at five different plants. An F value of 3.15 was obtained with a probability of .02. Because the probability is less than .05, the null hypothesis is rejected at $\alpha = .05$. Therefore, there is an overall difference between the mean weekly hours worked at the five plants. Which pairs of plants, if any, have significant differences between the means?

11.4 The randomised block design

A second experimental design is the **randomised block design**. The randomised block design not only focuses on one independent variable (treatment variable) of interest, but also includes a second variable, a blocking variable. A **blocking variable** is *a variable that the researcher wants to control but is not the treatment variable of interest*. The randomised block design divides the group of experimental units into homogeneous groups called blocks. The treatments are then randomly assigned to the experimental units in each block — one treatment to a unit in each block. As the randomised block design contains only one measure for each (treatment–block) combination, interaction cannot be analysed in randomised block designs.

For example, demonstration problem 11.2 showed how a completely randomised design could be used to analyse the effects of temperature on the tensile strengths of metal. However, other variables not being controlled by the researcher in this experiment, such as humidity, raw materials, machine and shift, may affect the tensile strength of metal. One way to control for these variables is to include them in the experimental design. The randomised block design can add one of these variables into the analysis as a blocking variable. Blocking can increase precision by removing one source of variation from experimental error.

One of the first people to use the randomised block design was Sir Ronald A Fisher. He applied the design to the field of agriculture, where he was interested in studying the growth patterns of varieties of seeds for a given type of plant. The seed variety was his independent variable. However, he realised that, as he experimented on different plots of ground, the block of ground might make some difference in the experiment. Fisher designated several different plots of ground as blocks, which he controlled as a second variable. All of the seed varieties were planted on all of the blocks. The main thrust of his study was to compare the seed varieties (independent variable). He merely wanted to control for the difference in plots of ground (blocking variable).

A special case of the randomised block design is the **repeated measures design**, which is a randomised block design in which each block level is an individual item or person, and that person or item is measured across all treatments. For example, a block level in a randomised block design may be night shift, and items produced under different treatment levels on the night shift are measured; in a repeated measures design, a block level might be an individual machine or person, and items produced by that person or machine are then randomly chosen across all treatments. Thus, a repeated measure of the person or machine is made across all treatments. This repeated measures design is an extension of the t test for dependent samples.

The sum of squares in a completely randomised design is:

$$\text{SST} = \text{SSC} + \text{SSE}$$

In a randomised block design, the sum of squares is:

$$\text{SST} = \text{SSC} + \text{SSR} + \text{SSE}$$

where:

SST = the total sum of squares
SSC = the sum of squares of columns (treatments)
SSR = the sum of squares of rows (blocks)
SSE = the sum of squares of error.

SST and SSC are the same for a given analysis whether a completely randomised design or a randomised block design is used. For this reason, SSR (blocking effects) comes out of SSE; that is, some of the error variation in the completely randomised design is accounted for in the blocking effects of the randomised block design, as shown in figure 11.5. By reducing the error term, it is possible that the value of F for treatment will increase (the denominator of the F value is decreased). However, if there is not sufficient difference between levels of the blocking variable, the use of a randomised block design can lead to a less powerful test than would a completely randomised design used for the same problem. Thus, the researcher should seek blocking variables that he or she believes are significant contributors to variation in measurements of the dependent variable.

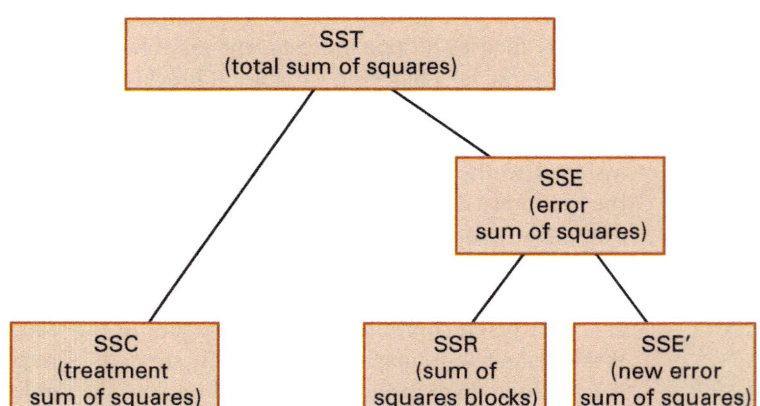

FIGURE 11.5 Partitioning the total sum of squares in a randomised block design

Figure 11.6 shows the layout of a randomised block design; at each of the intersections of independent variable and blocking variable, one measurement is taken. In the randomised block design, one measurement is taken for each treatment level under each blocking level.

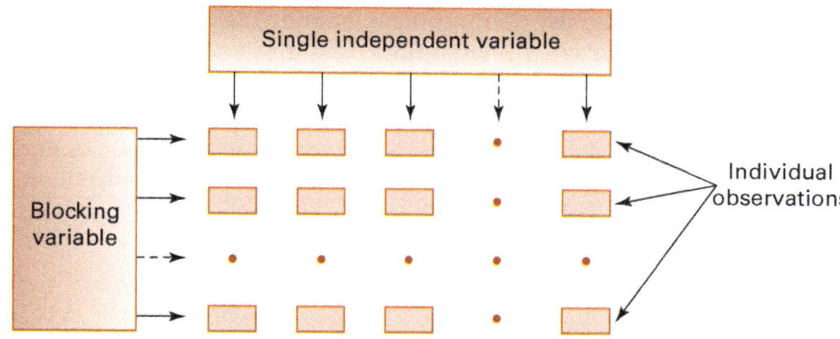

FIGURE 11.6 A randomised block design

The null and alternative hypotheses for the treatment effects in a randomised block design are:

H_0: $\mu_{\cdot 1} = \mu_{\cdot 2} = \mu_{\cdot 3} = \ldots = \mu_{\cdot C}$
H_a: At least one of the treatment means is different from the others.

For the blocking effects, the hypotheses are:

H_0: $\mu_{1\cdot} = \mu_{2\cdot} = \mu_{3\cdot} = \ldots = \mu_{R\cdot}$
H_a: At least one of the blocking means is different from the others.

Essentially, we are testing the null hypothesis that the population means of the treatment groups are equal. If the null hypothesis is rejected, at least one of the population means does not equal the others.

Refer to maths appendix

Since Excel is widely used for analysing a randomised block design, the formulas for computing a randomised block design are given in maths appendix 11.1 at the end of this chapter.

As before, the observed F value for treatments computed using the randomised block design formula is tested by comparing it with a table F value, which is found in table A.7 by using α, df_C (treatment) and df_E (error). If the observed F value is greater than the table value, the null hypothesis is rejected for that alpha value. Such a result would indicate that not all population treatment means are equal. At this point, the business researcher has the option of computing multiple comparisons if the null hypothesis has been rejected.

Some researchers also compute an F value for blocks, even though the main emphasis in the experiment is on the treatments. The observed F value for blocks is compared with a critical table F value determined from table A.7 by using α, df_R (blocks) and df_E (error). If the F value for blocks is greater than the critical F value, the null hypothesis that all block population means are equal is rejected. This result tells the business researcher that including the blocking in the design was probably worthwhile and that a significant amount of variance was drawn from the error term, thus increasing the power of the test between treatments. In this text, we have omitted F_{blocks} from the normal presentation and problem solving. We leave the use of this F value to the discretion of the reader.

An example of the application of the randomised block design is considered in demonstration problem 11.3.

DEMONSTRATION PROBLEM 11.3

PROBLEM: Suppose the ACCC studied the cost of groceries in the Melbourne metropolitan area during the summer of 2014. From experience, consumers believed there was a significant difference in the average cost of an ordinary week's grocery bill petrol between different geographical locations within Melbourne. To test this belief, they asked random shoppers to visit random supermarkets within the greater Melbourne area. In addition, the analysts realised that the supermarket chain might make a difference on pricing. They were mostly interested in the differences between areas, so they made 'geographical location' their treatment variable. To control for the fact that grocery pricing may vary with the supermarket chain, the analysts included supermarket chain as a blocking variable and selected six different supermarket chains to participate. The researchers randomly visited one of each supermarket chain in each geographical location, resulting in 30 measurements (five areas and six chains). The data are shown below. Test these data by using a randomised block design analysis to determine whether there was a significant difference in the average cost of a common basket of groceries between geographical locations. Let $\alpha = .01$.

	Geographical region$_j$					
Chain	South ($)	West ($)	North ($)	East ($)	North-west ($)	$\bar{x}_i$ ($)
A	133	135	146	143	137	138.8
B	131	135	147	150	142	141
C	145	138	145	152	145	145
D	135	132	148	149	146	142
E	128	135	139	145	138	137
F	128	128	132	138	142	133.6
$\bar{x}_j$	133.3	133.8	142.8	146.2	141.7	$\bar{x} = 139.6$

SOLUTION:

STEP 1. Set up H_0 and H_a
For treatments:

H_0: $\mu_{\cdot 1} = \mu_{\cdot 2} = \mu_{\cdot 3} = \mu_{\cdot 4} = \mu_{\cdot 5}$, where μ is the geographical region
H_a: At least one of the treatment means is different from the others.

For blocks:

H_0: $\mu_{1\cdot} = \mu_{2\cdot} = \mu_{3\cdot} = \mu_{4\cdot} = \mu_{5\cdot} = \mu_{6\cdot}$, where μ is the brand
H_a: At least one of the blocking means is different from the others.

STEP 2. Decide on the type of test
The appropriate statistical test is the F test in the ANOVA for randomised block designs.

STEP 3. Decide on the level of significance, α, and determine the critical value(s) and region(s)
Let $\alpha = 0.01$. There are four degrees of freedom for the treatment $(C - 1 = 5 - 1 = 4)$, five degrees of freedom for the blocks $(n - 1 = 6 - 1 = 5)$, and 20 degrees of freedom for the error $[(C - 1)(n - 1) = (4)(5) = 20]$. Using these, $\alpha = 0.01$, and table A.7, we find the critical F values:

$F_{0.01,\,4,\,20} = 4.43$ for treatments
$F_{0.01,\,5,\,20} = 4.10$ for blocks

STEP 4. Write down the decision rule
Reject the null hypothesis for treatments if the observed F value for treatments is greater than 4.43. Reject the null hypothesis for blocks if the observed F value for blocks is greater than 4.10.

STEP 5. Select a random sample and do relevant calculations
The sample data including row and column means and the grand mean were given above. The ANOVA output follows.

Source of variation	SS	df	MS	F
Treatment	782.2	4	195.55	15.65
Block	401.4	5	80.2733	6.43
Error	249.8	20	12.49	
Total	1433.4	29		

STEP 6. Draw a conclusion

Because $F_{treatment} = 15.65 > F_{0.01,\,4,\,20} = 4.43$, the null hypothesis is rejected for the treatment effects. There is a significant difference in the average price of groceries petrol between various geographical locations in the Melbourne metropolitan area.

The F value for the blocking effect is:

$$F = \frac{MSR}{MSE} = \frac{80.2733}{12.49} = 6.43$$

The value of F for blocks is also significant at $\alpha = .01$ ($F_{0.01,\,5,\,20} = 4.10$). This result indicates that the blocking portion of the experimental design also contributed significantly to the analysis.

USING EXCEL

Randomised block design or two-way ANOVA without replication

DP11-03

1. Access DP11-03.xls from the student website.
2. From the Data tab, select Data Analysis.
3. From the Data Analysis dialogue box, select Anova: Two-Factor Without Replication and click OK.
4. In the ANOVA: Two-Factor Without Replication dialogue box:
   a. enter the data range in the Input Range field.
   b. check Labels if you have included the column and row labels in the Input Range. If not, leave it unchecked.
   c. enter .01 for Alpha
   d. choose an output option.

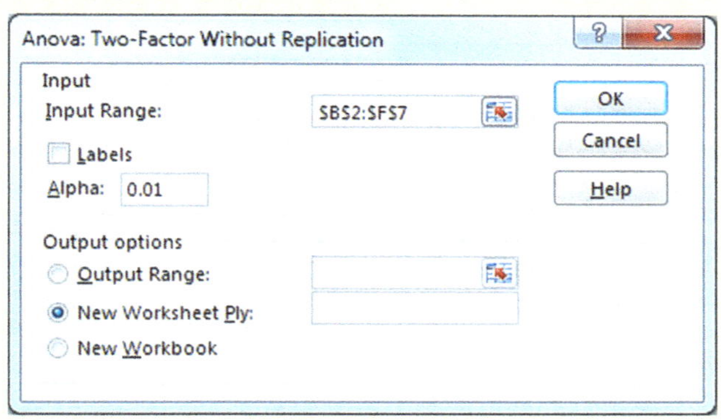

   e. Click OK.

The ANOVA from the Excel output follows.

	A	B	C	D	E	F	G
1	ANOVA						
2	*Source of Variation*	*SS*	*df*	*MS*	*F*	*P-value*	*F crit*
3	Rows	401.3667	5	80.27333	6.427008	0.00103	4.102685
4	Columns	782.2	4	195.55	15.65653	0.00001	4.43069
5	Error	249.8	20	12.49			
6							
7	Total	1433.367	29				
8							

PRACTICE PROBLEMS

Practising the calculations

P11-19 **11.19** The following data were gathered from a randomised block design. Use $\alpha = .01$ to test for a significant difference between the treatment levels. Establish the hypotheses and reach a conclusion about the null hypothesis.

	Treatment level		
Block	1	2	3
1	1.43	1.34	1.33
2	1.25	1.29	1.39
3	1.27	1.26	1.02
4	1.01	1.15	1.45

11.20 A randomised block design has a treatment variable with six levels and a blocking variable with 10 blocks. Using this information and $\alpha = .05$, complete the following table and reach a conclusion about the null hypothesis.

Source of variance	SS	df	MS	*F*
Treatment	2477.53			
Blocks	3180.48			
Error	11661.38			
Total				

Testing your understanding

P11-21 **11.21** Road safety is a high priority for all levels of government. Suppose a survey was conducted by the automobile associations in four Australian states to determine Australian motorists' views of the condition of their local roads. The association chose four states and randomly selected 10 motorists who drive an average of 1000 km a week on local roads. Each selected motorist was asked to rate their local roads on a scale from 0 to 100 to indicate how safe he or she felt driving on their particular roads. A score of 0 indicates feeling completely unsafe and a score of 100 indicates feeling perfectly safe. The scores are shown opposite. Test this randomised block design to determine whether there is a significant difference between the safety levels of roads in the four states. Use $\alpha = .05$.

Motorist	State 1	State 2	State 3	State 4
1	35	70	55	75
2	45	60	65	85
3	50	55	60	75
4	20	75	45	90
5	70	45	55	65
6	30	55	40	75
7	55	80	60	60
8	65	70	65	75
9	70	60	55	85
10	45	65	45	70

11.22 The CFO of a company is interested in determining whether the average length of long-distance calls by managers varies according to the type of telephone. A randomised block design experiment is set up in which long-distance calls by each of the five managers is sampled for four different types of telephones: mobile, computer, regular and cordless. The treatment is 'Phone type' and the blocks are 'Manager'. The partial results of analysis using Excel are shown below. Complete the missing values. Discuss the results and any implications they might have for the company.

	A	B	C	D	E
1	ANOVA				
2	*Source of Variation*	*SS*	*df*	*MS*	*F*
3	Phone type	35.761	*	****	****
4	Manager	144.336	*	****	****
5	Error	****	*	****	
6					
7	Total	188.209	**		
8					

11.5 A factorial design (two-way ANOVA)

Some experiments are designed so that *two or more treatments* (independent variables) *are explored simultaneously*. Such experimental designs are referred to as **factorial designs**. In factorial designs, *every level of each treatment is studied under the conditions of every level of all other treatments*. Factorial designs can be arranged such that three, four or *n* treatments or independent variables are studied simultaneously in the same experiment. As an example, consider the valve opening data in table 11.1. The mean valve opening for the 24 measurements is 6.34 cm. However, every valve but one in the sample measures something other than the mean. Why? Company management realises that the valves are made on different machines, by different operators, on different shifts, on different days, with raw materials from different suppliers. Business researchers who are interested in finding the sources of variation might decide to set up a factorial design that incorporates all five of these independent variables in one study. In this text, we explore the factorial designs with two treatments only.

Advantages of the factorial design

If two independent variables are analysed using a completely randomised design, the effects of each variable are explored separately (one per design). Thus, it takes two completely randomised designs to analyse the effects of the two independent variables. By using a factorial design, the business researcher can analyse both variables at the same time in one design, saving the time and effort of doing two separate analyses and minimising the experiment-wise error rate.

Some business researchers use a factorial design to control confounding or concomitant variables in a study. By building variables into the design, the researcher attempts to control for the effects of multiple variables *during* the experiment. In a completely randomised design, the variables are studied in isolation. In a factorial design, there is potential for increased power over the completely randomised design because the additional effects of the second variable are removed from the error sum of squares.

The researcher can explore the possibility of interaction between the two treatment variables in a two-factor factorial design if multiple measurements are taken under every combination of levels of the two treatments. Interaction will be discussed later.

Factorial designs with two treatments are similar to randomised block designs. However, whereas randomised block designs focus on one treatment variable and *control* for a blocking effect, a two-treatment factorial design focuses on the effects of both variables. Because the randomised block design contains only one measure for each (treatment–block) combination, interaction cannot be analysed in randomised block designs.

Factorial designs with two treatments

The structure of a two-treatment factorial design is featured in figure 11.7. Note that there are two independent variables (two treatments) and that there is an intersection at each level of each treatment. These intersections are referred to as *cells*. One treatment is arbitrarily designated as the *row* treatment (forming the rows of the design) and the other treatment is designated as the *column* treatment (forming the columns of the design). Although it is possible to analyse factorial designs with unequal numbers of items in the cells, the analysis of unequal cell designs is beyond the scope of this text. All factorial designs discussed here have cells of equal size.

Treatments (independent variables) of factorial designs must have at least two levels each. The simplest factorial design is a 2×2 factorial design, where each treatment has two levels. If such a factorial design is drawn in the manner of figure 11.7, it would include two rows and two columns, forming four cells.

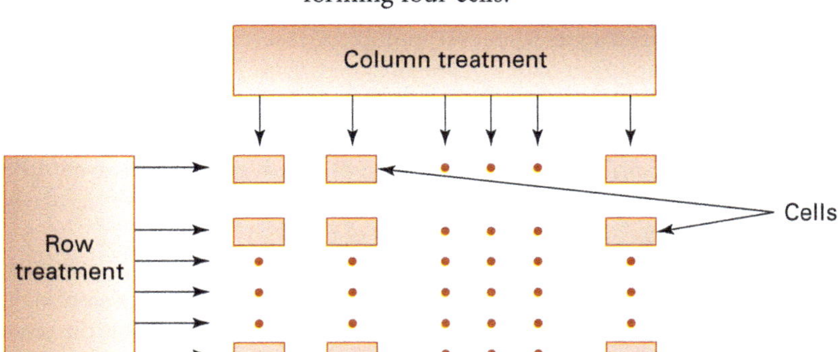

FIGURE 11.7 Two-way factorial design

In this section, we study only factorial designs with $n > 1$ measurements for each combination of treatment levels (cells). This approach allows us to attempt to measure the interaction between the treatment variables. As with the completely randomised design and the randomised block design, a factorial design contains only *one* dependent variable.

As an example of a factorial design, the natural gas industry can design an experiment to study usage rates and how they are affected by temperature and precipitation. Theorising that the outside temperature and type of precipitation affect natural gas usage, industry researchers can gather usage measurements for a given community over a variety of temperature and precipitation conditions. At the same time, they can make an effort to determine whether certain types of precipitation, combined with certain temperature levels, affect usage rates differently from other combinations of temperature and precipitation (interaction effects).

Statistically testing a factorial design

A **two-way analysis of variance (two-way ANOVA)** is used to analyse data for factorial designs with two factors (independent variables). The following hypotheses are tested using a two-way ANOVA.

Row effects:	H_0: Row means of the population data are all equal.
	H_a: At least one row mean is different from the others.
Column effects:	H_0: Column means of all the population data are all equal.
	H_a: At least one column mean is different from the others.
Interaction effects:	H_0: The interaction effects are zero.
	H_a: An interaction effect is present.

M *Refer to maths appendix*

As it is common practice to use Excel for computations for a randomised block design, the formulas for computing a two-way ANOVA are given in maths appendix 11.2 at the end of this chapter.

F values are determined for:

1. row effects
2. column effects
3. interaction effects.

Each of these observed F values is compared with a table F value. The table F value is determined by α, df_{num} and df_{denom}. The degrees of freedom for the numerator (df_{num}) are determined by the effect being studied. If the observed F value is for columns, the degrees of freedom for the numerator are $C - 1$. If the observed F value is for rows, the degrees of freedom for the numerator are $R - 1$. If the observed F value is for interaction, the degrees of freedom for the numerator are $(R - 1)(C - 1)$. The number of degrees of freedom for the denominator of the table value for each of the three effects is the same: the error degrees of freedom, $RC(n - 1)$. The table F values (critical F) for a two-way ANOVA are given in formula 11.4.

Table F values for a two-way ANOVA (11.4)

Row effects: $F_{\alpha, R-1, RC(n-1)}$

Column effects: $F_{\alpha, C-1, RC(n-1)}$

Interaction effects: $F_{\alpha, (R-1)(C-1), RC(n-1)}$

Interaction

As noted before, along with testing the effects of two treatments in a factorial design, it is possible to test for the interaction effects of the two treatments whenever multiple measures are taken in each cell of the design. **Interaction** occurs *when the effects of one treatment vary according to the levels of treatment of the other effect*. For example, in a study examining the impact of temperature and humidity on a manufacturing process, it is possible that temperature and humidity will interact in such a way that the effect of temperature on the process varies with the humidity. Low temperatures might not be a significant manufacturing factor when humidity is low but might be when humidity is high. Similarly, high temperatures might be a significant factor in low humidity but not in high humidity.

In design, interaction occurs when the pattern of cell means in one row (going across columns) varies from the pattern of cell means in other rows. This variation indicates that the differences in column effects depend on which row is being examined. Hence, an interaction between the rows and columns occurs. The same thing can happen when the pattern of cell means within a column is different from the pattern of cell means in other columns.

Interaction can be depicted graphically by plotting the cell means within each row (and can also be done by plotting the cell means within each column). The means within each row (or column) are then connected by a line. If the lines for the rows (or columns) are parallel, no interaction is indicated.

Figure 11.8 is a graph of the means of each cell in each row in a 2×3 (2 rows, 3 columns) factorial design with interaction. Note that the lines connecting the means in each row cross each other. In figure 11.9, the lines converge, indicating the likely presence of some interaction. Figure 11.10 depicts a 2×3 factorial design with no interaction.

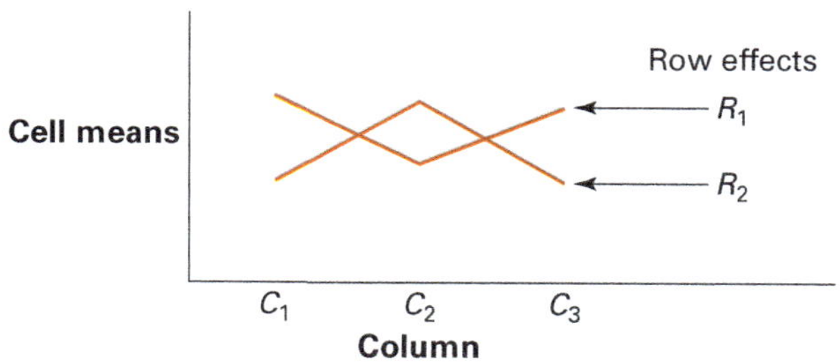

FIGURE 11.8 A 2×3 factorial design with interaction

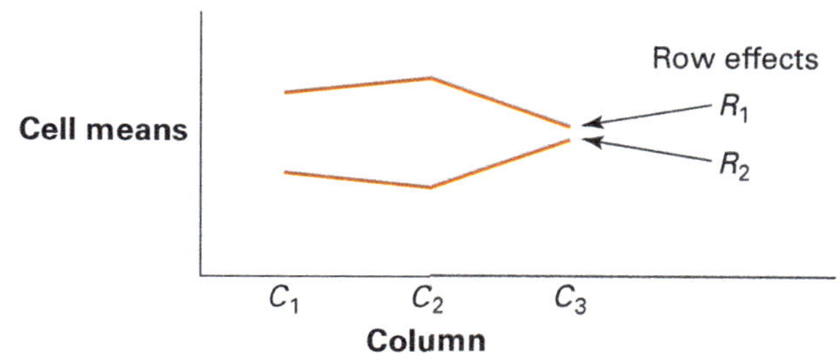

FIGURE 11.9 A 2×3 factorial design with some interaction

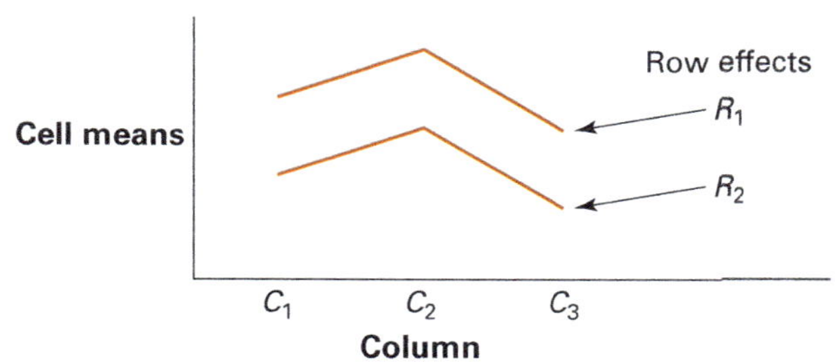

FIGURE 11.10 A 2×3 factorial design with no interaction

When the interaction effects are significant, the main effects (row and column) are confounded and should not be analysed in the usual manner. In this case, it is not possible to state unequivocally that the row effects or the column effects are significantly different because the difference between means of one main effect is affected by the level of the other main effect (interaction is present). Some specific procedures are recommended for examining main effects when significant interaction is present. However, these techniques are beyond the scope of material presented here. Hence, in this text, whenever interaction effects are present (F_{inter} is significant), the researcher should *not* attempt to interpret the main effects (F_{row} and F_{col}).

As an example of a factorial design, consider a perfume distributor who wishes to determine which stores were the most successful at selling his imported perfumes. The distributor is concerned that the type of store the perfumes are sold in (specialised stores, department stores and variety stores) might make a difference to sales. In addition, the distributor believes that where the store is located (street shopping centre in a major town or city or large complex or shopping centre) might affect the outcome of the experiment. Thus, a two-way ANOVA is set up with the type of store and location of the store as the two independent variables. The store type has three treatment levels, or classifications:

1. specialised stores
2. department stores
3. variety stores.

The store location has two treatment levels, or classifications:

1. street shopping centre in a major town or city
2. large complex or shopping centre.

The sale is the dependent variable in the experimental design. The distributor collected data from his records of 24 stores. This factorial design is a 2 × 3 design (2 rows, 3 columns) with four measurements per cell, as shown in the following table. The data are shown in thousands of dollars.

	Type of store			
Store location	**Specialised**	**Department**	**Variety**	$\bar{x}_i$
Street shopping centre	40	40	80	
	20	60	60	
	40	60	80	
	20	20	60	
	$\bar{x}_{11} = 30$	$\bar{x}_{12} = 45$	$\bar{x}_{13} = 70$	48.33
Large shopping complex	40	60	80	
	60	60	80	
	20	40	60	
	40	80	80	
	$\bar{x}_{21} = 40$	$\bar{x}_{22} = 60$	$\bar{x}_{23} = 75$	58.33
$\bar{x}_j$	35.0	52.5 $\bar{x} = 53.33$	72.5	

These data are analysed by using a two-way analysis of variance and $\alpha = .05$. The Excel output is given below.

	A	B	C	D	E
1	*Source of Variation*	*SS*	*df*	*MS*	*F*
2	Row	600.00	1	600.00	2.84
3	Column	5633.33	2	2816.67	13.34*
4	Interaction	100.00	2	50.00	0.24
5	Error	3800.00	18	211.11	
6	Total	10133.33	23		

*Denotes significance at $\alpha = .01$

The critical F value for the interaction effects at $\alpha = .05$ is:

$$F_{.05,\,2,\,18} = 3.55$$

The observed F value for interaction effects is 0.24, which is less than the critical table value (3.55). Therefore no significant interaction effects are evident. As the interaction effects are not significant, the main effects are now examined. The critical F value of the row effects at $\alpha = .05$ is $F_{.05,\,1,\,18} = 4.41$. The observed F value of 2.84 is less than the critical value. Hence, no significant row effects are present.

The critical F value of the column effects at $\alpha = .05$ is $F_{.05,\,2,\,18} = 3.55$. The observed F value for column effects (13.34) is greater than this critical value. Hence, a significant difference in column effects is evident at $\alpha = .05$.

A significant difference is noted in the sales according to type of shop. A cursory examination of the means of the three levels of the column effects (type of store) reveals that the lowest mean was for specialised stores. The highest mean sale was for variety stores. Using multiple comparison techniques, the distributor can statistically test for differences between the means of these three groups.

Because the sample sizes in each column are equal, Tukey's HSD test can be used to compute multiple comparisons. The value of MSE is 211.11 for this problem. When testing the column means with Tukey's HSD test, the value of n is the number of items in a column, which is eight. The number of treatments is $C = 3$ for columns, and $N - C = 24 - 3 = 21$.

With these two values and $\alpha = .05$, a value for q can be determined from table A.10:

$$q_{.05,\,3,\,21} = 3.58$$

From these values, the honestly significant difference can be computed:

$$\text{HSD} = q\sqrt{\frac{\text{MSE}}{n}} = 3.58\sqrt{\frac{211.11}{8}} = 18.39$$

The mean sales in the three columns are:

$$\bar{x}_1 = 35 \qquad \bar{x}_2 = 52.5 \qquad \bar{x}_3 = 72.5$$

The absolute values of differences between means are:

$$|\bar{x}_1 - \bar{x}_2| = |35.0 - 52.5| = 17.5$$
$$|\bar{x}_1 - \bar{x}_3| = |35.0 - 72.5| = 37.5$$
$$|\bar{x}_2 - \bar{x}_3| = |52.5 - 72.5| = 20.0$$

Note that only two differences are greater than 18.39 and are therefore significantly different at $\alpha = .05$ using the HSD test. In other words, sales in variety stores are different from those in other types of stores.

DEMONSTRATION PROBLEM 11.4

PROBLEM: Some theorists believe that training warehouse workers can reduce absenteeism. Suppose an experimental design is structured to test this belief. Warehouses in which training sessions have been held for workers are selected for the study. The four types of warehouses are general merchandise, commodity, bulk storage and cold storage. The training sessions are differentiated by length. Researchers identify three levels of training sessions according to the length of sessions: 1–20 days, 21–50 days and more than 50 days. Three warehouse workers are selected randomly for each particular combination of type of warehouse and session length. The workers are monitored for the next year to determine how many days they are absent. The resulting data are in a 4×3 design (4 rows, 3 columns) structure, as shown on the next page. Using this information, calculate a two-way ANOVA to determine whether there are any significant effects of type of warehouse or length of training sessions on absenteeism. Use $\alpha = .05$.

SOLUTION:

STEP 1. Set up H_0 and H_a

The following hypotheses are being tested.

For row effects:

H_0: $\mu_{1\cdot} = \mu_{2\cdot} = \mu_{3\cdot} = \mu_{4\cdot}$, where μ is the type of warehouse

H_a: At least one of the row means is different from the others.

For column effects:

H_0: $\mu_{\cdot 1} = \mu_{\cdot 2} = \mu_{\cdot 3}$, where μ is the length of training sessions

H_a: At least one of the column means is different from the others.

For interaction effects:

H_0: The interaction effects are zero.

H_a: There is an interaction effect.

STEP 2. Decide on the type of test

The two-way ANOVA with the F test is the appropriate statistical test.

STEP 3. Decide on the level of significance, α, and determine the critical value(s) and region(s)

Let $\alpha = .05$.

$$df_{rows} = 4 - 1 = 3$$
$$df_{columns} = 3 - 1 = 2$$
$$df_{interaction} = (3)(2) = 6$$
$$df_{error} = (4)(3)(2) = 24$$

STEP 4. Write down the decision rule

For row effects, $F_{.05,\,3,\,24} = 3.01$; for column effects, $F_{.05,\,2,\,24} = 3.40$; for interaction effects, $F_{.05,\,6,\,24} = 2.51$. For each of these effects, if any observed F value is greater than its associated critical F value, the respective null hypothesis will be rejected.

STEP 5. Select a random sample and do relevant calculations

	Length of training session (days)			
Type of warehouse	**1–20**	**21–50**	**More than 50**	$\bar{x}_i$
General merchandise	4	3	4	3.2222
	3.5	3.5	2	
	5	3	1	
Commodity	6	2	0	3.2222
	5	4	1	
	6	3	2	
Bulk storage	3	2	3.5	3.3333
	4	4	4.5	
	4	2	3	
Cold storage	3	6	5	5.0555
	3	5.5	6	
	4	7	6	
$\bar{x}_c$	4.2083	3.75	3.17	
		$\bar{x} = 3.7094$		

The Excel output for this problem is obtained as follows.

USING EXCEL

Two-way ANOVA with replication

DP11-04

1. Access DP11-04.xls from the student website.
2. From the Data tab, select Data Analysis.
3. From the Data Analysis dialogue box, select ANOVA: Two-Factor With Replication and click OK.
4. In the ANOVA: Two-Factor With Replication dialogue box:
   a. enter the data range, including the sample and column headings, in the Input Range field
   b. enter 3 in the Rows per sample field
   c. enter .05 for Alpha
   d. choose an output option

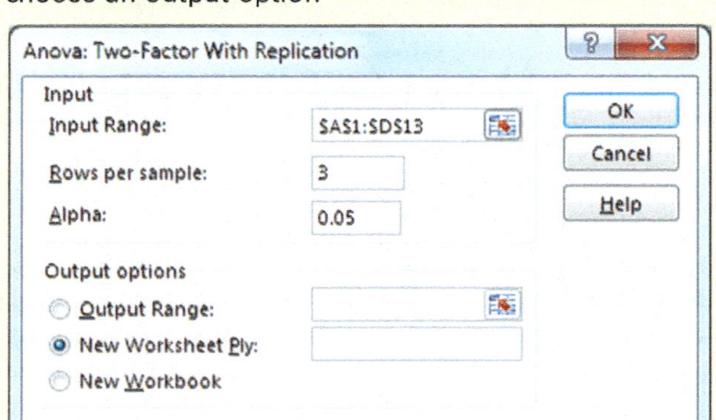

   e. click OK.

The Excel output follows.

	A	B	C	D	E	F	G
1	ANOVA: Two-Factor With Replication						
2							
3	SUMMARY	1 to 20	21 to 50	More than 50	Total		
4	*General merchandise*						
5	Count	3	3	3	9		
6	Sum	12.5	9.5	7	29		
7	Average	4.167	3.167	2.333	3.222		
8	Variance	0.583	0.083	2.333	1.382		
9							
10	*Commodity*						
11	Count	3	3	3	9		
12	Sum	17	9	3	29		
13	Average	5.667	3	1	3.222		
14	Variance	0.333	1	1	4.694		
15							
16	*Bulk storage*						
17	Count	3	3	3	9		
18	Sum	11	8	11	30		
19	Average	3.667	2.667	3.667	3.333		
20	Variance	0.333	1.333	0.583	0.813		
21							
22	*Cold storage*						
23	Count	3	3	3	9		
24	Sum	10	18.5	17	45.5		
25	Average	3.333	6.167	5.667	5.056		
26	Variance	0.333	0.583	0.333	2.028		
27							
28	*Total*						
29	Count	12	12	12			
30	Sum	41	45	38			
31	Average	4.208	3.75	3.167			
32	Variance	1.157	2.705	4.015			
33							
34							
35	ANOVA						
36	*Source of Variation*	*SS*	*df*	*MS*	*F*	*P-value*	*F crit*
37	Sample	21.85	3	7.29	9.89	0.000197	3.01
38	Columns	6.54	2	3.27	4.44	0.022818	3.40
39	Interaction	47.13	6	7.85	10.67	0.000081	2.51
40	Within	17.67	24	0.74			
41							
42	Total	93.1875	35				
43							

STEP **6. Draw a conclusion**

Looking at the ANOVA table, we must first examine the interaction effects. The observed *F* value for interaction is 10.67, which is greater than the critical *F* value. Therefore, the interaction effects are statistically significant at $\alpha = .05$. The *p*-value for interaction shown in the Excel output is .000081. Therefore, the interaction effects are significant at $\alpha = .0001$. In this case, the business researcher is not required to examine the main effects because the significant interaction confounds the main effects. The significant interaction effects indicate that certain warehouse types in combination with certain lengths of training session result in different absenteeism rates from other combinations of levels for these two variables. Using the cell means shown below, we can depict the interactions graphically as shown.

Type of warehouse	Length of training session (days)		
	1–20	21–50	More than 50
General merchandise	4.2	2.3	3.2
Commodity	5.7	3	1
Bulk storage	3.7	2.7	3.7
Cold storage	3.3	6.2	5.7

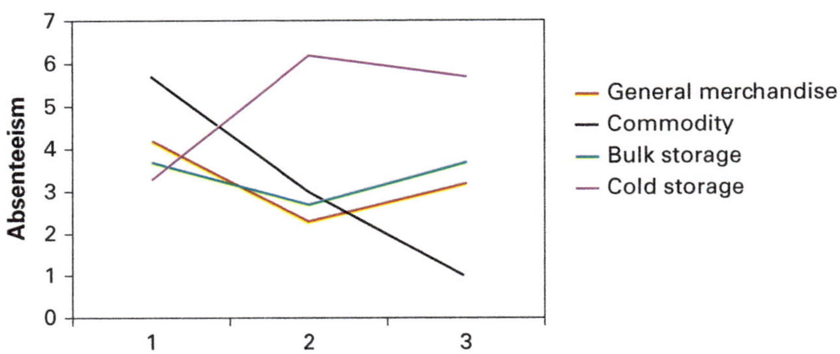

Note the intersecting lines, which indicate interaction. After the short training sessions (1), cold-storage workers had the lowest rate of absenteeism and workers at commodity warehouses had the highest. However, after medium-length sessions (2), cold-storage workers had the highest rate of absenteeism and general merchandise workers had the lowest. After the longest training sessions (3), commodity warehouse workers had the lowest rate of absenteeism, even though these workers had the highest rate of absenteeism after short sessions. Thus, the rate of absenteeism for workers at a particular type of warehouse depended on the length of the training session. There was an interaction between the type of warehouse and the length of sessions. This graph could be constructed with the row levels instead of column levels along the bottom axis.

PRACTICE PROBLEMS

Practising the calculations

11.23 Describe the following factorial design, with each data value represented by an *x*. How many independent and dependent variables are there? How many levels are there for each treatment? If the data are known, could interaction be determined from this design? Compute all degrees of freedom.

	Variable 1			
Variable 2	x_{111}	x_{121}	x_{131}	x_{141}
	x_{112}	x_{122}	x_{132}	x_{142}
	x_{113}	x_{123}	x_{133}	x_{143}
	x_{211}	x_{221}	x_{231}	x_{241}
	x_{212}	x_{222}	x_{232}	x_{242}
	x_{213}	x_{223}	x_{233}	x_{243}

11.24 Complete the following two-way ANOVA table. Determine the critical table *F* values and reach conclusions about the hypotheses for effects. Let $\alpha = .05$.

Source of variance	SS	df	MS	F
Row	126.98	3		
Column	37.49	4		
Interaction	380.82			
Error	733.65	60		
Total				

Testing your understanding

P11-25 **11.25** Suppose the following data have been gathered from a study with a two-way factorial design. 'Use $\alpha = .05$ and a two-way ANOVA to analyse the data. State your conclusions.

Treatment 2	Treatment 1	
	A	B
A	1.2	1.9
	1.3	1.6
	1.3	1.7
	1.5	2.0
B	2.2	2.7
	2.1	2.5
	2.0	2.8
	2.3	2.8
C	1.7	1.9
	1.8	2.2
	1.7	1.9
	1.6	2.0
D	2.4	2.8
	2.3	2.6
	2.5	2.4
	2.4	2.8

11.26 A mobile phone store retailer conducted a study to determine whether the number of contracts sold per day by stores is affected by the number of competitors within a 1 km radius and the location of the store. The company researchers selected three types of stores for consideration in the study: standalone suburban stores, shopping-centre stores and downtown stores. These stores vary in the numbers of competing stores within a 1 km radius, which have been reduced to four categories: 0, 1, 2, and 3 or more competitors. Suppose the following data represent the number of contracts sold per day in each of these types of stores with the given number of competitors. Use $\alpha = .05$ and a two-way ANOVA to analyse the data.

Store location	Number of competitors			
	0	1	2	3 or more
Standalone	41	39	87	65
	20	42	54	45
	50	38	52	43
Shopping centre	30	31	45	50
	35	38	52	43
	24	31	56	65
Downtown	20	21	34	27
	34	16	25	32
	32	28	27	34

11.27 Complete the computations in the ANOVA table shown below and determine the critical table *F* values. Interpret the analysis. Discuss this problem, including the structure of the design, sample sizes and decisions about the hypotheses.

Two-way ANOVA

Source of variation	df	SS	MS	*F*
Row	2	****	****	****
Column	2	1.852	****	****
Interaction	4	4.370	****	****
Error	**	14.000	****	
Total	26	20.519		

11.28 Consider the valve opening data displayed in table 11.1. Suppose the data represent valves produced on four different machines in three different shifts and that the quality controllers want to know whether there is any difference in the mean measurements of valve openings between shifts or machines. The data are given here, organised by machine and shift. In addition, Excel has been used to analyse the data with a two-way ANOVA. What are the hypotheses for this problem? Study the significant differences in the Excel output below. Discuss the results obtained. What conclusions might the quality controllers reach from this analysis?

Machine	Valve openings (cm)		
	Shift 1	Shift 2	Shift 3
1	6.56	6.38	6.29
	6.40	6.19	6.23
2	6.54	6.26	6.19
	6.34	6.23	6.33
3	6.58	6.22	6.26
	6.44	6.27	6.31
4	6.36	6.29	6.21
	6.50	6.19	6.58

	A	B	C	D	E	F	G
3	*Source of Variation*	*SS*	*df*	*MS*	*F*	*P-value*	*F crit*
4	Sample	0.00755	3	0.00252	0.20062	0.894	3.490
5	Columns	0.15048	2	0.07524	6.00100	0.016	3.885
6	Interaction	0.02519	6	0.00420	0.33488	0.906	2.996
7	Within	0.15045	12	0.01254			
8							
9	Total	0.33366	23				

11.29 A builder wants to predict the relationship between house size (as measured by number of rooms) and the selling price. Two different neighborhoods are compared. A random sample of 15 houses was selected, with the results as follows:

House	No. of rooms	Selling price ($000)	Neighbourhood
1	8	345	0
2	8	360	1
3	6	325	0
4	8	400	1
5	7	350	1
6	9	360	0
7	13	405	0
8	6	299	0
9	8	405	1
10	9	365	0
11	10	520	1
12	8	330	0
13	14	600	1
14	9	370	0
15	7	395	1

a. Is there a relationship between the selling price and two independent variables at the 0.05 level of significance?

b. Does the independent variable make a contribution to the regression model?

c. Add an interaction term to the model, and at the 0.05 level of significance, determine whether it makes a significant contribution to the model.

MISUSE OF STATISTICS

In theory, any phenomenon that affects the dependent variable in an experiment should be either entered into the experimental design or controlled in the experiment. Researchers will sometimes report statistical findings from an experiment but fail to mention the possible variables that were neither controlled by the experimental setting nor controlled by the experimental design. The findings from such studies are highly questionable and often lead to spurious conclusions. Scientifically, the researcher needs to conduct the experiment in an environment such that as many variables are controlled as possible. To the extent that they are not controlled, the researcher has an ethical responsibility to report that fact in the findings.

With experimental designs, selection of treatment levels should be done with fairness or even randomness in cases where several treatment levels are possible. A researcher can build in skewed views of the treatment effects by incorrect selection of treatment levels to be studied.

Another ethical consideration is making sample sizes equal. Sometimes this is done through the selection process or through attrition. It remains highly unethical to make up data values or to eliminate values arbitrarily to produce equal sample sizes.

CHAPTER CASE
REVISITED

Cyberbullying amongst Australian adolescents

1. The chapter case presents portions of a study on the cyberbullying experiences of young people in Australia based on their socioeconomic status. In particular, it studied whether there is a difference in cyberbullying experiences based on socioeconomic status. The researcher analysed the data using one-way ANOVA, with socioeconomic status being the dependent variable. The independent variables are higher socioeconomic, middle socioeconomic and lower socioeconomic. Excel output for socioeconomic status is given below.

   The results of the one-way ANOVA show that there is a significant difference in attitudes towards foreign-made goods between the three groups. The observed F value of 25.42 is greater than the critical F value of 3.40. Examining the average values for each group of people suggests that there might be a significant difference between socioeconomic background and cyberbullying experience.

	A	B	C	D	E	F	G
1	Anova: Single Factor						
2							
3	SUMMARY						
4	*Groups*	*Count*	*Sum*	*Average*	*Variance*		
5	Higher socioeconomic	8	263	32.875	3.553571		
6	Middle socioeconomic	9	349	38.77778	5.694444		
7	Lower socioeconomic	10	330	33	2.888889		
8							
9							
10	ANOVA						
11	*Source of Variation*	*SS*	*df*	*MS*	*F*	*P-value*	*F crit*
12	Between Groups	204.2361	2	102.1181	25.41553	0.000001	3.402826
13	Within Groups	96.43056	24	4.01794			
14							
15	Total	300.6667	26				
16							

2. Because there was an overall significant difference between the three groups, the next step is to use a multiple comparison test to determine which groups are significantly different. The sample sizes are unequal in the study; therefore, it is appropriate to use the Tukey–Kramer test.
3. Further analysis could be done to examine demographic independent variables such as gender or age of each of the respondents. Therefore, selecting gender and each of the three groups, a two-way ANOVA could be used to analyse the data. If more than one observation is taken in each cell (particular combination of gender and attitude of group), then interaction effects could also be analysed.

SUMMARY

1 Sound business research requires that the researcher plan and establish a design for the experiment before a study is undertaken. The design of the experiment should encompass the treatment variables to be studied, manipulated and controlled. These variables are often referred to as the independent variables. It is possible to study several independent variables and several levels, or classifications, of each of those variables in one design. In addition, the researcher selects one measurement to be taken from sample items under the conditions of the experiment. This measurement is referred to as the dependent variable because, if the treatment effect is significant, the measurement of the dependent variable depends on the independent variable(s) selected. This chapter explored three types of experimental designs: completely randomised design, randomised block design and the factorial experimental designs.

2 The completely randomised design is the simplest of the experimental designs because it has only one independent, or treatment, variable. Subjects are assigned randomly to treatments. If the treatment variable has only two levels, the design becomes identical to that used to test the difference between means of independent populations. The data from a completely randomised design are analysed using a one-way ANOVA. This produces an F value that can be compared with F values in table A.7 to determine whether the ANOVA F value is statistically significant. If it is, the null hypothesis that all population means are equal is rejected and at least one of the means is different from the others. Analysis of variance does not tell the researcher which means, if any, are significantly different from others. Although the researcher can visually examine means to determine which ones differ, statistical techniques called multiple comparisons must be used to determine statistically whether pairs of means are significantly different.

3 Two types of multiple comparison techniques are presented and used in this chapter: Tukey's HSD test and the Tukey–Kramer procedure. Tukey's HSD test requires that sample sizes are equal. The Tukey–Kramer procedure is used in the case of unequal sample sizes.

4 A second experimental design is the randomised block design, which contains a treatment variable (independent variable) and a blocking variable. The independent variable is the main variable of interest in this design. The blocking variable is a variable the researcher is interested in controlling rather than studying. A special case of randomised block design is the repeated measures design, in which the blocking variable represents subjects or items for which repeated measures are taken across the full range of treatment levels.

5 A third experimental design is the factorial design, which enables the researcher to test the effects of two or more independent variables simultaneously. In complete factorial designs, every treatment level of each independent variable is studied under the conditions of every other treatment level for all independent variables. This chapter focused on factorial designs with two independent variables. Each independent variable can have two or more treatment levels. These two-way factorial designs are analysed by a two-way ANOVA. This analysis produces an F value for each of the two treatment effects and for interaction. Interaction is present when the results of one treatment vary significantly according to the levels of the other treatment. At least two measurements per cell must be present in order to compute interaction. If the F value for interaction is statistically significant, the main effects of the experiment are confounded and should not be examined in the usual manner.

KEY TERMS

a posteriori p. 380
analysis of variance (ANOVA) p. 371
blocking variable p. 385
classification variable p. 370
completely randomised design p. 372
dependent variable p. 370
experimental design p. 370
***F* value (ANOVA)** p. 374
factorial designs p. 390
factors p. 370
independent variable p. 370
interaction p. 392
levels p. 371
multiple comparison tests p. 380
one-way analysis of variance (one-way ANOVA) p. 372
randomised block design p. 385
repeated measures design p. 386
treatment variable p. 370
Tukey–Kramer procedure p. 383
Tukey's honestly significant difference (HSD) test p. 380
two-way analysis of variance (two-way ANOVA) p. 392

KEY EQUATIONS

EQUATION	DESCRIPTION	FORMULA
11.1	**Formulas for computing a one-way ANOVA**	$\text{SSC} = \sum_{j=1}^{C} n_j(\bar{x}_j - \bar{x})^2$ $\text{SSE} = \sum_{i=1}^{n_j}\sum_{j=1}^{C}(x_{ij} - \bar{x}_j)^2$ $\text{SST} = \sum_{i=1}^{n_j}\sum_{j=1}^{C}(x_{ij} - \bar{x})^2$

EQUATION	DESCRIPTION	FORMULA
		$df_C = C - 1$ $df_E = N - C$ $df_T = N - 1$ $MSC = \frac{SSC}{df_C}$ $MSE = \frac{SSE}{df_E}$ $F = \frac{MSC}{MSE}$
11.2	Tukey's HSD test	$HSD = q_{\alpha, C, N-C}\sqrt{\frac{MSE}{n}}$
11.3	Tukey–Kramer formula	$q_{\alpha,C,N-C}\sqrt{\frac{MSE}{2}\left(\frac{1}{n_r}+\frac{1}{n_s}\right)}$
11.4	Table *F* values for a two-way ANOVA	Row effects: $F_{\alpha, R-1, RC(n-1)}$ Column effects: $F_{\alpha, C-1, RC(n-1)}$ Interaction effects: $F_{\alpha, (R-1)(C-1), RC(n-1)}$

REVIEW PROBLEMS

Practising the calculations

11.30 Complete the following ANOVA table.

Source of variance	SS	df	MS	F
Treatment				
Error	249.61	19		
Total	317.80	25		

11.31 You are asked to analyse a completely randomised design that has six treatment levels and a total of 42 measurements. Complete the following table, which contains some information from the study.

Source of variance	SS	df	MS	F
Treatment	210			
Error	655			
Total				

P11-32 **11.32** Compute a one-way ANOVA of the following data. Let α = .01. Use the Tukey–Kramer procedure to conduct multiple comparisons of the means.

Treatment 1	Treatment 2	Treatment 3
7	11	8
12	17	6
9	16	10
11	13	9
8	10	11
9	15	7
11	14	10
10	18	
7		
8		

11.33 Examine the structure of the following experimental design. Determine which of the three designs presented in the chapter would be most likely to characterise this structure. Discuss the variables and the levels of variables. Determine the degrees of freedom.

Person	Method 1	Method 2	Method 3
1	x_{11}	x_{12}	x_{13}
2	x_{21}	x_{22}	x_{23}
3	x_{31}	x_{32}	x_{33}
4	x_{41}	x_{42}	x_{43}
5	x_{51}	x_{52}	x_{53}
6	x_{61}	x_{62}	x_{63}

P11-34 **11.34** Analyse the following data, gathered from a randomised block design using α = .05. If the treatment effects are significant, use Tukey's HSD test to do multiple comparisons.

Blocking variable	Treatment			
	A	B	C	D
1	17	10	9	21
2	13	9	8	16
3	20	17	18	22
4	11	6	5	10
5	16	13	14	22
6	23	19	20	28

P11-35 **11.35** Compute a two-way ANOVA on the following data ($\alpha = .01$) using Excel.

Treatment 2	Treatment 1		
	A	B	C
A	5	2	2
	3	4	3
	6	4	5
B	11	9	13
	8	10	12
	12	8	10
C	6	7	4
	4	6	6
	5	7	8
D	9	8	8
	11	12	9
	9	9	11

Testing your understanding

P11-36 **11.36** A company conducted a consumer research project to ascertain customer service ratings from its customers. The customers were asked to rate the company on a scale from 1 to 7 on various quality characteristics. One question was concerned with the promptness of company response to a repair problem. The following data represent customer responses to this question. The customers were divided by location and by age. Use analysis of variance to analyse the responses. Let $\alpha = .05$. Compute multiple comparisons where they are appropriate. Graph the cell means and observe any interaction.

Age	Location			
	Sydney	Melbourne	Brisbane	Perth
21–35	3	2	3	2
	2	4	3	3
	3	3	2	2
36–50	5	4	5	6
	5	4	6	4
	4	6	5	5
Over 50	3	2	3	3
	1	2	2	2
	2	3	3	1

P11-37 **11.37** A major car manufacturer is trying to select the supplier with tyres of the greatest durability so wants to know whether there is any difference between the average lifetime of four different brands of tyres (A, B, C and D). The manufacturer selects comparable tyres from each company and tests them on comparable cars. The results are as follows.

A	B	C	D
31 000	24 000	30 500	24 500
25 000	25 500	28 000	27 000
28 500	27 000	32 500	26 000
29 000	26 500	28 000	21 000
32 000	25 000	31 000	25 500
27 500	28 000	26 000	27 500

Use $\alpha = .05$ to test whether there is a significant difference between the mean lifetime of these four brands. Assume tyre lifetime is normally distributed.

P11-38 **11.38** Agricultural researchers are studying three different ways of planting peanuts to determine whether significantly different yields will result. The researchers have access to a large peanut farm on which to conduct their tests. They identify six blocks of land. In each block of land, peanuts are planted in each of the three different ways. At the end of the growing season, the peanuts are harvested and the average number of kilograms per hectare is determined for peanuts planted using each method in each block. Using the following data and $\alpha = .01$, determine whether there is a significant difference in yield between the planting methods.

Block	Method 1	Method 2	Method 3
1	1310	1080	850
2	1275	1100	1020
3	1280	1050	780
4	1225	1020	870
5	1190	990	805
6	1300	1030	910

P11-39 **11.39** The US Construction Labor Research Council lists a number of construction labour jobs that seem to pay approximately the same wages per hour. Some of these are bricklaying, ironworking and crane operation. Suppose a labour researcher takes a random sample of workers from each of these types of construction jobs and from across the US and asks what their hourly wages are. If this survey yields the following data, is there a significant difference in mean hourly wages between these three jobs? If there is a significant difference, use the Tukey–Kramer procedure to determine which pairs of jobs, if any, are also significantly different. Let $\alpha = .05$.

Job type		
Bricklaying	**Ironworking**	**Crane operation**
19.25	26.45	16.20
17.80	21.10	23.30
20.50	16.40	22.90
24.33	22.86	19.50
19.81	25.55	27.00
22.29	18.50	22.95
21.20		25.52
		21.20

P11–40 **11.40** Are some unskilled office jobs viewed as having more status than others? Suppose a study is conducted in which eight unskilled, unemployed people are interviewed. The people are asked to rate each of five positions on a scale from 1 to 10 to indicate the status of the position, with 10 denoting most status and 1 denoting least status. The resulting data are given here. Use $\alpha = .05$ to analyse these repeated measures randomised block design data.

	Job				
Respondent	**Mail clerk**	**Typist**	**Recep-tionist**	**Secretary**	**Payroll assistant**
1	4	5	3	7	6
2	2	4	4	5	4
3	3	3	2	6	7
4	4	4	4	5	4
5	3	5	1	3	5
6	3	4	2	7	7
7	2	2	2	4	4
8	3	4	3	6	6

11.41 Analyse the following Excel output. Describe the design of the experiment. Using $\alpha = .05$, determine whether there are any significant effects. If so, explain why.

	A	B	C	D	E	F	G
1	Anova: Single Factor						
2							
3	SUMMARY						
4	*Groups*	*Count*	*Sum*	*Average*	*Variance*		
5	AD 1	6	108	18.00	3.20		
6	AD 2	6	106	17.67	3.87		
7	AD 3	6	68	11.33	11.87		
8	AD 4	6	54	9.00	9.20		
9	AD 5	6	92	15.33	9.47		
10							
11							
12	ANOVA						
13	*Source of Variation*	*SS*	*df*	*MS*	*F*	*P-value*	*F crit*
14	Between Groups	377.87	4	94.47	12.56	0.00	2.76
15	Within Groups	188	25	7.52			
16							
17	Total	565.87	29				

11.42 The following is Excel output for an ANOVA (two-factor without replication) problem. Describe the experimental design. The given value of alpha was .05. Discuss the output in terms of significant findings.

	A	B	C	D	E	F	G
1	ANOVA						
2	*Source of Variation*	*SS*	*df*	*MS*	*F*	*P-value*	*F crit*
3	Rows	24.33	2	12.17	3.07	0.09	4.10
4	Columns	212.50	5	42.50	10.71	0.00	3.33
5	Error	39.67	10	3.97			
6							
7	Total	276.50	17				

11.43 Study the following Excel output (for ANOVA, two-factor with replication) and graph. Discuss the meaning of the output.

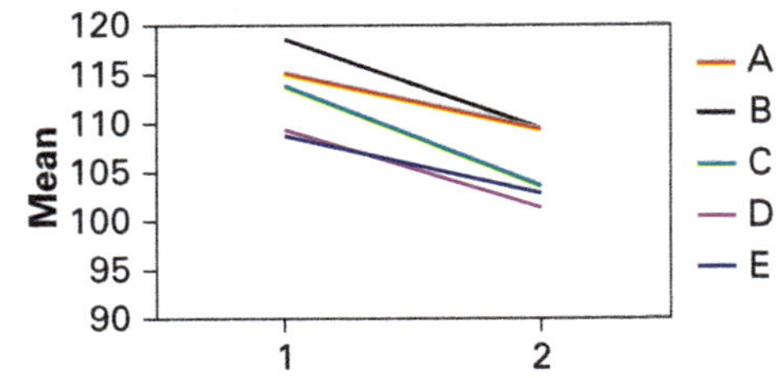

	A	B	C	D	E	F	G
1	ANOVA						
2	*Source of Variation*	*SS*	*df*	*MS*	*F*	*P-value*	*F crit*
3	Sample	215.70	4	53.93	6.27	0.01	3.48
4	Columns	288.80	1	288.80	33.58	0.00	4.96
5	Interaction	13.70	4	3.43	0.40	0.81	3.48
6	Within	86.00	10	8.60			
7							
8	Total	604.20	19				

MATHS APPENDIX

Formulas for computing a randomised block design

$$SSC = n\sum_{j=1}^{C}(\bar{x}_j - \bar{x})^2$$

$$SSR = C\sum_{i=1}^{n}(\bar{x}_i - \bar{x})^2$$

$$SSE = \sum_{i=1}^{n}\sum_{j=1}^{C}(x_{ij} - \bar{x}_j - \bar{x}_i + \bar{x})^2$$

$$SST = \sum_{i=1}^{n}\sum_{j=1}^{C}(x_{ij} - \bar{x})^2$$

$$df_C = C - 1$$

$$df_R = n - 1$$

$$df_E = (C-1)(n-1) = N - n - C + 1$$

$$MSC = \frac{SSC}{C-1}$$

$$MSR = \frac{SSR}{n-1}$$

$$MSE = \frac{SSE}{N-n-C+1}$$

$$F_{treatments} = \frac{MSC}{MSE}$$

$$F_{blocks} = \frac{MSR}{MSE}$$

where:

i = the block group (row)
j = the treatment level (column)
C = the number of treatment levels (columns)
n = the number of observations in each treatment level (number of blocks or rows)
x_{ij} = an individual observation
$\bar{x}_j$ = the treatment (column) mean
$\bar{x}_i$ = the block (row) mean
$\bar{x}$ = the grand mean
N = the total number of observations

Formulas for computing a two-way ANOVA

$$\text{SSR} = nC\sum_{i=1}^{R}(\bar{x}_i - \bar{x})^2$$

$$\text{SSC} = nR\sum_{j=1}^{C}(\bar{x}_j - \bar{x})^2$$

$$\text{SSI} = n\sum_{i=1}^{R}\sum_{j=1}^{C}(\bar{x}_{ij} - \bar{x}_i - \bar{x}_j + \bar{x})^2$$

$$\text{SSE} = \sum_{i=1}^{R}\sum_{j=1}^{C}\sum_{k=1}^{R}(x_{ijk} - \bar{x}_{ij})^2$$

$$\text{SST} = \sum_{i=1}^{R}\sum_{j=1}^{C}\sum_{k=1}^{n}(x_{ijk} - \bar{x})^2$$

$$\text{df}_R = R - 1$$

$$\text{df}_C = C - 1$$

$$\text{df}_I = (R-1)(C-1)$$

$$\text{df}_E = RC(n-1)$$

$$\text{df}_T = N - 1$$

$$\text{MSR} = \frac{\text{SSR}}{R-1}$$

$$\text{MSC} = \frac{\text{SSC}}{C-1}$$

$$\text{MSI} = \frac{\text{SSI}}{(R-1)(C-1)}$$

$$\text{MSE} = \frac{\text{SSE}}{RC(n-1)}$$

$$F_R = \frac{\text{MSR}}{\text{MSE}}$$

$$F_C = \frac{\text{MSC}}{\text{MSE}}$$

$$F_I = \frac{\text{MSI}}{\text{MSE}}$$

where:

n = number of observations per cell
C = number of column treatments
R = number of row treatments
i = row treatment level
j = column treatment level
k = cell member
x_{ijk} = individual observation
$\bar{x}_{ij}$ = cell mean
$\bar{x}_i$ = row mean
$\bar{x}_j$ = column mean
$\bar{x}$ = grand mean
N = total number of observations

CHAPTER

12 Chi-square tests

LEARNING OBJECTIVES

After studying this chapter, you should be able to:

1. understand the chi-square goodness-of-fit test, use it to test whether a given distribution is similar to a specified distribution (such as the Poisson distribution or normal distribution), and use it to test a hypothesis about a population proportion

2. understand the chi-square test of independence and use it to determine whether two variables are independent.

OPENING VIGNETTE

Social media is now crucial for business

Social media use is growing in leaps and bounds. Slightly more than half of the population of both Australia and New Zealand use Facebook, while relative newcomers such as Twitter, Tumblr and LinkedIn are among the fastest growing social media sites. Not surprisingly, businesses are beginning to enhance their social media presence as another means of reaching their customers. Suppose that a past survey of adult female social media users gave the following proportions: Facebook, 90%; LinkedIn, 3%; Twitter, 3%; Tumblr, 2%; Other, 2%. Suppose we now take a sample of male adult social media users and we obtain the following frequencies for the various categories.

Social media	Number of male users
Facebook	260
LinkedIn	37
Twitter	20
Tumblr	15
Other	18
Total	350

A marketing analyst wants to use the chi-square goodness-of-fit test to determine whether social media preferences of men and women are similar. This knowledge will help management better target their advertising campaigns to the two genders. The null hypothesis would be that there is no significant difference in social media preference between men and women. If this hypothesis cannot be rejected, it would imply that the same advertising strategy could be effective for both genders. The alternative hypothesis would be that there is a significant difference in social media preference. Nonrejection of the alternative hypothesis would imply that the company has to come up with a different strategy for each gender. Given that there are five social media categories, there are four degrees of freedom. The critical chi-square value, using an alpha of .05, is 9.4877. Therefore at the 5% level of significance, we would reject the null hypothesis if the observed chi-square goodness-of-fit statistic exceeds 9.4877. The observed chi-square statistic is 111.5, leading us to conclude that there is a significant difference in men and women's preferences for social media use. This result implies that the company should target different social media for each gender. For example, while Facebook is popular for most users, they may need to target other social media for male-oriented advertisements.

Introduction

This chapter explains hypothesis tests for categorical data based on one or two samples. We consider two techniques. The first is the *chi-square goodness-of-fit test.* It helps us to determine whether a sample could have come from a given type of population distribution. This is a useful test because we often encounter real-life data, which we need to check to determine what distribution it follows, such as normal, binomial or Poisson. The tests we have done so far assume that the variables are normally distributed. Nonparametric statistical techniques do not require the assumption of a normal distribution. Knowing the distribution of a given sample can help us to decide what type of hypothesis test to use.

The second technique we look at in this chapter is the *chi-square test of independence*, which tests whether there is a relationship (or dependence) between two categorical variables. There are instances in business when a manager may need to make a decision based on categorical data. For example, a bank manager may need to determine whether the credit risk of a customer depends on their home ownership status. Credit risk can be measured as good or poor, while home ownership can be measured as renting or buying a home. Since both variables are categorical, the techniques we have learnt so far cannot be used to analyse this problem. We therefore have to use the chi-square test of independence.

CHAPTER CASE

Job security at Combaro Ltd

The human resource (HR) manager at Combaro Ltd wanted to use the employment survey data to investigate issues related to job security at the company. With the switch from face-to-face processing of loan applications to online applications, the company has been able to keep its operating costs down, thereby enabling it to maintain profitability despite the sluggish economic growth since the 2008 global financial crisis (GFC). After extensive consultation between the workers and top management, a new enterprise bargaining agreement was implemented last year to improve worker productivity. One aspect of the agreement that the HR manager wanted to investigate was whether it had led to any significant change in the employees' perceptions of job security in the company. The company's strategic plan includes improving job security because that would also help to improve productivity. The manager also wanted to test whether the perception of job security in the company is related to gender. The company has recently put out a statement committing itself to a policy of non-discrimination in employee relations. If evidence of discrimination is found, appropriate policies would be devised to address the problem.

Respondents in the survey were asked to rate their perception of job security on a scale ranging from 1 (insecure) to 3 (very secure). The distribution of perceptions of job security from the employment survey follows.

Response	Frequency (f_o)
Insecure	14
Secure	20
Very secure	14
Total	48

The HR manager used these data to construct the following 2 × 3 contingency table relating gender and job security.

	Job security			
Gender	**Insecure**	**Secure**	**Very secure**	**Total**
Female	10	9	3	22
Male	4	11	11	26
Total	14	20	14	48

In a similar survey a few years earlier, the distribution of the responses to the job security question was: insecure, 52%; secure, 35%; very secure, 13%.

Questions to help managers make decisions

Combaro

1. What would be an appropriate statistical technique to use in analysing the data in the first table? Explain why you would recommend this technique.
2. From your analysis of these data, has there been a significant change in employees' perceptions of job security since the new workplace agreement was implemented? Explain your results.
3. What would be the appropriate statistical technique to analyse data such as those in the second table? Explain why you would use this approach.
4. Does employee perception of job security depend on gender? Interpret your results and show how management could use it to achieve the aims of the non-discrimination policy.

12.1 Chi-square goodness-of-fit test

In the binomial distribution only two possible outcomes can occur on a single trial in an experiment. An extension of the binomial distribution is the **multinomial distribution**, in which there can be more than two possible outcomes in a single trial. Suppose an electronics manufacturer wants to undertake a survey of customer satisfaction with a particular brand of its products in a particular city. The respondents are to indicate their level of satisfaction by selecting a single number on a scale of 1 (very dissatisfied) to 5 (very satisfied). Suppose that 100 customers are randomly selected to participate in the survey. This will be a multinomial experiment consisting of 100 identical trials, where each trial is to determine the satisfaction of each respondent. In each trial, only one outcome is possible because a person is not allowed to select more than one level of satisfaction. The trials are also independent because one respondent's selection does not affect that of any other respondent. The **chi-square goodness-of-fit test** can be used to determine whether the sample data conform to any kind of expected distribution. As the name suggests, the test determines whether the data 'fit' a given distribution. Suppose, in this example, the company has already conducted a national survey and wants to know whether customer satisfaction in this city has a pattern similar to the national pattern of satisfaction.

The chi-square goodness-of-fit test compares the *expected*, or theoretical, *frequencies* of categories from a population distribution with the *observed*, or actual, *frequencies* from a sample distribution to determine whether there is a significant difference between what was expected and what was observed. For example, in the customer satisfaction example, the sales manager might hypothesise that, because the age profile of the customers in this city is similar to that of the general population, the pattern of customer satisfaction is similar to the national pattern. To validate or reject this expected distribution, the observed results can be compared with the expected results using the chi-square goodness-of-fit test. This test can also be used to determine whether the customer satisfaction levels are normally distributed or Poisson distributed.

Formula 12.1 is used to compute a chi-square goodness-of-fit test.

Chi-square goodness-of-fit test (12.1)

$$\chi^2 = \sum \frac{(f_o - f_e)^2}{f_e}$$

$$\text{df} = k - 1 - m$$

where:

f_o = the frequency of observed values
f_e = the frequency of expected values
k = the number of categories
m = the number of parameters being estimated from the sample data

The idea behind the chi-square goodness-of-fit test is to compare how far the actual *observed frequency* is from the *expected* frequency. If the sales manager's hunch that customer satisfaction in the city is similar to the national customer satisfaction is correct, we would expect the squared difference between f_o and f_e to be zero or very small. Note that you could also compare them by looking at the absolute difference between the two but, because some deviations will be positive and others will be negative, the former will cancel out the latter and the sum of the deviations will be zero. So, as we learned in calculating the variance and the standard deviation, we square the deviations to ensure that the total deviation is positive. How significant the difference is between f_o and f_e is determined by comparing the test statistic with the critical value at a given level of significance. The degrees of freedom are obtained by first subtracting 1 from the sample size (n), as was the case for the t statistic. However, in addition, we also subtract m, the number of population parameters of the expected distribution that were estimated from the data. This is explained in the example opposite and in demonstration problem 12.1.

Looking at the numerator of the chi-square test statistic, we can see that, because we are squaring the deviations between f_o and f_e, the value of χ^2 can never be negative. As with the t distribution, the chi-square distribution belongs to a family of distributions, with each distribution uniquely defined according to its degrees of freedom (df). As can be seen from figure 12.1, the chi-square distribution is considerably skewed to the right (i.e. it has a strong positive skew) at low values of df. However, as df increases (i.e. as n gets larger), the chi-square distribution becomes more and more normal, as with the t distribution. Values for the chi-square distribution are given in table A.8. Because of space limitations, chi-square values are listed only for certain probabilities.

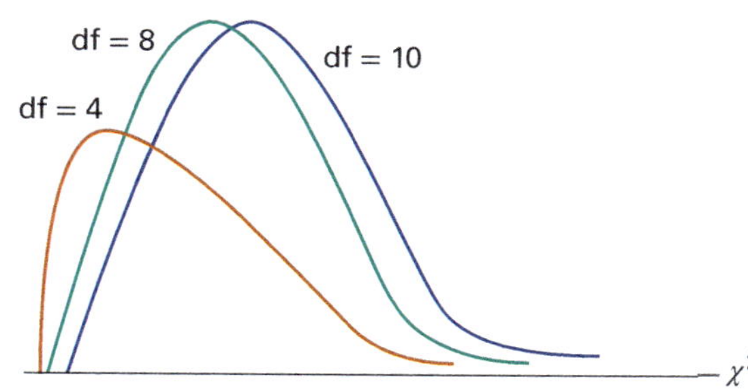

FIGURE 12.1 Family of chi-square distributions

The following example shows how the chi-square goodness-of-fit test can be applied to business situations. As part of a computer manufacturer's commitment to total quality control, it carefully monitors defective components, because this provides useful information for quality improvement. Defective components are placed into three categories according to the type of problem: defective chip, defective soldering point and defective circuit board. Based on past data collected from the assembly line, the quality control manager knows that the manufacturing process is under control if the distribution of defects is as follows: 14.2% defective chips, 60.5% defective soldering points and 25.3% defective circuit boards.

To test whether the process in a given week was under control, he randomly selected 50 defective components. The distribution of defects is shown in table 12.1. The manager can now use a chi-square goodness-of-fit test to determine whether the observed frequencies of responses from his survey are the same as the frequencies that would be expected if the quality control system is under control.

TABLE 12.1 Results of the quality control survey

Type of defect	Frequency (f_o)
Chip	9
Soldering point	35
Circuit board	6
Total	50

The test is carried out using the following steps.

STEP 1. Set up H_0 and H_a

H_0: The observed distribution is the same as the expected distribution.

H_a: The observed distribution is not the same as the expected distribution.

STEP 2. Decide on the type of test

The chi-square goodness-of-fit test is always one-tailed (or one-sided) because a chi-square value of zero (or close to zero) indicates that the observed and expected distributions are similar. Any deviation from a zero difference occurs only in the positive direction because chi-square is determined by a sum of squared values and can never be negative.

STEP 3. Decide on the level of significance, α, and determine the critical value(s) and region(s)

Let $\alpha = .05$. Given that there are three categories in this example (defective chip, defective soldering point and defective circuit board), $k = 3$. The value of m is 0 because the test does not require us to use the data to estimate any parameter values when using the χ^2 as a goodness-of-fit statistic. Therefore, the degrees of freedom are $k - 1 - m = 3 - 1 - 0 = 2$. For $\alpha = .05$ and df = 2, the critical chi-square value from table A.8 (reading from the second row and going across to the $\alpha = .05$ column) is:

$$\chi^2_{.05,\,2} = 5.9915$$

STEP 4. Write down the decision rule

If the chi-square value calculated from the survey data (i.e. the observed chi-square) is greater than 5.9915, then we reject the null hypothesis.

STEP 5. Select a random sample and do relevant calculations

The sample information (observed frequencies) was given on the previous page. To compute the chi-square goodness-of-fit test statistic, we first calculate the expected frequencies. The expected proportions are given below as .142, .605 and .263. The observed values from the sample data reported in table 12.1 sum to 50 (i.e. $n = 50$). Under the null hypothesis, the observed distribution is the same as the expected distribution. On that basis, we can calculate the expected frequencies by multiplying the expected proportions by the sample total of the observed frequencies ($n = 50$), as shown in table 12.2.

TABLE 12.2 Construction of expected values for the quality control problem

Type of defect	Expected proportion	Expected frequency (fe) (proportion × sample total)
Chip	.142	.142 × 50 = 7.10
Soldering point	.605	.605 × 50 = 30.25
Circuit board	.253	.253 × 50 = 12.65
Total		50.00

The chi-square goodness-of-fit test statistic is computed in table 12.3. This shows that the observed chi-square value is 4.75. We compare this with the critical value of 5.9915. In figure 12.2 (opposite), we reject H_0 if the computed test statistic falls in the rejection zone.

TABLE 12.3 Calculation of chi-square for the quality control problem

Type of defect	f_o	f_e	$\frac{(f_o - f_e)^2}{f_e}$
Chip	9	7.10	0.508
Soldering point	35	30.25	0.746
Circuit board	6	12.65	3.496
Total	50	50.00	$\chi^2 = 4.750$

STEP 6. Draw a conclusion

Because the observed chi-square of 4.75 is less than the critical value of 5.9915, we fail to reject the null hypothesis that the observed distribution is the same as the expected distribution. It is possible that the assembly line is producing defective components that match the historical 'in control' distribution, and therefore the observed differences between the two distributions could be due to chance. In this case, we do not have overwhelming evidence that the system is out of control and therefore we accept the possibility that it is still in control. The test result shows that the observed distribution is not significantly different from the expected distribution. On the basis of this evidence, we will recommend to the manager that there is no evidence that process has gone out of control and therefore no corrective measures would be necessary.

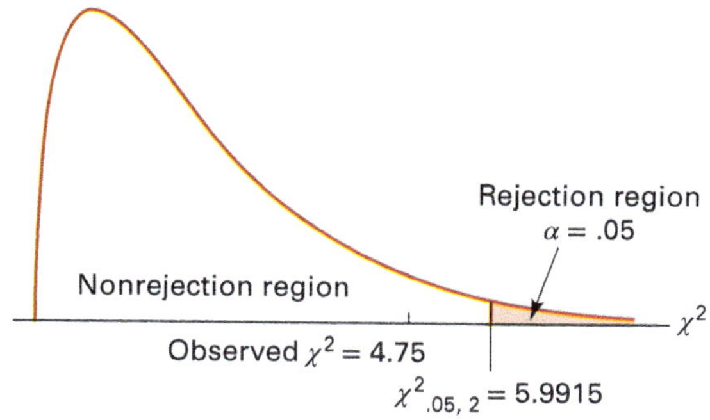

FIGURE 12.2 Graph of chi-square distribution for quality-control survey

DEMONSTRATION PROBLEM 12.1

PROBLEM: Roy Morgan Market Research regularly conducts surveys of registered Australian voters to determine their voting intentions. The following table shows the results of a telephone survey that asked voters which party they would vote for if an election were to be held on that day.

Party	Number
Liberal Party	241
National Party	14
Australian Labor Party	187
Greens	54
Others/Independents	46
Total	542

A previous survey had indicated the following distribution of voters' preferences: Liberal Party, 38%; National Party, 5%; Australian Labor Party, 38%; Greens, 13.5%; Others/Independents, 5.5%. Determine whether there has been a significant change in voters' preferences using $\alpha = .01$.

SOLUTION

STEP 1. Set up H_0 and H_a

H_0: Voters' preferences have not changed; i.e. voters' preferences in the recent poll are the same as in the previous poll.

H_a: Voters' preferences have changed; i.e. voters' preferences in the recent poll are not the same as in the previous poll.

STEP 2. Decide on the type of test

The chi-square goodness-of-fit test is one-tailed.

STEP 3. Decide on the level of significance, α, and determine the critical value(s) and region(s)

Let $\alpha = .01$. With four categories in this example, $k = 5$. The value of m is 0 because we did not use the data to estimate any parameters. Therefore, the degrees of freedom are $k - 1 - m = 4 - 1 - 0 = 3$. For $\alpha = .01$ and df = 3, the critical chi-square value from table A.8 is:

$$\chi^2_{.01,\,3} = 11.3449$$

STEP 4. Write down the decision rule

If the chi-square calculated from the recent survey data (i.e. the observed chi-square) is greater than 11.3449, we reject the null hypothesis.

STEP 5. Select a random sample and do relevant calculations

The expected proportions are those from the earlier poll, which were given on the previous page as .38, .05, .38, .135 and .055. The observed values from the sample data reported in the table on the previous page add up to 542. We can therefore calculate the expected frequencies by multiplying the expected proportions by the sample total of the observed frequencies ($n = 542$), as shown in the table below.

Party	Expected proportion	Expected frequency (f_e) (proportion × sample total)
Liberal Party	.38	$.38 \times 542 = 205.96$
National Party	.05	$.05 \times 542 = 27.10$
Australian Labor Party	.38	$.38 \times 542 = 205.96$
Greens	.135	$.135 \times 542 = 73.17$
Others/Independents	.055	$.055 \times 542 = 29.81$
Total		542.00

The chi-square test statistic can then be calculated using the table below.

Party	f_o	f_e	$\frac{(f_o - f_e)^2}{f_e}$
Liberal Party	241	205.96	5.961
National Party	14	27.10	6.332
Australian Labor Party	187	205.96	1.745
Greens	54	73.17	5.022
Others/Independents	46	29.81	8.793
			$\chi^2 = 27.853$

From the table above, our observed chi-square is 27.853. We compare this with the critical value of 11.3449. In the graph below, we reject H_0 if the computed test statistic falls in the rejection region.

STEP 6. Draw a conclusion

Given that the observed chi-square of 27.853 is greater than the critical value of 11.3449 in the following graph, we reject the null hypothesis and conclude that there has been a significant shift in voter preferences since the previous opinion poll. Specifically, there has been a significant shift from the Australian Labor Party to the Coalition, which is made up of the Liberal Party and the National Party.

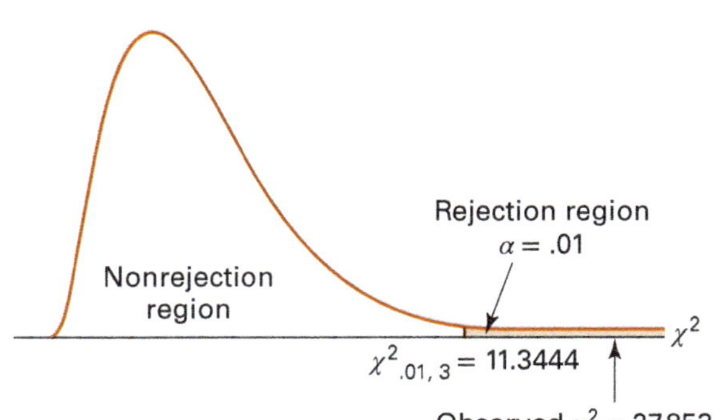

DEMONSTRATION PROBLEM 12.2

PROBLEM: The chi-square goodness-of-fit test can also be used to test whether a given distribution has a Poisson distribution. A Poisson distribution is identified by an average number of occurrences of events (λ) at a given location within a specified time period. This makes it useful for testing hypotheses about events such as waiting times in queues, the number of flaws in a manufactured item, and so on. Suppose the traffic manager of a city council believes traffic accidents at a busy intersection is Poisson distributed and sets out to test this hypothesis by gathering information. Confirmation of this distribution will help her to make a more informed recommendation to council regarding what response should be taken to deal with the problem. The following data represent a distribution of the frequency of traffic accidents at the location during daily intervals within the study period.

Use α = .05 to test whether the manager's belief is supported by the data.

Number of accidents	Observed frequencies
0	9
1	22
2	28
3	19
≥4	6

SOLUTION

STEP 1. Set up H_0 and H_a

H_0: The frequency distribution is Poisson.

H_a: The frequency distribution is not Poisson.

STEP 2. Decide on the type of test

The chi-square goodness-of-fit test is one-tailed.

STEP 3. Decide on the level of significance, α, and determine the critical value(s) and region(s)

Let α = .05. With five categories of accident occurrences, $k = 5$. The value of m is 1 because the mean accident occurrence (λ) was not given and would need to be estimated from the data. Therefore, the degrees of freedom are $k - 1 - m = 5 - 1 - 1 = 3$. For α = .05 and df = 3, the critical chi-square value from table A.8 is $\chi^2_{.05,\,3} = 7.8147$.

STEP 4. Write down the decision rule

If the chi-square value calculated from the data is greater than 7.8147, we reject the null hypothesis that the distribution is Poisson.

STEP 5. Select a random sample and do relevant calculations

We can calculate the expected frequencies in two steps. First, we compute the mean accident occurrence (λ) for the sample. The sample mean is actually a weighted average, which is obtained by multiplying each accident category number by the observed frequency in that category, adding up the product of the number of accidents and the frequency of those accidents, and dividing by the total number of observed frequencies; that is:

$$\lambda = \frac{0(9) + 1(22) + 2(28) + 3(19) + 4(6)}{84} = \frac{159}{84} = 1.89 \approx 1.9$$

Using $\lambda = 1.9$ as our estimate of the population mean, we now refer to the column for $\lambda = 1.9$ in the Poisson probabilities tables in table A.2 and read the probabilities of the various categories, where x = the number of accidents. For example, for zero accidents ($x = 0$), the probability is .1496; for one accident ($x = 1$), the probability is .2842. The remaining probabilities are given in the table on the following page.

In the second step (see column three of the following table), we compute the expected frequencies by multiplying the total number of accidents by the expected probabilities (column 2).

Accidents (x)	Expected probability	Expected frequency (f_e) (accidents × probability)
0	.1496	84 × .1496 = 12.57
1	.2842	84 × .2842 = 23.87
2	.2700	84 × .2700 = 22.68
3	.1710	84 × .1710 = 14.36
≥4	.1252	84 × .1252 = 10.52
Total		84.00

The chi-square test statistic can then be calculated using the following table.

Accidents	Observed frequencies	Expected frequencies	$\frac{(f_o - f_e)^2}{f_e}$
0	7	12.57	1.01
1	18	23.87	.15
2	25	22.68	1.25
3	17	14.36	1.50
4	12	10.52	1.94
Total	84	84.00	$\chi^2 = 5.85$

From the table above, our observed chi-square is 5.85. We compare this with the critical value of 7.8147. On the following graph, we reject H_0 if the computed test statistic falls in the rejection region.

STEP 6. Draw a conclusion

Because the observed chi-square of 5.85 is less than the critical value of 7.8147, we cannot reject the null hypothesis. That is, there is insufficient evidence to disprove the manager's claim that the frequency of accidents at the intersection follows a Poisson distribution.

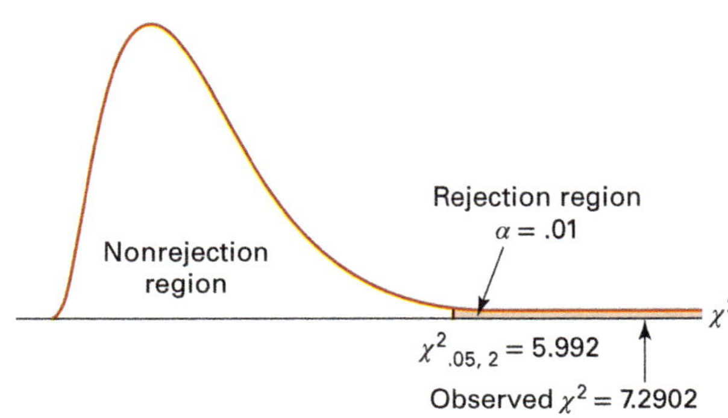

DEMONSTRATION PROBLEM 12.3

PROBLEM: Another application of the chi-square goodness-of-fit test is to determine whether a given distribution conforms to a normal distribution. (For continuous data, testing whether the data conform to a normal distribution could also be done using the Kolmogorov–Smirnov test, which is discussed elsewhere.) As an example, consider a business statistics lecturer who is interested in knowing whether the distribution of scores in her class is normal. This information is necessary because she wants to find out what proportion of the students in the course may have special needs. Suppose the lecturer has collected data consisting of a simple random sample of 300 scores in her first-year business statistics course. A previous study had determined that the average score in the course was 52.7%, with a standard deviation of 15.0%. A frequency distribution of the scores is found below.

Score (%)	Frequency
Under 30	10
30–under 40	35
40–under 50	97
50–under 60	78
60–under 70	38
70–under 80	30
80–under 90	8
90–under 100	4
Total	300

Based on the sample data, determine at the .01 level of significance whether the sample could have been drawn from a population in which the scores are normally distributed.

SOLUTION

STEP 1. Set up H_0 and H_a

H_0: The sample was drawn from a population of scores that are normally distributed.

H_a: The sample was drawn from a population of scores that are not normally distributed.

STEP 2. Decide on the type of test

The chi-square goodness-of-fit test is appropriate for testing this hypothesis.

STEP 3. Decide on the level of significance, α, and determine the critical value(s) and region(s)

Let $\alpha = .01$. With eight categories of scores, $k = 8$. The value of m is 0 because there was no need to estimate any parameters; the mean and standard deviation are given. Therefore, the degrees of freedom are $k - 0 - m = 8 - 0 - 1 = 7$. For $\alpha = .01$ and df = 7, the critical chi-square value from table A.8 is $\chi^2_{.01,\,7} = 18.4753$.

STEP 4. Write down the decision rule

Reject the null hypothesis if the chi-square value calculated from the data is greater than 18.4753.

STEP 5. Select a random sample and do relevant calculations

Under the null hypothesis, the distribution has a normal distribution. We can therefore calculate the expected frequencies as follows. First, we use the given mean and standard deviation to calculate the *z*-scores at the respective upper class limits (x). We then use table A.4 to find the areas under the standard normal curve to the left of each x. Next, we find the area or probability (p) for each class interval. Finally, we multiply each of these probabilities by the total number of observations to obtain the expected frequencies. If the expected frequency in any is less than five, we combine that class with an adjacent one that has more than five.

As an example, for the 'under 30' class, the *z*-score is calculated as:

$$z = \frac{30 - 52.7}{15} = -1.51$$

The area to the left of $z = -1.51$ is .065. The area of this class interval is also .065. The expected frequency in this class is given by $300_p = 300(.065) = 19.5$.

For the '30–under 40' class, the *z*-score is:

$$z = \frac{40 - 52.7}{15} = -.85$$

The area to the left of $z = -.85$ is .198. The area of this class interval is given by $.198 - .065 = .133$. The expected frequency is given by $300p = 300(.133) = 39.9$. The remaining expected frequencies are shown in the table overleaf.

Upper class limit (x)	$z = \frac{x - \mu}{\sigma} = \frac{x - 52.7}{15}$	Area under standard normal curve left of x	Area of class interval (p)	Expected frequency, $f_e = 300p$
30	−1.51	.065	.065	19.5
40	−.85	.198	.133	39.9
50	−.18	.429	.231	69.3
60	.49	.688	.259	77.7
70	1.15	.875	.187	56.1
80	1.82	.966	.091	27.3
90	2.49	.994	.028	8.4
100	3.15	1.000	.006	1.8
Total			1.000	300.0

The chi-square test statistic can then be calculated using the following table.

Upper class limit (x)	Observed frequencies (f_o)	Expected frequencies (f_e)	$\frac{(f_o - f_e)^2}{f_e}$
30	10	19.5	4.63
40	35	39.9	.60
50	97	69.3	11.07
60	78	77.7	.00
70	38	56.1	5.84
80	30	27.3	.27
90	8	8.4	.02
100	4	1.8	2.69
Total	300	300.0	$\chi^2 = 25.12$

From the above table, our observed chi-square value is 25.12. This is greater than the critical value of 18.4753.

STEP 6. Draw a conclusion

Because the observed chi-square value of 25.12 is greater than the critical value of 18.4753, we reject the null hypothesis; that is, the sample was not drawn from a population with a normal distribution.

DEMONSTRATION PROBLEM 12.4

A final application of the chi-square goodness-of-fit test is to test hypotheses about a population proportion. This could be used as an alternative technique to the z test. Using the z test of a population proportion, when the sample size is large enough ($np \geq 5$ and $nq \geq 5$), sample proportions are normally distributed and the following formula can be used to test hypotheses about p.

$$z = \frac{\hat{p} - p}{\sqrt{\frac{pq}{n}}}$$

The chi-square goodness-of-fit test can also be used to conduct tests about p; in this simple case, it can be viewed as a special case of the chi-square goodness-of-fit test where the number of classifications equals two (binomial distribution situation). The observed chi-square is computed in the same way as in any other chi-square goodness-of-fit test, but because the test contains only two classifications (success or failure), $k = 2$ and the degrees of freedom are $k - 1 = 2 - 1 = 1$.

As an example, we will solve the following problem from section 9.5 by using the chi-square methodology. This example tests the hypothesis that exactly 8% of a manufacturer's products are defective. The following hypotheses are being tested.

$$H_0\text{: } p = .08$$
$$H_a\text{: } p \neq .08$$

The value of alpha was given to be .10. To test these hypotheses, a business researcher randomly selected a sample of 200 items and determined that 33 of the items had at least one flaw.

In solving this problem using the chi-square goodness-of-fit test, we view it as a two-category expected distribution in which we expect .08 defective and .92 nondefective. The observed categories are 33 defective and 200 − 33 = 167 nondefective. Using the total number of observed items (200), we can determine an expected distribution as .08(200) = 16 and .92(200) = 184. Shown here are the observed and expected frequencies.

	f_o	f_e
Defective	33	16
Nondefective	167	184

Alpha is .10, the test is two-tailed and there is one degree of freedom. The critical table chi-square value is:

$$\chi^2_{.10,1} = 2.7055$$

An observed chi-square value greater than this value must be obtained to reject the null hypothesis. The chi-square for this problem is calculated as follows.

$$\chi^2 = \sum \frac{(f_o - f_e)^2}{f_e} = \frac{(33 - 16)^2}{16} + \frac{(167 - 184)^2}{184} = 18.06 + 1.57 = 19.63$$

Notice that this observed value of chi-square, 19.63, is greater than the critical table value, 2.7055. The decision is therefore to reject the null hypothesis; according to this analysis, the manufacturer does not produce 8% defective products. Observing the actual sample result in which .165 of the sample was defective indicates that the proportion of the population that is defective might be greater than 8%.

Note that the above results are approximately the same as those calculated using the z test. This can be explained by the interrelationship between the standardised normal distribution and a chi-square distribution with one degree of freedom. For example, using the z test, the observed z value is 4.43 and here our observed χ^2 value is 19.63. Notice that $\chi^2 \approx z^2$; that is, $19.63 \approx 4.43^2$. This relationship also applies to the critical values of the two test statistics at the .10 level of significance. For example, the critical value of χ^2 with one degree of freedom at $\alpha = .10$ is 2.7055, which is approximately equal to the square of the critical z value of 1.645. Furthermore, looking at the df = 1 row in table A.8, it can be seen that observed chi-square statistic of 19.63 has a p-value of less than .005, which is close to zero and roughly equal to the p-value of zero of the observed z statistic. This shows that, when doing a two-tailed test for the equality of two proportions, the z and the χ^2 tests are equivalent. However, if we are specifically interested in a one-tailed test, we must use the z test with the entire rejection region put into one tail of the standardised normal distribution.

PRACTICE PROBLEMS

Practising the calculations

12.1 Use a chi-square goodness-of-fit test to determine whether the observed frequencies have the same distribution as the expected frequencies ($\alpha = .05$).

Category	f_o	f_e
1	36	46
2	96	66
3	78	83
4	25	30
5	17	11

12.2 Are the following data Poisson distributed? Use $\alpha = .05$ and the chi-square goodness-of-fit test to answer this question. What is your estimated lambda?

Number of arrivals	f_o
0	28
1	17
2	11
3	5

12.3 Use the chi-square goodness-of-fit test to determine if the following observed data are normally distributed. Let $\alpha = .05$. What are the estimated mean and standard deviation?

Category	Observed
1 to less than 10	6
10 to less than 20	14
11 to less than 30	29
31 to less than 40	38
41 to less than 50	25
51 to less than 60	10
61 to less than 70	7

12.4 In one survey, female entrepreneurs were asked to select their personal definition of success from several categories. Thirty-nine per cent responded that happiness was their definition of success, 12% said sales/profit, 18% said helping others and 31% said achievements/challenge. Suppose you wanted to determine whether male entrepreneurs felt the same way and took a random sample of men, resulting in the following data. Use the chi-square goodness-of-fit test to determine whether the observed frequency distribution of data for men is the same as the distribution for women. Let $\alpha = .05$.

Definition	f_o
Happiness	42
Sales/profit	95
Helping others	27
Achievements/challenge	63

Testing your understanding

12.5 The general manager of a cosmetics marketing company believes the annual incomes of its clients are normally distributed. The following data represent the distribution of incomes for a random sample of the company's clients. Given a sample mean of \$67 000 and a standard deviation of \$24 000, use the chi-square goodness-of-fit test to determine whether this distribution is significantly different from the normal distribution. Assume that $\alpha = .05$. How could the result help the company to sell more cosmetics?

Annual income of client (\$)	Frequency
0–20 000	2
20 001–50 000	20
50 001–80 000	51
80 001–110 000	22
110 001–140 000	5

12.6 An emergency call service centre keeps records of emergency telephone calls. A study of 150 five-minute time intervals resulted in the following distribution of number of calls. For example, during 18 of the five-minute intervals, no calls were received. Use the chi-square goodness-of-fit test and $\alpha = .01$ to determine whether this distribution is Poisson. Explain your test result.

Number of calls (per 5-minute interval)	Frequency
0	18
1	28
2	47
3	21
4	16
5	11
6 or more	9

12.7 According to a recent survey, 66% of all computer companies are going to spend more on marketing this year than in previous years. Only 33% of other information technology companies and 28% of non-information technology companies are going to spend more than in previous years. Suppose a researcher wanted to conduct a survey of her own to test the claim that 28% of all non-information technology companies will spend more on marketing next year than this year. She randomly selects 270 companies and determines that 62 of the companies do plan to spend more on marketing next year. Use $\alpha = .05$, the chi-square goodness-of-fit test and the sample data to determine whether the 28% figure holds for all non-information technology companies.

12.2 Contingency analysis: chi-square test of independence

Hypothesis tests involving one and two population proportions are useful in many cases, but we will also encounter business situations where there will be a need to test hypotheses involving many proportions. For example, the manager of a superannuation fund that offers five different packages may wish to determine whether the proportion of customers selecting each package is related to the four sales regions in which the customers reside. Another example could be that of a campaign manager of a political party who wants to know whether party affiliation is related to educational level. In each of these cases, the proportions relate to characteristic categories of the variable of interest.

The goodness-of-fit test cannot be used to analyse these situations that involve two or more categorical variables. Such cases require a new statistical technique called the **chi-square test of independence** or **contingency analysis**. Contingency analysis is based on a **contingency table** and tests whether two events are independent. That test involved probabilities; here we will use the chi-square test of independence to determine whether two variables are related.

Suppose a business researcher is interested in determining whether investors' state or territory of residence is independent of the type of financial investment they have. On the survey questionnaire, the following two questions might be used to measure residence and type of financial investment.

In which state/territory do you reside?

1. New South Wales
2. Victoria
3. South Australia
4. Queensland
5. Northern Territory
6. Western Australia
7. Australian Capital Territory
8. Tasmania

Which type of financial investment are you most likely to make today?

1. Stocks
2. Government securities
3. Other

The business researcher would *tally the frequencies of responses* to these two questions in a two-way contingency table. Table 12.4 (overleaf) shows a contingency table for these two variables.

TABLE 12.4 Contingency table for the investment example

State/territory	Type of financial investment: Stocks	Government securities	Other
New South Wales			o_{13}
Victoria			
South Australia			
Queensland			
Northern Territory			
Western Australia			
Australian Capital Territory			
Tasmania	o_{81}		

The following notation will be used to describe entries in the table. Subscript i denotes the row and j the column. Thus, o_{13} is the observed frequency for the cell in the first row and third column of data, and o_{81} is the observed frequency for the cell in the eighth row and first column of data. The expected frequencies are denoted in a similar manner. The expected frequencies are calculated using:

$$e_{ij} = \frac{(\text{row } i \text{ total})(\text{column } j \text{ total})}{n}$$

where:

e_{ij} = the expected frequency in row i, column j

n = the total of all the frequencies (i.e. sum of the rows and columns).

Using these expected frequency values and the observed frequency values, we can compute a chi-square test of independence to determine whether the variables are independent using formula 12.2.

Chi-square test of independence (12.2)

$$\chi^2 = \sum_r \sum_c \frac{(f_o - f_e)^2}{f_e}$$

$$\text{df} = (r-1)(c-1)$$

where:

r = the number of rows

c = the number of columns

Note that the chi-square test of independence is one-tailed because we are again comparing f_o and f_e. If H_a is true, we would expect the absolute difference between the two to be significantly greater than zero. Also note that formula 12.2 is similar to formula 12.1, with the exception that the values are summed across both rows and columns and the degrees of freedom are different.

To illustrate this test, consider an insurance claims analyst who examined 100 motor vehicle insurance claims to determine whether the gender of a claimant is independent of the claimant's age. She grouped the ages of the claimants into the following three categories: less than 30 years, 30 to 50 years and more than 50 years. The resulting 3 × 2 contingency table is shown in table 12.5. Using α = .05, she can use the chi-square test of independence to determine whether gender is independent of age.

TABLE 12.5 Contingency table for the insurance claims example

	Gender		
Age	**Male**	**Female**	**Total**
< 30 years	32	25	57
30–50 years	18	5	23
> 50 years	17	3	20
Total	67	33	100

STEP 1. Set up H_0 and H_a

H_0: Gender is independent of age.

H_a: Gender is not independent of age.

STEP 2. Decide on the type of test

The chi-square test of independence is appropriate.

STEP 3. Decide on the level of significance, α, and determine the critical value(s) and region(s)

Let $\alpha = .05$. Here, there are three rows ($r = 3$) and two columns ($c = 2$). The degrees of freedom are $(3 - 1)(2 - 1) = 2$. The critical value of chi-square for $\alpha = .05$ from table A.8 is 5.9915.

STEP 4. Write down the decision rule

If the chi-square value calculated from the data is greater than 5.9915, we reject the null hypothesis and conclude that gender is not independent of age.

STEP 5. Select a random sample and do relevant calculations

The process of computing the test statistic begins by calculating the expected frequencies using the formula for e_{ij} given on the previous page. This formula multiplies the frequency of one category by the frequency of the other and divides the product by the total sample size (n). Notice that the numerator is similar to the multiplication rule for independent events. This rule says that, when two events are independent, the probability that they will *both* occur is equal to the product of their probabilities. Therefore, this equation for defining expected frequency expresses independence, in effect, by multiplying these probabilities.

$$e_{11} = \frac{\text{(row 1 total)(column 1 total)}}{\text{grand total}} = \frac{57(67)}{100} = 38.19$$

$$e_{12} = \frac{\text{(row 1 total)(column 2 total)}}{\text{grand total}} = \frac{57(33)}{100} = 18.81$$

$$e_{21} = \frac{\text{(row 2 total)(column 1 total)}}{\text{grand total}} = \frac{23(67)}{100} = 15.41$$

$$e_{22} = \frac{\text{(row 2 total)(column 2 total)}}{\text{grand total}} = \frac{23(33)}{100} = 7.59$$

$$e_{31} = \frac{\text{(row 3 total)(column 1 total)}}{\text{grand total}} = \frac{20(67)}{100} = 13.40$$

$$e_{33} = \frac{\text{(row 3 total)(column 3 total)}}{\text{grand total}} = \frac{20(33)}{100} = 6.60$$

We then list the expected frequencies in the cells of the contingency table (table 12.6) along with the observed frequencies. The expected frequencies are shown in parentheses beneath the observed frequencies.

TABLE 12.6 Contingency table of observed and expected frequencies (in brackets) for the insurance claims example

	Gender		
Age	**Male**	**Female**	**Total**
> 30 years	32 (38.19)	25 (18.81)	57
30–50 years	18 (15.41)	5 (7.59)	23
> 50 years	17 (13.40)	3 (6.60)	20
Total	67	33	100

Next, we compute the chi-square value by summing $\frac{(f_o - f_e)^2}{f_e}$ for all cells.

$$\chi^2 = \frac{(32-38.19)^2}{38.19} + \frac{(25-18.81)^2}{18.81} + \frac{(18-15.41)^2}{15.41} + \frac{(5-7.59)^2}{7.59} + \frac{(17-13.4)^2}{13.4} + \frac{(3-6.6)^2}{6.6}$$

$$= 1.0033 + 2.0370 + 0.4353 + 0.8838 + 0.9672 + 1.9636$$

$$= 7.2902$$

From the preceding calculation, the observed value of chi-square is 7.2902. We then compare this with the critical value of 5.9915. In the following graph, we reject H_0 if the computed test statistic falls in the rejection region.

STEP 6. Draw a conclusion

Since the observed chi-square of 7.2902 is greater than the critical value of 5.9915, we reject the null hypothesis and conclude that the gender of an insurance claimant is not independent of the claimant's age. Looking at the proportions in the cells, it can be seen that in all age groups women make fewer claims than men.

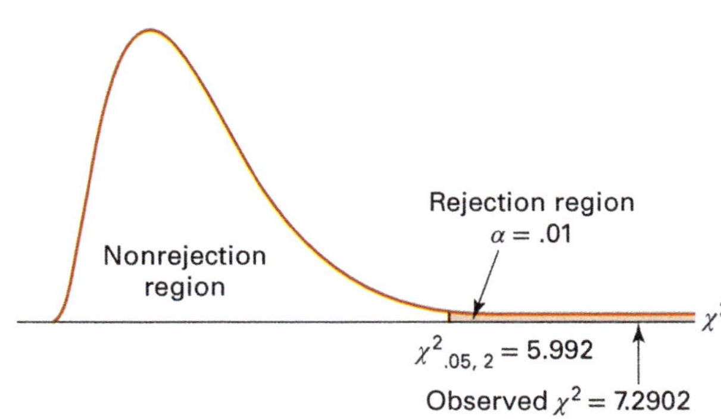

FIGURE 12.3 Graph of chi-square distribution for insurance claims example

DEMONSTRATION PROBLEM 12.5

PROBLEM: A popular supermarket chain routinely asks its customers whether they prefer paper or plastic bags with their purchases. A recent survey of customers recorded information on their bag preferences as well as their educational background. Using the information from the table below, can we conclude at the .01 level of significance that there is a relationship between educational background and type of bag preferred?

	Educational background		
Bag preference	**High school**	**Tertiary**	**Postgraduate**
Paper	20	40	80
Plastic	90	20	15
No preference	20	12	12

SOLUTION

STEP 1. Set up H_0 and H_a

H_0: Bag preference is independent of educational background.
H_a: Bag preference is not independent of educational background.

STEP 2. Decide on the type of test

Because we want to test the relationship between two variables (bag preference and educational preference) and the data are frequencies, the chi-square test of independence is appropriate.

STEP 3. Decide on the level of significance, α, and determine the critical value(s) and region(s)

The degrees of freedom are (3 – 1)(3 – 1) = 4, and the critical value is $\chi^2_{.01,\,4} = 13.2767$.

STEP 4. Write down the decision rule

If the chi-square value calculated from the data is greater than 13.2767, we reject the null hypothesis and conclude that bag preference is not independent of educational background.

STEP 5. Select a random sample and do relevant calculations

The expected frequencies are the products of the row and column totals divided by the grand total. The contingency table, with observed and expected frequencies (in brackets), follows.

	Educational background			
Bag preference	**High school**	**Tertiary**	**Postgraduate**	**Total**
Paper	20 (58.90)	40 (32.62)	80 (48.48)	140
Plastic	90 (52.59)	20 (29.13)	15 (43.28)	125
No preference	20 (18.51)	12 (10.25)	12 (15.24)	44
Total	130	72	107	309

The chi-square value is computed as follows.

$$\chi^2 = \frac{(20-58.90)^2}{58.90} + \frac{(40-32.62)^2}{32.62} + \frac{(80-48.48)^2}{48.48} + \frac{(90-52.59)^2}{52.59}$$
$$+ \frac{(20-29.13)^2}{29.13} + \frac{(15-43.28)^2}{43.28} + \frac{(20-18.51)^2}{18.51} + \frac{(12-10.25)^2}{10.25} + \frac{(12-15.24)^2}{15.24}$$
$$= 25.691 + 20.493 + 26.612 + 2.862 + 18.479 + 18.479 + 0.123 + 0.298 + 0.689$$
$$= 95.247$$

STEP **6. Draw a conclusion**

Because the observed chi-square of 95.247 is greater than the critical value of 13.2767, we reject the null hypothesis. Thus, there is sufficient evidence to conclude that there is a relationship between educational background and type of bag preferred. The relatively high value of the calculated chi-square statistic in relation to the critical value of chi-square suggests that, at $\alpha = .01$, the differences between the observed and expected frequencies are large enough to support the view that bag preference is related to the customers' educational background.

Please refer to 'Going further with KaddStat' for KaddStat instructions at www.johnwiley.com.au/highered/black4e/kaddstat.

MISUSE OF STATISTICS

In a chi-square goodness-of-fit or independence test, the chi-square distribution is used as an approximation for the true distribution. We use this approximation because the true distribution is difficult to compute in most cases. Nevertheless, the approximation may not hold if the expected frequency in one or more cells is small. In such cases, the calculated chi-square statistic tends to be inflated and may result in a wrong conclusion. It is generally recommended that where the expected frequency in a given cell is less than 5 it should be combined with an adjacent cell to get an expected frequency of more than 5.

PRACTICE PROBLEMS

Practising the calculations

P12-08 **12.8** Use the following contingency table to determine whether brand preference for breakfast cereal is independent of gender. Let $\alpha = .01$.

	Brand Preference			
Gender	**A**	**B**	**C**	**Total**
Male	18	25	17	60
Female	32	5	3	40
Total	50	30	20	100

P12-09 **12.9** Use the following contingency table and the chi-square test of independence to determine whether social class is independent of the number of children in a family. Let $\alpha = .05$.

	Social class		
Number of children	**Lower**	**Middle**	**Upper**
0	7	18	6
1	9	38	23
2 or 3	34	97	58
More than 3	47	31	30

P12-10 **12.10** A motor insurance company wanted to know whether the frequency of insurance claims by its customers was related to their age. Test the hypothesis at $\alpha = 0.1$ using the information below.

	Age of insured			
Action	**Under 25**	**25–35**	**36–55**	**Over 55**
Filed claim	85	92	100	65
Did not file claim	92	121	600	140

Testing your understanding

P12-11 **12.11** A computer manufacturer is considering sourcing supplies of an electrical component from four different manufacturers. The director of purchasing asked for 95 samples from each manufacturer. The numbers of acceptable and unacceptable components from each manufacturer are shown in the following table. Use a chi-square test to determine whether the quality of the component depends on the manufacturer. Let $\alpha = .05$. How does this help management to make decisions?

	Manufacturer				
Quality	**A**	**B**	**C**	**D**	**Total**
Unacceptable	12	8	5	11	36
Acceptable	83	87	90	84	344
Total	95	95	95	95	380

P12-12 **12.12** An accounting firm studied the time its accountants took to complete each client's tax return and related this to the amount of taxes paid by the client. The firm wanted to know whether a relationship exists between these two variables. It is thinking of introducing a new pricing policy that would depend on the time taken to complete a tax return. The following data were obtained from a survey. Perform an appropriate test using $\alpha = .05$. Would the proposed policy be justified based on your results? How could this information be used to improve the processing of tax claims?

No. of work hours	Amount of taxes paid		
	$0–3 000	$3 001–10 000	Over $10 000
0–2	52	55	27
3–4	47	55	31
Over 4	35	37	35

P12-13 **12.13** An investor wanted to know whether the distribution of weekly rental values in a certain location was normal. The results of her test were as shown.

Discuss the test used, the hypotheses, the results and the business implications. Use $\alpha = .05$.

Rental category	Observed frequency (f_o)	Expected frequency (f_e)	$(f_o - f_e)$	$(f_o - f_e)^2/f_e$
Under $400	6	4.68	1.32	0.37
$400–600	14	21.40	–7.40	2.56
$601–800	45	39.41	5.59	0.79
$801–1000	30	30.18	–0.18	0.001
Above $1000	10	9.20		0.07
Total	105	105	0.80	

CHAPTER CASE **REVISITED**

Job security at Combaro Ltd

1. The HR manager at Combaro Ltd wanted to analyse issues related to job security at the company using data from the employment survey. The first issue she wanted to address was whether the workplace agreement led to a significant change in employees' perceptions of job security. The chi-square goodness-of-fit test would be an appropriate technique to use to test this hypothesis because the data are presented as frequencies (or count data) organised into three categories. The null hypothesis would be that the observed distribution is the same as the expected distribution, against the alternative hypothesis that the observed distribution is not the same as the expected distribution. This test is one-tailed. Rejection of H_0 would imply that the new workplace agreement has led to a significant change in the employees' perceptions of job security in the company.
2. With three categories in this study, $k = 3$, and $m = 0$ because no parameters have had to be estimated to carry out the test. Therefore, the degrees of freedom are df $= k - 1 - m = 3 - 1 - 0 = 2$. Using $\alpha = .05$ and df $= 2$, the critical chi-square value from table A.8 is $\chi^2_{.05,\,2} = 5.9915$. Therefore, if the chi-square calculated from the survey data (i.e. the observed chi-square) is greater than 5.9915, we reject the null hypothesis. The expected frequencies calculated from the data are shown in the following table.

Response	Expected proportion	Expected frequency (f_e) (proportion × sample total)
Insecure	.52	.52 × 48 = 24.96
Secure	.35	.35 × 48 = 16.80
Very secure	.13	.13 × 48 = 6.24
Total	1.00	48.00

The observed chi-square goodness-of-fit test statistic is calculated as follows.

Response	f_o	f_e	$\frac{(f_o - f_e)^2}{f_e}$
Insecure	14	24.96	4.81
Secure	20	16.80	0.61
Very secure	14	6.24	9.65
Total	48	48.00	$\chi^2 = 15.07$

Since the observed chi-square value of 15.07 is greater than the critical value of 5.9915, we reject the null hypothesis and conclude that observed distribution is not the same as the expected distribution. This implies that the new workplace agreement has led to a significant change in the employees' perceptions of job security in the company. Before the workplace agreement, 52% of the employees felt insecure, while 13% felt very secure. After the workplace agreement had been implemented, the proportion feeling insecure had declined to 29%, while the proportion feeling very secure had increased by a similar percentage. Thus, the HR manager could conclude that there has been an improvement in perceptions of job security.

3. To determine whether perceptions of job security are related to gender, the HR manager could use the chi-square test of independence. This approach is appropriate because in this case we want to analyse two variables to see whether changes in one variable affects changes in the other. The null hypothesis would be that gender is independent of job security, against the alternative hypothesis that gender is not independent of job security.
4. The results of the chi-square test of independence using KaddStat are shown below. KaddStat gives a chi-square value of 7.059 with a *p*-value of .029. Given that the *p*-value is less than an alpha of .05, we can reject the null hypothesis at the 5% level in favour of the alternative hypothesis and conclude that gender is not independent of job security. There is some evidence to suggest that men tend to feel more secure in their jobs than women. For example, 21% of female employees felt insecure while 8% of men felt insecure. On the other hand, only 6% of female employees felt very secure whereas 23% of men felt very secure. The HR manager can therefore use this information to further probe factors responsible for this gender difference and propose measures to top management to address the issue.

	A	B	C	D	E	F	G	H	I
1		**Chi-square test statistic =**		7.059		**Number of:**			
2			***p*-value =**	0.029		**rows =**	2		
3						**columns =**	3		
4									
5				*Actual frequencies*					
6				**Variable B**					
7			Insecure	Secure	Very secure	Totals			
8	**Variable A**	Famale	10	9	3	22			
9		Male	4	11	11	26			
10		Totals	14	20	14	48			
11									
12				*Expected frequencies*					
13				**Variable B**					
14			Insecure	Secure	Very secure	Totals			
15	**Variable A**	Female	6.4167	9.1667	6.4167	22			
16		Male	7.5833	10.8333	7.5833	26			
17		Totals	14	20	14	48			
18	NOTE: Expected frequencies should not be less than 5.0								
19									
20					*Chi-square calculations*				
21					**Variable B**				
22				Insecure	Secure	Very secure			
23		**Variable A**	Female	2.0011	0.0030	1.8193			
24			Male	1.6932	0.0026	1.5394			
25									

SUMMARY

1 The chi-square goodness-of-fit test is used to determine whether a given set of data or a situation follows a particular distribution (e.g. normal or Poisson). We use a theoretical or expected distribution of measurements for several categories of a variable with the actual or observed distribution of measurements. If only two categories are used, the test offers the equivalent of a z test for a single proportion. The chi-square goodness-of-fit test for two categories is also equivalent to a z test of the equality of two population proportions against a two-sided alternative.

2 The chi-square test of independence is used to investigate whether there is dependence (a relationship) or independence (no relationship) between two categorical variables. The data used to conduct a chi-square test of independence are arranged in a two-dimensional table called a contingency table. For this reason, the test is sometimes referred to as contingency analysis. A chi-square test of independence is computed in a manner similar to that used with the chi-square goodness-of-fit test. Expected values are computed for each cell of the contingency table and then compared with the observed values using the chi-square statistic. Both the chi-square test of independence and the chi-square goodness-of-fit test require that expected values be greater than or equal to five in order to be confident that the results are sound.

KEY TERMS

chi-square goodness-of-fit test p. 412

chi-square test of independence p. 423

contingency analysis p. 423

contingency table p. 423

multinomial distribution p. 412

KEY EQUATIONS

EQUATION	DESCRIPTION	FORMULA
12.1	Chi-square goodness-of-fit test	$\chi^2 = \sum \frac{(f_o - f_e)^2}{f_e}$ $\text{df} = k - 1 - m$
12.2	Chi-square test of independence	$\chi^2 = \sum_r \sum_c \frac{(f_o - f_e)^2}{f_e}$ $\text{df} = (r-1)(c-1)$

REVIEW PROBLEMS

Practising the calculations

12.14 Use a chi-square goodness-of-fit test to determine whether the following observed frequencies represent a uniform distribution. Let $\alpha = .01$.

Category	f_o
1	20
2	17
3	13
4	14
5	18
6	21
7	19
8	18

P12-15 **12.15** Use the chi-square contingency analysis to determine whether variable 1 is independent of variable 2. Use a 5% level of significance.

	Variable 2		
Variable 1	12	23	21
	8	17	20
	7	11	18

P12-16 **12.16** Four investment companies were asked in a survey to rate the effect on their asset values of a 1 percentage point fall in stock market prices. The effect on asset values was rated using a 3-point scale, with 1 for no effect, 2 for a slight effect and 3 for a moderate effect. Actual (observed) counts of the responses are shown in the following table. Is the effect on asset values independent of the company? Let $\alpha = .01$.

	Effect on asset values			
Company	None	Slight	Moderate	Total
A	60	27	7	94
B	71	22	14	107
C	57	38	15	110
D	54	37	18	109
Total	242	124	54	420

P12-17 **12.17** The human resource manager of a large IT company collected data for days of the week on which employees were absent from work. The manager randomly selects 150 of the absences, which are shown in the table below. Use $\alpha = .05$ to determine whether the data indicate whether absences during the various days of the week are equally likely.

Day of week	Observed frequency
Monday	42
Tuesday	18
Wednesday	24
Thursday	27
Friday	39
Total	150

12.18 A researcher interviewed 2067 people and asked whether they were the primary decision makers in the household when buying a new car last year. Two hundred and seven were men who had bought a new car last year. Sixty-five were women who had bought a new car last year. Eight hundred and eleven of the responses were from men who did not buy a car last year. Nine hundred and eighty-four were from women who did not buy a car last year. Use these data to determine whether gender is independent of being a major decision maker in purchasing a new car last year. Let $\alpha = .05$.

Testing your understanding

12.19 Are random arrivals at a shoe store at the local mall Poisson distributed? A mall employee researched this question by gathering data for arrivals during one-minute intervals on a weekday between 6.30 pm and 8.00 pm. The data obtained follow. Use $\alpha = .05$ to determine whether the observed data seem to be from a Poisson distribution. How could this result help decision making?

Arrivals per minute	Observed frequency
0	26
1	40
2	57
3	32
4	17
5	12
6	8

P12-20 **12.20** As part of their infrastructure planning exercise, a city council analyst summarised annual household income and the number of motor vehicles owned for a random sample of households. The results are as follows. Using the chi-square test, determine whether the number of vehicles owned depends on the household's income. Use $\alpha = 0.05$. Explain your test result.

	Household income			
Number of vehicles	Under \$20 000	\$20 000–\$49 999	\$50 000–\$99 999	\$100 000 and above
0	20	12	10	8
1–2	9	18	30	80
3 or more	7	13	15	40

P12-21 **12.21** Are the types of professional jobs held in the computing industry independent of the number of years a person has worked in the industry? Suppose 246 workers are interviewed. Use the results below to determine whether the type of professional job held in the computer industry is independent of the number of years worked in the industry. Let $\alpha = .01$. What are the implications if any of your results for job retention in this industry?

	Professional position			
Years	Manager	Programmer	Operator	Systems analyst
0–3	6	37	11	13
4–8	28	16	23	24
More than 8	47	10	12	19

P12-22 **12.22** In the field of finance, the random walk hypothesis says that stock market prices follow what is described as a 'random walk'. This means that the price change today is expected to be independent of the price change yesterday. The table below shows price changes for a particular stock collected over 100 days. The price changes are categorised into three groups: up, no change and down. Test the hypothesis that the daily price changes for this stock are independent. Use $\alpha = .05$.

	Price change previous day		
Price change today	Up	No change	Down
Up	10	15	12
No change	5	10	5
Down	15	12	8

P12-23 **12.23** The following is a 3 × 2 contingency table for annual farm profit and the age of the farmer for a randomly selected sample of farmers in Fiji. Use an appropriate test to determine whether annual farm profit is related to a farmer's age. Comment on the results of your test.

	Annual farm profit		
Age category	**< $2000**	**$2000 or more**	**Total**
Less than 40 years	29	18	47
40–49 years	51	38	89
50 years or more	82	80	162
Total	162	136	298

CHAPTER

13 Simple regression analysis

LEARNING OBJECTIVES

After studying this chapter, you should be able to:

1. examine the strength and the shape of the relationship between two variables using scatter plots and the correlation coefficient
2. compute the equation of a simple regression line from a sample of data and interpret the slope and intercept of the equation
3. apply residual analysis to test the assumptions underlying regression analysis
4. compute a standard error of the estimate and interpret its meaning
5. compute a coefficient of determination and interpret it
6. test hypotheses about the slope of the regression model and interpret the results
7. estimate values of *y* using the regression model.

OPENING VIGNETTE

Teenage smoking in pregnancy and birth weight

Rates of smoking among Australian teenage mothers are among the highest in the world. According to a study of teenage smoking in pregnancy and birth weight, published by Chan and Sullivan in the *Medical Journal of Australia* (2008), approximately 42.1% of teenage mothers smoke in comparison to 17.3% for all mothers. Cigarette smoking among teenagers is one of the few risks that can be modified for low birth weight (LBW), and is more important in determining the birth weight of babies than maternal height, weight, previous pregnancies or gender of the baby. LBW is an important determinant of childhood development and a low LBW makes it more likely that a baby will develop chronic diseases later in life.

Chan and Sullivan's (2008) population study examined the association between smoking during pregnancy and the birth weight of babies born to teenage mothers in Australia. The study also examined the association between the number of cigarettes smoked during pregnancy and infant birth weight. Through regression analysis, Chan and Sullivan determined that the prevalence of LBW babies born to teenage smokers was 9.9%, compared to 6.0% in babies born to nonsmokers. Their study concluded definitively that babies whose mothers smoked during pregnancy were far more likely to have low LBW than babies whose mothers did not smoke.

Introduction

In business research (as in the sciences), understanding the relationships between two or more variables is often a key to successful decision making. For example, an account executive might find it useful to know how strong the relationship is between advertising dollars and sales dollars. An economist might be interested in whether the minimum hourly wage rate, the inflation rate or the producer price index could be used to predict the unemployment rate. In researching the behaviour of the bond market, a broker might find it useful to know whether the interest rate of bonds is related to the prime interest rate (in Australia, the cash rate set by the Reserve Bank). In an effort to predict the value of airline shares from day to day, a financial analyst might find it helpful to determine whether the price of an airline stock is related to the price of crude oil.

This chapter presents the method of regression analysis, in which mathematical models are developed to predict one variable from another. Using regression analysis, business researchers attempt to determine the functional relationship between the variables. Included also in this chapter are statistical tools for testing the validity, strength and predictability of the regression model.

CHAPTER CASE

Predicting the selling price of houses in the city of Baycoast

The city of Baycoast is a local government district within greater Melbourne. It is located on the bay (with part of the city stretching several kilometres along the bayside) but also stretches about three kilometres inland. There are three suburbs within the city of Baycoast and there is an eclectic mix of housing: some having bay views, others with no bay views; some in grand streets; some large, others quite small; some contemporary, others much older.

Baycoast City Real Estate Agents (BCREA) is a local real estate agency whose business has grown with the city. The principals are very interested in applying more modern techniques to assist in estimating the selling price of houses within the city. They are aware from their own experience that many factors influence the selling price; bay views, for example, will add considerably to the selling price. Other factors include: the size of the house, the size of the block and the design of and fittings in the property.

The estate agency commissioned the development of a database containing a large number of influencing factors together with the selling price of each house in the database. The commissioned firm developed the database by collecting a random sample of 120 houses of the total of 2513 within Baycoast that sold within the last year. As a first stage in the study, information was collected only about houses. A later stage might want to examine apartments.

BCREA is aware that a street considered to be more attractive is generally preferred by potential buyers and thereby attracts a higher selling price for houses. Hence, the company's agents are required to assess each street based on its perceived streetscape appeal, ranging from 0 (lowest appeal) to 10 (highest appeal). They would like to model the relationship between the street rating and the selling price to determine the extent to which it is a useful factor in determining price.

Questions to help managers make decisions

BCREA

1. Is there a relationship between the selling price of a house and its street rating? If there is a relationship, what type of relationship is there and how strong is it? Is it possible to develop a valid model to predict the selling price of a house based on the street rating?
2. If a valid model is possible, what information does it provide about the selling price of a house located in a street with a rating of 7?

13.1 Examining the relationship between two variables

Regression analysis is the process of constructing a mathematical model or function that can be used to predict the value of one variable using other variables. The most elementary regression model is called **simple regression**, which is *bivariate linear regression*, which means that it involves only two variables. One variable is predicted using the other. *The variable to be predicted* is called the *dependent variable* and is designated as y. *The predictor* is called the *independent variable*, or *explanatory variable*, and is designated as x. In simple regression analysis, only a straight-line relationship between two variables is examined. Nonlinear relationships and regression models with more than one independent variable can be explored by using multiple regression models.

As an example, consider whether the number of people attending a concert could be predicted using regression analysis. If so, what variables might be related to concert attendance? The most obvious factors would be those relating to the particular band or artist and their popularity. However, a few of the many other variables that can potentially contribute as well are: ticket prices, size and location of the venue, the time of year and time of day of the event, whether there are any age requirements and, perhaps, even the popularity of any support acts.

Suppose that an events manager, undertaking a study to develop a predictive model, recorded the attendances at twelve concerts at a particular (large) venue. She also knows how many CDs (singles and albums) these artists have sold in Australia in the year prior to the concert. Could the total number of CDs sold by an artist or band be used to predict how many people would turn up to a concert at the given venue? It seems reasonable that the number of CDs sold in the previous year, being a useful indicator of the popularity of the band or artist, might be a good indicator of the current interest in a concert given by this group. Accordingly, we would anticipate that higher sales implies greater popularity and, therefore, higher concert attendance. Demonstration problem 13.1 examines this problem.

Two introductory investigative tools of regression are **scatter plots** and Pearson's **correlation coefficient**. The Pearson correlation coefficient measures the strength of a linear relationship between two quantitative variables, the symbol for the sample correlation coefficient being r. The value of r can vary between -1 and $+1$; the closer in magnitude it is to 1, the stronger is the linear relationship. Although there is an expression for calculating the value of r, rarely would we try to calculate this value by hand. Rather, we would use an appropriate calculator, Excel or a statistical software package. Demonstration problem 13.1 explains how to solve the CD sales–concert problem using Excel.

DEMONSTRATION PROBLEM 13.1

Suppose the data displayed in table 13.1 are the twelve observations corresponding to concert attendance (in thousands) and the total Australian CD sales by the performing artist (or band) in the previous year (also in thousands). We will use these data throughout this chapter to investigate and develop a regression model to predict concert attendance using CD sales. Initially, we will explore whether CD sales might be a good predictor of concert attendance by using Excel to obtain the correlation coefficient and a scatter plot.

TABLE 13.1 CD sales and concert attendance

Artist/ band	Number of CD sales ('000)	Concert attendance ('000)
1	61	4.280
2	63	4.080
3	67	4.420
4	69	4.170
5	70	4.480
6	74	4.300
7	76	4.820
8	81	4.700
9	86	5.110
10	91	5.130
11	95	5.640
12	97	5.560

Obtaining the correlation coefficient and constructing a scattergram

We shall use Excel's Function feature to obtain the correlation coefficient.

DP13-01

1. Access DP13-01.xls from the student website.
2. Place the cursor in any empty cell (say, G4), and from the Formulas tab, select Insert Function.
3. In the Insert Function dialogue box, choose Statistical from the category drop-down menu, and CORREL (correlation) from the list of functions.
4. Click OK.
5. In the Function Arguments dialog box, enter the data ranges.

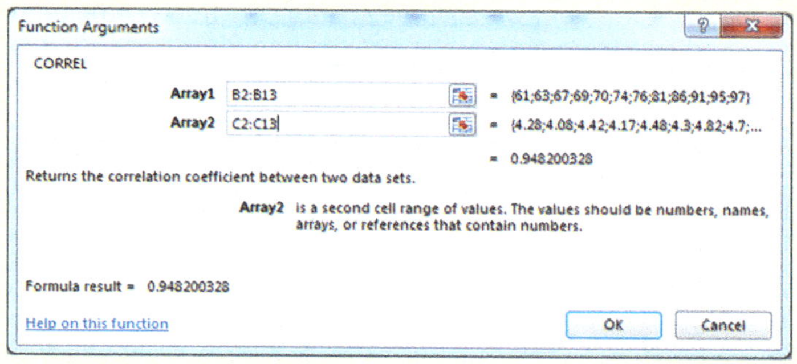

6. Click OK.

As we see, the correlation coefficient r is 0.948, which is very close to 1, indicating that the relationship is very strong. In addition, since the sign of r is positive, the relationship is also positive. This implies that, as the number of CDs sold increases, attendance at the concert will increase. At this stage, it looks as if we could develop the regression equation immediately.

However, there is a flaw in this conclusion. The correlation coefficient assumes a linear relationship. Thus, if the relationship is not linear (and we have not yet checked this), our regression output could be invalid. We need to check whether the relationship between CD sales and attendance is linear. How? We simply graph the actual relationship by constructing a scatter diagram; again, we use a software package, either Excel or a statistical package. Here, we shall again use Excel.

	B	C
1	Number of CD sales ('000)	Concert attendance ('000)
2	61	4.28
3	63	4.08
4	67	4.42
5	69	4.17
6	70	4.48
7	74	4.3
8	76	4.82
9	81	4.7
10	86	5.11
11	91	5.13
12	95	5.64
13	97	5.56

1. Highlight the two columns of data, including the headings as shown at right.
2. From the menu bar, choose the Insert tab. In the Charts group, click on the down arrow of the Scatter option and choose the top left-hand graph.
3. We need to format the axes to make the graph more presentable. Right-click the x axis and choose Format Axis.
4. In the Axis Options task pane, go to the Minimum option under Bounds and set it to 50. Press Return.
5. Right-click the y axis and choose Format Axis.
6. In the Axis Options task pane, go to the Minimum option under Bounds and set it to 4. Press Return.
7. Click on the Chart Elements button (the large plus sign) next to the chart and ensure Axis Titles is checked. Label the axes.

Figure 13.1 is a scatter plot of the data in table 13.1. We immediately see that, as CD sales increase, concert attendance increases. Is the relationship linear? Try to imagine a straight line passing through the points. Is a linear fit possible? Would a curve fit the data better? Of course, not all the data values will lie on any straight line that we might construct, but they will lie quite close to the line. Thus, the scatter plot provides us with some idea of how well a regression line fits the data. Later in the chapter, we present statistical techniques that can be used to determine more precisely how closely a regression line fits the data.

Note that the data we have used are only a sample; they do not include all concerts in the given venue, only a sample of concerts. Recall the conditions under which we can make an inference about a population based upon a random sample. Provided these conditions apply to our regression, we shall be able to construct a straight-line model that provides us with a good approximation of the straight line for the population.

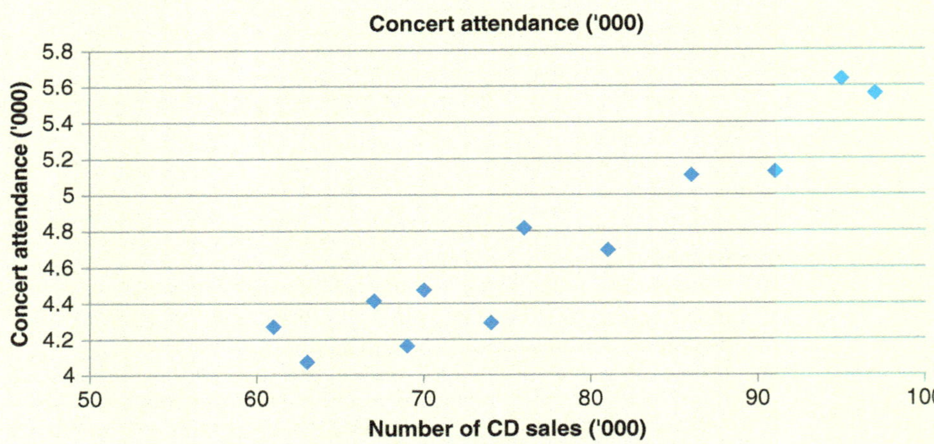

FIGURE 13.1 Scatter plot of CD sales and concert attendance data

13.2 Determining the equation of the regression line

This chapter deals only with simple linear (straight-line) regression. The aim is to find the 'best' straight line through the sample data points.

Now, from your high school maths, you will remember that the equation of a straight line is given by:

$$y = mx + c$$

where:

m = the slope of the line
c = the y intercept of the line

Data can be either population data (the total group of interest) or sample data (a subset of the population). In regression analysis, there again exist both a population and a sample regression line. Generally, we have access only to the sample data.

The equation of the regression line through the population points is given by:

$$\hat{Y} = \beta_0 + \beta_1 X$$

where:

$\hat{Y}$ = the predicted value of Y
β_0 = the intercept of the population line with the Y axis
β_1 = the slope of the population regression line

The observed values of the population, Y, will not necessarily all lie on this regression line. To account for this, we write the equation for a specific Y value as:

$$Y_i = \beta_0 + \beta_1 X_i + \varepsilon_i$$

where:

X_i = the ith value of the independent variable
Y_i = the ith value of the dependent variable
ε_i = the **error of prediction** $(\hat{Y}_i - Y_i)$

The ε (epsilon) term represents the fact that, even at the population level, not all data points lie on the population line. For example, suppose that we are trying to predict sales for a company using advertising as a predictor. Although advertising may affect sales, other factors also exist, such as the number of sales staff and the number of local competitors. Hence, even if we had the population data, a regression model to predict sales using advertising will involve some error.

Let's examine a graphical representation that will explain this more clearly. Figure 13.2 displays a population data set of weekly income vs age in years, together with the population regression line.

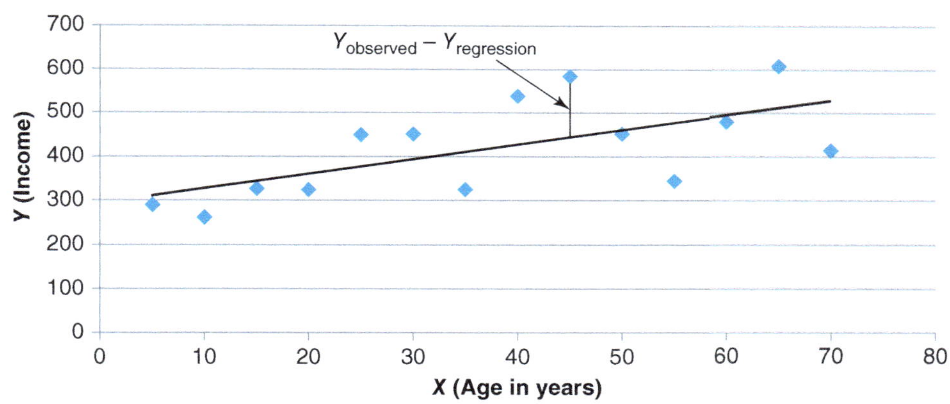

FIGURE 13.2 Population data set together with population regression line

We see that not all the observed Y values lie on this regression line. Some will lie (vertically) above the line and some below. For any given value of X, the difference between the observed value of Y and the value given by the regression line, depicted in figure 13.2 as the $(Y_{observed} - Y_{regression})$ line, is called the 'error term'. The error term is given the symbol ε (epsilon) and is written as:

$$\varepsilon = (Y - \hat{Y})$$

In figure 13.2, for an X value of 45, the predicted Y value is about 443, while the observed Y value is about 585. Thus the error term is (585 – 443) = 142.

Virtually all regression analysis involves sample data, rather than population data. Thus, β_0 and β_1 are unattainable and must be estimated. Hence, the equation of the regression line will be based on sample data (x_i, y_i) and will contain an intercept b_0 and a sample slope b_1. Just as we made inferences about the population mean μ based on the sample mean $\bar{x}$, we shall make inferences about the population coefficients (the β values), based on the sample coefficients (the b values). To enable us to make these inferences (and others), we need to make certain assumptions about the error term ε.

The assumptions we make about ε are as follows.

1. They are normally distributed with zero mean. Like the t test, regression is reasonably robust against departure from normality. Thus, inferences about β_0 and β_1 are not seriously affected if the departure from normality for each value of x is not extreme.
2. They have constant variance (homoscedasticity). Thus, the variability of y will be the same for low as for high values of x. The equal variance assumption is important when making inferences about β_0 and β_1. For serious departure, transformation of the data or weighted regression may assist.
3. They are independent of one another: a particularly important assumption when data are collected over a period of time, as errors in one period may be correlated with those in a previous period(s).

Inclusion of the term ε in the regression equation produces what is known as a **probabilistic model**.

Figure 13.3 shows four examples of the distribution of the Y values around the regression line; these distributions lie in a plane perpendicular to the page. Since the regression line depicts the predicted value $\hat{Y}$, the distributions are actually distributions of $\varepsilon = (Y - \hat{Y})$, and ε is usually referred to as the error term. Thus, the distributions represent the probabilities of observing a specific value of ε given a specific value of x; that is, they are conditional probabilities $P(\varepsilon|X)$, read as the probability of ε given a specific value of X.

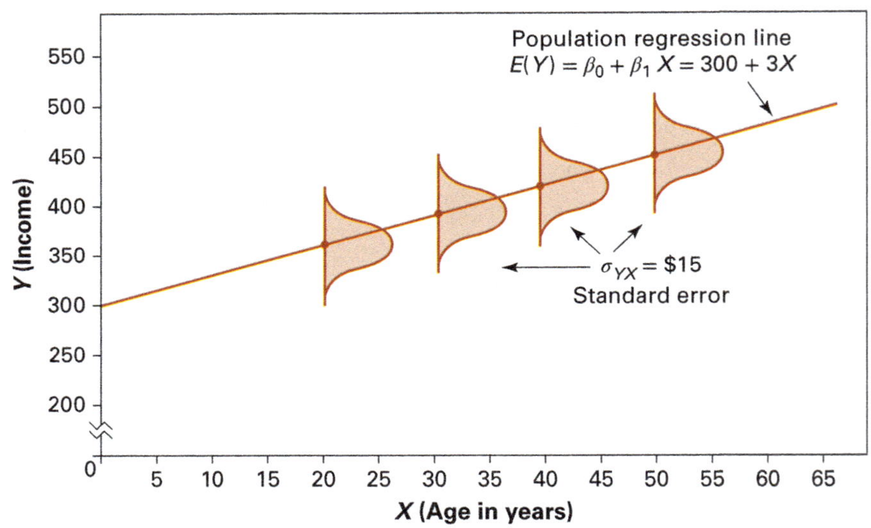

FIGURE 13.3 Population regression line together with distributions of observed values around the regression line

It is possible that, for given data, the assumptions listed are not valid and, hence, the regression is not valid. In section 13.3, we shall examine a method that will allow us to test whether the listed assumptions hold. There are also methods to mathematically transform data in an attempt to ensure that the assumptions are met.

The above discussion referred to population data. As we have only sample data, we cannot obtain the coefficients β_0 and β_1; hence, we cannot obtain the equation for the population line. Instead, using sample data, we obtain an estimate, which we write as:

Equation of the simple regression line (13.1)

$$\hat{y} = b_0 + b_1 x$$

where:

b_0 = the intercept of the sample line with the y axis
b_1 = the slope of the sample regression line
$\hat{y}$ = the predicted value of y

To determine the equation of the regression line for a sample of data, the researcher must determine the values of b_0 and b_1. The method by which these values are obtained is referred to as least squares analysis. Examine the regression line fitted through the points in figure 13.4. Observe that the line does not actually pass through any of the points (in practice, this may or may not be the case; the line could pass through some of the points). The vertical distance from each point to the line is the error of the prediction; that is, it is the difference between the sample (the observed value) and the value our model provides (the predicted value). In theory, an infinite number of lines could be constructed to pass through these points in some manner.

Least squares analysis is *a process whereby a regression model is developed by producing the minimum sum of the squares of the differences between the observed values of y and the predicted values (the squared error values); that is, the regression model minimises:*

$$\Sigma(y_i - \hat{y}_i)^2 \text{ for } i = 1 \text{ to } n$$

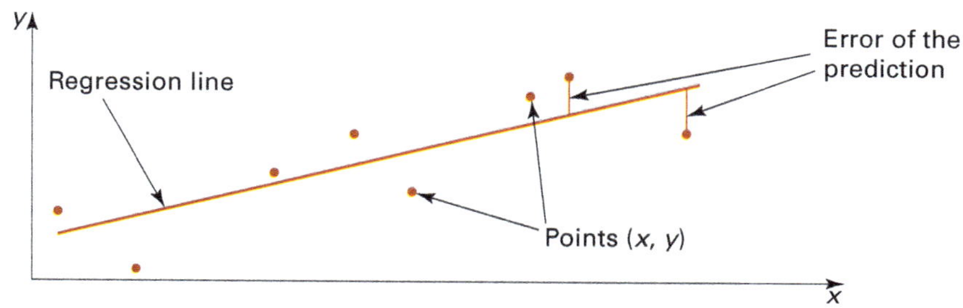

FIGURE 13.4 Plot of a regression line, data points and error of the prediction

On the basis of this criterion and a little calculus, a particular set of equations has been developed to produce formulas for the coefficients of the regression model. (Derivation of these formulas is beyond the scope of information being discussed here.) This produces what is called 'the line of best fit'.

Formula 13.2 is an equation for computing the value of the sample slope and intercept. Several versions of the equation are given to afford latitude in doing the computations.

Slope of the regression line **(13.2)**

$$b_1 = \frac{\Sigma(x-\bar{x})(y-\bar{y})}{\Sigma(x-\bar{x})^2} = \frac{\Sigma xy - n\bar{x}\bar{y}}{\Sigma x^2 - n\bar{x}^2} = \frac{\Sigma xy - \frac{(\Sigma x)(\Sigma y)}{n}}{\Sigma x^2 - \frac{(\Sigma x)^2}{n}}$$

Sum of squares **(13.3)**

The expression in the numerator of formula 13.2 appears frequently in this chapter and is denoted as SS_{xy} — the covariance between x and y:

$$SS_{xy} = \sum(x-\bar{x})(y-\bar{y}) = \sum xy - \frac{(\Sigma x)(\Sigma y)}{n}$$

Other sums of squares will also be useful in regression analysis. For example, later on we will use sum of squares of y (SS_{yy}), which is given by:

$$SS_{yy} = \sum y^2 - \frac{(\Sigma y)^2}{n}$$

Moreover, the expression in the denominator of formula 13.2 also appears frequently in this chapter and is denoted as SS_{xx}, the variance of x:

$$SS_{xx} = \sum(x-\bar{x})^2 = \sum x^2 - \frac{(\Sigma x)^2}{n}$$

With these abbreviations, the equation for the slope can be expressed as in formula 13.4.

Alternative formula for slope (13.4)

$$b_1 = \frac{SS_{xy}}{SS_{xx}}$$

Formula 13.5 is used to compute the sample y intercept. The slope must be computed before the y intercept.

***y* intercept of the regression line (13.5)**

$$b_0 = \bar{y} - b_1\bar{x} = \frac{\Sigma y}{n} - b_1\frac{\Sigma x}{n}$$

Formulas (13.2), (13.4) and (13.5) show that the following quantities are needed from the sample data to compute the slope and intercept: Σx, Σy, Σx^2 and Σxy, unless sample means are used. Table 13.2 contains the results of solving for the slope and intercept and determining the equation of the regression line for the data in table 13.1.

TABLE 13.2 Solving for the slope and the *y* intercept of the regression line for the CD sales and concert attendance example

CD sales ('000) *x*	Concert attendance ('000) *y*	x^2	*xy*
61	4.280	3 721	261.080
63	4.080	3 969	257.040
67	4.420	4 489	296.140
69	4.170	4 761	287.730
70	4.480	4 900	313.600
74	4.300	5 476	318.200
76	4.820	5 776	366.320
81	4.700	6 561	380.700
86	5.110	7 396	439.460
91	5.130	8 281	466.830
95	5.640	9 025	535.800
97	5.560	9 409	539.320
$\Sigma x = 930$	$\Sigma y = 56.690$	$\Sigma x^2 = 73\,764$	$\Sigma xy = 4\,462.220$

$$SS_{xy} = \sum xy - \frac{(\Sigma x)(\Sigma y)}{n} = 4462.22 - \frac{(930)(56.69)}{12} = 68.745$$

$$SS_{xx} = \sum x^2 - \frac{(\Sigma x)^2}{n} = 73\,764 - \frac{(930)^2}{12} = 1689$$

$$b_1 = \frac{SS_{xy}}{SS_{xx}} = \frac{68.745}{1689} = .0407$$

$$b_0 = \frac{\Sigma y}{n} - b_1\frac{\Sigma x}{n} = \frac{56.69}{12} - (.0407)\frac{930}{12} = 1.57$$

$$\hat{y} = 1.57 + .0407x$$

The least squares equation of the regression line for this problem is:

$$\hat{y} = 1.57 + .0407x$$

The slope of this regression line is .0407. For every unit increase in x (CD sales) there is an increase in y (concert attendance) of .0407. Since both x CD sales and y concert attendance are in thousands, we can say that, for every 1000 increase in CD sales, concert attendance increases, on average, by 40.7.

The constant term may be interpreted as the value of y when $x = 0$. In this case, the data do not include the value $x = 0$, and it is dangerous to suggest that the concert attendance would, on average, be 1570 if CD sales was zero. We simply have no information on how the regression line behaves at x values lower than $x = 61$ (the smallest available data value).

Superimposing the line representing the least squares equation for this problem on the scatter plot indicates how well the regression line fits the data points, as shown in figure 13.5.

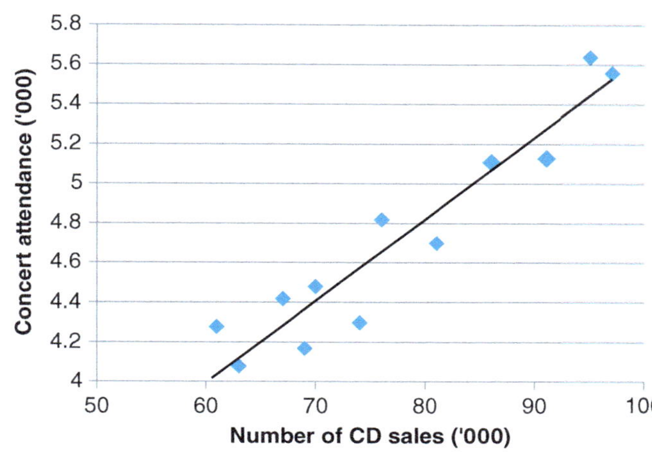

FIGURE 13.5 Graph of regression line for the CD–concert example

Clearly, it is unsatisfactory to have to complete the calculations shown in formulas (13.2) to (13.5) by hand. In the next section, we shall show how to use Excel to obtain the regression equation.

DEMONSTRATION PROBLEM 13.2

PROBLEM: An executive at a telecommunications company is interested in the relationship between an individual's income and their mobile phone usage. In particular, to help her in pricing and marketing strategies, she is interested in ascertaining whether she can use an individual's gross annual income to predict how much time they will spend on making National Direct Calls from their mobile phone per week.

She surveyed 12 mobile phone users and recorded their annual incomes and time (in minutes) spent each week making National Direct Calls. The data are presented in sequence, according to gross annual income.

Annual income ($000)	Weekly time on National Direct Calls (minutes)
23	69
29	95
29	102
35	118
42	126
46	125
50	138
54	178
64	156
66	184
76	176
78	225

SOLUTION: Using the Excel method explained in demonstration problem 13.1 and the data in the table, the correlation coefficient is obtained as 0.928, indicating a strong positive linear relationship (assuming that a linear relationship exists). We need to use a scatter plot to check whether the actual relationship is linear.

The following graph is a scatter plot of these data. Note the linear appearance of the data.

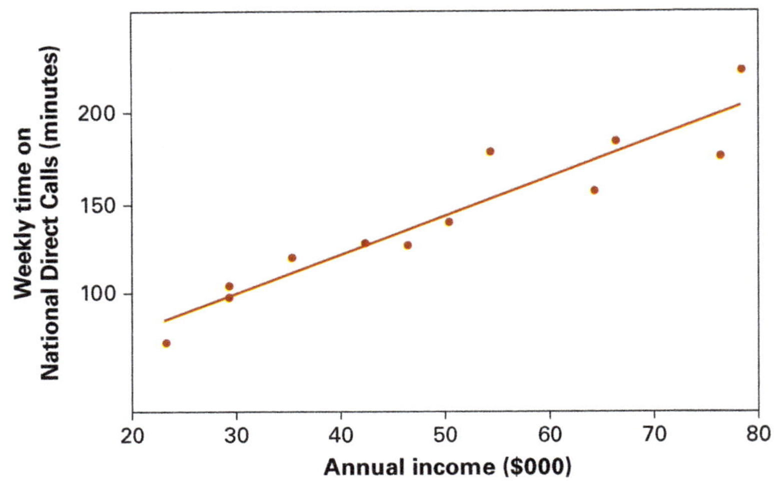

The least squares equation of the regression line may be obtained using the approach described in table 13.2 for the CD sales–concert example.

$$SS_{xy} = \sum xy - \frac{(\Sigma x)(\Sigma y)}{n} = 92\,038 - \frac{(592)(1692)}{12} = 8566$$

$$SS_{xx} = \sum x^2 - \frac{(\Sigma x)^2}{n} = 33\,044 - \frac{(592)^2}{12} = 3838.667$$

$$b_1 = \frac{SS_{xy}}{SS_{xx}} = \frac{8566}{3838.667} = 2.232$$

$$b_0 = \frac{\Sigma y}{n} - b_1\frac{\Sigma x}{n} = \frac{1692}{12} - (2.232)\frac{592}{12} = 30.888$$

The least squares equation of the regression line is obtained as:

$$\hat{y} = 30.888 + 2.232x$$

USING EXCEL

Finding the regression equation directly

While it is important to understand how the regression equation is obtained, Excel will provide the regression equation directly using the Data analysis tool. Using the mobile calls example, use the following instructions to obtain the regression equation directly.

DP13-02

1. Access DP13-02.xls from the student website. From the Data tab, select Data Analysis.
2. In the Data Analysis dialogue box, choose Regression and click OK.
3. In the Regression dialogue box, enter the range (include heading) for annual income in the Input X Range field, and enter the range (include heading) for the weekly time on calls in the Input Y Range field. Tick the Labels box.
4. Under output options, select New Worksheet Ply:
5. Click OK.

	A	B	C	D	E	F	G
1	SUMMARY OUTPUT						
2							
3	*Regression Statistics*						
4	Multiple R	0.941506					
5	R Square	0.886434					
6	Adjusted R Square	0.875077					
7	Standard Error	15.64908					
8	Observations	12					
9							
10	ANOVA						
11		*df*	*SS*	*MS*	*F*	*Significance F*	
12	Regression	1	19115.06	19115.06	78.05454	0.000005	
13	Residual	10	2448.937	244.8937			
14	Total	11	21564				
15							
16		*Coefficients*	*Standard Error*	*t Stat*	*P-value*	*Lower 95%*	*Upper 95%*
17	Intercept	30.91247	13.25422	2.332273	0.041888	1.380221	60.44472
18	Annual income ($000)	2.231504	0.25258	8.834848	0.000005	1.668721	2.794287
19							

The Excel output has three sections: the top is headed 'Regression Statistics'; the middle section is headed 'ANOVA'; the bottom section contains the regression coefficients. Note the terms 'Intercept' and 'Annual income ($000)'. The computer output of any regression software package will include the intercept term and the independent variable (in this case, annual income). Adjacent to the column containing this information is a column headed 'Coefficients'. The value of the intercept coefficient is 30.91247, while the coefficient of Annual income is given as 2.231504. We shall explain the remaining information contained in the output later.

The slope of the line $b_1 = 2.232$; this means that, for every unit increase of x (Annual income), y (Weekly time on National Direct Calls) is predicted to increase on average by 2.232 minutes per week. However, remember that annual income is in thousands of dollars, so a one 'unit' increase in annual income is actually $1000; thus, for every $1000 increase in annual income, we would predict that y will increase, on average, by 2.232 minutes a week.

PRACTICE PROBLEMS

Practising the calculations

These problems have very small samples to aid calculations. In practice these sample sizes would not be sufficient.

P13-01 **13.1** Sketch a scatter plot from the following data, and determine the equation of the regression line.

x	15	22	31	13	21
y	19	16	34	21	27

P13-02 **13.2** Sketch a scatter plot from the following data, and determine the equation of the regression line.

x	140	119	103	91	65	29	24
y	25	29	46	70	88	112	128

Testing your understanding

P13-03 **13.3** A corporation owns several companies. The strategic planner for the corporation believes dollars spent on advertising can to some extent be a predictor of total sales dollars. As an aid in long-term planning, she gathers the following sales and advertising information from several of the companies for 2012 ($ million).

Advertising	Sales
12.5	148
3.7	55
21.6	338
60.0	994
37.6	541
6.1	89
16.8	126
41.2	379

Use Excel to obtain the equation of the simple regression line to predict sales from advertising expenditures using these data. Interpret the slope and intercept.

P13-04 **13.4** Investment analysts generally believe that the price of fixed rate bonds is inversely related to the prime interest rate for loans; that is, bonds perform well when lending rates are down and perform poorly when interest rates are up. Can the bond rate be predicted by the prime interest rate? Use Excel to construct a least squares regression line to predict bond rates using the prime interest rate.

Bond rate %	Prime interest rate %
5	16
12	6
9	8
15	4
7	7

P13-05 **13.5** Is it possible to predict the sales price of a used car by using the mileage? One would expect that a higher mileage would indicate a lower resale value. The following data from a car auctioneer show the prices from one week's sales of 10 cars, along with their associated mileage. Use these data to develop the equation of a regression line to predict total domestic wine sales using the quantity of grapes crushed. Interpret the slope and intercept of the model.

Car	Odometer reading ('000 km)	Auction selling price ($'000)
1	48.5	16
2	76.3	9
3	28.4	25
4	30.4	22
5	65.2	12
6	38.3	18
7	112.2	6
8	15.1	30
9	68	13
10	34.2	20

P13-06 **13.6** The coaches and fans of basketball teams might be interested in predicting a player's average points scored per game using the number of attempted shots the player makes. The *New Zealand Breakers* are members of the National Basketball League. According to the National Basketball League, these *Breakers* players had the following average points per game and total number of attempted shots. Use these data to develop the equation of a regression line to predict average points per game from the number of shots attempted. Discuss the slope and intercept of the model.

Player	Attempts	Points per game
K. Penney	457	24.1
P. Jones	307	15.6
T. Ronaldson	253	11.8
O. Forman	229	9.1
R. Rickert	172	17.8
M. Vukona	150	7.8
O. Greene	142	13.6
D. Alston	109	13.8
W. Turner	95	12.4
P. Henare	68	3.7
P. Winitana	57	3.2
T. Behrendorff	53	3.4
R. Kersten	37	3.4
B. Charleton	6	0.6
C. Daniel	1	1.5
M. Townsend	1	0

P13-07 **13.7** Can the crime rate in an area be predicted by using the median income? Use the following data to develop the equation of a regression line to predict the number of crimes in an area based on its median income. Discuss the slope and intercept of the model. A region with a median income of \$100 000 with crimes is added to the sample. Do the results change? Why do you think the results do or do not change? Which of the two regression models do you prefer and why? Can you think of other variables that might also determine the crime rate in an area?

Area	Median income (\$)	Crimes (per 100 000 residents)
A	55 000	15
B	22 000	36
C	45 790	12
D	65 000	10
E	10 000	48
F	35 000	24
G	41 990	11
H	58 000	16
I	52 000	20
J	15 000	42

13.3 Residual analysis

How does a researcher test a regression line to determine mathematically whether the line is a close fit of the data and whether the regression assumptions are valid? One particularly popular approach is to use the *historical data* (x and y values used to construct the regression model) to test the model. With this approach, the values of the independent variable (x values) are inserted into the regression model and a predicted value ($\hat{y}$) is obtained for each x value. These predicted values ($\hat{y}$) are then compared with the actual y values to determine how much error the equation of the regression line produced. *Each difference between the actual y value and the predicted y value is the error of the regression line at a given point*, $(y_i - \hat{y}_i)$, and is referred to as the **residual**. It is the sum of squares of these residuals that is minimised to find the least squares line. (Technically, $y - \hat{y}$ pre-estimation is called the error (ε); post-estimation, $y - \hat{y}$ is called the residual (e). The residuals are calculated from the sample data.)

Let us first review what we mean by a residual. For each value of the independent variable (the x values), the sample data include a value for the dependent variable (the y values). That is, corresponding to each sample x_i there is an observed value y_i. Once we have developed the regression equation, we can calculate a predicted y value for each of the given x values; that is, we can calculate a $\hat{y}_i$ for each x_i. The residual, or error term, is simply the difference between the observed y value and the predicted y value: that is:

$$(y_i - \hat{y}_i)$$

Figure 13.6 (overleaf) displays the residuals for each of the data points. Table 13.3 (overleaf) shows $\hat{y}$ values and residuals for each pair of data values for the CD–concert regression model developed in section 13.2. The predicted values are calculated by inserting an x value into the equation of the regression line and solving for $\hat{y}$. For example, when $x = 61$, $\hat{y} = 1.57 + .0407(61) = 4.053$, as displayed in column 3 of table 13.3. Each of these predicted y values is subtracted from the actual y value to determine the error, or residual. For example, the first y value listed in the table is 4.280 and the first predicted value is 4.053, resulting in a residual of $4.280 - 4.053 = 0.227$. The residuals for this problem are given in column 4 of the table.

Note that the sum of the residuals in table 13.3 is approximately zero. The sum of the errors (ε) is always zero, but the sum of the residuals is not necessarily always zero, because we are using sample data.

Why are residuals important in regression? An examination of the residual values may provide the researcher with information on how well the regression line fits the historical data points.

For example, in absolute terms, the largest residual for the CD–concert example is –.282 and the smallest is .040. Because the objective of the regression analysis was to predict concert attendance in thousands, this value indicates an error of 282 when there are 74 000 CDs sold (3.8%) and an error of only 40 when CD sales are 86 000 (0.05%). This result presents the *best* and *worst* cases for the residuals. The researcher must examine other residuals to determine how well the regression model fits other data points.

TABLE 13.3 Predicted values and residuals for the CD–concert example

CD sales ('000) x	Concert attendance ('000) y	Predicted value $\hat{y}$	Residual $y - \hat{y}$
61	4.280	4.053	.227
63	4.080	4.134	–.054
67	4.420	4.297	.123
69	4.170	4.378	–.208
70	4.480	4.419	.061
74	4.300	4.582	–.282
76	4.820	4.663	.157
81	4.700	4.867	–.167
86	5.110	5.070	.040
91	5.130	5.274	–.144
95	5.640	5.436	.204
97	5.560	5.518	.042
			$\Sigma(y - \hat{y}) = -0.001$

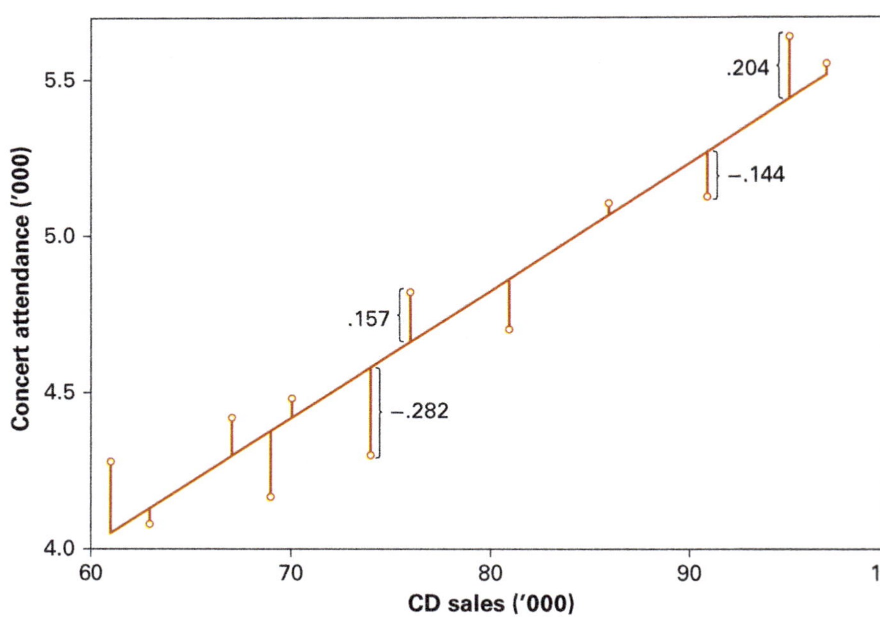

FIGURE 13.6 Close-up scatter plot with residuals for the CD–concert example

Sometimes residuals are examined to locate outliers. **Outliers** are *data points that lie apart from the rest of the points*. Outliers can produce large residuals and are usually easy to identify on scatter plots. Outliers can be the result of misrecorded or miscoded data, or they may simply be data points that do not conform to the general trend. The equation of the regression line is influenced by every data point used in its calculation in a manner similar to the arithmetic mean. Therefore, outliers sometimes can unduly influence the regression line by 'pulling' the line toward the outliers. The origin of outliers must be investigated to determine whether they should be retained or whether the regression equation should be recomputed without them. In the next section, we shall present a statistical measure of the residuals that will enable us to identify outliers.

The major use of residuals is to test the assumptions underlying regression.

1. The relationship between the variables is linear.
2. The error terms (ε) are independent of one another. This is particularly important if data are collected over time, as the errors in one time period may be correlated with errors at another time period; this is known as autocorrelation.
3. The errors are normally distributed with zero mean but, like the t test, regression is fairly robust against small departures from normality.
4. The variance of the errors is constant for all x. Thus, the variability of y is the same for high values of x as for low values.

To test these assumptions, residuals are plotted against the x values — the **residual plot**; figure 13.7 shows the residuals plotted against the x values for the CD–concert example.

For small sample sizes, residual plot analyses can be problematic and subject to over-interpretation. Hence, because the CD–concert example is constructed from only 12 pairs of data, one should be cautious in reaching conclusions from figure 13.7. The residual plots in figures 13.8, 13.9 and 13.10, however, represent large numbers of data points and therefore are more likely to depict overall patterns accurately.

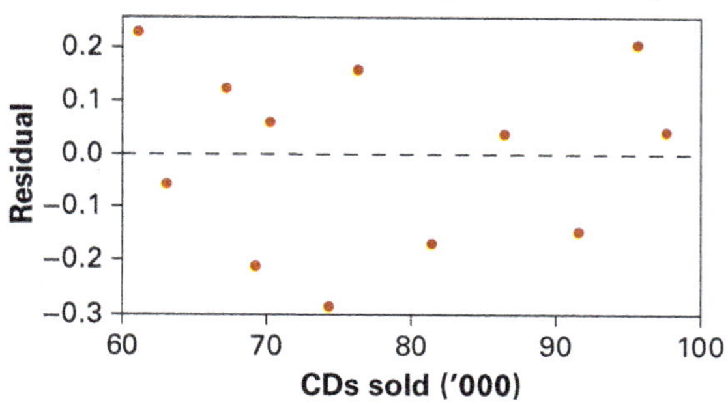

FIGURE 13.7 Graph of residuals for the CD–concert example

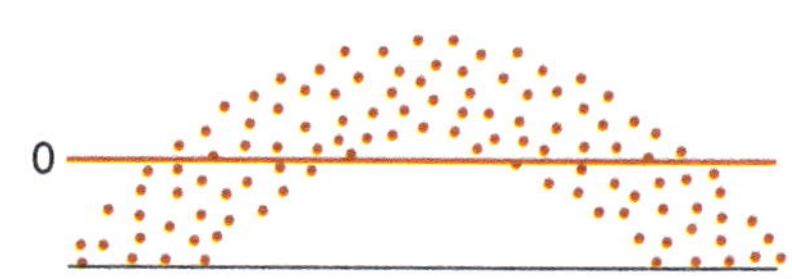

FIGURE 13.8 Nonlinear residual plot

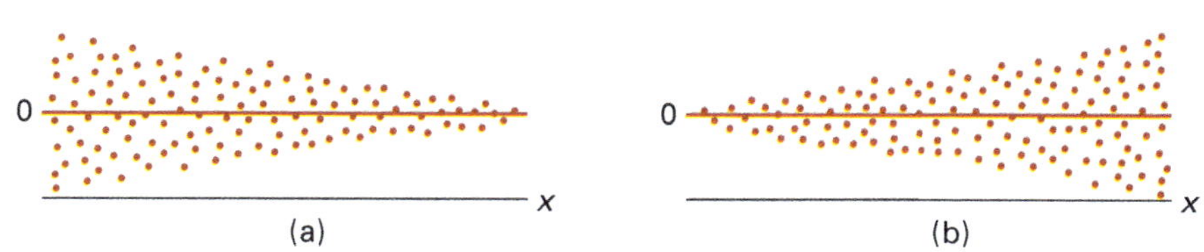

FIGURE 13.9 Nonconstant residual variance

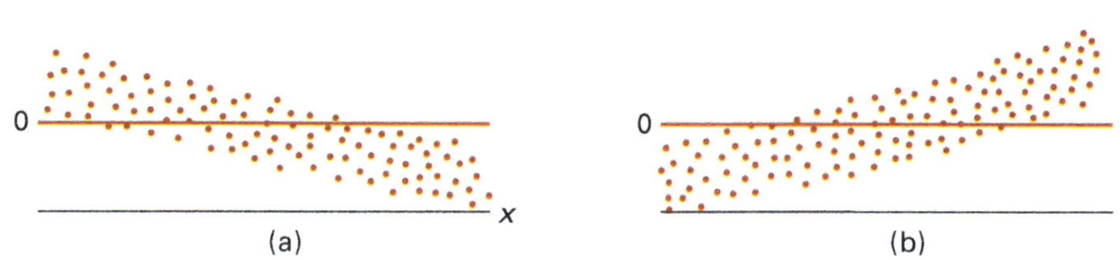

FIGURE 13.10 Graphs of non-independent residuals

Using residuals to test the assumptions of the regression model

One of the major uses of residual analysis is to test some of the assumptions underlying regression. The following are the assumptions of simple regression analysis.

1. The model is linear.
2. The error terms have constant variances.
3. The error terms are independent.
4. The error terms are normally distributed with zero mean.

Information about how well the regression assumptions are met by the particular regression model can be gleaned by examining the plots. For example, the residual plot in figure 13.8 indicates that the assumption that the model is linear does not hold. Note that the residuals are negative for low and high values of x and are positive for middle values of x. The graph of these residuals is parabolic, not random. The residual plot does not have to be shaped as a parabola for a nonlinear relationship to exist. Any significant deviation from an approximately horizontal residual plot may mean that a nonlinear relationship exists between the two variables.

The assumption of *constant error variance* is called **homoscedasticity**. If *the error variances are **not** constant* (called **heteroscedasticity**), the residual plots might look like one of the two plots in figure 13.9. Note in figure 13.9(a) that the error variance is greater for small values of x and smaller for large values of x. The situation is reversed in figure 13.9(b).

If the error terms are not independent, the residual plots could look like one of the graphs in figure 13.10. According to these graphs, instead of each error term being independent of the one next to it, the value of the residual is a function of the residual value next to it. For example, a large positive residual is next to a large positive residual and a small negative residual is next to a small negative residual.

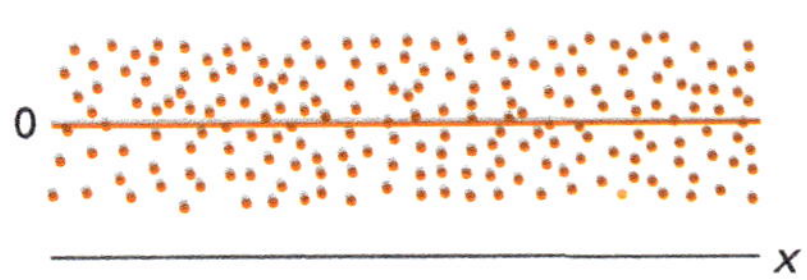

FIGURE 13.11 Healthy residual graph

The residual plot from a regression analysis that meets the assumptions might look like the graph in figure 13.11. The plot has random scatter around the x axis, the variances of the errors are about equal for each value of x, and the error terms do not appear to be related to adjacent terms.

DEMONSTRATION PROBLEM 13.3

Compute the residuals for demonstration problem 13.2 in which a regression model was developed to predict the weekly time spent making National Direct Calls on mobile phones. Analyse the residuals by using Excel graphic diagnostics.

USING EXCEL

Residual analysis

DP13-03

1. Access DP13-03.xls from the student website.
2. From the Data tab, select Data Analysis.
3. In the Data Analysis dialogue box, choose Regression and click OK.
4. In the Regression dialogue box:
   a. enter the data range for 'Weekly time on calls' in the Input Y range field
   b. enter the data range for 'Annual income' in the Input X range field
   c. check Labels if you have included the column headings in the input ranges. If not, leave it unchecked.
   d. choose an output option
   e. check Residuals and Residual Plots in the Residuals section

f. check Normal Probability Plots in the Normal Probability section

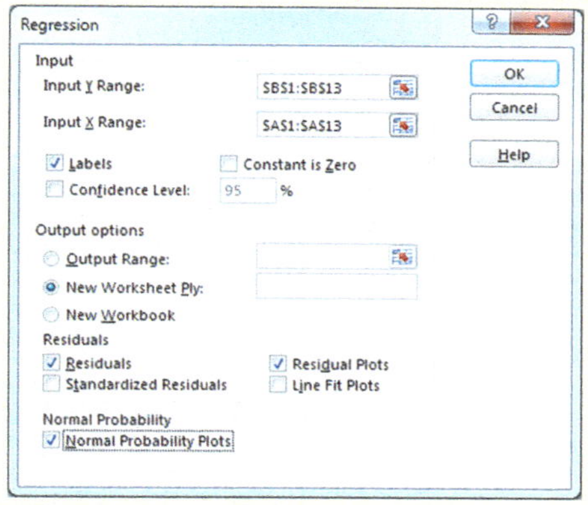

g. click OK.

The Excel output is shown on the next page. The Excel plots have been shown separately, below, for clarity. Note that, the Excel results will differ slightly from those calculated manually due to rounding errors.

From the Excel output on the next page, we can see that the regression model fits these data particularly well for observations (individuals) 2 and 5, as indicated by the small residual values of –0.63 and 1.36, respectively. For individuals 1, 8, 9, 11 and 12, the residuals are relatively large, indicating that the regression model does not fit the data well for these individuals.

From the residuals versus annual income plot (figure 13.12), it appears that the residuals increase (in absolute value) as income, x, increases, indicating a potential problem with heteroscedasticity.

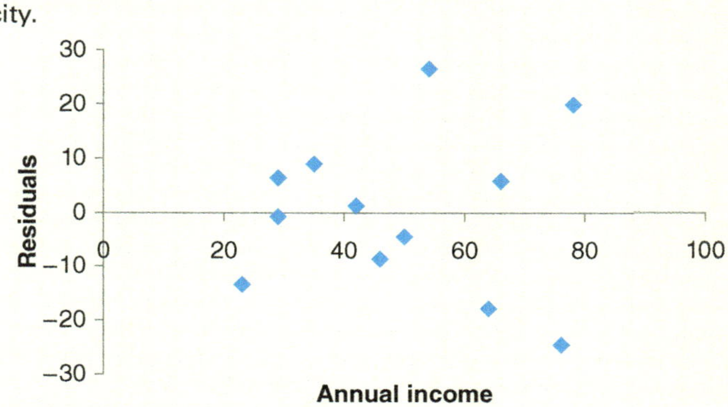

FIGURE 13.12 Plot of residuals versus annual income

The normal probability plot (figure 13.13) indicates that the residuals are very nearly normally distributed as they are close to lying on a straight line.

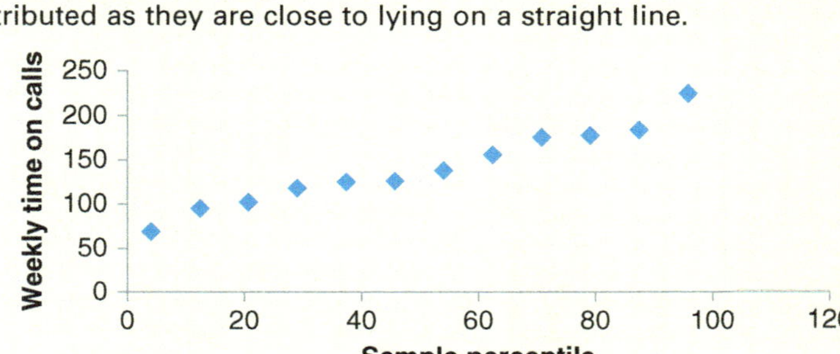

FIGURE 13.13 Normal probability plot

	A	B	C	D	E	F	G	H	I
1	SUMMARY OUTPUT								
2	*Regression Statistics*								
3	Multiple R	0.941506251							
4	R Square	0.88643402							
5	Adjusted R Square	0.875077422							
6	Standard Error	15.64907915							
7	Observations	12							
8									
9	ANOVA								
10		*df*	*SS*	*MS*	*F*	*Significance F*			
11	Regression	1	19115.06322	19115.06	78.05454	0.000005			
12	Residual	10	2448.936784	244.8937					
13	Total	11	21564						
14									
15		*Coefficients*	*Standard Error*	*t Stat*	*P-value*	*Lower 95%*	*Upper 95%*	*Lower 95.0%*	*Upper 95.0%*
16	Intercept	30.91246961	13.25422291	2.332273	0.041888	1.380220721	60.444718	1.380220721	60.44471849
17	Annual income ($000)	2.231503994	0.252579783	8.834848	0.000005	1.668721168	2.7942868	1.668721168	2.794286821
18									
19	RESIDUAL OUTPUT				PROBABILITY OUTPUT				
20	*Observation*	*Predicted Weekly time on National Direct Calls (minutes)*	*Residuals*		*Percentile*	*Weekly time on National Direct Calls (minutes)*			
21	1	82.23706148	−13.23706148		4.166667	69			
22	2	95.62608545	−0.626085446		12.5	95			
23	3	95.62608545	6.373914554		20.83333	102			
24	4	109.0151094	8.984890587		29.16667	118			
25	5	124.6356374	1.364362626		37.5	125			
26	6	133.5616534	−8.561653352		45.83333	126			
27	7	142.4876693	−4.48766933		54.16667	138			
28	8	151.4136853	26.58631469		62.5	156			
29	9	173.7287253	−17.72872525		70.83333	176			
30	10	178.1917332	5.808266759		79.16667	178			
31	11	200.5067732	−24.50677319		87.5	184			
32	12	204.9697812	20.03021883		95.83333	225			

PRACTICE PROBLEMS

Practising the calculations

13.8 Determine the equation of the regression line and the residuals for the following data. Comment on the residual values.

x	13	7	18	13	6
y	52	45	37	52	43	19

13.9 Solve for the predicted values of *y*, the residuals and the residual plot for the data in problem 13.3. The data are provided here again. Comment on the residual plot.

Advertising	15.3	4.8	24.2	65.0	40.3	4.6	20.9	45.1
Sales	170	43	360	1030	780	73	230	890

13.10 Solve for the predicted values of *y* and the residuals for the data in problem 13.4. The data are provided here again.

Bond rate	5%	12%	9%	15%	7%
Prime interest rate	16%	6%	8%	4%	7%

Testing your understanding

P13-11 **13.11** The equation of a regression line is:

$$\hat{y} = 50.506 - 1.64x$$

and the data are as follows:

x	5	7	11	12	19	25
y	47	38	32	24	22	10

Solve for the residuals and graph a residual plot. Do these data seem to violate any of the assumptions of regression?

P13-12 **13.12** A real estate agent researches the factors that influence house prices in Brisbane. She has collected data on recent sales and notes the size of each house in square metres. Suppose the house prices (and size in square metres) for the last ten sales are as follows.

Sales price ($'000)	Size (m^2)
$1 200	280
653	198
735	220
825	230
515	150
635	180
1 350	318
690	205

Develop a regression equation to predict the price of a house in Brisbane using the size in square metres. Compute residuals for this model. Obtain a graph of the residuals in the order of the *x* values. Comment on the shape of the residual graph.

P13-13 **13.13** Graph the following residuals and indicate which of the assumptions underlying regression analysis appear to be violated.

x	Residual	*x*	Residual
213	−11	237	6
216	−5	247	10
227	−2	263	12
229	−1		

P13-14 **13.14** Graph the following residuals and indicate which of the assumptions underlying regression analysis appear to be violated.

x	Residual	*x*	Residual
10	6	14	−3
11	3	15	2
12	−1	16	5
13	−11	17	8

13.15 Study the following residuals graph for a simple regression analysis. Comment on the residual evidence of lack of compliance with the regression assumptions.

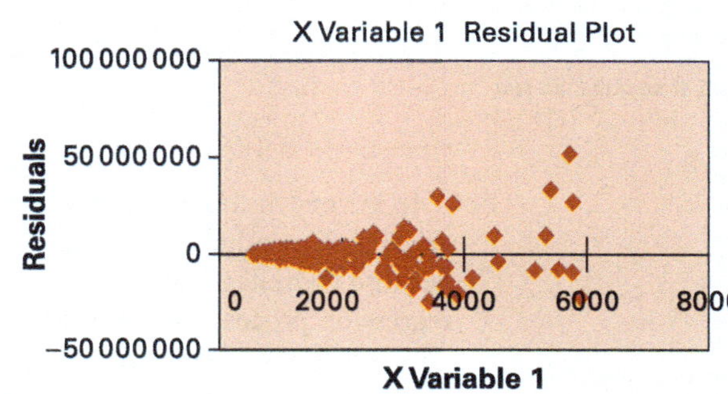

13.4 Standard error of the estimate

Residuals represent errors of estimation for individual points. With large samples of data, residual computations become laborious. Even with computers, a researcher sometimes has difficulty working through pages of residuals in an effort to understand the error of the regression model.

An alternative way of examining the error of the model is the standard error of the estimate, which provides a summary measure for the amount of error produced.

Because the sum of the residuals is approximately zero, attempting to determine the total amount of error by summing the residuals is fruitless. This zero-sum characteristic of residuals can be avoided by squaring the residuals and then summing them.

Table 13.4 contains the concert attendance and CD sales data from table 13.1, along with the residuals and the residuals squared. The *total of the residuals squared* column is called the **sum of squares of error (SSE)**.

TABLE 13.4 Determining SSE for the CD–concert example

Number of CD sales ('000) x	Concert attendance ('000) y	Residual $y - \hat{y}$	Residual squared $(y - \hat{y})^2$
61	4.280	.227	.05153
63	4.080	−.054	.00292
67	4.420	.123	.01513
69	4.170	−.208	.04326
70	4.480	.061	.00372
74	4.300	−.282	.07952
76	4.820	.157	.02465
81	4.700	−.167	.02789
86	5.110	.040	.00160
91	5.130	−.144	.02074
95	5.640	.204	.04162
97	5.560	.042	.00176
		$\Sigma(y - \hat{y}) = -.001$	$\Sigma(y - \hat{y})^2 = .31434$
	Sum of squares of error = SSE = .31434		

Sum of squares of error (13.6)

$$\text{SSE} = \Sigma\,(y - \hat{y})^2$$

In theory, infinitely many lines can be fitted to a sample of points. However, formulas (13.2) and (13.5) produce a line of best fit for which the SSE is minimised. This result is guaranteed because formulas (13.2) and (13.5) are derived from calculus to minimise SSE. For this reason, the regression process used in this chapter is called *least squares* regression.

A computational version of the equation for computing SSE is less meaningful for interpretation than

$$\text{SSE} = \Sigma(y - \hat{y})^2$$

but it is usually easier to compute. The computational formula for SSE follows.

Computational formula for SSE (13.7)

$$\text{SSE} = \Sigma y^2 - b_0\Sigma y - b_1\Sigma xy$$

For the CD–concert example:

$$\Sigma y^2 = (4.280)^2 + (4.080)^2 + (4.420)^2 + (4.170)^2 + (4.480)^2 + (4.300)^2 + (4.820)^2 + (4.700)^2 + (5.110)^2 + (5.130)^2 + (5.640)^2 + (5.560)^2 = 270.9251$$

$$b_0 = 1.5697928$$
$$b_1 = .0407016$$
$$\Sigma y = 56.69$$
$$\Sigma xy = 4462.22$$

$$\text{SSE} = \Sigma y^2 - b_0 \Sigma y - b_1 \Sigma xy = 270.9251 - (1.5697928)(56.69) - (.0407016)(4462.22) = .31405$$

Note: In previous sections, the values of the slope and intercept were rounded off for ease of computation and interpretation. They are shown here with more precision in an effort to reduce rounding error. The slight discrepancy between this value of SSE and the value computed in table 13.4 is due to rounding error.

The sum of squares of error is in part a function of the number of data points being used to compute the sum, which lessens the value of SSE as a measurement of error. A more useful measurement of error is the standard error of the estimate. The **standard error of the estimate (s_e)** is *the standard deviation of the error of the regression model* and has a more practical use than SSE. The standard error of the estimate follows.

Standard error of the estimate (s_e) **(13.8)**

$$s_e = \sqrt{\frac{\text{SSE}}{n-2}}$$

Using the value of SSE calculated in table 13.4, the standard error of the estimate for the CD–concert example is:

$$s_e = \sqrt{\frac{\text{SSE}}{n-2}} = \sqrt{\frac{.31434}{10}} = .1773$$

How is the standard error of the estimate used? As previously mentioned, the standard error of the estimate is a standard deviation of error. Thus, it can be interpreted as: on average, the model's errors are out, above and below, by this amount.

If data are approximately normally distributed, the empirical rule states that about 68% of all values are within $\mu \pm 1\sigma$ and that about 95% of all values are within $\mu \pm 2\sigma$. One of the assumptions for regression states that for a given x the error terms are normally distributed. Because the error terms are normally distributed, s_e is the standard deviation of error and the average error is zero, approximately 68% of the error values (residuals) should be within $0 \pm 1s_e$ and 95% of the error values (residuals) should be within $0 \pm 2s_e$. By having knowledge of the variables being studied and by examining the value of s_e, the researcher can often make a judgement about the fit of the regression model to the data by using s_e. How can the s_e value for the CD–concert example be interpreted?

The regression model in that example is used to predict concert attendance using the number of CD sales. Note that the range of the dependent variable in table 13.1 is from 4.08 to 5.64 (4080 to 5640). The regression model for the data yields an s_e of .1773. If the error terms were normally distributed about the given values of x, approximately 68% of the error terms would be within ±177.30 and 95% would be within ±2(177.30) = ±354.60. Examination of the residuals reveals that 100% of the residuals are within $2s_e$. The standard error of the estimate provides a single measure of error, which, if the researcher has enough background in the area being analysed, can be used to understand the magnitude of errors in the model. In addition, some researchers use the standard error of the estimate to identify outliers. They do so by looking for data that are outside $\pm 2s_e$ or $\pm 3s_e$.

DEMONSTRATION PROBLEM 13.4

PROBLEM: Compute the sum of squares of error and the standard error of the estimate for demonstration problem 13.2, in which a regression model was developed to predict mobile phone call times using annual income.

SOLUTION:

Individual	Annual income ($000) x	Weekly time on National Direct Calls (minutes) y	Residual $y - \hat{y}$	$(y - \hat{y})^2$
1	23	69	−13.22	174.77
2	29	95	−.62	0.38
3	29	102	6.38	40.70
4	35	118	8.99	80.82
5	42	126	1.37	1.88
6	46	125	−8.56	73.27
7	50	138	−4.49	20.16
8	54	178	26.58	706.50
9	64	156	−17.74	314.71
10	66	184	5.80	33.64
11	76	176	−24.52	601.23
12	78	225	20.02	400.80
	$\Sigma x = 592$	$\Sigma y = 1692$	$\Sigma(y - \hat{y}) = -.01$	$\Sigma(y - \hat{y})^2 = 2448.86$

$$SSE = 2448.8$$

$$s_e = \sqrt{\frac{SSE}{n-2}} = \sqrt{\frac{2448.86}{10}} = 15.65$$

In demonstration problem 13.2, we showed how to obtain the regression output using Excel. Below is the first section of the regression output (obtained using Excel) for the concert attendance problem. Note that the output includes a value for the standard error, 15.65. The use of Excel or a statistical package will provide us with the regression equation together with all relevant information.

An examination of the residuals for this problem reveals that 8 of 12 (67%) are within $\pm 1s_e$ and 100% are within $\pm 2s_e$. Is this size of error acceptable? Telecommunications executives can probably best answer that question.

	A	B
1	SUMMARY OUTPUT	
2	*Regression Statistics*	
3	Multiple R	0.941506
4	R Square	0.886434
5	Adjusted R Square	0.875077
6	**Standard Error**	**15.64908**
7	Observations	12

PRACTICE PROBLEMS

Practising the calculations

13.16 Use Excel to obtain the regression output (including residuals) for problem 13.1. Find the value of the standard error of the estimate (s_e) from the regression output. Determine how many of the residuals are within one standard error of the estimate. If the error terms are normally distributed, approximately how many of these residuals should be within $\pm 1s_e$?

13.17 Use Excel to obtain the regression output for problem 13.2. Find the value of s_e. Use the residuals computed to determine how many of them are within $\pm 1s_e$ and $\pm 2s_e$. How do these numbers compare with what the empirical rule says should occur if the error terms are normally distributed?

Testing your understanding

13.18 Determine the s_e for problem 13.3. Think about the variables being analysed in this problem and comment on the value of s_e.

13.19 Determine the s_e for problem 13.4. Examine the variables being analysed in this problem and comment on the value of s_e.

13.20 Use the data from problem 13.11 and determine the s_e.

13.21 Determine the s_e for problem 13.12. Comment on the size of s_e for this regression model, which is used to predict the price of a house in Brisbane.

P13-22 **13.22** To help determine how many beers to stock for the Ashes Cricket Test against England, the bar manager at the MCG wanted to know how the weather affects beer sales. Accordingly, he took a sample of 10 cricket matches and recorded the number of beers sold and the temperature in the middle of the day. Determine the equation of the regression line to predict the number of beers sold from the temperature. Compute the standard error of the estimate for this model. Does temperature appear to be a good predictor of the number of beers sold? Explain your reasoning.

Temperature (°C)	Beer Sales
25.0	6789
23.2	6210
28.5	8455
33.4	13432
26.2	8432
37.5	16453
28.0	9234
31.3	11237
27.8	9154
29.1	9265

13.5 Coefficient of determination

A widely used measure of fit for regression models is the **coefficient of determination** (**r^2**). The coefficient of determination is *the proportion of variability of the dependent variable (y) accounted for, or explained by, the independent variable (x).*

The coefficient of determination ranges from 0 to 1. An r^2 of zero means that the independent variable accounts for none of the variability of the dependent variable and that there is no regression prediction of y using x. An r^2 of 1 means that 100% of the variability of y is accounted for by x; hence, there is a perfect fit between y and x. Of course, generally r^2 has a value between the extremes. The researcher must interpret whether a particular r^2 is high enough or too low, depending on the use of the model and the context within which the model was developed.

In exploratory research where the variables are less well understood, low values of r^2 are likely to be more acceptable than they are in areas of research where the parameters are better developed and understood. A NASA researcher who uses vehicular weight to predict mission cost might hope for regression models which have an r^2 of .90 or higher. However, a business researcher who is trying to develop a model to predict the motivation level of employees might be pleased to get an r^2 near .50 in the initial research.

The dependent variable, y, being predicted in a regression model has a variation that is measured by the total sum of squares of y (SS_{yy}):

$$SS_{yy} = \sum(y - \bar{y})^2 = \sum y^2 - \frac{(\Sigma y)^2}{n}$$

and is the sum of the squared deviations of the y values from the mean value of y. This variation can be broken into two additive variations: the *explained variation*, measured by the sum of squares of regression (SSR), and the *unexplained variation*, measured by the sum of squares of error (SSE). This relationship can be expressed in equation form as:

$$SS_{yy} = SSR + SSE$$

where:

$SSR = \Sigma(\hat{y} - \bar{y})^2$

If each term in the equation is divided by SS_{yy}, the resulting equation is:

$$1 = \frac{SSR}{SS_{yy}} + \frac{SSE}{SS_{yy}}$$

The term r^2 is the proportion of the y variability that is explained by the regression model and is represented here as:

$$r^2 = \frac{SSR}{SS_{yy}}$$

Substituting this equation into the preceding relationship gives:

$$1 = r^2 + \frac{SSE}{SS_{yy}}$$

Solving for r^2 yields formula 13.9.

Coefficient of determination
(13.9)

$$r^2 = 1 - \frac{SSE}{SS_{yy}} = 1 - \frac{SSE}{\Sigma y^2 - \frac{(\Sigma y)^2}{n}}$$

Note: $0 \le r^2 \le 1$

The value of r^2 for the CD–concert example is solved as follows:

$$SSE = .31434$$

$$SS_{yy} = \sum y^2 - \frac{(\Sigma y)^2}{n} = 270.9251 - \frac{(56.69)^2}{12} = 3.11209$$

$$r^2 = 1 - \frac{SSE}{SS_{yy}} = 1 - \frac{.31434}{3.11209} = .899$$

That is, 89.9% of the variability in concert attendance is explained by variations in the artists' CD sales last year. This result also means that 11.1% of the variation in concert attendance, y, is unaccounted for by x or unexplained by the regression model. The coefficient of determination can be solved for directly by using:

$$r^2 = \frac{SSR}{SS_{yy}}$$

It can be shown through algebra that:

$$SSR = b_1{}^2 SS_{xx}$$

From this equation, a computational formula for r^2 can be developed. Note that this formula holds only for simple linear regression (i.e. with only one x variable).

Computational formula for r^2
(13.10)

$$r^2 = \frac{b_1^2 SS_{xx}}{SS_{yy}}$$

For the CD–concert example, $b_1 = .0407016$, $SS_{xx} = 1689$ and $SS_{yy} = 3.11209$. Using the computational formula for r^2 yields:

$$r^2 = \frac{(.0407016)^2(1689)}{3.11209} = .899$$

The middle portion of the regression output for the CD sales problem (ANOVA) is shown below. Under the heading 'SS', we see that the sum of squares of the regression is given as 2.798031, while the total sum of squares (SS_{yy}) is 3.112092 (as before). Dividing the regression sum of squares by the total sum of squares provides the value of r^2 as .899.

	A	B	C	D	E	F
1	ANOVA					
2		*df*	*SS*	*MS*	*F*	*Significance F*
3	Regression	1	**2.798031**	2.798031	89.09218	2.69E–06
4	Residual	10	0.31406	0.031406		
5	Total	11	**3.112092**			

DEMONSTRATION PROBLEM 13.5

PROBLEM: Compute the coefficient of determination (r^2) for demonstration problem 13.2, in which a regression model was developed to predict weekly mobile phone call times using a person's income.

SOLUTION:

$$\Sigma y^2 = 260\,136 \quad \Sigma y = 1692 \quad SSE = 2448.86$$

$$SS_{yy} = 260\,136 - \frac{(1692)^2}{12} = 21\,564$$

$$r^2 = 1 - \frac{SSE}{SS_{yy}} = 1 - \frac{2448.86}{21\,564} = .886$$

This regression model accounts for 88.6% of the variability in call times, leaving only 11.4% unexplained variation.

Using $SS_{xx} = 3838.667$ and $b_1 = 2.232$ from demonstration problem 13.2, we can solve for r^2 with the computational formula:

$$r^2 = \frac{b_1^2 SS_{xx}}{SS_{yy}} = \frac{(2.232)^2(3838.667)}{21\,564} = .886$$

This is also obtained, as shown below, using the Excel procedure described in demonstration problem 13.3.

	A	B
1	SUMMARY OUTPUT	
2	*Regression Statistics*	
3	Multiple R	0.941506
4	**R Square**	**0.886434**
5	Adjusted R Square	0.875077
6	Standard Error	15.64908
7	Observations	12

Relationship between r and r^2

The coefficient of correlation (introduced in chapter 3), r, is related to r^2, the coefficient of determination in linear regression. In simple linear regression, the coefficient of determination is the square of the coefficient of correlation. In demonstration problem 13.2, a regression model was developed to predict mobile phone call times using annual income. The r^2 value for the model was .886. Taking the square root of this value yields $r = .941$, which is exactly the sample correlation between call times and income. A word of caution here: because r^2 is always positive, solving for r by taking $\sqrt{r^2}$ gives the correct magnitude of r but may give the wrong sign. The researcher must examine the sign of the slope of the regression line to determine whether a positive or negative relationship exists between the variables and then assign the same sign to the correlation value.

PRACTICE PROBLEMS

Practising the calculations

13.23 Compute r^2 for problem 13.16 (problem 13.1). Interpret the value of r^2 obtained.

13.24 Compute r^2 for problem 13.17 (problem 13.2). Interpret the value of r^2 obtained.

13.25 Compute r^2 for problem 13.18 (problem 13.3). Interpret the value of r^2 obtained.

13.26 Compute r^2 for problem 13.19 (problem 13.4). Interpret the value of r^2 obtained.

13.27 Compute r^2 for problem 13.20 (problem 13.11). Interpret the value of r^2 obtained.

Testing your understanding

P13-28 **13.28** A health care provider wanted to test the link between childhood obesity and hours spent playing computer games per week. She took a sample of 15 8-year-old children. The number of kilograms a child was overweight was recorded, along with the number of hours of computer games played per week. Determine the equation of the regression line to predict the number of kilograms a child may be overweight depending on the number of hours playing computer games. Compute the standard error of the estimate (and r^2) for this model. Does number of hours of TV watched seem to be a good predictor of obesity? Why or why not?

Hours playing computer games	Overweight
41	8.5
36	5.2
24	0.4
37	7.1
39	8.2
41	9.5
29	2.4
30	2.8
20	–4
28	1.2
42	12
29	1.5
31	3.4
37	6.8
21	–2.1

13.6 Hypothesis tests for the slope of the regression model and testing the overall model

Testing the slope

In section 13.2, we saw how to calculate the coefficients of the regression equation, namely b_0 and b_1. These coefficients are sample statistics, as is $\bar{x}$, the sample mean. We can test whether a population mean could be equal to a given numerical value using hypothesis testing. We shall use hypothesis testing here to test whether the population parameters β_0 and β_1 could possibly be equal to zero. The null and alternative hypotheses are stated in the usual way:

$$H_0: \beta_1 = 0$$
$$H_a: \beta_1 \neq 0$$

Note that this test is two-tailed. Generally, we use a two-tailed test to test the population parameters. Testing the null hypothesis involves using either a t test or a p-value (both provide the same result).

t test of slope
(13.11)

$$t = \frac{b_1 - \beta_1}{s_b}$$

where:

$$s_b = \frac{s_e}{\sqrt{SS_{xx}}}$$

$$s_e = \sqrt{\frac{SSE}{n-2}}$$

$$SS_{xx} = \sum x^2 - \frac{(\Sigma x)^2}{n}$$

b_1 = the sample slope
β_1 = the hypothesised slope
df = $n - 2$

For the CD–concert regression model, the test with $\alpha = .05$ follows. The regression line derived from the data is:

$$\hat{y} = 1.57 + .0407x$$

The sample slope is $.0407 = b_1$. The value of s_e is .1773, $\Sigma x = 930$, $\Sigma x^2 = 73\,764$ and $n = 12$. The hypotheses are:

$$H_0\text{: } \beta_1 = 0$$
$$H_a\text{: } \beta_1 \neq 0$$

The df $= n - 2 = 12 - 2 = 10$. As this test is two-tailed, $\frac{\alpha}{2} = .025$ as shown in figure 13.14. The critical value from the table t value is $t_{.025,\,10} = \pm 2.228$. The observed t value for this sample slope is:

$$t = \frac{.0407 - 0}{.1773 \Big/ \sqrt{73764 - \frac{(930)^2}{12}}} = 9.43$$

As shown in figure 13.14, the t value calculated from the sample slope falls in the rejection region (shaded area). The null hypothesis that the population slope (β_1) is zero is rejected. If we reject the null hypothesis that β_1 is zero, then we retain the b_1 term in the regression equation. On the other hand, if we do not reject the null hypothesis, that is, we conclude that the population parameter is zero, then we must remove the β_1 term from the regression equation, which means that we do not have a regression.

We can test the intercept coefficient (β_0) in exactly the same manner. Nevertheless, we usually retain the intercept term even if the null hypothesis is not rejected.

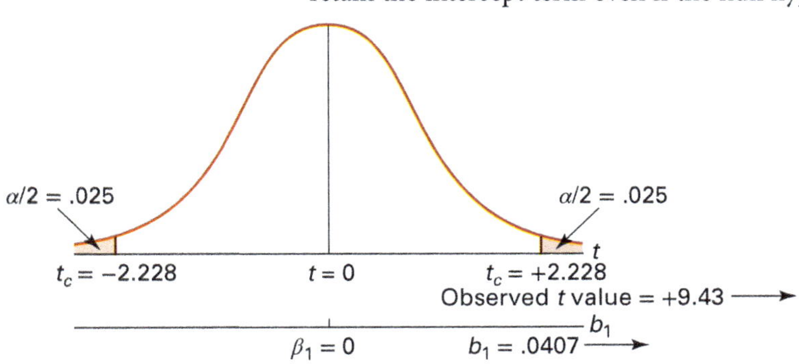

FIGURE 13.14 *t* test of slope from CD–concert example

Hypothesis testing can also be undertaken using **confidence intervals**, which are also of interest in their own right. Although a single estimate is often of interest to the researcher, the regression line is determined by a sample of points. If a different sample is taken, a different line will result, yielding a different single estimate for both b_0 and b_1. Confidence intervals take this inherent randomness of the sample into account. For example, a 95% confidence interval for β_1 means that, if we repeated the sampling exercise 100 times, 95 of these so-constructed confidence intervals can be expected to contain the true population parameter, β_1. However, we would usually interpret the interval as that we are 95% confident that the true population parameter lies in this range.

The confidence intervals can be applied to hypothesis testing; if the 95% confidence interval for β_1 does *not* contain zero (the hypothesised value of β_1 if H_0 is not rejected), we reject the null hypothesis (for a two-tailed test with α = .05). The expression for the confidence intervals is given as:

$$b_1 \pm t_{\alpha/2}\, s_{b_1}$$

where:

$$s_{b_1} = \frac{s_e}{\sqrt{SS_{xx}}}$$

As part of its regression output, Excel calculates these confidence intervals. Below is the bottom section of the regression output for the CD–concert example.

	A	B	C	D	E	F	G
1		*Coefficients*	*Standard Error*	*t Stat*	*P-value*	*Lower 95%*	*Upper 95%*
2	Intercept	1.569792777	0.338083	4.643218	0.000917	0.816497	2.323089
3	CD sales	0.040701599	0.004312	9.438865	2.69E–06	**0.031094**	**0.05031**

From the last two columns, we obtain the 95% confidence interval for number of CDs as (.03, .05). As this does not contain zero, we conclude that we are 95% confident that the population parameter is not zero, and we again reject the null hypothesis.

Before leaving this section, note the *p*-value associated with CD sales in the Excel output above. To test the null hypothesis that the population coefficient of CD sales is zero, we can check the *p*-value against the significance level (α) of .05. The rule is that if the *p*-value is less than the α value, we reject the null hypothesis. For the CD–concert example, since the *p*-value of 2.69E–0.6 (0.00000269) is less than .05, we reject the null hypothesis and retain the independent variable, CD sales, in the regression. This, of course, agrees with the *t* test calculated earlier. Finally, note that the *t* value of 9.438865 is also provided in the Excel output.

DEMONSTRATION PROBLEM 13.6

PROBLEM: In demonstration problem 13.2, we developed a regression model to predict a person's weekly mobile phone call times from their annual income. Test the slope of the estimated regression to determine whether there is a significant relationship between the two variables. Use α = .01.

SOLUTION: The hypotheses for this problem are:

$$H_0\text{: } \beta_1 = 0$$
$$H_a\text{: } \beta_1 \neq 0$$

Assume the level of significance is .01. With 12 pairs of data, df = 10. The critical *t* value is $t_{.01,\,10} = 3.169$. The regression line equation for this problem is:

$$\hat{y} = 30.888 + 2.232x$$

The sample slope, b_1, is 2.232, and $s_e = 15.65$, $\Sigma x = 592$, $\Sigma x^2 = 33\,044$ and $n = 12$. The observed *t* value for the sample slope is:

$$t = \frac{2.232 - 0}{15.65 \Big/ \sqrt{33044 - \frac{(592)^2}{12}}} = 8.84$$

The observed t value (8.84) is in the rejection region because it is greater than the critical t value of 3.169. The null hypothesis is rejected. The population slope for this estimated regression line is significantly different from zero.

In demonstration problem 13.2, we produced regression output directly using Excel. This output is repeated below.

	A	B	C	D	E	F	G
1	SUMMARY OUTPUT						
2							
3	*Regression Statistics*						
4	Multiple R	0.941506					
5	R Square	0.886434					
6	Adjusted R Square	0.875077					
7	Standard Error	15.64908					
8	Observations	12					
9							
10	ANOVA						
11		*df*	*SS*	*MS*	*F*	*Significance F*	
12	Regression	1	19115.06	19115.06	78.05454	4.89E–06	
13	Residual	10	2448.937	244.8937			
14	Total	11	21564				
15							
16		*Coefficients*	*Standard Error*	*t Stat*	*P-value*	*Lower 95%*	*Upper 95%*
17	Intercept	30.91247	13.25422	2.332273	0.041888	1.380221	60.44472
18	Annual income ($000)	2.231504	0.25258	8.834848	4.89E–06	1.668721	2.794287
19							

Examine the bottom section of this regression output. The first column contains the headings 'Intercept' and 'Annual income ($000)'. The second column contains the regression coefficients, b_0 and b_1. The third column displays the standard errors of the regression coefficients.

Dividing values in the second column by those in the third column provides the values in column four — the t statistics. Note the t statistic for the coefficient for 'Annual income ($000)', 8.834848, and compare it to that calculated above, 8.84 (the difference being due to rounding errors). We can also examine the p-values in the fourth column to test the hypotheses:

$$H_0\text{: } \beta_1 = 0$$
$$H_a\text{: } \beta_1 \neq 0$$

If the p-value is less than the critical value (usually .05 for a two-tailed test), the null hypothesis is rejected. As the p-value for b_1 is 0.00000489 (note that E-06 means multiply 4.89 by 10 to the power of −6, that is, move the decimal point 6 places to the left), which is less than .05, the null hypothesis is rejected and the b_1 term is retained in the regression equation. We would reach the same conclusion for $\alpha = .01$, as used earlier.

The sixth and seventh columns contain the 95% confidence intervals for the population coefficients. Thus, the 95% confidence interval for β_1 is provided as:

1.668721 to 2.794287

Again note that, as this interval does not contain zero, we are 95% confident that β_1 is not equal to zero.

PRACTICE PROBLEMS

Practising the calculations

13.29 Test the slope of the regression line determined in problem 13.1. Use $\alpha = .05$.

13.30 Test the slope of the regression line determined in problem 13.2. Use $\alpha = .01$.

13.31 Test the slope of the regression line determined in problem 13.3. Use $\alpha = .10$.

13.32 Test the slope of the regression line determined in problem 13.4. Use a 5% level of significance.

Testing your understanding

13.33 Shown here is an incomplete analysis of variance table for a simple regression analysis. Compute the coefficient of determination and interpret its value.

	A	B	C	D	E
10	ANOVA				
11	*Source*	*df*	*SS*	*MS*	*F*
12	Regression	1	5165		
13	Error	7	18554		
14	Total	8	23718		

13.34 Study the following analysis of variance table, which was generated from a simple regression analysis. Determine the coefficient of determination and interpret its value.

	A	B	C	D	E	F
10	ANOVA					
11		*df*	*SS*	*MS*	*F*	*Significance F*
12	Regression	1	116.65	116.65	8.26	0.021
13	Error	8	112.95	14.12		
14	Total	9	229.60			

13.7 Estimation and prediction

One of the main uses of regression analysis is as a prediction tool. If the regression function is a good model, the researcher can use the regression equation to determine values of the dependent variable for various values of the independent variable. For example, marketing managers would like to have a model with which they could predict the sales volume of a new store location using variables such as population density and number of competitors. The CD–concert example presents a regression model that has the potential to predict concert attendance from the number of prior CD sales.

In simple regression analysis, a point (or single) estimate prediction of y can be made by substituting the associated value of x into the regression equation and solving for y. From the CD–concert example, if the number of CD sales, in thousands, of a band is $x = 73$, the predicted concert attendance can be computed by substituting the x value into the regression equation determined in section 13.2:

$$\hat{y} = 1.57 + 0.0407x = 1.57 + .0407(73) = 4.5411$$

The point estimate of the predicted concert attendance is 4.5411 thousands, or 4541 people.

Confidence (prediction) intervals to estimate the conditional mean of y: $\mu_{y/x}$

Although a point estimate is often of interest to the researcher, the regression line is determined by a sample set of points; if a different sample is taken, a different line will result, yielding a different point estimate. Hence computing a confidence interval for the estimation is often useful. Because for any value of x (independent variable) there can be many values of y (dependent variable), one type of confidence interval is *an estimate of the average value of y for a given x.*

This average value of y is denoted $E(y_x)$ — the expected value of y — and can be computed using formula 13.12.

Confidence interval to estimate $E(y_x)$ for a given value of x
(13.12)

$$\hat{y} \pm t_{\alpha/2,n-2}\, s_e \sqrt{\frac{1}{n} + \frac{(x_0 - \bar{x})^2}{SS_{xx}}}$$

where:

x_0 = a particular value of x

$$SS_{xx} = \sum x^2 - \frac{(\Sigma x)^2}{n}$$

The application of this formula can be illustrated with the construction of a 95% confidence interval to estimate the average value of y (concert attendance in thousands) when x (CD sales in thousands) is 73. For a 95% confidence interval, $\alpha = .05$ and $\alpha/2 = .025$. The df $= n - 2 = 12 - 2 = 10$. The table t value is $t_{.025,10} = 2.228$. Other values needed for this problem, which were calculated previously, are:

$$s_e = .1773 \quad \Sigma x = 930 \quad \bar{x} = 77.5 \quad \Sigma x^2 = 73\,764 \quad SS_{xx} = 1689$$

For $x_0 = 73$, the value of $\hat{y}$ is 4.5411. The computed confidence interval for the average value of y, $E(y_{73})$, is:

$$4.5411 \pm (2.228)(.1773)\sqrt{\frac{1}{12} + \frac{(73 - 77.5)^2}{1689}} = 4.5411 \pm .1220$$

$$4.4191 \leq E(y_{73}) \leq 4.6631$$

That is, with 95% confidence the average value of y (in thousands) for $x = 73$ is between 4.4191 and 4.6631.

Table 13.5 shows confidence intervals computed for several values of x to estimate the average value of y. Note that, as x values get further from the mean x value (77.5), the confidence intervals get wider; as the x values get closer to the mean, the confidence intervals narrow. The reason is that the numerator of the second term in the square root term approaches zero as the value of x approaches the mean value of x, and increases as x departs from the mean. Intuitively, the further a particular value of x is away from its 'typical' value, the less confidence we have in using the regression line to predict y.

TABLE 13.5 Confidence intervals to estimate the average value of y for some x values in the CD–concert example

x	Confidence intervals	
62	4.0934 ± 0.1876	3.9058 to 4.2810
68	4.3376 ± 0.1461	4.1915 to 4.4837
73	4.5411 ± 0.1220	4.4191 to 4.6631
85	5.0295 ± 0.1349	4.8946 to 5.1644
90	5.2230 ± 0.1656	5.0674 to 5.3886

Prediction intervals to estimate a single value of y

A second type of interval in regression estimation is a **prediction interval** to *estimate a single value of y for a given value of x.*

Prediction interval to estimate *y* for a given value of *x*
(13.13)

$$\hat{y} \pm t_{\alpha/2, n-2} s_e \sqrt{1 + \frac{1}{n} + \frac{(x_0 - \bar{x})^2}{SS_{xx}}}$$

where:

x_0 = a particular value of x

$$SS_{xx} = \sum x^2 - \frac{(\Sigma x)^2}{n}$$

Formula 13.13 is virtually the same as formula 13.12, except for the additional value of 1 in the square root term. This additional value widens the prediction interval to estimate a single value of y from the confidence interval to estimate the average value of y. This result seems logical because the average value of y is toward the middle of a group of y values. Thus the confidence interval to estimate the average, which takes into account all the y values for a given x, need not be as wide as the prediction interval produced by formula 13.13.

A 95% prediction interval can be computed to estimate the single value of y for $x = 73$ from the CD–concert example by using formula 13.13. The same values used to construct the confidence interval to estimate the average value of y are used here.

$$t_{.025,\,10} = 2.228 \quad s_e = .1773 \quad \Sigma x = 930 \quad \bar{x} = 77.5 \quad \Sigma x^2 = 73\,764 \quad SS_{xx} = 1689$$

For $x_0 = 73$, the value of $\hat{y} = 4.5411$. The computed prediction interval for the single value of y is:

$$4.5411 \pm (2.228)(.1773)\sqrt{1 + \frac{1}{12} + \frac{(73 - 77.5)^2}{1689}} = 4.5411 \pm .4134$$

$$4.1277 \le y \le 4.9545$$

Figure 13.15 displays confidence intervals for various values of x for the average y value and the prediction intervals for a single y value. Note that the intervals flare out towards the ends, as the values of x depart from the average x value. Note also that the intervals for a single y value are always wider than the intervals for the average y value for any given value of x.

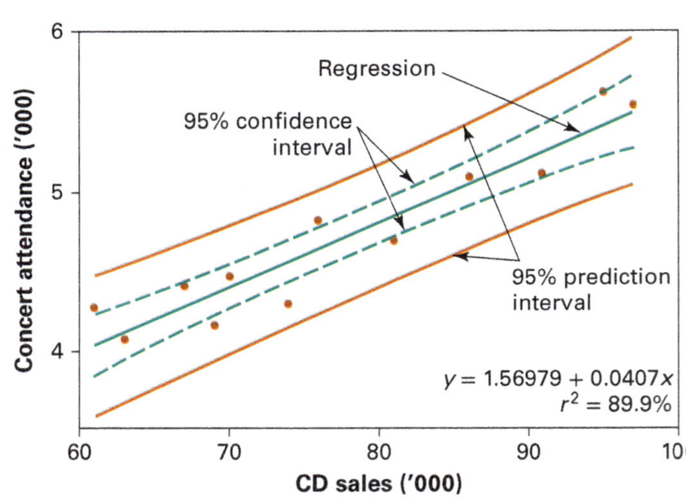

FIGURE 13.15 Intervals for estimation

An examination of the prediction interval formula to estimate y for a given value of x explains why the intervals flare out.

$$\hat{y} \pm t_{\alpha/2, n-2} s_e \sqrt{1 + \frac{1}{n} + \frac{(x_0 - \bar{x})^2}{SS_{xx}}}$$

As we enter different values of x_0 from the regression analysis into the equation, the only thing that changes in the equation is $(x_0 - \bar{x})^2$. This expression increases as individual values of x_0 lie further from the mean, resulting in an increase in the width of the interval. The interval is narrower for values of x_0 nearer to $\bar{x}$ and wider for values of x_0 further from $\bar{x}$. A comparison of formulas 13.12 and 13.13 reveals them to be identical except that formula 13.13 — to compute a prediction interval to estimate y for a given value of x — contains a 1 in the square root term. This distinction ensures that formula 13.13 will yield wider intervals than formula 13.12 for otherwise identical data.

Caution: A regression line is determined from a sample of points. The line, the r^2, the s_e and the confidence intervals change for different sets of sample points. That is, the linear relationship developed for a set of points does not necessarily hold for values of x outside the range of those used to establish the model. In the CD–concert example, the range of x values (number of CDs sold, in thousands) varied from 61 to 97. The regression model developed from these points may not be valid for sales of say 40, 50 or 100 because the regression model was not constructed with x values of those magnitudes. Beyond the sample data values, the relationship might be nonlinear. However, decision makers sometimes extrapolate regression results to values of x beyond the range of those used to develop the formulas (often in time-series sales forecasting). This must be undertaken with caution, and understanding the limitations of this type of use of regression analysis is essential.

DEMONSTRATION PROBLEM 13.7

PROBLEM: Construct a 95% confidence interval to estimate the average value of y (call times) for demonstration problem 13.2 when $x = 40$ (annual income in \$000). Then construct a 95% prediction interval to estimate the single value of y for $x = 40$ (annual income in \$000).

SOLUTION: For a 95% confidence interval, $\alpha = .05$, $n = 12$ and df = 10. The table t value is $t_{.025, 10} = 2.228$; $s_e = 15.65$, $\Sigma x = 592$, $\bar{x} = 49.33$, $SS_{xx} = 3838.667$ and $\Sigma x^2 = 33\,044$. For $x_0 = 40$, $\hat{y} = 120.17$. The computed confidence interval for the average value of y is:

$$120.17 \pm (2.228)(15.65)\sqrt{\frac{1}{12} + \frac{(40 - 49.33)^2}{3838.667}} = 120.17 \pm 11.35$$

$$108.82 \le E(y_{40}) \le 131.52$$

With 95% confidence, the average weekly mobile phone call times (in minutes) for a person with an annual income of \$40 000 is between 108.82 and 131.52.

The computed prediction interval for the single value of y is:

$$120.17 \pm (2.228)(15.65)\sqrt{1 + \frac{1}{12}\frac{(40 - 49.33)^2}{3838.667}} = 120.17 \pm 36.67$$

$$83.5 \le y \le 156.84$$

With 95% confidence, a single weekly call time in minutes for a person with a \$40 000 annual income is between 83.5 and 156.84. Obviously this interval is much wider than the 95% confidence interval for the average value of y for $x = 40$.

The graph overleaf depicts the 95% interval bands for both the average y value and the single y values for all 12 x values in this problem. Note once again the flaring out of the bands near the extreme values of x.

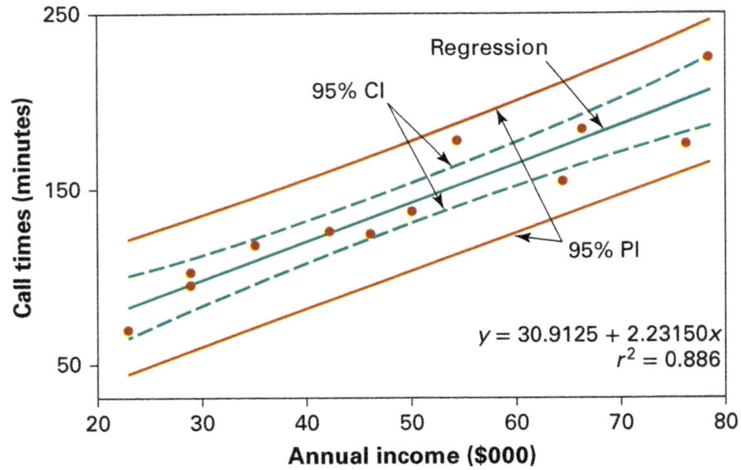

USING EXCEL

Obtaining the prediction interval

The prediction interval for a single value of y, and indeed the point estimate, can be obtained using Excel.[1]

DP13-02

1. Access DP13-02.xls from the student website.
2. Add an extra column to your data between the income and time columns. Label it 'Prediction' and fill it with zeros.
3. Add an extra row to your data. Enter the value of x for which you want to predict the single value of y (i.e. 40) in the income column, –1 in the prediction column and 0 for y in the time column.

	A	B	C	D
1	*Individual*	*Annual income ($000)*	*Prediction*	*Weekly time on National Direct Calls (minutes)*
2	1	23	0	69
3	2	29	0	95
4	3	29	0	102
5	4	35	0	118
6	5	42	0	126
7	6	46	0	125
8	7	50	0	138
9	8	54	0	178
10	9	64	0	156
11	10	66	0	184
12	11	76	0	176
13	12	78	0	225
14		40	–1	0

4. From the Data tab, select Data Analysis.
5. In the Data Analysis dialogue box, choose Regression and click OK.

1. This technique was devised by Professor Brett Inder, Monash University.

6. In the Regression dialogue box:
   a. enter the data range for 'Weekly time on National Direct Calls (minutes)', including the cell you added to the bottom of the column, in the Input Y Range field
   b. enter the data range for 'Annual income ($000)' and the 'Prediction' column in the Input X Range field, again making sure to include the extra row of data
   c. check Labels if you have included the column headings in the input ranges. If not, leave it unchecked.
   d. specify a 95% confidence interval
   e. choose an output option. (You do not need to check any of the Residuals or Normal Probability options.)

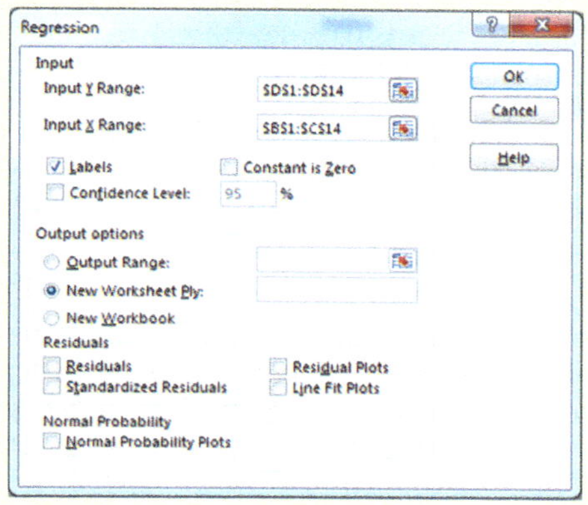

   f. click OK.

The relevant portion of the Excel output follows.

	A	B	C	D	E	F	G	H	I
16		*Coefficients*	*Standard Error*	*t Stat*	*P-value*	*Lower 95%*	*Upper 95%*	*Lower 95.0%*	*Upper 95.0%*
17	Intercept	30.91	13.25	2.33	0.0418876	1.38	60.44	1.38	60.44
18	Annual income ($000)	2.23	0.25	8.83	0.0000049	1.67	2.79	1.67	2.79
19	Prediction	120.17	16.46	7.30	0.0000260	83.50	156.84	83.50	156.84

The results for 'Prediction' give us the point estimate of 120.17 in the coefficients column, and the 'Lower 95%' and the 'Upper 95%' columns of 83.50 and 156.84 give us the 95% prediction interval, as obtained before.

PRACTICE PROBLEMS

Practising the calculations

13.35 Construct a 95% confidence interval for the average value of y for problem 13.1. Use $x = 25$.

Testing your understanding

13.36 Construct a 90% prediction interval for a single value of y for problem 13.2; use $x = 100$. Construct a 90% prediction interval for a single value of y for problem 13.2; use $x = 130$. Compare the results. Which prediction interval is greater? Why?

13.37 Construct a 98% confidence interval for the average value of y for problem 13.3; use $x = 20$. Construct a 98% prediction interval for a single value of y for problem 13.3; use $x = 20$. Which is wider? Why?

13.38 Construct a 99% confidence interval for the average bond rate in problem 13.4 for a prime interest rate of 10%. Discuss the meaning of this confidence interval.

Interpreting the output

Although manual computations can be done, most regression problems are analysed using a computer. In this section, computer output from Excel is discussed.

Refer back to the Excel regression output for demonstration problem 13.3. The regression equation is found under 'Coefficients' at the bottom of the ANOVA section. The slope or coefficient of x is 2.2315 and the y intercept is 30.9125. The standard error of the estimate is given as the fourth statistic under 'Regression Statistics' at the top of the output, 'Standard Error = 15.6491'. The r^2 value is given as .886 on the second line. The t test for the slope is found under 't Stat' near the bottom of the ANOVA section on the 'Annual Income ($000)' ($x$ variable) row, $t = 8.83$. Adjacent to the t statistic (or observed t value) is the p-value, which is the probability of obtaining the t statistic by chance if the null hypothesis is true. For this slope, the probability shown is 0.000 004 886. We would usually write this as 0.0000. The predicted values and the residuals are shown in the 'Residual Output' section.

MISUSE OF STATISTICS

Regression analysis can be misused in a number of ways. Knowingly violating the assumptions underlying statistical techniques is acting unethically. For example, regression analysis requires equal error variance and independence of error terms. Through the use of residual plots and other statistical techniques, a researcher can determine whether such assumptions are met. To present a regression model as fact when the assumptions underlying regression are not met is dishonest.

Another problem that occurs in regression analysis is attempting to predict values of the dependent variable lying outside the range of values used to develop the model. The concert attendance model used in this chapter was developed for data between 61 and 97 CD sales ('000). A linear relationship was evident between concert attendance and CD sales over this range. However, this model will not necessarily fit values outside the range of 61 to 97 CD sales ('000). Outside this range, the relationship may not be linear. It is unethical to make claims for a regression model outside the range of values for which the model was developed.

CHAPTER CASE **REVISITED**

Predicting the selling price of houses in the city of Baycoast

1. In the chapter case, questions were raised about the relationship between the price of a house and the rating of the street in which the house is located. Data were provided for a sample of 120 houses. As an initial investigation, the Pearson correlation coefficient, r, was computed to be 0.723. The p-value associated with the hypothesis test that the population correlation coefficient is zero is computed as 0.00000 which, being less than $\alpha = .05$, permits us to conclude that, at the 5% significance level, the population correlation coefficient is not zero and that we can use the sample coefficient as an estimate. This r value indicates that there is a relatively high correlation between the two variables and that developing a regression model to predict one variable using the other has potential. Constructing a scatter plot indicates that the relationship is linear.

   Designating selling price as the y or dependent variable and street rating as the x or predictor variable, the following regression output was obtained for these data using Excel and the Regression option in Data Analysis.

	A	B	C	D	E	F	G
1	SUMMARY OUTPUT						
2							
3	*Regression Statistics*						
4	Multiple R	0.72257					
5	R Square	0.522107					
6	Adjusted R Square	0.518058					
7	Standard Error	225.5847					
8	Observations	120					
9							
10							
11	ANOVA						
12		*df*	*SS*	*MS*	*F*	*Significance F*	
13	Regression	1	6560411	6560411	128.9174	1.21E–20	
14	Residual	118	6004839	50888.46			
15	Total	119	12565249				
16							
17							
18		*Coefficients*	*Standard Error*	*t Stat*	*P-value*	*Lower 95%*	*Upper 95%*
19	Intercept	183.2621	65.27645	2.807477	0.005844	53.99701	312.5273
20	Street	122.3153	10.77271	11.35418	1.21E–20	100.9824	143.6482
21							
22							

From this output, the regression model is:

Selling price = 183.262 + 122.315(Street)

The y intercept has no practical meaning in this analysis, as the data do not include the value $x = 0$. The slope (122.3153) indicates that, for every one point increase in Street, there is, on average, an increase of $122 315 in the selling price of a house (remember that price is in thousands). Both coefficients are statistically significant, as their p-values, relating to the hypothesis test that the population coefficient is zero, are both less than the critical value $\alpha = .05$.

The 95% confidence interval for β_1 is obtained from the regression output as:

100.9824 to 143.6482

The r^2 value is provided as .522107, indicating that 52.2% of the price of a house is explained by the variable street rating, leaving 47.8% unexplained.

Only one of the standardised residuals is greater than 2 (2.03), indicating that the normality assumption about the errors can be accepted.

2. Using this regression model, the average selling price of a house in a street with a rating of 7 is obtained as:

$$\text{Selling price} = 183.263 + 122.315(7) = 1039.467 = \$1\,039\,467$$

SUMMARY

1 Regression is a procedure that produces a mathematical model (function) that can be used to predict one variable using other variables. Simple regression is bivariate (two variables) and linear (only a straight-line fit is attempted). Simple regression analysis produces a model that attempts to predict a y variable, referred to as the dependent variable, using an x variable, referred to as the independent, or predictor, variable.

The shape of the relationship between two quantitative variables is checked using a scatter plot. The scatter plot is simply a two-dimensional display of the data, with the independent variable on the x axis and the dependent variable on the y axis. In order to develop a valid simple regression, the shape of the data display must be approximately linear.

2 Having confirmed that the relationship is approximately linear, the strength of the relationship is measured by the correlation coefficient. The closer in magnitude the correlation coefficient is to 1, the stronger the linear relationship. The scatter plot and the correlation coefficient are used together.

3 The general form of the equation of the simple regression line is the slope–intercept equation of a line. The equation comprises a constant (the y intercept value) and the slope of the line (the coefficient of x); the form of the equation is $y = b_0 + b_1x$. The coefficient b_1 is the slope of the line; the interpretation of this coefficient is that, for a one unit increase in x, the dependent variable, y, increases by b_1 units. If the data include the value $x = 0$, the coefficient b_0 is the intercept of the regression line with the vertical axis, and is the value of the dependent variable when the independent variable is zero. On the other hand, if the data do not include $x = 0$, the coefficient b_0 does not have any physical meaning; it is simply the intercept of the extension of the regression line with the vertical axis.

A residual analysis is used to test whether the assumptions underlying regression analysis are valid. The residual is the difference between the observed value of y and the predicted value of y: that is, $(y - \hat{y})$. Specifically, graphs of the residuals can reveal (1) lack of linearity, (2) lack of homogeneity of error variance and (3) dependence of error terms. Geometrically, the residuals are the vertical distances from the y values to the regression line. Because the equation that yields the regression line is derived in such a way that the line is in the geometric middle of the points, the sum of the residuals is zero.

4 A single value of error measurement called the standard error of the estimate, s_e, can be computed. The standard error of the estimate is the standard deviation of a model's residuals. The value of s_e can be used as a single guide to the magnitude of the error produced by the regression model as opposed to examining all the residuals. It is also used to develop a confidence interval for the predicted value of the dependent variable.

5 Another widely used statistic for testing the strength of a regression model is r^2, or the coefficient of determination. The coefficient of determination is the proportion of total variability of the y variable accounted for by, or predicted using, x. The coefficient of determination ranges from 0 to 1. The higher the value of r^2, the stronger is the predictability of the model.

6 Testing to determine whether the actual population slope of the regression line is different from zero is essential before accepting the regression model as valid. If the population slope of the regression line is not considered to be different from zero, we conclude there is no valid regression and no relationship. A t statistic, or a p-value, is used to test the significance of the slope.

7 One of the most prevalent uses of a regression model is to predict the values of y for given values of x. Predicted values of y (denoted as $\hat{y}$) can be calculated by inserting the given data values of x into the regression equation. Recognising that the predicted value is a sample result, a confidence interval can also be developed to provide a 95% confidence interval for the true population value of y. A prediction interval for a single y value for a given x value is also specified. This second interval is wider because it allows for the wide diversity of individual values, whereas the confidence interval for the mean y value reflects only the range of average y values for a given x.

KEY TERMS

coefficient of determination (r^2) p. 459
confidence interval p. 463
correlation coefficient p. 438
error of prediction p. 441
heteroscedasticity p. 452
homoscedasticity p. 452
least squares analysis p. 443
outliers p. 451
prediction interval p. 467
probabilistic model p. 442
regression analysis p. 437
residual p. 449
residual plot p. 451
scatter plot p. 438
simple regression p. 437
standard error of the estimate (s_e) p. 457
sum of squares of error (SSE) p. 456

KEY EQUATIONS

EQUATION	DESCRIPTION	FORMULA
13.1	Equation of the simple regression line	$\hat{y} = b_0 + b_1 x$
13.2	Slope of the regression line	$b_1 = \dfrac{\Sigma(x-\bar{x})(y-\bar{y})}{\Sigma(x-\bar{x})^2} = \dfrac{\Sigma xy - n\bar{x}\,\bar{y}}{\Sigma x^2 - n\bar{x}^2} = \dfrac{\Sigma xy - \frac{(\Sigma x)(\Sigma y)}{n}}{\Sigma x^2 - \frac{(\Sigma x)^2}{n}}$
13.3	Sum of squares	$SS_{xx} = \Sigma x^2 - \dfrac{(\Sigma x)^2}{n}$ $SS_{yy} = \Sigma y^2 - \dfrac{(\Sigma y)^2}{n}$ $SS_{xy} = \Sigma xy - \dfrac{(\Sigma x)(\Sigma y)}{n}$
13.4	Alternative formula for slope	$b_1 = \dfrac{SS_{xy}}{SS_{xx}}$
13.5	*y* intercept of the regression line	$b_0 = \bar{y} - b_1\bar{x} = \dfrac{\Sigma y}{n} - b_1\dfrac{\Sigma x}{n}$
13.6	Sum of squares of error	$SSE = \Sigma(y - \hat{y})^2$
13.7	Computational formula for SSE	$SSE = \Sigma y^2 - b_0\Sigma y - b_1\Sigma xy$
13.8	Standard error of the estimate (s_e)	$s_e = \sqrt{\dfrac{SSE}{n-2}}$
13.9	Coefficient of determination	$r^2 = 1 - \dfrac{SSE}{SS_{yy}} = 1 - \dfrac{SSE}{\Sigma y^2 - \frac{(\Sigma y)^2}{n}}$
13.10	Computational formula for r^2	$r^2 = \dfrac{b_1^2 SS_{xx}}{SS_{yy}}$
13.11	*t* test of slope	$t = \dfrac{b_1 - \beta_1}{s_b}$ $s_b = \dfrac{s_e}{\sqrt{SS_{xx}}}$
13.12	Confidence interval to estimate $E(y_x)$ for a given value of *x*	$\hat{y} \pm t_{\alpha/2,\,n-2}\, s_e \sqrt{\dfrac{1}{n} + \dfrac{(x_0 - \bar{x})^2}{SS_{xx}}}$
13.13	Prediction interval to estimate *y* for a given value of *x*	$\hat{y} \pm t_{\alpha/2,\,n-2}\, s_e \sqrt{1 + \dfrac{1}{n} + \dfrac{(x_0 - \bar{x})^2}{SS_{xx}}}$

REVIEW PROBLEMS

Calculating the statistics

P13-39 **13.39** Use Excel or a calculator to complete parts (a) to (f) for the following data.

x	7	9	2	18	13	8
y	10	11	13	32	16	14

a. Determine the equation of the least squares regression line to predict y using x.
b. Obtain the predicted values of y and the residuals.
c. Find the value of s_e and interpret it with respect to the regression assumptions.
d. Find the value of r^2.
e. Test the slope of the regression line. Use $\alpha = .05$.
f. Comment on the results determined in parts (b) to (e), and make a statement about the fit of the line.

P13-40 **13.40** Use Excel and the following data for parts (a) to (g).

x	56	48	39	53	62	65	48	64
y	7	9	6	3	12	14	4	13

a. Determine the equation of the simple regression line to predict y from x.
b. Obtain the predicted values of y and the residuals.
c. Find the value of SSE.
d. Obtain the standard error of the estimate.
e. Obtain the coefficient of determination.
f. Test the slope of the regression line. Assume $\alpha = .05$. What do you conclude about the slope?
g. Comment on parts (d) and (e).

P13-41 **13.41** If you were to develop a regression line to predict y using x, what value would the coefficient of determination have?

x	213	196	184	202	221	247
y	76	65	62	68	71	75

P13-42 **13.42** Obtain the equation of the least squares regression line to predict y from the following data.

x	47	94	68	73	80	49	52	61
y	14	40	34	31	36	19	20	21

a. Construct a 95% confidence interval to estimate the mean y value for $x = 60$.
b. Construct a 95% prediction interval to estimate an individual y value for $x = 70$.
c. Interpret the results obtained in parts (a) and (b).

Testing your understanding

P13-43 **13.43** A manager of a car dealership believes there is a relationship between the number of salespeople on duty and the number of cars sold. Suppose the following sample is used to develop a simple regression model to predict the number of cars sold using the number of salespeople. Obtain the value of r^2 and explain what r^2 means in this problem.

Week	Number of cars sold	Number of salespeople
1	79	6
2	64	6
3	49	4
4	23	2
5	52	3

P13-44 **13.44** A social scientist wanted to conduct research on whether having a university degree and staying in university longer meant that having children is postponed. The researcher obtained the following data.

Education	Age when first child was born
12 years	19
10 years	16
15 years	26
16 years	28
15 years	25
20 years	34
16 years	31
15 years	23
12 years	20
20 years	32
15 years	24
15 years	22
16 years	29
12 years	21
16 years	28
20 years	33
11 years	17
16 years	28

Develop a regression model to predict the number of children using years of education. Comment on the output.

P13-45 **13.45** You are the manager of a removalists company, and you want to develop a more accurate way of predicting the labour requirements for moving jobs. You decide to use the volume of goods (in cubic metres) that is being moved. You have the following data from the last 10 moves. Calculate the regression model for predicting the number of hours needed based on the volume of goods to be moved. Does the prediction seem plausible?

Hours	Cubic metres moved
18	60
14	40
27	90
9	20
22	70
15	34
18	56
15	42
4	10
14	39

13.46 Using the regression model developed in problem 13.45, predict the average labour hours for a moving job that consists of 90 square metres.

P13-47 **13.47** People in the aerospace industry believe that the cost of a space project is a function of the weight of the object being sent into space. Use the following data to develop a regression model to predict the cost of a space project using the weight of the space object. Determine the r^2 and s_e.

Weight (tonnes)	Cost ($ million)
1.897	53.6
3.019	184.9
0.453	6.4
0.988	23.5
1.058	33.4
2.100	110.4
2.387	104.6

13.48 People involved in the tourism industry are interested in many aspects of tourist behaviour. An aspect that may be of interest is whether there is a relationship between demand for tourists, as measured by the number of guest nights stayed, and the number of tourist accommodation establishments. Using the following data provided by Statistics New Zealand, develop a model to predict the number of guest establishments using the number of guest nights stayed. Interpret the slope and intercept of the model. Do they make sense? What do the p-value and r^2 suggest about the strength of the relationship? Suppose that there is a serious health scare in New Zealand and, as a result, guest nights stayed fall dramatically to 500 while number of guest establishments decreases slightly to 3850. If this extra observation is included in the estimation sample, how are the SSE, standard error and slope term affected? Is the new model appropriate for predicting the number of guest establishments? Why or why not?

Month	Number of establishments	Guest nights ('000)
Jan.	3863	4364
Feb.	3876	3493
Mar.	3877	3399
Apr.	3860	2814
May	3780	1942
June	3713	1809
July	3686	2205
Aug.	3723	2131
Sept.	3790	2286
Oct.	3878	2439
Nov.	3937	2795
Dec.	3970	3239

13.49 For the first regression model developed in problem 13.48, obtain the values of s_e and r^2. Assuming $\alpha = .05$, test the slope of the regression line. If the number of guest nights was 7500 (thousand) predict the number of establishments. Would you have any qualms in reporting this prediction to members of the New Zealand tourist industry?

13.50 Nowadays, there is a wide range of digital cameras available with many different features and price tags. The following table lists the prices and effective megapixels of some of these cameras. Suppose a potential buyer is interested in finding out if there is a positive relationship between effective megapixels and price. Using these data, perform a simple regression analysis to predict the price of a digital camera using the number of effective megapixels. Interpret the slope term and state whether it is consistent with the buyer's prior belief. Discuss the r^2 and s_e. Several of these cameras have a resolution of 10 effective megapixels, but their price varies significantly from $999 to $2199. Provide an intuitive explanation as to why this might be the case.

Model	Price ($)	Effective megapixels
Canon PowerShot S5IS	599	8
Canon EQS 400 D + 18–55 mm EFS	1199	10.1
Canon EQS 400 D + 17–85 mm EFS IS USM	2799	10.1
Fujifilm Finepix S8000fd	649	8
Kodak Easyshare ZD170	299	7.1
Nikon D80 DX 18–70 mm	2198	10
Nikon D40x Kit DX 18–55 mm EDII	999	10
Olympus E-140 Kit + 14–42 mm ED	999	10
Olympus E-510 Kit + 14–42 mm ED	1299	10
Olympus SP-560UZ	599	8
Panasonic Lumix DMC–L10 + Leica D14–50 mm	2199	10
Panasonic Lumix DMC-FZ18	769	8
Sony Alpha DSLR-A700 + 18–70 mm DT	2399	12.2

13.51 Study the following regression analysis to predict y using x.

a. What is the equation of the regression model?
b. What is the meaning of the coefficient of x?
c. What is the result of the test of the slope of the regression model? Let $\alpha = .10$. Why is the t statistic negative?
d. Comment on r^2 and the standard error of the estimate.
e. The correlation coefficient for these two variables is −.7918. Is this result surprising to you? Why or why not?

Regression analysis: y versus x

The regression equation is:
$y = 67.2 - 0.0565x$

Predictor	*Coef*	*SE Coef*	*t*	*p*
Constant	67.231	5.046	13.32	0.000
x	−0.05650	0.01027	−5.50	0.000

$S = 10.32$ $r^2 = 62.7\%$ $r^2(\text{adj}) = 60.6\%$

Analysis of variance

Source	*df*	*SS*	*MS*	*F*	*p*
Regression	1	3222.9	3222.9	30.25	0.000
Residual Error	18	1918.0	106.6		
Total	19	5141.0			

13.52 Study the following residual diagnostic graph. Comment on any possible violations of regression assumptions.

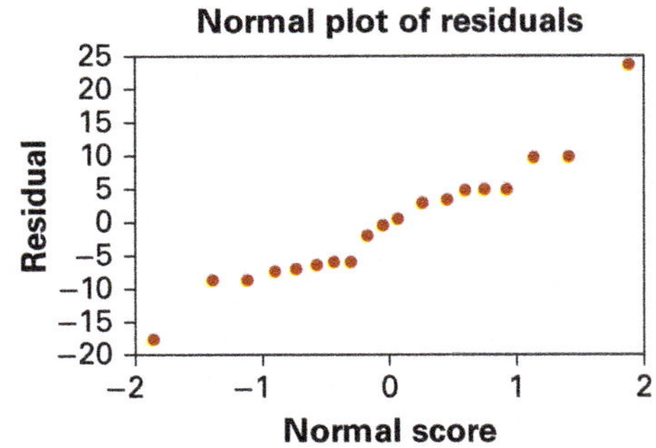

CHAPTER

14 Multiple regression analysis

LEARNING OBJECTIVES

After studying this chapter, you should be able to:

1. develop a multiple regression model using computer software
2. understand and apply significance tests appropriate to regression analysis; that is, the regression model and its coefficients
3. compute and interpret residuals, the standard error of the estimate and the coefficient of multiple determination
4. interpret multiple regression computer output.

OPENING VIGNETTE

Video gaming and gambling in Australian adolescents

Many young Australians like playing video games. However, research by Delfabbro, King, Lambos and Puglies in the *Journal of Gambling Studies* has discovered a link between video games and gaming machines.

In their study, 2669 teenagers between the ages of 13 and 17 were surveyed to obtain details of their involvement in video gaming and gambling. Even though the legal age for gambling in Australia is 18, the study found that 50–60% of young people aged between 15 and 17 gamble at least once per year, and the most popular activities are gambling on sports events and lottery products through online gambling websites, as well as virtual online casinos. The theory behind the study was that video games, gaming machines and online gambling sites all share a number of common characteristics:

- providing an interaction between players and technology
- maintaining patterns of reinforcement through punishment and rewards.

Griffiths (1995) argued that players of video games and gamblers also share a similar philosophy of remaining on their respective machine for as long as possible without losing.

Participants in the survey were asked how often they had engaged in each of the major forms of gambling during the past 12 months. The results were that 56.3% of those surveyed had gambled during the past 12 months, with boys at 61% more likely to gamble than girls at 51.7%.

Further multiple regression analyses were undertaken to examine whether pathological gambling was related to the frequency of video game playing after controlling for the influence of gender. In these analyses, gender was entered on the first step and the frequency was entered on the second. Each person's pathological gambling score was the dependent measure. It was discovered that the frequency with which young people played video games was only slightly related to their pathological gambling scores.

However, when the link between high-frequency video game playing and gambling was examined, it was found to be stronger.

Introduction

Simple regression analysis is known as bivariate linear regression, in which one dependent variable, y, is predicted using one independent variable, x. Examples of simple regression applications include models to predict retail sales using population density, crude oil production using energy consumption, or house price using the street rating. However, in many cases, other independent variables, taken in conjunction with these variables, can make the regression model a better fit in predicting the dependent variable. For example, retail sales could be predicted using the size of the store and the number of competitors, in addition to population density. A model to predict share price index could include, in addition to the prime interest rate, such predictors as yesterday's volume, the bond interest rate and the producer price index. A model to predict house prices could include the size of the house, the number of bedrooms, or whether it is one or two storeys.

As in simple regression, each of these examples still contains only one dependent variable, y: sales, share price index or house price. However, we now include multiple independent variables, x (predictors). *Regression analysis with two or more independent variables* is called **multiple regression** analysis.

CHAPTER CASE

Predicting the prices of houses in Baycoast: using additional variables

The principals at Baycoast City Real Estate Agents (BCREA) were pleased with the initial investigation of the relationship between the prices of houses in the Baycoast area and the street rating. The consultancy confirmed the principals' view that the quality of the street in which a house was located significantly influenced the price of the house. They reported that just over 52% of the variability of the prices of houses in Baycoast could be explained by the variability in the rating of the street. They also pointed out that this meant that about 48% of price variability remained unexplained. The BCREA principals have now asked the consultant to investigate which variables would explain most of this 48% unexplained variability. In particular, they have asked the consultant to concentrate, in addition to street rating, on the size or area of the house; whether the house is one or two storeys; whether the house has a good view of the bay; and the lot size.

Questions to help managers make decisions

BCREA-14

1. Several variables are presented that may be related to house prices. Which variables are strong predictors of house prices? Are the variables chosen by the estate agents the most suitable?
2. Is it possible to develop a valid mathematical model to predict house prices using the data given? If so, how strong is the model? With five independent variables, will we need to develop five different simple regression models and compare their results?

14.1 The multiple regression model

Multiple regression analysis is similar in principle to simple regression analysis. However, it is more complex conceptually and computationally. As with simple linear regression, here we are concerned only with models that are linear in the parameters. The equation of the probabilistic simple regression model is:

$$y = \beta_0 + \beta_1 x + \varepsilon$$

where:

y = the value of the dependent variable
β_0 = the population y intercept
β_1 = the population slope
ε = the error of prediction

Extending this notion to multiple regression gives the general equation for the probabilistic multiple regression model:

$$y = \beta_0 + \beta_1 x_1 + \beta_2 x_2 + \beta_3 x_3 + \cdots + \beta_k x_k + \varepsilon$$

where:

y = the value of the dependent variable
β_0 = the regression constant, or population y intercept
β_1 = the partial regression coefficient for independent variable 1
β_2 = the partial regression coefficient for independent variable 2
β_3 = the partial regression coefficient for independent variable 3
β_k = the partial regression coefficient for independent variable k
k = the number of independent variables
ε = the error of prediction (also known as the residual)

In multiple regression analysis, the dependent variable, y, is sometimes referred to as the **response variable**. The **partial regression coefficient** of an independent variable, β_j, *represents the increase that will occur in the value of y from a one-unit increase in that independent variable if all other variables in the regression are held constant*. The full (versus partial) regression coefficient of an independent variable is a coefficient obtained from the bivariate model (simple regression) in which the independent variable is the sole predictor of y. The partial regression coefficients occur because more than one predictor is included in a model.

In reality, the partial regression coefficients and the regression constant of a multiple regression model are population values and are unknown. In virtually all research, these values are estimated by using sample information (as we saw in simple regression). Shown here is the form of the equation for estimating y with sample information:

$$\hat{y} = b_0 + b_1 x_1 + b_2 x_2 + b_3 x_3 + \cdots + b_k x_k$$

where:

$\hat{y}$ = the predicted value of y
b_0 = the estimate of the regression constant
b_1 = the estimate of regression coefficient 1
b_2 = the estimate of regression coefficient 2
b_3 = the estimate of regression coefficient 3
b_k = the estimate of regression coefficient k
k = the number of independent variables

Multiple regression model with two independent variables (first-order)

Initially, we shall examine a multiple regression model containing only two independent variables. The population model is given as:

$$y = \beta_0 + \beta_1 x_1 + \beta_2 x_2 + \varepsilon$$

The constant and coefficients are estimated from sample information, resulting in the following sample model.

$$\hat{y} = b_0 + b_1 x_1 + b_2 x_2$$

Given one dependent variable and one independent variable, simple regression models yield a line of best fit through data points in the xy plane. In multiple regression analysis, the resulting model produces a response surface. Thus, with two first-order independent variables plus the dependent variable, the response surface is a response plane in a three-dimensional space (x_1, x_2, y).

Figure 14.1 is a three-dimensional graph of a series of points (x_1, x_2, y) representing values from three variables used in a multiple regression model to predict the price of a house using the number of square metres in the house and the age of the house.

If a response plane is fitted to the points shown in figure 14.1, the result is the graph in figure 14.2. Notice that most of the points are not on the plane, just as in simple regression, where not all the points lie on the line. As in simple regression, in multiple regression, errors in the fit of the model are usually present. The distances shown in the graph from the points to the response plane are the errors of fit, or residuals $(y-\hat{y})$. Multiple regression models with three or more independent variables involve more than three dimensions and cannot be depicted graphically. Notice that the plane, in this case, intercepts the y axis.

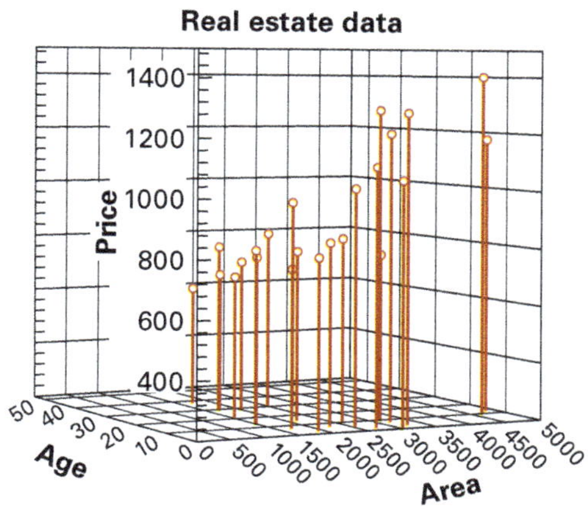

FIGURE 14.1 Points in a sample space

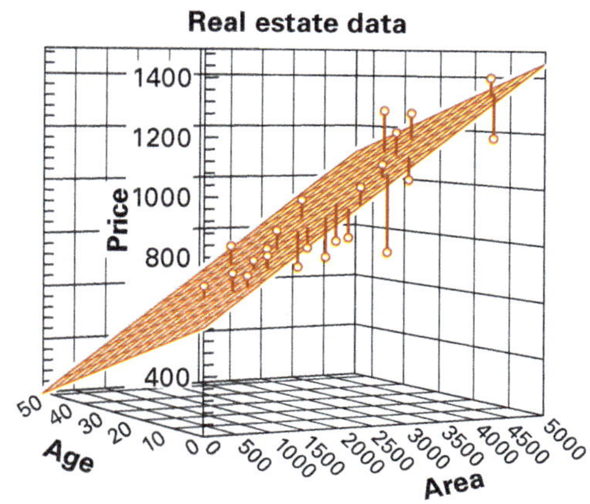

FIGURE 14.2 Response plane for a first-order, two-predictor multiple regression model

Determining the multiple regression equation

The simple regression equations for determining the sample slope and intercept are the result of using methods of calculus to minimise the sum of squares of error for the regression model. The procedure for developing these equations involves solving two simultaneous equations with two unknowns, b_0 and b_1. Finding the sample slope and intercept from these formulas requires the values of Σx, Σy, Σxy and Σx^2. Of course, even for simple regression, we would rarely, if ever, undertake these calculations manually.

The procedure for determining formulas to solve for multiple regression coefficients is similar. The formulas are established to meet an objective of *minimising the sum of squares of error for the model.* Hence, the regression analysis shown here is again referred to as least squares analysis. Methods of calculus are applied, resulting in $k+1$ equations with $k+1$ unknowns (b_0 and k values of b_j) for multiple regression analyses with k independent variables. Thus, a regression model with six independent variables will generate seven simultaneous equations with seven unknowns (b_0, b_1, b_2, b_3, b_4, b_5 and b_6).

For multiple regression models with two independent variables, the result is three simultaneous equations with three unknowns (b_0, b_1 and b_2).

$$b_0 n + b_1\Sigma x_1 + b_2\Sigma x_2 = \Sigma y$$
$$b_0\Sigma x_1 + b_1\Sigma x_1{}^2 + b_2\Sigma x_1 x_2 = \Sigma x_1 y$$
$$b_0\Sigma x_2 + b_1\Sigma x_1 x_2 + b_2\Sigma x_2{}^2 = \Sigma x_2 y$$

We stress that the process of solving these equations by hand is tedious and time consuming. Solving for the regression coefficients and regression constant in a multiple regression model with two independent variables requires Σx_1, Σx_2, Σy, $\Sigma x_1{}^2$, $\Sigma x_2{}^2$, $\Sigma x_1 x_2$, $\Sigma x_1 y$ and $\Sigma x_2 y$. In fact, these equations would be presented in matrix form and would be solved using matrix algebra. All business researchers use software to solve for the regression coefficients, the regression constant and other pertinent information. In this chapter, we will discuss computer output and assume little or no hand calculation. The emphasis will be on interpretation of the computer output.

USING EXCEL

A multiple regression model using Excel

The real estate study conducted in the city of Baycoast sought to determine which variables, if any, are related to the market price of a house in Baycoast. Several variables were explored, including the number of bedrooms, the number of bathrooms, the age of the house, the number of square metres of living space, the total number of square metres of space, the street rating, and the extent of the view of the bay. Suppose the researcher wants to develop a regression model to predict the market price of a house using just two variables: the age of the house and the street rating. The data for these three variables are contained in the file MR14-01.xls on the student website.

A number of statistical software packages can perform multiple regression analysis, including Excel.

MR14-01

1. Access MR14-01.xls from the student website.
2. From the Data tab, select Data Analysis.
3. From the Data Analysis dialogue box, select Regression and click OK.
4. In the Input Y Range field, enter the data range for Price ($'000), B1:B121.
5. In the Input X Range field, enter the data for both Age and Street, C1:D121.
6. Check Labels.
7. In Output options, choose New Worksheet Ply, and click OK.

The output for the Excel multiple regression analysis on the real estate data is given in figure 14.3.

	A	B	C	D	E	F	G
1	SUMMARY OUTPUT						
2							
3	*Regression Statistics*						
4	Multiple R	0.84730908					
5	R Square	0.71793269					
6	Adjusted R Square	0.71311102					
7	Standard Error	174.047988					
8	Observations	120					
9							
10	ANOVA						
11		*df*	*SS*	*MS*	*F*	*Significance F*	
12	Regression	2	9021003	4510502	148.8973	7.00869E–33	
13	Residual	117	3544246	30292.7			
14	Total	119	12565249				
15							
16		*Coefficients*	*Standard Error*	*t Stat*	*P-value*	*Lower 95%*	*Upper 95%*
17	Intercept	381.503485	54.9573	6.941817	2.31E-10	272.6634412	490.3435
18	Age	–14.7072765	1.631854	–9.01262	4.57E-15	–17.9390785	–11.4755
19	Street	130.297792	8.35865	15.58838	2.49E-30	113.7439241	146.8517

FIGURE 14.3 Excel output of regression for the real estate example

From figure 14.3, the regression equation for the real estate data in MR14-01.xls is:

$$\hat{y} = 381.503 - 14.707(\text{Age}) + 130.298(\text{Street})$$

The regression constant, 381.503, is the y intercept. The y intercept is the value of $\hat{y}$ if both x_1 (Age) and x_2 (Street) are zero. In this example, a practical interpretation of the y intercept is meaningless. It makes little sense to say that a house of zero age ($x_1 = 0$) and a zero street rating ($x_2 = 0$) would cost, on average, $381 503! This is another example of the intercept having no practical meaning if the original data do not include the origin.

The coefficient of x_1 (Age) is −14.707. The negative sign on the coefficient denotes an inverse relationship between the age of a house and the price of the house; in general, the older the house, the lower the price. Thus, a one-unit increase in age (one year) would result in a predicted decrease, on average, of 14.707 × $1000 = $14 707 in the price of the house, if street rating was held constant.

The coefficient of x_2 (Street) is 130.298. In this case, if the age of the house is kept constant, a one-unit increase in the street rating of the house will result in an increase, on average, of $130.298 × $1000 = $130 298 in the price.

In examining the regression coefficients, it is important to remember that the independent variables are often measured in different units. It is not wise to compare the regression coefficients of predictors in a multiple regression model and decide that the variable with the largest regression coefficient is the best predictor. In this example, the two variables are in different units, years and a unit of rating. Just because x_2 (Street) has the larger coefficient (130.298) does not necessarily make x_2 the stronger predictor of y.

The remaining portion of the computer output is discussed in section 14.2.

This regression model can be used to predict the price of a house in Baycoast. If the house is 10 years old and the street in which it is located has a rating of 6, then $x_1 = 10$ and $x_2 = 6$. Substituting these values into the regression model yields:

$$\begin{aligned}\hat{y} &= 381.503 - 14.707x_1 + 130.298x_2 \\ &= 381.503 - 14.707(10) + 130.298(6) = 1\,016\,221\end{aligned}$$

The predicted price of a house with these x values is $1 016 221, on average.

DEMONSTRATION PROBLEM 14.1

We have met the company Combaro Ltd before. It is based in Sydney, New South Wales, and is a subsidiary of a major Australian bank. It was established to provide low-cost loans for housing and other purposes, in competition with other low-cost lending institutions in Australia. Costs are contained by eliminating all face-to-face contact between Combaro staff and loan applicants. Instead, all applications are made online and all communication is by the internet, email, fax, letter or telephone.

The new enterprise bargaining agreement, which was implemented at the beginning of the last financial year, has now been in place for just over twelve months. A key feature of the agreement was the introduction of productivity performance measures. At the beginning of the year, each employee, in consultation with their manager, agrees to a set number of completed loans for the coming year, consistent with their position and experience. Their performance is measured as actual completed loans as a percentage of the agreed number. Thus, if they meet their agreed goal, their performance is 100%.

At the end of the just-completed financial year, a review of the productivity performance program was undertaken. A random sample survey of 48 of the company's full-time employees, which included results on a number of relevant variables, was completed. Initially, the company was interested in whether the amount of unpaid overtime and job satisfaction could be influencing productivity. The data for productivity, job satisfaction and unpaid overtime are contained in the file DP14-01.xls on the student website.

USING EXCEL

Multiple regression

DP14-01

Develop a multiple regression model and determine the expected productivity if job satisfaction (JobSat) is 12 and unpaid overtime (UOvTime) is 9. The following output shows the results of analysing the data by using the regression function of Excel, applying the procedure described in the previous Baycoast example. (Remember now to include both JobSat and UOvTime in the *x* range.)

	A	B	C	D	E	F	G
1	SUMMARY OUTPUT						
2							
3	*Regression Statistics*						
4	Multiple R	0.803087					
5	R Square	0.644948					
6	Adjusted R Square	0.629168					
7	Standard Error	2.835225					
8	Observations	48					
9							
10	ANOVA						
11		*df*	*SS*	*MS*	*F*	*Significance F*	
12	Regression	2	657.0842	328.5421	40.87107	7.61E-11	
13	Residual	45	361.7325	8.038499			
14	Total	47	1018.817				
15							
16		*Coefficients*	*Standard Error*	*t Stat*	*P-value*	*Lower 95%*	*Upper 95%*
17	Intercept	116.3905	5.24192	22.2038	7.01E-26	105.8328	126.9483
18	JobSat	–0.53301	0.280837	–1.89794	0.06413	–1.09864	0.032624
19	UOvTime	–1.47607	0.228269	–6.46636	6.33E-08	–1.93583	–1.01631

The regression equation is:

$$\hat{y} = 116.39 - 0.53(\text{JobSat}) - 1.47(\text{UOvTime})$$

where:

$\hat{y}$ = predicted productivity

The model indicates that, for every unit increase in job satisfaction rating (unpaid overtime being held constant), productivity reduces on average by 0.53 percentage points. This is an unexpected result: the more satisfied an employee is, the lower their productivity! As this result is counterintuitive, we would seek to investigate it in detail; however, this investigation requires a discussion of multicollinearity which is beyond the scope of this chapter. For each unit increase in unpaid overtime (one hour), productivity decreases by 1.47 percentage points. The inverse direction of this relationship is expected.

If job satisfaction is 15 and unpaid overtime is 4, the predicted productivity is given as:

$$\hat{y} = 116.39 - 0.53(12) - 1.47(9) = 96.8$$

Checking employee number 19, whose job satisfaction is 12 and unpaid overtime is 9, we see that the observed productivity (Prdtvty) is 96.6 compared with the predicted value of 96.8. This emphasises that regression is a predictive model, even though some relationships may be counterintuitive.

PRACTICE PROBLEMS

Practising the calculations

P14-01 **14.1** Use computer software to develop the equation of the regression model for the following data. Comment on the regression coefficients. Determine the predicted value of y for $x_1 = 200$ and $x_2 = 7$.

y	x_1	x_2
15	165	4
17	275	8
32	179	5
25	212	6
54	165	7
45	192	14
32	232	4
31	156	12
42	162	7
15	136	4

P14-02 **14.2** Use computer software to develop the equation of the regression model for the following data. Comment on the regression coefficients. Determine the predicted value of y for $x_1 = 33$, $x_2 = 29$ and $x_3 = 13$.

y	x_1	x_2	x_3
114	21	6	5
94	43	25	8
87	56	42	25
98	19	27	9
101	29	20	12
85	34	45	21
94	40	33	14
107	32	14	11
119	16	4	7
93	18	31	16
108	27	12	10
117	31	3	8

14.3 Using the following information, write the equation of the regression model. How many independent variables are there? Comment on the meaning of these regression coefficients.

Predictor	Coefficient
Constant	121.62
x_1	−0.174
x_2	6.02
x_3	0.00026
x_4	0.0041

Testing your understanding

14.4 Use the following information to determine the equation of the multiple regression model. Comment on the regression coefficients. Interpret the coefficients.

Predictor	Coefficient
Constant	31409.5
x_1	0.08425
x_2	289.62
x_3	−0.0947

Combaro **14.5** Use the data file Combaro.xls to complete the following exercises. Determine whether the relationship between productivity (Prdtvty) and days absent (DysAbsnt) is linear. Develop a regression model for productivity using days absent, job satisfaction (JobSat) and unpaid overtime (UOvTime). Is this a valid model? If not, why? Now include a new variable in the data set. Head this variable 'Days absent squared'. Obtain the data for this column by squaring the corresponding entry for 'Days absent'. (Do this for the first entry and simply copy down.) Rerun the regression with the previous three independent variables plus the new variable 'Days absent squared'. Check the t statistics and the p-values for all four independent variables. Based on the p-values, comment on the validity of the model.

P14-06 **14.6** Jensen, Solberg and Zorn investigated the relationship between insider ownership, debt and dividend policies in companies. One of their findings was that companies with high insider ownership choose lower levels of both debt and dividends. The following is a sample of data of these three variables for 11 different industries. Use the data to develop the equation of the regression model to predict insider ownership (expressed as a percentage) using debt ratio and dividend payout. Comment on the regression coefficients.

Industry	Insider ownership	Debt ratio	Dividend payout
Mining	8.2	14.2	10.4
Food and beverage	18.4	20.8	14.3
Furniture	11.8	18.6	12.1
Publishing	28.0	18.5	11.8
Petroleum refining	7.4	28.2	10.6
Glass and cement	15.4	24.7	12.6
Motor vehicle	15.7	15.6	12.6
Department store	18.4	21.7	7.2
Restaurant	13.4	23.0	11.3
Amusement	18.1	46.7	4.1
Hospital	10.0	35.8	9.0

14.2 Significance tests of the regression model and its coefficients

Multiple regression models can be developed to fit almost any statistical data set if the level of measurement is adequate and enough data points are available. Once a model has been constructed, it is important to test the model to determine whether it is a valid model — that is, whether the assumptions underlying regression analysis are met and whether it fits the data well. Assessing the validity of the regression model is undertaken by testing the overall significance of the model, studying the significance tests of the regression coefficients, analysing the residuals, examining the standard error of the estimate and observing the coefficient of determination. In this section, we examine an overall significance test of the regression model and a significance test of the individual coefficients. The other concepts are covered in section 14.3; residual analysis is pertinent to testing whether the assumptions of regression are met, and to do this we examine various graphs associated with the residuals.

Testing the overall model

With simple regression, a *t* test of the slope of the regression line is used to determine whether the population slope of the regression line is different from zero — that is, whether the independent variable contributes significantly to linearly predicting the dependent variable. The hypotheses for this test are:

$$H_0\text{: } \beta_1 = 0$$
$$H_a\text{: } \beta_1 \neq 0$$

The null hypothesis is rejected if the *p*-value is less than the critical alpha value (generally .05).

For multiple regression, an analogous test makes use of the *F* statistic. The overall significance of the multiple regression model is now tested with the following hypotheses.

$$H_0\text{: } \beta_1 = \beta_2 = \beta_3 = \ldots = \beta_k = 0\text{; all the population regression coefficients are zero}$$
$$H_a\text{: At least one of the population regression coefficients is} \neq 0$$

If we fail to reject the null hypothesis, we are stating that the regression model as a whole has no significant predictability for the dependent variable. A rejection of the null hypothesis indicates that at least one of the independent variables explains part of the variability in the dependent variable *y*.

This *F* test of overall significance is often printed as a part of the standard multiple regression output from statistical software packages. In Excel, the *F* test output appears in the analysis of variance (ANOVA) table. Shown here is the ANOVA table for the real estate example taken from the Excel output in figure 14.3 (p. 484).

	A	B	C	D	E	F
10	ANOVA					
11		*df*	*SS*	*MS*	*F*	*Significance F*
12	Regression	2	9021003	4510502	148.8973	7.00869E–33
13	Residual	117	3544246	30292.7		
14	Total	119	12565249			

The *F* value is 148.897 and $p = 7.00869 \times 10^{-33}$ (found under *Significance F* in the Excel output). Therefore, the *F* value is significant at $\alpha = .05$ (because $7.00869 \times 10^{-33} < .05$). The null hypothesis is therefore rejected, and we conclude that there is at least one significant predictor of house price in this analysis.

The ***F* value** is calculated by the following equation.

The *F* value
(14.1)

$$F = \frac{MS_{reg}}{MS_{err}} = \frac{\frac{SS_{reg}}{df_{reg}}}{\frac{SS_{err}}{df_{err}}} = \frac{\frac{SSR}{k}}{\frac{SSE}{n-k-1}}$$

where:

MS = mean square of either the regression (reg) or the residual (err)
SS = sum of squares of either the regression (reg) or the residual (err)
df = degrees of freedom of either the regression (reg) or the residual (err)
SSR = sum of squares of regression
k = number of independent variables (not the constant term)
SSE = error sum of squares
n = number of observations

Note that, in the ANOVA table for the real estate example, $df_{reg} = 2$. The degrees of freedom formula for regression is given by k: that is, the total number of independent (or x) variables. Note that k does not include the constant term. The real estate example uses two independent variables, so $k = 2$. Degrees of freedom error (residual) in multiple regression is given by the total number of observations minus the *total* number of regression coefficients estimated, or $n - k - 1$ (−1 refers to the estimated constant). For the real estate example, $n = 120$; thus, $df_{err} = 120 - 2 - 1 = 117$.

$MS = \frac{SS}{df}$. The F ratio is formed by dividing MS_{reg} by MS_{err}. In using the F distribution table to determine a critical value against which to test the observed F value, the degrees of freedom numerator is df_{reg} and the degrees of freedom denominator is df_{err}. The table F value is obtained in the usual manner. With $\alpha = .05$ for the real estate example, the critical value is (from the F table):

$$F_{.05,\,2,\,117} = 3.07$$

Comparing the observed F of 148.90 with this table value shows that the observed value lies in the rejection region; hence, our decision is to reject the null hypothesis. This same conclusion was reached above using the p-value method from the computer output (in the Excel regression output, the p-value for the F ratio is found under *Significance F*). It is much quicker and easier to use this p-value and compare it with our chosen value of α. Often we use $\alpha = .05$. If the p-value is less than α, we reject the null hypothesis.

If a regression model has only one linear independent variable, it is a simple regression model. In that case, the F test for the overall model is the same as the t test for significance of the population slope. The F value displayed in the regression ANOVA table is related to the t test for the slope in the simple regression case as follows.

$$F = t^2$$

In simple regression, the F value and the t value give equivalent information about the overall test of the model.

Most researchers who use multiple regression analysis will observe the value of F and its p-value rather early in the process. If F is not significant, then no population regression coefficient is significantly different from zero, and the regression model has no predictability for the dependent variable. That is, taken together, the x variables are not useful in predicting y.

Why do we use the F test when we can complete a series of t tests on the multiple coefficients? The F test combines all the t tests into a single test. The advantage of a single test is that the probability of a Type I error is controlled. If the t test for each population coefficient uses an α value of .05, then the probability of not making a Type I error is .95 for each individual coefficient. The probability of a Type I error for two coefficients combined is .9025 (= .95 × .95). Thus the probability of making a Type I error is 1 – .9025 = .0975, not .05 as we might expect. Clearly, this probability increases with the number of independent variables. For four independent variables, the probability of making a Type I error is .186.

To summarise, the *F* test is an efficient method of testing whether at least one population coefficient is non-zero.

Significance tests of the regression coefficients

Having completed the *F* test, and concluded that at least one variable in the model is useful, individual significance tests can be computed for each regression coefficient using a *t* test. Each of these *t* tests is analogous to the *t* test for the slope used for simple regression analysis. The hypotheses for testing the regression coefficient of each independent variable take the following form:

$$\begin{aligned} &H_0\text{: } \beta_1 = 0 \\ &H_a\text{: } \beta_1 \neq 0 \\ &H_0\text{: } \beta_2 = 0 \\ &H_a\text{: } \beta_2 \neq 0 \\ &H_0\text{: } \beta_k = 0 \\ &H_a\text{: } \beta_k \neq 0 \end{aligned}$$

Most multiple regression computer packages yield observed *t* values and *p*-values to test the individual regression coefficients as standard output. Shown here are the *t* values and their associated probabilities for the real estate example as displayed with the multiple regression output in figure 14.3.

	A	B	C	D	E
16		*Coefficients*	*Standard Error*	*t Stat*	*P-value*
17	Intercept	381.503485	54.9573	6.941817	2.31E–10
18	Age	–14.7072765	1.631854	–9.01262	4.57E–15
19	Street	130.297792	8.35865	15.58838	2.49E–30

At $\alpha = .05$, the null hypothesis is rejected for both variables because the probabilities (*p*-values) associated with their *t* values are less than .05. If the *t* statistic for any predictor variable is not significant (fail to reject the null hypothesis), the researcher would generally decide to drop that variable from the analysis as a nonsignificant predictor. Other factors can enter into this decision. There are also techniques for model building in which some variable sorting is required. It is worth noting, again, in the above regression output that the *t* statistic for each variable is equal to the coefficient divided by the standard error (as the hypothesised β value is 0).

The degrees of freedom for each of these individual *t* tests of regression coefficients is $n - k - 1$. In this particular example, because there are $k = 2$ predictor variables, the degrees of freedom is $120 - 2 - 1 = 117$. With $\alpha = .05$ and a two-tailed test (H_a: $\beta_j \neq 0$), the critical table *t* value is:

$$t_{.025,\,117} = \pm 1.98$$

Notice from the *t* ratios shown here that, if this critical table *t* value had been used as the hypothesis test criterion instead of the *p*-value method, the results would have been exactly the same. As a rough rule of thumb, if the *t* statistic is greater than 2, we would reject the null hypothesis (that the population independent variable was zero) at the .05 level of significance, and we would retain the independent variable in the regression. Again, it is usually much quicker to examine the p-values given in the output, as it is only necessary to check the p-values to see if they are above or below our chosen level of α; thus, if the p-value is below .05, you will generally find that the t statistic is 2 or more.

Note that Excel, as in the simple linear regression case, also calculates 95% confidence intervals for the estimated coefficients. These can be used in an identical manner as before, either as an alternative way to undertake hypothesis testing, or to provide the researcher with a likely range for the true population parameters, β_j.

PRACTICE PROBLEMS

Testing your understanding

14.7 Examine the Excel output shown here for a multiple regression analysis. How many predictors were there in this model? Comment on the overall significance of the regression model. Discuss the t ratios of the variables and their significance. Check the value of the t statistic for x_1 by manually calculating its value using the values of the coefficient and standard error provided in the table.

	A	B	C	D	E	F	G
1	SUMMARY OUTPUT						
2							
3	*Regression Statistics*						
4	Multiple R	0.741094					
5	R Square	0.549221					
6	Adjusted R Square	–0.35234					
7	Standard Error	2.392676					
8	Observations	10					
9							
10	ANOVA						
11		*df*	*SS*	*MS*	*F*	*Significance F*	
12	Regression	6	20.9253	3.487551	0.60919	0.723165	
13	Residual	3	17.1747	5.724898			
14	Total	9	38.1				
15							
16		*Coefficients*	*Standard Error*	*t Stat*	*P-value*	*Lower 95%*	*Upper 95%*
17	Intercept	–1.51951	3.763797	–0.40372	0.713474	–13.4976	10.45857
18	x1	0.409499	0.550443	0.743944	0.51088	–1.34226	2.161255
19	x2	0.527065	0.384211	1.371812	0.263709	–0.69566	1.749795
20	x3	0.288756	0.34776	0.830332	0.467255	–0.81797	1.395484
21	x4	–0.15804	0.391381	–0.4038	0.713419	–1.40359	1.08751
22	x5	–0.01265	0.371167	–0.03409	0.974946	–1.19387	1.168567
23	x6	0.165942	0.273952	0.605735	0.587447	–0.7059	1.037781

14.8 Following is the Excel output for a multiple regression analysis. Study the ANOVA table and the *t* ratios and use these to discuss the strengths of the regression model and the predictors. Does this model appear to fit the data well? From the information here, what recommendations would you make about the predictor variables in the model?

	A	B	C	D	E	F	G
1	SUMMARY OUTPUT						
2	*Regression Statistics*						
3	Multiple R	0.8364					
4	R Square	0.6996					
5	Adjusted R Square	0.6303					
6	Standard Error	639.5020					
7	Observations	17					
8							
9	ANOVA						
10		*df*	*SS*	*MS*	*F*	*Significance F*	
11	Regression	3	12382393.65	4127465	10.09252	0.001052147	
12	Residual	13	5316517.306	408962.9			
13	Total	16	17698910.96				
14							
15		*Coefficients*	*Standard Error*	*t Stat*	*P-value*	*Lower 95%*	*Upper 95%*
16	Intercept	157.5345	161.4060	0.9760	0.346871	−191.1619	506.2309
17	x1	0.7772	0.2996	2.5941	0.022254	0.1299	1.4245
18	x2	0.1406	0.3607	0.3899	0.702929	−0.6386	0.9199
19	x3	−1.5272	0.2971	−5.1407	0.00019	−2.1690	−0.8854

Combaro **14.9** Using the data in Combaro.xls on the student website, develop a multiple regression model to predict productivity (Prdtvty) using days absent (DysAbsnt), job satisfaction (JobSat) and unpaid overtime (UOvTime). Discuss the output and pay particular attention to the *F* test and *t* tests.

14.10 Using the data from problem 14.6, develop a multiple regression model to predict insider ownership using debt ratio and dividend payout. Comment on the strength of the model and the predictors by examining the ANOVA table and the *t* tests.

P14-11 **14.11** Use the data below to develop a multiple regression model to predict *y* using x_1, x_2 and x_3. Discuss the values of *F* and *t*.

y	x_1	x_2	x_3
6.4	45	13	309
2.5	76	32	216
4.9	21	15	400
2.1	98	42	389
6.9	45	5	456
9.5	76	6	432
2.1	21	21	299
7.4	56	26	379
5.9	18	57	224
7.1	56	23	309
2.1	23	54	276
7.4	16	25	213
7.3	85	10	362
9.1	32	14	420
3.6	86	6	421

P14-12 **14.12** Use the data below to develop a regression model to predict *y* using x_1 and x_2. Comment on the output. Develop a regression model to predict *y* using x_1 only. Compare the results of this model with those of the model using both predictors. What might you conclude by examining the output from both regression models?

y	x_1	x_2
28	12.6	134
43	11.4	126
45	11.5	143
49	11.1	152
57	10.4	143
68	9.6	147
74	9.8	128
81	8.4	119
82	8.8	130
86	8.9	135
101	8.1	141
112	7.6	123
114	7.8	121
119	7.4	129
124	6.4	135

14.13 Study the following Excel multiple regression output. How many predictors are in this model? How many observations? What is the equation of the regression line? Discuss the strength of the model in terms of *F*. Which predictors, if any, are significant? Why or why not? Comment on the overall effectiveness of the model.

	A	B	C	D	E	F
1	SUMMARY OUTPUT					
2						
3	*Regression Statistics*					
4	Multiple R	0.842				
5	R Square	0.710				
6	Adjusted R Square	0.630				
7	Standard Error	109.430				
8	Observations	15				
9						
10	ANOVA					
11		*df*	*SS*	*MS*	*F*	*Significance F*
12	Regression	3	321946.82	107315.6	8.96	0.0027
13	Residual	11	131723.20	11974.8		
14	Total	14	453670			
15						
16		*Coefficients*	*Standard*	*t Stat*	*P-value*	
17	Intercept	657.053	167.460	3.92	.0024	
18	X Variable 1	5.7103	1.792	3.19	.0087	
19	X Variable 2	−0.4169	0.322	−1.29	.2222	
20	X Variable 3	−3.4715	1.443	−2.41	.0349	

14.3 Residuals, standard error of the estimate and R^2

This section examines residual analysis, the principal method of checking the validity of the regression assumptions. We also introduce two methods for examining the strength of a regression model, namely, the standard error of the estimate and the coefficient of multiple determination, R^2.

Residuals

The **residual** of the regression model is *the difference between the observed y value and the predicted value, $\hat{y}$.*

$$\text{Residual} = y - \hat{y}$$

The residuals for a multiple regression model are solved for in the same manner as they are with simple regression. First, a predicted value, $\hat{y}$, is determined by entering the value for each independent variable for a given set of observations into the multiple regression equation and calculating $\hat{y}$. Next, the value of $y - \hat{y}$ is computed for each set of observations. Earlier we obtained the regression equation for house price using age and street rating as:

$$\hat{y} = 381.503 - 14.707(\text{Age}) + 130.298(\text{Street})$$

One of the houses in the data set was 15 years old and was in a street with a rating of 5; its selling price was $547 000. The predicted value of y, given Age = 15 and Street = 5, is:

$$\hat{y} = 381.50349 - 14.70727(15) + 130.29779(5) = 812.383$$

(We are using more decimal places to ensure agreement with the Excel output for the residual value.)

$$\text{Observed value of } y = 547.000$$
$$\text{Residual} = y - \hat{y} = 547.000 - 812.383 = -265.383$$

Note that, by checking Residuals in the Regression dialogue box, Excel will output both the predicted value of y and the calculated residual associated with this. For the real estate data, the regression model and residuals (including the standardised residuals) are displayed below (not all 120 residuals are shown).

	A	B	C	D	E	F	G
1	SUMMARY OUTPUT						
2							
3	*Regression Statistics*						
4	Multiple R	0.847309085					
5	R Square	0.717932686					
6	Adjusted R Square	0.713111022					
7	Standard Error	174.0479876					
8	Observations	120					
9							
10	ANOVA						
11		*df*	*SS*	*MS*	*F*	*Significance F*	
12	Regression	2	9021003.192	4510502	148.897	7.00869E−33	
13	Residual	117	3544246.133	30292.7			
14	Total	119	12565249.33				
15							
16		*Coefficients*	*Standard Error*	*t Stat*	*P-value*		
17	Intercept	381.5034855	54.95729755	6.94182	2.3E−10		
18	Age	−14.70727648	1.631854397	−9.01262	4.6E−15		
19	Street	130.297792	8.358650062	15.5884	2.5E−30		
20							
21	RESIDUAL OUTPUT					PROBABILITY OUTPUT	
22	*Observation*	*Predicted Price($'000)*	*Residuals*	*Standard Residuals*		*Percentile*	*Price($'000)*
23	1	812.3832984	−265.3832984	−1.537748		0.416666667	192
24	2	419.4222259	−6.422225941	−0.037213		1.25	290
25	3	667.3782298	−28.37822985	−0.164436		2.083333333	309
26	4	915.3342337	17.66576625	0.1023632		2.916666667	366
27	5	551.7877143	−93.7877143	−0.543447		3.75	413
28	6	736.7792196	30.2207804	0.1751125		4.583333333	430
29	7	463.5440554	−173.5440554	−1.005591		5.416666667	435
30	8	537.0804378	−228.0804378	−1.321599		6.25	437
31	9	900.6269573	261.3730427	1.5145107		7.083333333	448
32	10	814.4509947	−232.4509947	−1.346924		7.916666667	458
33	.	.	.	.		.	.
34	.	.	.	.		.	.
35	115	1465.939955	231.0600452	1.3388638		95.41666667	1492
36	116	915.3342337	100.6657663	0.5833018		96.25	1507
37	117	1014.149776	57.85022353	0.3352097		97.08333333	1599
38	118	1010.014384	85.98561621	0.4982386		97.91666667	1641
39	119	925.9061176	178.0938824	1.0319545		98.75	1697
40	120	1024.72166	101.2783397	0.5868514		99.58333333	1761

Having obtained the residuals, we need to use them to test whether the assumptions underlying the regression analysis are valid for this example. That is, we must check for:

1. linearity
2. independence of errors
3. normality of errors
4. equal variance.

Note, these four assumptions can be identified by the acronym LINE. These assumptions are tested using graphical output as follows:

1. a plot of residuals versus the predicted values of $y(\hat{y})$
2. a plot of residuals versus each independent variable
3. a plot of residuals versus observation order.

If a distinct pattern exists in the first plot, there may be a nonlinear relationship (perhaps quadratic) in at least one independent variable. The first plot will also detect nonconstant variance; if the band defining the extremes of the residuals is cone-shaped (instead of horizontal), the variance will be either increasing (a cone increasing in width) or decreasing (a cone decreasing in width). Patterns in the second set of plots will also detect nonlinearity. Normality and independence of the errors is checked using the third plot. Normality can also be checked using histograms, boxplots and the normal probability plot available in the Excel regression output.

Figure 14.4 shows the residuals versus predicted price. There is no evident pattern; this indicates that the errors are independent. We can see that the residuals lie within a fixed band, with no increase or decrease of the spread of the points; this indicates equal variance.

The two plots in figure 14.5 (overleaf) show the residuals versus each independent variable (Age and Street). Both plots show no pattern, thus confirming linearity.

Figure 14.6 (overleaf) shows the residuals versus observed order (time). Again, there is no evident pattern, indicating independence and constant variance.

Finally, figure 14.7 (p. 497) consists of a probability plot of the residuals. If this plot is approximately a straight line, the normality assumption is validated. The plot does not need to be exactly normal, as regression is robust and will permit reasonable deviation from normality. We can see that this normal plot is approximately a straight line.

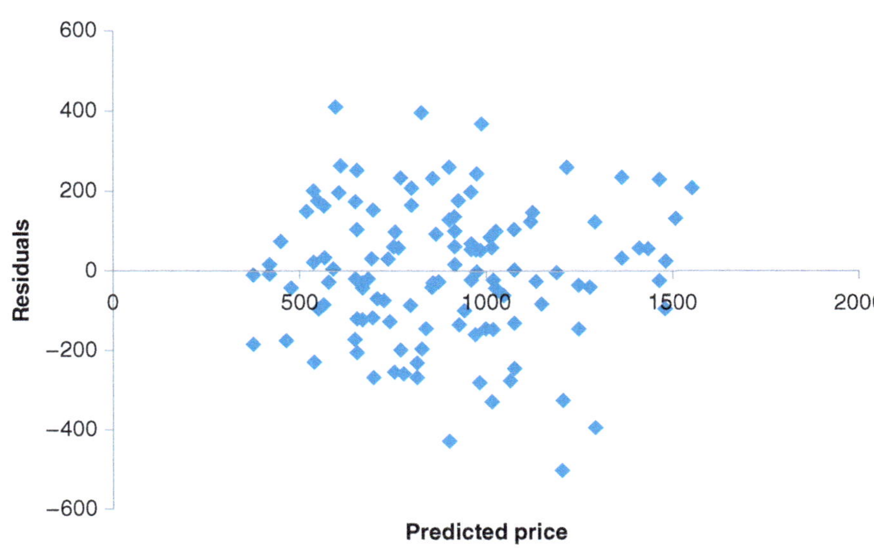

FIGURE 14.4 Excel plot of residuals vs predicted values of price ($'000)

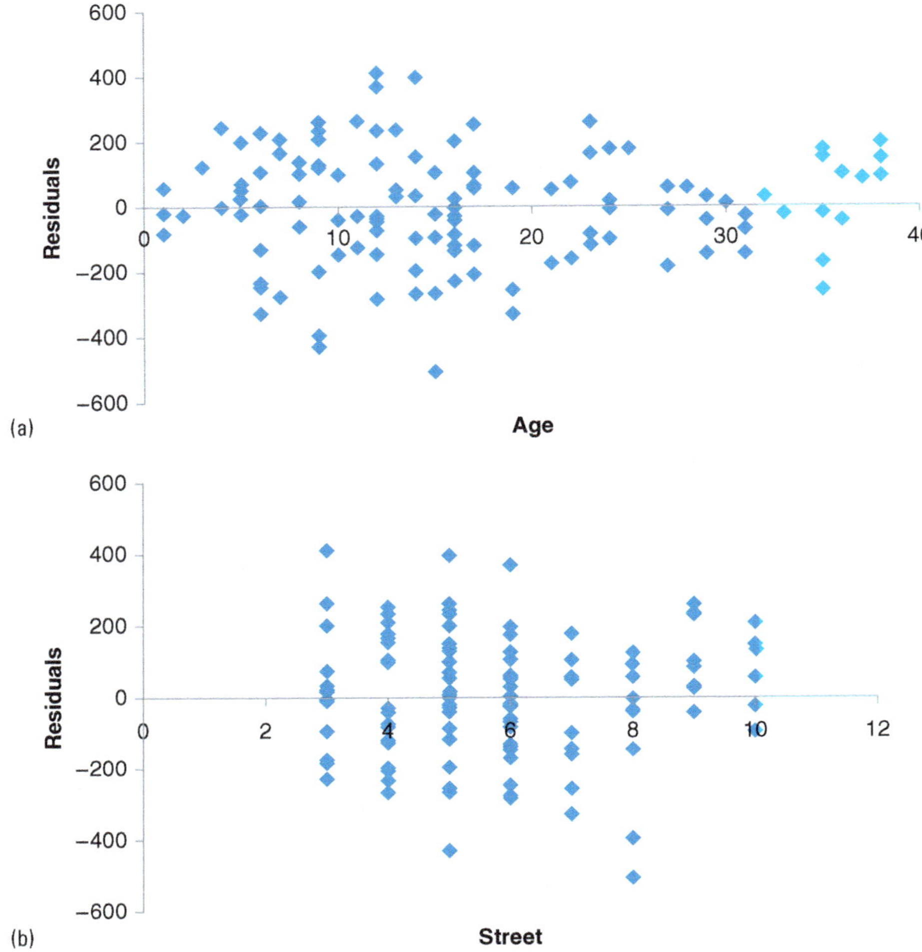

FIGURE 14.5 Excel plot of residuals versus (a) age and (b) street

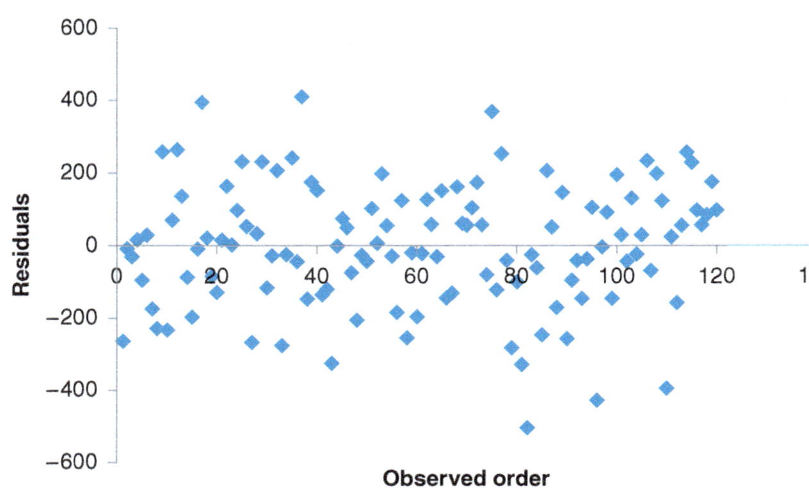

FIGURE 14.6 Excel plot of residuals versus observed order

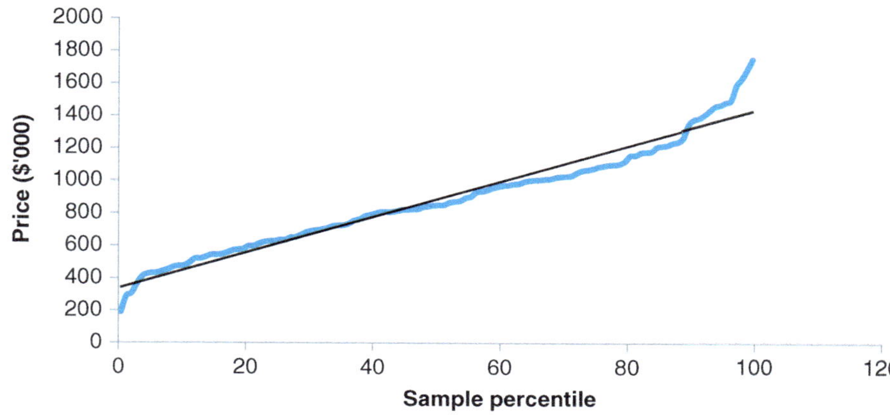

FIGURE 14.7 Excel normal probability plot of residuals

An examination of the residuals can reveal some information about the fit of the real estate regression model, as well as testing the appropriateness of the model. The business researcher can observe the residuals and decide whether they are small enough to support the accuracy of the model. House prices are often quoted within a ±10% band of a reasonable estimate of the selling price. An examination of the actual residuals reveals that about 75% of the predicted prices lie beyond 5% on either side of the selling price, indicating that more analysis needs to be undertaken to strengthen the predictive power of the regression.

Examination of residuals is also helpful in locating outliers. Outliers are *data points that are apart, or far, from the mainstream of the other data*. They are sometimes data points that were mistakenly recorded or measured. Because every data point influences the regression model, outliers can exert an overly important influence on the model based on their distance from other points. In examining figure 14.6 for outliers, the eighty-second residual listed is −504.277, which indicates that the regression model was not nearly as successful in predicting house price on this particular house as it was with others (an error of more than $504 277). For whatever reason, this data point stands apart from the other data points and may be considered an outlier, and should be checked further.

SSE and standard error of the estimate

One of the properties of a regression model is that the residuals sum, approximately, to zero. This property precludes the possibility of computing an 'average' residual as a single measure of error. In an effort to compute a single statistic that can represent the error in a regression analysis, the zero-sum property can be overcome by *squaring the residuals and then summing the squares*. Such an operation produces the sum of squares of error (SSE).

The formula for computing the sum of squares of error (SSE) for multiple regression is the same as it is for simple regression.

Sum of squares of error
(14.2)

$$SSE = \Sigma(y - \hat{y})^2$$

SSE can be obtained directly from the multiple regression computer output by selecting the value of 'SS' (sum of squares) listed beside 'Residual'. Shown overleaf are the Regression Statistics and the ANOVA portion of the multiple regression analysis model developed to predict house prices. Note that the SS for error shown in the ANOVA table equals 3 544 246.133.

	A	B	C	D
1	*Regression Statistics*			
2	Multiple R	0.84730908		
3	R Square	0.71793269		
4	Adjusted R Square	0.71311102		
5	Standard Error	174.047988		
6	Observations	120		
7				
8	ANOVA			
9		*df*	*SS*	*MS*
10	Regression	2	9021003.192	4510502
11	Residual	117	3544246.133	30293
12	Total	119	12565249.33	

SSE has limited usage as a measure of error. However, it is a tool used to solve for other, more useful, measures. One of these is the standard error of the estimate, s_e, which is essentially *the standard deviation of residuals (error) for the regression model.* An assumption underlying regression analysis is that the error terms are approximately normally distributed with a mean of zero. With this information and by the empirical rule, approximately 68% of the residuals should be within $\pm 1s_e$ and approximately 95% should be within $\pm 2s_e$. This property makes the standard error of the estimate a useful tool in estimating how accurately a regression model fits the data and also in identifying outliers.

The **standard error of the estimate** is computed by dividing SSE by the degrees of freedom of error for the model and taking the square root.

Standard error of the estimate (14.3)

$$s_e = \sqrt{\frac{\text{SSE}}{n-k-1}}$$

where:

n = number of observations

k = number of independent variables

The value of s_e can be computed for the real estate example as follows.

$$s_e = \sqrt{\frac{SSE}{n-k-1}} = \sqrt{\frac{3544246.133}{120-2-1}} = \sqrt{30293} = 174.05$$

Note that the values under the square root signs in the expression above are all available in the ANOVA section of the regression output. Also note that the final value of 174.05 is provided by the regression output, under the heading Regression Statistics.

The standard error of the estimate, s_e, is given as standard output from regression analysis by software packages. The regression output above contains the standard error of the estimate for the real estate example.

$$s_e = 174.047\,988$$

By the empirical rule, approximately 68% of the residuals should be within $\pm 1s_e = \pm 1(174.05) = \pm 174.05$. Because house prices are in units of \$1000, approximately 68% of the predictions should be within ± 174.05(\$1000), or $\pm$\$174 050. Examining the residual output displayed on p. 494

(Excel output) and in figure 14.6, 81/120, or about 67.5%, of the residuals are within this $\pm 1s_e$. According to the empirical rule, approximately 95% of the residuals should be within $\pm 2s_e$, or $\pm 2(174.05) = \pm 348.1$. Closer examination of the residual values, shown in figure 14.4, reveals that 114 of 120, or 95%, fall within this range. We may conclude that the residuals appear to be approximately normally distributed.

The business researcher can study the standard error of the estimate and these empirical rule-related ranges and decide whether the error of the regression model is sufficiently small to justify further use of the model. For the regression opposite, with a standard error of 174.05, developing a 95% confidence interval for an individual house would have a margin of error of approximately 2(174.05) = 348.1, or $348 100, a not very useful predictor.

Coefficient of multiple determination (R^2)

The **coefficient of multiple determination (R^2)** is analogous to the coefficient of determination (r^2). R^2 represents *the proportion of variation of the dependent variable, y, explained by the independent variables in the regression model.* The range of possible values for R^2 is from 0 to 1. An R^2 of 0 indicates no relationship between the predictor variables in the model and y. An R^2 of 1 indicates that 100% of the variability of y has been accounted for by the predictors. Of course, it is generally desirable for R^2 to be high, indicating the strong predictability of a regression model. The coefficient of multiple determination can be calculated by using formula 14.4.

Coefficient of multiple determination (14.4)

$$R^2 = \frac{\text{SSR}}{\text{SS}_{yy}} = 1 - \frac{\text{SSE}}{\text{SS}_{yy}}$$

Sum of squares of regression (14.5)

$$\text{SSR} = \Sigma(\hat{y} - \bar{y})^2$$

R^2 can be calculated in the real estate example by using the sum of squares of regression (SSR), sum of squares of error (SSE) and total sum of squares (SS_{yy}) from the ANOVA shown below:

SSR SSE

	A	B	C	D	E
1	*Regression Statistics*				
2	Multiple R	0.84730908			
3	R Square	0.71793269			
4	Adjusted R Square	0.71311102			
5	Standard Error	174.047988			
6	Observations	120			
7					
8	ANOVA				
9		*df*	*SS*	*MS*	
10	Regression	2	9021003.192	4510502	
11	Residual	117	3544246.133	30293	
12	Total	119	12565249.33		

SSyy

$$R^2 = \frac{\text{SSR}}{\text{SS}_{yy}} = \frac{9021003}{12565249} = .7179$$

Again, rather than calculate this value, virtually all statistical software packages give R^2 as standard output with multiple regression analysis. A re-examination of the regression output reveals that R^2 is given in the Regression Statistics section as:

.7179

This result indicates that a relatively high proportion, 71.8%, of the variation of the dependent variable, Price ($'000), is explained by the variation of the independent variables in this regression model.

Adjusted R^2

As additional independent variables are added to a regression model, the value of R^2 cannot decrease, and in most cases it will increase. In the formulas for determining R^2,

$$R^2 = \frac{\text{SSR}}{\text{SS}_{yy}} = 1 - \frac{\text{SSE}}{\text{SS}_{yy}}$$

the value of SS_{yy} for a given set of observations will remain the same as independent variables are added to the regression analysis because SS_{yy} is the sum of squares for the dependent variable. Because additional independent variables are likely to increase SSR at least by some amount, the value of R^2 will probably increase for any additional independent variables.

However, sometimes additional independent variables add no *significant* information to the regression model, yet R^2 increases. R^2 therefore may yield an inflated figure. Statisticians have developed an **adjusted R^2** *to take into consideration both the additional information each new independent variable brings to the regression model and the changed degrees of freedom of regression.* Standard statistical computer packages now compute and report adjusted R^2 as part of the output. The formula for computing adjusted R^2 is:

Adjusted R^2 **(14.6)**

$$\text{Adjusted } R^2 = 1 - \frac{\frac{\text{SSE}}{n-k-1}}{\frac{\text{SS}_{yy}}{n-1}}$$

The regression output above contains the value of the adjusted R^2. For the real estate example, this value is shown as:

.713

A comparison of R^2 (.718) with the adjusted R^2 (.713) for this example shows that the adjusted R^2 reduces the overall proportion of variation of the dependent variable accounted for by the independent variables by .005.

PRACTICE PROBLEMS

TESTING YOUR UNDERSTANDING

14.14 Study the Excel output shown in problem 14.7. Comment on the overall strength of the regression model in light of s_e, R^2 and adjusted R^2.

14.15 Study the Excel output shown in problem 14.8. Comment on the overall strength of the regression model in light of s_e, R^2 and adjusted R^2.

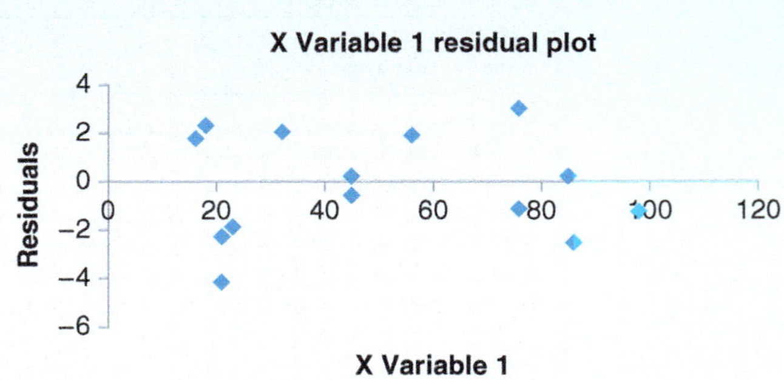

14.16 Using the regression output obtained in problem 14.2, comment on the overall strength of the regression model using s_e, R^2 and adjusted R^2.

14.17 Using the regression output obtained in problem 14.6, comment on the overall strength of the regression model using s_e, R^2 and adjusted R^2.

14.18 Using the regression output obtained in problem 14.11, comment on the overall strength of the regression model using s_e, R^2 and adjusted R^2.

14.19 Using the regression output obtained in problem 14.12, comment on the overall strength of the regression model using s_e, R^2 and adjusted R^2.

14.20 Study the Excel output shown in problem 14.13. Comment on the overall strength of the regression model in light of s_e, R^2 and adjusted R^2.

14.21 The plots shown at right represent the Excel output of the data presented in problem 14.11. Discuss any potential problems with meeting the regression assumptions for this regression analysis based on these residual graphics.

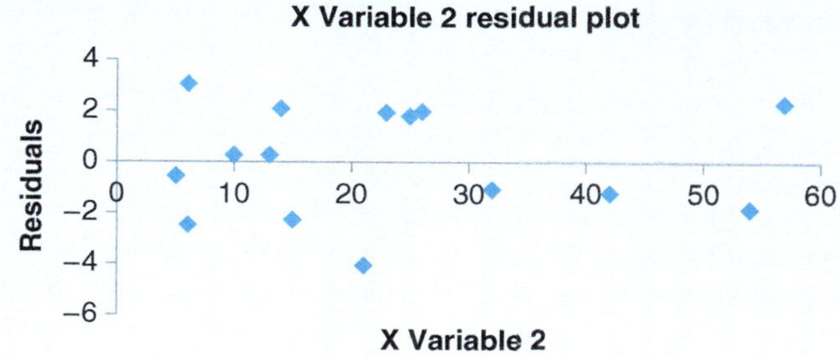

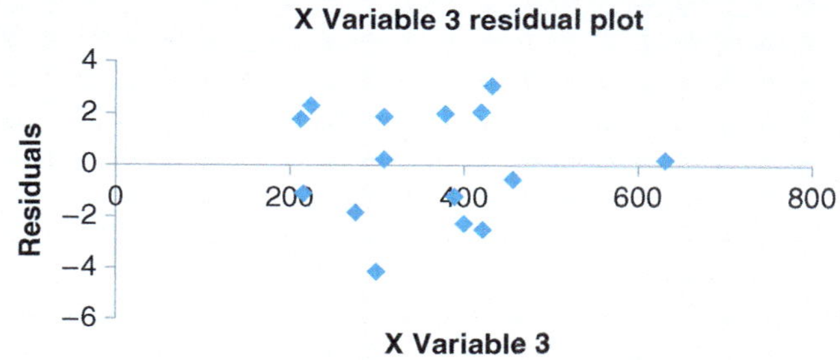

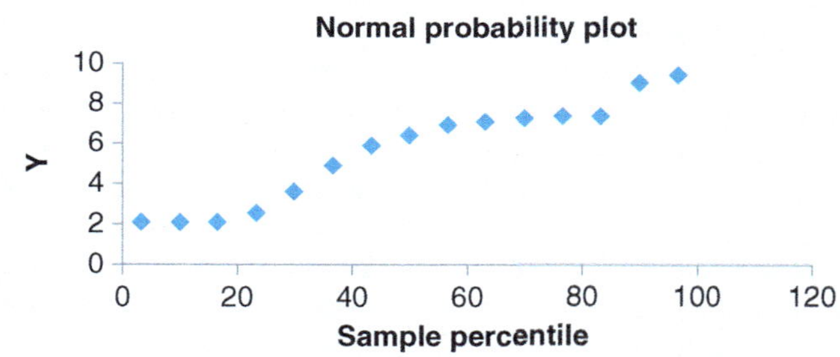

14.4 Interpreting multiple regression computer output

A re-examination of the multiple regression output

Figure 14.8 (overleaf) shows again the Excel multiple regression output for the real estate example. Many of the concepts discussed thus far in the chapter are highlighted. Note the following items:

1. the ANOVA table with the F value for the overall test of the model
2. the t ratios, which test the significance of the regression coefficients
3. the 95% confidence intervals for the true population parameters
4. the value of s_e
5. the value of R^2
6. the value of adjusted R^2
7. the sample size
8. the regression coefficients.

	A	B	C	D	E	F	G
1	SUMMARY OUTPUT						
2							
3	*Regression Statistics*						
4	Multiple R	0.84730908					
5	R Square	0.71793269					
6	Adjusted R Square	0.71311102					
7	Standard Error	174.047988					
8	Observations	120					
9							
10	ANOVA						
11		*df*	*SS*	*MS*	*F*	*Significance F*	
12	Regression	2	9021003.192	4510502	148.897302	7.00869E–33	
13	Residual	117	3544246.133	30293			
14	Total	119	12565249.33				
15							
16		*Coefficients*	*Standard Error*	*t Stat*	*P-value*	*Lower 95%*	*Upper 95%*
17	Intercept	381.503485	54.95729755	6.9418	2.30667E–10	272.6634412	490.34353
18	Age	–14.707276	1.631854397	–9.0126	4.57466E–15	–17.9390785	–11.475474
19	Street	130.297792	8.358650062	15.588	2.48817E–30	113.7439241	146.85166

FIGURE 14.8 Annotated version of the Excel output of regression for the real estate example

DEMONSTRATION PROBLEM 14.2

PROBLEM: Discuss the Excel multiple regression output for demonstration problem 14.1. Comment on the *F* test for the overall significance of the model, the *t* tests of the regression coefficients, and the values of s_e, R^2 and adjusted R^2. Obtain the confidence interval and predicted interval for a job satisfaction value of 15 and an unpaid overtime value of 4.

SOLUTION: This regression analysis was undertaken to predict the productivity of staff using the predictors job satisfaction (JobSat) and unpaid overtime (UOvTime). The equation of the regression model was presented in the solution of demonstration problem 14.1. The complete multiple regression output from the Excel analysis of the data is reproduced below.

	A	B	C	D	E	F	G
1	SUMMARY OUTPUT						
2							
3	*Regression Statistics*						
4	Multiple R	0.803087					
5	R Square	0.644948					
6	Adjusted R Square	0.629168					
7	Standard Error	2.835225					
8	Observations	48					
9							
10	ANOVA						
11		*df*	*SS*	*MS*	*F*	*Significance F*	
12	Regression	2	657.0842	328.5421	40.87107	7.61E-11	
13	Residual	45	361.7325	8.038499			
14	Total	47	1018.817				
15							
16		*Coefficients*	*Standard Error*	*t Stat*	*P-value*	*Lower 95%*	*Upper 95%*
17	Intercept	116.3905	5.24192	22.2038	7.01E-26	105.8328	126.9483
18	JobSat	–0.53301	0.280837	–1.89794	0.06413	–1.09864	0.032624
19	UOvTime	–1.47607	0.228269	–6.46636	6.33E-08	–1.93583	–1.01631

The value of F for this problem is 48.3, with a p-value of 6.3×10^{-12}, which is significant at $\alpha = .05$. On the basis of this information, the null hypothesis that all the population coefficients are zero would be rejected. Thus, we can proceed to testing each of the coefficients individually.

The t statistic for JobSat is −2.06 with an associated p-value of .046. Thus, as $.046 < .05$ (the alpha value), we would reject the null hypothesis that the population coefficient of JobSat is zero, and retain JobSat in the regression. Similarly, the t statistic for UOvTime is −7.08 with an associated p-value of 7.83×10^{-9}. Again, the p-value is less than the alpha value of .05; thus we would reject the null hypothesis that the population coefficient of UOvTime is zero and we will retain UOvTime in the regression. An equivalent method of determining this is to note that the 95% confidence intervals do not contain the value of zero.

The standard error of the estimate is $s_e = 2.53$, indicating that approximately 68% of the residuals should be within ±2.53. An examination of the Excel-produced residuals shows that actually 34 out of 48, or 70%, of the residuals fall in this interval. Approximately 95% of the residuals should be within $\pm 2(2.53) = \pm 5.06$, and an examination of the Excel-produced residuals shows that 100% of the residuals are within this interval. The residuals may be considered to be approximately normally distributed.

R^2 for this regression analysis is .68; that is, 68% of the total variability in productivity (Prdtvty) is accounted for by these two independent variables. Conversely, 32% of the total variability is unaccounted for by this model. The adjusted R^2 is .67 or 67%. The confidence interval for JobSat of 15 and UOvTime of 4 is obtained as 102.1 to 104.6. The predicted interval is 98.1 to 108.6. The confidence interval is the interval for all staff with a JobSat value of 15 and a UOvTime value of 4, whereas the prediction interval is for a single staff member with those values of the independent variables.

PRACTICE PROBLEMS

Testing your understanding

14.22 Study the Excel regression output that follows. How many predictors are there? What is the equation of the regression model? Using the key statistics described in this chapter, discuss the strength of the overall model and its individual predictors.

	A	B	C	D	E	F	G
1	SUMMARY OUTPUT						
2							
3	*Regression Statistics*						
4	Multiple R	0.976620872					
5	R Square	0.953788328					
6	Adjusted R Square	0.930682491					
7	Standard Error	0.518457226					
8	Observations	10					
9							
10	ANOVA						
11		*df*	*SS*	*MS*	*F*	*Significance F*	
12	Regression	3	33.28721263	11.09573754	41.27910876	0.000212099	
13	Residual	6	1.61278737	0.268797895			
14	Total	9	34.9				
15							
16		*Coefficients*	*Standard Error*	*t Stat*	*P–value*	*Lower 95%*	*Upper 95%*
17	Intercept	−7.842871616	3.67136107	−2.13622999	0.076547853	−16.82636853	1.140625297
18	X Variable 1	2.197732602	0.451077405	4.872185074	0.002788198	1.093985953	3.301479252
19	X Variable 2	0.057645441	0.020312024	2.837995923	0.029644833	0.007943709	0.107347173
20	X Variable 3	−0.001874043	0.001583831	−1.18323468	0.281469084	−0.005749538	0.002001451

14.23 Study the Excel regression output that follows. How many predictors are there? What is the equation of the regression model? Using the key statistics described in this chapter, discuss the strength of the model and its predictors.

	A	B	C	D	E	F	G
1	SUMMARY OUTPUT						
2							
3	*Regression Statistics*						
4	Multiple R	0.814					
5	R Square	0.663					
6	Adjusted R Square	0.636					
7	Standard Error	51.761					
8	Observations	28					
9							
10	ANOVA						
11		*df*	*SS*	*MS*	*F*	*Significance F*	
12	Regression	2	131567.0243	65783.5121	24.55	0.0000013	
13	Residual	25	66979.6543	2679.1862			
14	Total	27	198546.6786				
15							
16		*Coefficients*	*Standard Error*	*t Stat*	*P-value*		
17	Intercept	203.3937	67.5177	3.01	0.0059		
18	X1	1.1151	0.5278	2.11	0.0448		
19	X2	−2.2115	0.5667	−3.90	0.0006		

MISUSE OF STATISTICS

Multiple regression analysis can be used in inappropriate ways either intentionally or unintentionally. For example, consider a multiple regression using a number of independent variables. The output may show that some variables are not statistically significant, but some practitioners will use the regression coefficients of the significant variables from the multiple regression that contains the nonsignificant variables. The correct approach is to remove the nonsignificant variables (one at a time), and rerun the regression. Another reasonably common misuse of regression is to run a multiple regression without checking the linearity of the relationships between the independent and dependent variables. The use of scatter plots is essential, as they will also indicate the form of a nonlinearity. Although a residual analysis will generally reveal whether a nonlinear relationship exists, it is not always produced as part of the regression analysis. For this reason, it is essential to examine the scatter plots before developing the regression model. It is still important to examine the residuals in order to check the assumptions of regression. When comparing different multiple regressions, we must always use the adjusted R^2 value, as the R^2 value itself will increase with each additional independent variable. Another misleading aspect of multiple regression is the tendency of some researchers to assume cause-and-effect relationships between the dependent variable and predictors. Just because independent variables produce a high R^2 does not necessarily mean those variables are causing deviation of the y values. Indeed, some other force not in the model may be driving the independent variables and the dependent variable over the range of values being studied.

It is important to check for multicollinearity (correlation between two or more independent variables). The presence of multicollinearity raises several issues about the interpretation of other regression output. Researchers who ignore this problem are at risk of presenting spurious results.

Another danger in using regression analysis is in the extrapolation of the model to values beyond the range of values used to derive the model. A regression model that fits data within a given range does not necessarily fit data outside that range. One of the uses of regression analysis is in the area of forecasting. Users need to be aware that what has occurred in the past is not guaranteed to continue to occur in the future. Unscrupulous and sometimes even well intentioned business decision makers can use regression models to project conclusions about the future that have little or no basis. The receiver of such messages should be cautioned that regression models may lack validity outside the range of values in which the models were developed.

CHAPTER CASE
REVISITED

Predicting the selling price of houses in the city of Baycoast: using additional variables

1. The rating of the street in which a house is located in the city of Baycoast explains about 52% of the variability of the selling price of the house. In the chapter case, Baycoast City Real Estate Agents asserts that other factors also contribute to the selling price of a house, and that some of these might explain some or all of the 48% of the variability that remains unexplained. In particular, they asked the consultant to examine, in addition to the street rating (Street), the contribution of the size of the land on which the house sits (Area (sq m)), the total size of the house in square metres (Lot Size (sq m)), the number of storeys (Storeys) and the quality, if any, of the views of the bay (Bay Views).

   While the residual analysis will detect nonlinearities in the relationships between individual independent variables and the dependent variable, it is good practice to check for linearity by constructing a scatter plot for each independent variable versus the dependent variable. For this case, these plots confirm linearity with Price ($'000) for each of the five variables listed above. The correlation coefficients reveal the strength of the linear relationships. Shown at right are the correlation coefficients for those variables that have a significant correlation with Price ($'000). Also shown are the t statistics together with their p-values. As all the p-values are less than the alpha value of .05, we can conclude that the population correlation coefficients for these variables are not zero; hence, the sample correlation coefficients shown are a valid indication of the strength of the linear relationships. All five variables chosen by the estate agents are included within the table and may be used as possible predictors of Price ($'000).

	Correlation with Price($'000)		
Variable	r	t **statistic**	p**-value**
Age	−.363	−4.238	0.00004
Area (sq m)	.568	7.492	0.00000
Bathrooms	.331	3.813	0.00022
Bay Views	.676	9.970	0.00000
Bedrooms	.540	6.965	0.00000
Lot Size (sq m)	.411	4.895	0.00000
Rental Return %	−.404	−4.795	0.00000
Storeys	.565	7.440	0.00000
Street	.723	11.354	0.00000
Weekly Rent $	.666	9.688	0.00000

2. Using the five independent variables, the consultant produced the multiple regression shown overleaf (not all of the residuals are shown).

	A	B	C	D	E	F	G
1	SUMMARY OUTPUT						
2							
3	*Regression Statistics*						
4	Multiple R	0.979899					
5	R Square	0.960203					
6	Adjusted R Square	0.958457					
7	Standard Error	66.23069					
8	Observations	120					
9							
10	ANOVA						
11		*df*	*SS*	*MS*	*F*	*Significance F*	
12	Regression	5	12065187.9	2413038	550.105	4.8965E−78	
13	Residual	114	500061.433	4386.504			
14	Total	119	12565249.3				
15							
16		*Coefficients*	*Standard Error*	*t Stat*	*P-value*	*Lower 95%*	*Upper 95%*
17	Intercept	−342.497	32.6867766	−10.4782	2.12E−18	−407.2493105	−277.745
18	Lot Size (sq m)	0.101391	0.01769121	5.731128	8.28E−08	0.066344426	0.136437
19	Area (sq m)	1.794661	0.06611448	27.14474	1.4E−51	1.663688309	1.925633
20	Street	57.83986	4.40571831	13.12836	1.52E−24	49.11216865	66.56756
21	Storeys	149.1401	13.6087245	10.95915	1.59E−19	122.1812904	176.0988
22	Bay Views	376.7057	27.668323	13.61505	1.19E−25	321.894924	431.5164
23							
24	RESIDUAL OUTPUT						
25	*Observation*	*Predicted Price ($'000)*	*Residuals*	*Standard Residuals*			
26	1	621.868	−74.8679969	−1.154936252			
27	2	357.5459	55.4541035	0.855451691			
28	3	613.0929	25.9071403	0.399651343			
29	4	941.3578	−8.35775796	−0.12892929			
30	5	453.3624	4.6376399	0.071541629			
31	6	856.3233	−89.3233463	−1.377928822			
32	7	338.5854	−48.5853849	−0.749492769			
33	8	373.4647	−64.464691	−0.994451724			
34	9	1188.706	−26.7055496	−0.411967846			
35	10	566.0559	15.9440541	0.245957777			
36	11	942.4628	88.5371565	1.365800823			
37	12	907.5947	−32.5947282	−0.502816087			
38	13	1021.550	32.4496618	0.500578248			
39	14	765.9385	−53.9385363	−0.832072095			
40	15	509.1744	63.8255889	0.984592743			
41	115	1635.238	61.7618228	0.952756467			
42	116	1023.992	−7.99249738	−0.12329467			
43	117	1050.355	21.6449667	0.33390177			
44	118	1109.821	−13.8212159	−0.213210237			
45	119	1184.550	80.5498963	−1.242586943			
46	120	1139.069	−13.0694793	−0.20161372			

The F test examines whether at least one population coefficient is non-zero. The p-value associated with the F test is 4.8965×10^{-78}, which is less than the alpha value of .05. Thus we reject the null hypothesis that all the population coefficients are zero and accept that at least one is non-zero. The next step is to test each population coefficient using their t value and the associated p-value. Each of the p-values is less than alpha (.05), thus we accept that each population coefficient is non-zero. The R^2 value of .960 and the adjusted R^2 value of .958 indicate that about 96% of the total variability in the dependent variable (Price ($'000)) is explained by these five independent variables. The standard error of the estimate is 66.230; thus, approximately 95% of residual values will lie within 2(66.230) = ±$123 460. The standard error for the confidence interval of the average predicted value (for specified values of the independent variables close to their average values) is approximately $\frac{66.23}{\sqrt{120}} = 6.05$. Thus, a 95% confidence interval of the average predicted value (for values of the independent variables close to their average values) would have a margin of error of approximately 2(6.05) = 12.1, or $12 100. To obtain the predicted value of the dependent variable for values of the independent variables beyond the values close to their average values requires computer software.

Before accepting the multiple regression, it is essential to complete a residual analysis to test the assumptions of regression. For the Baycoast example, the assumptions are valid.

SUMMARY

1 Multiple regression analysis is a statistical tool in which a mathematical model is developed in an attempt to predict a dependent variable using two or more independent variables or in which at least one predictor is nonlinear. Because undertaking multiple regression analysis manually is extremely tedious and time consuming, it is always done using a computer.

The standard output from a multiple regression analysis is similar to that of simple regression analysis. A regression equation is produced with a constant that is analogous to the y intercept in simple regression, and with estimates of the regression coefficients that are analogous to the estimate of the slope in simple regression.

2 An F test for the overall model is computed to determine whether at least one of the regression coefficients is significantly different from zero. This F value is displayed in an ANOVA table, which is part of the regression output. If the F test indicates that at least one of the independent variables is significantly different from zero, then each of the independent variables is tested using the t test for the regression coefficient. If the magnitude of the t statistic for a particular independent variable is greater than the critical value (obtained from a table of t values), then the independent variable is not a valid predictor. The regression output also displays the p-value associated with this t test. If the p-value is greater than the alpha value (normally .05), we conclude that the independent variable is not a valid predictor.

3 The regression output also includes a value for the coefficient of multiple determination, which indicates the percentage of the total variability of the dependent variable explained by the independent variables. Because R^2 is inflated with the inclusion of additional independent variables, an adjusted R^2 should be used. Unlike R^2, adjusted R^2 takes into account the degrees of freedom and the sample size (number of observations).

Included also in the regression output is the standard error of the estimate, which is the standard deviation of the residuals. This value provides an indication of how well the model predicts the dependent variable. It provides a measure of average scatter around the regression. It is also used in developing confidence intervals for the predicted value. It is important to use residual analysis to test the assumptions associated with regression modelling. Computer software packages will facilitate this analysis by producing the required residual plots.

4 Computer regression output is generally of a standard format, and it is important to know your way around the regression output. In addition to the regression coefficients, the output includes: the ANOVA table, which displays the F value, together with the associated p-value, used for the overall test of the model; the t ratios, and their associated p-values, used to test the significance of the regression coefficients; the 95% confidence intervals for the population coefficients; the R^2 and adjusted R^2 values; and the standard error of the estimate.

KEY TERMS

adjusted R^2 p. 500
coefficient of multiple determination (R^2) p. 499
F value p. 489
multiple regression p. 481
partial regression coefficient p. 482
residual p. 493
response variable p. 482
standard error of the estimate p. 498

KEY EQUATIONS

EQUATION	DESCRIPTION	FORMULA
14.1	The *F* value	$F = \frac{MS_{reg}}{MS_{err}} = \frac{\frac{SS_{reg}}{df_{reg}}}{\frac{SS_{err}}{df_{err}}} = \frac{\frac{SSR}{k}}{\frac{SSE}{n-k-1}}$
14.2	Sum of squares of error	$SSE = \Sigma(y - \hat{y})^2$
14.3	Standard error of the estimate	$s_e = \sqrt{\frac{SSE}{n-k-1}}$
14.4	Coefficient of multiple determination	$R^2 = \frac{SSR}{SS_{yy}} = 1 - \frac{SSE}{SS_{yy}}$
14.5	Sum of squares of regression	$SSR = \Sigma(\hat{y} - \bar{y})^2$
14.6	Adjusted R^2	$\text{Adjusted } R^2 = 1 - \frac{\frac{SSE}{n-k-1}}{\frac{SS_{yy}}{n-1}}$

REVIEW PROBLEMS

Practising the calculations

P14-24 **14.24** Use the following data to develop a multiple regression model to predict y using x_1 and x_2. Discuss the output, including comments about the overall strength of the model, the significance of the regression coefficients and other indicators of model fit.

y	x_1	x_2
212	32	1.56
217	69	2.58
209	48	2.10
232	75	2.89
198	75	1.62
176	28	1.65
212	52	2.21
207	45	2.09
213	50	1.85
236	28	3.12
203	30	1.86

P14-25 **14.25** Given here are the data for a dependent variable, y, and three independent variables. Use these data to develop a regression model to predict y. Discuss the output.

y	x_1	x_2	x_3
14	51	16.4	56
17	48	17.1	64
29	29	18.2	53
32	36	17.9	41
54	40	16.5	60
86	27	17.1	55
117	14	17.8	71
120	17	18.2	48
194	16	16.9	60
203	9	18.0	77
217	14	18.9	90
235	11	18.5	67

Testing your understanding

P14-26 **14.26** What factors determine how happy workers are in their jobs? Use the following data and multiple regression to produce a model to predict employee satisfaction. Comment on the results of the process.

Job satisfaction	Relationship with supervisor	Overall quality of work environment	Total hours worked per week	Opportunities for advancement
60	2	7	56	3
15	1	1	75	1
95	5	9	40	5
56	4	8	69	4
40	2	3	55	3
80	4	8	40	5
10	1	1	90	1
90	5	9	35	5
30	3	6	55	2
65	3	6	55	2
75	3	6	54	3
15	2	1	55	1
80	5	8	42	5
70	3	9	35	4
50	2	5	50	4
95	5	10	40	5
80	2	9	60	3
50	3	5	40	2
60	2	8	50	2

P14-27 **14.27** A student researcher, Michael Larner, obtained the weight, height and various other physical measurements of 22 male subjects aged 16 to 30 years. Subjects were randomly chosen volunteers, all in reasonably good health. He collected measurements of mass (kg) and height (cm) and circumferences (cm) of biceps, chest, waist, thigh, head, forearm, neck, shoulder and calf. Use the data to predict a (16- to 30-year-old) male's mass from his height and the size of his biceps, chest, waist and thigh. Comment on the regression model and its strengths and weaknesses.

Mass (kg)	Height (cm)	Biceps (cm)	Chest (cm)	Waist (cm)	Thigh (cm)	Head (cm)	Forearm (cm)	Neck (cm)	Shoulder (cm)	Calf (cm)
77	178	33.5	100	85	53	58	28.5	38.5	114	37.5
85.5	187	36.5	107	90.5	52	59	29.5	39	119	40
63	175	31	94	80.5	49	57	25	36.5	102	33
80.5	183	34	104	91.5	50	60	28.5	39	114	38
79.5	174	36.5	107	92	53	59	28.5	39	114	40
94	180	38	112	101	57.5	59	30.5	39	121	39.5
66	177.5	29	93	76	50	58.5	26.5	35	105	38.5
69	182.5	31	95	84	49	60	27	37	108	36
65	178.5	29	93	74	47	55.5	26.5	35	112	34
58	168.5	31	96	76	46	58	26.5	35	103	35
69.5	170	37	109.5	80	50	58.5	28.5	39	118	38
73	180	33	102	86	49	59	27.5	38.5	113	36
74	186.5	36	101	82	49	60	29.5	38.5	115.5	38
68	188	30	98.5	82	49.5	57	25	37	108	37
80	173	36	103	95.5	52.5	58	29.5	40	117	37
66	171	32.5	89	81	48	56.5	26.5	35	104.5	38
54.5	169	30	92.5	76	42	57	24	35.5	102	32
64	181	28.5	87.5	84	42	58	25.5	35	109	35.5
84	188	34.5	99	88	50.5	56	30	40.5	119	39
73	173	34.5	97	82	49	58	28	37	104	38
89	179	35.5	106	96	51	58.5	29	39	118	39.5
94	184	33.5	106	99.5	55	57	31	39	120	42

14.28 In light of your results in problem 14.27, experiment with various combinations of all of the variables in an attempt to better predict mass. Comment on your preferred model. If you are a male aged 16–30 years, use the results of your preferred model to predict your mass using the appropriate measurements required; otherwise, try to obtain some measurements from someone who is in this age range and predict his mass. How good is your prediction?

P14-29 **14.29** Before heading to the beach in the afternoon in mid winter, hardy Sydney surfers are very interested in what the temperature is likely to be given the temperature at breakfast time. Afternoon temperatures, however, are also likely to be affected by other meteorological factors, such as precipitation and sunshine. The following data relate to daily temperatures in a recent winter month in Sydney at 9.00 am and 3.00 pm, as well as rainfall in the 24 hours to 9.00 am, evaporation in the 24 hours to 9.00 am and the hours of bright sunshine in the 24 hours to midnight the day before. Using these data, develop a regression model to predict the 3.00 pm Sydney temperature in July using the predictor variables of the temperature at 9.00 am and the amounts of rainfall, evaporation and sunshine. Discuss the results, highlighting both the significant and insignificant predictors.

Date	Day	Rain (mm)	Evaporation (mm)	Sun (hours)	9.00 am temperature (°C)	3.00 pm temperature (°C)
1	Fri.	50.2	0	8	13.1	17.2
2	Sat.	0	4.4	7.4	13.8	17.7
3	Sun.	2.2	3.4	9.6	11.3	18.4
4	Mon.	0	1.6	9.6	9.9	19.2
5	Tues.	0	1.4	6.5	12	18.6
6	Wed.	0	2.4	9.8	10.8	20.5
7	Thurs.	0	2.2	3.6	11.1	16.5
8	Fri.	0	1.8	0.1	12.3	16.2
9	Sat.	2.4	0.4	8	12.5	16.9
10	Sun.	1.6	1.4	2.2	10.6	14.5
11	Mon.	3.4	3.4	7.4	12.9	16.4
12	Tues.	0	2.8	0	9.2	13.1
13	Wed.	1	0	6.9	11.1	17.8
14	Thurs.	0	2.4	5.1	11.2	18.3
15	Fri.	0	2.8	5.5	10.6	16.6
16	Sat.	2	0.8	9.8	11.7	17.2
17	Sun.	0	4	10	12.1	15.6
18	Mon.	0	3.6	9.8	8.5	17.4
19	Tues.	0	2.8	8.1	8.5	17.1
20	Wed.	0	3.2	9.4	11	17.6
21	Thurs.	0	1.8	8.7	9.4	16.6
22	Fri.	0	2.2	10	9.3	20.7
23	Sat.	0	2.2	10	8.9	19.2
24	Sun.	0	2.8	9.9	10.5	21.4
25	Mon.	0	4.6	9.8	16.5	21
26	Tues.	0	4	3.4	15.3	19.5
27	Wed.	0	3.8	10.2	14.1	20
28	Thurs.	0	2.6	10.2	12.2	19.7
29	Fri.	0	3.2	10.2	10.5	20.1
30	Sat.	0	3	10.2	13	22.7
31	Sun.	0	3	10.1	11.9	21.8

P14-30 **14.30** Shown here are the data for y and three predictors, x_1, x_2 and x_3. A multiple regression analysis has been done on these data and the Excel results are given. Comment on the outcome of the analysis in light of the data.

y	x_1	x_2	x_3
94	21	1	204
97	25	0	198
93	22	1	184
95	27	0	200
90	29	1	182

y	x_1	x_2	x_3
91	20	1	159
91	18	1	147
94	25	0	196
98	26	0	228
99	24	0	242

y	x_1	x_2	x_3
90	28	1	162
92	23	1	180
96	25	0	219

	A	B	C	D	E	F	G
1	SUMMARY OUTPUT						
2							
3	*Regression Statistics*						
4	Multiple R	0.969885147					
5	R Square	0.940677198					
6	Adjusted R Square	0.920902931					
7	Standard Error	0.850310731					
8	Observations	13					
9							
10	ANOVA						
11		*df*	*SS*	*MS*	*F*	*Significance F*	
12	Regression	3	103.1850526	34.39502	47.57077378	7.61E–06	
13	Residual	9	6.50725505	0.723028			
14	Total	12	109.6923077				
15							
16		*Coefficients*	*Standard Error*	*t Stat*	*P-value*	*Lower 95%*	*Upper 95%*
17	Intercept	87.89042155	3.445413204	25.50944	0.000000001	80.09635	95.684494
18	x1	–0.256115006	0.083165889	–3.07957	0.013149139	–0.444249	–0.067981
19	x2	–2.713717739	0.730602364	–3.71436	0.004812438	–4.366456	–1.060979
20	x3	0.070605574	0.013531635	5.217815	0.0005508	0.039995	0.1012163

14.31 Residual diagnostic output from the multiple regression analysis for the data given in problem 14.30 is shown below. Discuss any potential problems with meeting the regression assumptions for this regression analysis based on the residual graphics.

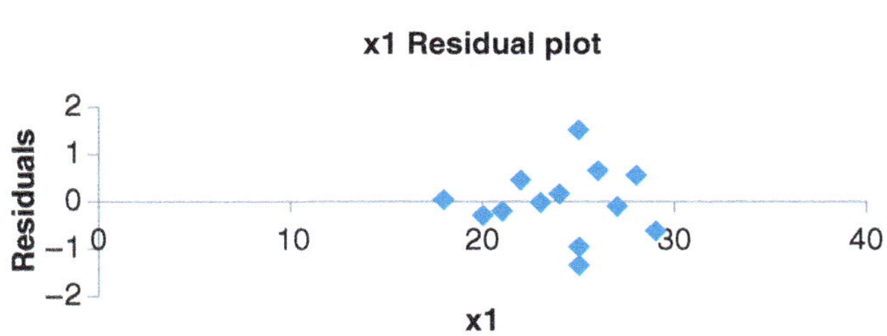

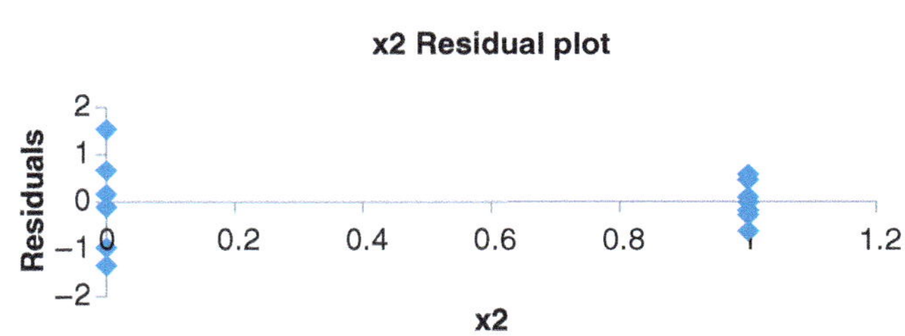

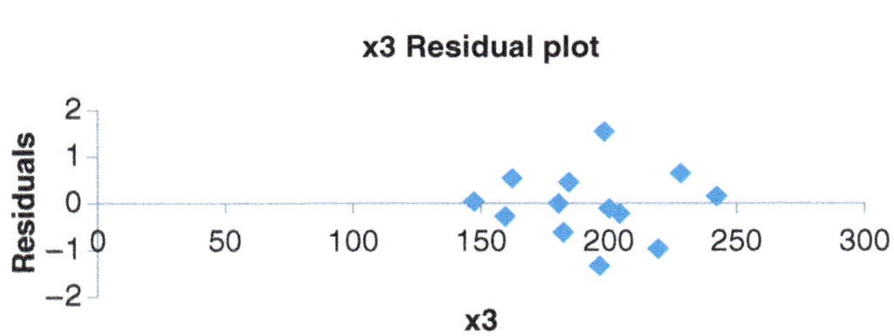

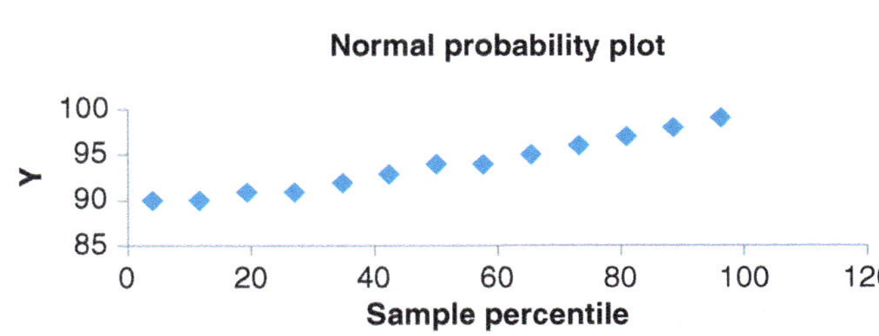

CHAPTER

15 Time-series forecasting and index numbers

LEARNING OBJECTIVES

After studying this chapter, you should be able to:

1. identify the four possible components of time-series data
2. understand how to use time-series smoothing methods
3. understand how to estimate least squares trend-based forecasting models
4. understand how to estimate autoregressive trend-based forecasting models and test for autocorrelation
5. evaluate alternative forecasting models by computing the forecast error
6. construct and interpret price indices.

OPENING VIGNETTE

The power of tourism

Although both the Australian and New Zealand economies are known to be mainly dependent on natural resource exports, the tourism sector has established itself as a powerful performer in both countries in recent years. In the 2011–12 financial year, tourism contributed over A$87 billion to Australia's economy, equivalent to about 6% of its GDP. In New Zealand tourism contributed NZ$17 billion to the economy in 2012–13, equivalent to 8.7% of GDP. In addition, tourism accounts for about 8% of total employment in Australia and about 6% of total employment in New Zealand.

One of the fastest growing tourism markets in both countries is China. This has come about as a result of the phenomenal growth of the Chinese economy and the emergence of a fast-growing middle class. Figure 15.1 shows a time-series plot of short-term visitor arrivals in Australia from China for the period January 1991 to May 2014.

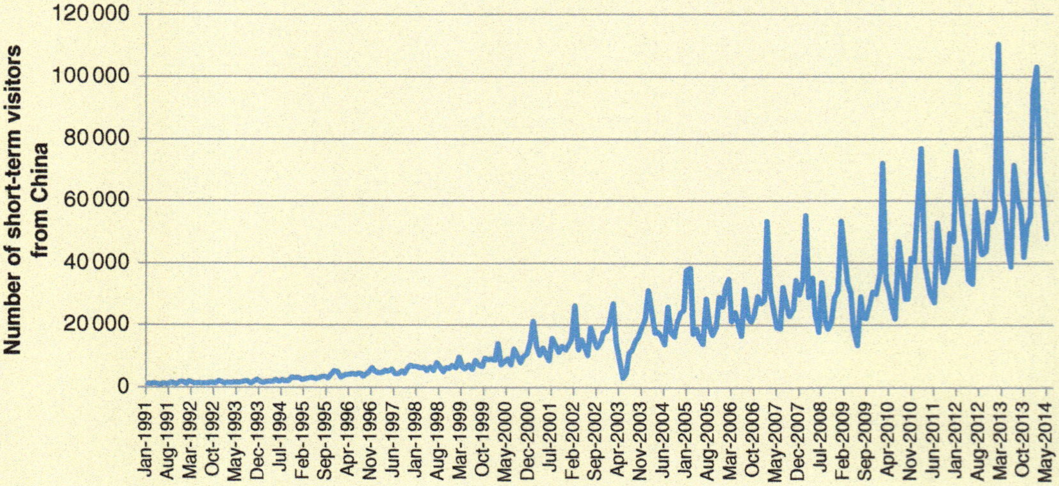

FIGURE 15.1 Short-term tourist arrivals in Australia from China, January 1991 to May 2014

Suppose you are a financial analyst advising a client about potential investments in the tourism industry. Your initial assessment of the tourist arrivals data from China clearly shows that there is a strong seasonal element. One course of action you could take would be to smooth the series so that you could properly observe the underlying trends in the series. Since these are monthly data, you could use a 12-month moving average to smooth and produce a forecast of future growth in visitor arrivals from China. The smoothed visitor arrivals series in figure 15.2 shows that there has been exponential growth in tourist arrivals from China since January 1991. The forecast points to further growth in the future, which is consistent with predictions from international institutions such as the International Monetary Fund for further growth in the Chinese economy.

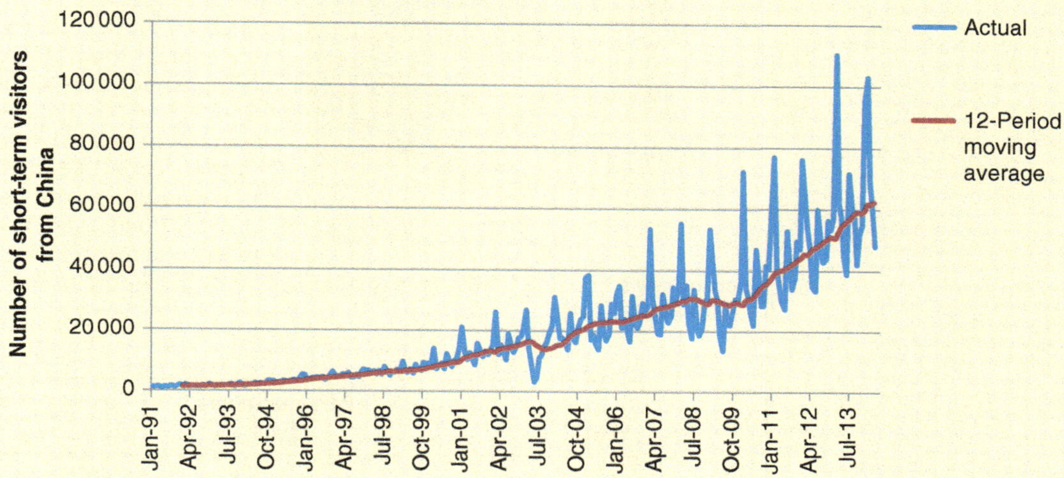

FIGURE 15.2 Graph of actual and smoothed visitor arrivals

Introduction

Regression analysis can be used to make inferences and build models. In this chapter, we will use regression analysis and other statistical techniques to forecast **time-series data**. In addition, we will learn how to construct and use index numbers. Time-series data are numerical data that are collected over time. In decision situations, it is often necessary to make a forecast, which is *the art or science of predicting the future*. For example, the marketing manager of a manufacturing company would need to make timely forecasts of product demand, stock flows and so on to ensure that the company meets its growth targets. Analysts in a government's treasury department would need to make forecasts of government revenues, inflation, unemployment, gross domestic product and other economic variables to help with budget preparation and development of economic policies. Time-series analysis allows us to identify patterns and trends in the data that help explain variations in past values of the given variable. This in turn enables us to forecast future values more reliably. In that sense, cross-sectional data are not very good for forecasting because they are collected at a given point in time and lack the historical properties of time-series data. For example, unlike cross-sectional data, time-series data can be used to identify the trend, which can then be used for **forecasting**.

There are two broad forecasting methods: *qualitative* and *quantitative*. Qualitative forecasting methods are based on expert opinion and judgement and are often used when historical data are not available. Quantitative forecasting methods are based on statistical methods and use quantitative historical data. This chapter focuses on quantitative forecasting methods.

CHAPTER CASE

Forecasting at Combaro Ltd

Over the years, Combaro Ltd has implemented innovative strategies, such as the use of online applications and communicating with clients via internet, email, fax, letter and telephone. These strategies have enabled the company to reduce its operating costs and offer competitive lending rates. Consequently, the business has grown from strength to strength and the workforce has expanded from a staff of 15 to the current complement of 1040 full-time employees. Shown here are time-series data for the value of personal loans and housing loans for the years 2003 to 2013. It can be seen that over this period personal loans have roughly quadrupled from $18 000 in 2003 to $70 000 in 2013. On the other hand, the company's housing loans have increased twenty-three-fold from $17 300 in 2003 to $401 500 in 2013.

Year	Personal loans ($000)	Housing loans ($000)
2003	18	17.3
2004	22	32.6
2005	27	47.5
2006	31	77.4
2007	35	111.2
2008	43	146.2
2009	47	180.5
2010	51	234.8
2011	57	285.8
2012	65	343.5
2013	70	401.5

Top management is planning for further expansion in the company's operations as part of a long-term strategy to increase its market share. However, to help it plan effectively, the company requires reliable forecasts on how much the value of lending could be in the future.

Combaro Ltd has built its reputation on its ability to provide low-cost loans for housing and other purposes, in competition with other low-cost lending institutions in Australia. However, to continue doing so and to maintain profitability, it needs to be able to develop both short- and long-term forecasts of what the Reserve Bank of Australia's cash rate is likely to be.

The table opposite lists historical data for RBA cash rates from May 2006 to April 2014. The RBA steadily increased the cash rate between May 2006 and September 2008. Thereafter, however, it began to cut interest rates in response to the global financial crisis (GFC) and the recession that followed.

Month/year	Cash rate (%)	Month/year	Cash rate (%)	Month/year	Cash rate (%)
May 2006	5.73	Jan. 2009	4.25	Sept. 2011	4.75
June 2006	5.75	Feb. 2009	3.35	Oct. 2011	4.75
July 2006	5.75	Mar. 2009	3.25	Nov. 2011	4.50
Aug. 2006	5.99	Apr. 2009	3.06	Dec. 2011	4.25
Sept. 2006	6.00	May 2009	3.00	Jan. 2012	4.25
Oct. 2006	6.00	June 2009	3.00	Feb. 2012	4.25
Nov. 2006	6.19	July 2009	3.00	Mar. 2012	4.25
Dec. 2006	6.25	Aug. 2009	3.00	Apr. 2012	4.25
Jan. 2007	6.25	Sept. 2009	3.00	May 2012	3.75
Feb. 2007	6.25	Oct. 2009	3.21	June 2012	3.50
Mar. 2007	6.25	Nov. 2009	3.48	July 2012	3.50
Apr. 2007	6.25	Dec. 2009	3.74	Aug. 2012	3.50
May 2007	6.25	Jan. 2010	3.75	Sept. 2012	3.50
June 2007	6.25	Feb. 2010	3.75	Oct. 2012	3.25
July 2007	6.25	Mar. 2010	3.98	Nov. 2012	3.25
Aug. 2007	6.45	Apr. 2010	4.22	Dec. 2012	3.00
Sept. 2007	6.50	May 2010	4.48	Jan. 2013	3.00
Oct. 2007	6.50	June 2010	4.50	Feb. 2013	3.00
Nov. 2007	6.70	July 2010	4.50	Mar. 2013	3.00
Dec. 2007	6.75	Aug. 2010	4.50	Apr. 2013	3.00
Jan. 2008	6.75	Sept. 2010	4.50	May 2013	2.75
Feb. 2008	6.96	Oct. 2010	4.50	June 2013	2.75
Mar. 2008	7.22	Nov. 2010	4.73	July 2013	2.75
Apr. 2008	7.25	Dec. 2010	4.75	Aug. 2013	2.50
May 2008	7.25	Jan. 2011	4.75	Sept. 2013	2.50
June 2008	7.25	Feb. 2011	4.75	Oct. 2013	2.50
July 2008	7.25	Mar. 2011	4.75	Nov. 2013	2.50
Aug. 2008	7.25	Apr. 2011	4.75	Dec. 2013	2.50
Sept. 2008	7.02	May 2011	4.75	Jan. 2014	2.50
Oct. 2008	6.18	June 2011	4.75	Feb. 2014	2.50
Nov. 2008	5.33	July 2011	4.75	Mar. 2014	2.50
Dec. 2008	4.35	Aug. 2011	4.75	Apr. 2014	2.50

Questions to help managers make decisions

Combaro

1. Plot the time-series data for both personal and housing loans and use the plot to recommend an appropriate least squares trend-based model that could be used to provide forecasts for each of these variables. Explain your choice in each case.
2. Estimate and report the models you have selected for each of the series and comment on the statistical fit of each model. Predict the value of personal and housing loans for 2014. Compare the exponential trend model with the quadratic model to see which provides a more accurate forecast for the value of housing loans. Explain your results.
3. Management would like to know whether seasonal fluctuations are an issue in the cash rate data. Suggest an approach that could be used to determine whether indeed there is seasonal influence in the series and use it to smooth the series. Comment on your results.
4. Determine whether there is evidence of autocorrelation in the cash rate series. Based on your results, suggest an appropriate method that could be used to forecast the series. Explain your reasons. Use the method to predict the cash rate for May 2014.
5. On the basis of the forecasts you have developed in questions 1, 2 and 3, what can you say to Combaro management regarding the possible short-term direction of personal loans, housing loans and interest rates?

15.1 Components of a time series

In general, data are made up of one or more of the following components:

- trend
- seasonal
- cyclical
- irregular.

Each of these components is explained in this section.

Trend component

The **trend component** is the long-term upward or downward movement in a given variable over time. The trend can be linear or nonlinear. A linear trend describes a situation where the variable increases (or decreases) by a fairly constant amount. In a nonlinear trend, the percentage change in the variable is not constant. For example, figure 15.3 shows a graph of average full-time weekly earnings of adults in Australia for the period February 2000 to May 2014. It can be seen that, over this period, there has been an upward trend in average weekly earnings. Figure 15.4 shows beer production in Australia. Here, it can be seen that there is no discernible trend in beer production; that is, beer production neither increases nor decreases over the period. Finally, figure 15.5 shows the total number of new houses approved for construction over the period January 1983 to May 2014 in Australia. In this case, a slight downward trend is evident.

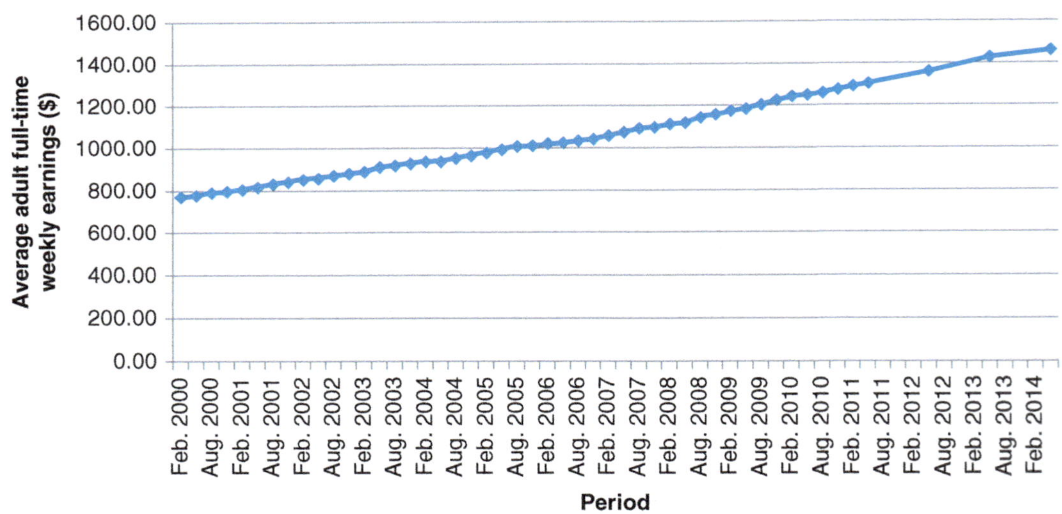

FIGURE 15.3 Excel plot of average full-time adult weekly earnings in Australia (February 2000 to May 2014)

Seasonal component

In some cases, time series show a repeating pattern or fluctuation over time. If such fluctuations occur over periods of one year or less, they are referred to as the **seasonal component**. For example, in a given year, sales of bathing suits and electric fans are higher during summer and lower during winter; supermarket sales may be higher during periods of celebrations, such as Christmas and Easter, and lower during other periods. The Australian beer production data (figure 15.4) show evidence of seasonality. It can be seen that there is always a spike in beer production in the December quarter due to increased demand during the festive period. The housing approval data (see figure 15.5) also show signs of seasonal behaviour in the sense that several highs and lows can be observed in the number of approvals within a given year.

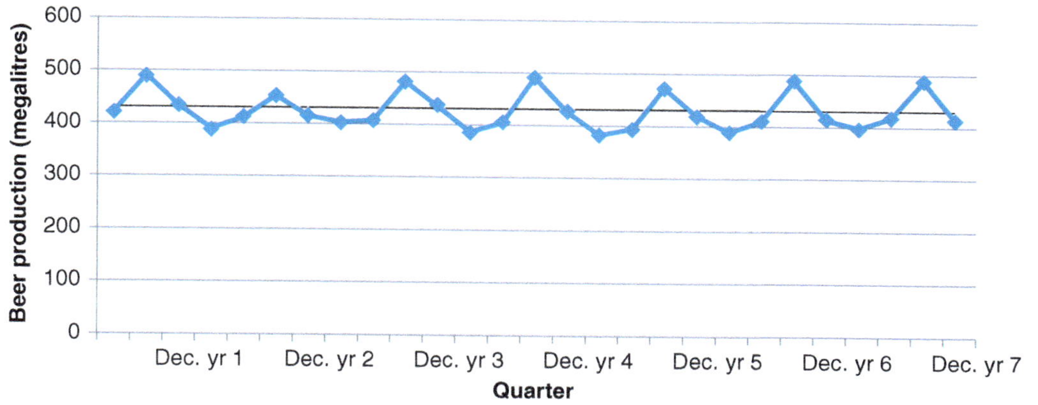

FIGURE 15.4
Excel plot of quarterly beer production in Australia

Cyclical component

The **cyclical component** refers to the fluctuations in the time series (called cycles) that generally occur over periods of more than one year. The cycles are characterised by troughs (or lows) and peaks (or highs). The time-series data for house approvals (figure 15.5) provide clear evidence of cyclical behaviour because there is a peak about every five or six years, followed by a trough of approximately the same duration. Other economic and business variables that tend to exhibit cyclical patterns include economic growth (measured by GDP), inflation and long-term product demand.

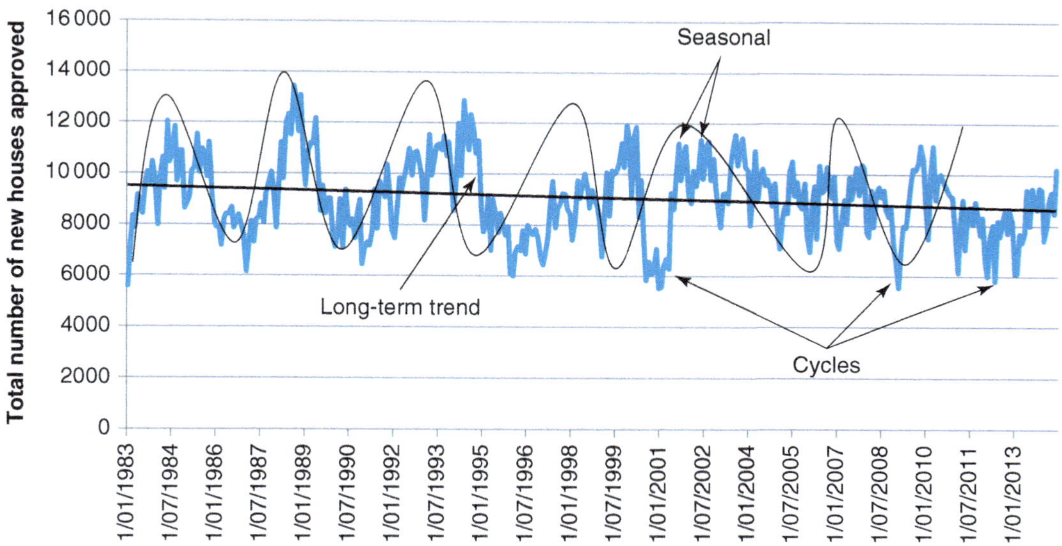

FIGURE 15.5
Graph of house approvals for the total number of new houses (per month) (January 1983 to May 2014)

Irregular (or random) component

The **irregular** or **random component** is caused by irregular or unpredictable changes in the time series that are caused by components other than those we have already described. Such components tend to be completely unpredictable and are probably nonrecurring random events, such as fads in fashion, equipment malfunction, strikes, natural disasters and wars. Because such random components exist in all time-series data, one of the aims of this chapter is to introduce techniques to reduce the random variation to help us describe and measure the other components. By doing so, we hope to be able to increase the accuracy of our forecasts.

15.2 Time-series smoothing methods

When we analyse time-series data such as those shown in figure 15.5, our visual impression of the overall long-term trend is often obscured by the amount of variation from year to year. This makes it difficult to identify the long-term upward or downward trend in the series. In this section, we introduce two techniques: *moving averages* and *exponential smoothing*. These techniques can be used to 'smooth' a time series (i.e. remove as much of the irregular component as possible) and thereby provide an overall impression of the pattern of movement in the series over time.

The moving average method

TABLE 15.1 Australian production of red meat

Year	Production of red meat ('000s of tonnes)
1	3009
2	3031
3	3200
4	3067
5	3090
6	3000
7	3142
8	3092
9	3292
10	3178
11	3082
12	3014

As the name suggests, **moving averages** are 'moving' because we successively compute new averages by adding a more recent time-series value to a group of such values and dropping the oldest values in the group. Table 15.1 presents data for the production of red meat in Australia over a 12-year period. Figure 15.6 shows a graph of these data.

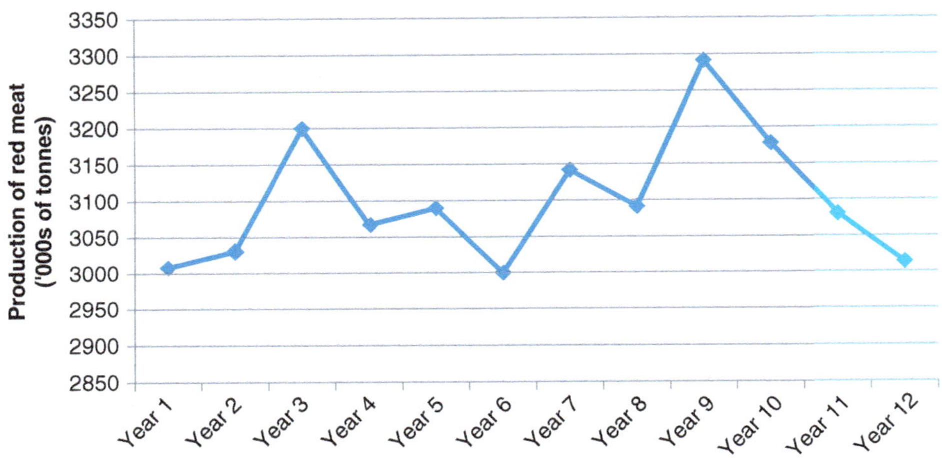

FIGURE 15.6 Excel plot of Australian production of red meat

Suppose we want to forecast red meat production using a 3-period (or 3-year) moving average (MA). The number of periods to use for the moving average depends on the frequency of the data. For quarterly data, use a 4-period MA; for monthly data, use a 12-period MA. The choice for annual data is left to the discretion of the analyst, who could use two, three or four periods depending on the sample size. In this example, it would be impossible to produce a forecast for the first three years because of a lack of data. Therefore, the first forecast is for Year 4 using the average of the first three years of production. Therefore, the first moving average (MA_1) is:

$$MA_1 = \frac{3009 + 3031 + 3200}{3}$$
$$= 3080$$

We then compute the second moving average by finding the average of the three years starting at Year 2. Thus, the second moving average is:

$$MA_2 = \frac{3031 + 3200 + 3067}{3}$$
$$= 3099$$

The process continues as shown in the table below.

Year	Production of red meat ('000s of tonnes)	3-year MA
1	3009	–
2	3031	–
3	3200	–
4	3067	3080
5	3090	3099
6	3000	3119
7	3142	3052
8	3092	3077
9	3292	3078
10	3178	3175
11	3082	3187
12	3014	3184

When the purpose of the moving average is to smooth the data rather than to produce a forecast, we centre the moving averages. That is, we place the first moving average between the first and third years, the second moving average between the second and fourth years and so on. In this case, the moving averages are as follows.

Year	Production of red meat ('000s of tonnes)	Centred 3-year MA
1	3009	–
2	3031	3080
3	3200	3099
4	3067	3119
5	3090	3052
6	3000	3077
7	3142	3078
8	3092	3175
9	3292	3187
10	3178	3184
11	3082	3091
12	3014	–

Figure 15.7 shows a plot of the original time series along with the centred moving average series. It can be seen that the moving average line displays considerably fewer fluctuations than the original series. This explains why the moving average method is called a smoothing technique, as it dampens or 'averages out' the fluctuations in the time series.

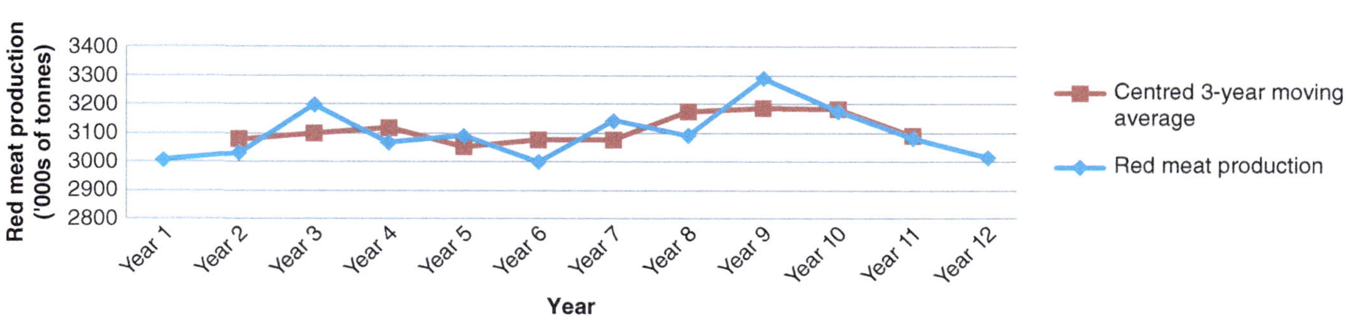

FIGURE 15.7 Excel plot of Australian production of red meat and centred 3-year moving averages

DEMONSTRATION PROBLEM 15.1

DP15-01 **PROBLEM:** Data on Australia's gross domestic product (GDP) are shown in the table below and in the Excel file DP15-01.xls for the period March 2010 to March 2014. Compute a 4-quarter moving average forecast for the series.

Quarter	Gross Domestic Product ($ billions)
Mar. 10	328.27
June 10	336.94
Sept. 10	343.59
Dec. 10	348.76
Mar. 11	354.45
June 11	361.15
Sept. 11	366.61
Dec. 11	370.20
Mar. 12	372.36
June 12	374.40
Sept. 12	376.54
Dec. 12	378.93
Mar. 13	382.05
Jun. 13	386.15
Sept. 13	390.76
Dec. 13	395.64
Mar. 14	400.56

SOLUTION: The first moving average forecast for March 2011 is the average of the first four values:

$$MA_1 = \frac{328.27 + 336.94 + 343.59 + 348.76}{4} = 339.39$$

The second moving average is found by dropping the first value and finding the average of the next four values:

$$MA_2 = \frac{336.94 + 343.59 + 348.76 + 354.45}{4} = 345.94$$

The remaining moving averages are shown in the table below.

Quarter	GDP ($ billions)	4-quarter moving average
Mar. 10	328.27	–
June 10	336.94	–
Sept. 10	343.59	–
Dec. 10	348.76	–
Mar. 11	354.45	339.39
June 11	361.15	345.94
Sept. 11	366.61	351.99
Dec. 11	370.20	357.74
Mar. 12	372.36	363.10
June 12	374.40	367.58
Sept. 12	376.54	370.89
Dec. 12	378.93	373.38
Mar. 13	382.05	375.56
June 13	386.15	377.98
Sept. 13	390.76	380.92
Dec. 13	395.64	384.47
Mar. 14	400.56	388.65

These calculations can be tedious. Please refer to 'Going further with KaddStat' for KaddStat instructions at www.johnwiley.com.au/highered/black4e/kaddstat.

The exponential smoothing method

The moving average method which we have just discussed has two main disadvantages. First, it involves the loss of the first and last sets of time periods. This could be a significant loss of information if there are few observations in the time series. Second, the process of dropping the last observation in one set when calculating the next moving average causes the moving average to ignore some of the previous time-series values. For example, in calculating a 5-year moving average as described in demonstration problem 15.1, the moving average for year 4 reflects years 2, 3, 4, 5 and 6 but is not affected by year 1. Similarly, the moving average for year 5 does not consider years 1 and 2. **Exponential smoothing** addresses both of these problems. Exponential smoothing also has another advantage over moving averages in that it can be used to compute short-term (e.g. one period ahead) forecasts when it is not clear whether there is any long-term trend in the time series. In this section, we consider a simple form of exponential smoothing. There are more sophisticated methods (not discussed here) that specifically deal with trends.

Exponential smoothing derives its name from the fact that it involves a series of *exponentially weighted* moving averages. The weights are exponential because the values become smaller over time, with the most recent observation receiving the highest weight and the weights decreasing as we go back further into time. The exponential smoothing model is given in formula 15.1.

Exponential smoothing (15.1)

$$F_{t+1} = \alpha x_t + (1 - \alpha)F_t$$

where:

F_{t+1} = the forecast for the next time period $(t + 1)$
F_t = the forecast for the current time period (t)
x_t = the actual value for the current time period (t)
α = alpha, the smoothing constant, which is between 0 and 1

In applying the exponential smoothing model, the forecast for the next period is equal to the actual value for the current time period weighted by an adjustment factor, plus the forecast for the current time period weighted by one minus the adjustment factor. It can be seen from formula 15.1 that the higher the value of alpha, the higher is the weighting given to recent values and the lower is the weighting given to distant values. On the other hand, the lower the value of alpha, the higher is the weighting given to distant values and the lower is the weighting given to recent values. As an example, suppose we want to apply exponential smoothing to the Australian production of red meat data in table 15.1. The procedure is as follows.

1. Select the value of alpha, the smoothing constant. In this example, we will select α = .3, because we are interested in smoothing the series and, therefore, are wanting to apply less weight to recent observations than past ones.
2. Forecast for Year 1, F_1: We have no data prior to Year 1 and so we cannot make a forecast for Year 1.
3. Forecast for Year 2, F_2: Because we did not have a forecast for Year 1, we cannot compute a forecast for Year 2. Instead, we use the actual value for Year 1 as the forecast for Year 2. Therefore, the forecast for Year 2 is $F_2 = x_1 = 3009$.
4. Forecast for Year 3, F_3: This is calculated as follows.

$$\begin{aligned} F_{t+1} &= \alpha x_t + (1 - \alpha)F_t \\ F_3 &= .3x_{t2} + (1 - \alpha)F_2 \\ &= .3(3031) + .7(3009) \\ &= 3015.6 \end{aligned}$$

5. Forecast for Year 4, F_4: This is calculated as follows.

$$F_{t+1} = \alpha\, x_t + (1 - \alpha)F_t$$
$$F_4 = .3x_3 + (1 - \alpha)F_3$$
$$= .3(3200) + .7(3015.6)$$
$$= 3070.9$$

6. The forecasts for all the periods are shown in the table below.

Year	Production of red meat ('000s of tonnes)	Forecast using $\alpha = .3$
Year 1	3009	–
Year 2	3031	3009
Year 3	3200	3015.6 = .3(3031) + .7(3009)
Year 4	3067	3070.9 = .3(3200) + .7(3015.6)
Year 5	3090	3069.7 = .3(3067) +.7(3070.9)
Year 6	3000	3075.8 = .3(3090) + .7(3069.7)
Year 7	3142	3053.1 = .3(3000) + .7(3075.8)
Year 8	3092	3079.8 = .3(3142) + .7(3053.1)
Year 9	3292	3083.5 = .3(3092) + .7(3079.8)
Year 10	3178	3146.1 = .3(3292) + .7(3083.5)
Year 11	3082	3155.7 = .3(3178) + .7(3146.1)
Year 12	3014	3133.6 = .3(3082) + .7(3155.7)
Year 13		3097.7 = .3(3014) + .7(3133.6)

DEMONSTRATION PROBLEM 15.2

DP15-02 PROBLEM: The data in the table below show recent data for Australian consumption of unleaded petrol measured in megalitres. Use exponential smoothing to forecast the values for each time period. Work out the problem using alpha values of .2 and .8.

Period	Consumption of unleaded petrol (megalitres)
1	11 560
2	12 426
3	13 466
4	14 522
5	15 214
6	16 308
7	18 874
8	19 962
9	19 876
10	19 048
11	19 251
12	19 234

SOLUTION: We begin with $\alpha = .2$. The forecasts for the first three periods are as follows.

$$F_1 = \text{no forecast}$$
$$F_2 = x_1 = 11\,560$$
$$F_3 = .2(12\,426) + .8(11\,560) = 11\,733.2$$
$$F_4 = .2(13\,466) + .8(11\,733.2) = 12\,079.8$$

The remainder of the forecasts are shown in the table opposite. Also shown are forecasts using $\alpha = .8$. Notice that forecasts for $\alpha = .8$ are higher than for $\alpha = .2$. This is due to the fact, in the forecasting mode, we place more emphasis on more recent values of the variable of interest.

Period	Consumption of unleaded petrol (megalitres)	$\alpha = .2$	$\alpha = .8$
1	11 560	–	–
2	12 426	11 560.0	11 560.0
3	13 466	11 733.2	12 252.8
4	14 522	12 079.8	13 119.4
5	15 214	12 568.2	14 033.6
6	16 308	13 097.4	14 684.8
7	18 874	13 739.5	15 665.9
8	19 962	14 766.4	17 847.1
9	19 876	15 805.5	18 922.9
10	19 048	16 619.6	19 061.9
11	19 251	17 105.3	18 562.3
12	19 234	17 534.4	18 821.9
13		17 874.3	19 235.5

Please refer to 'Going further with KaddStat' for KaddStat instructions at www.johnwiley.com.au/highered/black4e/kaddstat.

Seasonal indices

As we saw in figure 15.4, some time-series variables may exhibit strong seasonal patterns for certain time periods within a given year. The **seasonal index** is a factor that adjusts the trend value of a time series to compensate for the effect of a pattern that repeats over a period of one year or less. It helps us to identify the relative influence of various months or quarters in a time series, and this information can be used to smooth or 'deseasonalise' the time series. The techniques for isolating the seasonal elements in a time series by calculating seasonal indices are referred to as **decomposition** methods. One such technique used here is the **ratio-to-moving average method**. This method assumes that the time-series data can be represented as a product of the four components of time series: trend, seasonal, cyclical and irregular. This is also referred to as the multiplicative time-series model. It can be written as:

$$y_t = T \times C \times S \times I$$

where:

y_t = time-series data value at time t
T = trend value
C = cyclical value
S = seasonal value
I = irregular or random value.

We will illustrate how to calculate seasonal indices using the ratio-to-moving average method. We will use the beer production data for Australia shown in figure 15.4. The approach involves removing the seasonal (S) and irregular (I) components from the data to isolate the combined trend and cyclical components, T and C. The procedure is as follows.

STEP 1. Compute 4-period moving averages, because we are dealing with quarterly data. The first moving average is given by:

$$MA_1 = \frac{435 + 380 + 421 + 490}{4} = 431.5$$

Table 15.2 shows the remaining moving averages.

TABLE 15.2 Development of 4-period moving averages for the Australia beer production data

Period	Actual value (*TCSI*)	4-period MA	Centred moving average (*TC*)	Ratio to moving average (*SI*)
Mar. yr 1	435		–	–
		–		
June yr 1	380		–	–
		431.5		
Sept. yr 1	421		431.5	0.976
		431.5		
Dec. yr 1	490		432.8	1.132
		434.0		
Mar. yr 2	435		432.9	1.005
		431.8		
June yr 2	390		427.3	0.913
		422.8		
Sept. yr 2	412		420.4	0.980
		418.0		
Dec. yr 2	454		419.6	1.082
		421.3		
Mar. yr 3	416		420.6	0.989
		420.3		
June yr 3	403		423.8	0.951
		427.3		
Sept. yr 3	408		430.0	0.949
		432.8		
Dec. yr 3	482		430.7	1.119
		428.5		
Mar. yr 4	438		428.2	1.023
		427.8		
June yr 4	386		428.9	0.900
		430.0		
Sept. yr 4	405		428.7	0.945
		427.3		
Dec. yr 4	491		426.9	1.150
		426.5		
Mar. yr 5	427		425.2	1.004
		423.8		
June yr 5	383		421.6	0.908
		419.3		
Sept. yr 5	394		418.4	0.942
		417.5		
Dec. yr 5	473		418.4	1.130
		419.3		
Mar. yr 6	420		421.4	0.997
		423.5		
June yr 6	390		425.4	0.917
		427.3		
Sept. yr 6	411		426.7	0.963
		426.0		
Dec. yr 6	488		427.0	1.143
		428.0		

Period	Actual value ($TCSI$)	4-period MA	Centred moving average (TC)	Ratio to moving average (SI)
Mar. yr 7	415		429.0	0.967
		430.0		
June yr 7	398		430.0	0.926
		430.0		
Sept. yr 7	419		429.9	0.975
		429.8		
Dec. yr 7	488		426.8	1.143
		423.8		
Mar. yr 8	414		–	–
		–		
June yr 8	374		–	–

STEP 2. Because we have an even number of periods, the computed moving averages do not correspond to any of the original time periods. To correct this problem, we calculate *centred moving averages* by averaging each successive pair of moving averages. This can be seen in the third column of table 15.2. The centred moving average process isolates the T and C components through the process of averaging.

STEP 3. On the basis of the assumption that the time series (y_t) comprise the product of the four components, in this step we estimate the $S \times I$ component by dividing the original time-series value for each quarter by the corresponding centred moving average (which is a combination of the trend and cycle components). The result is called a *ratio-to-moving average*, which gives this method its name. That is,

$$\frac{y_t}{T \times C} = \frac{T \times C \times S \times I}{T \times C} = S \times I$$

As an example, let us consider the September year 1 quarter. The production value of 421 is divided by the centred moving average of 431.5 to give a ratio-to-moving average of 0.976. The remaining ratio-to-moving averages are shown in column 5 of table 15.2.

STEP 4. The final step in determining the seasonal indices is to calculate the mean ratio-to-moving average for each period. Each quarter's ratio-to-moving average is averaged over the years to produce the seasonal index for that quarter. Table 15.3 shows the seasonal indices obtained by averaging the ratio-to-moving averages for each quarter. For example, the average seasonal index for the December quarter is 1.128. This indicates that beer production in Australia during December is 12.9% above the average for the year.

TABLE 15.3 Seasonal indices for the Australia beer production data

Year	March quarter	June quarter	September quarter	December quarter
1	–	–	0.976	1.132
2	1.005	0.913	0.980	1.082
3	0.989	0.951	0.949	1.119
4	1.023	0.900	0.945	1.150
5	1.004	0.908	0.942	1.130
6	0.997	0.917	0.963	1.143
7	0.967	0.926	0.973	1.143
Total	5.985	5.515	6.730	7.899
Seasonal index (average)	0.998	0.919	0.961	1.128

One important rule to note about seasonal indices is that the sum of the seasonal indices must equal the number of time periods. When this condition is not met, the seasonal indices must be *normalised* (i.e. adjusted). For example, since the beer production data are quarterly, the indices should sum to 4.0. However, as can be seen by totalling each row in table 15.3, they do not sum exactly to 4.0. The seasonal indices can be normalised by multiplying each seasonal index by the number of time periods (4 in this case) and dividing by the sum of the unadjusted seasonal indices. For example, the normalised index for the March quarter is given by:

$$\frac{0.998 \times 4.00}{4.006} = 0.996$$

TABLE 15.4 Normalised indices for the Australia beer production data

Quarter	Index
March	0.997
June	0.918
September	0.960
December	1.126

The remaining normalised indices are shown in table 15.4 and are seen to sum to 4.00.

Deseasonalising time series

After the normalised seasonal indices are determined, the original data can be **deseasonalised**. A strong seasonal component may mask a trend in the time-series data, and the removal of the seasonal effect allows us to identify the trend. The deseasonalisation of actual values is relatively common with data published by the ABS and other agencies. The data can be deseasonalised by dividing the actual values, which consist of *TCSI*, by the normalised seasonal indices. For example, the deseasonalised data value for the March year 1 quarter in table 15.5 is given by 435/0.997 = 436.3. Table 15.5 gives the deseasonalised data for this example for all quarters, while figure 15.8 is a graph of the deseasonalised data. Although Excel can be used to deseasonalise time-series data, such as the Australian beer production data, KaddStat is faster and easier to use.

TABLE 15.5 Deseasonalised Australia beer production data

Period	Actual value (*TCSI*)	Seasonal index (*S*)	Deseasonalised value (*TCI*)
Mar. yr 1	435	0.997	436.3
June yr 1	380	0.918	413.9
Sept. yr 1	421	0.960	438.5
Dec. yr 1	490	1.126	435.2
Mar. yr 2	435	0.997	436.3
June yr 2	390	0.918	424.8
Sept. yr 2	412	0.960	429.2
Dec. yr 2	454	1.126	403.2
Mar. yr 3	416	0.997	417.3

Period	Actual value (*TCSI*)	Seasonal index (*S*)	Deseasonalised value (*TCI*)
June yr 3	403	0.918	439.0
Sept. yr 3	408	0.960	425.0
Dec. yr 3	482	1.126	428.1
Mar. yr 4	438	0.997	439.3
June yr 4	386	0.918	420.5
Sept. yr 4	405	0.960	421.9
Dec. yr 4	491	1.126	436.1
Mar. yr 5	427	0.997	428.3
June yr 5	383	0.918	417.2
Sept. yr 5	394	0.960	410.4
Dec. yr 5	473	1.126	420.1
Mar. yr 6	420	0.997	421.3
June yr 6	390	0.918	424.8
Sept. yr 6	411	0.960	428.1
Dec. yr 6	488	1.126	433.4
Mar. yr 7	415	0.997	416.2
June yr 7	398	0.918	433.6
Sept. yr 7	419	0.960	436.5
Dec. yr 7	488	1.126	433.4
Mar. yr 8	414	0.997	415.2
June yr 8	374	0.918	407.4

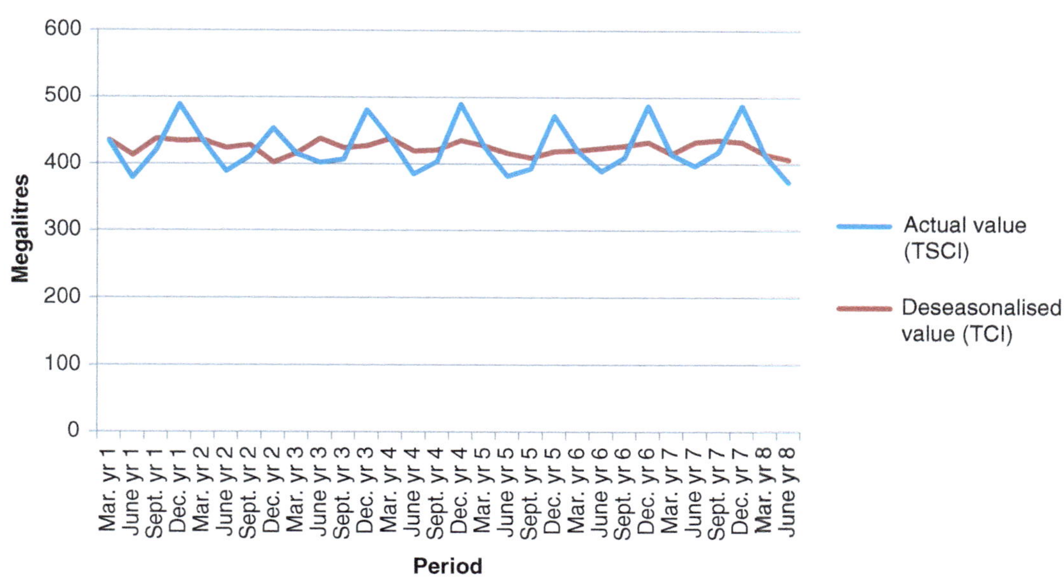

FIGURE 15.8 Graph of the original and deseasonalised data for the Australia beer production data

PRACTICE PROBLEMS

Practising the calculations

P15-01 **15.1** Use the following time-series data to answer the given questions.

Period	Time series	Period	Time series
1	48	7	43
2	41	8	52
3	37	9	60
4	34	10	48
5	36	11	41
6	31	12	30

a. Develop forecasts for periods 5 to 12 using a 3-period moving average.
b. Develop forecasts for periods 5 to 12 using a 4-period weighted moving average. Weight the most recent period by a factor of 4, the previous period by 2, and the two periods prior to that by 1.
c. Compute the errors of the forecasts in parts (a) and (b) and observe the differences between the errors forecast by the two different techniques.

P15-02 **15.2** Following are time-series data for eight different periods. Use exponential smoothing to forecast the values for periods 3 to 8. Use the value for the first period as the forecast for the second period. Compute forecasts using two different values of alpha: $\alpha = .1$ and $\alpha = .8$. Compute the errors for each forecast and compare the errors produced using the two different exponential smoothing constants.

Period	Value	Period	Value
1	211	5	242
2	228	6	227
3	236	7	217
4	241	8	203

P15-03 **15.3** Following are time-series data for nine time periods. Use exponential smoothing with constants of .3 and .7 to forecast time periods 3 to 9. Let the value for time period 1 be the forecast for time period 2. Compute additional forecasts for time periods 4 to 9 using a 3-month moving average. Compute the errors for the forecasts and discuss the size of the error under each method.

Period	Value	Period	Value
1	9.4	6	11.0
2	8.2	7	10.3
3	7.9	8	9.5
4	9.0	9	9.1
5	9.8		

P15-04 **15.4** The ABS publishes statistics on the exports of various types of agricultural commodities by month. Shown here are the export figures on fresh, chilled or frozen beef and veal (tonnes) for January of a recent year to December of the next year. Use these data to compute 12-month centred moving averages (*TC*) and the seasonal effects (*SI*) for March of year 1 to March of year 2.

1st year	Beef and veal exports (t)	2nd year	Beef and veal exports (t)
Jan.	39 173	Jan.	49 515
Feb.	71 306	Feb.	72 861
Mar.	80 859	Mar.	94 422
Apr.	69 911	Apr.	82 366
May	79 716	May	82 559
June	78 897	June	96 323
July	86 977	July	87 157
Aug.	77 677	Aug.	88 790
Sept.	79 661	Sept.	90 889
Oct.	97 070	Oct.	86 613
Nov.	87 287	Nov.	71 330
Dec.	81 264	Dec.	70 555

P15-05 **15.5** The following table shows ABS quarterly data for household consumption expenditure in Australia for the period March 2010 to December 2013. Compute the seasonal indices and use them to deseasonalise the data.

Quarter	Household consumption expenditure($ millions)
Mar. 10	175 572
June 10	181 119
Sept. 10	185 345
Dec. 10	195 724
Mar. 11	186 434
June 11	191 547
Sept. 11	196 142
Dec. 11	205 567
Mar. 12	196 002
June 12	201 425
Sept. 12	206 861
Dec. 12	216 642
Mar. 13	205 026
June 13	210 605
Sept. 13	216 790
Dec. 13	227 954

Testing your understanding

P15-06 **15.6** The data below show ABS retail turnover data for supermarkets and grocery stores in New South Wales for the period August 2012 to June 2014.

a. Use these data to develop forecasts for the above period using a 3-period moving average.

b. Use these data to develop forecasts for the above period using a 3-period weighted moving average.

c. Plot the forecasts of the two types of moving averages and the original time series. Comment on your results.

Year	Turnover ($ millions)
Aug. 12	2 167.7
Sept. 12	2 111.5
Oct. 12	2 200.2
Nov. 12	2 188.8
Dec. 12	2 425.6
Jan. 13	2 231.5
Feb. 13	2 021.8
Mar. 13	2 267.2
Apr. 13	2 117.1
May 13	2 186.5
June 13	2 104.6
Jul. 13	2 155.7
Aug. 13	2 244.2
Sept. 13	2 157.0
Oct. 13	2 299.5
Nov. 13	2 271.3
Dec. 13	2 612.8
Jan. 14	2 423.2
Feb. 14	2 157.3
Mar. 14	2 371.2
Apr. 14	2 287.6
May 14	2 339.4
June 14	2 238.0

P15-07 **15.7** The following data show the number of issues of initial public offerings for a 13-year period. Use these data to develop forecasts for the years 3 to 13 using exponential smoothing techniques with α values of .2 and .9. Let the forecast for year 2 be the value for year 1. Compare the results and comment on any differences.

Year	Issues
1	332
2	694
3	518
4	222
5	209
6	172
7	366
8	512
9	667
10	571
11	575
12	865
13	609

P15-08 **15.8** The ABS publishes census information on manufacturing. Included in these figures are quarterly production figures for electricity (million kilowatt hours) for five years. Use the data in the P15-08.xls file from the student website to analyse the effects of seasonality, trend and cyclicality. Comment on your results.

P15-09 **15.9** Shown below are Statistics New Zealand quarterly data for the total number of people employed in New Zealand for the period March 2010 to December 2013. Calculate seasonal indices for the data. Deseasonalise the data and plot a graph of the original series and the deseasonalised series. Comment on your results.

Period	Number employed (000s)
Mar. 10	2 170.6
Jun. 10	2 165.6
Sept. 10	2 181.9
Dec. 10	2 203.0
Mar. 11	2 209.9
June 11	2 208.3
Sept. 11	2 206.5
Dec. 11	2 237.0
Mar. 12	2 230.9
June 12	2 220.4
Sept. 12	2 208.1
Dec. 12	2 205.1
Mar. 13	2 239.8
June 13	2 236.5
Sept. 13	2 261.8
Dec. 13	2 311.2

15.3 Least squares trend-based forecasting models

In general, the most important component of a time series and, therefore, the most often studied component is trend. We most often are interested in the trend because it can help us to make short- and long-range forecasts. As we saw in section 15.2, one way to identify the trend is to smooth the time series using either the moving average or exponential smoothing technique. In this section, we will consider another method of estimating the trend, which is to use least squares regression techniques to fit a trend line to the data. We will consider methods for estimating *linear* and *non-linear* trends. It is highly recommended that the data are first plotted with the time-series values as the data on the y axis (dependent variable) and the time periods on the x axis (independent variable). This gives us a visual impression of the long-term trend and allows us to determine whether a linear or nonlinear trend-based technique is appropriate. Here, we consider the linear trend model and two nonlinear methods: the quadratic and exponential trend models.

The linear trend model

The linear trend model may be stated as:

$$y_t = \beta_0 + \beta_1 x_t + \varepsilon_t$$

where:

y_t = the data value at time period t
x_t = the time period t
β_0, β_1 = the intercept and slope parameters, respectively
ε_t = the error term in period t.

Let us revisit the average full-time adult weekly earnings data shown in figure 15.3, which are reproduced in table 15.6. The scatter plot in figure 15.3 shows that a linear trend model would be appropriate for these data.

TABLE 15.6 Average full-time adult weekly earnings for Australia, February 2000 to May 2014

Period	Average adult full-time weekly earnings ($)	Period	Average adult full-time weekly earnings ($)
Feb. 2000	772.10	May 2007	1076.80
May 2000	779.10	Aug. 2007	1093.10
Aug. 2000	794.10	Nov. 2007	1098.60
Nov. 2000	798.10	Feb. 2008	1113.10
Feb. 2001	805.90	May 2008	1119.60
May 2001	818.80	Aug. 2008	1144.50
Aug. 2001	833.00	Nov. 2008	1158.00
Nov. 2001	842.60	Feb. 2009	1175.60
Feb. 2002	853.90	May 2009	1187.80
May 2002	860.10	Aug. 2009	1204.20
Aug. 2002	872.40	Nov. 2009	1226.80
Nov. 2002	882.10	Feb. 2010	1243.90
Feb. 2003	892.50	May 2010	1250.10
May 2003	912.80	Aug. 2010	1258.80
Aug. 2003	920.50	Nov. 2010	1275.20
Nov. 2003	929.10	Feb. 2011	1291.30
Feb. 2004	937.90	May 2011	1304.70
May 2004	939.00	Aug 2011	1316.85
Aug. 2004	952.00	Nov. 2011	1329.00
Nov. 2004	965.00	Feb 2012	1341.15

Period	Average adult full-time weekly earnings ($)	Period	Average adult full-time weekly earnings ($)
Feb. 2005	980.60	May 2012	1353.30
May 2005	993.80	Aug 2012	1373.05
Aug. 2005	1009.20	Nov 2012	1392.80
Nov. 2006	1011.80	Feb. 2013	1356.65
Feb. 2006	1023.30	May 2013	1420.50
May 2006	1025.80	Aug 2013	1428.95
Aug. 2006	1037.10	Nov 2013	1437.40
Nov. 2006	1044.10	Feb 2014	1445.65
Feb. 2007	1058.50	May 2014	1453.90

To estimate the trend line using least squares, we first generate the x_t values by replacing the years with discrete time periods: $x_t = 1, 2, 3, \ldots, 58$. We then regress the time-series values (y_t) against the time periods (x_t). The Excel output is shown below.

	A	B	C	D	E	F
1	SUMMARY OUTPUT					
2						
3	*Regression Statistics*					
4	Multiple R	0.997				
5	R Square	0.994				
6	Adjusted R Square	0.994				
7	Standard Error	16.522				
8	Observations	58				
9						
10	ANOVA					
11		*df*	*SS*	*MS*	*F*	*Significance F*
12	Regression	1	2430200	2430200	8902.981	2.06E-63
13	Residual	56	15286.02	272.9647		
14	Total	57	2445486			
15						
16		*Coefficients*	*Standard Error*	*t Stat*	*P-value*	
17	Intercept	732.837	4.395515	166.7237	0.0000	
18	*x*	12.227	0.129588	94.35561	0.0000	

The Excel output shows that the linear trend forecasting equation is given by:

$$\hat{y}_t = 732.837 + 12.227x_t$$

The intercept on the y axis, $b_0 = 732.837$, is the trend value of average adult weekly earnings for the origin year (November 1999), as predicted by the model. The slope, $b_1 = 12.227$, indicates that average adult weekly earnings are expected to increase by an average of $12.23 per quarter.

The slope coefficient has a p-value of 0.000, which indicates that a significant linear trend is present in the data. In addition, the R^2 of .994 indicates that a linear trend model provides a good fit for the data. To find the trend estimate for August 2014, substitute $x_t = 59$ into the linear trend forecasting equation as follows.

$$\hat{y}_t = 732.837 + 12.227(59) = 1454.23$$

Thus, average adult weekly earnings for August 2014 has an expected value of $1454.23.

DEMONSTRATION PROBLEM 15.3

The table below shows the total volume of wine consumed in Australia (in thousands of litres) for the period 1999 to 2013. Use Excel to fit a linear trend model to the data. Plot the estimated trend and forecast sales for 2014.

USING EXCEL

Linear trend analysis

DP15-03

Year	Total volume of wine consumed ('000s litres)
1	46 540
2	48 624
3	49 708
4	50 261
5	52 872
6	55 122
7	57 275
8	58 311
9	62 263
10	62 807
11	65 600
12	68 451
13	68 000
14	69 044
15	68 719

1. Access DP15-03.xls from the student website.
2. Code the periods as years $t = 1, 2, \ldots, 15$.
3. Create a scatter plot of the data.
4. To add a linear trend line, right-click on one of the data points on the scatter plot and choose Add Trendline . . . from the menu that appears.
5. In the Format Trendline task pane, choose Linear from the Trendline Options.
6. Click Close.

The scatter plot with the fitted trend line is shown below.

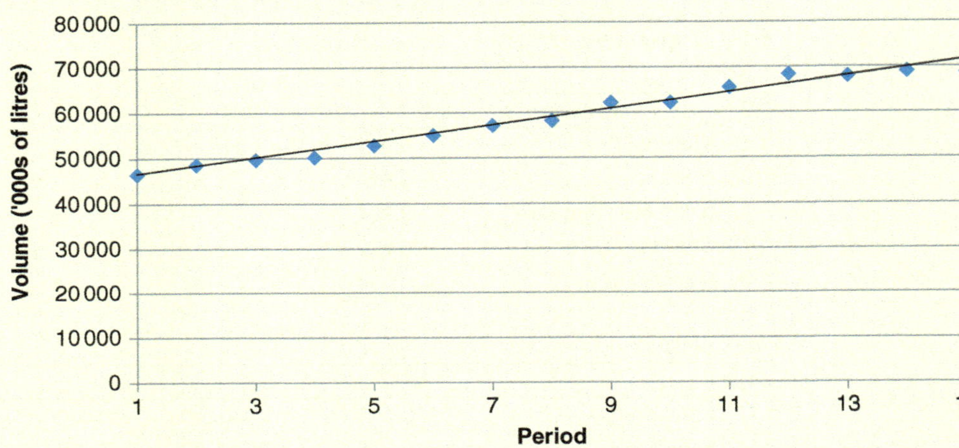

7. Perform a regression analysis with Volume as y_t, the dependent variable, and Year as x_t, the independent variable.

The Excel output is shown below.

	A	B	C	D
1				
2				
3	*Regression Statistics*			
4	Multiple R	0.988		
5	R Square	0.977		
6	Adjusted R Square	0.975		
7	Standard Error	1274.863		
8	Observations	15		
9				
10		*Coefficients*	*Standard Error*	*t Stat*
11	Intercept	44605.467	692.707	64.393
12	x_t	1787.625	76.188	23.463

The estimated equation is:

$$\hat{y}_t = 44605.467 + 1787.625x_t$$

The intercept on the y axis, $b_0 = 44\,605.467$, is the trend value of sales for the origin year, Year 1, as predicted by the model. The slope $b_1 = 1\,787.625$, indicates that the volume of wine consumed in Australia increases by an average of 1 787 625 litres per annum.

A forecast for the volume of wine consumed in Year 16 can be obtained by substituting $x_t = 16$ into the estimated equation and calculating a predicted value for y_t as follows.

$$\hat{y}_t = 44605.467 + 1787.625(16) = 73\,207.467 \times 10^3 = 73\,207\,467 \text{ litres.}$$

The quadratic trend model

A linear trend equation is used to represent the time series when it is believed that the data are increasing (or decreasing) by equal amounts, on average, from one period to the next. As shown in demonstration problem 15.3, this can be ascertained by plotting a scatter diagram and fitting a trend line to the data. A time series in which the data increase (or decrease) by nonconstant amounts indicates that the trend is curvilinear. In such cases, a quadratic or exponential model may be appropriate. A **quadratic model** is *a multiple regression model in which the predictors include a variable and that same variable squared.* The quadratic model is nonlinear with respect to the variables because we include a squared term for the time period (x^2_t). However, it is linear with respect to the parameters. The quadratic model can be stated as follows.

$$Y_t = \beta_0 + \beta_1 x_t + \beta_2 x^2_t + \varepsilon_t$$

where:

y_t = the data value in time period t

x_t = the time period t

x_t^2 = the square of time period t

β_0 = the intercept parameter

β_1, β_2 = the slope parameters

ε_t = the error term in period t.

This model can be implemented in time-series trend analysis by using the time period squared as an additional predictor. For example, figure 15.9 shows a scatter plot of Australian 90-day treasury bills. It can be seen that the trend is not strictly linear and therefore fitting a linear trend model to this data may not be appropriate.

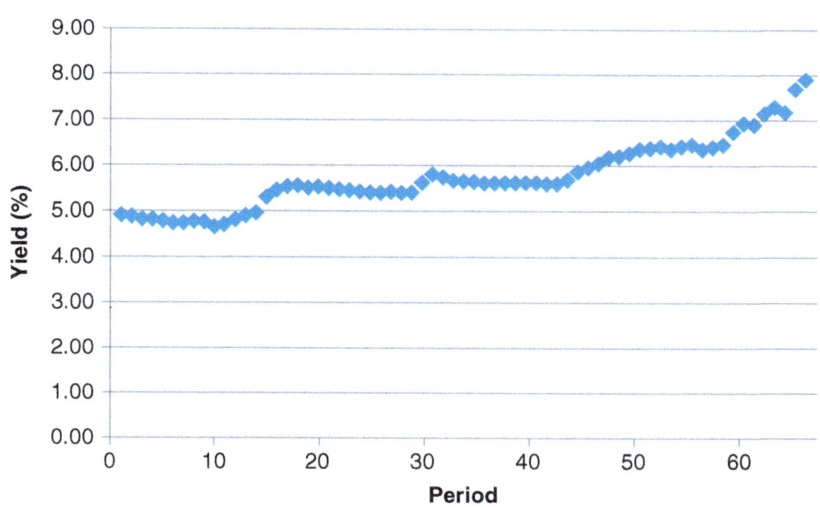

FIGURE 15.9 Scatter plot of Australian 90-day treasury bills

Thus, in this example, besides using $x_t = 1, 2, 3, 4, \ldots, 67$ as an explanatory variable in the model, we would also add $x_t^2 = 1, 4, 9, 16, \ldots, 4489$ as an additional explanatory variable. The Excel output for this quadratic trend regression analysis is shown in figure 15.11. We see that the quadratic trend model produces an adjusted R^2 of .91 and a standard error of the estimate of .23. For comparison, the results of the linear trend model are shown in figure 15.12. The linear trend model produces an adjusted R^2 of .87 and a standard error of the estimate of .27. Thus, it can be seen that, in this case, the quadratic trend model provides a better fit than the linear trend model. Figure 15.10 shows a plot of the original and predicted series for the quadratic trend model.

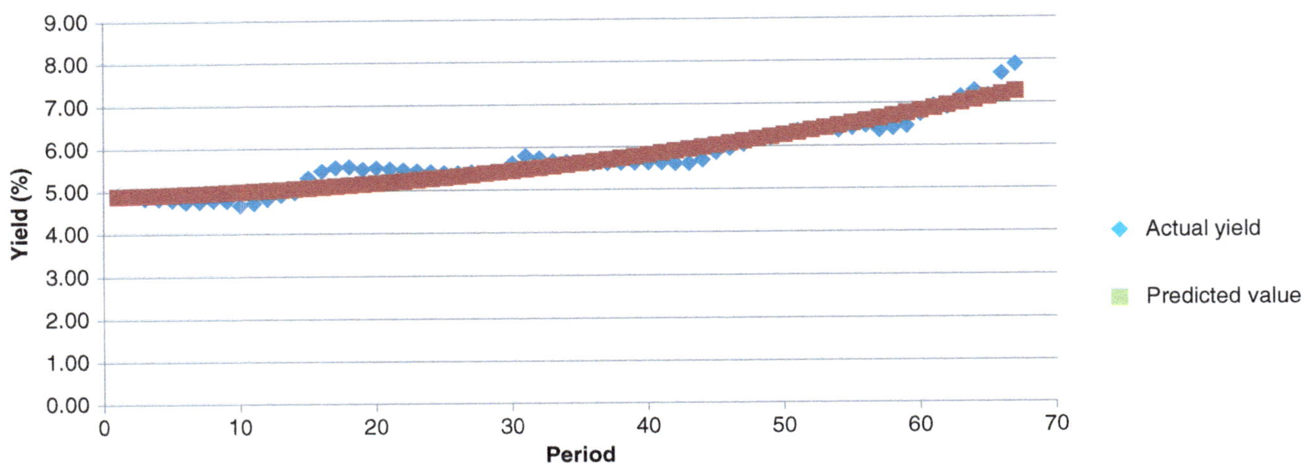

FIGURE 15.10 Excel plot of actual and predicted Australian 90-day treasury bills using the quadratic model

Output for quadratic trend model is shown in figure 15.11.

	A	B	C	D	E
1	SUMMARY OUTPUT				
2					
3	*Regression Statistics*				
4	Multiple R	0.955			
5	R Square	0.913			
6	Adjusted R Square	0.910			
7	Standard Error	0.225			
8	Observations	67			
9					
10		*Coefficients*	*Standard Error*	*t Stat*	*P-value*
11	Intercept	4.8971	0.0848	57.7197	0.0000
12	Period	0.0053	0.0058	0.9285	0.3566
13	Period Sq	0.0004	0.0001	5.4763	0.0000

FIGURE 15.11 Results for the quadratic trend model estimate of the Australian 90-day treasury bills data

Output for the linear trend model is shown in figure 15.12.

	A	B	C	D	E
1	SUMMARY OUTPUT				
2					
3	*Regression Statistics*				
4	Multiple R	0.934			
5	R Square	0.872			
6	Adjusted R Square	0.870			
7	Standard Error	0.270			
8	Observations	67			
9					
10		*Coefficients*	*Standard Error*	*t Stat*	*P-value*
11	Intercept	4.5457	0.0667	68.1093	0.0000
12	Period	0.0359	0.0017	21.0424	0.0000

FIGURE 15.12 Results for the linear trend model estimate of the Australian 90-day treasury bills data

The exponential trend model

When a time series tends to increase such that the percentage change from one value to the next is constant, an exponential trend is said to be present. In such cases, fitting an exponential trend model is more appropriate. The exponential trend model can be defined as:

$$y_t = \beta_0 \beta_1^{x_t} + \varepsilon_t$$

where:

y_t = the data value in time period t
x_t = the time period t
β_0 = the intercept parameter
β_1 = the model parameter related to the percentage of growth of the series
ε_t = the error term in period t.

The model as expressed above is nonlinear and we would need to transform it into a linear equation in order to use the least squares regression estimation method. We can do this by using a base-10 logarithmic transformation. Taking the logarithm of both sides of the equation, we can write the expected value of the dependent variable as:

$$\log y_t = \log(\beta_0 \beta_1^{x_t})$$
$$\log y_t = \log \beta_0 + \log(\beta_1^{xt})$$
$$\log y_t = \log \beta_0 + x_t \log \beta_1$$

We can then use least squares regression with $\log y_t$ as the dependent variable and x_t as the independent variable. Once we find the estimates of $\log \beta_0$ and $\log \beta_1$, we take antilogs to provide estimates for them.

DEMONSTRATION PROBLEM 15.4

The table overleaf shows the annual sales data (in millions of dollars) for an internet start-up company for the period 2003 to 2013. Predict the company's sales for 2014 using an exponential trend model.

Year	Sales ($ millions)
2003	2.55
2004	2.93
2005	3.50
2006	3.90
2007	4.00
2008	3.90
2009	4.88
2010	5.85
2011	6.70
2012	8.40
2013	9.83

USING EXCEL

Exponential trend analysis

DP15-04

1. Access DP15-04.xls from the student website.
2. Code the years as time periods $t = 1, 2, \ldots, 11$.
3. Calculate a new variable, log Sales, the logarithms of the sales values. (Use the Excel log function. Type = LOG(y_t)), where y_t is Sales or a reference to the cell that contains the sales. Do this for each value to produce the logarithms of the sales values.)
4. Perform a regression analysis with the log of y_t as the dependent variable, and the time period as x_t, the independent variable.

   The Excel output follows.

	A	B	C	D	E	F
1	SUMMARY OUTPUT					
2						
3	*Regression Statistics*					
4	Multiple R	0.979				
5	R Square	0.959				
6	Adjusted R Square	0.954				
7	Standard Error	0.040				
8	Observations	11				
9						
10	ANOVA					
11		*df*	*SS*	*MS*	*F*	*Significance F*
12	Regression	1	0.332	0.332	209.857	0.000
13	Residual	9	0.014	0.002		
14	Total	10	0.346			
15						
16		*Coefficients*	*Standard Error*	*t Stat*	*P-value*	
17	Intercept	0.343	0.026	13.335	0.000	
18	x_t	0.055	0.004	14.486	0.000	

The estimated exponential trend equation can be written as:

$$\log \hat{y}_t = 0.343 + 0.055x_t$$

Note that, since we have taken the log of the intercept and slope parameters, the estimated coefficients, 0.343 and 0.055, are not to be taken as estimates of β_0 and β_1, respectively. To get the actual estimates, we have to take their antilog:

$$\hat{\beta}_0 = \text{antilog}(0.343) = 10^{0.343} = 2.203$$

This means that predicted costs for the year 2003 (i.e. the origin) is \$2.203 million. The predicted slope is given by:

$$\hat{\beta}_1 = \text{antilog}(0.055) = 10^{0.055} = 1.135$$

The exponential trend forecasting equation can therefore be written as:

$$\hat{y}_t = 2.203(1.135)^{x_t}$$

The value 1.135 tells us that the underlying percentage growth in annual sales is 13.5%.

For forecasting purposes, we can substitute the corresponding time periods into the above equation. For example, to predict costs for 2014 (period 12), substitute $x_t = 12$ into the equation and work out the value of y_t as follows.

$$\hat{y}_t = 2.203(1.135)^{12} = 10.069$$

We can also use the log $\hat{y}_t$ equation to make the forecast as follows.

$$\log \hat{y}_t = 0.343 + 0.055(12) = 1.003$$

Therefore, $\hat{y}_t$ = antilog (1.003) = $10^{1.003}$ = 10.069. An Excel plot of the actual versus predicted costs is shown in figure 15.13.

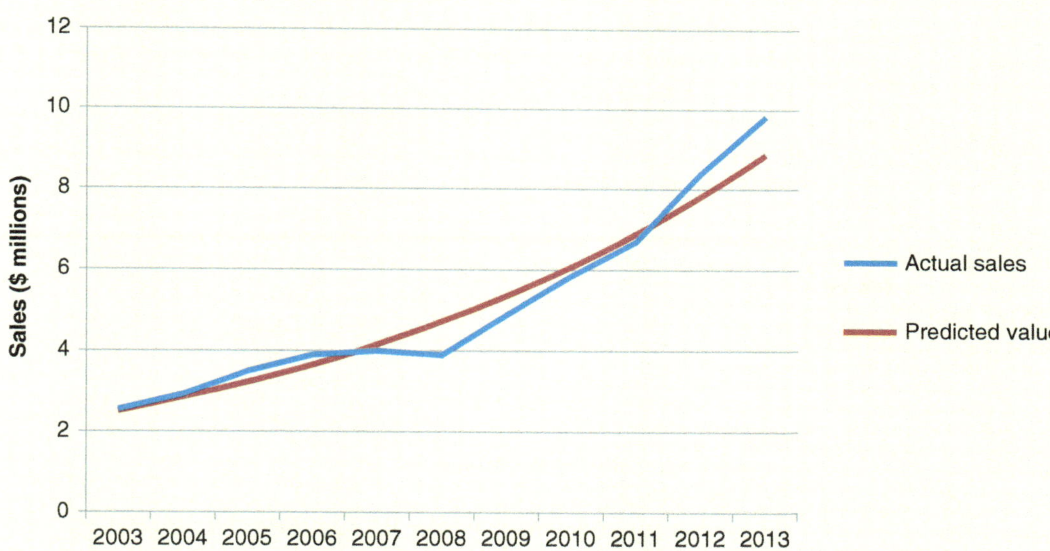

FIGURE 15.13 Excel plot of actual and predicted annual costs for the exponential trend model

15.4 Autoregressive trend-based forecasting models

Among the key assumptions underlying the linear regression model is that the error terms (or residuals) are independent of each other. When using regression with time-series data, the assumption of independent error terms could be violated; that is, the error terms may be correlated over time. This is referred to as *serial correlation*, or *autocorrelation*. The presence of autocorrelation can be determined visually by observing a scatter plot of the regression residuals. A randomly distributed residual plot would indicate the absence of autocorrelation. However, autocorrelation is said to exist if we can observe a nonlinear pattern in the distribution of the residuals. This pattern could be in the form of a series of negative residuals followed by positive ones and then negative ones, and so on. In this section, we introduce a formal test for autocorrelation.

Testing for autocorrelation

Autocorrelation occurs in data when the error terms of a regression forecasting model are correlated. When autocorrelation occurs in a regression analysis, several possible problems might arise. First, the estimates of the regression coefficients no longer have the minimum variance property and may be inefficient. Second, the variance of the error terms may be greatly underestimated by the mean square error value. Third, the true standard error of the estimated regression coefficient may be seriously underestimated. Fourth, the confidence intervals and tests using the t and F distributions are no longer strictly applicable.

First-order autocorrelation results from correlation between the error terms of adjacent time periods (rather than two or more previous periods). If first-order autocorrelation is present, the error for one time period, e_t, is a function of the error of the previous time period, e_{t-1}, as follows.

$$e_t = \rho e_{t-1} + v_t$$

The first-order autocorrelation coefficient, ρ, measures the correlation between the error terms. It is a value that lies between −1 and +1, as does the coefficient of correlation, v_t, which is a normally distributed independent error term. If positive autocorrelation is present, the value of ρ is between 0 and +1. If the value of ρ is 0, $e_t = v_t$, which means there is no autocorrelation and e_t is just a random, independent error term.

One way to determine whether autocorrelation is present in a time-series regression analysis is by using the **Durbin–Watson test** for autocorrelation. Formula 15.2 is used as a Durbin–Watson test for autocorrelation.

Durbin–Watson test
(15.2)

$$D = \frac{\sum_{t=2}^{n}(e_t - e_{t-1})^2}{\sum_{t=1}^{n} e_t^2}$$

where:

n = the number of observations
e_t = the residual at time t
e_{t-1} = the residual at time $t-1$ (i.e. the one-period lagged residual)

Note from formula 15.2 that the Durbin–Watson test involves finding the difference between successive values of error ($e_t - e_{t-1}$). If errors are positively correlated, this difference will be smaller than with random or independent errors. Squaring this term eliminates the cancellation effects of positive and negative terms.

The null hypothesis for this test is that there is *no* autocorrelation. For a two-tailed test, the alternative hypothesis is that there *is* autocorrelation.

$$H_0: \rho = 0$$

$$H_a: \rho \neq 0$$

Most business and economic forecasting autocorrelation tends to be positive autocorrelation. In the Durbin–Watson test, D is the observed value of the Durbin–Watson statistic using the residuals from the regression analysis. A critical value for D can be obtained from the values of α, n and k by using table A.9, where α is the level of significance, n is the number of data items and k is the number of predictors.

Table A.9 in the appendix gives two Durbin–Watson tables; one table with values for $\alpha = .05$ and the other for $\alpha = .01$. Table A.9 includes values for d_U and d_L, which range from 0 to 4. If the observed value of D is above d_U, there is no significant autocorrelation so we do not reject the null hypothesis. If the observed value of D is below d_L, there is autocorrelation and we reject the null hypothesis. Sometimes the observed statistic, D, is between the values of d_U and d_L. In this case, the Durbin–Watson test is inconclusive.

As an example, consider the table below, which lists data for a country's GDP over a 27-year period. Suppose we want to fit a least squares trend based model to the data.

Year	GDP ($ billion)
1	431.32
2	445.00
3	434.45
4	454.77
5	478.98
6	500.27
7	512.37
8	538.80
9	558.73
10	580.72
11	576.98
12	577.25
13	598.62
14	623.17
15	651.01
16	677.81
17	704.43
18	736.00
19	774.11
20	804.95
21	820.56
22	851.47
23	878.31
24	913.67
25	939.69
26	967.45
27	998.27

The resulting errors of prediction can be tested using the Durbin–Watson statistic for the presence of significant positive autocorrelation by using $\alpha = .05$. The hypotheses are:

$$H_0: \rho = 0$$

$$H_a: \rho > 0$$

The regression results are shown in figure 15.14.

	A	B	C	D	E	F	G
1							
2	*Regression Statistics*						
3	Multiple R	0.987548					
4	R Square	0.975251					
5	Adjusted R Square	0.974262					
6	Standard Error	28.55837					
7	Observations	27					
8							
9	ANOVA						
10		*df*	*SS*	*MS*	*F*	*Significance F*	
11	Regression	1	803478.854	803478.9	985.1618	1.32747E–21	
12	Residual	25	20389.51536	815.5806			
13	Total	26	823868.3694				
14							
15		*Coefficients*	*Standard Error*	*t Stat*	*P-value*	*Lower 95%*	*Upper 95%*
16	Intercept	357.6777	11.30475706	31.63957	1.09E–21	334.3951093	380.96028
17	X Variable 1	22.14778	0.705629126	31.38729	1.33E–21	20.69451349	23.601054

FIGURE 15.14 Regression results for the Australian GDP data

Figure 15.15 shows the Durbin–Watson test results that can be produced together with the regression results:

	A	B
1	Durbin-Watson Calculations	
2		
3	Sum of Squared Difference of Residuals	3360.070
4	Sum of Squared Residuals	20389.721
5		
6	Durbin-Watson Statistic	0.165

FIGURE 15.15 Durbin–Watson test results for the GDP data

According to the output, $D = 0.165$. Because we used a simple linear regression, the value of k is 1. The sample size, n, is 27, and $\alpha = .05$. The critical values in table A.9 are:

$$d_U = 1.47 \text{ and } d_L = 1.32$$

Because the computed D statistic, 0.165, is less than the value of $d_L = 1.32$, the null hypothesis is rejected. A positive autocorrelation is present in this example. The residual plot in figure 15.16 shows that the error terms are not randomly distributed. They follow a distinct inverted U-curve, which indicates the presence of autocorrelation.

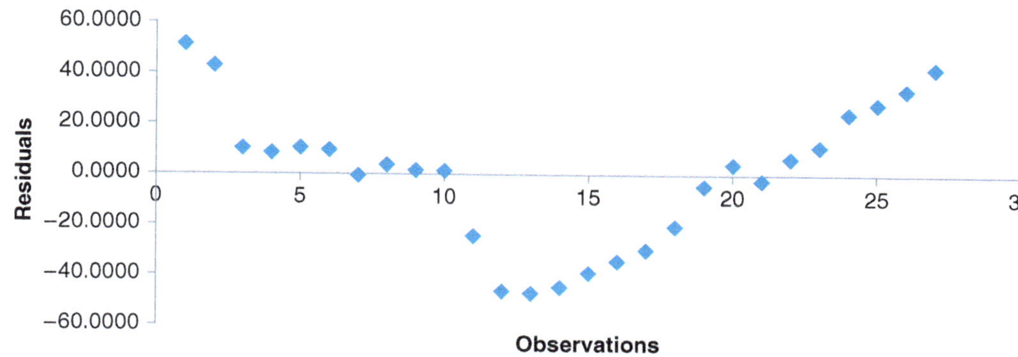

FIGURE 15.16 Residual plot for the GDP data

Ways to overcome the autocorrelation problem

Several approaches to data analysis can be used when autocorrelation is present. One uses additional independent variables and the other transforms the independent variable.

Addition of independent variables

Often the reason that autocorrelation occurs in regression analyses is that one or more important predictor variables are left out of the analysis. For example, suppose a researcher develops a regression forecasting model that attempts to predict sales of new homes using data on previous house sales. Such a model might contain significant autocorrelation. The exclusion of the variable 'prime mortgage interest rate' might be a factor driving the autocorrelation between the other two variables. Adding this variable to the regression model might significantly reduce the autocorrelation.

Transforming variables

When the inclusion of additional variables is not helpful in reducing autocorrelation to an acceptable level, transforming the data in the variables may help to solve the problem. One such method is the **first-differences approach**. With the first-differences approach, each value of x is subtracted from each succeeding time period value of x; these 'differences' become the new and transformed x variable. The same process is used to transform the y variable. The regression analysis is then computed on the transformed x and transformed y variables to produce a new model that is hopefully free of significant autocorrelation effects. Another way is to generate new variables by using the percentage changes from period to period and doing a regression analysis on these new variables. A third way is to use autoregressive models, which is what we consider in this chapter.

The existence of significant autocorrelation implies that, until we correct the violated error assumptions of the regression model, it will not provide a satisfactory fit and hence the forecast will be invalid. However, autocorrelation also provides us with a good opportunity to develop another forecasting technique. If we have strong grounds to believe that the error terms are correlated over time, the **autoregressive model** may be the most effective.

The autoregressive model is *a multiple regression model in which the independent variables are time-lagged versions of the dependent variable*, which means we try to predict a value of y from its past values. The independent variable can be lagged for one, two, three or more time periods. An autoregressive model containing independent variables for three time periods looks like this.

$$\hat{y}_t = b_0 + b_1 y_{t-1} + b_2 y_{t-2} + b_3 y_{t-3} + e_t$$

DEMONSTRATION PROBLEM 15.5

PROBLEM: The data below show ABS data for total income taxes (in millions of dollars) paid by individuals in Australia for the period March 2005 to March 2014. Develop a two-lag autoregressive model and use it to forecast total individual income tax for April 2014.

Period	Total income tax (y_t)	One-period lagged (y_{t-1})	Two-period lagged (y_{t-2})
Mar. 05	41 542	–	–
June 05	40 756	41 542	–
Sept. 05	41 273	40 756	41 542
Dec. 05	45 348	41 273	40 756
Mar. 06	46 173	45 348	41 273
Jun. 06	45 233	46 173	45 348
Sept. 06	43 947	45 233	46 173
Dec. 06	48 026	43 947	45 233
Mar. 07	47 827	48 026	43 947
June 07	53 841	47 827	48 026
Sept. 07	43 123	53 841	47 827
Dec. 07	49 663	43 123	53 841
Mar. 08	49 776	49 663	43 123
June 08	58 134	49 776	49 663
Sept. 08	45 978	58 134	49 776
Dec. 08	50 296	45 978	58 134
Mar. 09	46 545	50 296	45 978
June 09	53 443	46 545	50 296
Sept. 09	39 717	53 443	46 545
Dec. 09	47 647	39 717	53 443
Mar. 10	47 144	47 647	39 717
June 10	54 513	47 144	47 647
Sept. 10	45 001	54 513	47 144
Dec. 10	53 170	45 001	54 513
Mar. 11	51 948	53 170	45 001
June 11	59 006	51 948	53 170
Sept. 11	51 369	59 006	51 948
Dec. 11	58 949	51 369	59 006
Mar. 12	58 040	58 949	51 369
June 12	66 255	58 040	58 949
Sept. 12	53 756	66 255	58 040
Dec. 12	60 851	53 756	66 255
Mar. 13	61 273	60 851	53 756
June 13	69 198	61 273	60 851
Sept. 13	58 239	69 198	61 273
Dec. 13	67 534	58 239	69 198
Mar. 14	66 437	67 534	58 239

SOLUTION: The autoregressive model can be specified as follows.

$$y_t = b_0 + b_1 y_{t-1} + b_2 y_{t-2} + e_t$$

As shown earlier, the independent variables are the first and second lags of the dependent variable.

USING EXCEL

Two-lag autoregressive model

DP15-05

1. Access DP15-05.xls from the student website.
2. Perform a regression analysis with y_t as the dependent variable and use the first and second lags of y_t as the independent variables. Note that, as a result of taking the first and second lags of y_t, we lose the first two periods of data. The data for the regression therefore start from September 2005.

The Excel output is shown below.

	A	B	C	D	E	F
1	SUMMARY OUTPUT					
2						
3	*Regression Statistics*					
4	Multiple R	0.794				
5	R Square	0.630				
6	Adjusted R Square	0.607				
7	Standard Error	4889.713				
8	Observations	35				
9						
10	ANOVA					
11		*df*	*SS*	*MS*	*F*	*Significance F*
12	Regression	2	1302665308	651332653.8	27.24182	0.00000
13	Residual	32	765097477.1	23909296.16		
14	Total	34	2067762785			
15						
16		*Coefficients*	*Standard Error*	*t Stat*	*P-value*	
17	Intercept	5691.742	6566.200	0.867	0.392	
18	1-lag	0.226	0.132	1.713	0.096	
19	2-lag	0.688	0.138	4.987	0.000	

The estimated autoregressive model is:

$$\hat{y}_t = 5691.742 + 0.226y_{t-1} + 0.688y_{t-2}$$

The overall regression is significant at the 0.5% level and the R^2 value of 63% indicates that the model provides a reasonable level of predictability. A forecast of income taxes for April 2014 is given by:

$$\hat{y}_t = 5691.742 + 0.226(66437) + 0.688(67534) = 67169.9$$

According to the model, total individual income tax in April 2014 will be $67 169.9 million.

Autoregression can be a useful tool in locating seasonal or cyclical effects in time-series data. For example, if the data are given in monthly increments, autoregression using variables lagged by as much as 12 months can search for the predictability of previous monthly time periods. If data are given in quarterly time periods, autoregression of up to four periods removed can be a useful tool in locating the predictability of data from previous quarters. When the time periods are in years, lagging the data by yearly periods and using autoregression can help in locating cyclical predictability.

PRACTICE PROBLEMS

Practising the calculations

P15-10 **15.10** The following table shows monthly ABS data for approvals for residential buildings in Queensland for the period January 2011 to June 2014. Estimate the data using a linear trend model. Forecast the number of building approvals in July 2014.

Period	Number of building approvals	Period	Number of building approvals
Jan. 11	1035	Oct. 12	1624
Feb. 11	1272	Nov. 12	1493
Mar. 11	1708	Dec. 12	1161
Apr. 11	1356	Jan. 13	1262
May 11	1557	Feb. 13	1346
June 11	1546	Mar. 13	1367
July 11	1200	Apr. 13	1494
Aug. 11	1661	May 13	1660
Sept. 11	1481	June 13	1549
Oct. 11	1413	Jul. 13	1853
Nov. 11	1673	Aug 13	1684
Dec. 11	1293	Sept. 13	1654
Jan. 12	1279	Oct. 13	1753
Feb. 12	1673	Nov. 13	1597
Mar. 12	1770	Dec. 13	1208
Apr. 12	1286	Jan. 14	1515
May 12	1769	Feb. 14	1651
June 12	1756	Mar. 14	1713
Jul. 12	1766	Apr. 14	1528
Aug. 12	1817	May 14	1955
Sept. 12	1484	June 14	1783

P15-11 **15.11** Data for the number of internet subscribers (in thousands) in Australia for June 2009 to December 2013 are shown below. Fit a quadratic trend model to the data and predict the number of internet subscribers in January 2014.

June 09	8 420
Dec. 09	8 950
June 10	9 502
Dec. 10	10 446
June 11	10 906
Dec. 11	11 596
June 12	12 036
Dec. 12	12 161
June 13	12 358
Dec. 13	12 397

P15-12 **15.12** Time-series data for the number of owner–managers of unincorporated businesses in Australia ('000s) are shown in the table below. Fit an exponential trend model to the data and forecast the number of owner–managers for period 14.

Period	Number of owner–managers ('000s)
1	335.7
2	350.3
3	399.3
4	393.4
5	468.3
6	409.4
7	464.6
8	483.6
9	475.1
10	510.9
11	501.3
12	535.3
13	544.3

P15-13 **15.13** The table below shows annual time-series data for New Zealand exports taken from the World Bank's *World Development Indicators*. Use the data to develop an autoregressive forecasting model with a two-year lag. Predict exports in year 24.

Year	Real GDP
1	72.100
2	74.445
3	77.660
4	79.787
5	83.723
6	84.368
7	86.135
8	86.492
9	86.376
10	86.862
11	86.847
12	85.701
13	86.646
14	92.233
15	97.114
16	101.129
17	104.697
18	106.248
19	106.673
20	111.866
21	114.842
22	118.605
23	123.832

Testing your understanding

P15-14 **15.14** ABS monthly time-series data for the number of people employed on a full-time basis are shown in the table below. Plot the data. Estimate the following forecasting models: linear trend, quadratic trend and exponential trend. Compute a forecast for the number of people employed in July 2014 with each model. Compare the three models using appropriate measures and choose the best forecasting model, giving your reasons.

Period	Number employed ('000s)
Jan. 11	7839
Feb. 11	7938
Mar. 11	7902
Apr. 11	7849
May 11	7831
June 11	7870
July 11	7907
Aug. 11	7809
Sept. 11	8014
Oct. 11	7891
Nov. 11	7907
Dec. 11	8041
Jan. 12	7922
Feb. 12	7988
Mar. 12	7938
Apr. 12	7912
May 12	7984
June 12	7924
July 12	7988
Aug. 12	7896
Sept. 12	8135
Oct. 12	8007
Nov. 12	8042
Dec. 12	8133
Jan. 13	8002
Feb. 13	8047
Mar. 13	7967
Apr. 13	7997
May 13	8010
June 13	7974
July 13	8024
Aug. 13	7926

Period	Number employed ('000s)
Sept. 13	8127
Oct. 13	7952
Nov. 13	8009
Dec. 13	8063
Jan. 14	7958
Feb. 14	8091
Mar. 14	7992
Apr. 14	8012
May 14	8061
June 14	8018

P15-15 **15.15** The following table shows quarterly data for the amount of motor vehicle taxes collected by the federal government in Australia for the period March 2007 to March 2014.

a. Develop 2-lag and 4-lag models.
b. Determine the forecast for the June 2014 quarter.
c. Compute a Durbin–Watson statistic to determine whether significant autocorrelation is present in the models. Use an alpha of .05.
d. Comment on the appropriateness of the models based on your results in (a) and the goodness-of-fit measures.

Period	Motor vehicle taxes ($ millions)	Period	Motor vehicle taxes ($ millions)
Mar. 07	1 454	Dec. 10	1 819
June 07	1 557	Mar. 11	1 784
Sept. 07	1 598	June 11	1 956
Dec. 07	1 539	Sept. 11	2 006
Mar. 08	1 541	Dec. 11	1 891
June 08	1 707	Mar. 12	1 894
Sept. 08	1 705	June 12	2 094
Dec. 08	1 575	Sept. 12	2 163
Mar. 09	1 502	Dec. 12	2 078
June 09	1 677	Mar. 13	2 011
Sept. 09	1 760	June 13	2 216
Dec. 09	1 714	Sept. 13	2 259
Mar. 10	1 656	Dec. 13	2 148
June 10	1 787	Mar. 14	2 121
Sept. 10	1 903		

15.5 Evaluating alternative forecasting models

How does a decision maker know which forecasting technique is doing the best job in predicting the future? One way is to compare forecast values with actual values to determine the **error of a forecast** using formula 15.3. The error measures how closely the model fits the actual data at each point and is defined as the difference between the actual value and the forecast of that value.

Error of a forecast (15.3)

$$e_t = x_t - F_t$$

where:
e_t = the error of the forecast
x_t = the actual value
F_t = the forecast value

A perfect model would lead to errors (or residuals) of zero for each time period. Several techniques can be used to measure overall error, including mean error, mean absolute deviation (MAD), mean square error (MSE), mean percentage error (MPE) and mean absolute percentage error (MAPE). Here we will consider MAD and MSE.

The **mean absolute deviation (MAD)** is the mean, or average, of the absolute values of the errors. Formula 15.4 is used to calculate MAD.

Mean absolute deviation (15.4)

$$\text{MAD} = \frac{\sum |y_t - F_t|}{n}$$

where:
y_t = the actual value at time t
F_t = the forecast value at time t
n = the number of time periods

The **mean square error (MSE)** is also a measure of the variability in the forecast errors and is similar to the MSE we encounter in regression and analysis of variance. It is *computed by squaring each error (thus creating a positive number) and averaging the squared errors*. Formula 15.5 is used to calculate MSE.

Mean square error (15.5)

$$\text{MSE} = \frac{\sum (y_t - F_t)^2}{n}$$

where:
y_t = the actual value at time t
F_t = the forecast value at time t
n = the number of time periods

DEMONSTRATION PROBLEM 15.6

DP15-06 PROBLEM: The table below shows annual data for total international trade in goods and services for Australia for the period 1985–86 to 2010–11. Calculate MAD and MSE for the linear trend model forecasts for total international trade in goods and services.

SOLUTION: The following table shows the MAD and MSE calculations.

Period, x_t	Total trade, y_t	Predicted total trade, F_t	Error $(y_t - F_t)$	Error^2 $(y_t - F_t)^2$	Absolute deviation, $\lvert(y_t - F_t)\rvert$
1	39.059	15.322	23.74	563.45	23.74
2	44.264	24.750	19.51	380.79	19.51
3	51.78	34.178	17.60	309.82	17.60
4	55.675	43.606	12.07	145.65	12.07
5	61.17	53.035	8.14	66.18	8.14
6	66.571	62.463	4.11	16.88	4.11
7	70.511	71.891	−1.38	1.90	1.38
8	77.916	81.319	−3.40	11.58	3.40

Period, x_t	Total trade, y_t	Predicted total trade, F_t	Error $(y_t - F_t)$	Error² $(y_t - F_t)^2$	Absolute deviation, $\|(y_t - F_t)\|$
9	83.838	90.748	−6.91	47.74	6.91
10	88.583	100.176	−11.59	134.39	11.59
11	99.895	109.604	−9.71	94.26	9.71
12	106.448	119.032	−12.58	158.36	12.58
13	115.314	128.460	−13.15	172.83	13.15
14	113.837	137.889	−24.05	578.48	24.05
15	128.409	147.317	−18.91	357.51	18.91
16	155.995	156.745	−0.75	0.56	0.75
17	155.771	166.173	−10.40	108.21	10.40
18	151.493	175.601	−24.11	581.22	24.11
19	146.48	185.030	−38.55	1 486.08	38.55
20	166.805	194.458	−27.65	764.68	27.65
21	195.944	203.886	−7.94	63.08	7.94
22	216.795	213.314	3.48	12.12	3.48
23	233.813	222.743	11.07	122.56	11.07
24	284.571	232.171	52.40	2 745.79	52.40
25	253.762	241.599	12.16	147.94	12.16
26	297.84	251.03	46.81	2 191.25	46.81
				Sum = 11263.31	Sum = 422.18
				$\text{MSE} = \frac{(y_t - F_t)^2}{n} = 433.20$	$\text{MAD} = \frac{\|y_t - F_t\|}{n} = 16.23$

KaddStat can be used to compute forecast errors. Please refer to 'Going further with KaddStat' for KaddStat instructions at www.johnwiley.com.au/highered/black4e/kaddstat.

PRACTICE PROBLEMS

Practising the calculations

P15-16 **15.16** The following table gives forecast errors from a linear trend model used to forecast a company's annual sales. Use these forecast errors to compute MAD and MSE. Discuss the information yielded by each type of error measurement.

Year	Error
2005	3.0
2006	2.8
2007	−2.0
2008	1.4
2009	0.5
2010	−1.1
2011	−2.3
2012	−1.7
2013	1.6

P15-17 **15.17** Determine the error for each of the following forecasts. Compute MAD and MSE.

Period	Value	Forecast
1	202	–
2	191	202
3	173	192
4	169	181
5	171	174
6	175	172
7	182	174
8	196	179
9	204	189
10	219	198
11	227	211

Testing your understanding

P15-18 **15.18** Using the following data, determine the values of MAD and MSE. Explain any similarities and differences between the two measures.

Period	Value	Forecast
1	19.4	16.6
2	23.6	19.1
3	24.0	22.0
4	26.8	24.8
5	29.2	25.9
6	35.5	28.6

P15-19 **15.19** The following are data for job vacancies in the mining industry in Australia for the period November 2009 to May 2014. Use the data to answer the following questions.

a. Compute a 4-period moving average to forecast job vacancies for the given period.

b. Compute a 4-year weighted moving average to forecast job vacancies for the given period. Weight the most recent period by 4, the next most recent period by 3, the next period by 2 and the last period of the four by 1.

c. Determine the errors for parts (a) and (b). Compute the MSE for parts (a) and (b). Compare the MSE values and comment on the effectiveness of the moving average versus the weighted moving average for these data.

Period	Job vacancies ('000s)
Nov. 09	4.1
Feb. 10	5.2
May 10	6.2
Aug. 10	7.1
Nov. 10	7.7
Feb. 11	8.1
May 11	9.5
Aug. 11	9.9
Nov. 11	10.3
Feb. 12	9.9
May 12	9.6
Aug. 12	8.0
Nov. 12	8.3
Feb. 13	6.7
May 13	5.1
Aug. 13	4.9
Nov. 13	4.7
Feb. 14	5.0
May 14	4.2

15.6 Index numbers

This chapter has presented various methods to analyse and forecast time series. In this section, we introduce the concept of index numbers. An **index number** is a percentage that expresses a measurement in a given period in terms of the corresponding measurement for a selected **base period**. The base period is a particular point in time (often in the past), against which all comparisons are made. Index numbers are widely used in economics and business to provide a basis for making comparisons of changes in a given variable (or variables) over time. There are numerous indices in use today which consider prices, values, quantities, sociological conditions and other factors. One of the most common is the consumer price index (CPI), which describes the change in prices from one time period to another for a fixed market 'basket' of items. Therefore, an increase in the CPI from month to month indicates that the cost of living is increasing. Other popular indices include the Australian All Ordinaries (All Ords) Index, the Australian Securities Exchange (ASX) Index, the Dow Jones Industrial Average, the Nikkei Index and the Standard & Poor's Index of 500 Stocks. In this section, we will consider only price indices.

In addition to allowing us to compare prices at different points in time, we can use price indices to deflate the effect of inflation on time-series data in order to compare values in real dollar terms instead of in actual dollars. We begin our discussion with the simple price index, followed by the unweighted and weighted aggregate price indices.

Simple price index

Formula 15.6 is used to calculate a **simple price index**.

Simple price index
(15.6)

$$I_i = \frac{P_i}{P_0}(100)$$

where:

P_0 = the quantity, price or cost in the base year
P_i = the quantity, price or cost in the year of interest
I_i = the index number for the year of interest

TABLE 15.7 Average prices of unleaded petrol in the Brisbane metropolitan area, 2000–2010

Period	Average price (cents/litre)
2000	79.3
2001	79.9
2002	79.5
2003	82.0
2004	90.4
2005	103.2
2006	118.3
2007	118.5
2008	134.8
2009	117.6
2010	127.5

As an example of the simple price index, consider the average price per litre of unleaded petrol in the Brisbane metropolitan area for the years 2000 to 2010 as shown in table 15.7.

Suppose we want to compute price indices for the time series using the year 2000 as the base year. Using formula 15.6, the simple price index for 2010 is:

$$I_{2010} = \frac{P_{2010}}{P_{2000}} = \frac{127.5}{79.3}(100) = 160.8$$

The value of 160.8 indicates that the price of petrol in the Brisbane area in 2010 was 60.8% higher than in 2000. Table 15.8 displays all the price indices for the data in table 15.7, with 2000 as the base year, along with the raw data. A cursory glance at these index numbers reveals that petrol price rises in Brisbane were fairly small from 2000 to 2003. Petrol prices began to escalate in 2005, reaching a peak in 2008 as a result of supply-related issues, combined with the GFC. Although prices declined in 2009, 2010 saw a resurgence of petrol prices. This example shows that index numbers allow us to make quicker price comparisons than the actual prices themselves.

TABLE 15.8 Price indices for unleaded petrol in the Brisbane metropolitan area, 2000–2010

Period	Average price (cents/litre)	Index
2000	79.3	100.0
2001	79.9	100.8
2002	79.5	100.2
2003	82.0	103.4
2004	90.4	114.0
2005	103.2	130.1
2006	118.3	149.1
2007	118.5	149.4
2008	134.8	170.0
2009	117.6	148.3
2010	127.5	160.8

Aggregate price indices

Although simple index numbers can be useful, as we saw in the previous example, they have a major limitation in the sense that they can be used only for a single item or commodity. However, there are instances where we might be interested in comparing prices of a collection of items, say a market basket of goods and services. In such cases, we can use an aggregate price index. There are two main types of aggregate price indices: unweighted aggregate price index and weighted aggregate price index.

Unweighted aggregate price index

An **unweighted aggregate price index** puts equal weight or importance on all the items in the market basket. Formula 15.7 is used to calculate an unweighted aggregate price index.

Unweighted aggregate price index number (15.7)

$$I_i = \frac{\Sigma P_i}{\Sigma P_0}(100)$$

where:

P_i = the price of an item in the year of interest (i)
P_0 = the price of an item in the base year (0)
I_i = the index number for the year of interest (i)

Suppose a state's department of social services wants to compare the cost of family food over several years. Department officials decide that, instead of using a single food item to do this comparison, they will use a food basket that consists of five items: eggs, milk, bananas, potatoes and sugar. They gathered price information on these five items for the years 2005, 2010 and 2015. The items and the prices are listed in table 15.9.

TABLE 15.9 Prices of a basket of food items

Item	2005	2010	2015
Eggs (dozen)	1.28	1.60	2.09
Milk (2 litres)	1.50	1.90	2.49
Bananas (per kg)	1.05	1.10	1.98
Bread (per loaf)	2.00	2.60	3.42
Potatoes (per kg)	0.70	1.67	2.98
Total	**6.53**	**8.87**	**12.96**

Using the data in table 15.9 and formula 15.7, the unweighted aggregate price indices for the years 2005, 2010 and 2015 can be computed by using 2005 as the base year. The first step is to add, or aggregate, the prices of all the food basket items in a given year. These totals are shown in the last row of table 15.9. The index numbers are constructed by using these totals, rather than the individual item prices: $\Sigma P_{2005} = 6.53$, $\Sigma P_{2010} = 8.87$, $\Sigma P_{2015} = 12.96$. From these figures, the unweighted aggregate price index for 2010 is computed as follows.

$$\text{For 2010: } I_{2010} = \frac{\Sigma P_{2010}}{\Sigma P_{2005}}(100) = \frac{8.87}{6.53}(100) = 135.8$$

This index means that prices in 2010 were 35.8% higher than in 2005.

Weighted aggregate price index

An unweighted aggregate price index has two major limitations. First, by placing equal weights on all commodities in the market basket, it is implied that each commodity is equally important. However, this means that, per unit, more expensive commodities will have more influence on the index. Secondly, because not all the commodities are consumed at the same rate, changes in the price of the least consumed commodity will have undue influence on the index. A **weighted aggregate price index** addresses these problems by accounting for differences in the levels of prices per unit and differences in the levels of consumption in the market basket. Formula 15.8 is used to calculate a weighted aggregate price index by using quantity weights in each time period (year).

Weighted aggregate price index number (15.8)

$$I_i = \frac{\Sigma P_i Q_i}{\Sigma P_0 Q_0}(100)$$

where:

Q_0 = the quantity in the base year
Q_i = the quantity in the year of interest
P_0 = the price in the base year
P_i = the price in the year of interest

Two common weighted aggregate price indices are used in business and economics. These are the Laspeyres index and the Paasche index.

Laspeyres price index

The **Laspeyres price index** is *a weighted aggregate price index computed by using the quantities of the base period (year) for all other years*. The advantages of this technique are that the price indices for all years can be compared, and new quantities do not have to be determined for each year. Formula 15.9 is used to calculate a Laspeyres price index.

Laspeyres price index (15.9)

$$I_L = \frac{\sum P_i Q_0}{\sum P_0 Q_0}(100)$$

where:

Q_0 = the quantity in the base year
P_0 = the price in the base year
P_i = the price in the year of interest

Notice that formula 15.9 requires the base period quantities (Q_0) in both the numerator and the denominator.

The food basket presented in table 15.9 consists of eggs, milk, bananas, bread and potatoes. Aggregate price indices were computed for these items by combining (aggregating) the prices of all items for a given year. The unweighted aggregate price indices computed for these data gave all items equal importance.

Suppose that policy analysts realise that applying equal weight to these five items is probably not a representative way to construct this food basket and so they consequently ascertain quantity usage weights for each food item for one year's consumption. Table 15.10 lists these five items, their prices and their quantity usage weights for the base year (2005).

TABLE 15.10 Food basket items with quantity usage weights

	Price		Base year (2005)	
Item	**2010**	**2015**	**Price**	**Quantity**
Eggs (dozen)	1.60	2.09	1.28	45
Milk (2 litres)	1.90	2.49	1.50	50
Bananas (per kg)	1.10	1.98	1.05	25
Bread (per loaf)	2.60	3.42	2.00	50
Potatoes (per kg)	1.67	2.98	0.70	48

From these data, the policy analysts can compute Laspeyres price indices. For example, the Laspeyres price index for 2010 with 2005 as the base year is:

$$I_{2010} = \frac{\sum P_i Q_0}{\sum P_0 Q_0}(100) = \frac{\sum P_{2010} Q_{2005}}{\sum P_{2005} Q_{2005}} \times 100$$

$$= \frac{(1.60 \times 45) + (1.90 \times 50) + (1.10 \times 25) + (2.60 \times 50) + (1.67 \times 48)}{(1.28 \times 45) + (1.50 \times 50) + (1.05 \times 25) + (2.00 \times 50) + (0.70 \times 48)} \times 100$$

$$= \frac{404.7}{292.5} \times 100 = 138.4$$

The Laspeyres price index of 138.4 indicates that the cost of buying this food basket in 2010 was 38.4% more than in 2005. This is higher than the unweighted index of 135.8 we found earlier, reflecting the fact that the prices of the most consumed goods (milk and bread) rose more than those of the less consumed goods during this period.

Paasche price index

The **Paasche price index** is *a weighted aggregate price index computed by using the quantities for the year of interest in computations for a given year*. The advantage of this technique is that it incorporates current quantity figures in the calculations. One disadvantage is that ascertaining quantity figures for each time period is expensive. Formula 15.10 is used to calculate a Paasche price index.

Paasche price index (15.10)

$$I_P = \frac{\Sigma P_i Q_i}{\Sigma P_0 Q_i}(100)$$

where:

Q_i = the quantity in the year of interest
P_0 = the price in the base year
P_i = the price in the year of interest

Suppose the yearly quantities for the basket of food items listed in table 15.10 are determined. The result is the quantity usage weights and prices shown in table 15.11 for the years 2005 and 2010, which can be used to compute Paasche price index numbers.

TABLE 15.11 Food basket items with yearly quantity usage weights for 2005 and 2010

Item	P_{2005}	Q_{2005}	P_{2010}	Q_{2010}
Eggs (dozen)	1.28	45	1.60	42
Milk (2 litres)	1.50	50	1.90	48
Bananas (per kg)	1.05	25	1.10	26
Bread (per loaf)	2.00	50	2.60	50
Potatoes (per kg)	0.70	48	1.67	40

The Paasche price index for 2010 can be determined by using a base year of 2005 as follows.

$$I_{2010} = \frac{\Sigma P_i Q_i}{\Sigma P_0 Q_i}(100) = \frac{\Sigma P_{2010} Q_{2010}}{\Sigma P_{2005} Q_{2010}} \times 100$$

$$= \frac{(1.60 \times 42) + (1.90 \times 48) + (1.10 \times 26) + (2.60 \times 50) + (1.67 \times 40)}{(1.28 \times 42) + (1.50 \times 48) + (1.05 \times 26) + (2.00 \times 50) + (0.70 \times 40)} \times 100$$

$$= \frac{383.8}{281.1} \times 100 = 136.5$$

The value of 136.5 means that prices rose by 36.5% between 2005 and 2010.

DEMONSTRATION PROBLEM 15.7

PROBLEM: A survey was carried out in a popular supermarket at the same time over two periods to study price trends. The prices of five items were examined in the survey. Shown below are the items, their prices and the quantities used weekly by a typical household for the years 2010 and 2014. Use these data to develop unweighted aggregate price indices for 2014 with a base year of 2010. Compute the Laspeyres price index for the year 2014 using 2010 as the base year. Compute the Paasche index number for 2014 using 2010 as the base year.

	2010		2014	
Item	**Price**	**Quantity**	**Price**	**Quantity**
Beef steak (1 kg)	15.50	4	18.00	5
Bread (680 g)	4.35	3	5.10	5
Milk (1 litre)	1.40	4	1.5	6
Potatoes (1 kg)	1.80	2	2.90	4
Coffee (150 g)	9.20	2	10.00	2

SOLUTION: Unweighted aggregate index for 2014:

$$I_{2014}=\frac{\Sigma P_{2014}}{\Sigma P_{2010}}(100)=\frac{37.50}{32.25}(100)=116.3$$

The Laspeyres index for 2014 is calculated as follows.

$$\begin{aligned}I_{2014}&=\frac{\Sigma P_{2014}Q_{2010}}{\Sigma P_{2010}Q_{2010}}\times 100\\&=\frac{(18.00\times 4)+(5.10\times 3)+(1.50\times 4)+(2.90\times 2)+(10.00\times 2)}{(15.50\times 4)+(4.35\times 3)+(1.40\times 4)+(1.80\times 2)+(9.20\times 2)}\times 100\\&=\frac{119.10}{102.65}\times 100\\&=116.0\end{aligned}$$

The Paasche index for 2014 is calculated as follows.

$$\begin{aligned}I_{2014}&=\frac{\Sigma P_{2014}Q_{2014}}{\Sigma P_{2010}Q_{2014}}\times 100\\&=\frac{(18.00\times 5)+(5.10\times 5)+(1.50\times 6)+(2.90\times 4)+(10.00\times 2)}{(15.50\times 5)+(4.35\times 5)+(1.40\times 6)+(1.80\times 4)+(9.20\times 2)}\times 100\\&=\frac{156.1}{133.25}\times 100\\&=117.2\end{aligned}$$

According to these results, between 2010 and 2014, the cost of this basket of groceries increased by 16.3% based on the unweighted aggregate price index, 16% based on the Laspeyres index, and 17.2% based on the Paasche index.

Laspeyres and Paasche indices compared

Given that the Laspeyres index uses a fixed-weight formula, it is convenient to use because new expenditure weights do not have to be specified every time the index is calculated. Thus, expensive surveys are avoided. The fixed-weight approach is reasonable if there is not much change in consumption patterns. On the other hand, the Paasche index uses different expenditure weights in each period, which means that it can be used only to make comparisons between the current and base periods. For these reasons, the Laspeyres index tends to be preferred to the Paasche index. In a period of price rises and therefore changing demand patterns, the Laspeyres index will tend to overestimate the overall price rise, while the Paasche index will underestimate it. **Fisher's Ideal index** minimises both kinds of errors by using the geometric mean of the Laspeyres and Paasche index numbers as shown in formula 15.11.

Fisher's Ideal index
(15.11)

$$I_F=\sqrt{\frac{\Sigma P_iQ_0}{\Sigma P_0Q_0}(100)\frac{\Sigma P_iQ_i}{\Sigma P_0Q_i}(100)}$$

where:

Q_0 = the quantity in the base year
P_0 = the price in the base year
P_i = the price in the year of interest

Using the data in demonstration problem 15.7, Fisher's Ideal index is:

$$I_{2014} = \sqrt{\frac{\sum P_{2014}Q_{2010}}{\sum P_{2010}Q_{2010}}(100)\frac{\sum P_{2014}Q_{2014}}{\sum P_{2010}Q_{2014}}(100)}$$

$$= \sqrt{\frac{119.10}{102.65}(100) \times \frac{156.10}{133.25}(100)}$$

$$= \sqrt{(116.0)(117.2)}$$

$$= 116.6$$

Changing the base period

Very often, statistical agencies such as the ABS change the base period of a given index number series. This happens because of the need to update the base period to a more recent period. Suppose, for example, that 1990 was used as the base year for data collected in the 1990s; however, the base year was changed to 2000 for data from the year 2000. This results in two different series that are not comparable. To be able to compare prices between 1990 and 2009, it would be necessary to form a single continuous index, sometimes referred to as a *chained index*.

DEMONSTRATION PROBLEM 15.8

PROBLEM: The following are two series of house price indices for Australia. The first series has 1990 as the base year (1990 = 100), and the second has 2000 as the base year (2000 = 100). Construct a new house price index for Australia with 2000 as the base year.

Year	Series 1 (1990 = 100)	Series 2 (2000 = 100)
1997	101.6	
1998	102.9	
1999	104.0	
2000	105.0	100.2
2001		100.0
2002		100.1
2003		100.6
2004		100.7
2005		102.2
2006		110.2
2007		122.0

SOLUTION: To construct a single series, first find the year in which the two series overlap. This is 2000, where the index number is 105.0 with 1990 as the base year, and 100.2 with 2000 as the base year.

The new index number for 1999 is:

$$I_{1999} = 104.0 \times \frac{100.2}{105.0} = 99.2$$

In the same manner, the new index number for 1998 is:

$$I_{1998} = 102.9 \times \frac{100.2}{105.0} = 98.2$$

Finally, the index number for 1997 is:

$$I_{1997} = 101.6 \times \frac{100.2}{105.0} = 97.0$$

The new series is shown in the following table.

Year	Series 1 (1990 = 100)	Series 2 (2000 = 100)	Combined series (2000 = 100)
1997	101.6		97.0
1998	102.9		98.2
1999	104.0		99.2
2000	105.0	100.2	100.2
2001		100.0	100.0
2002		100.1	100.1
2003		100.6	100.6
2004		100.7	100.7
2005		102.2	102.2
2006		110.2	110.2
2007		122.0	122.0

Applications of price indices

As indicated earlier, the CPI is used as a key measure of inflation. The CPI, published quarterly, is a weighted aggregate price index based on a variation of the Laspeyres index. As is the case with all price indices, the base period (i.e. the period in which the index is set equal to 100.0) is changed periodically. Numerous other indices are used widely in the public and private sectors. They include several producer price indices, which measure industry outputs and inputs; the House Price Index, which measures inflation or deflation in the price of the stock of houses over time; and the Pensioner and Beneficiary Living Cost Index, which is designed to assess the impact of changes in out-of-pocket living expenses of households whose principal source of income is from government pensions and benefits.

An important use of a price index is as a price deflator to convert nominal or actual dollars into real dollars by taking inflation into account. For example, table 15.12 shows time-series data for average weekly earnings in Australia from 2005 to 2010. Based on these data, we can see that average weekly earnings in this period increased from $1083.60 to $1362.50, an increase of 26%. However, this is a nominal increase because we have not taken into account the fact that the CPI increased from 150.6 to 174.0, which is equivalent to an increase of 23% in inflation. To obtain the increase in real wages during this period, we can deflate the actual average weekly earnings for each year by dividing by the corresponding CPI and multiplying by 100; for example:

$$\text{Real average weekly earnings in 2005} = \frac{1083.60}{150.6} \times 100 = \$719.52$$

The remaining real average weekly earnings are shown in the last column of table 15.12. It can be seen that, in real terms, average weekly earnings increased by 8.7% between 2005 and 2010. Such information could be used by unions when bargaining with businesses or the government for wage increases.

TABLE 15.12 Actual and real average weekly earnings in Australia

Year	Average weekly earnings ($)	CPI	Real weekly earnings ($)
2005	1083.60	150.6	719.52
2006	1125.90	155.5	724.05
2007	1175.40	160.1	734.17
2008	1232.30	166.0	742.35
2009	1311.20	169.5	773.57
2010	1361.50	174.0	782.47

PRACTICE PROBLEMS

Practising the calculations

P15-20 **15.20** The following table gives the price of a basket of groceries in a certain city from 2008 to 2014. Find the simple index numbers for the data.

a. Let 2008 be the base year.
b. Let 2010 be the base year.

Year	Price ($)
2008	60.50
2009	65.03
2010	70.05
2011	80.55
2012	92.80
2014	112.10

P15-21 **15.21** Using the following price data collected from Brisbane supermarkets, compute the unweighted aggregate price index numbers for the four types of meat. Let 2005 be the base year for this market basket of goods.

	Year		
Item	2005	2010	2015
Sausages (per kg)	3.99	4.50	4.98
Pork chops (per kg)	8.99	9.98	13.49
Beef steak (per kg)	12.85	13.99	18.99
Roast lamb (per kg)	4.05	4.98	6.95

P15-22 **15.22** Calculate Laspeyres price indices for 2013–2015 from the following data. Use 2005 as the base year.

Item	2005 quantity	2005 price ($)	2013 price ($)	2014 price ($)	2015 price ($)
1	21	0.50	0.67	0.68	0.71
2	6	1.23	1.85	1.90	1.91
3	17	0.84	.75	.75	.80
4	43	0.15	.21	.25	.25

P15-23 **15.23** Calculate Paasche price indices for 2014 and 2015 using the following data and 2005 as the base year.

Item	2005 price ($)	2014 price ($)	2014 quantity	2015 price ($)	2015 quantity
1	22.50	27.80	13	28.11	12
2	10.90	13.10	5	13.25	8
3	1.85	2.25	41	2.35	44

Testing your understanding

P15-24 **15.24** The following table summarises the unit sales and prices for a food manufacturer from 2012 to 2015.

	Cashew nuts		Macadamia nuts	
Year	Quantity (kg)	Price ($/kg)	Quantity (kg)	Price ($/kg)
2012	560	9.50	40	14.00
2013	590	10.50	180	16.00
2014	635	16.00	230	19.50
2015	885	18.00	380	23.00

Using 2012 as the base year, construct an unweighted price index, a Laspeyres index and a Paasche index. Interpret each index and explain any differences that you find in your results.

P15-25 **15.25** From 2010 to 2015, the average hourly earnings of production workers in a certain factory went from $9.85 to $17.36, and the consumer price index went from 82.4 to 152.4. What was the percentage increase or decrease in the average worker's real earnings? Explain your result.

P15-26 **15.26** The following table presents two price index series, one with 2001 = 100 for the period 2001 to 2009, and the other with 2009 = 100 for the period 2009 to 2015. Construct a single series for the period 2001 to 2015, using 2009 as the base year. How much have prices risen during this period?

Year	Series 1 (2001 = 100)	Series 2 (2009 = 100)
2001	100.0	
2002	103.0	
2003	108.1	
2004	110.0	
2005	117.2	
2006	120.1	
2007	122.0	
2008	122.5	
2009	130.5	100.0
2010		104.3
2011		106.5
2012		110.0
2013		112.9
2014		118.5
2015		120.5

MISUSE OF STATISTICS

Time-series methods use historical data to extrapolate future values. Their main advantage is that they require fewer assumptions than other econometric methods, and they do not require knowledge of independent variables to predict changes in the dependent variable. The key assumption here is that the past trends in a variable's movement will continue into the future. This assumption has been criticised for being mechanical and this may be justified in some cases because various business and economic factors may underlie changes in a given variable.

Choices made by the analyst could affect the value and accuracy of the forecast. Examples include the choice of parameters, such as the value of a smoothing constant and the length of the forecast horizon. In general, the longer the forecast horizon, the less reliable is the forecast. It is recommended that time-series methods be used in tandem with other forecasting methods, including the use of business judgement, to inform business decision making. It is also a good idea to present forecasts with additional information such as the forecast error (e.g. MAD and MSE) and the model diagnostics to support the appropriateness of the model (or models) employed.

CHAPTER CASE **REVISITED**

Forecasting at Combaro Ltd

1. A plot of the series for personal and housing loans is provided in the figure at right. It can be seen that the linear trend model would be appropriate to use in forecasting personal loans because the series is roughly linear, with personal loans growing by approximately the same amounts every year. On the other hand, a quadratic model or exponential model could be more appropriate for forecasting housing loans, because the series is nonlinear, with housing loans growing by increasing amounts every year. For the same reason, an exponential trend model could also be used for forecasting housing loans.

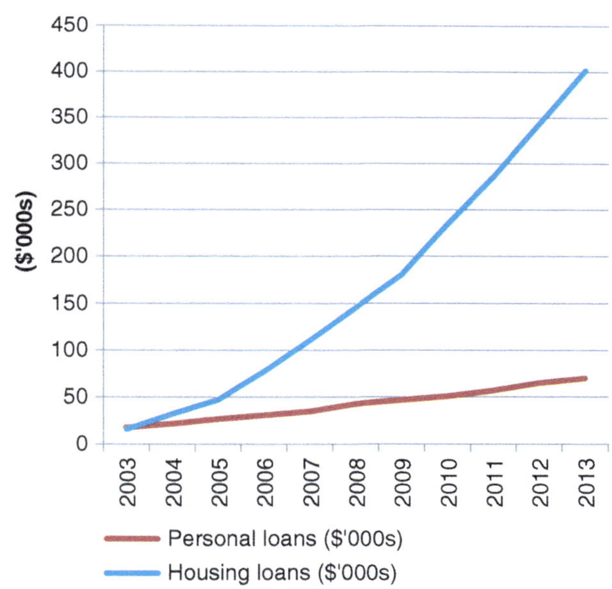

Year	Personal loans ($000)	Housing loans ($000)
2003	18	17.3
2004	22	32.6
2005	27	47.5
2006	31	77.4
2007	35	111.2
2008	43	146.2
2009	47	180.5
2010	51	234.8
2011	57	285.8
2012	65	343.5
2013	70	401.5

2. The linear trend model estimate for personal loans is:

$$\hat{y}_t = 11.055 + 5.218x_t;$$

adjusted $R^2 = .993$,

where $x = 0$ in 2002

The quadratic trend model estimate for housing loans is:

$$\hat{y}_t = 6.219 + 7.364x_t + 2.616x_t^2;$$

adjusted $R^2 = .9998$,

where $x = 0$ in 2002

The exponential trend model estimate for housing loans is:

$$\log \hat{y}_t = 1.281 + .131x_t$$

The adjusted R^2 is 99.3% for the linear trend model and 99.9% for the quadratic model. It is not meaningful to compare the R^2 of the exponential trend model with that of the quadratic model because the dependent variable in the former is a logarithm. As can be seen later, we make this comparison using the forecast errors. In general, the linear and quadratic models fit their respective time series very well. The graph below shows actual personal loans data versus the fitted linear trend line; it confirms the observation that a linear trend regression model provides a close fit to the data. However, the graph on the following page showing actual housing loans versus the fitted linear trend line suggests that forecasts based on a linear trend regression model would tend to underestimate actual housing loans.

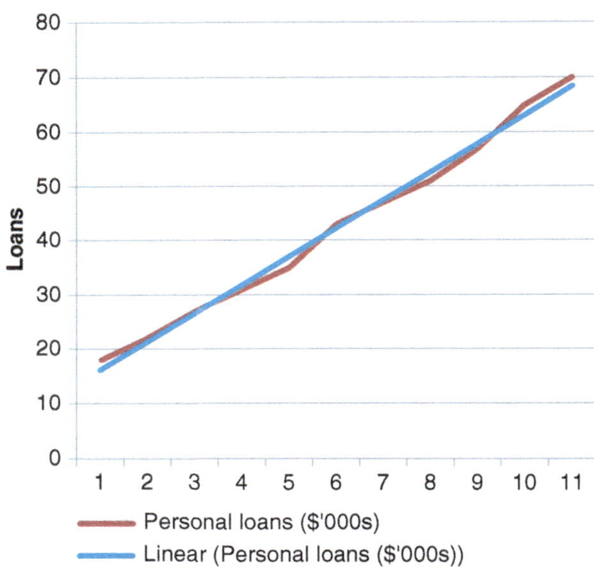

Predictions for 2014 ($t = 12$) using the linear trend model for personal loans and the quadratic and exponential trend models for housing loans, respectively, are:

$$\hat{y}_{12} = 11.055 + 5.218(12) = 73.671$$
$$\hat{y}_{12} = 6.219 + 7.364(12) + 2.616(144) = 471.291$$
$$\log \hat{y}_{12} = 1.281 + .131(12) = 2.853$$
$$\hat{y}_{12} = 10^{2.853} = 712.853$$

According to the results, the value of personal loans in 2014 is predicted to be $73 671 using the linear trend model. The value of housing loans is predicted to be $471 291 using the quadratic trend model, and $712 853 using the exponential trend model.

Forecast accuracy for the quadratic and exponential trend models can be compared using MAD and MSE. The results are summarised in the table below. The quadratic model produces a more accurate forecast because its MAD and MSE are much smaller than those of the exponential trend model.

Model	MAD	MSE
Quadratic trend	2.229	7.078
Exponential trend	27.584	2516.889

3. Because the cash rate data are monthly data, the 12-month ratio-to-moving average model could be used to compute seasonal indices to deseasonalise the data. The following output shows a comparison of the actual and deseasonalised data. It can be seen that the actual and deseasonalised data are a close fit. This suggests that fluctuations in the cash rate were not excessive. There was a steady increase in the cash rate from May 2006 (period 1) to August 2008 (period 27), followed by a rapid decline between September 2008 (period 28) and May 2009 (period). There was a brief recovery from that period to October 2011 (period 65). However, the cash rate has been on a downward trend since then.

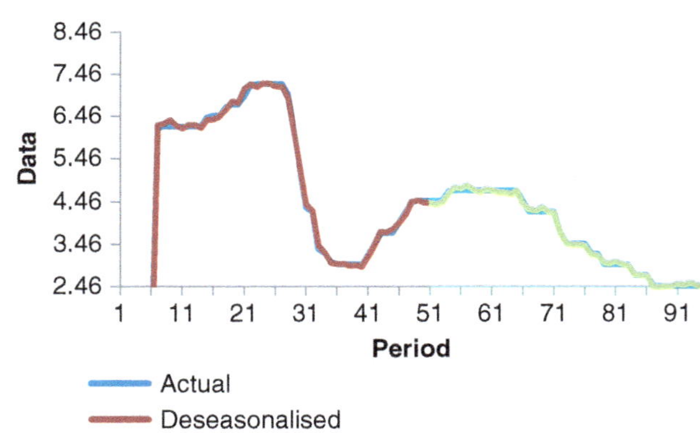

4. The plot of the regression residuals opposite shows a curvilinear pattern, which indicates that autocorrelation is present in this data series. The Durbin–Watson test statistic is $D = .06$. Given a d_L of 1.64 for $k = 1$, the null hypothesis that there is no autocorrelation can be rejected at $\alpha = .05$. This result means that least squares trend-based forecasting models would not be reliable tools to use for forecasting the cash rate.

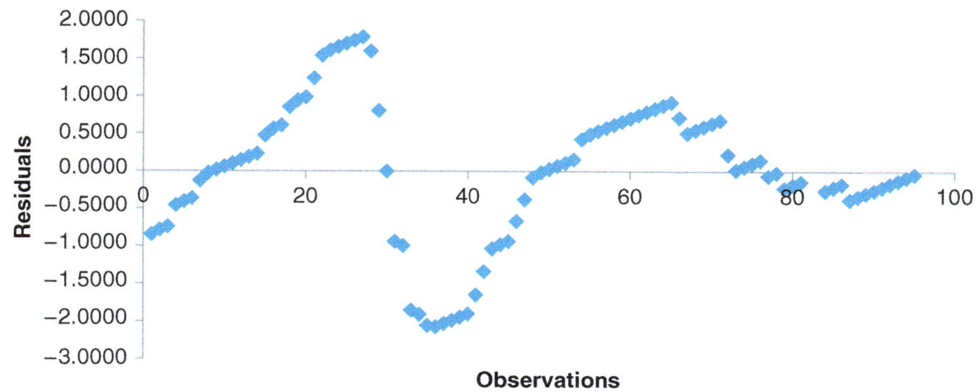

With the presence of autocorrelation, it would be more appropriate to use the autoregressive forecasting model. Since these are monthly data, lags of up to 12 months could be used if the sample size permits. Excel output for a 6-lag autoregressive model is shown below.

	A	B	C	D	E	F
1	SUMMARY OUTPUT					
2						
3	*Regression Statistics*					
4	Multiple R	0.993				
5	R Square	0.986				
6	Adjusted R Square	0.985				
7	Standard Error	0.184				
8	Observations	89				
9						
10	ANOVA					
11		*df*	*SS*	*MS*	*F*	*Significance F*
12	Regression	6	195.541	32.590	959.784	0.000
13	Residual	82	2.784	0.034		
14	Total	88	198.326			
15						
16		*Coefficients*	*Standard Error*	*t Stat*	*P-value*	
17	Intercept	0.109	0.070	1.560	0.123	
18	1-lag	1.368	0.110	12.416	0.000	
19	2-lag	–0.083	0.187	–0.442	0.659	
20	3-lag	–0.378	0.186	–2.039	0.045	
21	4-lag	0.111	0.184	0.600	0.550	
22	5-lag	0.026	0.185	0.142	0.887	
23	6-lag	–0.070	0.110	–0.638	0.525	

The model performs well with a high R^2 of .99. The coefficients of the first and third lags are statistically significant, while the others are not. However, the F-statistic is significant, suggesting that at least one of the slope coefficients is non-zero. To forecast the cash rate for May 2014, we use the respective lagged values of y_t from November 2013 (y_{t-6}) to April 2014 (y_{t-1}) as follows.

$$\hat{y}_t = .109 + 1.368y_{t-1} - .083y_{t-2} - .378y_{t-3} + .111y_{t-4} + .026y_{t-5} - .070y_{t-6}$$

$$\begin{aligned}\hat{y}_t &= .109 + 1.368(2.5) - .083(2.5) - .378(2.5) + .111(2.5) + .026(2.5) - .070(2.5) \\ &= .109 + 3.420 - .208 - .945 + .278 + .065 - .175 \\ &= 2.54\%\end{aligned}$$

According to the autoregressive model, the cash rate for May 2014 is forecast to be 2.54%.

5. On the basis of all the forecasts, Combaro management will be informed that, in 2014, personal and housing loans are likely to reach levels of \$73 671 and \$471 291, respectively. These are equivalent to increases of 5% and 17%, respectively. However, the cash rate is likely to remain unchanged in May 2014. Nevertheless, the trend suggests that it could rise in the medium to long term.

SUMMARY

1 Time-series data are defined as data that have been gathered over a period of time. Time-series data can comprise four key components: trend, cyclical, seasonal and irregular (or random). Trend is the long-term general direction of time-series data. The cyclical component refers to the business and economic cycles that occur over periods of more than one year. The seasonal component refers to the patterns or cycles of data behaviour that occur over time periods of less than one year. The irregular component refers to irregular or unpredictable changes in the time series that are caused by components other than trend, cyclical and seasonal movements in the series.

2 One way to develop an accurate forecast is to identify the components of the time series and incorporate this information into the forecast. However, the existence of random variation in the data makes this task very difficult. There are a number of ways to smooth a time series to reduce random variation in the data to reveal the trend. The first is the moving average method, which is a time period average that is revised for each time period by including the most recent value(s) in the computation of the average and deleting the value or values that are farthest away from the present time period. Although a useful method, the process of deleting distant values leads to loss of information. We therefore considered the exponential smoothing method in which all the data are used, but the data from previous time periods are weighted exponentially to forecast the value for the present time period. The forecaster has the option of selecting how much to weight more recent values versus those of previous time periods.

Seasonal indices can be computed using the ratio-to-moving average method. Seasonal indices help us to identify the relative influence of various months or quarters in a time series and this information can be used to smooth or 'deseasonalise' the time series. The ratio-to-moving average method assumes that the time-series data can be represented as a product of its four components, and it tries to isolate these effects in the time series.

3 The trend in a time series can also be estimated using least squares trend-based forecasting models. We considered three ways of fitting trend equations to a time series using least squares techniques: linear, quadratic and exponential trend models. These models make a number of assumptions about the error terms, including the assumption that they are independent. When this assumption is violated, autocorrelation is said to exist. In such cases, these models will not provide a satisfactory fit and hence the forecast will be poor. One way to test for autocorrelation is to use the Durbin–Watson test.

4 The presence of autocorrelation presents an opportunity to use the autoregressive model for forecasting. Autoregression is a forecasting technique in which time-series data are predicted by independent variables that are lagged versions of the original dependent variable data. A variable that is lagged one period is derived from values of the previous time period. Other variables can be lagged two or more periods.

5 The accuracy of the forecasts of two or model models can be assessed by calculating the forecast error using two criteria: mean absolute deviation (MAD) and mean square error (MSE). The forecast error is the difference between the actual value of the variable and the forecast value.

6 Index numbers allow decision makers to compare changes in a variable over time. We considered three types of index numbers: simple price index, unweighted aggregate price index and weighted aggregate price index. Simple index numbers are constructed by calculating the ratio of the raw data value for a given time period to the raw data value for the base period and multiplying the ratio by 100. The index number for the base time period is designated to be 100. Unweighted aggregate price index numbers are constructed by summing the prices of several items for a time period and comparing that sum with the sum of the prices of the same items during a base time period and multiplying the ratio by 100. Weighted aggregate price indices are index numbers that use the prices of several items, and the items are weighted by their quantity usage. Examples of weighted aggregate price indices are Laspeyres price index, Paasche price index and Fisher's Ideal index.

KEY TERMS

- **autocorrelation** p. 540
- **autoregressive model** p. 543
- **base period** p. 550
- **cyclical component** p. 519
- **decomposition** p. 525
- **deseasonalised** p. 528
- **Durbin–Watson test** p. 540
- **error of a forecast** p. 547
- **exponential smoothing** p. 523
- **first-differences approach** p. 543
- **Fisher's Ideal index** p. 555
- **forecasting** p. 515
- **index number** p. 550
- **irregular component** p. 519
- **Laspeyres price index** p. 553
- **mean absolute deviation (MAD)** p. 548
- **mean square error (MSE)** p. 548
- **moving averages** p. 520
- **Paasche price index** p. 554
- **quadratic model** p. 535
- **random component** p. 519
- **ratio-to-moving average method** p. 525
- **seasonal component** p. 518
- **seasonal index** p. 525
- **simple price index** p. 550
- **time-series data** p. 515
- **trend component** p. 518
- **unweighted aggregate price index** p. 551
- **weighted aggregate price index** p. 552

KEY EQUATIONS

EQUATION	DESCRIPTION	FORMULA
15.1	Exponential smoothing	$F_{t+1} = \alpha x_t + (1-\alpha)F_t$
15.2	Durbin–Watson test	$D = \dfrac{\sum_{t=2}^{n}(e_t - e_{t-1})^2}{\sum_{t=1}^{n} e_t^2}$
15.3	Error of a forecast	$e_t = X_t - F_t$
15.4	Mean absolute deviation	$\text{MAD} = \dfrac{\sum \lvert y_t - F_t \rvert}{n}$
15.5	Mean square error	$\text{MSE} = \dfrac{\sum (y_t - F_t)^2}{n}$
15.6	Simple price index	$I_i = \dfrac{P_i}{P_0}(100)$

EQUATION	DESCRIPTION	FORMULA
15.7	**Unweighted aggregate price index number**	$I_i = \frac{\sum P_i}{\sum P_0}(100)$
15.8	**Weighted aggregate price index number**	$I_i = \frac{\sum P_i Q_i}{\sum P_0 Q_0}(100)$
15.9	**Laspeyres price index**	$I_L = \frac{\sum P_i Q_0}{\sum P_0 Q_0}(100)$
15.10	**Paasche price index**	$I_p = \frac{\sum P_i Q_i}{\sum P_0 Q_i}(100)$
15.11	**Fisher's Ideal index**	$I_F = \sqrt{\frac{\sum P_i Q_0}{\sum P_0 Q_0}(100)\frac{\sum P_i Q_i}{\sum P_0 Q_i}(100)}$

REVIEW PROBLEMS

Practising the calculations

P15-27 **15.27** The ABS data below show monthly time series data for short-term visits to the United Kingdom and its territories by Australian residents.

Period	Number	Period	Number
Jan. 07	19 000	Oct. 10	27 100
Feb. 07	16 400	Nov. 10	23 500
Mar. 07	25 400	Dec. 10	43 200
Apr. 07	32 700	Jan. 11	17 400
May 07	52 700	Feb. 11	16 500
June 07	58 900	Mar. 11	27 500
July 07	44 700	Apr. 11	46 100
Aug. 07	46 300	May 11	62 100
Sep. 07	52 200	June 11	75 500
Oct. 07	27 100	July 11	53 700
Nov. 07	22 400	Aug. 11	57 600
Dec. 07	45 000	Sept. 11	57 700
Jan. 08	20 100	Oct. 11	25 600
Feb. 08	16 300	Nov. 11	24 100
Mar. 08	28 300	Dec. 11	46 900
Apr. 08	37 300	Jan. 12	18 500
May 08	52 500	Feb. 12	16 900
June 08	55 200	Mar. 12	33 100
July 08	44 100	Apr. 12	43 700
Aug. 08	50 300	May 12	62 200
Sept. 08	50 300	June 12	68 700
Oct. 08	24 900	July 12	47 000
Nov. 08	20 300	Aug. 12	51 300

Period	Number	Period	Number
Dec. 08	42 700	Sept. 12	59 100
Jan. 09	18 500	Oct. 12	28 900
Feb. 09	15 700	Nov. 12	24 700
Mar. 09	26 600	Dec. 12	56 700
Apr. 09	35 000	Jan. 13	18 200
May 09	53 500	Feb. 13	15 700
June 09	57 300	Mar. 13	32 900
July 09	52 300	Apr. 13	47 000
Aug. 09	52 100	May 13	69 000
Sept. 09	52 000	June 13	80 300
Oct. 09	27 000	July 13	64 900
Nov. 09	24 500	Aug. 13	58 800
Dec. 09	45 300	Sept. 13	64 300
Jan. 10	18 600	Oct. 13	26 900
Feb. 10	15 100	Nov. 13	25 500
Mar. 10	29 400	Dec. 13	58 800
Apr. 10	33 100	Jan. 14	18 800
May 10	57 200	Feb. 14	15 600
June 10	70 800	Mar. 14	28 500
July 10	51 500	Apr. 14	46 200
Aug. 10	54 100	May 14	60 600
Sept. 10	56 200		

a. Explore trends in these data by using linear and quadratic trend models. Comment on the performance of these models.

b. Use a 10-month moving average to forecast values for January 2008 to May 2014.

c. Use simple exponential smoothing to forecast values for January 2008 to May 2014. Let $\alpha = .3$ and then let $\alpha = .7$. Which weight produces better forecasts?
d. Compute the MAD for the forecasts obtained in parts (b) and (c) and compare the results.
e. Determine seasonal effects using decomposition on these data. Let the seasonal effects have four periods. After determining the seasonal indices, deseasonalise the data.

P15-28 **15.28** Using the following data, compute index numbers for 2010 to 2013 using 1999 as the base year.

Year	Quantity	Year	Quantity
1999	2073	2007	2520
2000	2290	2008	2529
2001	2349	2009	2483
2002	2313	2010	2467
2003	2456	2011	2397
2004	2508	2012	2351
2005	2463	2013	2308
2006	2499		

P15-29 **15.29** Compute unweighted aggregate price index numbers for each of the given years using 2005 as the base year.

Item	2005	2010	2014
Pork sausage (per kg)	5.20	8.15	10.00
Beef roast (per kg)	12.50	15.50	20.00
Chicken breast (per kg)	5.50	8.50	10.50
Chicken legs (per kg)	3.10	4.50	5.20

P15-30 **15.30** Using the following data and 2006 as the base year, compute the Laspeyres price index for 2009 and the Paasche price index for 2008.

	2006		2007	
Item	Price ($)	Quantity	Price ($)	Quantity
1	2.75	12	2.98	9
2	0.85	47	0.89	52
3	1.33	20	1.32	28

	2008		2009	
Item	Price ($)	Quantity	Price ($)	Quantity
1	3.10	9	3.21	11
2	0.95	61	0.98	66
3	1.36	25	1.40	32

P15-31 **15.31** The following are data on two CPI series for food. The first is for the period 1997 to 2003 with 1990 = 100, and the second is for the period 2003 to 2007 with 2003 = 100. Combine the two into a single series for the period 1997 to 2007, using 2003 as the base year.

Year	Series 1 (1990 = 100)	Series 2 (2003 = 100)
1997	122.8	
1998	128.8	
1999	134.9	
2000	141.4	
2001	149.3	
2002	153.5	
2003	160.6	100.0
2004		104.9
2005		106.3
2006		108.8
2007		110.2

Testing your understanding

P15-32 **15.32** Shown in the table below are 16 years of data on company profits of Australian manufacturing industries.

a. Use a 3-year moving average to forecast the profits for years 8 to 16 for these data. Compute the error of each forecast and then determine the mean absolute deviation of error for the forecast.
b. Use exponential smoothing and $\alpha = .2$ to forecast the data for years 8 to 16. Compute the error of each forecast and then determine the mean absolute deviation of error for the forecast.
c. Compare the results obtained in parts (a) and (b) using MAD. Which technique performs better? Why?

Year	Profit ($ million)	Year	Profit ($ million)
1	4 657	9	12 481
2	5 689	10	12 446
3	7 889	11	9 811
4	8 964	12	10 812
5	6 381	13	11 488
6	5 175	14	10 905
7	7 293	15	11 161
8	9 568	16	11 068

P15-33 **15.33** The ABS publishes a series on Australia's international merchandise imports and exports. The following table displays a portion of the data for imports of chemicals and related products from January of year 1 to December of year 5.

Time period	Chemical and related products imports ($ million)	Time period	Chemical and related products imports ($ million)	Time period	Chemical and related products imports ($ million)
(Year 1)		(Year 3)		(Year 5)	
January	986	January	1301	January	1218
February	1048	February	1223	February	1198
March	1226	March	1245	March	1408
April	996	April	1401	April	1386
May	1162	May	1273	May	1290
June	1087	June	997	June	1343
July	1102	July	1259	July	1393
August	1114	August	1201	August	1383
September	1201	September	1281	September	1497
October	1174	October	1237	October	1422
November	1181	November	1180	November	1388
December	1035	December	1146	December	1433
(Year 2)		(Year 4)			
January	1152	January	1259		
February	1120	February	1294		
March	1315	March	1344		
April	1385	April	1347		
May	1261	May	1327		
June	1156	June	1148		
July	1177	July	1205		
August	1285	August	1214		
September	1108	September	1173		
October	1319	October	1474		
November	1245	November	1039		
December	1061	December	1112		

a. Use time-series decomposition methods to develop the seasonal indices for these data.
b. Use the seasonal indices to deseasonalise the data.
c. Fit linear, quadratic and exponential trend models to the data.
d. Which of the models would you recommend as giving the best forecast? Explain your answer.

P15-34 **15.34** The following table shows exports of machinery and transport equipment (in millions of dollars) from September of year 1 to April of year 4. Use these data to develop autoregressive models for a 1-month lag and a 4-month lag. Compare the results of these two models. Which model seems to yield better predictions? Why? Under what conditions would these models be more appropriate for forecasting than least squares methods? Explain.

Time period	Machinery and transport equipment exports ($ million)
(Year 1)	
Sept.	1199
Oct.	1128
Nov.	1223
Dec.	1270
(Year 2)	
Jan.	704
Feb.	1027
Mar.	1226
Apr.	1178
May	1171
June	1138
July	1071
Aug.	1173
Sept.	1102
Oct.	1316

Time period	Machinery and transport equipment exports ($ million)
Nov.	1275
Dec.	1461
(Year 3)	
Jan.	762
Feb.	1049
Mar.	1425
Apr.	1153
May	1086
June	1287
July	1127
Aug.	1193
Sept.	1150
Oct.	1254
Nov.	1344
Dec.	1367
(Year 4)	
Jan.	805
Feb.	1009
Mar.	1153
Apr.	1006

P15-35 **15.35** The following table gives ABS data for finance provided for the construction of dwellings in New South Wales for January 2012 to May 2014.

a. Evaluate how well the following trend models fit the data: linear, quadratic and exponential.

b. Plot the residuals over time and comment on the results.

c. At the .05 level of significance, is there evidence of autocorrelation in the residuals?

d. Based on your results in parts (a)–(c), do you have any grounds to question the validity of the model?

Period	Finance for construction of dwellings in NSW ($'000s)
Jan. 12	321.9
Feb. 12	309.0
Mar. 12	311.7
Apr. 12	297.5
May 12	318.9
June 12	315.6
July 12	306.8
Aug. 12	317.7
Sept. 12	310.1
Oct. 12	309.2
Nov. 12	309.5
Dec. 12	318.1
Jan. 13	292.7
Feb. 13	305.5
Mar. 13	309.5
Apr. 13	321.5
May 13	308.5
June 13	312.2
July 13	310.5
Aug. 13	314.5
Sept. 13	313.0
Oct. 13	297.8
Nov. 13	313.0
Dec. 13	311.0
Jan. 14	305.1
Feb. 14	307.2
Mar. 14	318.0
Apr. 14	309.3
May 14	309.2

P15-36 **15.36** The following data give monthly figures for standard variable interest rates in Australia over a 4-year period. Use these data to develop an autoregressive model with a 6-month lag. Discuss the strength of the model.

Period	Standard variable interest rate (%)
(Year 1)	
Jan.	8.05
Feb.	7.55
Mar.	7.30
Apr.	6.80
May	6.80
June	6.80
July	6.80
Aug.	6.80
Sept.	6.55
Oct.	6.30
Nov.	6.30
Dec.	6.05
(Year 2)	
Jan.	6.05
Feb.	6.05
Mar.	6.05
Apr.	6.05
May	6.30
June	6.55
July	6.55
Aug.	6.55
Sept.	6.55
Oct.	6.55
Nov.	6.55
Dec.	6.55
(Year 3)	
Jan.	6.55
Feb.	6.55
Mar.	6.55

Period	Standard variable interest rate (%)
Apr.	6.55
May	6.55
June	6.55
July	6.55
Aug.	6.55
Sept.	6.55
Oct.	6.55
Nov.	6.80
Dec.	7.05
(Year 4)	
Jan.	7.05
Feb.	7.05
Mar.	7.05
Apr.	7.05
May	7.05
June	7.05
July	7.05
Aug.	7.05
Sept.	7.05
Oct.	7.05
Nov.	7.05
Dec.	7.05

P15-37 **15.37** The values of purchasing power for the minimum wage in 1997 dollars for the years 1980 to 1997 are shown in the table. Use these data and exponential smoothing to develop forecasts for the years 1981 to 1997. Use α = .1, .5 and .8, and compare the results using MAD. Discuss your findings. Select the value of α that gave the best result, and use the results of exponential smoothing to predict the purchasing power in 1998. Construct a simple index for the purchasing power of wages. Comment on how much it has changed in this period.

Year	Purchasing power ($)	Year	Purchasing power ($)
1980	6.04	1992	4.86
1981	5.92	1993	4.72
1982	5.57	1994	4.60
1983	5.40	1989	4.34
1984	5.17	1990	4.67
1985	5.00	1991	5.01
1986	4.91	1995	4.48
1987	4.73	1996	4.86
1988	4.55	1997	5.15

APPENDIX

TABLE A.1 Binomial probability distribution 570
TABLE A.2 Poisson probabilities 579
TABLE A.3 The e^{-x} table 584
TABLE A.4 Areas of the standard normal distribution $\mu = 0, \sigma = 1$ 585
TABLE A.5 Cumulative normal probabilities 586
TABLE A.6 Critical values of t 587
TABLE A.7 Percentage points of the F distribution 590
TABLE A.8 The chi-square table 600
TABLE A.9 Critical values for the Durbin–Watson test 601
TABLE A.10 Critical values of the studentised range (q) distribution 603

TABLE A.1 Binomial probability distribution

					n = 1				
					Probability				
x	.1	.2	.3	.4	.5	.6	.7	.8	.9
0	.900	.800	.700	.600	.500	.400	.300	.200	.100
1	.100	.200	.300	.400	.500	.600	.700	.800	.900

					n = 2				
					Probability				
x	.1	.2	.3	.4	.5	.6	.7	.8	.9
0	.810	.640	.490	.360	.250	.160	.090	.040	.010
1	.180	.320	.420	.480	.500	.480	.420	.320	.180
2	.010	.040	.090	.160	.250	.360	.490	.640	.810

					n = 3				
					Probability				
x	.1	.2	.3	.4	.5	.6	.7	.8	.9
0	.729	.512	.343	.216	.125	.064	.027	.008	.001
1	.243	.384	.441	.432	.375	.288	.189	.096	.027
2	.027	.096	.189	.288	.375	.432	.441	.384	.243
3	.001	.008	.027	.064	.125	.216	.343	.512	.729

					n = 4				
					Probability				
x	.1	.2	.3	.4	.5	.6	.7	.8	.9
0	.656	.410	.240	.130	.063	.026	.008	.002	.000
1	.292	.410	.412	.346	.250	.154	.076	.026	.004
2	.049	.154	.265	.346	.375	.346	.265	.154	.049
3	.004	.026	.076	.154	.250	.346	.412	.410	.292
4	.000	.002	.008	.026	.063	.130	.240	.410	.656

					n = 5				
					Probability				
x	.1	.2	.3	.4	.5	.6	.7	.8	.9
0	.590	.328	.168	.078	.031	.010	.002	.000	.000
1	.328	.410	.360	.259	.156	.077	.028	.006	.000
2	.073	.205	.309	.346	.313	.230	.132	.051	.008
3	.008	.051	.132	.230	.313	.346	.309	.205	.073
4	.000	.006	.028	.077	.156	.259	.360	.410	.328
5	.000	.000	.002	.010	.031	.078	.168	.328	.590

$n = 6$									
	Probability								
x	.1	.2	.3	.4	.5	.6	.7	.8	.9
0	.531	.262	.118	.047	.016	.004	.001	.000	.000
1	.354	.393	.303	.187	.094	.037	.010	.002	.000
2	.098	.246	.324	.311	.234	.138	.060	.015	.001
3	.015	.082	.185	.276	.313	.276	.185	.082	.015
4	.001	.015	.060	.138	.234	.311	.324	.246	.098
5	.000	.002	.010	.037	.094	.187	.303	.393	.354
6	.000	.000	.001	.004	.016	.047	.118	.262	.531

$n = 7$									
	Probability								
x	.1	.2	.3	.4	.5	.6	.7	.8	.9
0	.478	.210	.082	.028	.008	.002	.000	.000	.000
1	.372	.367	.247	.131	.055	.017	.004	.000	.000
2	.124	.275	.318	.261	.164	.077	.025	.004	.000
3	.023	.115	.227	.290	.273	.194	.097	.029	.003
4	.003	.029	.097	.194	.273	.290	.227	.115	.023
5	.000	.004	.025	.077	.164	.261	.318	.275	.124
6	.000	.000	.004	.017	.055	.131	.247	.367	.372
7	.000	.000	.000	.002	.008	.028	.082	.210	.478

$n = 8$									
	Probability								
x	.1	.2	.3	.4	.5	.6	.7	.8	.9
0	.430	.168	.058	.017	.004	.001	.000	.000	.000
1	.383	.336	.198	.090	.031	.008	.001	.000	.000
2	.149	.294	.296	.209	.109	.041	.010	.001	.000
3	.033	.147	.254	.279	.219	.124	.047	.009	.000
4	.005	.046	.136	.232	.273	.232	.136	.046	.005
5	.000	.009	.047	.124	.219	.279	.254	.147	.033
6	.000	.001	.010	.041	.109	.209	.296	.294	.149
7	.000	.000	.001	.008	.031	.090	.198	.336	.383
8	.000	.000	.000	.001	.004	.017	.058	.168	.430

(continued)

TABLE A.1 *(continued)*

				$n = 9$					
				Probability					
x	.1	.2	.3	.4	.5	.6	.7	.8	.9
0	.387	.134	.040	.010	.002	.000	.000	.000	.000
1	.387	.302	.156	.060	.018	.004	.000	.000	.000
2	.172	.302	.267	.161	.070	.021	.004	.000	.000
3	.045	.176	.267	.251	.164	.074	.021	.003	.000
4	.007	.066	.172	.251	.246	.167	.074	.017	.001
5	.001	.017	.074	.167	.246	.251	.172	.066	.007
6	.000	.003	.021	.074	.164	.251	.267	.176	.045
7	.000	.000	.004	.021	.070	.161	.267	.302	.172
8	.000	.000	.000	.004	.018	.060	.156	.302	.387
9	.000	.000	.000	.000	.002	.010	.040	.134	.387

				$n = 10$					
				Probability					
x	.1	.2	.3	.4	.5	.6	.7	.8	.9
0	.349	.107	.028	.006	.001	.000	.000	.000	.000
1	.387	.268	.121	.040	.010	.002	.000	.000	.000
2	.194	.302	.233	.121	.044	.011	.001	.000	.000
3	.057	.201	.267	.215	.117	.042	.009	.001	.000
4	.011	.088	.200	.251	.205	.111	.037	.006	.000
5	.001	.026	.103	.201	.246	.201	.103	.026	.001
6	.000	.006	.037	.111	.205	.251	.200	.088	.011
7	.000	.001	.009	.042	.117	.215	.267	.201	.057
8	.000	.000	.001	.011	.044	.121	.233	.302	.194
9	.000	.000	.000	.002	.010	.040	.121	.268	.387
10	.000	.000	.000	.000	.001	.006	.028	.107	.349

					$n = 11$				
					Probability				
x	.1	.2	.3	.4	.5	.6	.7	.8	.9
0	.314	.086	.020	.004	.000	.000	.000	.000	.000
1	.384	.236	.093	.027	.005	.001	.000	.000	.000
2	.213	.295	.200	.089	.027	.005	.001	.000	.000
3	.071	.221	.257	.177	.081	.023	.004	.000	.000
4	.016	.111	.220	.236	.161	.070	.017	.002	.000
5	.002	.039	.132	.221	.226	.147	.057	.010	.000
6	.000	.010	.057	.147	.226	.221	.132	.039	.002
7	.000	.002	.017	.070	.161	.236	.220	.111	.016
8	.000	.000	.004	.023	.081	.177	.257	.221	.071
9	.000	.000	.001	.005	.027	.089	.200	.295	.213
10	.000	.000	.000	.001	.005	.027	.093	.236	.384
11	.000	.000	.000	.000	.000	.004	.020	.086	.314

					$n = 12$				
					Probability				
x	.1	.2	.3	.4	.5	.6	.7	.8	.9
0	.282	.069	.014	.002	.000	.000	.000	.000	.000
1	.377	.206	.071	.017	.003	.000	.000	.000	.000
2	.230	.283	.168	.064	.016	.002	.000	.000	.000
3	.085	.236	.240	.142	.054	.012	.001	.000	.000
4	.021	.133	.231	.213	.121	.042	.008	.001	.000
5	.004	.053	.158	.227	.193	.101	.029	.003	.000
6	.000	.016	.079	.177	.226	.177	.079	.016	.000
7	.000	.003	.029	.101	.193	.227	.158	.053	.004
8	.000	.001	.008	.042	.121	.213	.231	.133	.021
9	.000	.000	.001	.012	.054	.142	.240	.236	.085
10	.000	.000	.000	.002	.016	.064	.168	.283	.230
11	.000	.000	.000	.000	.003	.017	.071	.206	.377
12	.000	.000	.000	.000	.000	.002	.014	.069	.282

(continued)

TABLE A.1 *(continued)*

				n = 13					
				Probability					
x	.1	.2	.3	.4	.5	.6	.7	.8	.9
0	.254	.055	.010	.001	.000	.000	.000	.000	.000
1	.367	.179	.054	.011	.002	.000	.000	.000	.000
2	.245	.268	.139	.045	.010	.001	.000	.000	.000
3	.100	.246	.218	.111	.035	.006	.001	.000	.000
4	.028	.154	.234	.184	.087	.024	.003	.000	.000
5	.006	.069	.180	.221	.157	.066	.014	.001	.000
6	.001	.023	.103	.197	.209	.131	.044	.006	.000
7	.000	.006	.044	.131	.209	.197	.103	.023	.001
8	.000	.001	.014	.066	.157	.221	.180	.069	.006
9	.000	.000	.003	.024	.087	.184	.234	.154	.028
10	.000	.000	.001	.006	.035	.111	.218	.246	.100
11	.000	.000	.000	.001	.010	.045	.139	.268	.245
12	.000	.000	.000	.000	.002	.011	.054	.179	.367
13	.000	.000	.000	.000	.000	.001	.010	.055	.254

				n = 14					
				Probability					
x	.1	.2	.3	.4	.5	.6	.7	.8	.9
0	.229	.044	.007	.001	.000	.000	.000	.000	.000
1	.356	.154	.041	.007	.001	.000	.000	.000	.000
2	.257	.250	.113	.032	.006	.001	.000	.000	.000
3	.114	.250	.194	.085	.022	.003	.000	.000	.000
4	.035	.172	.229	.155	.061	.014	.001	.000	.000
5	.008	.086	.196	.207	.122	.041	.007	.000	.000
6	.001	.032	.126	.207	.183	.092	.023	.002	.000
7	.000	.009	.062	.157	.209	.157	.062	.009	.000
8	.000	.002	.023	.092	.183	.207	.126	.032	.001
9	.000	.000	.007	.041	.122	.207	.196	.086	.008
10	.000	.000	.001	.014	.061	.155	.229	.172	.035
11	.000	.000	.000	.003	.022	.085	.194	.250	.114
12	.000	.000	.000	.001	.006	.032	.113	.250	.257
13	.000	.000	.000	.000	.001	.007	.041	.154	.356
14	.000	.000	.000	.000	.000	.001	.007	.044	.229

					n = 15				
					Probability				
x	**.1**	**.2**	**.3**	**.4**	**.5**	**.6**	**.7**	**.8**	**.9**
0	.206	.035	.005	.000	.000	.000	.000	.000	.000
1	.343	.132	.031	.005	.000	.000	.000	.000	.000
2	.267	.231	.092	.022	.003	.000	.000	.000	.000
3	.129	.250	.170	.063	.014	.002	.000	.000	.000
4	.043	.188	.219	.127	.042	.007	.001	.000	.000
5	.010	.103	.206	.186	.092	.024	.003	.000	.000
6	.002	.043	.147	.207	.153	.061	.012	.001	.000
7	.000	.014	.081	.177	.196	.118	.035	.003	.000
8	.000	.003	.035	.118	.196	.177	.081	.014	.000
9	.000	.001	.012	.061	.153	.207	.147	.043	.002
10	.000	.000	.003	.024	.092	.186	.206	.103	.010
11	.000	.000	.001	.007	.042	.127	.219	.188	.043
12	.000	.000	.000	.002	.014	.063	.170	.250	.129
13	.000	.000	.000	.000	.003	.022	.092	.231	.267
14	.000	.000	.000	.000	.000	.005	.031	.132	.343
15	.000	.000	.000	.000	.000	.000	.005	.035	.206

					n = 16				
					Probability				
x	**.1**	**.2**	**.3**	**.4**	**.5**	**.6**	**.7**	**.8**	**.9**
0	.185	.028	.003	.000	.000	.000	.000	.000	.000
1	.329	.113	.023	.003	.000	.000	.000	.000	.000
2	.275	.211	.073	.015	.002	.000	.000	.000	.000
3	.142	.246	.146	.047	.009	.001	.000	.000	.000
4	.051	.200	.204	.101	.028	.004	.000	.000	.000
5	.014	.120	.210	.162	.067	.014	.001	.000	.000
6	.003	.055	.165	.198	.122	.039	.006	.000	.000
7	.000	.020	.101	.189	.175	.084	.019	.001	.000
8	.000	.006	.049	.142	.196	.142	.049	.006	.000
9	.000	.001	.019	.084	.175	.189	.101	.020	.000
10	.000	.000	.006	.039	.122	.198	.165	.055	.003
11	.000	.000	.001	.014	.067	.162	.210	.120	.014
12	.000	.000	.000	.004	.028	.101	.204	.200	.051
13	.000	.000	.000	.001	.009	.047	.146	.246	.142
14	.000	.000	.000	.000	.002	.015	.073	.211	.275
15	.000	.000	.000	.000	.000	.003	.023	.113	.329
16	.000	.000	.000	.000	.000	.000	.003	.028	.185

(continued)

TABLE A.1 *(continued)*

	n = 17								
	Probability								
x	.1	.2	.3	.4	.5	.6	.7	.8	.9
0	.167	.023	.002	.000	.000	.000	.000	.000	.000
1	.315	.096	.017	.002	.000	.000	.000	.000	.000
2	.280	.191	.058	.010	.001	.000	.000	.000	.000
3	.156	.239	.125	.034	.005	.000	.000	.000	.000
4	.060	.209	.187	.080	.018	.002	.000	.000	.000
5	.017	.136	.208	.138	.047	.008	.001	.000	.000
6	.004	.068	.178	.184	.094	.024	.003	.000	.000
7	.001	.027	.120	.193	.148	.057	.009	.000	.000
8	.000	.008	.064	.161	.185	.107	.028	.002	.000
9	.000	.002	.028	.107	.185	.161	.064	.008	.000
10	.000	.000	.009	.057	.148	.193	.120	.027	.001
11	.000	.000	.003	.024	.094	.184	.178	.068	.004
12	.000	.000	.001	.008	.047	.138	.208	.136	.017
13	.000	.000	.000	.002	.018	.080	.187	.209	.060
14	.000	.000	.000	.000	.005	.034	.125	.239	.156
15	.000	.000	.000	.000	.001	.010	.058	.191	.280
16	.000	.000	.000	.000	.000	.002	.017	.096	.315
17	.000	.000	.000	.000	.000	.000	.002	.023	.167

	n = 18								
	Probability								
x	.1	.2	.3	.4	.5	.6	.7	.8	.9
0	.150	.018	.002	.000	.000	.000	.000	.000	.000
1	.300	.081	.013	.001	.000	.000	.000	.000	.000
2	.284	.172	.046	.007	.001	.000	.000	.000	.000
3	.168	.230	.105	.025	.003	.000	.000	.000	.000
4	.070	.215	.168	.061	.012	.001	.000	.000	.000
5	.022	.151	.202	.115	.033	.004	.000	.000	.000
6	.005	.082	.187	.166	.071	.015	.001	.000	.000
7	.001	.035	.138	.189	.121	.037	.005	.000	.000
8	.000	.012	.081	.173	.167	.077	.015	.001	.000
9	.000	.003	.039	.128	.185	.128	.039	.003	.000
10	.000	.001	.015	.077	.167	.173	.081	.012	.000
11	.000	.000	.005	.037	.121	.189	.138	.035	.001
12	.000	.000	.001	.015	.071	.166	.187	.082	.005
13	.000	.000	.000	.004	.033	.115	.202	.151	.022
14	.000	.000	.000	.001	.012	.061	.168	.215	.070
15	.000	.000	.000	.000	.003	.025	.105	.230	.168
16	.000	.000	.000	.000	.001	.007	.046	.172	.284
17	.000	.000	.000	.000	.000	.001	.013	.081	.300
18	.000	.000	.000	.000	.000	.000	.002	.018	.150

				$n = 19$ Probability					
x	.1	.2	.3	.4	.5	.6	.7	.8	.9
0	.135	.014	.001	.000	.000	.000	.000	.000	.000
1	.285	.068	.009	.001	.000	.000	.000	.000	.000
2	.285	.154	.036	.005	.000	.000	.000	.000	.000
3	.180	.218	.087	.017	.002	.000	.000	.000	.000
4	.080	.218	.149	.047	.007	.001	.000	.000	.000
5	.027	.164	.192	.093	.022	.002	.000	.000	.000
6	.007	.095	.192	.145	.052	.008	.001	.000	.000
7	.001	.044	.153	.180	.096	.024	.002	.000	.000
8	.000	.017	.098	.180	.144	.053	.008	.000	.000
9	.000	.005	.051	.146	.176	.098	.022	.001	.000
10	.000	.001	.022	.098	.176	.146	.051	.005	.000
11	.000	.000	.008	.053	.144	.180	.098	.017	.000
12	.000	.000	.002	.024	.096	.180	.153	.044	.001
13	.000	.000	.001	.008	.052	.145	.192	.095	.007
14	.000	.000	.000	.002	.022	.093	.192	.164	.027
15	.000	.000	.000	.001	.007	.047	.149	.218	.080
16	.000	.000	.000	.000	.002	.017	.087	.218	.180
17	.000	.000	.000	.000	.000	.005	.036	.154	.285
18	.000	.000	.000	.000	.000	.001	.009	.068	.285
19	.000	.000	.000	.000	.000	.000	.001	.014	.135

				$n = 20$ Probability					
x	.1	.2	.3	.4	.5	.6	.7	.8	.9
0	.122	.012	.001	.000	.000	.000	.000	.000	.000
1	.270	.058	.007	.000	.000	.000	.000	.000	.000
2	.285	.137	.028	.003	.000	.000	.000	.000	.000
3	.190	.205	.072	.012	.001	.000	.000	.000	.000
4	.090	.218	.130	.035	.005	.000	.000	.000	.000
5	.032	.175	.179	.075	.015	.001	.000	.000	.000
6	.009	.109	.192	.124	.037	.005	.000	.000	.000
7	.002	.055	.164	.166	.074	.015	.001	.000	.000
8	.000	.022	.114	.180	.120	.035	.004	.000	.000
9	.000	.007	.065	.160	.160	.071	.012	.000	.000
10	.000	.002	.031	.117	.176	.117	.031	.002	.000
11	.000	.000	.012	.071	.160	.160	.065	.007	.000
12	.000	.000	.004	.035	.120	.180	.114	.022	.000
13	.000	.000	.001	.015	.074	.166	.164	.055	.002
14	.000	.000	.000	.005	.037	.124	.192	.109	.009
15	.000	.000	.000	.001	.015	.075	.179	.175	.032
16	.000	.000	.000	.000	.005	.035	.130	.218	.090
17	.000	.000	.000	.000	.001	.012	.072	.205	.190
18	.000	.000	.000	.000	.000	.003	.028	.137	.285
19	.000	.000	.000	.000	.000	.000	.007	.058	.270
20	.000	.000	.000	.000	.000	.000	.001	.012	.122

(continued)

TABLE A.1 *(continued)*

					$n = 25$				
					Probability				
x	.1	.2	.3	.4	.5	.6	.7	.8	.9
0	.072	.004	.000	.000	.000	.000	.000	.000	.000
1	.199	.024	.001	.000	.000	.000	.000	.000	.000
2	.266	.071	.007	.000	.000	.000	.000	.000	.000
3	.226	.136	.024	.002	.000	.000	.000	.000	.000
4	.138	.187	.057	.007	.000	.000	.000	.000	.000
5	.065	.196	.103	.020	.002	.000	.000	.000	.000
6	.024	.163	.147	.044	.005	.000	.000	.000	.000
7	.007	.111	.171	.080	.014	.001	.000	.000	.000
8	.002	.062	.165	.120	.032	.003	.000	.000	.000
9	.000	.029	.134	.151	.061	.009	.000	.000	.000
10	.000	.012	.092	.161	.097	.021	.001	.000	.000
11	.000	.004	.054	.147	.133	.043	.004	.000	.000
12	.000	.001	.027	.114	.155	.076	.011	.000	.000
13	.000	.000	.011	.076	.155	.114	.027	.001	.000
14	.000	.000	.004	.043	.133	.147	.054	.004	.000
15	.000	.000	.001	.021	.097	.161	.092	.012	.000
16	.000	.000	.000	.009	.061	.151	.134	.029	.000
17	.000	.000	.000	.003	.032	.120	.165	.062	.002
18	.000	.000	.000	.001	.014	.080	.171	.111	.007
19	.000	.000	.000	.000	.005	.044	.147	.163	.024
20	.000	.000	.000	.000	.002	.020	.103	.196	.065
21	.000	.000	.000	.000	.000	.007	.057	.187	.138
22	.000	.000	.000	.000	.000	.002	.024	.136	.226
23	.000	.000	.000	.000	.000	.000	.007	.071	.266
24	.000	.000	.000	.000	.000	.000	.001	.024	.199
25	.000	.000	.000	.000	.000	.000	.000	.004	.072

TABLE A.2 Poisson probabilities

					λ					
x	**.005**	**.01**	**.02**	**.03**	**.04**	**.05**	**.06**	**.07**	**.08**	**.09**
0	.9950	.9900	.9802	.9704	.9608	.9512	.9418	.9324	.9231	.9139
1	.0050	.0099	.0196	.0291	.0384	.0476	.0565	.0653	.0738	.0823
2	.0000	.0000	.0002	.0004	.0008	.0012	.0017	.0023	.0030	.0037
3	.0000	.0000	.0000	.0000	.0000	.0000	.0000	.0001	.0001	.0001
x	**.1**	**.2**	**.3**	**.4**	**.5**	**.6**	**.7**	**.8**	**.9**	**1.0**
0	.9048	.8187	.7408	.6703	.6065	.5488	.4966	.4493	.4066	.3679
1	.0905	.1637	.2222	.2681	.3033	.3293	.3476	.3595	.3659	.3679
2	.0045	.0164	.0333	.0536	.0758	.0988	.1217	.1438	.1647	.1839
3	.0002	.0011	.0033	.0072	.0126	.0198	.0284	.0383	.0494	.0613
4	.0000	.0001	.0003	.0007	.0016	.0030	.0050	.0077	.0111	.0153
5	.0000	.0000	.0000	.0001	.0002	.0004	.0007	.0012	.0020	.0031
6	.0000	.0000	.0000	.0000	.0000	.0000	.0001	.0002	.0003	.0005
7	.0000	.0000	.0000	.0000	.0000	.0000	.0000	.0000	.0000	.0001
x	**1.1**	**1.2**	**1.3**	**1.4**	**1.5**	**1.6**	**1.7**	**1.8**	**1.9**	**2.0**
0	.3329	.3012	.2725	.2466	.2231	.2019	.1827	.1653	.1496	.1353
1	.3662	.3614	.3543	.3452	.3347	.3230	.3106	.2975	.2842	.2707
2	.2014	.2169	.2303	.2417	.2510	.2584	.2640	.2678	.2700	.2707
3	.0738	.0867	.0998	.1128	.1255	.1378	.1496	.1607	.1710	.1804
4	.0203	.0260	.0324	.0395	.0471	.0551	.0636	.0723	.0812	.0902
5	.0045	.0062	.0084	.0111	.0141	.0176	.0216	.0260	.0309	.0361
6	.0008	.0012	.0018	.0026	.0035	.0047	.0061	.0078	.0098	.0120
7	.0001	.0002	.0003	.0005	.0008	.0011	.0015	.0020	.0027	.0034
8	.0000	.0000	.0001	.0001	.0001	.0002	.0003	.0005	.0006	.0009
9	.0000	.0000	.0000	.0000	.0000	.0000	.0001	.0001	.0001	.0002
x	**2.1**	**2.2**	**2.3**	**2.4**	**2.5**	**2.6**	**2.7**	**2.8**	**2.9**	**3.0**
0	.1225	.1108	.1003	.0907	.0821	.0743	.0672	.0608	.0550	.0498
1	.2572	.2438	.2306	.2177	.2052	.1931	.1815	.1703	.1596	.1494
2	.2700	.2681	.2652	.2613	.2565	.2510	.2450	.2384	.2314	.2240
3	.1890	.1966	.2033	.2090	.2138	.2176	.2205	.2225	.2237	.2240
4	.0992	.1082	.1169	.1254	.1336	.1414	.1488	.1557	.1622	.1680
5	.0417	.0476	.0538	.0602	.0668	.0735	.0804	.0872	.0940	.1008
6	.0146	.0174	.0206	.0241	.0278	.0319	.0362	.0407	.0455	.0504
7	.0044	.0055	.0068	.0083	.0099	.0118	.0139	.0163	.0188	.0216
8	.0011	.0015	.0019	.0025	.0031	.0038	.0047	.0057	.0068	.0081
9	.0003	.0004	.0005	.0007	.0009	.0011	.0014	.0018	.0022	.0027
10	.0001	.0001	.0001	.0002	.0002	.0003	.0004	.0005	.0006	.0008
11	.0000	.0000	.0000	.0000	.0000	.0001	.0001	.0001	.0002	.0002
12	.0000	.0000	.0000	.0000	.0000	.0000	.0000	.0000	.0000	.0001

(continued)

TABLE A.2 *(continued)*

	λ									
x	3.1	3.2	3.3	3.4	3.5	3.6	3.7	3.8	3.9	4.0
0	.0450	.0408	.0369	.0334	.0302	.0273	.0247	.0224	.0202	.0183
1	.1397	.1304	.1217	.1135	.1057	.0984	.0915	.0850	.0789	.0733
2	.2165	.2087	.2008	.1929	.1850	.1771	.1692	.1615	.1539	.1465
3	.2237	.2226	.2209	.2186	.2158	.2125	.2087	.2046	.2001	.1954
4	.1733	.1781	.1823	.1858	.1888	.1912	.1931	.1944	.1951	.1954
5	.1075	.1140	.1203	.1264	.1322	.1377	.1429	.1477	.1522	.1563
6	.0555	.0608	.0662	.0716	.0771	.0826	.0881	.0936	.0989	.1042
7	.0246	.0278	.0312	.0348	.0385	.0425	.0466	.0508	.0551	.0595
8	.0095	.0111	.0129	.0148	.0169	.0191	.0215	.0241	.0269	.0298
9	.0033	.0040	.0047	.0056	.0066	.0076	.0089	.0102	.0116	.0132
10	.0010	.0013	.0016	.0019	.0023	.0028	.0033	.0039	.0045	.0053
11	.0003	.0004	.0005	.0006	.0007	.0009	.0011	.0013	.0016	.0019
12	.0001	.0001	.0001	.0002	.0002	.0003	.0003	.0004	.0005	.0006
13	.0000	.0000	.0000	.0000	.0001	.0001	.0001	.0001	.0002	.0002
14	.0000	.0000	.0000	.0000	.0000	.0000	.0000	.0000	.0000	.0001
x	4.1	4.2	4.3	4.4	4.5	4.6	4.7	4.8	4.9	5.0
0	.0166	.0150	.0136	.0123	.0111	.0101	.0091	.0082	.0074	.0067
1	.0679	.0630	.0583	.0540	.0500	.0462	.0427	.0395	.0365	.0337
2	.1393	.1323	.1254	.1188	.1125	.1063	.1005	.0948	.0894	.0842
3	.1904	.1852	.1798	.1743	.1687	.1631	.1574	.1517	.1460	.1404
4	.1951	.1944	.1933	.1917	.1898	.1875	.1849	.1820	.1789	.1755
5	.1600	.1633	.1662	.1687	.1708	.1725	.1738	.1747	.1753	.1755
6	.1093	.1143	.1191	.1237	.1281	.1323	.1362	.1398	.1432	.1462
7	.0640	.0686	.0732	.0778	.0824	.0869	.0914	.0959	.1002	.1044
8	.0328	.0360	.0393	.0428	.0463	.0500	.0537	.0575	.0614	.0653
9	.0150	.0168	.0188	.0209	.0232	.0255	.0281	.0307	.0334	.0363
10	.0061	.0071	.0081	.0092	.0104	.0118	.0132	.0147	.0164	.0181
11	.0023	.0027	.0032	.0037	.0043	.0049	.0056	.0064	.0073	.0082
12	.0008	.0009	.0011	.0013	.0016	.0019	.0022	.0026	.0030	.0034
13	.0002	.0003	.0004	.0005	.0006	.0007	.0008	.0009	.0011	.0013
14	.0001	.0001	.0001	.0001	.0002	.0002	.0003	.0003	.0004	.0005
15	.0000	.0000	.0000	.0000	.0001	.0001	.0001	.0001	.0001	.0002

	λ									
x	**5.1**	**5.2**	**5.3**	**5.4**	**5.5**	**5.6**	**5.7**	**5.8**	**5.9**	**6.0**
0	.0061	.0055	.0050	.0045	.0041	.0037	.0033	.0030	.0027	.0025
1	.0311	.0287	.0265	.0244	.0225	.0207	.0191	.0176	.0162	.0149
2	.0793	.0746	.0701	.0659	.0618	.0580	.0544	.0509	.0477	.0446
3	.1348	.1293	.1239	.1185	.1133	.1082	.1033	.0985	.0938	.0892
4	.1719	.1681	.1641	.1600	.1558	.1515	.1472	.1428	.1383	.1339
5	.1753	.1748	.1740	.1728	.1714	.1697	.1678	.1656	.1632	.1606
6	.1490	.1515	.1537	.1555	.1571	.1584	.1594	.1601	.1605	.1606
7	.1086	.1125	.1163	.1200	.1234	.1267	.1298	.1326	.1353	.1377
8	.0692	.0731	.0771	.0810	.0849	.0887	.0925	.0962	.0998	.1033
9	.0392	.0423	.0454	.0486	.0519	.0552	.0586	.0620	.0654	.0688
10	.0200	.0220	.0241	.0262	.0285	.0309	.0334	.0359	.0386	.0413
11	.0093	.0104	.0116	.0129	.0143	.0157	.0173	.0190	.0207	.0225
12	.0039	.0045	.0051	.0058	.0065	.0073	.0082	.0092	.0102	.0113
13	.0015	.0018	.0021	.0024	.0028	.0032	.0036	.0041	.0046	.0052
14	.0006	.0007	.0008	.0009	.0011	.0013	.0015	.0017	.0019	.0022
15	.0002	.0002	.0003	.0003	.0004	.0005	.0006	.0007	.0008	.0009
16	.0001	.0001	.0001	.0001	.0001	.0002	.0002	.0002	.0003	.0003
17	.0000	.0000	.0000	.0000	.0000	.0001	.0001	.0001	.0001	.0001
x	**6.1**	**6.2**	**6.3**	**6.4**	**6.5**	**6.6**	**6.7**	**6.8**	**6.9**	**7.0**
0	.0022	.0020	.0018	.0017	.0015	.0014	.0012	.0011	.0010	.0009
1	.0137	.0126	.0116	.0106	.0098	.0090	.0082	.0076	.0070	.0064
2	.0417	.0390	.0364	.0340	.0318	.0296	.0276	.0258	.0240	.0223
3	.0848	.0806	.0765	.0726	.0688	.0652	.0617	.0584	.0552	.0521
4	.1294	.1249	.1205	.1162	.1118	.1076	.1034	.0992	.0952	.0912
5	.1579	.1549	.1519	.1487	.1454	.1420	.1385	.1349	.1314	.1277
6	.1605	.1601	.1595	.1586	.1575	.1562	.1546	.1529	.1511	.1490
7	.1399	.1418	.1435	.1450	.1462	.1472	.1480	.1486	.1489	.1490
8	.1066	.1099	.1130	.1160	.1188	.1215	.1240	.1263	.1284	.1304
9	.0723	.0757	.0791	.0825	.0858	.0891	.0923	.0954	.0985	.1014
10	.0441	.0469	.0498	.0528	.0558	.0588	.0618	.0649	.0679	.0710
11	.0244	.0265	.0285	.0307	.0330	.0353	.0377	.0401	.0426	.0452
12	.0124	.0137	.0150	.0164	.0179	.0194	.0210	.0227	.0245	.0263
13	.0058	.0065	.0073	.0081	.0089	.0099	.0108	.0119	.0130	.0142
14	.0025	.0029	.0033	.0037	.0041	.0046	.0052	.0058	.0064	.0071
15	.0010	.0012	.0014	.0016	.0018	.0020	.0023	.0026	.0029	.0033
16	.0004	.0005	.0005	.0006	.0007	.0008	.0010	.0011	.0013	.0014
17	.0001	.0002	.0002	.0002	.0003	.0003	.0004	.0004	.0005	.0006
18	.0000	.0001	.0001	.0001	.0001	.0001	.0001	.0002	.0002	.0002
19	.0000	.0000	.0000	.0000	.0000	.0000	.0001	.0001	.0001	.0001

(continued)

TABLE A.2 *(continued)*

	λ									
x	**7.1**	**7.2**	**7.3**	**7.4**	**7.5**	**7.6**	**7.7**	**7.8**	**7.9**	**8.0**
0	.0008	.0007	.0007	.0006	.0006	.0005	.0005	.0004	.0004	.0003
1	.0059	.0054	.0049	.0045	.0041	.0038	.0035	.0032	.0029	.0027
2	.0208	.0194	.0180	.0167	.0156	.0145	.0134	.0125	.0116	.0107
3	.0492	.0464	.0438	.0413	.0389	.0366	.0345	.0324	.0305	.0286
4	.0874	.0836	.0799	.0764	.0729	.0696	.0663	.0632	.0602	.0573
5	.1241	.1204	.1167	.1130	.1094	.1057	.1021	.0986	.0951	.0916
6	.1468	.1445	.1420	.1394	.1367	.1339	.1311	.1282	.1252	.1221
7	.1489	.1486	.1481	.1474	.1465	.1454	.1442	.1428	.1413	.1396
8	.1321	.1337	.1351	.1363	.1373	.1381	.1388	.1392	.1395	.1396
9	.1042	.1070	.1096	.1121	.1144	.1167	.1187	.1207	.1224	.1241
10	.0740	.0770	.0800	.0829	.0858	.0887	.0914	.0941	.0967	.0993
11	.0478	.0504	.0531	.0558	.0585	.0613	.0640	.0667	.0695	.0722
12	.0283	.0303	.0323	.0344	.0366	.0388	.0411	.0434	.0457	.0481
13	.0154	.0168	.0181	.0196	.0211	.0227	.0243	.0260	.0278	.0296
14	.0078	.0086	.0095	.0104	.0113	.0123	.0134	.0145	.0157	.0169
15	.0037	.0041	.0046	.0051	.0057	.0062	.0069	.0075	.0083	.0090
16	.0016	.0019	.0021	.0024	.0026	.0030	.0033	.0037	.0041	.0045
17	.0007	.0008	.0009	.0010	.0012	.0013	.0015	.0017	.0019	.0021
18	.0003	.0003	.0004	.0004	.0005	.0006	.0006	.0007	.0008	.0009
19	.0001	.0001	.0001	.0002	.0002	.0002	.0003	.0003	.0003	.0004
20	.0000	.0000	.0001	.0001	.0001	.0001	.0001	.0001	.0001	.0002
21	.0000	.0000	.0000	.0000	.0000	.0000	.0000	.0000	.0001	.0001
x	**8.1**	**8.2**	**8.3**	**8.4**	**8.5**	**8.6**	**8.7**	**8.8**	**8.9**	**9.0**
0	.0003	.0003	.0002	.0002	.0002	.0002	.0002	.0002	.0001	.0001
1	.0025	.0023	.0021	.0019	.0017	.0016	.0014	.0013	.0012	.0011
2	.0100	.0092	.0086	.0079	.0074	.0068	.0063	.0058	.0054	.0050
3	.0269	.0252	.0237	.0222	.0208	.0195	.0183	.0171	.0160	.0150
4	.0544	.0517	.0491	.0466	.0443	.0420	.0398	.0377	.0357	.0337
5	.0882	.0849	.0816	.0784	.0752	.0722	.0692	.0663	.0635	.0607
6	.1191	.1160	.1128	.1097	.1066	.1034	.1003	.0972	.0941	.0911
7	.1378	.1358	.1338	.1317	.1294	.1271	.1247	.1222	.1197	.1171
8	.1395	.1392	.1388	.1382	.1375	.1366	.1356	.1344	.1332	.1318
9	.1256	.1269	.1280	.1290	.1299	.1306	.1311	.1315	.1317	.1318
10	.1017	.1040	.1063	.1084	.1104	.1123	.1140	.1157	.1172	.1186
11	.0749	.0776	.0802	.0828	.0853	.0878	.0902	.0925	.0948	.0970
12	.0505	.0530	.0555	.0579	.0604	.0629	.0654	.0679	.0703	.0728
13	.0315	.0334	.0354	.0374	.0395	.0416	.0438	.0459	.0481	.0504
14	.0182	.0196	.0210	.0225	.0240	.0256	.0272	.0289	.0306	.0324
15	.0098	.0107	.0116	.0126	.0136	.0147	.0158	.0169	.0182	.0194
16	.0050	.0055	.0060	.0066	.0072	.0079	.0086	.0093	.0101	.0109
17	.0024	.0026	.0029	.0033	.0036	.0040	.0044	.0048	.0053	.0058
18	.0011	.0012	.0014	.0015	.0017	.0019	.0021	.0024	.0026	.0029
19	.0005	.0005	.0006	.0007	.0008	.0009	.0010	.0011	.0012	.0014
20	.0002	.0002	.0002	.0003	.0003	.0004	.0004	.0005	.0005	.0006
21	.0001	.0001	.0001	.0001	.0001	.0002	.0002	.0002	.0002	.0003
22	.0000	.0000	.0000	.0000	.0001	.0001	.0001	.0001	.0001	.0001

	λ									
x	9.1	9.2	9.3	9.4	9.5	9.6	9.7	9.8	9.9	10.0
0	.0001	.0001	.0001	.0001	.0001	.0001	.0001	.0001	.0001	.0000
1	.0010	.0009	.0009	.0008	.0007	.0007	.0006	.0005	.0005	.0005
2	.0046	.0043	.0040	.0037	.0034	.0031	.0029	.0027	.0025	.0023
3	.0140	.0131	.0123	.0115	.0107	.0100	.0093	.0087	.0081	.0076
4	.0319	.0302	.0285	.0269	.0254	.0240	.0226	.0213	.0201	.0189
5	.0581	.0555	.0530	.0506	.0483	.0460	.0439	.0418	.0398	.0378
6	.0881	.0851	.0822	.0793	.0764	.0736	.0709	.0682	.0656	.0631
7	.1145	.1118	.1091	.1064	.1037	.1010	.0982	.0955	.0928	.0901
8	.1302	.1286	.1269	.1251	.1232	.1212	.1191	.1170	.1148	.1126
9	.1317	.1315	.1311	.1306	.1300	.1293	.1284	.1274	.1263	.1251
10	.1198	.1210	.1219	.1228	.1235	.1241	.1245	.1249	.1250	.1251
11	.0991	.1012	.1031	.1049	.1067	.1083	.1098	.1112	.1125	.1137
12	.0752	.0776	.0799	.0822	.0844	.0866	.0888	.0908	.0928	.0948
13	.0526	.0549	.0572	.0594	.0617	.0640	.0662	.0685	.0707	.0729
14	.0342	.0361	.0380	.0399	.0419	.0439	.0459	.0479	.0500	.0521
15	.0208	.0221	.0235	.0250	.0265	.0281	.0297	.0313	.0330	.0347
16	.0118	.0127	.0137	.0147	.0157	.0168	.0180	.0192	.0204	.0217
17	.0063	.0069	.0075	.0081	.0088	.0095	.0103	.0111	.0119	.0128
18	.0032	.0035	.0039	.0042	.0046	.0051	.0055	.0060	.0065	.0071
19	.0015	.0017	.0019	.0021	.0023	.0026	.0028	.0031	.0034	.0037
20	.0007	.0008	.0009	.0010	.0011	.0012	.0014	.0015	.0017	.0019
21	.0003	.0003	.0004	.0004	.0005	.0006	.0006	.0007	.0008	.0009
22	.0001	.0001	.0002	.0002	.0002	.0002	.0003	.0003	.0004	.0004
23	.0000	.0001	.0001	.0001	.0001	.0001	.0001	.0001	.0002	.0002
24	.0000	.0000	.0000	.0000	.0000	.0000	.0000	.0001	.0001	.0001

TABLE A.3 The e^{-x} table

x	e^{-x}	x	e^{-x}	x	e^{-x}	x	e^{-x}
0.0	1.0000	3.0	0.0498	6.0	0.00248	9.0	0.00012
0.1	0.9048	3.1	0.0450	6.1	0.00224	9.1	0.00011
0.2	0.8187	3.2	0.0408	6.2	0.00203	9.2	0.00010
0.3	0.7408	3.3	0.0369	6.3	0.00184	9.3	0.00009
0.4	0.6703	3.4	0.0334	6.4	0.00166	9.4	0.00008
0.5	0.6065	3.5	0.0302	6.5	0.00150	9.5	0.00007
0.6	0.5488	3.6	0.0273	6.6	0.00136	9.6	0.00007
0.7	0.4966	3.7	0.0247	6.7	0.00123	9.7	0.00006
0.8	0.4493	3.8	0.0224	6.8	0.00111	9.8	0.00006
0.9	0.4066	3.9	0.0202	6.9	0.00101	9.9	0.00005
1.0	0.3679	4.0	0.0183	7.0	0.00091	10.0	0.00005
1.1	0.3329	4.1	0.0166	7.1	0.00083		
1.2	0.3012	4.2	0.0150	7.2	0.00075		
1.3	0.2725	4.3	0.0136	7.3	0.00068		
1.4	0.2466	4.4	0.0123	7.4	0.00061		
1.5	0.2231	4.5	0.0111	7.5	0.00055		
1.6	0.2019	4.6	0.0101	7.6	0.00050		
1.7	0.1827	4.7	0.0091	7.7	0.00045		
1.8	0.1653	4.8	0.0082	7.8	0.00041		
1.9	0.1496	4.9	0.0074	7.9	0.00037		
2.0	0.1353	5.0	0.0067	8.0	0.00034		
2.1	0.1225	5.1	0.0061	8.1	0.00030		
2.2	0.1108	5.2	0.0055	8.2	0.00027		
2.3	0.1003	5.3	0.0050	8.3	0.00025		
2.4	0.0907	5.4	0.0045	8.4	0.00022		
2.5	0.0821	5.5	0.0041	8.5	0.00020		
2.6	0.0743	5.6	0.0037	8.6	0.00018		
2.7	0.0672	5.7	0.0033	8.7	0.00017		
2.8	0.0608	5.8	0.0030	8.8	0.00015		
2.9	0.0550	5.9	0.0027	8.9	0.00014		

TABLE A.4 Areas of the standard normal distribution $\mu = 0, \sigma = 1$

The entries in this table are the probabilities that a standard normal random variable is between 0 and z_1 (the shaded area).

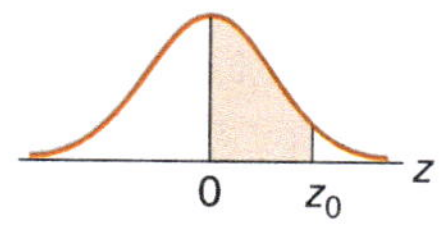

z_1	0.00	0.01	0.02	0.03	0.04	0.05	0.06	0.07	0.08	0.09
0.0	.0000	.0040	.0080	.0120	.0160	.0199	.0239	.0279	.0319	.0359
0.1	.0398	.0438	.0478	.0517	.0557	.0596	.0636	.0675	.0714	.0753
0.2	.0793	.0832	.0871	.0910	.0948	.0987	.1026	.1064	.1103	.1141
0.3	.1179	.1217	.1255	.1293	.1331	.1368	.1406	.1443	.1480	.1517
0.4	.1554	.1591	.1628	.1664	.1700	.1736	.1772	.1808	.1844	.1879
0.5	.1915	.1950	.1985	.2019	.2054	.2088	.2123	.2157	.2190	.2224
0.6	.2257	.2291	.2324	.2357	.2389	.2422	.2454	.2486	.2517	.2549
0.7	.2580	.2611	.2642	.2673	.2704	.2734	.2764	.2794	.2823	.2852
0.8	.2881	.2910	.2939	.2967	.2995	.3023	.3051	.3078	.3106	.3133
0.9	.3159	.3186	.3212	.3238	.3264	.3289	.3315	.3340	.3365	.3389
1.0	.3413	.3438	.3461	.3485	.3508	.3531	.3554	.3577	.3599	.3621
1.1	.3643	.3665	.3686	.3708	.3729	.3749	.3770	.3790	.3810	.3830
1.2	.3849	.3869	.3888	.3907	.3925	.3944	.3962	.3980	.3997	.4015
1.3	.4032	.4049	.4066	.4082	.4099	.4115	.4131	.4147	.4162	.4177
1.4	.4192	.4207	.4222	.4236	.4251	.4265	.4279	.4292	.4306	.4319
1.5	.4332	.4345	.4357	.4370	.4382	.4394	.4406	.4418	.4429	.4441
1.6	.4452	.4463	.4474	.4484	.4495	.4505	.4515	.4525	.4535	.4545
1.7	.4554	.4564	.4573	.4582	.4591	.4599	.4608	.4616	.4625	.4633
1.8	.4641	.4649	.4656	.4664	.4671	.4678	.4686	.4693	.4699	.4706
1.9	.4713	.4719	.4726	.4732	.4738	.4744	.4750	.4756	.4761	.4767
2.0	.4772	.4778	.4783	.4788	.4793	.4798	.4803	.4808	.4812	.4817
2.1	.4821	.4826	.4830	.4834	.4838	.4842	.4846	.4850	.4854	.4857
2.2	.4861	.4864	.4868	.4871	.4875	.4878	.4881	.4884	.4887	.4890
2.3	.4893	.4896	.4898	.4901	.4904	.4906	.4909	.4911	.4913	.4916
2.4	.4918	.4920	.4922	.4925	.4927	.4929	.4931	.4932	.4934	.4936
2.5	.4938	.4940	.4941	.4943	.4945	.4946	.4948	.4949	.4951	.4952
2.6	.4953	.4955	.4956	.4957	.4959	.4960	.4961	.4962	.4963	.4964
2.7	.4965	.4966	.4967	.4968	.4969	.4970	.4971	.4972	.4973	.4974
2.8	.4974	.4975	.4976	.4977	.4977	.4978	.4979	.4979	.4980	.4981
2.9	.4981	.4982	.4982	.4983	.4984	.4984	.4985	.4985	.4986	.4986
3.0	.4987	.4987	.4987	.4988	.4988	.4989	.4989	.4989	.4990	.4990
3.1	.4990	.4991	.4991	.4991	.4992	.4992	.4992	.4992	.4993	.4993
3.2	.4993	.4993	.4994	.4994	.4994	.4994	.4994	.4995	.4995	.4995
3.3	.4995	.4995	.4995	.4996	.4996	.4996	.4996	.4996	.4996	.4997
3.4	.4997	.4997	.4997	.4997	.4997	.4997	.4997	.4997	.4997	.4998
3.5	.4998									
4.0	.49997									
4.5	.499997									
5.0	.4999997									
6.0	.499999999									

TABLE A.5 Cumulative normal probabilities

The entries in this table are the cumulative probabilities that a standard normal random variable is between $-\infty$ and z_1 (the shaded area).

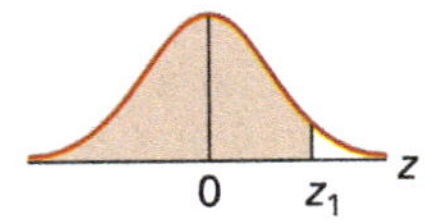

z_1	0.00	0.01	0.02	0.03	0.04	0.05	0.06	0.07	0.08	0.09
0.1	0.5000	0.5040	0.5080	0.5120	0.5160	0.5199	0.5239	0.5279	0.5319	0.5359
0.1	0.5398	0.5438	0.5478	0.5517	0.5557	0.5596	0.5636	0.5675	0.5714	0.5753
0.2	0.5793	0.5832	0.5871	0.5910	0.5948	0.5987	0.6026	0.6064	0.6103	0.6141
0.3	0.6179	0.6217	0.6255	0.6293	0.6331	0.6368	0.6406	0.6443	0.6480	0.6517
0.4	0.6554	0.6591	0.6628	0.6664	0.6700	0.6736	0.6772	0.6808	0.6844	0.6879
0.5	0.6915	0.6950	0.6985	0.7019	0.7054	0.7088	0.7123	0.7157	0.7190	0.7224
0.6	0.7257	0.7291	0.7324	0.7357	0.7389	0.7422	0.7454	0.7486	0.7517	0.7549
0.7	0.7580	0.7611	0.7642	0.7673	0.7704	0.7734	0.7764	0.7794	0.7823	0.7852
0.8	0.7881	0.7910	0.7939	0.7967	0.7995	0.8023	0.8051	0.8078	0.8106	0.8133
0.9	0.8159	0.8186	0.8212	0.8238	0.8264	0.8289	0.8315	0.8340	0.8365	0.8389
1.0	0.8413	0.8438	0.8461	0.8485	0.8508	0.8531	0.8554	0.8577	0.8599	0.8621
1.1	0.8643	0.8665	0.8686	0.8708	0.8729	0.8749	0.8770	0.8790	0.8810	0.8830
1.2	0.8849	0.8869	0.8888	0.8907	0.8925	0.8944	0.8962	0.8980	0.8997	0.9015
1.3	0.9032	0.9049	0.9066	0.9082	0.9099	0.9115	0.9131	0.9147	0.9162	0.9177
1.4	0.9192	0.9207	0.9222	0.9236	0.9251	0.9265	0.9279	0.9292	0.9306	0.9319
1.5	0.9332	0.9345	0.9357	0.9370	0.9382	0.9394	0.9406	0.9418	0.9429	0.9441
1.6	0.9452	0.9463	0.9474	0.9484	0.9495	0.9505	0.9515	0.9525	0.9535	0.9545
1.7	0.9554	0.9564	0.9573	0.9582	0.9591	0.9599	0.9608	0.9616	0.9625	0.9633
1.8	0.9641	0.9649	0.9656	0.9664	0.9671	0.9678	0.9686	0.9693	0.9699	0.9706
1.9	0.9713	0.9719	0.9726	0.9732	0.9738	0.9744	0.9750	0.9756	0.9761	0.9767
2.0	0.9772	0.9778	0.9783	0.9788	0.9793	0.9798	0.9803	0.9808	0.9812	0.9817
2.1	0.9821	0.9826	0.9830	0.9834	0.9838	0.9842	0.9846	0.9850	0.9854	0.9857
2.2	0.9861	0.9864	0.9868	0.9871	0.9875	0.9878	0.9881	0.9884	0.9887	0.9890
2.3	0.9893	0.9896	0.9898	0.9901	0.9904	0.9906	0.9909	0.9911	0.9913	0.9916
2.4	0.9918	0.9920	0.9922	0.9925	0.9927	0.9929	0.9931	0.9932	0.9934	0.9936
2.5	0.9938	0.9940	0.9941	0.9943	0.9945	0.9946	0.9948	0.9949	0.9951	0.9952
2.6	0.9953	0.9955	0.9956	0.9957	0.9959	0.9960	0.9961	0.9962	0.9963	0.9964
2.7	0.9965	0.9966	0.9967	0.9968	0.9969	0.9970	0.9971	0.9972	0.9973	0.9974
2.8	0.9974	0.9975	0.9976	0.9977	0.9977	0.9978	0.9979	0.9979	0.9980	0.9981
2.9	0.9981	0.9982	0.9982	0.9983	0.9984	0.9984	0.9985	0.9985	0.9986	0.9986
3.0	0.9987	0.9987	0.9987	0.9988	0.9988	0.9989	0.9989	0.9989	0.9990	0.9990
3.1	0.9990	0.9991	0.9991	0.9991	0.9992	0.9992	0.9992	0.9992	0.9993	0.9993
3.2	0.9993	0.9993	0.9994	0.9994	0.9994	0.9994	0.9994	0.9995	0.9995	0.9995
3.3	0.9995	0.9995	0.9995	0.9996	0.9996	0.9996	0.9996	0.9996	0.9996	0.9997
3.4	0.9997	0.9997	0.9997	0.9997	0.9997	0.9997	0.9997	0.9997	0.9997	0.9998

TABLE A.6 Critical values of t

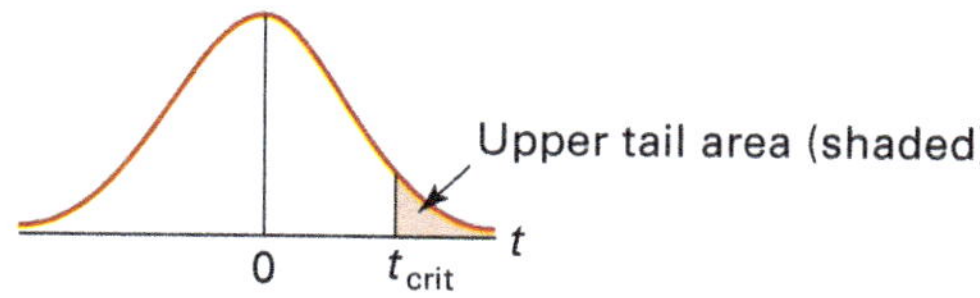

	Upper tail areas					
df	$t_{.10}$	$t_{.05}$	$t_{.025}$	$t_{.01}$	$t_{.005}$	$t_{.001}$
1	3.078	6.314	12.706	31.821	63.657	318.309
2	1.886	2.920	4.303	6.965	9.925	22.327
3	1.638	2.353	3.182	4.541	5.841	10.215
4	1.533	2.132	2.776	3.747	4.604	7.173
5	1.476	2.015	2.571	3.365	4.032	5.893
6	1.440	1.943	2.447	3.143	3.707	5.208
7	1.415	1.895	2.365	2.998	3.499	4.785
8	1.397	1.860	2.306	2.896	3.355	4.501
9	1.383	1.833	2.262	2.821	3.250	4.297
10	1.372	1.812	2.228	2.764	3.169	4.144
11	1.363	1.796	2.201	2.718	3.106	4.025
12	1.356	1.782	2.179	2.681	3.055	3.930
13	1.350	1.771	2.160	2.650	3.012	3.852
14	1.345	1.761	2.145	2.624	2.977	3.787
15	1.341	1.753	2.131	2.602	2.947	3.733
16	1.337	1.746	2.120	2.583	2.921	3.686
17	1.333	1.740	2.110	2.567	2.898	3.646
18	1.330	1.734	2.101	2.552	2.878	3.610
19	1.328	1.729	2.093	2.539	2.861	3.579
20	1.325	1.725	2.086	2.528	2.845	3.552
21	1.323	1.721	2.080	2.518	2.831	3.527
22	1.321	1.717	2.074	2.508	2.819	3.505
23	1.319	1.714	2.069	2.500	2.807	3.485
24	1.318	1.711	2.064	2.492	2.797	3.467
25	1.316	1.708	2.060	2.485	2.787	3.450
26	1.315	1.706	2.056	2.479	2.779	3.435
27	1.314	1.703	2.052	2.473	2.771	3.421
28	1.313	1.701	2.048	2.467	2.763	3.408
29	1.311	1.699	2.045	2.462	2.756	3.396
30	1.310	1.697	2.042	2.457	2.750	3.385
31	1.309	1.696	2.040	2.453	2.744	3.375
32	1.309	1.694	2.037	2.449	2.738	3.365
33	1.308	1.692	2.035	2.445	2.733	3.356
34	1.307	1.691	2.032	2.441	2.728	3.348
35	1.306	1.690	2.030	2.438	2.724	3.340
36	1.306	1.688	2.028	2.434	2.719	3.333
37	1.305	1.687	2.026	2.431	2.715	3.326
38	1.304	1.686	2.024	2.429	2.712	3.319
39	1.304	1.685	2.023	2.426	2.708	3.313
40	1.303	1.684	2.021	2.423	2.704	3.307

(continued)

TABLE A.6 *(continued)*

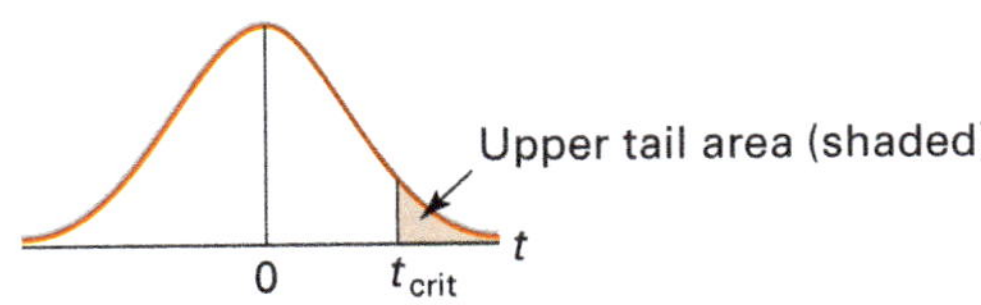

df	Upper tail areas					
	$t_{.10}$	$t_{.05}$	$t_{.025}$	$t_{.01}$	$t_{.005}$	$t_{.001}$
41	1.303	1.683	2.020	2.421	2.701	3.301
42	1.302	1.682	2.018	2.418	2.698	3.296
43	1.302	1.681	2.017	2.416	2.695	3.291
44	1.301	1.680	2.015	2.414	2.692	3.286
45	1.301	1.679	2.014	2.412	2.690	3.281
46	1.300	1.679	2.013	2.410	2.687	3.277
47	1.300	1.678	2.012	2.408	2.685	3.273
48	1.299	1.677	2.011	2.407	2.682	3.269
49	1.299	1.677	2.010	2.405	2.680	3.265
50	1.299	1.676	2.009	2.403	2.678	3.261
51	1.298	1.675	2.008	2.402	2.676	3.258
52	1.298	1.675	2.007	2.400	2.674	3.255
53	1.298	1.674	2.006	2.399	2.672	3.251
54	1.297	1.674	2.005	2.397	2.670	3.248
55	1.297	1.673	2.004	2.396	2.668	3.245
56	1.297	1.673	2.003	2.395	2.667	3.242
57	1.297	1.672	2.002	2.394	2.665	3.239
58	1.296	1.672	2.002	2.392	2.663	3.237
59	1.296	1.671	2.001	2.391	2.662	3.234
60	1.296	1.671	2.000	2.390	2.660	3.232
61	1.296	1.670	2.000	2.389	2.659	3.229
62	1.295	1.670	1.999	2.388	2.657	3.227
63	1.295	1.669	1.998	2.387	2.656	3.225
64	1.295	1.669	1.998	2.386	2.655	3.223
65	1.295	1.669	1.997	2.385	2.654	3.220
66	1.295	1.668	1.997	2.384	2.652	3.218
67	1.294	1.668	1.996	2.383	2.651	3.216
68	1.294	1.668	1.995	2.382	2.650	3.214
69	1.294	1.667	1.995	2.382	2.649	3.213
70	1.294	1.667	1.994	2.381	2.648	3.211
71	1.294	1.667	1.994	2.380	2.647	3.209
72	1.293	1.666	1.993	2.379	2.646	3.207
73	1.293	1.666	1.993	2.379	2.645	3.206
74	1.293	1.666	1.993	2.378	2.644	3.204
75	1.293	1.665	1.992	2.377	2.643	3.202
76	1.293	1.665	1.992	2.376	2.642	3.201
77	1.293	1.665	1.991	2.376	2.641	3.199
78	1.292	1.665	1.991	2.375	2.640	3.198
79	1.292	1.664	1.990	2.374	2.640	3.197
80	1.292	1.664	1.990	2.374	2.639	3.195

df	Upper tail areas $t_{.10}$	$t_{.05}$	$t_{.025}$	$t_{.01}$	$t_{.005}$	$t_{.001}$
81	1.292	1.664	1.990	2.373	2.638	3.194
82	1.292	1.664	1.989	2.373	2.637	3.193
83	1.292	1.663	1.989	2.372	2.636	3.191
84	1.292	1.663	1.989	2.372	2.636	3.190
85	1.292	1.663	1.988	2.371	2.635	3.189
86	1.291	1.663	1.988	2.370	2.634	3.188
87	1.291	1.663	1.988	2.370	2.634	3.187
88	1.291	1.662	1.987	2.369	2.633	3.185
89	1.291	1.662	1.987	2.369	2.632	3.184
90	1.291	1.662	1.987	2.368	2.632	3.183
91	1.291	1.662	1.986	2.368	2.631	3.182
92	1.291	1.662	1.986	2.368	2.630	3.181
93	1.291	1.661	1.986	2.367	2.630	3.180
94	1.291	1.661	1.986	2.367	2.629	3.179
95	1.291	1.661	1.985	2.366	2.629	3.178
96	1.290	1.661	1.985	2.366	2.628	3.177
97	1.290	1.661	1.985	2.365	2.627	3.176
98	1.290	1.661	1.984	2.365	2.627	3.175
99	1.290	1.660	1.984	2.365	2.626	3.175
100	1.290	1.660	1.984	2.364	2.626	3.174
150	1.287	1.655	1.976	2.351	2.609	3.145
200	1.286	1.653	1.972	2.345	2.601	3.131
∞	1.282	1.645	1.960	2.326	2.576	3.090

TABLE A.7 Percentage points of the *F* distribution

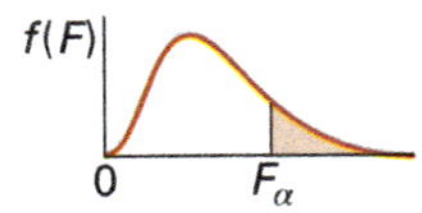

v_2 \ v_1	$\alpha = .10$ Numerator degrees of freedom 1	2	3	4	5	6	7	8	9
Denominator degrees of freedom 1	39.86	49.50	53.59	55.83	57.24	58.20	58.91	59.44	59.86
2	8.53	9.00	9.16	9.24	9.29	9.33	9.35	9.37	9.38
3	5.54	5.46	5.39	5.34	5.31	5.28	5.27	5.25	5.24
4	4.54	4.32	4.19	4.11	4.05	4.01	3.98	3.95	3.94
5	4.06	3.78	3.62	3.52	3.45	3.40	3.37	3.34	3.32
6	3.78	3.46	3.29	3.18	3.11	3.05	3.01	2.98	2.96
7	3.59	3.26	3.07	2.96	2.88	2.83	2.78	2.75	2.72
8	3.46	3.11	2.92	2.81	2.73	2.67	2.62	2.59	2.56
9	3.36	3.01	2.81	2.69	2.61	2.55	2.51	2.47	2.44
10	3.29	2.92	2.73	2.61	2.52	2.46	2.41	2.38	2.35
11	3.23	2.86	2.66	2.54	2.45	2.39	2.34	2.30	2.27
12	3.18	2.81	2.61	2.48	2.39	2.33	2.28	2.24	2.21
13	3.14	2.76	2.56	2.43	2.35	2.28	2.23	2.20	2.16
14	3.10	2.73	2.52	2.39	2.31	2.24	2.19	2.15	2.12
15	3.07	2.70	2.49	2.36	2.27	2.21	2.16	2.12	2.09
16	3.05	2.67	2.46	2.33	2.24	2.18	2.13	2.09	2.06
17	3.03	2.64	2.44	2.31	2.22	2.15	2.10	2.06	2.03
18	3.01	2.62	2.42	2.29	2.20	2.13	2.08	2.04	2.00
19	2.99	2.61	2.40	2.27	2.18	2.11	2.06	2.02	1.98
20	2.97	2.59	2.38	2.25	2.16	2.09	2.04	2.00	1.96
21	2.96	2.57	2.36	2.23	2.14	2.08	2.02	1.98	1.95
22	2.95	2.56	2.35	2.22	2.13	2.06	2.01	1.97	1.93
23	2.94	2.55	2.34	2.21	2.11	2.05	1.99	1.95	1.92
24	2.93	2.54	2.33	2.19	2.10	2.04	1.98	1.94	1.91
25	2.92	2.53	2.32	2.18	2.09	2.02	1.97	1.93	1.89
26	2.91	2.52	2.31	2.17	2.08	2.01	1.96	1.92	1.88
27	2.90	2.51	2.30	2.17	2.07	2.00	1.95	1.91	1.87
28	2.89	2.50	2.29	2.16	2.06	2.00	1.94	1.90	1.87
29	2.89	2.50	2.28	2.15	2.06	1.99	1.93	1.89	1.86
30	2.88	2.49	2.28	2.14	2.05	1.98	1.93	1.88	1.85
40	2.84	2.44	2.23	2.09	2.00	1.93	1.87	1.83	1.79
60	2.79	2.39	2.18	2.04	1.95	1.87	1.82	1.77	1.74
120	2.75	2.35	2.13	1.99	1.90	1.82	1.77	1.72	1.68
∞	2.71	2.30	2.08	1.94	1.85	1.77	1.72	1.67	1.63

$\alpha = .10$ Numerator degrees of freedom ν_1: 10	12	15	20	24	30	40	60	120	∞	ν_2 (Denominator degrees of freedom)
60.19	60.71	61.22	61.74	62.00	62.26	62.53	62.79	63.06	63.33	1
9.39	9.41	9.42	9.44	9.45	9.46	9.47	9.47	9.48	9.49	2
5.23	5.22	5.20	5.18	5.18	5.17	5.16	5.15	5.14	5.13	3
3.92	3.90	3.87	3.84	3.83	3.82	3.80	3.79	3.78	3.76	4
3.30	3.27	3.24	3.21	3.19	3.17	3.16	3.14	3.12	3.10	5
2.94	2.90	2.87	2.84	2.82	2.80	2.78	2.76	2.74	2.72	6
2.70	2.67	2.63	2.59	2.58	2.56	2.54	2.51	2.49	2.47	7
2.54	2.50	2.46	2.42	2.40	2.38	2.36	2.34	2.32	2.29	8
2.42	2.38	2.34	2.30	2.28	2.25	2.23	2.21	2.18	2.16	9
2.32	2.28	2.24	2.20	2.18	2.16	2.13	2.11	2.08	2.06	10
2.25	2.21	2.17	2.12	2.10	2.08	2.05	2.03	2.00	1.97	11
2.19	2.15	2.10	2.06	2.04	2.01	1.99	1.96	1.93	1.90	12
2.14	2.10	2.05	2.01	1.98	1.96	1.93	1.90	1.88	1.85	13
2.10	2.05	2.01	1.96	1.94	1.91	1.89	1.86	1.83	1.80	14
2.06	2.02	1.97	1.92	1.90	1.87	1.85	1.82	1.79	1.76	15
2.03	1.99	1.94	1.89	1.87	1.84	1.81	1.78	1.75	1.72	16
2.00	1.96	1.91	1.86	1.84	1.81	1.78	1.75	1.72	1.69	17
1.98	1.93	1.89	1.84	1.81	1.78	1.75	1.72	1.69	1.66	18
1.96	1.91	1.86	1.81	1.79	1.76	1.73	1.70	1.67	1.63	19
1.94	1.89	1.84	1.79	1.77	1.74	1.71	1.68	1.64	1.61	20
1.92	1.87	1.83	1.78	1.75	1.72	1.69	1.66	1.62	1.59	21
1.90	1.86	1.81	1.76	1.73	1.70	1.67	1.64	1.60	1.57	22
1.89	1.84	1.80	1.74	1.72	1.69	1.66	1.62	1.59	1.55	23
1.88	1.83	1.78	1.73	1.70	1.67	1.64	1.61	1.57	1.53	24
1.87	1.82	1.77	1.72	1.69	1.66	1.63	1.59	1.56	1.52	25
1.86	1.81	1.76	1.71	1.68	1.65	1.61	1.58	1.54	1.50	26
1.85	1.80	1.75	1.70	1.67	1.64	1.60	1.57	1.53	1.49	27
1.84	1.79	1.74	1.69	1.66	1.63	1.59	1.56	1.52	1.48	28
1.83	1.78	1.73	1.68	1.65	1.62	1.58	1.55	1.51	1.47	29
1.82	1.77	1.72	1.67	1.64	1.61	1.57	1.54	1.50	1.46	30
1.76	1.71	1.66	1.61	1.57	1.54	1.51	1.47	1.42	1.38	40
1.71	1.66	1.60	1.54	1.51	1.48	1.44	1.40	1.35	1.29	60
1.65	1.60	1.55	1.48	1.45	1.41	1.37	1.32	1.26	1.19	120
1.60	1.55	1.49	1.42	1.38	1.34	1.30	1.24	1.17	1.00	∞

(continued)

TABLE A.7 *(continued)*

ν_2 \ ν_1 ($\alpha = .05$, Numerator degrees of freedom; rows: Denominator degrees of freedom)	1	2	3	4	5	6	7	8	9
1	161.45	199.50	215.71	224.58	230.16	233.99	236.77	238.88	240.54
2	18.51	19.00	19.16	19.25	19.30	19.33	19.35	19.37	19.38
3	10.13	9.55	9.28	9.12	9.01	8.94	8.89	8.85	8.81
4	7.71	6.94	6.59	6.39	6.26	6.16	6.09	6.04	6.00
5	6.61	5.79	5.41	5.19	5.05	4.95	4.88	4.82	4.77
6	5.99	5.14	4.76	4.53	4.39	4.28	4.21	4.15	4.10
7	5.59	4.74	4.35	4.12	3.97	3.87	3.79	3.73	3.68
8	5.32	4.46	4.07	3.84	3.69	3.58	3.50	3.44	3.39
9	5.12	4.26	3.86	3.63	3.48	3.37	3.29	3.23	3.18
10	4.96	4.10	3.71	3.48	3.33	3.22	3.14	3.07	3.02
11	4.84	3.98	3.59	3.36	3.20	3.09	3.01	2.95	2.90
12	4.75	3.89	3.49	3.26	3.11	3.00	2.91	2.85	2.80
13	4.67	3.81	3.41	3.18	3.03	2.92	2.83	2.77	2.71
14	4.60	3.74	3.34	3.11	2.96	2.85	2.76	2.70	2.65
15	4.54	3.68	3.29	3.06	2.90	2.79	2.71	2.64	2.59
16	4.49	3.63	3.24	3.01	2.85	2.74	2.66	2.59	2.54
17	4.45	3.59	3.20	2.96	2.81	2.70	2.61	2.55	2.49
18	4.41	3.55	3.16	2.93	2.77	2.66	2.58	2.51	2.46
19	4.38	3.52	3.13	2.90	2.74	2.63	2.54	2.48	2.42
20	4.35	3.49	3.10	2.87	2.71	2.60	2.51	2.45	2.39
21	4.32	3.47	3.07	2.84	2.68	2.57	2.49	2.42	2.37
22	4.30	3.44	3.05	2.82	2.66	2.55	2.46	2.40	2.34
23	4.28	3.42	3.03	2.80	2.64	2.53	2.44	2.37	2.32
24	4.26	3.40	3.01	2.78	2.62	2.51	2.42	2.36	2.30
25	4.24	3.39	2.99	2.76	2.60	2.49	2.40	2.34	2.28
26	4.23	3.37	2.98	2.74	2.59	2.47	2.39	2.32	2.27
27	4.21	3.35	2.96	2.73	2.57	2.46	2.37	2.31	2.25
28	4.20	3.34	2.95	2.71	2.56	2.45	2.36	2.29	2.24
29	4.18	3.33	2.93	2.70	2.55	2.43	2.35	2.28	2.22
30	4.17	3.32	2.92	2.69	2.53	2.42	2.33	2.27	2.21
40	4.08	3.23	2.84	2.61	2.45	2.34	2.25	2.18	2.12
60	4.00	3.15	2.76	2.53	2.37	2.25	2.17	2.10	2.04
120	3.92	3.07	2.68	2.45	2.29	2.18	2.09	2.02	1.96
∞	3.84	3.00	2.60	2.37	2.21	2.10	2.01	1.94	1.88

$\alpha = .05$

Numerator degrees of freedom (v_1)

10	12	15	20	24	30	40	60	120	∞	v_2 (Denominator degrees of freedom)
241.88	243.90	245.90	248.00	249.10	250.10	251.10	252.20	253.30	254.30	1
19.40	19.41	19.43	19.45	19.45	19.46	19.47	19.48	19.49	19.50	2
8.79	8.74	8.70	8.66	8.64	8.62	8.59	8.57	8.55	8.53	3
5.96	5.91	5.86	5.80	5.77	5.75	5.72	5.69	5.66	5.63	4
4.74	4.68	4.62	4.56	4.53	4.50	4.46	4.43	4.40	4.36	5
4.06	4.00	3.94	3.87	3.84	3.81	3.77	3.74	3.70	3.67	6
3.64	3.57	3.51	3.44	3.41	3.38	3.34	3.30	3.27	3.23	7
3.35	3.28	3.22	3.15	3.12	3.08	3.04	3.01	2.97	2.93	8
3.14	3.07	3.01	2.94	2.90	2.86	2.83	2.79	2.75	2.71	9
2.98	2.91	2.85	2.77	2.74	2.70	2.66	2.62	2.58	2.54	10
2.85	2.79	2.72	2.65	2.61	2.57	2.53	2.49	2.45	2.40	11
2.75	2.69	2.62	2.54	2.51	2.47	2.43	2.38	2.34	2.30	12
2.67	2.60	2.53	2.46	2.42	2.38	2.34	2.30	2.25	2.21	13
2.60	2.53	2.46	2.39	2.35	2.31	2.27	2.22	2.18	2.13	14
2.54	2.48	2.40	2.33	2.29	2.25	2.20	2.16	2.11	2.07	15
2.49	2.42	2.35	2.28	2.24	2.19	2.15	2.11	2.06	2.01	16
2.45	2.38	2.31	2.23	2.19	2.15	2.10	2.06	2.01	1.96	17
2.41	2.34	2.27	2.19	2.15	2.11	2.06	2.02	1.97	1.92	18
2.38	2.31	2.23	2.16	2.11	2.07	2.03	1.98	1.93	1.88	19
2.35	2.28	2.20	2.12	2.08	2.04	1.99	1.95	1.90	1.84	20
2.32	2.25	2.18	2.10	2.05	2.01	1.96	1.92	1.87	1.81	21
2.30	2.23	2.15	2.07	2.03	1.98	1.94	1.89	1.84	1.78	22
2.27	2.20	2.13	2.05	2.01	1.96	1.91	1.86	1.81	1.76	23
2.25	2.18	2.11	2.03	1.98	1.94	1.89	1.84	1.79	1.73	24
2.24	2.16	2.09	2.01	1.96	1.92	1.87	1.82	1.77	1.71	25
2.22	2.15	2.07	1.99	1.95	1.90	1.85	1.80	1.75	1.69	26
2.20	2.13	2.06	1.97	1.93	1.88	1.84	1.79	1.73	1.67	27
2.19	2.12	2.04	1.96	1.91	1.87	1.82	1.77	1.71	1.65	28
2.18	2.10	2.03	1.94	1.90	1.85	1.81	1.75	1.70	1.64	29
2.16	2.09	2.01	1.93	1.89	1.84	1.79	1.74	1.68	1.62	30
2.08	2.00	1.92	1.84	1.79	1.74	1.69	1.64	1.58	1.51	40
1.99	1.92	1.84	1.75	1.70	1.65	1.59	1.53	1.47	1.39	60
1.91	1.83	1.75	1.66	1.61	1.55	1.50	1.43	1.35	1.25	120
1.83	1.75	1.67	1.57	1.52	1.46	1.39	1.32	1.22	1.00	∞

(continued)

TABLE A.7 *(continued)*

v_2 \ v_1 ($\alpha = .025$, Numerator degrees of freedom)	1	2	3	4	5	6	7	8	9
1	647.79	799.48	864.15	899.60	921.83	937.11	948.20	956.64	963.28
2	38.51	39.00	39.17	39.25	39.30	39.33	39.36	39.37	39.39
3	17.44	16.04	15.44	15.10	14.88	14.73	14.62	14.54	14.47
4	12.22	10.65	9.98	9.60	9.36	9.20	9.07	8.98	8.90
5	10.01	8.43	7.76	7.39	7.15	6.98	6.85	6.76	6.68
6	8.81	7.26	6.60	6.23	5.99	5.82	5.70	5.60	5.52
7	8.07	6.54	5.89	5.52	5.29	5.12	4.99	4.90	4.82
8	7.57	6.06	5.42	5.05	4.82	4.65	4.53	4.43	4.36
9	7.21	5.71	5.08	4.72	4.48	4.32	4.20	4.10	4.03
10	6.94	5.46	4.83	4.47	4.24	4.07	3.95	3.85	3.78
11	6.72	5.26	4.63	4.28	4.04	3.88	3.76	3.66	3.59
12	6.55	5.10	4.47	4.12	3.89	3.73	3.61	3.51	3.44
13	6.41	4.97	4.35	4.00	3.77	3.60	3.48	3.39	3.31
14	6.30	4.86	4.24	3.89	3.66	3.50	3.38	3.29	3.21
15	6.20	4.77	4.15	3.80	3.58	3.41	3.29	3.20	3.12
16	6.12	4.69	4.08	3.73	3.50	3.34	3.22	3.12	3.05
17	6.04	4.62	4.01	3.66	3.44	3.28	3.16	3.06	2.98
18	5.98	4.56	3.95	3.61	3.38	3.22	3.10	3.01	2.93
19	5.92	4.51	3.90	3.56	3.33	3.17	3.05	2.96	2.88
20	5.87	4.46	3.86	3.51	3.29	3.13	3.01	2.91	2.84
21	5.83	4.42	3.82	3.48	3.25	3.09	2.97	2.87	2.80
22	5.79	4.38	3.78	3.44	3.22	3.05	2.93	2.84	2.76
23	5.75	4.35	3.75	3.41	3.18	3.02	2.90	2.81	2.73
24	5.72	4.32	3.72	3.38	3.15	2.99	2.87	2.78	2.70
25	5.69	4.29	3.69	3.35	3.13	2.97	2.85	2.75	2.68
26	5.66	4.27	3.67	3.33	3.10	2.94	2.82	2.73	2.65
27	5.63	4.24	3.65	3.31	3.08	2.92	2.80	2.71	2.63
28	5.61	4.22	3.63	3.29	3.06	2.90	2.78	2.69	2.61
29	5.59	4.20	3.61	3.27	3.04	2.88	2.76	2.67	2.59
30	5.57	4.18	3.59	3.25	3.03	2.87	2.75	2.65	2.57
40	5.42	4.05	3.46	3.13	2.90	2.74	2.62	2.53	2.45
60	5.29	3.93	3.34	3.01	2.79	2.63	2.51	2.41	2.33
120	5.15	3.80	3.23	2.89	2.67	2.52	2.39	2.30	2.22
∞	5.02	3.69	3.12	2.79	2.57	2.41	2.29	2.19	2.11

Denominator degrees of freedom

$\alpha = .025$ Numerator degrees of freedom ν_1										Denominator degrees of freedom ν_2
10	12	15	20	24	30	40	60	120	∞	
968.63	976.72	984.87	993.08	997.27	1001.40	1005.60	1009.79	1014.04	1018.00	1
39.40	39.41	39.43	39.45	39.46	39.46	39.47	39.48	39.49	39.50	2
14.42	14.34	14.25	14.17	14.12	14.08	14.04	13.99	13.95	13.90	3
8.84	8.75	8.66	8.56	8.51	8.46	8.41	8.36	8.31	8.26	4
6.62	6.52	6.43	6.33	6.28	6.23	6.18	6.12	6.07	6.02	5
5.46	5.37	5.27	5.17	5.12	5.07	5.01	4.96	4.90	4.85	6
4.76	4.67	4.57	4.47	4.41	4.36	4.31	4.25	4.20	4.14	7
4.30	4.20	4.10	4.00	3.95	3.89	3.84	3.78	3.73	3.67	8
3.96	3.87	3.77	3.67	3.61	3.56	3.51	3.45	3.39	3.33	9
3.72	3.62	3.52	3.42	3.37	3.31	3.26	3.20	3.14	3.08	10
3.53	3.43	3.33	3.23	3.17	3.12	3.06	3.00	2.94	2.88	11
3.37	3.28	3.18	3.07	3.02	2.96	2.91	2.85	2.79	2.72	12
3.25	3.15	3.05	2.95	2.89	2.84	2.78	2.72	2.66	2.60	13
3.15	3.05	2.95	2.84	2.79	2.73	2.67	2.61	2.55	2.49	14
3.06	2.96	2.86	2.76	2.70	2.64	2.59	2.52	2.46	2.40	15
2.99	2.89	2.79	2.68	2.63	2.57	2.51	2.45	2.38	2.32	16
2.92	2.82	2.72	2.62	2.56	2.50	2.44	2.38	2.32	2.25	17
2.87	2.77	2.67	2.56	2.50	2.44	2.38	2.32	2.26	2.19	18
2.82	2.72	2.62	2.51	2.45	2.39	2.33	2.27	2.20	2.13	19
2.77	2.68	2.57	2.46	2.41	2.35	2.29	2.22	2.16	2.09	20
2.73	2.64	2.53	2.42	2.37	2.31	2.25	2.18	2.11	2.04	21
2.70	2.60	2.50	2.39	2.33	2.27	2.21	2.14	2.08	2.00	22
2.67	2.57	2.47	2.36	2.30	2.24	2.18	2.11	2.04	1.97	23
2.64	2.54	2.44	2.33	2.27	2.21	2.15	2.08	2.01	1.94	24
2.61	2.51	2.41	2.30	2.24	2.18	2.12	2.05	1.98	1.91	25
2.59	2.49	2.39	2.28	2.22	2.16	2.09	2.03	1.95	1.88	26
2.57	2.47	2.36	2.25	2.19	2.13	2.07	2.00	1.93	1.85	27
2.55	2.45	2.34	2.23	2.17	2.11	2.05	1.98	1.91	1.83	28
2.53	2.43	2.32	2.21	2.15	2.09	2.03	1.96	1.89	1.81	29
2.51	2.41	2.31	2.20	2.14	2.07	2.01	1.94	1.87	1.79	30
2.39	2.29	2.18	2.07	2.01	1.94	1.88	1.80	1.72	1.64	40
2.27	2.17	2.06	1.94	1.88	1.82	1.74	1.67	1.58	1.48	60
2.16	2.05	1.94	1.82	1.76	1.69	1.61	1.53	1.43	1.31	120
2.05	1.94	1.83	1.71	1.64	1.57	1.48	1.39	1.27	1.00	∞

(continued)

TABLE A.7 *(continued)*

$\alpha = .01$

Numerator degrees of freedom (v_1); Denominator degrees of freedom (v_2)

v_2 \ v_1	1	2	3	4	5	6	7	8	9
1	4052.18	4999.34	5403.53	5624.26	5763.96	5858.95	5928.33	5980.95	6022.40
2	98.50	99.00	99.16	99.25	99.30	99.33	99.36	99.38	99.39
3	34.12	30.82	29.46	28.71	28.24	27.91	27.67	27.49	27.34
4	21.20	18.00	16.69	15.98	15.52	15.21	14.98	14.80	14.66
5	16.26	13.27	12.06	11.39	10.97	10.67	10.46	10.29	10.16
6	13.75	10.92	9.78	9.15	8.75	8.47	8.26	8.10	7.98
7	12.25	9.55	8.45	7.85	7.46	7.19	6.99	6.84	6.72
8	11.26	8.65	7.59	7.01	6.63	6.37	6.18	6.03	5.91
9	10.56	8.02	6.99	6.42	6.06	5.80	5.61	5.47	5.35
10	10.04	7.56	6.55	5.99	5.64	5.39	5.20	5.06	4.94
11	9.65	7.21	6.22	5.67	5.32	5.07	4.89	4.74	4.63
12	9.33	6.93	5.95	5.41	5.06	4.82	4.64	4.50	4.39
13	9.07	6.70	5.74	5.21	4.86	4.62	4.44	4.30	4.19
14	8.86	6.51	5.56	5.04	4.69	4.46	4.28	4.14	4.03
15	8.68	6.36	5.42	4.89	4.56	4.32	4.14	4.00	3.89
16	8.53	6.23	5.29	4.77	4.44	4.20	4.03	3.89	3.78
17	8.40	6.11	5.19	4.67	4.34	4.10	3.93	3.79	3.68
18	8.29	6.01	5.09	4.58	4.25	4.01	3.84	3.71	3.60
19	8.18	5.93	5.01	4.50	4.17	3.94	3.77	3.63	3.52
20	8.10	5.85	4.94	4.43	4.10	3.87	3.70	3.56	3.46
21	8.02	5.78	4.87	4.37	4.04	3.81	3.64	3.51	3.40
22	7.95	5.72	4.82	4.31	3.99	3.76	3.59	3.45	3.35
23	7.88	5.66	4.76	4.26	3.94	3.71	3.54	3.41	3.30
24	7.82	5.61	4.72	4.22	3.90	3.67	3.50	3.36	3.26
25	7.77	5.57	4.68	4.18	3.85	3.63	3.46	3.32	3.22
26	7.72	5.53	4.64	4.14	3.82	3.59	3.42	3.29	3.18
27	7.68	5.49	4.60	4.11	3.78	3.56	3.39	3.26	3.15
28	7.64	5.45	4.57	4.07	3.75	3.53	3.36	3.23	3.12
29	7.60	5.42	4.54	4.04	3.73	3.50	3.33	3.20	3.09
30	7.56	5.39	4.51	4.02	3.70	3.47	3.30	3.17	3.07
40	7.31	5.18	4.31	3.83	3.51	3.29	3.12	2.99	2.89
60	7.08	4.98	4.13	3.65	3.34	3.12	2.95	2.82	2.72
120	6.85	4.79	3.95	3.48	3.17	2.96	2.79	2.66	2.56
∞	6.63	4.61	3.78	3.32	3.02	2.80	2.64	2.51	2.41

$\alpha = .01$

Numerator degrees of freedom

10	12	15	20	24	30	40	60	120	∞	ν_1 / ν_2
6055.93	6106.68	6156.97	6208.66	6234.27	6260.35	6286.43	6312.97	6339.51	6366.00	1
99.40	99.42	99.43	99.45	99.46	99.47	99.48	99.48	99.49	99.50	2
27.23	27.05	26.87	26.69	26.60	26.50	26.41	26.32	26.22	26.13	3
14.55	14.37	14.20	14.02	13.93	13.84	13.75	13.65	13.56	13.46	4
10.05	9.89	9.72	9.55	9.47	9.38	9.29	9.20	9.11	9.02	5
7.87	7.72	7.56	7.40	7.31	7.23	7.14	7.06	6.97	6.88	6
6.62	6.47	6.31	6.16	6.07	5.99	5.91	5.82	5.74	5.65	7
5.81	5.67	5.52	5.36	5.28	5.20	5.12	5.03	4.95	4.86	8
5.26	5.11	4.96	4.81	4.73	4.65	4.57	4.48	4.40	4.31	9
4.85	4.71	4.56	4.41	4.33	4.25	4.17	4.08	4.00	3.91	10
4.54	4.40	4.25	4.10	4.02	3.94	3.86	3.78	3.69	3.60	11
4.30	4.16	4.01	3.86	3.78	3.70	3.62	3.54	3.45	3.36	12
4.10	3.96	3.82	3.66	3.59	3.51	3.43	3.34	3.25	3.17	13
3.94	3.80	3.66	3.51	3.43	3.35	3.27	3.18	3.09	3.00	14
3.80	3.67	3.52	3.37	3.29	3.21	3.13	3.05	2.96	2.87	15
3.69	3.55	3.41	3.26	3.18	3.10	3.02	2.93	2.84	2.75	16
3.59	3.46	3.31	3.16	3.08	3.00	2.92	2.83	2.75	2.65	17
3.51	3.37	3.23	3.08	3.00	2.92	2.84	2.75	2.66	2.57	18
3.43	3.30	3.15	3.00	2.92	2.84	2.76	2.67	2.58	2.49	19
3.37	3.23	3.09	2.94	2.86	2.78	2.69	2.61	2.52	2.42	20
3.31	3.17	3.03	2.88	2.80	2.72	2.64	2.55	2.46	2.36	21
3.26	3.12	2.98	2.83	2.75	2.67	2.58	2.50	2.40	2.31	22
3.21	3.07	2.93	2.78	2.70	2.62	2.54	2.45	2.35	2.26	23
3.17	3.03	2.89	2.74	2.66	2.58	2.49	2.40	2.31	2.21	24
3.13	2.99	2.85	2.70	2.62	2.54	2.45	2.36	2.27	2.17	25
3.09	2.96	2.81	2.66	2.58	2.50	2.42	2.33	2.23	2.13	26
3.06	2.93	2.78	2.63	2.55	2.47	2.38	2.29	2.20	2.10	27
3.03	2.90	2.75	2.60	2.52	2.44	2.35	2.26	2.17	2.06	28
3.00	2.87	2.73	2.57	2.49	2.41	2.33	2.23	2.14	2.03	29
2.98	2.84	2.70	2.55	2.47	2.39	2.30	2.21	2.11	2.01	30
2.80	2.66	2.52	2.37	2.29	2.20	2.11	2.02	1.92	1.80	40
2.63	2.50	2.35	2.20	2.12	2.03	1.94	1.84	1.73	1.60	60
2.47	2.34	2.19	2.03	1.95	1.86	1.76	1.66	1.53	1.38	120
2.32	2.18	2.04	1.88	1.79	1.70	1.59	1.47	1.32	1.00	∞

Denominator degrees of freedom

(continued)

TABLE A.7 *(continued)*

v_2 \ v_1	$\alpha = .005$ Numerator degrees of freedom								
Denominator degrees of freedom	1	2	3	4	5	6	7	8	9
1	16212.46	19997.36	21614.13	22500.75	23055.82	23439.53	23715.20	23923.81	24091.45
2	198.50	199.01	199.16	199.24	199.30	199.33	199.36	199.38	199.39
3	55.55	49.80	47.47	46.20	45.39	44.84	44.43	44.13	43.88
4	31.33	26.28	24.26	23.15	22.46	21.98	21.62	21.35	21.14
5	22.78	18.31	16.53	15.56	14.94	14.51	14.20	13.96	13.77
6	18.63	14.54	12.92	12.03	11.46	11.07	10.79	10.57	10.39
7	16.24	12.40	10.88	10.05	9.52	9.16	8.89	8.68	8.51
8	14.69	11.04	9.60	8.81	8.30	7.95	7.69	7.50	7.34
9	13.61	10.11	8.72	7.96	7.47	7.13	6.88	6.69	6.54
10	12.83	9.43	8.08	7.34	6.87	6.54	6.30	6.12	5.97
11	12.23	8.91	7.60	6.88	6.42	6.10	5.86	5.68	5.54
12	11.75	8.51	7.23	6.52	6.07	5.76	5.52	5.35	5.20
13	11.37	8.19	6.93	6.23	5.79	5.48	5.25	5.08	4.94
14	11.06	7.92	6.68	6.00	5.56	5.26	5.03	4.86	4.72
15	10.80	7.70	6.48	5.80	5.37	5.07	4.85	4.67	4.54
16	10.58	7.51	6.30	5.64	5.21	4.91	4.69	4.52	4.38
17	10.38	7.35	6.16	5.50	5.07	4.78	4.56	4.39	4.25
18	10.22	7.21	6.03	5.37	4.96	4.66	4.44	4.28	4.14
19	10.07	7.09	5.92	5.27	4.85	4.56	4.34	4.18	4.04
20	9.94	6.99	5.82	5.17	4.76	4.47	4.26	4.09	3.96
21	9.83	6.89	5.73	5.09	4.68	4.39	4.18	4.01	3.88
22	9.73	6.81	5.65	5.02	4.61	4.32	4.11	3.94	3.81
23	9.63	6.73	5.58	4.95	4.54	4.26	4.05	3.88	3.75
24	9.55	6.66	5.52	4.89	4.49	4.20	3.99	3.83	3.69
25	9.48	6.60	5.46	4.84	4.43	4.15	3.94	3.78	3.64
26	9.41	6.54	5.41	4.79	4.38	4.10	3.89	3.73	3.60
27	9.34	6.49	5.36	4.74	4.34	4.06	3.85	3.69	3.56
28	9.28	6.44	5.32	4.70	4.30	4.02	3.81	3.65	3.52
29	9.23	6.40	5.28	4.66	4.26	3.98	3.77	3.61	3.48
30	9.18	6.35	5.24	4.62	4.23	3.95	3.74	3.58	3.45
40	8.83	6.07	4.98	4.37	3.99	3.71	3.51	3.35	3.22
60	8.49	5.79	4.73	4.14	3.76	3.49	3.29	3.13	3.01
120	8.18	5.54	4.50	3.92	3.55	3.28	3.09	2.93	2.81
∞	7.88	5.30	4.28	3.72	3.35	3.09	2.90	2.74	2.62

$\alpha = .005$

Numerator degrees of freedom (ν_1)

10	12	15	20	24	30	40	60	120	∞	ν_2 (Denominator degrees of freedom)
24221.84	24426.73	24631.62	24836.51	24937.09	25041.40	25145.71	25253.74	25358.05	25465.00	1
199.39	199.42	199.43	199.45	199.45	199.48	199.48	199.48	199.49	199.50	2
43.68	43.39	43.08	42.78	42.62	42.47	42.31	42.15	41.99	41.83	3
20.97	20.70	20.44	20.17	20.03	19.89	19.75	19.61	19.47	19.32	4
13.62	13.38	13.15	12.90	12.78	12.66	12.53	12.40	12.27	12.14	5
10.25	10.03	9.81	9.59	9.47	9.36	9.24	9.12	9.00	8.88	6
8.38	8.18	7.97	7.75	7.64	7.53	7.42	7.31	7.19	7.08	7
7.21	7.01	6.81	6.61	6.50	6.40	6.29	6.18	6.06	5.95	8
6.42	6.23	6.03	5.83	5.73	5.62	5.52	5.41	5.30	5.19	9
5.85	5.66	5.47	5.27	5.17	5.07	4.97	4.86	4.75	4.64	10
5.42	5.24	5.05	4.86	4.76	4.65	4.55	4.45	4.34	4.23	11
5.09	4.91	4.72	4.53	4.43	4.33	4.23	4.12	4.01	3.90	12
4.82	4.64	4.46	4.27	4.17	4.07	3.97	3.87	3.76	3.65	13
4.60	4.43	4.25	4.06	3.96	3.86	3.76	3.66	3.55	3.44	14
4.42	4.25	4.07	3.88	3.79	3.69	3.59	3.48	3.37	3.26	15
4.27	4.10	3.92	3.73	3.64	3.54	3.44	3.33	3.22	3.11	16
4.14	3.97	3.79	3.61	3.51	3.41	3.31	3.21	3.10	2.98	17
4.03	3.86	3.68	3.50	3.40	3.30	3.20	3.10	2.99	2.87	18
3.93	3.76	3.59	3.40	3.31	3.21	3.11	3.00	2.89	2.78	19
3.85	3.68	3.50	3.32	3.22	3.12	3.02	2.92	2.81	2.69	20
3.77	3.60	3.43	3.24	3.15	3.05	2.95	2.84	2.73	2.61	21
3.70	3.54	3.36	3.18	3.08	2.98	2.88	2.77	2.66	2.55	22
3.64	3.47	3.30	3.12	3.02	2.92	2.82	2.71	2.60	2.48	23
3.59	3.42	3.25	3.06	2.97	2.87	2.77	2.66	2.55	2.43	24
3.54	3.37	3.20	3.01	2.92	2.82	2.72	2.61	2.50	2.38	25
3.49	3.33	3.15	2.97	2.87	2.77	2.67	2.56	2.45	2.33	26
3.45	3.28	3.11	2.93	2.83	2.73	2.63	2.52	2.41	2.29	27
3.41	3.25	3.07	2.89	2.79	2.69	2.59	2.48	2.37	2.25	28
3.38	3.21	3.04	2.86	2.76	2.66	2.56	2.45	2.33	2.21	29
3.34	3.18	3.01	2.82	2.73	2.63	2.52	2.42	2.30	2.18	30
3.12	2.95	2.78	2.60	2.50	2.40	2.30	2.18	2.06	1.93	40
2.90	2.74	2.57	2.39	2.29	2.19	2.08	1.96	1.83	1.69	60
2.71	2.54	2.37	2.19	2.09	1.98	1.87	1.75	1.61	1.43	120
2.52	2.36	2.19	2.00	1.90	1.79	1.67	1.53	1.36	1.00	∞

TABLE A.8 The chi-square table

Values of χ^2 for selected probabilities

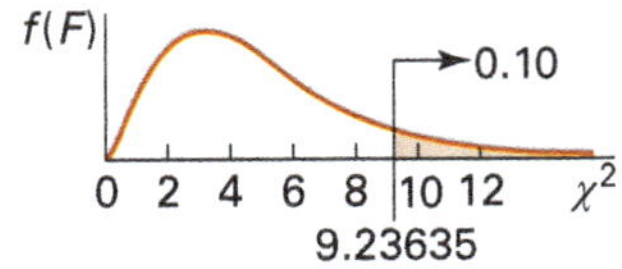

Example: df (number of degrees of freedom) = 5, the tail above χ^2 = 9.23635 represents 0.10 or 10% of the area under the curve.

Degrees of freedom	Area in upper tail									
	.995	.99	.975	.95	.9	.1	.05	.025	.01	.005
1	0.0000393	0.0001571	0.0009821	0.0039322	0.0157907	2.7055	3.8415	5.0239	6.6349	7.8794
2	0.010025	0.020100	0.050636	0.102586	0.210721	4.6052	5.9915	7.3778	9.2104	10.5965
3	0.07172	0.11483	0.21579	0.35185	0.58438	6.2514	7.8147	9.3484	11.3449	12.8381
4	0.20698	0.29711	0.48442	0.71072	1.06362	7.7794	9.4877	11.1433	13.2767	14.8602
5	0.41175	0.55430	0.83121	1.14548	1.61031	9.2363	11.0705	12.8325	15.0863	16.7496
6	0.67573	0.87208	1.23734	1.63538	2.20413	10.6446	12.5916	14.4494	16.8119	18.5475
7	0.98925	1.23903	1.68986	2.16735	2.83311	12.0170	14.0671	16.0128	18.4753	20.2777
8	1.34440	1.64651	2.17972	2.73263	3.48954	13.3616	15.5073	17.5345	20.0902	21.9549
9	1.73491	2.08789	2.70039	3.32512	4.16816	14.6837	16.9190	19.0228	21.6660	23.5893
10	2.15585	2.55820	3.24696	3.94030	4.86518	15.9872	18.3070	20.4832	23.2093	25.1881
11	2.60320	3.05350	3.81574	4.57481	5.57779	17.2750	19.6752	21.9200	24.7250	26.7569
12	3.07379	3.57055	4.40378	5.22603	6.30380	18.5493	21.0261	23.3367	26.2170	28.2997
13	3.56504	4.10690	5.00874	5.89186	7.04150	19.8119	22.3620	24.7356	27.6882	29.8193
14	4.07466	4.66042	5.62872	6.57063	7.78954	21.0641	23.6848	26.1189	29.1412	31.3194
15	4.60087	5.22936	6.26212	7.26093	8.54675	22.3071	24.9958	27.4884	30.5780	32.8015
16	5.14216	5.81220	6.90766	7.96164	9.31224	23.5418	26.2962	28.8453	31.9999	34.2671
17	5.69727	6.40774	7.56418	8.67175	10.08518	24.7690	27.5871	30.1910	33.4087	35.7184
18	6.26477	7.01490	8.23074	9.39045	10.86494	25.9894	28.8693	31.5264	34.8052	37.1564
19	6.84392	7.63270	8.90651	10.11701	11.65091	27.2036	30.1435	32.8523	36.1908	38.5821
20	7.43381	8.26037	9.59077	10.85080	12.44260	28.4120	31.4104	34.1696	37.5663	39.9969
21	8.03360	8.89717	10.28291	11.59132	13.23960	29.6151	32.6706	35.4789	38.9322	41.4009
22	8.64268	9.54249	10.98233	12.33801	14.04149	30.8133	33.9245	36.7807	40.2894	42.7957
23	9.26038	10.19569	11.68853	13.09051	14.84795	32.0069	35.1725	38.0756	41.6383	44.1814
24	9.88620	10.85635	12.40115	13.84842	15.65868	33.1962	36.4150	39.3641	42.9798	45.5584
25	10.51965	11.52395	13.11971	14.61140	16.47341	34.3816	37.6525	40.6465	44.3140	46.9280
26	11.16022	12.19818	13.84388	15.37916	17.29188	35.5632	38.8851	41.9231	45.6416	48.2898
27	11.80765	12.87847	14.57337	16.15139	18.11389	36.7412	40.1133	43.1945	46.9628	49.6450
28	12.46128	13.56467	15.30785	16.92788	18.93924	37.9159	41.3372	44.4608	48.2782	50.9936
29	13.12107	14.25641	16.04705	17.70838	19.76774	39.0875	42.5569	45.7223	49.5878	52.3355
30	13.78668	14.95346	16.79076	18.49267	20.59924	40.2560	43.7730	46.9792	50.8922	53.6719
40	20.70658	22.16420	24.43306	26.50930	29.05052	51.8050	55.7585	59.3417	63.6908	66.7660
50	27.99082	29.70673	32.35738	34.76424	37.68864	63.1671	67.5048	71.4202	76.1538	79.4898
60	35.53440	37.48480	40.48171	43.18797	46.45888	74.3970	79.0820	83.2977	88.3794	91.9518
70	43.27531	45.44170	48.75754	51.73926	55.32894	85.5270	90.5313	95.0231	100.4251	104.2148
80	51.17193	53.53998	57.15315	60.39146	64.27784	96.5782	101.8795	106.6285	112.3288	116.3209
90	59.19633	61.75402	65.64659	69.12602	73.29108	107.5650	113.1452	118.1359	124.1162	128.2987
100	67.32753	70.06500	74.22188	77.92944	82.35813	118.4980	124.3421	129.5613	135.8069	140.1697

TABLE A.9 Critical values for the Durbin–Watson test

Entries in the table give the critical values for a one-tailed Durbin–Watson test for autocorrelation. For a two-tailed test, the level of significance is doubled.

	Significant points of d_L and d_U: $\alpha = .05$ Number of independent variables									
k	1		2		3		4		5	
n	d_L	d_U	d_L	d_U	d_L	d_U	d_L	d_U	d_L	d_U
15	1.08	1.36	0.95	1.54	0.82	1.75	0.69	1.97	0.56	2.21
16	1.10	1.37	0.98	1.54	0.86	1.73	0.74	1.93	0.62	2.15
17	1.13	1.38	1.02	1.54	0.90	1.71	0.78	1.90	0.67	2.10
18	1.16	1.39	1.05	1.53	0.93	1.69	0.82	1.87	0.71	2.06
19	1.18	1.40	1.08	1.53	0.97	1.68	0.86	1.85	0.75	2.02
20	1.20	1.41	1.10	1.54	1.00	1.68	0.90	1.83	0.79	1.99
21	1.22	1.42	1.13	1.54	1.03	1.67	0.93	1.81	0.83	1.96
22	1.24	1.43	1.15	1.54	1.05	1.66	0.96	1.80	0.86	1.94
23	1.26	1.44	1.17	1.54	1.08	1.66	0.99	1.79	0.90	1.92
24	1.27	1.45	1.19	1.55	1.10	1.66	1.01	1.78	0.93	1.90
25	1.29	1.45	1.21	1.55	1.12	1.66	1.04	1.77	0.95	1.89
26	1.30	1.46	1.22	1.55	1.14	1.65	1.06	1.76	0.98	1.88
27	1.32	1.47	1.24	1.56	1.16	1.65	1.08	1.76	1.01	1.86
28	1.33	1.48	1.26	1.56	1.18	1.65	1.10	1.75	1.03	1.85
29	1.34	1.48	1.27	1.56	1.20	1.65	1.12	1.74	1.05	1.84
30	1.35	1.49	1.28	1.57	1.21	1.65	1.14	1.74	1.07	1.83
31	1.36	1.50	1.30	1.57	1.23	1.65	1.16	1.74	1.09	1.83
32	1.37	1.50	1.31	1.57	1.24	1.65	1.18	1.73	1.11	1.82
33	1.38	1.51	1.32	1.58	1.26	1.65	1.19	1.73	1.13	1.81
34	1.39	1.51	1.33	1.58	1.27	1.65	1.21	1.73	1.15	1.81
35	1.40	1.52	1.34	1.58	1.28	1.65	1.22	1.73	1.16	1.80
36	1.41	1.52	1.35	1.59	1.29	1.65	1.24	1.73	1.18	1.80
37	1.42	1.53	1.36	1.59	1.31	1.66	1.25	1.72	1.19	1.80
38	1.43	1.54	1.37	1.59	1.32	1.66	1.26	1.72	1.21	1.79
39	1.43	1.54	1.38	1.60	1.33	1.66	1.27	1.72	1.22	1.79
40	1.44	1.54	1.39	1.60	1.34	1.66	1.29	1.72	1.23	1.79
45	1.48	1.57	1.43	1.62	1.38	1.67	1.34	1.72	1.29	1.78
50	1.50	1.59	1.46	1.63	1.42	1.67	1.38	1.72	1.34	1.77
55	1.53	1.60	1.49	1.64	1.45	1.68	1.41	1.72	1.38	1.77
60	1.55	1.62	1.51	1.65	1.48	1.69	1.44	1.73	1.41	1.77
65	1.57	1.63	1.54	1.66	1.50	1.70	1.47	1.73	1.44	1.77
70	1.58	1.64	1.55	1.67	1.52	1.70	1.49	1.74	1.46	1.77
75	1.60	1.65	1.57	1.68	1.54	1.71	1.51	1.74	1.49	1.77
80	1.61	1.66	1.59	1.69	1.56	1.72	1.53	1.74	1.51	1.77
85	1.62	1.67	1.60	1.70	1.57	1.72	1.55	1.75	1.52	1.77
90	1.63	1.68	1.61	1.70	1.59	1.73	1.57	1.75	1.54	1.78
95	1.64	1.69	1.62	1.71	1.60	1.73	1.58	1.75	1.56	1.78
100	1.65	1.69	1.63	1.72	1.61	1.74	1.59	1.76	1.57	1.78

(continued)

TABLE A.9 *(continued)*

	Significant points of d_L and d_U: $\alpha = .01$									
	Number of independent variables									
k	1		2		3		4		5	
n	d_L	d_U	d_L	d_U	d_L	d_U	d_L	d_U	d_L	d_U
15	0.81	1.07	0.70	1.25	0.59	1.46	0.49	1.70	0.39	1.96
16	0.84	1.09	0.74	1.25	0.63	1.44	0.53	1.66	0.44	1.90
17	0.87	1.10	0.77	1.25	0.67	1.43	0.57	1.63	0.48	1.85
18	0.90	1.12	0.80	1.26	0.71	1.42	0.61	1.60	0.52	1.80
19	0.93	1.13	0.83	1.26	0.74	1.41	0.65	1.58	0.56	1.77
20	0.95	1.15	0.86	1.27	0.77	1.41	0.68	1.57	0.60	1.74
21	0.97	1.16	0.89	1.27	0.80	1.41	0.72	1.55	0.63	1.71
22	1.00	1.17	0.91	1.28	0.83	1.40	0.75	1.54	0.66	1.69
23	1.02	1.19	0.94	1.29	0.86	1.40	0.77	1.53	0.70	1.67
24	1.04	1.20	0.96	1.30	0.88	1.41	0.80	1.53	0.72	1.66
25	1.05	1.21	0.98	1.30	0.90	1.41	0.83	1.52	0.75	1.65
26	1.07	1.22	1.00	1.31	0.93	1.41	0.85	1.52	0.78	1.64
27	1.09	1.23	1.02	1.32	0.95	1.41	0.88	1.51	0.81	1.63
28	1.10	1.24	1.04	1.32	0.97	1.41	0.90	1.51	0.83	1.62
29	1.12	1.25	1.05	1.33	0.99	1.42	0.92	1.51	0.85	1.61
30	1.13	1.26	1.07	1.34	1.01	1.42	0.94	1.51	0.88	1.61
31	1.15	1.27	1.08	1.34	1.02	1.42	0.96	1.51	0.90	1.60
32	1.16	1.28	1.10	1.35	1.04	1.43	0.98	1.51	0.92	1.60
33	1.17	1.29	1.11	1.36	1.05	1.43	1.00	1.51	0.94	1.59
34	1.18	1.30	1.13	1.36	1.07	1.43	1.01	1.51	0.95	1.59
35	1.19	1.31	1.14	1.37	1.08	1.44	1.03	1.51	0.97	1.59
36	1.21	1.32	1.15	1.38	1.10	1.44	1.04	1.51	0.99	1.59
37	1.22	1.32	1.16	1.38	1.11	1.45	1.06	1.51	1.00	1.59
38	1.23	1.33	1.18	1.39	1.12	1.45	1.07	1.52	1.02	1.58
39	1.24	1.34	1.19	1.39	1.14	1.45	1.09	1.52	1.03	1.58
40	1.25	1.34	1.20	1.40	1.15	1.46	1.10	1.52	1.05	1.58
45	1.29	1.38	1.24	1.42	1.20	1.48	1.16	1.53	1.11	1.58
50	1.32	1.40	1.28	1.45	1.24	1.49	1.20	1.54	1.16	1.59
55	1.36	1.43	1.32	1.47	1.28	1.51	1.25	1.55	1.21	1.59
60	1.38	1.45	1.35	1.48	1.32	1.52	1.28	1.56	1.25	1.60
65	1.41	1.47	1.38	1.50	1.35	1.53	1.31	1.57	1.28	1.61
70	1.43	1.49	1.40	1.52	1.37	1.55	1.34	1.58	1.31	1.61
75	1.45	1.50	1.42	1.53	1.39	1.56	1.37	1.59	1.34	1.62
80	1.47	1.52	1.44	1.54	1.42	1.57	1.39	1.60	1.36	1.62
85	1.48	1.53	1.46	1.55	1.43	1.58	1.41	1.60	1.39	1.63
90	1.50	1.54	1.47	1.56	1.45	1.59	1.43	1.61	1.41	1.64
95	1.51	1.55	1.49	1.57	1.47	1.60	1.45	1.62	1.42	1.64
100	1.52	1.56	1.50	1.58	1.48	1.60	1.46	1.63	1.44	1.65

Source: Critical values for the Durbin–Watson test. From *Biometrika* Trustees from Durbin, J & Watson, GS 1951, 'Testing for serial correlation in least square regression II', *Biometrika*, vol. 38, pp. 159–78.

TABLE A.10 Critical values of the studentised range (q) distribution

$\alpha = .05$

Degrees of freedom	Number of populations																		
	2	3	4	5	6	7	8	9	10	11	12	13	14	15	16	17	18	19	20
1	18.0	27.0	32.8	37.1	40.4	43.1	45.4	47.4	49.1	50.6	52.0	53.2	54.3	55.4	56.3	57.2	58.0	58.8	59.6
2	6.08	8.33	9.80	10.9	11.7	12.4	13.0	13.5	14.0	14.4	14.7	15.1	15.4	15.7	15.9	16.1	16.4	16.6	16.8
3	4.50	5.91	6.82	7.50	8.04	8.48	8.85	9.18	9.46	9.72	9.95	10.2	10.3	10.5	10.7	10.8	11.0	11.1	11.2
4	3.93	5.04	5.76	6.29	6.71	7.05	7.35	7.60	7.83	8.03	8.21	8.37	8.52	8.66	8.79	8.91	9.03	9.13	9.23
5	3.64	4.60	5.22	5.67	6.03	6.33	6.58	6.80	6.99	7.17	7.32	7.47	7.60	7.72	7.83	7.93	8.03	8.12	8.21
6	3.46	4.34	4.90	5.30	5.63	5.90	6.12	6.32	6.49	6.65	6.79	6.92	7.03	7.14	7.24	7.34	7.43	7.51	7.59
7	3.34	4.16	4.68	5.06	5.36	5.61	5.82	6.00	6.16	6.30	6.43	6.55	6.66	6.76	6.85	6.94	7.02	7.10	7.17
8	3.26	4.04	4.53	4.89	5.17	5.40	5.60	5.77	5.92	6.05	6.18	6.29	6.39	6.48	6.57	6.65	6.73	6.80	6.87
9	3.20	3.95	4.41	4.76	5.02	5.24	5.43	5.59	5.74	5.87	5.98	6.09	6.19	6.28	6.36	6.44	6.51	6.58	6.64
10	3.15	3.88	4.33	4.65	4.91	5.12	5.30	5.46	5.60	5.72	5.83	5.93	6.03	6.11	6.19	6.27	6.34	6.40	6.47
11	3.11	3.82	4.26	4.57	4.82	5.03	5.20	5.35	5.49	5.61	5.71	5.81	5.90	5.98	6.06	6.13	6.20	6.27	6.33
12	3.08	3.77	4.20	4.51	4.75	4.95	5.12	5.27	5.39	5.51	5.61	5.71	5.80	5.88	5.95	6.02	6.09	6.15	6.21
13	3.06	3.73	4.15	4.45	4.69	4.88	5.05	5.19	5.32	5.43	5.53	5.63	5.71	5.79	5.86	5.93	5.99	6.05	6.11
14	3.03	3.70	4.11	4.41	4.64	4.83	4.99	5.13	5.25	5.36	5.46	5.55	5.64	5.71	5.79	5.85	5.91	5.97	6.03
15	3.01	3.67	4.08	4.37	4.59	4.78	4.94	5.08	5.20	5.31	5.40	5.49	5.57	5.65	5.72	5.78	5.85	5.90	5.96
16	3.00	3.65	4.05	4.33	4.56	4.74	4.90	5.03	5.15	5.26	5.35	5.44	5.52	5.59	5.66	5.73	5.79	5.84	5.90
17	2.98	3.63	4.02	4.30	4.52	4.70	4.86	4.99	5.11	5.21	5.31	5.39	5.47	5.54	5.61	5.67	5.73	5.79	5.84
18	2.97	3.61	4.00	4.28	4.49	4.67	4.82	4.96	5.07	5.17	5.27	5.35	5.43	5.50	5.57	5.63	5.69	5.74	5.79
19	2.96	3.59	3.98	4.25	4.47	4.65	4.79	4.92	5.04	5.14	5.23	5.31	5.39	5.46	5.53	5.59	5.65	5.70	5.75
20	2.95	3.58	3.96	4.23	4.45	4.62	4.77	4.90	5.01	5.11	5.20	5.28	5.36	5.43	5.49	5.55	5.61	5.66	5.71
24	2.92	3.53	3.90	4.17	4.37	4.54	4.68	4.81	4.92	5.01	5.10	5.18	5.25	5.32	5.38	5.44	5.49	5.55	5.59
30	2.89	3.49	3.85	4.10	4.30	4.46	4.60	4.72	4.82	4.92	5.00	5.08	5.15	5.21	5.27	5.33	5.38	5.43	5.47
40	2.86	3.44	3.79	4.04	4.23	4.39	4.52	4.63	4.73	4.82	4.90	4.98	5.04	5.11	5.16	5.22	5.27	5.31	5.36
60	2.83	3.40	3.74	3.98	4.16	4.31	4.44	4.55	4.65	4.73	4.81	4.88	4.94	5.00	5.06	5.11	5.15	5.20	5.24
120	2.80	3.36	3.68	3.92	4.10	4.24	4.36	4.47	4.56	4.64	4.71	4.78	4.84	4.90	4.95	5.00	5.04	5.09	5.13
∞	2.77	3.31	3.63	3.86	4.03	4.17	4.29	4.39	4.47	4.55	4.62	4.68	4.74	4.80	4.85	4.89	4.93	4.97	5.01

(continued)

TABLE A.10 *(continued)*

Degrees of freedom	$\alpha = .01$ Number of populations 2	3	4	5	6	7	8	9	10	11	12	13	14	15	16	17	18	19	20
1	90.0	135.	164.	186.	202.	216.	227.	237.	246.	253.	260.	266.	272.	277.	282.	286.	290.	294.	298.
2	14.0	19.0	22.3	24.7	26.6	28.2	29.5	30.7	31.7	32.6	33.4	34.1	34.8	35.4	36.0	36.5	37.0	37.5	37.9
3	8.26	10.6	12.2	13.3	14.2	15.0	15.6	16.2	16.7	17.1	17.5	17.9	18.2	18.5	18.8	19.1	19.3	19.5	19.8
4	6.51	8.12	9.17	9.96	10.6	11.1	11.5	11.9	12.3	12.6	12.8	13.1	13.3	13.5	13.7	13.9	14.1	14.2	14.4
5	5.70	6.97	7.80	8.42	8.91	9.32	9.67	9.97	10.2	10.5	10.7	10.9	11.1	11.2	11.4	11.6	11.7	11.8	11.9
6	5.24	6.33	7.03	7.56	7.97	8.32	8.61	8.87	9.10	9.30	9.49	9.65	9.81	9.95	10.1	10.2	10.3	10.4	10.5
7	4.95	5.92	6.54	7.01	7.37	7.68	7.94	8.17	8.37	8.55	8.71	8.86	9.00	9.12	9.24	9.35	9.46	9.55	9.65
8	4.74	5.63	6.20	6.63	6.96	7.24	7.47	7.68	7.87	8.03	8.18	8.31	8.44	8.55	8.66	8.76	8.85	8.94	9.03
9	4.60	5.43	5.96	6.35	6.66	6.91	7.13	7.32	7.49	7.65	7.78	7.91	8.03	8.13	8.23	8.32	8.41	8.49	8.57
10	4.48	5.27	5.77	6.14	6.43	6.67	6.87	7.05	7.21	7.36	7.48	7.60	7.71	7.81	7.91	7.99	8.07	8.15	8.22
11	4.39	5.14	5.62	5.97	6.25	6.48	6.67	6.84	6.99	7.13	7.25	7.36	7.46	7.56	7.65	7.73	7.81	7.88	7.95
12	4.32	5.04	5.50	5.84	6.10	6.32	6.51	6.67	6.81	6.94	7.06	7.17	7.26	7.36	7.44	7.52	7.59	7.66	7.73
13	4.26	4.96	5.40	5.73	5.98	6.19	6.37	6.53	6.67	6.79	6.90	7.01	7.10	7.19	7.27	7.34	7.42	7.48	7.55
14	4.21	4.89	5.32	5.63	5.88	6.08	6.26	6.41	6.54	6.66	6.77	6.87	6.96	7.05	7.12	7.20	7.27	7.33	7.39
15	4.17	4.83	5.25	5.56	5.80	5.99	6.16	6.31	6.44	6.55	6.66	6.76	6.84	6.93	7.00	7.07	7.14	7.20	7.26
16	4.13	4.78	5.19	5.49	5.72	5.92	6.08	6.22	6.35	6.46	6.56	6.66	6.74	6.82	6.90	6.97	7.03	7.09	7.15
17	4.10	4.74	5.14	5.43	5.66	5.85	6.01	6.15	6.27	6.38	6.48	6.57	6.66	6.73	6.80	6.87	6.94	7.00	7.05
18	4.07	4.70	5.09	5.38	5.60	5.79	5.94	6.08	6.20	6.31	6.41	6.50	6.58	6.65	6.72	6.79	6.85	6.91	6.96
19	4.05	4.67	5.05	5.33	5.55	5.73	5.89	6.02	6.14	6.25	6.34	6.43	6.51	6.58	6.65	6.72	6.78	6.84	6.89
20	4.02	4.64	5.02	5.29	5.51	5.69	5.84	5.97	6.09	6.19	6.29	6.37	6.45	6.52	6.59	6.65	6.71	6.76	6.82
24	3.96	4.54	4.91	5.17	5.37	5.54	5.69	5.81	5.92	6.02	6.11	6.19	6.26	6.33	6.39	6.45	6.51	6.56	6.61
30	3.89	4.45	4.80	5.05	5.24	5.40	5.54	5.65	5.76	5.85	5.93	6.01	6.08	6.14	6.20	6.26	6.31	6.36	6.41
40	3.82	4.37	4.70	4.93	5.11	5.27	5.39	5.50	5.60	5.69	5.77	5.84	5.90	5.96	6.02	6.07	6.12	6.17	6.21
60	3.76	4.28	4.60	4.82	4.99	5.13	5.25	5.36	5.45	5.53	5.60	5.67	5.73	5.79	5.84	5.89	5.93	5.98	6.02
120	3.70	4.20	4.50	4.71	4.87	5.01	5.12	5.21	5.30	5.38	5.44	5.51	5.56	5.61	5.66	5.71	5.75	5.79	5.83
∞	3.64	4.12	4.40	4.60	4.76	4.88	4.99	5.08	5.16	5.23	5.29	5.35	5.40	5.45	5.49	5.54	5.57	5.61	5.65

Source: Critical values of the studentised range (q) distribution. From Pearson, ES & Hartley, HO 1956, 'Tables for statisticians', *Biometrika*, vol. 1, no. 3, pp. 176–7. Reproduced with permission of Oxford University.

Chapter 1

opening vignette, p. 2: internetlivestats.com 2014, 'Google search statistics', www.internetlivestats.com; Net Applications.com 2014, 'Desktop search engine market share', www.netmarketshare.com; 2012, 'What do statisticians do at Google?', *Forbes*, www.forbes.com; **p. 9:** Siddhartha, RD, Fowlkes, EB & Hoadley, B 1989, 'Risk analysis of the space shuttle: pre-Challenger prediction of failure', *Journal of the American Statistical Association*, vol. 84, no. 408, pp. 945–57; **p. 9:** Scheurer, V 2011, 'Convicted on statistics?', *Understanding uncertainty*, http://understandinguncertainty.org; Green, P 2002, 'Letter from the President to the Lord Chancellor regarding the use of statistical evidence in court cases', Royal Statistical Society, www.rss.org.uk; Byard, RW 2004, 'Unexpected infant death: lessons from the Sally Clark case', *Medical Journal of Australia*, vol. 181, no. 1, pp. 52–4; Pallister, D 2007, 'Solicitor wrongly jailed for killing sons died from excess alcohol', *The Guardian*, 8 November, www.guardian.co.uk; **p. 10:** Squire, P 1988, 'Why the 1936 *Literary Digest* poll failed', *Public Opinion Quarterly*, vol. 52, no. 1, pp. 125–33.

Chapter 2

opening vignette, p. 14: Statistics New Zealand 2014, *Business operations survey*, www.stats.govt.nz; **chapter case, p. 15:** Brand, JE, Lorentz, P & Mathew, T 2014, *DA14 Digital Australia*, Interactive Games & Entertainment Association, www.igea.net; **demonstration problem 2.1, p. 18:** Top Yields 2014, www.topyields.nl; **problem 2.1, p. 21:** NationMaster.com 2014, 'Cost of living: average monthly disposable salary: after tax: countries compared', www.nationmaster.com; **problem 2.2, p. 21:** Public Transport Victoria 2014, 'Train station patronage', www.ptv.vic.gov.au; **figures 2.1–2.3, pp. 22–3:** CIA 2011, 'Country comparison: public debt', *The World Fact Book*, www.cia.gov; **p. 32:** Cleveland, WS 1985, *The elements of graphing data*, Wadsworth Advanced Books and Software, Monterey, CA; **demonstration problem 2.5, p. 32:** Insolvency and Trustee Service Australia 2011, *Profiles of debtors*, p. 16, www.afsa.gov.au; **problems 2.10 and 2.11, p. 38:** Department of Foreign Affairs and Trade 2014, *Trade statistics*, www.dfat.gov.au; **problem 2.12, p. 38:** Bureau of Infrastructure, Transport and Regional Economics 2014, *Domestic on time performance*, Department of Infrastructure and Transport, www.bitre.gov.au; **problem 2.15, p. 41:** Statistics New Zealand, 'Overseas student numbers studying in New Zealand' and 'Overseas visitor arrivals', www.stats.govt.nz, tables 2.03–4 and 2.04; **opening case revisited, p. 42:** Brand, JE, Lorentz, P & Mathew, T 2014, *DA14 Digital Australia*, Interactive Games & Entertainment Association, www.igea.net; **problem 2.27, p. 44:** Visa Solutions 2014, *Costs of living in Australia*, www.australia-migration.com.

Chapter 3

opening vignette, p. 48: Bruner, J 2013, 'Tweet loud and quiet', *Radar*, O'Reilly, www.radar.oreilly.com; Beevolve Inc. 2012, 'An exhaustive study of Twitter users across the world', www.beevolve.com; **problem 3.21, p. 84:** Home Price Guide 2007.

Chapter 4

opening vignette, p. 94: The Gemba Group 2014, *Gemba sports and entertainment report: gym workouts and group exercise*, www.thegembagroup.com.

Chapter 5

opening vignette, p. 136: Australian Institute of Health and Welfare; Australian Government Department of Health, *National binge drinking campaign*, www.drinkingnightmare.gov.au; **chapter case, p. 137:** Sawyer, MG, Arney, FM, Baghurst, PA, Clark, JJ, Graetz, BW, Kosky, RJ, Nurcombe, B, Patton, GC, Prior, MR, Raphael, B, Rey, J, Whaites, LC & Zubrick, SR 2000, *Mental health of* *young people in Australia*, Child and adolescent component of the National Survey of Mental Health and Well-being, www.health.gov.au; **problem 5.10, p. 155:** Statistics New Zealand 2008, *Accommodation survey: August 2008*, media release, Statistics New Zealand, www.stats.govt.nz; **problem 5.12, p. 155:** Kachor, K 2007, 'Industry split over audit standards', *InvestorDaily*, 5 December, www.investordaily.com.au.

Chapter 6

pp. 172–4: Ingram, JA & Monks, JG 1989, *Statistics for business and economics*, Harcourt Brace Jovanovich, Publishers, San Diego; Kirk, RE 1972, *Statistical issues: a reader for the behavioural sciences*, Brooks/Cole Publishing Co., Monterey, CA.

Chapter 7

p. 202: Australian Bureau of Statistics, *2006 Census data by location*, ABS, www.censusdata.abs.gov.au.

Chapter 8

opening vignette, p. 228: Australian Medical Association Queensland 2014, *Lighten your load*, www.amaq.com.au; **p. 238:** Dudycha, AL & Dudycha, LW 1972, 'Behavioral statistics: an historical perspective', in R Kirk (ed.), *Statistical issues: a reader for the behavioral sciences*, Brooks/Cole, Monterey, CA; **p. 240:** Kirk, RE 1968, *Experimental design: procedures for the behavioural sciences*, Brooks/Cole, Belmont, CA.

Chapter 9

opening vignette, p. 262: Bita, N 2013, 'Babies in childcare crisis', *The Australian*, 20 January, www.theaustralian.com.au; 'Childcare agencies struggling to find staff in Australia looking offshore', 14 September 2013, www.news.com.au; 'Childcare shortage a hurdle for paid parental leave', *The Australian*, 29 April 2014, www.theaustralian.com.au; Department of Employment 2014, 'Child care worker, Tasmania, September 2014', ANZSCO 4211-11, www.docs.employment.gov.au; **pp. 272–3:** Robin Boyle; **p. 274:** Flaherty, DJ, Zimmerman, RA & Murray, MA 1995, 'Benchmarking against the best', *Journal of Accountancy*, July, pp. 85–8.

Chapter 10

opening vignette, pp. 312–13: Unisuper, www.unisuper.com.au; REST Industry Super, www.rest.com.au; **table 10.3, p. 334:** Whitlark, D & Geurts, M 1998, 'Phone surveys: how well do respondents represent average Americans?', *Marketing Research*, Fall, pp. 13–17; **problem 10.23, p. 345:** ANZ 2014, 'Job advertisement series', www.media.anz.com; **problem 10.25, p. 346:** Australian Bureau of Statistics, www.abs.gov.au; **demonstration problem 10.6 p. 350:** RedBalloon 2009, 'Reward & recognition survey results Australia & New Zealand, November 2009', www.redballoon.com; **p. 352:** Australian Bureau of Statistics 2011, *Household expenditure survey, Australia: summary of results, 2009–10*, cat. no. 6530.0, ABS, Canberra, www.abs.gov.au; **problem 10.37, p. 360:** Jones, G, Noble, ADL, Schauer, B & Cogger, N 2009, 'Measuring the attenuation in a subject-specific random effect with paired data', *Journal of Data Science*, vol. 7, pp. 179–88.

Chapter 11

opening vignette, p. 368: Elliott, R & Leonard, C 2004, 'Peer pressure and poverty : exploring fashion brands and consumption symbolism among children of the "British poor"', *Journal of Consumer Behaviour*, vol. 3, no. 4, pp. 347–59; Phau, I & Yip, SL 2008, 'Attitudes toward domestic and foreign luxury brand apparel: a comparison between status and non status seeking teenagers', *Journal of Fashion Marketing and Management: An International Journal*, 2008, vol. 12, no. 1, pp. 68–9; **chapter case, p. 369:** Headspace: National Youth Mental Health Foundation, wwww.headspace.org.au; Due, P, Merlo, J, Harel-Fisch, Y, Damsgaard, MT, Holstein, BE, Hetland, J, Currie, C, Gabhainn, SN, de Matos, MG & Lynch, J 2009, 'Socioeconomic inequality in exposure to bullying during adolescence: a comparative, cross-sectional, multilevel study in 35 countries', *American Journal of Public Health*, May, vol. 99, no. 5, pp. 907–14; Price, M & Dalgleish, J 2010, 'Cyberbullying: experiences, impacts and coping strategies as described by Australian young people', *Youth Studies Australia*, vol. 29, no. 2, pp. 51–9.

Chapter 12

opening vignette, p. 410: Adcorp 2013, 'Social media statistics January 2013, Australia and New Zealand', www.adcorp.com.au; **demonstration problem 12.1, p. 415–16:** Roy Morgan Research 2012, *Morgan Poll trends: federal voting intention trend (2011 to 2012) — House of Representatives*, www.roymorgan.com.

Chapter 13

opening vignette, p. 436: Chan, DL & Sullivan, EA 2008, 'Teenage smoking in pregnancy and birthweight: a population study, 2001–2004', *The Medical Journal of Australia*, vol. 188, no. 7, pp. 392–6; **problem 13.6, p. 460:** National Basketball League, www.nbl.com.au.

Chapter 14

opening vignette, p. 480: Delfabbro, PH, King, DL, Lambos, C & Puglies, S 2009, 'Is video-game playing a risk factor for pathological gambling in Australian adolescents?' *Journal of Gambling Studies*, vol. 25, pp. 391–405; Griffiths, MD 1995, Adolescent gambling. London: Routledge; **problem 14.6, p. 487:** Jensen, RG, Solberg, DP & Zorn, TS 1992, 'Simultaneous determination of insider ownership, debt and dividend policies', *Journal of Financial and Quantitative Analysis*, vol. 27, no. 2; **problem 14.27, p. 509:** Larner, M 1996, 'Mass and its relationship to physical measurements', *MS305 data project*, Department of Mathematics, The University of Queensland, St Lucia, Qld; **problem 14.29, p. 510:** Bureau of Meteorology.

Chapter 15

opening vignette, pp. 514–15: Australian Bureau of Statistics, www.abs.gov.au; **chapter case, pp. 516–17:** Reserve Bank of Australia 2014, *Interest rates and yields — money market — monthly*, RBA, www.rba.gov.au; **figure 15.3, p. 518:** Australian Bureau of Statistics 2014, *Average full-time adult weekly earnings*, cat. no. 6302.0, ABS, Canberra; **figure 15.4, p. 519:** Australian Bureau of Statistics 2010, *Manufacturing production Australia*, cat. no. 8301.0.55.001, ABS, Canberra; **figure 15.5, p. 519:** Australian Bureau of Statistics 2014, *Building approvals, Australia*, cat. no. 8731.0, ABS, Canberra; **table 15.1, p. 520:** Australian Bureau of Statistics 2012, *Livestock products*, cat. no. 7215.0, ABS, Canberra; **figure 15.6, p. 520:** Australian Bureau of Statistics 2012, *Livestock products*, cat. no. 7215.0, ABS, Canberra; **demonstration problem 15.2, p. 524:** Australian Bureau of Agricultural and Resource Economics and Sciences 2011, 'Statistics', www.abare.gov.au; **problem 15.9, p. 530:** Statistics New Zealand, *Key labour force measures by qualification, age and sex*, www.nzdotstat.stats.govt.nz; **table 15.6, pp. 531–2:** Australian Bureau of Statistics, www.abs.gov.au; **demonstration problem 15.4, p. 533:** Australian Bureau of Statistics 2011, *Business indicators, Australia*, cat. no. 5676.0, ABS, Canberra; **figure 15.9, p. 534:** Reserve Bank of Australia 2011, *Interest rates and yields — money market — monthly*, RBA, www.rba.gov.au; **p. 540:** Australian Bureau of Statistics, www.abs.gov.au;

demonstration problem 15.6, p. 543: Australian Bureau of Statistics 2014, *Business indicators, Australia*, cat. no. 5676.0, ABS, Canberra; **problem 15.10, p. 602:** Australian Bureau of Statistics 2011, *Production of selected construction materials*, cat. no. 8301.0, ABS, Canberra; **problem 15.13, p. 545:** World Bank, *World development indicators*, www.worldbank.org; **table 15.7, p. 550:** Australian Automobile Association, 'Petrol prices', www.aaa.asn.au; **table 15.12, p. 556:** Australian Bureau of Statistics 2010, *Average weekly earnings, Australia*, cat. no. 6302.0, ABS, Canberra; **problems 15.32–15.36, pp. 564–7:** Australian Bureau of Statistics, www.abs.gov.au.

Glossary

a posteriori after the experiment; pairwise comparisons made by the researcher *after* determining that there is a significant overall *F* value from an ANOVA; also called *post hoc p. 380*

adjusted R^2 a modified value of R^2 in which the degrees of freedom are taken into account, thereby allowing the researcher to compare models with different numbers of variables *p. 500*

alpha (α) the probability of committing a Type I error; also called the level of significance *p. 267*

alternative hypothesis a statement that the 'alternate' condition exists: that is, there is a change in the parameter; the new theory is true; there are new standards; the system is not performing as specified. Usually, this is the hypothesis that a researcher is interested in testing *p. 264*

analysis of variance (ANOVA) a technique for analysing whether there is a significant difference in a dependent variable in two or more independent groups *p. 371*

arithmetic mean the average of a set of numbers *p. 53*

autocorrelation a problem that arises in regression analysis when data occur over time and the error terms are correlated; also called *serial correlation p. 540*

autoregressive model a multiple regression forecasting technique in which the independent variables are time-lagged versions of the dependent variable *p. 543*

base period a point in time against which all comparisons are made *p. 550*

Bayes' rule a method of calculating conditional probability that takes into account new information *p. 126*

beta (β) the probability of committing a Type II error *p. 271*

bimodal data sets that have two modes *p. 51*

binomial distribution a discrete distribution in which there are only two possible outcomes in any one trial *p. 143*

blocking variable a variable that the researcher wants to control but is not the treatment variable of interest *p. 385*

box and whisker plot a diagram that uses the first, second and third quartiles along with the two extreme values not deemed to be outliers to depict a distribution graphically; sometimes called a *box plot p. 76*

categorical data non-numerical data that are labels or identifiers *p. 4*

census a collection of data on the whole population *p. 3*

central limit theorem regardless of the shape of a population distribution, the sample means are approximately normally distributed for sufficiently large sample sizes ($n \geq 30$) *p. 210*

Chebyshev's theorem a theorem stating that at least $1-\frac{1}{k^2}$ values fall within $\pm k$ standard deviations of the mean, regardless of the shape of the distribution *p. 66*

chi-square distribution a continuous distribution determined by the sum of the squares of *k* independent random variables *p. 249*

chi-square goodness-of-fit test a statistical test used to analyse probabilities of multinomial distribution trials along a single dimension; it compares expected, or theoretical, frequencies of categories from a population distribution with the observed, or actual, frequencies from a distribution *p. 412*

chi-square test of independence a statistical test used to analyse the frequencies of two variables with multiple categories to determine whether the two variables are independent *p. 423*

class mark the midpoint of a class interval *p. 17*

class midpoint the midpoint of a class interval *p. 17*

classical method of assigning probabilities assigning probabilities assuming that each outcome is equally likely to occur, with no assumed knowledge or historical basis for what will occur *p. 97*

classification variable the independent variable of an experimental design that was present prior to the experiment and is not the result of the researcher's manipulations or control *p. 370*

cluster (or area) sampling a type of random sampling in which the population is divided into non-overlapping areas or clusters, and elements are randomly sampled from the areas or clusters *p. 203*

coefficient of determination (r^2) the proportion of variability of the dependent variable explained by the independent variable in a regression model *p. 459*

coefficient of multiple determination (R^2) the proportion of variation of the dependent variable accounted for by the independent variables in a regression model *p. 499*

coefficient of skewness a coefficient that compares the mean and median in light of the magnitude of the standard deviation *p. 75*

coefficient of variation (CV) the ratio of the standard deviation to the mean, expressed as a percentage *p. 72*

collectively exhaustive events a list containing all possible elementary events for an experiment *p. 104*

complement all the elementary events of an experiment that occur when a specified event does not occur *p. 104*

complement of a union the probability that neither of two events of interest will occur *p. 113*

completely randomised design an experimental design where independent random samples of experimental units are assigned to treatments *p. 372*

conditional probability the probability of occurrence of one event given that another event has occurred *p. 107*

confidence interval a range of values within which the analyst can declare, with a specified degree of confidence, that the population parameter lies; also known as *interval estimate pp. 230, 463*

contingency analysis another name for the chi-square test of independence *p. 423*

contingency table a table that presents the frequency with which two events occur and co-occur *pp. 106, 423*

continuous distributions distributions associated with random variables that can take values at every point over a given interval *p. 170*

continuous random variable a random variable that takes all possible values within an interval *p. 138*

convenience sampling a nonrandom sampling technique in which items for the sample are selected for the convenience of the researcher *p. 204*

correlation a measure of the degree of relatedness of two or more variables *p. 80*

correlation coefficient *see* Pearson product–moment correlation coefficient *p. 438*

critical value the value that divides the nonrejection region from the rejection region *p. 267*

critical value method a method of testing hypotheses where a sample test statistic is compared with a critical value. This allows a conclusion to be reached to reject or not reject the null hypothesis *p. 267*

cross-sectional data data that are collected at a fixed point in time *p. 5*

cumulative frequency running total of frequencies through the classes of a frequency distribution *p. 17*

cyclical component patterns of highs and lows through which data move over time periods, usually of more than one year *p. 519*

data snooping occurs when a given data set is used more than once for making a statistical inference. It may involve changing the decision rule, hypotheses and/or critical values after the first inspection of the data *p. 350*

decomposition breaking down the effects of time-series data into the four components: trend, cyclical, seasonal and irregular *p. 525*

degrees of freedom (df) a mathematical adjustment made to the size of a sample; used along with α to locate values in statistical tables *p. 240*

dependent samples two or more samples selected in such a way as to be dependent or related. Each item or person in one sample has a corresponding matched or related item in the other samples; also called *related samples p. 337*

dependent variable the variable of interest *p. 370*

deseasonalised removed the effects of seasonality from time-series data *p. 528*

deviation from the mean the difference between a number and the average of the set of numbers of which the number is a part *p. 62*

discrete random variable a random variable that takes a finite or countably infinite number of values *p. 137*

disproportionate stratified random sampling a type of stratified random sampling in which the proportions of items selected from the strata for the final sample do not reflect the proportions of the strata in the population *p. 202*

Durbin–Watson test a statistical test for determining whether significant autocorrelation is present in a time-series regression model *p. 540*

elementary events events that cannot be decomposed or broken down into other events *p. 100*

empirical rule a guideline that states the approximate percentage of values that fall within a given number of standard deviations of a mean of a set of data that are normally distributed or approximately normal *p. 65*

error of a forecast the difference between an actual value and the forecast value *p. 547*

error of estimation the absolute difference between the point estimate (used to estimate a parameter) and the parameter *p. 230*

error of prediction the difference between the observed value and the predicted value *p. 441*

event an outcome of an experiment *p. 100*

experiment a process or activity that produces outcomes *p. 100*

experimental design a plan and structure to test hypotheses in which the researcher either controls or manipulates one or more variables *p. 370*

exploratory data analysis (EDA) graphical and numerical summaries of data to highlight key aspects of data *p. 3*

exponential distribution a continuous distribution, closely related to the Poisson distribution, that describes the times between random occurrences *p. 186*

exponential smoothing a forecasting technique in which a weighting system is used to determine the importance of previous time periods in the forecast *p. 523*

***F* distribution** the probability distribution of the ratio of two sample variances *p. 354*

***F* value** the ratio of two sample variances, used to reach statistical conclusions regarding the null hypothesis *pp. 354, 489*

***F* value (ANOVA)** the ratio of the treatment variance (MSC) to the error variance (MSE) *p. 374*

factorial design experimental design in which two or more independent variables are studied simultaneously and every level of each treatment is studied under the conditions of every level of all other treatments; also called *factorial experiment* *p. 390*

factors another name for the independent variables of an experimental design *p. 370*

finite population correction (fpc) factor a statistical adjustment made to the *z* formula for sample means to account for the fact that a population is finite and the population size is known *p. 215*

first-differences approach a transformation process in which each value of a variable is subtracted from each succeeding time period value of the variable *p. 543*

Fisher's Ideal index an index which minimises errors in both the Laspeyres and Paasche price indices by using the geometric mean of the Laspeyres and Paasche index numbers *p. 555*

forecasting the art or science of estimating the future value of a given variable *p. 515*

frequency distribution a tabular summary of the data presented as non-overlapping class intervals covering the entire data range and their corresponding frequencies *p. 16*

frequency polygon a graph constructed by plotting a dot for the frequencies at the class midpoints and connecting the dots *p. 28*

grouped data data that have been organised into a frequency distribution *p. 16*

heteroscedasticity the condition that occurs when the error variances produced by a regression model are not constant *p. 452*

histogram a vertical bar chart where the area of each bar is equal to the frequency of the corresponding class interval *p. 22*

homoscedasticity the condition that occurs when the error variances produced by a regression model are constant *p. 452*

hypothesis testing hypothesis testing is a statistical technique that uses a set of well-defined steps. It requires a null and alternative hypothesis statement to be specified as the first step that involves a population parameter. By using representative sample data, the hypothesis procedure arrives at a conclusion about the particular population parameter of interest *p. 263*

independent events events such that the occurrence or non-occurrence of one has no effect on the occurrence of the other(s) *p. 103*

independent samples two or more samples in which the selected items are not related *p. 316*

independent variable the factors that influence the variable of interest *p. 370*

index number a percentage that expresses a measurement in a given period in terms of the corresponding measurement for a selected base period (a particular point in time, often in the past, against which all comparisons are made) *p. 550*

interaction effects of one treatment in an experimental design varying according to the levels of treatment of the other effect(s) *p. 392*

interpolation a prediction of the value of something that is hypothetical or unknown based on other values that are known *p. 58*

interquartile range (IQR) the distance between the first and the third quartiles *p. 61*

intersection the portion of outcomes that contains elements that occur in both or all groups of interest *p. 102*

interval estimate a range of values within which the analyst can declare, with some confidence, the population parameter lies; also known as *confidence interval* *p. 230*

irregular component changes in a time series that are unpredictable and not associated with trend, seasonal or cyclical components; also called *random component* *p. 519*

joint probability the probability that two events will co-occur as an outcome of an experiment *p. 107*

judgement sampling a nonrandom sampling technique in which items selected for the sample are chosen by the judgement of the researcher *p. 204*

kurtosis a measure that reflects the amount of peakedness and tail weight of a distribution *p. 76*

Laspeyres price index a type of weighted aggregate price index in which the quantity usage values used in the calculations are from the base year *p. 553*

least squares analysis the process by which a regression model is developed by producing a minimum sum of the squared error values *p. 443*

leptokurtic describes distributions with a higher and thinner peak and longer tails relative to a normal distribution with the same variance *p. 76*

level of confidence the amount equal to 100% $\times$ $(1 - \alpha)$, where α is the area under the normal curve in the tails of the distribution; i.e. outside the area defined by the confidence interval *p. 231*

level of significance the probability of committing a Type I error; also known as alpha, α *pp. 231, 267*

levels the subcategories of the independent variable used by the researcher in the experimental design; also called *classifications* *p. 371*

lower control limit (LCL) the bottom line of a control chart, usually situated approximately three standard deviations of the mean below the centreline; data points below this line indicate quality-control problems *p. 106*

margin of error (ME) the amount added to or subtracted from the point estimate to form the confidence interval. It equals half the width of the confidence interval. It can also be viewed as the maximum specified value for the error of estimation used to construct a confidence interval *p. 230*

marginal probability the overall probability of one event totalled over all combinations of every other event *p. 106*

mean absolute deviation (MAD) the average of the absolute values of the deviations around the mean for a set of numbers *p. 548*

mean or expected value the long-run average of occurrences *p. 140*

mean square error (MSE) the average of all errors squared of a forecast for a group of data *p. 548*

measures of central tendency measures used to yield information about the centre of a set of numbers *p. 51*

measures of location measures used to yield information about certain sections of a set of numbers when ranked into as ascending array *p. 56*

measures of shape tools that can be used to describe the appearance of a data distribution *p. 74*

measures of variability summary measures that describe the spread or dispersion of a set of data *p. 61*

median the middle value in an ordered array of numbers *p. 51*

mesokurtic describes distributions that are normal in shape; that is, not very high or very flat *p. 76*

mode the most frequently occurring value in a set of data *p. 51*

moving average an average of data from previous time periods used to smooth the value for following time periods. This average is modified at each new time period by including more recent values not in the previous average and dropping values from the more distant time periods, which were in the previous average. It is updated at each new time period *p. 520*

multimodal data sets that contain two or more modes *p. 51*

multinomial distribution a distribution in which there are more than two possible outcomes in a single trial *p. 412*

multiple comparison tests statistical techniques used to compare pairs of treatment means when an analysis of variance yields an overall significant difference in the treatment means *p. 380*

multiple regression regression analysis with one dependent variable and two or more independent variables *p. 481*

mutually exclusive events events such that the occurrence of one precludes the occurrence of the other(s) *p. 103*

nonrandom sampling a sampling method in which not every unit of the population has a known probability of being selected for the sample *p. 198*

nonrejection region any portion of a distribution that is not in the rejection region. If a test statistic falls in the nonrejection region, the decision is not to reject the null hypothesis *p. 267*

nonsampling error error other than a sampling error *p. 206*

normal distribution a continuous distribution that is bell-shaped in appearance and often used in statistics to model a variety of real-world observations *pp. 65, 172*

normal probability plot a graphical technique for assessing whether a dataset has a normal distribution (at least approximately). The data are plotted against a theoretical normal distribution, and departures in the plot away from a straight line indicate departures from normality *p. 327*

null hypothesis a statement that the 'status quo' condition has been maintained: that is, there is no change in the parameter; the existing theory is still true; the existing standard is correct; the system is performing as intended *p. 264*

numerical data data that take numerical values from either counting (discrete) or measurement (continuous) *p. 5*

ogive a cumulative frequency polygon *p. 30*

one-tailed test a statistical test interested in testing deviations from the null hypothesis in one direction only *p. 265*

one-way analysis of variance (ANOVA) the process used to estimate and compare the effects of the different treatments of an outcome or dependent variable *p. 372*

operating characteristic (OC) curve in hypothesis testing, a graph of probabilities of Type II error for various possible values of an alternative hypotheses *p. 301*

outliers data points that lie apart from the rest of the points *pp. 22, 66, 451*

Paasche price index a type of weighted aggregate price index in which the quantity usage values used in the calculations are from the year of interest *p. 554*

paired *t* test a *t* test to test the differences between two related or matched samples; sometimes called the '*t* test for related measures' or the 'correlated *t* test'; also known as the *matched-pairs test* *p. 338*

parameter a descriptive measure of a population *p. 3*

Pareto chart a vertical bar chart ordered with respect to frequency from highest to lowest *p. 35*

partial regression coefficient the coefficient of an independent variable in a multiple regression model; it represents the increase in the value of the dependent variable resulting from a one-unit increase in the independent variable if all other variables are held constant *p. 482*

Pearson product–moment correlation coefficient (r) a correlation measure used to determine the degree of association of two variables that are quantitative *p. 80*

percentiles measures of location that divide a set of data into two parts of a known proportion *p. 57*

pie chart a circular display of data where the area of each slice is proportional to the percentage contribution of the corresponding sublevel *p. 32*

platykurtic describes distributions that are flat and spread out with shorter tails relative to a normal distribution with the same variance *p. 76*

point estimate a single estimate of a population parameter based on a sample statistic *p. 230*

Poisson distribution a discrete distribution that describes the probability of occurrence of events over an interval; it focuses on the number of occurrences over some interval or continuum *p. 155*

population a collection of people, objects or items of interest *p. 3*

power the probability of rejecting a null hypothesis when the null hypothesis is false. The power of a statistical test is $1 - \beta$ *p. 271*

power curve a graph that plots power values against various values of the alternative hypothesis *p. 302*

prediction interval a confidence interval used to predict a single value of a dependent variable given a specific value of the independent variable *p. 467*

primary data data collected to address a specific need *p. 6*

probabilistic model a model that includes an error term that allows for various values of *y* to occur for a given value of *x* *p. 442*

probability-based sampling a sampling method in which every unit of the population has a known probability of being selected for the sample *p. 198*

probability matrix a table that displays the marginal and joint probabilities of a given problem in a table *p. 107*

proportionate stratified random sampling a type of stratified random sampling in which the proportions of the items selected for the sample from the strata reflect the proportions of the strata in the population *p. 202*

***p*-value** the area in the tail(s) of a distribution beyond the calculated sample test statistic. This area represents the probability of finding another test statistic, using a different sample, at least as extreme as the calculated test statistic computed under the assumption that the null hypothesis is true *p. 267*

quadratic model a multiple regression model in which the predictors include a variable and that same variable squared *p. 535*

quartiles measures of location that divide a set of data into four equal subgroups or parts *p. 58*

quota sampling a nonrandom sampling technique in which the population is stratified on some characteristic and then elements selected for the sample are chosen by nonrandom processes *p. 205*

random component changes in a time series that are unpredictable and not associated with trend, seasonal or cyclical components; also called *irregular component* *p. 519*

random sampling a sampling method in which every unit of the population has a known probability of being selected for the sample *p. 198*

random variable a variable that contains the outcomes of a chance experiment *p. 137*

randomised block design an experimental design in which there is one independent variable of interest and a second variable, known as a blocking variable *p. 385*

range the difference between the largest and smallest data values *pp. 16, 61*

ratio-to-moving-average method a decomposition method that assumes that time-series data can be represented as a product of the four components: trend, cyclical, seasonal and irregular *p. 525*

raw data data that have not been summarised in any way *p. 16*

regression analysis the process of constructing a mathematical model or function that can be used to predict one variable using another variable *p. 437*

rejection region the portion of a distribution in which a test statistic must lie to reject the null hypothesis *p. 267*

relative frequency the ratio of the frequency of a class interval to the total frequency *p. 17*

relative frequency of occurrence method assigning probability based on cumulated historical data *p. 98*

repeated measures design a randomised block design in which each block level is an individual item or person, measured across all treatments *p. 386*

residual the difference between the actual *y* value and the *y* value predicted by the regression model; the error of the regression model in predicting each value of the dependent variable *pp. 449, 493*

residual plot a graph in which the residuals for a particular regression model are plotted along with their associated values of *x* *p. 451*

response variable the dependent variable in a multiple regression model; the variable that the researcher is trying to predict *p. 482*

robust describes a statistical technique that is relatively insensitive to minor violations in one or more of its underlying assumptions *p. 239*

sample a subset of units in a population *p. 3*

sample proportion the ratio of the frequency at which a given characteristic occurs in a sample to the number of items in the sample *p. 218*

sample size estimation an estimate of the size of a sample necessary to fulfil the requirements of a particular level of confidence and to be within a specified margin of error *p. 252*

sample space a complete roster or listing of all elementary events for an experiment *p. 101*

sampling error the difference between the value computed from a sample (a statistic) and the corresponding value for the population (a parameter) *p. 205*

sampling frame a list, map, directory or some other source that is used to represent the population being sampled *p. 197*

scatter plot a graph of pairwise data of two continuous variables *pp. 39, 438*

seasonal component a pattern that is repeated throughout a time series for periods of one year or less *p. 518*

seasonal index a factor that adjusts the trend value of a time series to compensate for the effect of a pattern that repeats over a period of one year or less *p. 525*

secondary data data that were collected for some other purpose and are already available *p. 6*

set notation the use of mathematical symbols to define a group or set of events and describe outcomes relating to their occurrence with other sets of events *p. 102*

simple price index a price, expressed as a percentage, determined by computing the ratio of a price for a particular year of interest to the price for a base year *p. 550*

simple random sampling a sampling method in which every (possible) sample has the same probability of being sampled;

consequently, every unit of the population has an equal probability of being selected in the sample *p. 198*

simple regression bivariate, linear regression *p. 437*

skewness the lack of symmetry of a distribution of values *p. 74*

snowball sampling a nonrandom sampling technique in which survey subjects who fit a desired profile are selected based on referral from other survey respondents who also fit the desired profile *p. 205*

standard deviation the square root of the variance *p. 64*

standard error of the estimate (s_e) the standard deviation of the error of a simple linear regression model *pp. 457, 498*

standard error of the mean the standard deviation of the distribution of sample means *p. 211*

standard error of the proportion the standard deviation of the distribution of sample proportions *p. 218*

standardised normal distribution a specifically defined normal distribution that has a mean of 0 and a standard deviation of 1. This is called the *z* distribution and tabulated *z*-scores are used to calculate probabilities *p. 175*

statistic a descriptive measure of a sample *p. 3*

statistical hypotheses a formal hypothesis structure consisting of the null hypothesis and the alternative hypothesis, which together contain all the possible outcomes of the experiment or study *p. 264*

statistical inference use of sample data to reach conclusions about the population from which a sample was drawn *p. 3*

stem and leaf plot a display of continuous data where the rightmost digit is the leaf and the rest of the digits form the stem *p. 33*

stratified random sampling a type of random sampling in which the population is divided into various non-overlapping strata and then a simple random sample is taken from each stratum *p. 201*

subjective probability method a probability assigned based on the intuition or reasoning of the person determining the probability *p. 99*

sum of squares of error (SSE) the sum of the residuals squared for a regression model *p. 456*

sum of squares of *x* the sum of the squared deviations from the mean for a set of values *p. 64*

systematic sampling a random sampling technique in which every *k*th item or person is selected from the population *p. 203*

***t* distribution** a distribution that describes the standardised sample mean in small samples when the standard deviation is unknown and the population is normally distributed *p. 238*

time-series data data gathered on a given characteristic over a period of time *pp. 5, 515*

treatment variable the independent variable of an experimental design that the researcher either controls or modifies *p. 370*

tree diagram a graphical representation of the outcomes of an experiment *p. 124*

trend component the long-term upward or downward movement in a given variable over time *p. 518*

Tukey–Kramer procedure a modification of the Tukey HSD multiple comparison procedure; used when there are unequal sample sizes *p. 383*

Tukey's honestly significant difference (HSD) test a technique used for pairwise a posteriori multiple comparisons to determine if there are significant differences between the means of any pair of treatment levels in an experimental design *p. 380*

two-stage sampling cluster sampling done in two stages: a first round of samples is taken and then a second round of samples is taken from within the first *p. 203*

two-tailed test a statistical test interested in testing deviations from the null hypothesis in either direction *p. 265*

two-way analysis of variance (two-way ANOVA) the process used to statistically test the effects of variables in factorial designs with two independent variables *p. 392*

Type I error an error committed in hypothesis testing when the decision is to reject the null hypothesis H_0 when in reality it is true and it should not have been rejected. The probability of making this type of error is α *p. 269*

Type II error an error committed in hypothesis testing when the decision is not to reject the null hypothesis H_0 when in reality it is false and should have been rejected. The probability of making this type of error is β *p. 270*

ungrouped data data that have not been summarised in any way *p. 16*

uniform distribution a simple continuous distribution that has the same height over a range of values (also called the rectangular distribution) *p. 184*

union a new set of unique elements formed by combining the elements of two or more other sets *p. 102*

union probability the probability of one event occurring or the other event occurring or both occurring *p. 106*

unweighted aggregate price index a price index that puts equal weight or importance on all items in a market basket *p. 551*

variance the average of the squared deviations from the mean for a set of numbers *p. 63*

Venn diagram a graphical representation of how any event may occur in terms of its occurrence with any other event *p. 102*

weighted aggregate price index a price index, expressed as a percentage, computed by multiplying quantity usage weights and item prices, summing the products to determine a market basket's worth in a given year, and then determining the ratio of the market basket's worth in the year of interest to the same value computed for a base year *p. 552*

***z*-score** the number of standard deviations a value is above or below the mean of a set of numbers *p. 71*

Index

a posteriori pairwise comparisons 380
100(1 – α)% confidence interval to estimate μ 231
accounting fraud, detecting 194
addition laws 109–16
adjusted R_2 500–1
aggregate price indices 551
alpha (α) 267, 271
alternative hypotheses 264
analysis of variance (ANOVA) 371
area sampling 203–4
arithmetic mean 53
association, measures of 80–4
Australian Bureau of Statistics (ABS) 6
autocorrelation, testing for 540–3
autocorrelation problem, overcoming 543–5
autoregressive trend-based forecasting models 539–47

bar charts 22
base period, changing 556–7
Bayes' rule 126–7
beta (β) 271
bimodal data 51
binge drinking, survey 136
binomial distributions
- assumptions 143–4
- graphing 152–4
- mean 150–2
- misuse of statistics 164
- standard deviation 152

binomial formula 146
binomial problems, solving 144–7
binomial tables, using 147–9
birth weight, and teenage smoking in pregnancy 436
bivariate linear regression 437
blocking variables 385
body temperature 170
box and whisker plots 76–8

categorical data 4–5
- graphical representation 15, 32

causation, and correlation 85
census 3, 197
central limit theorem 210–13, 230
central tendency, measures of 51–6
Challenger space shuttle 9
Chebyshev's theorem 66–7
chi-square distributions 249–50, 428
chi-square goodness-of-fit tests 410, 412–23, 428
chi-square test of independence 410, 423–9, 428
childcare industry 262
Clark, Sally 9
class midpoint/marks 17, 18
classical method of assigning probabilities 97–8
classification variables 370
cluster (or area) sampling 203–4
coefficient of determination (r_2) 459–62
coefficient of determination (r_2), relationship between r and r_2 462
coefficient of multiple determination (R_2) 499–500
coefficient of skewness 75–6
coefficient of variation (CV) 72–3
collectively exhaustive events 103
column graphs 22
complement of a union 113
complementary events 104
completely randomised design (one-way ANOVA) 372–80
conditional probability 107, 120–9
confidence intervals 230–5, 241–4
- difference between related populations 343
- difference between two means
- t statistic, population variances unknown 322–7
- z statistic, population variances unknown 333–4
- to estimate conditional mean of y: $\mu_{y/x}$ 466–70
- two population proportions 351–2
- two population variances 359–60

confidence intervals formula
- ratio of two population variances 360
- to estimate difference between related populations 343
- to estimate $E(y_x)$ for given value of x 467
- to estimate p 246
- to estimate $p_1 - p_2$ 352
- to estimate population variance 249
- to estimate μ
- population standard deviation unknown and population normally distributed 241
- using finite population correction factor 235
- to estimate $\mu_1 - \mu_2$ 322
- assuming similar variance 333

contingency analysis 423–9
contingency tables 105–6
continuous data
- frequency distributions 16
- graphical representation 15, 22–39, 33

continuous distributions
- nature and application 170
- nature of
- versus discrete distributions 137–8

continuous random variables 137–8
convenience sampling 204
correlation 80–4
- and causation 85

correlation coefficient 438
critical value 267
critical value method of hypothesis testing 267, 276–8
cross-sectional data 5
cumulative frequency 17, 18
cumulative frequency polygons 230
customer surveys 7
cyberbullying amongst adolescents 369–70, 401
cyclical component 519

$\bar{d}$, formula for 338
data
- graphical display 22–39
- obtaining 6–7
- types 4–5

data collection agencies 6
data snooping 361
decomposition methods 525
degrees of freedom 240
dependent samples 337
dependent variables 370, 437
descriptive statistics 95
deseasonalising time series 528–30
deviation from the mean 62–3
discrete distributions
  describing 138–42
  mean or expected value 140, 141
  misuse of statistics 164
  standard deviation 140–1
  variance 140, 141
  versus continuous distributions 137–8
  see also binomial distributions
discrete random variables 137–8
disproportionate stratified random sampling 202
Durbin–Watson test 540

electronic games, marketing survey analysis 15–16, 41–2
elementary events (probability) 100–1
empirical rule, standard deviation 65–6
error of estimation 230
error of a forecast 548
error of prediction 441
events (probability) 100
Excel, using for statistical analysis
  add-ins 7–9
  binomial problems 148, 149–50
  confidence intervals 234
  correlation 83–4
  correlation coefficients and scattergrams 439–40
  descriptive statistics 54–5
  F-test two-sample for variances 359
  frequency polygons 28–9
  frequency tables 18–21
  histograms 24–7
  hypothesis testing for single populations 280–1, 286
  linear trend analysis 543–5
  multiple regression 486
  multiple regression model 484–5
  normal distribution 179
  ogives 30–1
  one-way ANOVA 378
  Pareto charts 36–7
  pie charts 32–3
  Poisson distributions 159–60
  prediction intervals 470–1
  random number generation 200–1
  random sample selection 200
  randomised block design 389
  regression equation, finding directly 446–7
  residual analysis 452–3
  scatterplots 40
  t confidence interval for population mean 243–4
  t-test: paired two sample for means 342
  t-test: two-sample assuming equal variances 332–3
  two-way ANOVA with replication 396–7
  two-way ANOVA without replication 389
  z-test: two-sample means 321–2
expected values 140
experimental design
  ethical considerations 400
  introduction to 370–2
  treatment levels 400
experiments (probability) 100
explanatory variables 437
exploratory data analysis (EDA) 3, 14
exponential distributions 170, 186–9
  probabilities for 187–8
exponential probability density function 187
exponential smoothing method 523–5
exponential trend model 537–9

F distribution, determining lower-tail critical value 355
F distribution table, reading 376–7
F test for two population variances 354
F value 354, 374, 489
F-distribution 354
factorial designs (two-way ANOVA) 390–400
  advantages 391
  interaction 392–6
  statistically testing 392
  with two treatments 391–2
finite population correction (fpc) factor 215–17, 235–6
Fisher's Ideal index 555–6
forecasting 515, 516–17, 559–62
forecasting errors 548, 559
forecasting models
  autoregressive trend-based models 539–47
  evaluating 547–50
  least squares trend-based models 532–9
frequency distributions 16–18
frequency polygons 28–9
frequency tables, using Excel 18–21

gambling, and video gaming 480
general law of addition 109–14
general law of multiplication 116–17
geometric mean 366
Google 2
grouped data 16
gym workouts 94

histograms 22–7
house prices, predicting 437, 472–3, 480–1, 505–7
hypothesis testing
  choosing level of significance 273
  fundamentals 263–72
  p-value method 278
  proportions 288–92
  rejection and nonrejection regions 266–8
  six-step approach 272–3
  Type I errors 269–70
  Type II errors 270–1, 296–304
  variance 292–6
hypothesis testing for population means
  critical value method 276–8
  finite populations 276
  large sample case (*z* statistic, σ unknown) 274–82
  small sample case (*t* statistic, σ unknown) 282–7
hypothesis testing for two populations
  difference between two means, *t* statistic, population variances unknown 326–36
  with paired observations 337–42
  proportions 347–51
  variances 354–9
  z statistic, population variances unknown 315–26

incorrect analysis, consequences 9–10
independent events
  assessing 122–4
  and probability 103–4
independent samples 316
independent variables 370–1, 437
index numbers 550–9
inferential statistics, probability in process of 95
interpolation 58
interquartile range (IQR) 61–2
intersections (probability) 102
interval estimates 230
irregular component 519

job security 411, 429–30
joint probability 107
judgement sampling 204–5

k (sampling cycle), determining value of 203
KaddStat 7, 8, 9
kurtosis 76

Laspeyres price index 553, 555
law of conditional probability 120
leptokurtic distributions 76
level of confidence 231
level of significance 231, 267, 361
life insurance premiums 314–15, 361

linear trend model 532–5
location, measures of 56–60
luxury brands, and teenagers 368

margin of error (ME) 230
marginal probability 106
matched pairs test 337
mean 53, 56
  binomial distributions 150–2
  discrete distributions 140
  Poisson distributions 160
  uniform distributions 184
mean absolute deviation (MAD) 548
mean square error (MSE) 548
measures of association 80–4
measures of central tendency 51–6
measures of location 56–60
measures of shape 74–9
measures of variability 61–74
median 51–3
  and skewness 75
mental health and young people 137, 165
mesokurtic distributions 76
misuse of statistics
  chi-square tests 428
  decision rule and significance level 361
  descriptive summary measures 85
  discrete distributions 164
  level of significance in hypothesis testing 273
  multiple regression analysis 504–5
  normal distributions 181
  probability information 129
  regression analysis 472
  sample statistics 256
  sampling distributions 220
  time series methods 559
  and use of jargon 361
  variance and experimental design 400
mode 51
  and skewness 75
moving average method 520–2
multimodal data 51
multinominal distributions 412
multiple comparison tests 380–5
multiple regression computer output, interpreting 501–4
multiple regression equation, determining 483
multiple regression model 481–2
  residuals 493–7
  significance tests of regression coefficients 490–1
  SSE and standard of error of estimate 497–9
  testing overall model 488–90
  with two independent variables (first-order) 482–3
multiplication laws 116–19
mutually exclusive events 103

national statistics agencies 6
nonrandom sampling
  characteristics 198
  versus random sampling 198–205
nonrandom sampling techniques 204–5
nonrejection region 267–8
nonsampling errors 205–6
normal distribution problems, solving 177–80
normal distributions 23, 170
  applications 172
  approximation to binomial distribution 181–4
  chi-square goodness-of-fit test 418–20
  history and characteristics 172–4
  misuse of statistics 181
  probability density function of 173
  standardised 175–7
normal probability plots 327–8
null hypothesis 264
numerical data 5

ogives 30–1
one-tailed test 265
one-way analysis of variance (one-way ANOVA) 372
  formulas for computing 374
one-way ANOVA, formulas for computing 374
operating characteristic (OC) curves 301–2
organisational restructures 96, 129–30
outliers 22, 23, 451

p-value method of hypothesis testing 267, 278
Paasche price index 554, 555
paired *t* test 338
parameters 3–4
Pareto charts 36–7
partial regression coefficient 482
Pearson product–moment correlation coefficient 80–2
Pearsonian coefficient of skewness 75–6
Pearson's correlation coefficient 438
percentiles 57–8
pie charts 32–3
platykuric distributions 76
point estimates 230
Poisson distributions
  approximation of binomial distribution 161–2
  characteristics and applications 155–6
  chi-square goodness-of-fit test 417–18
  graphing 160–1
  mean and standard deviation 160
  misuse of statistics 164
Poisson formula 156
Poisson problems, solving by formula 156–60

population mean estimation
  t confidence intervals 241–4
  t statistic (σ unknown) 238–45
  z statistic (σ known) 229–37
  z statistic with small samples 236
population parameters, ethical concerns 256
population proportion
  chi-square goodness-of-fit test 420–1
  estimating 245–8
population standard deviance 64, 70
population variance
  estimating 248–51
  formula 63, 70
  formula for testing hypotheses about 293
populations 3
power curves 301–2
prawn farm
  growth 171, 189
  quality control 195–6, 221–2
  quality of product on arrival 228–9, 256–7
  weight of prawns 262–3, 304–5
prediction intervals, to estimate single value of *y* 467–70
pregnancy, smoking and birth weight 436
price indices 500–9
  aggregate price indices 551–6
  applications 557
  changing base period 556–7
  simple price index 550–1
primary data
  collection 6–7
  nature of 6
probabilistic models 442
probabilities
  addition laws 109–16
  conditional probability 120–9
  contingency tables and probability matrices 105–9
  exponential distribution 187–8
  methods of determining 97–100
  misuse of statistics 129
  multiplication laws 116–19
  in process of inferential statistics 95
  range possible 98
  revising 126
  of right tails of exponential distribution 186
  structure of 100–4
  use of 'or' 112–13
probability of the complement of *A* 104
probability density function
  exponential distributions 187
  normal distributions 173
  uniform distributions 184
probability matrices 107–8
probability-based sampling 198
proportionate stratified random sampling 202

proportions
hypothesis testing 288–92
see also two population proportions

quadratic models 535
quadratic trend model 535–7
quartiles 58–60
quota sampling 205

r_2, computational formula for 461
random component 519
random sampling
characteristics 198
versus nonrandom sampling 198–205
random sampling techniques 198–204
random variables 137–8
randomised block design 385–90
formulas 406
repeated measures design 386
range 16–17, 61
range of possible probabilities 98
ratio-to-moving average method 525
raw data 16
real estate, location 49–50, 85–6
regression analysis 437, 472
regression coefficients, significance tests 490–1
regression lines
alternative formula 444
determining equation of 440–9
slope 443
y intercept 444
regression model, hypothesis tests for slope 462–6
regulatory compliance 14
rejection region 267–8, 302–3
relative frequency 17, 18
relative frequency of occurrence method, assigning probabilities 98–9
repeated measures design 386
research services 6–7
Reserve Bank of Australia 6
residual analysis 449–55
residual plot 451
residuals
multiple regression model 493–7
regression model 449
using to test assumptions of regression model 452
response variables 482
robustness, of statistical techniques 239
rural obesity in Queensland 228

sample means, *z* formula for difference between 316
sample proportion 218
sample size
effect of increasing on rejection limits 302–3
ethical considerations 400
when estimating *p* 254
when estimating μ 252
sample size estimation
when estimating *p* 254
when estimating μ 252–3
sample space (probability) 101
sample standard deviation 68, 70
sample statistics, misuse 256
sample variance 68, 70
samples 3
sampling
applications 196
from finite population 215–17
reasons for 196–7
sampling distribution
central limit theorem 210–13
finite population correction factor 215–17
misuse of statistics 220
of sample mean $\bar{x}$ 207–17
of sample proportion $\hat{p}$ 218–19
sampling errors 205–6
sampling frames 197
scatter plots 39–40, 438
s_d, formula for 338
seasonal component, time series 518
seasonal indices 525–8
secondary data
collection 6
nature of 6
set notation (probability) 102
shape, measures of 74–9
simple price index formula 550–1
simple random sampling 198–201
simple regression 437
simple regression analysis 480
estimation and prediction 466–72
interpreting output 472
introduction 437–40
simple regression line, equation of 442
skewness 74–6
smoking in pregnancy 436
snowball sampling 205
social media 48, 410
special law of addition 114–15
special law of multiplication 117–18
standard deviation 62, 64–8
in binomial distributions 150–2
computational formulas 69–71
in discrete distributions 140–2
Poisson distributions 160
population versus sample variance 68–9
uniform distributions 184
and variability 62–74
standard error of the estimate 455–9
standard error of the mean 211
standard error of the proportion 218
standardised normal distributions 175–7
statistical analysis, using Excel 7–9
statistical hypotheses 264
statistical inference 3, 4
statistical software packages 7
statistical techniques, robustness of 239
statistics
basic concepts 3–4
definition 3
Statistics New Zealand 6
stem and leaf plots 33–4
stratified random sampling 201–2
subjective probability method, assigning probabilities 99
sum of squares 443
sum of squares of errors (SSE) 456
sum of squares of regression 499
sum of squares of *x* 64
summation notation 91–2
superannuation funds, choosing 312–13
surveys 7
systematic sampling 202–3

t distribution
characteristics 239–40
formula 238
t distribution tables, reading 240–1
t formula
misapplication 256
to test difference between means 327
t formula to test difference between two dependent populations 338
t test of slope 463
t test for μ 283
time series
components of 518–19
smoothing methods 520–31
time-series data 5, 515
deseasonalising 528–30
tourism industry 514–15
treatment variables 370
tree diagrams 124–6
trend component, time series 518
trend-based forecasting models
autoregressive trend-based forecasting models 539–47
least squares 1, 532–9
Tukey–Kramer formula 384
Tukey–Kramer procedure, unequal sample sizes 383–5
Tukey's honestly significant difference (HSD) test
equal sample sizes 380–3
formula 381
two population proportions
confidence intervals 351–2
hypothesis testing 347–51
statistical inferences 347–53
two population variances
confidence intervals 359–60
hypothesis testing 354–9
statistical inferences 353–61

two populations with paired observations
hypothesis testing 337–42
statistical inferences 337–46
two-stage sampling 203
two-tailed test 265
two-variable continuous data, graphical representation 39–40
two-way analysis of variance (two-way ANOVA) 392
formulas for computing 407
Table *F* values 392

μ, formula to test hypotheses about, with finite population 276
ungrouped data 16
uniform distributions 170, 184–6
probability density function 184
union probability 106–7
unions (probability) 102
United States, 1936 presidential election 10
unweighted aggregate price index 551–2

variability, measures of 61–74
variance 63–4
computational formulas 69–71
in discrete distributions 140–2
hypothesis testing 292–6
population versus sample variance 68–9
and standard deviation 62–74
see also two population variances
Venn diagrams 102
video gaming, and gambling 480
voluntary response bias 10
voluntary response surveys 7

weighted aggregate price index 552–6

z formula for difference between two population proportions 347
z formula for sample means 213, 230
difference between two means (independent samples and population variance known) 316
finite population 215
z formula for sample proportions, when $np > 5$ and $nq > 5$ 218
z formula to test difference between two population proportions 348
z test of population proportion 288
z test for a single mean 274
z-scores 71–2

Fundamental symbols and abbreviations

Samples, populations and probability

CV	coefficient of variation
E_i	event of interest
$\cap$	intersection, elements common to both sets
λ	mean number of occurrences in the interval in a Poisson distribution; say *lambda*
$\mu_{\bar{x}}$	mean of the sample means; say *mu x bar*
A'	not A; not in A; say *A complement*
n_i	number of outcomes in which the event of interest could occur
z-score	number of standard deviations that the variable x is above or below the mean (when the population mean is known)
x_i	number of times the event of interest has occurred
r	Pearson correlation coefficient
s_k	Pearsonian coefficient of skewness
μ	population mean; say *mu*
p	population proportion
N	population size
σ	population standard deviation; say *sigma*
σ^2	population variance
$f(x)$	probability density function
q	probability of failure in a binomial distribution
p	probability of success in a binomial distribution
$P(X\|Y)$	probability of X given Y
$P(E_i)$	probability that an event of interest occurs
$\bar{x}$	sample mean; say *x bar*
$\hat{p}$	sample proportion; say *p hat*
n	sample size; number of observations or total number of items
s	sample standard deviation
s^2	sample variance
$SE_{\bar{x}}$ or $\sigma_{\bar{x}}$	standard error of the mean or standard deviation of the sample means
Σx	summation of all the numbers in a grouping; say *sigma x*
N_E	total number of outcomes
$\cup$	union, combined elements of both sets

Inference and hypothesis testing

H_a	alternative hypothesis
χ^2	chi-square ratio or chi-square distribution; say *ki square*
z_{crit}	critical value of the test statistic
df	degrees of freedom
F	F value; ratio of two sample variances
α	level of significance; probability of Type I error; say *alpha*
ME	margin of error of the confidence interval
μ_D	mean population difference between related samples
$\bar{d}$	mean sample difference
H_0	null hypothesis
$1 - \beta$	power of the test
β	probability of Type II error; say *beta*
s_d	standard deviation of sample difference
$SE_{\hat{p}}$	standard error of the proportion

Analysis of variance

ANOVA	analysis of variance
MSR	mean block sum of squares (randomised block design)
MSC	mean square of columns
MSE	mean square of errors
MST	mean square of totals
SSE	sum of squares of error
SSR	sum of squares of rows (randomised block design)
SST	sum of squares of totals
SSC	sum of squares of treatments
HSD	Tukey's honestly significant difference test

Decision making

d_i	decision alternative i
EMV	expected monetary value
$P_{i,j}$	payoff for decision i under state j
s_j	state of nature

Regression and forecasting

x_t	actual value for current time period (t)
α	alpha, the exponential smoothing constant, which is between 0 and 1; say *alpha*
r^2	coefficient of determination
R^2	coefficient of multiple determination
SS_{xy}	covariance between x and y
C	cyclical value
df	degrees of freedom
b_k	estimate of regression coefficient k
$E(y_x)$	expected value of y
F_t	forecast value for current time period (t)
F_{t+1}	forecast for the next time period ($t + 1$)
I_i	index number for the year of interest
β_0	intercept of the population line with the Y axis
b_0	intercept of the sample line with the y axis
I	irregular or random value
Y_i	ith value of the dependent variable
X_i	ith value of the independent variable
I_L	Laspeyres price index
d_L	lower critical value of Durbin–Watson statistic
MAD	mean absolute deviation
MSE	mean square error
MS_{reg}	mean square of the regression
MS_{err}	mean square of the residual
MA	moving average
k	number of independent variables (not including the constant term)
n	number of observations
D	observed value of Durbin–Watson statistic
I_P	Paasche price index
β_k	partial regression coefficient for independent variable k
ε	population error term
$\hat{Y}$	predicted value of Y (for population data)
$\hat{y}$	predicted value of y (for sample data)
P_i	price in a given year (i)
P_0	price in base year (0)
e	sample error term
S	seasonal value
β_1	slope of the population regression line
b_1	slope of the sample regression line
s_e	standard error of the estimate
SSE	sum of squares of error
SS_{reg}	sum of squares of regression
SS_{err}	sum of squares of residual
SS_{xx}	sum of squares of x
SS_{yy}	sum of squares of y
y_t	time-series data value at time t
T	trend value
d_U	upper critical value of Durbin–Watson statistic
VIF	variance inflation factor

Nonparametric statistics

d	differences in ranks of each pair (in a Spearman's rank correlation analysis)
D	Kolmogorov–Smirnov test statistic
K	Kruskal–Wallis test statistic
U	Mann–Whitney U test statistic
M_d	median (in a Wilcoxon matched-pairs signed rank test)
n_1	number of items in sample with characteristic 1 (in a runs test)
n_2	number of items in sample with characteristic 2 (in a runs test)
S	number of plus signs in n matched pairs with non-zero differences (in a sign test)
R	number of runs
T	smallest sum of ranks (in a Wilcoxon matched-pairs signed rank test)
r	Spearman's rank correlation coefficient
W_1	sum of ranks for values from group 1 (in a Mann–Whitney U test)
W_2	sum of ranks for values from group 2 (in a Mann–Whitney U test)

Quality control

$\overline{p}$	average of sample proportions; say *p bar*
$\overline{\overline{x}}$	average sample mean for all samples; say *x double bar*
$\overline{R}$	average sample range for all samples; say *R bar*
$\overline{s}$	average sample standard deviation for all samples; say *s bar*
LCL	lower control limit
$\overline{x}$	sample mean; say *x bar*
TQM	total quality management
UCL	upper control limit

Wiley The manufacturer's authorized representative according to the EU General Product Safety Regulation is Wiley-VCH GmbH, Boschstr. 12, 69469 Weinheim, Germany, e-mail: Product_Safety@wiley.com.

Printed and bound by CPI Group (UK) Ltd, Croydon, CR0 4YY
15/09/2026
02217276-0001